MO☾N HANDBOOKS

PANAMA

WILLIAM FRIAR

Puerto Limón

C a r i b b e a n   S e a

Uatsi

Sixaola
Guabito
Changuinola
Bocas ⊙
Almirante
Parque
Internacional
La Amistad
Parque Nacional
Bastimentos

BOCAS
DEL TORO

Laguna de
Chiriquí

Chiriquí Grande

Golfo de los
Mosquitos

COLÓN

COSTA
RICA

PN
Volcán Barú

Río
Sereno
Volcán
Boquete

Bosque
Protector de
Palo Seco

Parque Nacional
Omar Torrijos H
(El Copé)

El Copé

COCLÉ

VERAGUAS

CHIRIQUÍ

La Concepcion

COMARCA
NGÖBE-BUGLÉ

Santa Fé

Penonomé

David

Puerto
Armuelles

Boca Chica

Las
Lajas

Tolé

San Francisco

Aguadulce

Antón

Bahía de
Parita

PN
Sarigua

Parque Nacional
Golfo de Chiriquí

Bahía de
Charco Azul

Divisa

Santiago ⊙

HERRERA

Ocú

Chitré

Golfo de Chiriquí

Golfo de
Montijo

Las
Minas

Las Tablas

LOS
SANTOS

Isla de
Coiba

Parque
Nacional
Coiba

Refugio de Vida
Silvestre Isla de Cañas

Tonosí

Arenas

Parque Nacional
Cerro Hoya

P A C I F I C   *O C E A N*

© AVALON TRAVEL

PANAMA

Parque Nacional
Portobelo

El Porvenir

Portobelo

Cartí

Parque Nacional
Chagres

COMARCA
GUNA YALA

Sabanitas

Lago
Alajuela

Colón

El Llano

Lago
Bayano

Chepo

COMARCA
GUNA DE
MADUGANDÍ

Panama
Canal

1

PANAMA CITY

PANAMA

COMARCA
GUNA DE
WARGANDÍ

Lago
Gatún

PN Altos de
Campana

Santa Fé

Puerto
Obaldía

El Valle
de Antón

Chame

COMARCA
EMBERÁ

San Carlos

Archipiélago
de las Perlas

San Miguel

La Palma

Isla del
Rey

Río
Tuira

Yaziva

El Real de
Santa María

Golfo de Panamá

DARIÉN

COMARCA
EMBERÁ

Parque Nacional Darién

Pocrí

Pedasí

Jaqué

COLOMBIA

Juradó

Cupica

Golfo de
Cupica

0   25 mi

0   25 km

Contents

Discover Panama

Panama is hard to beat. It has incredible natural beauty, a modern infrastructure, good roads, clean water, a booming economy, year-round warm weather, a peaceful atmosphere, a rich history, and excellent health conditions.

Travelers are beginning to discover all the country has to offer. It's not yet overrun with hordes of tourists, unlike some of its neighbors, but people have come to realize that Panama is more than just a canal.

Democracy and prosperity haven't squeezed all the intrigue out of this intriguing country, which has been the plaything of empires for half a millennium. To its boosters, Panama is still "the crossroads of the world"; to jaded locals, "a racket with a flag." To a Panamanian poet, it's the "heart of the universe"; to a spy novelist, "Casablanca without heroes." But there's one thing nobody calls it: boring.

Panama City alone can keep travelers plenty busy. It is by far the most sophisticated and vibrant city in Central America. You can literally see it grow: The skyline changes almost daily, and new roads, bridges, and a metro system are on the way.

The natural wonders of Panama are just as overwhelming. A quarter of the country is protected wilderness, much of which has never seen a road. Even in Panama's busiest towns, the tropical night air vibrates with the calls of a thousand frogs, and you wake to the songs of hundreds of brilliant birds. Where else can you find a national park so close to the capital that you can pop over to watch wild kinkajous, capybaras, and coatimundis, then be back in time for lunch at a fancy French restaurant?

There's always something new to learn about a country with more biodiversity per square meter than the Amazon, not to mention a diverse mix of indigenous people and immigrants. Panama attracts adventurers and misfits, entrepreneurs and schemers, dreamers and full-on nutcases. If you don't encounter a colorful character during your stay, you aren't getting out enough.

And then there's that famous canal, which is in the middle of a multi-billion-dollar expansion program that should make it as much an engineering marvel for the 21st century as it was for the 20th.

There's an old saying that visitors who drink water from the Chagres, the powerful river that feeds the canal, are bound to return. It's Panama's largest source of drinking water; you'll inevitably drink some during your stay. Don't expect your first trip to Panama to be your last.

Planning Your Trip

▶ WHERE TO GO

Panama City
Panama City is by far the most cosmopolitan city in Central America, yet it is also rich in history. The heart of this burgeoning metropolis of soaring skyscrapers, sophisticated restaurants, and international banks and businesses is Casco Viejo, a charming and well-preserved neighborhood that dates from the 16th century.

The Panama Canal and Central Isthmus
In addition to seeing and transiting the Panama Canal, visitors can explore the historic townsites and tropical forests of the Pacific side of the canal, as well as the Spanish ruins and tranquil waters of the Caribbean side.

Bocas del Toro
The Bocas archipelago is a bohemian playground of white-sand beaches, big surf, pristine coral reefs, and interesting creatures. The humans are pretty fascinating, too, with a rich mix of diverse peoples that includes indigenous and Afro-Caribbean inhabitants who've called Bocas home for hundreds of years.

Central Panama
The central provinces contain Panama's most accessible highlands and popular beaches. From any of the beaches it's easy to head for the hills and escape the heat in the town of El Valle de Antón, nestled at the bottom of an extinct volcano and known for its waterfalls, square trees, golden frogs, and a popular Sunday crafts market.

Western Highlands and Beaches
The cool highlands of western Panama are home to the country's highest mountain, Volcán Barú. The dormant volcano's fertile soil produces gourmet coffee, gorgeous

IF YOU HAVE . . .

Panama City skyline

- **ONE WEEK:** Visit Panama City, the Panama Canal, and either Bocas del Toro or Boquete, in the western highlands.
- **TWO WEEKS:** This is enough time to visit both Bocas del Toro and the western highlands.
- **THREE WEEKS:** Add Guna Yala or a visit to the islands and beaches of Parque Nacional Marino Golfo de Chiriquí or the Golfo de Montijo, the gateway to Parque Nacional Isla Coiba.
- **FOUR WEEKS:** Add the Azuero Peninsula and, if possible, Parque Nacional Darién.

flowers, and delicious oranges and strawberries. But its sprawling protected areas, most notably the gigantic Parque Internacional La Amistad, are what really set the region apart.

The western Pacific beaches and islands are equally inviting. Here you'll find two massive offshore national parks, Parque Nacional Marino Golfo de Chiriquí and Parque Nacional Coiba. Their waters teem with 760 species of fish, not to mention aquatic giants such as humpback whales and whale sharks. The equally lovely islands and beaches of the Golfo de Montijo are gradually becoming more accessible to travelers, especially Playa Santa Catalina, home to the most famous surf break in Latin America.

The Azuero Peninsula

The Azuero Peninsula, Panama's heartland, is the most culturally rich region of the country, with Spanish colonial towns that time has forgotten. The Azuero, known for its festivals, hosts the country's most important Carnaval celebration. The peninsula also has beaches that offer good surfing, snorkeling, and fishing.

Guna Yala

Only about 40 of the nearly 400 islands in Guna Yala, commonly known as the San Blas Archipelago, are inhabited. On these live the Guna, the most fascinating and intact indigenous culture in the Americas. The uninhabited islands are palm-covered paradises of white sand and clear blue water.

The Darién

The legendary Darién jungle has long attracted adventurers. Parque Nacional Darién is one of the largest and most vital tropical forests in the western hemisphere. The forested coast offers a completely different experience, including astonishingly abundant sealife just offshore. The Darién is also home to three nations of indigenous people who cling to the rugged ways of life they've sustained for centuries.

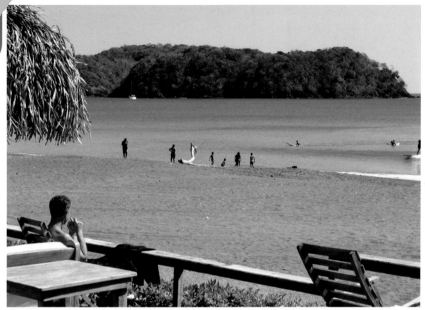

Playa Venao, on the Azuero Peninsula, is a favorite with surfers.

▶ WHEN TO GO

Panama has two seasons, rainy and dry. The dry season lasts mid-December–mid-April and is Panama's "summer." This is the high season for tourism. The weather can be especially lovely at the beginning of the dry season.

The rainy season lasts mid-April–mid-December. During most of the rainy season, storms pass through quickly, leaving much of the day and evening clear. Storms tend to start earlier and last longer in the final months of the rainy season; this is not a great time to go on long hikes or drive on rough roads, as the countryside turns to mud and routes can be impassable.

The rain never stops completely in some parts of the country. Be prepared for some precipitation year-round along the Caribbean coast, in the western highlands, and on the islands of Bocas del Toro. September-October

and February-March are the driest times in Bocas. Late February-March is considered the best time to visit the islands of Guna Yala.

Temperatures in Panama don't change much during the year. In the lowlands, expect a high of about 32°C (90°F) in the day, down to 21°C (70°F) in the evening. It never gets cold in the lowlands, and the dry-season breezes in the evening are pleasant. It gets considerably cooler in the highlands. Panama can be quite humid year-round, but especially so in the rainy season.

Panama's biggest holiday is Carnaval, held each year in the four days leading up to Ash Wednesday. The country comes to a complete halt during those days. November is filled with *fiestas patrias* (national-independence holidays).

Carnaval reveler

► BEFORE YOU GO

Passports, Tourist Cards, and Visas

Citizens of the United States, Canada, most of western Europe, much of Latin America, and a few other countries do not need a visa to enter Panama, but their passport must be valid for at least six months beyond their date of entry. Tourists from these countries are normally allowed to stay in Panama for up to 90 days. Nationals of other countries must apply for a stamped visa or authorized visa, which is available through a Panamanian consulate or embassy.

Vaccinations

All visitors should make sure their routine immunizations are up to date. The CDC recommends that travelers to Central America be vaccinated against hepatitis A and, in some cases, hepatitis B. A typhoid fever vaccination is also recommended, though the chance of contracting the disease in Panama is slim. A rabies vaccination is only recommended for those who come into direct contact with carnivores, bats, or other mammals.

Those planning to travel to rural parts of Panama should probably be vaccinated against yellow fever and may want to consider antimalarial medication. Yellow-fever vaccinations are recommended, but no longer required, for those arriving in Panama from a country where yellow fever is endemic. This includes much of South America.

Explore Panama

The suggested itineraries in this chapter include specific mentions of restaurants, accommodations, and other businesses to convey a sampling of what's available to you in Panama. There are many other good options for each destination, indicated in each chapter by 🌙.

▶ THE SEVEN-DAY BEST OF PANAMA

Day 1: Panama City

Arrive at Tocumen International Airport in the morning and take a cab to Casco Viejo, dropping your bags off at Canal House or Magnolia Inn. Fuel up at René Café, just a short walk away.

Tour the Panama Canal, particularly the Miraflores Locks, then enjoy lunch on the balcony of the visitors center, where you can watch ships transit while you dine. Cross the canal at the Puente Centenario (Centennial Bridge) for views of Gaillard Cut, where canal builders cleaved the mountains of the Continental Divide in two.

Visit the former Canal Zone townsites of Balboa and Balboa Heights. In Balboa, find the Goethals Monument, which pays tribute to the chief engineer of the canal. From there, head to Amador Causeway (Calzada de Amador) and admire the sweeping views of Panama Bay and the parade of ships coming through the canal.

Work up an appetite for dinner by browsing for handicrafts at Balboa's Centro de Artesanías Internacional. Return to Casco Viejo for dinner at one of its many atmospheric restaurants, such as Restaurant Las Bóvedas, which was originally a dungeon.

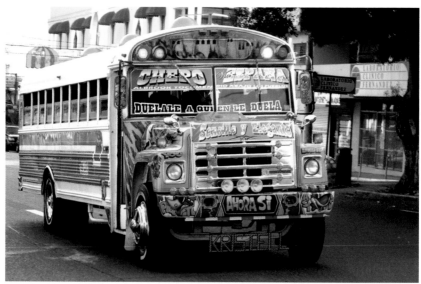

colorful bus in Panama City

Red Frog Beach in Bocas del Toro

Day 2

Today, make visits to Panamá La Vieja and Casco Viejo to get a sense of Panama City's rich, colorful history. Meander around Casco Viejo's Plaza de la Independencia and admire the architectural variety of the buildings nearby. Pop in to the Museo de la Historia de Panamá to get a sense of Panamanian history beyond the canal.

Stay on for dinner in Casco Viejo at Manolo Caracol, where you can experience Panama's seasonal best in 10 courses. Make it an early night and head back to your hotel, as you've got a long trek ahead of you tomorrow.

Day 3: Boquete

Make the seven-hour trip to Boquete, starting out as early as you can. In the evening, head to the bar at Panamonte Inn and Spa to enjoy a quiet drink in a sleek, yet cozy atmosphere. Check in to the pleasant and affordable Pensión Marilós.

Day 4

In the morning, get breakfast and a cup of famous Boquete coffee at Café Ruiz. Spend the day on a guided hike with Coffee Adventures, a tour outfit that will take you along Sendero Los Quetzales. The truly fit can plan a night ascent of Volcán Barú, arriving in time to catch the dawn and a view of both oceans.

Travelers looking for lower-impact activities can enjoy the gardens and the changing face of Volcán Barú throughout the day, or get their thrills with a zipline ride from Boquete Tree Trek.

Head to Big Daddy's Grill for dinner, being sure to get seated in the garden terrace. Order the fish tacos, and stay for the excellent margaritas. Head back to Pensión Marilós for the night.

Day 5: Bocas del Toro

Take the hour-long flight to Bocas del Toro. Stop at Lili's Café for a sample of Lili's delicious French toast. Take a boat tour around Isla Colón with outfitter Transparente Tours. You'll return to shore in the evening, so get your land legs back by strolling the souvenir kiosks in town, or taking an evening yoga class at Bocas Yoga.

For dinner, head back to Bocas town to Restaurante Guari-Guari, where you're guaranteed the best food in the area. Enjoy the nightlife by starting out at low-key La Iguana Bar, then party into the wee hours at El Barco Hundido. Tuck in for the night at Isla Colón's Hotel Bocas del Toro.

Day 6: Isla Bastimentos

In the morning, prepare for another adventure-packed day by heading to Isla Bastimentos. The island's north shore beaches, such as Red Frog Beach, are a fantastic way to idle away a day. If you look hard enough, you should be able to spot the beach's namesake.

Those looking to spend their time under water should make for Cayo Crawl, on the southern end of Bastimentos. Order lunch at one of the restaurants on stilts, then go snorkeling until your food is ready.

Once you've sunned, frogged, and snorkeled yourself out, check in at Eclypse de Mar, where you can rent your own bungalow over the water, and enjoy the sea breeze and the beautiful views. The bungalows even feature glass panels in the floor, so you can see the fish swimming below you.

Day 7: Panama City

Head back to Panama City after you've enjoyed a morning walking the beaches of Isla Bastimentos. It's time to do some last-minute shopping, so make your way to Imagen, Panama's best art gallery. There, enjoy the offerings from the local art scene. Next, visit one of the two Reprosa stores for a unique jewelry piece.

Once you've stocked up on gifts and keepsakes, take a cab to Tocumen International Airport, but not before saying goodbye to Panama.

▶ SEE IT ALL IN 21 DAYS

Those determined to touch on every part of Panama during a three-week trip can do it, but just barely. It means covering a lot of ground and, most likely, spending quite a bit of cash. Those with limited money can take it more slowly and rely more on buses and their own planning and less on planes and tour operators, but in that case, travelers should build about a week more into the itinerary. The Darién section of the itinerary assumes officials have lifted travel restrictions to the national park.

Day 1

Arrive at Tocumen International Airport and check in to Canal House in Panama City. Once you're settled in, go up to the roof and check out the fascinating view of the surrounding city. Those up for a drink at a funky club should head to Relic Bar in the basement of the Luna's Castle hostel.

Day 2

Get an early start and visit the ruins of Panamá La Vieja, then go for a walking tour of Casco Viejo. Grab lunch at René Café, where you'll be stuffed to the gills for not much money.

After lunch, make a visit to the Church of the Golden Altar and the nearby Flat Arch at Iglesia de Santo Domingo. Have dinner at La Mar in the El Cangrejo neighborhood, where you can dine on ceviche made from the freshest of seafood.

Day 3

Visit the Panama Canal, first touring the Miraflores Locks, then the impressive Gaillard Cut. Make at least a brief stop to see the wildlife

EXPLORING THE PANAMA CANAL

the Panama Canal

Some save for years to afford a Panama Canal cruise. But those already in Panama can make a day transit of the canal for a tiny fraction of what the luxury liners charge. Two companies on the Pacific-side of the isthmus offer passenger service. (The adventurous, especially those short of cash, can sometimes get a free transit by working as a line-handler on a yacht.)

From January to March, day transits are offered only on Thursday, Friday, and Saturday. They're offered only on Saturday the rest of the year. Most are partial transits, although even these take nearly a full day. Plan accordingly. The partial transit takes 4-5 hours and costs US$115 for adults, US$60-65 for children, including transfers. Full transits are offered one Saturday a month (US$165 for adults, US$75 for children).

One of the companies also offers a partial Friday-night transit, which gives a very different perspective on the canal. The locks are brightly lit by high-mast lighting, turning night into day.

Nearly as storied as the Panama Canal is the Panama Railroad, which ferried 49ers across the isthmus during the California gold rush. Its descendant is the **Panama Railway,** which offers passengers an incredibly scenic early-morning ride from the Pacific to the Atlantic along the banks of the canal. The coast-to-coast ride lasts only an hour, but creates memories that will last a lifetime.

You can hire a taxi to meet you on the Caribbean side and explore the Spanish ruins. **Portobelo** and **Fuerte San Lorenzo** transport visitors back to the days of pirates and conquistadors, and the mile-long **Gatún Locks** bring them back to the high-tech present. If time allows, squeeze in a wildlife-viewing tour, by boat or kayak, down the lower reaches of the **Río Chagres,** a storied river where one can spot the occasional caiman or crocodile. Finish up in time to catch the train back to Panama City, or take one of the frequent buses.

the banks of the Panama Canal

at Gamboa and Parque Nacional Soberanía, a true tropical rainforest just a short drive from downtown Panama City. End the day with a ramble along the Amador Causeway, a good place to stop for a drink as the Panama City skyline lights up across the bay. Have dinner at Mi Ranchito, then head back to your room at Canal House for the night.

Day 4

Take an early morning ride across the isthmus on the Panama Railway and explore the Caribbean entrance to the canal. The Spanish ruins of Castillo San Gerónimo in Portobelo and Fuerte San Lorenzo transport visitors back to the days of pirates and conquistadors, and the mile-long Gatún Locks bring them forward again to the high-tech present. If time allows, squeeze in a wildlife-viewing tour, by boat or kayak, down the lower reaches of the Río Chagres. Finish up in time to take the train back to Panama City, and enjoy traditional Panamanian food and folkloric dance at Restaurante y Cafetería El Trapiche.

Day 5

Take a charter flight to Santa Cruz de Cana, the remotest and most spectacular wildlife destination in enormous Parque Nacional Darién. Hike the Machinery Garden Trail, a species-rich jungle trail that passes by the overgrown, rusted remains of gold-mining equipment. Spend the night in Cana's rustic lodge.

Day 6

Hike up the The Pirre Mountain Trail to Cana's cloud-forest camp, a journey of four to five hours, where you're likely to encounter all sorts of wildlife. At the camp, temperatures cool off, and the night is alive with the sounds of forest animals.

Day 7

Hike back down the mountain and take a return flight to Panama City. Spend a few hours shopping for souvenirs or meandering through the ritzy Metro Mall.

Take in some classical music at Teatro Nacional, or hit the clubs along Calle Uruguay, then dine on French-inspired dishes in a former dungeon at Restaurante Las Bóvedas.

Days 8-11

Reward yourself for all that exercise by flying off for a few days of Caribbean sun and sea. Choose between one of two stunning tropical archipelagos: the booming bohemia of Bocas del Toro or the more rustic but culturally fascinating attractions of Guna Yala. Travelers with a few extra days can visit both locales. The best way to explore Guna Yala is from the deck of a hired yacht; travelers on a limited budget can stay in simple Guna hotels and get around by motorboat. This is a place for snorkeling off remote cays, walks through traditional island villages, and forest hikes to powerful waterfalls and sacred cemeteries on the mainland.

A visit to Panama's other great Caribbean archipelago, Bocas del Toro, can be split between funky Bocas town and the unspoiled beaches and coral reefs around Isla Bastimentos and its neighbors.

Days 12-14

Head for the highlands of western Panama. Fly to David (travelers coming from Guna Yala must go through Panama City) and take a bus or car to Boquete. Spend an afternoon exploring the town, famous throughout Panama for its flowers, oranges, and rainbows, and its views of Volcán Barú, Panama's tallest mountain. Take a tour of Café Kotowa, a charming boutique coffee producer. Choose the full three-hour tour, or the shorter 45-minute one.

More active types can summit Volcán Barú in hopes of seeing both oceans at once, hike through Parque Nacional Volcán Barú on the famous Sendero Los Quetzales, or book a half-day kayaking tour with Mirador Adventures. Afterward, grab a drink at Zanzibar, before a quick dinner at Machu Picchu.

In Portobelo, you can visit ancient Spanish fortresses like Castillo San Gerónimo.

HISTORIC SITES

The historic Casco Viejo neighborhood is a must-see in Panama City.

If you're fascinated by Panama's role as a crossroads of the world, you can cover 500 years of history in less than a week. A visit that concentrates on the human efforts to conquer the isthmus by trail, railway, and canal is an especially economical and speedy introduction to the country, since most sights are within 100 kilometers of the capital.

- **Colonial Panama City:** Panamá La Vieja, Casco Viejo, Avenida Central, and Plaza Santa Ana.

- **Conquistadors, Pirates, and 49ers:** Portobelo, Fuerte San Lorenzo, Río Chagres, and the Camino de Cruces.

- **The Path Between the Seas:** Miraflores Locks, Gaillard Cut, Panama Railway, Ancón, and Balboa.

Days 15-17

To see how the Pacific side of the isthmus compares with the Caribbean, head back down the mountain to the Parque Nacional Marino Golfo de Chiriquí. Another option is to go surfing at Playa Santa Catalina and the Golfo de Montijo, the best surfing spot in the country.

Next, visit the most impressive island off Panama's Pacific coast, the enormous Isla Coiba. It's a former Devil's-Island-style prison colony whose isolation has kept it among the most unspoiled spots in the country. Here, you can take snorkeling or diving trips, and submerge yourself in the fish-filled waters.

Days 18-19

Return to the mainland at David, Santiago, or Panama City and arrange transportation to the Azuero Peninsula. Learn about Panama's history, crafts, and folkloric traditions in Chitré, La Arena, Parita, La Villa de Los Santos, Guararé, and Las Tablas, and

Parque Nacional Cerro Hoya has some of the most unspoiled wilderness in Panama.

enjoy the sparsely inhabited coastline between Pedasí and Playa Cambutal. Alternatively, be among the first pioneering travelers discovering the Western Azuero Peninsula, which provides surprisingly easy access to the mountainous, magnificent Parque Nacional Cerro Hoya, the most unexplored of Panama's national parks.

Day 20

Head back to Panama City by land or air for last-minute shopping, sightseeing, and a 10-course farewell dinner at Manolo Caracol.

Day 21

Transfer to Tucumen International Airport for the flight home.

▶ FAMILY FUN

Learn About Wildlife
EL CENTRO DE EXHIBICIONES MARINAS

This marine exhibition center, located toward the end of the Amador Causeway, is run by the Smithsonian Tropical Research Institute. Kids will enjoy the outdoor aquarium, and the whole family can visit the dry forest nearby, where a plethora of wildlife can be spotted.

PARQUE MUNICIPAL SUMMIT

Explore the grounds of the Parque Municipal Summit, also known as the Summit Botanical Gardens and Zoo. Created in 1923 to study tropical plants, the gardens now feature more than 350 species of plants. There's a small zoo here, and a harpy eagle compound, where kids can get an up-close view of this powerful bird of prey.

FOR THE BIRDS

the toucan sanctuary at Casa Mariposa Boutique Hotel, Santa Fé

Panama doesn't just attract bird-watchers: It creates them.

It's smaller than South Carolina, but has more bird species than the United States and Canada put together. That means beautiful birds are everywhere all the time and impossible to ignore. There's always something singing, crying, croaking, flitting, flapping, or soaring overhead. More than likely it's something you've never seen before, flashing colors you thought only existed in a box of crayons.

Birders have counted 972 species in Panama so far. Migrants visit from North and South America, and more than 100 species are endemic. Twelve are found nowhere else on earth. Hundreds of species are easy to find without much effort.

Important areas for endemics are the **Caribbean and Pacific lowlands and islands,** the **Darién,** and especially the **western highlands,** the last of which also happen to be among the most accessible, lovely, and comfortable areas for visitors.

Panama offers good birding year-round, though the isthmus is hopping September–April, as that's when North American migrants (avian and human) arrive to escape the cold. A special event during this time is the spectacular raptor migration of millions of **broad-winged hawks, Swainson's hawks,** and **turkey vultures,** which takes place October–mid-November and March–early April. They pass overhead in flocks that can number in the many thousands. The former Canal Zone is the best place to witness this extraordinary phenomenon. June and July are the toughest times to spot birds.

Long-established lodges and inns are dotted around the top birding areas, with knowledgeable owners who can supply expert naturalist guides and detailed birding information. Some of these are world famous, ranging from the upscale Canopy Tower (in the former **Canal Zone,** close to Panama City) to the rustic lodge at Cana (on the remote **Cerro Pirre,** in the Darién), which has been called one of the world's top-10 birding destinations.

Many lodges are simply great places to stay, even for those with no interest in anything with wings. They are listed throughout this guidebook, as are recommended naturalist guides and birding areas. For detailed birding itineraries and tips, the up-to-date *A Bird-Finding Guide to Panama,* by George R. Angehr, Dodge Engleman, and Lorna Engleman, is an indispensable resource. The classic *A Guide to the Birds of Panama,* by Robert S. Ridgely and John A. Gwynne, is an encyclopedic, beautifully illustrated list of species found in Panama.

CENTRO DE VISITANTES DE MIRAFLORES

Take a tour of Miraflores Locks and visit its four-story museum, housed in the Centro de Visitantes de Miraflores. Kids will likely enjoy the 2nd floor, with its flora and fauna displays, and the 3rd floor, with its full-scale pilot-training simulator, the most.

Explore the Rainforest
GAMBOA RAINFOREST RESORT

Enjoy bird-watching walks and night safaris on the lake, even if your family isn't staying here. The resort's aerial tram takes you up and away through a forest canopy, then you can climb up an observation tower for views of the landscape surrounding you.

LAGO GATÚN

Take a boat trip to Lago Gatún in order to visit the surrounding islands' primate sanctuary, where you'll be sure to spot several species of monkeys, most of which have been rescued from illegal captivity.

CANOPY ADVENTURE

For older kids (10 and up), a zipline tour may be the most exciting part of your trip to Panama. The Canopy Adventure in El Valle starts with a nature hike, then a zipline ride through the forest, past a roaring waterfall.

Take to the Water
AQUABUS

See the major sights of Panama City, including Casco Viejo and the Amador Causeway, and keep kids interested by taking a tour via Aquabus, which makes its way into the water three times throughout the length of the tour.

PACIFIC BEACHES

Relax at one of the resorts or smaller hotels at Coronado, Farallón, or Santa Clara, all of which are within a two-hour drive of Panama City. Spend a couple of days playing in the surf and splashing in the pool, or arrange for a banana-boat ride on the ocean.

▶ HIKING OCEAN TO OCEAN

The ultimate Panama destination for hardcore outdoor adventurers is the Darién, and the ultimate Darién adventure is a trek through the jungle between the Atlantic and Pacific oceans. But trans-Darién expeditions are grueling, expensive, and not always available, depending on the security situation near the Colombian border.

Still, there is a safer, easier, and far cheaper way to hike from (close to) the Pacific Ocean to the Atlantic. This suggested itinerary crosses the isthmus on the west side of the Darién. Note that this itinerary is intended only for the highly energetic and fit.

For those who truly want to immerse themselves in the Darién, Ancon Expeditions offers an intense two-week trek that takes in

the rivers, rainforests, and highlands of the region. Custom-designed trips are also possible.

Day 1

Arrive at Tocumen International Airport and transfer to a hotel in Panama City.

Day 2

Head east in the early morning to the Bayano area, about 90 kilometers from Panama City. If time allows, take a boat across Lago Bayano, a large artificial lake, to explore the Bayano Caves on the far side. This will probably only be possible if the tour includes transportation up to Burbayar. Otherwise, begin hiking up to the Continental Divide from El Llano, on the El Llano–Cartí Road.

GO GREEN

The pristine Parque Nacional Cerro Hoya has only recently become accessible by land.

Although all tourism affects the environment, it's getting easier to travel around Panama in reasonable comfort and with a moderately clear conscience. Here are some tips for those who want to stray from the beaten path without beating down a new one.

VISIT THE AZUERO PENINSULA

The Azuero Peninsula sees relatively few foreign visitors and was deforested generations ago. It's unlikely a trip here will do much harm, and it's a way to get to know what Panamanians consider the "real" Panama.

VOLUNTEER

It's increasingly easy for foreigners to volunteer with community and environmental projects in Panama. Hostels and language schools can often arrange volunteer work, sometimes offering discounts as incentives. Local nonprofits and ecolodges also sometimes accept volunteers. All these are listed throughout the book.

THINK SMALL

Every day seems to bring a new luxury hotel tower or beach mega-resort to the isthmus. But it's the little places that add more to their natural surroundings and local community than they take. For the first time, it's possible to go from one end of Panama to the other and stay only at these charming little places, with hosts that go out of their way to make you feel at home. Here are some of the best:

· **Azuero Peninsula:** Casa de Campo Pedasí

· **Bocas del Toro:** Al Natural Resort, Bluff Beach Retreat, Eclypse de Mar, La Loma Jungle Lodge, Soposo Rainforest Adventures, Tesoro Escondido, Dolphin Island Lodge

· **Boquete:** La Montaña y El Valle, The Coffee Estate Inn, Tinamou Cottage

· **Cerro Punta and Vicinity:** Hostal Cielito Sur Bed and Breakfast

· **El Valle:** Golden Frog Inn, Park Eden

· **Former Canal Zone:** Dos Palmitos

· **Fortuna Road:** Lost and Found Eco-Resort

· **Pacific Beaches:** Tógo B&B

· **Playa Santa Catalina:** La Buena Vida

· **Santa Fé:** Hostal La Qhia, Casa Mariposa Boutique Hotel

Panama City

Spend the night in Burbayar Lodge, in a lush tropical forest about 15 kilometers north of the Interamerican Highway.

Day 3

Explore the forest around Burbayar Lodge, then head over the Continental Divide, through Guna territory, toward the coastal town of Cartí on the Caribbean coast, 22 kilometers from Burbayar. Camp in the forest along the way.

Days 4-5

Arrive in Cartí early in the morning and hire a boat to one of the nearby inhabited islands. Snorkel around the crystal-clear waters of Achutupu, an uninhabited islet with its own little shipwreck. Spend a night or two in Hotel Kuna Niskua, a rustic Guna hotel.

Day 6

Fly back to Panama City. Spend the day sightseeing and resting.

Day 7

Transfer to Tocumen International Airport for the flight home; your feet will be glad for the rest.

Emberá-Wounaan baskets

The **Emberá-Wounaan** of the Darién are renowned for their artistic abilities. This is especially true of the Wounaan, who are generally thought to produce the finest works. Three crafts are popular with travelers and are a major source of income for the Emberá-Wounaan. These can be bought directly from their makers in the **Darién** or one of the villages up the **Río Chagres** close to the canal. But some of the best examples can be found at the handicrafts market near the YMCA in the townsite of **Balboa.**

DECORATIVE BASKETS

A variety of baskets are painstakingly crafted from the fine leaf fibers of the *chunga* (black palm). Traditional baskets are plain or contain black-and-white geometrical patterns. But brightly colored ones depicting detailed scenes of butterflies, macaws, and forest animals have become popular, and the artisans are always experimenting with new ideas. The most sought-after baskets use natural dyes for the vivid colors.

The finest baskets are so tightly woven it's been said they can hold water, although there's no indication the baskets were ever actually used for that purpose. You won't want to spoil yours by testing the theory.

CARVED TAGUA NUTS

The tagua nut, also known as the "ivory nut" or "vegetable ivory," is the seed of a variety of palm tree that grows throughout the tropics. The Emberá-Wounaan learned to carve beautiful and delicate miniature sculptures of forest animals out of the nut, depicting everything from ants to jaguars. These can be remarkably detailed and lifelike. They are made by the men, who primarily use the particularly hard nut of *Phytelephas see-mannii*, often leaving the bottom half of the nut intact as a base. Because a good crop of tagua nuts requires healthy tagua trees, this is a particularly sustainable, environmentally friendly source of income for the Emberá-Wounaan.

COCOBOLO STATUES

Cocobolo (*Dalbergia retusa*) is a kind of rosewood that Emberá-Wounaan men carve into sculptures. As with the tagua nuts, these usually depict forest animals. When polished, the wood is a deep, lustrous red.

PANAMA CITY

Panama City surprises newcomers. It is by far the most cosmopolitan city in Central America, which becomes obvious as soon as one sees its densely packed towers. But its vibrant modernity really shouldn't be surprising, given the capital's status as an international banking center and its location next to the Pacific entrance of the Panama Canal, the crossroads of the world. Panama City has been important to world commerce since its founding nearly 500 years ago.

It's also an international city. The shops of Indian and Chinese merchants have been city institutions for generations. Any given day might find Colombian émigrés having a drink in a British pub, Japanese businesspeople making a deal in an Argentine steak house, and North American retirees looking for their place in the tropical sun.

The city's rich diversity can be seen in its houses of worship: Along with its Roman Catholic churches are synagogues, mosques, one of the world's seven Baha'i Houses of Worship, the Greek Orthodox Metropolitanate of Central America, a prominent Hindu temple, and gathering houses for every conceivable Protestant congregation.

The one faith that draws all these people together is business. Deals are being made everywhere at all times, from kids hawking cell-phone accessories at congested intersections to developers determined to build on every square centimeter of open space. Life is

© WILLIAM FRIAR

HIGHLIGHTS

LOOK FOR **(** TO FIND RECOMMENDED SIGHTS, ACTIVITIES, DINING, AND LODGING.

(**Panamá La Vieja:** Founded nearly 500 years ago, this original Panama City was the first Spanish city on the Pacific coast of the Americas. Its stone ruins transport you back to the time of gold-hungry conquistadors and pillaging buccaneers (page 34).

(**Casco Viejo:** This charming colonial neighborhood is the cornerstone of modern Panama City. An ambitious renovation project has brought restaurants, theaters, and clubs to its historic buildings, sidewalk cafés to its quaint plazas, and new life to its crumbling churches (page 35).

(**Avenida Central:** The walking street that extends from Plaza Cinco de Mayo to Parque Santa Ana is one of the most vibrant parts of town, a bustling commercial center that draws a cross section of Panamanian society (page 44).

(**Parque Natural Metropolitano:** More than a city park, this 265-hectare tropical forest within the city limits offers a glimpse of Panama's flora and fauna (page 50).

(**Bella Vista and Marbella:** Panama City's most dynamic nightlife lies along Calle Uruguay, where trendy new restaurants and clubs open and close constantly (page 55).

fast-paced compared with the rest of Panama, and the city's residents are comparatively assertive, street-savvy, and no-nonsense. Panama City is to, say, the Azuero Peninsula as New York City is to rural Nebraska. Everyone on the road is in a great hurry, and skyscrapers pop up overnight.

Still, by the standards of many other countries' capitals, Panama City is a mellow, fun-loving place. Any excuse for a party will do, and big celebrations, especially Carnaval, shut down the whole city.

Those who come to Panama solely for its natural treasures will be tempted to blast right through the capital on their way to the country's forests, mountains, islands, and beaches. But it'd be a shame not to spend some time in Panama City. Hundreds of years of history live on in its streets, and its more modern attractions are especially appealing after roughing it in the wilderness for a while. Besides, it has its very own tropical forest. Even city streets aren't far removed from nature; an entire book has been written on the birds of Panama City.

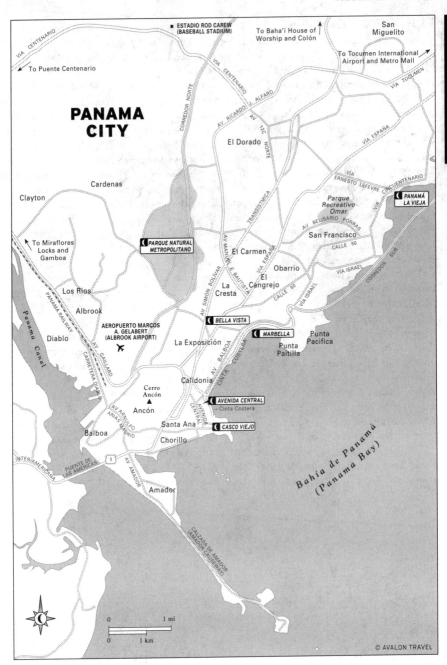

PANAMA CITY

ESTADIO ROD CAREW
(BASEBALL STADIUM)

To Baha'i House of
Worship and Colón

San
Miguelito

To Tocumen International
Airport and Metro Mall

VÍA CENTENARIO

To Puente Centenario

VÍA CENTENARIO

CORREDOR NORTE

AV. RICARDO J. ALFARO

VÍA TOCUMEN

El Dorado

AV. 12C NORTE

VÍA ESPAÑA

VÍA
ERNESTO LEFEVRE

VÍA CINCUENTENARIO

Cardenas

Clayton

Parque
Recreativo
Omar

PANAMÁ
LA VIEJA

TRANSÍSTMICA

AV. BELISARIO PORRAS

To Miraflores
Locks and
Gamboa

PARQUE NATURAL
METROPOLITANO

San Francisco

CALLE 50

Los Rios

Albrook

AV. MANUEL E. BAUTISTA

El Carmen

AV. SIMÓN BOLÍVAR

VÍA ESPAÑA

Obarrio
El
Cangrejo

CALLE 50

VÍA ISRAEL

CORREDOR SUR

La
Cresta

VÍA ISRAEL

Diablo

PANAMA RAILWAY

AV. GAILLARD

BELLA VISTA

MARBELLA

Punta
Pacifica

AEROPUERTO MARCOS
A. GELABERT
(ALBROOK AIRPORT)

La Exposición

AV. BALBOA

CINTA COSTERA

Punta
Paitilla

P
a
n
a
m
a

C
a
n
a
l

CARRETERA DIABLO

Calidonia

Cerro
Ancón

AVENIDA
CENTRAL

AVENIDA CENTRAL
—Cinta Costera

AV. ARNULFO
ARIAS MADRID

Ancón

Santa Ana

CASCO VIEJO

Balboa

Chorillo

INTERAMERICANA

PUENTE DE
LAS AMÉRICAS

1

AV. AMADOR

Bahía de Panamá
(Panama Bay)

Amador

CALZADA DE AMADOR
(AMADOR CAUSEWAY)

0   1 mi

0   1 km

© AVALON TRAVEL

PLANNING YOUR TIME

Those in a big hurry can see Panama City's main tourist attractions, from Casco Viejo to Panamá La Vieja, in a single day, traffic permitting. But try to spend at least a couple of days in the capital. That's the only way to get a sense of its rhythms and to experience its less-showy charms: feeling a tropical evening breeze at a sidewalk café, splurging on dinner at an elegant restaurant, bargaining for *molas* (handcrafted blouses) with a Guna, dancing at an all-night club, or just people-watching on the streets.

The ruins of **Panamá La Vieja** can be explored in about two hours. Plan on a half day for a walking tour of the historic quarter of **Casco Viejo** that includes visits to its major museums and churches.

Those compelled to see and do it all should count on about four full days in Panama City. Most, however, will be content to hit the highlights over the course of two or three days. Try not to be in too great a rush, as traffic in Panama City is bad and is expected to get worse until at least 2014. Streets and entire blocks are being dug up to make way for the city's new metro, and the Bridge of the Americas spanning the canal is undergoing major repairs. Allow extra time to get around, and try to travel outside commuting hours.

Consider spending a day wandering around the city's more colorful **shopping districts.** If time and budget allow, plan on at least one evening out on the town. Good areas to combine dinner and nightlife include the **Calle Uruguay** area, **Casco Viejo,** and **Calle 53 in Marbella.**

Parque Natural Metropolitano offers a chance for those who can't make it to the national parks to enjoy a true tropical nature walk within the city limits. It's a short drive from downtown, and the longest trail takes two hours to walk.

Because downtown Panama City is so close to the Panama Canal, many visitors prefer to extend their stay in the city and make day trips to explore the canal area rather than shift their home base to lodging in the former Canal Zone. In that case, plan on an extra day or two to see the major sights on the Pacific side of the canal, and at least another day or two to explore the Caribbean side.

The climate in Panama City is hot and humid in the dry season (approximately mid-December to mid-April) and hot, very humid, and wet in the rainy season. But for most of the rainy season, storms don't sweep in until mid-afternoon and generally come down in short, powerful bursts that race on as quickly as they arrive. Because of the high ratio of concrete to trees, midday can be wiltingly hot. Explore in the early mornings and reserve the afternoons for relaxing. Sunday is by far the quietest time in the city, with the fewest cars on the road. Keep in mind, however, that many places are closed on Sunday.

Sights

ORIENTATION

Panama City is a growing metropolis of 813,000 people, or more than 1.2 million if you include the greater metropolitan area. Streets and public transportation have not kept pace with the city's growth, and the roads are usually busy and during morning and evening rush hours can become absolutely jammed. In recent years the city has grown east toward Tocumen International Airport, and with its absorption of the former U.S. Canal Zone, urban sprawl has been creeping north and west as well.

Panamanians typically drop the "city" when referring to the capital and just call it "Panama." As with the country, the accent is on the last syllable—Panamá (pah-nah-MA)—when speaking Spanish. Formally, it's La Ciudad de Panamá.

The city is bounded by the Bahía de Panamá (Panama Bay) and the Pacific Ocean to the south and the Panama Canal to the west. The terrain is fairly flat—the United States dug the canal nearby because the Continental Divide is particularly low-lying here—though a few isolated hills, most notably Cerro Ancón, jut up near the canal's Pacific entrance.

The section of the city of most interest to visitors runs along the coast from Casco Viejo, the cornerstone of modern Panama City, east to the ruins of Panamá La Vieja, eight kilometers away. Most of the cosmopolitan parts of the capital lie between these two landmarks.

An exception to this rule is **Costa del Este,** a new city within (or, more accurately, on the outskirts of) Panama City. It's a rapidly growing mini-metropolis of upscale homes and condos whose skyline is beginning to rival downtown's in its concentration of skyscrapers. It's a new frontier for privileged Panamanians escaping the city's congestion and noise and for international jet-setters adding to their portfolio of vacation homes. But it doesn't yet hold enough interest to the average visitor to justify making the long trip from the city center.

Getting one's bearings can be tricky in Panama City, given its confusing mass of winding streets and its topsy-turvy geography (some never get used to seeing the Pacific Ocean lying to the south, for instance).

The city is organized into a series of loosely defined neighborhoods. The only ones most travelers will be concerned with are **Punta Pacífica, Punta Paitilla, Marbella, Bella Vista, El Cangrejo, Calidonia/La Exposición, Santa Ana,** and **San Felipe/Casco Viejo.** There are also a few places of note a bit farther east, in **Obarrio** and **San Francisco.**

Vía España, a busy commercial street, has long been the heart of modern Panama City. In recent years, though, the action has spread just north to El Cangrejo and south to Bella Vista and Marbella. Most of Panama's upscale hotels, restaurants, and shops are in these areas.

An area of about three square blocks between Bella Vista and Marbella, centered on **Calle Uruguay,** is a booming nightlife destination of restaurants and clubs, as is, to a lesser degree, the main strip through Marbella, **Calle 53.** The Calle Uruguay nightlife area is being eroded by the building boom, with clubs and restaurants being knocked down to put up yet another skyscraper, but there's still enough going on here to justify a visit.

An older commercial center is found along **Avenida Central** in the Calidonia and Santa Ana districts. Bordering it is the district of **San Felipe,** which contains the historic neighborhood of **Casco Viejo,** tucked away on a small peninsula.

Avenida de los Mártires, formerly known as **Fourth of July Avenue,** used to mark the boundary between Panama City and the former Canal Zone.

A major artery is the **Cinta Costera** (Coastal

CENTRAL PANAMA CITY

VÍA RICARDO J. ALFARO

CORREDOR NORTE

CAMINO DE LA AMISTAD

TEATRO ABA ■
RIBA SMITH ■

ICON CLUB ▼
TEATRO EN CÍRCULO ■

VÍA BRASIL

BLG ■

AV. 12 NORTE

PARQUE NATURAL METROPOLITANO

CLAYTON

U.S. EMBASSY ■

LA GOTA FRÍA ▼

INSTITUTO GEOGRÁFICO NACIONAL TOMMY GUARDIA ■

EL CANGREJO

AV. JUAN PABLO II

AV. SIMÓN BOLÍVAR

UNIVERSIDAD DE PANAMÁ

LA CRESTA

To Puente Centenario, Miraflores Locks and Gamboa

CURUNDÚ

VÍA ESPAÑA

BELLA VISTA

PANAMA RAILWAY

ALBROOK

AEROPUERTO MARCOS A. GELABERT (ALBROOK AIRPORT) ✈

AV. ASCANIO VILLALAZ

DIABLO

AV. GAILLARD

GRAN TERMINAL DE TRANSPORTES ■

LA EXPOSICIÓN

CARRETERA DIABLO

AV. ROOSEVELT

CALIDONIA

AV. BALBOA

CINTA COSTERA

Panama Canal

BALBOA

ANCÓN

MI PUEBLITO ■

Cerro Ancón ▲

SANTA ANA

SEE "CALIDONIA AND LA EXPOSICIÓN" MAP

AV. MADRID (BALBOA RD)

▌ AVENIDA CENTRAL

AV. DE LOS MÁRTIRES

CHORILLO

CASCO VIEJO

SEE "CASCO VIEJO" MAP

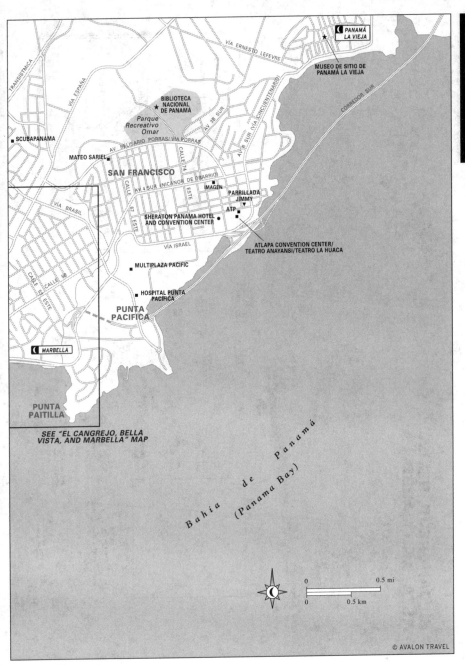

EL CANGREJO, BELLA VISTA, AND MARBELLA

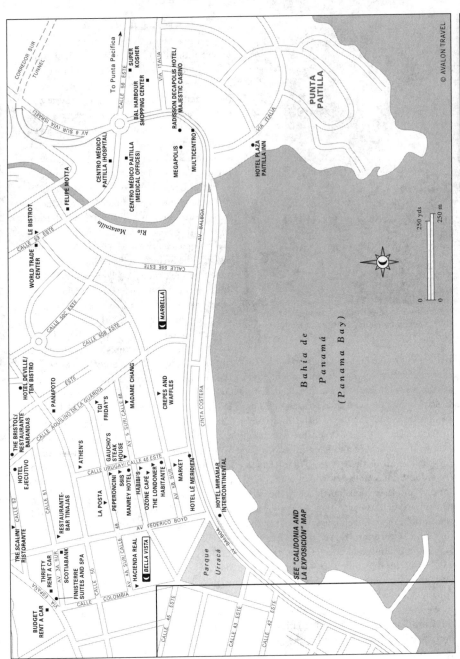

© AVALON TRAVEL

To Punta Pacifica

CORREDOR SUR TUNNEL

AV 6 SUR (VIA ISRAEL)

CALLE 56 ESTE

SUPER KOSHER

BAL HARBOUR SHOPPING CENTER

VIA ITALIA

RADISSON DECAPOLIS HOTEL/ MAJESTIC CASINO

CENTRO MÉDICO PAITILLA (HOSPITAL)

CENTRO MÉDICO PAITILLA (MEDICAL OFFICES)

MEGAPOLIS

MULTICENTRO

VIA ITALIA

PUNTA PAITILLA

HOTEL PLAZA PAITILLA INN

FELIPE MOTTA

Río Matarillo

AV. BALBOA

CALLE LE BISTROT

CALLE 53 ESTE

WORLD TRADE CENTER

CALLE 50E ESTE

CALLE 50C ESTE

CALLE 50B ESTE

🏨 MARBELLA

Bahía de Panamá (Panama Bay)

250 yds
250 m
0
0

HOTEL DEVILLE/ TEN BISTRO

CALLE AQUILINO DE LA GUARDIA

ESTE

PANAFOTO

THE BRISTOL/ RESTAURANTE BARANDAS

HOTEL EJECUTIVO

CALLE 51

ATHEN'S

TGI FRIDAY'S

CALLE 48

MADAME CHANG

AV. 5 SUR/CALLE 48

CREPES AND WAFFLES

CINTA COSTERA

TRE SCALINI RISTORANTE

CALLE 52

LA ESPAÑA

THRIFTY RENT A CAR

SCOTIABANK

AV. 3A SUR

RESTAURANTE-BAR TINAJAS

LA POSTA

GAUCHO'S STEAK HOUSE

S6IS

PEPERONCINI

CALLE URUGUAY/CALLE 48 ESTE

HABIBI'S

MANREY HOTEL

AV. 5B SUR

OZONE CAFÉ

THE LONDONER

HABITANTE

AV. 5B SUR

MARKET

HOTEL LE MERIDIEN

HOTEL MIRAMAR INTERCONTINENTAL

AV. BALBOA

BUDGET RENT A CAR

FINISTERRE SUITES AND SPA

CALLE 50

COLOMBIA

AV. 4A SUR/CALLE

🏨 HACIENDA REAL

🏨 BELLA VISTA

AV. FEDERICO BOYD

Parque Urracá

SEE "CALIDONIA AND LA EXPOSICION" MAP

CALLE 45 ESTE

CALLE 43 ESTE

CALLE 42 ESTE

© WILLIAM FRIAR

the cathedral tower of the original Panama City, sacked by Henry Morgan in 1671

Belt), a multilane highway built on landfill at the edge of Panama Bay. It runs roughly parallel to **Avenida Balboa,** which extends from Casco Viejo to the posh condo towers of Punta Paitilla and Punta Pacífica. The bustling commercial street of **Calle 50** runs between and parallel to Vía España and Avenida Balboa.

North of all of these is the **Transístmica (Avenida Simón Bolívar),** which cuts across the city and then heads north across the isthmus. However, those planning to drive toward the Caribbean are much better off taking the toll road, **Corredor Norte,** which extends across the isthmus and ends close to the city of Colón. Another toll road, **Corredor Sur,** leads from Tocumen International Airport to Panama City, where it meets Avenida Balboa. A project to extend the Corredor Norte to meet the Corredor Sur, near the international airport, may finally be completed by the time you read this.

◖ PANAMÁ LA VIEJA

Known in English as Old Panama, these extensive ruins (8:30 A.M.–6:30 P.M. Tues.–Sun., US$4 adults, US$2 students) are all that's left of the original Panama City. The ruins are on the eastern outskirts of the modern-day city, an easy drive east along Vía Cincuentenario. The Corredor Sur arcs right by it, making for an especially impressive sight at night, when the ruins are illuminated. The site is commonly known as Panamá Viejo, though that's not its proper name.

The city was founded on August 15, 1519, by the notorious conquistador Pedro Arias de Ávila, better known as Pedrarias, and burned down during a battle with the equally notorious Welsh pirate Henry Morgan in 1671. After that disaster, the Spanish moved Panama City to a more defensible site a few kilometers southwest, in the area now known as Casco Viejo.

Since most of Panamá La Vieja was made of wood, only the partial remains of a relatively few stone buildings were left standing. Two of the best-preserved structures are near the main entrance. The first is the **cathedral tower,** which is largely intact. It's one of Panama's national symbols and was built between 1619 and 1626. The cathedral was known officially as La Catedral de Nuestra Señora de la Asunción, a name that was later transferred to its replacement in Casco Viejo. The other well-preserved structure, a bit farther in, is the Casa Alarcón, also known as the **Casa del Obispo** (Bishop's House). Built in the 1640s, it was a three-story building with a wooden top floor. It's the largest and most intact house on the site, but it's still just fragments of walls. There are other ruins worth exploring, but try not to wander too far—the more distant structures border a neighborhood plagued by crime and gangs.

For that same reason, visitors should come only during regular opening hours, even though parts of the site can be explored anytime. It's also the only time visitors can climb to the top of the cathedral tower.

A restoration project is buttressing the crumbling, rough-hewn stone walls with red bricks completely out of keeping with the original architecture. There are signs in English and Spanish that explain the history of some of the ruins.

There are lots of souvenir kiosks in the buildings next to the ruins that sell devil masks, *molas* (handcrafted blouses), Ngöbe-Buglé necklaces, and various other trinkets. There's a cafeteria inside as well. An ATP information booth is on the premises, but you'll have a better chance turning up lost pieces of eight than finding anyone actually working there.

Museo de Sitio de Panamá La Vieja

During the restoration archaeologists found Spanish pots, plates, and utensils dating from the 16th and 17th centuries, as well as a much older cemetery with bones dating from 50 B.C. These and other relics are kept in the Museo de Sitio de Panamá La Vieja (tel. 226-9815 or 224-6031, www.panamaviejo.org, 9 A.M.–5 P.M. Tues.–Sun., US$3 adults, US$0.50 students), about a kilometer before the ruins themselves. It's one of Panama's best museums, a modern, two-story place with attractively presented displays. If you stop here first, be sure to buy a ticket that includes entry to the ruins; it's cheaper than buying them separately.

Start on the top floor and work your way down. Displays include indigenous artifacts from the hundreds of years before the Spanish conquest, when the site was a fishing village. One of the more haunting exhibits is the skeleton of a woman believed to have died at about age 40; she was apparently an important figure, whose grave also included the skulls of nine males. Other displays include items from the early Spanish colonial days, such as shards of cooking pots, coins, lead musket balls, trinkets, and so on. There's also a model of the city as it looked before Morgan's incendiary visit. The ground floor has details on the restoration of the site. There is limited information in English; there are no English-speaking guides.

◖ CASCO VIEJO

Casco Viejo has always had a romantic look, but for decades the romance has been of the tropical-decadence, paint-peeling-from-the-walls variety. Since the 1990s, though, it's been undergoing a tasteful and large-scale restoration that's giving the old buildings new luster and has turned the area into one of the city's most fashionable destinations for a night out. Elegant bars, restaurants, and sidewalk cafés have opened. Hotels and hostels are arriving. Little tourist shops are popping up. Amazingly, this is being done with careful attention to keeping the old charm of the place alive. Unfortunately, the renovation is squeezing out the poorer residents who've lived here for ages.

The "Old Part," also known as Casco Antiguo or the San Felipe district, was the second site of Panama City, and it continued to be the heart of the city during the first decades of the 20th century. UNESCO declared it a World Heritage Site in 1997. It's a city within the city—940 buildings, 747 of which are houses—and one from a different age. It's a great place for a walking tour. You can wander down narrow brick streets, sip an espresso at an outdoor café, visit old churches, and gaze up at wrought-iron balconies spilling over with bright tropical plants. Its buildings feature an unusual blend of architectural styles, most notably rows of ornate Spanish and French colonial houses but also a smattering of art deco and neoclassical buildings.

In some respects Sunday is a good day for exploring Casco Viejo. For one thing, it's the likeliest time to find the churches open and in use. However, though more bars and restaurants are now staying open on Sunday, most aren't, and even some of the museums are closed. Several places are also closed on Monday. Getting a look inside historic buildings and museums is easiest during the week, especially since some are in government offices open only during normal business hours. Churches open and close rather erratically.

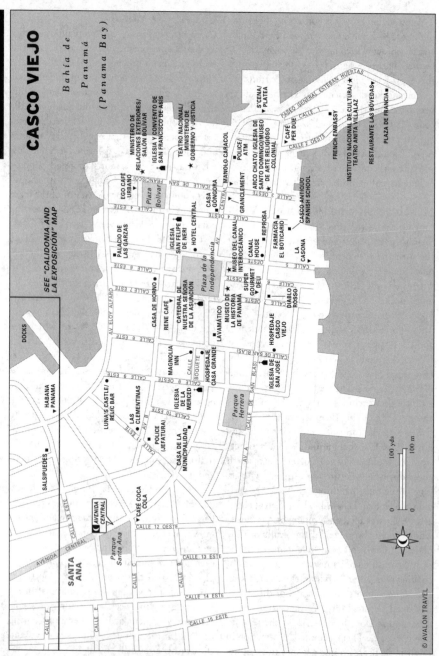

CASCO VIEJO

*Bahía de
Panamá
(Panama Bay)*

SEE "CALIDONIA AND
LA EXPOSICIÓN" MAP

DOCKS

SALSIPUEDES ■

HABANA
▼ PANAMA

SANTA
ANA

*Parque
Santa Ana*

AVENIDA CENTRAL

CAFÉ COCA
COLA ●

AVENIDA
CENTRAL

CALLE 11 ESTE

CALLE 12 OESTE

CALLE 13 ESTE

CALLE 14 ESTE

CALLE 15 ESTE

CALLE F

CALLE E

CALLE D

CALLE C

CALLE B

LUNA'S CASTLE/
RELIC BAR ●

LAS
CLEMENTINAS ●

POLICE
(JEFATURA) ■

CASA DE LA
MUNICIPALIDAD ■

AV. B

CALLE 10 ESTE

IGLESIA
DE LA
MERCED ■

Calle
BOQUETE

MAGNOLIA
INN ●

HOSPEDAJE
CASA GRANDE ●

Calle
BOQUETE

AV. ELOY ALFARO

CALLE 8 ESTE

CASA DE HORNO ●

RENE CAFÉ ●

CATEDRAL DE
NUESTRA SEÑORA
DE LA ASUNCIÓN ■

*Plaza de la
Independencia*

LAVAMATICO ■

MUSEO DE
LA HISTORIA
DE PANAMÁ ★

CALLE 7 ESTE

PALACIO DE
LAS GARZAS ■

CALLE 6 ESTE

CALLE 4 ESTE

IGLESIA
SAN FELIPE
DE NERI ■

HOTEL CENTRAL ●

AV. (CALLE DE SAN FRANCISCO)

EGO CAFÉ
URBANO ●

*Plaza
Bolívar*

MINISTERIO DE
RELACIONES EXTERIORES/
SALÓN BOLÍVAR ■

IGLESIA Y CONVENTO DE
SAN FRANCISCO DE ASÍS ■

(CALLE DE SAN FRANCISCO)

CASA
GÓNGORA ■

CALLE 1 OESTE

MANOLO CARACOL

GRANCLEMENT

AV. CENTRAL

TEATRO NACIONAL/
MINISTERIO DE
GOBIERNO Y JUSTICIA ■

POLICE/
ATM ■

ARCO CHATO/ IGLESIA DE
SANTO DOMINGO/MUSEO
DE ARTE RELIGIOSO
COLONIAL ■

CALLE 3 OESTE

MUSEO DEL CANAL
INTEROCEÁNICO ★

CANAL
HOUSE ●

REPROSA ●

FARMACIA
EL BOTICARIO ●

LA
CASONA ●

CALLE 5 OESTE

CASCO ANTIGUO
SPANISH SCHOOL

SUPER
GOURMET
DELI ●

CALLE 6 OESTE

DIABLO
ROSSO ●

HOSPEDAJE
CASCO
VIEJO ●

CALLE 8 OESTE

IGLESIA DE
SAN JOSÉ ■

AV. (CALLE DE SAN BLAS)

*Parque
Herrera*

CALLE DE SAN BLAS

AV. A

S'CENA/
PLATEA ▼

CAFÉ
PER DUE ●

PASEO GENERAL ESTEBAN HUERTAS

CALLE 1

CALLE 2 OESTE

FRENCH EMBASSY ■

INSTITUTO NACIONAL DE CULTURA/
TEATRO ANITA VILLALAZ ★

RESTAURANTE LAS BÓVEDAS ▼

PLAZA DE FRANCIA ■

0   100 yds

0   100 m

© AVALON TRAVEL

Safety Considerations

Even with the makeover, Casco Viejo is not the safest part of Panama City. Ironically, the area's renaissance seems to be driving crime: With more tourists and affluent residents in Casco Viejo, there's more appeal for criminals.

There's no reason to be overly concerned, but use common sense and try not to stand out. If you're pale and gringo, try to look as though you're a resident foreigner. Don't wander around at night, and be cautious when venturing beyond the major hubs of activity (Plaza Bolívar, Plaza de la Independencia, and Plaza de Francia). Look at the map of Casco Viejo and mentally draw a line from Luna's Castle to Parque Herrera: At night, do not venture west of this area on foot. Also avoid the block of Calle 4 between Avenida Central and Avenida B at night. Parque Herrera is still on the edge of a sketchy area.

© JIM GUY

Panama City's cathedral, on Plaza de la Independencia, is a good place to start touring Casco Viejo.

The neighborhood is well patrolled by the *policía de turismo* (tourism police), who cruise around on bicycles and are easy to spot in their short-pants uniforms. They've been trained specifically to serve tourists, and they're doing an impressive job. It's not unusual for them to greet foreign tourists with a handshake and a smile and offer them an insider's tour of the area or help with whatever they need. Don't hesitate to ask them for help or directions. Their station is next to Manolo Caracol and across the street from the Ministerio de Gobierno y Justicia (Avenida Central between Calle 2 Oeste and Calle 3 Este, tel. 211-2410 or 211-1929). It's open 24 hours, and the officers will safely guide you to your destination night or day.

There's a heavy police presence around the presidential palace, but those police are stern and no-nonsense. Their job is to protect the president, not help tourists.

Plaza de la Independencia

In the center of Casco Viejo is the Plaza de la Independencia, where Panama declared its independence from Colombia in 1903. This area was the center of Panama City until the early 20th century. The buildings represent a real riot of architectural styles, from neo-Renaissance to art deco. Construction began on the cathedral, the **Catedral de Nuestra Señora de la Asunción,** in 1688, but it took more than 100 years to complete. Some of the stones used come from the ruins of Panamá La Vieja. It has an attractive marble altar and a few well-crafted stained-glass windows, though otherwise the interior is rather plain. The towers are inlaid with mother-of-pearl from the Perlas Islands. The bones of a saint, Santo Aurelio, are contained in a reliquary hidden behind a painting of Jesus near the front of the church, on the left as one faces the altar.

Museo del Canal Interoceánico

The Museo del Canal Interoceánico (Avenida

Central between Calle 5 Oeste and Calle 6 Oeste, tel. 211-1995 or 211-1649, www.museodelcanal.com, 9 A.M.–5 P.M. Tues.–Sun, US$2 adults, US$0.75 students) is dedicated to the history of the Panama Canal. The museum is housed in what started life as the Grand Hotel in 1874, then became the headquarters of the French canal-building effort, and later spent the early part of the 20th century as the capital's central post office. It's worth a visit, but be prepared for some frustration if you don't speak Spanish. Everything is Spanish only, which is significant since the exhibits often consist more of text than anything else. However, an audio guide in English, Spanish, and French is available. The displays tell the story of both the French and American efforts to build the canal, and throw in a little bit of pre-Columbian and Spanish colonial history at the beginning. There's some anti-American propaganda, and most of what's written about the canal from the 1960s on should be taken with a big chunk of salt. There's a good coin collection upstairs, as well as a few Panamanian and Canal Zone stamps. There's also a copy of the 1977 Torrijos-Carter Treaties that turned the canal over to Panama. You can tour the whole place in about an hour.

Museo de la Historia de Panamá

The Museo de la Historia de Panamá (Avenida Central between Calle 7 Oeste and Calle 8 Oeste, tel. 228-6231, 8 A.M.–4 P.M. Mon.–Fri., US$1 general admission, US$0.25 children) is a small museum containing artifacts from Panama's history from the colonial period to the modern era. It's in the Palacio Municipal, a neoclassical building from 1910 that is now home to government offices. At first glance it seems like just another one of Panama's woefully underfunded museums housing a few obscure bits of bric-a-brac. But anyone with some knowledge of Panama's history—which is essential, since the Spanish-only displays are

poorly explained—will find some of the displays fascinating.

Among these are a crudely stitched Panama flag, said to have been made by María Ossa de Amador in 1903. She was the wife of Manuel Amador Guerrero, a leader of the revolutionaries who conspired with the Americans to wrest independence from Colombia. The flag was hastily designed by the Amadors' son, and the women in the family sewed several of them for the rebels; the sewing machine they used is included in the display. If the revolution had failed, this quaint sewing circle might have meant death by hanging for all of them. Instead, Manuel Amador became the first president of Panama.

On a desk by the far wall is the handwritten draft of a telegram the revolutionaries sent to the superintendent of the Panama Railroad in Colón, pleading with him not to allow Colombian troops from the steamship *Cartagena* to cross the isthmus and put down the revolution. This was one of the tensest moments in the birth of Panama. In the end, they didn't cross over, and the revolution was nearly bloodless. The telegram is dated November 3, 1903, the day Panama became independent, and those who sent it are now considered Panama's founding fathers.

Other displays include a stirrup found on the storied Camino de Cruces, a plan for the fortifications built at Portobelo in 1597, 17th-century maps of the "new" Panama City at Casco Viejo (note the walls that originally ringed the city, now all but gone), and the sword of Victoriano Lorenzo, a revered hero of the War of a Thousand Days.

Western Fringes of Casco Viejo

The church with the crumbling brown facade and whitewashed sides near the corner of Avenida Central and Calle 9 Oeste is **Iglesia de la Merced,** which was built in the 17th century from rubble salvaged from the ruins of

Panamá La Vieja. It's worth a quick stop for a look at its wooden altars and pretty tile floor. The neoclassical building next to it, the **Casa de la Municipalidad,** is a former mansion now used by the city government.

The little park, **Parque Herrera,** was dedicated in 1976. The statue of the man on horseback is General Tomás Herrera, an early hero of Panama's complex independence movements. Some of the historic buildings ringing the park are undergoing major renovation, with at least three hotels planned for the area.

Church of the Golden Altar

The massive golden altar *(altar de oro)* is a prime tourist attraction at **Iglesia de San José** (Avenida A between Calle 8 and Calle 9, 7 A.M.–noon and 2–8 P.M. Mon.–Sat., 5 A.M.–noon and 5–8 P.M. Sun.). Legend has it that the altar was saved from the rapacious Welsh pirate Henry Morgan during the sacking of the original

© WILLIAM FRIAR

Church of the Golden Altar, Panama City

Panama City when a quick-thinking priest ordered it painted black, hiding its true value.

The Flat Arch

The original **Iglesia de Santo Domingo** (Avenida A and Calle 3 Oeste) was built in the 17th century, but it burned twice and was not rebuilt after the fire of 1756. It remains famous for one thing that survived, seemingly miraculously: the nearly flat arch (Arco Chato). Since it was built without a keystone and had almost no curve to it, it should have been a very precarious structure, yet it remained intact even as everything around it fell into ruins. One of the reasons a transoceanic canal was built in Panama was that engineers concluded from the intact arch that Panama was not subject to the kinds of devastating earthquakes that afflict its Central American neighbors.

On the evening of November 7, 2003, just four days after Panama celebrated its first centennial as a country, the arch finally collapsed into rubble. It has since been rebuilt, but its main appeal, its gravity-defying properties through the centuries, can never be restored. The church itself is undergoing a slow restoration.

Plaza de Francia

The Plaza de Francia (French Plaza) has seen a great deal of history and was among the first parts of Casco Viejo to be renovated, back in 1982.

The obelisk and the marble plaques along the wall commemorate the failed French effort to build a sea-level canal in Panama. The area housed a fort until the beginning of the 20th century, and the *bóvedas* (vaults) in the seawall were used through the years as storehouses, barracks, offices, and jails. You'll still hear gruesome stories about dungeons in the seawall, where prisoners were left at low tide to drown when the tide rose. Whether this actually happened is still a subject of lively debate among amateur historians. True or not, what you will find there now is one of Panama's more colorful restaurants, Restaurante Las Bóvedas. Also in the plaza are the French Embassy, the headquarters of the **Instituto Nacional de Cultura** (INAC, the National Institute of Culture) in what had been Panama's supreme court building, and a small theater, **Teatro Anita Villalaz.** Tourists are not allowed into the grand old building that houses INAC, but it's worth peeking into from the top of the steps or the lobby, if you can get that far. Note the colorful, if not particularly accomplished, mural depicting idealized versions of Panama's history. (The building was used as a set for the 2008 James Bond film *Quantum of Solace,* as were the ruins of the old Union Club.) Next to the restaurant is an **art gallery** (tel. 211-4034, 9:30 A.M.–5:30 P.M. Tues.–Sat.) run by INAC that displays works by Panamanian and other Latin American artists.

Walk up the staircase that leads to the top of the vaults. This is part of the old seawall that protected the city from the Pacific Ocean's dramatic tides. There's a good view of the Panama City skyline, the Bridge of the Americas, and the Bay of Panama, and the breeze is great on a hot day. The walkway, **Paseo General Esteban Huertas,** is shaded in part by a bougainvillea-covered trellis and is a popular spot with smooching lovers. Along the walkway leading down to Avenida Central, notice the building on the waterfront to the right. For years this has been a ruin, though there have long been plans to turn it into a hotel. This was once the officers' club of the Panamanian Defense Forces; it was largely destroyed during the 1989 U.S. invasion. Before that, it was the home of the Union Club, a hangout for Panama's oligarchy that's now on Punta Paitilla.

Casa Góngora

Built in 1756, the stone house of Casa Góngora (corner of Avenida Central and Calle 4, tel. 212-0338, 8 A.M.–4 P.M. Mon.–Fri., free) is the oldest house in Casco Viejo and one of the oldest in Panama. It was originally the home of a Spanish pearl merchant. It then became a church and has now been turned into a small, bare-bones museum. It's had a rough history—it has been through three fires and the current wooden roof is new. A 20th-century restoration attempt was botched, causing more damage. There isn't much here, but the staff can give free tours (in Spanish) and there have been noises about making it more of a real museum in the future. There's an interesting, comprehensive book on the history of the house and neighborhood (again, in Spanish) that visitors are welcome to thumb through, containing rare maps, photos, and illustrations. Ask for it at the office. The museum hosts jazz and folkloric concerts and other cultural events in the tiny main hall on some Friday and Saturday nights, and occasionally hosts art shows.

Iglesia San Felipe de Neri (corner of Avenida B and Calle 4) dates from 1688 and, though it has also been damaged by fires, is one of the oldest standing structures from the Spanish colonial days. It was renovated in 2003, but is seemingly never open to the public.

The National Theater

The intimate Teatro Nacional (National Theater, between Calle 2 and Calle 3 on Avenida B, 9:30 A.M.–5:30 P.M. Mon.–Fri.) holds classical concerts and other posh events. It was built in 1908 on the site of an 18th-century monastery. It's housed in the same building as the **Ministerio de Gobierno y Justicia** (Ministry of Government and Justice), which has its entrance on Avenida Central.

Inaugurated on October 1, 1908, the neo-baroque theater is worth a brief visit between concerts to get a glimpse of its old-world elegance. The public can explore it during the week but not on weekends. The first performance here was a production of the opera *Aida,* and for about 20 years the theater was a glamorous destination for the city's elite. Note the bust of the ballerina Margot Fonteyn in the lobby; she married a Panamanian politician in 1955 and lived out the last part of her life in Panama.

The ceiling is covered with faded but still colorful frescoes of cavorting naked ladies, painted by Roberto Lewis, a well-known Panamanian artist. Leaks in the roof destroyed about a quarter of these frescoes, and the roof partially collapsed. The roof was restored and the theater reopened in 2004. Be sure to walk upstairs to take a look at the opulent reception rooms.

Plaza Bolívar

Plaza Bolívar (on Avenida B between Calle 3 and Calle 4) has been undergoing a charming restoration. It's especially pleasant to hang out on the plaza in the evening, when tables are set up under the stars. It's a good rest stop for a drink or a bite. A good café to check out is Restaurante Casablanca.

The plaza was named for Simón Bolívar, a legendary figure who is considered the father of Latin America's independence from Spain. In 1826 Bolívar called a congress here to discuss forming a union of Latin American states. Bolívar himself did not attend and the congress didn't succeed, but the park and the statue of Bolívar commemorate the effort.

The congress itself was held in a small, two-story building that has been preserved as a museum, now known as the **Salón Bolívar** (Plaza Bolívar, tel. 228-9594, 9 A.M.–4 P.M. Tues.–Sat., 1–5 P.M. Sun., US$1 adults, US$0.25 students).

While the museum is designed attractively, there's not much in it. The room upstairs contains the text of the protocols of different congresses called during the independence movement. There's also a replica of Bolívar's jewel-encrusted sword, a gift from Venezuela (the original is now back in Venezuela). The actual room where the congress took place is on the ground floor.

The little museum is entirely enclosed by glass to protect it and is actually in the courtyard of another building, the massive **Palacio Bolívar,** which was built on the site of a Franciscan convent that dates from the 18th century. The building that houses the Salón Bolívar was originally the *sala capitula* (chapter house) of that convent, and is the only part of it that is still intact. The *palacio* dates from the 1920s and was a school for many years. Now it's home to the Ministerio de Relaciones Exteriores (Foreign Ministry). During regular business hours (about 8 A.M.–3 P.M. Mon.–Fri., 9 A.M.–1 P.M. Sat.), it's possible, and well worthwhile, to explore the huge inner courtyard, which has been outfitted with a clear roof that's out of keeping with the architecture, but protects it from the elements. The courtyard is open to the surf in the back, where part of the original foundation can be seen. Be sure to notice the beautiful tilework and the posh chandelier at the entrance.

Next door but still on the plaza is a church and former monastery, **Iglesia y Convento de San Francisco de Asís.** The church dates from the early days of Casco Viejo, but was burned during two 18th-century fires, then restored in 1761 and again in 1998. It's an attractive confection on the outside, particularly its soaring tower, which is partly open-sided. It resembles a gothic wedding cake. It is not currently open to the public.

The Presidential Palace

The presidential palace, **El Palacio de las Garzas** (Palace of the Herons), is on the left at Calle 5 Este, overlooking Panama Bay. It's an attractive place that houses the presidential office and residence. Visitors are not permitted, and the palace and the neighboring streets are surrounded by guards. Everyone walking past the front of the palace must now go through a metal detector; they're set up at either end of the street. Guards may ask for your passport, but more likely they will just wave you through after the cursory search. Be polite and deferential—they should let you walk by the palace. As

© JIM GUY

The presidential palace, El Palacio de las Garzas, is named for the herons wandering its courtyard.

you pass, sneak a peek at the courtyard through the palace's front door, visible from the street, and try to spot the herons around the fountain.

Vicinity of Casco Viejo

A pedestrian path with great views links Casco Viejo to the city markets, running through the dockyard area known as known as the **Terraplén.** This is one of the more colorful and lively parts of the city. The path is part of the Cinta Costera along the Bay of Panama. Pedestrians, cyclists, and runners can enjoy great views of the bay, skyline, and fishing fleet while exploring the waterfront area. Four wide, busy lanes of the Cinta Costera separate the path from the densely packed and rather squalid streets of the Santa Ana and Santa Fé districts, making the path appealing even to the more safety-conscious.

For hundreds of years, small fishing boats have off-loaded their cargo around the Terraplén. These days fish is sold through the relatively clean, modern fish market, the two-story **Mercado de Mariscos** (5 A.M.–5 P.M. daily), on the waterfront just off the Cinta Costera on the way to Casco Viejo, right before the Mercado Público. This is an eternally popular place to sample ceviche made from an amazing array of seafood, sold at stalls around the market. There's usually a line at Ceviches #2 (4:30 A.M.–5 P.M. daily), though whether it's because the ceviche is truly better or because it's simply closer to the entrance and open later than the other stalls is something I'll leave to true ceviche connoisseurs. The large jars of pickled fish don't make for an appetizing scene, but rest assured that ceviche is "cooked" in a pretty intense bath of onions, limes, and chili peppers. Prices for a Styrofoam cup of fishy goodness range from US$1.25 for corvina up to US$3.50 for *langostinos*. You shouldn't leave Panama without at least trying some ceviche, whether here or somewhere a bit fancier.

Other stands, some with seating areas, are next to the main market building closer to the dock, but they tend to be smellier than the market. Those with sensitive noses will want to visit the area early in the morning, before the sun ripens the atmosphere.

Meat and produce are sold at the nearby **Mercado Público** (public market) on Avenida B, just off Avenida Eloy Alfaro near the Chinese gate of the Barrio Chino. The market is plenty colorful and worth a visit. It's gated and has a guard at the entrance.

The meat section, though cleaner, is still not fully air-conditioned, and the humid, cloying stench of blood in the Panama heat may convert some to vegetarianism. The *abarrotería* (grocer's section) is less overwhelming and more interesting. Shelves are stacked with all kinds of homemade *chichas* (fruit juices), hot sauce, and honey, as well as spices, freshly ground coconut, duck eggs, and so on. The produce section is surprisingly small.

© WILLIAM FRIAR

Panama City's Mercado de Mariscos (fish market) is just outside Casco Viejo.

There's a **food hall** (4 A.M.–3 or 4 P.M. daily) in the middle of the market. The perimeter is ringed with *fondas* (basic restaurants) each marked with the proprietor's name. A heaping plateful costs a buck or two.

Lottery vendors set up their boards along the walls by the entrance, and across the gated parking lot is a line of shops selling goods similar to and no doubt intended to replace those on the Terraplén. These include hammocks, army-surplus and Wellington boots, machetes, camping gear, and souvenirs such as Ecuadorian-style Panama hats. Each store keeps different hours, but most are open 8 A.M.–4 P.M. Monday–Saturday, and some are open Sunday mornings.

The market is staffed with friendly, uniformed attendants who can explain what's going on, especially if you speak a bit of Spanish. There's a Banco Nacional de Panamá ATM near the entrance.

Up Calle 13 is the crowded shopping area of Salsipuedes (a contraction of "get out if you can"). The area is crammed with little stalls selling clothes, lottery tickets, and bric-a-brac. Just north of this street is a small **Chinatown,** called Barrio Chino in Spanish. Most of the Chinese character of the place has been lost through the years; the ornate archway over the street is one of the few remaining points of interest.

Practicalities

There is one ATM in Casco Viejo, next to the tourism police station on Avenida Central near Calle 2. It's best to come to Casco Viejo with sufficient cash.

Farmacia El Boticario (Avenida A and Calle 4 Oeste, tel. 202-6981, 8:30 A.M.–7 P.M. Mon.–Fri., 9 A.M.–6 P.M. Sat.) is Casco Viejo's only pharmacy.

Getting Around

A good way to explore the area is to come with a knowledgeable guide or taxi driver who can drop you in different areas to explore on foot.

You'll probably save time this way, as the streets are confusing and it's easy to get lost. Do major exploring only during the daytime; those who come at night should taxi in and out to specific destinations. Restaurant and bar owners can call a cab for the trip back.

Even locals get lost here. Watch out for narrow one-way streets and blind intersections. Street parking is hard to find in the day and on weekend nights. There's a paid lot with an attendant on the side of the Teatro Nacional that faces Panama Bay. It's open 24 hours a day.

◖ AVENIDA CENTRAL

The west end of Avenida Central, from Plaza Cinco de Mayo to Parque Santa Ana, is a busy walking street lined with shops. Except for the handicraft stalls on Plaza Cinco de Mayo, the shops won't interest foreign visitors much, as they deal mainly in cheap clothes and jewelry, electronics, and photo-development services.

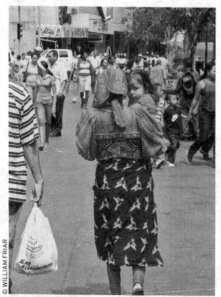

People-watching on Avenida Central is always fun.

© WILLIAM FRIAR

But the people-watching on the street is fun. The area provides a real sense of daily life in an older, humbler section of Panama City. The walk along Avenida Central goes through the heart of the Santa Ana district to the outskirts of San Felipe/Casco Viejo.

To take a walking tour, start at the highly congested **Plaza Cinco de Mayo.** Note the massive building. It was inaugurated in 1912 as the terminus of the Panama Railroad and had an on-again, off-again life as Panama's anthropology museum until the museum was finally moved to the Curundu area. To the east is the rather unattractive Palacio Legislativo, which houses the Asamblea Legislativa (Panama's national legislature). A new home for the Asamblea is being built next to the current one.

Now head down Central. The area is a photographer's dream. On a typical stroll one can spot Guna women going about their business in traditional clothing, juice vendors squeezing tropical fruit or crushing sugarcane in hand-cranked presses (try some!), and hawkers luring customers into stores by clapping their hands. The crumbling old buildings reflect a real mishmash of architectural styles, including neoclassical, neo-baroque, and art deco. Some are quite striking. When you come to the major intersection, note the art deco building on the corner, the one housing the **Banco Nacional de Panamá.** Also check out the facade of the old building right next to it on the walking street. Its tiles are covered with pretty murals depicting the history of Panama from the conquest to the building of the Panama Canal.

Be sure to walk all the way to **Parque Santa Ana.** The twice weekly lottery drawings were held here for many years, and it's like a place from another, very Spanish era. It's very pleasant to get here before 8 A.M., when it's still cool under the ancient shade trees, and eavesdrop on the old men sitting around reading newspapers or arguing politics while getting a spectacularly vigorous shoeshine.

Slip into the maze of side streets if you want to do some more exploring. A good spot is the major intersection with Calle I; head uphill to Calle Estudiante, where you'll find Pizzeria Napoli and the **Instituto Nacional.** The latter was built in 1911 and has a rather heroic, neoclassical yellow facade. Students here are known for frequent participation in demonstrations, most notably the Flag Riots of 1964, which had as its main battleground the nearby Avenida de los Mártires (Martyrs' Avenue, which until the riots was called Fourth of July Avenue).

MUSEUMS

You'd never get a sense of the rich history of Panama if all you had to go on were the museums of its capital city. They are neglected and underfunded, and what few exhibits they contain are generally poorly presented and contain almost no explanation of their significance.

Panama has paid more attention to its cultural treasures in recent years. The city's anthropology museum, Museo Antropológico Reina Torres de Araúz, has a new home. The modern art museum, Museo de Arte Contemporáneo, once an art gallery more than anything else, has emerged as a respectable repository of Panama's better-known and emerging contemporary artists. And one day the ambitious new Museum of Biodiversity, designed by Frank O. Gehry, may actually be completed. The latest estimate is that it will finally open in the first half of 2013.

El Museo Antropológico Reina Torres de Araúz

Panama's anthropology museum (Avenida Juan Pablo II and Calle Curundu, tel. 501-4731, 9 A.M.–4 P.M. Tues.–Sun., US$2,50 adults, US$1 students) has a troubled history, including a dramatic robbery in 2003 and funding shortages that forced it into a moribund existence for years. As of 2006, the Museo Antropológico Reina Torres de Araúz (sometimes known by

the acronym MARTA) is a cement monolith from the exposed-duct school of modern design. The museum's permanent collection is comprised of 15,000 pieces.

Most intriguing are the pieces from the **Barriles culture,** believed to be Panama's earliest major civilization. The figures on display came from a ceremonial center that dates from around 60 B.C. and consist of about a dozen and a half carvings of stone figures and fragments.

The museum's **gold collection** includes figures of animals, armor plates, ceramics, jewelry, breastplates, a crown, and other items made by ancient indigenous peoples and recovered from archaeological sites around the country. Most of these items are *huacas,* ceremonial treasures buried with prominent indigenous people. The oldest item, a copper and gold nose ring found on Cerro Juan Díaz on the Azuero Peninsula, dates from 180 B.C.

El Museo de Arte Contemporáneo

The Contemporary Art Museum (Avenida San Blas, in Ancón, next to the old Ancón Elementary School, tel. 262-3380 or 262-8012, www.macpanama.org, 9 A.M.–5 P.M. Tues.–Sun., US$5 adult, US$3 students, US$2 children) is one of Panama's best and best-maintained museums. It more resembles an art gallery than a museum (many of the pieces are for sale). But it does present a reasonable cross section of Panama's best-known and emerging modern artists as well as some work from other parts of Latin America. It sometimes presents film series.

El Museo de Ciencias Naturales

Panama City's Natural Sciences Museum (Avenida Cuba and Calle 29 Este, tel. 225-0645, 9 A.M.–3:30 P.M. Tues.–Sat., US$1 adults, US$0.25 students) is a modest place consisting of four rooms mainly containing some stuffed and mounted animals and geological specimens. It's worth a quick visit, at least if you're in the neighborhood, to get a

CALIDONIA AND LA EXPOSICIÓN

BELLA VISTA

SEE "EL CANGREJO, BELLA VISTA, AND MARBELLA" MAP

RESTAURANTE MASALA ▼
RESIDENCIAL LOS ARCOS ●

HOTEL CALIFORNIA ●

HOTEL COSTA INN ■

HOSPITAL NACIONAL ■

HOTEL ÁVILA ●
PENSIÓN LAS TORRES ●

EURO HOTEL ●

MAMALLENA ■

BANCO NACIONAL DE PANAMA ■
BBVA ■

HOTEL ANDINO ●
FONDA5 ▼
WESTERN UNION ■

CENTRAL POST OFFICE/ STAMP MUSEUM ■

CASA MUSEO BANCO NACIONAL ★
HOTEL CENTROAMERICANO ●

FARMACIA MILANI ■
HOTEL ROMA PLAZA ■

Parque Belisario Porras

RESTAURANTE BOULEVARD BALBOA ▼

HOTEL ARENTEIRO ■

National Lottery Plaza
RESTAURANTE RINCÓN TABLEÑO ▼

SEE DETAIL

BALBOA MONUMENT ★

CINTA COSTERA

LA EXPOSICIÓN

AV CHILE
AV 3A SUR
AV 4A SUR
AV JUSTO AROSEMENA (AV 3 SUR)
AV CUBA (AV 2A SUR)
AV PERÚ (AV 1 SUR)
AV CENTRAL
AV 1 NORTE
AV 2A NORTE
AV SIMÓN BOLÍVAR
AV 3A NORTE
AV 4A NORTE
VÍA ESPAÑA
AV 1A NOBLE
AV 2A NOBLE
AV BALBOA
AV ECUADOR

CALLE 44 ESTE
CALLE 43 ESTE (CALLE FELIPE MOTTA C)
CALLE 42 ESTE
CALLE 41 ESTE
CALLE 40 ESTE
CALLE 39 ESTE
CALLE 38 ESTE
CALLE 37 ESTE
CALLE 36 ESTE
CALLE 35 ESTE
CALLE 34 ESTE
CALLE 33 ESTE
CALLE 32 ESTE
CALLE 31 ESTE
CALLE 30 ESTE
CALLE 29 ESTE
CALLE 38 OESTE
CALLE 36 OESTE
CALLE 26

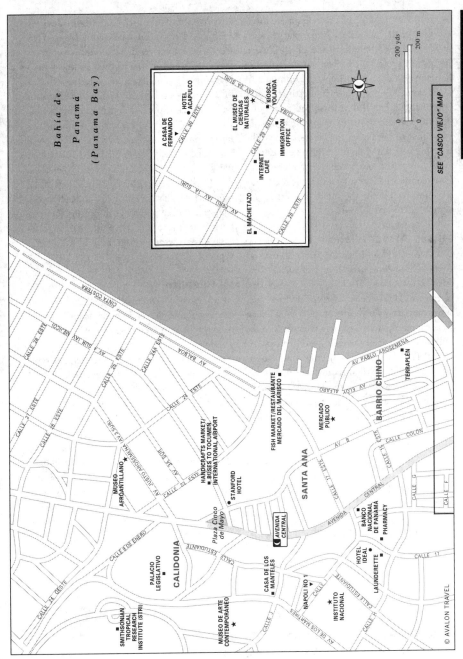

Bahía de Panamá (Panama Bay)

SEE "CASCO VIEJO" MAP

200 yds
200 m

A CASA DE FERNANDO
HOTEL ACAPULCO
EL MUSEO DE CIENCIAS NATURALES
KIOSCA YOLANDA
INTERNET CAFE
IMMIGRATION OFFICE
EL MACHETAZO
CALLE 36 ESTE
AV 2A SUR
AV 1A SUR
AV PERÚ
AV CUBA
CALLE 29 ESTE
CALLE 28 ESTE

CINTA COSTERA
AV BALBOA
CALLE 26 ESTE
AV SUR (AV MÉXICO)
CALLE 25 ESTE
CALLE 24A ESTE
CALLE 24 ESTE
CALLE 23 ESTE
CALLE 22 ESTE
CALLE 21 ESTE
AV JUSTO AROSEMENA
AV 3A SUR

MUSEO AFROANTILLANO

HANDICRAFTS MARKET/
BUSES TO TOCUMEN
INTERNATIONAL AIRPORT

STANFORD HOTEL

FISH MARKET/RESTAURANTE
MERCADO DEL MARISCO

MERCADO PÚBLICO

AV PABLO AROSEMENA
AV ELOY ALFARO
BARRIO CHINO
TERRAPLÉN

SANTA ANA
AV B
CALLE 17 ESTE
CALLE 15 ESTE
CALLE COLÓN
CALLE 13 ESTE
CALLE G
CALLE F

Plaza Cinco de Mayo
AVENIDA CENTRAL
AVENIDA CENTRAL

CALLE ESTUDIANTE
CALLE 8 DE ENERO
CALLE 24 OESTE

PALACIO LEGISLATIVO
CALIDONIA

CASA DE LOS MANTELES
NAPOLI NO 1
INSTITUTO NACIONAL

BANCO NACIONAL DE PANAMÁ
PHARMACY
HOTEL IDEAL
LAUNDERETTE
CALLE 17

SMITHSONIAN TROPICAL RESEARCH INSTITUTE (STRI)

MUSEO DE ARTE CONTEMPORÁNEO

CALLE 3
AV DE LOS MÁRTIRES
CALLE ESTUDIANTE
CALLE H

© AVALON TRAVEL

close-up look at some of Panama's more interesting animals, including a jaguar, harpy eagle, howler and spider monkeys, and a huge iguana. It's also fun to get a close look at the amazing hanging nest of an oropendola (a common bird in Panama). But the most interesting display is probably a handful of fossilized bones of a 50,000-year-old sloth (*Eremotherium rusconi*), estimated to have been four meters long. The remains were found on the Azuero Peninsula in 1991. Only the geology and paleontology room is air-conditioned, ensuring that the rocks stay nice and cool while the snake exhibit, for instance, is hot and humid.

Museo Afroantillano

The Afro-Antillean Museum (Calle 24 Este off Avenida Justo Arosemena/Avenida 3 Sur, tel. 262-5348, 262-1668, or 501-4130, 8:30 A.M.–3:30 P.M. Tues.–Sat., US$1 adults, US$0.25 children) preserves the memory of the thousands of West Indian workers, mostly from Barbados, who supplied the bulk of the labor for the building of the Panama Canal. These workers, who had the most dangerous and grueling jobs during canal construction, are often little more than a footnote in accounts of the building of the canal. Their descendants today make up a significant part of the population of the country.

The museum is tiny and worth a quick visit. However, be aware that its location is on a dicey street. If you do come, take a taxi and have the driver wait outside the entrance for you; you can see everything the museum has to offer in about a half hour.

The museum is installed in an old wooden house stocked with canal construction-era furnishings and photos meant to give a sense of what life might have been like for these workers, though it is certainly much more comfortable than the shacks many of the workers had to make do with in those days.

Casa Museo Banco Nacional

This elegant little house (Calle 34 Este and Avenida Cuba, tel. 225-0640, 8 A.M.–12:30 P.M. and 1:30–4:30 P.M. Mon.–Fri., free), the former residence of a doctor, dates from 1925 and is now owned by the Banco Nacional de Panamá. It has rotating exhibits of arts and crafts for sale, though those I've seen have been quite poor. It does have a tiny but interesting collection of Panamanian commemorative coins, including a silver 20 balboa piece about the size of a fist, a small gold 100 balboa piece, and a tiny 2.5 centavo piece. Other coins date from 1904, some of the earliest days of the republic. It's worth visiting just to see how the well-heeled lived in early-20th-century Panama City. The house is lovely, with marble staircases, ornate wrought-iron fixtures, and several types of tile floors.

Mi Pueblito

Also known as Los Pueblitos, Mi Pueblito (off the westbound side of Avenida de los Mártires near the base of Cerro Ancón, 9 A.M.–9 P.M. Tues.–Sun., US$1), literally, "my little town," is a charming, if idealized, re-creation of a typical Panamanian town on the Azuero Peninsula, Panama's heartland. The architecture is Spanish colonial, which is especially notable in the red-tile roofs and whitewashed walls, the mission-style church, and the central plaza and fountain. The builders have included lots of small, loving touches, from the lesson plan on the blackboard of the schoolhouse to the telegraph office that looks as though the operator has just left for a siesta. There's even a rustic outhouse behind the buildings. Nearby is a small *pollera* (traditional embroidered dress) museum.

The Mi Pueblito complex has been expanded to recognize the traditional dwellings of some of the other peoples of Panama. These are directly across the street from the Spanish colonial village. The first site honors the West Indian immigrants who provided most of the labor force for the building of the Panama Canal. The brightly painted two-story wooden buildings are an extremely fanciful take on what the laborers' accommodations were really like. A walk through a little forest takes you to more accurate re-creations of the way three indigenous peoples—the Guna, Emberá-Wounaan, and Ngöbe-Buglé—lived, and in many cases still do.

CHURCHES AND SHRINES

Panama City's cathedral and most of its historically significant Catholic churches are in Casco Viejo. A couple of other prominent churches are scattered around modern Panama City.

Despite being an overwhelmingly Catholic country, Panama has a live-and-let-live attitude toward the many minority faiths brought by immigrants from around the world or still practiced by its indigenous peoples. The Baha'i House of Worship and Hindu Temple are especially prominent and draw curious visitors.

Santuario Nacional del Corazón de María

The National Sanctuary (on Calle Manuel María Icaza near Calle 53 Este, tel. 263-9833) was dedicated on August 22, 1949. It's a relatively simple church with pretty stained-glass windows and a modern interior, but atmosphere is provided by a riot of peacocks. Other domesticated birds wander around a fountain near the crypts. The crypts themselves are a bit creepy but worth a look; they're out the side entrance to the right as one faces the altar. Masses are held several times daily. The church's facade is attractive at night, when it's illuminated and provides a striking contrast to the glittery modern buildings that surround it. It's not worth making a special trip for, but given its central location it might be convenient to pop in briefly.

Iglesia del Carmen

The Iglesia del Carmen (at Vía España and Avenida Federico Boyd, across the street from the Hotel El Panamá, tel. 223-0360) is the most conspicuous church in modern Panama City. A cream-colored, neogothic confection with tall twin towers, built in 1947, it's a Panamanian landmark and worth a quick peek for those in the neighborhood.

Baha'i House of Worship

Panama's Baha'i House of Worship (tel. 231-1191, 9 A.M.–6 P.M. daily, free), the only one in Latin America and one of only seven in the world, is an impressive structure that resembles an egg, with huge, open arched entrances that let the breezes blow through but keep the rain out. The temple interior is entirely unadorned. It has an unusual panoramic view of the city, the Pacific Ocean, and the surrounding countryside.

The temple is northeast of Panama City, near Las Cumbres. To get there, head east and then north on the Transístmica (Avenida Simón Bolívar) from downtown Panama City. After about 15 kilometers there's a big intersection with Tumba Muerto (Avenida Ricardo J. Alfaro). Continue north on the Transístmica. About four kilometers past the intersection there should be a Bacardi rum factory on the left. Turn left here and head uphill for 1.5 kilometers to the temple.

Hindu Temple

The Hindu Temple (7:30 A.M.–noon and 4–8 P.M. daily, free) is less impressive than the Baha'i House of Worship, but easier to get to. It's a rather modern, spartan place that looks more imposing from a distance than it does close up. The most interesting thing about it, at least when worshippers are around, is the sense it gives you of how extensive and well-established Panama's South Asian community is.

The temple is off Tumba Muerto (Avenida Ricardo J. Alfaro). Head east a couple of kilometers past Calle de la Amistad (Friendship Highway) and make a left turn. Visitors must sign in at the gate. The temple is a short drive uphill.

PARKS

Other than Parque Natural Metropolitano, Panama City isn't blessed with much in the way of impressive or well-tended open spaces. Even little plazas are hard to find outside of Casco Viejo and the walking section of Avenida Central—they're one bit of the city's Spanish heritage that, sadly, is slipping away.

The Cinta Costera and Avenida Balboa

Panama City's newest and grandest avenue also offers some of its most dramatic views. Built on landfill, the Cinta Costera (coastal belt) sweeps along the edge of Panama Bay from Casco Viejo to ritzy Punta Paitilla and Punta Pacífica. It offers good views of the modern skyline of Panama City, Panama Bay, and the old seawall, churches, and historic buildings of Casco Viejo. The original concept for the promenade called for huge expanses of parkland and lovely facilities to attract families and tourists down to the sea edge.

The reality is far more pedestrian and far less pedestrian-friendly. While there are some playing fields and such, most of the common spaces are simply large fields of grass that turn brown in the dry season. Getting to these spaces isn't that easy, either. The few pedestrian overpasses are spaced widely apart.

These caveats aside, it's still a pleasant place for a morning or evening stroll or jog. Try to time your visit to coincide with high tide, when the view is nicer and the smell less potent. (Panama City has always dumped its untreated sewage into the bay, though an extensive and massively expensive new sewage treatment system is finally in the works after years of delay.) The Cinta Costera has recently been extended from the seafood market to the outskirts of Casco Viejo, a particularly scenic and colorful stretch of waterfront. The pedestrian path is wide and pleasant here.

The Cinta Costera runs parallel to Avenida Balboa, which for decades was the city's bayside promenade, lined with high-rises that hugged the edge of the sea. But with the advent of the Cinta Costera, Avenida Balboa is no longer on the waterfront, to the consternation, no doubt, of those who own property along it. About midway along Avenida Balboa is a little park that contains an enormous statue of Balboa "discovering" the Pacific, though these days he's so far from the water he looks like he's trying to hail a cab.

Parque Belisario Porras

Though it's not worth a special trip, those staying in Calidonia who need a little open space can visit Parque Belisario Porras, between Calle 33 Este and Calle 34 Este and Avenida Perú and Avenida Cuba. It's an austere, formal plaza with a monument to Porras, thrice president of Panama and one of its founding fathers, looking rather dapper and jaunty. The plaza is surrounded by attractive old buildings, housing various government offices and the Spanish embassy. A line of kiosks serves greasy fast food to office workers on Avenida Perú near Calle 35, next to the Ministerio de Economía y Finanzas.

Parque Urracá

This is just a small city park off Avenida Balboa and Avenida Federico Boyd, but it's often filled with people, and it's fun to wander from here north and west through the hilly backstreets of Bella Vista. This is the edge of the *area bancaria* (banking area), so-called because of its many banks, often built into old houses. They're fast disappearing thanks to the construction boom, but it's still possible to walk down tree-lined streets and see beautiful Spanish colonial mansions with red-tiled roofs and stone walls.

◖ Parque Natural Metropolitano

Amazingly enough, you don't even have to leave the limits of Panama City to find a tropical forest. This 232-hectare park (entrance on Avenida Juan Pablo II in the Curundu district, www.parquemetropolitano.org, tel. 232-6713 or 232-5516, trails open 5 A.M.–6 P.M. daily, free, donations encouraged) is just minutes from downtown, and it's a lovely little place with a surprising amount of wildlife given its location and size.

Most of the park is dry lowland Pacific forest, now rare in Central America because of deforestation, and it's home to about 45 species of mammals, 36 of reptiles, and 14 of amphibians. These include such colorful creatures as two- and three-toed sloths, *monos tití* (Geoffroy's tamarin), and boa constrictors. As usual, however, don't be surprised if you see only birds during a hike. The park has recorded 227 bird species.

Having an urban center this close to a nature park has its drawbacks: A highway, Corredor Norte, cuts right through the park's eastern edge, and other busy streets run by its borders. You're never far from the roar of the road. Sadly, there have also been reports of occasional muggings. Don't wander on a trail alone.

There are about four kilometers of trails spread among three main loops. Not surprisingly, the most strenuous one, **La Cienaguita,** also offers the best chance of seeing animals. It takes about two hours to walk. It's an interpretive trail; the visitors center sells an informative booklet about it for US$2. The **Mono Tití Road** is a wide trail which ascends 150 meters to **Cerro Cedro** (Cedar's Hill), which offers views of Panama City. The easiest trail is **Los Momótides,** across an extremely busy road—be careful crossing the street. It's short and level, designed for people in a hurry or who have difficulty walking, and it is a nice little walk.

The **visitors center** (8 A.M.–4 P.M. Mon.–Fri., 8 A.M.–1 P.M. Sat.) offers a free brochure, but ask for the glossy color trail guide, which has a much-needed map. Guided tours in English and Spanish are sometimes available, but you have to arrange this at least a day or two in advance.

Cerro Azul

This hilly area about an hour east of Panama City has long been popular with more affluent city dwellers looking to escape the hot lowlands—the elevation reaches 950 meters, high enough to cool things off significantly. Attempts have been made to attract tourists to the area, but only serious birders are likely to find it of great interest. They come for the foothill species, including some that are otherwise found only in the Darién. There are some stretches of elfin forest, but getting to the less-developed areas requires four-wheel drive with high clearance, and some places can only be approached on foot. Birders should go with a knowledgeable naturalist guide. Other than that, this is mostly an area of suburban homes and little else.

To get to Cerro Azul, take the Corredor Sur toll road toward the international airport. When the road ends at the Riande Aeropuerto Hotel and Resort, turn left onto the Interamerican Highway. Make another left at the Super Xtra supermarket and follow the Cerro Azul signs. Casa de Campo is about a 20-minute drive up the hill. Turn left at Urbanización Las Nubes and follow the signs. To get to Cerro Azul by public transportation, take any bus going to 24 de Diciembre. Get off at the Super Xtra supermarket and transfer to a Cerro Azul bus.

There is one nice place to stay on Cerro Azul. **Hostal Casa de Campo Country Inn and Spa** (39 Avenida Los Cumulos, Panama City tel. 226-0274, Cerro Azul tel. 297-0067, cell 6677-8993, infor@panamacasadecampo.com, www.panamacasadecampo.com, starts at US$77 s/d) is a large, upscale country home that's been turned into a pleasant, well-maintained inn with lots of character and extensive grounds. All rooms are different, and some are considerably nicer than others. Despite the name, this is not a hostel. There's a small swimming pool, a full-service spa, and good views of the surrounding forested hills and Lago Alajuela. The inn offers a variety of spa,

STRIP CLUBS, BROTHELS, AND BATHHOUSES

Prostitution is legal and regulated by the Panamanian government, but it's hardly free from exploitation. And AIDS and other sexually transmitted diseases are serious risks for those who engage in casual or commercial sex.

Consider the following: An estimated 20,000 people in Panama are living with HIV, and epidemiologists believe the true number could be twice that. Given the country's small population, that gives Panama one of the highest rates in Central America. More people die of AIDS in Panama than in any other Central American country; it is the country's seventh leading cause of death. And the rate of HIV infection is on the rise.

The prevalence of HIV/AIDS is especially high in Panama City and other metropolitan areas, but the United Nations' AIDS agency reports a high concentration of cases among poor indigenous peoples as well, especially the Guna.

While Panama has made some progress with its HIV/AIDS programs, much more needs to be done. The UN estimates that fewer than half the prostitutes in Panama have been reached by an AIDS-prevention program. It also has found that more than 10 percent of men who have sex with men are now HIV-positive. Many of these men also have sex with women. And there are plenty of other sexually transmitted diseases out there.

Panama has several "gentlemen's clubs" or "nightclubs" with strip shows and the like. These usually have fancy names with words such as "elite" or "palace" in them. Those interested will have no trouble finding advertisements in tourist-oriented publications.

Panama City has had gay bathhouses in the past, including one that was quite upscale. However, that one recently closed down and I'm not aware of any that have taken its place. Again, those who are determined will likely find any new ones, most likely through contacts at gay bars or the Internet.

The area around the public market in San Felipe and the backstreets near Avenida Central have lots of rough and seedy bars, including some bars catering to a gay clientele and places that are more or less brothels. This area can be quite dangerous, though, and one of the toughest Panamanians I know thinks it's a dumb move for a gringo to barhop around here—there's an excellent chance of getting mugged on the way home. You've been warned.

tour, and outdoor adventure packages, including bird-watching trips. Meals are available for an extra charge. The inn can arrange round-trip transportation from Panama City, about an hour away. The staff speak English, Spanish, and Italian.

Entertainment and Events

NIGHTLIFE

Panama City has experienced a nightlife boom in recent years, concentrated in a handful of streets and neighborhoods around the city.

The most popular area is a densely packed grid of restaurants, clubs, cafés, and bars bounded by the **Bella Vista** district to the west and **Marbella** to the east. The center of this area is **Calle Uruguay.** Businesses come and go overnight, but there's always someplace worth

visiting. If the long-awaited Buddha Bar franchise ever opens an outlet in Panama, it will instantly be the hottest nightspot in the city. It's allegedly going up on Vía Brasil, but the estimate of when or if it might actually arrive keeps getting pushed back.

Calle 53 Este, the main street through the upscale business district of Marbella, draws young singles and couples to its music clubs. The renovation of **Casco Viejo** has made it an ideal place for clubs, sidewalk cafés, and bars, at least on the weekends. The most popular entertainment area in Panama City is not actually in the city proper, but along the Calzada de Amador (Amador Causeway) in the old Canal Zone.

Clubs have traditionally opened very late in Panama City. Typically they didn't really get going until midnight or later, and the partying often lasted all night. However, in late 2011 a new law, commonly known as the *ley zanahoria* (carrot law), came into effect that prohibits the sale of alcohol between 3 A.M. and 9 A.M. Thursday–Saturday and between 2 A.M. and 9 A.M. Sunday–Wednesday. Enforcement of the controversial law has been uneven, and it remains to be seen whether it will stick.

Cover charges at prominent clubs on a big night can be US$10–20, though there are all kinds of promotions to offset this. Many clubs don't charge a cover during the week or early in the evening, usually before 11 P.M. Women can get in free and/or get free drinks at least once a week, and some clubs have all-you-can-drink open bar specials before 11 P.M. Less-trendy spots typically have cover charges of US$5 or less.

Oddly, in a country where kids learn to dance to salsa and merengue as soon as they can walk, and where partying is virtually a civil right, it's not unusual to see little or no dancing at a Panama City club these days. Even if the place is packed and the music deafening, most people may just be talking, flirting, and drinking.

Don't ask a taxi driver to take you to a good nightclub unless what you're looking for is a strip club or brothel. What gringos call "nightclubs" or "clubs" are usually still known as "discos" or *discotecas* in Panama.

Clubs and bars come and go fast in Panama City, and what's popular one week can be dead or out of business the next, so it's best to aim for a neighborhood rather than a specific bar or club. If you want a nice quiet bar, upscale hotels are a good option. The **Sparkles Bar,** on the fifth floor of the InterContinental Miramar, has a terrific view of the skyline and Panama Bay.

Internet entertainment listings in Panama are getting a bit better, but including addresses, hours, and phone numbers is still an alien concept, and entertainment-listings websites are constantly abandoned without warning. Try cocoas. net, www.dealante.com, or www.elcuara.com.

Casco Viejo

Something of a bohemian, international art scene has begun to bubble up from the underground, fueled by the arrival of young backpackers and, especially, European and South American expats. Most of the more mainstream action is concentrated around Plaza Bolívar, though nightspots pop up from time to time on the streets leading up to Plaza de Francia. The Parque Herrera area looks poised to take off in the next couple of years. Be careful in this area at night, particularly around Parque Herrera. It's best to come and go by taxi; ask the bar or club to call one for you.

Relic Bar (at Luna's Castle: Calle 9 Este and Avenida Eloy Alfaro, tel. 262-1540, www. relicbar.com, Mon.–Sat. nights) is a funky bar with an underground vibe. It's on the lowest level of the Luna's Castle hostel, so patrons must be buzzed in through the security gate. The bar opens onto a huge patio that looks up into the homes of residents of Casco Viejo, who no doubt find the shenanigans of the tourists below at least as interesting as the tourists do the *Rear Window* peek into locals' lives. The bar itself is cave-like and contains part of the old wall that used to ring Casco Viejo.

The bar's most prominent neighbor has stopped by at least once: Panama's president, Ricardo Martinelli, and assorted ministers showed up unexpectedly to an event at the bar a couple of years ago.

La Casona (end of Calle 5, off Avenida A, cell 6706-0528, http://cascoviejo.com, hours vary Wed.–Sat.) is a combination bar/cultural center/DJ club. It has inspired more affection and excitement since it opened in 2005 than

GAY AND LESBIAN BARS AND CLUBS

Panama City is still a place where gay bars have to keep a low profile, but you don't hear horror stories of police raids, gay bashings outside of clubs, and so on—not, at least, among the relatively affluent. It's more a matter of people wanting to be cautious and discreet. Gay bars and clubs are either in remote locations or hidden in plain sight—it's possible to walk right past one and not know anything's there at all.

Like other clubs, they come and go quickly. A mega-club on the outskirts of Panama City, known variously over the years as Boy Bar, Box, Glam, etc., has closed down. That leaves BLG as the longest-established of the prominent gay clubs, though a newer one, Lips Club, has the busiest events calendar. The Internet is the best source for current information, though websites are underfunded, often out of date, and go bust constantly. Start with www.farraurbana.com and www.gaypty.com. Facebook searches can often turn up current information (in Spanish), though usually written for those already familiar with the clubs and lacking in detail.

The three clubs listed here are the most prominent and popular spots that are most likely to still be around when you read this. They draw mostly a gay male clientele (the one lesbian bar closed many years ago), but lesbians and straight singles or couples are welcome. Lesbians seem particularly well-represented at Lips Club. Regardless of one's sexual orientation, visitors will likely find the vibe at these places friendlier, more low-key, more inclusive, and less macho than at many of the city's straight bars and clubs.

There are also so-called "camouflage" bars—ostensibly straight bars that draw closeted gays—and rough dives. Neither kind is included here, for reasons of privacy and safety.

BLG (Transístmica and Avenida Brasil, tel. 393-6298, www.blgpanama.net, 10 P.M.-late Wed.-Sun.), also known as Balagan's, is the most upscale gay bar in Panama. It moved a couple of years back from the Calle Uruguay area to a spot that's much less convenient for visitors, along the Transístmica near the Colpan Ford dealership. Even though it's relatively new, it's already had a renovation and a grand reopening in March 2012. Look for the "BLG" out front. The club draws men, women, and some straight couples. The music is mostly electronica. It has *transformista* (drag) shows, comedians, and other special events on some nights.

La Gota Fría/Lips Club (Avenida Manuel Espinosa Batista near the intersection of Avenida Simón Bolívar/Transístmica and Avenida Ricardo J. Alfaro/Tumba Muerto, no phone, 10 P.M.-late Wed. and Fri.-Sun., US$5-10 cover) has the most organized club schedule. It has a stage and frequently hosts *transformista* (drag) shows and other events. Foam parties are a popular shtick these days, which fit nicely with the car-wash motif. It hosts special shows throughout Carnaval. The club manages the neat trick of being in one of the most visible spots in the city but staying well hidden. It's on the 2nd floor of a building behind the Splash car wash, which is next to the large roundabout at the intersection of the Transístmica and Tumba Muerto. Everyone in the city knows this area, even if they don't know the club.

Icon Club (Tumba Muerto and Avenida Juan Pablo II, cell 6230-0378, www.iconclub-panama.com, 9 P.M.-3 A.M. Thurs.-Sun.), formerly called Oxen, is the massive warehouse club of choice these days. Like its predecessors, it can be bloody hard to find the first time. To get there from Tumba Muerto, first look for Plaza Edison, the distinctive cone-shaped office building. The cross street is Avenida Juan Pablo II; turn west onto it. The club is in the commercial complex on the right side of the road. The club hosts especially elaborate *transformista* (drag) shows from time to time. These can be entertaining even (or especially) when they're not particularly skilled.

any new place I can remember, having filled a major gap in the nightlife scene. People love its informal vibe—it's one of the few hot spots in Panama that doesn't have a dress code—as well as the mixture of people it attracts, from backpackers to the hipster art crowd to overdressed yuppies. There's an art gallery, and La Casona occasionally hosts films, artists' talks, live concerts, and traveling exhibitions. This place keeps moving from one derelict building to another in Casco Viejo, keeping one step ahead of the wave of gentrification. Double-check its current location before venturing out.

Platea (near the intersection of Avenida Central and Avenida A, tel. 228-4011, www.scenayplatea.com, 8 P.M.–3 A.M. Wed.–Sat.) is a cozy cave of a bar on the ground floor of the same building that houses S'Cena, a Mediterranean restaurant, across from the ruins of the old Union Club. There's music every night, from live jazz, salsa, or world music to karaoke.

The bar at **Restaurante Las Bóvedas** (Plaza de Francia, tel. 228-8058 or 228-8068, 5:30 P.M.–late Mon.–Sat.) hosts live jazz Friday and Saturday after about 9:30 P.M.

The fairly new **Habana Panama** (Calle Eloy Alfaro and Calle 12 Este, tel. 212-0152, cell 6628-4189 or 5780-2183, www.habanapanama.com, usually Thurs.–Sat. nights) is an attempt to bring actual dancing back to Panama City clubs and to play something other than the same old *típico* and reggaeton. It's a Cuban music hall that quite accurately bills itself as *el bunker de la música cubana*. Bunker indeed: It's just down from the entrance to Casco Viejo, in an area that can be dangerous to wander around at night. Huge spotlights beam down onto the street from the entrance to the surprisingly upscale club. The proprietors are going for old Havana romance and old Havana sounds. The club manages to attract surprisingly big-name international acts, from salsa great Willie Colón to Los Van Van, one of the most venerable Cuban bands still playing.

◖ Bella Vista and Marbella

Most of the popular clubs and bars in this area are on or near Calle Uruguay, Panama City's major nightlife destination. Places fold and new ones pop up at lightning speed, so it's impossible to say what will be there when you visit. The best bet is just to stroll around late on a Thursday, Friday, or Saturday night and follow the crowds, particularly on Avenida 5B, Avenida 5 Sur/Calle 48, and Calle Uruguay itself, and see what looks appealing. Big venues tend to surface across the street from Crepes and Waffles (Avenida 5B between Calle Uruguay and Calle Aquilino de la Guardia) and next to the Panama City Hooters (Calle 49 and Calle Uruguay).

Street names are confusing around here. Calle Uruguay is also sometimes known as Calle 48 Este, and the cross streets have all kinds of names and are often called simply Calle 45, 46, 47, and so on, even though they are officially low-numbered avenues.

S6is (Calle Uruguay between Avenida 4A and 5A, tel. 264-5237, Tues.–Sun. nights until late), pronounced *seis* (the number six), is a DJ bar/cocktail lounge in an old house that projects the air of a party in a pleasant, minimalist apartment. It attracts a mid-twenty-something and older crowd.

T.G.I. Friday's (Avenida 4A Sur near Calle Aquilino de la Guardia/49 Este, tel. 269-4199) is a perennially popular destination for young singles on the prowl or just hanging with their friends. There's another one attached to the Country Inns and Suites on the Calzada de Amador (Amador Causeway).

As a Panama kid who now lives in London, there was no way I'd skip a Panama pub called **The Londoner** (Calle Uruguay between Avenida 5A Sur and Avenida 5B Sur, tel. 214-4883, 5 P.M.–late daily). Its owner is South African, it doesn't have beer on tap, and the Panamanian bartenders were puzzled by the concept of a gin and tonic, in any language.

On the other hand, they were gracious and eager to learn. That's service you rarely find in Panama. Bottled imports include Guinness, Newcastle Brown Ale, and Strongbow cider. The Londoner is a homey place with a pool table and a less gringo-heavy crowd than other expat magnets: It's a good place to encounter Brits and Commonwealth types. It's where to head to watch a soccer game on a big screen, rather than resort to a sports bar. The English pub grub (US$5–11.50) includes shepherd's pie, bangers and mash, and fish and chips.

El Cangrejo and Vicinity

Nightlife in El Cangrejo centers on the big hotels and casinos and a handful of venerable restaurants. It's popular with some Panamanians and resident expats, but many of its nightspots are overrated and/or overpriced.

A good place in the area is the **Istmo Brew Pub** (Avenida Eusebio A. Morales, tel. 265-5077, 4 P.M.–3 A.M. Mon.–Sat., 4 P.M.–12:30 A.M. Sun.). It's an open-air venue, right across the street from Wine Bar and Las Vegas Hotel Suites, with a friendly atmosphere, a pool table, and a big-screen TV showing whatever game happens to be on. This is the only place in Panama I know of that makes its own beer. It only makes three kinds, and on any given day only one may be in stock. The beer definitely tastes homemade rather than artisanal, and at nearly $5 a pint is steep for Panama, where a local bottle is easy to find for a tenth of that price. Still, the home brew is light and refreshing, and this is a comfortable spot to hang out and people-watch. They serve no domestic beers, only mass-market imported beers along the lines of Amstel Light, Corona, and Budweiser. As these cost nearly $4 a bottle, the pints are a far better value. There's a daily happy hour until 8 P.M. The pub also serves bar food.

CASINOS

Gambling is legal in Panama, and casinos are scattered throughout the city, primarily in the better hotels around Vía España. Centrally located ones include the **Royal Casino,** next to the Marriott (Calle 52 at Calle Ricardo Arias, tel. 210-9100); the **Majestic Casino** (tel. 215-5151) in the Multicentro Mall on Avenida Balboa; and the **Fiesta Casino** (tel. 208-7250) behind the Hotel El Panamá. The **Veneto Hotel and Casino** is the glitziest (Vía Veneto between Avenida 2 Norte/Eusebio A. Morales and Calle D, tel. 340-8888). The hotel itself is a 17-story, 300-room Vegas knockoff with decor that's an odd mix of the garish and the generic—more Atlantic City than Panama City.

CINEMAS

There are plenty of movie theaters in Panama City. Mostly these are multiplexes showing recent Hollywood spectacles and are generally in English with Spanish subtitles rather than dubbed. This is indicated in the listings: looks for "SUB" for subtitled films and "DOB" for dubbed films. The standard ticket prices are US$4–4.50 for adults, US$3.50 for students, US$3 for kids. Tickets are generally about half price on Tuesday or Wednesday.

The daily newspapers carry a list of current movies, locations, and show times. A good online list is at www.cine.com.pa/, or try the *La Prensa* newspaper's online listings: www.prensa.com.

The fancy Mexican-owned cinema chain **Cinépolis** (Multiplaza Pacific Mall, tel. 302-2463) has arrived in Panama, with its first beachheads in the upscale Multiplaza Pacific Mall and the newish Metro Mall (though the latter doesn't have VIP seats). It offers two kinds of movie experiences: the usual multiplex theater at usual multiplex prices, or Cinépolis VIP, which allows patrons to choose their (overstuffed, reclining) seat in advance. Moviegoers can order food and drink to be delivered to their seats. It's pretty posh. Tickets for this cost US$12.50, which strikes the average Panamanian as extortionate.

The **Diablo Rosso café/art gallery** (#11,

Avenida A and Calle 7, tel. 228-4833 or 228-4837, www.diablorosso.com) in Casco Viejo hosts an indie film night on Wednesday, a welcome addition to the movie scene for culture-starved residents.

CONCERTS AND THEATER

Panama City has an active theater scene, with regular productions featuring offerings by Panamanian playwrights as well as classic and contemporary plays from other countries. The easiest music performance to find on any given night is a *típico* combo, though salsa, Latin pop/rock, reggaeton, and other high-energy music forms are also popular. Most of these are local acts that perform in clubs, but with the opening of more modern, high-capacity venues such as the **Figali Convention Center** at the Panama Canal Village, the city is beginning to attract more big-name international pop acts.

Big concerts are sometimes held in the

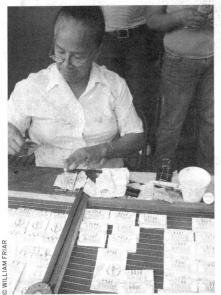

© WILLIAM FRIAR

There are nearly 10,000 lottery vendors in Panama.

baseball stadium, **Estadio Nacional Rod Carew,** as well. Classical music and dance groups come through less often. Tickets for major concerts and other events are usually available through Blockbuster outlets or online at www.blockbusterpanama.com or through Ticket Plus outlets or online at hwww.ticketplus.com.pa. Official ticket outlets are constantly in flux in Panama and may change by the time you arrive. Make sure you're buying from a legitimate source. Also, official online outlets restrict sales by region, so you probably won't be able to buy tickets for a hot show until you're actually in Panama.

Panama's elegant old **Teatro Nacional** (Avenida B between Calle 3 and Calle 4 in Casco Viejo, tel. 262-3525 or 262-3582) hosts visiting classical music ensembles and other arts events. **Teatro en Círculo** (Avenida 6C Norte near Vía Brasil, tel. 261-5375), near Scubapanama, in a quiet residential area east of downtown, presents many of the city's highest-profile plays, from Spanish-language renditions of Shakespeare to well-received original productions by Panamanian playwrights. The small **Teatro Anita Villalaz** (Plaza de Francia in Casco Viejo, tel. 211-4017 or 211-2040) is another prominent playhouse. Performance groups often rent out the **Teatro ABA** (Avenida Simón Bolívar/Transístmica near Avenida de los Periodistas, tel. 260-6316) for their productions. It's near the Chinese restaurant Palacio Lung Fung and not far from Teatro en Círculo.

LOTTERY

The Lotería Nacional de Beneficencia, or national lottery, is a tenacious carryover from a time when Panamanians had fewer entertainment options. The first lottery was held in 1882, and the current system dates from 1919. It's still hugely popular.

Every Sunday and Wednesday at 1 P.M., a crowd gathers for the drawing, broadcast live throughout the country on TV and radio. Drawings are held in Plaza Víctor Julio Gutiérrez, which is covered by an open-sided shed that takes up an entire block between Avenida Perú and Avenida Cuba and Calle 31 and Calle 32. Anyone can drop by to watch.

The ritual is solemn and unwavering. First, the lottery balls are turned incessantly back and forth in a shiny steel cage by a designated official. This seems to last for hours. At last, the cage is stopped and a ball is extracted by a child dressed in his or her very best. The ball is twisted apart to reveal a number printed inside, which is held up for all to see, read aloud by the emcee, and then carefully recorded on a board behind the stage. Three sets of four numbers are chosen, corresponding to the first, second, and third prize. A ticket holder must have all four numbers in the correct order to win one of the three prizes, though there are small prizes (US$1–50) for getting some of the numbers right.

Going through this process 12 times turns the drawing into an event long enough to allow for all kinds of sideshows: beauty queens in *polleras,* folkloric dances, musical performances, visiting dignitaries, and so on.

All this for a first prize of US$2,000. Second prize is US$600 and third US$300. That's still a lot of money for the average hardworking Panamanian. And people often buy multiple tickets with the same numbers; theoretically, the maximum prize is US$570,000—if one bought 285 winning tickets.

There are also special drawings that pay more. *Gorditos del Zodíaco* (little fat ones of the Zodiac) are held on the last Friday of each month. First prize is US$4,000 (for a maximum of US$900,000 if one bought many, many winning tickets). A newer gimmick, the *sorteo de oro* (gold drawing), increases the payout if a winning ticket has certain letters printed on it. To purists, though, adding this alphabet soup to the mix ruins the charm of those three rows of numbers, which are posted diligently around the country on bus station chalkboards and other public spots twice a week, year in and year out.

Four-number tickets cost US$1. If that's too expensive, a two-number *chance* (CHON-seh) goes for US$0.25. These pay out if the numbers correspond to the last two numbers of any of the winning combinations. First prize for these is US$14, second prize is US$3, and third prize is US$2. The maximum for multiple tickets is US$280.

Tickets are sold by freelance vendors around the country. You can find vendors on any street with lots of foot traffic. A whole battalion has stalls set up on the Avenida Perú side of the lottery plaza, between Calle 31 and Calle 32. There are nearly 10,000 vendors in Panama.

Shopping

Panama has no shortage of shopping malls and commercial centers—at last count there were more than two dozen of various sizes. Many of these, however, look better stocked than they are, and the city is not the best place to look for the latest fashions. However, those in the market for cosmetics and perfumes can find better deals than they would in the United States at the nicer department stores, such as the **Stevens, Collins, Felix B. Maduro,** and **Dante**

chains. There are branches of these on Vía España, on Tumba Muerto (Avenida Ricardo J. Alfaro) in El Dorado, and in some of the malls.

One of the newer and glitzier malls is the upscale **Multiplaza Pacific,** in Punta Pacífica. The youth-oriented **Multicentro** is on the west end of Avenida Balboa near Punta Paitilla. There's a food court on the top floor that has a great view of the city and the bay. A particularly massive and constantly growing complex is the **Albrook**

BOUTIQUE BREEBAART: A DASH OF PARIS IN PANAMA

© WILLIAM FRIAR

Helèné Breebaart with one of her creations

The small fashion house **Boutique Breebaart** (Calle Abel Bravo, Casa #5, Obarrio, tel. 264-5937, 9 A.M.-6 P.M. Mon.-Fri., open weekends by appointment) is housed in the home of its owner and designer, the warm and utterly charming Helèné Breebaart, an artist who first came to Panama as the local representative for Christian Dior perfumes. Try to chat with her, in any of her several languages, if she's around: She is a relentlessly creative and upbeat person, and she has some great stories of her years in Panama, ranging from life as a clothing designer during the military dictatorship to dressing Rosalynn Carter for a gala evening of former and current U.S. first ladies. This may not be easy, though, as Helèné is a human dynamo and very busy; she's never still for long.

The boutique offers unusual dresses, bathing suits, cushions, place settings, tablecloths, handbags, napkins, and other items. Recurring motifs include butterflies, hibiscuses, hummingbirds, pineapples, coral, and other tropical-Panama flora and fauna, usually appliquéd onto the dresses and other items. But most of all, her signature work is inspired by the colorful *molas* of the Gunas, who are the ones who actually stitch the clothing and other pieces she designs. Those staying in high-end hotels may recognize her work (or in some cases poorer-quality rip-offs) from the pillows and other furnishings in their rooms. Her collections appear from time to time in upscale department stores in the United States.

Much of the work is quite lovely and elegant; some is rather kitschy and works best on the beach. Each piece is handmade and can cost anywhere from US$10 to thousands of dollars. Tablecloths alone start at around US$300, or US$1,000 and up for custom-made ones.

Women of considerable means who'd like a one-of-a-kind dress or jacket can meet with Helèné and brainstorm a colorful creation. Simple shifts start at about US$400. Producing the final article can take weeks and the boutique would like to do at least one fitting, but these can be created with extra material and shipped to the purchaser for final adjustments back home if time is short. Those on a more modest budget can pick up one of her butterfly, hibiscus, or hummingbird patches, starting at around US$10, and later pin or sew them onto an article of clothing, or even use them as drink coasters. The patches come in attractive wrapping and make nice little gifts.

A few items are on display, as are some jewelry, hats, and other accessories made by other designers. If you visit, peek in the back to see the dozen Guna sewers at work.

Mall, sometimes also called Los Pueblos II, next to the Gran Terminal de Transportes, the main bus terminal, which is near the domestic airport in Albrook. It's the favorite of many locals.

A newer ritzy shopping center is **Metro Mall,** about halfway between downtown and the international airport on Vía Tucumen, the old road (not the highway) to the airport. However, it's too far from town to be of much interest to visitors. Other upscale shopping destinations include the **Bal Harbour** mini-mall (mainly for food, especially kosher food) in the Punta Paitilla area, the designer-name shops along **Calle 53 in Marbella** (especially in the **World Trade Center**), and the tony jewelry stores and galleries on **Avenida 2 Sur/Samuel Lewis** in Obarrio. More bargain-oriented stores are on **Vía España** and in the malls and strip malls of the **El Dorado** neighborhood, though both places have higher-end shops as well.

ART GALLERIES

Panama's best high-end art gallery is **Imagen** (Calle 50 and Calle 77, tel. 226-8989, 9 A.M.–1 P.M. and 2–6 P.M. Mon.–Sat.). It's in a lovely old building, and the staff are gracious. It's small, but it's a good place to go just to get a sense of what's happening in the local art scene. **Habitante** (Calle Uruguay, tel. 264-6470, 9 A.M.–6 P.M. Mon.–Sat.), in the Calle Uruguay nightlife area, is also small, but less interesting, though it's certainly more central. **Mateo Sariel** (Vía Porras and Calle 66 Este, tel. 270-2404, 9 A.M.–6 P.M. Mon.–Fri.), though also well known, often feels more like a framing shop than an art gallery, though those willing to rummage around the piles of paintings sometimes unearth a find.

The hippest of the new art galleries sprouting up in Casco Viejo is the **Diablo Rosso café/art gallery** (#11, Avenida A and Calle 7, tel. 228-4833 or 228-4837, www.diablorosso.com, 11 A.M.–8:30 P.M., Tues.–Sat.). It frequently hosts after-hours art shows and events.

BOOKSTORES

Panama City is not a great town for readers, but the bookstore selections have gotten somewhat better in recent years. Don't expect bargains, though—shipping heavy books to Panama is expensive, and that's reflected in the prices. Both the Gran Morrison department store and the Farmacia Arrocha drugstore chains carry books and magazines. Offerings are hit-or-miss, though occasionally a rare find surfaces. The Gran Morrison on Vía España is particularly promising.

Librería Argosy (Vía Argentina near Vía España, tel. 223-5344, 10 A.M.–6 P.M. Mon.–Sat.), run by a friendly Greek émigré named Gerasimos (Gerry) Kanelopulos, has been a Panama City institution for more than three decades. It's a small, crowded place. Be sure to dig below the piles—a lot of books are buried under each other. The shop carries a substantial collection of works about Panama or written by Panamanian authors. Note Gerry's extensive collection of autographed photos: Pride of place belongs to Dame Margot Fonteyn, who spent her twilight years in Panama.

There are several outlets of **El Hombre de la Mancha** (www.hombredelamancha.com), a local bookstore/café chain, mostly in shopping malls. They typically have a small English-language book selection with a few best sellers and a lot of bulk discount books, as well as a reasonable selection of Spanish-language books by Panamanian authors. The branch near the Country Inns and Suites in El Dorado (Central Comercial Camino de Cruces, tel. 360-2063, 10 A.M.–10 P.M. Mon.–Sat., 11 A.M.–8 P.M. Sun.) has the best selection, at least in Spanish, but it's also the least conveniently located for most tourists. There are branches in the Multiplaza Pacific, Multicentro, Metro, Albrook shopping malls, and the domestic airport at Albrook.

Exedra Books (Vía España and Vía Brasil, tel. 264-4252, www.exedrabooks.com, noon–7 P.M. Mon.–Sat.) is modeled after U.S. chains such as Borders, minus the books. For such a large, attractive store, most of its offerings are odd and very limited. The English-language books in particular seem to consist of by-the-pound leftovers. It does have a decent selection of Spanish-language fiction, though, and it seems to be making a genuine effort to become a real bookstore. It also carries some used books at better prices. Upstairs there's an Internet café that actually has a café. It's also a ticket outlet for local concerts and other events. Literary talks, in Spanish, are given on Monday night at 7 P.M.

CRAFT SHOPS AND BOUTIQUES

The jewelry store **Represa** (Avenida 2 Sur/ Samuel Lewis and Calle 54 Este, tel. 271-0033, www.represa.com, 9 A.M.–6 P.M. daily) is a Panama institution. It's a great place to go for unique presents or souvenirs. There's a second Represa store (9 A.M.–5 P.M. daily) in Casco Viejo. Represa is most famous for its reproductions of gold and silver *huacas,* figures recovered from pre-Columbian graves. The figures are created by using molds made through the so-called "lost wax" process, which creates exact replicas, including the imperfections in the original. This process is virtually the same as that used to produce the ancient original pieces.

Prices at Represa are very reasonable—some pieces start at less than US$10, though the cost goes straight up from there depending on the purity of the gold or silver. Pieces include replicas of some of the finest and oldest *huacas* in the collection of Panama's anthropology museum. The store carries other jewelry as well, including replicas of pieces of eight and the pearl-encrusted brooches known as *mosquetas,* the latter traditionally worn with the *pollera.* Represa offers tours of its factory near Panamá La Vieja; email tours@represa.com for details.

Casa de los Manteles (Avenida de los Mártires near Calle J, tel. 262-0822, 9 A.M.–6 P.M. Mon.–Sat.), is known for its lovely embroidered tablecloths, napkins, and other linens. It also carries good-quality *guayabera* (the semiformal traditional Latin American shirt). The store has a parking lot behind the building.

There is a **handicrafts market** in Plaza Cinco de Mayo, behind the anthropology museum, that offers hats, *mola* blouses, hammocks, sandals, and the like. Hats are especially well represented. Most stalls open by 9 A.M. daily and stay open until sundown. If you have trouble finding this market, ask for the *artesanía* near Plaza Cinco de Mayo. Better handicrafts markets are in Balboa, in the old Canal Zone.

ELECTRONICS AND PHOTO SUPPLIES

Panafoto (Calle 50 and Calle 49A Este, tel. 263-3000, www.panafoto.com, 9 A.M.–7:30 P.M. Mon.–Sat., noon–6 P.M. Sun.) is a modern, glass-enclosed consumer electronics store and the first stop for camera buffs. There's an espresso bar upstairs.

TAILORED SUITS

La Fortuna (Vía España at Calle 55 Este near Vía Argentina, tel. 302-7890 or 263-6434, 9 A.M.–6 P.M. Mon.–Sat.) is Panama's best-known destination for tailored men's suits. It's been around since 1925 and has dressed ambassadors and presidents. A custom-made suit or tuxedo in high-quality imported fabric can be had for around US$500; knock US$100–200 off that estimate for less-expensive material. One of the nifty things about having a suit made here is that the tailors sew a panel inside the suit with the buyer's name and the statement that it was made *exclusivo* for him. If you don't care for any of their styles, you can bring in a photo of what you'd like and they'll create it for you. They carry a range of fabric from famous European and North American designers.

This is the tailor of choice for many high-ranking politicians, and it's said owner José Abadí was one of the inspirations for Le Carré's book *The Tailor of Panama*, about a tailor to powerful Panamanian officials who is forced by a British agent to spy on his customers.

Visitors should place an order at the start of their travels, as the process requires two fittings, and the shop normally needs at least 10 days to make a suit (more during peak seasons, such as before the independence holidays in November). Those pressed for time can sometimes have a suit made in 24 hours, but don't expect a perfect fit.

Sports and Recreation

Panama City is really not the best spot for either spectator or participant sports. Generally only the most expensive hotels have tennis courts, pools big enough to swim laps in, or decent gyms. Most sports clubs are upscale places open to members and their guests.

The best options for those interested in golf are Summit Golf, Hotel and Spa in the former Canal Zone or, for those going to the Pacific beaches, the course at the Coronado Hotel and Resort or the newer El Mantaraya Golf Club at the Royal Decameron Resort. They are well-maintained, championship courses with good facilities.

BASEBALL

Panama produces a disproportionate number of U.S. Major League baseball players for its size. *Fútbol* (soccer) is beginning to nudge *beisbol* from its pedestal as the country's favorite team sport, but it is still Panama's national pastime, has a passionate following, and produces some of the best players in the world.

The national baseball stadium **Estadio Nacional Rod Carew** (Corredor Norte, Camino de la Amistad, and Transístmica in Cerro Patacón on the northwest outskirts of the city, tel. 230-4255, www.estadionacional.com.pa or www.fedebeis.com, US$4), named after native son and Hall of Famer Rod Carew, is easy to get to. The stadium seats 26,000, but during a routine game between provincial teams, it may be nearly empty, making it easy to get close to the action and possibly see a major-leaguer in the making. Baseball is played only during Panama's summer (the dry season), though in season the stadium may host several games a week. The baseball season ends in May. Big concerts featuring international stars are sometimes held at the stadium.

HORSE-RACING

Panama has a well-established horse-racing industry. The national racetrack, **Hipódromo Presidente Remón** (tel. 217-6060, www.hipodromo.com, races Thurs., Sat., Sun., and holidays) is on the outskirts of the city about eight kilometers east of Punta Paitilla in the Juan Díaz area, on the way to the international airport. The quickest way to get there is via the Corredor Sur. It's also accessible from Vía España, which becomes Vía José Agustín Arango east of the city. The racecourse is just past the 45,000-seat national *fútbol* stadium, Estadio Rommel Fernández.

SNORKELING AND DIVING

Scubapanama (Avenida 6C Norte, tel. 261-3841 or 261-4064, www.scubapanama.com), Panama's largest dive operator, also rents and sells snorkeling and diving gear. Those who plan to do a fair amount of snorkeling should know that most of the equipment available on Panama's beaches and islands is mediocre at best. This is a decent place to buy some if you didn't bring your own.

Accommodations

Panama City offers good lodging options for most budgets. Finding an available room has gotten harder and harder in the last several years, but the city's hotel supply has finally caught up with the boom in tourism and business.

Advance reservations are a good idea, especially for midrange and luxury hotels. Try to book as far ahead of time as possible if visiting during holidays and the dry season. Panama City hotels tend to be terrible about answering email and responding to reservation-request forms on their websites. This is especially true of the lower-end lodgings. If you don't hear back in a few days, your best bet is to call.

WHAT TO EXPECT

Hotels often charge the same for one or two guests. Those traveling solo can sometimes save money by buddying up with fellow travelers, though often hotels charge more for two beds in a room. A third or fourth guest in a room is typically just a nominal additional charge, so small groups can often find deals even at the higher end of the scale. The midrange and high-end hotels often offer corporate rates and promotional deals that can be significantly cheaper than their standard rates. It never hurts to ask for the discount, which you can often get without so much as a business card. All prices listed include Panama's 10-percent room tax.

Hostels

Panama City is seeing a surge in hostels, and these tend to be the safest of the bare-bones accommodations. The best can be surprisingly pleasant, but dispel any notion of European- or even American-style youth hostels: Panama City hostels tend to be grungy, makeshift affairs installed in converted apartments. Many hostels are now serving as de facto travel agencies, helping guests with area tours and travel throughout Panama and to Colombia and Costa Rica. Wireless access and use of Internet-enabled computers, luggage storage, and a modest, do-it-yourself breakfast are standard free extras at the city's hostels. Some hostels have air-conditioning, at least at night. They also increasingly have private rooms that can be pretty decent, especially for the price; these are popular and tend to fill up fast.

Panama City hostels are often on the move. Real estate is so expensive in the city that hostels often take up residence in an old apartment building that's waiting to be bought up, torn down, and replaced with a skyscraper. When that happens, the hostel owner packs up and moves on to the next building. Make sure you know where your hostel really is before you show up!

US$10-25

At the low end of the scale, every US$10 extra can mean dramatically better digs. For US$13, don't expect much more than a bare hostel room with a fan, though often even these places offer air-conditioning for a couple of bucks more.

US$25-50

Air-conditioning is universally available once the price gets up to around US$40–50 s/d per night; hot water kicks in at less than that. It's getting harder to find clean, safe, and comfortable rooms at this price, but it's still possible.

US$50-100

For US$60 s/d, it's possible to find some pleasant, clean hotels with reliable air-conditioning, hot-water bathrooms, and sometimes wireless Internet and satellite TV. Three-star hotel territory starts at around US$100 s/d. At that price, it's possible to find attractive rooms with good beds and amenities such as satellite TV, in-room telephones, free wireless Internet, in-room safes, a decent restaurant/bar, a small swimming pool (often on the rooftop), and so on. Some of these places are in high demand and should be booked several days or even weeks in advance if possible.

US$100-150

Many of the options for US$100–150 a night are so-called *aparthotels,* which offer furnished, usually large studio and one-bedroom apartments with a full kitchen and utensils, telephone, and washer and dryer either in the apartment or in a laundry facility on the premises. These also sometimes have a business center and small pool. They typically offer price breaks for long stays. These have proved popular and prices have climbed accordingly, but they still get booked solid with long-term visitors doing business in or moving to Panama.

Over US$150

Rack rates for luxury hotels are US$200–300 a night per couple. Guests may find these rates a good-value splurge at the very best places and excessive at others. Prices can vary wildly from day to day, and deals are often available. Booking far enough in advance—a good idea since these places are in great demand—can knock about US$100 off the rack rate. Luxury hotels universally offer high-speed wired or wireless Internet, but expect to pay at least US$15 a day for the privilege.

Panama City has begun to introduce a couple of closely related kinds of hotels: high-end apartment-style suites and condo hotels. The first are basically *aparthotels* for the luxury market. The second are time-share–style condos that can be rented out as hotel rooms when the owner is out of town.

CASCO VIEJO

A couple of hostels, a few lovely boutique hotels, and luxury apartments call Casco Viejo home. Apartments in Casco Viejo can often be rented for short periods, including by the night. The websites www.loscuatrotulipanes.com and www.arcoproperties.com are good places to start looking.

US$10-25

◖ Luna's Castle (Calle 9 Este and Avenida Eloy Alfaro, tel. 262-1540, www.lunascastle-hostel.com, US$13 pp in dorms, US$15 pp in a/c dorms, US$30 s/d in private rooms, breakfast included) opened in 2008 and has quickly become the Hilton of Panama's hostels. It's owned by the same guys who made Mondo Taitu (now under new ownership) and Hostel Heike in Bocas popular. Luna's Castle is in a lovely three-story colonial house with high ceilings and ornate balconies. French doors on the 2nd and 3rd floor open onto million-dollar views of Casco Viejo, Panama Bay, and the downtown skyline. Original fixtures include tile floors and a handsome wooden staircase.

On the ground floor is Relic Bar, a Casco Viejo hot spot that is open to all. For security in the evening, only hostel guests with wristbands are allowed upstairs into the hostel itself. The wristbands also entitle guests to discounts at some area restaurants.

The hostel has both dorms and private rooms. One dorm has four beds. The rest have 6–12 beds. All are mixed sex. Dorm rooms 7, 10, and 12 have ocean views. Number 10 is the most spacious. There are seven private rooms. A movie theater downstairs shows current releases to hostel guests, who can recline on three tiers of mattresses that serve as stadium-style seats. There's a lounge area, table tennis, and computers with free Internet access, as well as free wireless access for those with their own electronics. The included breakfast consists of (make-your-own) pancakes, bananas, coffee, and tea. The hostel also occasionally hosts art exhibitions and other cultural events.

Luna's Castle has a binder that contains up-to-date information for budget travelers on where to go and how to get around in Panama City and other backpacker destinations. The hostel also has maps of Casco Viejo and the rest of Panama City. They can help make arrangements for stays in other parts of Panama, including land transits to Guna Yala. Guests have access to lockers, free luggage storage, a book exchange, guitars, games, a communal kitchen, local and international calling, taxi shuttles to the international airport, a bar, parking, tour bookings, etc.

This is a top choice for budget travelers who want to spend time exploring Casco Viejo, meet other travelers, and get help with onward travel. On the other hand, it's a big, self-contained backpacker enclave, and it's not terribly convenient to other parts of the city. Travelers who want to meet locals and see other parts of the city on the cheap may find it easier to stay in more centrally located places such as Mamallena, La Jungla, or Pensión Las Torres.

This place is popular, so try to make reservations early. Luna's Castle only takes reservations two weeks in advance, but you can reserve through www.hostelworld.com earlier than that. The hostel does not take reservations for private rooms, the air-conditioned dorms, or for those arriving after 8 P.M.

Opened in 2005, **Hospedaje Casco Viejo** (Calle 8 and Avenida A, tel. 211-2027, www.hospedajecascoviejo.com, dorm beds US$11 pp, US$22 s/d with shared bath, US$25 s/d with private bath) offers 16 rooms in an old three-story house behind the Iglesia de San José (Church of the Golden Altar). All the rooms have ceiling fans only. None of the bathrooms has hot water. Some of the bedrooms have balconies. There's a tiny interior patio and a TV room for hanging out, a shared kitchen, a gated entrance with 24-hour reception, free wireless Internet, and lockers. This place could be great, but it tends toward the grungy side. In any case, the location can't be beat.

US$50-100

Magnolia Inn (Calle 8 and Calle Boquete, tel. 202-0872, cell 6073-2773 or 6711-7108, U.S. tel. 786/375-9633, www.magnoliapanama.com, dorm beds US$16.50, private rooms start at US$88 s/d/t) opened in January 2012 offering "luxury" dorm beds and the most economical upscale rooms in Casco Viejo. It's a terrific addition to the neighborhood. The inn is the creation of a friendly gringo couple, Cherie and Reggie, and their teenage kids. They clearly love this place, which is housed in a gorgeous, listed house built circa 1900 and surprisingly intact, with marble floors, high ceilings, and period features such as an art deco staircase. The dorms are "luxurious" in that they have soft but thick mattresses, bedside plugs to charge one's electronics, air-conditioning, steps leading to the top bunks, lockers, and no more than 4–6 beds per room. They are certainly among the more civilized hostel accommodations in the country. The dorm rooms share clean toilets and hot-water showers. There's also a pleasant shared kitchen and lounge. There's a ballroom upstairs with a view of the cathedral towers. The inn sometimes offers ballroom dance classes there.

The inn has six private rooms with air-conditioning, TV, and private baths. These start at US$88 for rooms that sleep up to three people. The three nicest and biggest rooms are on the top floor and go for US$148.50 each. Room 3C has views of the cathedral, the rooftops of Casco Viejo, and the ocean.

Over US$150

A truly boutique hotel, **Canal House** (Avenida A and Calle 5 Oeste, tel. 228-1907 or 228-8683, toll-free U.S./Canada tel. 888/593-5023, www.canalhousepanama.com, starts at US$210 s/d including breakfast) offers some of the handsomest accommodations in the country. It is owned by the same company behind Las Clementinas. A four-story, 4,000-square-foot house built in 1893 and beautifully restored in 2005, it has just two suites and one guest room. The opulent furnishings manage to be both contemporary and in keeping with the colonial feel of the building. As its name suggests, the Canal House pays homage to the Panama Canal, down to the books in the library and the photos on the walls.

The master suite is the Miraflores (US$340), which features a huge bedroom with a king-size bed and walk-in closet, a sitting/dining area, a wraparound balcony, and a spiral staircase that leads to a loft study with a daybed, desk, and library. The Gatun Suite (US$270), on the top floor, has a king-size bed and a separate sitting room. The Pedro Miguel Room (US$210) is dramatically smaller, little bigger than its queen-size bed, but guests have access to the same common areas and services as other guests.

All three accommodations feature high-gloss hardwood floors, plasma-screen TVs with satellite TV, free wireless Internet, use of an iPad, and French doors that open onto wrought-iron balconies with fascinating views of the surrounding neighborhood. (Be sure to check out the view from the roof.) Management prides itself on personalized, attentive service, and it offers many extras for an additional fee, ranging from airport transfers and tours to secretarial services. This place books up well in advance, especially the least-expensive room (Pedro Miguel).

Casa de Horno (Avenida B and Calle 8, tel. 212-0052, cell 6561-3078, www.casadelhorno. net, starts at US$275 s/d, including breakfast) offers eight modern, spacious rooms in a historic, compact building. The designers have done an admirable job of striking a balance between preserving the old character of the place and fitting it with contemporary comforts. The original stone walls are exposed throughout, but the rooms have luxury features such as a modern kitchen with minibar and wine cooler, a sitting area, and 40-inch flat-screen TVs. All the rooms have balconies, and some look out of the cathedral. However, the rooms are not high enough up to have much of a view. The rooms

and common areas are filled with the rather romantic Portobelo portraits of Sandra Eleta, one of Panama's best-known photographers.

◀ **Las Clementinas** (Calle 11 and Avenida B, tel. 228-7613, http://lasclementinas.com, US$308–341 s/d) is another beautiful boutique hotel, though this one is on the very edge of what is normally considered Casco Viejo. It borders the considerably less charming part of the Santa Ana district. It is owned by the same company behind the Canal House. Housed in a 1930s-era apartment building, it features six large suites decorated in elegantly simple good taste. Each suite has somewhat different furnishings and art, but all have handsome hardwood floors and fully equipped kitchens. Like the Canal House, Las Clementinas offers many services for an extra fee.

This place is extremely popular and muchloved, so make bookings as far in advance as possible. Attached to the hotel is an attractive café (tel. 228-7617, 7 A.M.–11 P.M. Tues.–Sat., 7 A.M.–3 P.M. Sun.) that offers a two-course lunch for US$8.50.

CALIDONIA, LA EXPOSICIÓN, AND SANTA ANA

Most of the budget hotels are in and around the Calidonia/La Exposición district. This is a busy, older neighborhood near Panama Bay, with a high concentration of cheaper hotels, most of them in a 10-block area between Avenida Perú and Avenida Cuba.

Though a somewhat poor neighborhood, Calidonia is a bustling area and travelers generally feel safe enough here. Adventurous types can try one of the rock-bottom pensions along the pedestrian section of Avenida Central, but these are known hangouts for prostitutes and their customers and are not recommended. That area is busy day and night, which can add a sense of safety but makes for a noisy night's sleep. It's unquestionably a colorful place to stay, though.

In 2012, roadwork and the building of the

first phase of the new metro system were turning a significant chunk of Calidonia into a construction zone. Local businesses and residents were working around the chaos, but some of the places listed below may be affected by noise during your stay.

Some of the cheaper options in this neighborhood, especially those with the word "pension" or *"residencial"* in their names, are often used by local couples needing, shall we say, a little quality alone time. This isn't necessarily as tawdry as it sounds. While some twosomes are engaging in a financial transaction or adulterous liaison, others simply live in small houses with large families and never get any privacy at home.

US$10-25

The well-established ◖ **Mamallena** (Casa 7-62, Calle 38 Oeste just off Avenida Central, cell 6676-6163, mamallenapa@yahoo.com, www.mamallena.com, starts at US$13 pp, a/c 9 P.M.–8 A.M.) has moved to a cool old, two-story house with a terrace. It's in a relatively quiet residential area of Calidonia and has good security. The hostel, which is partnered with the newer, instantly popular hostel of the same name in Boquete, is better-looking than most: The ceilings are high, the tile floors are lovely, and there's art on the walls. Movies are shown on a big-screen TV in the front living area. Facilities include two 8-bed dorms and one 12-bed dorm (the 12-bedder is actually less crowded). Stays include the ubiquitous pancake breakfast. There are also a dozen small private rooms with shared bathrooms (US$33 s/d) that are dark and a bit cell-like but basically okay, with semi-orthopedic mattresses, in a separate building set in a "rock garden" (i.e., gravel backyard), which also has attractive, custom-made wooden picnic tables and hammocks and serves as a common area for the hostel. The private rooms are popular and fill up fast. The hostel also offers good-value tours through its own travel agency, **Panama Travel Unlimited**

(tel. 395-5014, info@panamatravelunlimited, www.panamatravelunlimited.com). These include Panama City tours (US$25/pp) and day trips to Caribbean-side attractions (US$40/pp for either Portobelo and Isla Grande or Gatún Locks and Fuerte San Lorenzo). The agency also can arrange chartered sailboat cruises around Guna Yala for US$125–150 per person. There's a book exchange and shared kitchen. Airport transfers are available for US$30 per person for up to four people; the return trip to the airport is US$5 less.

It's a miracle the neighborhood institution that is **Pensión Las Torres** (Calle 36 and Calle Perú, tel. 225-0172, starts at US$15 s/d) still exists. How much longer can it possible endure? It consists of 24 rooms in a converted house, built in 1931, that retains its original Spanish tile and other old touches that give the place character and an almost Moroccan air. Prices have not gone up here in several years. A tiny fan-cooled room with shared bathroom goes for US$15 s/d. Large rooms with air-conditioning, satellite TV, and private hot-water bathroom are also available starting at US$18 s/d. Rooms are spartan but funky, and the beds are decent. If you think of it as a hostel that has only private rooms, you'll probably be pleasantly surprised. The staff are very friendly. This is a good budget place away from the normal tourist haunts. However, the rooms with private baths don't have bathroom doors, which can be awkward if you're sharing a room. The entrance to Pensión Las Torres is a bit hard to find, as it's hidden behind bushes.

The five-story **Hotel Ideal** (Calle 17 near Calle I, tel. 262-2400, $22–24 s/d) is one of the last remnants of a certain strain of wackiness that used to flourish in Panama City. The hotel remains a popular, if ramshackle, budget-lodging option. The ceiling and walls of the lobby are covered with mirrored discs. The rooms are old and a bit shabby (ask to see several), but they have good air-conditioning, private bathrooms with hot water, and TVs. Lockers in the lobby are US$0.25. There's a basic cafeteria and, next door, a self-service launderette (US$0.50–US$1 wash, US$1–1.50 dry, 7:30 A.M.–7:30 P.M. daily). The hotel is right across the street from a large public clinic, Policlínica President Remón, which contains a pharmacy (7 A.M.–7 P.M. Mon.–Fri.).

Hotel Andino (Calle 35 Este between Avenida Perú and Vía España, tel. 225-1162 or 225-0702, info@hotelandino.net, www.hotelandino.net, US$54 s, US$60.50 d) has 43 large, spartan air-conditioned rooms with satellite TV and wireless Internet access. The hotel was recently renovated and is now much more cheerful but twice as expensive as it was a couple of years ago. It's tucked away on a quiet street close to the bustle around Parque Belisario Porras. There's a bar/restaurant on the premises.

US$25-50

The three-story **Residencial Los Arcos** (Avenida 3 Sur and Calle 44 Este, tel. 225-0569, 225-0570, or 225-0571, US$44 s/d, a/c) offers simple but clean and tasteful modern rooms in a quiet neighborhood close to the action. Rooms can also be rented by the hour, but the place does not have a tawdry atmosphere.

The six-story **Hotel San Remo** (Calle 31 Este near Avenida Perú, tel. 227-0958 or 227-2840, www.hotelsanremopanama.com, US$36 s/d, a/c), across the street from Plaza Víctor Julio Gutiérrez (the national lottery plaza), opened in early 2003 and offers 60 simple but clean, modern rooms with decent beds and free wireless Internet access. The hotel also has a restaurant/bar, secure parking, and Internet and laundry service. This place is a good value, even if some of the rooms are quite small and look out on brick walls.

Hotel Centroamericano (Avenida Ecuador between Avenida Cuba and Avenida Perú, tel. 227-4555, www.hotelcentroamericano.com, US$55 s/d, a/c) was renovated in 2011. Its 61

rooms are much spruced up, if still quite simple. All rooms have satellite TV, wireless Internet, and in-room safes. They're proud here, for some reason, of having ice machines on every floor.

The only real problem with the **Hotel Arenteiro** (Calle 30 Este between Avenida Cuba and Avenida Perú, tel. 227-5883 or 225-3175, www.hotelarenteiropanama.com, US$30 s/d, a/c) is that it's five stories high but has no elevator. If you have a lot of luggage, ask for a lower floor. It offers 58 small, minimalist rooms with thin mattresses. It may remind you of a European pension. All rooms have satellite TV and phones. There's a restaurant/bar and a protected parking lot. Prices here have actually dropped dramatically recently, which may have something to do with the metro station being dug just a block away.

The **Hotel Acapulco** (Calle 30 Este between Avenida Cuba and Avenida Perú, tel. 225-3832, US$38.50 s/d, including breakfast and a/c) is an older but well-maintained six-story place with 55 clean, pleasant rooms, efficiently run by a proud, friendly staff. The beds are on the soft side but acceptable. All rooms have satellite TV and some have little balconies. There's a 24-hour restaurant. This is a decent option in its price range.

Euro Hotel (Vía España next to Hotel Bella Vista, tel. 263-0802 or 263-0927, info@eurohotelpanama.com, http://eurohotelpanama.com, US$55 s/d), the successor to the old Hotel Europa, opened at the end of 2004. It was spruced up by a renovation but is not terribly different-looking from its older self. It offers 103 rooms, a small pool, a bar, and a roomy cafeteria. Rooms are simple, plain, and dark but otherwise perfectly okay. The furnishings are older but in good shape, and the beds are firm. Don't waste money on the suites, which are just connecting rooms featuring bedrooms barely big enough to contain the bed.

The 60-room, five-story ⬛**Hotel California** (Vía España and Calle 43, tel. 263-7736, hotelcalifornia@cwpanama.net, www.hotelcaliforniapanama.net, starts at US$44 s, US$49.50 d, a/c) has been known for many years as a place to get a decent room at a great price. Beds are somewhat hard, but rooms are nicely maintained, clean, and cheerful and have hot-water bathrooms, free wireless Internet access, safes, telephones, and satellite TV. Some have a bay view partly obstructed by high-rises. Rooms are somewhat small. The hotel is on loud, crowded Vía España and is not conveniently close to much, at least for pedestrians. Try to get a room at the back of the building, away from the road. There's a small gym and whirlpool tub on the roof. There's also laundry service and a bar/restaurant.

US$50-100

Hotel Roma Plaza (Calle 33 Este and Avenida 3 Sur, tel. 227-3844, reservas@hotelromaplaza.net, www.hotelromaplaza.net, US$71.50 s/d including breakfast) would be considered a decent two- or (on a good day) three-star hotel, if Panama used such ratings. Its rooms are light and airy and have dressing tables, satellite TV, and mini-bars. Some of the rooms smell of smoke, and a few are windowless; try to arrive early enough so you can switch rooms if you don't like the one you're shown. There's a pleasant 24-hour cafeteria, restaurant, bar, safe-deposit boxes, an attractive rooftop pool with a good view, a small gym, and free wireless Internet access. This place fills up. The hotel offers airport transfers for US$25 for two people, which is a few dollars less than the average taxi fare.

Hotel Costa Inn (Avenida Perú and Calle 39 Este, tel. 227-1522, costainn@cwpanama.net, www.hotelcostainn.com, US$66 s, US$77 d, including airport pickup and breakfast, a/c) is a seven-story hotel offering 87 rooms, a 24-hour bar/restaurant, a parking lot, room service, and a small rooftop pool with a good view of the city and the Bay of Panama. It was remodeled a few years back, and the rooms are now cheerful,

with good beds and modern furnishings, satellite TV, and free wireless Internet. This place often has promotional deals, and the standard rates have not gone up in two years. It's popular with Latin American businesspeople. Free airport pickup at either the international or domestic airport is included. The hotel also runs a free shuttle that drops guests off at the airport (though only a couple of times a day, which may or may not coincide with your flight times). Both are unusual pluses for a hotel in this category. More recently the hotel has added a free shuttle service between the hotel and both the Albrook Mall and Multiplaza Pacific Mall.

The **Stanford Hotel** (off Plaza Cinco de Mayo, tel. 262-4933 or 262-4948, www.hotelstanfordpanama.com, US$47 s, US$62 d, including breakfast) now occupies what for many, many years had been the Hotel Internacional. It's been renovated and, though still a rather spartan place, it's spruced up and more comfortable than it's been in years. The beds are cheap but firm, and the rooms are fairly clean except for the smudged walls, which could use a lick of paint. Service is a bit disorganized, but friendly. The hotel's main appeal is its location right by Plaza Cinco de Mayo, at the entrance to the pedestrian section of Avenida Central, a plus for guests who want to be in the thick of an older, commerce-driven section of Panama City and away from the more touristy areas. There's a restaurant, a rooftop terrace, Internet-enabled computers in the lobby, and a neighboring casino.

US$100-150

Eco Inn Avila (Avenida Perú between Calle 36 Este and Calle 37 Este, tel. 394-1155 or 394-1160, www.ecoinnhotels.com, US$110 s/d, including buffet breakfast) was a good deal when it opened a couple of years back, but it has since been acquired by a small Latin American chain and prices have climbed steeply. It's now overpriced, especially given its scruffy neighborhood on the edge of Calidonia, close to

© WILLIAM FRIAR

A massive bust of Albert Einstein is a handy landmark in El Cangrejo.

Bella Vista, and a couple of blocks down from Hospital Nacional. Still, it's a clean, friendly, modern place in a newish six-story building. It's worth considering if special deals are being offered. Rooms are simple but attractive, with flat-screen TVs, in-room safes, and free wireless Internet access. There's basement parking and a restaurant (7:30 A.M.–10 P.M. daily).

EL CANGREJO AND VICINITY

Most of the midrange hotels, including nearly all the *aparthotels,* are in or around El Cangrejo, in the center of Panama City. They are mainly clustered together on busy Avenida Eusebio A. Morales/2 Norte or the rather quieter Calle D. Higher-end hotels are also beginning to appear.

US$10-25

La Jungla Hostel (Calle 49 Oeste between Vía Argentina and Vía Veneto, tel. 214-8069 www.hostallajungla.com, starts at $13 pp) is one of the city's more appealing hostels, not to

mention one of the cleanest. Run by the same folks who have Hostal Nomba in Boquete, it occupies the top two floors of a six-story apartment building in a relatively quiet residential section of El Cangrejo, three buildings up from Hotel Las Huacas (which is more familiar to taxi drivers). It sleeps up to 56 people in 6–10 person mixed-sex dorms with thin mattresses and four private rooms. Beds are US$13 in a fan-cooled room, US$3 more for air-conditioning. Women who'd like a single-sex dorm pay US$14. Private rooms start at US$32 s and US$43 d for a decent bedroom with shared bath; they cost a bit more with air-conditioning. Room 10, a curved room with lots of windows, is particularly popular. The nicest dorms and private rooms are downstairs, in the more chic part of the hostel. Baggage storage and towel rental are available for a buck a day. There's free wireless Internet access. The hostel also has snorkel equipment to rent and an in-house washer/dryer. There's a 10 percent discount for those who do local volunteer work (which the hostel can arrange). This is a laid-back, friendly place. There's a security gate, closed-circuit video cameras, 24-hour staffing, a shared kitchen, and a large terrace to hang out on. La Jungla may not be well-marked. If there's no sign, check the labels on the door buzzer.

US$50-100

Hotel Marbella (Calle D near Avenida Eusebio A. Morales, tel. 263-2220, www.hmarbella. com, US$88 s/d), near the Hotel Granada, is generally considered one of the better economy hotels. It's a clean, modern, five-story place on a pleasant residential street but close to a lot of urban action. The rooms are dark and austere, and most look out on blank walls. There's a restaurant on-site.

Hotel Las Huacas (Calle 49 Oeste, about halfway between Vía Veneto and Vía Argentina, tel. 213-2222, www.lashuacashotel.com, starts at US$80 s/d) is a pleasant, reasonably priced surprise tucked away on the backstreets of El Cangrejo. A renovation in mid-2010 replaced most of its rather kitschy safari trappings, and its 33 rooms now have a sleek, modern look. The rooms vary in size but all feature a mini-bar, free wireless Internet access, and a safe. Most have a small balcony.

The 53-room, seven-story **Hotel Milan** (Avenida Eusebio A. Morales, tel. 263-6130, hotelmilan@cwpanama.net, US$77 s/d) has the same ownership as the Euro Hotel. Built in 2004, it's nothing fancy and the mattresses are cheap, but it's clean, well maintained, and in a central and reasonably quiet location (at least as of this writing). Standard rooms are fairly large and have in-room safes. Small "economical" rooms are $11 cheaper but cannot be reserved in advance. It has a restaurant/bar.

US$100-150

Aparthotel Torres de Alba (Avenida Eusebio A. Morales, tel. 300-7130, www.torresdealba.

com.pa, starts at US$99 s/d) offers what are essentially small modern apartments, each of which has a bedroom, sitting room, full kitchen, safe, and washer and dryer. The place consists of twin 13-story towers and is mainly aimed at short-term residents. But even tourists who don't need all that stuff might consider staying here; it's simple but quite nice. There's a small gym, a pool that's borderline big enough for lap swimmers, and a parking garage in the building.

Rooms at **Sevilla Suites Apart-Hotel** (Avenida Eusebio A. Morales, tel. 213-0016 or 213-1312, fax 223-6344, www.sevillasuites. com, starts at US$110 s/d, including breakfast), built in 2000, are smaller and darker than those at the Torres de Alba, but the furnishings are quite nice. Accommodations lie closer to the hotel end of the apartment-hotel spectrum, but all the suites have mini-kitchens and wireless Internet access, and some have terraces. There's a small gym and pool. Two of Panama's best restaurants, Restaurante 1985 and Rincón Suizo, are right across the street, and several others are very close.

Coral Suites Apart-Hotel (Calle D, tel. 269-2727, fax 269-0083, coralsuites@coral-suites.net, www.coralsuites.net, US$132 s, US$154 d including continental breakfast) is a modern, nicely maintained place built in 2001. It features 63 rooms with very firm beds, full kitchenettes, satellite TV, in-room safe, ironing board, and a sitting area with table. There's room service, but no restaurant. There's a decent-size rooftop pool without much of a view and a small but reasonably equipped gym. Service is rather disorganized, but this is otherwise a good place.

A more recent addition to the row of business hotels on Calle D is the six-story ◖ **Toscana Inn** (Calle D, tel. 265-0018 or 265-0019, www. toscanainnhotel.com, US$121 s/d, including breakfast). The rooms are decorated simply with a rather old-fashioned aesthetic, but the furnishings are new (the hotel opened in late

2009) and each room is equipped with a flat-screen TV, a minifridge, a safe, and firm beds. The corporate rate is about 10 percent cheaper; be sure to ask. Service is friendly and attentive. There's a small restaurant and bar, but no pool.

The three-story **Metro Hotel** (Calle D, tel. 202-5050, ventas@metrohotelpanama.com, www.metrohotelpanama.com, US$75 s/d, including continental breakfast) opened in November 2010 offering simple but clean and cheerful rooms. This place has a modern, colorful decor but is deliberately simple: it's for people who want a decent room in the center of town without paying a fortune. Entry-level rooms are little wider than the full-size bed, but the mattresses are good and the rooms feature a minifridge, safe, free wireless Internet access (guests are also welcome to use computers in the lobby), and tidy bathrooms. Another US$24 buys a room nearly twice as big, with two full beds. The hotel also offers parking and a laundry service.

The 166-room **Hotel Riande Granada** (Avenida Eusebio A. Morales near Vía España, tel.204-4444, granada@riandehotels.com, www.riandehoteles.com, starts at US$148.50 s/d) is one of the stalwarts of the Panama City hotel scene. Known universally as the Hotel Granada, for decades it was a top choice among the midrange hotels. It's needed a renovation for several years, and in 2011 it finally got it. A handsome makeover has resulted in more elegant, modern rooms but has also launched the Granada into a higher price bracket. The hotel has a casino, cafeteria, and swimming pool. It's part of the Riande chain, which also owns the Riande Aeropuerto Hotel and Resort near the international airport.

Over US$150

Victoria Hotel and Suites (Calle D, tel. 395-9000, fax 395-9001,info@victoriahotelandsuites.com, www.victoriahotelandsuites.com, rack rates start at US$193 s/d) is a modern, nine-story business hotel that opened across the street from the Veneto Hotel and Casino in the autumn of 2010. It features 127 spotless rooms in a modern minimalist style with dark woods, blown-up photos of Casco Viejo, and all the amenities one would expect of a contemporary hotel in this class (32-inch flat-screen TVs, iPod docking stations, and 24-hour room service). The least expensive accommodations are the "deluxe rooms," which are spacious and have comfortable king-size beds. Request a room on a higher floor to get a view of the cityscape and a glimpse of the Pacific behind the towers. There's a tiny rooftop pool and gym, a lobby bar, and a restaurant. Service is friendly.

BELLA VISTA AND MARBELLA

Most of Panama's luxury hotels and a few hostels are found on or south of Vía España in the *area bancaria* (banking area) and the surrounding districts of Bella Vista and Marbella. Streets here are alive 24 hours a day.

Being conveniently close to both Vía España and the Calle Uruguay nightlife area makes this a popular location for travelers, who will definitely feel they're in the throbbing heart of Panama City. However, a great deal of skyscraper construction is going on in the area, increasing noise levels and generally disrupting the neighborhood.

US$50-100

Formerly a hostel, **San Roque Guesthouse** (Calle Ricardo Arias and Avenida 3 Sur, tel. 390-9554 or 390-9592, booking@hotelsanroquepanama.com, www.hotelsanroquepanama.com, starts at US$60.50 s/d, a/c) has been given a cheerful sprucing up and is now a pleasant if cramped 20-room guesthouse squeezed between tower blocks right next to Restaurante Costa Azul. Prices vary depending on demand, but count on around US$60.50 for a stark, windowless, but clean and modern room with satellite TV and wireless Internet access. Three people can share a room for $75, and up to six people can shoehorn themselves into a room with three beds for US$100. There's a small, enclosed patio with a waterfall, which is a nice touch. Thick walls make this a relatively quiet oasis in the middle of a busy part of town. The owners are expanding, and a terrace restaurant was in the works in 2012. Given its location, this place is a good value, especially for small groups.

US$100-150

The corncob-shaped **Hotel Plaza Paitilla Inn** (Vía Italia in Punta Paitilla, tel. 208-0600, www.plazapaitillainn.com, US$126.50 s/d) was originally a rather upscale Holiday Inn. It's now at the upper end of the midrange hotels, and though it has aged considerably, it was renovated a few years back making rooms look rather spiffy, with new floor-to-ceiling windows that replaced fragile balconies. Many of the 272 rooms have dramatic views of Panama Bay and the city skyline, though skyscraper construction is eating away at these. The hotel has a casino and pool. The rates quoted here are technically promotional, but they're more likely to be on offer than the nominal rack rates. There is not much of interest to travelers within easy walking distance.

◖**Hotel Ejecutivo** (Avenida Aquilino de la Guardia between Calle 51 and Calle 52, tel. 265-8011 or 264-3989, toll-free U.S./Canada tel. 866/876-0915, www.executivehotel-panama.com, US$104.50 s/d) has been a favorite with Latin American businesspeople for more than 30 years, and it's easy to see why. The Ejecutivo (eh-HEC-oo-TEE-voh), known as the Executive in English, is a solid value. (Several kinds of promotional discounts are routinely available—corporate, weekend, booking by Internet—that lower the cost by about 20–25 percent.) Rooms are similar to what you'd expect at a Best Western–style hotel: clean, pleasant enough, but nothing fancy. All come equipped with a refrigerator,

TV, coffeepot, telephone, desk, free Internet access, and balcony.

The hotel is centrally located just down from Vía España, and some rooms have terrific views of the lights of the city and Panama Bay, although these are disappearing thanks to the skyscraper-construction epidemic. The coffee shop offers big portions at low prices, and it's open 24 hours Thursday–Sunday. It's a popular place for breakfast. Guests are allowed to use some of the business center's facilities for free. Amenities include a tiny pool and fitness center.

Over US$150

Hotel Esplendor (Avenida Samuel Lewis and Calle Gerardo Ortega, tel. 209-9600, www.esplendorpanama.com, rack rates start at US$217 s/d) opened in late 2010 with 100 suites spread out over 42 floors. A number of newer towers in Panama City were intended to be condo towers and ended up being converted to hotels at the last minute, and this definitely feels like one of them. It's already showing signs of wear, and the service is less than gracious. On the other hand, suites have good beds, full kitchens, and are decorated in an understated, handsome style with all the usual amenities. They're spacious as well, ranging from 90 square meters for one-bedroom suites (US$217 for up to four people) to 110 for two-bedroom ones. Those on the higher floors have spectacular views of Panama City and the ocean; if you stay here, try for a place as high up as possible. One of the new arrivals on the city's culinary scene, Rausch Restaurant, is in the hotel. There's a small pool.

The 363-room **Hotel Continental and Casino** (Vía España and Calle Ricardo Arias, tel. 263-9999, www.continentalhotel.com, starts at US$130.30 s/d), right on busy Vía España, is another old Panama City landmark, but it's benefited from a tasteful remodeling that transformed it into an upscale business hotel. All the rooms are nice, but some are bigger and more elegantly appointed than others. There are quite a few categories (and prices) to choose from, so if you're not happy with what you booked, ask to see other options. The hotel has a restaurant, cafeteria, small pool, and casino. There are often promotional deals of various kinds here.

The ◖ **Panama Marriott Hotel** (Calle 52 at Calle Ricardo Arias, tel. 210-9100, fax 210-9110, www.marriott.com, starts at US$192.50 s/d) is quite an elegant place, with 295 rooms, a fitness center, a spa, and a pleasant, upscale cafeteria, but no formal restaurant. There's also a deli with sandwiches and salads. Ask for a corner room; they're the largest of the standard rooms, which come with the usual business-hotel amenities. Corporate and other special rates are often available. There are six wheelchair-accessible rooms on the lower floors. This place is one of the most popular of the higher-end hotels. It's an attractive place in a central location, with lots of dining, shopping, and entertainment options an easy walk away.

Hotel Lé Meridien (Avenida Balboa and Calle Uruguay, tel. 297-3200, www.starwoodhotels.com, starts at US$196.90 s/d) is a member of the ever-expanding hotel portfolio of local developer Empresas Bern that also includes the InterContinental Miramar next door and the Gamboa Rainforest Resort. This one goes for a hipster-chic ambience reminiscent of a W Hotel, down to the electronic lounge beats pulsating through the shiny lobby. Its 111 rooms feature modern, minimalist furnishings that suggest a nicely appointed frequent-fliers lounge. There's a restaurant, a spa, and a small pool that, at least until the surrounding buildings are completed, may not be the most comfortable spot for female sunbathers, as it draws unwelcome attention from construction workers next door. The location is convenient for those with business in the financial district or who want to explore the Calle Uruguay nightspots, but it's a bit isolated otherwise, especially at night. If you ask reception to call you a cab, you'll get a tourist taxi that is authorized to charge several times the street-taxi rate. It should be easy to catch a cab on Avenida Balboa or up Calle Uruguay if you prefer.

Built in 1951, the **Hotel El Panamá** (Vía España next to Iglesia del Carmen, tel. 215-9000 or 215-9181, www.elpanama.com, starts at US$148.80 s/d) was for many years Panama's premier hotel. It has 330 rooms, including some cabanas by the large, attractive pool. The hotel has changed hands and been renovated repeatedly over the years, but one thing remains constant: The service is lousy. Because of its international name recognition, it still draws a lot of guests, many of whom are on package holidays. For the money, you can do better elsewhere without the potential hassle. However, frequent promotional offers can make the rates tempting, and the hotel is centrally located.

◖**Hotel DeVille** (Calle Beatriz M. de Cabal near Calle 50, tel. 206-3100 or 263-0303, www.devillehotel.com.pa, starts at US$231 s/d, including breakfast) is an elegant, rather formal boutique hotel with four types of rooms: deluxe rooms, junior suites, two-bedroom duplex suites, and grand luxury suites. The "deluxe" is a spacious room with the simplest furnishings. It features a marble-tiled bathroom, high ceilings, a high-speed Internet connection, sitting area, and in-room safe. The junior suite is quite opulent, with highly polished dark woods, antique Vietnamese furniture inlaid with mother-of-pearl, a large bathroom with two sinks, a fax machine, and so on. The duplex suite resembles the junior suite but has an upper level with a bedroom and second bath. The grand luxury suite, oddly, isn't quite as luxurious as the duplex suites. Amusingly enough, given the ambivalent feelings toward Teddy Roosevelt in Panama, one of the suites is named for him. Even the fanciest suites, though more luxurious than the average overnight guest would need during a short stay, can be a decent value for families or groups. Art from local galleries is displayed in the lobby.

The ultramodern **◖ Radisson Decapolis Hotel** (behind the Multicentro Mall on Avenida Balboa, tel. 215-5000, toll-free U.S./ Canada tel. 800/395-7046, www.radisson. com, rack rates start at US$163.90 s/d) is inspired by Europe and North America's trend-setting hotels. It's quite an impressive place that will appeal to those who prefer the sleek and streamlined over old-world elegance.

Opened in 2004, it's a 29-story concoction of brushed stainless steel and glass, including a glass elevator that goes to the 14th floor and is worth the ride just for the view. Traditional Panamanian elements—*mola* patterns, devil masks, ships—inform the modern decor. The standard rooms are quite large, sleek, attractive, and minimalist, with photo blowups of Panama's indigenous peoples over the beds and large windows looking out on the view. The view is spectacular on the ocean side, particularly on the higher floors, offering a panorama that encompasses Panama Bay, the towers of Paitilla, and, in some rooms, Casco Viejo.

Each room at the Decapolis has a safe, ironing board, hair dryer, coffeemaker, Internet connection, satellite TV, and English- and Spanish-language newspapers are delivered daily. Other features include the equally striking Fusion restaurant, a martini/sushi lobby bar, a tiny pool on the 4th floor with a hot tub and bar, and several executive floors, including two exclusively for businesswomen. The hotel's spa, Aqua, has some exercise machines and offers a full range of spa services, including facials, sauna, and steam baths. The hotel connects through a walkway with the glitzy Majestic Casino and the Multicentro Mall.

◖ Hotel Riu Plaza (Calle 50, tel. 378-9000, US$208 s/d) is my favorite among the latest crop of the high-end hotels. Opened in September 2010, it has 645 rooms spread over 34 floors. Rooms are spacious and well maintained, with bright but elegant decor, comfy beds, and nicely appointed bathrooms.

They remind me very much of the rooms in the Hotel Ciudad de David in, um, the city of David. Rooms look out over either Avenida Balboa or Calle 50. There's an inviting pool area with a decent-size pool and an artificial waterfall, a gym that for a change doesn't seem like an afterthought, an attractive bar/sushi lounge which is a nice spot to hang out in the evenings, a cafeteria, and a fancy Panamanian-fusion restaurant, Tastes. The lobby area is quite dramatic, with high ceilings and ornate furnishings that suggest a cross between a retro-modern train station and a business-class airport lounge. Front desk and concierge staff are prompt and professional.

From the outside, the **Bristol** (Calle Aquilino de la Guardia between Calle 51 and Calle 52, just down from the Hotel Ejecutivo, tel. 264-0000 or 265-7844, www.thebristol. com, rack rates start at US$390 s/d) is a non-descript, salmon-colored building that's easy to overlook, especially now that bigger buildings are going up all around it. Inside, however, the Bristol is a lovely boutique hotel. It's quite a luxurious place. Standard rooms are "deluxe," and they truly are. The furnishings are elegant, with local touches such as *mola* pillows and lamp bases made from Ngöbe-Buglé sandstone figurines. The attached Restaurante Barandas is attractive and one of Panama City's most ambitious. Service can be erratic here.

The **Hotel InterContinental Miramar Panama** (Avenida Balboa, tel. 206-8888, fax 223-4891, www.miramarpanama.com, starts at US$181.50 s/d) is on the middle of Avenida Balboa and has great views of the Pacific and the Panama City skyline. With the building of the Cinta Costera, however, it's no longer on the edge of the bay but rather on a landfill island between these two major traffic arteries. It's a 185-room luxury hotel that's part of the InterContinental chain and comes with the works: two restaurants, a largish pool, a health spa, tennis court, several bars, and so on. It's about due for an upgrade but is still a comfortable place to stay. All rooms have an executive desk, three phones, broadband access, minibar, safe, and other amenities. The best things about the hotel are its views and attractive pool.

The **Marriott Executive Apartments Finisterre** (Avenida 3A Sur and Calle Colombia, tel. 214-9200, www.marriott.com, starts at US$130 s/d for an executive suite) consists of 126 suites in a new tower built in 2010 just off Vía España across from the Iglesia del Carmen. The smallest and least expensive of these is the 600-square-meter executive suite, which features a king or two double beds, a couple of sofa beds, a 32-inch LCD TV, a dining area, and a fully equipped kitchen. The decor is understated and modern. Most of the suites have a view of Cerro Ancón (Ancon Hill). There's a three-story parking garage right in the building, a small fitness center, and a spa. There's a small restaurant and a fairly large pool, both located on lower floors. This is the sort of place affluent Latin American expat families might stay while shopping around for a luxury home.

EAST PANAMA CITY
Over US$150

Sheraton Panama Hotel and Convention Center (Vía Israel and Calle 77 across the street from the Atlapa Convention Center, tel. 305-5100, www.starwoodhotels.com, starts at US$141.90 s/d) has long had the most loyal clientele of the Panama luxury hotels. It's a huge complex with 362 rooms, three restaurants, a shopping gallery, an appealing casino that has expanded in recent years, an athletic club, a pool, a spa, and so on. This is the second-oldest luxury hotel in the city, after Hotel El Panamá, and it's changed hands several times through the years; it used to be called the Caesar Park, and its incarnation as a Sheraton is relatively recent. The hotel is on the eastern outskirts of town, quite a hike from everything but the

Atlapa Convention Center, the ruins of Old Panama, and the international airport. The popular indoor/outdoor grill **Restaurante y Parrillada Jimmy** (Vía Cincuentenario, tel. 224-1096, most items under US$10) is on the far side of the Atlapa Convention Center from the hotel. A counterpart to the plainer Restaurante Jimmy near the Hotel Continental downtown, it serves no-nonsense pastas, Greek dishes, seafood, and sandwiches. It's not worth making a special trip from elsewhere in the city, but it's one of the few options for those staying in this remoter part of town.

Amid great fanfare, controversy, funding crises, and an international incident or two, the **Trump Ocean Club International Hotel and Tower** (Calle Punta Colón, tel. 215-8800, U.S./Canada toll-free tel. 855/225-9640, www.trumphotelcollection.com, starts at US$251.90 s/d) has finally arrived. Sort of. Designed to resemble a gigantic sail—quite reminiscent of the Burj al Arab luxury hotel in Dubai—it was supposed to become a skyline-defining landmark for Panama City.

That might have happened, too, except it was erected in Punta Pacífica, just east of Punta Paitilla. So many other massive towers have already sprouted up all around the Trump building that it's barely visible from most angles. This also means that "rooms with an ocean view" might more accurately be described as "rooms with a view of skyscrapers and slivers of ocean." The rooms are spacious and luxurious, with all kinds of bells and whistles and deep, fluffy duvets on the beds. The hotel also buys into the current trend of putting bathtubs in the bedroom rather than in the, you know, bathroom.

Whether you love it, hate it, or feel a bit of both, it's definitely an impressive edifice. The hotel starts high up in the building, with the hotel's three-story "sky lobby." The public areas are attractive and dramatic, paying homage to Panama with touches like tables made from petrified wood extracted from Lago Gatún,

© WILLIAM FRIAR

The Trump Ocean Club International Hotel and Tower was designed to resemble a gigantic sail.

the bottom of which is filled with trees left standing when forests were flooded to create the artificial lake during the construction of the Panama Canal.

It's entirely possible never to speak a word of Spanish in the tower, as management appears to have cornered the market on employees who speak at least a semblance of fluent English.

Service fluctuates between friendly but slow to confused incompetence.

One of the snazziest things about the place is the large, open pool deck on the 13th floor. It features five swimming pools, including a couple of infinity pools. Other features include a good-size gym and spa and several restaurants.

Food

WHAT TO EXPECT

The restaurants are among the best things about Panama City. It's easy to find good food, pleasant surroundings, and a surprisingly wide variety of cuisine. Overall, Panama City is still waiting for a truly great restaurant, but there are quite a few good ones. There are plenty of solid options in every price range to keep short-term visitors happy.

Look out for the 10 percent service charge on the bill; it's easy to double tip. The fad of placing bottled water on the table appears to be on the wane. These bottles are neither free nor necessary: Tap water in Panama is clean. If you're offered bottled water and don't want it, smile, shake your head, and ask for "Chagres" (CHA-gress) instead. (The Río Chagres is the source of Panama City's drinking water.)

For the higher-end restaurants, expect to pay about what you would for a similar place in the

United States. But it's also quite possible to stuff yourself on tasty, simple food for about US$2–3, if ambience means nothing to you. Panamanian *comida corriente* (literally, current food, meaning typical dishes of the day served cafeteria style) venues are scattered around the city, as are all kinds of American fast-food franchises.

Many of the upscale restaurants are found in two general areas on either side of Vía España: El Cangrejo to the northeast of the Hotel El Panamá, and the booming nightlife area around Calle Uruguay (also known as Calle 48 Este).

Make reservations at the fancier places, if only to be sure the restaurant is actually open. Even the best restaurants can be surprisingly empty, especially in the early evening. Things tend to get busier at lunchtime, when the upscale establishments draw a business clientele. Many restaurants are closed for lunch on Saturday and all day on Sunday or Monday.

Vegetarians may have to rely on the limited options at meat-eaters' restaurants. The safest bets are usually Asian or Italian places. Vegetarian restaurants tend to be low-end *comida corriente* places, serving food for a pittance. Vegans have especially limited options—Middle Eastern and Asian places are the best bet, followed by supermarkets. Those who eat kosher, though, have a few good options.

Restaurants are coming and going faster than ever in Panama these days. A good source of information (in Spanish) for new and notable restaurants is www.degustapanama.com.

CASCO VIEJO

Places to eat come and go especially quickly in Casco Viejo. It can be hard to find a decent place to eat on Sunday and Monday, and breakfast is tough any day. The **Super Gourmet Deli** (Avenida A between Calle 5 Oeste and Calle 6 Oeste, 8 A.M.–5 P.M. Mon.–Sat., 10 A.M.–4 P.M. Sun.) is a good option for breakfast or to grab a

René Café

sandwich or salad to go before a walking tour. Guests can sit outside or in.

Cafés

◖ **René Café** (Calle 7 Este on the north side of the cathedral, tel. 262-3487 or 228-3487, www.renecafe.com, 10 A.M.–3 P.M. and 6–10 P.M. Mon.–Sat.) has survived for several years now in a spot that has seen many cafés come and go. It's a pleasant little air-conditioned oasis with just six table-clothed tables and a gracious and attentive staff. Lunch here is a great deal: two starters (e.g., a large salad and crepes), a choice of main course (chicken, fish, pork, or veggies) and dessert (e.g., coconut flan) for less than US$10. The set dinner menu consists of more than double the number of items—at more than double the price.

Diablo Rosso café/art gallery (#11, Avenida A and Calle 7, tel. 228-4833 or 228-4837, www.diablorosso.com, café 11 A.M.–8:30 P.M. Tues.–Sat., US$5–8) is a café, but more important, it has quickly turned into an arts and culture hub for Casco Viejo. Owned by the popular Panamanian rock band Señor Loop, it displays modern works by local artists, hosts after-hours art openings and events, and holds a movie night on Wednesdays, showing the more ambitious of Hollywood movies as well as independent films and documentaries. The café is part of an emerging arts scenes that includes Relic Bar/Luna's Castle, Super Gourmet, and La Casona. It has a hipster vibe, with thrift-store furniture and arty books and magazines for sale. The café serves soup, sandwiches, quesadillas, and the like.

◖ **Caffe Per Due** (Avenida A, tel. 228-0547, 8:30 A.M.–10 P.M. Mon.–Sat., 9:30 A.M.–10 P.M. Sun.) offers tasty thin-crust pizzas and delicious homemade desserts in a friendly, casual atmosphere. Most pizzas are US$6–9 and range from gourmet experiments (roquefort, bacon, and walnut) to more conventional fare. The Italian owner, Manuela, knows what she's doing, so trust her recommendations. If she offers you *chocolatina,* her homemade brownie cake made with local chocolate, order it. The menu also includes salads and pastas. The place is quite small; try to snag a table on the back terrace if you can.

Granclement (Avenida Central between Calle 3 Oeste and Calle 4 Oeste, tel. 223-6277, 11:30 A.M.–8 P.M. Mon.–Thurs., 11:30 A.M.–9:30 P.M. Fri.–Sat., 12:30–8 P.M. Sun.) serves gourmet ice cream and sorbet by the scoop or the tub in flavors that range from the tropical (mango, *guanábana,* passion fruit) to the exotic (basil, lavender, spearmint), as well as more conventional choices. It's pricey for Panama, but hard to resist on a hot day.

International

Ego Café Urbano (Plaza Simón Bolívar, tel. 262-2045, noon–3 P.M. and 6 P.M.–11 P.M. Mon.–Fri., 6–11 P.M. Sat. and Sun.), sometimes known as Ego y Narciso, is a stylish café and bar with two nonconnecting dining areas as well as outdoor tables set along a corner of Plaza Simón Bolívar. It offers a small menu of pastas, meats, and fish for about US$10–15, as well as a bar menu of brochettes, salads, and such. It's been a popular place for several years. The safest bets are the appetizers and desserts. In any case, it's a pleasant spot for an evening drink. Service can be sluggish, particularly if you're seated in the more formal dining room, which is sort of an annex to the main café. The bar stays open after the kitchen closes so long as there are customers.

◖ **Manolo Caracol** (Calle 3 and Avenida Central, tel. 228-4640, 228-9479, or 228-0109, www.manolocaracol.net, 6–11 P.M. Mon.–Fri., 6:30–10 P.M. Sat., US$30) is the namesake restaurant of Manolo Maduño. Manolo promises *cocina con amor* (food made with love) and he delivers. There is one multicourse menu each night (if you talk to Manolo ahead of time he'll try to accommodate vegetarians), and food starts arriving as soon as you sit down. The menu changes with the season, but a typical offering might include seafood salad, portobello mushrooms, grilled shrimp, mussels, marinated tomatoes, red snapper, tuna, and something exotic for dessert. A typical meal consists of 10 courses. You definitely have to be in a receptive mood for this kind of food bombardment, but if you're willing to surrender to the experience, it offers one of the more entertaining dining options in Panama City.

Manolo's open kitchen sits right in the dining room, under a copper smoke hood and behind mounds of fresh produce set on a counter. In front of this is a dugout canoe filled with bottles of Spanish wine (the only kind served). Modern art hangs on the walls. The restaurant is a stone and concrete box, so when it's crowded, it's loud. Manolo himself, a Spaniard by way of Colombia, is a kinetic character likely to be the loudest person there. He presides over everything: He'll likely greet you as a long-lost friend with a crushing hug, and slip you a glass of wine on the house if he sees your cup is empty—just because you're such a terrific person.

Restaurante Las Bóvedas (Plaza de Francia, tel. 228-8058 or 228-8068, 5:30 P.M.–late Mon.–Sat., US$20) is built right into the historic stone vaults (*bóvedas*) of the old city's seawall, so you're dining in what was once a dungeon. The ambience alone is reason enough to stop by for a meal or at least a drink. The French-inspired main dishes have always been a secondary reason to visit, though it seems to have been on an upswing lately. The second room in the place is a bar called Los Piratas. The house drink is the caipirinha, a potent Brazilian concoction. There's live jazz in the bar on Friday and Saturday nights after about 9:30 P.M.

Mediterranean
S'Cena (near the intersection of Avenida A and Avenida Central, tel. 228-4011, www.scenayplatea.com, noon–3:30 P.M. and 7 P.M.–midnight Mon.–Sat., noon–4 P.M. Sun., mains average around US$20) is on the 2nd floor of an old two-story house just across the street from the ruins of the old Union Club. It's a small place with a great location, though the view of the ocean a few steps away is severely limited. A couple of narrow French doors lead out onto a balcony; be sure to take a look. The food is pricey and the decor is simple, but the service is friendly. Try the *mero a la brasa con fondo de romesco* (grilled grouper with romesco sauce). Note the exposed ancient wall made of bits of brick and stone. The restaurant is affiliated with the Platea Bar downstairs, which means you'll be hearing live jazz Thursday–Saturday, like it or not.

CALIDONIA, LA EXPOSICIÓN, AND SANTA ANA
Cafeterias and Diners
Restaurante Boulevard Balboa (Avenida Balboa and Calle 33, tel. 225-0914, 6:30 A.M.–1 A.M. Mon.–Sat., US$5) was a Panama institution that opened in 1958 and attracted a mix of power-breakfasting politicians and regular joes, waited on by servers who'd been there almost since the beginning. Its most notorious moment came in July of 2001, when a prominent lawyer, Roque Alberto Pérez Carrera, was assassinated there by a man who shot him twice before escaping by taxi.

The original diner finally fell victim to Panama's construction boom just shy of its 50th birthday, but it has reopened two blocks away with the same staff and clientele, but a significantly spiffier modern look. It'll never have the same cozy coffee-shop vibe, but it does have free wireless Internet and a terrace overlooking Avenida Balboa. This is the place to come for breakfast Panama City style, such as eggs with beefsteak. It's known for its grilled sandwiches and its *batidos* (milk shakes).

Café Coca Cola (Calle C and Calle 12 Oeste, tel. 228-7687, 7:30 A.M.–11 P.M. daily, US$5),

© WILLIAM FRIAR

produce market, Calidonia

across the street from Parque Santa Ana, is a slightly grungy air-conditioned diner and a Panama City institution. This place has been here forever—the building it's housed in was erected in 1907, just four years after Panama became a country—and is a good spot for people-watching and soaking up the atmosphere of a slower, quainter Panama City from an earlier era. Food ranges from sandwiches to chop suey to pasta. The espresso drinks are palatable, and I've heard good things about the *sancocho*.

A Casa de Fernando (Calle 30 Este between Avenida Perú and Avenida Cuba, tel. 225-2378, 24 hours daily, under US$10) is a pleasant tavern likely to be of interest to those staying in the Calidonia/La Exposición area, mainly because it's got a central location and is open 24 hours. It serves an absurdly ambitious variety of food, including salads, soups, sandwiches, and all the usual meats, seafood, and pasta. It's not air-conditioned, but there are ceiling fans. This is a good find.

Indian

Indian restaurants have been slow to catch on in Panama City, despite a significant South Asian population. There are usually only one or two places in the entire city, and they don't tend to stick around long. They also tend to lay off the chilies in deference to the Panamanian palate, so ask for food to be prepared *picante* if you want it with a bit of a bite and *muy picante* if you prefer it moderately hot. Those who like it fiery are probably out of luck.

Restaurante Masala (Avenida 3 Sur and Calle 45, tel. 225-0105, 11:30 a.m.–3 p.m. and 6–10:30 p.m. Mon.–Sat., under US$15) offers the usual North Indian dishes, including ample vegetarian offerings. Food here is similar to an average takeout place in the United States or the United Kingdom. The kitchen must lack a proper tandoori oven, however, as the naan is more like fried bread. Its old home, a charming Bella Vista house, was bulldozed for yet another skyscraper, and its new digs are small and dark, but pleasant buying ceviche at the Restaurante Mercado de Marisco

enough and decorated with the expected Indian flourishes. Both table and floor seating is available. It's right next to Residencial Los Arcos.

Panamanian

Fast-food stands on Avenida Perú and Calle 35, near the Ministerio de Economía y Finanzas, cater to office workers who want cheap deep-fried goodies. They're convenient to those staying in Calidonia.

Restaurante Rincón Tableño #5 (Avenida Cuba near Calle 31 Este, tel. 227-5649, 5:30 A.M.– 4:30 P.M. Mon.–Sat., 5:30 A.M.–2:30 P.M. Sun., under US$5) is a basic *comida corriente* cafeteria except that the waitresses wear pretty *pollera*-style blouses. The menu changes daily.

Pizzerias

Panama City has two branches of the beloved Napoli pizzeria. Napoli is famous for its clam pizza, but I've always been partial to its wonderfully charred, greasy pepperoni pies. There

are plenty of pastas and such on the menu, but people come here for the wood-oven–baked pizza. Plate-size individual pizzas are available for about five bucks.

The older and much plainer **Napoli** (Calle Estudiante and Calle I, one block from Avenida de los Mártires, tel. 262-2446 or 262-2448, 11:30 A.M.–11:30 P.M. Wed.–Mon.) is a good place to grab lunch during a walking tour of Avenida Central. It's a short walk up from the heart of Central. This branch has been around since 1962 and is an institution. It has an air-conditioned interior and an outdoor seating area where you can look out on what's left of the street life in this once bustling, now declining, area. The second branch is in Obarrio.

Seafood

Restaurante Mercado de Marisco (Avenida Balboa, tel. 377-0379, 11 A.M.–6 P.M. daily, closed the first Mon. of each month, mains around US$10) is just upstairs from the city fish market, which is at the west end of Avenida Balboa. It boasts that it has the "best and freshest fish and seafood in Panama," and one would hope so, given its downstairs neighbor. (The fish market is modern and fairly clean.) It's reasonably priced and offerings include ceviche, seafood soup, corvina, jumbo shrimp, and octopus in garlic sauce. The ceviche is particularly popular. If you don't see anything on the menu you like, buy your own fish downstairs and have it cooked here. The restaurant is a spartan place with little atmosphere, but there's a partial view of the bay and the Panama City skyline. The waitstaff are friendly and speak a little English. Since the area is a bit rough, it's best to come here at lunch. Come early or late to avoid the lunch rush, as this place fills up.

EL CANGREJO AND VICINITY

Some of the city's most established restaurants are in El Cangrejo, particularly along Avenida Eusebio A. Morales. Vía Argentina is mostly known as a relatively quiet place to go for breakfast, a cup of coffee and a snack, or typical Panamanian food.

Cafés

It's about time Panama City got a place like the **New York Bagel Café** (off Vía Argentina, next to Einstein's Head, tel. 390-6051, 7 A.M.–8 P.M. Mon.–Fri., 8 A.M.–8 P.M. Sat., 8 A.M.–3 P.M. Sun.). It serves more than half a dozen decent coffees by the cup in a fittingly shabby coffeehouse atmosphere that's more San Francisco than New York, with thrift-store furniture and art on the walls. Full breakfasts are served all day for around US$6. The bagels actually taste like bagels, they try their hand at Tex-Mex, and US$4 gets diners wireless Internet access with no time limit.

Cafeterias and Diners

If you're just looking for a simple place for breakfast or a snack, try **Churrería Manolo** (Vía Argentina 12 at Avenida 2B Norte, tel. 264-3965, 7 A.M.–1 A.M. daily, US$5). Though it's been given a rather austere remodeling, it still has an unpretentious coffee-shop atmosphere that has attracted both locals and resident foreigners for years. It's hard to explain the fondness for this place. The food quality goes up and down; the only things you can really count on are the churros. The yummiest churro is the *manjar blanco*—the filling is similar to condensed milk and looks disgusting, but it's so tasty it'll curl your toes. For a real sugar buzz, order the churros along with *chocolate a la española* (Spanish hot chocolate), which is thick and delicious. Mainly, though, Manolo is just a relaxing place to hang out on one of the few streets in the city that strike a nice balance between bustle and mellowness. After breakfast, sandwiches are the best bet. Other offerings include pasta, meat, and seafood.

East Asian

Panama City's longest-established Japanese restaurant is **Matsuei** (Avenida Eusebio A. Morales, tel. 264-9562 or 264-9547, www.matsueipanama.com, noon–11 P.M. Mon.–Sat., 5:30–10:30 P.M. Sun. and holidays, most items US$7–9), a small, simple place with a sushi bar that's been around since 1978. It has an extensive menu of sushi and sashimi, but far from budget prices. Cooked options include corvina prepared "Japanese style," tempura, and so on. The sushi's okay, but nothing special. This place is pretty consistent for Panama, where sushi places come and go. The *ebi* (shrimp) is tasty, but I don't recommend the California rolls. Imported fish is more expensive.

International

Restaurante 1985 (Avenida Eusebio A. Morales near Vía Veneto, tel. 263-8571 or 263-8541, www.1985.com, noon–11 P.M. Mon.–Fri., 6–11 P.M. Sat.–Sun.) is one of Panama's best restaurants, and one of its most expensive. It's under the command of Chef Willy Diggelmann, a long-established chef with an ever-expanding empire that includes Rincón Suizo, Caffé Pomodoro, and a rather pedestrian wine bar called the Wine Bar. It specializes in French cuisine and seafood but also offers German, Swiss, Spanish, and gourmet vegetarian dishes. The atmosphere is kind of floral country French, and not at all stuffy. This is a nice place for a splurge, as most dishes are in the double digits. If you're going by taxi, tell the driver you want to go to *restaurante mil noveciento ochenta y cinco,* or just point to this entry.

Rincón Suizo (Avenida Eusebio A. Morales near Vía Veneto, tel. 263-8310, www.1985. com, noon–11 P.M. Mon.–Fri., 6–11 P.M. Sat.–Sun.) is upstairs from Restaurante 1985, in the same building, and serves good Swiss and German food in a darker, cozier atmosphere. Offerings include raclette, *berner rösti* (fried potatoes), and cheese fondue. The food tends to be a bit cheaper here than at 1985.

Panamanian

Restaurante y Cafetería El Trapiche (Vía Argentina, tel. 269-2063 or takeout 269-4353, 7 A.M.–11 P.M. daily, US$4–9) has long been a local favorite for traditional Panamanian fare such as *mondongo* (tripe), *hojaldres* (fry bread), tortillas, tamales, and *ropa vieja* (shredded beef with rice). Those who want to sample a variety of things can go for the Fiesta Panameña (US$11). Breakfast is served until 11:30 A.M. and includes such hearty fare as scrambled eggs, steak, white cheese, and *carimañola* (a fried, meat-stuffed roll) for around US$5. There's an air-conditioned interior as well as seating outside on Vía Argentina.

Peruvian

The first time I visited **◼ La Mar** (Calle Guatemala next to the PowerClub Gym near Vía Argentina, tel. 209-3323, www.lamarcebicheria.com, noon–3 P.M. and 7–11 P.M.

Mon.–Fri., 12:30–11 P.M. Sat., 1–9 P.M. Sun., mains US$10–20) none of the six types of ceviche on the menu were available. This might seem like a problem for a place that calls itself a *"cebichería Peruana"* (Peruvian ceviche) restaurant. But the seafood here is so good one imagines the chef just hadn't found anything suitable in the market that day. Part of the growing culinary empire of the celebrated Peruvian chef Gastón Acurio, La Mar offers an extensive menu of Peruvian specialties, many of which will be unfamiliar to non-Peruvians. (The restaurant's website offers a Peruvian gastronomic dictionary, for Spanish speakers.) Originally opened as the high-end Astrid and Gastón, it has been reopened as a more casual but still sleek place with gray slate walls, shiny black tabletops, a ceviche bar, and a glassed-in kitchen. Service is also casual, for better or worse.

The waitstaff can make suggestions if you get overwhelmed, though unless you like organ meats beware of anything with *corazon de ternera* (calf heart), a Pervuian delicacy but not to everyone's taste. Seafood is definitely the way to go here, as the preparation is outstanding. The *especial macho,* for instance, is a butter-soft fillet of whatever mild fish is fresh that day on a bed of mashed potatoes and topped with tender calamari and shrimp that actually tastes like shrimp. It's delicious. The pisco sours are sweet and potent but very tasty. The desserts are also good, but so rich and sugary you can get diabetes just looking at them.

Machu Picchu (Calle Eusebio A. Morales, tel. 264-9308, noon–3 P.M. and 6–11 P.M. Mon.–Sat., noon–9 P.M. Sun.) is a pleasant, cozy, and moderately priced Peruvian restaurant with friendly service and decent seafood, which is its specialty. A good value here is to share a number of appetizers, which average around US$5. Try the Peruvian ceviche, which is prepared quite differently from Panamanian ceviche. The house wine is good, but consider sampling a pisco sour if you've never had one and are willing to risk a drink made with raw egg. Machu Picchu has a sister restaurant of the same name in Boquete.

Seafood

My favorite place for seafood is **◖Siete Mares** (Calle Guatemala near Vía Argentina, tel. 264-0144, 11:30 A.M.–11:30 P.M. daily, US$16–24). One of the most consistent and consistently popular restaurants in the city, it's a cozy, tranquil place, and the service is good. An unusual house specialty is fried ceviche, a light and tangy appetizer. The fish is so tasty you won't need to order anything fancier than *corvina a la plancha* (grilled corvina). The restaurant has a modern look reminiscent of an upscale hotel lobby, including an artificial waterfall near the entrance. It does have one peculiar touch: chairs on rollers, like those you might find in a plush conference room. A pianist performs in the evening.

Steak Houses

Martín Fierro (Avenida Eusebio A. Morales, tel. 264-1927 or 223-1333, noon–3 P.M. and 6–11 P.M. Mon.–Sat., noon–10 P.M. Sun.) is a brightly lit place where decor runs a distant second to simply serving slabs of meat—grilled beef, chicken, and pork, either domestic or imported from Omaha, Nebraska. Expect to pay upward of US$25 for imported beef. The restaurant also serves pasta, seafood, and fish, but that's not why anyone comes here. Meals include access to a meager salad bar. If you really feel like punishing your heart, try the tasty *mozzarella frita* (fried mozzarella)—oh, go ahead, you're on vacation. Then try the quite good *tres leches* (three-milk) cake.

BELLA VISTA, MARBELLA, AND OBARRIO
Cafés

Crepes and Waffles (Avenida 5B between Calle Uruguay and Calle Aquilino de la Guardia, tel. 269-1574 or 305-6536, www.crepesywaffles. com.pa, noon–11 P.M. Mon.–Sat., 9 A.M.–11 P.M. Sun., US$10) is a popular Latin American chain that serves—guess what?—in a sunny, modern, brick-and-glass building with an air-conditioned interior, outdoor terrace, and yuppie vibe. Only the 1970s soft rock mars the pleasant atmosphere. Its large selection of savory and sweet crepes include some vegetarian options. Other offerings include lots of coffee drinks, a salad bar, pita sandwiches, and other café goodies. There are newer branches in the Multiplaza Pacific and Albrook malls.

The menu at **Ozone Café** (Calle Uruguay near Calle 48, tel. 214-9616, www.ozonecafepanama.com, 11 A.M.–3 P.M. and 6–10 P.M. or so daily, mains average US$15) is almost comically eclectic: Among other things it features Indian, Iraqi, Indonesian, German, Lebanese, Senegalese, Italian, Tunisian, and Alabaman(!) cuisine. Of these, the Middle Eastern fare is probably the safest bet, and you'd probably also do okay with the pastas, salads, and grilled meats. The food is tasty, but the chef has a fondness for oil. This is a cozy, popular little place with a low slanting ceiling and little lamps that hang above the tables. The servers are gracious and attentive.

Cafeterias and Diners

The small Vía España branch of the **Niko's Café** chain is centrally located (Vía España to the side of the El Rey supermarket, tel. 223-0111, www.nikoscafe.com, 24 hours daily). These cafeterias have proven to be quite popular because of their wide selection of simple and tasty food, fast service, cleanliness, long hours, and cheap prices. A few dollars buy heaps of meat, starches, and some veggies from long rows of steam tables. Niko's also offers fresh sandwiches, soups, individual pizzas, and desserts. Most breakfast items are US$3 or less.

There are several cafeterias within a five-minute walk of the Hotel Continental, some of which are open 24 hours a day. The best known of these, though no longer open 24 hours, is **Restaurante Jimmy** (Calle Manuel María Icaza, tel. 223-1523, 7 A.M.–11 P.M. Mon.–Sat., US$5–7, many mains under US$10), just down from the hotel. It's a neighborhood institution with a spartan but clean and modern diner atmosphere since its 2003 move to new digs. It serves a wide range of items, including its own take on Greek food (pita, tzatziki, fried eggplant, *keftedakia*, and so on), which can be odd but rather tasty. Other possibilities include *sancocho* (a local stew), pasta, sandwiches, seafood, pizza, and various meats. There's another branch across the street from the Atlapa Convention Center on the way to the international airport.

The coffee shop of the **Hotel Ejecutivo** (Avenida Aquilino de la Guardia between Calle 51 and Calle 52, 24 hours Thurs.–Sat.) serves breakfast 24 hours a day in an unpretentious, friendly atmosphere. Offerings range from a full Panamanian-style breakfast with lots of fried things bad for your health to an all-you-can-eat breakfast buffet.

Rock Burger (Calle 53 Este, tel. 233-0725, 8:30 A.M.–10 P.M. daily) is a fast-food place offering decent burgers made to order for US$3.50 for a quarter pounder up to US$8.75 for a whole pound of beef. Those with more modest appetites can order "mini-rockers," or sliders, as gringos might know them as. The menu also includes a variety of sandwiches, including some served in pita or as wraps for US$3.50–6. Breakfast goes for US$3 or less. This place is popular with families. There are also Rock Burger outlets on Calle 50 and in Costa del Este.

There's a newer, rather sleek outlet of **Churrería Manolo** (Avenida 1D Sur and Calle Juan Ramón Poll C., tel. 214-3986, 7 A.M.–1 A.M. daily) in Obarrio. Check out this well-loved chain for its great churros, Spanish hot chocolate (*chocolate a la española*), breakfast, and sandwiches.

East Asian

Madame Chang (Calle 48 near Calle Uruguay, tel. 269-1313 or 269-9654, noon–3 P.M. and 6–10 P.M. Mon.–Sat., noon–10 P.M. Sun., US$15) has long been considered Panama's best and most upscale Chinese restaurant. But it appears to be going through a rocky period. It's still worth a go, particularly at lunch. Try the clams in black bean sauce to start. The *guabina* (a mild-flavored fish) steamed in soy sauce and Chinese vegetables, when done right, is light and delicious. The atmosphere is pleasant, with tile floors and peach walls and tablecloths, but it's not particularly dressy.

Sushi Itto (Calle 55 Este near Avenida 2 Sur/Samuel Lewis, tel. 265-1222 or 265-1136, noon–10 P.M. Mon.–Thurs., noon–11 P.M. Fri. and Sat., 12:30–10:30 P.M. Sun.), right next to the Reprosa jewelry store, is part of a Mexican sushi chain (yep, Mexican). It's a modern place with an extensive sushi menu as well as tempura, rice dishes, pastas, soups, and even a few Thai dishes. The sushi's okay. There's a second outlet in the Multiplaza Pacific Mall.

Guatemalan

◀ **Hacienda Real** (Calle 49 and Calle Colombia, tel. 264-0311, www.hacienda-real.com, noon–midnight daily, mains starting at around US$17), which opened in January 2010, is a bright new star on the Panama City dining scene. Though part of a Guatemala-based group of restaurants with branches around Central America, it doesn't feel like a chain restaurant at all. Decorating the place reportedly cost millions, and it shows. Great care has been taken beyond the decor as well. One of the waiters told me the parent company even has a kind of exchange program: Waiters from Guatemala were sent down to help get the Panama City branch off the ground, and the Panamanian staff were sent to Guatemala City to learn a bit about Guatemalan food and culture.

The food is tasty rather than outstanding, but the restaurant alone is lovely enough to justify a visit. It takes up three floors and has the feel of a Guatemalan coffee baron's opulent home. It specializes in grilled meats. Be sure to try the typically Guatemalan black beans with thick tortillas. The *choricero* starter includes these along with (delicious) french fries, a heap of chorizo sausage, and guacamole. It can easily feed two people with no need for a main course. The house flan is exceptional.

The colorful basement dining room shares its space with an open-plan kitchen, but the vaulted brick ceiling makes this room noisy, especially when filled with the business crowd holding power lunches. The glassed-in terrace two floors up is a quieter option, and it has a view of the leafy neighborhood and a sliver of sea. There are many other nooks and private rooms to choose from, as well as an attractive front patio with ceiling fans for those who'd prefer to dine alfresco.

International

La Posta (Calle 49 just west of Calle Uruguay, tel. 269-1076, www.lapostapanama.com, noon–2:30 P.M. and 6:30–10:30 P.M. Mon.–Sat., US$15–30) has become one of Panama City's favorite restaurants in the last few years. It serves imported and local seafood and meats along with a number of pastas. Some of us find the food uneven, but that's no reason not to visit it. It's in a sprawling old Bella Vista home, and it's been restored and decorated in a style very different from the much-missed Eurasia, which had a similar idea. La Posta is going for tropical elegance, with bamboo and wicker chairs, ceiling fans, old tile floors, and a long, elegant bar. Somerset Maugham and Hemingway would have felt right at home.

As its name suggests, **Fusion** (Radisson Decapolis Hotel, behind the Multicentro Mall on Avenida Balboa, tel. 215-5000, 6:30–10:30 A.M., noon–3 P.M., and 6–10:45 P.M. daily, most mains US$12–28) offers a fusion of different cuisine, especially Asian and Peruvian. This is easily the most striking-looking restaurant in Panama City. Be sure to sit inside the cone-shaped room, which shoots up for three floors and is dominated by a seven-meter bust that vaguely resembles an Easter Island statue and supposedly is meant to represent the fusion of the world's different races. The hotel's swimming pool is on the floor above it. The pool has a partial glass bottom, which allows light to stream through and gives the feel of dining in an underwater temple in Atlantis. Avoid the house wine. The passion fruit dessert is delicious.

Le Bistrot (Calle 53 Este, tel. 264-5587 or 269-4025, 11:30 A.M.–11:30 P.M. daily), tucked away in a nondescript office building across from the World Trade Center in Marbella, is a Panama institution that's been around for nearly 30 years. Year after year it's been one of the city's more consistent spots for fine dining and good service, especially compared to some of its trendier (and more expensive) rivals. The chairs on rollers may remind you of Siete Mares, which makes sense since they're both owned by the same folks. The decor is dated, but this is still a good place for a romantic dinner, as the banquettes and mood lighting offer lots of privacy. Food tends toward the usual array of seafood, fish, and meats, but it's quite well prepared. The *calamari a la plancha* (grilled squid) is a bit oily but delicious. Also try the *langostinos a la thermidor* (prawns thermidor), or the very tender *filete a la pimienta* (pepper steak). The *flan de queso* (cheesecake flan) is good if you still have room.

Italian

Tre Scalini Ristorante (Calle 52 in Bella Vista, tel. 269-9951 or 269-9952, www.trescalinipanama.com, noon–3:30 P.M. and 6–11 P.M. daily, mains around US$15) offers decent Italian food and friendly service in a cozy faux-Italian atmosphere. It's been around for more than two decades and is an old standby for many a Panama City dweller. There's a second Tre Scalini in the El Dorado district (Boulevard El Dorado and Calle Miguel Brostella, tel. 260-0052 or 236-5303), if you happen to find yourself out that way. Avoid the house wine at either place.

◖**Vinoteca** (Calle 57 and Avenida 1 Sur, tel. 223-7734 or 223-4676, http://vinotecapanama.com, noon–3 P.M. and 7–11 P.M. Mon.–Fri., noon–11 P.M. Sat., mains US$15–20) is a newer Italian restaurant that has risen from the ashes of one of Panama City's most venerable ones, Restaurante de las Americas. The new place is far more contemporary, both in ambience and service, and in my opinion the food is better. The service is good here: attentive, warm, and knowledgeable. The chef himself is often in the dining room, chatting with the young, affluent international crowd and helping with service.

"Vinoteca" roughly translates to wine cellar or wine collection, and the restaurant's own offerings include a decent and reasonably priced selection of Argentinean, Chilean, and Spanish wines kept in a glass-walled room visible from the dining room. The waitstaff know their wines and are helpful in recommending good pairings with food, which is a rarity in Panama. Wine is available by the bottle, glass, or *quartino,* a mini-carafe equivalent to a large glassful. The food is not out of the world or beautifully presented, but both the pasta and risotto are good. Seafood fans should try the *risotto di frutti mare.* The restaurant is small but has lots of hard surfaces (no tablecloths, tile floors), so it can get pretty noisy when full.

Napoli No. 2 (Calle 57 and Avenida 1D Sur, tel. 263-8799 or 263-8800, noon–midnight Tues.–Sat.) is the somewhat more upscale younger sister of the original Napoli pizzeria in the much more upscale neighborhood of Obarrio. It's air-conditioned and pleasant. The service is not so hot, but the food comes fast once you finally get to order.

Mediterranean

◖**Restaurante Beirut** (Calle Ricardo Arias and Avenida 3 Sur, tel. 214-3815, noon–3 A.M. daily) has quickly become one of Panama City's favorite restaurants. Huge amounts of yummy, moderately priced Lebanese food are whisked to your table by the waitstaff, whether you sit in the air-conditioned interior or outside on the breezy covered terrace, which has fake stalactites dripping from its ceiling, creating a cave-like effect. The latter is the louder option, since the restaurant sits on a busy street across from the Marriott, but, especially in the evening—and most especially on a Friday evening—that's where the action is, and the people-watching is fun. The most economical way to eat here is to share. Go for one of the combination platters for around US$14; it consists of eight tasty items that can feed two reasonably hungry people. Even the pita is fresh and piping hot. The prices attract a younger crowd than one normally finds at this kind of restaurant, but everyone loves this place.

Habibi's (Calle Uruguay and Calle 48, tel. 264-3647, www.habibispanama.com, 11:30 A.M.–1 A.M. daily, US$10 or less) is a Lebanese café in a lovely old home that's been given an attractive modern makeover. It offers tasty Middle Eastern food, complete with hot pita bread. It's a popular place with a large front terrace for those who'd rather dine alfresco—a good option on dry-season evenings. This is also a good place for drinks and appetizers before a meal elsewhere.

The inexpensive **Athen's** (Calle 50 and Calle Uruguay, tel. 265-4637, 11 A.M.–11:30 P.M. Thurs.–Tues., under US$10) is a popular place for pizzas and for Greek salads, gyros, souvlaki, and other Greek dishes. It's a casual, fast-food kind of place with an air-conditioned interior and an outdoor terrace overlooking Calle 50 and Calle Uruguay. Each table has a phone customers can use to place an order, a gimmick undercut by the fact that the servers come around unprompted. The pizzas are just so-so. The pita sandwiches are huge and drowned in yogurt sauce but otherwise tasty. There's a second Athen's in the Obarrio neighborhood (Calle 57, tel. 223-1464) that's open on Wednesday when this branch is closed; its night off is Tuesday. A third one recently opened up in El Dorado, far away from the usual tourist haunts.

Panamanian

Restaurante-Bar Las Tinajas (Calle 51 near Avenida Federico Boyd, tel. 263-7890 or 269-3840, www.tinajaspanama.com, 11 A.M.–11 P.M. daily, US$10–15) is an unabashed tourist restaurant. It's worth checking out for its folkloric dance performances at 9 P.M. Tuesday–Saturday. Reservations are required for the show. The cuisine is Panamanian (and rather bland), and the restaurant is decorated to suggest a traditional town on the Azuero Peninsula. The quality of both the food and service can vary wildly here. Those who don't have time to travel around Panama to sample traditional Panamanian food and folklore can get a sense of it here, but those who plan to travel extensively around the country can have a less touristy experience elsewhere.

The upscale █ **Restaurante Barandas** (Calle Aquilino de la Guardia between Calle 51 and Calle 52, tel. 264-0000 or 265-7844, 6:30 A.M.–11 P.M. daily) in the Bristol hotel is noted for its nouvelle Panamanian cuisine. Traditional Panamanian fixtures such as *carimañolas* (fried, meat-stuffed rolls), corvina, and yuca are given the fusion treatment, with unusual sauces and generally lighter, healthier recipes. The executive chef is Coquita Arias de Calvo, who has her own local cooking show, books, and magazine. She is sort of Panama's answer to Martha Stewart or Nigella Lawson. The dining room is formal and quite pleasant. Food is not always consistent here.

Tastes Fusion Restaurant (Hotel Riu Plaza, Calle 500, tel. 378-9000, 6:30–10:30 P.M. daily, mains US$14–31), in the Hotel Riu, is a newer place taking a stab at

Panamanian-fusion cuisine, and for the most part they do a good job with it. It's a surprisingly small restaurant for such a massive hotel, which helps the staff give gracious and attentive service. The atmosphere aims at modern and sophisticated without being too formal. Food presentation is fancy and a bit fussy—lots of deconstructed dishes assembled at the table—but it's a pleasant place to eat. The food can be hit or miss. It's open only for dinner.

Seafood

One of Panama City's old standbys has once again become a destination restaurant thanks to a recent move to flashy new digs. █ **Casa de Mariscos** (Calle Manuel María Icaza, tel. 223-7755 or 264-2644, www.lacasadelmarisco-acha.com, noon–11 P.M. daily, most US$20–30) is an impressive-looking place with a polished stone facade, two-story ceilings, a plate-glass wall overlooking a small illuminated garden, and big, colorful paintings on its walls. The restaurant is still affectionately known to regulars as Acha in honor of its Spanish owner, Ramón Martínez Acha, who founded the original Casa de Mariscos in 1965 with his wife, Claudia Vásquez de Martínez. The seafood is well-prepared and delicious. For such a stylish and modern place, the restaurant holds on to some old ways it should have ditched by now, such as a pedestrian wine list and hairnets for some of its waitstaff. But it's still a good bet for a fancy night out.

Steak Houses

Market (Calle Uruguay and Calle 47, tel. 264-9401, noon–2:30 P.M. and 6:30–11 P.M. Mon.–Wed., 11:30 A.M.–11 P.M. Thurs.–Sat., 11:30 A.M.–9 P.M. Sun.), by the owner of the popular Restaurante La Posta, has been a favorite among Panamanian, gringo, and European meat lovers for the last few years. Market is known for its steaks (around US$30 for imported U.S. beef; about half that for tougher local beef from Chiriquí) and burgers (about US$7 for most, or more than double that for a colossal Angus beef burger). Burgers and beer are the best value. Market also does a pretty tasty Cobb salad and maracuya (passion fruit) pavlova. This is a fairly casual place with a large, high-roofed bar area, separated by walls of wine bottles from a slightly more formal dining area. The sound can be deafening when it's busy, such as a Sunday night, which is the traditional family night out for Panamanians who can afford it. Market also serves brunch on Saturday and Sunday.

An old standby, **Gaucho's Steak House** (Calle Uruguay and Calle 48, tel. 263-4469 or 263-1406, noon–3 P.M. and 6–10:30 P.M. daily) serves decent steaks for those who don't expect much more in a dining experience. Both the atmosphere (brightly lit, chain-steak-house vibe) and the food (this is a place for meat: you won't find much green outside the potted plants) are unadorned. The service tends to be fast and perfunctory. Though ostensibly an Argentine steak house, Gaucho's imports its meat from the United States. Expect to pay upward of US$25 for imported beef. Chicken and seafood are also on the menu, but that's not why people come here. For starters, try the *picado de chorizo* (a plate of sliced sausages); it's delicious.

Vegetarian

Me Gusta Comida Vegetariana (Calle Ricardo Arias, no phone, 7:30 A.M.–8 P.M. Mon.–Sat., portions US$0.60/each) has an ambience as plain as its no-frills food. It serves *comida corriente* cafeteria items and a few other goodies such as soy milk and veggie burgers. Its name, by the way, translates to the suitably plain "I like vegetarian food." It's near Restaurante Costa Azul, but probably not for much longer. It's a miracle it's survived the wrecking ball so far, as towers are sprouting all around it.

SUPERMARKETS AND SPECIALTY FOODS

Supermarkets are everywhere in Panama City, and in recent years their selections have vastly improved. They now more closely resemble mega-markets in the United States, with an array of imported and local goods, including a better choice of fresh produce (difficult growing conditions make much beyond tropical fruit hard to come by in the tropics).

Panama's biggest grocery-store chain is **El Rey.** It has close to a dozen stores in the greater Panama City area alone. The one on Vía España (tel. 223-7850, 24 hours daily) is centrally located and has a pharmacy and many other services. The more upscale **Riba Smith** supermarket has four locations in Panama City at last count. The most convenient for visitors are in Bella Vista (Calle 45, tel. 225-6247, 7:30 A.M.–9 P.M. Mon.–Sat., 8 A.M.–8 P.M. Sun.), on the Transístmica (tel. 299-3999, 7:30 A.M.–9 P.M. Mon.–Sat., 8 A.M.–8 P.M. Sun.), and in the Multiplaza Pacific shopping center (tel. 302-3793, 7:30 A.M.–9 P.M. Mon.–Sat., 8 A.M.–8 P.M. Sun.). The stores have buffet-style cafeterias as well. Riba Smith also does home (and presumably hotel!) deliveries with 24 hours notice and a modest minimum purchase.

Foodie Market (Bal Harbour shopping center in Punta Paitilla, 7:30 A.M.–8:30 P.M. Mon.–Fri., 8 A.M.–7 P.M. Sat., 9 A.M.–8 P.M. Sun.) is a small market that has good veggies and fruit.

Some of Panama's best coffee is at **Café Ruiz** (World Trade Center on Calle 53, tel. 265-0779, www.caferuiz.com, 7:30 A.M.–6 P.M. Mon.–Fri.). It's a café and shop that carries all kinds of roasts and flavors of coffee, both whole bean and ground. Attractive gift packages and mugs are available. Café Ruiz coffee is also available at some supermarkets, but the gourmet roast is available only at the Café Ruiz shops.

Felipe Motta in Marbella (Calle 53, tel. 269-6633, 9 A.M.–7 P.M. Mon.–Fri., 9 A.M.–6 P.M. Sat.) has a good selection of wines at prices comparable to what you'd find in the United States. It also has some gourmet foods and fresh bread and pastries.

Kosher Food

There's a kosher cafeteria/bakery, a kosher supermarket, and occasionally a kosher restaurant clustered together in Punta Paitilla. These have good, unusual (for Panama) offerings that may be of interest even to those who don't keep kosher. They are great options on Sunday, when many other places are closed, but expect crowds. **Pita-Pan Kosher** (Vía Italia, tel. 264-2786 or 265-1369, 7 A.M.–9 P.M. Mon.–Thurs., 7 A.M.–5 P.M. Fri., 9 A.M.–9 P.M. Sun., US$3.50–6) is an air-conditioned kosher cafeteria in the upscale Bal Harbour shopping center just off Avenida Balboa. It serves fish, salads, pasta, sandwiches, pizza, quiche, hummus with falafel, and so on. It even has kosher sushi. The food here is tasty. Another plus is that it serves pita and other fresh bread by the loaf. It's closed Friday evening through Sunday morning for the Sabbath.

Super Kosher (Calle 56 Este, tel. 263-5253, 8:30 A.M.–8:30 P.M. Sun.–Thurs., 8:30 A.M.–4:30 P.M. Fri.) is an upscale kosher supermarket one street north of the Bal Harbour shopping center. It has good veggies and products from the United States. There's a cafeteria inside that serves breakfast items, sandwiches, and other goodies, all kosher.

Information and Services

TOURIST INFORMATION

Panama's government tourism ministry, the Autoridad de Turismo Panamá (ATP), has its administrative headquarters at the Atlapa Convention Center next to the Sheraton Panama Hotel and Convention Center off Vía Israel, but it's not set up to deal with actual visitors. If you're eternally optimistic, you can try calling the office at 226-3544 or 226-7000. Until recently it was known as IPAT (Instituto Panameño de Turismo).

You will occasionally see ATP information booths around town, including ones at the ruins of Old Panama. There's also an information booth between Immigration and Customs at Tocumen International Airport that's sometimes staffed, though don't expect much more than a handful of hotel flyers. (Grab the business cards, if there are any—some of these offer 10 percent off at restaurants and businesses you might actually want to visit.)

Taxi drivers often double as tour guides. Don't expect a scholarly lecture on the sights, but it can be a reasonable way to cover a lot of ground. Agree on a price ahead of time.

MAPS

Tourist maps of Panama City are still a half-hearted affair. They tend not to be widely available, user-friendly, or terribly accurate or up-to-date, and they often seem little more than a guide to advertisers who paid to be put on the map, literally. Your best bets are the fold-outs that come with the free *Focus Magazine,* copies of which are easy to find in hotels and tourist-oriented sights around the city. City maps are sometimes for sale at bookstores, pharmacies, and Gran Morrison department stores. The stores also may carry one of several pictorial maps of Casco Viejo that have popped up in the last few years; these can make navigating around its maze of streets a bit easier.

HOSPITALS, POLICE, AND EMERGENCIES

Panama has begun offering free health insurance to tourists who enter the country by air. An explanatory leaflet should be distributed to passengers upon their plane's arrival.

The emergency number for the police (*policía*

nacional) is 104. The emergency number for the fire department *(bomberos)* is 103. Directory assistance *(asistencia al directorio)* is 102. The national operator can be reached at 101. To reach the international operator, dial 106.

The Panamanian government has a hotline for tourists who are lost, have been robbed, or are having any other problems (including with the police). The hotline's operators should be able to help tourists who speak English, Spanish, French, and Portuguese. The hotline number is 178.

The fire department *(bomberos)* has a reputation for arriving on the scene of an emergency before the police. Panama City finally has an official emergency medical response service. Dial 911 to call an ambulance (this is only for medical help; dial 104 for the police). This service, **Sistema Único de Manejo de Emergencias** (Unified System for the Management of Emergencies, www.sume911.pa), is slowly being rolled out around the country. This is a relatively new service. If an ambulance doesn't come quickly, your best bet may be to grab a taxi and get to the closest hospital.

Hospital Punta Pacífica and Hospital Nacional would be my first choices in an emergency, and both are central. There are private ambulance services in Panama City, though these are really aimed at already-existing subscribers. One to try is **SEMM** (tel. 366-0122 for emergencies, tel. 366-0100 for office, http://semmpanama.net).

Panama City has excellent medical facilities and excellent doctors and dentists, many of whom were trained in the United States and speak English. Even those without medical insurance can receive good care for far less than in the United States. It is illegal for foreigners to use government-funded *seguro social* (social security) hospitals and clinics, unless they work in Panama and have an employer who pays into the *seguro social* system. Attempting to do so is insurance fraud, which is a serious crime.

Centro Médico Paitilla (Calle 53 and Avenida Balboa, tel. 265-8800 or 269-0333, www.centromedicopaitilla.com) has long been considered Panama's best medical center. The **Hospital Nacional** (Avenida Cuba between Calle 38 and Calle 39, tel. 207-8100 or 207-8102, emergency room tel. 207-8110, 207-8136, or 306-3310, ambulance tel. 207-8119, www.hospitalnacional.com) opened a facility in 1998 and has been positioning itself as catering to the expatriate and foreign tourist market. The glittery new kid in town is **Hospital Punta Pacífica** (Punta Pacífica, tel. 204-8000, emergencies tel. 204-8184 or 204-8185, www.hospitalpuntapacifica.com). The hospital is affiliated with Johns Hopkins Medicine International, which provides advice and training from the acclaimed medical center in Baltimore, Maryland.

The pharmacy at the centrally located **El Rey supermarket** (tel. 223-1243) on Vía España is open 24 hours a day. **Farmacia Milani** (Calle 33 and Avenida Justo Arosemena/Avenida 3 Sur, tel. 225-0065), across the street from Hotel Roma Plaza in Calidonia, is also open 24 hours a day. **Farmacia Arrocha** is a large drugstore chain. Centrally located branches include one just off Vía España (Calle 49 Este, tel. 223-4505, 7 A.M.–9:45 P.M. daily), about midway between the Hotel Ejecutivo and the Hotel El Panamá, and one in the Albrook Mall (tel. 315-1728).

NEWSPAPERS AND PERIODICALS

All of Panama's daily newspapers are published in Panama City and are widely available at newsstands and in shops. Most are in Spanish (there are also long-established Chinese-language papers for the Chinese immigrant population). There are currently no stand-alone English-language daily newspapers, though some of the Spanish-language dailies are flirting with running stories in English, both in print and online.

Focus Magazine, a free magazine published twice yearly in English and Spanish, contains brief, enthusiastic articles on various attractions around the country, as well as maps, hotel and restaurant listings, and general tourist information. The same folks put out *The Visitor* (www.thevisitorpanama.com), a free, twice-monthly, bilingual tourist newspaper. Both are widely available at hotels and other locations that cater to travelers.

NATIONAL LIBRARY

Panama's national library, the four-story **Biblioteca Nacional de Panamá** (Parque Recreativo Omar off Vía Porras, tel. 224-9466 or 221-8360, 9 A.M.–6 P.M. Mon.–Fri., 9 A.M.–5 P.M. Sat.), may be of interest to those who want in-depth information on Panama. The collections include books by Panamanian authors or about Panama, and newspaper morgues dating from the 19th century. A wall of filing cabinets contains biographical information on prominent Panamanians and expatriates. The library is open to the public, but the stacks can't be browsed: Visitors search the electronic catalog on the 3rd floor and then request their selection from a librarian. All books must be perused on the premises; borrowing privileges have been suspended because too many people did not return books. There are several quiet, comfortable areas to read inside the library.

NAUTICAL CHARTS

Islamorada Internacional (Bldg. 808, Avenida Arnulfo Arias Madrid/Balboa Road, tel. 228-4348 or 228-6069, www.islamorada.com, 8 A.M.–5 P.M. Mon.–Fri.) is the place to go in Panama for nautical charts, books, software, instruments, flags, and pendants. It's actually in Balboa, in the former Canal Zone, across the street from the huge fountain of Arnulfo Arias. It lays claim to being the largest nautical bookstore in Panama. It also has general guidebooks to the Caribbean and elsewhere. Yachters can reach it in Balboa harbor at VHF channels 12

and 16; in Cristóbal try VHF 65 and 85, Radio Balboa. The staff speak fluent English here.

MONEY

Strangely enough for an international banking capital, until recently there were only two places in and around Panama City where visitors could exchange currencies. New places have begun to pop up around Plaza Concordia on Vía España and Vía Veneto next to Hotel El Panamá. But these deal mainly in euros and Colombian pesos, and they tend to be a bit casual and borderline shady, the kind of places where you can also cash checks and buy cheap watches.

Those who must exchange currency are much better off going to **Panacambios** (Vía España, tel. 223-1800, 8 A.M.–5 P.M. Mon.–Fri.), toward the back of the Plaza Regency next to Plaza Concordia. It's a Panama institution that's been in the same place since 1990. It's set back from the street and comes equipped with an armed guard and security gate. Panacambios carries every currency you can think of. How good the exchange rate will be depends on the currency: There's not much of a market to buy Colombian pesos, for instance, so you're probably better off spending them in Colombia than selling them here. The staff here are good-natured pros, and if you ask, they'll probably tell you if they can offer a good rate for whatever currency you have or want. Rates for euros and colones are more competitive, but in general they will be no better than those at a U.S. airport exchange counter—in other words, not a steal. Panama is dollar country.

The **Banco Nacional de Panamá** branch (7 A.M.–11 P.M. daily) in Tocumen International Airport has traditionally exchanged some major currencies, but in 2012 they had at least temporarily suspended this service.

The centrally located **Scotiabank** (Avenida Federico Boyd and Calle 51, 8 A.M.–3:30 P.M. Mon.–Fri., 9 A.M.–12:30 P.M. Sat.) in Bella Vista cashes travelers checks, something that can be quite a hassle in Panama.

Banks with ATMs are all over Panama City. For those staying in the Calidonia area, branches of **Banco Nacional de Panamá** (BNP) and **BBVA** (hours for both: 8 A.M.–3 P.M. Mon.–Fri., 9 A.M.–noon Sat.) are centrally located on a busy street. They both have 24-hour ATMs. The **HSBC** (10:30 A.M.–6 P.M. Mon.–Fri., 9 A.M.–3 P.M. Sat.) at the Multicentro Mall has unusually long hours during the week. Avoid the main BNP branch on Vía España; it gets absolutely packed.

Those who need to send or receive money the old-fashioned way can find **Western Union** (www.westernunion.com) outlets just about anywhere in Panama City. The main office is in the Plaza Concordia shopping complex (Vía España, tel. 800-2224, 8 A.M.–7 P.M. Mon.–Fri., 8 A.M.–5 P.M. Sat.). Other centrally located offices include a large center in the Albrook Mall (tel. 269-1055, 10 A.M.–7 P.M. daily), as well as an outlet next door in the Gran Terminal de Transportes. There's an outlet in the Super Empeñas San Ramón store in Calidonia (Calle 34 near Avenida Perú, tel. 225-1952, 7:30 A.M.–5:30 P.M. Mon.–Sat.). **MoneyGram** has about three dozen outlets in Panama City. The one at the Plaza Concordia is in the Bambi Empeños stores (Vía España, tel. 263-4293, 8 A.M.–6 P.M. Mon.–Fri., 8 A.M.–3 P.M. Sat.).

POST OFFICE

Panama's main post office is in Calidonia (Avenida Central between Calle 33 and Avenida Perú, 7 A.M.–5:45 P.M. Mon.–Fri., 7 A.M.–5 P.M. Sat.), across from the Basílica Don Bosco. There's a small **stamp museum** (tel. 512-0601, 8:30 A.M.–4:30 P.M.) in the complex that consists of a few recent first-day covers stuck on the wall of an office. Other post office branches include ones in the Plaza Concordia shopping center on Vía España and next to Restaurante Boulevard Balboa (Avenida Balboa near Calle 31). All are open the same hours as the main post office.

COMMUNICATIONS

Free wireless Internet has sprung up everywhere in Panama—in hotels, hostels, restaurants, cafés, you name it—and nowhere is this more true than in the capital. Often, for better and worse, there's no password protection, and it's just a matter of firing up your computer or phone and logging on. Even if you find a place that isn't yet wireless equipped, chances are you'll have a half dozen other signals from neighboring establishments to choose from, with proprietors who don't care if you piggyback. The Panamanian government is also rolling out a program of free Wi-Fi hotspots in public parks, hospitals, and schools around the country.

Internet cafés open and close constantly in Panama City, and the proliferation of free access throughout the city is bound to make the attrition rate even worse. Most are just bare-bones air-conditioned rooms with terminals, but the rates are good—usually around US$0.50–0.75 an hour. It's often possible to pay for just a half hour or 15 minutes. Some offer international calling at competitive rates (about US$0.20 a minute to Costa Rica or the United States, for instance). A few also send and receive faxes; domestic faxes tend to be reasonable, but sending an international fax can cost US$5 a page or more. Be sure to ask for rates ahead of time.

There are plenty of Internet cafés in the Calidonia area, where most of the budget hotels are. Many of these hotels also have Internet computers, often dollar-fed ones. A convenient Internet café is between the immigration office and Restaurante Pizzeria Romanaccio (Calle 29 Este between Avenida Perú and Avenida Cuba, no phone, 8 A.M.–midnight daily).

The Plaza Concordia shopping complex on Vía España has several places to access the Internet, the nicest of which is next to Western Union in the Cable and Wireless international call center (8 A.M.–9:30 P.M. Mon.–Sat., 9:30 A.M.–8 P.M. Sun.), which also charges standard rates for international phone calls. The Multicentro Mall also has call centers and Internet cafés. Passport-photo shops are in the same complex. There are plenty of other Internet places in the heart of Vía España. Centro Comercial Vía Veneto, the shopping center to the side of the Hotel El Panamá on Vía Veneto, has several 24-hour Internet cafés/international call centers. Names and ownership change seemingly overnight. Other Internet cafés in the Vía España area include a couple on Calle Ricardo Arias off Vía España, just south of the Hotel Continental.

Bytes Café/Sepia Restaurant (Vía Argentina, no phone, 7 A.M.–11 P.M. Mon.–Sat.) is across the street from and just north of the Vía Argentina branch of Churrería Manolo. It also places international calls.

Enterprising street vendors are now offering use of their cell phones to make local calls for around US$0.20, which can be more convenient than hunting for a pay phone. These are easiest to find in working-class commercial areas such as Calidonia, La Exposición, and Santa Ana.

However, those expecting to make lots of local calls are better off buying a local mobile phone that can be recharged with prepaid phone cards. Surprisingly good ones with clear sound and long battery life are widely available in shops throughout Panama for about $15–20, including a local SIM card, immediate activation, and US$2 in phone credit.

Internet cafés have been slow to come to Casco Viejo. But free wireless access is increasingly common in the area's lodgings and restaurants.

VISAS AND OFFICIALDOM

Panama City's main **Migración y Naturalización** (Immigration and Naturalization, Avenida Cuba and Calle 29 Este, tel. 207-1800, 777-7777, or 227-1077, tel./fax 227-1227, 8 A.M.–3 P.M. Mon.–Fri.) office is in Calidonia, close to most of the budget hotels. Visitors who need to change or extend their visa should come here (and be prepared for a long day).

LAUNDRY

Lavamáticos (launderettes) are harder and harder to find in central Panama City (as opposed to *lavanderías,* which are comparable to dry-cleaning places in the United States). Hostels and both budget and business-oriented hotels often provide laundry service at quite reasonable rates; be sure to ask for prices ahead of time. Some hotels, especially *aparthotels,* have self-service washers and dryers. *Lavamáticos* generally charge around US$5–6 total to wash and dry a load. Washing in cold water is often a bit cheaper.

Lavandería Dry Clean (Calle Ricardo Arias near Avenida 3 Sur, 7:30 A.M.–7:30 P.M. Mon.–Sat.) is right next to Restaurante Costa Azul in Bella Vista.

Lavandería Fan Clean (tel. 399-2108, 7 A.M.–8:30 P.M. Mon.–Sat., 7:30 A.M.–5 P.M. Sun.) is across the street from Einstein's Head, about a block north of Vía Argentina in El Cangrejo.

Launderettes are scarce in Calidonia/La Exposición, but the midrange hotels often have laundry service. There's a *lavamático* in Casco Viejo (Avenida Central near Calle 8 Este, 7 A.M.–7 P.M. Mon.–Sat., 7 A.M.–3 P.M. Sun.) next to the cathedral. It charges US$0.50–$1 to wash, US$1 to dry.

SPANISH LANGUAGE COURSES

The Canadian-run **Spanish Panama** (Vía Argentina and Avenida 3B, tel. 213-3121, www.spanishpanama.com) is a well-established school in El Cangrejo that offers a range of private and group classes. In April 2010 it moved to new digs a few blocks away from its old home, which had been plagued by construction noise. Group classes that include airport pickup, lodging, breakfast, and (optional) salsa dance classes start at US$400/week. A one-week crash course (language instruction only) is US$180. Free weekly cultural and orientation activities are also available. Spanish Panama is on Vía Argentina near the turnoff for Einstein's Head.

Casco Viejo now has a Spanish-language school. Run by former Peace Corps volunteers, **Casco Antiquo Spanish School** (Avenida A and Calle 4, tel. 838-5592, www.cascospanish. com) is in a crumbling old building with lots of character that houses several nongovernmental organizations that give the place the feel of a lively community center. Group lessons with two to three people are US$9.50/hour. Private lessons tailored to individual needs are US$12/ hour. Intensive courses in groups of no more than six people start at US$195/week. Business-Spanish tutorials are US$18/hour. The school can arrange lodgings in local hostels and volunteer opportunities with the nongovernmental organizations in the building.

Getting There

Panama City, not surprisingly, is the country's transportation hub. It has its major international and domestic airports, its biggest bus terminal, its main ship ports, and plenty of rental car companies. Most travelers come to and leave the country through Tocumen International Airport, 25 kilometers east of Panama City. (It's pronounced "toe-COO-men," not "TOC-you-men," as many tourists and expats think.) The nearest cruise-ship port is at the end of the Calzada de Amador, which is near the Pacific entrance to the Panama Canal a few kilometers from downtown. The national bus terminal, for international, regional, and local buses, is the Gran Terminal de Transportes in Albrook. It's quite close to Panama City's domestic airport, Aeropuerto Marcos A. Gelabert, also in Albrook.

No roads or ferry service currently link Panama and Colombia; only airlines provide regular passenger service between the two countries.

DOMESTIC FLIGHTS

Panama City's small domestic airport, officially called **Aeropuerto Marcos A. Gelabert,** is near the Gran Terminal de Transportes in Albrook, a former U.S. Air Force base. It's just a couple of kilometers northwest of the heart of Panama City. Flights generally leave Panama City early in the morning, though some popular destinations have multiple daily departures scattered throughout the day.

Most taxi drivers won't know the airport by name: Ask to go to the Aeropuerto de Albrook. Emphasize that you want to go to Albrook to avoid being taken to Tocumen, the international airport. The fare from most parts of Panama City should be only a few dollars. It will generally make more sense, and even be more economical overall, to take a taxi directly to the airport than fool with making the short ride from downtown to Albrook by bus.

Air Panama (tel. 316-9000, www.flyairpanama.com) is the country's one remaining domestic carrier, following the sudden collapse of Aeroperlas in February 2012. Unless and until a new enterprise takes off, this is the only option for in-country flights. Air Panama was so inundated with new business following the demise of Aeroperlas that passengers were having to go to the airport to make and pay for bookings; the phone lines and website weren't coping. Air Panama flies to Bocas del Toro, Guna Yala, the Darién, David, the Islas Perlas, and a few other mainland destinations.

The airport terminal was undergoing a major overhaul in 2012, which in the short run was making for lots of noise, dust, and heat (the air-conditioning was switched off) but hopefully will improve facilities in the long run.

REGIONAL BUSES

Buses are the backbone of Panama's public transit system. They're frequent, fast, and cheap—at least by the standards of visitors. One-way fares from Panama City to most places in Panama are less than US$10. The longest and most expensive fare, to Bocas del Toro, is still less than US$30.

Most long-distance buses leave from the capital's **Gran Terminal de Transportes.** It's pretty *gran,* all right—huge and two stories high. Buses arrive on the top floor and leave from street level, which is where all the ticket booths are. Destinations are posted on each booth, and a schedule of hours and intermediate destinations is sometimes posted behind the ticket seller. The Gran Terminal now has a website (www.grantnt.com) listing details and prices for all destinations, which would be super swell if the list wasn't two years out of date.

There may be more than one bus headed to your destination at any given time. If a bus that has your destination as a final stop isn't convenient, look for one that has it as an interim stop. Those heading to Santiago, for instance, can buy a ticket at the Santiago booth or, say, the David booth since Santiago is on the way to David.

There's a US$0.10 departure fee for long-distance bus service. This fee can no longer be paid in cash. Passengers must get a rechargeable *Rapipass* smartcard at one of the booths near the exit turnstiles. There is no charge for the card (other than the US$0.10 exit fee), but passengers must present their passport or local identity card to the attendant, who will record the details. Card readers at the turnstiles deduct the US$0.10 fee from the *Rapipass* as passengers exit. Using the bathrooms in the terminal costs US$0.25.

Panama City and local area buses also operate from the terminal, including buses to Tocumen International Airport (look for the Tocumen, Corredor Sur bus). They leave from the ground floor, on the side facing the shopping mall. Destinations are signposted.

The ground floor has shops, pharmacies, a half-dozen banks and ATMs, a branch of the low-cost Niko's Café cafeteria, two U.S.-style food courts, places to take passport-size photos and laminate ID cards, a clinic, places selling cheap mobile phone and phone cards, and other businesses likely to be of interest to travelers.

Global Bank (10 A.M.–6 P.M. Mon.–Fri., 9 A.M.–2:30 P.M. Sat) has a 24-hour ATM. So does **HSBC bank** (9:30 A.M.–5:30 P.M. Mon.–Fri., 9 A.M.–1 P.M. Sat.), which is just opposite. There are now lots of ATMs in the terminal, but if there are crowds or you'd rather not withdraw money at a bus terminal, use one of the ATMs in the shopping mall next door. **Telxpress** (tel. 269-1055, 8 A.M.–8 P.M. daily) offers international phone call service at prices that tend to be excessive.

Schedule

Below are some bus destinations likely to be of interest to visitors. Bus schedules stay pretty stable, though the first and last bus of the day often change. Try to travel so you arrive at your destination during daylight hours, when it will be much easier to find local transport. Aim for *expresso* buses to your destination, as these can shave considerable time off a journey.

Almirante (port for Bocas del Toro archipelago) and Changuinola: One daily bus, at 8 P.M., though if that one fills up the company sometimes runs a second one at 8:30 P.M. The bus sells out so get to the station and buy tickets early. The ride takes about 10 hours. The company that runs this route has been adding and dropping a second departure, in the morning, for years now. If it's available and scheduled to leave later than about 7 A.M., any delay will mean you stand an excellent chance of missing the last water taxi to the islands and have to spend the night in either Almirante or Changuinola, or at a more attractive, but more remote and expensive, hotel called La Escapada. The last water taxi leaves at 6:30 P.M., and it sometimes fills up. It's safer to overnight on the bus and get to the islands during the day. It arrives at about 6 A.M. the next morning at the Almirante crossroads (US$27.80) and 7 A.M. at Changuinola (US$29). There's a two-suitcase maximum included in the fare.

Bayano: Every 40 minutes or so 3:20 A.M.–6 P.M. (US$3 to Lago Bayano, 2.5 hours).

Chitré: About once an hour 6 A.M.–11 P.M. (US$9.05, 3.5 hours).

Colón: Every 20 minutes or less 4:50 A.M.–10:10 P.M. for air-conditioned bus (US$3.15 for express, about 1.5 hours; the non-express bus using the toll road is US$2.15 but can be far slower). Look for the names ULTRACOLPA or EPACOC, the two companies that run the fancy air-conditioned buses. Avoid the cheaper but incredibly slow buses that skip the toll road and stop everywhere. Be very careful at the Colón bus station. Those who want to go to Portobelo or Isla Grande by public transportation should take a Colón-bound bus and transfer at Sabanitas, on the Transístmica (Boyd-Roosevelt Highway), well before reaching Colón.

Coronado: Every 15 minutes 6 A.M.–9 P.M. (US$2.80, 1.5 hours).

Darién: 4 A.M. and 4:15 P.M. Because of road conditions, Metetí (US$9, 6 hours) is usually the last stop. In the dry season, early morning buses sometimes make it all the way to Yaviza (US$14, about 7 hours). Add at least an hour to these estimates if the road is bad. For current road conditions, call the bus company that makes this run at cell 6792-9493 (Panama City) or cell 6841-4767 (Metetí).

David: Two well-established companies run large, long-haul, air-conditioned buses between Panama City and David. The fare is US$15.20 one-way, or US$18.15 for a one-way express bus. The trip theoretically takes about 6.5 hours, but buses frequently run late; express buses can shave up to an hour off that time. Buses generally stop at provincial towns along the Interamerican Highway, most notably Aguadulce, Penonomé, and Santiago. Other stops are made by request. In Santiago, buses

usually take a half-hour break at the Pyramidal or Los Tucanes complex, both of which have a cafeteria, restaurant, bathrooms, pharmacy, ATM, and other services. Seats are assigned, and passengers can request seat assignments. For safety's sake, avoid seats at the front of the bus. Avoid sitting near the bathroom in the back. The companies frequently tinker with their schedules, so don't count on precise timing. However, buses leave virtually around the clock, and there is usually more than one option per hour during daylight hours. A third company, **Panafrom,** was running this route in 2012. They have six daily departures.

The largest of the three companies, with the most frequent trips, is **Terminales David-Panama** (tel. 314-6228, tel. 314-6395 for cargo, terminal@cwpanama.net). Buses leave every 60–90 minutes 5:30 A.M.–midnight. The last two buses, at 10:45 P.M. and midnight, are expresses.

Padafront (tel. 314-6264) has departures to David about every 1–2 hours approximately 6:45 A.M.–midnight. The last two buses, at 10:45 P.M. and midnight, are expresses.

El Copé: Every half hour 5 A.M.–6 P.M. (US$6.50, 3 hours).

El Valle: Every 30 minutes 7 A.M.–7 P.M. (US$4.25, 2.5 hours).

Farallón and Santa Clara: Every 20 minutes 5:30 A.M.–8 P.M. (US$3.95 to Santa Clara, US$4.70 to Farallón, 2 hours).

Las Tablas: About once an hour 6 A.M.–7 P.M. (US$9.70, 4 hours).

Paso Canoa (border crossing with Costa Rica): One of the companies that makes the Panama City–David run, Padafront, continues west to Paso Canoa, the main border crossing with Costa Rica. The trip takes 8–9 hours, slightly less for an express. Most travelers will be better off taking one of the international buses that continue to Costa Rica and beyond. But if you just need to make it to the border, Padafront leaves Panama City more frequently. Another possibility is to take any bus to David and switch to one of the small regional buses that run constantly between that city and the border.

Penonomé and La Pintada: Every 20–30 minutes 4:45 A.M.–10:45 P.M. (US$5.25 to Penonomé, 2 hours; US$6 to La Pintada, 2.5 hours).

San Carlos: Every 30 minutes 7 A.M.–7 P.M. (US$3.25, 2 hours).

Santiago: About every 30 minutes 2 A.M.– midnight (US$9.10, about 4 hours). Two companies, Expreso Veraguense and Sanpasa, work this route and compete aggressively with each other. Be prepared for *boleteros* (ticket touts) trying to get your business as you approach their counters.

Soná (for those going to Playa Santa Catalina): 8:20 A.M., 10:20 A.M., 12:45 P.M., 2:20 P.M., 4:20 P.M., and 5:45 P.M. (US$9.70, about 4.5 hours). Get a Santa Catalina bus or taxi in Soná. The last bus for Santa Catalina leaves Soná at 4 P.M.

BY CAR

The **Corredor Norte,** a toll highway with several entrances on the north and west outskirts of the city, leads north across the isthmus, ending at Sabanitas, not far from the outskirts of Colón, on the Caribbean coast. This is a far better option than taking the old, slow potholed Transístmica (also known as the transisthmian highway, officially it's the Boyd-Roosevelt Highway, though no one calls it that).

The **Corredor Sur,** another toll highway that begins just east of Punta Paitilla, leads to Tocumen International Airport, where it links with the Interamerican Highway. There, at a cloverleaf intersection next to Hotel Riande Aeropuerto Hotel and Resort, the Interamerican Highway (really just a two-lane road) continues east toward Cerro Azul and the Darién. This road passes through the Darién and finally ends at Yaviza, the beginning of the Darién Gap, through which no road has ever been built.

To all points west of Panama City— the beaches, mountains, Azuero Peninsula, Bocas del Toro, Costa Rican border, and the rest—there are only two ways to begin the journey by land: by crossing the **Puente de las Américas** (Bridge of the Americas) near the Pacific entrance to the Panama Canal or by taking the newer **Puente Centenario** (Centennial Bridge) across the canal near Pedro Miguel.

The Puente de las Américas is aging dramatically and has not been well maintained. There is also much more and much heavier traffic rumbling across it than it was ever meant to handle. As a result, it is literally falling apart. The Panamanian government launched a huge and enormously expensive repair project in early 2012, but it caused so much traffic chaos it was temporarily suspended. The project is expected to take until at least 2014 to complete. Try to avoid this bridge and take the Puente Centenario instead, especially during rush hours and at the start or end of the weekend.

West of either bridge, the road eventually connects with another toll highway, the **Autopista Arraiján-La Chorrera.** This is now a divided highway for much of the way to the western frontier, though most of the stretch between Santiago and David is still a two-lane road. Nevertheless, this entire ribbon of road is officially part of the Interamerican Highway.

Most Pacific-side destinations in the former Canal Zone are accessible from Panama City by taking **Gaillard Highway** (now officially known as Avenida Omar Torrijos Herrera), which borders the east bank of the canal and runs past the domestic airport at Albrook, the Panama Railway terminal at Corozal, Clayton, Miraflores and Pedro Miguel Locks, and so on. The road forks outside Gamboa. Left leads to the attractions around Gamboa before Gaillard Highway dead-ends in Gamboa itself. Right leads through part of Parque Nacional Soberanía, including part of the historic Las Cruces Trail, before intersecting the Transístmica, the old road linking Panama City with Colón.

Getting Around

Traffic in Panama City is bad and getting worse all the time. There are an estimated 450,000 cars here, which comes to one for every other man, woman, and child. Skyscraper construction, excavation work for the new metro system, flooded streets during bad weather, and major repair work on the main bridge spanning the Panama Canal have turned a congested city into one that comes to a near standstill at times.

If possible, avoid car trips during morning and evening rush hours, especially 8–9 A.M. and 4:30–6:30 P.M. A couple of toll roads that cut through the city—Corredor Norte and Corredor Sur—are a quick escape from some of the congestion, since they're priced out of reach of the average Panama City driver. Most tolls are less than US$2, so you'll save a lot of time and aggravation by taking them.

Taxis are inexpensive and easy to find at all hours, making them the transportation of choice even for Panamanians of modest means. Buses are frequent and even cheaper, but they are a far slower and less convenient way to get around most parts of the city. Panama City's new bus system, Metro Bus, is bringing modern mass transit to the city.

I don't recommend that those unfamiliar with Panama City, especially those unaccustomed to Latin American roads, attempt to drive in the city. It's a good way to spoil your day, if not your whole trip. Drivers are aggressive, streets are confusing and poorly marked, and there's a severe shortage of traffic signals, which most drivers treat merely as friendly suggestions in any case. Streets have been known to change from two-way to one-way literally overnight, without anyone bothering to change the signs. Other nuisances include the occasional stolen manhole cover.

Traffic in the former Canal Zone remains more orderly, but it too is increasingly showing the effects of chaotic road expansion and urban sprawl. Taxis, and in some cases buses, are convenient options for trips into the canal area, particularly for Pacific-side destinations such as the Calzada de Amador (Amador Causeway), Albrook, Miraflores Locks, and Balboa.

Adding to the confusion of getting around is the fact that many streets have multiple names. The names used in this chapter are generally those most likely to be recognized by taxi drivers and other locals. Some destinations, especially in the former Canal Zone, are much more likely to be known by proximity to landmarks than by any street name.

BY TAXI

Taxis offer by far the easiest way to get around the city. Panama reportedly has 40,000 taxis, and most of them are in Panama City jockeying for your business. Most are small Japanese cars that will take an individual just about anywhere in town for US$2 or less. Don't be put off by taxi drivers beeping their horns at you; it can be annoying, but it's just their way of finding out if you want a ride. All legal taxis in Panama, except tourist taxis with license plates that start with the letters "SET," must be painted yellow.

Taxis are not metered in Panama City (or anywhere else in the country), though they're being tested in the city and may eventually be installed. In the meantime, taxis charge according to a government-mandated zone system. The city is carved up into seven zones; fares are based on the number of zones crossed. The minimum fare is US$1.20, and each zone crossed is another US$0.40. The maximum standard fare for a single passenger traveling across all zones—from the Amador Causeway to Costa del Este, which is a very long ride—should be no more than US$3.60.

Each additional passenger adds US$0.50 to the fare, regardless of the distance. There's also a US$0.30 surcharge on Sunday, holidays, and late at night (10 P.M.–5 A.M.). Phoning for a taxi adds US$0.50 to the fare. Most taxi drivers are honest and decent, even if their driving is a bit nuts.

Asking the fare ahead of time is one way to know what you're in for, but it also betrays your ignorance of the going rate to your destination. Another common strategy for trips within the city limits is just to hand the driver US$2 at the end of the ride; if the legitimate fare is more than that, they'll most definitely let you know, but they're less likely to think they can scam you. Taxi drivers are required to present the zone chart on demand, though anyone likely to rip you off is likely to have a fake zone chart as well.

A bigger concern recently has been taxi drivers who refuse to take a fare because the destination is not convenient or profitable. Such a tactic is understandable, but it's illegal. The government has been cracking down on the so-called *no voy* ("I'm not going that way"). If this happens to you, report the culprit at tel. 502-0591.

Don't be alarmed if your driver stops to pick up another fare heading the same way. It's a normal practice, but tell the driver not to do it if it makes you uncomfortable (though expect to pay extra for the privilege of a private ride).

The bashed-up bodies of the average cab will give you some sense of how these Mad Maxes drive. Pulse-pounding near misses are common; think of it as local color. Fortunately, traffic congestion and moderate speeds mean most actual mishaps end up as fender benders.

Fares for rides outside the central city, for instance into the former Canal Zone, go up according to distance, but not as quickly as one might think. A ride as far as Gamboa, on the Panama Canal about halfway across the entire isthmus, costs around US$30. Taxis can also be hired for day tours, but bear in mind that few taxi drivers speak much English or are particularly knowledgeable tour guides, though

all know the city well. There are no standard rates—it depends on the distance, the mood of the driver, and your bargaining skills, but about US$7–8 an hour is a decent rule of thumb.

A few larger, air-conditioned cabs lurk around the more upscale hotels and are allowed to charge several times what the smaller guys do. They are tourist taxis, recognizable by the "SET" license plates. You can always just walk down the street to find a cheaper ride if you can do without air-conditioning and the sense of safety that comes from riding in a bigger hunk of metal.

Taxis are almost always easy to find, but radio taxis can be called as well. Hotels and restaurants will usually be happy to make the call for you.

BY RENTAL CAR

The major U.S. car rental agencies have outlets scattered around Panama City as well as at the international and domestic airports. Several outlets are within a few blocks of the Hotel Continental and Hotel El Panamá on or near Vía España.

Driving is likely to be the best way of getting to the beaches within a couple hours of the city. And for exploring both the nearby canal area and distant locations, it's a reasonable alternative to taxis, buses, and organized tours. Most of the rental agencies are within easy walking distance of each other near the Hotel El Panamá.

Avis Rent A Car (Calle D, tel. 278-9444, www.avis.com, 7 A.M.–9 P.M. daily) is near the El Cangrejo branch of Churrería Manolo, not far from the Hotel El Panamá. At last count it had five other branches in the Panama City and Panama Canal areas.

Budget Rent A Car (central reservations tel. 263-8777, www.budgetpanama.com) has two branches in the Vía España area. The larger one is on the western end of Vía España itself (tel. 263-9190, 7 A.M.–10 P.M. daily), just before Calle Gabrielle Mistral in Bella Vista. The other is at the entrance to the Hotel El Panamá (tel. 214-6806, 8 A.M.–5 P.M. daily).

© WILLIAM FRIAR

Panama City's colorful *diablos rojos* buses are being phased out.

Hertz (tel. 210-9213, www.hertz.com, 8 A.M.–5 P.M. Mon.–Fri., 8 A.M.–4 P.M. Sat.) has an office at the Marriott Hotel. Including the international airport, Hertz at last count had five outlets in Panama City. For other locations, check their website.

National Car Rental (Vía Veneto and Avenida 2A Norte, tel. 265-5092, www.nationalcar.com, 8 A.M.–5 P.M. Mon.–Sat.) has an office in El Cangrejo, but the main outlet and car park is some distance away on Calle 50 (tel. 265-3333, 7 A.M.–10 P.M. daily). For other locations, check their website.

There's a **Thrifty Car Rental** (Vía España, tel. 214-7677) near the southern end of Vía España, opposite Budget Rent A Car.

ORGANIZED TOURS

All of Panama's major tour operators have their headquarters in Panama City, and they all offer Panama City tours. They're more of an afterthought for the ecotourism outfits, though, so those looking for a group tour might consider going with a more traditional tour company that offers city tours as a more or less daily business, or simply book through your hotel.

Because Panama City is a relatively compact place, half-day and full-day tours typically give an overview of the entire city, including the ruins of Panamá La Vieja (Panamá Viejo), parts of the reviving colonial district of Casco Viejo, and at least a drive through the major sections of modern, central Panama City. The full-day tours in particular usually find time for a visit to the area of the Panama Canal close to the city. This part of the tour inevitably includes a visit to Miraflores Locks and sometimes throws in stops at the handicrafts market next to the YMCA in Balboa and the Panama Canal Authority's Administration Building, a historic structure perched on a hill that has impressive murals depicting canal construction days in its rotunda and offers dramatic views of the former Canal Zone. All three canal stops are worthwhile, so look for tours that include more than just Miraflores Locks.

Pesantez Tours (tel. 366-9100, 223-5374, or 263-7577, www.pesantez-tours.com) is a long-established tour operator with a reputation for dependable service. Other possibilities include **Panoramic Panama** (tel. 314-1581 or 314-1604, www.bedandbreakfastpanama.com), which is affiliated with La Estancia, a popular bed-and-breakfast in the former Canal Zone; **Ecocircuitos** (tel. 315-1305, U.S./Canada toll-free tel. 800/830-1521, www.ecocircuitos.com); and **Gray Line Panama** (tel. 323-2333 or 323-3328, www.grayline-panama.com).

Expect to pay US$80–110 per person for a half-day tour and US$110–165 for a full-day tour. Larger groups pay less per person. Lunch is sometimes included. The exception is Panoramic Panama, which charges the same rate, US$110, for half-day city and canal tours for either one or two people, which is more reasonable. The company also offers a half-day tour for those just passing through Panama with a layover of at least seven hours. The rate for one or two people is US$180, including pickup and drop-off at the international airport.

City Sightseeing Panama (office: Avenida Justo Arosemena and Calle 29 Este, tel. 392-6000 or 392-9999, www.city-sightseeing.com) is the first company to offer a hop-on, hop-off bus service in Panama. Introduced in early 2012, the double-decker bus covers quite a lot of ground, from the Cinta Costera and the financial district in the east to Casco Viejo, the Amador Causeway, Albrook, and Miraflores Locks to the west and south. A recorded audio commentary of the tour is available in six languages. The top deck is covered but the bus is open-air, and as soon as the tour launched, in the dry season, locals were already wondering how watertight the ride might be in the rainy season. Take rain gear just in case.

The stops are at Multicentro Mall, the Bella Vista branch of Tre Scalini Ristorante (central to a number of hotels), Parque Urracá, Albrook Mall, Miraflores Locks, the Biomuseo, Isla Flamenco at the end of the Amador Causeway, and the entrance to Casco Viejo. A ninth stop, at El Pueblito, is the works.

A map with exact locations of the stops is on the company's website. Some of the stops have kiosks where passengers can get information and buy tickets; otherwise, buy tickets on the bus. The cost is US$29 for a 24-hour ticket or US$38 for a 48-hour ticket. Kids pay US$5 less for either ticket. The bus runs every half hour from 9 A.M.–6 P.M. An optional add-on pedestrian tour of Casco Viejo leaves from that stop at 3:30 P.M. This can be a relatively efficient way to combine shopping with a bit of sightseeing. The entire loop takes about two hours if one chooses not to get off anywhere.

Another new way to explore the city and its surroundings is by the **Aquabus** (tel. 226-8917, www.pmatours.net, 10:30 A.M. or 2 P.M. Tues.–Sun., US$39 adults, US$29 kids 3–12), introduced in 2012 by Panama Marine Adventures, one of two companies that offer local transits of the Panama Canal. This is an amphibious bus that picks passengers up at the Albrook Mall for a ride along the Cinta Costera, Casco Viejo, and the Amador Causeway, going for three dips along the way before returning to Albrook Mall. The tour lasts two hours.

BY BUS

Until very recently, bus service in Panama City was provided by privately owned buses known locally as *diablos rojos* (red devils) because of the way they often barrel recklessly through traffic, racing rival buses to get to waiting customers first. The highly photogenic buses were old converted school buses covered in hand-painted images, often depicting pop-culture icons. For better or worse, the *diablos* rojos are scheduled to disappear almost completely from Panama City's streets by the time you read this, replaced by the new Metro Bus system.

Metro Bus

The new Metro Bus system features modern, air-conditioned buses run by the city, a part of a radical attempt to create a centralized, orderly mass-transit system, a first for Panama. The Metro Bus system runs according to a timetable (theoretically, at least), and picks up and drops off passengers only at designated stops. The buses and stops are recognizable by their distinctive white-and-orange color scheme.

Despite the huge investment in setting up this system and changing an entire transportation culture, many months after the launch of Metro Bus, there were still no comprehensive route maps, either in print or online. New routes are being introduced with no warning, sometimes literally overnight, to the surprise of commuters with no way to get to work, as the new buses take only prepaid electronic cards, not cash.

All main Metro Bus routes begin and end

either in Albrook or Calidonia. A sign on the front of the bus flashes the final destination and the main artery taken (e.g., by way of Corredor Norte/Corredor Sur/Transísmica, etc.).

The stop in Calidonia is known as **Pediátrica,** because it's in front of the massive social security hospital on Avenida 3A Sur, between Calle 23 Este and Calle 24 Este. The stop in Albrook is at the **Gran Terminal de Transportes,** which is also the terminus for buses to the canal area and long-distance buses to just about every part of the country.

The main Metro Bus arteries connect downtown via either the Corredor Norte or Corredor Sur. These are meant to shuttle commuters to and from the suburbs. In the outlying areas, there are additional Metro Bus *troncales* (trunk routes) that take passengers to and from the main routes. These routes will be of limited interest to visitors.

The Corredor Sur buses make stops between Paitilla and Pediátrica and/or Albrook that may be useful for some visitors. All the Corredor Sur buses make the same downtown stops, in a loop running close to Panama Bay: Calle 26 Este, Calle 32 Este, Calle 41 Este, Calle 49 Este, Paitilla, Parque Urraca, Hospital del Niño, Calle 39 Este, and Boulevard. Eastbound passengers should be sure to get off no later than Paitilla, or else be prepared for a long ride on the Corredor Sur.

Those on a limited budget may also be interested in the Tocumen–Albrook route. This picks up and drops off passengers outside the international airport at Tocumen, making all the stops listed above. The terminus is the Gran Terminal de Transportes in Albrook, but the bus also stops at Pediátrica. The catch here is that the bus does not go all the way to the airport but rather stops at a roundabout half a kilometer away. Those with a lot of luggage may want to think twice about taking this option, particularly since there are no luggage racks on the bus.

In April 2012, two new rush-hour routes were introduced to reduce congestion: Balboa–Vía España–Albrook Directo and Gran Estación–Transístmica–Albrook Directo. The first route is likely to be of most interest to visitors, since it connects central Panama City with Balboa and Albrook. However, these routes run only on weekdays 4:30–8:30 A.M. and 3–7 P.M., which is the busiest time to be on the road. All bus routes operate in a circle; if you stay on the bus, you'll eventually end up back where you started.

Bus fares for *troncales* rides are currently US$0.25, but are scheduled to rise to US$0.45. The fare for rides that use the Corredor Norte or Corredor Sur is US$1.25. Cash is not accepted on Metro buses. Passengers must buy a rechargeable Metro Bus card, which is sold in more than 1,000 stores throughout the city (look for the orange-and-white Metro Bus sign). The card itself costs US$2, but this does not include any fare credit. The minimum credit that can be loaded onto the cards is US$0.50; the maximum is US$50.

Upon boarding a Metro Bus, touch the card against the yellow machine next to the driver. *Transbordos* (transfers) are available for no extra fee. Passengers can ride up to three buses for no extra fee, provided the trip is in the same direction and each transfer is made within 40 minutes of the last. Passengers who want to transfer must touch their card against the green machine by the exit when stepping off the bus.

Canal-Area Buses

Buses are a more reasonable option for destinations outside the central city, especially into the former Canal Zone. These buses are not a part of the Metro Bus system. Most are still non-air-conditioned school buses, and they only take cash.

Buses to various points in the canal area leave from the Gran Terminal de Transportes in Albrook. It's easy to miss these buses because they're hidden away in a little nook of the Albrook terminal. As you face Niko's Café, the entrance to this little sub-terminal will be on the right. Look for a sign that says SACA or COOP SACA.

Clayton: Every half hour 5:30–10 A.M., noon, every half hour 1:30–5 P.M., 6:30 P.M., and 8 P.M. Monday–Friday. On weekends the bus leaves at 6:45 A.M., 8 A.M., 10 A.M., noon, 2 P.M., 6:30 P.M., 9 P.M., and 10:45 P.M. The price is US$0.35.

Amador: Every half hour from about 6 A.M.–8 P.M. The price is US$0.25; US$0.50 in the evenings or on weekends and holidays.

Gamboa: Roughly every 1–2 hours 5 A.M.–10:45 P.M. Monday–Friday and 6:45 A.M.–10:45 P.M. Saturday and Sunday. The price is US$0.65. This bus can drop passengers off at Pedro Miguel Locks, Paraíso, Parque Nacional Soberanía, Summit Botanical Gardens, and other destinations en route to Gamboa for US$0.25–0.65.

Miraflores Locks (take the Paraíso, Gamboa, or Clayton bus): Buses run on the same schedule as the Clayton bus. Most buses do not go all the way to the locks—they only do so at shift changes for canal workers, which means the 5:30 A.M., 6:30 A.M., and 2:30 P.M. buses. All other buses stop along the main road, and passengers must walk about one kilometer to get to and from the locks. The schedule is inconvenient for visitors since they are not allowed into Miraflores until 9 A.M. and the visitors center closes at 5 P.M. In other words, plan to hoof it. Fortunately, it's a scenic walk.

BY METRO

You're likely to see many torn-up streets throughout Panama City during your visit, some of which cause major detours and traffic congestion. In the works is a modern metro system, Panama City's most ambitious transportation project yet. Line 1 of the Metro is expected to be completed sometime in 2014. Additional lines will be added in coming years.

The Line 1 stops will be Albrook (connecting with the Gran Terminal de Transportes), Curundu, Plaza Cinco de Mayo, Marañon, Santo Tomás, Iglesia del Carmen, Vía Argentina, Fernandez de Cordoba, 12 de Octubre, Pueblo Nuevo, San Miguelito, Pan de Azucar, and Los Andes. (Station names may change.) The stops between Albrook and Vía Argentina are likely to be of most interest to visitors, since they cover the heart of Panama City.

East of Fernandez de Cordoba, the Metro emerges from underground and runs on an elevated track through the suburbs to Los Andes, where the line ends at a shopping mall. Officials promise a ride along the entire line will take just 23 minutes. The fare price had not been announced at the time of writing.

THE PANAMA CANAL AND CENTRAL ISTHMUS

The Panama Canal is one of the most awe-inspiring of all human endeavors. Built across the isthmus of Panama at one of its narrowest and lowest points, it is 80 kilometers (50 miles) long, extending from Panama City on the Pacific Ocean to the city of Colón on the Caribbean Sea. To the bafflement of many a visitor, the Caribbean entrance is northwest of the Pacific entrance.

What was once the Canal Zone ran the length of the canal, extending eight kilometers on either side of it. The U.S. civilian townsites and military bases are now abandoned or being engulfed by the surrounding urban centers, though some of the forested lands have been set aside as protected areas.

The canal itself is so impressive it's easy to overlook nature's equally astonishing handiwork on its banks and in its waters. Parque Nacional Soberanía is one of the most accessible tropical forests in the world. It and the surrounding forests have some of the best bird-watching in the country. There's also a surprisingly decent chance of coming across largish mammals, including three species of monkeys (white-faced capuchins, Geoffroy's tamarins, and howlers), sloths, kinkajous, coatimundis, and capybaras (the largest rodent in the world) in the extensive moist tropical forests still standing here. Even jaguars and harpy eagles are not unheard of, but the chances of spotting either are extremely slim. You may also see a green iguana or two.

COURTESY OF THE AUTORIDAD DEL CANAL DE PANAMÁ

HIGHLIGHTS

© AVALON TRAVEL

LOOK FOR 🌙 **TO FIND RECOMMENDED SIGHTS, ACTIVITIES, DINING, AND LODGING.**

🌙 **Miraflores Locks:** The most accessible set of locks at the Panama Canal offer a close-up look at one of the world's great engineering feats (page 110).

🌙 **Balboa:** This historic townsite offers a glimpse of what life in the former Canal Zone was like (page 113).

🌙 **Amador Causeway:** This beautiful breakwater has spectacular views of Panama City and the Panama Canal (page 115).

🌙 **Panama Canal Transit:** One of the world's top cruising destinations is also an affordable day trip (page 117).

🌙 **Panama Railway:** Travel from ocean to ocean in an hour on this historic and highly scenic rail line (page 118).

🌙 **Parque Nacional Soberanía:** This species-rich tropical forest is just a few minutes' drive from downtown Panama City (page 130).

🌙 **Portobelo Ruins:** Wander the battered remains of one of the most important, pirate-pestered ports in the Spanish Empire (page 149).

THE PANAMA CANAL

Though less visited than the Pacific side, the Caribbean end of the Panama Canal and the nearby coastline are rich in history and even richer in natural beauty. Evidence of the former includes the well-preserved ruins of Spanish forts, built to protect looted Incan treasure, and some of the most awe-inspiring structures of the canal. The area's natural attractions can be found among the mangroves, coral reefs, beaches, and forests that still abound with wildlife. Scuba diving and snorkeling are popular and easily accessible in the warm Caribbean waters, home to brilliant tropical fish and ancient shipwrecks. All this begins within a two-hour drive of Panama City.

PLANNING YOUR TIME

It's possible to visit **Miraflores Locks, Pedro Miguel Locks, Gaillard Cut,** and the townsites of **Balboa** and **Ancón** in a single day. A good way to end that day is with an evening walk and a meal or a drink on the **Amador Causeway (Calzada de Amador).** A quick visit to **Gamboa** can be tacked on, but really exploring that area takes a second day. A **Panama Canal transit** is an all-day event; taking the **train** across the isthmus requires a half day to a full day, depending on the return trip. **Isla Taboga** is better for a day trip than an overnight visit, and those planning to see other islands can skip it altogether.

Most visitors to the Caribbean side go just

THE PANAMA CANAL AND CENTRAL ISTHMUS

Caribbean Sea

To **PORTOBELO RUINS**

Parque Nacional Portobelo

FUERTE SAN LORENZO

Colón

Bahía Limón

Río Chagres

Sabanitas

Área Protegida San Lorenzo

GATÚN DAM

Gatún
GATÚN LOCKS

COLÓN PROVINCE

Lago Gatún

Lago Alajuela (Madden Lake)

Parque Nacional Chagres

To Achiote and Escobal

Monumento Nacional Isla Barro Colorado

PARQUE NACIONAL SOBERANÍA

CORREDOR NORTE

TRANSISTMICA

Río Chagres

Chilibre

Panama

Gamboa

Canal

SUMMIT BOTANICAL GARDENS AND ZOO

TRANSISTMICA

PANAMA PROVINCE

Parque Nacional Camino de Cruces

Paraíso

PUENTE CENTENARIO

PANAMA CANAL TRANSIT

VIA CENTENARIO

Pedro Miguel

MIRAFLORES LOCKS

Lago Miraflores

PANAMA RAILWAY

Clayton

Diablo

Arraiján

Ancón

BALBOA

La Chorrera

La Boca

Cerro Ancón

Playa Kobbe (Playa Blanca)

AMADOR CAUSEWAY

INTERAMERICANA

CORREDOR NORTE

INTERAMERICANA

CORREDOR SUR

PN Metropolitano

PANAMA CITY

Bahía de Panamá
(Panama Bay)

0   5 mi

0   5 km

Isla Taboga

© AVALON TRAVEL

for the day and return to Panama City at night. It's possible to take in **Portobelo,** the attractions near the Caribbean entrance to the Panama Canal (most notably **Gatún Locks** and **Gatún Dam**), and **Fuerte San Lorenzo** in a single day. However, it would be a long day, with lots of driving, and it's probably too ambitious for those relying solely on public transportation. Consider striking either Portobelo or Fuerte San Lorenzo off the itinerary; it'd be hard to do both. If at all possible, take the train across the isthmus at least one way. It's the most scenic and pleasant way to make the trip.

The Panama Canal is in the middle of a multibillion-dollar expansion that will include two new sets of giant locks, one on the Pacific and one on the Caribbean side of the isthmus. It's expected to be completed in 2015.

Spending the night somewhere on the Caribbean side is pretty much a must for those who want to add an outdoor activity such as scuba diving, birding, or boating to a visit. One approach for a longer visit is to stay a night or two on **Isla Grande,** stopping at Portobelo on the way over and visiting San Lorenzo and the canal-area attractions on the way back to Panama City.

Rainfall is far heavier on the Caribbean than the Pacific side of the isthmus. It averages 3.2 meters in Colón, nearly twice as much as in Panama City. For those not metrically inclined, that's more than 10 *feet* of rain a year. The dry season is also not as well-defined on the Caribbean as it is on the Pacific side. In Portobelo, one of the wettest spots in Panama, it rains nearly year-round.

The Former Canal Zone

The Pacific side of the former Canal Zone contains two of the Panama Canal's three sets of locks and the beginning of the approximately 14-kilometer Gaillard Cut through the Continental Divide, the toughest part of the canal to dig and the most dramatic to see. One of the new post-Panamax locks is also being built here.

The area also contains most of the former zone townsites, as they were known, which were home to the civilian employees of the canal and their families. These include Ancón, Balboa, La Boca, and Diablo. It's home also to what were once its most important U.S. military bases, including Howard Air Force Base, Fort Clayton, Fort Amador, Quarry Heights, Albrook Air Force Base, and Rodman Naval Station.

The Amador Causeway has become a major nightlife and tourism destination. Albrook is now a fairly upscale suburban residential area (and home to Panama City's domestic airport and bus terminal). Parts of Clayton have been converted into something called La Ciudad del Saber (The City of Knowledge), which attracts international academic and research institutions. The latest area to see development is Howard, which is gradually being rebranded as Panama Pacifico. Business parks, condominiums, an airport (there's already a huge airfield from its U.S. Air Force days), and more are being planned for the area.

But much of the former zone has become a series of ghost towns awaiting a development plan, or are being plowed under to make way for suburban housing, port facilities, highways, and industrial complexes.

SIGHTS

The Canal Zone attractions run along the east bank of the canal and are easily accessible from Panama City.

Pacific Side Locks

Work on the new post-Panamax locks on the

THE PANAMA CANAL

NEW LOCKS FOR A "POST-PANAMAX" WORLD

COURTESY OF THE AUTORIDAD DEL CANAL DE PANAMÁ

Giant locks and new access channels are being added to the canal.

The Panama Canal is in the middle of a multibillion-dollar expansion program due to be completed in 2015. Its centerpiece will be two new sets of locks, one near each ocean, located to the west of the current ones.

The chambers of the existing locks are enormous: each is almost 305 by 34 meters. The new ones will be colossal: nearly 427 by 55 meters. Each set of the new locks will contain three chambers, beside which will run basins in tiers meant to capture and reuse water used during transits. (The existing locks lose millions of gallons of freshwater to the sea with each lockage; the canal's watershed would have to be greatly expanded to use a similar system for the new locks.) New access channels are also being dug, and existing ones widened and deepened.

Expansion work is well under way; though until the new locks are finished, there won't be much to see but giant holes in the ground.

The project is meant to allow "post-Panamax" ships to transit the canal (Panamax ships are specifically designed to fit through the existing canal). But not everyone is convinced the project will succeed, or even that it's necessary. Of course, the first time around there were plenty of doubters, too.

Pacific side of the canal had not even begun as this book went to press. But presuming work is completed on schedule, they should be finished and hard at work raising and lowering colossal ships by 2015.

◖ MIRAFLORES LOCKS

Miraflores Locks (Esclusas de Miraflores), completed in May 1913, stand at the Pacific entrance to the Panama Canal. They link the Pacific Ocean with the artificial Miraflores

© KAREN FRIAR

The original locks controls have been replaced by a computerized system, but the old control boards have been left in place.

and theater. The 1st floor of the museum contains a history of the canal, starting with the failed French effort and continuing through its completion by the United States. The 2nd floor is an ecological exhibit that stresses the importance of the Panama Canal watershed and displays on the flora and fauna found within it. The 3rd floor shows the operation of the canal and includes a full-scale pilot-training simulator and a topographical canal map. The 4th floor has route maps that stress the importance of the canal to world commerce.

The restaurant has a terrace right on the edge of the locks, making it a great place to come for lunch or dinner. There's also an outdoor snack bar on the ground floor.

PEDRO MIGUEL LOCKS AND GAILLARD CUT
The Pedro Miguel Locks, about a 10-minute drive farther down Gaillard Highway from Miraflores, raise and lower ships in one 9.5-meter step, linking Miraflores Lake and Gaillard Cut. These locks are not open to the public, but they're visible through a chain-link fence. Those in the area may want to stop briefly and take a peek. There's also a partial view of the beginning of Gaillard Cut (also called Culebra Cut), where the canal was dug right through the Continental Divide. It's a dramatic sight, though the widening of the cut has made it a bit less so by pushing back and lowering the rocky peaks through which the waterway runs. Farther up the road is the Puente Centenario, an elegant suspension bridge over the canal that was inaugurated in 2004. There are good, if quick, views of the cut from the bridge.

Cerro Ancón
ADMINISTRATION BUILDING
The agency that runs the Panama Canal, now known as the Autoridad del Canal de Panamá (Panama Canal Authority), is headquartered in an imposing building perched on a small

Lake, raising and lowering ships 16.5 meters in two impressive steps. Of the canal's three sets of locks, these are the easiest to reach from Panama City and the best equipped to handle visitors. Recently, guards have become strict about not letting visitors onto the grounds until the visitors center opens at 9 A.M.

The massive **Centro de Visitantes de Miraflores** (Miraflores Visitors Center, tel. 276-8325, www.pancanal.com, 9 A.M.–5 P.M. daily, including holidays, entire complex: US$8, US$5 for kids ages 5–17, younger kids free, ground terrace and shops only: US$5, US$3 for kids) is an out-of-place monolith from the outside, but inside it's rather impressive. It contains a four-story museum, an observation deck, a theater that shows documentaries on the canal in English and Spanish, and a restaurant with good views of the locks. Hold on to your ticket to be admitted to the museum

© JIM GUY

The Administration Building on Cerro Ancón is the headquarters of the Autoridad del Canal de Panamá, which runs the Panama Canal.

hill on the side of Cerro Ancón. Known simply as the Administration Building (Edificio de Administración), it's worth visiting for a couple of reasons. First, there are dramatic murals inside the building's rotunda that depict the construction of the canal. These were painted by William B. Van Ingen, a New York artist who also created murals for the Library of Congress and the U.S. Mint in Philadelphia. They were installed in January 1915 and underwent a restoration in 1993. The four major panels of the mural show excavation at Gaillard Cut and the construction of Miraflores Locks, the Gatún Dam spillway, and a set of lock gates. They give a sense of what a staggering task the building of the canal was.

Second, there's a sweeping view of part of the former Canal Zone, especially the townsite of Balboa, from the back of the building. Walk through the doors at the rear of the rotunda, but they may lock behind you; in that case just

walk around the outside of the building to get back to the front entrance.

In the foreground are what were once Balboa Elementary School (on the left) and Balboa High School (on the right). The marble monolith between them is the Goethals Monument. The long, palm-lined promenade is the Prado. Each section of the Prado has the exact dimensions of a lock chamber: 1,000 by 110 feet. In the distance are the Bridge of the Americas and Cerro Sosa (Sosa Hill). Those feeling energetic can walk down the long flight of stairs and explore the townsite of Balboa.

Note the large bronze plaque at the foot of the steps. It's dedicated to David D. Gaillard, who led the excavation of Gaillard Cut. The plaque was moved here from the side of a mountain that was leveled during widening work. It was designed by the sculptor James Earle Fraser, who also designed the Buffalo Nickel and is best known for his moving sculpture *End of the Trail.* There's a replica of the plaque at the Miraflores Visitors Center.

Visitors are free to explore the rotunda any time of the day or night, but other parts of the building are off-limits without an appointment. Sign in with the guard at the door.

ADMINISTRATOR'S HOUSE

The Administrator's House, a wooden mansion set in a well-tended garden, is a short drive or an easy, pleasant walk farther up the road from the Administration Building. When the road forks, head left. During construction days this was the home of the canal's chief engineer. It originally sat overlooking what is now Gaillard Cut, allowing the chief engineers (first John F. Stevens, then George W. Goethals) to keep an eye on the excavation even when they were home. In 1914 it was taken apart and moved by train to its present location. It has been the home of the canal's chief executive ever since. Visitors are not allowed in the house, but they can walk around the front entrance. It's also pleasant to walk down Lion Hill Road, the winding, jungle-shrouded road to the right as you face the house. The grounds are enclosed by a green chain-link fence for security.

TOP OF CERRO ANCÓN

There's an impressive view of Casco Viejo, Panama Bay, and the modern city skyline from the top of Cerro Ancón (Ancon Hill). Walk behind the communications tower to get a look at the entrance to the Panama Canal, the Bridge of the Americas, Miraflores Locks, and the townsite of Balboa. It's also possible to walk up to the giant Panamanian flag, which was one of the first things to go up in the former Canal Zone after the ratification of the treaties that turned the canal over to Panama. This spot has the best view of the Panama City skyline. The U.S. military dug a tunnel into the heart of the hill, the entrance to which still stands in Quarry Heights, as a secure command post during times of crisis.

The road to the top starts at the entrance to Quarry Heights, once the headquarters of the U.S. Southern Command. Those driving should head up the road that goes past the Administration Building, then take a right when the road forks at the Administrator's House. Go past the guard house, then make a left past the headquarters of the environmental nonprofit ANCON. Access from this point on is by a one-way road. Guards at either end of the road tell you when it's safe to go, but honk the horn around curves anyway. The top of Cerro Ancón is two kilometers up from the Quarry Heights gate.

◖ Balboa

Those who want a sense of what life was like in the former Canal Zone should consider spending an hour or two wandering around the townsite of Balboa. The unofficial capital of the Canal Zone, it was the most formally planned of the zone communities. Today it's being squeezed between a container port and highway overpasses, and many of the old apartments are either unoccupied or have been converted into offices, but it retains much of its peculiar utilitarian elegance.

GOETHALS MONUMENT

This marble monolith at the base of the Administration Building was erected in honor of George W. Goethals, the chief engineer of the canal from 1907 to its completion in 1914. The three tiers of the fountain symbolize the three sets of locks. The monument was controversial when it was erected; some complained it didn't fit into the community's design.

CENTRO DE CAPACITACIÓN ASCANIO AROSEMENA

Along the palm-lined promenade of the **Prado** are what were once **Balboa Elementary School** and **Balboa High School.** Both are now offices used by the Panama Canal Authority. Parts of

THE OTHER SIDE

In the old Canal Zone days, those on the Pacific side of the canal spoke of the area around the Caribbean entrance as "the Other Side." (Naturally, those "other siders" in turn tended to apply that term to those on the Pacific side.) The Atlantic side felt like another world, even though it was less than 80 kilometers away. There were just two ways to get there by land: by the railroad or by a pothole-riddled highway known as the Transístmica. As kids, many Pacific siders, including this one, rarely made what seemed like an epic journey to the Caribbean side: swim meets and the annual football jamboree against our archrival, Cristóbal High School, were about it.

In those days we all thought in terms of the Atlantic rather than the Caribbean side, though the latter is more accurate. Even in a tiny world, the Atlantic side was minuscule, and it got less attention. The canal's headquarters was on the Pacific coast, close to Panama City, and that's where the action was. As a result, the Caribbean communities tended to be tight and socially active. With fewer diversions, Atlantic siders had to find ways to entertain themselves.

Residents lived in townsites with names such as Cristóbal, Gatún, Coco Solo (birthplace of John McCain), Margarita, and Rainbow City, dotted among which were U.S. military bases, such as Fort Sherman, Fort Gulick, and Fort Davis. Cristóbal was literally across the street from Colón, and partly for that reason the boundaries between the Canal Zone and Panama were especially fluid on this side.

When the gringos left, much of the Canal Zone became a virtual ghost town, and this is especially true of the Caribbean side. Whole townsites have grown silent, and in some places the tropical forest is taking over again.

---

the old high school, now known as the Centro de Capacitación Ascanio Arosemena (tel. 272-1111, 7 A.M.–4:15 P.M. Mon.–Fri.), are open to visitors. Outside is a breezeway dedicated to the Panamanians who died during the 1964 Flag Riots; their names are inscribed on the pillars. Just inside the building is a display that attempts to walk a delicate line between the still-polarized views on what exactly happened during the riots, the bloodiest and most controversial conflict between the United States and Panama until the 1989 U.S. invasion.

Lining the halls on this floor and the one above is a wealth of rare artifacts from both the French and U.S. canal efforts, including railroad ties and pickaxes, clippings from 19th-century newspapers, bonds sold to finance the disastrous French effort, fascinating black-and-white prints dating from the 1880s, maps, Canal Zone stamps and seals, and historic china and silverware from the Canal Zone governor's house. On the 2nd floor is the

Biblioteca Roberto F. Chiari (10 A.M.–4 P.M. Mon.–Fri. for researchers). This is the library of the Autoridad del Canal de Panamá (Panama Canal Authority), housed in what was once the high school library. It contains all kinds of technical and historical books and documents on the Panama Canal and Panama. It's not technically open to the general public, but those who fancy themselves researchers can certainly stop by and sign in.

STEVENS CIRCLE

Farther down the Prado is Stevens Circle, a rather drab monument to John Stevens, the canal's chief engineer between 1905 and 1907 and its master designer. On the left is the **Balboa post office.** Directly across the main road is what's left of a cafeteria that used to feed canal workers around the clock. Next to it is the **Teatro Balboa,** once a movie theater and now host to occasional concerts and other performances. Across the street from that is the former commissary for canal employees, now offices.

BALBOA ROAD

Heading down Avenida Arnulfo Arias Madrid (also known as Balboa Road) in the direction of Amador and Panama City, you'll see the **Union Church,** an ecumenical church still in use. Just past it is an enormous and rather weird **fountain** built in honor of Arnulfo Arias Madrid, who was elected (and overthrown) president of Panama four times. It was built by Mireya Moscoso, Arias's widow, after she became president in 1999, and depicts Arnulfo flashing a "V for victory" sign at figures representing the Panamanian people, who are struggling to their feet.

◀ Amador Causeway

The beautiful breakwater known as the Amador Causeway (Calzada de Amador) extends more than three kilometers into the Pacific, calming the waters at the entrance of the Panama Canal and preventing that entrance from silting up. It was built from soil dug from the canal and connects three islands: **Naos, Perico,** and **Flamenco.**

The causeway has gorgeous views. On one side the majestic Bridge of the Americas spans the Pacific entrance to the canal, so there's always a parade of ships gliding underneath it or waiting their turn in the anchorage. On the other side is the half-moon of Panama Bay, ringed by the ever-growing Panama City skyline.

The causeway is a nightlife destination for locals, and huge amounts of money are being poured into it in the hopes it will lure international visitors. In the last few years, restaurants, bars, and shopping centers have gone up in this area, as have a hotel, cruise-ship terminal, marina, convention hall, and amphitheater. Most of these have been built on Isla Flamenco on one end of the causeway and in Amador proper on the other. (Amador was formerly a U.S. army base called Fort Amador.)

The causeway itself has gotten an

THE PANAMA CANAL

© THOMAS GORISSEN/WWW.THOMASGORISSEN.COM

The Amador Causeway is popular with families, especially on the weekend.

understated and elegant makeover, with new streetlights and a renovated walking path that left the palm trees along it intact but added benches for those who need a rest. Near the entrance to the causeway is a row of flags of many countries, though the U.S. one is conspicuously absent; flying the stars and stripes anywhere in Panama, especially at a former gringo army base, would be loaded with controversial symbolism.

Amador and the causeway can get packed with visitors on the weekends, particularly dry-season Sundays. The popularity of the bars and restaurants causes traffic jams on the two-lane road on weekend nights.

For those without cars, the main way to get around here is on foot, though it can be a long walk in the sun from one end of the causeway to another. Fortunately, most of the attractions are clustered at the end of the causeway, on or near Isla Flamenco. There's a bike and scooter rental place at the entrance to the causeway. It may also be possible to flag down a passing taxi or bus for a quick ride up or down the causeway.

Avoid the taxi concession at the Flamenco Shopping Plaza. It's aimed at cruise-ship passengers and their prices are outrageous. (The hourly rate is nearly 10 times the norm.)

MUSEO DE LA BIODIVERSIDAD (MUSEUM OF BIODIVERSITY)

Designed by architect Frank O. Gehry, who is married to a Panamanian, this ambitious museum project (www.biomuseopanama.org) is meant to do for Panama what Gehry's Guggenheim did for Bilbao, Spain. The overly exuberant even maintain it will one day be a greater draw than the canal. This level of hype is a lot for any building to live up to, let alone one that is more modest in scale than the Bilbao Guggenheim and some other Gehry projects.

The museum's completion has been delayed for years by funding shortages, and the expected opening date has been pushed back several times. The museum should finally open its doors during the life of this book, but I'll believe it when I see it.

In the meantime, the museum has been offering talks and a look at scale models of what the finished product will be like. The schedule varies, but in the dry season has included visits at noon and 5 P.M. on Saturdays and Sundays and talks in English at 1 P.M. on Sundays. Entrance fee is US$2.

For safety reasons, visitors younger than 18 are not allowed, and adults must wear long trousers and closed-toe shoes. Construction can cause the cancellation of planned visits.

EL CENTRO DE EXHIBICIONES MARINAS

There's a long-established little museum, El Centro de Exhibiciones Marinas (Punta Culebra on Naos, tel. 212-8000, ext. 2366, rainy season hours: 1–5 P.M. Tues.–Fri., 10 A.M.–6 P.M. Sat. and Sun.; dry season hours: 10 A.M.–6 P.M. Tues.–Sun., US$5 adults, US$1 children), toward the end of the causeway, that's well worth a visit. Try to call ahead of time, as opening and closing hours shift erratically.

This nicely designed marine exhibition center is run by the Panama-based Smithsonian Tropical Research Institute. Exhibits set up along a beachside path explain the extensive natural and human history of the area and touch on that of Panama in general. There's a small outdoor aquarium and an air-conditioned observation building. Free telescopes are set up along the path; check out the ships waiting to transit the canal. At the end of the path are a few hundred square meters of dry forest, once common all along the Pacific coast of Central America, but now mostly wiped out since it's easy to burn. It's amazing what you may find in this little patch of forest. There are lots of iguanas, and the last time I was there I saw a shaggy three-toed sloth walking upside down along a branch just a few meters above my head.

The center is on Punta Culebra toward the

COURTESY OF THE AUTORIDAD DE CANAL DEL PANAMÁ

The Panama Canal is one of the world's great engineering feats.

end of the causeway. At the public beach on the first island, Naos, make a right when the road forks. There should be large signs.

☾ Panama Canal Transit

A transit of the Panama Canal is unforgettable, and you don't have to buy a cruise to have the experience. These days the most popular way to do it is with **Panama Marine Adventures** (tel. 226-8917, www.pmatours.net, adults US$115–165, children under 12 US$65–75) on the *Pacific Queen*. This is an air-conditioned 119-foot vessel equipped with a snack bar, souvenir shop, and television monitors on which cruisers can watch documentaries on the canal when they need a break from the action on deck. Transits take place on Thursdays, Fridays, and Saturdays during the high season (January through March). The rest of the year transits are Saturday only. Transits do not normally go all the way through the canal from ocean to ocean. Instead, they go through two

sets of locks, Miraflores and Pedro Miguel, and Gaillard Cut. Transits begin or end at Gamboa, depending on whether it's a northbound or southbound transit. (Direction of the transit is marked on the company's website calendar.) Customers check in at Isla Flamenco on the Amador Causeway at 9 A.M. The tour includes land transportation between Isla Flamenco and Gamboa. The partial transit takes 4–5 hours. The price includes pickup at the Flamenco marina on the causeway, lunch and soft drinks, and a bilingual guide.

One Saturday a month the company offers a full transit. This starts at Flamenco at 7:30 A.M. and goes through the entire canal, ending at Colón, after exiting Gatún Locks. The transit takes 8–9 hours. It includes all the partial transit services plus a continental breakfast and land transportation back from Colón and Isla Flamenco.

Another group that offers transits is **Canal and Bay Tours** (tel. 209-2009 or 209-2010, www.canalandbaytours.com), with a similar schedule and identical prices (except for the partial-transit kids' fare—it's US$5 cheaper). It uses the 96-foot-long *Isla Morada* and 115-foot-long *Fantasia del Mar,* old ferryboats that made the run to Taboga for many years. The company has spruced them up. They recently introduced a partial Friday-night transit, which gives a very different perspective on the canal. The locks are brightly lit by high-mast lighting, turning night into day, and the rest of the canal is lit well enough to see what's going on.

Transits generally start early in the morning, but it's impossible for either company to promise exact end times. Scheduling is entirely up to the Panama Canal Authority.

C Panama Railway

The Panama railway (tel. 317-6700, www.panarail.com, adults US$25 one-way, children 12 and under US$15 one-way), the descendant of the famed Panama Railroad built for the 49ers during the California gold rush, ran constant daily trips back and forth across the isthmus during the Canal Zone days. It ran along and sometimes over stretches of the Panama Canal, was billed as the world's fastest and cheapest transcontinental journey, and was used as a commuter and cargo train.

Currently, the train makes one daily passenger trip, leaving the Pacific side of the isthmus at 7:15 A.M. and returning at 5:15 P.M. It's quite a step up from the utilitarian train of the old Canal Zone days: The cars in this one have dark wood paneling, leather banquettes set around tables, large observation windows, and waitresses in conductors' outfits who serve coffee and muffins. Seats are limited and most are set aside for daily commuters, so make reservations if possible. If not, show up early. Be sure to ask if there's space in the glass observation car. Sometimes there is only standing room on the between-car platforms available, which is actually quite pleasant since the ride is short and the spacious platforms offer great views and nice breezes.

The train doesn't quite go from ocean to ocean. The Pacific terminus is at the old Canal Zone townsite of Corozal, about a 15-minute drive away from downtown Panama City. The Caribbean terminus is at Colón. The train is an express and makes no stops en route. The trip lasts about an hour.

Those who take the train from Panama City to Colón can either hire a taxi and spend the day exploring Caribbean-side attractions, such as the nearby Gatún Locks, Fuerte San Lorenzo, and the Colón Free Zone, until it's time for the return train, or else catch a bus back to Panama City at the Terminal de Buses in Colón. However, the logistics of this are a bit dicey. Those who can afford it should instead arrange a tour that includes the train trip and a car that meets your group at the Colón station. Typically, not many taxis meet the train; beware of phony cabs. Only get into a licensed taxi, which will be painted bright yellow and have a license plate that matches the number painted on its side.

The bus terminal is a five-minute walk straight past the end of the rail line. It may be possible to find a cab there as well. Do not cross the road into Colón, as it is unsafe.

ENTERTAINMENT AND EVENTS

Amador Causeway has become a nightlife destination for Panama City dwellers, and on the weekends traffic there can be a nightmare. Panama's biggest concert venue is also in Amador, and there are a few other places to see live music and theater. During the dry season, a **concert series** is held on the steps of the Panama Canal Administration Building in Balboa on Tuesday and Thursday evenings.

Bars and Clubs

There are plenty of places to booze and schmooze in Amador. **Flamenco Shopping Plaza,** the shopping and dining center on Isla Flamenco, has several shoebox-size bars/nightclubs on the ground floor at the back of the complex. Each has a different theme—e.g., sports pub, Egyptian, *ciber*—but they're pretty interchangeable. Sometimes people dance a bit, but the clubs are usually too crowded for that. These are mostly places to have a drink and hook up.

Some of the restaurants on the 2nd floor of Flamenco Plaza have live music groups on weekend nights and Sunday afternoons. Chances of hearing "Margaritaville" are good, though the combos I've heard haven't actually been that bad. A folkloric dance group sometimes performs in the plaza when a ship is in port.

More ambitious clubs come and go elsewhere on the causeway and on the mainland around the Figali Convention Center, but these rarely last long. Those with their own transportation or a patient taxi should just trawl along and follow the crowds.

Performing Arts

Amador's glitzy **Panama Canal Village** (tel. 314-1414) contains the Figali Convention Center, Panama's largest venue for extravaganzas. It hosts major international rock and pop acts—ones that have gotten local fans revved up in the last few years include Metallica, the Red Hot Chili Peppers, Shakira, Paulina Rubio, and the Jonas Brothers.

Teatro Balboa (tel. 228-0327), an aging former movie house off Stevens Circle in the heart of the former Canal Zone townsite of Balboa, hosts concerts and the occasional play and special event.

The **Theatre Guild of Ancon** (tel. 212-0060, www.anconguild.com) is the only English-language playhouse in the country. It somehow survived the demise of the Canal Zone's once-thriving community theater scene and still puts on the occasional play. The rickety old wooden playhouse is next to the police station at the base of Cerro Ancón, just off Avenida Frangipani and Manzanillo Place. Jennifer Aniston's dad, John Aniston, was an actor at the theater in the 1950s.

SHOPPING

Balboa has a couple of good places to buy handicrafts. The first is the **Centro de Artesanías Internacional** (behind the YMCA on Avenida Arnulfo Arias Madrid/Balboa Road, 9 A.M.–6 P.M. Mon.–Sat., 10 A.M.–5 P.M. Sun.). It houses many stalls selling handicrafts from all over Panama—including tagua carvings, *molas,* cocobolo figurines, handwoven baskets, and Panama hats—as well as some from other parts of Latin America.

The tagua carvings, cocobolo figurines, and handwoven baskets are made by the Emberá and, especially, the Wounaan. They're incredibly labor-intensive, so don't expect good-quality ones to come cheap. This is especially true of the baskets, which are internationally famous. A so-so basket about the size of a softball costs at least US$25. Rainforest Art, a Wounaan-run stall at the very back of the center, is the first place to look for high-quality works.

Those who won't feel satisfied with a visit to Panama unless they buy a Panama hat (actually made in Ecuador) will find some good-quality ones here. Ask for the stall of Segundo Reyes. His best ones sell for US$100–200. He also has some coarser ones that start at a tenth of that. All hats come in attractive balsa boxes and make good presents. They need blocking, but you can have it done at home.

A newer *artesanía* is in the YMCA building itself, and those who work there aggressively lure in lost visitors who've heard there's a handicrafts hall nearby. By all means take a look, but don't be confused and miss out on the much bigger and better selection at the main artisans' center.

Farther up Avenida Arnulfo Arias Madrid/ Balboa Road, on the right as one heads toward Avenida de los Mártires, is the **Centro Municipal de Artesanías Panameñas** (8 A.M.–6 P.M. daily). It's run by Gunas and has a wider and better selection of *molas.* You can probably strike a better bargain here, since they see less business. The Guna women sewing *molas* and wearing *mola* blouses aren't doing it for show. That's really how they dress and what they do.

Most of the original shops at the **Flamenco Shopping Plaza,** at the end of the causeway, closed down in the last couple of years. Little wonder: The shops were hidden behind the plaza's restaurants and many visitors didn't even know they were there. Optimistic newcomers may have taken their place by the time you visit. The small cruise-ship terminal across the parking lot has a few services, including a duty-free shop that's open only to cruise-ship passengers in transit.

SPORTS AND RECREATION
Amador Causeway
The Amador Causeway is a popular place for walking, running, or biking. It's especially pleasant to ramble about in the morning and early evening, when the weather is cool and the light is gorgeous.

A well-run bike-rental place, **Bicicletas Moses** (tel. 211-2579, 8 A.M.–9 P.M. daily), is at the beginning of the causeway, where the international flags are flown. It's right next to Restaurante Pencas. It rents mountain bikes, tandem bikes, fun cycles (they resemble Hot Wheels–style tricycles), and other wheeled transport by the half hour and hour. Expect long lines on dry-season weekends. They also rent scooters. There's a nearby ATM if you need cash. They also rent baby carriers.

You may see people splashing around in the little beaches along the causeway; don't join them. These days it's such a health hazard it's actually illegal, as nearby signs warn visitors.

Cruises
Canal and Bay Tours (tel. 209-2009 or 209-2010, www.canalandbaytours.com) offers three-hour cruises of Panama Bay once a month, generally on a Friday or Saturday. The trip departs from the Amador cruise-ship terminal on Isla Flamenco. The fare is US$25.

Marinas
The **Flamenco Yacht Club** (Isla Flamenco, tel. 314-0665) is a well-equipped marina that offers moorings, repairs, maintenance, and supplies for everything from small pleasure boats to mega-yachts.

Golf
Summit Golf and Resort (tel. 232-4653, www.summitgolfpanama.com), 14 kilometers north of Balboa, is an upscale golf course, hotel, and spa that welcomes nonmembers. It's a 6,626-yard, par-72 course that was given a major makeover a few years back. It has a modern circular clubhouse with pretty views of rolling countryside, as well as a restaurant and bar. Greens fees are US$120 for 18 holes including cart, though they sometimes offer twilight fees for those willing to play as it's getting dark. Club rental is about US$50. Summit is 7.5 kilometers north of Miraflores Locks. The turnoff is on the right 1.5 kilometers before the left turn toward Gamboa.

ACCOMMODATIONS
Hotels and B&Bs are coming at last to the Pacific side of the canal area. There are now a few appealing places, but many travelers still prefer to stay in downtown Panama City, which is quite close by.

Ancón and Balboa
Simple but pleasant and quiet B&Bs are beginning to pop up in the old Canal Zone towns of Balboa and Ancón. The latter is on the side of Cerro Ancón and now includes the former U.S. Army base of Quarry Heights, formerly the headquarters of the U.S. Southern Command. Evidence of the latter still exists in the form of The Tunnel, a high-security command post drilled straight into the side of Cerro Ancón that was used for strategic planning in times of crisis.

These areas have the advantage of remaining quiet, tree-shrouded residential neighborhoods that are right next door to the urban chaos of

Panama City. Tranquil as this area is, it's important to exercise some caution, especially at night. Streets can be dark and deserted, and the incidence of home break-ins has shot up with the demise of the Canal Zone. Violent crime is unlikely, however. The places listed here all have good security, including locked gates.

US$50-100

◖ **Dos Palmitos** (532B Guayacan Terrace, Ancón, tel. 391-0994, cell 6581-8132, in Europe: 331/4542-4007, Skype: Dos Palmitos, www.dospalmitos.com, US$82.50 s, US$96.80 d, including breakfast) is an appealing B&B in former Canal Zone housing of the older, two-story wooden variety. It features four small rooms, all of which are clean and have a simple but attractive decor, new bathrooms, comfortable beds, flat-screen TVs, free wireless Internet, hardwood floors, and air-conditioning.

This is not a posh place; it's a home that's been converted into a simple B&B. But it's immaculate and run well by a hands-on owner and is a good base for independent travelers who want to explore this part of Panama. It's a hidden gem. The neighborhood is not as well tended as it was in the old Canal Zone days, but this is still a quiet residential area, especially given that the crowded streets of Panama City are just a short walk away. There's a shared kitchen and common area with an Internet computer. Breakfast is served on a back terrace overlooking a walled garden. You're more likely to hear birdsong than traffic.

Dos Palmitos is owned and run by Angeline, a Dutch journalist with an interest in the history of Panama and the canal—be sure to notice the historic photos on the wall, as well as the framed newspapers and stock certificate from the era of the French canal fiasco. She speaks French, Dutch, English, Spanish, and German. She lives on the ground floor of the house, so she's often around. She can arrange tours at very reasonable prices, including day

trips to El Valle and Santa Clara and Gamboa. Best of all is a tour that overcomes the problem of getting back from the Caribbean side after taking the Panama Railway across the isthmus. For US$130 for two people (not including the US$25 per person train fare), guests are dropped off at the train in Corozal, picked up in Colón at the end of the ride, taken to Portobelo and Fuerte San Lorenzo, and then driven back to Dos Palmitos. (Guests can request a side trip to visit Gatún Locks, which they should definitely do.) That's a good price for a very full day.

The well-established and very popular **La Estancia** (Casa 35, Calle Amelia Denis de Icaza, tel. 314-1581 or 314-1604, www.bedandbreakfastpanama.com, starts at US$82.50 s/d, including continental breakfast, a/c) is a 12-room bed-and-breakfast in Quarry Heights, the former headquarters of the U.S. Southern Command, on the side of Cerro Ancón. The building was once used as apartments for military personnel and thus is a bit stark and utilitarian, but the owners have made attempts to soften the place.

Rooms have telephones and private bathrooms. Three have their bathrooms down the hall but come with a balcony and hammock to make up for that slight inconvenience. Most rooms have a queen-size bed. There's a common area for guests to relax in and free wireless Internet. The place is surrounded by trees, and there's a partial view of the Panama Canal and the Bridge of the Americas from some of the balconies. Two of the rooms are actually fair-size apartments with sitting rooms, kitchenettes, and a small patio. These go for US$108.90 a night, including breakfast. Guests can use the washer and dryer.

The owners can arrange tours through their own tour company, Panoramic Panama. To get to La Estancia, take the first left up the hill after passing the guardhouse at the entrance to Quarry Heights. The bed-and-breakfast is 400 meters past the guardhouse in a peach-colored, three-story building on the right.

Opened in 2008, the **C Balboa Inn** (2311a Calle Las Cruce, Balboa, tel. 314-1520, www.thebalboainn.com, $85 s, $95 d, including breakfast, a/c) is in what had once been a house for Panama Canal employees in the old Canal Zone days. The area is still a quiet residential neighborhood where you can hear the sounds of chirping birds in the surrounding trees rather than squealing traffic and construction. Security includes a locked gate in the front. Since the inn is near the base of Cerro Ancón, the occasional cute little *ñeque* shows up in the backyard. This is a good option for those who are happy to be somewhere in-between both the canal and the city. It has nine rooms, all with private bath, TV/DVDs, safes, and free wireless Internet. Rooms are simple with rather thin mattresses, but each has been decorated with cheerful nature murals. A couple of the rooms upstairs have windows on two sides that let in lots of light. The friendly and competent staff can help arrange tours and give restaurant advice. Guests are welcome to use the kitchen. English, Spanish, and German are spoken here. This is a good find.

La Boca

La Boca means "the mouth," an apt name for a town bordering the Pacific entrance to the Panama Canal. There is not much to interest visitors in this former Canal Zone residential area.

US$50-100

The **Canal Inn** (opposite the campus of Universidad Marítima Internacional de Panamá, tel. 314-0112, cell 6612-7168, franzwald1@cwpanama.net, www.canal-inn.com, US$77 s, US$88 d, including breakfast, a/c) is an old Canal Zone building that has been converted into a pleasant B&B. It's across the street from what used to be Canal Zone College, at the foot of the Bridge of the Americas and near the banks of the canal.

It offers 17 simple but cheerful rooms of different sizes, all with wireless Internet access. There's a breakfast nook and common lounge area, and the whole place has been painted in bright colors and decorated to make it as homey and cozy as the old utilitarian Zone architecture will allow. It's cute. There's a small swimming pool out front.

This is a very quiet, almost deserted area, but heavy traffic rumbling over the bridge keeps it from ever being entirely silent. To get there, take the turnoff to La Boca in Balboa between the Union Church and the police station. Continue straight, then make the first left after the gas station. Continue on to the old Canal Zone College, which is now a maritime university. The Canal Inn will be on the right.

Albrook

Albrook is a former U.S. Air Force station that has become a popular destination for reasonably well-off Panamanians and foreign expats to live, mainly because it was quiet and not too built-up. It's much more developed now, especially around its main entrance, but it's still pretty quiet and leafy. That also makes it a rather isolated spot for most visitors, though it's also home to Panama City's domestic airport, main bus terminal, and one of its largest malls. There is one place to stay, though hotels are also in the works for the mall/bus terminal area.

US$50-100

Albrook Inn (14 Calle Hazelhurst, tel. 315-1789 or 315-1975, www.albrookinn.com, starts at US$99 s/d, including continental breakfast, a/c) is a two-story, 30-unit hotel opened in 2003 in a peaceful middle-class suburban neighborhood next to what had been the Albrook Officers' Club back when Albrook was a U.S. Air Force base. The standard rooms are small and simple with very firm beds and cable TV. Larger junior suites with a sitting room and sink start at US$110 s/d. There's a restaurant/bar in a backyard *rancho* (thatched-roof hut), a pool with hot tub, and both laundry service and a self-service washer and dryer. This is a good place if you can find a room with beds that aren't slabs of rock; try several.

Amador

Big, ambitious hotels have long been planned for Amador and the Amador Causeway (Calzada de Amador). They've been slow to come, but there are a couple of smaller, appealing options.

US$100-150

The well-established **Country Inn and Suites** (Amador, tel. 211-4500, fax 211-4501, www.panamacanalcountry.com/amador, starts at US$127 s/d including breakfast) is popular with visitors who want familiar surroundings close to both Panama City and the Panama Canal. You can't get much closer to the canal: It's literally on the edge of its Pacific entrance. It is on the water just past the entrance to Amador, before the causeway. It's a four-story, 159-unit hotel that resembles the other nondescript members of the chain. Standard rooms include cable TV, telephone, iron and ironing board, coffeemaker, free wireless Internet, and a balcony. It's worth paying the extra US$16.50 to get the view of the Pacific entrance to the canal and the Bridge of the Americas, the proximity to which is the most distinctive thing about this place. The hotel also has 53 suites of various kinds. There's a T.G.I. Friday's, an attractive swimming pool on the edge of the canal, a tennis court, a spa, and a business center. Tours of Panama City, the canal, and other attractions are easy to arrange from here.

OVER US$150

The Beach House (Isla Naos, Amador Causeway, tel. 380-1200, www.thebeachhousepanama.com, rack rates start at US$247.50 s/d, including breakfast) is a more upscale hotel that opened on the causeway itself in 2011. Tucked between Mi Ranchito and the ferry landing for Isla Taboga, it overlooks a little marina. It's quite small and has attractive modern rooms with good beds, well-appointed bathrooms, and balconies that face toward the city or Taboga. The city-facing rooms have spectacular views of the Bay of Panama and the skyline. Because it's so far up the causeway, the Beach House is quite isolated from Panama City and the rest of the former Canal Zone. It's a very quiet spot except on weekends, when the causeway is clogged with exercisers in the daytime and partiers at night.

Those without their own transportation will have to take taxis to get to and from the causeway. But there couldn't be a more convenient spot for those who want to visit Taboga, the Smithsonian's Centro de Exhibiciones Marinas, and, of course, the Amador Causeway itself. It is also convenient to the Museo de la Biodiversidad, whenever that finally opens. Stays include breakfast at the neighboring Mi Ranchito and access to a small swimming pool.

Clayton and Ciudad del Saber (City of Knowledge)

What was formerly known as Fort Clayton, a U.S. Army base, is now simply Clayton. The section of it closest to the canal is the Ciudad del Saber, known in English as the City of Knowledge. This is an ambitious, even admirable, plan to create a kind of research and academic park with institutions from around the world, and it has met with some success.

The rest of Clayton was largely abandoned in the last decade, but now development is coming fast.

US$25-50

The **Hostal de Clayton** (Building 605 B, tel. 317-1634 or 317-1264, cell 6631-0281 or 6572-5966, www.hostaldeclayton.com, starts at US$15 pp, including breakfast) consists of four rooms in old U.S. Army quarters in a particularly deserted part of Clayton. The rooms aren't terribly clean and the mattresses are thin, but the staff are friendly, the area is quiet, and the rates are good. Dorm rooms are US$15–19.95. Couples can share a private room for US$44.60. Free wireless Internet access, air-conditioning during the night, a rather barren backyard, and a basic breakfast are included. The hostel is about two kilometers from the main Clayton entrance. Taxis should charge US$5 from Albrook or US$25 from Tocumen. This place is far away from just about everything except Miraflores Locks.

OVER US$150

You are likely to encounter plenty of determined smiles at the newish **Holiday Inn City of Knowledge** (tel. 317-4000, www.holiday-inn.com, US$151.80 s/d). That's because it was built in conjunction with a hotel-management program, the Panama International Hotel School, at the Ciudad del Saber in Clayton, and its students and graduates run the place. The service can be a bit confused at times, but they definitely try hard. This Holiday Inn is an attractive, seven-story version, with good-size rooms that have minifridges, free broadband, and modern furnishings. There's a small pool behind the hotel, and a restaurant and bar. It's literally across the street from the canal and a short drive from Miraflores Locks. Expect to pay a bit more for canal-view rooms, the best of which are on the 6th floor. However, the hotel is not quite close enough to the canal to see much, especially since there are trees partly obscuring the view. The best views are from the stark event rooms on the top floor. The hotel is just off Gaillard Highway, about 10 kilometers from Balboa. It'll be on the right shortly before the main entrance to the City of Knowledge and the turnoff to Miraflores Locks.

West Bank of Canal and Playa Bonita

The area just over the Bridge of the Americas is beginning to see tourist development. This is particularly true of the area that used to be known as Fort Kobbe, a U.S. Army base now known simply as **Kobbe** (sometimes spelled Koby, which is how it's pronounced), which hotel developers are trying to recast as Playa Bonita. A couple of big, fancy resorts have gone up here as have the beginning of what will likely be a number of condo towers.

Nonguests are not allowed on the grounds of the resorts. Locals and the backpacking crowd hang out instead in **Veracruz,** right next door, which has a few basic places to eat and drink and not much else, other than a reputation as a home to *maleantes* (thugs) which the resorts are anxious to keep as far away from their stretch of beach as possible. To do so, they've ringed their properties with gates and guards. Critics also argue that all beaches in Panama are public by law but these resorts' fences have cut off public access, effectively privatizing them.

These are the closest proper beaches to Panama City, and the only ones where you might feel safe sticking your toe into the water without the fear of pollution. The shoreline is pretty here, but the beaches are rocky and small, so don't expect vast expanses of gorgeous sand.

OVER US$150

The 300-room **◖ InterContinental Playa Bonita Resort and Spa** (tel. 206-8880 Panama City reservations, tel. 316-1463 at the hotel, www.playabonitapanama.com, US$265 s/d), which opened in 2005, is a fancy resort hotel in a spectacular spot near the Pacific entrance to the canal. It's part of a hotel group that includes the Miramar InterContinental and the Gamboa Rainforest Resort, among others.

This one is on a beach just west of the Bridge of the Americas. Guest rooms are in two five-story buildings designed so each room has a view of the sea, the ships waiting to transit the canal, and the islands of Taboga and Taboguilla in the distance. The beautifully landscaped grounds include a terraced fountain that flows down into five lagoon-shaped swimming pools of various sizes. These end in a small, rocky, half-moon beach. Now called Playa Bonita (formerly Kobbe Beach), the beach is not the greatest, but it's pleasant. This is the closest beach hotel from Panama City. It's an appealing, if pricey, place.

Standard rooms are attractive, with two double beds or one king bed, a safe, minibar, balcony, cable TV, coffeemaker, and wireless Internet access (US$10/day). The resort has three restaurants, including one in a large *rancho* by the beach. Bars are in the lobby and by the pool. A large, modern gym with plate-glass windows facing the ocean is open 24 hours a day. There's also an elegant full-service spa with a Southeast Asian tropical motif.

The resort is a short drive from Panama City, but it's quite secluded and there's nothing much around it. Only guests are allowed through the gatehouse, which is guarded more zealously than Panama's border crossings.

The ginormous **Westin Playa Bonita** (tel. 304-6600, www.starwoodhotels.com, starts at US$269.50 s/d) offers 600 rooms in three conjoined towers overlooking a strip of rocky beach. It has three swimming pools and an absolutely gigantic *rancho* bar restaurant on the grounds by the beach. Rooms are nice but rather plain, and the small bathtub in the bedroom is an odd touch. Room amenities include packets of bug repellent, a reminder that the *chitras* out here are ferocious, since the property is surrounded by mangroves. Not all rooms have an ocean view; getting one can involve a hefty upgrade fee. Service can be a bit chaotic, and the hotel is showing signs of wear and lack of maintenance.

It's definitely an attractive resort with sleekly modern public areas and inviting pools and grounds. Also, at least some among the concierge staff are impressively helpful and friendly; one makes it a point to remember the names of every guest he encounters.

FOOD

Despite all the development in the former Canal Zone, it's far from becoming a culinary destination.

Fortunately, downtown Panama City is quite close if the restaurants here aren't appealing.

There are plenty of places to eat on and near the causeway, though I've yet to have a memorable meal at any of them.

The **Balboa Yacht Club** (tel. 228-5196 or 228-5794) has risen from the ashes after a fire some years ago. It's roughly in its old location—despite the name, it's in Amador, above the water near the Country Inn and Suites. At this point it's a big *rancho* with a deck serving burgers, buckets of beer, and the like and blasting classic rock. It's popular with die-hard Zonians and yachters.

American chain restaurants (T.G.I. Friday's, Bennigan's, Subway) are also making inroads. Flamenco Plaza on Isla Flamenco and a newer complex on Isla Perico have an impressive number of theme restaurants squeezed into cramped spaces. Oddly, both have been designed so the parking lot is on the best real estate, with a view of Panama Bay and the Panama City skyline, while the restaurants are set so far back they really only have a view of the parking lot. Most are indoor/outdoor places. It's pleasant to sit outside in the evenings and enjoy the tropical breeze. There are also places to eat at the Gran Terminal de Transportes/Albrook Mall.

The food at ◖ **Centro de Visitantes de Miraflores** (Miraflores Locks Visitors Center, tel. 276-8325, noon–11 p.m. daily, US$10–15) is decent. It includes sandwiches, pastas, seafood, salads, and so on. But that's not the reason to come here. Dining on a terrace just a few meters from the locks of the Panama Canal is, to say the least, a novel experience. Diners can watch ships transiting day or night (high-mast lighting turns night into day at the locks). Come early or reserve a table against the railing, where the view is best. Service charge is included.

Niko's Café (tel. 228-8888, 7 a.m.–11 p.m. daily), at the end of the Prado next to Stevens Circle in Balboa, is one of a small chain of successful cafeterias in Panama City that offer simple, tasty food at rock-bottom prices. This one is in the heart of the old Canal Zone, between what was once the high school football stadium and the employee commissary, built on the site of a bowling alley. Reflecting its location, the cafeteria displays great panoramic black-and-white photos of the Canal Zone, U.S. military bases, and parts of Panama dating from the 1920s and 1930s. Much to the amazement of old Zonians, the seal of the Canal Zone is above the counter. About US$4 will get you heaps of food, which includes traditional Panamanian fare, sandwiches, soups, individual pizzas, and desserts. The café now has wireless Internet access.

Lum's Bar and Grill (tel. 317-6303, 11 A.M.–midnight daily, US$10–15), just off Gaillard Highway across the tracks from the railroad station in Corozal, is one of the last bastions of meat-and-potatoes Zonian spirit. Turn off the highway at the lovingly preserved Panama Railroad train cars. It's a converted warehouse that features a restaurant in the main room with pastas, salads, sandwiches, and the like. Attached to it is a sports bar with pool tables, ESPN, and, on some nights, live local bands. A favorite is a blues-rock outfit called Bitches Ghost, composed of Panamanians and gringo expats. These include Rod Richards, the original lead guitarist for the late 1960s/early 1970s rock band Rare Earth.

Restaurante Pencas (Amador, tel. 211-3671, www.pencas.com, noon–11 P.M. Mon.–Thurs., 12:30 P.M.–12:30 A.M. Fri.–Sat., noon–10 P.M. Sun.) is just past the Panama Canal Village. It's a large open-air place with tables on a raised deck near the water, and it has a view of the ocean and the Panama City skyline. The menu tends toward American comfort food and includes baby back ribs and other grilled meats, sandwiches, burgers, fajitas, pasta, and seafood. The *filete de canal frances* is a small but tender cut of beef. Restaurante Pencas sometimes hosts live music performances.

Mi Ranchito (Isla Naos, Amador Causeway, tel. 228-4909, 8:30 A.M.–midnight Mon.–Thurs., 8:30 A.M.–1 A.M. Fri.–Sat., mains US$7–12) is a simple but clean open-air place under a thatched roof on Naos, just past the turnoff to the Centro de Exhibiciones Marinas. It's the most popular place to eat on the Amador Causeway. It serves traditional Panamanian food, with an emphasis on fish and seafood at reasonable prices. It also has—wonder of wonders—a view of the bay. While many people have good experiences here, I've found the food to be just so-so—the corvina is not very flavorful and is drowned in sauce, and the soup is thin. Still, the location is good and a *típico* meal in pleasant surroundings can be had for less than US$10. The *patacones* (fried green plantains) are tasty.

INFORMATION AND SERVICES

The **Smithsonian Tropical Research Institute** (tel. 212-8000, www.stri.org) has its headquarters, the Earl S. Tupper Research and Conference Center, in Ancón. It's a large building on Roosevelt Avenue across Avenida de los Mártires from the Palacio Legislativo. It has a small **research library** (9 A.M.–5 P.M. Mon., Wed.–Fri.; 8 A.M.–5 P.M. Tues.; 9 A.M.–noon Sat.) that contains science periodicals and older research books and a **bookstore** (10 A.M.–4:30 P.M. Mon.–Fri.) with some hard-to-find books on Panama's natural history. Both are worth a visit for detailed information on Panama's flora and fauna. They are open to the public, but visitors must present an ID and sign in to get into the center. The center also has a cafeteria that serves lunch for less than US$5.

GETTING THERE AND AROUND

Taxis are the most convenient way to get from downtown Panama City to most of the destinations in the former Canal Zone, though they're easy to explore by rental car as well. Many tour operators offer day tours that include stops in

Balboa, Miraflores Locks, and the handicrafts market next to the YMCA. Exploring by bus requires a lot of connections.

By Taxi

Taxis from central Panama City to any of these destinations should cost less than US$5. But to explore more than one, it makes more sense to arrange a taxi tour. Agree on a price ahead of time.

By Bus

There are many buses from Panama City to specific canal-area destinations, but trying to explore the whole area by bus is time-consuming, and the fares quickly add up. Taxis are a more practical alternative. Those who want to stick with public transportation can take one of the SACA buses from the Gran Terminal in Albrook.

By Car

The Administration Building is in Altos de Balboa (Balboa Heights), a short drive from downtown Panama City. It's hard to miss. Balboa begins just down the hill from it.

Miraflores Locks are about a 20-minute drive from Panama City, just off Gaillard Highway. The entrance to Miraflores Locks is on the left past Clayton, which is less than 10 kilometers from Balboa. Pedro Miguel Locks are about five kilometers farther on. Just beyond Pedro Miguel is the beginning of Gaillard Cut, now sometimes referred to by its original name, Culebra Cut.

Amador begins near the east end of the Bridge of the Americas. Drivers coming from downtown Panama City can reach Amador by two roads. The older route is to drive through Balboa on Avenida Arnulfo Arias Madrid (also called Balboa Road) and onto the road between the YMCA and the huge statue of Arnulfo Arias. This leads straight to Amador. A faster and more direct route is to take a newer access road that links Avenida de los Mártires directly with Amador near the entrance to the Bridge of the Americas; follow the signs and stay alert—the intersections come up quickly and can be dangerous. Once in Amador, stay straight to get to the causeway.

ISLA TABOGA

Taboga is the most easily accessible island from Panama City. It's just 12 nautical miles away, a trip that takes about an hour by ferry. It's a pretty, quaint little island. If you squint, its whitewashed walls, curving staircases, and flowering trees may remind you of a Greek island.

Taboga is home to a full-time population and attracts many weekend visitors. It's an appealing place that inspires a nostalgic affection somewhat out of proportion to its modern-day charms, especially for those who like deserted, pristine shores. Beaches here are okay, if a bit rocky, but they can get relatively crowded on dry-season weekends, and some trash washes up from Panama City.

Since Taboga's attractions can be explored in a day and there aren't many facilities on the island, you may not want to spend the night. But it is a good place for a day trip.

The ferry ride over is half the fun of a Taboga visit. It leads past the Pacific entrance to the Panama Canal, under the Bridge of the Americas, and along the causeway. You can occasionally see dolphins on the way over, and if you're very, very lucky, you may spot a humpback whale.

An awful lot of history has passed through Taboga since the Spaniards first came calling in the early 16th century. The current town was founded in 1524, and it claims to have the second-oldest church in the western hemisphere. Francisco Pizarro is said to have planned the destruction of the Incan Empire on Taboga. Its visitors have also included pirates, 49ers, and workers on both the French and American canals. Canal workers recovered from their illnesses at a convalescent hospital here that has long since disappeared.

There are no ATMs or banks on the island, so take all the cash you think you'll need.

Isla Taboga is known as "the island of flowers."

Sights

The main beaches are on either side of the floating pier, where the ferries arrive. The more attractive one, **Playa La Restinga,** faces Panama City. A right turn as you leave the pier leads along an ocean path shaded by tamarind trees. Avoid the stretch of beach on the far left as you face the ocean; the smell of sewage will tell you why. At low tide it's possible to walk across a sandbar from Playa La Restinga to the neighboring islet of El Morro. The sandbar disappears at high tide.

The town itself is quite attractive and worth exploring. There are two main roads, a high street and a low street, which are easy to walk on since there are few cars on the island. Both roads are to the left of the pier as you leave the ferry. When the jasmine, oleander, bougainvillea, and hibiscus are in bloom, you'll understand why Taboga is called "the Island of Flowers." Houses tend to be well-maintained and quaint.

When Paul Gauguin first left Europe for the tropics, he was so taken with Taboga that he tried to buy land here. However, he was broke and ended up having to help dig the Panama Canal instead, a job he detested. He never could afford Taboga's prices and soon sailed on. He eventually found Tahiti, and the rest is art history. There's a plaque commemorating his stay, from May to July 1887, up the high street by some picturesque Spanish ruins. Don't miss the lovely garden filled with a rainbow of flowering plants.

The cute whitewashed church in the center of town, **Iglesia San Pedro,** was originally made out of wood, erected after the founding of Taboga in 1524. It's supposedly the second-oldest church in the western hemisphere. Taboga is a hilly island that lends itself to walks past old gravesites, abandoned U.S. military bunkers, and the overgrown remains of Spanish fortifications. The cemetery, on the edge of the ocean toward the end of the road, makes for a picturesque amble.

It's possible to take a moderately strenuous

walk to the top of **Cerro de la Cruz,** which, as the name implies, is topped by a cross. There's a good view of the ocean from here. The south side of the island, together with neighboring Isla Urabá, is part of a national wildlife refuge that protects the nesting area of an important brown pelican colony.

Accommodations and Food

Until recently Taboga lacked decent places to spend the night; most people are content with a day trip. There are once again a few options, the most popular of which is **El Cerrito Tropical** (tel. 390-8999, cell 6489-0074, www.cerritotropicalpanama.com, starts at US$77 s/d, including breakfast, a/c), which is on a hill about a 10-minute walk from the ferry pier. El Cerrito is a B&B with three "B&B rooms" and three apartments. The apartments range from a one-bedroom for up to two people (US$110) up to a three-bedroom that can sleep six (US$297). The rooms are due for a sprucing up, but the place has a relaxed vibe, like staying at a friend's beach house. The B&B rooms are simple but cheerfully decorated, with private bathrooms and a shared balcony. These range in price US$77–104.50. Your hosts are Cynthia Mulder, a Canadian, and her husband Hiddo, who is from the "Dutch Caribbean." They can organize a range of tours, including fishing, snorkeling, and exploring the island. El Cerrito's website has good information on the island and how to get around. Also check out www.taboga.panamanow.com.

The B&B has an attractive two-terrace restaurant (7:30–9 A.M., noon–2 P.M., 5:30–7 P.M.) with lovely views of the ocean and ships at anchor waiting to transit the canal. Most items are US$7.50–12.50.

Vereda Tropical (tel. 250-2154, www.hotelveredatropical.com, starts at US$71.50 s/d) is a surprisingly attractive if rather peculiar-looking hotel. It's sort of a cross between a mock Spanish colonial and a nautical-themed building. Rooms are pleasant and clean, and the more expensive ones have air-conditioning and balconies with a view of the ocean. It's worth springing a bit more to get the ocean view. The place is perched at the top of a hill, which gives its terrace restaurant, which is shaded by bougainvilleas, great ocean views. It's open 7:30–10:30 A.M., 12:30–4 P.M., and 6:30–9 P.M. Most dishes are US$11–16, and include pizza, seafood, and pasta. It's the only pizzeria on the island, but it's not very good. The view makes up for a lot, though.

Mundi's (cell 6476-0610, 8:30 A.M.–4 P.M. daily, US$8–13) serves the best food on Taboga. It's a simple little open-air place right above the water, to the right as one exits the ferry ramp. It has good yuca, good corvina, and friendly service.

Restaurante Acuario (cell 6801-6394 or 6763-8896, 8:30 A.M.–9 P.M. daily, most US$8–13) is on a balcony of a house above Playa Honda, to the left as one leaves the ferry pier. It's a basic seafood place with prices that aren't basic enough. It charges US$10, for instance, for a not very tasty shrimp cocktail.

Getting There and Around

Ferries to Isla Taboga leave from Isla Naos on the Amador Causeway. A taxi from Panama City to the pier should cost about US$4–5. There is parking near the pier for those who drive.

El Calypso (tel. 314-1730 or 390-2403) uses two ferries of different size, the *Calypso Queen* and *Calypso Princess.* The fare is US$7 one way and US$12 round-trip.

El Calypso ferries make the trip to Taboga at 8:30 A.M. Monday–Friday, with a second ferry at 3 P.M. Monday and Friday. On weekends and holidays they leave at 8 A.M., 10:30 A.M., and 4 P.M.

Trips from Taboga back to Amador are at 9:30 A.M. Monday and Friday, with a second ferry at 4:30 P.M. Monday–Friday. The weekend and holiday schedule is 9 A.M., 3 P.M., and 5 P.M.

Ferry schedules are more theoretical than real; service is erratic. Make a reservation or show up early on dry-season weekends and holidays to be sure of getting a ticket—this is a popular day-trip destination for Panamanians. The ferry requires passengers to arrive at least an hour ahead of time. Also, since there's no assigned seating, board early to claim a spot out of the sun—it's easy to get fried before even reaching the beach. There are few vehicles of any kind on the island, and it's easy to get around on foot. But if the heat or the climbs get to be too much, a taxi ride anywhere costs no more than US$1.50.

Gamboa and Vicinity

The townsite of Gamboa, on the banks of the Panama Canal about halfway across the isthmus, is surrounded by extraordinary natural beauty, especially given how close it is to Panama City. It's a gateway to world-famous birding trails, the tropical rainforest of Parque Nacional Soberanía, the powerful Río Chagres, botanical gardens and a zoo, and the huge, artificial Lago Gatún. That lake is at the heart of the canal and contains Barro Colorado Island, one of the world's foremost natural laboratories for the study of tropical nature.

Though Emberá and Wounaan people still live up the Río Chagres, Gamboa is the headquarters of the canal's engineering and dredging divisions and has a modern infrastructure. Gamboa today has few services, accommodations, or places to eat.

Lago Alajuela (formerly Madden Lake) is a second artificial lake northeast of Gamboa that supplies water for the canal. Some people like to visit its impressive Madden Dam, but because it's not entirely safe, tourists should avoid it.

SIGHTS
Parque Municipal Summit (Summit Botanical Gardens and Zoo)
These gardens (off Gaillard Highway a few kilometers before Gamboa, tel. 232-4854, 9 A.M.–5 P.M. daily, US$5) are worth a quick side trip on the way to or from Gamboa. They were created by the Panama Canal Company in 1923 for the study of tropical plants and turned over to the Panamanian government in 1985. The place has deteriorated in recent years, but some efforts are being made to fix it up. At last count there were 4,000 plants representing 366 species still growing in the gardens.

Summit Gardens also has a small zoo that contains tapirs, caimans, jaguars, and other large animals. Many of their cages are tiny and antiquated, which will disturb many visitors.

The harpy eagle compound, Summit's showcase, is more encouraging. The harpy eagle is the world's most powerful bird of prey; it can grow up to a meter long from bill to tail. Sadly, it's also endangered. The bird is indigenous to Panama, and a major purpose of the compound is to try to get the birds to reproduce in captivity. The specimens here are magnificent, with thick plumage, fearsome hooked bills, and steely talons. They look like stoic high chiefs.

◪ Parque Nacional Soberanía
This is a true tropical forest, and it's one of the most accessible in the world. Its 22,000 hectares extend along the east bank of the Panama Canal, ending at Lago Gatún near the town of Limón. The wildlife is amazing, especially considering how close the park is to population centers. Among its inhabitants are 525 species of birds, 105 species of mammals, 55 species of amphibians, and 79 species of reptiles.

All its well-maintained trails are a short drive from Panama City on the Gaillard Highway, making it quite feasible to go for a morning hike during which there's a chance of encountering such tourist-pleasing critters as sloths, coatimundis, toucans, and kinkajous, and then be back in the heart of the city in time for lunch in an air-conditioned restaurant.

A section of the famous **Camino de Cruces (Las Cruces Trail),** which has a history dating to the 16th century, runs through the park. To reach it by car, continue straight when the Gaillard Highway forks just past the railroad overpass with "1929" carved in it. The road, now Madden Road (don't expect a street sign), will pass through a forest, which, sadly, is often strewn with litter. There's a parking area and picnic tables on the left after 6.3 kilometers. The trailhead is well marked. It's possible to hike this trail for about five or six hours to the Chagres and even camp along it. For just a glimpse of this storied trail, walk at least five minutes along it and you'll come to a section where the ancient paving stones that once lined the trail have been restored. In the dry season, you may have to brush aside dead leaves to find them. (Use your boot to do this, not your hand, as there are still some poisonous snakes in the forest.)

All the other trails are on the road to Gamboa. Back near the 1929 overpass, turn off the Galliard Highway toward Gamboa. The first major trail will be the wide, flat **Plantation Road.** It's a right turn off the highway; follow the Canopy Tower signs. The entrance to the trail is on the left at the base of the road leading to the Canopy Tower.

Farther along the main road is **Sendero El Charco** (literally, pond trail), also on the right. This is a very short (844 meters) trail with a little waterfall near the entrance. A barbecue area on the premises attracts hordes of families on the weekends.

The best trail for viewing birdlife is the famous **Pipeline Road (Camino del Oleoducto).** To get there, cross over the one-lane bridge leading into Gamboa. Continue straight. After about three kilometers the road will fork; take the left fork onto the gravel road. The swampy area to the right, just before Pipeline Road, is worth checking out on the way back from an early-morning birding trip. At around 8–9 A.M., as the forest warms up, there's an excellent chance of spotting capybaras, the world's largest rodents, on the far side of the clearing. A couple of kilometers past this area there's a Parque Nacional Soberanía sign indicating you've reached Camino del Oleoducto. Make a right here and park.

For the first six kilometers or so, the forest is mostly secondary growth. You'll see dozens of species of birds if you arrive early. There's a slight chance of finding anteaters, howler monkeys, white-faced capuchins, Geoffroy's tamarin, green iguanas, agoutis, coatimundis, or two- and three-toed sloths. Serious birders will want to continue past this area into old-growth forest, where there's a possibility of seeing such rare specimens as yellow-eared toucanets, crimson-bellied woodpeckers, sirystes, and other gorgeous birds that will impress even those who don't know a russet antshrike from a slaty-winged foliage-gleaner. The unbelievably lucky may see an endangered harpy eagle, but don't count on it. Pipeline Road continues for many kilometers, but the bridges over streams are not well-maintained these days. Bridge collapses can curtail a long hike. Get here by dawn to see this famous birding road in all its feathered glory.

About 1.6 kilometers in from the entrance to Pipeline Road is the **Panama Rainforest Discovery Center** (tel. 264-6266 in Panama City, tel. 314-9386 or 314-9388 in Gamboa, www.pipelineroad.org, 6 A.M.–4 P.M. daily), a new interpretive center and observation tower in the middle of the forest. The tower is a modern steel structure 30 meters high, with rest platforms on the way up and a top platform that's just above the canopy. There is a kilometer of developed trails in the immediate area. The visitors center has restrooms and a gift shop that sells drinks and snacks. Admission to the complex is a whopping US$30 for adults and US$4 for kids younger than 12 during the premium time of 6–10 A.M., when one is most likely to see wildlife. The price drops to US$20 for adults and US$2 for kids after 10 A.M. But to have the best chance of seeing interesting wildlife, particularly birds, visitors should try to be on-site as soon as the tower opens. The center is open daily except for Christmas Day and New Year's Day. Recently it has been offering late afternoon hikes (4–6 P.M.), when the forest starts to come back to life.

Other than the Panama Rainforest Discovery Center, the rest of the Pipeline Road area, and the national park generally, is open to the public at a much more modest fee. Hiking and camping permits are available at the ANAM office at the edge of the park, inconveniently located well before any of the trails. It's on Gaillard Highway at the fork just past the narrow overpass; you can't miss the huge Parque Nacional Soberanía sign. The office is officially open 8 A.M.–4 P.M. weekdays, but the staff live in the little house behind the office so there should always be someone there to take your money. Entrance fee is US$5, which gives visitors access to all the trails for the day. The camping fee is another US$5.

Bear in mind there are no developed camping sites in the park (though there are some facilities at Sendero El Charco) and this is a tropical forest. Those planning an early-morning hike can probably pay on the way back without a problem. But otherwise ask about the conditions of the trails, especially Pipeline Road, before venturing out. The Camino de Cruces is quite a hike from the other trails; Gamboa-bound buses take passengers only as far as the fork to Gamboa, after which you'll have to hoof it for six kilometers unless you can flag down a ride. It's much more convenient to take a taxi from Panama City or go with a tour group.

Lago Gatún

Once the largest artificially made lake in the world, at 422 square kilometers Lago Gatún is still a plenty impressive body of water. It was formed by damming the Río Chagres near its mouth, at Gatún, and is an integral part of the Panama Canal. Transiting ships still follow the submerged riverbed of the Chagres, since it's the deepest part of the lake. It's long been a popular spot with boaters, water-skiers, anglers, and even scuba divers. The diving here is unusual, to say the least. A Belgian locomotive and 8 of its 40 train cars, abandoned during construction days, were recently salvaged from the bottom of the lake, and submerged trees and remnants of old towns are still there. Not surprisingly, however, the water is murky and in some places choked with vegetation. Divers find the experience rather spooky.

Caimans have always shared the lake with people, but there are a lot more of them now. The lake now also has crocodiles, so diving may not be the best idea.

The fishing here is terrific—the peacock bass population, accidentally introduced decades ago, is so out of control anglers are actually encouraged to catch them to restore some kind of ecological balance. It's not uncommon for an angler who knows the good spots to catch dozens of fish an hour.

A highlight of a Lago Gatún boat trip is a visit to the **primate sanctuary** scattered among more than a dozen islands in the lake, known collectively as the Islas Tigre and Islas Las Brujas. Here visitors can spot tamarins, spider monkeys, white-faced capuchins, howlers, and night monkeys swinging or peering from trees just a few meters from the boat.

Only visit the sanctuary on a tour led by a responsible naturalist group such as Ancon Expeditions. Do not feed or have any physical contact with the monkeys. All but the night monkeys have been rescued from illegal captivity, and the project is trying to reintroduce them to the wild. The last thing they need is more human contact. Besides, some can be

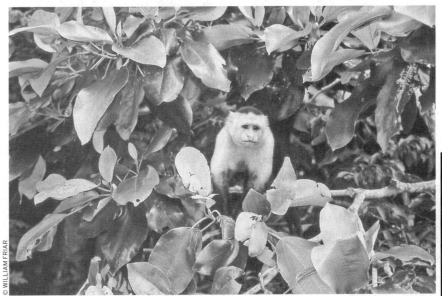

© WILLIAM FRIAR

a white-faced capuchin at the primate sanctuary in Lago Gatún

pretty aggressive, so don't get too close. Some boat tours of the area include walks through small, forested islands, some of which have spooky ruins from the old Canal Zone days. Douse yourself with insect repellent before exploring them; the mosquitoes can be voracious.

Barro Colorado Island

BCI, as it's commonly known, is one of the world's most famous biological reserves. Part of what makes it exceptional is that it's been left alone so long: It was declared a protected area in 1923, when such reserves in the neotropics were almost unheard of. Since then its flora and fauna have been more intensely studied than those of any other tropical area of comparable size. The island is administered by the **Smithsonian Tropical Research Institute** (STRI, tel. 212-8951, fax 212-8026, www.stri.org), which is based in Panama.

Barro Colorado Island was actually a hill until 1914, when the damming of the Chagres River to create Lago Gatún made that hill an island. The flooding of the lake left only 15 square kilometers of tropical forest on the island, but they contain 480 species of trees (more than in all of Europe), 70 species of bats, 384 species of birds, 30 species of frogs, 47 species of snakes, and on and on. Just accounting for the insects on the island is an overwhelming task. Take ants, for instance: More than 200 species have been identified so far.

Day visitors, as opposed to research scientists, can walk on only some trails, usually an interpretive loop that takes 2–3 hours to traverse at an easy clip. It's fairly flat most of the way, but it does get muddy at times. There's a short side trail off the main loop that's well worth taking. It leads to the aptly named Big Tree, a kapok *(Ceiba pentandra)* so huge other trees are growing on its branches.

Visitors are not allowed on the trails without an authorized guide. But consider buying *A Day on Barro Colorado Island* (Smithsonian), by Marina Wong and Jorge Ventocilla, anyway. It contains a trail guide and information on the island's flora and fauna that will help you get much more out of your visit. It's sold in a few places in Panama, including the little bookshop at STRI's main office in Panama City. The Gamboa Rainforest Resort may have it as well.

BCI has the kind of wildlife many visitors come to the tropics to see, including tapirs, coatimundis, sloths, ocelots, anteaters, collared peccaries, and three species of monkeys. Day visitors expecting a jungle crawling with creatures will likely be disappointed. One may see almost no animal life during a short visit to BCI.

The only mammals one is likely to encounter are agoutis and howler monkeys. It's actually hard not to stumble upon howlers. A 1977 census found 65 troops on the island, each with about 19 monkeys. Their numbers haven't changed much since.

Access to the island is strictly controlled. Visitors must arrange a tour through STRI or an STRI-approved tour operator, and the few spaces get booked up early. Cancellations are not uncommon, however, so last-minute trips are sometimes possible. Some tour operators offer trips to Barro Colorado Nature Monument, which includes the surrounding mainland as well as the island itself. Make sure the tour actually goes to the island if that's important to you.

STRI offers **tours** (tel. 212-8951, fax 212-8026, www.stri.org, Tues., Wed., and Fri. at 7:15 A.M.; Sat. and Sun. at 8 A.M.; US$70 pp, US$40 students). The cost includes the launch from Gamboa to BCI, a 2–3-hour hike with a naturalist guide, a tour of the visitors center, and lunch at the field-research station (vegetarian food is available). It may be possible to chat up a research scientist over lunch. Reservations should be made as far ahead of time as possible.

The launch to the island leaves from a pier in Gamboa, about an hour's drive from Panama City. It's imperative that visitors arrive early, as the launch to the island leaves on the dot

and there's no other way to get there. Visitors are responsible for their own transportation to Gamboa. A taxi from Panama City costs around US$30. The STRI website now has detailed information about the trip and a schematic map explaining how to get to the pier.

Río Chagres

This powerful river supplies most of the water for the Panama Canal and much of the drinking water for Panama City. It once flowed unimpeded across the isthmus, emptying into the Caribbean below the ruins of Fuerte San Lorenzo near the city of Colón. The damming of the river near Gatún Locks created the massive Lago Gatún, and today the river disappears into the lake at Gamboa and doesn't resurface until it approaches the Caribbean. But the upper reaches of the Chagres still wind their way through lovely rainforest. In the dry season, stretches of the river become little more than glorified puddles. In the rainy season, however, the Chagres can rise many meters in a single hour. Flash floods are not unknown.

The Emberá and Wounaan have been relocated from the Darién jungle in recent decades to live in communities along the banks of the river surprisingly close to Panama City. The one most visited by tourists is Parara Puru. While these are true Emberá who cling to some of their traditional ways, visitors should note that the village is rather touristy and the elaborate traditional costumes the people wear are put on for their benefit. Even the concept of a village is not a traditional part of Emberá culture; historically, families lived in relative isolation from each other.

Still, the trip up the river is beautiful and encounters with Emberá and Wounaan people are always interesting. Visits to the community include dance demonstrations, a walk through a botanical garden, and a chance to buy cocobolo figurines, tagua nut carvings, woven baskets, and other handicrafts. Those inclined can have themselves painted with traditional *jagua* (a kind of vegetable dye) designs, but bear in mind the dye takes up to two weeks to fade and can't be washed off. Several tour operators offer trips up the Chagres to Parara Puru. **Aventuras Panama** (tel. 260-0044 or 236-5814, www.aventuraspanama.com) offers an all-day excursion for US$110. The trip includes lunch in the community. River rafting is also possible on the Chagres.

SPORTS AND RECREATION
Canopy Tower

Unless the Canopy Tower (tel. 264-5720, U.S. toll-free tel. 800/930-3397, www.canopytower.com) is packed with guests, it offers day tours to anyone. There's a decent chance of seeing good-size mammals (other than your fellow visitors) and an excellent chance of spotting lots of birds. Possibilities include an early-morning (6:30–11 A.M.) or lunch (12:30–5 P.M.) visit for

COURTESY OF THE CANOPY TOWER

The Canopy Tower is a unique eco-lodge in Parque Nacional Soberanía.

US$95 that includes a two-hour guided walk and wildlife viewing from the tower.

Gamboa Rainforest Resort

You don't have to be a guest at the Gamboa Rainforest Resort (tel. 314-5000, www.gamboaresort.com) to use its **activities center** (8 A.M.–6 P.M. daily) or book its tours, which include bird-watching walks and night safaris on the lake. The resort rents kayaks, bicycles, and other toys. You can also charter fishing boats here, but expect to pay for it.

The **aerial tram** (7:30 A.M., 9:15 A.M., 10:30 A.M., 1:30 P.M., and 3 P.M. Tues.–Sun., US$40 pp) is one of the star attractions of the resort. It's sort of like a ski lift that takes passengers up about 80 meters to a hill, passing through the canopy of a patch of secondary forest along the way. A bilingual naturalist guide travels along in each four- or five-person gondola to spot and describe flora and fauna. Passengers can get off at the top and climb a 30-meter observation tower that offers panoramic views of the canal, the Chagres, and the surrounding forest. The trip takes a little over an hour, not including the stop at the observation platform. Don't get your hopes up about seeing too much wildlife; these canopy trams are a comfortable way to experience tropical forest, but a quick zip through the trees is unlikely to net many encounters with animals. For the best chance of seeing anything, take the first tram of the day, before most birds and jungle critters have slipped away. The rate is excessive for what you get, but if you're lucky enough to glimpse something special, you might feel it's worth it. Contact Gamboa Rainforest Resort for reservations and information.

Before or after a tram ride, it's worth wandering around the resort's **flora and fauna exhibits,** though combining this with the tram ride is an additional US$10 pp. They're housed in a series of structures on the road leading up to the tram and include an orchid nursery, a

THE PANAMA CANAL

serpentarium with impressive native and non-native species, a butterfly house, and a small freshwater aquarium that also contains crocodiles, caimans, and turtles. The model Emberá village nearby is rather hokey, but it's a chance to meet a few Emberá and buy their tightly woven baskets and other handicrafts.

Fishing, Boating, and Adventure Tours

There's a small **marina** just outside Gamboa, near the one-lane bridge across the Río Chagres, where boatmen offer fishing tours on their basic *pangas.* Stop by at least a day ahead of time to work out a deal. Anglers need to be on the lake just before dawn; by midmorning the peacock bass stop biting. A morning of fishing costs about US$50. The captains can also take visitors on an exploratory cruise around Lago Gatún and/or the Chagres River. The price depends on distance.

A group called **Panama Canal Fishing** (tel. 315-1905, cell 6678-2653, www.panama-canalfishing.com) offers a higher-end, all-inclusive fishing experience on Lago Gatún. Trips are made on a roomy and comfortable Hurricane Fundeck 201. The cost is US$445 per boat and includes round-trip transfers between Panama City and Gamboa, a fishing guide and captain, picnic lunch and drinks, and all fishing equipment, bait, and lures. Boats can accommodate up to six anglers, at US$25 extra per person after the first two. Prices do not include sales tax.

Panama Canal Fishing is run by Richard Cahill and his wife, Gaby. Rich has worked for years as an accomplished naturalist guide with Ancon Expeditions, and is highly recommended. He's knowledgeable, reliable, enthusiastic, fun, and an all-around good guy. He's fluent in English and Spanish. The company also offers tours of the lake's primate sanctuary and the Panama Canal, usually as an add-on to the fishing trip.

Aventuras Panama (tel. 260-0044 or 236-5814, cell 6679-4404, www.aventuraspanama.com) offers rafting trips on the Río Chagres. The rafting is usually quite gentle, with mostly Class II rapids and a few Class IIIs. It's not intended for those who need big white water. However, this is still a long, fairly rigorous trip, and the Chagres, like any other powerful river, has seen its share of accidents and needs to be approached with respect. Clients are picked up from their hotel at 5 A.M. and driven into the highlands above Cerro Azul. From there, it's a 1.5-hour hike through the forest to the put-in spot. Rafters spend all day on the river, ending up in Lago Alajuela (also called Madden Lake) in the late afternoon. Clients are dropped back at their hotel around 7 P.M. The trip costs US$175 per person and includes breakfast, lunch, and transfers. Clients must be between the ages of 12 and 70. The company offers many other tours, including rafting trips on the Mamoní and Río Grande and a boat ride up the Chagres to visit the Emberá community of Parara Puru.

ACCOMMODATIONS AND FOOD

The few hotels in the Gamboa area are impressive, if expensive, places that are destinations in themselves. The only restaurants open to non-guests are at the Gamboa Rainforest Resort, though the Canopy Tower sometimes offers day passes that include a meal. There are also basic fast-food stands near the entrance to the main Gamboa pier that are open during work hours to feed Panama Canal dredging division workers.

Other lodging is beginning to come to this area. Three B&Bs have opened up in old Zone housing in Gamboa. **The Canopy B&B** (Harding Ave. and Jadwin Ave., tel. 833-5929, U.S. toll-free 800/930-3397, www.canopytower.com, US$88 s, US$132 d, including breakfast), not to be confused with the Canopy Tower, is meant as a more affordable alternative.

Ivan's Beds and Breakfast (111 Jadwin

Ave., tel. 6981-4583, cell 6981-4583, www.gamboaecotours.com, US$45 pp, including breakfast) is aimed at birders and other nature lovers, as it's quite close to Pipeline Road. **Mateo's Gamboa B&B** (131A Calle Humberto Zárate, cell 6690-0664, www.gamboabedandbreakfast.com, US$35 s/d, including breakfast) is run by a retired Panamanian couple.

It's also possible to camp in Parque Nacional Soberanía, but there are no facilities and this is a true tropical forest, with all the potential discomfort that that implies.

Canopy Tower

The Canopy Tower (tel. 264-5720, U.S. toll-free tel. 800/930-3397, www.canopytower.com, high-season Canopy Room packages US$229 pp, including meals and one bird tour, three-day minimum stay) is an old U.S. military radar tower that has been cleverly transformed into an impressive 12-room hotel and wildlife observation platform, high above the floor of the protected Parque Nacional Soberanía. Visitors can look out the window of their room right into the forest.

The rooms are simple but cheerful and comfortable, with teak louvered doors and other touches that soften the utilitarian feel of the structure. Each room has two single beds with ceiling fans and a good hot-water bathroom. Five single rooms have been added on the level below the canopy rooms, about 5.5 meters above the hilltop. Formerly guides' quarters, they are quite small (eight square meters, less than half the size of the canopy rooms), have a single bed, and share a bathroom.

The Blue Cotinga Suite (US$259 s/d in high season) is a large room (34 square meters) that can sleep three and has a private balcony with a hammock swing. This is the fanciest place to stay at the tower. The Harpy Eagle Suite, one floor down, is a bit smaller (27 square meters) and plainer, but the rates are the same for one or two people. It can sleep up to four.

The tower is not air-conditioned so as not to scare away wildlife and separate guests from the sound of the forest. However, the elevation is high enough that, with the screened windows open and the ceiling fan on, it's quite comfortable. The tower is made of metal and sound carries easily, so don't expect to sleep in late.

The rooms, however, are only a small part of a visit to the tower. Stays include all meals and a daily, guided tour into the national park on well-maintained trails. The food here is good, concentrating on simple but tasty local dishes.

One flight up from the canopy rooms are the dining and living room, which offer a near 360-degree view. Guests can continue up to the roof, which is a great place to watch the sun rise and set over the forest, listen to the roar of howler monkeys, and watch for owls and other nocturnal creatures at night.

The chances of spotting birds and wildlife can plummet during a rain, though they come out to dry afterwards. But the migration season, which occurs late in the rainy season, can be an exciting time to visit. This is when literally millions of raptors pass through Panama on their annual migration. Rates at this time (mid-September to mid-December) are higher than "green season" rates but lower than high-season ones.

Guests are likely to see more wildlife while lounging in the tower than they would on long hikes in remoter areas. Within five minutes of my first visit several years ago I saw a tití monkey (Geoffroy's tamarin) and a host of other creatures. By the end of my second visit a few years later, I had seen a kinkajou, a dozen coatimundi moms and babies, a sloth, an unidentified snake, and innumerable birds (short-tailed hawk, three toucans in a single tree, dusky-capped flycatcher, white-whiskered puffbird, white-shouldered tanager, blue-crowned manakin, and on and on). At last count, bird-watchers had identified 283 species of birds just from the tower and Semaphore Hill Road.

The Canopy Tower is 25 kilometers from

THE PANAMA CANAL

Panama City, about a half-hour drive. Those driving must take the left fork off Gaillard Highway after the railroad bridge and follow the road toward Gamboa. The well-marked turnoff to the Canopy Tower will be on the right 1.6 kilometers past Summit Botanical Gardens. There's a gate across the entrance to the tower road that you may have to open. Go up the one-lane, well-maintained road 1.7 kilometers to the tower. The tower is not wheelchair-accessible. Access to the top of the tower is by stairs—five dozen of them.

Make reservations, even for day trips, as far in advance as possible; the tower is world-famous and extremely popular.

Gamboa Rainforest Resort

The resort (tel. 314-5000, U.S. toll-free tel. 877/800-1690, www.gamboaresort.com, starts at US$198 s/d), which opened in 2000, is a peculiar mixture of an ecotourism resort, luxury spa, and theme park. Spread over its 137 hectares are a slice of tropical forest with an aerial tram running through the canopy, a full-service spa, a 107-room hotel, an entire neighborhood of one- and two-bedroom historic apartments converted from old Canal Zone housing, a huge swimming pool, tennis courts, three restaurants, traditionally dressed Emberá selling handicrafts at a pseudo-model village, an orchid nursery, a snake house, an amphibian exhibit, several aquariums, a butterfly house, and a marina.

The location couldn't be better: The resort was built right on the banks of the Chagres, one of Panama's most important rivers, and it is only a stroll away from Lago Gatún, where one can watch ships transiting the Panama Canal. It's bordered by Parque Nacional Soberanía, the major trails of which are just a few kilometers away, as is the Canopy Tower.

There are two basic kinds of accommodations. Those in the main building start at US$231 for a room with a balcony, air-conditioning, minibar, safe, cable TV, iron and ironing board, coffeemaker, and so on. Room quality is on a par with what one would find at a midlevel business hotel in the United States.

The price for the one-bedroom historic apartment is a comparative bargain at US$198 s/d. Whereas the rooms in the hotel are generic, these have character. They consist of renovated wooden buildings dating from the 1930s that actually housed Panama Canal employees and their families in the old Canal Zone days. The decor is simple and cheerful, from the rattan furniture to the historic canal clippings and sketches on the walls. All have sitting rooms and kitchenettes with microwaves, minifridges, and coffeemakers. They don't have a view of the river, but they're surrounded by trees.

All kinds of multiday packages are available that combine stays with golfing, bird-watching, spa treatments, ecotours, and so on. The resort's activities center rents mountain bikes, kayaks, pedal boats, and other gear.

The food at the resort is hit or miss. Of the three restaurants, **Restaurante Los Lagartos** (tel. 276-6812, 11:30 A.M.–5 P.M. daily) is the best option because of its terrific location. It's down the hill from the main hotel, built onto an attractive, open-walled wooden terrace that juts into the Río Chagres near where it empties into Lago Gatún. From their tables diners can sometimes see turtles, caimans, and the odd iguana sunbathing on the same log, peacock bass and tilapia nosing about in the shallows, and little blue herons and jacanas hunting for food among the floating vegetation. Even here the food tends to be mediocre, but the show put on by nature is exceptional.

The spa at the Gamboa Rainforest Resort is also open to nonguests and offers a wide assortment of treatments and packages at U.S. prices, varying from manicures and massages to a full day of pampering. The Gamboa Rainforest Resort is about a 45-minute drive from downtown Panama City.

GETTING THERE AND AROUND

The end of the road in Gamboa is about a 45-minute drive from Panama City. Taxis charge around US$30 one-way. Buses leave from the SACA bus section of the Gran Terminal de Transportes in Albrook. Gamboa-bound buses take passengers within reasonable walking distance of every attraction in the area except the Camino de Cruces. They're not close to each other, though, so it's not feasible to walk from one attraction to the next. Buses to and from Gamboa stop at designated bus stops along Gaillard Highway about every half hour during daylight hours, but this can be a time-consuming way to visit the various spots. Those who can afford it should consider hiring a taxi for a half-day or full-day tour.

Those driving from Panama City should head west on Gaillard Highway. Just past Pedro Miguel the road summits a small hill and then crosses under a narrow underpass, a railroad bridge with "1929" carved into it. The ANAM office that sells hiking and camping permits is at the fork. Going straight leads into Madden Forest, a part of Parque Nacional Soberanía. Here's where you'll find the Camino de Cruces (Las Cruces Trail). A left turn at the fork keeps you on Gaillard Highway and leads to Summit Botanical Gardens, Plantation Road, the Canopy Tower, and Sendero El Charco, in that order. Cross the one-lane bridge (caution—be sure to stop if the red light is on) into the town of Gamboa, where the road ends. An immediate right turn leads up to the Gamboa Rainforest Resort. Staying straight leads to the Isla Barro Colorado launch and Pipeline Road.

Colón and the Costa Abajo

The Colón province lies along the central Caribbean coast of Panama. Its capital is Colón, historically Panama's second-most important city. Though this area starts just 80 kilometers north of Panama City, it has long been neglected and has significantly fewer resources and facilities than the Pacific side of the isthmus. A few tour operators, especially dive operators, specialize in the area, but it is still relatively off the beaten track for most tourists. This is slowly changing, with new hotels, cruise-ship departures, and commercial projects in the works. These plans are serious enough to worry environmentalists, who fear especially for the important mangrove forests along the coastline. There is even talk of building a fanciful Dubai-style offshore city stuffed with high-rises next to Colón.

The coastline west of Colón is known as Costa Abajo ("lower coast"). It is a still a lightly developed area with rough roads and few visitors other than avid bird-watchers.

But it offers the well-preserved ruins of a Spanish fort and lush tropical forest surrounding the mouth of the storied Río Chagres. These are all on the west side of the canal, across the swing bridge at Gatún Locks that is the only land link between western and eastern Panama on the Caribbean side of the isthmus.

The area is worth adding as a side trip on the way to or from, say, Portobelo or Isla Grande, or for those taking the Panama Railway across the isthmus. As a destination in itself, it's likely to be most appealing to those with an especially keen interest in the Panama Canal or Panama's piratical past.

The area's few main sights—Gatún Locks, Gatún Dam, and Fuerte San Lorenzo—are all clustered close together in a relatively small area southwest of Colón. So are its natural attractions, the mouth of the Río Chagres and the bird-watching spots around Achiote and Escobal.

THE PANAMA CANAL

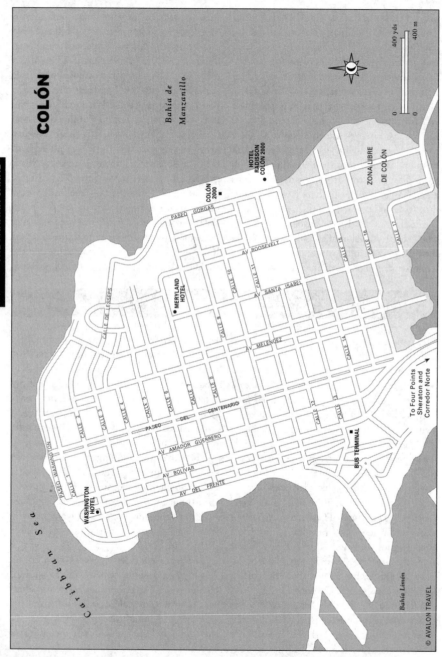

COLÓN

Bahía de Manzanillo

Caribbean Sea

Bahía Limón

PASEO GORGAS

COLÓN 2000

HOTEL RADISSON COLÓN 2000

AV. ROOSEVELT

CALLE 15

CALLE 16

CALLE 17

ZONA LIBRE DE COLÓN

CALLE DE LESSEPS

MERYLAND HOTEL

CALLE 10

CALLE 11

AV. SANTA ISABEL

CALLE 9

AV. MELENDEZ

CALLE 14

PASEO WASHINGTON

CALLE 3

CALLE 4

CALLE 5

CALLE 6

CALLE 7

CALLE 8

PASEO DEL CENTENARIO

AV. AMADOR GUERRERO

AV. BOLIVAR

AV. DEL FRENTE

CALLE 1

CALLE 2

CALLE 12

CALLE 13

WASHINGTON HOTEL

BUS TERMINAL

To Four Points Sheraton and Corredor Norte

0 400 yds
0 400 m

© AVALON TRAVEL

SAFETY CONSIDERATIONS

Though the city of Colón (pop. 42,133, co-LONE in Spanish and kah-LAWN in English) has a long, colorful history, it should be avoided. It has little to offer tourists, and you can see all the region's sights without ever stopping here. More importantly, extreme unemployment and poverty give this crumbling city a terrible reputation as a place where muggings are common.

There's always talk about revitalizing Colón, but little ever seems to change for its poor residents. For the foreseeable future, sadly, visitors should stay well away from the city.

For those who insist on visiting, do not walk around Colón: Drive or take taxis everywhere. Shopping at the Colón Free Zone and Colón 2000 is reasonably safe.

HISTORY

For most of its history, Colón has been known as a place to avoid. Even the intrepid Columbus decided to steer clear of the area when he and his crew became the first Europeans to see Isla Manzanillo. All they saw was a pestilential swamp filled with mosquitoes, snakes, caimans, and who knows what else.

Throughout the Spanish colonial era, the Colón area was largely ignored. The Spanish built their forts at San Lorenzo to the west and Portobelo and Nombre de Dios to the east.

It wasn't until an American company began work on the Panama Railroad in 1850 that people started living and working on the island and built the foundations of the city of Colón. The railroad had its Caribbean terminus nearby, and a settlement sprang up to house the employees and cater to the 49ers, who were on their way to the California goldfields.

The town did not even merit a name until 1852, when it was dubbed Aspinwall in honor of one of the founders of the railroad. Panama was still a part of Colombia at the time, and officials in Bogotá rejected the name, insisting it be called Colón, the Spanish name for

Columbus. A feud over the name erupted between the Panama Railroad Company and Bogotá, resulting in much confusion until 1890, when the Colombian government began rejecting any letters with "Aspinwall" on the envelope. The railroad company finally gave in.

Colón's fortunes declined following the gold rush, but they revived again in the 1880s when the French began their doomed attempt to build a sea-level canal. Colón residents would later reminisce about this as a time when champagne was in far greater supply than the suspect local water. Then Colón burned to the ground in 1885 during the so-called Prestán Uprising and was rebuilt, primarily by the Panama Railroad Company. It wasn't until the French effort collapsed and the U.S. effort began that Colón began to be cleaned up and transformed into a modern city. The gringos installed sewers and plumbing, paved the streets, drained the swamps, and sanitized the whole place.

For the first half of the 20th century, Colón became a rather picturesque little city of three-story wooden buildings with long verandas, and white, neoclassical concrete buildings erected by the Isthmian Canal Commission. Front Street, which faced the railroad tracks and the port of Cristóbal, boasted elegant shops. As Panama City and the Pacific side of the isthmus grew in importance, Colón again deteriorated.

SIGHTS
Gatún Locks

On the Pacific side of the Panama Canal it takes two sets of locks to raise or lower ships 26 meters. Gatún Locks (visiting hours: 9 A.M.–4 P.M. daily), on the Caribbean side west of Colón, do the job by themselves. Each lock chamber is the same size as those on the Pacific—almost 305 by 34 meters—but there are three pairs of them on this side. That makes Gatún Locks absolutely massive, a little more than 1.5 kilometers from end to end. It's an impressive sight. It will probably still be impressive even when the new

AMINTA MELENDÉZ: COLÓN'S FAVORITE DAUGHTER

One special day in Colón's history is November 5. On that day in 1903, separatists in Colón used a young woman, 18-year-old Aminta Melendéz, to smuggle a message to conspirators in Panama City about a plot to disarm Colombian troops that had landed in Colón to put down Panama's incipient revolution. Melendéz was the daughter of Porfirio Melendéz, Colón's police chief and one of the separatists. To do so, she had to walk right past swarms of heavily armed troops, and capture would likely have meant her execution.

The plot was never acted upon, but Aminta's bravery is still celebrated every November 5 as part of Colón's independence festivities. Throughout her life, it was traditional for the president of Panama to visit her home to pay homage. Oddly, for a country that loves celebrations, this is not a national holiday, something that annoys Colón boosters.

post-Panamax locks are completed just east of these. They're scheduled to begin service in 2015.

As dramatic as the locks are, most visitors based on the Pacific side of the isthmus are satisfied with seeing Miraflores and perhaps Pedro Miguel without making a special trip just to see these.

An observation platform up a long flight of stairs gives an excellent view of the locks, the Caribbean entrance to the canal, and Lago Gatún. There's another observation spot downstairs. It has a small-scale model of the entire canal. Bathrooms for tourists are in the building behind the model.

The number of tourists visiting the locks is increasing, but free bilingual talks, like the ones offered at Miraflores, are still sporadic here. The best bet to catch a talk is when a cruise ship disgorges its passengers for a tour.

Gatún Dam

The huge (nearly 2.5 kilometers long) earthen Gatún Dam was built to create Lago Gatún (Gatún Lake), a vital part of the Panama Canal. It was the largest such structure in the world when the canal opened in 1914. The dam controls the flow of the mighty Río Chagres, a major obstacle to canal builders, and supplies electricity used at the locks and the surrounding communities. It's an awesome sight when the spillway is opened and the water comes roaring out. A small bridge runs right by the spillway, behind which there's a good view of the canal.

To get to the dam, cross over the swing bridge that spans the north end of Gatún Locks. The wait can be up to half an hour if a ship is transiting, but the bridge provides a fascinating fish's-eye view of the locks, since one actually drives through a lock chamber. Take the first left after the bridge and head up the road for about two kilometers.

There is a free car ferry across the channel that runs 5 A.M.–9 P.M. daily. But the wait can be as long as an hour, depending on ship traffic, for the three-minute ride. For safety reasons you're not even allowed out of the car. The ferry is meant primarily for heavy equipment and trucks too big for the swing bridge, which is far more interesting and comparatively speedy.

Fuerte San Lorenzo and Área Protegida San Lorenzo

This is one of Panama's newest protected areas. Its 12,000 hectares include a former U.S. military base (Fort Sherman), the impressive ruins of the Spanish fort of San Lorenzo, and four types of forest, including mangroves and freshwater wetlands. The United States left most of this forest standing, and with the departure of the military, all kinds of wildlife have returned even to formerly populated areas. The big question is what happens next.

Conflicting demands are being made on the area. On the one side are those who want to preserve this vital ecosystem, restricting its use as much as possible to ecotourism and scientific research. This area is a crucial link in the biological corridor that runs the length of Panama, especially since so much of the land to the east and west of it has already been deforested. That also makes it a linchpin in the even more important Mesoamerican Biological Corridor, which runs the entire length of Central America.

It seems likely that those pushing for conservation will be at least partly successful. In the short term, only organized groups are being allowed into most of the protected area. That's probably just as well for now, because visitors really wouldn't want to wander around here by themselves. Besides the usual hazards found in a tropical forest, there is unexploded ordnance in the area. The U.S. military conducted jungle-warfare training and had a firing range here.

The ruins of Fuerte San Lorenzo (full name: Castillo de San Lorenzo el Real de Chagres) are impressive and surprisingly intact. They sit on the edge of a cliff with a commanding view of the Caribbean coast and the mouth of the Río Chagres, which the Spaniards built the fort to protect. The Welsh buccaneer Henry Morgan won a bloody battle here in 1671, destroying the then-wooden fort before crossing the isthmus to sack Panama City. San Lorenzo was rebuilt as a strong stone fort in 1680, but the British admiral Edward Vernon still managed to destroy it in 1740. It was rebuilt yet again in 1768, with more fortifications added in 1779. These are the ruins visible today. The ruins, along with those at Portobelo, were declared a UNESCO World Heritage Site in 1980. Be careful wandering around the fort. There are few guardrails, and it's easy to walk right off a roof or a cliff.

The entrance to the area is 12 kilometers past Gatún Locks in the former U.S. military base of Fort Sherman; stay straight after crossing over the swing bridge at the locks. Fuerte San Lorenzo is another 11 kilometers up a rough but passable road. It's a left turn past the entrance to Fort Sherman. On the way to Fort Sherman, look for a water-filled channel near the road. This is the French Cut, a remnant of the doomed French effort to build a sea-level canal.

Once-popular Shimmy Beach, to the right as one enters Sherman, is covered in trash washed up from Colón—not the best spot for a swim. The turnoff to San Lorenzo is on the left. It's a 20-minute drive on a sometimes-rough road from here. Those without a four-wheel drive can ask about road conditions at the gate.

From this point on the road is surrounded by beautiful rainforest. It's easy to feel transported back in time and imagine conquistadors and pirates hacking their way through this jungle in their relentless pursuit of treasure. Follow the signs to the fort, which is where the road ends. Road conditions get fairly rough toward the end.

SHOPPING
Zona Libre de Colón

The Zona Libre de Colón (Colón Free Zone, most shops 8 A.M.–5 P.M. Mon.–Fri., a few open on Sat.–Sun.) is the world's second-largest free-trade zone, after Hong Kong. A free zone is an area where goods can be imported and exported free from customs duties. Each year about US$10 billion worth of goods move through its 1,000 companies, which employ an estimated 15,000 permanent workers and thousands more temporary ones. It opened in 1948.

This isn't just some sort of oversize shopping mall: It's a shopping city within a city, one far wealthier and better maintained than the real city that surrounds it. It's huge—400 hectares—and is one of the most important contributors to Panama's GNP. Goods come mainly from Hong Kong, Japan, and the United States and go mainly to Central and South America.

The Zona Libre is primarily aimed at international wholesalers, not consumers.

Individuals can shop at some stores there, but getting in and around the place, and getting purchases out, is a hassle. Think twice before going to the trouble: Many goods are just as cheap and far easier to get at airport duty-free stores or even at discount houses back home.

Private cars and taxis are not allowed inside the free zone, which is just as well because the streets inside it are permanently gridlocked with trucks. There are fairly safe parking lots just outside the zone.

Visitors need a permit to enter the Zona Libre. The office is on the right as you face the main gate. Have passports and return flight information handy. Be prepared for a long wait in line.

Good values inside the zone include 10-, 14-, and 18-karat gold, jewelry, cosmetics, liquor, and high-end handbags, scarves, watches, and stereo equipment. Gold jewelry is sold by weight depending on the purity.

One store worth checking out is **Motta International** (tel. 431-6000, www.motta-int.com), not far from the main entrance. Motta carries a little bit of a lot of things, including watches, perfume, liquor, electronics, clothing accessories, and crystal. Sample brand names: Cartier, Lalique, Montblanc, CK, Fendi, Limoges Castel, Baccarat, and Camusso. The atmosphere is pleasant and the service gracious.

Once you've made a purchase, you can't just waltz outside the Zona Libre with it. Remember, this is a free-trade zone and purchases are meant for export only. For those flying out of the country, stores will deliver purchases to the airport for pickup on the day of the flight. Stores tend to charge a minimum of at least US$15 for delivery and need at least two days.

Everyone leaving the zone is subject to search, and anyone caught with *contrabando* can be charged with a crime.

Colón 2000

This cruise port/shopping mall is on the eastern edge of Colón, close to the Free Zone. It opened in 2000 and was supposed to attract fleets of cruise ships to Colón and breathe life into the local economy. This has been slow to happen.

Since 2007, Royal Caribbean Cruise Lines has been making Colón 2000 a home port, with its *Enchantment of the Seas* offering cruises originating from the port. Some other cruise ships stop at the port as well. Besides a handful of duty-free shops and some souvenir-trinket stores, most of which are only open during cruise season, the complex includes an enormous Super 99 grocery store, a Western Union branch, Hertz and Budget car rental offices, an ATM, and a couple of places to eat. During the main cruise season (approximately Oct.–May), folkloric dancers perform for the tourists when a ship is in port. The place is pretty deserted when ships don't show up.

In spoken Spanish this place is called Colón Dos Mil.

SPORTS AND RECREATION
Bird-Watching

The central Caribbean coast is prime bird-watching country. The Audubon Society once identified 350 species on a single day during its annual Christmas Bird Count. Especially popular spots for birding include what is now the **Área Protegida San Lorenzo** and the **Achiote and Escobal Roads,** in Costa Abajo, west of Colón. The roads to Achiote and Escobal start just past Gatún Dam, though they can be tough to drive, particularly in the rainy season. Birdwatchers should go with an experienced guide.

Tours

Nattur Panama (tel. 442-1340, fax 442-8485, www.natturpanama.com) offers a popular tour, the Conquerors' Path, that includes a boat trip down the lower Río Chagres to Fuerte San Lorenzo, a tour of the fort, and a trip to Gatún Locks. The cost is US$85 per person with a four person minimum. It also offers tours of Portobelo, Gatún Locks, and Colón, as well as

© WILLIAM FRIAR

The view from the pool at the Washington Hotel is rather unusual: ships at anchor on the other side of the seawall.

fishing and birding trips. The group has a nature lodge in Sabanitas.

ACCOMMODATIONS AND FOOD

Be prepared to be rather isolated, as it is not safe to wander far outside the hotels in and around Colón, and there's nothing much around the safer but more remote spots. It's generally a better idea to make the Pacific side your base and just make day trips around here.

Colón

There are several places to stay in or on the outskirts of Colón. The four listed here are the best and safest. Those staying in Colón should eat at their hotel. Otherwise, a reasonably safe dining option away from downtown Colón is **Café Iguana** (in Colón 2000, tel. 447-3570 and 447-3956, 10 A.M.–10 P.M. Mon.–Sat., US$5–12). In the Colón 2000 cruise port/shopping center, the café is upstairs and on the right as one faces

the complex. It's a simple but pleasant place to eat if the air-conditioner is working, with photos from the Panama Canal construction era on the wall and Middle Eastern music on the stereo. People come here for the Lebanese food, but other options include Mexican food, sandwiches, burgers, fish, meats, and pastas. If nothing on the menu looks appealing, there's also a Subway sandwich shop in the Colón 2000 complex, as well as a few other restaurants and cafés.

The **Meryland Hotel** (corner of Calle 7 and Santa Isabel next to Parque Sucre, tel. 441-7055, 441-5309, or 441-7127, www.hotelmeryland.com, US$44 s, US$55 d, a/c) was built in 2000 in a quiet, sparsely settled part of town. There's a long, narrow park outside and lots of schoolkids passing by on school days. It definitely feels like the safest spot to stay in town. It's a modern, clean place with cheerful neo-Spanish colonial decor, featuring lots of glossy tile and ornate iron fixtures. Amazingly, the paint in the rooms started peeling soon after the hotel opened. All rooms have cable TV and phones. The hotel has parking and an Internet café. There's room service from the restaurant (open until 10 P.M. Sun.–Fri., later on Sat.) on the premises. Rooms are dark and the beds need replacing, but this is still a decent value in an okay neighborhood if you need to spend the night in Colón. Some of the houses near the hotel used to be quarters for Panama Canal employees during the Canal Zone days.

The **Washington Hotel** (2nd St. at the northwest end of Colón, tel. 441-7133, US$61 s/d) is now officially known as the New Washington Hotel, but no one will ever call it that. Built by the United States in 1913 at the order of President William H. Taft, a frequent visitor to Panama during canal construction days, first as Secretary of War and then as president, on the site of a Panama Railroad Company guesthouse erected in 1870, it was once one of Panama's grand hotels. It has hosted two American presidents (Taft and Warren Harding), a British prime minister (David Lloyd George), Will Rogers, Bob Hope, Al Jolson, and others. Those glory days are long gone. The Spanish-inspired colonial building and common areas are still lovely, if tattered, with brass railings, wrought ironwork, chandeliers, painted wooden beams, and marble stairs. And the hotel is built right on the edge of the sea, with a view of ships at anchor waiting to transit the canal. But the new rooms are still drab and musty, with spongy beds. They're large, however, and come with a minifridge. Amenities include a bar, casino, nightclub, and a large pool right next to the seawall; sea spray sometimes splashes close to the pool. It's definitely worth a quick visit for those in the neighborhood, but most would probably prefer staying in the less historic but more comfortable surroundings of the Meryland Hotel, which has comparable rates.

The six-story, 103-room **Hotel Radisson**

Colón 2000 (Colón 2000, www.radisson.com, tel. 447-1135, US$152.90 s/d) is the most upscale place to stay in downtown Colón and the most convenient for those with a cruise to catch. It has good security and is in Colón 2000, which is kind of the city's Green Zone. The rooms are pleasant enough, if a bit musty, and there's a restaurant, bar, and small gym and pool, but the whole place gives off a kind of sluggish, sullen Caribbean vibe. Two rooms on the 2nd floor are available, for an extra fee, with a stark balcony that looks out over the pool, but I advise avoiding these: the pool fills up with partiers blasting music, making these potentially the loudest rooms in the hotel. Try for a room that faces away from the pool and the waterfront if peace and quiet are important to you.

The newish **C Four Points by Sheraton Colón** (Avenida A. Waked, Millennium Plaza, on the outskirts of Colón, tel. 447-1000, www.starwoodhotels.com, starts at US$137.50) is the fanciest place to stay on the Caribbean side of the canal area. It's a 15-story tower in a gated shopping complex, just off the main road leading into downtown Colón. It's in an industrial area right next to the Free Zone and close to nothing else, but it's certainly the most secure location you could hope for. The 230 rooms are spacious, attractive, and comfortable, with floor-to-ceiling windows, but not much to look out on (though some of us find it interesting to get a bird's-eye view on the city-within-a-city that is the Colón Free Zone). Service is friendly and attentive. Some of the rooms have a distant view of Limón Bay and the entrance to the canal. There's a restaurant, bar, and a small pool that's right next to the polluted Río Manzanillo. Good deals can be had here, depending on when you visit. It's a significantly nicer hotel than the Radisson, and when there's a deal available, it might even be cheaper.

Outside Colón
C Sierra Llorona Panama Lodge (tel.

442-8104, cell 6614-8191, www.sierrallorona. com, starts at US$55 s/d, including breakfast and a hike with local guide) is a lodge south of Colón that's popular with bird-watchers: Approximately 200 species of resident and migratory birds have been spotted in the surrounding forest. Hikes led by a local guide are available in the surrounding area, which includes the lodge's own private reserve. These are included with stays. Day-trippers can visit the lodge for a hike, lunch, and use of the facilities for US$20 for one or two people.

Sierra Llorona means "crying mountain," an apt name for a place that sees rain 286 days a year. Expect predawn rains even in the so-called dry season here. The plus side of all that precipitation is evident in the lushness of the 200 hectares of private primary and secondary rainforest surrounding the lodge. There are four kilometers of well-maintained trails that start about a 10-minute walk from the lodge. Scientists frequent the area to study its flora and fauna, some of which is not found elsewhere. A new species of frog, *Atelopus limosus,* was discovered here in 1995. This is its only known habitat.

The lodge is really a sprawling private house with a separate building a short walk down the hill. There are seven rooms of various sizes; none is anything fancy, but they're clean, cheerful, and comfortable. They do not have air-conditioning, TV, or telephones. The lodge sits on a ridge 300 meters above sea level. Even this modest elevation is enough to give the place pleasant breezes in the morning and evening and views of the Caribbean, Limón Bay, and, at night, the lights of Colón.

Sierra Llorona is near the small community of Santa Rita Arriba (not to be confused with nearby Santa Rita). If you're coming from Panama City, it's reached by a right turn off the Transístmica a couple of kilometers before Sabanitas.

The **Hotel Meliá Panama Canal** (Avenida de Las Naciones Unidas, tel. 470-1100 or 470-1916, www.solmelia.com, US$126.50 s/d), a Spanish-owned 258-room resort, has a striking location on the forested banks of Lago Gatún near the Área Protegida San Lorenzo in Espinar (formerly Fort Gulick), close to Colón and Gatún Locks. But it's not yet an area that attracts many tourists, and the base itself is still largely a ghost town.

The hotel was built from the remains of the U.S. military's notorious School of the Americas, which had a reputation for training Latin American dictators and torturers. Its parentage notwithstanding, it's quite an attractive hotel, with bright and cheerful Spanish-Mediterranean decor that tosses in a splash of Italian rococo. Rooms are large, with Spanish tile floors, cable TV, tasteful decoration, lots of dark wood, a minibar, and incredibly hard beds. Guests have also complained of wafer-thin walls, indifferent or rude service, and musty, poorly maintained rooms. Amenities include an impressive swimming pool, pleasant restaurant, piano bar, casino, business center, and so on. Its restaurant is wildly inconsistent.

The hotel offers tours to Gatún Locks, motorboat and kayak rentals on Lago Gatún, fishing trips, and other activities. Package deals, especially on the weekend and during the rainy season, are often available.

The hotel is not far from Gatún Locks. To get here from Panama City, turn left before the Cuatro Altos overpass outside Colón. Stay straight on this road, which snakes to the right, then back left, for about 1.5 kilometers. Take the second left onto Avenida de Las Naciones Unidas. Look for the Sol Meliá sign.

INFORMATION AND SERVICES

The Colón 2000 cruise port/shopping center has a few facilities of interest to tourists. The **Super 99** supermarket has a Citibank outlet and ATM, a cafeteria, and a pharmacy (10 A.M.–6 P.M. Mon.–Fri., 11 A.M.–3 P.M. Sat.). The store also carries everything from phone cards and cheap mobile phones to camping supplies.

The complex also has a **Western Union office**

(tel. 441-7308, 9 A.M.–5 P.M. Mon.–Sat.). The **Colombian consulate** (tel. 441-6170 or 441-0114) is in an upstairs office nearby. **Budget** (tel. 441-7161) and **Hertz** (tel. 441-3272) rental car offices are open approximately 8 A.M.–5 P.M. Monday–Saturday. Duty-free shops (cruise passengers only) and souvenir shops may only be open during cruise-ship season.

There is a marina, **Shelter Bay** (tel. 433-3581, www.shelterbaymarina.com), at Fort Sherman, just west of the canal entrance. It has a simple restaurant/bar serving burgers and such with nothing more than US$10. There's a small pool/whirlpool tub, table tennis, and free wireless Internet access, but there's little reason for anyone other than yachters to go all the way out there.

GETTING THERE AND AROUND

A quick and easy trip coast to coast is literally a 500-year-old dream. The dream has finally been realized with the completion of the Corredor Norte from Panama City to Sabanitas, not far from Colón. Depending on Panama City and Colón traffic off the highway, the trip should take no more than 1.5 hours, probably less. Expect it to take nearly twice that long via the old Transístmica. It's not worth it just to avoid the minimal toll.

Most visitors explore the area with a taxi guide or a tour operator. Look for tours that include at least a one-way train trip.

By Bus

The **Terminal de Buses de Colón** (on Avenida Bolívar, Colón's major shopping drag, and Calle 13) is a busy place and should be relatively safe, at least during the day, but be alert for pickpockets and backpack thieves. Any bus marked Costa Abajo can take you to Gatún Locks and the attractions west of them, including the bird-watching areas around Achiote (fare: US$1). For La Guaira and Nombre de Dios, look for buses that say Costa Arriba,

though be sure to confirm the bus is really going all the way to your destination. Below are details on a few of the more popular routes.

La Guaira: 9:30 A.M., 11:30 A.M., 1:30 P.M., 3:30 P.M., 4:30 P.M., and 5:30 P.M. The fare is US$2.85. Return buses leave La Guaira every hour or two 5:30 A.M.–1 P.M. The Sunday schedule is different, with buses running at 9:30 A.M., 12:30 P.M., and 3:30 P.M., returning at 10 A.M., 11 A.M., noon, 1 P.M., 2 P.M., and 4 P.M. This schedule changes a lot, so use these times only as general guidelines.

Nombre de Dios: 6 A.M., 9 A.M., 10 A.M., 11 A.M., noon, 1 P.M., 3 P.M., 4 P.M., and 5:45 P.M. Monday–Saturday; 9 A.M., 11 A.M., 1 P.M., 3 P.M., and 5:45 P.M. Sunday. The fare is US$2.75. Return buses run once an hour 4 A.M.–3 P.M.

Panama City: Buses leave every 20 minutes or so 4:30 A.M.–10 P.M. The fare is US$1.80, or US$2.50 for the express bus. Try to get the express, which takes about 1.5 hours. The slower buses can take up to twice as long to cover the same ground when traffic is bad.

Portobelo: 16 buses daily 6:15 A.M.–9 P.M. The fare is US$1.30. Return buses run about every half hour 4:30 A.M.–6 P.M.

By Taxi

A taxi anywhere within Colón should cost about US$1. Take taxis everywhere. To visit area tourist attractions, consider hiring a taxi by the hour. Watch out for fake taxis: Real taxis are yellow, and their license plate numbers match those painted on their doors.

Now that more cruise ships stop at Colón 2000, the taxis have organized into cooperatives and have established standard fares for tours, which they carry around as a laminated sheet. It's easy to find a taxi at Colón 2000 during cruise-ship season, though it may be difficult at other times. Fares are excessive, but there's some semblance of order and all rates are negotiable; you can make a deal for less if there are more taxis than passengers around.

Taxi cooperative fares are US$3 for trips within Colón or to the Free Zone; Gatún Locks tour for US$80, or US$160 for Gatún Locks and Portobelo (1–4 people), US$180 for a tour of the Pacific-side attractions, including Miraflores Locks, Casco Viejo, and Old Panama (1–3 people); and transfers to Tocumen International Airport (US$100 for one person, US$120 for two).

By Car

To get to Colón and Costa Abajo from Panama City, take the **Corredor Norte** toll highway to the end of the line. Cars have to finish the journey north on the old **Transístmica** (also known as the Transisthmian Highway or the Boyd-Roosevelt Highway).

At the Cuatro Altos (literally, four stops) intersection, turn west (left) to get to Gatún Locks, Gatún Dam, and the Costa Abajo attractions. Stay straight for Colón. Roads aren't well marked, and highway construction, especially the new overpass at Cuatro Altos, has jumbled things up considerably.

Portobelo and the Costa Arriba

The stretch of coast east of Colón is known as Costa Arriba, which includes Portobelo, Nombre de Dios and its neighboring villages, and La Guaira, the jumping-off point for Isla Grande. For most of the way this is a lovely drive: It's quite striking to zip along the lush, quiet coastline and suddenly come upon the ruins of ancient Spanish forts.

Though the Spanish ruins scattered all over this seaside town hint at its long history, it still may be hard to believe that Portobelo (pop. 3,867) was one of the most important ports in the Spanish Empire. Today it's sleepy and impoverished, the decaying houses of its current residents built near or in some cases into the crumbling stone ruins. It truly comes alive only on October 21, for the celebration of the Festival del Cristo Negro (the Black Christ Festival).

The town's poverty can be a bit intimidating, but visitors shouldn't have any problems if they come here during the day and stay alert. Portobelo is one of the wettest spots on the isthmus.

A large swath of this area is part of Parque Nacional Portobelo, whose boundaries extend into the surrounding waters. The park is under increasing development pressure, however, as are the natural treasures that are not even nominally protected. Settlers are rapidly cutting down much of the lush forest in this area, and cookie-cutter suburban housing is going up along the beautiful coastline.

SIGHTS
◖ Portobelo Ruins

During the Spanish colonial era, the Costa Arriba became one of the most strategically important areas in the entire Spanish Empire. It was here that most of the incredible treasure of the Incas was brought after being shipped up from South America. All that wealth made the Caribbean coast a target of pirates and buccaneers for hundreds of years. The Spanish fortresses were constantly under siege and were captured several times.

Entering Portobelo from the west, the first Spanish structure you'll encounter is **Castillo Santiago de la Gloria,** on the left side of the road. It's the last incarnation of a fort that was built, destroyed, rebuilt, and tinkered with for more than 150 years and never ended up defending the town particularly well. These ruins date from 1753.

In the town itself is **Castillo San Gerónimo,** which dates from the same period. The nearby customs house, the **Real Aduana de Portobelo,** was restored in February 1998 by the Spanish government. The little museum inside the

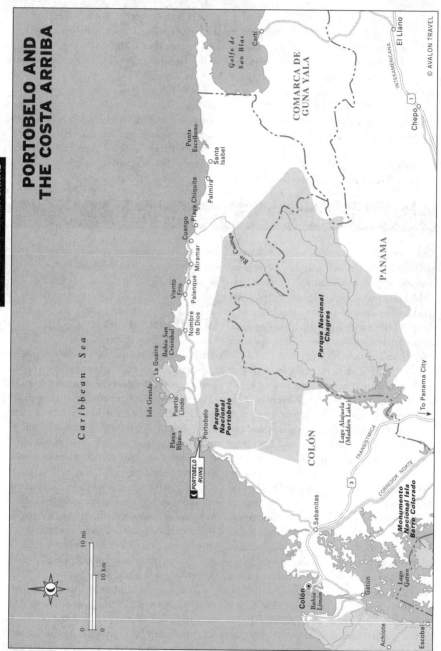

PORTOBELO AND
THE COSTA ARRIBA

© AVALON TRAVEL

building has recently been spiffed up with a few modern displays and a film on the history of the area. There's a small model of Portobelo's fortifications just outside the entrance. On the other side of the model is a second room where one can see a bit of the original foundation, but exhibits consist mainly of a few old tools, cannonballs, and mortars. There are also replicas of pre-Columbian tools and weapons mixed in with a few pieces of real pottery shards.

Admission to the **museum** (8 A.M.–4 P.M. Mon.–Fri., 8:30 A.M.–3 P.M. Sat.–Sun.) and to the neighboring Museo del Cristo Negro de Portobelo is US$1 for adults, US$0.25 for children. The price includes a guided tour of the displays, though the guides speak only Spanish.

Church and Museum of the Black Christ

The large white church nearby is the **Iglesia de San Felipe,** which is still in use. It dates from 1814, but its tower wasn't completed until 1945. It's famous as the home of the life-size effigy of the Nazarene of Portobelo, better known as the Black Christ. The effigy, depicting Christ carrying the cross, normally resides on a podium to the left of the altar, but it is brought out to the center of the church for the Black Christ Festival (Festival del Cristo Negro), by far Portobelo's biggest event. The handsome altar of the church is adorned with gold images depicting various emblems of the crucifixion, including nails, instruments of torture, and the dice the Roman soldiers cast for Christ's robe. Small wooden carvings ringing the walls depict the stages of the cross.

Behind this church is the recently renovated **Iglesia de San Juan de Dios,** home to the new **Museo del Cristo Negro de Portobelo,** which displays several of the robes donated by Panamanians for the festival, some of which are more than 100 years old. It's well worth a visit. Among the more famous robes is the one donated by the champion boxer Roberto "Manos de Piedra" (literally, hands of stone) Durán.

© WILLIAM FRIAR

THE PANAMA CANAL

Portobelo was one of the Spanish Empire's most important ports.

The Black Christ figurine's robes are changed twice a year, and each is used just once. The statue is adorned with a red wine–colored robe for the Black Christ Festival held each October 21. This is changed to a purple one for Holy Week. Many of the robes are donated anonymously. Some are simple and others are quite ornate, done up in gold trim and the like, and cost thousands of dollars to make.

If this museum is locked, walk over to the museum at the *aduana* and ask the attendant to open it for you.

Other Forts

If exploring these ruins and buildings doesn't satisfy your historical urges, hire a water taxi near Castillo Santiago de la Gloria for US$2 per person to take you across the bay to visit what's left of **Castillo San Fernando,** which was designed in the 1750s to replace Castillo San Felipe, demolished in 1739 by Edward

THE PANAMA CANAL

THE BLACK CHRIST FESTIVAL

© KAREN FRIAR

the Black Christ

Every October 21, Portobelo comes back to life at the Festival del Cristo Negro (Festival of the Black Christ). It's quite a spectacle. Thousands throng the Church of San Felipe, home to the life-size wooden effigy of the Nazarene of Portobelo, otherwise known as the Black Christ. Some come by foot from distant parts of Panama. Others come crawling on their hands and knees, their friends sweeping the ground in front of them free of debris or rocking a small shrine before their faces to keep the pilgrims' eyes on the prize. Still others let their companions pour candle wax on them as they crawl, as a further act of penance.

What's this all about? There are several legends of the origin of the statue and its festival. One has it that the statue arrived in Portobelo on a ship bound for Cartagena, Colombia. A storm arose each time the ship tried to continue on, and the crew members decided the effigy wanted to stay in Portobelo. Variations on the story have the ship either sinking in the storm and the statue washing up on shore or the crew members throwing the statue overboard in fright. Then, the story goes, on October 21, 1821, Portobelo residents prayed to the Black Christ to be spared from a cholera epidemic sweeping the isthmus; they were.

Each October 21 since, people from all over Panama who have prayed to the Black Christ for help with an illness or other problem give thanks by making a pilgrimage to Portobelo, often performing some act of devotion or penance along the way. Most find just walking here from Sabanitas in the heat and humidity to be

sacrifice enough. That's a walk of nearly 40 kilometers; health stations are set up along the way for those who need them. There are no portable toilets anywhere, so you can imagine what Portobelo is like by the end of the night.

Devotees often wear purple robes in emulation of the Christ statue. Those who have asked for a major favor make the pilgrimage for several years. Each year they cut a bit of cloth off the hem of their robes. Some of the robes end up awfully short, presenting the interesting paradox that the most pious also have the most scandalous attire.

The festival is a blend of the sacred and profane in other ways as well. For many, it's an excuse to get very drunk and dance all night. It's not unusual to see a pilgrim in resplendent purple robes making his way to town carrying a beer. The whole vibe is sort of spring-break-with-self-flagellation.

Once in Portobelo, pilgrims crowd into the church to worship before the Black Christ. Many offer necklaces, which are draped around the effigy. Mass is held, and devotees burn hundreds of votive candles and sing songs about the festival and the effigy. Late at night the statue is carried out of the church and paraded through the streets on a litter. The procession takes a long time, as the statue is carried with a peculiar rocking, back-and-forth gait: three steps forward, two steps back.

Those in Panama on October 21 should make an effort to attend the festival. It's a fascinating spectacle. But be forewarned it's also a major mob scene. Be prepared for epic traffic jams and stay alert for pickpockets. Traffic is generally stopped several kilometers outside of Portobelo, forcing even non-pilgrims to walk in. It's best to drive or come with a tour operator. Trying to get a return bus is a nightmare; many pilgrims go back home right after they arrive, so the line for the bus is hours long even in the morning. One strategy is to hire a boat near Portobelo and motor into town, skirting the traffic. Suggest this to your tour guide ahead of time, or call a hotel, restaurant, or dive operator to arrange it.

© BONNIE KAY SPINDLER

Pilgrims walk to the Black Christ Festival from all over Panama.

first **Portobelo Triathlon** (www.triathlon.org.pa) was held in 1997, and it has become an annual event. It is slated for March or April and increasingly attracts world-class athletes. The event includes a 1,800-meter swim from La Guaira to Isla Grande and back, a 35-kilometer bike ride to Portobelo, and a 10-kilometer off-road run in the Portobelo area.

Playa Blanca

Playa Blanca is a pretty little beach, by far the nicest in the area, situated on a remote cove at the tip of a forested peninsula 20 minutes by boat from Portobelo. There are no roads leading to it, and it is accessible only by sea, which gives it the feel of an island. Day-trippers can hire a water taxi to the beach from the ruins of Castillo Santiago de la Gloria in Portobelo for about US$30 per couple.

Diving and Snorkeling

There are 16 dive spots around the Portobelo area, with attractions that vary from coral reefs and 40-meter-deep walls to a small airplane and a cargo ship. The best diving in the area is off the rocky Farallones Islands, a fair boat ride away. There's a chance of seeing nurse sharks, spotted eagle rays, and schools of barracudas there. But any honest dive operator will be the first to admit the diving around Portobelo is for the most part just average: Expect no more than 10 meters of visibility on a typical day. And visibility is quite volatile: up to 30 meters on a great day, and down to 3 when it rains (several rivers empty into the ocean here; the diving is better in the dry season). As always when you dive, bring evidence of certification and ask to see the dive master's credentials.

Scubaportobelo (tel. 448-2147 in Portobelo or 261-4064 and 261-3841 at the main office in Panama City, www.scubapanama.com) is five kilometers west of Portobelo. The spot is pleasant, with a wooden mirador built on rocks over the ocean. This is the Portobelo division

Vernon, a British admiral. Unfortunately, American builders used rock from the fort in the construction of the canal, further damaging what little that time, war, and pirates had spared. Also, a short, steep hike above town leads to some fortifications with a good view of the bay; if you're heading east, it'll be on the hill to the right just before town. Drivers can park by the side of the road.

SPORTS AND RECREATION

Portobelo has long been a popular spot for scuba divers and yachters. There are also appealing spots for beach lounging. It's possible to hike in the forests of Parque Nacional Portobelo, but this should be attempted only with an experienced guide.

In 1996, John Collins, the creator of the original Ironman triathlon in Hawaii, visited the Portobelo area on a yacht and decided it would be a perfect place for a triathlon. The of Scubapanama, Panama's largest dive operation. Divers pay for everything separately here. Complete equipment rental is US$20, including one full tank. The second tank costs US$6, and additional tanks US$4.50. Boat transport is about US$7–20, depending on the destination. Dive tours that include transportation from Panama City are also available.

Other Activities

Selvaventuras (tel. 442-1042, cell 6680-7309) is a shoestring operation started in 2001 by four eager guys from Colón. They no longer have an office, but they still offer excursions. These include jungle hikes to waterfalls, overnight camping in the forest, horseback riding, fishing trips, and boat transport to nearby beaches. Prices vary depending on the destination and length of trip. For instance, a tour of the closest forts (which you can really do yourself) costs US$2 per person; a half-day hike is around US$20 per person. The guides speak a little English.

There's a **zipline ride** west of Portobelo in an area called Río Piedra. It's operated by a group called **Panama Outdoor Adventures** (cell 6605-8171, http://panamaoutdooradventures.com), west of Portobelo. It consists of nine cables strung between platforms that are up to 30 meters above the forest floor. The tour lasts about 2.5 hours, including a forest walk. On the way to Portobelo, the group has signs posted shortly after the turnoff to María Chiquita and before Río Piedra. Panama Outdoor Adventures offers other excursions, such as river tubing for US$25 and nature walks for US$10.

ACCOMMODATIONS

El Otro Lado (tel. 202-0111, info@elotrolado.com.pa, www.elotrolado.com.pa, US$539 s/d, including breakfast and round-trip boat transportation from Portobelo) translates to "the other side," which in this case refers to the fact that the property is across Drake's Bay from the

Portobelo ruins and accessible only by boat. It's only a five-minute boat ride, but this is enough to give this place a sense of seclusion. El Otro Lado describes itself as a "private retreat," and it consists of only four houses, one with two bedrooms and the others with one, each decorated differently. There's an infinity pool and a large gazebo that houses the restaurant, bar, and common areas. The whole place looks like it has an appealing retro-modern Caribbean vibe. The staff can take guests to a nearby beach and arrange tours. Food and service are good here.

Sunset Cabins are part of Scubaportobelo (tel. 448-2147, http://panamaportobelocabins.com, starts at US$52.80 s/d), which is the local branch of Scubapanama. The cabins are meant primarily for divers, but during the frequent slow periods landlubbers can get a room here too. The rooms are basic, small, with low ceilings and crammed with beds. But they have air-conditioning. Up to four people can be squeezed into each room, but you'd better really like each other. There's a basic restaurant on the premises.

Coco Plum Eco-Lodge (tel. 448-2102 or 448-2309, US$45 s, US$55 d) offers more attractive accommodations. It's just before Restaurante La Torre on the way to Portobelo. It's a cheerful place, with conch shells ringing the door frames of the rooms and murals of fish painted on the walls inside. Rooms are clean and pleasant, though a bit dark. There are a dozen rooms, most with air-conditioning. This place used to be quite friendly, but lately there have been some complaints of unfriendly service.

FOOD

Seafood is the attraction around here, particularly dishes done in a Caribbean style (usually spicier than Pacific-side food, often with coconut milk). Simple but cute, moderately priced places are dotted along the coast on the way to Portobelo.

◖ Restaurante Los Cañones (about six kilometers before Portobelo, tel. 448-2980,

11 A.M.–10 P.M. Mon.–Fri., 8 A.M.–10 P.M. Sat.–Sun.) is a charming little open-air place on a small bay. Looking out at the Caribbean, it's easy to imagine Sir Francis Drake's ships gliding past on the way to a sneak attack. Seafood is the specialty at this popular place. The food is good. Try the *pulpo en leche de coco* (octopus in coconut milk).

A little farther down the road is **Restaurante Las Anclas** (tel. 448-2102, 10 A.M.–8 P.M. daily), at the Coco Plum Eco-Lodge. It's a cute place entirely decorated with detritus recovered from the sea, including sewing machines, the wheel of a boat, wheelbarrow parts, gas containers, and so on. Seafood is again the specialty here. The chef is Colombian, so be sure to order the enormous, Colombian-style *patacones* (fried green plantains).

Restaurante La Torre (tel. 448-2039, 10 A.M.–7 P.M. Mon.–Fri., 7:30 A.M.–7 P.M. Sat.–Sun.) is a little open-air restaurant just beyond Restaurante Las Anclas. It's easy to spot because of the stone tower that gives the place its name. Again, seafood is its main thing. The service is friendly and courteous. There's an illustrated capsule history of Portobelo, in Spanish and English, along one of the wooden walls.

INFORMATION AND SERVICES

Just as you enter Portobelo there's a large, unmarked wooden building, one of the biggest structures in town, at a fork in the road. This is yet another CEFATI building (tel. 448-2200, 8:30 A.M.–4:30 P.M. Mon.–Fri.), a tourist center run by ATP, Panama's government tourism institute. It's usually rather barren, but the last time I was there it had a few devil masks used in the *congos* dances and entries in a competition to design a new bus stop.

The last gas station on this entire stretch of road is at María Chiquita, roughly halfway between Sabanitas and Portobelo.

GETTING THERE
By Bus

Portobelo is about 100 kilometers from Panama City. Those coming by Colón-bound bus from Panama City will have to change buses in Sabanitas. Do not go all the way to Colón, and make sure ahead of time that the bus stops in Sabanitas, which is on the Transístmica 60 kilometers from Panama City. Passengers are let off near the El Rey supermarket. Buses between Sabanitas and Portobelo run only during daylight hours. The fare is US$1.25.

The main bus stop in Portobelo is next to the Iglesia de San Felipe. Colón-bound buses leave Portobelo every half hour 4:30 A.M.–6 P.M. To get from Portobelo to Panama City, take a bus to Sabanitas (Colón-bound buses stop there). Get off at Sabanitas, cross the highway, and take any of the frequent long-distance buses running from Colón back to Panama City.

By Car

Take the Sabanitas exit off the Corredor Norte. The turnoff to Portobelo is at Sabanitas, on the right side of the Transístmica just past the El Rey supermarket as you head north, in the direction of Colón. Stay on this road to Portobelo, about 35 kilometers away.

GETTING AROUND

Portobelo is a small town and easily walkable, though be alert and try not to wander around alone.

A **water taxi** (tel. 448-2266; ask for Carlos) is on the edge of the bay next to Castillo Santiago de la Gloria, the first fort as you enter Portobelo from the west. It's next to the Restaurante Santiago de la Gloria. A trip across the bay to the ruins of Castillo San Fernando is US$2 per person. Prices to area beaches range from US$10 per couple to nearby Playa Huerta up to US$30 per couple for a trip to Playa Blanca. Prices are likely negotiable if business is slow.

NOMBRE DE DIOS AND VICINITY

Eight tiny towns—villages really—run along the coast east of Isla Grande. Five of these are linked by a road, which is in remarkably good condition.

All look pretty dismal and deserted, especially during the day, when their inhabitants are out working in the fields or fishing in the ocean.

The first five—**Nombre de Dios, Viento Frío, Palenque, Miramar,** and **Cuango**—are lined up one after another on a lonesome, 30-kilometer stretch of road that runs along the edge of the sea. The last three—**Playa Chiquita, Palmira,** and **Santa Isabel**—are even more isolated, separated from the others by the Río Cuango. This river is known for gold, and it still attracts wishful-thinking prospectors. The road ends at the river, and those final three towns are accessible only by boat. Santa Isabel is the last town before the Comarca de Guna Yala (the San Blas Islands). All these towns are so sleepy they're practically comatose.

There isn't much reason for tourists to come to this part of Panama, at least these days. The beaches aren't that great, the area is in the middle of the boonies, and the lovely tropical forest covering its rolling hills is being hacked and burned as quickly as possible to make way for cattle farms.

Historically, this is the home of so-called Afro-Colonials, the descendants of escaped African slaves from the Spanish era. These escaped slaves, known as *cimarrones,* slipped away and established hidden towns called *palenques.* They would emerge from the forest from time to time to raid Spanish mule trains along the Camino Real, more to harass their former captors than for treasure that was useless to them. It's fun to think that the anglers chatting with you about the tides may very well be descended from *cimarrones* who helped Drake in one of his famous exploits.

In modern times, Costa Arriba has attracted settlers from Los Santos province. They are famous or notorious, depending on your perspective, for their prowess at cutting down trees. Having mostly deforested their own province, they're diligently working on doing the same to this area, which borders a vitally important national park.

Sights

The first, largest, and most famous of the little towns is **Nombre de Dios** (pop. 1,053), about 25 kilometers east of Portobelo. It was the original Caribbean terminus for the Camino Real, the overland route used by the conquistadors to transport plunder from the destruction of the Incan Empire. The first European to lay eyes on the area was Rodrigo de Bastidas during his voyage of discovery of the isthmus of Panama in 1501. Columbus rode out a terrible storm here in 1502. Legend has it that Nombre de Dios (name of God) got its name when the unlucky Spanish explorer Diego de Nicuesa ordered his beleaguered and starving crew to take refuge in the harbor, shouting, "Let us stop here, in the name of God!"

Nombre de Dios was a poor, shallow harbor and proved nearly impossible to defend. Sir Francis Drake attacked it in 1572, though a wound forced him to retreat. He returned in 1595 and sacked it. The Spanish abandoned Nombre de Dios and moved the Caribbean end of the Camino Real to the far better and more defensible harbor of Portobelo in 1597. Nombre de Dios quickly faded away.

Today it is a poor, out-of-the-way, oceanside settlement of squat cinderblock buildings connected by dirt roads, as are the other towns along this road. There's nothing to recall its rich past except a modern-era sign that reminds you this humble place is one of the oldest surviving towns in the Americas. The left fork leads to the old part of town, inhabited mainly by anglers. The right fork leads to the new side, which is where most of the settlers from Los Santos province live. There's an artificial water channel that runs right through the middle of town; the builders of the Panama Canal scooped up sand from Nombre de Dios to build Gatún Locks after the Gunas turned them away from beaches in the San Blas Islands.

Festivals and Events

These sleepy towns live for festivals, especially Carnaval and their *fiestas patronales,* the saint's day corresponding to the anniversary of the town's founding. These dates are the best bet to catch the colorful, African-derived dances known as *congos*. Some *fiestas patronales* and other local celebrations in the region include April 27 (Nombre de Dios), June 8 (Santa Isabel), June 19 (Playa Chiquita), June 24 (Palmira), July 31 (Viento Frío), September 8 (Palenque), and September 24 (Río Indio). It's not worth making a trip all the way out here just for one of the celebrations, but those who plan to visit anyway should bear those dates in mind.

On October 12, Viento Frío celebrates a big **Día de la Raza festival,** the Latin American version of Columbus Day. In recent years, of course, attitudes toward that day have become ambivalent throughout the Americas, with some seeing it as a more appropriate time for mourning than celebration. It could be fascinating to attend such an unusual Columbus Day commemoration in an area Columbus actually visited.

Water Activities

Water sports are the main attraction. If you go for a swim, beware of the undertow and rip currents. There is also some scuba diving in the waters off the coast. Wrecks of Spanish ships are still being found out here, including a 500-year-old one discovered in 1998 just off Nombre de Dios that some believe is the *Vizcaina,* one of the four ships used by Columbus on his fourth and final voyage to the Americas. It's well documented that the *Vizcaina* was in fact abandoned in these waters, but studying this wreck and establishing its identity has been a slow process mired in controversy and red tape. However, the ship appears to date from the early 16th century, which makes it exceptionally rare whoever its captain was. Shipwrecks are off-limits to divers, and scavenging around them is a serious crime.

It's possible to hire local boatmen in these towns for trips to Guna Yala, but it's not recommended. The trip takes a minimum of 1–2 hours in small, open boats on a sea that can quickly turn rough. Bear in mind that some of the greatest navigators in history have lost ships in these waters.

Skilled, safety-conscious captains with well-maintained boats are in short supply in this area, and it may very well be risky to make the trip. At the very least, go with a captain who has life jackets, or bring your own.

Practicalities

There are few services of any kind in this remote, neglected part of the country. Most visitors arrange tours from Portobelo or Panama City. There's a pay telephone in each town, but that's about it. There are no banks or ATMs. The best chance of finding official help if one encounters trouble is in Palenque, the administrative headquarters of the district.

There are a few basic places to stay in this area, and as usual camping on the beach is free. This area doesn't get many foreigners, though, so people may wonder what you're up to. It's probably a good idea to let the police and townspeople know you come in peace.

As always, camp only in a tent. *Chitras* (sand flies) are likely to be the least of your troubles. This is cattle country, which means vampire bats, and it's poor and neglected, which means a risk of disease-carrying mosquitoes.

There is a small, open-air seaside restaurant in Miramar that offers heaps of fried seafood and other simple fare for a couple of dollars.

Getting There

To get to this area by car, first drive through Portobelo, making sure you have a full fuel tank. After about eight kilometers there'll be a crossroads known, logically enough, as El Cruce. Turn right here.

After about 13 kilometers there's a rickety suspension bridge. Grit your teeth and drive over it. The first sizable settlement is Nombre de Dios (15 kilometers from El Cruce, about

THE PANAMA CANAL

25 minutes). The paved road ends a little past Nombre de Dios, turning into a rocky dirt road that's passable in a regular car most of the way. The road continues through Viento Frío (8 kilometers past Nombre de Dios), and then through nearby Palenque, Miramar, and Cuango, which are bunched together within a few kilometers of each other toward the end of the road. The road gets rough beyond Miramar, requiring a four-wheel drive in the rainy season, before coming to a sudden end at the especially run-down Cuango, on the edge of the wide mouth of the Río Cuango.

A small gas station just east of Miramar is the only one in the entire region east of María Chiquita.

Getting to these remote areas by bus can be a hassle, as service is neither frequent nor speedy. Those coming from Panama City can take a Colón-bound bus to Sabanitas and get off at the El Rey supermarket. Look for buses with Costa Arriba or the name of the particular destination painted on the windshield. Buses also run between Nombre de Dios and the Colón bus terminal. It's also possible to hire a taxi in Sabanitas or Colón, but the fare will probably be rather steep, depending on the destination.

Isla Grande

This is the closest of the Caribbean islands to the mainland. It's mainly a place for locals who want a quick dose of natural Caribbean beauty and tranquility and don't mind that the hotels and restaurants are generally mediocre at best and the place a noisy party scene at times. Those planning to go to Bocas del Toro or the San Blas Islands can easily give Isla Grande a miss; those archipelagos have much more to offer. It's also quite a humid place; be prepared for some serious afternoon napping.

Isla Grande is not really all that grand—it's about five kilometers long and 1.5 kilometers wide and has around 1,000 inhabitants, most of whom live in the small town that runs along a single waterfront path facing the mainland. It consists mainly of a handful of simple hotels, some run-down houses, and a few tiny stores and open-air restaurants. The island is only a few hundred meters from the mainland.

Though Isla Grande has a couple of small beaches, this is not the place for vast expanses of sand. What the island mostly offers is the chance to laze about and enjoy some beautiful views of the forested mainland, clear blue ocean, and palm-covered nearby islands.

Isla Grande tends to be dead during the week, especially in the rainy season. At these times, there are few dining options, and some of the hotels may be closed. Those who visit during a dry-season weekend, however, will likely find plenty of people having a rowdy good time and blasting music late into the night. Bear that in mind when considering a hotel in town.

SIGHTS

The best, and most popular, stretch of beach on the island is in front of the Hotel Isla Grande. A better and less crowded beach is on Isla Mamey, a tiny, uninhabited private island with relatively calm, shallow waters. It's possible to snorkel or scuba dive here. This is a popular destination for boat tours. These tours usually include a trip near the mainland through a channel lined with beautiful mangroves. This channel has come to be known locally as the Tunnel of Love.

West of Isla Cabra is **Bahía Linton,** one of the safest anchorages between Colón and Cartagena, Colombia. (There's another anchorage at **José del Mar,** better known as José Pobre. It's in a cove next to the isolated village of Cacique, between Portobelo and Isla Grande.)

PRIVATE ISLANDS

On the boat ride over from the mainland to Isla Grande, there's a developed island that's largely deforested except for palm trees. This is **Isla Cabra,** a private island. It is not open to visitors, but those with binoculars should keep their eyes open for macaw nests.

At the entrance to **Bahía Linton** is **Isla Linton,** another private island one should not set foot on. However, boat tours of the waters near Isla Linton are popular because of the monkeys that have been introduced here, which can be summoned by clapping. Be careful: Tourists often feed the monkeys (something you should *not* do), which has made them bold around people. A monkey bit a woman in 2002.

The owners of Isla Linton, Allan and Rosalind Baitel, are conservationists working in conjunction with Florida State University to create a research facility on the island.

The Baitels also run an animal rescue and rehabilitation program behind their home on the mainland (again, this is not open to the public). Here they try to heal animals wounded by hunters or otherwise injured or interfered with, after which they return them to the forest. In some cases, all they can do is give the animals a safe home, as is the case with a couple of jaguars that some people kept as pets before the couple rescued them. These jaguars would no longer be able to survive in the wild. Unfortunately, Panama has no program for breeding jaguars in captivity, so the Baitels have been trying to find a way to export the big cats to a country that does have such a program. Ironically, the international CITES treaty, created to protect endangered species, prohibits the export of animals that were not actually bred in captivity, which has proved to be a major obstacle.

ACCOMMODATIONS AND FOOD

For such a small place, there's quite a range of places to stay, though no great bargains. Only the lucky or the easy-to-please will think they're getting their money's worth, at any budget. In the hoteliers' defense, it's not cheap to offer big-city amenities in such a remote area. And the cheaper places tend to cater not to foreign couples on a budget but rather to Panamanian weekend partiers who shoehorn as many people as possible into a room.

Most of the cheap hotels are clustered close together along the main strip overlooking the water. On dry season weekends, good luck getting a quiet night's sleep if you stay in any of these. Sister Moon is farther along still, on an isolated bluff accessible by a rocky path. Bananas Village Resort is clear on the other side of the island, secluded from everything.

At mealtimes, count yourself lucky just to find a place that's open, especially during a rainy-season weekday. The hotels are the best bet for food. Several of the ones along the main drag have

simple, open-air restaurants right on the water's edge. What they may lack in quality they somewhat make up for in rustic island ambience.

❰ Hotel Sister Moon (cell 6948-1990 or 6789-4336, www.hotelsistermoon.com, US$25 pp in dorms, US$69 s/d) sits by itself on the hills of a palm-covered point overlooking a picture-postcard bay, rolling surf, and the emerald green mainland. The main accommodations consist of a series of thatched-roof cabins on stilts, dotted along the hillside. Each has a double bed. The cabins are rustic but pleasant. It's like staying in a tree house, and the breeze here is a welcome respite from the island's humidity. The bathrooms are cold water only, and the cabins are not air-conditioned and do not have screens on the windows. Dorm rooms with bunk beds go for US$25 a bed, including breakfast. Day guests can use the pool and other facilities for US$20 a day, including two drinks.

A small, rocky beach with a good surf break is close by. A sundeck juts out right over the surf break, and next to it is a little restaurant and a pub with a billiard table and dartboard. There's also a small, murky swimming pool that's more scenic than inviting. An odd thing about this place is that it seems to live a perpetual twilight existence. There's something perpetually unfinished about it. That can be great for those seeking seclusion, but those who make reservations far in advance should confirm before arrival that everything's up and running.

Bananas Village Resort (Panama City reservations tel. 263-9510, resort tel. 448-2252 or 448-2959, www.bananasresort.com, rates start at US$152.90 s/d, including breakfast) is the fanciest place on Isla Grande. It's on the north side of the island, tucked away in a lovely, isolated spot facing the ocean. It's accessible only by boat or forest trails. A variety of different, confusing packages are available. Rates go up on the weekends. Rates for day visitors are available.

The place, which opened in 1998, is nicely designed, cheerful, and small. The rooms are in eight A-frame cottages on stilts. Each cottage has three units: two large rooms below and one very large room above. They're the same price, but the upstairs ones are nicer. All have balconies, hammocks, and air-conditioners. There's a swimming pool, and guests have free access to sea kayaks, snorkeling equipment, beach chairs, and so on. Boat excursions to the surrounding area are extra. Though the resort is attractive, the service is bad, and the place is not well-maintained. Guests can't count on hot water, for example.

The open-air restaurant is the most expensive on the island, with entrées that reach the double figures. The food is okay, but tends to be deep-fried with heavy sauces.

INFORMATION AND SERVICES

There is no tourist office on the island. The island also lacks banks, ATMs, or much in the way of services at all. Bring cash. Tours and recreational activities are generally arranged through the hotels.

GETTING THERE AND AROUND

Access to Isla Grande is from the down-at-the-heels village of La Guaira, 120 kilometers from Panama City. La Guaira is 20 kilometers from Portobelo. Those with their own car just drive through town and continue along the same road. The trip from Panama City takes about two hours.

The road is often riddled with potholes. At the entrance to La Guaira look for a sign that reads Isla Grande. Take the left turn indicated. Park by the dock for free, or in the partially fenced-in area on the left, behind Doña Eme's kiosk, for US$3 a day. Obviously, don't leave anything valuable in the car. When you come back, one or more teenagers may hit you up for change for watching the car. It's up to you whether to give one of them anything, but they can be unpleasant if you don't.

Those coming by bus from Panama City should take a Colón-bound bus and make sure it stops in Sabanitas. Get off at the El Rey supermarket in Sabanitas, which is right on the highway, and switch to a bus bound for La Guaira. These don't come often, and the schedule changes frequently. Get an early start, as buses between Sabanitas and La Guaira run more often in the morning. Even then, be prepared to wait a long time, cough up the money for a cab, or ditch the whole idea and visit Portobelo instead.

Any of the boatmen hanging around the dock at La Guaira will take you to the island (don't expect life jackets). The ride takes about five minutes. The fee is US$3.50 per person (depending on fuel prices) to be dropped off in what passes for downtown Isla Grande. Expect to pay more at night, which you should avoid since few boats in these waters have lights. Boatmen may ask for more if they think you're a clueless gringo. Settle on a price ahead of time, and clarify whether the rate is per person or per group.

Nearly every place on Isla Grande is easily

@ DANIEL HO/ISTOCKPHOTO.COM

Isla Grande

accessible by foot. Those who want to visit Sister Moon or Bananas and don't feel like hoofing it can hire a boatman down by the town waterfront for a couple of dollars. Your hotel can probably arrange for a boat back to the mainland at the end of your trip, but if not, it should be easy to find one along the waterfront.

BOCAS DEL TORO

It's hard to leave Bocas. It's a terribly relaxing place, and at the same time it exudes a funky, romantic charm that has something untamed about it. The place is filled with colorful characters nursing drinks in dilapidated wooden bars or running rustic hotels on remote beaches. It's the kind of Caribbean hideaway one expects to find only in old Bogart films.

And it's just gorgeous. It has emerald islands, pristine beaches, turquoise waters, dense forests, barely explored mountains and rivers, sprawling coral gardens, spooky mangrove channels, and exotic wildlife. Four species of endangered sea turtles still visit the waters of Bocas, coming ashore by the hundreds during nesting season to lay their eggs. Little Swan's Cay, really just a rock in the ocean, is the only Panamanian nesting site of the beautiful red-billed tropicbird. That's just one of more than 350 species of birds attracted to the region. Sloths, caimans, dolphins, neon-colored frogs, and, of course, lots of small tropical fish are easy to spot in the archipelago. No wonder more than a dozen countries have shot their versions of the *Survivor* TV series here.

The people help make Bocas special. More ethnicities and nationalities are represented on the islands than anywhere in the country outside of Panama City. And you are more likely to hear English spoken here than anywhere in the country, period. The islands have long been home to the Ngöbe-Buglé, as well as the

© WILLIAM FRIAR

HIGHLIGHTS

LOOK FOR ☾ TO FIND RECOMMENDED SIGHTS, ACTIVITIES, DINING, AND LODGING.

☾ **Swan's Cay:** This picture-postcard islet is one of the last stands of the red-billed tropicbird (page 174).

☾ **Cayo Crawl:** This is the quintessential Bocas scene: rustic restaurants float just above the surface of a glassy sea, with tropical fish swimming just below (page 205).

☾ **Isla Bastimentos's North Shore Beaches:** The island's north shore beaches offer pristine sand, monster waves, and brilliant red frogs (page 206).

☾ **Parque Nacional Marino Isla Bastimentos:** The Cayos Zapatillas, which offer cave diving and a pair of undeveloped islands, are the highlight of this marine park (page 211).

☾ **Río Teribe and the Naso:** Explore the beautiful forest world of a little-known indigenous people who are fighting for their survival (page 225).

BOCAS DEL TORO

descendants of Afro-Caribbean immigrants from the English-speaking islands of Jamaica, San Andrés, and Providencia, many of whom came down to work on the region's enormous banana plantations. Most of the hotels and restaurants on the islands are owned by Europeans and North Americans. And the mostly young and boho tourists Bocas attracts are coming from all over the world.

For most visitors, Bocas del Toro means the archipelago that stretches about 100 kilometers from Boca del Drago in the west to Isla Escudo de Veraguas in the east. For them the mainland is just a place to fly over or drive through on the way to the islands. But the rest of the province

of Bocas del Toro has plenty of spectacular natural beauty, including the Caribbean side of the enormous Parque Internacional La Amistad and the wetlands of San San Pondsack. Lucky hikers, at least those who venture far up into the mainland forests, may encounter endangered mammals such as Baird's tapirs. All five species of cats found on the isthmus, including jaguars, are hanging on in the most remote reaches of the forest, but the chance of coming across one is slim. The forests are also still home to indigenous peoples trying to hold on to their culture and ancestral lands. This includes the little-known Naso, who welcome visitors to their communities up the Río Teribe.

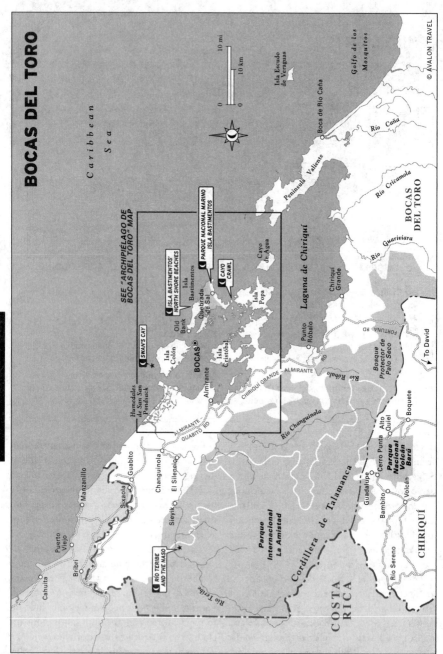

More than just about anyplace else in Panama, the Bocas archipelago has taken off as a tourist destination. Backpackers spill over from Costa Rica, and more affluent expatriates from the United States and Canada have bought up beachfront property to build their fantasy tropical getaways. Everyone is in the real-estate business these days, and condos and big resorts are in the works. But the funk factor is still strong and the islands are not yet a tourist trap. Long-term residents grumble that Bocas isn't what it used to be, but so far the new arrivals have mainly just brought more international flavor and a broader range of lodging, dining, entertainment, and activity possibilities. For now, backpackers and surfers can still find a decent bed for US$10 and a full meal for US$3, and those with more money to spend can stay in relatively luxurious surroundings and dine on surprisingly good international cuisine.

Bocas is one of the wettest regions in Panama. The rain never completely stops even in the dry season, but even in the rainy season storms usually blow through quickly. Rainfall tends to be heaviest in December and July.

The islands are evolving rapidly from a great backpackers' secret into a more upscale destination. Two bits of advice for those contemplating a visit: 1) Hurry and visit while they still have that quirky, rustic Bocas charm and beauty, and 2) do your part to make sure the charm and beauty survive.

PLANNING YOUR TIME

Given both the area's remoteness and its many attractions, getting anything out of Bocas requires a bare-minimum stay of two nights. Three or four is better. There is enough to keep visitors happy for a full week, especially since the Caribbean heat and pace of life have a tendency to slow everyone down and make hammock time pretty appealing. Consider staying a bit longer than you think you'll need. Weather is unpredictable in Bocas, and it's not unheard

of for it to rain virtually nonstop for three days. It'd be a shame if you had to leave just as the sun finally came out.

The **Archipiélago de Bocas del Toro** is only part of the province of Bocas del Toro, but it's the part that the great majority of visitors come to explore. The islands have far better accommodations, food, and attractions and a more pleasant climate than the mainland towns.

Most visitors stay in **Bocas town** on **Isla Colón.** Nearly everyone has to at least pass through Bocas town, since it has the only airport in the archipelago, and water taxis from the mainland come only here. (It's easy to make day trips from the islands to mainland destinations, though visitors who head up the Río Teribe to visit the Naso or Parque Internacional La Amistad should plan to spend at least one night in the forest.)

Here's where the names start getting confusing. The town, the archipelago, and the province share the same name, often shortened simply to Bocas. And just to really mess you up, the whole of Isla Colón is sometimes referred to as Isla Bocas.

The other commonly visited islands are east of Isla Colón, which is the point of departure to all of them. The services diminish the father east you go. **Isla Carenero** is the second-most developed island, and it's just a few minutes by boat from Isla Colón. The western tip of **Isla Bastimentos** has the second-biggest town in the archipelago, **Old Bank.** Most of the rest of the island, the largest in the archipelago, is sparsely populated, but its natural attractions draw many visitors. **Isla Solarte,** though it starts just 10 minutes by boat from Isla Colón, still mainly draws visitors just to Hospital Point, a snorkeling/diving spot at its western tip. The other islands are more remote and still largely undeveloped, though a few secluded little hotels, ecolodges, and guesthouses are scattered among them, usually in relatively undeveloped spots. So far only Isla Colón has cars.

Those who want to cover a lot of ground or

have any kind of nightlife should probably stay in Bocas town or on Isla Carenero. Carenero is so close to Bocas town it's actually easier and quicker to get to and from town from there than it is from other parts of Isla Colón.

Getting back and forth to Bocas town from other parts of Isla Colón and the other islands can easily become time-consuming and expensive, though some hotel packages in the remoter areas include daily trips. Those staying in the remote parts of Bastimentos should plan on spending most of their time in that general area, as Bocas town is a long boat ride away. One strategy is to stay in Bocas town part of the time and spend a night or two in a more distant spot before or afterward.

Afternoons and evenings are the best time to explore Bocas town, which is generally dead during the day; many restaurants do not open for lunch. The restaurants and few nightspots start to wake up as the sun goes down.

Throughout the archipelago, the great beaches and pounding surf tend to be on the north side of the islands, where there's nothing but ocean until Jamaica. Generally the sea is too rough for safe swimming. The water tends to be glassy on the southern side of the islands and in sheltered bays on the eastern sides, and that is where the good snorkeling is.

High season on the islands is November or December–April, but this traditionally can be the wettest time to visit the islands. Weather in Bocas is usually best during the mini dry seasons of September–October and February–March. Turtles nest on the beaches from about March to late September.

SAFETY CONSIDERATIONS

The archipelago is a friendly, mellow place, and violent crime is rare. But the increase in tourism has brought an increase in petty theft. Don't leave valuables unattended, particularly on the north shore beaches of Bastimentos.

Land scams are a problem in Bocas. Be skeptical of great deals on beachfront property or get-rich-quick plantation schemes. Legitimate cheap land in Bocas is a thing of the past. Also, establishing land ownership is tricky in Bocas, and Panamanian land-use laws are complicated. Do plenty of research and get legal and technical advice from trustworthy sources.

ENVIRONMENTAL CONCERNS

Bocas del Toro is one of the loveliest parts of Panama, and it's still relatively unspoiled. The protected areas of the mainland include a large chunk of the enormous Parque Internacional La Amistad and the buffer forest that surrounds it, as well as the wetlands of San San Pondsack. The islands are home to an important national park, Parque Nacional Marino Isla Bastimentos. Bocas is a crucial link in the Mesoamerican Biological Corridor that extends from southern Mexico to eastern Panama.

Even the unprotected parts of the province are still largely undeveloped. Most of the land remains covered with forest, including primary evergreen forests with century-old trees that soar above 30 meters. The hundreds of animal and thousands of plant and insect species here include many that are endangered and some that are found nowhere else on earth.

But Bocas del Toro is under increasing human pressure. Developments are coming to Bocas, and coming fast. New roads are allowing subsistence farmers and cattle ranchers into formerly inaccessible areas. A vivid example of rapid deforestation can be seen along the Chiriquí Grande–Almirante Highway, where lush evergreen forests started disappearing as soon as it was completed. The waters are also being overfished, with lobster in particular locally threatened. The national mania for teak farming has spread to Bocas; there have been reports of acres of diverse, species-rich native trees being illegally cut down to plant this nonnative tree, which local wildlife has little use for as a habitat. And there is a strong push to dam the

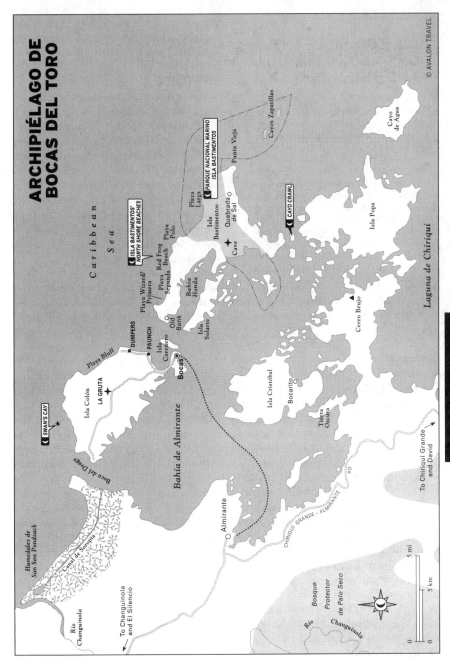

ARCHIPIÉLAGO DE
BOCAS DEL TORO

© AVALON TRAVEL

Caribbean Sea

SWAN'S CAY

Isla Colón

LA GRUTA

Playa Bluff

DUMPERS

PAUNCH

Isla Carenero

Bocas

Old Bank

Isla Solarte

Playa Wizard/Primera

Playa Segunda

Red Frog Beach

Playa Polo

ISLA BASTIMENTOS'
NORTH SHORE BEACHES

Bahía Honda

Playa Larga

Isla Bastimentos

Cave

Quebrada de Sal

PARQUE NACIONAL MARINO
ISLA BASTIMENTOS

Punta Vieja

Cayos Zapatillas

Cayo de Agua

CAYO CRAWL

Isla Popa

Cerro Brujo

Bocarito

Isla Cristóbal

Tierra Oscura

Laguna de Chiriquí

Bahía de Almirante

Boca del Drago

Humedales de
San San Pondsack

Canal de Soropta

Río Changuinola

To Changuinola
and El Silencio

Almirante

CHIRIQUÍ GRANDE - ALMIRANTE RD

To Chiriquí Grande
and David

Bosque
Protector
de Palo Seco

Río
Changuinola

0   5 mi

0   5 km

BOCAS DEL TORO

DID YOU HEAR THE ONE ABOUT THE BOA AND THE MONKEY?

When I was in Bocas a couple of years ago, everyone was talking about a rather dramatic episode involving a 2.5-meter boa constrictor and an adult howler monkey. The boa had tried to swallow the howler, but it was too big for him and was slowly choking him to death. Reinier Plooijer, the co-owner of Playa Bluff Lodge, had raised exotic reptiles in his native Holland, so he was the closest to a snake vet around. His solution? He stuck his hand down the boa's throat, extracted the now-deceased monkey, flushed out the boa's digestive tract, then resuscitated it with an air hose. After a few days and a course of antibiotics, the boa was well enough to slip back into the forest, where it has hopefully learned to eat more modest portions.

Don't believe it? The story, with photos, is here, in the local *Bocas Breeze* newspaper: http://bit.ly/greedyboa.

powerful mainland rivers, which have the highest hydroelectric potential in the country but which run through land that is home to both indigenous peoples and important ecosystems.

On the islands at least, the greatest human impact is caused by tourists and resident expatriates. Seeing tourism come to an area as relatively untouched as Bocas del Toro always provokes mixed feelings. It's so easy to destroy what attracts people to a place like this in the first place. But ecologically sensitive tourism might, with luck, help preserve its natural beauty and maybe even help its people.

It's encouraging to see new tourism operations popping up that try hard not only to be low-impact but to help restore the land and water around them to a healthy state, and who support neighboring indigenous communities. During your stay, please do your part to keep

Bocas beautiful and wild for generations to come by seeking these places out and treading as lightly as possible.

HISTORY

When Christopher Columbus sailed into what is now Bahía Almirante in 1502, on his fourth and final voyage, he likely would have found a land long settled by several indigenous peoples. Columbus barely mentions the area, however, and he soon pushed on east with his worm-eaten ships and exhausted, demoralized crew. He was intrigued to find natives wearing large gold discs around their necks, who told him there were rich goldfields on the mainland. Today's indigenous peoples still talk of lost gold mines in the remote highlands.

It's often said that Columbus gave the Bocas islands and other geographical features their names, but there is no evidence of this. It appears they were later named in his honor, such as Isla Colón (i.e., Columbus Island), Isla Cristóbal (Christopher Island), and Bahía Almirante (Admiral's Bay). Columbus does refer to a place called Bastimentos, but this is believed to be the name he gave to Nombre de Dios in eastern Panama.

The earliest evidence of habitation on the coast and along the river valleys dates from 600 B.C. For years the best-known archaeological site was Cerro Brujo on Peninsula Aguacate, an oddly shaped peninsula that juts out between Isla Cristóbal and Isla Popa. It appears to have been a small village whose inhabitants subsisted on farming and fishing, including the hunting of manatees. But in 2002 archaeologists discovered evidence of what appears to have been a large and culturally sophisticated settlement at Boca del Drago on Isla Colón. They believe it was occupied in A.D. 900–1150. Excavation is ongoing, and the significance of the site is still being determined.

During the days of Spanish exploration and conquest, the Naso people, also known

A FEW ECO-FRIENDLY SUGGESTIONS

- Do not touch coral. Coral is alive and can take years to recover from even minimal contact. Some coral is endangered and protected by international law: To be on the safe side, don't buy coral jewelry.

- Hire local boatmen and guides. This offers them an alternative to fishing and hunting and gives the local community a stake in preserving their surroundings. Encourage them to take it slow and not toss anchors into coral fields.

- Stay at small, low-impact places such as the environmentally friendly La Loma Jungle Lodge and Tesoro Escondido.

- Team up with others for boat tours. It saves money and lessens the disturbance caused by boats that motor through the same popular spots day after day.

- Do not take souvenirs of any kind from the beaches or forests.

- Stick to established trails.

- Do not eat sea turtle meat or eggs, or any other endangered species. For one thing, it's illegal. Avoid lobster, which is overfished and locally endangered. There are more decent vegetarian alternatives on the islands than in most parts of Panama.

- Buy indigenous handicrafts directly from the makers.

- Visit community-development projects such as Proyecto ODESEN, Soposo Rainforest Adventures, and the Ngöbe restaurant in Bahía Honda.

- Consider volunteering locally, or making a donation to legitimate projects. U.S. residents can make a tax-deductible contribution to the nonprofit Nature Conservancy, which works in Bocas del Toro and elsewhere in Panama. Contributions can be made online (http://nature.org) or by mail (The Nature Conservancy, Attn: Treasury, 4245 N. Fairfax Dr., Suite 100, Arlington, VA 22203, U.S.A., tel. 800/628-6860).

- Report poaching or signs of environmental destruction to ANAM's hotline (tel. 500-0855, ext. 1111). These *denuncias* can also be made online (www.anam.gob.pa/denuncia_web/default.asp). If enough visitors complain, it may have an impact.

- Don't litter. Pick up and pack out trash left by others.

- A group of local businesses called The Bocas Sustainable Tourism Alliance (cell 6086-2231, info@discoverbocasdeltoro.com, www.discoverbocasdeltoro.com) is getting off the ground. Contact them for more information and suggestions on how you can help.

as the Térraba or Teribe, appear to have been the dominant group, living by the rivers of the mainland, along the coast of Bahía Almirante, and even as far north as Isla Colón. Today they are barely hanging on, with a population of just 3,800 in Panama and a few hundred over the border in Costa Rica. They are now vastly outnumbered by the Ngöbe-Buglé, the largest indigenous group, not just in Bocas but in all of Panama. Tiny populations of Bri Bri and Bokota also remain.

Pressure from the Spanish, tribal warfare, and the introduction of European diseases decimated the indigenous populations. Some, including the Dorasque, were wiped out altogether. But the Spanish never consolidated their hold on Bocas del Toro. That allowed the incursion of enterprising pirates and traders from England and other countries, the beginning of the international mix the region retains to this day. Early traders dealt in such items as the shell of the hawksbill turtle and coconut, but bananas eventually became the region's most important commodity.

The descendants of English-speaking Afro-Caribbean immigrants are among the longest-established residents of the islands. The earliest of these were brought over as slaves by English traders, but later arrivals came to work for the banana companies. Most trace their ancestry to Jamaica and the Colombian-owned Caribbean islands of San Andrés and Providencia. They are still a dominant cultural force in both Bocas town and, especially, Old Bank on Isla Bastimentos, where Guari-Guari, a Bocas-specific variety of so-called Panamanian Creole English, is still widely spoken.

The banana business began to take off in Bocas toward the end of the 19th century, attracting American and German planters. In 1899 the giant United Fruit Company (now known as Chiquita Brands International; the local division was called the Bocas Fruit Company) took over the whole show. It established its headquarters in Bocas town, which was founded in 1826 but until that point was a sleepy village. The company built a hospital on the tip of Isla Solarte, an isolated area now known as Hospital Point, to quarantine patients with infectious diseases such as yellow fever and malaria. The hospital is long gone, but a headquarters building the company constructed in 1905 became Hotel Bahía, which was recently renovated but retains a few reminders of its history.

The early 20th century was a boom time for Bocas del Toro. Bocas town became a hub for international commerce and one of the most important cities in Panama. It was prosperous enough to attract foreign consulates and support three (by some counts five) newspapers.

The islands' prosperity didn't last long, however. A fungus wilt that came to be known as Panama disease decimated the banana plantations on the islands and coastline. The company was forced to shift its operations to the mainland, to the area between the Changuinola and Sixaola Rivers, and over the border into Costa Rica. By 1920 the importance of the islands had declined dramatically. Even the hospital was shut down, as it was too far a trek for company employees on the mainland. The mainland banana plantations continue to thrive, however.

The province is one of the most seismically active parts of Panama. On April 22, 1991, the border area between Costa Rica and Panama was struck by an earthquake, measuring 7.5 on the Richter scale, that was felt as far away as El Salvador. Costa Rica was hardest hit, but Bocas del Toro suffered greatly. The earthquake killed two dozen people in the province, injured hundreds more, and left thousands homeless. Changuinola and Almirante, on the mainland, sustained most of the damage. There have been other sizable earthquakes since then, but none nearly as damaging.

For most of the 20th century, though, Bocas remained a rather placid place. It has long been seen in Panama as a backwater province, and it still feels culturally and geographically quite separate from the rest of the country. It is now experiencing its second major boom, though this time the lucrative crops are tourists and retirees rather than bananas.

Isla Colón

By far the most developed island in the archipelago is Isla Colón, and by far the most developed part of Isla Colón is the town of Bocas del Toro, at the southeast tip of this large (61 square kilometers) island. Bocas town is nearly an island in its own right; it's connected to the rest of Isla Colón by a slender isthmus.

Almost all the archipelago's hotels, restaurants, tour outfits, and visitor services are in Bocas town. Most of the action is on either side of Calle 3, the broad main street that runs along the water's edge on the east side of town. (It's officially Calle Ephraim S. Alphonse, though no one calls it that.) The busiest section extends from the town plaza, Parque Bolívar, down to the ferry pier. The area west of Calle 3 is mainly residential, as is the section on the northwest waterfront, which is known locally as Saigon.

Bocas town is laid out in a grid pattern, with numbered streets running more-or-less north to south and lettered avenues running more-or-less west to east. But the streets aren't well marked, and there isn't even universal agreement on which road is which: The avenues above Avenida D are called different things on different maps. Fortunately, the town is small enough it's hard to get lost.

A road leads north out of town, past the fairgrounds where the annual sea festival, La Feria Internacional del Mar, is held, and over an isthmus. This isthmus, known locally as *cabaúas,* has some beaches, but they're too close to town to be nice, and there's a reason the bay here is named *Bahía Sand Fly.*

The road forks north of the isthmus. The fork is known locally as the *i griega* (literally Greek i, Spanish for the letter "y," pronounced ee-gree-EG-a). The east fork heads up the east coast of the main island, becoming increasingly rough but leading to the island's best beaches. The west fork leads to a road that cuts diagonally across the island. About halfway along the road is La Gruta, a cave popular with those into bats. The road dead-ends at Boca del Drago, a little beach area on the northwest side of the island about 14 kilometers from Bocas town.

SIGHTS

Several of the sights on and around Isla Colón are most easily—or only—accessible by boat. Except for those who bring a car over by ferry, which is rarely worth it, getting around on land usually requires hiring a taxi, renting a bike, or hoofing it, though a bus now makes a few daily trips between Bocas town and Boca del Drago.

Isla Colón has forests and other caves to explore, but don't attempt this without a knowledgeable guide. Night trips to turtle-nesting spots are popular during nesting season, from about March to October. Just wandering around little Bocas town night or day can be a colorful experience in multicultural people-watching. Be sure to venture beyond Calle 3 to get a feel for the non-touristy parts of town.

Playa Bluff

The nicest beach is Playa Bluff, about a 25-minute drive from town. It's absolutely gorgeous and often deserted during the week. This is also an important nesting site for endangered sea turtles. The surf can get rough here and is usually too dangerous for swimming, or even for wading above one's knees, though it's a good spot for surfers. Around September–October, however, the winds die down and the water turns to glass; you can even snorkel during this calm spell.

The road ends just past Playa Bluff, after which the only way farther up the coast is by foot. About an hour hike away is **La Piscina** (the swimming pool), a protected lagoon on the north side of the

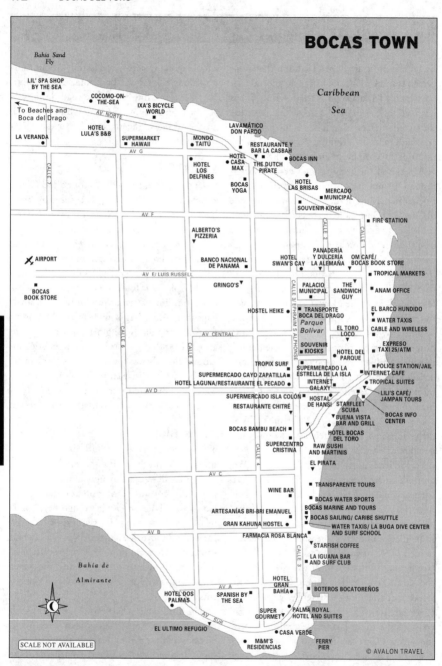

BOCAS TOWN

Bahía Sand Fly

Caribbean Sea

LIL' SPA SHOP BY THE SEA

COCOMO-ON-THE-SEA

IXA'S BICYCLE WORLD

To Beaches and Boca del Drago

AV. NORTE

HOTEL LULA'S B&B

LA VERANDA

SUPERMARKET HAWAII

AV. G

MONDO TAITÚ

LAVAMÁTICO DON PARDO

RESTAURANTE Y BAR LA CASBAH

HOTEL LOS DELFINES

HOTEL CASA MAX

THE DUTCH PIRATE

BOCAS INN

BOCAS YOGA

HOTEL LAS BRISAS

MERCADO MUNICIPAL

SOUVENIR KIOSK

AV. F

FIRE STATION

ALBERTO'S PIZZERIA

CALLE 2

CALLE 1

AIRPORT

BANCO NACIONAL DE PANAMÁ

HOTEL SWAN'S CAY

PANADERÍA Y DULCERÍA LA ALEMAÑA

OM CAFÉ/ BOCAS BOOK STORE

AV. E/ LUIS RUSSELL

TROPICAL MARKETS

BOCAS BOOK STORE

GRINGO'S

PALACIO MUNICIPAL

THE SANDWICH GUY

ANAM OFFICE

HOSTEL HEIKE

TRANSPORTE BOCA DEL DRAGO

Parque Bolívar

EL BARCO HUNDIDO

WATER TAXIS

CABLE AND WIRELESS

CALLE 6

CALLE 5

CALLE 3/ EPHRAIM S. ALPHONSE

AV. CENTRAL

EL TORO LOCO

SOUVENIR KIOSKS

HOTEL DEL PARQUE

EXPRESO TAXI 25/ATM

TROPIX SURF

SUPERMERCADO CAYO ZAPATILLA

HOTEL LAGUNA/RESTAURANTE EL PECADO

SUPERMERCADO LA ESTRELLA DE LA ISLA

INTERNET GALAXY

POLICE STATION/JAIL

INTERNET CAFE

TROPICAL SUITES

AV. D

SUPERMERCADO ISLA COLÓN

RESTAURANTE CHITRÉ

HOSTAL DE HANSI

STARFLEET SCUBA

BUENA VISTA BAR AND GRILL

LILI'S CAFÉ/ JAMPAN TOURS

BOCAS INFO CENTER

BOCAS BAMBU BEACH

HOTEL BOCAS DEL TORO

CALLE 4

SUPERCENTRO CRISTINA

RAW SUSHI AND MARTINIS

EL PIRATA

AV. C

TRANSPARENTE TOURS

WINE BAR

BOCAS WATER SPORTS

BOCAS MARINE AND TOURS

ARTESANÍAS BRI-BRI EMANUEL

BOCAS SAILING/ CARIBE SHUTTLE

GRAN KAHUNA HOSTEL

WATER TAXIS/ LA BUGA DIVE CENTER AND SURF SCHOOL

AV. B

FARMACIA ROSA BLANCA

STARFISH COFFEE

CALLE 3

LA IGUANA BAR AND SURF CLUB

Bahía de Almirante

HOTEL GRAN BAHÍA

BOTEROS BOCATOREÑOS

HOTEL DOS PALMAS

SPANISH BY THE SEA

AV. A

SUPER GOURMET

PALMA ROYAL HOTEL AND SUITES

AV. SUR

EL ULTIMO REFUGIO

CASA VERDE

M&M'S RESIDENCIAS

FERRY PIER

SCALE NOT AVAILABLE

© AVALON TRAVEL

© WILLIAM FRIAR

building a pier, Bocas style

island. If you go without a guide, ask for directions at Playa Bluff Lodge, on Playa Bluff.

Taxis sometimes charge a premium to make the run up to Playa Bluff. They're not trying to rip you off: Part of the road here is really just a path along the beach and through estuaries. Sometimes only four-wheel-drive vehicles can make it out there, and even they often have a punishing ride. Expect to pay about US$8–10 per carload, one way, to get to the beginning of the nice beaches, near La Coralina (an inn with an attractive public restaurant/bar on a ridge). The cost to get to the end of Playa Bluff will probably be at least US$10–12. Prices go up or down depending on the state of the road. Taxis don't cruise this area looking for rides, but if you have a drink or a meal at one of the restaurants, the staff should be able to call a taxi for you when you're ready to leave.

Bocas del Toro Research Station

The Smithsonian Tropical Research Institute (STRI) offers a free half-hour tour of its Bocas del Toro Research Station (tel. 757-9794, Panama City tel. 212-8564 or 212-8082, www. stri.org) on Thursday and Friday 3–5 P.M. Call ahead to confirm a time, as drop-ins occasionally get turned away, especially if a school group is touring the facility. The station is on the narrow isthmus that separates Boca town from the rest of Isla Colón and contains laboratories, teaching facilities, and accommodations for researchers and visitors. During the tour, guests can see scientists at work on experiments and some of the specimens they have gathered, including an impressive collection of some of the 70 species of sponge found in the archipelago. There is also an aquarium that contains sea urchins, five types of starfish, sea cucumbers, coral, sea anemones, lobsters, and a green sea turtle. The station is built right in the middle of what the scientists are studying, so the guide can, for instance, point out living examples of red, black, and white mangroves near the dock and the different species of caiman living in the brackish pond in front of the station. Bring bug spray, as the *chitras* here can be brutal. The research station is a US$0.70–taxi ride from downtown.

Botanical Gardens

Finca Los Monos (tel. 757-9461, cell 6729-9943, www.bocasdeltorobotanicalgarden.com, US$10 pp) is a 23-acre tropical garden just north of the isthmus that separates Bocas town from the larger part of the island. Tours of the garden are given 1 P.M. Monday and 8:30 A.M. Friday, or by appointment. It's beautiful, with carefully tended grounds. Howler monkeys, sloths, and lots of birds also like to visit the garden.

The turnoff is on the left between the Smithsonian and the *i griega* intersection. It's close to town, a short bike ride away. It should be possible to get a taxi from Bocas town for around US$1. Bring binoculars and sturdy footwear.

La Gruta

Halfway across the island on the road to Boca del Drago is La Gruta (literally, the cavern), home to zillions of bats. It's at the little settlement of Colonia Santeña, near the Coca-Cola sign. If your idea of fun is to wade through guano in a claustrophobic cave and inhale disease-carrying particulates, then by all means walk through the thing. The rest of us will be happy with a snapshot of the highly photogenic entrance to the cave, a green grotto with a little statue of the Virgin standing guard. Round-trip taxi fare from Bocas town is US$20. The shuttle bus that runs between Bocas town and Boca del Drago can drop you there, but check the return schedule to avoid getting stranded.

Boca del Drago

This is another popular beach area, mainly because it's easily accessible by boat. It lies on the northwest side of the island. Boca del Drago is also the name of the canal separating this part of Isla Colón from the mainland. The water is tranquil, so landing a boat is not a problem; many of the island tours include a stop here. It's also possible to take a scenic drive across the island from Bocas town.

This beach isn't as nice as Playa Bluff, but it's much better for swimming and splashing about. Many people who come here don't realize that beaches continue past the little beach restaurant about a 10-minute walk away. The most popular is Playa Estrella (Star Beach), named for its abundance of starfish. This is included on many boat tours, so don't expect to have it all to yourself. It's also popular with partying Panamanian tourists, who come with their blaring sound systems. There are coral gardens close by that extend all along the west side of the island. The snorkeling can be decent, but the coral is not in great shape and visibility isn't always the best.

There's a little thatch-roofed, sand-floored seafood restaurant on the beach called **Restaurante Yarisnori** (no phone, 8 A.M.–6:30 P.M. Wed.–Mon.). The mixed ceviche is pretty good. Other items include red snapper, shrimp, octopus, lobster, and prawns. Most seafood costs around US$14–19; other dishes average around US$9.

Access to Boca del Drago is by boat, bus, car, or bike. One road extends across the island from Bocas town to Boca del Drago, about 14 kilometers away. Most people coming from Bocas town take the shuttle bus that leaves from the side of the town park every two or three hours during the day (cell 6492-6166 or 6708-8419, US$5 round-trip). A round-trip taxi ride costs US$30 for two people, including a stop at La Gruta for those interested. The bike ride is hilly, and tiring in the heat.

◀ Swan's Cay

A standard boat tour around Isla Colón includes a stop at lovely Swan's Cay, a craggy rock that juts out of the ocean north of the island, about a half hour by motorboat from Bocas. It's impossibly picturesque. Swan's Cay is also called **Isla de los Pájaros** (Bird Island) for reasons that become obvious when you visit it. Most notably, it's the only known nesting grounds in Panama for the red-billed tropicbird, an elegant white bird with tail feathers about a meter long. Do not disturb the birds by walking on the island; you can, however, snorkel around it. The current isn't too strong, but the water can get pretty churned up at times, drastically reducing visibility.

The boatman may offer to motor through the narrow cleft in the western crag. It's possible if the boatman times the waves right. It's a fun thing to do—you can see crabs scuttling along the rocky walls centimeters from the boat. Go for it if you trust his boating skills.

Isla Solarte and Hospital Point

Also known as **Nancy's Cay,** Solarte is a seven-kilometer-long island situated two kilometers east of Isla Colón. The boat ride from Bocas town takes about 10 minutes. Its western tip, Hospital Point, is one of the most popular diving and snorkeling spots in the archipelago. There are coral reefs just a few meters from the surface, but there's also a wall that drops about 13 meters. A diving or snorkeling trip to Hospital Point is usually included as part of a tour of the islands.

The point is named for the hospital the United Fruit Company built here in 1900 for its labor force, which was being decimated by malaria, yellow fever, and other tropical diseases. The house on the point is the home of Clyde Stephens, who for 32 years was a banana researcher for United Fruit. He gives lectures on the history of the banana industry, and his books include a history of Hospital Point, which he bought in 1970. His books are available in Bocas town.

Laguna Bocatorito

Otherwise known as **Dolphin Bay,** this lagoon,

formed by the east side of Isla Cristóbal and an odd-shaped peninsular blob that juts from the mainland, starts about 10 kilometers south of Isla Colón. A labyrinth of shallow channels formed by mangroves screens its northern entrance, helping to make it a kind of giant natural aquarium, six kilometers across at its widest. Day trips to Laguna Bocatorito are popular because of the possibility of spotting bottlenose dolphins (*delfines*) close up. The best chance of seeing them is from June to July, when rough seas drive them into the calm waters of the bay. They tend to hang around an unusually long time, which isn't surprising when one considers what a smorgasbord the bay offers them: The mangroves act like a kind of net, drawing fish into the bay.

Tours to this area should only be done with a responsible, eco-oriented group like Ancon Expeditions, which will keep a respectful distance from the dolphins.

Canal de Soropta

If you're looking for a break from the beaches and snorkeling, a boat trip up the Canal de Soropta, on the mainland east of the town of Changuinola, is an interesting off-the-beaten-track jaunt. The 12-kilometer canal was built in 1903 by Michael T. Snyder, a pioneering plantation owner, to shelter his banana barges from the open sea on their way between the mainland and the islands. Sometimes referred to as the Changuinola Canal, it parallels the coastline from the mouth of the Río Changuinola to Almirante Bay.

When the canal was bordered by forest on either side, it was a prime birding spot. Unfortunately, slash-and-burn farmers and cattle ranchers have cut away much of the forest in recent years. But it still attracts quite an array of birds. Manatees are occasionally spotted here as well. It makes for a tranquil jungle cruise, though the boats motoring up and down the canal probably don't make the local fauna very happy; ask the boatman to take it slow.

BOCAS DEL TORO

It takes about a half hour by boat to reach the entrance to the canal from Bocas town. Heading all the way up to the Río Changuinola takes about 45 minutes at a leisurely pace, but you don't have to go that far to get a good look at the wildlife; there are tons of birds at the very entrance of the canal. Early morning or late afternoon is the best time to go. You may want to include this as part of an Isla Colón tour, since the entrance to the canal is just opposite Boca del Drago. Expect to pay an extra charge, but agree on a price ahead of time.

Sea Turtles

During some months of the year, lucky visitors may get a chance to see sea turtles laying their eggs. Four species of endangered sea turtles find Bocas as attractive as the tourists do: the hawksbill *(Eretmochelys imbricata)*, leatherback *(Dermochelys coriacea)*, green *(Chelonia mydas)*, and loggerhead *(Caretta caretta)*. Most lay their eggs on the beaches between March and September.

Night trips to the beach are popular during nesting season. The most accessible site is Playa Bluff on the east side of Isla Colón. Other good places are Playa Larga on Isla Bastimentos and the Cayos Zapatillas. An important spot on the mainland is the strip of coast between the mouth of the Río Changuinola and Peninsula Soropta, just across from Boca del Drago. Sometimes called Playa Changuinola, it's part of the protected wetlands of San San Pondsack.

Female turtles lay eggs several times in a season. The incubation period lasts about 60 days. Only one in 1,000–10,000 baby turtles survives to adulthood.

Only the leatherbacks and hawksbill are easy to find. Few greens nest in Bocas; those that do come from about June to August, their numbers peaking in July. Loggerheads rarely nest anywhere in the tropics. When they're spotted, it's usually as they're swimming by.

Bocas was once the most important nesting ground in the Caribbean for the relatively small hawksbill (about a meter long, up to 80 kilograms), especially on the remote Playa Chiriquí, a vast beach on the mainland east of Peninsula Valiente. They nest from June to October, peaking in August and September. Hawksbills *(carey* in Spanish) are what first drew traders to Bocas. Because they're prized for their meat and shell, their populations are critically endangered worldwide. The majority of hawksbills that come to the islands nest on the Cayos Zapatillas.

The enormous leatherbacks, known locally as the *baula* or *canal*, are the largest of all sea turtles (up to 2.5 meters and 900 kilograms). They nest from March to June, peaking in April and May. Though most numerous on Playa Chiriquí, believed to be the most important leatherback rookery in Central America, they nest on beaches throughout the archipelago and coast.

Turtles are legally protected, but enforcement is lax and they're still poached for their meat, eggs, and shells. Conservation projects and protected areas are having a positive impact. The **Sea Turtle Conservancy** (www.conserveturtles.org), formerly called the Caribbean Conservation Corporation, has been working with local communities to help the recovery of the hawksbill population on Chiriquí Beach, on the Bocas mainland. For information, and to track the progress of Bocas turtles that have been tagged with a satellite transmitter, visit www.conserveturtles.org.

Eating turtle eggs and meat is illegal, as is possessing anything made of tortoiseshell. Do not use flashlights, take flash photos, or even wear light-colored clothing near nesting spots. This can scare away nesting females or disorient baby turtles trying to make it to the sea. Stay out of sight while the turtles lay their eggs. Never touch them, which disturbs them and can be dangerous—some have strong jaws and a nasty bite. Don't handle eggs or disturb the nests. This can introduce bacteria or damage the eggs.

To ensure a responsible visit and support

conservation efforts, go with qualified local guides. It is against the law for taxi drivers to conduct turtle tours; do not try to hire one. Consider donating money or time to a conservation project, such as those supported by the Sea Turtle Conservancy.

Chocolate Tour

The half-day **Oreba Chocolate Tour** (cell 6649-1457, US$30 pp) has proved to be a popular activity for those looking for a break from sun and surf. The tour includes a guided tour of a cacao farm on the mainland, land transport to and from Almirante (the water taxi fare is extra), a forest hike, a demonstration of traditional chocolate-making, and a simple Ngöbe lunch. The hike to the farm is uphill and fairly strenuous. Wear sturdy shoes. Trips can also be booked through the Bocas Info Center and some hotels and hostels.

ENTERTAINMENT AND EVENTS

Part of the charm of Bocas del Toro is that there's so little to do besides splash around in the water or laze in a hammock. In the daytime, Bocas town is more or less deserted, since most visitors are out snorkeling, boating, surfing, and so on. Things liven up a bit in the evening, though the action is generally confined to the restaurants and bars.

Nightlife

El Barco Hundido (Calle 1 between Avenida Central and Avenida E, near Cable and Wireless, 8 P.M.–12:30 A.M. Sun.–Thurs., 8 P.M.–3 A.M. Fri.–Sat.) is a lively and funky bar whose name, Spanish for shipwreck, comes from the sunken boat just offshore. Some people call it the Wreck Deck. The bar is an open-sided wooden patio with a view of the *barco hundido,* which is illuminated at night. Semi-competent DJs spin on busy nights, and there's actually dancing. It gets packed and has become popular with locals. A popular feature of

the place is the Barco Loco (crazy boat), a party boat onto which the bar scene sometimes spills over for cruises around the islands when the bar's owner is so moved.

The open-air **Bocas Bambu Beach** (Calle 3, tel. 757-9062, 5 P.M.–midnight or 1 A.M. daily) consists of a large deck with tables under open-sided tents on bamboo poles, a stage area, a long bar, and a ginormous TV screen showing music videos and movies. This is not a place to come for food or cocktails—consuming anything more ambitious than a beer is a recipe for disappointment—but the ambience is cool. Entertainment in the past has included a fire dancer.

El Toro Loco (Avenida Central just east of the park, open daily) manages to please both the old gringos and the more urbane European expats, who concede it's a fun place to hang out. Basically a large funky shack with TVs tuned to big games, it's popular with just about everyone. Part of the reason for that is a friendly bar staff that serve some of the cheapest booze in Bocas. It has a dartboard, free wireless Internet, and serves bar food.

La Iguana Bar (Calle 3 between Avenida A and B, evenings–late daily) has a friendly, surfer-shack ambience on the edge of the water. It's a popular yet low-key place for those who feel like doing a little dancing or a lot of drinking. It attracts a nice mix of people and way too much reggae.

The **Buena Vista Bar and Grill** (Calle 1 between Avenida C and Avenida D, tel. 757-9035, noon–9:30 P.M. Wed.–Mon.) remains a popular hangout, especially for gringos who like to talk real estate and watch U.S. ball games. Older visitors will feel comfortable here. The Buena Vista was for sale in 2012.

Festivals and Events

The biggest annual party in Bocas is the **Feria Internacional del Mar** (International Festival of the Sea), held for about four days in the second half of September (dates vary). It can feature such activities as a beauty contest, boat races, fireworks, volleyball and other games, various cultural events and displays, and, of course, lots of drinking and dancing.

Those planning to be in Bocas on the New Year's holiday should contact Al Natural Resort (tel./fax 757-9004, cell 6496-0776, 6576-8605 or 6640-6935, www.alnaturalresort.com) on Isla Bastimentos for details and reservations for their famous **New Year's Eve beach party.**

Other celebrations include:

• May 1: **Palo de Mayo.** Maypole dance in Bocas town and Isla Bastimentos.

• July 16: **Día de la Virgen del Carmen.** Parade in honor of the patron saint of Isla Colón. *La Peregrinación a la Gruta,* a pilgrimage to the virgin's shrine at La Gruta, halfway across the island, takes place on the following Sunday.

• October 12: **Columbus Day.** Though the date commemorates Columbus's discovery of America in 1492, Bocas has borrowed it to remember his visit to the archipelago in 1502.

• November 16: **Founding Day** of the province of Bocas del Toro.

SHOPPING

Souvenir kiosks at the north end of Calle 3 have some cheap jewelry, *molas,* and other knickknacks. Oddly, there are few Ngöbe-Buglé crafts there. These kiosks may be moved to the new Mercado Municipal by the time you visit. Other souvenir kiosks are around the town park, mostly on its south end.

Organic chocolate bars made by local companies are sold at a few spots around town, including Super Gourmet and Starfish Coffee. They cost about US$4 for a 100-gram bar. The chocolate is intense, crumbly, and delicious, more like brownies than a typical chocolate bar. They can make for nice little gifts for folks back home, as long as they don't get too hot and you get home quickly enough; they have no preservatives, so they only last about a week in transit. Oreba Chocolate makes a variety of chocolate products, including baking chocolate, hot-chocolate mix, and a delicious chocolate bar that tastes like dark fudge.

Pure Tree Natural Body Products (cell 6607-8962 and 6570-8277, www.upinthehill. com) are made by a couple who use plants and fruit grown on their farm in Bastimentos. They make all kinds of delicious-smelling oils, balms, salves, and skin-care products in attractive bottles. Three will be of special interest to Bocas visitors at war with the *chitras:* Cococitronella and Fight the Bite to ward them off, and Stop Scratchin' to control the maddening itch.

Bocas Book Store (Avenida E near Calle 1, cell 6452-5905 or 6739-0693, 9 a.m.–4 p.m. Mon.–Sat.) has a bar and a Ping-Pong table that see more action than the bookshelves. It's on the ground floor of the same building that houses Om Café. Most of the books are used best sellers, but there's a little bit of a lot of things. Don't expect a bargain, though: paperbacks are US$5–7, hardbacks are US$8, and travel books are US$10.

Artesanías Bri-Bri Emanuel (Calle 3 between Avenida B and Avenida C, tel. 757-9652, 10 a.m.–8 p.m. Mon.–Sat.), right across the street from Bocas Marine and Tours, seems to carry more Guatemalan souvenirs than Panamanian ones, but it does have a few things, such as devil masks and traditional Ngöbe-Buglé dresses and handbags.

SPORTS AND RECREATION

Few leave the archipelago without taking at least one boat tour, which is by far the most popular outdoor activity. These tours usually include snorkeling, but those not interested in that can just splash around in the water or sun themselves on the boat or the beach during snorkeling stops. Scuba diving and surfing are also popular, and as tourism takes off in Bocas, more and more outfitters with more and more toys are showing up. Though of interest to just a minority of visitors, forest hikes and camping are also possible. Nearly all the guides and outfitters in the archipelago are in Bocas town, and most of these are found along Calle 3.

Diving and Snorkeling

Diving and snorkeling in Bocas can be good, but well-traveled divers may not find it as spectacular as other parts of the Caribbean. Several rivers empty into the sea here, so visibility tends to be 15 meters on a good day, 22 meters on an excellent day. It's a good place for beginning divers and snorkelers because there's so much calm, accessible water and lots to explore at shallow depths. Bocas also has a reputation as being one of the cheapest places in the world to get open-water certification.

Bocas has extensive coral and sponge gardens that are easy for even novice snorkelers to explore. There is also more challenging cave, wall, and wreck diving for experienced scuba divers. Popular spots include **Hospital Point,** the **Cayos Zapatillas, Cayo Crawl,** and **Cristóbal Light** (a reef marked by a navigation light on the north side of Isla Cristóbal). A **ferry boat wreck** is off the tip of Bocas town, and nurse sharks can sometimes be spotted there. More ambitious spots include **Cayos Tigre (Tiger Rock),** off the north tip of Peninsula Valiente, more than 40 kilometers southeast of Bocas town, and **Isla Escudo de Veraguas,** which is more than twice as far away. Dive operators sometimes offer trips to Cayos Tigre, but a trip to Escudo de Veraguas is a major undertaking and the sea is too rough to attempt it much of the year.

The best snorkeling tends to be in the placid, protected waters on the south side of the islands. The north sides are open to the sea and pounding surf. Because of this, the most satisfying spots for snorkelers tend to be Hospital Point and the area near Cayo Crawl, which are quite calm and have lots to see near the surface. There's also some snorkeling between **Boca del Drago** and **Big Bight** on the west side of Isla Colón, but the coral isn't that healthy and the visibility can be poor.

There are now several scuba operations to choose from, with similar offerings and prices. Expect to pay around US$35 (one tank) or US$60 (two tanks) for half-day scuba trips. Scuba classes range from half-day Discover Scuba courses (around US$60–75) to open-water certification (US$250–300) to divemaster certification (around US$500) and beyond.

The scuba operations also offer snorkeling trips for $15–30, depending on the destination and whether the trip is a half day or full day. Snorkeling trips tend of leave around 9:30 A.M. Snorkel trips are also a central part of many boat tours offered by other tour operators.

Those who'd rather arrange their own dive or snorkel trips can rent gear and fill scuba tanks at some of the dive shops. La Buga Dive Center has a wide range of gear for rent or sale, including underwater cameras. Some other spots around town also rent snorkel gear, including Ixa's Bicycle World (Avenida Norte between Calle and Calle 6, tel. 757-9585). Expect to pay US$10 per day for mask, snorkel, and fins.

Starfleet Scuba (Calle 1, tel./fax 757-9630, www.starfleetscuba.com) is one of the dive operators in the area. They speak English, Spanish, and German here. **Bocas Water Sports** (Calle 3 and Avenida A, near the ferry dock, tel. 757-9541, www.bocaswatersports.com) is another reputable operator. They offer instruction in English or Spanish. **La Buga Dive Center and Surf School** (Calle 3, tel. 757-9534, cell 6781-0755, www.labugapanama.com) is half a block south of Bocas Water Sports. They speak English and Spanish here. **The Dutch Pirate** (Avenida Norte, cell 6567-1812, www.thedutchpirate.com) has an office on the north end of town, near La Casbah. They offer instruction in English, Spanish, French, German, and Dutch.

Surfing

Bocas del Toro has good surfing, some of the best in the country. Waves are best December–March

sanding a surfboard, Bocas town

and least consistent August–October. There are three well-known breaks on Isla Colón, as well as some less-famous ones that local surfers try to keep to themselves. The three main spots, all of which are along the east coast, are listed here, in order of their distance from town.

Paunch breaks left and right. It has long, rippable waves that are appropriate for all levels and attract beginners. It's a reef break, so wear booties.

Dumpers (also known as Dumps) is a reef-bottom left break with big tubes and short but dramatic rides. This is a dangerous break that should be attempted only by advanced surfers. Waves can get up to three meters. The reef is sharp, so wear booties. There's also an inner break known, logically enough, as **Inner Dumps**. It's another left-breaking, reef-bottom wave. It's faster and longer than the outside wave, but not as big.

Playa Bluff is a gorgeous, several-kilometer-long beach at the end of the road. It's a powerful beach break known for destroying surfboards. It features fast-breaking waves and long tubes. Those who know it well say the waves are best when they're no more than about 1–2 meters high. Even when the swell isn't big, the waves are too powerful for beginning surfers and swimmers.

Several places in Bocas rent surfboards, often fairly battered ones. Hostel Heike, Mondo Taitu, and Hostel Gran Kahuna also rent them. Expect to pay about US$10–15 for short boards and US$15–20 for long boards per day.

Surfing lessons are easy to come by. **Bocas Surf School** (office in Hotel Lula's Bed and Breakfast, tel. 757-9057, cell 6852-5291, www.bocassurfschool.com) is run by Dez and Garret Bartelt, retired professional athletes who also own Rincón Surf and Board in Puerto Rico. Classes range from a half-day (US$59) or full-day introduction (US$89) to a five-day immersion (US$369), board included. **La Buga Dive Center and Surf School** (Calle 3, tel. 757-9534, cell 6781-0755, www.labugapanama.

com) offers group surf lessons for US$49 for a half day or US$89 for a full day.

Tropix Surf (Calle 3 between Avenida D and Avenida Central, near the southwest end of the park, tel. 757-9727, 9 A.M.–noon and 3–7 P.M. daily) sells custom-made surfboards produced on the premises.

Kayaking

Some hotels offer kayaks to guests, either included with stays or for an extra charge.

Bocas Water Sports (Calle 3 and Avenida A, near the ferry dock, tel. 757-9541, www.bocaswatersports.com) rents single kayaks for US$3/hour, US$10/half day, and US$18/full day. Do not go out on open water without a life jacket.

Hiking

There are undeveloped forest trails on Isla Colón and other islands in the archipelago, but as usual only hike in the forest with a knowledgeable guide. Certainly don't hike alone. Be especially careful on any hike in the forests of Isla Popa, which still has fer-de-lance and other venomous snakes.

Boat Tours

There is no shortage of boatmen offering tours of the islands and snorkeling spots. Usually these are organized as day trips with fairly standardized itineraries at similar prices. Rates go up as fuel prices increase.

Expect to pay about US$25 per person for most trips. Clients have to pay additional per person entrance fees of US$3 for Red Frog Beach (the surrounding land is private property) and US$10 for the Zapatillas (it's in a national park).

One tour takes clients around Isla Colón to Swan's Cay for bird-watching and snorkeling, stops for lunch and a swim at Boca del Drago, then stops down the west side of Isla Colón for at least one snorkeling spot, usually the popular Playa Estrella (Star Beach).

Another standard trip is to the Cayos Zapatillas, with a stop for lunch and a splash at one of the Cayo Crawl restaurants. A cheaper tour goes to Red Frog Beach, the popular snorkeling spot of Hospital Point on Isla Solarte, and the town of Old Bank on Bastimentos. Red Frog Beach is the most popular beach on Bastimentos because it's both attractive and accessible. Expect to pay about US$10 per person, plus the Red Frog Beach entrance fee.

There are several established tour operators along the water in Bocas town offering sightseeing and snorkeling trips. Tours generally include snorkeling equipment, but it may not be in the best shape, so it's best to bring your own if possible. The most professional operators carry emergency radios, and all should provide life jackets; be sure to check. Trips generally start midmorning and return to Bocas town before dark. Private tours are possible, but expect to pay more if your group has fewer than six people, the minimum for most tours.

Transparente Tours (Calle 3 near Avenida C, tel. 757-9915, transparentetours@hotmail.com, www.bocas.com) has been offering snorkeling and sightseeing boat tours for years now. (It joined forces with the competing J&J Tours a few years back, and it's sometimes listed as J&J Transparente.) Tours start at 9:30 A.M. and return around 4:30–5:30 P.M. They include snorkeling equipment and an ice chest for any drinks/snacks guests bring.

Boteros Bocatoreños (tel. 757-9760, boterosbocas@yahoo.com, www.bocas.com), also called Boatmen United, is a group composed of boatmen who have organized to stay afloat amid growing competition from tour operators.

Bocas Water Sports (Calle 3 and Avenida A, near the ferry dock, tel. 757-9541, www.bocaswatersports.com) and **Starfleet Scuba** (Calle 1, tel./fax 757-9630, www.starfleetscuba.com), though primarily scuba outfits, also offer snorkeling trips.

Jampan Tours (Calle 1 next to Starfleet Scuba, tel. 757-9619, http://jampantours.com)

offers more unusual tours, including forest walks and visits to an indigenous village, in addition to the usual suspects. It's one of the few places able to offer tours of a small chocolate farm run by a couple of gringo expats who live in the Dolphin Bay area (US$25 per person, plus a US$5 entrance fee).

Those willing to pay a bit more may want to consider taking a tour on a sailboat rather than a bumpy *lancha* with noisy outboard motor. **Bocas Sailing** (Calle 3, tel. 757-7048, cell 6464-4242, http://bocassailing.com) offers the standard tours for US$45 per person. It's a more ecofriendly option, and less likely to traumatize the *delfines* on a Laguna Bocatorito (Dolphin Bay) trip. The Belgian-run **Odin Sailing** (cell 6795-5123, www.odinsailingpanama.com) also offers US$45 sailboat trips, on a 60-foot trimaran.

It's also possible to work out a deal with one of the many freelance boatmen offering tour guide services, but use caution and judgment when going this route. However, these guys are generally not licensed. Two boatmen I can recommend are Gallardo "Cabrioli" Livingston and Bola Smith. Ask for them at Boteros Bocatoreños.

Yoga

The sun, the surf, and the laid-back lifestyle make Bocas a natural magnet for yogis and yoginis, who come to the island on yoga retreats and to teach classes. **Bocas Yoga** (Calle 4 near Avenida G, cell 6658-1355, www.bocasyoga.com, sweetlaurakay@msn.com, Mon.–Sat.) is a well-established studio run in a large wooden house that is also the home of Laura Kay, a yoga teacher who takes her work seriously, yet seems to have a playful bohemian streak as well. Her studio is modern, spacious, and well designed. It has hardwood floors, air-conditioning, good natural lighting, and new yoga mats and equipment. Because Bocas town can get noisy even on the edge of town, the studio is soundproofed. Laura occasionally hosts guest classes taught by highly respected yoga teachers from Colombia and Costa Rica. Morning group classes are held at 9:15 A.M. Monday–Friday. There are frequent evening and Saturday classes as well. Group classes are US$5 a session. Private classes are also available, for US$35 for the first person, US$5 more for each additional person.

Spas

Spa services come and go in Bocas, but one that seems destined to stick around is **Starfleet Spa** (Calle 1, tel./fax 757-9630, www.starfleetscuba.com), upstairs from and run by the same couple that owns Starfleet Scuba. It offers massages, facials, waxing, and various skin treatments in pleasant and comfortable rooms, though some street noise inevitably spills over. One of the owners, Georgina, was trained as a massage therapist in London and gives excellent massages. The most expensive massage is US$65 for 75 minutes. The spa offers a range of other services as well, including waxing and facials.

Lil' Spa Shop by the Sea (Avenida H and Calle 7, cell 6591-3814, www.spashopbythesea.com, 10 A.M.–6 P.M. by appointment) is on the northwest edge of town near Cocomo-on-the-Sea. It offers good massages either in the loft of the little wooden spa or on a covered pier over the water. Prices range from US$30 for a 30-minute massage up to US$80 for a 90-minute one. Other services include facials, waxing, haircuts, coloring, manicures, and pedicures. The spa also rents out simple but clean cabins without air-conditioning for US$25 per person. Guests are welcome to use a little Jacuzzi on the property.

ACCOMMODATIONS

Most of the hotels in the archipelago are in Bocas town, and most of these are built right on the water. But there are more and more options around Isla Colón and on the other major islands of the archipelago. There's quite a variety of accommodations, ranging from simple but clean hostels to modern midrange hotels to bed-and-breakfasts to rather upscale and exotic bungalows. All have hot water unless otherwise indicated.

Many of the hotels have websites that are accessible through www.bocas.com. A lot of the lodgings, especially the cheaper ones, are not diligent about keeping their websites up to date or alive at all, and many are bad about answering email. A phone call is often the best way to go.

Bocas town has been experiencing a boom in hostels lately. If everything in the center of town is filled up, try hunting along Calle 3 north of town. Hostels—some more legitimate-looking than others—come and go along this stretch of road.

Until recently, Bocas town did not allow the construction of any building taller than three stories. This helped keep the town funky and charming even as tourists discovered it. But four-story buildings are beginning to pop up, changing the look of the area.

Bocas Town
US$10-25

The current owners of the very popular **Hostel Heike** (Calle 3 just west of the park, tel. 757-9667 or 757-9708, U.S. 925/465-6167, www.hostelheike.com, dorm beds start at US$10 pp, including pancake breakfast) are a trio of guys from the San Francisco Bay Area who also own Luna's Castle in Panama City and have a knack for giving the backpacker set exactly what it wants. If you stay here, you'd better like company: Nearly 60 beds are squeezed into dorm rooms with 4–10 bunks. The hostel has shared hot-water bathrooms, free wireless Internet access and Internet computers, free Spanish lessons three times a week, lockers, a book exchange, communal kitchen, and other handy hostel extras. Rooms are basic but cheerful—they're brightly painted, designed to let light in, and feature lots of pretty wood. Some have

air-conditioning; the others have fans. Private rooms are US$22 (double occupancy) or US$33 (triple occupancy). There's a mirador on the top floor strung with hammocks.

Casa Verde (Avenida Sur near Calle 4, cell 6633-8050, cvbocas@gmail.com, www.casaverdebocas.com, US$12.50 for dorm beds) is my favorite among the new crop of hostels. Dorms are small and windowless but are clean and have good beds. It's just around the corner from the Ferry Pier and Super Gourmet at the south edge of town. It's on the water's edge and shares space with a popular bar and grill, **La Mama Loca,** built onto a pier. The restaurant offers a cheeseburger, beer, and fries combo for US$6.50 and hosts happy hours 11 A.M.–6 P.M. daily.

Mondo Taitu (north end of Calle 5, tel. 757-9425, www.mondotaitu.com, dorm beds start at US$10 pp, US$12 with a/c) is a funky, friendly place with 4–8 person rustic wooden dorms. The hostel also has some double rooms for US$24 and a tree house triple for US$36. It has a communal kitchen, free loaner bikes (including a couple of tandem bikes), a bar, and a library of free DVDs guests can watch in one of the common areas. Hammocks for napping are strung around the joint; it's hard to find one that's not already occupied. Conditions here are not always the cleanest.

❿ **Hostal de Hansi** (Avenida D and Calle 1, tel. 757-9085, http://hostalhansi.bocas.com, starts at US$12 s, US$25 d) is a two-story wooden place run by Heike, the former owner of Hostel Heike. (That's right: Heike owns Hansi, not Heike.) The place is immaculate and an excellent deal. A small single room is US$12 with a shared bathroom, or US$15 with a private bathroom. If you want a TV (local channels) it's US$2 more. A double room with private bath, TV, and balcony is US$25–30. Triples are US$30–36. All the rooms have ceiling fans and orthopedic mattresses. Guests are welcome to use the communal kitchen and dining area, and there's free wireless Internet. Reservations are not accepted here.

an Kahuna Hostel (Calle 3 near , tel. 757-9038, www.grankahunab- US$10–12 pp) works hard to try to keep their place clean by Panama hostel standards, and it shows. A two-story, bright orange and yellow old-style Bocas house, the Gran Kahuna is hard to miss. Opened in 2008, it features 49 beds with thin foam mattresses and a veranda that looks out over the sea. The hostel also has a little dock right across the street that's just for its guests to hang out. There are lockers, free wireless Internet, a washer/dryer, shared kitchen, cold-water shared bathrooms, and big flat-screen TV in the common areas. It's a mellow, friendly place. Surfboards are US$15 per day and the managers can arrange surf tours and lessons.

US$25-50

Hotel Casa Max (Avenida G near the north end of Calle 4, about a block west of the Bocas Inn, tel. 757-9120, casamax1@hotmail.com, starts at US$33 s/d) is a bright and cheerful Dutch-owned place in a wooden building that's been going strong since the mid-1990s. An attached annex has brought the room total to 14. The original rooms (US$33 s/d) are simple but clean and have private baths, fans, hot water, and firm beds. The newer rooms (US$44 s/d) have air-conditioning and TV. The place has a colorful facade that's hard to miss, even at night, when it's lit up prettily. A restaurant on the premises, Rum Runners, serves breakfast and dinner, specializing in Indonesian food.

Hotel del Parque (Calle 2, on the southeast side of the park, tel. 757-9008, delparque35@hotmail.com, US$37.50 s, US$45 d, a/c) offers eight rooms—four doubles and four triples—in an attractive wooden house right on the park and surrounded by flowering trees. Rooms are simple but pleasant with okay mattresses, satellite TV, and private bathrooms. There's a view of the park from the veranda and a nice little garden on the property. Guests are welcome to use the kitchen. This is a friendly place.

La Veranda (Calle H near the corner of Calle 7, tel./fax 757-9211, http://laverandapanama.tripod.com, US$29–55.50 s/d) is a Caribbean-style wooden house with a wraparound veranda that gives the place its name. It's at the north edge of town about a block southwest of Cocomo-on-the-Sea. It offers seven pleasant rooms of various quality. The cheapest rooms (US$29 s/d) have shared bathrooms and somewhat thin mattresses. The nicest rooms (US$55.50 s/d) are cheerful and large, with private bathrooms and air-conditioning. Air-conditioning may not be necessary since this place often gets a nice breeze, though sometimes the neighbors insist on blasting their music. All the rooms have mosquito nets. Guests are welcome to use the kitchen, and there's free wireless Internet.

US$50-100

Hotel Los Delfines (Calle 5 and Avenida G, tel. 757-9963, www.posadalosdelfines.net, US$45 s/d), on the northern outskirts of town, is a clean place built circa 2001 that has 12 pleasant rooms with colorful Peruvian bedspreads, satellite TV, and wireless Internet. Some of the rooms are quite dark, and the ones on the top floor have low, slanting ceilings. There is a bar/dining area downstairs.

Hotel Lula's Bed and Breakfast (Avenida Norte and Calle 6, tel. 757-9057, cell 6629-0836, information@lulabb.com, www.lulabb.com, starts at US$55 s/d, including breakfast, a/c) is a pleasant, clean bed-and-breakfast that features lots of handsome wood and rooms with attractive bathrooms. The place has two doubles with double beds (US$55 s/d) and four rooms with a double bed, single bed, and fold-out-chair bed (US$66 d, US$77 t, US$88 q). The nicest rooms are the two triples that overlook the balcony.

Hotel Bahía (south end of Calle 3, across from the ferry landing, tel. 757-9626, www.ghbahia.com, US$73 s, US$80 d, a/c) is the grand old lady of Bocas. Built in 1905, it was once the headquarters building for the United Fruit Company. A renovation a few years ago preserved the building's historical character (the fruit company's massive old safe still sits in the office), while cheering up the place considerably. The 16 rooms are simple, bordering on stark, with lukewarm-water bathrooms, TV, and lots of attractive wood. However, it is not being terribly well-maintained or cleaned. A basic breakfast is served on the terrace downstairs.

Cocomo-on-the-Sea (Avenida Norte between Calle 6 and Calle 7, tel./fax 757-9259, www.cocomoonthesea.com, US$66 s, US$82.50 d, including breakfast), is right on the water, about a five-minute walk northwest of the town center, and offers four large, simple rooms in a wooden building surrounded by a lush tropical garden. Once one of the most comfortable places to stay in Bocas, it's overdue for a renovation and maintenance work and is now borderline rustic. The location is still pleasant, and it's away from the bustle of downtown Bocas. The two rooms in front, Calypso and La Palma, have an ocean view, but all four rooms have access to a comfortable veranda and sundeck, strung with hammocks, that juts into the water. A third person in any room is an additional US$11. Guests have free use of sea kayaks.

Hotel Laguna (Calle 3 about a block south of the park, tel. 757-9091, www.thehotellagunabocas.com, starts at US$85 s/d, a/c) offers 22 modern, clean rooms in the center of downtown. Rooms are dark but cheerful with wood paneling and colorful bedspreads. All have satellite TV, firm beds, and telephones. The attractive deluxe junior suite (US$160) is simply a larger room with a balcony. Other suites of various size and furnishings are available. The attached indoor/outdoor restaurant is a nice place to watch the passing scene on Calle 3, and it's the home of El Pecado, long one of the best restaurants in Bocas.

The **Bocas Inn** (north end of Calle 3, Bocas tel./fax 757-9600, Panama City tel. 269-9415, fax 264-3713, www.anconexpeditions.com, US$99 s/d, including breakfast, a/c) is an attractive, two-story wooden lodge set in a lush garden. It's owned by Ancon Expeditions, which has its field office in the building. The place is meant primarily for visitors who've arranged package tours with Ancon Expeditions, generally but not necessarily through Ancon's main office in Panama City, but it's also available for those who just want a room. The nicest rooms face the ocean. These open out on a terrace with hammocks (the terrace can be used by all guests). On the ground floor is a breezy veranda/pier that has a dining room and bar right on the water and quiet jazz and modern lounge music playing on the stereo. It's a good place to stop for a drink even if you're not staying at the inn.

The **Hotel Swan's Cay** (Calle 3 just north of Parque Bolívar, tel. 757-9316 or 757-9090, tel./fax 757-9027, www.swanscayhotel.com, rooms start at US$79 s/US$93.50 d in the main building) was the first fancy hotel in Bocas, built smack in the middle of town. The whole place is thoroughly air-conditioned and features such city-style touches as a carpeted lobby with wood-paneled walls. Rooms have satellite TV, telephones, and Italian furniture, but the smaller ones are cramped and the whole place is dark. There are two swimming pools, one of which is a rather uninviting aboveground pool a few minutes' walk from the main hotel. Many find the hotel staid and out of sync with the bohemian ambience of the rest of Bocas. Its formal, air-conditioned restaurant is usually empty.

US$100-150

▐ **Hotel Bocas del Toro** (Calle 1, tel. 757-9771, www.hotelbocasdeltoro.com, starts at US$141.90 s/d, a/c) strikes a good balance between being attractive and comfortable, while retaining traditional Bocas charm. It's easily the best-run hotel in town. Like every other place in Bocas, things can go wrong here, but if they do, the staff immediately set about fixing it. The hotel features 11 clean, modern rooms in a Caribbean-style wooden building built right on the water. All the rooms have TVs, telephones, in-room safes, and hair dryers. The most expensive rooms have balconies that look out on the ocean. These latter are US$218.90 s/d, for a "premium room," or US$302.50 s/d, for a huge "premium luxury" room.

Hotel Bocas del Toro is a handsome place, featuring nine kinds of dark, polished wood. The restaurant needs some work, but fortunately it was recently taken over by the hotel management and is gradually improving. Lunch and dinner options include burgers, seafood, various meat dishes, and pasta, with mains running about US$7–12.

M&M's Residencias (Avenida Sur, past the ferry dock, tel. 757-9004, cell 6596-6076, al-naturalbocas@cwpanama.net, starts at US$120 s/d, a/c) is the new project from some of the people behind Al Natural on Isla Bastimentos. Its feel might be termed tropical minimalism. It consists of two rooms available for short-term rentals, above which are two full apartments for longer stays. All four are part of an unusual enclosed complex that includes the Al Natural office and dock. They are built over the water, and everything is made from tropical oak, a handsome, light-colored wood. The two short-term rooms are angled so that their terraces face open water, with the mainland mountains in the distance. You'd never know you were in Bocas town here, and the complex is big enough to muffle much of the sound from the street. The rooms have high ceilings and comfortable beds. The sea-front studio (US$120 s/d) has a kitchenette with new stainless-steel appliances. The sea-front one bedroom apartment (US$150 s/d) has a living area, full kitchen, and larger terrace. Those staying at Al Natural get a discount, and, for those who can afford it, staying at both places is an easy way to experience both town life in Bocas and its remoter attractions.

OVER US$150

Tropical Suites (Calle 1 near Avenida D, tel. 757-9880 or 757-9081, cell 6689-9451, www.bocastropical.com, starts at US$192.50 s/d, a/c) is a three-story apartment building near the CEFATI office that offers 16 modern, spacious, somewhat stark studio apartments that can be rented by the day, week, or month. Those looking for the funky, Caribbean side of Bocas won't find it here, but it will probably appeal to those who want something more than a hotel room, particularly those who need a long-term place to stay. Each apartment has a queen bed, a double sofa bed, a balcony, fully equipped kitchen, satellite TV, bathrooms with two sinks and whirlpool bath, wireless Internet connection, and so on. Utilities and daily maid service are included. Amenities include a coin laundry, security cameras, a marina, and a tiny restaurant nook that's open for breakfast, lunch, and dinner and provides room service. Regular daily rates are US$192.50 s/d for apartments that look out on the street, or US$247.50 s/d for a much more appealing sea view. Add US$20 for each additional person. Tropical Suites has the distinction of being the first place in the archipelago with an elevator.

The four-story **Palma Royale Hotel and Suites** (Calle 3, tel. 757-9979, suites US$203.50) is across from the ferry dock and offers 15 bright, handsome modern rooms of various sizes. The cheapest is an economy studio on the ground floor (US$88 s/d), which has a queen bed but lacks the view of the larger rooms. Most of the other accommodations are suites with private balconies and sitting rooms (US$203.50 for two–four adults). Sea views are great on the 3rd and 4th floor, the latter of which houses a lovely penthouse suite with a wraparound veranda.

Playa Bluff and Vicinity

Taxi transport to this area tends to be pricey because of the distance and road conditions. The

© WILLIAM FRIAR

Tesoro Escondido has one of the best views on the islands.

going rate for taxis from town is about US$8–10 to get as far as La Coralina, and US$10–12 to get to the places farther up the beach. However, each of the lodgings here works hard to get their guests free or discounted rides, giving them lifts when they can or organizing groups to go together. It's also possible to ride bikes back and forth into town, but it's a bit of a workout on a hot day. Bikes are the quickest way to travel within the Playa Bluff area itself, though not necessarily the easiest, as the road is hilly and sandy. Places to stay generally have bikes that guests can borrow.

Places up here are still off the grid, having to supply their own electricity and water, which generally means captured rainwater. Tesoro Escondido, Bluff Beach Retreat, and Playa Bluff Lodge are all on solar power, an ecofriendly solution that also means they don't have air-conditioning. All the places are right next to the ocean and often get a pleasant sea breeze.

US$50-100

Tesoro Escondido (cell 6749-7435 or 6711-9594, bocasbluff@yahoo.com, www.bocaste-soroescondido.com, starts at US$38.50 s/d) is Spanish for hidden treasure, and that's the perfect name for this place, which is between La Coralina and Bluff Beach Retreat. You wouldn't notice it if you didn't know it was there. It consists of a wooden house built on a bluff about 10 meters above the surf. The house is on four levels; from the terrace/dining room/kitchen level there's a spectacular view of the ocean and two beaches, one on either side of the house. You'd better like dogs if you stay at this place: the owner, Monique, has five, not including the occasional visiting pooch of a guest or worker, nor her cat. They're all good-natured, but watch out when they stampede at once.

Rooms are simple and rustic. In lieu of a minifridge, each room has a camping cooler; instead of air-conditioning, there's a clip-on fan over the bed. (There is, however, free wireless

Internet.) But they've all got a bohemian chic feel and are perfectly comfortable. There are whimsical touches everywhere. The tabletops and paving stones are decorated with images of dragonflies, dolphins, and iguanas made from colored glass. The pattern is repeated in colorful glass walls made from salvaged bottles, which are lovely when the sun shines through; birds make nests in these. In fact, whenever possible Monique and her staff have tried to use recycled materials—glass, tile, driftwood, bits of old houses.

There are six rooms in the main house. Rooms 5 and 6 (US$49.50 s/d) are on the top floor, reached by a spiral staircase made from a tree trunk. They open out onto a balcony with hammocks and feel a bit like a tree house. Rooms 1 and 2 (US$38.50 s/d) are on the level below the dining/bar area, but are perfectly quiet because they're toward the back of the building, which also means only the bathrooms have a view of the sea. All the rooms have access to shared kitchens.

There are also three cabins set in a tropical garden (39 kinds of heliconia!) on the edge of the bluff. The Turtle (US$71.50) and Dolphin (US$82.50 s/d) are next to each other and similar: one-bedroom cabins with private baths, a deck from which to watch the sea from a hammock, and a kitchenette. The Turtle has a ceiling fan. The Dragonfly cabin (US$82.50) is a bit farther away and a bit bigger, with two decks. It's the only cabin with a fridge. It's set back closer to the road, but it's right above a cove with its own little beach. The Dolphin has a stunning view of the waves breaking on the edge of the cove. More recently, a one-bedroom apartment, the Butterfly, has become available (US$104.50). It has a living area and a full kitchen with fridge.

Tesoro Escondido can arrange various tours and activities, including scuba lessons and trips, boat tours, and horse hire.

♦US$100-150

☾ Playa Bluff Lodge (cell 6798-8507, www.playablufflodge.com, US$104.50 s/d, including breakfast and transportation from town) opened in 2009 near the far end of Playa Bluff and the end of the road. At first glance, it seems to be a modern but unremarkable two-story house—albeit one built right in front of a lovely stretch of beach. But a closer look reveals it to be something quite remarkable indeed. The Dutch owners have turned it into their own tropical nature preserve. They have built a lush artificial pond in their backyard that attracts reptiles, amphibians, birds, and other jungle creatures. These include incredibly cute red-eyed tree frogs, basilisks, opossums, Amazon parrots, parakeets, and oropendolas. Howler monkeys, white-faced capuchins, anteaters, and sloths stop by from time to time, as do the occasional boa constrictor and green vine snake. Needless to say, this is not a place for those afraid of snakes, though it's worth noting that in five years of living out here, they have never seen a venomous snake. Beyond the pond are 23 hectares of forest with extensive trails that are rather muddy and hilly; one leads to a waterfall.

The owner, Reinier, bred exotic reptiles in the Netherlands, so he really knows what he's doing. The lodge has a terrarium filled with a whole rainbow of Bocas's poison-dart frog, but he keeps them strictly segregated so they don't mix with the naturally occurring varieties in the area.

The lodge runs turtle tours for interested guests from the end of March through the end of June; this usually means camping out on the beach near the house. The lodge can also help arrange other tours and activities, including hiring horses, which is one way to get to the quiet snorkeling spot of La Piscina, about 45 minutes north.

The lodge has five spacious, modern, and spotlessly clean rooms. The rooms have ceiling fans, not air-conditioning, but are surprisingly cool even in the daytime. Stays include breakfast, and free use of bikes and local mobile phones. The owners speak English, Spanish, German, and Dutch. This a great find for families or anyone with an interest in nature.

A new restaurant, **Playa Bluff Lounge** (cell 6798-8507, 11 A.M.–8:30 P.M., US$8 or less), opened in a large *rancho* on the property at the end of 2011. It's right between the lodge and the ocean. But even though surfers congregate here when the waves are good, and families bring their young children to play in a separate kids' area, the restaurant has been designed carefully so that it doesn't intrude upon the lodge at all. Restaurant clients are not allowed onto the grounds of the lodge, and all one can hear from its garden is the sound of breaking surf. The menu includes sandwiches, salads, burgers, and bar food such as nachos.

◖ **La Coralina** (cell 6788-8992 or 6786-9823, www.lacoralina.com, starts at US$88 s/d) is on a bluff above an isolated cove with pounding surf. The main building is a two-story, Spanish colonial–style building with an airy interior and lots of balconies. The three rooms in the building have either one queen and one twin bed (US$121 s/d) or two queen beds (US$143 s/d), with attractive bathrooms, ceiling fans, and air-conditioning. There are also three less-expensive rooms in a courtyard behind the building. All have two double beds and air-conditioning. Two of them have shared bathrooms (US$88 s/d), but they're close to the rooms, spotless, attractive, and designed with real flair. The third room has a private bathroom (US$99 s/d). All the rooms in the building are simply but cheerfully decorated and painted in bright tropical colors, and the mattresses are good. It's breezy on the top of the hill, which keeps the *chitras* down and air-conditioning easier to do without.

The four large suites (US$176 s/d; except for the Bamboo Suite, which is US$198 s/d) next to the main building are luxurious and gorgeous, with loving attention given to the inventive decor, king beds, large showers, air-conditioning, satellite television, safes, and private patios. The Ocean Suite has a view of the ocean from the patio, and the Garden Suite looks out on the garden. The Hammock Suite has a private covered balcony with double hammocks; the Bamboo Suite has an outside tub on the private walled-patio.

The bar and restaurant are housed in an attractive *rancho* on the edge of the bluff. The food here is delicious. Those who are here on Mexican Food Sunday should try the taco salad, which is huge and made with fresh tuna. The restaurant is open 8 A.M.–9 P.M. daily. Last call at the bar is at 10 P.M. Nonguests are welcome.

Recent additions include a deck with a great view and a day spa offering open-air massages above the crashing surf. A swimming pool is in the works. There's a large gift shop selling good-quality crafts from Panama and other Central American countries. The realistic-looking rock wall surrounding the base of the bar is actually made of foam and was part of a set for the *Miami Vice* movie. The owner and her gracious staff are among the best things about this place. There's plenty to do at the hotel, and the owner is constantly coming up with new ideas. For surfers, Bluff, Dumpers, and Paunch are within easy walking distance. There are 6.5 acres of trails to walk, and horses, bikes, and surfboards are available for hire.

OVER US$150

Bluff Beach Retreat (cell 6677-8867, www.bluffbeachretreat.com, starts at US$150–250 for up to four adults, three night minimum) consists of a large, lovely beach house and two casitas set in four acres of tropical garden. The beach house is built from handsome, highly polished dark wood and features a wraparound lanai. The whole place is designed to be as open to its beautiful surroundings as possible without sacrificing comfort. It features three immaculate bedrooms, a large kitchen, and a dining and bar area. A large and attractive lap pool was added recently.

The whole house can accommodate up to nine people for US$425–795, but rooms are also rented out individually. The house, roomy as it is, doesn't have a whole lot of privacy for people who want to be off by themselves. The two casitas run US$150–325. La Piña can sleep two guests and Las Palmas can handle four. Both have kitchens and are clean and nicely appointed. There's a three-night minimum stay in any of the rooms.

Yoga retreats are sometimes held here. This place and its grounds are lovely. Families or groups traveling together would love this place, but couples or solo travelers may feel a bit isolated.

Vicinity of Isla Colón

There are a few places to stay and eat just north of Bocas town in Saigon, among the mangroves on the south side of the island, and in and around Boca del Drago.

OVER US$150

The three-story, 118-room **Playa Tortuga** (tel. 302-5424 Panama City reservations, tel. 757-9050 at the hotel, www.hotelplayatortuga.com, starts at $191 s/d, including breakfast) is located just past the *i griega* (the turnoff to Boca del Drago), it's the first large-scale hotel in the archipelago, and when it opened in 2008 it instantly doubled the number of hotel rooms on Isla Colón. Owned by the same group that operates Country Inns and Suites in Panama, it has the feel of a motel and looms over its narrow strip of beach, which isn't wide enough even to lay out a beach towel. Rooms have firm beds, minifridges, in-room safes, satellite TV, free wireless Internet, and balconies overlooking the sea. They are clean and new but aging rapidly. The hotel has a pool that's not nearly as big as it looks on the hotel website, plus a kids' pool, which makes the place popular with families. The hotel also features two restaurants, a

gym, and music that's pumped throughout the open common areas. Service is slow. The hotel is north of town but the road is good, making it a fairly quick drive. There's a free shuttle service into town three times a day.

✒ The Spanish-owned **Punta Caracol Acqua Lodge** (cell 6612-1088 or 6676-7186, www.punta-caracol.com, starts at US$405 s, US$465 d, including breakfast, dinner, and transfers) consists of nine bungalows built off the west side of Isla Colón, right on the calm waters of Almirante Bay. Boardwalks link the bungalows to each other and to an attractive open-air restaurant where at night guests dine by the light of kerosene lanterns. That's all that's out there: The little resort feels as though it's floating off by itself in the shallow sea. The place is run on solar power, and there's a septic system (toilet paper must be disposed of in a trash can, not the toilet).

Its five Punta Caracol Suites are cheerful, spacious, two-story wooden bungalows with thatched roofs. Upstairs is a large master bedroom with mosquito nets over a king-size bed. A window is cut into the thatch to give a view of the water, but it can get stuffy up there at night. Downstairs is a sitting room with a couch that converts into a bed. This leads onto a back terrace with a landing from which guests can go snorkeling or swimming right from their rooms. The clear, shallow sea is your backyard, and there's nothing between you and the mainland mountains in the far distance.

The three Luna Suites (US$476 s, US$573 d), are similar to the others but have larger terraces and bathing platforms, plus a hammock and hanging chair. All eight bungalows can sleep up to four people, but the price goes up accordingly. There's also a Master Suite that's twice as big as the Punta Caracol Suites (US$496 s, US$625 d). It can accommodate up to six people, but again, there's a substantial per-person charge.

Rates include a welcome cocktail, snorkeling gear, and use of kayaks. Food can be delicious here, and a huge breakfast is served in the morning.

The staff are casual here, sometimes to

WATER QUALITY AND QUANTITY

Bocas del Toro is one of the few places in Panama that can't depend on safe drinking water coming out of the tap. Bocatoreños cite it as an example of how the central government neglects this remote province, which despite the tourism boom remains one of the poorest in Panama. For more than a decade, protests, sometimes violent ones, have flared up over the need for new waterworks and improved schools, roads, bridges, hospitals, and schools. It doesn't help that the aging infrastructure is occasionally damaged by earthquakes in this seismically active area, and pretty much annually by floods during the rainy season.

Water remains iffy even on the rapidly developing islands. Water is now allegedly safe, but it can still taste funky. Some establishments on the islands filter their water. Consider erring on the side of caution and bringing a water purifier or buying bottled water. Local shops sell water for about US$1 a liter. Avoid the temptation to rely on beer as a thirst quencher, as that's a great way to get dehydrated in this hot, sweaty climate.

The islands occasionally experience serious water shortages (and, increasingly, power outages). At the height of tourist season in early 2007, Isla Colón endured a shortage that lasted nearly three months and sometimes forced residents and tourists to get by on a half hour of water daily. The problem abated when the United States quietly sent a military ship with a portable desalination plant to the rescue. There have been less-drastic shortages in more recent years.

Generally, though, there's plenty of water, and after recent crises some businesses installed their own water storage tanks. Ironically, the remotest hotels, which are off the grid, usually have the most dependable water supplies. As for mainland Bocas, many communities are constantly promised better conditions but suffer from a permanent lack of potable water.

---

the point of near rudeness. There's a whiff of mangrove stench when the wind blows from shore. Despite the proximity of the mangroves, though, the *chitras* aren't too bad. If you stay here, you really have to be in the mood for isolation without too much entertainment. Expenses accumulate quickly if you want to explore. It's a long boat trip back to town, and the resort charges US$15–30 round-trip to ferry you. Tours of the surrounding area are extra.

FOOD

Bocas town offers a fair range of cuisine, considering its size and location. A number of fast-food stalls are set around the perimeter of the park. Many restaurants are closed for lunch, when the tourists are usually out snorkeling and sunbathing.

Avoid any restaurant that serves sea turtle meat or eggs or any other endangered species protected by law.

There are two places beyond Bocas town that are worth making a trip for: Restaurante Guari-Guari and La Coralina. Guari-Guari is just north of town and is described below. La Coralina is a little hotel up at Playa Bluff with an appealing restaurant/bar right above the surf that's open to the public.

Restaurants and Cafés

The best place to eat in the archipelago is ◖**Restaurante Guari-Guari** (cell 6627-1825, 5:30–10 P.M. Thurs.–Tues., US$16). It's a short US$0.50 cab ride north of town, past the Feria del Mar on the isthmus that connects Bocas town with the rest of Isla Colón. The restaurant offers a single fixed-price menu each night: six courses for US$16. The food is gourmet and can include delicious takes on fare such as apple and pecan salad, carpaccio with shaved parmesan, a shot of asparagus crème, breaded prawns, and *filete* in red wine sauce. The restaurant is run by a friendly European couple; the chef is Spanish, and her German partner is host and waiter. It's a nicely decorated open-air place within earshot of pounding surf. The bathrooms are spotless. It's the place to go for a special night out.

⟨ Restaurante El Pecado (Hotel Laguna, Calle 3, tel. 757-9091, 5–10 P.M. Tues.–Sat., US$10–15) is now in its third home, on the terrace of the Hotel Laguna, so it's a pleasant place to sit and watch the passing scene on Calle 3. The food is good and includes French, Thai, Mexican, Lebanese, and Panamanian dishes. The Thai soup is to die for, as is the fried camembert. Starters tend to be big and filling enough to make a meal out of. The French-Canadian owners are colorful characters and at this point practically Bocas institutions. In the last couple of years, the restaurant has gotten on a pizza kick, but even though the plate-size pies are thick and piled with toppings, they don't have much flavor. Dinner is a safer bet than lunch because the owners are more likely to be in the kitchen. The sangria is delicious.

⟨ Restaurante y Bar La Casbah (near the intersection of Avenida Norte, Avenida G, and Calle 4, cell 6477-4727, around 6–10 P.M. Tues.–Sat., US$10–15) is a consistently good choice for great food in a funky atmosphere. The restaurant is shoehorned into the open-air wooden porch of a small, ramshackle building (which also houses a hidden, bottom-of-the-barrel hostel). It has a friendly bohemian vibe, and it's a popular hangout for European expat residents. The owner-chef, Christopher, is an excellent cook who makes the best possible use of available ingredients. The French-influenced menu is small but changes daily. A growing demand in Bocas for vegetarian food has led to more salads and meat-free options such as falafel and gazpacho. But the beef fillet is especially good here—it's tender, full of flavor, and cooked perfectly. It's the best steak in town. If there are fresh mushrooms, the chef offers his fillets with a cognac and cream sauce that is absolutely delicious. The bacon shrimp rolls may sound odd, but the combination

works and makes for a surprisingly light and fresh appetizer. Vegetables are cooked exactly right; if you don't think you like eggplant, it's only because you haven't had it here. The bananas flambé is delicious, too.

⟨ Wine Bar (Calle 3, cell 6627-5906, 5–11 P.M. Mon.–Sat.) is a new place that recaptures the old romantic charm of Bocas town, which is getting harder to find. It has, bar none, the best wine selection in Panama. Christin Fjeld, a Norwegian expat and Bocas veteran, has established her Wine Bar on the second floor of an old Caribbean house. A veteran of two Sonoma wineries and a former caterer for Hollywood film shoots, she is a serious oenophile and gourmand. There is no wine list. Selection varies constantly and include wines from Argentina, Chile, Italy, France, Spain, and California. Tell Christin or the waitstaff what you like, and they'll pour a glass (US$4 and up) or bottle (US$16 and up) to suit your taste. You can choose from a small but eclectic tapas menu (US$4–10).

Dinner is offered to 10 guests a night, Monday–Friday. Reservations are a must. Diners have two options a night (US$12–15), which will vary depending on whatever happens to look good and fresh that morning. One of the best things about Wine Bar are the vegetable side dishes, which are fresh, good quality, and cooked perfectly. Desserts include a variety of homemade flavored truffles made from local organic chocolate. Imbibe in the main room, which is decorated with old-fashioned upholstered furniture, or sip and sup out on the veranda overlooking the Third Street action.

⟨ Raw Sushi and Martinis (Calle 1 across the street from Hotel Bocas del Toro, cell 6938-8473, noon–10 P.M. Tues.–Sun., less than US$10) is a small place that serves outstanding sushi and martinis, two things which are invariably disappointing elsewhere in Panama. For dessert try the banana and chocolate spring rolls. In the evenings a young Argentine woman plays jazz sax.

Gringo's (Avenida Central between Calle

4 and 5, cell 6852-1370, 12:30–9 P.M. Mon.– Sat., under US$8), as one might expect, is run by a gringo, but the food is Mexican. Gringo's serves quite tasty grub in a friendly, festive atmosphere. There are cozy booths inside, or you can sit out front on the sheltered porch. It offers among the better Mexican food you're likely to find in Panama. Everything is homemade, including the yummy chips and salsa. Gringo's is just west of the main street, in a residential area.

Alberto's Pizzeria (Calle 5 between Avenida E/Luis Russell and Avenida F, tel. 756-9066, 11 A.M.–3 P.M. and 5–11 P.M. Mon.–Sat., US$6–8) has the best pizza on the island. Ingredients are fresh, and the pizzas are lovingly made by the dedicated staff. A pizza feeds two moderately hungry people. The only drawback of this place at lunchtime is that, even though the dining area is open-sided, it doesn't have fans and can't catch a breeze, so it can be blazingly hot. Fortunately, Alberto's offers fresh lemonade and orange juice. There's also a full bar.

El Ultimo Refugio (cell 6726-9851, 5 P.M.–late Mon.–Fri., US$12–14) is easy to miss because it's at the far south of town, all the way down Calle 3 past the ferry pier. The eclectic menu changes daily, but can include such tempting dishes as tangy, delicious shrimp in passion fruit cream sauce, pork tenderloin with balsamic onion reduction, and chicken and shrimp Asian noodle salad. Popular starters include homemade chips and black bean dip, hummus, and pesto crostini. The food is good, the drinks are strong and well mixed, and the owner, Catherine, is a warm and friendly host. What's not to love?

Restaurante Chitré (Calle 3 near Avenida D, no phone, 6 A.M.–9 P.M. Mon.–Sat., 10 A.M.–9 P.M. Sun.) is not just the best *fonda* in town, but it also serves some of the tastiest food, period. Meat, rice, and a soda will set you back US$3. Try the *polla en salsa;* it's delicious. The place is a hole in the wall, but it has a front porch that's good for people-watching.

Om Café and Bar (Avenida E/Luis Russell and Calle 3, cell 6624-0898, generally 8 A.M.–noon 6–10 P.M. Fri.–Tues., full meals US$11–13) has long been one of the most appealing restaurants in town. Most people sit on the large, 2nd-floor veranda, but there's also a lively bar scene with hipster music playing on the sound system. The owner is Indian-Canadian, and when she runs the kitchen, expect delicious Indian home cooking. When she's not around, quality suffers. To be on the safe side, ask if Sunanda is there. The menu focuses on Northern Indian food, including pakoras, samosas, seekh kebabs, and tikkas. Vegetarians can choose from several options. Non-veg types should try the shrimp tikka, which is great. So are the inventive cocktail concoctions, such as the intense Tajmatini, made with vodka, lychee liqueur, and cranberry juice. The Bollywood (vodka, triple sec, and passion fruit) is refreshing and not too sweet. Cocktails go for around US$4–6. The bar is open until around midnight.

Many locals' favorite place for cheap *típico* food these days is **Beso de Dragón** (cell 6083-5746, 11 A.M.–9 P.M. day), a rustic open-air place across from the beach in the Feria del Mar isthmus. A big, surprisingly tasty *plato del día* (plate of the day) of meat, rice, *patacones*, lentils, and macaroni salad runs US$3.50–5. Seafood dishes are also available for US$8 and up. This place is popular with Panamanian tourists. It's a fair hike or US$0.60 taxi from downtown Bocas. It's a good place to stop on the way to or from Playa Bluff or Boca del Drago.

The Pirate (Calle 3 near Avenida C, no phone, 7 A.M.–11 P.M. daily, US$13–20) is a bar/restaurant on the water next to the downtown water-taxi piers. It serves so-so food, mostly seafood, and is relatively expensive. The best deal is its executive lunch, a full plate of *típico* food for less than US$6.

A good bet for breakfast is **Lili's Café** (Calle 1 and Avenida D, next to Tropical Suites,

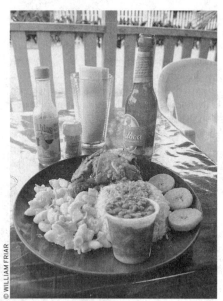

© WILLIAM FRIAR

lunchtime at Beso de Dragón

cell 6501-5487, www.kodiakbocas.com, 7 A.M.–4 P.M. Mon.–Tues. 7 A.M.–10 P.M. Wed.–Sat., 7 A.M.–noon Sun., US$5–10). It's a Bocas favorite as much for Lili's food as for her famous smile. Breakfast is served all day; omelets more closely resemble frittatas, but are tasty nonetheless. The French toast is delicious. Other offerings include sandwiches, seafood, salad, lasagna, *gallo pinto* (a rice-and-bean dish), and various daily specials. Be sure to try Lili's own Killin' Me Man hot sauce.

Starfish Coffee (Calle 3 near Avenida B, no phone, 8 A.M.–6:30 P.M. Tues.–Fri., 9 A.M.–6:30 P.M. Sat.) has been going through a rough patch lately, but it's still the closest thing to a real coffeehouse in Bocas. It traditionally has been a good bet for breakfast, which it serves 8 A.M.–noon. Most full breakfasts are around US$5–6. Attention Brits: They don't call it that, but they serve a Bocas version of a full English breakfast here, substituting chipotle for baked beans and adding an extra helping of

grease. There's a large selection of hot and cold coffee, tea, and chocolate drinks (made with organic Bocas chocolate). Lunch and dinner options include sandwiches, salads, tapas, and fish and chips. There's a book exchange and a newsstand that carries new and used magazines to buy or borrow.

Panadería y Dulcería La Alemaña (Calle 2 near Avenida E/Luis Russell, tel. 757-9436, 7 A.M.–8 P.M. daily), across the street from Om Café, offers so-so fresh bread and tasty buns at cheap prices.

Markets

Super Gourmet (Calle 3 near the ferry pier, 9 A.M.–7 P.M. Mon.–Sat.) is a godsend for expatriates hungering for something beyond the usual local fare. It has a nice selection of goodies, including fresh bread, cheese, fruit, organic Bocas chocolate, gourmet Boquete coffee, and many items that only in the backwaters of Bocas would be considered "gourmet" (Old El Paso salsa, ramen noodles, Vienna sausages). It also carries pricey but not necessarily good wine. The best things about the place are its new chocolate bar and its deli counter, which offers salads and sandwiches for around US$3–6, lasagna, quiches, pastries, and so on. The sandwiches are only so-so, but they're big. The cookies, many made with Bocas chocolate, are killer.

Tropical Markets (Calle 1 and Avenida E/Luis Russell, 9 A.M.–6 P.M. Mon.–Sat.) is a series of food stalls in an odd two-story building on the east side of town. The stalls carry meat, seafood, produce, wine, and other groceries, with a more upscale selection than is normally found in Bocas stores.

It's said there are now nearly two dozen *chinos* (mini-supermarkets) in Bocas town alone. Certainly you're never more than a short walk from one anywhere in town. Several are on Calle 3, just north and south of Avenida D. **Supermercado La Estrella de la Isla** (Calle 3, 7 A.M.–midnight daily) is next door to Hotel

Bocas town has many colorful dining options, like The Pirate.

Laguna. **Supermercado Cayo Zapatilla** (Calle 3) is a similar place across the street. Both have produce stands on the street. The newer Supercentro Cristina is bigger but not really better. **Supermercado Isla Colón** (7:30 A.M.–11 P.M. daily) is on the southeast corner of Calle 3 and Avenida D.

The basic **Supermarket Hawaii** (Calle 6 and Avenida G, 7:30 A.M.–10:30 P.M. daily) is more convenient for those staying north of downtown.

INFORMATION AND SERVICES
Tourist Information and Maps

The Bocas Info Center (Calle 1 between Jampan Tours and Starfleet Scuba, no phone, 10 A.M.–8 P.M.) is an attempt by local business owners to provide visitors with basic tourist information. The staff speak English and Spanish and can answer a range of questions about Bocas.

The tiny **ANAM** office (Calle 1, on the water northeast of the park, tel. 757-9244, 8 A.M.–noon and 1–4 P.M. Mon.–Fri.) issues park permits and sometimes has marginally useful maps and brochures of Parque Nacional Marino Isla Bastimentos. Entrance to the marine park is US$10 per person. The fee to camp is another US$5 per tent. The fees can also be paid to the ranger on the Cayos Zapatillas, but those planning to camp there should check in with ANAM in any case to check on current conditions and rules. The office sometimes has information on other natural attractions of the area, including San San Pondsack. It's one block east of Parque Bolívar.

Medical Services

Farmacia Rosa Blanca (Calle 3 next to Bocas Marine and Tours, tel. 757-9560, 8:30 A.M.–9 P.M. Mon.–Sat., 10 A.M.–noon and 7–9 P.M. Sun.) is a full-service pharmacy and general store. It also carries a range of electronics and accessories (USB sticks, cables) and basic snorkeling gear.

Money

A branch of **Banco Nacional de Panamá** (Avenida E/Luis Russell and Calle 4, 8 A.M.–3 P.M. Mon.–Fri., 9 A.M.–noon Sat.) is in Bocas town on the way to the airport. It has a 24-hour ATM (the only one on the island, which sometimes goes out of service) and cashes travelers checks.

While credit cards are increasingly accepted in Bocas, many transactions are still cash only. This can be a big hassle for those who want to book hotels ahead of time. Some places charge a fee for credit-card use; be sure to ask. It's usually best to bring all the cash you think you might need during a stay.

Post Office

The post office (8 A.M.–4 P.M. Mon.–Fri., 8 A.M.–noon Sat.) is in the Palacio Municipal.

Internet Access

With the proliferation of free wireless Internet

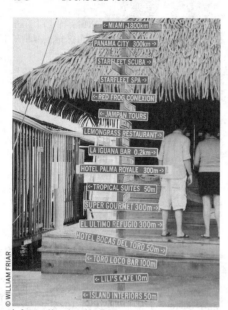
information booth, Bocas town

just about everywhere, those with laptops or smartphones may have little need for Internet cafés, which are increasingly thin on the ground. Hostels and some of the hotels also tend to have computers that guests can use to connect to the Internet.

Internet Galaxy (Calle 2 and Avenida D, 9 A.M.–8 P.M. daily) offers Internet access for US$1.50/hour. There's another, nameless Internet place around the corner on Calle 1 across the street from the police station that is open 9 A.M.–10 P.M. It charges US$1.61/hour and offers Skype calls.

Visas and Officialdom

There is an Immigration and Naturalization office, **Migración y Naturalización** (tel./fax 757-9263, 8 A.M.–4 P.M. Mon.–Fri.), in the Palacio Municipal at the north end of the park. But for most immigration concerns, foreigners still have to go to the main office in Changuinola, which is on the mainland, a lengthy bus or taxi trip away, or to David or Panama City.

Laundry

Lavamático Don Pardo (Avenida Norte, 8 A.M.–8 P.M. Mon.–Sat.), between Casa Max and Restaurante y Bar La Casbah, charges US$5 to wash and dry.

Marinas

The archipelago, long a haven for yachters, now supports three marinas. **Bocas Yacht Club and Marina** (tel. 757-9800, fax 757-9801, www.bocasmarina.com) is just southwest of Bocas town, across a small bay. It has floating docks that accommodate boats up to 100 feet long. The marina also offers some boat maintenance, laundry, charter, and brokerage services. There's an open-air bar.

Marina Carenero (tel./fax 757-9242, www.careeningcaymarina.com), on the west side of Isla Carenero close to Bocas town, accommodates boats up to 60 feet long. Laundry, boat maintenance, and Internet services are also available. There's a marina near the entrance to Red Frog Beach, and others are in the works.

Educational Courses

Spanish by the Sea (Calle 4 and Avenida A, tel. 757-9518, cell 6592-0775, www.spanishatlocations.com) is a flexible Spanish-language program run by a friendly staff that operates out of a home in the heart of Bocas town. Prices depend on course length, size of group, and hours per day of instruction. For instance, a five-day group course, with four hours a day of instruction, is US$180 per person. An intensive, 40 hour per week private course would cost US$440.

Students can spend part of their course at the school's sister facilities in Boquete, Panama City, and Turrialba, Costa Rica. The school can also arrange tours and outdoor adventures for an extra fee. It's also possible to combine courses with volunteer work, including help with a sea-turtle conservation project March–June, for those who want to practice their Spanish in meaningful situations or just help out.

Students can stay at the school's hostel for

US$10 pp for a shared room with shared bath, US$18 pp for a private room with shared bath, or US$25–30 s/d for a private room with private bath. The school also offers accommodations in town, ranging from homestays to vacation rentals.

Habla Ya (Avenida G and Calle 9, tel. 757-7352, www.hablayapanama.com), the younger sister of the Habla Ya language school in Boquete, recently opened up north of town in Saigon near the Centro de Salud and the cemetery, shortly before the road forks on the way to the Feria del Mar. Group lessons are US$175–255 per week; private lessons are US$275–355. Hourly rates are also available. The school can arrange homestays, hotels for any budget, and vacation rentals. The school also offers a wide range of activities and outdoor adventures.

A Florida-based nonprofit called the **Institute for Tropical Ecology and Conservation (ITEC)** (U.S. tel. 352/367-9128, www.itec-edu.org) has a biological field station in Boca del Drago. It's a private outfit unaffiliated with any university, but it draws its faculty from various U.S. and Latin American universities. It offers three-week winter and four-week summer courses in tropical ecology. Tuition is US$1,850 and US$2,050 respectively. The fee includes room and board.

GETTING THERE

Regardless of their final destination in the archipelago, travelers must first get to Bocas town, on Isla Colón. There are two ways to do this—by plane or by land and water taxi/ferry.

By Air

There are a couple of daily flights between Panama City and Bocas del Toro (US$113 each way, about 1.25 hours). The sudden collapse of Aeroperlas in 2012 meant there are no longer flights between David and Bocas, unless Air Panama or a new airline picks up the route.

Flight schedules change more frequently for Bocas than other domestic destinations in Panama. Flights can also fill up fast, especially during holidays. Book as far in advance as possible, and double-check departure times a day or two before your flight.

A small Costa Rican airline, Nature Air, flies between Bocas and several destinations in Costa Rica, including San José.

The only airport in the archipelago is on Isla Colón, on the edge of Bocas town. The little airport is on the west side of town, along Avenida E. Those without much luggage will probably find it easy to walk to most of the town's hotels, but a taxi or *transporte cooperativa* van between the airport and town costs US$1 per person.

Air Panama (tel./fax 316-9000, www.fly-airpanama.com) has two daily flights from Panama City to Bocas: 6:45 A.M. and 3:30 P.M. Monday–Saturday, and 8 A.M. and 3:30 P.M. Sunday. Flights from Bocas to Panama City are 8 A.M. and 4:45 P.M. Monday–Saturday, and 9:15 A.M. and 4:45 P.M. Sunday.

The Costa Rica–based **Nature Air** (Costa Rica tel. 506/2299-6000, U.S./Canada toll-free tel. 800/235-9272, www.natureair.com) offers three weekly nonstop flights between Bocas and San José, Costa Rica, as well as connecting service to and from other Costa Rican destinations. The schedule varies depending on the time of year.

By Land and Water

The logistics of getting to and from the islands from the mainland aren't that complicated, but they can be confusing to those unfamiliar with the area. Almirante is the mainland port for the Bocas archipelago. The water taxis and the car ferry leave from there. The last water taxis of the day leave Almirante for the islands at 6:30 P.M. After that, travelers will have to spend the night on the mainland, most likely in Changuinola or Almirante. Changuinola has a broader range of accommodations and services;

© WILLIAM FRIAR

A slow car ferry runs between Bocas town and Almirante.

neither town is the safest place at night. A better option for those who can afford it is La Escapada, 64 kilometers east of Almirante.

Getting to the islands by water taxi often involves fending off *boleteros* (ticket touts) who work for commissions from specific hotels and water-taxi operations. They may offer to carry travelers' luggage to the water-taxi pier for a small tip. Those who want to help local people can find many better ways than handing over spare change to these kids, which is just going to mean more hassle for the next tourist who wanders through.

Taxi drivers sometimes steer passengers to a particular water-taxi service or try to overcharge passengers, for instance by charging as much per person as locals would pay per carload. Be sure to clarify the deal before getting in the cab.

Some enterprising characters sometimes offer a kind of tourist shuttle service at the Costa Rican border in which they meet travelers—sometimes before they even cross over to Panama—and offer to usher them all the way to the islands by taxi and water taxi. They charge significantly more for this service than you'd pay on your own, and they'll steer you to places that pay them commission.

ALMIRANTE VIA OTHER PARTS OF PANAMA

There are frequent minibuses between Almirante and David, and one daily bus between Almirante and Panama City. A second daily bus is sometimes added.

For those driving, the land link between the islands and the rest of Panama is the Fortuna Road. It connects Chiriquí, a small Pacific-side town on the Interamericana about 15 kilometers east of David, with Chiriquí Grande, about 100 kilometers away on the Caribbean coast. The route takes travelers over the Continental Divide and the huge Fortuna Dam and hydroelectric plant. It's a scenic drive on a good road, but be careful as it averages more than one auto accident a week. Driving the length of the Fortuna Road takes a little under two hours.

The road descends the Caribbean slope quickly and soon reaches the hot and humid flatlands near the coast. Pass the village of Punta Peña. There'll be a crossroads ahead, with a 24-hour gas station and restaurant. Straight leads to the oil-port town of Chiriquí Grande, which has nothing to offer travelers since a ferry service to the islands stopped running years ago.

Instead, turn left at the gas station onto the new road to Almirante. This is a lovely, 70-kilometer drive that takes about an hour. But slash-and-burn farmers and subsistence ranchers have followed the road, and the lush tropical evergreen forest along this entire strip of coast is disappearing fast. Entire hillsides are sliding down into the road, so be careful. It's a disturbing example of how quickly nature can be devastated in the tropics; at this rate, the land here will be of little value to anyone in a few years.

There's a bridge between kilometer markers 8 and 9. This is a good place for a rest stop. Pull over on the right just after the bridge, or turn left and park near the bank of the little river. About five minutes upriver is a massive boulder in the middle of the stream with **petroglyphs** near the top. If the weather is dry, bring a water container to splash river water on the boulder; it's much easier to make out the petroglyphs when they're wet. There are trails on both sides of the river; the petroglyphs are easiest to see from the east side. Cross back over the bridge on foot and follow the path down by the river. When the trail gets very rocky, head uphill, which allows one to look down on the boulder. If you can't find it, and a local is hanging around, ask him or her to show the way. A tip of US$0.25–0.50 for this would be appreciated. The trail on the west side of the river leads into some lovely forest and a waterfall about a half hour away.

ALMIRANTE VIA COSTA RICA

For those coming from or going to Costa Rica, the closest border crossing is a rickety bridge over the Río Sixaola that connects the flyspeck town of Guabito (Panama side) with the flyspeck town of Sixaola (Costa Rica side). Travelers must be sure to go through customs and immigration on both sides of the border. Try to avoid arriving at the border at lunchtime, when the offices on both sides can close at different times, stranding travelers for up to two hours. Taxis and buses wait for passengers right below the border crossing in Guabito.

There are no direct buses between Costa Rica or the border and Almirante, the port for water taxis to the islands. They instead run to and from Changuinola, which is the closest transportation hub to the border. However, buses and taxis run constantly between Changuinola and Almirante, making for easy connections.

There is now a simpler way to deal with all these logistics. The **Caribe Shuttle** (pier next to La Buga Dive Center in Bocas town, tel. 757-7048, Costa Rica tel. 506/2750-0626, www.caribeshuttle.com) is a service that runs travelers between Bocas and hotels in Costa Rica. Space is limited, so advance reservations are a must. Surfers can bring boards up to nine feet long for a US$7 fee.

In Bocas, the Caribe Shuttle transports passengers by boat from the company's pier in Bocas town to the mainland, where they continue by bus to the Guabito-Sixaola border crossing and then on to Puerto Viejo, Cahuita, or Manzanillo in Costa Rica. The shuttle leaves Bocas at 8 A.M. and 12:30 P.M. daily. The company no longer offers hotel pickup in Bocas; passengers must make their own way to the pier.

For the trip from Costa Rica to Bocas, hotel pickup takes place 7–7:30 A.M. and 11:30 A.M.–noon, depending on the hotel.

In either direction, the trip costs US$32 each way between Bocas and Puerto Viejo. Add US$6 each way for pickup/drop-off in the Costa Rican towns of Cahuita or Manzanillo. The company also offers transfers to or from other parts of Costa Rica, including Arenal/La Fortuna, Monteverde, Tortugero, and San

José, but these are not timed to link up with the Costa Rica–Bocas leg; expect to spend a night in one of the intermediate Costa Rica stops.

ALMIRANTE VIA BOCAS TOWN WATER TAXIS

Two—sometimes three—water-taxi companies run between the mainland town of Almirante and Bocas town on Isla Colón. All have daily departures for Almirante roughly every 30–45 minutes, depending on demand, 6 A.M.– 6:30 P.M. The trip takes about 25 minutes. The fare is US$5 each way at either place. Water-taxi prices stay pretty stable, but fuel costs occasionally bump them up a bit.

Boats sometimes fill to capacity. Those with a tight schedule should book their departure from Bocas the night before they intend to leave, but this can only be done in person. Don't plan tight transfers, as water taxis' schedules are loose.

Bocas Marine and Tours (Almirante tel. 758-4085, Bocas town tel./fax 757-9033, www.bocasmarinetours.com) is the first place you'll come to in Almirante. In Bocas town, its pier is midway down Calle 3, near Transparente Tours and Restaurante Le Pirate.

Expreso Taxi 25 (Almirante tel. 758-3498, Bocas town tel. 757-9028) is farther down the street in Almirante. In Bocas town, its pier is near the police station.

In Almirante, those with their own vehicle can park in guarded parking for US$3–5 per day at Leiza's, on the road just before the water-taxi piers. There's a sign.

ALMIRANTE VIA BOCAS TOWN FERRY

Few will want to fool with the painfully slow **Ferry Palanga** (tel. 391-0350, 261-0350, 229-1742, or 229-1639, cell 6615-6674) that runs between Almirante and Bocas town. It doesn't run often in any case. Only those who insist on bringing a vehicle to Bocas town—something there is very little reason to do—should bother with the ferry. It runs Monday–Saturday,

leaving Almirante at 8 A.M. and returning from Isla Colón at 4 P.M. The trip takes 1.5 hours. The fare is US$1.50 for foot passengers, US$0.75 for kids, US$2 for a bike, US$10 for a motorcycle, US$15 for a car, and US$30 for a four-wheel drive. The ferry pier in Almirante is past the turnoff to the water taxis; look for the Texaco sign. The Bocas town ferry dock is at the southern end of Calle 3, across the street from the Hotel Bahía.

GETTING AROUND
By Water

Many places on Isla Colón are more cheaply and easily reached by boat, which is also the only way to get to the other islands in the archipelago. Fares are standardized to most destinations. Rising gas prices may push these rates up. Freelance boats operate a casual water-taxi service between the islands, though with each passing year the service becomes more organized and comfortable. Any legitimate taxi boat should be equipped with life jackets and a sun canopy. These boats stop constantly throughout the day at the town piers. Boats operate less frequently at night, and the lack of proper lighting on most can make it a riskier prospect; try to travel in daylight. Boats leave when they fill up. Less-common destinations may require hiring the whole boat; it may be more economical and efficient to visit these places as part of a full-fledged boat tour.

A water-taxi collective operates in downtown Bocas town. It's just to the right as you face Bocas Marine and Tours. It focuses on Bocas-Bastimentos transport, but will find you a boat to wherever you want to go. Another cooperative operates from a landing right next to the Barco Hundido. As you face the bar, the boardwalk to the landing will be on your right. Standard prices are posted, including rates to popular surf spots.

The standard per-person fare is US$1 to the nearest point on Isla Carenero, US$3 to Old

Bank and US$6 to Red Frog Beach on Isla Bastimentos, and US$3 to Solarte. Carenero is less than 5 minutes away; it takes about 10 minutes to get to Solarte or Old Bank. Boats can sometimes drop clients on the beaches on the east side of Isla Colón. The surf can sometimes be quite rough, though. Expect to pay more if you're the only one in the boat, or wait until there's at least one other passenger. Rates double to Red Frog Beach and other more distant locations at night.

By Land

There are only two major roads beyond Bocas town: one that extends up the east coast of Isla Colón, dead-ending at Playa Bluff, and a second that cuts diagonally across the island to Boca del Drago. There's no need to ferry a car over, as it's easy to get around the island by taxi, bus, or rented bike or motorcycle.

There is a minibus service, **Brisas del Mar** (cell 6492-6166 or 6708-8419, US$5 round-trip) connecting Bocas town and Boca del Drago. It leaves from the northwest end of Parque Bolívar Monday–Friday at 7 A.M.,

10 A.M., noon, 2 P.M., 4 P.M., and 6 P.M., returning at 8 A.M., 11 A.M., 1 P.M., 3 P.M., 5 P.M., and 7 P.M. This schedule changes from time to time, depending on demand. This is a slow ride, as the bus picks up locals all along the route. It usually takes about an hour.

Taxis constantly trawl Calle 3 looking for customers. The fare to or from the airport and anywhere in town, including all the way to the northern waterfront at Saigon, is US$1 per person. Fares within town are US$0.50. The one-way fare to the end of Playa Bluff is US$10–12, depending on the condition of the road and mood of the driver. A round-trip ride to Boca del Drago is US$30 and to La Gruta US$20. *Transporte colectiva* vans operate in town and to the airport, also for US$1 per person. Flag them down just as you would a taxi.

Bike and scooter rental places come and go, but there are always several to choose from. A popular place that has been around a surprisingly long time is **Ixa's Bicycle World** (Avenida Norte between Calle 5 and Calle 6, tel. 757-9585, 8 A.M.–7 P.M.). It rents bikes for US$8 for a half day, US$12 per day, or US$15 for 24 hours.

BOCAS DEL TORO

Isla Carenero

This little island is just a banana's throw across the water from Bocas town. Because it's so close to the busy waterfront and is pretty built up itself, it's not a popular tourist destination, it's more like a suburb of Bocas town. But it's home to a couple of appealing places to stay.

The side of the island facing Isla Colón is rather densely populated, with lots of basic houses squeezed next to each other on the waterfront. The side that faces Bastimentos is more deserted; there's little there except for a couple of small hotels and a bit of beach. The north side of the island has pounding surf, but the coastline is rather rugged and more mud and farmland than beach. Actually, the whole

island is ringed by just a narrow band of sandy beach. Visitors have to travel to one of the other islands for big, spectacular beaches. The island is notorious for especially voracious *chitras* (sand flies).

SIGHTS AND RECREATION

It's possible to walk around the entire perimeter of the island, but be prepared for a bit of an adventure rather than a leisurely walk. It can take up to two hours to go the whole way around, and there are sections that require scrambling up muddy hills, dropping several feet, slipping through barbed-wire fences, avoiding pounding surf, and negotiating slippery, jagged rocks.

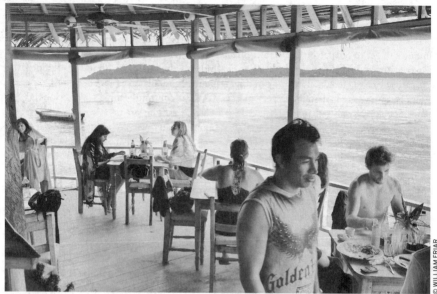

© WILLIAM FRIAR

Bibi's on the Beach, Isla Carenero

Carenero is popular with surfers thanks to a long, barreling reef break off the north side of the island that's considered one of the best waves in Bocas. Called simply Carenero, it's just a five-minute boat ride from Bocas town and thus can get crowded. The reef is shallow; wear booties.

SHOPPING

Carenero has the best gift shop on the islands. **Treasures of the Turquoise Crab** (tel. 757-9157, www.careeningcay.com) at the Careening Cay Resort is an air-conditioned store selling good quality local and imported jewelry and souvenirs. These include tagua carvings, Emberá-Wounaan masks, and so on. The *chaquiras* (Ngöbe-Buglé necklaces) here are among the best I've seen in Panama, with the most elaborate going for about US$50. The owner is a professional jeweler, so there are original creations as well.

ACCOMMODATIONS AND FOOD

Places to stay on Carenero vary from hostel dorms to fairly upscale little hotels. Most have a restaurant attached. A walking path along the water links all of them.

The **Careening Cay Resort** (tel. 757-9157, www.careeningcay.com, starts at US$42.90 s/d, including breakfast) is set in a garden near the water overlooking Isla Colón. It is composed of six wooden bungalows and an open-air restaurant, the Cosmic Crab Café, over the water. Three of the bungalows (US$97.90 s/d) have two rooms, with a queen-size bed, twin-size bunk beds, and a fully equipped kitchenette with gas stove, microwave, and fridge. The room divider doesn't reach the ceiling, limiting privacy. There is also a one-room bungalow with queen bed (US$75.60 s/d). A newer bungalow is twice the size of the two-bedroom ones and sleeps six or more people (US$141.60). All the bungalows have a TV and DVD player and hot-water bathrooms, and all stays include a buffet breakfast and free use of kayaks. Additional people in all bungalows are US$11 per person.

There are also more basic cabins, ranging from US$42.90 s/d for a small room without air-conditioning to US$53.90 s/d for a bigger one that does have air-conditioning. The owners have recently added some small budget cabins on a boardwalk right on the water. These are basic and little bigger than their queen beds, but they have private bathrooms, wall fans, and a view over the water (US$64.90 s/d). Stays in all these economy accommodations include breakfast and free use of kayaks. A pool is in the works.

The restaurant attached to the resort is the ☾ **Cosmic Crab Café** (tel. 757-9157, www. careeningcay.com, noon–9 P.M. Tues.–Sun., US$6–10), a friendly place that's especially popular with the gringo crowd. The bar and main dining area is in a large *rancho* over the water, connected by a boardwalk to a line of small private *ranchos* which are gradually being converted into simple cabins for overnight guests.

Offerings include seafood, salads, soups, and burgers. The restaurant is known for its crab cakes, at least when crab is available. At other times they make the cakes with other fish, such as red snapper, which is delicious, as are the conch fritters. This is also a good place to go for hummus and falafel. The wife in the couple that own the place is a mixologist and is always creating new concoctions, which are enormous and start around US$5. Her ginger snap martini is refreshing and potent. There's a whole line of ice-cream-based drinks with names like Sex in the Mud (vanilla vodka, Kahlua, crème de cacao, chocolate ice cream, and a frozen banana). There's a sunset dinner three-course special from 4–6 P.M. for US$8, and this is a place where you can actually see the sun set.

The **Aqua Lounge Hostel & Bar** (cell 6456-4659 or 6929-4863, bocasaqualounge@gmail. com, www.bocasaqualounge.info, US$11 pp, including breakfast) is built onto a dock strung with hammocks, and when it gets too warm, guests can roll right into the sea for a swim or a bounce on the water trampoline. The shared bathrooms have hot-water showers. The two dorm rooms have a total of 11 beds, and though they're pleasant enough, some may find them dark and a bit claustrophobic. But all the extras make this place more like a tropical bohemian playground than a backpackers' crash pad. Those on a tight budget can string a hammock for US$6. Private rooms are US$25. Stays include breakfast and the use of the communal kitchen.

Guests need to be comfortable sharing their surroundings with partying hordes, as the attached **Aqua Lounge Bar** is a popular nightspot. It opens around 10 A.M. and stays open late every night. The big nights here are Saturday (reggae night) and Wednesday (ladies' night). The Aqua Lounge is directly across from the Barco Hundido in Bocas town, making it easy to bar hop.

Casa Acuario (tel. 757-9565, casaacuario@ aol.com, www.casaacuario.com, US$88–99 s/d, a/c) is a house built right over the water that offers five cute, spacious, and sunny wood-paneled rooms with modern bathrooms, and satellite TV. It has its own small stretch of beach. There's a balcony upstairs with a view of the ocean, Isla Colón, and the mountains on the distant shore. Guests are welcome to use the kitchen. A third and fourth person in the room are another US$11 each. The place has a family vibe and not a whole lot of privacy, so pray that your neighbors are *simpático*.

Hotel Tierra Verde (tel. 757-9903, cell 6615-5911, www.hoteltierraverde.com, starts at US$71.50 s/d, including breakfast, a/c) is a three-story, surfer-oriented hotel set back from the beach. Built in 2001, it has seven rooms with dark-wood paneling, all with hot-water bathrooms. A two-bedroom suite (US$165 s/d) was added a couple of years ago. It occupies the 3rd floor and has a private balcony, sitting room, minifridge, and cable TV. It's quite attractive. Rates for the other rooms are

US$71.50 s/d with a garden view and US$82.50 for an ocean view. Additional guests are US$11 each. Stays include a continental breakfast, use of kayaks, and wireless Internet access. Guests can also use the Internet-connected computer in the lobby. The hotel arranges a variety of tours.

Doña Mara (tel. 757-9551, donamara10@hotmail.com, www.hoteldonamara.com, US$75 s/d, a/c), on the east side of the island, facing Bastimentos, is a cinderblock building with six simple but pleasant and brightly painted rooms, all with satellite TV and tile floors. The place is well-maintained. It's on a small beach and has a bar and restaurant.

Bibi's on the Beach (tel. 757-9137, 8 A.M.–9 P.M. daily, US$5–10) is a good-size split-level *rancho* right above breaking surf, with a soul-soothing view of the ocean, Bastimentos, and Solarte. Bibi's inspires a lot of affection locally. It offers a few traditional Caribbean dishes as well as salads, sandwiches, pastas, and a variety of Italian- and French-influenced dishes. "Bibi's ceviche" is an unusual and zippy take on ceviche, made with pineapple, passion fruit, and yuca chips. It's refreshing on a hot afternoon. Main dishes, such as the tasty chicken *criollo*, are large and filling.

The **Pickled Parrot** (tel. 757-9093, 11 A.M.–late daily, US$5–6), near the end of the path on the east side of Carenero, consists of a large *rancho* built onto a pier where one can watch waves crashing under one's feet. The sea view is terrific. It serves bar food and half-pound burgers (US$5.25). It's a relaxing place to drink a beer or a quite good blended cocktail with fresh tropical fruit and meditate on the islands and sea. It's run by a colorful gringo whose mercurial mood swings are part of the entertainment (one local describes him as a "disgruntled pirate"). Wednesday is karaoke night, a popular time to visit for many and an excellent time to stay away for others. The kitchen closes at 9 P.M., but the bar stays open until the last customer teeters out. The last water taxi to Isla Colón (US$1.50) leaves at around midnight. The joint has a few rooms for rent if you get stranded, or you can make your way to the other side of the island and try to flag down a boat running between the Aqua Lounge and Bocas town if the bars are still open.

GETTING THERE

There are few services of any kind on Carenero, but it's less than five minutes by boat from Bocas town. Water taxis run frequently between Carenero and the two town piers. To get to Bastimentos from Carenero, it's easier to take a boat back to Bocas town and get a Bastimentos-bound boat from there.

Isla Bastimentos

This big, beautiful island (52 square kilometers) has a lot to offer nature lovers. The north shore has pounding surf and miles of gorgeous sandy beaches, some of which attract sea turtles in nesting season. The protected waters on the southeast side of the island, between Cayo Crawl and Punta Vieja, are shallow and glassy, making it easy to explore a large underwater playground of coral and sponges. To the southwest are mangrove islands. And the island itself is home to forest that harbors many exotic and endangered species, including the famous red poison-dart frog *(Oophaga pumilio),* that many come to the island to see. The midsection of the island and some of its surrounding waters are part of a national marine park, Parque Nacional Marino Isla Bastimentos.

Though about 1,350 people live on the island, most are concentrated in the largely Afro-Caribbean town of Old Bank on its western tip, and in the Ngöbe village of Quebrada de Sal (Salt Creek). They're rather ragged places and there isn't much to see, but they're both culturally interesting and worth a visit.

The attractions on Bastimentos are spread widely apart. The town of Old Bank, just 10 minutes by boat from Bocas town, is the closest to Isla Colón. Cayo Crawl is at the southern tip, separated by a shallow channel from Isla Popa. The southeast side is sheltered, with glassy water, coral gardens, the Ngöbe village of Quebrada de Sal, and access to the Cayos Zapatillas. Lovely beaches with pounding surf, the famous red frogs, and turtle-nesting spots are on the northern side. Exploring the forested interior, part of which belongs to the marine park, requires a guide to reach caves and a freshwater lake.

SIGHTS
Old Bank
The hot and humid town of Old Bank, known to many simply as Bastimentos, is on the western tip of the island, not far from Isla Carenero and Bocas town. Most of its residents live close to each other in crumbling, zinc-roofed homes perched on the waterfront or on the hillside behind it. Its residents are mostly descendants of West Indian immigrants, and the place has a mellow, strongly Caribbean vibe. There's always loud music playing—sometimes live, if you're lucky.

The town is poor, trash-strewn, and has little to see, but it still has lots of local color, and it's the best place in the islands to hear Guari-Guari, a Bocas-specific variety of so-called Panamanian Creole English. It's fascinating to listen to and nearly impossible for the uninitiated to make much sense of, even though it derives primarily from English.

Old Bank is not for everyone, especially as a place to stay. Some people love it, particularly backpackers and surfers who want to experience the real Bocas. Two parallel concrete paths extend the length of town. A trail to the north-side beaches starts at the east end of town.

Bahía Honda
This mangrove-ringed bay on the southern side of Bastimentos has become popular in recent years with travelers interested in exploring the long, mysterious jungle **cave** near its shore. But there's more there than that, including the Ngöbe community of Bahía Honda, which totals about 200 people in 40 families and welcomes visitors. It has a few attractions of possible interest, including a new restaurant and a unique jungle lodge.

The Ngöbe's rustic, thatched-roof **Bahía Honda Restaurant** (cell 6726-0968, 6619-5364, or 6592-5162; ask for Rutilio Milton, US$5) on the shoreline caters to travelers and supports the local community. The restaurant is open for lunch only, and only with advance notice. Call ahead of time or arrange a visit through your hotel.

There is no real village as such and the Ngöbe have lost many of their traditional ways, but Ngöbe women can often be seen making traditional *nagua* dresses, *chakara* woven bags, and *chaquira* beaded necklaces. These are for sale. A child's *nagua* makes a cute present for young girls (US$10; the adult-size ones are US$30). Visitors can hike surrounding trails or try their luck in a *cayuco* (dugout canoe). Be careful—they're very easy to flip.

The boat trip up the windy creek to the Bahía Honda bat cave is pretty cool, especially if you travel with a guide who takes it slow and is good at spotting wildlife. Be patient and you may see three-toed sloths, iguanas, and caimans. The vegetation is striking as well. Black, red, and white mangroves grow on either side, and where the boat ties up, there are enormous stands of bamboo and absolutely massive gnarled old trees. The cave is a short walk away, with its bats, stalactites, and water that in places can come up to your neck.

◖ Cayo Crawl
Boats from Isla Colón that approach Bastimentos

from the south pass a series of idyllic mangrove islands, protected as part of the marine park, before coming to Cayo Crawl, a shallow channel between Isla Bastimentos and Isla Popa. Cayo Crawl is sometimes called Cayo Coral, and in English it's called Crawl Cay or Coral Cay. It's about a half hour by boat from Bocas town.

The water here is a luminous light green, smooth as glass, and in some places only a meter deep before hitting sandy bottom. The area attracts lots of tropical fish. It's an easy, relaxing place to snorkel or splash around.

Some tour operators, wanting to save on gas, take snorkelers only as far as Cayo Crawl and call it a day. Given that coral gardens don't start until one rounds the point and heads up the southeast coast of Bastimentos—at which point there are kilometers of them—you should find out ahead of time exactly where the boat is heading.

The channel harbors a few rustic thatched-hut restaurants, built on stilts over the water, that are tourist destinations in their own right. Tours to Cayos Zapatillas and around Bastimentos usually include a stop at one of these photogenic spots. These are bare-bones establishments, but at least you know the seafood is fresh. Expect to pay around US$8–10 for fish, or more than twice that for lobster.

The water is so shallow and clear that diners can watch slender needlefish and brilliant parrotfish, angelfish, snapper, and other aquatic life cavort just off the boardwalk. The fish in the area are so spoiled by free feedings that Restaurante Cayo Crawl attracts a couple of tame barracuda.

For those who want to eat at any of these places, since service tends to proceed at a languorous Caribbean pace, place your orders ahead of time and then go snorkeling until the food's ready.

Cayo Crawl to Punta Vieja

The sheltered waters from Cayo Crawl to Punta Vieja, a point about eight kilometers up the southeast coast of Bastimentos, offer some colorful snorkeling. The sea here is so shallow and

calm it's like swimming in a tropical aquarium. There's a variety of coral and sponges and lots of small but dazzling fish. However, the visibility can be disappointing. A few small hotels have been built along the coast, but this is still a remarkably isolated and tranquil spot. Waves are so gentle here that fish swim right up to the narrow strips of sandy beach.

C North Shore Beaches

The sea along the northern side of Bastimentos is generally much too rough to do more than get one's feet wet. Swimmers should be aware of the risk of riptides. But there are several spectacularly beautiful beaches here. The one most popular with sea turtles is **Playa Larga,** to the east in Parque Nacional Marino Isla Bastimentos. The one most popular with tourists is **Red Frog Beach,** which is also the easiest to get to, as a road connects it to a yacht marina on the tranquil southern side of the island. There have been reports of thefts from these beaches. Do not leave valuables unattended.

The sea is often too choppy to land boats on the beaches. An exception is **Playa Polo,** which is partly protected because waves break on rocks about 100 meters offshore. This means it's easier to go for a swim here, but it also means it's more likely to have visitors than some of the other beaches, and it's far too small to accommodate many people comfortably. There are nicer beaches farther west.

If the sea is rough, the best way to get to these beaches is from the southern side of Bastimentos, where the waters are protected, and walk to the northern shore. A couple of paths, including a wide road, lead from a yacht marina about 10 minutes by boat east of Old Bank. This is the most popular way to get to Red Frog Beach.

A scenic but more strenuous way to go is to walk over the hills from Old Bank. This trail starts toward the eastern edge of town, just past the soccer field and trash pile. There are now signs pointing to the start of the trail, but ask

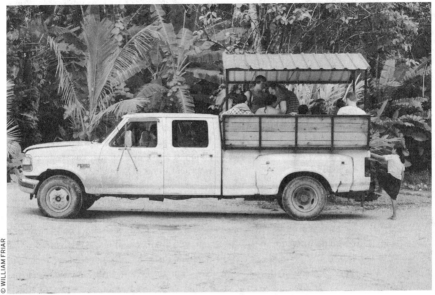

© WILLIAM FRIAR

Red Frog Beach shuttle

for directions to the beach (*playa,* pronounced PLY-yah) if you can't find the way. It's a very pretty walk over a hill to the beach, with panoramic views from the summit. The walk takes half an hour at a moderate pace. Part of the trail leads through private property; if the landowner is around, it's a good idea to pay a US$1 toll to pass through it. The trail can get muddy and slippery near the beach.

The first beach you'll come to is called, logically enough, **Playa Primera (First Beach),** though these days most people know it by its other, more intriguing name, **Playa Wizard.** It's a wide, stunning stretch of sand, big rollers, and, if you're lucky, very few people. Again, beware of the strong surf here. Walk east to get to **Playa Segunda (Second Beach)** and Red Frog Beach.

Silverbacks, the biggest surf break in Bocas, is west of these beaches and is accessible by boat. It's a huge, barreling reef-bottom right break that is often compared to big Hawaiian waves such as Backdoor. Wave faces can exceed seven meters. It's strictly for expert surfers. There are beach breaks off Wizard/First Beach and Red Frog Beach that are appropriate for intermediate surfers.

RED FROG BEACH

Red Frog Beach is the most popular beach in Bocas, partly because of the red frogs, but mainly because there's practically a conveyor belt depositing tourists there. Water taxis run frequently between Bocas town and a yacht marina on the southern shore of Bastimentos, and from there a wide road leads straight north to Red Frog Beach. A pickup-truck shuttle service transports those who don't relish a 10–15 minute walk to the beach, though there's often a long wait for it.

Private developers have set up a booth to collect a US$3 fee at the southern road entrance (all beaches in Panama are public property; the fee is ostensibly for keeping the beach clean and maintaining the infrastructure surrounding it). The fee includes the round-trip shuttle transport.

Red Frog Beach's namesake is a tiny creature also called the strawberry poison-dart frog (*Oophaga pumilio*) that's easier to spot here than anywhere else in Panama. The toxins in its skin are only a danger to animals who try to eat it. The frog comes in a variety of vibrant colors besides red.

It can be hard to spot red frogs at first, though once you see one, they suddenly seem to be everywhere. Look among the fallen leaves at the end of the road near the beach. If a local is around, ask him or her for help in finding the *rana roja* (RAH-na ROH-ha).

The beach itself is pretty, but as on the other north shore beaches, the breakers can get pretty big and rough. On the eastern side of the beach is a boardwalk which wraps around a rock outcropping for those who'd rather look at the surf from above than splash around in it.

West of and parallel to the main road is a narrower forest trail that runs between Red Frog and the south shore. It's easier to find red frogs, as well as many other frog species, along this less-developed trail. The noise they make is amazing; it's like a huge frog convention.

There are some filthy public bathrooms at both ends of the road, and a bar and grill with rather sullen service and customers at the beach itself. The marina on the south shore has a restaurant/bar that's sometimes open. There's a large, busy open-air restaurant, Kayukos Restaurant and Island Lounge, a five-minute walk up the trail, at the Bocas Bound hostel.

A water-taxi ride from Bocas town to the entrance of the road leading to Red Frog Beach is US$5 each way. Jampan Tours also runs a water shuttle, the Red Frog Conexion, between their pier in Bocas town and the Red Frog Beach road entrance for US$4 one-way or US$7 round-trip. It only makes the trip six to eight times a day, though, so saving a few bucks over a regular water-taxi fare by taking the shuttle may mean a long wait if you don't time it right.

Quebrada de Sal (Salt Creek)

This village of 450 people is not terribly scenic, but it's worth a visit, at least for those already on Bastimentos. It's approached by water on the southeastern side of the island, between Cayo Crawl and Punta Vieja. The approach can be one of the best parts of the trip, as the boat has to pass through dense mangrove channels where there's a chance of spotting sloths. The boat docks next to a concrete path that peters out at the edge of the village. Visitors must pay US$1 a head to enter and sign a registry. There's a modest souvenir shop that has crude, painted wooden figures of animals, some *chácaras* (traditional woven Ngöbe-Buglé handbags), and a few other things, but nothing too memorable.

The center of the community is a spacious field with a cinderblock school house, a dining hall, and a dance hall. A lot of the traditional Ngöbe culture has disappeared from the village, though there are still some thatched-roof houses on stilts and residents who still adhere to their traditional religion. The villagers are courteous if a bit reserved; but if you speak some Spanish, you should have little trouble finding someone to chat with.

There isn't much else in the village, but there's a nice forest hike from here that leads to Playa Larga. The trail starts at the far side of the village. It's a good idea to hire a villager to lead the way and point out the flora and fauna. It's also possible to do this hike without a guide, but as always, don't head off into the forest alone. The walk takes about an hour each way, and there's a chance of spotting armadillos, *conejos pintados,* and other small creatures. The community now has its own website with some basic information about Quebrada de Sal and its attractions: www.aliatur.bocas.com.

ENTERTAINMENT AND EVENTS

Entertainment is mostly confined to the bars and restaurants along the waterfront in Old Bank. **Roots Bar and Restaurant** (no phone, 11:30 A.M.–9:30 P.M. Wed.–Mon.) is a friendly place to hang out. **Cantina La Feria** is

MOST RED FROGS AREN'T RED

What is locally called the red frog is more widely referred to as the strawberry poison-dart frog. But neither name does justice to a species that comes in a jewel box of colors. Though in its best-known form it is red with blue legs, the tiny frog can be green, yellow, purple, orange, black, white, or a combination of these and other colors, with or without spots.

A safer bet is to call it by its scientific name, *Oophaga pumilio*. (It was reclassified in 2006, before which it was known as *Dendobates pumilio*.) It lives along the Caribbean coast from Nicaragua to Panama. Though it's common throughout Bocas del Toro, Bastimentos is famous for containing a remarkable number of forms, or morphs, on a single island.

The frogs can be hard to spot because of their small size: just 18–25 millimeters, or less than half as big as a man's thumb. They live in the forests of the islands and mainland but don't mind disturbed areas and are easiest to spot in dry leaf litter or near the forest edge. The males have a surprisingly loud call.

Though its skin produces toxins for defense, *Oophaga pumilio* doesn't pose a threat to humans, particularly those who don't eat one. It's nowhere near as potent as the golden poison-dart frog of Colombia, the aptly named *Phyllobates terribilis*. The skin of a single specimen of these is said to have enough toxin to kill 20,000 mice or a gruesome number of humans. Indigenous hunters of the Colombian rainforest traditionally tipped their blowgun darts with the deadly stuff.

Compared to these formidable creatures, *Oophaga pumilio* is positively cuddly. But their own poison, or pumiliotoxin, is still potent. A group of visiting researchers discovered in 2004 how they get it: from munching a type of small ant.

a nightlife option for adventurous folks staying in Old Bank. It has all the rough Caribbean character you could want. It's a basic cantina over the water that serves *seco* (a sugarcane liquor) and beer at locals-friendly prices. The scene can be kind of intimidating at first, especially when the cops come around checking IDs, but the vibe is generally low-key. Use common sense, go with a group, and be respectful.

Notable annual events, and excuses for a party, in Old Bank include **Palo de Mayo,** a Maypole dance on May 1 that's also held in Bocas town, and **Founding Day** on November 23.

The place to be on New Year's Eve is the Al Natural Resort, which throws an all-night **New Year's Eve beach party.** For a quite reasonable price, the staff provide boat transportation, refreshments, and DJs who are flown down from overseas for the occasion. Everyone eventually crashes wherever he or she likes.

SHOPPING

Destination shopping is a novel concept for Bocas, but **Up in the Hill** (cell 6607-8962 and 6570-8277, www.upinthehill.com, 8 A.M.–dark daily) is worth the effort. And the effort is considerable: As its name implies, it's up on the hill above Old Bank, about a 15-minute walk that begins in residents' backyards and continues through a secondary-growth forest. You're rewarded at the top by a refreshing breeze, lovely views of the ocean and surrounding islands, and a friendly welcome from the expat couple (he's from Argentina, she's from Scotland) who live on a farm up here with their young child. They're the makers of Pure Tree products, all of which are composed from natural ingredients found on the farm. These are available in stores around Bocas, so don't come up here just for that; however, there are lots of reasons to visit. One is a tour of the farm and an explanation of how the plants and fruits are used, including chocolate-making.

The family's house is also a shop with local crafts, mosaic art, and handmade lamps and furniture. There's a rustic but clean cabin (US$55 s/d, two-night minimum; weekly and

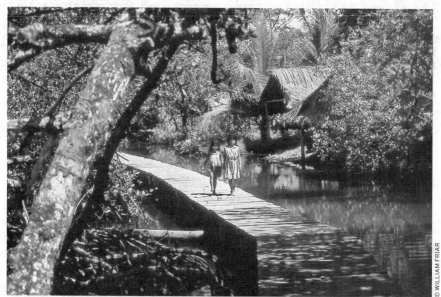

© WILLIAM FRIAR

the entrance to Quebrada de Sal, a Ngöbe village

monthly rates available) with an outside hot-water shower, composting toilet, kitchen, and spectacular views on the edge of a cliff; be sure to check out the bird's-eye view of Silverback, Bocas's best surf break. To get to Up in the Hill, face the police station (with one's back to the ocean) and take the path that starts to the right of it. Then follow the signs up the hill. The trail continues down to First (also Wizard) Beach, making this a nice place to take a break. Allow up to a week for responses to email, as this is a rather isolated spot without Internet access.

SPORTS AND RECREATION

Most people out here arrange tours through their hotels, which also tend to supply any needed sports gear. Other options include **Scuba 6 Diving** (cell 6793-2722, info@scuba6diving.com, www.scuba6diving.com), based in room number six of Pension Tío Tom (hence the name). Run by a friendly Dutch couple, Roberto and Debby, it opened in December 2010 and offers instruction in English, German, Spanish, or Dutch. Their equipment is new and well-maintained, and there's a letter of commendation from PADI on the wall that's positively gushing. A two-tank, two-site dive runs about US$70 per person. Dive groups are kept small; no more than four people per instructor.

Up in the Hill (cell 6607-8962 and 6570-8277, www.upinthehill.com) offers surfing lessons for US$40 for two hours, including a longboard. Surf tours are US$100 for a half day and US$150 for a full day. They also rent surfboards for US$10 for a half day, or US$15 for a full day. **Hostal Bastimentos** (tel. 757-9053) rents surfboards for US$10 per day. Those staying at the hostel can use its kayaks for free. **Pension Tío Tom** (tel. 757-9831, tiotomscabin@gmail.com) rents snorkeling gear (US$4 for snorkel, mask, and flippers), boogie boards (US$10), booties (US$2). It also has kayaks for US$2.50/hour up to US$20 day.

◪ **Parque Nacional Marino Isla Bastimentos**

This 13,226-hectare park is shaped like a bridge, and most of it is underwater. It starts among the mangrove islands on the southwestern side of Bastimentos, arcs across its midsection, and curves down to two lovely little islands. These islands, the **Cayos Zapatillas,** are the most visited parts of the park thanks to the good snorkeling and diving among the nearby coral gardens and underwater caves, which start about 12 meters down. It's quite dramatic even to snorkel around here; the shallow waters suddenly give way to deep canyons. The coral heads inside the reef are in good shape, and there is a large variety and abundance of fish. Nurse sharks live in this area, as well as two different species of lobsters. The water is turbulent around here, which can make visibility cloudy. It's not a good place for snorkelers who aren't fairly strong swimmers. There's an attractive beach on the western island for those who prefer to lounge, but the *chitras* (sand flies) can get nippy. The Zapatillas are about an hour by fast boat from Isla Colón.

There is an interpretive trail called **El Bosque Detrás del Arrecife** (literally, the forest behind the reef) on the more easterly of the Zapatillas (farther away from Bastimentos). It starts behind the ranger station.

Most visitors to Isla Bastimentos come only for the beach, but the **inland forest** is a natural treasure trove, which is why a big swath of it is included in the marine park. For one thing, it is home to 28 species of reptiles and amphibians, more than half of which are threatened or endangered. There's a good chance of spotting sloths, monkeys, and many species of birds in a trip through the forest, especially in the early morning. The **Laguna de Bastimentos,** near the northern coast midway across the island, is home to freshwater turtles, caimans, and crocodiles. Do not attempt a hike through the forest without a guide.

Playa Larga, which is part of the park, is an important sea-turtle nesting area, attracting four species of endangered turtles from about April or May through September. Admission to the park is US$10 per person. Even those just snorkeling or diving in the waters around the Cayos Zapatillas must pay this fee. Ask the tour operator if the fee is included in the tour price. Camping on either island is possible for US$5 more per tent.

ACCOMMODATIONS AND FOOD

Most places to stay and eat are in Old Bank, and most of these are budget options. Residents often rent out rooms in their houses to travelers for a few dollars. This is definitely a way to become immersed in the local culture, but these rooms are generally super basic and the surroundings noisy. Residents willing to rent rooms post signs on their houses, making it easy to wander around until something looks appealing. The most upscale accommodations are quite a ways away, between Cayo Crawl and Punta Vieja on the southeast side of the island.

Cayo Crawl has a couple of restaurants that serve mainly those on boat tours.

Old Bank

All the places to stay and eat in Old Bank (Bastimentos town) are either right along the waterfront or along a concrete path on the hillside above it.

Pension Tío Tom (tel. 757-9831, tiotomscabin@gmail.com, starts at US$22 s/d) is a fun place to stay for anyone with a bohemian bent. Accommodations are basic and aimed at the backpacking set, but the place is spotless and oozes rustic, piratical charm. The pension has four double rooms and one triple (US$22–27). The nicest of the accommodations is a little bungalow set apart from the others which the owners jokingly refer to as the "honeymoon suite." It's actually quite charming, with a big window overlooking the water and a balcony strung with a hammock (US$34 s/d). Rooms

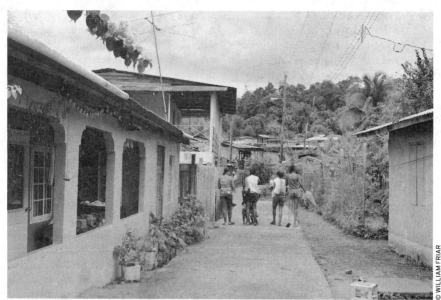

© WILLIAM FRIAR

Old Bank is the largest community on Isla Bastimentos.

have free wireless Internet access. The pension has a simple restaurant that specializes in Asian and Caribbean food and can also do vegetarian fare, some of which is drawn from the pension's new hydroponic garden. Most main dishes are around US$5–10. Nonguests can eat here if it's not too busy. Breakfast is served 8–11 A.M., with a continental breakfast going for US$3.50.

Tío Tom is built over the water, on a pier that attracts 38 species of colorful fish. The tree in the dining area is said to have 72 species of orchids growing on it. It's now also home to Tom's menagerie of indigenous frogs. Though Pension Tío Tom has a secluded feel, bear in mind it's in the middle of the town's rather crowded waterfront, and trash along the shore and loud music played by neighbors are part of the local color. The pension is the home of the friendly, easygoing German owners, Tom and Ina Reichelt. They've lived on Bastimentos for well over a decade and know the area well. The couple speaks English, German, and some Spanish. This place is a good find, and a great deal.

Hostal Bastimentos (tel. 757-9053, starts at US$18 s/d) offers 28 clean rooms in a sprawling, Caribbean-style yellow wooden building with lots of character. Small, rustic rooms with rotary fans are US$18 s/d. Slightly bigger and nicer rooms are US$20 s/d. The nicest rooms are US$40 s/d with air-conditioning and private bathrooms. The best of these are quite appealing and airy. There are two communal kitchens, lots of balcony space for lazing in hammocks, and Internet access for US$1 per hour. This is an attractive, well-maintained place. It's set back from town on a little hill, giving it a view of the town and ocean.

Roots Bar and Restaurant (no phone, 11:30 A.M.–9:30 P.M. Wed.–Mon., US$3–10) is a pleasant thatched-roof place over the water with a warm Caribbean vibe and smiling proprietors. This is a good place to try traditional Caribbean food with coconut rice and Caribbean sauces (ask for the secret Roots sauce). Dishes run toward seafood, including lobster and octopus.

Built in 2004, **Hotel Caribbean View** (tel. 757-9442, hotelcaribbeanview@yahoo.com, www.bocas.com, US$55–71 s/d, a/c) is in a two-story, Caribbean-style building, white with gold trim, that's right on the water and has 11 rooms with modern hot-water bathrooms, local TV, telephones, and free wireless Internet. The rooms are small but clean and in good shape. The nicest are the six rooms upstairs with private balconies. There's a small restaurant on the water.

Bahía Honda and Vicinity

Bahía Honda is a long, deep bay between Isla Bastimentos and Isla Solarte that starts a few minutes by boat east of Old Bank. Opened in November 2009, **Bocas Bound** (tel. 757-8021, cell 6521-0637, www.bocasbound.com, US$13 pp in dorm, a/c) is a large hostel about a five-minute walk up the hill from the beginning of the main Red Frog Beach trail, where most boats drop off day-trippers. There are 80 hostel beds and four private rooms. The place is a bit odd and utilitarian because the accommodations were built as a workers' dormitory for an ill-fated construction project. Each dorm has 10 bunk beds, tile floors, and lockers. The (cold-water) showers and toilets are in individual stalls with doors, but they are separated from the bedroom only by a doorway draped with a curtain. It feels a bit like bedding down in a dressing room, and it may be a bit awkward to share with strangers. The private rooms (starting at US$22 s/d) have exactly the same layout except with double and single beds, rather than bunks, and dividers that don't go all the way to the ceiling separating each dorm unit into separate "rooms." Unless you have the entire unit to yourself, these are about as private as an office cubicle. The staff try to rent these out to families. The private rooms also have water, a minifridge, and a seating area.

Backpackers stay here mainly because of its proximity to Red Frog Beach, which guests can visit without paying the entrance fee. However it's isolated from the rest of Bocas, and going back and forth to Bocas town and other parts of the archipelago adds up quickly. The hostel is not actually on Red Frog Beach, though it is just a five-minute walk away. It is on a hill and faces south, overlooking a marina and Bahía Honda.

Down the hill from the rooms is a huge open-air restaurant/bar/lounge, Kayukos Restaurant and Island Lounge, that is the social hub of the place. There's table tennis, a widescreen TV and DVD player, a giant chessboard, and free wireless Internet. Bathrooms are clean, and the place is well-run. New surfboards can be rented for US$20 a day, kayaks for US$15 a day, and snorkel gear for US$7 a day.

Palmar Tent Lodge (cell 6880-8640, www.palmartentlodge.com, US$44 s/d) is a nifty, ecofriendly tent camp which opened in September 2010 on the west end of Red Frog Beach, away from most of the touristy hordes. It's run by the same people who have the Casa Verde hostel in Bocas town. Comfortable, safari-style tents are set in a grove of tall trees just back from the surf. Private tents (US$44 s/d) have two single or one double bed, private outdoor showers, lockers, mosquito nets, and solar-powered lamps and fans. The showers use rainwater heated by the sun. There are also shared "dorm" tents for US$15/person. Behind these relatively fancy tents are six campsites set in a circle, where campers can pitch their own tent for US$9 or rent one for US$15. There's an open-air bar/restaurant. Guests have access to a common kitchen and a fire pit.

The very cool ◖ **Eclypse de Mar** (cell 6511-4581, www.eclypsedemar.com, bungalows start at US$198 s/d, including breakfast) is one of my favorite places in Bocas. Run well by a friendly Argentinean couple, Malena Trevisan and Chango Castro, it shares the same concept as Punta Caracol (bungalows over the water that are linked by boardwalks), but has a very different feel. The bungalows are beautiful, made

ished nispero and cedar. They
...ss panel in the floor so guests
...swimming under their feet;
... the water at night. Bungalows
are tastefully designed with modern fixtures,
very firm beds, ceiling fans, warm-water bathrooms, and in-room safes. Each has a private
deck with a staircase leading right into the
water. The four standard bungalows (US$198
s/d, US$264 t, $308 q) are plenty nice, but the
two honeymoon suites (US$275 s/d) are even
nicer. The bedrooms are bigger and feature
king beds, and they have a desk nook and a
small living room with a glass-topped coffee
table fixed above another opening in the floor.
It's fun to have breakfast here while keeping
an eye out for curious fish. The least expensive
accommodations are two rooms in the main
lodge. These are small but comfortable, with
full beds, in-room safes, private baths, and a
balcony strung with hammocks.

Eclypse de Mar is off the grid, powered by solar
electricity and with clean, filtered water provided
from a spring onshore. There's no air-conditioning,
but there are ceiling fans, and it's breezy enough
over the water you're unlikely to miss air-conditioning. There are lights only when the sun goes down,
and toilet paper is deposited in a bin next to the toilet. The vibe here is friendly and familial, so you'll
enjoy your stay more if you're at least somewhat social. The staff are warm and make you feel at home.

The food is the only thing that's still a work
in progress. It's tasty and plentiful, but don't
expect gourmet. The coconut bread is a nice
touch but doesn't have much flavor, and the
seafood can be overcooked. But they make a
delicious pumpkin soup, and food is nicely
presented and reasonably priced. There's good
wine as well. There's free wireless Internet in
the restaurant area and kayaks and basic snorkeling gear are free to guests (visitors can rent
kayaks for US$5/hour). The lodge arranges
boat tours to all the usual destinations, plus a
few that are lesser known.

Staying here, you feel secluded without being
cut off from everything. Old Bank is a stone's
throw away, and there's a 2.5-hectare nature
preserve onshore, just behind the lodge. This
used to be pastureland, but the lodge has re-
planted it and is trying to restore mangroves
that have been cut away and start an iguana-
breeding project.

Easy walking trails run through the preserve, the centerpiece of which is a series of in-
geniously designed lush artificial lagoons on
different levels. The water flows slowly from
one level to the next, which prevents mosquitoes from breeding, but provides a home to a
family of caimans. Some Mayan statue replicas, salvaged from one of the many *Survivor*
programs filmed here, are dotted around the
preserve, which adds a nice Indiana Jones feel.

**La Loma Jungle Lodge and Chocolate
Farm** (cell 6619-5364 or 6592-5162, www.
thejunglelodge.com, US$104/person, includ-
ing all meals, transfers, and day trips) bucks
the trend toward generic, resource-gulping
resorts with a unique, low-impact, but comfortable little hideaway in harmony with its
beautiful surroundings. It's one of my favorite spots in Panama. A 23-hectare former farm
right next to the border of Parque Nacional
Marino Isla Bastimentos, La Loma is set back
from the mangrove-covered shoreline of Bahía
Honda and features secondary-growth forest,
a cacao (chocolate) growing and processing operation, and coconut and banana groves. The
main lodge has a dining area and an upstairs
mirador and is bordered by a creek that ends
in a little wading hole and waterfall. The three
guest *ranchos* (and a fourth on the way) are on
the side of a hill behind the lodge. This may be
the most environmentally friendly place to stay
in Panama. Visitors are welcome even if they
don't spend the night.

Beaches are a short boat ride away, but
there are no beaches on the property itself.
Accommodations put guests as close to nature

as possible without sacrificing comfort. The spacious, immaculate Ngöbe-inspired ranchos are rustic in the sense of being simple and open-air, but they're quite lovely. Made from handsome wood from fallen trees and sustainably harvested lumber, they are designed to let in evening breezes and look out on the forest and bay. The first rancho is close to the main lodge and is best for those who'd have trouble with the rather aerobic climb to the other ones. The second one is a 149-step climb from the lodge, which can be a bit strenuous for those unused to humidity. The third is a bit farther up the hill. (Look carefully at the hill trail; there are tons of red frogs all around it.)

The second rancho has panoramic views of the bay, but the third is surrounded by trees that sometimes attract curious white-capuchin and night monkeys. An armadillo may come sniffing around, too. Each rancho has one double and one single bed with mosquito nets, hot-water showers, and flush toilets. They are spaced far apart from each and are quite private. Nights here are wonderfully peaceful, especially with the moon shining on the sea and forest.

Among the best things about the place are the owners: Margaret, who's English, and her husband, Henry, a Peruvian-American. They are delightful people who make guests feel like welcome visitors to their home, which is what this place is. Their small staff are warm and friendly.

Stays include round-trip transportation from Bocas town (about 20 minutes away), all meals, day trips to Red Frog Beach, and tours of the garden. Part of the proceeds support community projects among the Ngöbe in Bahía Honda. The food is delicious and features produce from the lodge's organic gardens.

Other activities are easily arranged for an extra fee, including tours of the Bahía Honda cave, forest hikes with Ngöbe guides, fishing or snorkeling trips, surfboard rental, and so on. The lodge can arrange for guests to participate in or observe a number of activities with members of the nearby Ngöbe community, including cooking lessons, cacao-processing, and craft-making.

Cayo Crawl to Punta Vieja

There are three resorts on the nearly 10 kilometers of beautiful curving coastline between Cayo Crawl and Punta Vieja. Each is quite secluded, both from each other and from everything else. Depending on boat speed, from Isla Colón it can take up to an hour to reach these places.

Tranquilo Bay (tel. 380-6952, U.S. tel. 713/589-6952, www.tranquilobay.com, multiday all-inclusive packages start at US$1,445 s, US$2,230 d for three nights, a/c) has the only truly industrialized-world-style accommodations on Bastimentos. Perched on a hill just around the point from Cayo Crawl, it's a small all-inclusive resort that opened in 2004 after several years of construction and planning. The resort isn't on a beach. The hill is set above mangroves, but attractive beaches are a short boat ride away.

The resort is on 100 acres of land that was a banana plantation for 100 years, but which is now being allowed to revert to forest. It offers six large, modern cabanas, set in a clearing at the top of the breezy hill and linked with each other and the main lodge by a paved path that's shaded by lush tropical vegetation and illuminated at night. The cabanas are attractive and well-appointed, with comfortable beds, a sitting area, and large hot-water bathrooms with handsome granite countertops. There are no phones or TVs, and free wireless Internet is available only in the main lodge. Cabanas look out on either the ocean or the surrounding forest. Each has a front porch with hammocks, Adirondack chairs, and ceiling fans. The two-story main lodge has a large dining room and bar with a broad deck where one can sit and watch the ocean and colorful oropendolas as they flit back and forth to their hanging nests.

Even those who don't need all its creature comforts may be interested in the place for its tours. The resort offers trips not only to the

it also to remoter parts of the east-
⁾ and mainland not easily accessi-
ᴗ travelers. Excursions include jungle
ᴧ.ᴋes, kayak trips, scuba and snorkeling, surfing, fishing, and lounging on secluded beaches.

Packages range 3–7 nights, either with or
without daily excursions. All packages include
transfers, the round-trip domestic flight from
Panama City to Bocas, all meals, nonalcoholic
and some alcoholic beverages, and water and
land activities around the resort. These activities include kayaking, snorkeling, swimming,
hikes, and access to Tranquilo Bay's library and
video library. Without daily excursions, rates
range from US$1,445 s, US$2,230 d for three
nights up to US$2,564 s, US$3,920 d for seven
nights. Add about US$100 per person per day
for packages that include excursions. Excursions
can also be booked à la carte at the resort.

The semi-rustic but attractive **Casa Cayuco**
(no phone, www.casacayuco.com, starts at
US$247.50 s, US$302.50 d, all-inclusive, three
night minimum) is on the beach between
Tranquilo Bay and Al Natural. It consists of a
three-story lodge with an open-air dining room,
bar, kitchen and sitting area, and four cabins a
short walk away. Three of the cabins are on the
beach, and one is set back from the water but surrounded by tropical forest. There's also a room
on the 2nd floor of the lodge. This is another
remote spot surrounded by tropical forest and
little else. Electricity is supplied by solar power.

Made primarily from nispero wood, the
cabins are airy and attractive, with private
bathrooms and ceiling fans. The wooden-
shuttered windows don't have screens, but the
beds have mosquito nets. Rates for the cabins
are US$247.50 s, US$335.50–375.50 d. Up
to five or six people can stay in cabins for an
extra per person fee. Rates in the lodge room
are US$247.50 s, US$302.50 d. The room can
accommodate up to four people for an extra
per person fee. There is a three-night minimum stay in any of the accommodations. Rates

include all meals, transfers to and from Bocas,
and use of sports equipment, including snorkel gear, kayaks, paddleboards, Hobie Cat sailboats, and surfboards.

This is a pleasant, ecofriendly place that caters primarily to groups—yoga, surf, school, and
so on—interested in adventure travel and service projects in the neighboring communities.
It's owned by an American couple, Tom and
Linda Kimbrell, who have considerable experience in this kind of work. Guided excursions
range from snorkeling tours of nearby reefs to a
boat trip all the way out to the tip of Peninsula
Valiente, where there's a secluded beach. Rates
for most of these are US$50–100 per person.

Al Natural Resort (tel./fax 757-9004,
cell 6496-0776 or 6576-8605, www.alnatur-
alresort.com, starts at US$214.50 s, US$281.45
d, including all meals, transfers, and use of
recreation equipment) has long been one of
my favorite places to stay in Panama. It consists of just seven bungalows (the warm and
friendly Belgian owners never plan to build
more than nine) on a secluded, pristine beach
just below Punta Vieja on the southeastern side
of Isla Bastimentos. The bungalows are based
on the traditional Ngöbe-Buglé house design:
They're round, thatched-roofed wooden structures on stilts perched on the edge of the clear
blue water. Inside, they're remarkably comfortable and well-appointed for such a remote spot.
They have private, hot-water showers (a modern flush toilet is in a clean, well-maintained
stall just outside each bungalow), good queen-
or king-size beds with mosquito netting fine
enough to keep out *chitras* (sand flies), and an
electrical system powered by solar panels.

The bungalows are designed to put guests
as close to the lovely natural surroundings as
possible. The entire front of each is an open
deck with gorgeous views of the sea, the Cayos
Zapatillas, and the distant mainland. The
backs are partly open to the tropical forest behind the resort. But the area is so isolated, and

the bungalows so well designed, that each has a great deal of privacy. They also tend to be surprisingly free of creepy-crawlies.

The bungalows are set on nine hectares of land, a former coconut plantation that is reverting to forest. Three species of primates, armadillos, boas, opossums, raccoons, and caiman have been spotted back here. A short, wide trail leads through this patch of secondary-growth forest to a north-shore beach. Guests have free use of sea kayaks, snorkeling gear, and fishing tackle in the calm, protected waters in front of the resort.

The heart of the resort is a large, three-story building—also wooden and thatch-roofed. The bottom floor is the dining/bar area. The 2nd floor houses an open-air games area. There's an observation deck with expansive views on the top floor. Meals are served family-style; the food is simple, but good wine is included with dinners. Some of the food—including bananas, pineapples, and ducks—is grown or raised at the resort. Occasionally a guest chef cooks; when that happens, the quality of the food soars.

This is a great option for couples looking for a romantic spot, for adventurous families, or even for students of ingenious and environmentally appropriate architecture. It's fun to note all the little touches. The showers are lined with pebbles laid out to form traditional Ngöbe-Buglé designs. The bungalows use a great deal of driftwood, with shapes carefully selected to fit into the overall design instead of being cut to fit.

Bungalows have either one or two stories. They come in two basic flavors: Natural House or Superior Natural House. The Natural House has a queen-size bed and 12-volt electrical system. The Superior Natural House is larger, with a king-size bed, one or two single beds, and a 110-volt electrical system, sufficient to run a ceiling fan. It's well worth spending the extra money for a Superior Natural House, which is significantly nicer. The two-story houses can accommodate more people for an

additional fee. One of t⊦ hexagonal and has three b⊾ cleverly closed off for privacy.

Given how remote this spot ⊾ prising maintenance can sometime⊾ cern. During one of my stays, for i⊾ there were glitches with the hot water an⊾ of the boats. These problems were quickly ⊾ solved, but anyone who stays here should not expect everything to run like clockwork; it's still a bohemian Caribbean place, even given the exclusive prices.

High-season rates start at US$214.50/ US$281.45 s/d for the first night in a Natural House. Rates drop to US$146.48/195.30 s/d on subsequent nights. All-inclusive packages adding daily half-day tours and all drinks are also available; there's a two-night minimum for these.

Camping

It's possible to camp in **Parque Nacional Marino Isla Bastimentos** for US$5 per tent in addition to the US$10 per-person park entrance fee. Entrance fees for both can be paid at the ANAM office in Bocas town. This entitles you to pitch a tent anywhere in the park. That includes the forest on Bastimentos itself, but as always it's not a great idea to camp in a tropical forest without a qualified guide. Most campers prefer to stay on one of the **Cayos Zapatillas,** which are part of the park, for a romantic, deserted-island experience. It's theoretically possible to buy permits directly from the ranger stationed on the Zapatillas. However, check at the ANAM office in Bocas town about current camping conditions and restrictions before venturing out that far. You'll also need to hire a boatman you can trust to come pick you up when you're ready to return.

INFORMATION AND SERVICES

La Loma, Tranquilo Bay, Casa Cayuco, and Al Natural generally arrange all food, transportation, and activities for their guests. Make sure

BOCAS DEL TORO

rify exactly what is being provided ahead
_me, because there's little to buy way out
_e. Even Old Bank is a significant boat ride
way. In Old Bank there is a *minisuper* (convenience store) near Roots Bar and Restaurant
and a police post, health clinic, and phone
booth behind Pension Tío Tom. Some of the
places to stay have Internet access for guests,
but there are no Internet cafés.

GETTING THERE

Isla Colón is a 10-minute water-taxi ride from
Old Bank; flag down passing boats. The fare
is US$3 per person.

ELSEWHERE IN THE ARCHIPELAGO

New places to stay are beginning to pop up
elsewhere in the islands. Some of these are nice
and have surprisingly modern infrastructures
given their location. They tend to be off by
themselves, and the nearest population center
or place to eat (besides your lodging) is likely
to be a Ngöbe-Buglé village. Popa Paradise
Resort, which is right above an attractive beach
on Isla Popa, sometimes lets day visitors use
its pool, clubhouse, and other facilities for a
US$10 entrance fee.

There's a quite appealing place to stay in
Laguna Bocatorito (Dolphin Bay), near the
village of Bocatorito, about 20 minutes by boat
from Bocas town. **Dolphin Bay Hideaway** (cell
6417-7351 or 6772-9917, erika@dolphinbayhi-
deaway.com, www.dolphinbayhideaway.com,
starts at US$137.50 s/d, including transfers,
breakfast, and dinner) opened in 2006 with
three attractive, cheerful, and spotless rooms
in a two-story Caribbean-style house. All have
four-poster beds, fans, and stylish modern bathrooms with hot water. None has air-conditioning or TVs: This is a place for people who like to
be close to nature. There is free wireless Internet
and use of *cayucos* (dugout canoes), however.

Two rooms are downstairs. The smallest
room has a queen bed and looks out on the
garden (US$137.50 s/d). The corner room is
larger, with a king bed and view of the bay
(US$176 s/d). The room upstairs (US$154 s/d)
is also quite large and has the most traditional
charm, with a queen bed and spacious bathroom. It opens onto the large shared veranda,
so it's not as private as the other two rooms.
Lunch and candlelit dinners are served on the
veranda, which is a pleasant place to hang out
or lounge in hammocks.

Guests need to be comfortable around animals, as
the owners have friendly dogs, a restless parrot, chickens, and have been known to get the visits from the
odd kinkajou or howler monkey. There's no beach
on the property, but snorkeling and dolphin-watch-
ing spots are close by, and boat rides to sandy beaches
are easy to arrange. The owners can arrange tours to
all the surrounding attractions for an extra fee.

Popa Paradise Beach Resort (cell 6550-
2505, www.popaparadisebeachresort.com,
starts at US$176 s/d, including breakfast) is the
pioneering lodging on Isla Popa, and it didn't
start small. Opened in January 2009, the resort occupies 25 acres of what once was a farm.
Only the front five acres have been developed;
the rest is being left to return to forest as best
it can, helped by the planting of hundreds of
trees by the staff. There are eight casitas dotted
around the property on a ridge above a good-
size crescent beach. The casitas are linked
by cement paths that lead to the large clubhouse, which has a dining terrace, a small spa,
a lounge with a giant-screen TV, and a kidney-
shape infinity-edge pool with a swim-up bar.

The casitas (US$385 s/d) are individual bun-
galows with balconies and attractive Balinese
furniture and porches that look out onto the
ocean. They either have a four-poster, a queen, or
two twin beds, and all are air-conditioned, have
satellite TV and DVD players, and hot-water
bathrooms. Ocean-front casita number 10 has
an extra little cement veranda and is nicest of all.

There are also two junior suites, also known

as the executive suites (US$550 s/d), on a point above the resort's dock, but they don't have as much charm as the casitas and look a bit worn. They do, however, have kitchenettes and sliding-glass doors that open onto a lovely view. For those who want a truly opulent experience, above these is the master suite, also known as the penthouse (US$693 s/d), which features 20-foot ceilings, a large bathroom with separate tub (the only room that has one), a full kitchen, a master bedroom, a second bedroom, a stereo, and so on. All three of these have air-conditioning and flat-screen satellite TVs.

There are also four simpler and more economical rooms (US$176 s/d and US$275 s/d) in the main clubhouse. They're attractive and have air-conditioning, private bathrooms, and porches, though those who want to watch TV have to rely on the big-screen television in the lounge. Guests in these have access to all the facilities at the resort.

The restaurant's menu features such fusion dishes as yuca gnocchi. The fancier main dishes go for around $16–21. There is free wireless Internet in the clubhouse, which has a pool table, Ping-Pong table, library, spa, and a big-screen TV.

There are kayaks and snorkeling gear for guest use. There's a coral reef a few hundred meters offshore, but when the water's not clear, the staff can arrange transport to other snorkeling spots. Other boat and walking tours are also available. Isla Popa is still mostly covered with tropical forest, and it does have venomous snakes. Guests should take care if they go on forest hikes, just as they would in a tropical forest on the mainland. However, snakes do not hang out in areas that have been cleared, and all the facilities of the resort are on absolutely manicured lawns.

With all the upscale facilities, and upscale prices, it'd be easy for potential guests to forget they're on a lightly populated, remote tropical island. This is a place for people who like the idea of being far away from everything and are into outdoor activities. If it rains, there's not a whole lot to do (though the staff do try to come up with creative ideas during long rainy spells—cooking classes, anyone?). And guests will need at least a slight sense of adventure, especially when making the 40-minute ride over from Bocas town in a small boat.

If the resort isn't too busy, it sometimes allows day guests to use the pool and other facilities for US$10 per person 9 A.M.–5 P.M.

Those who stay three nights or more get free round-trip transfers between the resort and Bocas town at the beginning and end of their stay. Otherwise, it's US$100 per person round-trip.

Mainland Bocas

Most visitors spend little time on the mainland of the province. Towns here have a bit of a rough, frontier feel and should be approached with some caution, at least at night, but, like most places, you can also meet kind people. Mainland Bocas outside the towns holds more appeal, thanks mainly to the gigantic Parque Internacional La Amistad and increasingly accessible trips up the Río Teribe. Powerful rivers and magnificent evergreen forests lead down from the highlands, where indigenous peoples work to survive both physically and culturally. Important wetlands line the coast, including the—at least nominally—protected San San Pondsack.

ALMIRANTE

You'd have to be bananas to choose to stay in the small, ramshackle banana-port town of Almirante (pop. 12,430) rather than on the islands, but those who miss the last water taxi from town may end up stranded here for the night. The main street into Almirante leads from the highway and parallels the railroad tracks as it reaches town. The water-taxi piers are to the right, across the train tracks and not visible from the road. There's a grungy hotel, Hospedaje San Francisco, and a general store on the left side of the road and a bus terminal to the right. A second road crosses the main street just past the bus terminal. Most of the town's services are on or near this road, including a Banco Nacional de Panamá with an ATM. Be careful in Almirante, especially after dark.

Accommodations and Food

La Hotel Preferida (Almirante crossroads, tel. 758-3968, cell 6411-3828, starts at US$18 s/d) would not be a preferred hotel most places, but it's the best bet if you're stuck around Almirante. It's on the highway next to the stop for long-distance buses and near the road leading into town. It offers 34 basic but fairly clean, okay rooms with decent mattresses on the 2nd floor of a commercial building which also houses a Chinese restaurant and a *comida corriente* place. Rooms vary in quality, so ask to see several. Rooms with air-conditioning, which may be tough to do without, are US$27.50. The manager is friendly. It's possible to get your clothes washed here for US$3.50 wash/dry.

Stranded folks who can afford it should consider trying to spend the night at **La Escapada** (cell 6698-9901 or 6618-6106, www.laescapada.net, US$77 s/d, US$93.50 with two double beds, a/c), located about 64 kilometers east of the Costa Rican border on the Almirante–Chiriquí Grande Road. It's between kilometer markers 48 and 49 and is easily the best place to stay along the Bocas coastline. Run by a couple from Florida who live on the property with a couple of big, friendly dogs, guest accommodations consist of four rooms in a wooden building set on a 12.5-acre former cattle ranch that is being allowed to revert to forest. Rooms are simple but clean and modern, with comfortable beds and screened back porches for those who

want to commune with nature while avoiding the *chitras* (sand flies). The rooms aren't close enough to the water to have a view, but they are surrounded by trees. A short walk leads down to a dock, at the end of which is the hotel's screened-in terrace bar/restaurant, which appears to float above the glassy water and which has a spectacular view of the ocean and islands.

Breakfast, lunch, and dinner are available, with American and Italian main dishes going for around US$10. Electricity is supplied by a generator, at least until the grid finally reaches this remote spot. Kayaks and snorkeling gear are available for guests. This place is popular with those who need to take their vehicles to the island, as it's not too far from the Almirante ferry, which leaves early.

The property is down the hill from the highway and is reached by a long, steep, dirt-and-gravel road that is only accessible by a powerful four-wheel drive or by fairly fit pedestrians with sure footing. Walking up the hill is quite a workout. Any bus heading to or from Changuinola and Almirante can drop or pick up passengers at the entrance to the property.

Getting There and Around
BY BUS
Try to arrive in Almirante well before the last water taxi leaves for the islands at 6:30 P.M. Remember that buses often run late and water taxis can fill up. Long-haul buses from David, Panama City, and other parts of Panama still do not go into Almirante itself. They drop passengers at the crossroads outside of town and then head on to Changuinola. It's a long walk, especially with luggage, from the crossroads to the water-taxi piers. It's worth the US$0.50 per person to take a taxi to the pier area.

There are no direct buses between the Costa Rican border crossing at Guabito-Sixaola and Almirante. Travelers must instead switch buses halfway, at the Changuinola bus terminal.

Guabito–Changuinola buses run every 25

minutes or so 5:30 A.M.–8 P.M. The trip takes a half hour and costs US$1.45.

Changuinola–Almirante buses have a similar schedule: about every 25 minutes from about 5:40 A.M.–7:45 P.M. The trip also takes a half hour and costs US$1.45.

The water-taxi companies in Almirante aren't visible from the bus terminal but are within easy walking distance. Look for the train tracks. Cross over them and head left along the waterfront.

Buses from Almirante to David and Panama City leave from the crossroads at the edge of town. Take a taxi (US$0.50 per person) to get there. There is one direct daily bus to Panama City, leaving Almirante at 8 A.M. A second bus, at around 7–8 P.M., has been added and dropped over the years. The fare is US$27.80, and the ride takes roughly 10 hours. Passengers are limited to two bags each; additional luggage is charged as cargo.

David-bound buses leave Almirante every half hour or so 5 A.M.–7 P.M. The fare is US$8.45, and the trip takes about four hours.

Buses from Almirante to Changuinola leave from the Almirante bus terminal every 25 minutes from 6 A.M. until late in the evening. The trip takes a half hour and costs US$1.45.

BY CAR

Those with their own transportation will need 9–10 hours from Panama City or 3.5 hours from David to drive straight through to Almirante. Those coming from Panama City should consider breaking the trip somewhere along the way and spending the night. Lost and Found Eco-Resort is a good option along the Fortuna Road. Another possibility is Santiago, the provincial capital of Veraguas, on the Interamericana a little under four hours from Panama. It has a range of services and places to stay but is not exactly a scenic or exciting town.

Coming up the Fortuna Road, continue west on the Chiriquí Grande–Almirante Road for about 60 kilometers. The turnoff to Almirante is on the right and comes up quickly. The main road continues to Changuinola and the Costa Rican border. After the turn, the road will fork. Be sure to take the gravel road to the right. Stay straight, with the train tracks on the right, and turn right just before the bus terminal—it should be the first right after the old Bocas Fruit Company sign. The water-taxi piers are up this road.

You'll probably encounter a *boletero* (ticket tout) eager to show you the way and take you to the water-taxi service he works for, for a tip. Park at the fenced-in lot at **Leiza's** for US$3–5 a day.

CHANGUINOLA

This congested, unlovely provincial town (pop. 39,896) is not exactly what you'd call a tourist destination. It's little more than a single strip of road—Avenida 17 de Abril, commonly known as Calle Central—that's lined with shops offering cheap goods and basic services, plus a few hotels and restaurants. It's not even particularly colorful—it's a hot, humid, nondescript little town surrounded by banana plantations. But it is a commerce and transportation hub.

Those who haven't experienced this part of Panama may be curious to pass by for a quick visit. It's a crossroads for those traveling between Costa Rica and the islands or heading up into Naso country and the Bocas entrance to Parque Internacional La Amistad. Only those who end up stranded on the way to or from those places will likely want to spend the night.

Central Changuinola is about a kilometer long from north to south, and nearly everything of interest is on or within a block of Avenida 17 de Abril, which runs parallel to the train tracks. Because of that, the town is easily walkable. But Changuinola isn't particularly safe after dark; take taxis instead of walking (less than US$1 in town). The streets are packed with them. Unless otherwise noted, all the places listed are on Avenida 17 de Abril.

BOCAS DEL TORO

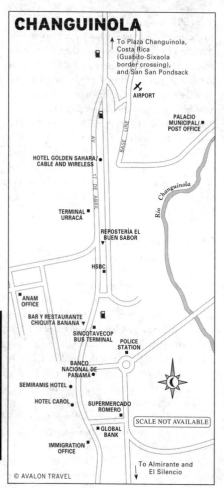

CHANGUINOLA

To Plaza Changuinola,
Costa Rica
(Guabito-Sixaola
border crossing),
and San San Pondsack

AIRPORT

PALACIO
MUNICIPAL/
POST OFFICE

HOTEL GOLDEN SAHARA/
CABLE AND WIRELESS

AV 17 DE ABRIL

BASE LINE

Río Changuinola

TERMINAL
URRACÁ

REPOSTERÍA EL
BUEN SABOR

HSBC

ANAM
OFFICE

BAR Y RESTAURANTE
CHIQUITA BANANA

SINCOTAVECOP
BUS TERMINAL

POLICE
STATION

BANCO
NACIONAL DE
PANAMÁ

SEMIRAMIS HOTEL

HOTEL CAROL

SUPERMERCADO
ROMERO

SCALE NOT AVAILABLE

GLOBAL
BANK

IMMIGRATION
OFFICE

To Almirante and
El Silencio

© AVALON TRAVEL

Accommodations
US$10-25

Hotel Carol (tel. 758-8731, starts at US$25 s/d, a/c), near the south end of Avenida 17 de Abril, offers 37 rooms, which are dark and basic, but okay, with smudged walls and concrete floors. The cheapest rooms are cold-water only and have no TV. The more expensive rooms are nicer, with cable TV, hot water, and tile floors, though they're still not the cleanest. This is the best bet among the cheaper hotels.

Hotel Golden Sahara (tel. 758-7478, 758-7908, or 758-7910, hotelgoldensahara@yahoo.com, US$44 s/d, a/c), toward the north end of town, has 28 modern rooms with hot water and cable TV. Rooms are clean if a bit sterile. The rooms vary quite a bit—some are dark, and others are quite a bit cheerier. The hotel is well run, and the staff members are attentive. They're happy to recommend places to eat and give other tips. This place is a good deal.

US$25-50

Semiramis Hotel (tel. 758-6006, 758-6009, or 758-6013, US$30–35 s/d, a/c), near the heart of town, across the street from the Banco Nacional de Panamá, has fairly nice, clean rooms with cable TV and attractive bathrooms. It has a bar and restaurant that's open 7 A.M.–11 P.M. daily.

Food

Bar y Restaurante Chiquita Banana (tel. 758-8215, 7 A.M.–11 P.M. daily, US$6 or less) is the best place to eat in town, which isn't saying a whole lot. It serves an extensive menu of Chinese and *criollo* food. The *arroz con pollo* (chicken and rice) is tasty, cheap, and plentiful. There's a daily special—be sure to ask about it, since it's not written down anywhere. Most people eat on the enclosed front patio, which looks out on the busy street, but there's a fancier air-conditioned dining room inside, with a somewhat more upscale menu. This place has been here forever, and it'll probably still be serving greasy grub come doomsday.

Repostería El Buen Sabor (tel. 758-8422, 8 A.M.–10 P.M. Mon.–Sat., 10 A.M.–9 P.M. Sun.), across the street and a bit south of Terminal Urracá, is a bakery and pastry shop that offers local specialties such as the *bon de Bastimentos,* which tastes like dry gingerbread, as well as fruit drinks, ice cream, and other goodies.

Information

The local **ANAM office** (tel. 758-6603,

8 A.M.–4 P.M. Mon.–Fri.) may have information on San San Pondsack and Parque Internacional La Amistad, but it's not really set up for travelers, so don't get your hopes up. It's in a residential neighborhood a couple of blocks west of the center of town. Head west on the road that runs past the Hotel El Gran Hong Kong. Turn left after two blocks. The office is a block down this road.

The **police station** is on an unmarked road east of the railroad tracks. It's parallel to and one block east of Avenida 17 de Abril. It's around the corner from the Hotel Alhambra and the Banco Nacional de Panamá.

Services

There are several banks along Avenida 17 de Abril that have 24-hour ATMs in addition to regular banking hours (8 A.M.–3 P.M. Mon.–Fri., 9 A.M.–noon Sat.). **Global Bank** is about a block north of and across the street from the immigration office on the south side of town. The **Banco Nacional de Panamá** is right next to the Hotel Alhambra. **HSBC** is a couple of blocks south of the bus terminal on the east side of the street. The **Multi-Credit Bank** is farther up Avenida 17 de Abril.

The **post office** is in the Palacio Municipal de Changuinola, on an unmarked road east of the airstrip on the north side of town.

Supermercado Romero (8 A.M.–10 P.M. Mon.–Sat., 8 A.M.–6 P.M. Sun.), one block east of the south end of Avenida 17 de Abril, next to the Global Bank, has a pharmacy and ATM.

The local **Cable and Wireless office** (8 A.M.–noon and 1–4 P.M. Mon.–Fri.) is next to the Golden Sahara. It sells telephone cards.

An **immigration office** (tel. 775-4515, 7:30 A.M.–noon and 1–3 P.M. Mon.–Fri.) is at the south end of town.

There are three **gas stations** on Avenida 17 de Abril.

Getting There and Around

Changuinola is a regional transit hub, with two

bus terminals and a small airstrip. Sadly, the dilapidated train that used to link Changuinola and Almirante is no more. Those traveling between the Costa Rican border and the islands must pass through this town.

BY AIR

The Changuinola airport is on the north end of town, just east of Avenida 17 de Abril. Taxi fare to and from town is US$0.70.

Air Panama (tel./fax 316-9000, www.flyairpanama.com) offers 1–2 daily flights from the Albrook airport in Panama City to Changuinola (6:45 A.M. and 3:30 P.M. Mon.–Sat., 3:30 P.M. Sun.), and return flights from Changuinola to Panama City (7:15 A.M. and 4 P.M. Mon.–Sat., 4 P.M. Sun.). There is often an intermediate stop in Bocas town; make sure you get off in the right place. The flight takes roughly an hour for nonstops or an hour and a half, sometimes more, if there's a stop in Bocas town. It costs US$113.

BY BUS

Changuinola has two bus terminals. Long-distance buses to Panama City and David leave from Terminal Urracá. Local and regional buses, including those to the Guabito-Sixaola border crossing, leave from the SINCOTAVECOP bus terminal.

Terminal Urracá is on the north end of town between the Hotel Golden Sahara and the Multi-Credit Bank. There is one direct daily bus each way between Panama City and Changuinola. It leaves Changuinola at 7:30 A.M., arriving in Panama City at least 11 hours later. The fare is US$29. An evening bus, usually leaving around 6 P.M., has been added and dropped over the years. Two pieces of luggage are allowed; additional luggage is an extra charge.

Buses from Changuinola to David leave every half hour 3 A.M.–7 P.M. The trip takes about 4.5 hours and costs US$10. Local and regional buses leave from the **SINCOTAVECOP bus terminal,**

BOCAS DEL TORO

across the street from Bar y Restaurante Chiquita Banana. Destinations include:

Almirante: Every 25 minutes, 5:40 A.M.–7:45 P.M. The trip takes 30 minutes and costs US$1.45.

Guabito/Costa Rican border crossing at Sixaola: Every 25 minutes or so, 5:30 A.M.–8 P.M. The trip takes 30 minutes and costs US$1.45. There's also a *colectivo* taxi that works like a bus and runs between Changuinola and Guabito.

El Silencio: Every 20 minutes, 5:30 A.M.–9 P.M. The trip takes 20 minutes and costs US$0.80.

San José, Costa Rica: There is one direct bus a day from Changuinola to San José, Costa Rica. It leaves at 9:55 A.M. and, depending on road and weather conditions, arrives around 4 P.M. Costa Rican time. The fare is US$14. These buses leave from the side of the bus station.

BY TAXI OR CAR

It shouldn't be hard to find a taxi on Avenida 17 de Abril. Expect to pay US$0.70 to the airport, US$8 to El Silencio, US$7 to Guabito, and US$20 to Almirante (up to five passengers).

To reach Changuinola by car from eastern Panama, stay left on the main road when it forks at Almirante. Changuinola is 21 kilometers farther west, on a scenic and curvy road. Watch out for speeding traffic.

HUMEDALES DE SAN SAN PONDSACK

These wetlands, established as a wildlife refuge in 1994, encompass a strip of coast that extends east and south from the Río Sixaola to the Caribbean. It comprises 16,125 hectares, but only a small part of it is easily accessible. The wetlands are managed by a local group called AAMVECONA (www.aamvecona. com), whose acronym translates to "Friends and Neighbors of the Coast and Nature." They run a turtle and manatee conservation project which also does reforestation. The project accepts volunteers.

Walking along the boardwalk gives visitors a close-up look at this otherworldly place. Animals found in the wetlands include an important population of manatees and leatherback and hawksbill sea turtles, but the manatees are shy and the turtles seasonal, so as usual don't get your hopes up. Birders come here for the 67 known avian species it attracts. The only things visitors are guaranteed to see, however, are mangroves, palms, and eerie, brackish water.

The wetlands can be visited either as part of a boat tour from the islands or by taxi from Changuinola. The visitors center at the entrance to the wetlands is just off the road leading to Guabito. Arrange for the taxi either to wait or to pick you up for the return trip. To be sure the taxi will show up at the appointed time, don't pay until the return to Changuinola.

There is not yet a consensus on how to spell the wetlands' funky name. You may see it as San San Pondsock, San San Pond Soc, San-San Pondsack, and so on. It's all the same place, but don't confuse it with Punta Pondsack, also known as Punta Pond Soc, east of Almirante.

GUABITO

Even by the modest standards of mainland Bocas del Toro, the down-at-the-heels border town of Guabito (pronounced wah-BEE-toe, pop. 14,360) has little to offer visitors. It's simply a place to pass through on the way to or from Costa Rica. There are no hotels and no appealing places to eat. The nearest spot with significant services is Changuinola, about a 20-minute drive away.

The border crossing is on an elevated railway trestle on the edge of the Río Sixaola. The combination immigration, customs, and ATP office is right on the train tracks next to the bridge that crosses the river.

The border runs right down the middle of the Río Sixaola. Travelers must cross the railroad bridge on foot or in a vehicle. The bridge

© WILLIAM FRIAR

Crossing over the Río Sixaola in Guabito is a memorable way to enter Panama from Costa Rica.

was built in 1908 and has been deteriorating ever since. Pedestrians should watch their step, as there are large gaps between ties, and a long drop to the river. Crossing the bridge is not the most inviting way to enter a country, but it makes for a memorable photo. A new bridge is being erected, slowly, right next to the old one. The border crossing is quite casual, and anyone who wants to can wander out on the bridge to take a look. Buses and taxis are available downstairs from customs and immigration.

Access to the Bocas del Toro archipelago is by water taxi from Almirante. There are no direct buses from Guabito to Almirante, Panama City, David, or anywhere else you're likely to want to go. Take a bus to the Changuinola bus terminal and change there. Buses to Changuinola run about every 25 minutes, 5:30 A.M.–8 P.M. The trip takes 30 minutes and costs US$1.45.

Taxis should charge around US$7 to Changuinola and US$25 to Almirante. This is

per ride, *not* per person. Taxi drivers and tour guides sometimes try to take advantage of clueless new arrivals at the border, so be polite but firm and don't get ripped off.

Buses from Sixaola, on the Costa Rican side, leave for San José, Costa Rica, at 6 A.M., 8 A.M., 10 A.M., and 3 P.M. The ride takes 6.5–8 hours. (Remember that Costa Rican time is one hour earlier than Panamanian time.) Another option is to take a bus from Sixaola to Puerto Limón and transfer to a San José bus from there.

◖ RÍO TERIBE AND THE NASO

A trip up the Río Teribe is one of the most memorable experiences Bocas del Toro has to offer, and it makes for a nice change of scene for those getting island fever in the archipelago. This is the homeland of the Naso, an indigenous people who live near the river in 11 communities surrounded by beautiful forest. It's a reasonable and accessible trip for those with the slightest sense of adventure, an interest in indigenous cultures, and a desire to explore a bit of tropical forest in rustic but relatively comfortable conditions. The climate is quite different from that on the islands and doesn't fit preconceived notions of a tropical rainforest. It can be rather mild and pleasantly breezy upriver.

Wekso

Wekso is about 40 minutes to an hour up the Río Teribe from El Silencio. It has a grim history as the former site of Pana-Jungla, a jungle-warfare/survival school that put elite Panamanian and foreign troops through legendarily difficult training. It was closed in 1990, but spooky remnants of the camp include a cage that once housed a black panther, the ruins of barracks and officers' quarters, and a serpentarium that once held Panama's deadliest snakes. Today, however, it has been transformed into an ecotourist camp used by the Naso nonprofit **ODESEN** (cell 6574-9874 or 6569-2844, turismonaso_odesen@hotmail.com, http://odesen.bocas.com).

The Wekso camp is on a small hill overlooking the river. The dining area is on the edge of the hillside and has a great view of the river below and the forest beyond. At the back of the camp is a large guest bungalow that resembles an oversize version of a traditional Naso thatched-roof house. It's rustic but perfectly acceptable and tidy, with foam-rubber mattresses, mosquito nets over the beds, and inviting hammocks on the front porch. There's an outhouse with flush toilets. Snakes are not unheard of around the camp; watch your step.

Just below the camp is a ranger station for Parque Internacional La Amistad. This area is not technically in the park but rather in the buffer forest around it. But guests must pay the US$5 park entrance fee anyway.

There is a good chance of spotting a variety of colorful birds in this area, including the white-fronted nunbird, blue-headed parrot, king vultures, long-tailed tyrants, Amazon kingfishers, snowy cotingas, and snowcap and green thorntail hummingbirds. As always, mammals in tropical forests are hard to find, but possibilities include water opossums, white-lipped peccaries, and neotropical river otters. Frogs are generally easy to spot, including red-eyed tree frogs (*Agalychnis callidryas*) and poison-dart frogs (*Oophaga pumilio*).

A pretty loop trail that starts at the camp takes about two hours to walk at a slow pace. A second trail forks off it about 40 minutes in. The forest alternates between primary and secondary growth. The patches of primary forest contain some huge, impressive trees, including bongo, almond, and ceiba. The trail can be good for birding, including crowd pleasers such as toucans, and there's a chance of spotting sloths. This area is too close to well-settled areas to draw much wildlife, however.

Sieyik

About an hour upriver from Wekso is Sieyik, the Naso capital, which is home to the king. It's a village of about 500 people who live in houses scattered around a lovely hillside overlooking the river.

The center of the village is a clearing that contains the royal residence, a school, and the health post, all of which are very simple buildings made from cinderblocks.

A visit to Sieyik with a tour operator will likely include a walk around the village and a visit to a traditional home, which may include lunch. Traditional Naso homes are built on stilts of one kind of palm (*jira*) and the roofs are thatched with another kind (*palenquilla*). Residents sleep on the soft bark of a rubber tree. Newer homes use wooden planks for walls and floor, and sometimes have corrugated zinc roofs.

Visits may also include the chance to buy handicrafts, including objects carved from cedar, which are interesting but rarely achieve

ABOUT THE NASO

The Naso are better known in Panama as the Teribe or Naso-Teribe. Some Naso say that "Teribe" is a mispronunciation of *tjer di,* which means "river of the Grandmother," the ancestral guiding spirit of the people. They are also sometimes known as the Térraba. The Naso are the last people in the Americas to still have a monarch.

Spanish records suggest that in the 16th century the Naso were already well-established in the region, including Almirante Bay as far north as Isla Colón, and may in fact have been the dominant power of the time. The Naso were gradually squeezed out of the area and by the latter half of the 19th century had retreated far up the Río Teribe in the highlands near the Costa Rican border, to communities known as *palenques* (Spanish for palisade or stockade, the name given by the Spaniards to hidden villages).

By their own account, the Naso have fought just about all the indigenous people in the region at one time or another. By the 17th century their numbers had declined. A tuberculosis epidemic in the early 20th century killed many, including the king.

Today the Naso are among the most beleaguered of Panama's eight surviving indigenous peoples. The cultural identity of the few Naso who remain is being eroded on all sides: by the dominant Latin culture, by missionaries, by intermarriage with other indigenous peoples, and so on.

There are about 3,800 Naso left in Panama. As a Naso man once said to me with a sad smile, "*Estamos en peligro de extinción*" ("We are in danger of extinction").

They are working hard to cling to their traditions and land, however. They still speak their ancestral language, along with Spanish. The men tend to wear nondescript white shirts and black slacks, but many women still wear distinctive dresses. These are cotton-print outfits in a single bright, bold color such as blue or yellow. They have puffy blouses and a tiny floral pattern that from a distance can look like polka dots.

The Naso still do not have *comarca* (reservation) status for their land. This is in stark contrast to their far more populous neighbors,

the Ngöbe-Buglé, who now have a *comarca* that covers a huge chunk of western Panama. The Naso continue to tangle with them and others over land ownership.

The biggest threat to their existence today, though, is a Colombian consortium's project to dam the Teribe and a tributary river for a hydroelectric dam project. Environmentalists and indigenous-rights activists say the Bonyik dam (sometimes spelled Bonyic), would displace thousands of people and cause serious environmental damage. UNESCO has expressed "serious concern" over the possible environmental impact of the project.

The Naso and the Ngöbe-Buglé have staged nationwide protests against the project, some of which have ended in violence and death of indigenous people amid accusations of excessive force by government authorities.

The Naso are ruled by a king (or occasionally a queen), who is assisted by a *consejo* (board of advisers) drawn from the communities. The Naso reserve the right to switch kings if they become unhappy with him. They can vote him out, but the replacement has to come from the royal family. They did just that in 2004 when the then-king, Tito Santana, came out in support of the Bonyik dam. The *consejo* deposed him and named a new king, Valentín Santana, who is Tito's uncle. But Tito Santana continued to be supported by some nontraditional Naso and recognized by the Panamanian government. This internal conflict complicated the struggle to create a Naso *comarca*.

The Naso elected a new king from the royal family, Alexis Santana, in 2011, and the Panamanian government has recognized him. In March 2012 the new king signed an agreement with the Panamanian government to reopen negotiations about the project. One provision of the initial agreement allows the dam builders to re-enter Naso territory and resume work.

A bill to create a 130,000-hectare *comarca* for the Naso, which would give them greater self-determination, has been moving through the Panamanian national assembly at a glacial pace.

NASO TALES

The Naso have great folktales. Some of the most evocative stories involve the *indios conejos* (rabbit Indians). They were nocturnal, had stripes down their backs, could see well in the dark, and could run superhumanly fast. Sometimes they ran through the forest at night bearing torches. They were also fierce and wild warriors who favored bows and arrows. The Naso say they waged wars with them near Palenque in the time of their grandparents. The only way the Naso could get the upper hand was to attack at daybreak, while their enemy slept.

What makes these tales especially intriguing is that the other indigenous peoples of western Panama have similar stories of going to war with *indios conejos*. Some versions are even more fanciful, describing them as white and just a meter tall, like mutant rabbits. One theory is that these stories are based on real battles with Miskito Indians. Some Naso don't believe the stories, but others are convinced the *indios conejos* did and still do exist, though today they're hidden away in the Chiriquí highlands.

Other tales are of lost cities and gold mines far up the Teribe beyond Palenque. Again, other indigenous people have similar stories. These may be purely fanciful, of course, but there is evidence the ancient inhabitants of this area had plenty of gold. Columbus was fascinated by the indigenous people he encountered during his brief visit to Bocas del Toro who wore mirror-like discs of gold around their necks. And some believe there was once a quite developed civilization in the highlands. A Panamanian guide told me that a park ranger, looking for survivors of a plane crash, once stumbled upon stone houses 40 kilometers upriver from Palenque.

Tales of evil spirits and sinister encounters are also popular with the Naso. One involves Dö (pronounced "DOO"), a spirit that takes the shape of a monkey but has a scorpion's tail. It's said that he abducts people, keeps them in his cave for eight days, and then drowns them in the river. Ask your hosts about this; on the way back down the river, they can point out the mouth of the cave where the spirit lives. The cave is supposedly hugely long, leading between the Sixaola and Changuinola Rivers. The tale gets even better: They say an American found treasure in the cave 50 years ago. He took it, which would have been okay if he'd left something else behind in exchange. He didn't, and he didn't meet a happy end.

Then there's Älu, the spirit of the bongo tree, which takes the form of a monkey without a head. Its eyes are in its armpits, so in order to see it must raise its arms into the air. When Älu appears, blood gushes from around the bongo tree.

By the by, Wekso, where many visitors spend the night, is a Naso word that means "the place of bongo trees."

the level of artistry one sees with Emberá-Wounaan and Guna works.

Parque Internacional La Amistad

The Río Teribe is the Caribbean gateway of Parque Internacional La Amistad (PILA) and the Palo Seco Buffer Forest that borders it. Far up in the headlands of the Teribe there are still jaguars, harpy eagles, tapirs, and macaws. That's because it's brutally hard to get to this area. The Caribbean side of PILA is far less accessible than the Pacific side, which lies in Chiriquí province and has some developed trails close to population centers. Anyone who wants to enter the park from the Caribbean slope is in for a serious trek and needs a skilled guide and boatmen and considerable supplies. The terrain is steep, there are no trails, and the boat has to fight an increasingly fast and powerful river. Even for the Naso, the upper reaches of the Teribe are becoming a distant memory. Getting to the Naso homeland of Palenque, a long-abandoned village, requires a full day on the river.

Getting There and Around

Just getting to Naso country is a fun little

© WILLIAM FRIAR

the royal residence and graveyard, Sieyik

adventure. In the days of the jungle-warfare school, there was a forest road that led as far as the Pana-Jungla, but it has disappeared back into the forest and the ever-shifting river. Today visitors come mainly by boat up the Río Teribe, though some areas can be reached on horseback or on foot on rough, narrow trails.

The departure point for the river journey is El Silencio, a tiny community about 10 kilometers from Changuinola, where the Río Teribe meets the Río Changuinola. River transport is by motorized *piragua* (dugout canoe). It's a beautiful trip. Small rapids ripple the river, and the air feels incredibly fresh and clean after the humidity of the towns and coast. Farm country at the beginning gives way to lush countryside and a view of the Talamanca Mountains in the distance. The trip downriver is twice as fast. Tour operators sometimes let guests return the old-fashioned way: on disposable balsa-wood rafts that follow the current and are abandoned once the destination is reached.

As all this suggests, getting up the Río Teribe and exploring the area requires a fair amount of planning and is usually done through a tour operator or directly through one of two Naso groups, Soposo Rainforest Adventures or ODESEN. Both groups offer single- and multiple-day trips that include transportation, food, accommodations, and guided walks.

Soposo Rainforest Adventures (cell 6631-2222, www.soposo.com) is run by a former Peace Corps worker, Demecia, and her Naso husband, Celestino. Their operation is professional and well organized. It's based in Soposo, which is on the Río Teribe about five minutes downriver from Wekso. They have built traditional-style huts for guests with double beds, mosquito nets, porches, and hammocks. There is no electricity; lanterns are used at night. Stays include guided hikes and, depending on the length of stay, visits to Sieyik and other communities. Trips include round-trip transportation from Almirante, accommodations, guided hikes, cultural activities, and all meals.

A one-night stay is US$140 per person. For those under time pressure, they also offer single-day trips (9 A.M.–4:30 P.M.) to Soposo, for US$90 per person, that feature a traditional lunch and a hike. A two-night stay (US$275 pp) includes a visit to Sieyik and an optional homestay with a Naso family. A five-night stay (US$400 pp) allows time for longer hikes and homestays.

An older ecotourism project is run by a Naso nonprofit called **ODESEN** (cell 6574-9874 or 6569-2844, turismonaso_odesen@hotmail.com, http://odesen.bocas.com). It's a Spanish acronym that translates to Organization for Naso Sustainable Ecotourism Development. Assisted by Conservation International, the group uses proceeds from tourist visits to help the community. ODESEN currently houses most guests at the Wekso camp.

Visits can be arranged directly through ODESEN or through tour operators who work with the group. Visitors who book through ODESEN are charged cafeteria-style according to the services they need. The boat ride between El Silencio and Wekso is US$50 round-trip for up to six people. Lodging is US$20 per person. Food is US$3 for breakfast, US$6 for lunch, and US$5 for dinner. A guided hike of the trails near Wekso is US$20 per group. Add to this the US$5 per person entrance fee for the national park and the cost of traveling between Almirante or Changuinola and El Silencio, and a couple should count on spending around US$80 per person total for the whole overnight adventure, including all transportation, or less if traveling in a group. No one should come all this way without visiting at least one of the upriver communities, though, so add US$85 per person for a guided trip upriver to Sieyik or Sieykin, the site of the Naso capital and royal residence; again, this is significantly cheaper if done with a group.

There is no electricity at any of the facilities used by either ODESEN or Soposo; candles and flashlights provide the only illumination at night. Traditional meals are generally simple and can include such dishes as *palmito* and *plosón* salad. *Palmito* is heart of palm. *Plosón* is a fern that contains a tiny amount of cyanide—it's quite tasty.

Day trips are definitely worthwhile, but it'd be a shame to make this much effort and not spend at least a night; it really deepens the experience.

It rains year-round up the Río Teribe, but less so in January–March and August–October. March is the driest month. Bring rain gear, a light jacket, and waterproof bags for electronics and passports regardless of when you come. It can get cooler and breezy during the summer (January–March). It's also a good idea to bring bottled water or water-purification tablets or filters.

CENTRAL PANAMA

The section of Panama that stretches roughly from Altos de Campana in the east to the Fortuna Road in the west contains Panama's most popular beaches, its most accessible highlands, and some of its most important and historic provincial towns. The Cordillera Central, Panama's central mountain range, forms the backbone of most of this long stretch of land. Its steep, sawtoothed peaks create a fortress-like wall between the Pacific and Caribbean slopes, making it especially easy to discern the Continental Divide here.

The Pacific side contains some of the longest-settled parts of Panama. Significant population centers include the quaint provincial town of Penonomé, the industrial outpost of Aguadulce, and the major transportation hub of Santiago. These and most of the other sizable towns are in the lowlands right on the Interamerican Highway—also known as the Pan-American Highway or, in Spanish, the Interamericana—and most of the beaches are just a couple of kilometers south of it.

These beaches are among the nicest and most accessible in the country, and they're in a part of Panama that sees less rain than average. As a result, the area is booming, with major resorts and condo developments going up at an alarming speed.

Lovely beaches are also found on the Archipiélago de las Perlas, an archipelago of more than 90 Pacific islands that begins just a 15-minute plane ride or hour boat trip from Panama City.

HIGHLIGHTS

LOOK FOR ◖ TO FIND RECOMMENDED SIGHTS, ACTIVITIES, DINING, AND LODGING.

◖ **Farallón:** Enjoy the sun at Panama's fastest-growing Pacific beach destination (page 243).

◖ **Sunday Market:** El Valle's market is a popular weekend destination for Panama City residents in search of crafts, plants, and an excuse to enjoy the cool weather and natural attractions (page 252).

◖ **El Copé:** This little-visited park is an eastern outpost of Panama's rugged western highlands, with good facilities for campers (page 264).

◖ **Natá de los Caballeros:** A little town with a long history, Natá has a 500-year-old church, one of the oldest in the Americas (page 268).

◖ **Santa Fé:** This peaceful mountain town recalls a pre-boom Boquete (page 275).

The highlands are all north of the highway, though many of them are easy to get to on good roads. The most popular of these spots is El Valle de Antón. More isolated places are not much farther away, and their beauty makes it worth the trouble to get there. All are dotted along the Cordillera Central, which means visitors at the higher elevations get to experience both Pacific and Caribbean flora and fauna.

At the Continental Divide, most roads end and the only way forward is on foot through dense tropical forest. Much of the Caribbean slope is less well known and more lightly settled than some remote parts of the Darién. Exploring it requires a serious organized trek through rugged wilderness.

PLANNING YOUR TIME

Which destinations in central Panama to choose will depend on your taste and where else in Panama you're planning to go. Those who want a little beach time within easy driving distance of Panama City have lots of options. Plan to spend at least a couple of nights to have time to truly relax.

For big full-service resorts with lots of facilities, go for **Coronado** or the resorts in and around **Santa Clara** and **Farallón.** The resorts at the latter are newer, and though a construction explosion is rapidly transforming it, the area is still not as densely developed as long-established Coronado. Their white-sand beaches are also among the prettiest on the coast, though

CENTRAL PANAMA

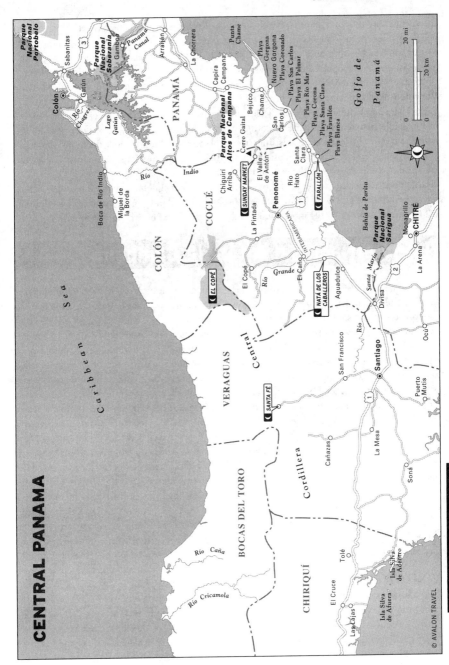

CENTRAL PANAMA

Parque Nacional Portobelo

Sabanitas

Colón

Río Chagres

Lago Gatún

Gatún

Parque Nacional Soberanía

Gamboa

Panamá Canal

3

Arraiján

La Chorrera

Punta Chame

Playa Chame

Capira

Campana

Parque Nacional Altos de Campaña

Cerro Gaital

Bejuco

Chame

San Carlos

Playa Gorgona

Nuevo Gorgona

Playa San Carlos

Playa El Palmar

Playa Río Mar

Playa Corona

Santa Clara

Playa Santa Clara

Playa Farallón

Playa Blanca

Golfo de Panamá

PANAMÁ

Boca de Río Indio

Río

Indio

Chiguirí Arriba

SUNDAY MARKET

El Valle de Antón

Penonomé

Río Hato

FARALLÓN

1

INTERAMERICANA

COCLÉ

La Pintada

Bahía de Parita

Parque Nacional Sarigua

Monagrillo

CHITRÉ

La Arena

2

COLÓN

Miguel de la Borda

EL COPÉ

El Copé

Río

Grande

El Caño

NATÁ DE LOS CABALLEROS

Aguadulce

Santa María

Río

Divisá

Ocú

Caribbean Sea

San Francisco

Santiago

Puerto Mutis

1

VERAGUAS

Central

SANTA FÉ

Cordillera

Cañazas

La Mesa

Soná

BOCAS DEL TORO

Río Caña

Tolé

El Cruce

CHIRIQUÍ

Río Cricamola

Las Lajas

Isla Silva de Afuera

Isla Silva de Adentro

20 mi

20 km

© AVALON TRAVEL

CENTRAL PANAMA

the surf can be rough. The other beach spots generally offer cheaper but less attractive places to stay, on beaches that have calmer surf but aren't going to grace a postcard anytime soon.

It's easy to add a day or overnight trip to **El Valle de Antón** from any of these beach spots; Santa Clara and Farallón are especially close to it. If possible, plan to visit El Valle on a Sunday, when its famous little market is bustling.

El Valle has the largest selection of lodgings, restaurants, and activities in the central highlands, and it's the easiest to get to of the mountain spots. **Parque Nacional Omar Torrijos H. (El Copé),** by contrast, is the most remote and

wild of these spots, but it has better visitor facilities than any other national park in the country. It's a good place to spend the night and enjoy some evening and morning hiking and bird-watching. It can get surprisingly chilly in the highlands—take a windbreaker and rain gear at any time of year. As attractive as the central highlands are, those short on time and planning to head to the wilder and even more beautiful western highlands won't miss too much by skipping them.

The **Archipiélago de las Perlas** is the closest major island group to Panama City. It offers beautiful beaches and lots of aquatic activities.

Parque Nacional Altos de Campana

Established in 1966, Altos de Campana is Panama's oldest national park. Its 4,817 acres are spread over hillsides that range from 400 meters above sea level to the 850-meter-high Cerro Campana. Birders come up here for a chance to see the gorgeous orange-bellied trogon and other striking species. But the countryside is heavily settled, with only fragments of intact tropical and premontane forest left. There's a mirador just up from the park's ranger station, on the left, though the view is plenty dramatic just from the road. That view is the main reason to come up here; this place will appeal to most people more as a highway vista point than as a park to hike and camp in. It offers a breathtaking panorama of the Pacific Ocean, Punta Chame, craggy hills, an estuary that snakes up through the green countryside, and, on a clear day, Isla Taboga in the far distance.

VISITOR INFORMATION

The **ANAM ranger station** is four kilometers uphill from the turn off the Interamericana, on the left. Pay the US$5 entrance fee here, plus US$5 more to camp. For US$15, you may be able to rent a bunk in a cabin on a ridge behind the

station. It's meant for ANAM staff, but if there's room, you're welcome to stay. The cabin has two basic rooms, each with four bunk beds, a common room, and a shared cold-water bathroom. Bring bedding. It's nothing special, but the price is right and you can't beat the location: perched right above a steep, craggy valley, with sweeping views all the way down the hills and out to sea.

The ranger at the station can answer basic questions (in Spanish only) about the area and the single developed trail, **Sendero La Cruz.** Five kilometers up from the ANAM station, or nine kilometers from the turnoff, you'll see a *senderos* sign on the right. Turn there onto a brutal road that requires a four-wheel drive with high clearance and a good warranty. Head up toward the towers as far as possible, then park. The trail leads through mostly secondary forest to a cross 700 meters away and 800 meters above sea level. The hike up and back takes about two hours.

GETTING THERE

The turnoff to Altos de Campana is less than an hour west of Panama City. The right turn up from the westbound side of the Interamericana,

STAYING SAFE ON PANAMA'S HIGHWAYS

Drivers should take it easy on the windy, hilly stretch of the Interamericana that heads west past Altos de Campana. The curves are deceptively sharp, and many cars lose control. Take the speed signs seriously – they're really not being conservative.

All the mainland areas mentioned in this chapter are well served by buses from Panama City. Try to travel in the morning, when service is more frequent and it's easier to find your way around. It's much tougher to get transportation to remoter areas after dark. For beach and lowland areas, it's not necessary to take a bus that has your destination on the windshield; any bus plying the Interamericana that goes at least as far as your stop will drop you off. Buses to highland destinations are generally less frequent, though it's easy to get a bus to El Valle.

Renting a car is also a reasonable option, especially to get to the beaches. The road from Panama City is good the whole way, if more than a bit dangerous. Speeding is a problem on the Interamericana, so drive defensively. It's possible to get to El Valle, La Pintada, Santa Fé, and San Francisco in a regular car; just about every other highland spot described in this chapter requires a powerful, high-clearance four-wheel-drive vehicle.

Avoid driving through the countryside at night, when visibility is poor and help harder to find if you get into trouble. Note that there's a toll booth about 30 kilometers from Panama City, at the start of the Autopista Arraiján-La Chorrera.

about six kilometers west of Capira, comes up fast. Be careful, and approach the turn very slowly. The drive starts steep, and it sometimes requires a four-wheel drive.

To get to the park from Panama City by public transportation, take a bus that goes at least as far as Capira, which is where you'll switch buses. Buses make the trip from Capira up to Altos de Campana every day 8 A.M.–6:30 P.M. Look for Capira-Chicá on the windshield—Altos de Campana is an intermediate stop. Buses make the run every hour or two; service is erratic. Buses head back down to Capira 5 A.M.–4 P.M. It's also possible to get a taxi from Capira, but expect to pay around US$25.

Beach Towns and Resorts

Wide, sandy, and accessible beaches start a little under an hour's drive from Panama City and stretch west for 50 kilometers. This strip of coast is where most people who live in and around Panama City, at least those who can afford it, go for a weekend at the beach. These beaches are great for swimming, bodysurfing, and lazing about. Some offer decent surfing. Those interested in diving and snorkeling need to head farther west or to the Caribbean side of the isthmus. One spot, Punta Chame, is known for windsurfing and kitesurfing.

The area has undergone major development in the last couple of decades, however, and now the most popular beaches have condo towers looming over them. You sometimes have to contend with weekend personal-watercraft riders, all-terrain-vehicle riders, and boombox blarers, though some effort has been made to control these nuisances. But it's still quite possible to find clean, secluded spots without another soul on the beach for as far as you can see, especially if you come during the week.

With the exception of the stretch of coast from Santa Clara to Farallón, which has light-sand beaches, the sand mostly comes in shades of

CENTRAL PANAMA

brown, gray, and even black. But those who can get beyond their postcard preconceptions of a tropical beach will find these quite inviting. They're wide, long, and sandy, and the water is warm.

Many of the places to stay along the beach have restaurants attached. There are lots of other simple places to eat along the side of the road on the way to or from the beaches. But those with their own cars should consider doing what local weekenders do: Pack a cooler. Some of the accommodations have kitchen facilities. The most popular beach areas have small grocery stores with basic supplies. Playa Coronado has a large 24-hour supermarket.

The big resorts cater primarily to package and charter groups from outside Panama, but in the rainy season they sometimes offer special deals for people already in Panama. Keep an eye out for ads online and in Panamanian newspapers. These can be a good deal, but bear in mind that the resorts can get packed with partiers blaring music night and day.

There are still (thankfully) few places along the coast to rent boats, ATVs, Jet Skis, and other recreational toys. Those who want a little boat ride can always hire a fisherman and putter around. Campesinos all along the beaches rent horses, especially on the weekends. If you have trouble finding a likely candidate, ask for help at your hotel. Except at resorts, it shouldn't cost more than a few dollars an hour. Please be considerate about where you ride; horses muck up the beach for sunbathers.

The Pacific coast of Panama is completely different from the Caribbean coast. For one thing, where the Caribbean tides average 30 centimeters, the Pacific's massive tides range about 3.5–5.5 meters. Some of the beaches have strong rip currents and pounding surf, so watch out. The beaches are listed in order of their distance from Panama City, with the closest described first.

PUNTA CHAME

Punta Chame (POON-tah CHA-meh) is at the end of a dry and rather barren peninsula

> # A ROADSIDE ATTRACTION
>
> **Artesanías Típicas Panameñas** (tel. 248-5313, 8 A.M.-6 P.M. daily) on the westbound side of the Interamericana, east of Capira, near kilometer marker 50, has long been a convenient place to stretch one's legs and do a little shopping on the way to and from the beach. It's a large, open building with a moderate selection of fancy hammocks (the most elegant of which are the white ones from Nicaragua, which sell here for about US$150), tooled-leather chairs, traditional Azuero ceramics and devil masks, and other souvenir possibilities. With enough warning, they can make hand-painted ceramic signs with house numbers, family name, or personalized messages. Those with their own transportation can place an order when heading west and pick up the completed sign on the way back east.

that curves up toward the mainland to the east, forming Bahía de Chame, a long, narrow bay that from shore looks like a quiet strait. Getting here by car from Panama City takes less than 1.5 hours. This is a popular windsurfing spot. In the middle of the bay, between the tip of Punta Chame and the mainland, is Isla Taborcillo, which was once owned by John Wayne. It's a rather forlorn spot.

Despite various plans over the years to develop Punta Chame for tourism, it has traditionally appealed mainly to avid sailboarders. The beaches aren't as nice as those farther along the coast, there are few facilities, and the village is nondescript. But the area does offer solitude and lovely views of the sea, islands, and hilly mainland. And there are now more and better places to stay than ever before, and more ways for outdoorsy types to entertain themselves.

There are few services in Punta Chame itself. The town of Chame, near the Interamericana, has a branch of the Banco Nacional de Panamá and a little store with basic supplies next to a soccer field.

Accommodations and Food

All the places to stay and eat listed below are on a divided avenue which starts at the entrance of town and ends a couple of kilometers farther on at the beach.

The French-owned ◖**Hostal Casa Amarilla** (cell 6032-6738, www.hostalcasaamarilla.com, standard rooms US$70 s/d, cabins US$25 s, US$30 d) is at the beginning of the main avenue leading into Punta Chame. It is one of several places in Panama with the word "hostal" in the name that are far nicer than that term implies to an English speaker. As the rest of the name suggests, the main building is a yellow house, but is only part of a compound that includes a restaurant on an attractive covered terrace, well-tended gardens, a small L-shaped swimming pool, a pool table, and a few wooden cabins. The compound is not on the water, but the beach is 300 meters away.

Rooms in the main house are pleasant, with cheerful decor, teak floors, air-conditioning, and private bath, and wooden cabins are intended for travelers on a tighter budget. They're small and much simpler but still attractive, with fans and shared bathrooms. The beds in all the accommodations have good, semi-orthopedic mattresses. The whole place is spotless.

The terrace bar/restaurant (7–10:30 A.M. breakfast, noon–4 P.M. lunch, 6:30–9:30 P.M. daily, US$15) serves French and French-Antillean fare. There's free wireless Internet.

Nitro City (tel. 202-6875 or 223-1747, http://nitrocitypanama.com, kite/skate season rates start at US$289 s/d including breakfast, kids under 12 free) feels like a place that was built based on the doodlings of a teenage boy after he'd had too much soda and candy. It's an upscale extreme-sports resort that opened in December 2011, focusing on kiteboarding, which is what Punta Chame is best known for, but also including surfing, motocross, wakeboarding in a practice park with an artificial pond, skateboarding, and just about any other rough-and-tumble activity a kid might be interested in. You don't have to stay here to take advantage of the facilities. Day-use passes are US$30.

There's a large, lagoon-shaped pool and a warehouse of a restaurant that is open to the public (8 A.M.–9 P.M. daily, mains US$14–19). The small menu includes kid-friendly fare such as pasta, pizza, and barbecued meats.

There are several categories of rooms, all of which are in two-story buildings abutting the beach. In fact, everything at this place abuts the beach, which is long and attractive, with white-and-gray sand and a great view of the ocean and Isla Taborcillo. "Champion Rooms" (US$342 s/d) aren't that big, and feature bathrooms with peculiarly tiny whirlpool bathtub. There's a hot tub on the deck. "Partner Rooms" (US$289 s/d) have no hot tub. The fanciest is the Nitro Suite (US$462 s/d), which among other things includes an arcade video game. All rooms feature absolutely massive flat-screen TVs. If after all this your kids still claim to be bored, you can send them to the video game room. All these rates are for the kiteboarding seasons from late December to the end of April and the beginning of July to the middle of August. Prices drop around US$66 a night at other times.

Punta Chame Villas (tel. 240-5590, cell 6006-7265, www.hotelpuntachamevillas.com, US$150 s/d including breakfast, a/c) is a four-story, 15-room hotel that opened in 2010 with an attractive swimming pool, a restaurant/bar, and a little Internet café. Rooms are simple but modern and clean, with flat-screen TVs, balconies, and soft but okay mattresses. The restaurant is open 7:30 A.M.–9 P.M., or later on the weekend. The hotel can arrange car rentals and transfers to or from the international airport in Panama City.

Getting There

The turnoff to Punta Chame is about 70 kilometers west of Panama City. The drive takes a little under an hour. Don't confuse the turnoff to Punta Chame with the town of Chame, which is a few kilometers farther west along the Interamericana. If you see a sign for Chame, you've gone too far. From the Punta Chame turn-off it's another 25 kilometers down to the beach on a potholed road that's unpaved in sections.

To get to Punta Chame from Panama City by public transportation, take a bus that goes at least as far as Bejuco (beh-HOO-coh), about a kilometer past the Punta Chame turn-off. The fare is US$2.60. Get off at Bejuco, which is little more than a way station on the Interamericana, and take either a "bus" (really a pickup truck, US$1.25) or a taxi (asking US$15, but try bargaining) to Punta Chame. The pickup-buses are by the Texaco station; the taxis are a little farther west, near an underpass. Buses run every hour or so from approximately 6 A.M.–7 P.M. from Bejuco to Punta Chame and 5 A.M.–4:30 P.M. from Punta Chame to Bejuco.

PLAYA GORGONA

The next beach area along the coast is Playa Gorgona, about seven kilometers past the Punta Chame turnoff. Gorgona has the feel of a modest weekend beach destination that's past its prime and hovering on the brink of abandonment—which is exactly what it is. There are better hotels and nicer beaches farther west.

The place will be of interest mainly to surfers. **Playa Malibu,** right next to Gorgona, has a reputation for offering the best and most reliable ride along this whole stretch of coast. To get there, take the Gorgona turnoff from the Interamericana and head straight down to the beach. The break is to the left, near the mouth of a river. Those traveling by car should take a four-wheel drive and park it on the beach near the break. Otherwise, there's a good chance someone may break into the car while you're surfing.

Accommodations and Food

Casa Sin Punto (Calle Los Pescadores, tel. 832-6447, cell 6780-5495, www.casasinpunto. com, US$72 s/d, including breakfast, a/c) offers three simple but clean and pleasant rooms in a house a few hundred meters from the ocean. There's free wireless Internet, and the friendly German owner can make dinner if requested.

Rincón Catracho (tel. 240-5807, noon–9 P.M. on weekends, call ahead of time during the week) has a friendly sidewalk café ambience in the middle of this down-at-the-heels village. The chef offers a small menu of international cuisine.

The aptly named ◖ **La Ruina** (tel. 240-5126, cell 6527-8462, www.laruinatavern.com, noon–late Thurs.–Sun., under US$10) is a restaurant and bar built into what had been a U.S. military beer hall during World War II (an antiaircraft battery was nearby; the United States feared a Japanese attack on the Panama Canal). It's the dream project of Frank Marcheski, a retired U.S. Army sergeant from New Jersey, who admired the ruin when he was stationed in Panama in the late 1970s and always wanted to buy it. He and his Panamanian wife, Dilcia, who grew up in a house next to the ruin, now do. It's a large, airy two-story place with two long bars downstairs and staircases that snake about the place to create lots of private nooks upstairs. The fare tends toward burgers, lasagna, seafood, and *arroz con pollo* (chicken and rice). It's a simple place but incredibly atmospheric. Old photos are on the walls, and the couple has lots of information on the interesting but little-known history of this area. Frank was a card dealer in Atlantic City, and he's set up a card table upstairs for fun. There's sometimes live music on the weekends.

Getting There

The turnoff to Playa Gorgona is on the Interamericana about seven kilometers west of the turnoff to Punta Chame and four kilometers east of the Coronado turnoff. La Ruina and Rincón Catracho are in downtown Gorgona, which is a right turn before the beach as you head toward Cabaña Playa Gorgona. Follow the prominent signs to La Ruina. Rincón Catracho is right across the street from it. Those without their own wheels will probably have to hoof it from the Interamericana to any of these places. Alternatively, if there are no taxis around, visitors can get off the bus at the Coronado turnoff and get a taxi back to Gorgona from there.

PLAYA CORONADO

Playa Coronado, about 10 kilometers past the Punta Chame turnoff, is the most developed beach in Panama. Because the beach is a long sweep of pure (blackish) sand, this has long been a favorite place for those living in Panama City to build a weekend beach house. Growth here has exploded in the last couple of decades. Coronado has condo towers, mansions, several places to eat, an equestrian club, and a major resort hotel. Every centimeter of beachfront property has been built on, but even here there's a good chance of not having to deal with crowds.

Accommodations and Food

A moderate deal in pricey Coronado is **Hotel Gaviota** (Panama City reservations tel. 224-9053 or 224-9056, Coronado tel. 240-4526, http://hotelgaviotapanama.com, US$60.50 s/d, a/c). Head down the main road from the Coronado guardhouse and make a right at the new Ibiza Coronado apartment building. It's about a kilometer past the white condo towers toward the end of Paseo George Smith (also called Paseo Lajas). It offers 10 rooms, most of which are in a motel-style building set back from the beach with no view. The ones in this building are simple, and pleasant. Each has two good double beds and attractive warm-water bathrooms. Avoid rooms 1 and 2, which are old and small, set in a separate building. Main dishes in the simple restaurant run US$7–15. The restaurant is officially open 8 A.M.–5 P.M. daily, but that's likely only the case on dry-season weekends. The place has two swimming pools set in a well-tended, flower-filled garden

on a rise overlooking the ocean. Amenities include a bar on the premises and a large new open-air dining room. Warning: Day-trippers from Panama City are shipped in by the busload on dry-season weekends. Day passes that allow use of all facilities except the rooms are US$18. Room prices drop during the week. Packages that include all meals are available.

The small, upscale **Corowalk Inn** (tel. 240-1516 or 240-1517, www.hostalesdelpacifico.com, US$77 s/d, a/c), in the El Rey shopping complex on the Interamericana, is a 14-room hotel built in 2002. It offers 14 modern, attractive rooms with good beds. The rooms are small and simple but pleasant. Some rooms have no windows, and others are on a terrace overlooking the El Rey parking lot. The staff are refreshingly friendly. This place is on the highway, not the beach.

Coronado Hotel and Resort (Avenida Punta Prieta, Panama City reservations tel. 264-3164 or 264-2724, U.S. toll-free tel. 866/465-3207, www.coronadoresort.com, starts at US$300 s/d), a short drive past the Coronado guardhouse, is one of the biggest resort hotels outside of Panama City. It has a health spa, 18-hole golf course, four tennis courts, three bars, three restaurants, a large swimming pool, and so on. Its latest addition is a huge equestrian club on a separate property, with its own steak house, **Restaurante Estribos de Plata.** Its 76 rooms (all suites) are modern and cheerful, ranging in size from large to gigantic. The least expensive are the standard suites, which have a king-size bed, a sitting room with two sofa beds, minibar, telephone, hot-water bathroom, and TV. Package deals are sometimes available. Guests can rent bicycles, golf carts, ATVs, horses, and more. All kinds of tours are available.

This place is not actually on the beach. A frequent shuttle bus runs between the hotel and its private beach club on the water two kilometers away. A nice place to grab a simple lunch at the hotel (hotel guests only) is **La Terraza,** a

CENTRAL PANAMA

casual open-air place near the pool. The food is nothing special, but the atmosphere is pleasant.

El Rincón del Chef (tel. 240-1941, cell 6676-4834, http://elrincondelchefpanama.com, 8 A.M.–9 P.M. Mon.–Thurs., 8 A.M.–10 P.M. Fri.–Sat., 7 A.M.–9 P.M. Sun., under US$10) is a cute, Spanish mission–style open-air restaurant offering an ambitious range of dishes, from (rather greasy) corvina wontons to Thai food to imported beef. It's the best bet for a decent meal. They rent coolers (US$7.50/day) and sell ice (US$0.50/bag). It's on the right as you head toward the Coronado gaurdhouse.

Information and Services

There's a modern shopping complex at the turnoff to Coronado that has a huge 24-hour **El Rey** supermarket, whose sign on a tall pole is visible for kilometers. There's a **pharmacy** inside the supermarket.

The complex also includes the Corowalk Inn, a **gas station,** a **Global Bank** (8:30 A.M.–3 P.M. Mon.–Fri., 9 A.M.–2:30 P.M. Sat.), and other stores. Global Bank has an ATM.

Two newer shopping malls have been built along the Interamericana next door. Most of the stores are unlikely to interest the average traveler—don't expect upscale clothing shops, for instance—but there is now a choice of supermarkets, pharmacies, banks, and U.S. fast-food outlets. There's also a **Felipe Motta wine store** (9 A.M.–6 P.M. Sun.–Thurs., 9 A.M.–9 P.M. Fri. and Sat.) It's in the mall on the west side of the Interamericana, just past the turnoff to Coronado.

Getting There and Around

The turnoff to Coronado is well marked; look for the El Rey supermarket sign. There's a guardhouse at the entrance to the area. Those who arrive without a hotel reservation or an invitation from a resident have to stop at the Coronado *sala de ventas* (sales office) in a building shortly before the guardhouse, to be issued a free day pass. This process is a nuisance,

especially since all beaches in Panama are open to the public, but it does keep the crowds down. Just say you are taking a look at the area. Gringos should have no trouble getting a pass.

Buses run constantly between Coronado and Panama City, about 80 kilometers east (US$2.80). From the turnoff you can take a taxi or minibus to the beach or your hotel for a few dollars.

A taxi from the shopping complex on the Interamericana to the beach, three kilometers away, costs around US$3. Minibuses make the same run from in front of the hardware store on the road leading into Coronado, across from the shopping complex, for US$0.50.

BETWEEN PLAYA CORONADO AND PLAYA CORONA

The 15 kilometers of beach between Coronado and Corona are relatively undeveloped and have few facilities. The area is most popular with surfers. All beaches are a left turn off the Interamericana, then a couple of kilometers drive or hike to the beach.

The best known spots are **Playa Teta,** about three kilometers west of the Coronado turnoff onto an unmarked dirt road; **Playa El Palmar,** just after the town of San Carlos; and **Playa Río Mar,** two kilometers past San Carlos onto a well-marked road. The sea bottom tends to be rocky in this area, so booties are a must. (Non-surfers will not find most stretches of these beaches very attractive.) There are 2–3 breaks at each spot. Teta and Río Mar are the most popular.

San Carlos, 11 kilometers west of the Coronado turnoff, is the only sizable town along the Interamericana between Coronado and Corona. It's about at the midpoint of the surfing beaches along this part of the coast. There's little of interest in town; the main significance of San Carlos for tourists is that buses run frequently between it and the highland town of El Valle de Antón. However, these buses pick up and drop off passengers right on the Interamericana, not in the town itself.

Accommodations

The few simple places to stay in this area will likely be of most interest to surfers. (There are also surf camps in El Palmar, Spain, which can cause some confusion when researching on the Internet.) A surf school aimed at beginners is **Panama Surf School** (cell 6673-0820, www.panamasurfschool.com), run by an Argentinean named Flor Villareal. Surf lessons in English or Spanish start at US$40 per adult. Groups and kids get a discount. Experienced surfers can rent boards for US$15 per day. Transportation from Panama City and a variety of land and sea tours are also available.

Villa Sanchez Barry (cell 6667-0808, www.villasanchezbarry.com, starts at US$27.50 s, US$35 d) is on the road to El Valle, not on the beach, but good beaches are a short drive away and it's high enough up in the hills to catch a breeze and offer great views of the coast and ocean. Lodging is in a home that offers a tiny but pleasant and air-conditioned backpackers' room. An entire apartment in the house with two bedrooms, two bathrooms, a kitchen, and a solarium is also available (US$66 s/d, three-night minimum). There's also a separate two-bedroom cottage (US$55 s/d, three-night minimum). All accommodations have access to kitchens. You definitely feel like you're living in the owners' house here, so it's a good thing they're a friendly and welcoming Panamanian and American couple. There's an attractive swimming pool. Rates provided are for "bareboat" accommodations. Packages that include meals, transfers, and/or tours are also available.

Getting There

Surfers without their own transportation will probably have to hoof it with their boards at least a kilometer or two from the bus stop on the Interamericana to any of these beaches. Bus fare from Panama City to any of these turnoffs is no more than US$3.25.

Buses between San Carlos and El Valle run constantly during daylight hours. The fare is US$1. The last bus down from El Valle leaves at 8 P.M. Bus fare between San Carlos and Panama City is US$3.25.

SANTA CLARA AND VICINITY

The days of Santa Clara being the prettiest area beach with inexplicably little tourism development are rapidly coming to an end. The secret's finally out, and all-inclusive resorts, condos, and golf courses are moving in. Fortunately, a few smaller-scale places are still around. Especially during the week and the rainy season, you probably won't have to deal with crowds, at least not yet. The short road from the highway to the beach has lots of potholes, but is drivable in a regular car if you're careful.

Accommodations and Food

There are a few pleasant places to stay in Santa Clara. None of them is a bargain, however. This is also the best area on this part of the coast for camping. There are still a few places where backpackers can pitch a tent in secure surroundings with good facilities for a few dollars. You can also just claim any open stretch of beach for free, but keep an eye on your gear.

A new bed-and-breakfast, **Villa Botero B&B** (tel. 993-2708 or cell 6616-4991, www.villaboterobb.com, juanpepas2@hotmail.com, US$137.50 s/d, including breakfast, a/c) has only two guest rooms, both of which face a swimming pool and have minimalist modern decor, flat-screen TVs, in-room safe, minifridge, and free wireless Internet. Besides the swimming pool, the main house has a barbecue, kitchen, and laundry facilities, which guests are welcome to use. The B&B is a 10-minute walk to the beach. To get to Villa Botero, follow the main road into Santa Clara. Take the unpaved road on the right about 100 meters past the police post. The B&B is the fourth house down, with the large black gate.

Restaurante y Balneario Santa Clara

(tel. 993-2123, 11 A.M.–6 P.M. Mon.–Fri., 9 A.M.–7 P.M. Sat.–Sun. in the dry season, under US$10) is a restaurant, bar, and campsite that gets packed on dry-season weekends. During the week, you're likely to have it all to yourself. Campers can stay here for US$3–5 per person. The rate includes use of a *rancho*—a little open-air thatched-roof hut—and hammock right on the beach, clean bathrooms, and outdoor showers. Day visitors can use these facilities for US$1 each. There's a guard on duty at night. This is by far the best place to camp along this entire stretch of coast.

The restaurant is little more than a large thatched hut on the beach. The food isn't memorable, but it'll do in a pinch and the location is cool. The place is on the beach near Cabañas Las Sirenas. The restaurant specializes in seafood and pizzas. *Pulpo a ajillo* (octopus in garlic sauce) is chewy but tasty.

Restaurante y Balneario Santa Clara also arranges horse rental for about US$6 an hour on the weekends. Motorboat rentals may also be possible.

■ **Cabañas Las Sirenas** (Panama City reservations, through Pesantez Tours tel. 263-7577, Cabañas Las Sirenas office, Spanish only tel. 993-3235 or cell 6550-2500, www.lasirenas.com, starts at US$143 for one-bedroom cottage) is my favorite place to stay on my favorite Pacific coast beach. It offers the quietest, coziest, and most secluded lodging around. To get there, head down the paved main road from the Santa Clara turnoff and follow the Las Sirenas signs, which will lead you onto a dirt road. Both roads are potholed but drivable. Las Sirenas has added cheerful new furnishings, and the place is better than ever. It's not luxurious, but it offers quite comfortable and large beach cottages. The cottages above the beach all have sitting rooms, well-equipped kitchens, barbecue areas, air-conditioned bedrooms, patios with hammocks, in-room safes, TVs, and a view of the ocean. The ones on the beach, numbers 6–10, are similarly equipped. These

are more private and the porch looks out on the beach a few steps away. Number 10 is closest to the ocean. The grounds are well cared for, with bougainvillea and other beautiful flowering bushes. One-bedroom cottages are US$143 and can sleep four. Two-bedroom cottages go for US$198 and can sleep six.

XS Memories (tel. 993-3096, fax 993-3069, www.xsmemories.com, US$60.50 s/d, US$2–4 tent camping, US$6–10 RVs) is a secure and comfortable place to pitch a tent, park the RV, or rent a room. It's run by a friendly couple from Las Vegas who have built a tidy walled compound with a pool, set on well-tended grounds.

Campers should note that the site is a couple of kilometers from the ocean, on the other side of the Interamericana from the Santa Clara turnoff. Motor home rates include water, electricity, septic service, and access to a small shop for repairs. Campers and RVers are also welcome to use the pool, shower, and all other facilities. This place is popular with gringos and is well-known among the RV crowd, who stop here on their quest to drive the Interamerican Highway from North America to the end of the road in the Darién.

XS Memories also offers three wheelchair-accessible cabins, each with air-conditioning and hot water. One of the cabins has a kitchenette. Rooms are simple but clean, though the mattresses are thin. There's a restaurant and sports bar with a big-screen TV. The restaurant (8 A.M.–8 P.M. Mon.–Thurs., 8 A.M.–10 P.M. Fri.–Sun., US$3–10) concentrates on simple, hearty American fare and bar food, such as hamburgers, chips with guacamole, and a variety of chicken, beef, and pork dishes. There's a tiny zoo on the premises. Bikes can be rented for US$6 a day. XS Memories is on the north side of the Interamericana opposite the turnoff to Santa Clara. The turn is well marked.

♪ The **Sheraton Bijao Beach Resort** (tel. 908-3600, www.starwoodhotels.com, starts at US$350 s/d, including food, drink, and activities) opened in 2009. It is the most attractive and sophisticated-looking of the Pacific beach all-inclusive resorts. It features 294 rooms, four restaurants, three swimming pools, a spa, a disco, designated areas for kids and teens, and plenty of places to celebrate with premium alcohol.

Most of the rooms are in the multistory main hotel, which is built into the side of a hill and looks out on the ocean and the pool complex, which cascades in tiers down to the beach like a cross between a series of artificial lagoons and a water park. Rooms are attractive and modern, though the "deluxe" rooms are not especially luxurious. All rooms include the usual amenities of places at this level (flat-screen satellite TV, air-conditioning, and in-room safes). Try to get a room facing the ocean and pool, as the views are lovely, much more appealing than the "garden-view" rooms. There are also 20 suites in separate structures right above the beach.

The designers have done a good job with the decor, which is rather elegant, and the layout of the whole resort, which includes huge, dramatic public spaces with sweeping views. It's also done with something of a sense of history, as many of the facilities are named after people and places associated with the Canal Zone or the building of the Panama Canal, including Coco Solo, Gaillard, Rodman, Balboa, and even De Lesseps. There is a resemblance between the main hotel building and the late, lamented Tivoli Hotel, Panama City's first grand hotel.

The turnoff from the Interamericana is at kilometer marker 108. It's about 2.5 kilometers to the hotel, which is in an isolated spot past a gated community with a golf course. To get onto the grounds requires going through two checkpoints: one for the gated community and then one for the hotel itself.

Getting There and Around

The poorly marked turnoff to Playa Santa Clara is 13 kilometers past Corona. It's about a 1.5-hour drive from Panama City, 108 kilometers east. Buses from Panama City make the trip every 20 minutes or so from early morning until mid-evening, though it's best to go during daylight hours. The fare is US$3 and the trip takes around two hours. Any westbound bus heading to Río Hato, Antón, Penonomé, or points farther west can let passengers off here. Buses will often drop passengers off at the beach for an extra US$1; be sure to ask the driver ahead of time. Otherwise passengers will have to walk 1.5 kilometers from the highway to the beach, unless a taxi happens to be hanging around.

The Santa Clara turnoff is about seven kilometers east of the depressed town of Río Hato. Next to that town is a huge old airstrip built by the U.S. military. It's being restored to accommodate charter flights. Next to this is the growing beach resort of Farallón. The closest large town is Penonomé, 36 kilometers west.

Those who want to do a bit of exploring under their own steam can rent bikes at **XS Memories** (tel. 993-3096, www.xsmemories.com).

◖ FARALLÓN

The Farallón (far-ah-YONE) area, which starts about three kilometers west of the Santa Clara turnoff, didn't get much attention until the Colombian-owned Decameron hotel chain built a mammoth resort there in late 2000.

Before then, Farallón was just a quiet fishing village with a pretty beach that attracted some weekenders. Next door is a large airstrip built years ago by the U.S. military, since this is one of the driest places in Panama. In the 1980s it was the site of a Panamanian military base that housed some of Noriega's elite troops. U.S. forces wiped out the base during the 1989 Just Cause invasion.

Now, suddenly, it's the hot beach destination. The new beach resorts often refer to this area as Playa Blanca, the name of one stretch of beach here, but most everyone in Panama still thinks of the area simply as Farallón. New condominium buildings are sprouting up as far

BEACH CAMPING

Campers considering sleeping on the beach along this strip of coast should be careful. As usual, sleep in a tent as a precaution against the small but real chance of being bitten by vampire bats, which carry rabies. Locals also warn about *maleantes* (thugs). Given that there are several guarded, inexpensive places with good facilities on or near the beach, you're better off pitching your tent there than on a secluded stretch of beach. The best camping facilities are at Santa Clara.

as the eye can see. The days of Farallón and the other sleepy beach villages around here are numbered. The beach resorts are generally not open to day visitors; most of them have gated entrances with security guards.

As with its neighbor, Santa Clara, the beach is lovely, and it's a wonder it was neglected for so long. There are a few other simpler and cheaper places to stay and eat in the village of Farallón and around the town of Río Hato, back on the Interamericana, a few kilometers farther west. Río Hato is the nearest semi-urban center, but has little to offer other than a few services.

Accommodations and Food

My favorite place to stay along the whole Pacific coast these days is **C Tógo B&B** (cell 6613-5233, www.togopanama.com, starts at US$121 s/d). Opened in October 2009, it's just down the hill from the Decameron resort, but is light-years away from it in scale and style. This place has been created with a keen eye for comfort and the budget and taste to do things right.

Named for its owners, Antonio (a Panamanian) and Gordon (from Argentina), Tógo is in a long-established beach neighborhood a two-minute drive west of the Decameron. It is not actually on the beach and doesn't have an ocean view, but it is literally

across the road from it. This stretch of beach is just far enough from the resorts that guests, especially during the week and the rainy season, are unlikely to have to compete with hordes of other sunbathers.

Tógo is a beach house that was redesigned as a cozy, comfortable B&B. Everything here has been thought out carefully. Though houses surround Tógo on all sides, a high wall encloses the 2,000-square-meter property, creating a quiet compound with rooms that look out on the B&B's lovely garden, which features mature trees and hammocks from which to admire them. There's even a little artificial water feature.

You need to be at least somewhat social to stay here, as the owners live in the compound and share their large, open living, dining, and kitchen areas with their guests. Antonio and Gordon can offer good tips about what to do and where to go not only in the region but in Panama City as well. The walls are decorated with appealing abstract art painted by Gordon, who is a graphic designer.

The house was built in 1976, but was thoroughly renovated and redesigned to be as open to the garden as possible without sacrificing comfort. The decor is an attractive blend of the modern, traditional Miami-style tropical, and even a touch of classic Canal Zone (which is where the handsome wooden beams came from). There are five rooms, four of which have a queen bed and an outside sitting area. The largest is an upstairs room with a queen bed, sofa bed, kitchenette, and private balcony. A third person in any of the rooms is US$27.50 extra.

Rooms are immaculate and spacious, with understated modern furnishings, air-conditioning (which you may not need if the sea breezes are blowing), and attractive bathrooms with high-quality fixtures. A welcome cocktail, breakfast, bike use, and wireless Internet access are included with stays. Other meals can be arranged for an extra fee. This is an appealing alternative to the mega-resorts. The B&B is adults only.

The name of the **Royal Decameron Beach**

Tógo B&B is cozy and comfortable.

Resort and Villas (Panama City reservations tel. 214-3535, resort tel. 993-2255, www.decameron.com, all-inclusive packages start at around US$200 s/d) keeps mutating, but most know it simply as the Decameron. It's an enormous beach resort—600 rooms set in three-story units above a large, gorgeous stretch of beach. All rooms have the same layout and feature either two full beds or a king-size bed. The rooms are medium-size, cheerful, and modern, if fairly nondescript, and the beds are comfortable. The resort features 10 restaurants and cafés, 11 bars, nine pools, a duty-free shop, and so on. It was built in 2000, which by the standards of this area makes it the grand old hotel. But it remains popular and many locals like it because it was designed and landscaped to blend in with its surroundings rather than dominate them.

The Decameron is an all-inclusive place that features unlimited consumption of food and domestic booze, including taxes and tips. Also included are daily activities, performances, and use of nonmotorized water-sports equipment, such as ocean kayaks and snorkeling gear. Other goodies include a free scuba-diving minicourse and aerobics and dance classes. Tours, fishing trips, use of the 18-hole Mantarraya golf course, and other activities are available for an extra charge. Rates can fluctuate by US$100 depending on if you come during the rainy season.

Transportation to and from Panama City is sometimes included in package deals arranged through travel agents. The resort caters mainly to large Canadian, European, and South American groups.

The **Playa Blanca Resort and Spa** (Panama City reservations tel. 264-6444, fax 264-3972, hotel tel. 993-2910 or 993-2911, www.playablancaresort.com, starts at US$153 s/d) is two kilometers farther west down the beach. It's part of a huge residential development that also includes condo towers, sports and convention centers, and what is billed as the second-largest swimming pool in the world (in reality, a 17-acre artificial seawater lagoon).

© WILLIAM FRIAR

The Bristol Buenaventura is Panama's most beautiful big resort.

The all-inclusive hotel itself is on the edge of all this, on the beach. It features 222 rooms in seven three- and four-story buildings set around an attractive swimming pool. The decor is kind of faux-Mediterranean, with the buildings done up in white with blue trim. Facilities include two main restaurants (one seafood, one buffet) plus a sailboat-shaped outdoor restaurant on the beach that's open on the weekends, a spa/beauty parlor, an Internet café, a small open-air theater, gift shops, a nine-hole putting course, a late-night disco, and so on. An activities center offers personal watercraft, ATVs, kayaks, mountain bikes, sailboarding gear, surfing lessons, fishing trips, sailboats, and tours of El Valle, Panama City, and other sights.

Rates include all meals, domestic liquor, use of nonmotorized aquatic gear (kayaks, pedal boats), and daily activities. The simple but pleasant rooms have one queen-size or two double beds, safes, satellite TV, and balconies. Try to get a room in buildings 600 or 700, which are right on the edge of the beach; the others are set around the swimming pools. Day passes are sometimes available. There have been some complaints about service and maintenance lately.

The most luxurious beach resort in Panama is the new **《 Bristol Buenaventura** (tel. 908-3333, www.thebristol.com, starts at US$434 s/d, a/c), which is under the same ownership as the Bristol Hotel in Panama City. This place is something else. Even those who don't go for big resorts are likely to be impressed by the ambition of the place, and the taste with which it has been realized.

Opened in February 2009, the resort is in the middle of the new Buenaventura gated development, which starts about 6.5 kilometers from the Interamericana, on the same road as, but past, the other resorts.

The hotel itself consists of a three-story main building with 114 rooms and a growing number of villas. The villas are two-story, four-bedroom fully furnished houses that go for US$2,000 a night.

The resort is done up in Spanish colonial style, with pretty fountains and terraces, an artificial lagoon/canal, and an elegant swimming pool in a garden setting. There's a spa and fitness center, and even a mission-style church for weddings.

Inside, the rooms and common areas are decorated in exquisite modern taste. Even the least-expensive rooms are among the most opulent in Panama. These are large (50 square meters), with hardwood floors, an iPod docking station, a desk, 42-inch LCD flat-screen TVs, marble bathroom with spacious showers and a separate tub, and Egyptian cotton linens. Only rooms on the 3rd floor have a good view of the ocean, but the view of the artificial lagoon and the grounds of this fantasy mini-city of luxury are eye-pleasing as well. With relatively few guests, the atmosphere is quiet and serene.

There is one main formal restaurant, as well as three casual cafés and grills, a handsome indoor bar, and a swim-up bar at the pool. A separate clubhouse, El Faro, is named for its lighthouse tower, which overlooks a second long swimming pool that ends in a lovely stretch of beach.

Service at the resort is gracious and attentive. This place is several cuts above the other beach resorts. This is not an all-inclusive: prices include just the room and taxes. Food, drinks, tours, and spa services are charged separately. Transfers from Panama City to the resort in a Lincoln Town Car are US$250, or more for a fancier car.

The turnoff to the hotel is just before the town of Río Hato. The hotel is three kilometers from the highway, surrounded by new condo developments.

My choice for a good hangout spot in this area is **Pipa's Beach Bar and Restaurant** (tel. 223-0975, cell 6575-7386, www.pipasbeach.com, 11 A.M.–8 or 9 P.M. daily, US$10–20), two kilometers past the Decameron. It's a relaxed, friendly place which offers a small menu of seafood and bar food and tapas. There's beach volleyball and private tables set out under canopies. Visitors get there by just walking west

along the beach past the Decameron. It's also possible to drive right to the place by turning right toward the Decameron and going straight, but this involves navigating through the yards of local fisherfolk who live in the area, so be polite and drive slowly. After two kilometers the road turns to sand. The bar will be up ahead on the left, on the beach.

Information and Services

There's an **ATP office** (tel. 993-3241, 8:30 A.M.–4:30 P.M. Mon.–Fri.) on the road that runs past the west side of the airstrip leading from the Interamericana to the Decameron.

Just about anything guests at the Decameron or Playa Blanca Resort could want is provided at the resorts. A couple of the services at the Decameron are also available to nonguests. These include **CB Tours** (tel. 993-2255, ext. 3067, 8 A.M.–6 P.M. daily), in the parking lot of the Decameron. It rents mountain bikes with helmets for US$5 for 1.5 hours or US$20 for a two-hour bike tour. Visitors can also rent ATVs for US$25 for a half hour, US$35 for an hour, US$50 for two hours, and US$70 for three hours. Guided tours by ATV are also available. Near the entrance to the Decameron parking lot is a **Banco Nacional de Panamá** ATM.

There are also a few services in the town of Río Hato, which is divided by the Interamericana, four kilometers west of the Decameron turnoff. **Plaza Río Hato,** in the center of town on the south side of the Interamericana, is a mini-mall with a grocery store, bakery, and, occasionally, an Internet café.

Getting There and Around

To get to this area from the direction of Panama City, continue west past the Santa Clara turnoff for three kilometers. On the far (west) side of the airstrip, turn left. The road runs past an ATP office, then to the Decameron resort on the beach two kilometers from the highway. A right turn at the resort leads to the fishing village of Farallón.

Buses to Farallón from Panama City, about 110 kilometers to the east, cost US$4 and leave every 20 minutes or so, 5:30 A.M.–8 P.M. The trip takes around two hours. Buses drop passengers off at the Decameron or Playa Blanca Resort by request.

A **National Car Rental** (tel. 265-2222, 8 A.M.–1 P.M. and 2–5 P.M. Mon.–Sat., 8 A.M.–4 P.M. Sun.) is in the parking lot of the Decameron.

El Valle de Antón

When the steamy heat of Panama City is too much even for locals, they head to the hills of El Valle de Antón, which everyone simply calls El Valle. It's a pleasant little town nestled in the valley of a huge extinct volcano. The valley floor is about 600 meters above sea level, high enough to make this area significantly cooler and fresher than the lowlands. This is one of the few places in Panama where you'll find houses with fireplaces.

El Valle proper lies along the wide, flat valley floor, and most of the sights are within town or on gentle slopes not far away. That makes it easy to go almost anywhere on foot or by bicycle, a pleasant way to get around given the mild climate and the flower-lined streets.

The first thing you see upon entering El Valle is a *supermercado* (supermarket) with a gas station, to the right. This and the **public market** in the center of town are common landmarks, and most of the directions in this section will use them as starting points. A single main road, sometimes called **Avenida Central** or Calle Central, but not marked in any case, runs through the town from the *supermercado* past the public market, ending in a fork at the west end of town.

Several of El Valle's biggest attractions— the Chorro El Macho waterfall, the **Canopy Adventure,** and the petroglyphs of **La Piedra Pintada**—are a few minutes' drive past this fork.

You'll hear talk of **La India Dormida** (the sleeping Indian girl) during your stay. This refers to the silhouette some see along a section of the hilltops ringing the valley. From the correct angle and with enough imagination, you may see it too.

El Valle is famous for its nearly extinct golden frogs and its square trees. Even though the area is heavily settled, there is still wildlife in the protected forests. There's also a small zoo, **El Níspero,** with indigenous and nonnative species.

Those who want to get the old heart pounding should try the Canopy Adventure zipline ride. Other popular nature activities in El Valle include hiking, horseback riding, and splashing around under waterfalls. If you come early in the week, especially Monday or Tuesday, you'll likely have El Valle all to yourself. This is nice in some ways, but some may find the place a bit too sleepy. To see the public market in full swing, come on a Sunday morning. Saturday is also a pretty active day, and typically the only busy night. Most visitors leave El Valle by midday Sunday. On holiday weekends in the dry season, every room in El Valle can fill up.

It's also possible to do El Valle as a day trip from Panama City, either on your own or through a tour operator. Many of these offer packages that include transportation, a visit to the market, and sometimes the Canopy Adventure.

SIGHTS
El Níspero
Though it's usually considered a zoo, El Níspero (no phone, 7 A.M.–5 P.M. daily, US$2 adults, US$1 children) is really more of a plant nursery with caged creatures. Even if you have qualms about animals confined in small places—and some of the cages here are vry small—consider visiting this one. For one thing, it's a good place to see Panama's all-but-extinct **golden frogs.**

EL VALLE DE ANTÓN

To Interamericana

To Chorro El Macho, Canopy
Adventure, and El Valle Lodge

To La Piedra
Pintada

GOLDEN
FROG INN

HOTEL
CAMPESTRE

HORSE
RENTAL

CALLE CLUB CAMPESTRE

Río Antón

CRATER VALLEY
RESORT

CENTRO COMERCIAL
EL VALLE

LOS
MANDARINOS
BOUTIQUE SPA
AND HOTEL

LA CASA DE
LOURDES

PINOCCHIO'S

CALLE EL CICLO

CALLE RANITA DE ORO

SERPENTARIUM

CALLE CAPIRITA

CABAÑAS
GYSELL

CALLE EL HATO

AV. CENTRAL

HOTEL Y
RESTAURANTE
LOS CAPITANES

CASA DE
JUAN

INTERNET CAFÉ/
MI FARMACIA/
LAVAMATICO

EL VALLE GOURMET
AND COFFEE SHOP

CALLE DE LOS SAUCES

CENTRO DE
PRODUCCIÓN DE
ORQUÍDEAS DE EL
VALLE Y CABUYA

HOTEL RINCÓN VALLERO

AV DE LOS GUAYACANES

CALLE DE LOS MILLONARIOS

PARK EDEN

EL NÍSPERO

ATM

ARTASH

CALLE DE LOS MILLONARIOS

VÍA ESPAVÉ

RESTAURANTE
SANTA LIBRADA #2

SUPERCENTRO YIN

HOTEL DON PEPE/
ARTESANÍAS PEPE/
RESTAURANTE MAR DE PLATA

HOTEL PEKIN/
MI FARMACIA/
MINISUPER

HOTEL RESIDENCIAL EL VALLE/
TIERRA Y MAR/DAVID'S SHOP

RESTAURANTE Y
REFREQUERÍA MASSIEL

CALLE MARIAGAR

PANADERÍA Y
DULCERÍA CANO

MINISUPER
PUEBLO

CALLE DEL MERCADO

POST
OFFICE

PUBLIC MARKET
ATP BOOTH

SUNDAY MARKET

CALLE LA COMPAÑÍA

ANTON VALLEY HOTEL
BRUSCHETTA

LIBRARY

LAUNDERETTE

MUSEUM

HEALTH CLINIC

AV DE LOS MILLONARIOS

CALLE LOS POZOS

LOS POZOS TERMALES

CALLE DEL MACHO

CABAÑAS
POTOSÍ

CALLE LA REFORMA

CALLE LA PINTADA

Chorro las Mozas

500 yds

500 m

0

0

WAVING GOODBYE TO THE GOLDEN FROG?

golden frog

Panama's famous golden frog, *Atelopus zeteki,* is native to El Valle. Seeing these frogs is supposed to bring good luck, and they have a special place in the heart of Panamanians. They're practically a national symbol, and golden frog *huacas* (ceremonial figurines buried with the dead) are common in pre-Columbian graves.

It's hard to believe something this color can exist in nature. Sadly, it may not. Golden frogs were endangered even before the chytrid fungus, which is devastating amphibian populations throughout Central America, came to El Valle in 2006. The fungus coats the skins of frogs, suffocating them. In 2007, David Atten-

borough's BBC series *Life in Cold Blood* came to El Valle to film them and their behavior – they are believed to communicate by waving one arm. At the end of the shoot, scientists collected the wild specimens for their own protection; Attenborough declared that this would be the last time the frogs would be filmed in nature, as they are believed to be extinct in the wild. Let's hope not. For now, they're being kept alive in zoos and rescue projects. This includes the **El Valle Amphibian Conservation Center,** El Valle's little El Níspero zoo. Hopefully one day they can be returned to the wild to thrive again.

Today they are being cared for by the El Valle Amphibian Conservation Center, a kind of Noah's ark for the little critters and about 40 other critically endangered species. Supported by the Houston Zoo, half of the facility is open to the public and is well worth a visit.

Other indigenous creatures here include the capybara, the world's largest rodent—it can grow up to a meter long and weigh up to 45 kilograms; several species of primates, including Geoffroy's tamarin and the white-faced capuchin; sleepy-looking sloths; a tapir; and

El Valle's little zoo, El Níspero, has some striking native species.

two species of felines, the margay and ocelot. Among the decidedly nonindigenous critters here are some emus, of all things. The zoo also has a greenhouse stuffed with orchids, extensive gardens, and a fish-filled wishing well.

To get to El Níspero, continue west along Avenida Central 1.4 kilometers past the *supermercado* at the entrance to town. Take a right turn at the sign that says El Níspero. Follow the winding road 1.1 kilometers. The road is rough but doesn't require a four-wheel drive. El Níspero is on the left.

La Piedra Pintada

El Valle has an impressively large boulder covered with petroglyphs that is locally known as La Piedra Pintada (literally, the painted rock). No one is sure what all the squiggly designs carved (not painted) into the face of this boulder mean, or even who made them, though everyone has a theory. Maybe it's just the doodling of the gods. The boulder is easy to get to

and thus worth a visit. It's just a five-minute walk up a trail that follows a pretty little stream.

Drive west on the main road, Avenida Central, past the public market and out of town. Take a left after the bridge. Make the first real right, then follow the road until it ends at a cul-de-sac at a small church. (The whole way is well marked.) Small boys will mysteriously appear, eager to show you the rock—for a fee, of course. Being surrounded by a swarm of tykes can be intimidating, but you shouldn't have a problem. As soon as you choose one, the others will back off. He'll probably be pleased with a quarter. By the way, they're not leading you astray if they steer you left rather than straight up, as the misleading sign would have you go.

Square Trees

Behind and to the right of the Hotel Campestre is a trail, often muddy, that runs by a brook and a bit of secondary-growth forest. The trail isn't well marked and has forks, but if you follow your intuition about the main trail, you should be okay. After 5–10 minutes, you should see a collapsing bamboo fence on the right. Walk over it into the little clearing. The most convincing specimens are more trapezoidal than square, but at least you can say you've seen El Valle's famous square trees.

El Serpentario

This small serpentarium (cell 6569-2676, theoretically 8 A.M.–at least 5 P.M. Mon.–Sat., US$3) is next to a stream north of Avenida Central and east of Calle El Hato. Creepy-crawlies here include a variety of boas (rainbow, constrictor), an eyelash viper, a tarantula, several fer-de-lance, coral snakes both true and false, and a *patoca* (jumping pit viper). Come here *after* you've done all your Panama forest hikes. It's the pet project of a respected local biologist, Mario Urriola, who can also provide tour-guide services. Don't count on the serpentarium being open during posted hours; instead try to call ahead of time to make sure Mario is actually going to be around.

To get there, turn right at the gas station near the entrance to town and follow the signs. There's a parking area about 200 meters down a rough road. From there it's about another 100 meters on foot.

Centro de Producción de Orquídeas de El Valle y Cabuya

This small, voluntary conservation association (no phone, 9 A.M.–2 P.M. daily) has about 100 native orchid species on display in greenhouses about 200 meters south of Avenida Central, near the ANAM office. It's a left turn past Cabañas Gysell, not far from the entrance to town.

SHOPPING
◖ Sunday Market

Some visitors come to El Valle just for the public market, which got a makeover a few years back. Here you'll find crafts from many parts of Panama, in addition to fresh fruit, vegetables, and plants. While the kind and quality of crafts vary week to week, this is usually a good place to buy Panama hats. These are not the elegant, tightly woven hats that most people think of—those Panama hats are actually Ecuadorian. The ones here aren't usually even the relatively finely woven ones made in some parts of the Azuero Peninsula. These are more coarsely woven, usually of white and black fibers, and are the most common kind worn in Panama. Prices range about US$15–50. You should expect to pay about US$30 for a decent one. Other items to consider include carved soapstone figures. The limiting factor isn't the price but the weight you have to lug around. The market is quaint and lively, but not big. While a popular weekend destination for lots of Panama City residents and the old Canal Zone crowd, and much-trumpeted by tour outfits, it's unlikely to blow your socks off.

The public market is 1.7 kilometers down the main road as you enter El Valle. You can't miss it—it's smack in the center of town. The market operates on a limited scale during the week, but it's in full swing on Saturdays and especially Sundays. There are also a few souvenir kiosks directly across the street.

Other Craft Shops

Two souvenir shops are just east of the market, on the ground floor of Hotel Don Pepe and Hotel Residencial El Valle. **David's Shop** (tel. 983-6536, 7 A.M.–7 P.M. Sun.–Thurs., 7 A.M.–10 P.M. Fri.–Sat.) has a better selection of crafts than the market itself. There's a little workshop at the back where you can peek in at artisans at work. The shop can also dispense tourist information, arrange horse rentals and trips to the Canopy Adventure, and rent bikes. It's affiliated with Hotel Residencial El Valle upstairs.

Artesanías Pepe (tel. 983-6425, 7 A.M.–7 P.M. daily) next door, below Hotel Don Pepe, is a similar place, though the quality and selection is better at David's Shop.

SPORTS AND RECREATION

El Valle is popular with middle-class and wealthy Panamanians as a weekend getaway. As such, most entertainment takes place inside people's weekend homes. There is almost nothing in the way of nightlife in El Valle. Hiking, horseback riding, and bird-watching are the main things to do around here. These can often be arranged through one's hotel. **David's Shop** (tel. 983-6536, 7 A.M.–7 P.M. Sun.–Thurs., 7 A.M.–10 P.M. Fri.–Sat.) rents bikes. It's possible to take hikes and horseback trips up into the mountains, but these tend to be on old forest paths used for years as commute routes rather than on developed trails and shouldn't be attempted without a knowledgeable guide. Be sure to bring rain gear, warm clothing, and long-sleeved shirts (to avoid getting cut up by the brush).

Canopy Adventure

The outdoor activity that's gotten the most attention in recent years is the Canopy Adventure (El Valle tel. 983-6547, Panama City tel. 264-5720, http://adventure.panamabirding.com, open approximately 8 A.M.–5 P.M. daily). It's a lot of fun, as long as you're comfortable with heights. The Canopy Adventure is sort of a cross between a nature hike and a zipline thrill ride. The hike comes at the beginning, when you head uphill through steamy forest on a trail that's steep and slick at times. The hike takes about 30–45 minutes. You're walking through protected private land that borders a private forest reserve, so there's a good chance of seeing some wildlife.

Now for the really fun part: the zipline ride. Riders are attached by harness and pulley to four cables strung between trees. Cables are at a gentle downward angle, so you go flying back down to the trailhead in stages. You're about 30 meters above the base of the lovely El Chorro waterfall at the beginning. The ride goes right past the roaring falls.

Riders zip through the trees under their own power. The first run is the most dramatic, when you're also the most nervous about slamming into a tree.

The whole ride costs US$50. Clients can also opt to do just the last stage for US$12.50. Those who don't care for heights can opt instead for a four-kilometer guided walk (US$35) or a swim in the pool below the waterfall (US$3.50). For US$125 the Canopy Adventure provides transportation to and from Panama City, lunch, and a tour of El Valle in addition to the ride. Part of the proceeds goes to maintaining the nature preserve. The prices do not include sales tax.

You will get muddy. Wear long pants to protect your legs and sturdy, closed shoes with decent traction. The guides offer water and insect repellent during the hike. Sunday is the busiest day, so show up before 10 A.M. to avoid long lines. Allow two hours for the whole thing.

The Canopy Adventure is three kilometers past the public market (heading west) on the main road. Follow the blue signs reading El Macho. At the west end of town, the road forks after a bridge. Take the right fork, which is Calle El Macho. The ride's office, a thatched-roof hut, will be on the left.

Horseback Riding

There's a long-established **horse rental** (cell 6646-5813, 8 A.M.–6 P.M. daily, US$8/hour) outfit next to the chapel at the fork in the road. It's one kilometer up Calle El Hato. The price includes a Spanish-speaking guide. You can request a destination or just take the staff's advice; many trails lead up through the wooded hills.

Adventure Tours

Nature tours can often be arranged through your hotel. **Hotel y Restaurante Los Capitanes** (tel. 983-6080, cell 6687-8919, www.los-capitanes.com), for instance, offers a variety of hikes guided by local schoolkids for US$2–3, including a two-hour hike to the top of La India Dormida, stopping at three waterfalls along the way.

© WILLIAM FRIAR

It's easy to rent horses in El Valle.

The **Panama Explorer Tours (PEX)** (Panama City tel. 215-2328, www.crater-valley.com), which operates Crater Valley Resort and Adventure Center, offers a range of outdoor activities in El Valle and the surrounding area. These include hikes, treks, rock climbing, rappelling, ropes courses, rafting, and mountain biking. These are quite reasonably priced, starting at US$7 per person to try the climbing wall and up to US$88 for rafting.

ACCOMMODATIONS

Hotel options used to be quite limited in El Valle, but now visitors can choose among simple but pleasant budget accommodations, quaint bed-and-breakfasts, an ecolodge, and resort spas. The high season runs approximately November–March.

US$10-25

Backpacker accommodations don't last long in El Valle. One that is defying the odds at the moment is **La Casa de Juan** (No. 4, Calle de Los Millonarios, cell 6453-9975, lacasadejuanpanama@gmail.com, www.lacasadejuanpanama.blogspot.com, US$10 pp in dorms, US$20–25 s/d). It's in a private home with a cluttered, junk-filled patio and dark, rather dingy rooms. The dormitory has a zinc roof but no fans, so guests may have the rare distinction of feeling hot and stuffy in cool and fresh El Valle. Basic private rooms are US$20 s/d with shared bathroom, US$5 more for private bath. Guests have access to a TV, kitchen, and laundry facilities. This place isn't great, but it may suit those on a tight budget. It's within reasonable walking distance of the market and other downtown attractions. Ironically enough, it's on Calle de Los Millonarios (the street of the millionaires), about 200 meters south of Cabañas Gysell.

US$25-50

Cabañas Gysell (Calle El Hato near Avenida Central, tel. 983-6507, US$25 s, US$35 d) is a cute little place run by friendly folks who've decorated it with lots of love—something that's always a treat in Panama, where so many budget accommodations are functional at best. Rooms are painted blue and white and are decorated with nice touches, such as hand-painted murals on the walls. Its eight rooms are set in a garden with an outdoor kitchen, hammocks, and rocks scattered about with words of wisdom inscribed on them. The rooms are simple but clean and perfectly okay, with good beds and hot-water bathrooms. Some rooms are more attractive than others, so ask to see a few. Rooms are US$5 cheaper in the low season.

Cabañas Potosí (Calle La Reforma, tel. 983-6181 in El Valle, cell 6941-6148, www. vrbo.com/162797, most US$49 s/d) has been around forever. It's owned by relatives of Mario Bernal, a well-known birding guide, who lives across the street. As a result, this place is popular with birders. It offers four cabanas and one room in the family house, all set on two well-tended hectares just west of town. Each cabana has a double and a single bed, hot-water bathrooms, and wall fans. They're quite simple but have high ceilings and porches with a good view of the hills. Cabañas Potosí is one kilometer west of town on the main road. At the end of town, take the first two lefts you come to. The place will be on the right.

US$50-100

The centrally located **Hotel Residencial El Valle** (Avenida Central, tel. 983-6536, cell 6615-9616, www.hotelresidencialelvalle.com, starts at US$55 s/d) is above David's Shop, a souvenir store near the market that's affiliated with the hotel. It offers 17 simple but fine rooms with new beds, hardwood floors, local TV, free wireless Internet, and hot-water bathrooms. The rooms have fans and are cheerful, clean, and quite nice. The friendly general manager, Luis Enrique Tiban, speaks some English, can help arrange guides, and has a map for guests.

His talented family constructed the building, the beds, even the room mirrors with butterflies and birds painted around their borders. The place has a spacious terrace with a view of the mountains, including Cerro Gaital and Cerro Cara Iguana, and a good profile of La India Dormida. Use of the kitchen is included with your stay. This place is a good value.

The Hotel Pekin (Avenida Central, tel. 908-7066, cell 6799-2268hotelpekinelvalle@gmail. com, US$50 s/d, a/c) is an odd-looking place which opened in early 2012 on the main road not far from the market. It consists of what by El Valle standards is a massive motel complex, with a Chinese gate over its entrance that's impossible to miss. Shops and a parking lot are downstairs, and 28 rooms are upstairs. Rooms are basic but clean—one is tempted to say sterile-looking—with hot water, wireless Internet, and rock-hard beds. Some of the rooms are huge and have ceilings two stories high. Though the place is sorely lacking in charm, it'd be a reasonable option if the beds were better.

Hotel y Restaurante Los Capitanes (Calle El Ciclo, tel. 983-6080, www.los-capitanes.com, starts at US$44 s, US$66 d, including breakfast) is set on lovingly tended grounds in the heart of the valley. There's not much else around it, so you get sweeping views of the mountains ringing the valley. The cheapest rooms are in a long, one-story building next to the main hotel. They're pretty simple and a bit dark. The best rooms are the family suites upstairs in the tower (US$121 for up to three adults). They have lofts and balconies. There's a common lounge area equipped with satellite TV.

To get to Los Capitanes, head down the main road into town 0.8 kilometers past the *supermercado.* Turn right at the big anchor. (There should also be a sign.) You'll soon see the hotel on your left. The hotel can arrange pickup and drop-off in Panama City. Prices can go down significantly during the week.

The **Hotel Rincón Vallero** (off Calle de Los

Millonarios, El Valle tel. 983-6175, Panama City tel. 271-5935, www.hotelrinconvallero.com, starts at US$83 s/d, including breakfast, a/c) is surrounded by flowering trees and has an artificial waterfall and fish-filled stream that runs through an enclosed patio containing the dining room and lobby. All rooms have color TVs and hot water. Most of the rooms are in cabins set around a garden with an artificial duck and fishpond. There are 14 rooms. The standard rooms are on the small side and rather dark. The junior suites (US$105) are large rooms, and there are also full suites (US$138). All these prices are for double occupancy. A third person in any of the rooms costs US$11 more.

Directions to the hotel are well marked. As you enter El Valle, make a left turn off the main road 0.2 kilometers past the *supermercado*. Follow the road 0.6 kilometers, then make a left. Follow that road another 0.2 kilometers. The hotel is on the left.

The **⟨ Anton Valley Hotel** (Avenida Central across from the church, tel. 983-6097, cell 6383-5978, http://antonvalleyhotel.com, starts at US$71.50 s/d) is a nine-room inn opened in 2007 and its rooms are comfortable and well-maintained. It's on the main road, within easy walking distance of the market and most of the available services. The rooms are the most attractive in downtown El Valle. They're simple but cheerful, with a queen or two twin beds with orthopedic mattresses, minifridges, ceiling fans, and satellite TV. The popular Bruschetta's restaurant is right next door.

US$100-150

The popular **⟨ Golden Frog Inn** (tel. 983-6117, cell 6565-8307, www.goldenfroginn.com, US$55–137.50 s/d) is in a pretty former villa set on a hectare of well-tended gardens filled with flowering plants. It's owned by a gringo couple who moved down from Washington State with their two friendly dogs. The inn, known in Spanish as Hostal Rana Dorada,

offers six rooms of different size and quality. The three largest rooms have lovely terraces, and a 2011 renovation added small kitchens. This is part of a shift in emphasis by the owners toward longer-term vacation rentals, aimed at those considering a move to El Valle. However, short-term stays are also available. Two of these rooms are US$121 s/d. The largest (US$137.50 for up to four people) has two bedrooms, one of which has a queen bed and the other a double bed. These rooms have flat-screen, satellite TV.

The three other rooms (US$55–77) are much smaller and simpler. One of them has a private bath, and the other two share a bathroom. All have access to a communal kitchen by the pool. All the rooms are clean and decorated in simple good taste. Discounts are available for weekly and long-term rentals.

There's a popular, complimentary happy hour for guests at sunset every evening. It's hosted on the terrace of the owner's house, which also has a lending library for guests. The inn is near Crater Valley Adventure Spa. Upon entering El Valle, turn right at the Texaco station and follow the signs.

⟨ Park Eden (Vía Espavé, tel. 983-6167, cell 6695-6190, www.parkeden.com, starts at US$121 s/d, including full breakfast and afternoon tea) is a charming bed-and-breakfast in a lovely garden setting. For 18 years it was the country home of Lionel Alemán Toledano and his wife Mónica, who turned it into a bed-and-breakfast in 2000. Both speak fluent English and Spanish. Staying with them is like visiting your favorite country aunt and uncle: They couldn't be more friendly and attentive.

There are six places to stay, all quite different. Breakfast and afternoon tea are served in a cozy glassed-in porch in the main house, where the couple lives. It has a view of the garden. La Vie en Rose (US$121) is in the front of the main house and has a private terrace and a full and twin bed. As befits its name, it's rose-colored and frilly. La Casita (US$121) is the designated honeymooners' room. The Linda Vista (US$264) is a two-story house with two bedrooms upstairs and a downstairs living room and sunny kitchen. It features big windows that let in a lot of light, a sofa bed, outdoor fountain, and a large terrace with a barbecue grill. Guests usually book the entire house, but the individual bedrooms are also available by themselves. There are lovely views of the garden and Cerro Gaital and other mountains from the upstairs rooms. Los Limoneros (US$132) has a queen bed, sleeper couch, and small private terrace.

Most rooms have some combination of TV/VCR, coffeemaker, small fridge, and microwave. All are decorated with quaint and sometimes quirky knickknacks and homey touches.

Crater Valley Adventure Spa (Calle Capirita at the corner of Calle Ranita de Oro, tel. 215-2328, www.crater-valley.com, weekend rates start at US$134 s/d, including breakfast) is a spa resort built into an elegant old Spanish-style villa that belonged to a grandmother of one of the current owners. To get there, upon entering El Valle make the first right past the *supermercado* and follow the signs. Pass the two asphalt roads on the right. The spa will be on the left.

Amenities include an attractive swimming pool with tanning deck, a sauna, a large and amazingly turbulent hot tub, spa services, yoga classes, small library, and a souvenir shop. Its large, attractive grounds have a view of Cerro Gaital and are filled with trees, flowering plants, and three fishponds. There's a bar and dining area.

The spa has eight modern rooms with good beds, hot-water bathrooms, and satellite TV. Each of the rooms is completely different. Some are surprisingly plain and others are large and tastefully appointed.

Over US$150

My favorite place to stay in El Valle is **Canopy Lodge** (U.S. toll-free tel. 800/930-3397, El Valle tel. 264-5720, www. canopylodge.com and www.canopytower.com, US$159–229 pp including meals and birding tour), the younger sister to the famed Canopy Tower near Gamboa. Bird-watchers are drawn by the chance of spotting foothill species, such as the rufous-crested coquette, dull-mantled antbird, rufous-vented ground cuckoo, and black-crowned antpitta.

This is still an appealing place to stay even if you're not a birder. Opened in 2005, it's set in a lush garden on the Río Guayaco, a rushing river fed by Chorro El Macho. Guests walk through a bower and over a bridge to get to the lodge. The rooms are large, airy, and spotless, with balconies overlooking the river, forest, and Cerro Pajita. Rooms have either one king- or two queen-size comfortable, orthopedic beds. The rooms and bathrooms are modern and deliberately minimalist. There's an observatory on the 3rd floor of the lodge and an outdoor bar/dining area where guests are served simple but tasty meals. The lodge is in a 75-acre private nature reserve owned by the family of the owner, who also owns the Canopy Adventure, 400 meters uphill. Follow the road to El Chorro; the gate and parking lot are on the left.

Per-person prices in the double rooms are set to match those of the canopy rooms at the Canopy Tower: US$229 in high season (Dec. 16–April 15), US$159 in the green season (April 16–Sept. 15), and US$179 during the migration season (Sept. 16–Dec. 15). Prices include lodging, a daily birding tour, and all meals. Current prices and packages that combine stay at both the Canopy Tower and Canopy Lodge are listed on the Canopy Tower website.

Los Mandarinos Boutique Spa and Hotel (tel. 983-6645, U.S. toll-free 888/281-8413, www.losmandarinos.com, starts at US$173.29 s/d) is just uphill from La Casa de Lourdes and is owned by members of the same family. It continues the restaurant's semi-Italian aesthetic with 12 double rooms and four suites set in two-story buildings with stone walls and red-tile roofs. The executive rooms (US$173.29 s/d) are the most economical, with air-conditioning you're unlikely to need, decent beds, satellite TV, and large bathrooms with showers. Some of the rooms have stone-walled showers, which are a hit with guests. Larger "deluxe" rooms with whirlpool bath are US$235.62 s/d. The suites (US$300.30 s/d) are large, with a kitchenette, a sitting/dining room, and a small balcony with a view of the mountains. There's a two-night minimum on the weekends. During national holidays, rates are higher and there's a three-night minimum. The hotel has a full-service spa.

FOOD

◖ **Bruschetta's** (Avenida Central at the Anton Valley Hotel, tel. 983-6097, cell 6383-5978, 11:30 A.M.–8 P.M. daily, most mains US$11–14) developed a devoted following in the last few years. It serves pasta, seafood, and various meats in a pleasant garden setting. The chef here takes pride in his food and is an attentive host, often serving guests himself. The pesto pasta is reasonably tasty, made with homemade pesto. As one might hope, the bruschetta is good.

Restaurante y Refrequería Massiel (Avenida Central, cell 6710-4587, 6 A.M.–6 P.M. Mon.–Thurs., 6 A.M.–8 P.M. Fri.–Sun., US$4.50–7.50) is a simple open-air place that serves *típico* Panamanian food that appeals both to locals and to foreign visitors. The menu of the day can include fish, grilled chicken, *ropa vieja* (traditional dish of shredded beef), as well as burger combos for less than US$5. It's on the right side of the main road less than 100 meters past the market as one head toward the church.

Restaurante Santa Librada (Avenida Central, tel. 983-6376 or 645-5310, 7 A.M.–9 P.M. daily, under US$8) is another popular locals' hangout for simple Panamanian fare at good prices. The decor is nothing fancy, but it's a pleasant open-air place. Seafood and grilled meats top out at less than US$8. The big bowl of *sancocho de gallina* (chicken stew) has a nice flavor but is a little light on the chicken and veggies. The papaya *batido* (shake), however, is killer. The restaurant is on the right as you head into town, down Avenida Central about 1.5 kilometers from the first *supermercado*. Santa Librada also rents out a few basic rooms.

Pinocchio's (Calle El Hato, tel. 983-6715, noon–9 P.M. Mon.–Sat., noon–8 P.M. Sun.) serves quite tasty if somewhat greasy thin-crust pizzas. Individual pizzas cost around US$6–8 and are actually big enough to feed two reasonably hungry people. The English-speaking owner is friendly and takes a justifiable pride in his cooking. Other items on the menu include chicken, pork chops, burgers, tacos, shakes, and fruit juices. It is in an attractive building about 500 meters down from the horse rentals.

El Valle Gourmet and Coffee Shop is across Avenida Central from the Internet café on the way into town, and is only open on the weekends.

Stop by **Rincón Vallero** (off Calle de Los Millonarios, tel. 983-6175, 7 A.M.–9 P.M. Mon.–Thurs., 7 A.M.–11 P.M. Fri.–Sun., under US$15) for a meal even if you're not staying there. It's pleasant to eat on its enclosed patio, which has an artificial waterfall and a fish stream running through it. It's a cute place, and the decor is attractive. Fortunately, the food is good, too. You can make a meal just on the appetizers. Try the *plato típico*, which consists of favorite Panamanian finger food: *patacones, carimañolas*, chorizos, and *bollas*—all tasty and worth experiencing at least once. Also go for the fried ceviche, which is a rarity in Panama and quite delicious. Main dishes run the range of meat, chicken, fish, and seafood.

◖ **Artash** (Calle La Planta, cell 6980-2734, 9 A.M.–6 P.M. Mon., Wed., Thurs., and Fri., 8 A.M.–6 P.M. Sat. and Sun., US$5–8) is a welcome addition to the limited El Valle culinary scene. Opened in 2011, it's a casual but pleasant café on the front terrace of a yellow house shared by the Panamanian chef and his

ANOTHER ROADSIDE ATTRACTION

Restaurante Los Camisones (tel. 993-3622, 11 A.M.-close daily, US$10), also known as El Rincón de los Camisones, is a pleasant and popular open-air place that gets absolutely packed on a dry-season Sunday. It's near kilometer marker 104, which is about 7 kilometers west of the turnoff to El Valle and about 10 kilometers east of Santa Clara. The place isn't visible from the road, but the turnoff is marked. As you head west, it's a steep right (north) turn up a narrow road – slow down as you approach the turn, and watch out for cars coming down from the restaurant. It's set back from the road and has no view, but it catches a welcome breeze. It serves a range of typical Panamanian dishes. The food's not bad, but the restaurant's popularity stems more from being part of many families' weekend-getaway ritual than for the quality of its fare. The brave – at least, those carrying pepper spray – can try the *"creeps de la casa"* for dessert.

Canadian girlfriend, who is the restaurant's manager/host. The menu includes light and tasty fare such as Vietnamese crepes, ginger chicken, and tandoori wraps, as well as all-day breakfasts. The frappés are delicious.

La Casa de Lourdes (off Calle El Ciclo, tel. 983-6450, noon–11 P.M. daily, depending on reservations) is El Valle's first gourmet restaurant. It's the latest project of Lourdes de Ward, the celebrated owner-chef of one of Panama City's favorite upscale restaurants, the now-closed Golosinas. The menu is small and changes seasonally. It features French- and Asian-influenced Panamanian nouvelle cuisine such as blackened fish in tamarind sauce and yuca croquettes. Food here can be quite good, though it depends on who's in the kitchen, and service is warm and attentive. It's one of the loveliest-looking places to eat in the country—it somewhat resembles a salmon-colored Italian villa, with a colonnade that leads to a terrace with a fireplace, reflecting pool, and hillside garden.

La Casa de Lourdes sits by itself in a relatively undeveloped area north of the town center. Head north on Calle El Ciclo, pass Hotel y Restaurante Los Capitanes, and make a left at the next major intersection. Make another left and wind your way down to the restaurant. The last few hundred meters are on a rough gravel and dirt road. This is a small place, so it's a good idea to make reservations; if no one is around, they sometimes close early.

Panadería y Dulcería Cano (Avenida Central, tel. 983-6420, generally 7:30 A.M.–8 P.M. daily) is a bakery and pastry shop across the street from the church.

INFORMATION AND SERVICES

There's an **ATP kiosk** at the west end of the public market, though it quite likely won't be staffed. If it is, the staff may not speak any English or have much information.

There are two outlets of the **Mi Farmacia** (7 or 8 A.M.–8 P.M. Sun.–Thurs., 7 or 8 A.M.–9 P.M. Fri.–Sat.), a small pharmacy. The first (tel. 983-5096) is on the grounds of the Hotel Mi Pekin. The second (tel. 983-6072) is on the main street on the way into town, in a building that also houses an Internet café and launderette.

There are no banks in El Valle, but there is a **Banco Nacional de Panamá** ATM near Restaurante Santa Librada on Avenida Central.

The **post office** (9 A.M.–2:45 P.M. Mon.–Fri., 7 A.M.–noon Sat.) is behind the public market, off Calle del Mercado.

A **public library** (no phone, 8:45 A.M.–3:15 P.M. Mon.–Sat.) with Internet computers is right next to the church and across the street from the Anton Valley Hotel. It charges US$1 per hour. The orchid cooperative also has an Internet café. There's another **Internet place** (tel. 983-6688, 8 A.M.–noon and 1:30–6 P.M.

Mon.–Fri., 8 A.M.–5 P.M. Sat., 11 A.M.–3 P.M. Sun.) on the north side of Avenida Central, one block west of Calle El Ciclo, the street that leads up to Hotel y Restaurante Los Capitanes. (It's in the same building as the pharmacy.) It also charges US$1 an hour.

In the same building is a *lavamático* (8 A.M.–4 P.M. Mon.–Sat.) that charges US$0.75 to wash, US$1 to dry a load, and US$0.30 for detergent.

Supercentro Yin (7 A.M.–7 P.M. daily) is a basic grocery store across the street from Hotel Residencial El Valle. There's a similar store next to the gas station at the entrance to El Valle.

Both **Los Mandarinos Boutique Spa and Hotel** (tel. 983-6645, U.S. toll-free 888/281-8413, www.losmandarinos.com) and the **Crater Valley Adventure Spa** (Calle Capirita at the corner of Calle Ranita de Oro, tel. 215-2328, www.crater-valley.com) have spa services that include massages, facials, manicures/pedicures, saunas, hot tubs, and so on, at prices comparable to similar facilities in the United States. You do not have to be staying at either place to use the spas.

GETTING THERE AND AROUND

El Valle is 120 kilometers from Panama City, a drive that takes a little under two hours. If you're driving, head west on the Interamerican Highway for 95 kilometers, which takes about an hour and a quarter. The turnoff to El Valle will be on the right. It's better marked than it used to be, but keep an eye open. If you're coming from Panama City and you get to Playa Corona, you've gone too far. Double back at the first turnoff.

Head north off the Interamericana up the winding two-lane road over the hills and into the valley. The road leads straight into El Valle, about 25 kilometers from the highway. It's a lovely drive, with a craggy ring of lush, forested hills before you and a good view of the Pacific behind. This road used to have more craters than the moon but is now in great shape, though it floods in heavy rains. Watch out for tire-eating roads in the town itself.

Buses to El Valle from Panama City leave every half hour or so, 7 A.M.–7 P.M. every day except Sunday, when they run 6:45 A.M.–9 P.M. The fare is US$3.50. The ride takes about 2.5 hours.

Taxis are near the public market, or you can ask your hotel to track one down; US$1.50 or less should get you just about anywhere, though you'll usually find it just as easy to walk around the central part of the town.

To get to other parts of Panama (besides Panama City) by bus, you'll probably have to take a bus to San Carlos and transfer there. Buses between San Carlos and El Valle run constantly during daylight hours. The fare is US$1.

Penonomé and Vicinity

PENONOMÉ

There isn't much to see in Penonomé (pop. 15,840), the capital of the province of Coclé. Most of it is not even very pretty, but somehow it remains one of Panama's quainter towns. It has given way to modern commerical bustle and congestion without entirely giving up its quiet Spanish colonial charm, at least in the heart of town. Penonomé rewards those who take the time to explore its backstreets with glimpses of what it must have looked like a hundred years ago.

Penonomé is in the middle of wide expanses of flat, humid lowland, with the Interamericana curving north to meet it before dropping back down south on its way west. Visible off to the distant north are the tantalizingly lush highlands.

Sights

In the evenings it's pleasant to wander around the town plaza, which sometimes attracts a surprisingly cool breeze and, more often, the neighborhood skater kids. The plaza has a gazebo and (miraculously) a few shade trees. It faces the **Catedral de Penonomé,** whose most distinctive features are its small, modern stained-glass windows, which look pretty when the sun is right. To the side is the **Casa de Gobierno,** the municipal government offices, which has some fine wrought-iron grillwork on the outside. This is all ringed by a few old, sloping red-tile-roofed buildings, some of which feature bright green doors that somehow fit into the scene. There is also a small museum, **El Museo de Penonomé** (Calle San Antonio near Parque Ruben Dario Carles, tel. 997-8490, 9 A.M.–4 P.M. Mon.–Sat., 9 A.M.–noon Sun., US$1 adults, US$0.25 children) several blocks from the plaza in the direction of the Interamericana.

Shopping

Penonomé has two main commercial drags: Avenida Juan Demóstenes Arosemena, which leads up to the Interamericana a kilometer or so away, and about three kilometers of the Interamericana itself that skirts the edge of town. The first is mainly a busy shopping street for cheap goods. The latter strip has the better hotels and restaurants, plus street vendors selling (real) Panama hats. Those interested should find a good selection of hats outside the Restaurante Universal, which is near Hotel y Suites Guacamaya.

Mercado de Artesanías Coclé (Interamericana, 9 A.M.–4 P.M. Mon.–Fri.) is across the Interamericana from the Hotel y Suites Guacamaya. It has a decent, though hardly exceptional, selection of Ngöbe-Buglé bags, assorted ceramics, and small souvenirs.

Accommodations

Hotel y Suites Guacamaya (Interamericana,

tel. 991-0117, US$47 s/d, a/c), on the Interamericana just east of the entrance to town, is a modern 40-room hotel built in 2001. Rooms are simple but pleasant and have satellite TV.

On the western outskirts of town is the modern **Hotel La Pradera** (Interamericana, tel. 991-0106, www.hotelpradera.net, US$34.40 s/d, a/c). Built in 2001, it has 30 clean rooms with hot water, satellite TV, and good beds. Half the rooms have one double bed, and the other half have two double beds. There's a restaurant and bar and a small pool set in a backyard. It's the best hotel in Penonomé.

Food

Bohemio's Coffee and More (tel. 908-5852, 10 A.M.–9 P.M. Mon.–Sat., under US$5) has a couple of tables outside in a little strip of garden with a tiny fountain are actually a pleasant oasis in this busy town even if the food is nothing special. To get there, head down the main shopping street, Avenida Juan Demóstenes. When you reach a store called Casa Peter, look on the right side of the street for a doorway framed by wrought-iron fencing. Bohemio's is down this passageway. It's right next to a building called Edificio Don Bosco.

Panadería y Refresquería Romellini (Avenida Juan Demóstenes Arosemena, 7 A.M.–10 P.M. daily), just down from Hotel Dos Continentes on the way toward downtown Penonomé, offers sandwiches for a couple of bucks and delicious smells for free.

There are five outlets of the local **Gallo Pinto** chain (6 A.M.–9 P.M. Mon.–Sat., 6 A.M.–2 P.M. Sun.) in the area. Each serves basic *comida corriente* (fast food) in an equally basic atmosphere. Full meals here cost a couple of dollars. The ones likely to be most convenient are Gallo Pinto #1, on Calle Nicanor Rosas near the center of town, and Gallo Pinto #2, on Avenida Juan Demóstenes Arosemena near its intersection with the Interamericana.

Restaurante Las Tinajas (Interamericana,

tel. 997-9606, 7 a.m.–10 p.m. daily, US$2–3) is a cafeteria with a quaint thatch-roofed dining area with traditional Panamanian designs on the walls.

There's a **public market** between Calle Damian Carles and Avenida Juan Demóstenes Arosemena near the town plaza. A large Super 99 grocery store is on the Interamericana just west of Penonomé.

Information and Services

Super Farmacia Coclé (Avenida Juan Demóstenes Arosemena near its intersection with the Interamericana, tel. 997-9849, 8:30 a.m.–7:30 p.m. Mon.–Sat., 8:30 a.m.–12:30 p.m. Sun.) is a pharmacy just down from the Hotel Dos Continentes. There's a supermarket, **Supercentro Coclé,** next door.

There are several banks with ATMs down Avenida Juan Demóstenes Arosemena on the way into town. **HSBC bank** (8 a.m.–3:30 p.m. Mon.–Fri., 9 a.m.–noon Sat.) is just a bit farther down on the way into town. There are also a couple of Internet places that charge about US$1 per hour. **Hobby Chat Internet Café** (9 a.m.–10 p.m. daily) is upstairs from the Delta gas station.

The **post office** (Calle Damian Carles, 7 a.m.–5:45 p.m. Mon.–Fri., 7 a.m.–4:45 p.m. Sat.) is about a block south of the town plaza.

Getting There and Around

Penonomé is 143 kilometers west of Panama City, a drive that takes about two hours.

Buses leave from different places in Penonomé depending on the destination. Buses to Panama City leave from the large building with the Utrapep Terminal de Transporte de Penonomé sign emblazoned on the front. It's across the Interamericana from the Hotel Dos Continentes. They depart every 20–30 minutes, 4 a.m.–7 p.m. Fare is US$5.25.

Regional buses (such as to Santiago, Chitré, and Las Tablas) stop at the Restaurante Universal, near Hotel y Suites Guacamaya on the Interamericana. Buses to David have to be flagged down at bus stops on the Interamericana.

Most of the local area buses leave from a loosely defined terminal area near the public market between Calle Damian Carles and Avenida Juan Demóstenes Arosemena just south of the public market. Buses cluster in different stretches of these streets according to destination, which as always are written on the windshield. You may need to ask someone where yours is. If you don't speak Spanish, just ask, "buses a [destination]?" ("boo-sez ah...?"). Destinations of possible interest include La Pintada, Chiguirí Arriba, El Copé, and Aguadulce.

LA PINTADA

Because it's so close to Penonomé, those in the area should consider a half-day trip to La Pintada (pop. 3,700), in the foothills northwest of town. It's a pleasant, mellow place ringed by hills, including some big ones by Panamanian standards. The most storied of these is Cerro Orarí, a low, jagged-toothed peak that has inspired Panamanian poets and musicians but would go unnoticed by those from a truly mountainous country.

It's a pleasant, quiet town with some nearby petroglyphs, a pretty little river, and a cigar factory. The hatmakers in this district are famous for a variety of Panama hat called a *sombrero pintado* (painted hat), named for the rings of black fibers woven into it.

Sights

The artisans' market, *mercado de artesanías* (7 a.m.–3 p.m. Mon.–Fri.), has a decent selection of hats of different weaves made in the surrounding area. The best ones cost US$100 and up, though fairly respectable ones can be had for a fraction of that. A few pieces of pottery and some bric-a-brac are also on sale. It may be possible to hire a guide here for a few dollars.

There are now signs pointing the way to the *piedras pintadas* (petroglyphs). They are on private land, so you may be asked to pay a small fee to visit them. Getting to them involves a

© THOMAS GORISSEN/WWW.THOMASGORISSEN.COM

Culecos, in which partiers are doused with water, are a daily ritual during La Pintada's Carnaval celebration.

short walk and a little scrambling over rocks. The closest are across a *quebrada* (brook) that only has water in the rainy season. They consist of a few dim figures of some kind of animals, though they're too abstract to identify. The other sets are farther upstream. The most interesting thing about all of these is trying to guess what they might have once signified to the pre-Columbian indigenous people who carved them. Are they maps? Messages? Simple artistic expression? No one knows.

The **Río Coclé del Sur** is a pretty little river that runs by the edge of town. To get there, make a right turn past the church as you head into town and look for the *balneario* sign. You can hire a little painted boat and captain to paddle you around for US$0.50 at Balneario J. Los Algarrobos, the river's popular waterhole.

Those interested in seeing how Panamanian cigars get made can visit **Cigarros Joyas de Panamá** (tel. 692-2582 or 634-4437), a small

factory right before town on the way up from Penonomé. To get there, look for a sign on the outskirts of town. Make a hard left turn, which will double back onto a side road in the direction from which you just came. Stay right at the fork. The cigar factory is a couple hundred meters down on the right.

Festivals and Events

Popular festivities in La Pintada include the district's famous **El Topón procession,** a Christmas-day parade featuring effigies of Mary and the baby Jesus; **Carnavalito,** a mini-Carnaval celebration held the month before the actual Carnaval; and October 19, the anniversary of the town's founding.

Food

There are no places to stay, just a couple of places to eat, and few services of any kind in La Pintada. **Restaurante Casa Vieja** (tel.

CENTRAL PANAMA

983-0646, 11 A.M.–7 P.M. Mon.–Thurs., 11 A.M.–9 P.M. Fri.–Sat., most mains US$5–10) is a new and surprisingly attractive place to eat, by far the swankiest spot in a town that until now has really not had anything qualifying as a restaurant. There's a breezy, open-air dining room with exposed stone walls and hacienda-style furnishings as well as a smaller, air-conditioned room. The food, sadly, is flavorless and bland. Imported beef is available (US$14–19), but it's hard to imagine it'd be worth the expense. Still, it's a nice spot for a break. The restaurant is just off the main road, on the right 200 meters past the police station. It's opposite the town church.

Getting There

To get to La Pintada by car, take the road leading west from the plaza in downtown Penonomé and stay straight for 13 kilometers. The road ends at La Pintada. The road to the petroglyphs is two kilometers before town, on the left.

Buses from Penonomé to La Pintada leave from near the town market every 20 minutes, 6:20 A.M.–8 P.M. The fare is US$1.05, and the trip takes 15 minutes. A taxi from Penonomé is US$7 each way.

CERRO LA VIEJA

Posada Ecológica del Cerro la Vieja (Panama City tel. 263-4278, lodge tel. 983-8905, www.posadalavieja.com, starts at US$82.50 s, US$98 d, including breakfast) is a pleasant surprise. It's a combination mountain inn and off-the-beaten-path spa resort in a spot you wouldn't expect to find either. Those with limited time who are heading up to the western highlands can give it a miss, but it has several things to recommend it. It's perched atop a 470-meter ridge with a terrific view of a huge forested valley and the green peak of the 520-meter-high Cerro La Vieja (literally, old lady mountain), which looks close enough to touch. The breezes here blow strong and cool, but when they stop,

it can be as hot and humid as the lowlands. The surrounding land is heavily settled by farmers—the drive up will give a real flavor of Panamanian country life—but the lodge is attempting to bring back native vegetation on its 250 hectares.

The lodge's owner, Alfonso Jaén C., also owns the tourist restaurant Las Tinajas in Panama City. He takes understandable pride in this place. There are 22 rooms, all with hot water, and some are definitely nicer than others. The best are in the pair of modern two-story cabanas perched right on the edge of the ridge. Rooms on the top floor are best of all, but all have balconies and hammocks.

Spa services are available at reasonable rates. A 50-minute massage, for instance, is US$50. The lodge offers many different excursions for its guests, most of which cost US$15–25 per person.

The food is simple but tasty, and the restaurant has a spectacular view of the valley and Cerro La Vieja.

Getting There

The lodge is 28 kilometers northeast of Penonomé on the Chiguirí Arriba road. Those driving from Panama City should turn right off the Interamericana at the Hotel Dos Continentes. Look for a sign reading Caimito and turn right. Continue straight up into the hills. The paved road ends at the town of Caimito. Continue straight on the dirt road to the lodge. The drive takes about 45 minutes. Buses (really pickup trucks with benches) leave from the public market in Penonomé every 60–90 minutes during daylight hours (US$1.75). Look for the Chiguirí Arriba bus. You can also come by taxi from Penonomé, which will cost you US$25–30 depending on the condition of the road and the driver's mood.

EL COPÉ

This somewhat hard-to-reach park consists of more than 25,000 hectares of forested highlands stretching down the Pacific and Caribbean sides of the Continental Divide. Its full name is **Parque Nacional General de División Omar Torrijos Herrera,** but most people know it simply as El Copé, and that's how it'll be referred to here.

The park was created to honor the late military dictator Omar Torrijos, who died in a plane crash in these mountains on July 31, 1981. Supposedly some charred remains of the plane are still intact on Cerro Marta, a peak you'll see to the right as you enter the park, but you'd have to be a major bushwhacking mountain climber to prove it.

Because this park is hard to get to, it's filled with thousands of acres of primary forest you'll likely have to yourself. It's a beautiful place with sweeping vistas, as long as it's not too foggy. Even when it is, the morning mist rising off the mountains is quite dramatic.

El Copé is about as far east as the birds of the western highlands venture. If you're not an experienced bird-watcher or guided by one, however, you may not spot many species. El Copé is well known as a place to see hummingbirds, especially the snowcap and green thorntail. The rare bare-necked umbrellabird—which looks as though it's wearing a thatch roof—has been spotted here in the last few years. Its call sounds like the roar of a bull. All the feline species of Panama are still found in the park, but chances are slim you'll bump into any. Ditto for Baird's tapirs, white-lipped peccaries, and collared peccaries. Yes, there are venomous snakes, but you're unlikely to see one. Regardless, watch where you step and sleep.

This area gets rain and fog year-round and is quite a bit cooler than the lowlands, so bring warm, waterproof clothes.

Hiking

Several good, wide trails start from the entrance to the park. Facing into the park, with the visitor shelter and park sign to your right,

you'll see two. The one to the left heads straight up to the top of a mountain with views of both oceans (about a half-hour's walk). The one to the right heads down toward the Caribbean slope (endless). The latter trail is rocky and rutted, and you'll have to cross several streams. Be prepared for ankle-deep mud. An hour into it there's a far more rugged, strenuous trail that leads back to the shelter. The umbrellabird has been spotted here (as have venomous snakes). Do not take this trail without a guide: You will get lost. It takes about an hour to get back to the shelter. There is also a half-kilometer interpretive trail that starts behind the shelter. There's a rudimentary trail map posted on a signboard. The ranger may be available to guide you; as always, a small tip is appreciated.

Practicalities

The **ranger station** is on the left just as you come to the official entrance to the park at the crest of the hill. The park entrance fee is US$5, another US$5 to camp in a tent, and US$20 per person in the modern cabin. There's also an **ANAM administrative station** in the small town of El Copé, below the park, that's theoretically open 8 A.M.–3 P.M. Monday–Friday.

In 2002 the glorified toolshed that served as a visitors shelter was replaced with what may be the nicest cabin in the entire Panama national parks system. It's simple but pleasant and has a bathroom with running water.

Just 128 paces behind the shelter is an attractive **visitors center** that's allegedly open 8 A.M.–5 P.M. daily. It's on a ridge with an awe-inspiring view of mountains, the valley, and the Caribbean.

Since my last visit to the park, several community-run projects have gotten off the ground in the area, with some help from volunteers. **Alberque Navas** (tel. 983-9130, around US$30/night pp, including meals) is run by the local Navas family in Barrigón. Their house is on the right as one heads up toward El Copé; this is where the road usually turns rough:

Look for the small Navas sign on the front of their house. For years they have allowed visitors to park here and provided a shuttle service up to the park. This has become less necessary as the road has improved. They host overnight visitors in their house and offer visits to their forest cabin in a remote area called La Rica, where those who don't mind roughing it a bit can hike, bird-watch, and splash about in a waterfall. They speak only Spanish, but they are experienced in making themselves understood to monolingual gringos.

A newer project is **La MICA Biological Station** (cell 6707-8900, la.mica@yahoo.com, www.lamica.org), directed by Julie Ray, a gringa biologist who did her PhD research up here and then stuck around to make the natural attractions of the area more accessible to visitors and other researchers, and to give the local community new sources of income.

The project and its guest facilities are in the town of El Copé, about five kilometers from the park. There's a cabin and a dormitory that sleeps up to 25 people for US$10/person. Food is an additional US$15 a day for all meals. Campers can pitch a tent for US$5.

It opens the door to a beautiful part of Panama still little known even to most Panamanians. They offer logistical support at quite reasonable prices, putting isolated communities and wild nature within reach of even the most ill-equipped visitor. The project can supply transportation from and to Panama City (US$90 each way), Santa Clara (US$75 round-trip), Penonomé (US$35 round-trip), and Aguadulce (US$40 round-trip). Rates are for up to four people, except for Panama City, which is an additional US$10/person after the first passenger. La MICA can also supply porters (US$10/day), equipment rental, and guided tours of the park and other attractions, such as Chorro Las Yayas, a waterfall in Barrigón that is also maintained as a community project. The Las Yayas project offers a cabin for visitors interested in spending the night (US$10–15 pp).

Getting There

The turnoff to El Copé is 20 kilometers west of Penonomé. It wasn't marked on my last visit. If you're coming from the direction of Penonomé, turn right just before the pedestrian bridge that spans the Interamericana. From here it's a 33-kilometer drive into the mountains. The last seven kilometers are on a dirt road that used to be horrendous. It's now much improved, but it's still a rough, bumpy drive that requires a four-wheel drive. The trip can take more than an hour from Penonomé even with a powerful vehicle, depending on road conditions.

Direct buses from Panama City to El Copé run once or twice an hour 6 A.M.–7 P.M. The trip takes about three hours and costs US$6.50. If you're coming from Penonomé, you can take an El Copé bus (US$2) from there as well. In either case, switch at the little town of El Copé to the Barrigón bus (US$0.50). From Barrigón hike uphill into the park, a rocky four kilometers that takes about an hour. You can also ask someone in Barrigón for a ride; this is a common practice, and the fee should be less than US$10 if the road isn't too bad.

Aguadulce and Vicinity

AGUADULCE

The industrial town of Aguadulce (pop. 7,700), 53 kilometers east of Santiago in Coclé province, lies on a vast, dusty, sun-blasted and none of the few sights, restaurants, or hotels here are anything special. The area is known for producing salt, shrimp, and sugar, and there's a big dairy on the edge of town.

Sights

Museo de la Sal y el Azúcar (Avenida Sebastián Sucre, tel. 997-4280, 8:30 A.M.–noon and 1–4 P.M. Tues.–Fri., 8:30 A.M.–12:30 P.M. Sat., US$1 adults, US$0.25 children) is a tiny museum housed in a turn-of-the-20th-century building that was once the town post office. It's on the plaza, facing the cathedral. An earnest, Spanish-speaking guide will explain the simple displays and tell you more than you're likely to want to know about how salt and sugar are produced in the area. Salt has been harvested in the province since pre-Columbian times using much the same method: Seawater is diverted into artificially made channels near the shore and allowed to evaporate. The current elaborate, mazelike channel system has been used for more than 100 years. The staff here try hard to make do with very limited resources.

Las Piscinas is one of those surreal, only-in-Panama projects. Because the beach around here is really gooey mudflats, the community has seen fit to build four tile swimming pools, the largest of which is about 15 meters long, smack in the middle of a rocky part of those flats. At low tide the pools drain out. At high tide during the dry season, local folks splash around in them. Others come here to check out the plentiful shorebirds.

To get to the pools, take the unmarked road to the left of the church in Aguadulce. The road runs past some shrimp farms. After about

two kilometers there'll be a big mirador on the left over the water. Shortly after that will be a kiosk with a Coca-Cola sign. Turn left here and park. Mangroves will be in front of you, on the left. Walk about 200 meters until the path turns rocky. The pools are up ahead on the right. A taxi here costs about US$5 each way. By the way, if instead of parking by the kiosk you stay straight on the main road, in 1.4 kilometers you'll come to a landing beach for fishing boats. It's a colorful spot with good photo possibilities.

Accommodations and Food

There isn't much in Aguadulce to warrant spending the night, but if you do, the best place in town is the **Hotel Carisabel** (Calle Eduardo Pedreshi, tel. 997-3800, www.hotelcarisabel.com, US$27 s, US$32.40 d, a/c). It's a 21-room motel with TVs and a bathtub-size swimming pool. It's a modern but spartan place, and the walls are a bit smudged. Some of the beds are good, some aren't—shop around.

Pannito's Café (Avenida Abelardo Herrera, tel. 997-5555, 6:30 A.M.–10:30 P.M. Mon.–Sat., 7:30 A.M.–10:30 P.M. Sun., less that US$5) is a popular and friendly cafeteria next to the church (take the street on the right as you face the front of the church). Offerings include traditional Panamanian breakfasts, whole grilled chickens, sandwiches, pizzas, and baked goods. It may close for a few hours in the late afternoon.

Information and Services

There are no tourist offices in Aguadulce. The best bet for general information is to ask a staffer at the Museo de la Sal y el Azúcar.

Aguadulce has several banks with ATMs, all on Avenida Rodolfo Chiari, the main road that leads to the cathedral. The closest to the church is HSBC. INAC, Panama's ministry of culture,

CENTRAL PANAMA

has opened a surprisingly big cultural center, **Centro Cultural Anel Omar Rodríguez Barrera** (tel. 997-4389) that sometimes hosts concerts, art shows, and other high-toned happenings. It's right across the street from Hotel Carisabel.

Getting There and Around

It's a couple of kilometers from the Interamericana to the center of town, an awfully long walk in the hot sun. If you get dropped off by the highway, consider a cab into town. It costs US$1.25.

Regional buses leave from the town plaza. Buses to Panama City, David, and other distant spots don't come into the city; go to the Interamericana to catch one of these.

Buses to El Copé leave from the side of the museum every 45 minutes, 6 A.M.–6 P.M. The fare is US$2. Buses heading in the direction of Penonomé (US$2) can drop you off at Natá (US$0.75).

Minibuses to Santiago leave every 15 minutes, 5:45 A.M.–7 P.M. from the town plaza. Large, David-bound buses stop at Santiago, but these must be caught on the Interamericana.

Taxis to Natá are US$5. A trip all the way to Penonomé is around US$30.

VICINITY OF AGUADULCE
◖ Natá de los Caballeros

The Spanish founded Natá on May 20, 1522, which makes it the oldest surviving town in Panama and one of the oldest in the Americas. Its origins go back further than that, however—it was the center of an important indigenous chiefdom. Its last leader was named Natá; the Spanish took his name for their new town, then used the town as a base from which to conquer the native peoples of western Panama. Legend has it that it got its full name, Natá de los Caballeros, when the king of Spain sent 100 *caballeros* (knights) to help in these wars. The town remained an important regional center of Spanish power throughout the colonial period.

Natá's past is far more interesting than its present, however. Today it's a sleepy village of onion and tomato farmers. Pretty much the only attraction left is its famous, ancient church, the **Basílica Menor Santiago Apostól de Natá.** Though built over several decades after the founding of the town, it lays claim to being the oldest church along the entire Pacific littoral of the Americas. While of interest to historians, it's actually a rather simple if attractive stucco church with a plain wooden ceiling and red-tile roof. Its most notable features are its elaborate carved wooden altars. It was renovated in 1998. Every July 25, a statue of Santiago Apostól, the patron saint of Natá, is paraded through the streets of the town for the faithful. The nearby chapel, **Capilla de San Juan de Dios,** is supposed to be renovated eventually. The church is in the heart of town, less than a kilometer from the Interamericana.

El Caño

This little town nine kilometers northeast of Natá has an important **archaeological dig** (9 A.M.–noon and 12:30–4 P.M. Tues.–Sat., 9 A.M.–1 P.M. Sun., US$1 adults, US$0.25 children) that's open to visitors, but there isn't much to see today. Its centerpiece was a ring of carved stone columns, about six meters high, in the shape of human and animal figures. In the 1920s a North American adventurer, A. Hyatt Verrill, removed nearly all of them, 150 in total, and shipped them to museums in the United States along with gold and ceramics found at the site. Only the stone pedestals from which the figures were cut remain in the field today. Nearby is an excavated cemetery where five exposed skeletons can still be seen at the bottom of a four-meter-deep pit. The site dates to approximately A.D. 800–1100.

There's a small museum on the site in the quaint house with the red-tile roof. It's worth a quick visit. While most of the few pieces not taken out of the country aren't displayed here, for security reasons, there are a few small stone

© WILLIAM FRIAR

stone pedestals at El Caño's archaeological dig

statues and ceramics, photos of statues that were removed, a crude model of the site, and some pieces that date from the Spanish era.

The complex is three kilometers from the Interamericana and is accessible by a dirt road that runs by the left side of El Caño's church, Iglesia San Lorenzo, as one faces it. Keep left at the fork. The site is kind of isolated. Those without their own transport are probably best off hiring a taxi in Natá. In the rainy season, the site is a swamp swarming with ferocious mosquitoes. If possible, wear rubber boots and douse yourself with insect repellent.

Getting There

Both Natá and El Caño are just off the Interamericana on the way to Penonomé and Aguadulce and can be visited as a side trip from either of those larger towns in a couple of hours. Rather than fool with buses, those without their own transportation should consider hiring a cab in Aguadulce (or Penonomé—it's just 21 kilometers east of Natá). However, any bus running between Aguadulce and Natá can drop visitors off along the Interamericana at the edge of these towns.

CENTRAL PANAMA

Santiago

Though it's one of Panama's major cities and the provincial capital of Veraguas, most people treat Santiago (pop. 32,480) as a place to break their journey to somewhere else. Usually that somewhere else is David or Panama City, since Santiago falls just about midway between the two. It's about a 3.5–4-hour drive to either city.

Santiago is a homely commercial and transportation hub on the Interamerican Highway with little to offer tourists. But it does have the facilities and bus connections one would expect of a growing Panamanian town with such a strategic location. And it has a real town life, some decent places to stay, and even some entertainment possibilities. It's a good place to stop for the night on cross-country trips.

The Interamericana forks at the eastern outskirts of town. Taking the left fork off the Interamericana leads into town via Avenida Central, also known as Avenida Hector A. Santacoloma, though few call it that. The road leads through a busy commercial stretch before splintering by the town church, the Catedral Santiago Apóstol. Roads from here lead down to the surfing beaches of Playa Santa Catalina and to Puerto Mutis, a launching point for trips to Parque Nacional Coiba.

Most of the hotels, restaurants, shops, and services of interest to visitors are not in Santiago proper but rather on the Interamericana. Instead of turning in to Santiago at the fork, stay right; facilities are on either side of the Interamericana.

A little farther west, the Interamericana is intersected by Calle 10A Norte, also called Calle Polidoro Pinzón. This cuts southwest into Santiago (a left turn, if coming from the direction of Panama City) and is where the main bus terminal and a few other facilities for visitors can be found.

Celebrations in Santiago include the religious festivals of Jesús de la Misericordia on April 8 and the Virgen del Carmen on July 16; the Patronales de Santiago Apóstol (patron saint's day) on July 25; and the Grito de Separación de Panamá de Colombia (the town's call for independence from Colombia) on November 9.

SIGHTS

A self-guided walking tour of Santiago's few sights shouldn't last longer than a couple of hours, including people-watching. The **Catedral Santiago Apóstol,** on the west end of Avenida Central, contains the remains of General José de Fábrega, a key figure in Panama's decision to declare independence from Spain and become a part of Gran Colombia in 1821. As always, it's interesting to see how lively churches in Panama can get

© WILLIAM FRIAR

La Escuela Normal Superior Juan Demóstenes Arosemena is noted for its ornate architectures and murals.

on a given day, but it's unadorned by Catholic standards and isn't worth a special trip. The plaza, however, has recently been spruced up and looks rather nice.

Across the plaza from the church is the **Museo Regional de Veraguas** (tel. 998-4543, 9 A.M.–4 P.M. Tues.–Sat.). It attempts in very little space to cover just about the entire history of the province of Veraguas. Displays include fossils, prehistoric stone tools, pottery that dates back up to 2,000 years, replicas of pre-Columbian gold *huacas,* and displays that show traditional regional crafts, such as the building of mud houses. By Panama museum standards, this place isn't bad and is worth a quick visit.

La Escuela Normal Superior Juan Demóstenes Arosemena (Avenida 5A Norte between Calle 6B Norte/Calle Domingo García and Calle 8A Norte/Calle Eduardo Santo, tel. 998-4295) is an imposing teachers' college and pretty much the proud symbol of Santiago. It's worth a quick look if you're in the neighborhood, which is several blocks northeast of the cathedral.

It's a bulky structure with a red-tile roof, but what will grab your attention is the flamboyantly ornate entrance, which features nudes frolicking up the columns and across the arch. Visitors are welcome to peek inside, where there are more ornate columns and, across the hall, a theater with murals painted by Roberto Lewis, a famous Panamanian artist who also painted the ceiling of the Teatro Nacional in Panama City. They're not in great condition and, frankly, aren't terribly impressive, but you've got to admire the ambition: The murals depict key moments from pretty much the whole span of human history, from the discovery of fire to the Code of Hammurabi to the crucifixion of Christ to Copernicus. He tossed in the Spanish enslavement of Native American peoples for good measure.

SPORTS AND RECREATION

Santiago's de facto port, **Puerto Mutis** (MOO-tees) is a jumping-off point for boats to Coiba and other fishing and diving spots.

Some sportfishing and diving operations still operate out of here, though Santa Catalina is supplanting it as the port of choice. It's also possible to work out cheap trips to Coiba with local fishermen, but it's a risky proposition and is not recommended. These are small, open boats on seas that can quickly turn rough. The boats are unlikely to have a backup motor, life jackets, or a radio, let alone sportfishing gear.

Puerto Mutis is 24 kilometers southwest of Santiago on a good road and is easily accessible from Santiago by bus or taxi. The town is just a few houses, hole-in-the-wall restaurants, gas stations, and shops lining the road, which ends at a pier on an estuary.

Right at the end of the road is **Montijo's Bay Restaurante, Bar, y Gasolinera** (tel. 999-8174), where you can dine right across from a huge gasoline tank. It's a surprisingly pleasant, modern, open-air place on stilts that looks out on a pretty view of the estuary.

The road to Puerto Mutis is not well marked. To get there by car, follow Avenida Central (Avenida Hector A. Santacoloma) toward the cathedral and take the left fork once you reach it. Turn left behind the church onto Calle 2 Norte. The Hotel Santiago will be on the left. Take the second right (it's Avenida 5B Sur, but it's not marked) and then stay straight all the way to Puerto Mutis.

ACCOMMODATIONS

Santiago has a range of accommodations, most of which are on the Interamericana just outside of town.

US$10-25

Santiago has its very own hostel, **Hostal Veraguas** (tel. 958-9021, cell 6669-6126, www.hostalveraguas.com, dorm bed for US$6–8, private rooms start at US$12). The hostel is in a small private house in a nondescript suburb, Barriada San Martín, north of the Interamericana. Rooms are bare but clean. Common areas include the home's living room and a little *rancho* in a garden that also has a small aboveground swimming pool. There's a book exchange, laundry facilities, and a kitchen for guests. Your host is Lidia Jaramillo, a Santiago native who speaks decent English and some French. Opened in 2006, the hostel is still taking shape, and new features are added from time to time. Everything is flexible here, so price breaks and even free stays may be possible for longer stays or help around the hostel.

The hostel is a bit hard to find. Starting at the Centro Los Tucanes on the Interamericana, turn north at the overpass onto the road that leads to San Francisco and Santa Fé. (If you're starting from the main Santiago bus terminal, you're already on this road; just head north.) Turn right at the gas station two blocks down. Make an immediate left. The Universidad de Panamá branch should be on the left and Instituto Urracá on the right. Go three blocks and turn right. The hostel is on the right five blocks down. You may have to call or ask for "la casa de Lidia Jaramillo." For those on foot, it's about 2 kilometers from Centro Los Tucanes and 2.5 kilometers from Centro Pyramidal. This hostel is sometimes referred to as Hostel Santiago or Hostel Backpackers.

Hotel Gran David (Interamericana, tel. 998-4510, US$42 s, US$55 d), easily confused with the nearby Hotel Plaza Gran David, is on the north side of the Interamericana, just past the turnoff to Santiago as you head toward David. A long-established and popular budget hotel, it underwent a major renovation in 2012. It's definitely worth checking out if you arrive in town without a reservation.

US$50-100

Hotel Galeria (Interamericana, tel. 958-7950 or 958-7951, US$66 s/d, a/c) is on the north side of the Interamericana, just east of the Hotel Gran David. It's next to a small mall and offers 40 rooms, a bar, and a restaurant. It's not a fancy place, but it's long been popular with

business travelers and tourists who can afford it because it offers clean and modern rooms with comfortable beds, hot showers, and satellite TV. There's even a weight room. The restaurant is open for breakfast, lunch, and dinner.

The ◖ **Hotel La Hacienda** (Interamericana, tel. 958-8580 or 958-5477, fax 958-8579, US$77 s, US$94 d, a/c) is the best hotel in Santiago, at least until the renovations at the other hotels are finished and whatever is being built at the new Mykonos mall opens. On the Interamericana less than three kilometers west of town, it offers 42 bright and cheerful rooms decorated with furnishings that seem imported directly from Puebla, Mexico. There's a small gym, a small but attractive swimming pool, laundry facilities, a restaurant and bar, and an Internet café. A casino has been added recently. Rooms come with double, queen, or king beds. All rooms have free wireless Internet and satellite TV. Though there's hot water in the shower, there's none in the sink, which is a bit odd for a hotel in this price range. It's also a bit peculiar that windows only look into the hallway, which gives the place a certain claustrophobic feel. Day passes and special deals are often available.

About eight kilometers west of Hotel La Hacienda is the **Hotel Vista Lago Ecoresort** (tel. 954-9916, Panama City office tel. 393-9405, www.hotelvistalago.net, starts at US$60 s/d), which opened in mid-2009. It's a pretty odd place. It has 24 unadorned rooms with satellite TV, free wireless Internet, and a view of the water. It's in the middle of absolutely nothing, so the only reason to stay here is to get a bed as far as possible from town. However, the common areas are open and cheerful, and there's an attractive L-shaped pool. Day passes (US$5 adults, US$3 children) to use the pool and other facilities are available from 9 A.M.–6 P.M. The hotel is less than 10 minutes by cab from Santiago, so a day trip might be worth it on a hot day with nothing else to do. It's also an okay place to take a break during a long road trip. There's a restaurant.

FOOD

The restaurant at the **Hotel Gran David** (Interamericana, tel. 998-4510 or 998-2622, 6:30–11:30 A.M., noon–2 P.M., and 6–10 P.M. Mon.–Sat., 6:30 A.M.–3 P.M. Sun.) is ambitious for Santiago these days, meaning you might see a dish or two featuring balsamic vinegar and the like. The reality doesn't live up to the promise, but the food's okay and the portions are huge. A caprese salad, for instance, could easily work as a starter for three or four people. The tables aren't always the cleanest here.

Terrazas (Interamericana, tel. 933-1600, 6 A.M.–midnight Sun.–Thurs, 6 A.M.–2 A.M. Fri.–Sat., US$5–10), right across the Interamericana from the Hotel Gran David, is a passable grill with an air-conditioned interior, a covered terrace right on the highway, and incredibly slow service. A big and okay plate of *arroz con pollo* is US$6. There's free wireless Internet access.

The restaurant at **Hotel Galeria** (Interamericana, tel. 958-7950 or 958-7951, under US$10) has an ambitious menu of meats, seafood, and pasta, but this is a place to keep things simple. The food is okay, but nothing special by any means. It's open for breakfast, lunch, and dinner.

◖ **Restaurante Puerto Perú** (across the Interamericana from the Centro Pyramidal, tel. 998-1264, noon–3 P.M. and 6–10 P.M. Tues.–Fri., noon–10 P.M. Saturday, noon–5 P.M. Sun., US$11–14), formerly Restaurante Delicias del Mar, specializes in Peruvian seafood, of all things, and offers a range of other ambitious fish and meat dishes. It's generally acknowledged to be the best restaurant in Santiago.

Restaurante Los Tucanes (Interamericana, tel. 998-6490, 11:30 A.M.–10:30 P.M. daily, US$10), is in a gas-station plaza on the Interamericana just west of the Hotel Gran David. It's a quiet, pleasant air-conditioned place with tablecloths that takes a stab at both international cuisine and local food. Offerings include meat, pasta, chow mein, conch, and rice every which way. The *filete a la plancha en salsa chimi-churry* is a chewy but tasty piece of grilled steak in a brown sauce, served with green peas. The service is gracious.

The food at the **Hotel La Hacienda** (Interamericana, tel. 958-8580, 6 A.M.–10 P.M. daily, US$11–16) is passable but no great shakes, and it's overpriced for what it offers. This is especially true at breakfast, which averages US$8 a dish. It features Mexican and Peruvian dishes as well as the usual meat and seafood offerings. The guacamole is bland, though the chips are homemade. The enchiladas are the best bet among the Mexican offerings. Don't order anything too ambitious here. The restaurant itself is attractive, in a bright and kitschy kind of way.

INFORMATION AND SERVICES

The **ATP office** (Avenida Central, also called Hector A. Santacoloma, tel. 998-3929, fax 998-0929, 8:30 A.M.–4:30 P.M. Mon.–Fri.) is in Plaza Palermo, a small strip mall across and down the street from Restaurante Tropicalismo. The staff here are friendly, understand a couple of words of English, and may have a little more marginally useful printed material than other offices.

There are late-night **pharmacies** at the transportation centers on the Interamericana (Los Tucanes and Pyramidal). The Galeria has a 24-hour one.

Los Tucanes and Pyramidal have ATMs. There's a **Banco Nacional de Panamá** (9:30 A.M.–5:30 P.M. Mon.–Fri., 9 A.M.–noon Sat.) across the street from Los Tucanes that has a drive-through ATM. A few banks with ATMs are clustered along Avenida Central in the blocks leading up to the cathedral, starting with **Global Bank** (Calle Rogelio Girón R., 8 A.M.–3 P.M. Mon.–Fri., 9 A.M.–noon Sat.). There are plenty of **grocery stores** in Santiago, including a 24-hour Super 99; look for the high signpost.

Internet cafés that stay open late are all over the place. There are several near the main bus terminal and on Avenida Central.

The **Galeria** on the Interamericana resembles any small strip mall in the United States, complete with American fast food and American blockbusters playing at the little multiplex, Cines Moderno. There's also a 24-hour pharmacy and ATM.

A new mall, **Mykonos** was under construction in 2012 on the Interamericana two kilometers east of Santiago, and it may be finished by the time you read these. It looked like it was going to be quite substantial and feature an upscale hotel and restaurant.

GETTING THERE AND AROUND

Because Santiago is about midway between Panama City and David, it's an important transportation hub with excellent, frequent connections to many destinations. The Interamericana is four lanes of divided highway from Panama City all the way to Santiago. West of Santiago it narrows to two lanes of somewhat rougher road until David, though in mid-2010 it was in better shape than ever before and there are now occasional passing lines. It takes about 3.5 hours to drive the 250 kilometers between Panama City and Santiago at a safe clip, and, depending on road conditions, about 3–4 hours to drive from Santiago to David. Those heading west should note there are few gas stations west of Santiago. Fill up here.

By Bus

Santiago has three bus depots: the main terminal, in Santiago itself, and the Centro Pyramidal and Centro Los Tucanes, on the Interamericana near the east and west entrances to town, respectively.

The two *centros* on the Interamericana are where large, long-haul buses (Padafront, Terminales David-Panama) bound to and from Panama City and David stop. International buses take a break there as well.

Terminales David-Panama (tel. 998-4006, 6:30 A.M.–9:30 P.M. Mon.–Sat., 7 A.M.–8 P.M.

Sun.), the larger long-haul carrier, has an office on the west end of the Pyramidal complex. It sells tickets and (grudgingly) dispenses information.

Its buses to David leave every hour or so, 8:30 A.M.–11:30 P.M. There are also three express buses, at 2 A.M., 3 A.M., and 8 A.M. Fare is US$9.05.

Buses to Panama City leave approximately every hour or 1.5 hours 6 A.M.–11 P.M. There are also two express buses, at 2 A.M. and 3 A.M. The fare is US$9.05. Local buses to Panama City leave more frequently from the bus terminal in downtown Santiago, but some of them are smaller and less comfortable minibuses, and there's less metal between you and the dangers of the road.

The Pyramidal also has a hotel, air-conditioned restaurant, outdoor cafeteria, ATM, gas station, pharmacy (8 A.M.–midnight daily), call center (9 A.M.–10 P.M.) and gas station.

The main city bus terminal, the **Terminal de Transporte de Veraguas,** is on Calle 10A Norte, also called Calle Polidoro Pinzón. It has a small bakery and pharmacy and a left-luggage place (look for the *Guarda Equipaje* sign; starts around US$1 per day, more for bigger and more valuable items). There's a 24-hour supermarket and Internet cafés across the street. There are ATMs and a couple of basic places to eat in the terminal itself.

Those heading to Playa Santa Catalina should note that there are no direct buses from Santiago. Take the bus to Soná and transfer to a Santa Catalina bus there. There are only four daily buses from Soná to Santa Catalina, at 5 A.M., 11 A.M., 2 P.M., and 4 P.M. (US$4.85).

There's a large sign at the entrance to the terminal that indicates the parking place where you can find your bus. Destinations are also painted on the wall in front of the parking places. The following are some popular routes:

Chitré: Every 30 minutes, 5:30 A.M.–8 P.M.; US$3. The trip takes about 1.5 hours.

Ocú: Every 20–30 minutes, during daylight hours; US$2. The trip takes a little less than an hour.

Panama City: Every 30 minutes, 24 hours a day; US$9.05. The trip takes 3.5 hours. (Some of these are now big buses versus the old minibuses that usually run from here. However, the David–Panama City long-haul bus companies don't stop here; for these, go to the Centro Pyramidal or Centro Los Tucanes on the Interamericana.)

Puerto Mutis: Every 15–20 minutes, 7 A.M.–10 P.M. Monday–Friday. The last bus on Saturday is at 8 P.M., on Sunday at 6:45 P.M.; US$1.30. The trip takes a little less than an hour.

Santa Fé: Every 30 minutes, 5 A.M.–6:30 or 7 P.M., returning 4:40 A.M.–6 P.M.; US$2.90. The trip takes about an hour. The bus stops by San Francisco (US$0.90) on the way.

Soná: Every 20 minutes, 5:30 A.M.–9:15 P.M.; US$2.10. The last bus leaves at 8 P.M. on weekends. The trip takes a little less than an hour.

By Taxi

Those who want to take a taxi to Playa Santa Catalina should be prepared to pay US$90, but this may be negotiable—this isn't a common trip, and taxi drivers don't have a fixed idea of the price. Taxis to Puerto Mutis are US$15 each way. Taxis within town should cost less than US$2 for most destinations.

Santa Fé and San Francisco

◖ SANTA FÉ

Santa Fé is a bit like Boquete before the gringo invasion: a humble little highland town with its own simple charm, beautiful surroundings, and almost no tourists. A road down to the Caribbean coast, the first for this entire region, is coming, and it will undoubtedly lead to more deforestation and settlement. It's an appealing destination for those who want to experience a peaceful country town from another time, as long as they don't mind simple accommodations and know how to make their own entertainment.

Santa Fé (pop. 2,800) is 54 kilometers north of Santiago. Founded around 1557, it and the surrounding hills were the scene of fierce battles between the Spanish and indigenous peoples under the command of Urracá, an especially skilled warrior who managed to beat back the conquistadors for a time and today is commemorated on Panama's one *centavo* coin.

Santa Fé is 470 meters above sea level, which is high enough to get some cool breezes and fog. It scores low on the quaintness scale: It's a sprawl of nondescript houses and little else. The charm is to be found in the slower, simpler pace of life of its inhabitants. This is a town where people still ride horses down main street, and young couples gather in the plaza to flirt and hold hands.

The countryside is pretty, and the drive up is stunning. There are sweeping vistas of rolling hills and pasturelands, and in the distance the mountains of the Continental Divide, still green with dense forests (for now) as they spill down toward the Caribbean slope.

The main road up from the south forks just as it enters town. Staying straight leads into the heart of town, where there are a couple of markets, the town church and plaza, a couple of places to eat, and not much else. The left (west) fork leads up to the trail head to Alto de Piedra.

Tours

The owners of **Hostal La Qhia** (tel. 954-0903, www.panamamountainhouse.com) are the best source for tourist information. The hostel works with local cooperatives and indigenous people to offer a variety of tours and hikes, including half-day and full-day **forest hikes** to area waterfalls, waterholes, and river areas. Note: the hostel was for sale in 2012; hopefully, the new

CENTRAL PANAMA

management will retain its contacts with local guides and area attractions. Other places to stay in town may also be able to help set up tours.

The best-known hiking spot is **Alto de Piedra,** which is now easily accessible because a road has been built from Santa Fé to Alto de Piedra and is gradually being extended to the Caribbean slope. There's a waterfall in this area about seven kilometers from Santa Fé. It's a 10-minute walk from the road, but it is not sign-posted so you'll need either to go with a guide or ask for directions to *la cascada de Alto de Piedra* (the Alto de Piedra waterfall). There are plenty of other hikes and waterfalls in the area, but these should not be attempted without a guide.

Cesar Miranda (tel. 954-0807, cell 6792-0571 or 6666-4251, aventurascesamo@hotmail.com, http://aventurascesamo.blogspot.com) is a local guide who has been offering trips for several years now and has earned a reputation for running a pretty professional operation. He's available for horse tours, guided hikes, and birding trips to all the area attractions. Trips are US$20/person for nearby locations up to US$35/person for an all-day trip to more distant spots. Horseback riding trips are around US$20 per person. He doesn't speak English but he's experienced working with clients who speak no Spanish.

The coffee cooperative, **Beneficio de Café El Tute,** offers casual tours of its coffee-roasting facilities for US$5 a person. It is just uphill from Hostal La Qhia. At certain times of the day, you can just follow the delicious smell of roasting coffee to find the place.

A tour of a local farm noted for its huge collection of **orchids** (US$5 pp) is also available. It's in the community of La Mula alongside the Río Santa María, a 45-minute walk from the hostel, but the hostel can arrange transport for those who want it. Lunch at the farm is another US$3 per person for those interested.

Santa Fé is known for its orchids, and the person most responsible for that is **Berta de Castrellón** (tel. 954-0910), an orchid grower who lives in town. She's the head of the Asociación de Orquideología de Veraguas, which puts on a three-day **orchid festival** here in mid-August. She and her brother, Mariano Gonzalez, are also birding guides. Berta lets visitors tour the huge collection of orchids at her house, but she's often away these days.

The hard core may be interested in a hike over the Continental Divide down to the Caribbean coast. This is a difficult trek that would likely take at least a couple of days and cost a considerable amount of money. The building of the road is making the trip easier, but this is still not something to attempt it unless you're in excellent shape and are prepared to supply all the necessary camping gear. Parts of the Caribbean coast in this region of Panama are remoter and more difficult to traverse than the Darién jungle. There's a good chance of stumbling upon drug runners along this remote coast who will be none too pleased to see you. For those who insist on making the trip, the recommended route is to travel the unpaved road which is being built between Alto de Piedra and Guabal, 20 kilometers to the north. A *chiva* (a pickup with benches for passengers) makes the trip four times a day. The drive takes about an hour and a half and costs US$4. From Guabal it's a five-hour hike to Río Luis, where one can hire a boat and captain to head downriver to the Caribbean for about US$20. That trip takes about two hours. Hikers will then have to find a place to camp. They can then retrace their steps to get back to civilization. The boat trip back upriver will likely cost twice as much, as it's traveling against the current.

If **inner-tubing** down a river is more your style, there's a local guy named William (cell 6583-5944), by the Río Mulabá, who rents inner tubes and life jackets for US$7. This trip is not suitable for small children, and the river can be too rough at times in the rainy season. The float takes about 2–3 hours, not including land transport. William speaks some English. Book through your hotel or call him at his cell. He has a stand set up by the side of the road on the far side of the Bulaba Bridge.

Accommodations and Food

Santa Fé is a town in flux, very much like Bocas and Boquete in their early days as a tourist destination. There are no real grocery stores and the restaurants are none-too-pristine *fondas* (cafeterias). If you plan to spend any length of time up here, bring food.

◖ The Blue Iguana (no phone, noon–10 P.M. Tues.–Sun., US$5–7), on the right just as one drives into town, is housed in a building which more resembles a cavernous warehouse than a place to eat. Opened in 2011, it's run by a couple from Austin, Texas, who live in Santa Fé with their two sons. The burgers here are likely to be the best you'll find in Panama. They're juicy and flavorful, served on homemade buns with spicy fries. Other gringo comfort food includes nachos, chicken wings, and pizza, and there's a good selection of international bottled beers by Panama standards, ranging from Belgian to Japanese. The owners were planning to open a bakery, which would be a godsend. As one would expect from good Austinites, there's an electic mix of good music on the sound system. The place has an attractive bar and a Ping-Pong table. The side terrace has a great view of the surrounding hills.

◖ Hostal La Qhia (tel. 954-0903, cell 6592-5589 www.panamamountainhouse. com, US$11 dorm beds, private room with shared bath US$33, private room with private bath $38.50) is the most attractive hostel in the country. It's set in a garden at the end of town, just up from the bus station, and has a breathtaking view of the mountains. The hostel itself is a pretty, wide-open house with stone walls and floors and a bohemian-chic vibe. The dorm is now in a separate building with eight beds and attractive tilework. Next to it in the

same building is the nicest of the private rooms, which has a private bath. The building also has a pleasant open-air communal kitchen. Private rooms with shared bath are upstairs in the main house. The walls are made of lacquered cane, so splintered sunlight streams in and pleasant mountain breezes blow through. There's also a long balcony for those who want to hang out and enjoy the view. Downstairs is a bar/dining area that opens onto a large terrace strung with hammocks. Breakfast is around US$3. There's a book exchange and lots of written information on local attractions and tours, including hike descriptions and maps. An attractive private house may be available to rent for longer stays.

The **Hotel Santa Fé** (tel. 954-0941, info@ hotelsantafepanama.com, www.hotelsantafepanama.com, starts at US$20 s, US$25 d), a 16-room motel 500 meters south of the town entrance, has gone through many ups and downs over the years. Managers Greg, a gringo who has lived in Panama for years, and Leslie, a Panamanian environmental lawyer from Santiago have put in new mattresses and sheets, installed wireless Internet, spruced the place up, vastly improved the restaurant and common areas, and added such customer-oriented touches such as greeting guests with a welcome drink and planting an attractive little garden. The managers' improvements have made a significant difference, but this is still a pretty rustic place in need of a major renovation by the owners. The cheapest rooms are tiny, lack hot water, and are cooled by fans. Larger rooms with air-conditioning, satellite TV, and hot water are US$38–42. All the rooms have private bathrooms, though they need a makeover. You may not need air-conditioning or even fans in Santa Fé.

The little restaurant at Hotel Santa Fé is much improved and is now one of the best options. The hotel is on the main road, on the left as one heads toward town. One can now dine along the terrace by candlelight in the evenings. The menu is small and simple, with

CENTRAL PANAMA

mains running about US$6–8. Fried chicken with ginger is a popular dinner option; it's a bit greasy but tasty.

A clean, simple vegetarian restaurant, with the suitably plain name **Restaurante Vegetariano** (cell 6638-0939, hours vary) is on the 2nd floor of a house with a balcony overlooking the town church (look for the sign by the right side of the main road as one passes the town plaza). Run by a Swiss-Panamanian couple, it offers a small assortment of veggie options including *rosti* potatoes with fried egg, pesto pasta, nachos, and hummus for US$4.50–7. It is open for dinners Wed.–Sun., and at other times upon request.

⬛ Casa Mariposa Boutique Hotel (cell 6791-5092 or 6097-9987, www.casamariposasantafe.com, starts at US$64.90 s/d, a/c) comes as quite a surprise. Talk about a hidden gem: located about four kilometers east of Santa Fé, it opened in December 2011 with just two bungalows (the owners call them "villas") set on two hectares of land with sweeping views of the surrounding highlands and valleys. Two more villas should be completed by the time you read this. There is also a good-size (24 feet by 13 feet) swimming pool, a restaurant was nearing completion when I visited, and a spa was in the works. A naturalist/cook, Graham, and a massage therapist, Rachel, were already living and working on the premises. Breakfast fixings are included with stays, delivered to the bungalows for guests to prepare themselves. Lunch and dinner are available in the restaurant. Lunch goes for around US$5–6 and dinner for about US$8–12. The sandwiches ar delicious, made with home-baked bread.

The villas are tastefully appointed and immaculate, each with a full modern kitchen, a flat-screen TV with DVD player, an in-room safe, and a porch overlooking the view. The

The lovely Casa Mariposa Boutique Hotel offers some of the most upscale accommodations in central Panama.

© WILLIAM FRIAR

Motmot (US$75.90 s/d) is somewhat bigger than the Tucán (US$64.90).

You would not expect to find anything this upscale anywhere in central Panama, let alone around Santa Fé. The bungalows are extraordinarily good value. Within days of its opening, it was already getting booked up. Make reservations as far in advance as possible.

The Canadian owners, Erica and Kevin, are reforesting the property, which was formerly farmland, and already the grounds are quite attractive. There's a small pond, and a *quebrada* (brook) borders it on two sides. What really makes this place special, though, is that it is a toucan sanctuary. Erica and Kevin have nine toucans, including stunning fiery-billed and collared aracaris. They are breeding them through a Panamanian-government sanctioned program, and releasing the offspring into the wild.

Those not staying at Casa Mariposa are welcome to come for a two-course lunch and feed the toucans on Tuesdays, Thursdays, and Saturdays. The cost is US$15 per person. To maintain the peace and quiet of the toucan sanctuary, overnight guests must be 21 years old or older and no more than two people can share a bungalow. This is not a place for partiers.

The road leading up to Casa Mariposa is 3.7 kilometers east of the Santa Fé bus terminal. To get there, cross over the Río Mulabá bridge and continue on for just over two kilometers. You should see a Casa Mariposa sign on the right. From here it's another 500 meters on a road which is due to be paved by the time you read this. If it's not, you may need to park here and have the owners drive you up in their truck, as this last bit is rough even for the average 4WD to climb.

Mercado Agricola y Artesanal Santa Fé (in the center of town, on the east side near the church, no phone, 7:30 A.M.–6:30 P.M. daily) is an open-air market with some fruits and vegetables for sale, as well as a few handicrafts, mostly Ngöbe-Buglé.

The **Centro de Mercadeo de Productos Agropecuario, Orgánico, y Artesenal** (no phone, 6 A.M.–7 P.M. daily, closed during lunchtime) has a name bigger than its building. It's a cooperative that sells a few veggies and beans, straw hats, Ngöbe-Buglé handicrafts, and the local coffee. To get there, keep right at the fork as the road leads into town. Continue up to the northern edge of town, then turn right onto the dirt road. The cooperative is on the right, next to the bus station. The restaurant (no phone, 5:30 A.M.–9 P.M. daily) below it is pleasant and breezy, and the food is basic and cheap. A substantial lunch here costs less than US$3. There is also a greasy spoon next to the bus terminal that is open during daylight hours.

Information and Services

An **Internet café** (no phone, 8 A.M.–6 P.M. daily) is in the Fundacion Hector Gallego, about 100 meters uphill from Hostal La Qhia, just down from the coffee plant. It charges US$0.75/hour.

SAN FRANCISCO

The small town of San Francisco (pop. 2,220) is on the road to Santa Fé about 20 kilometers north of Santiago. It's not very scenic, but its stunning church makes it well worth a stop on the way to or from Santa Fé.

The church, **Iglesia San Francisco de la Montaña** (9:30 A.M.–4 P.M. Tues.–Sun.), is my favorite in all of Panama. It dates from 1727, more than 100 years after the town was founded. The building itself is charming, but what makes the church special are its baroque cedar altars, pulpit, and pillars. There are eight altars, all quite different and all painted in rich reds, golds, blues, and greens. Take time to look carefully at the carvings on the altars and the pillars, which reveal unusual syncretisms that fuse European and indigenous images and traditions. Note, for instance, the tropical fruits carved into the pillars at the front of the

San Francisco's church is filled with fascinating and colorful baroque altars and ornamentation.

church. My favorite bits are the extraordinarily elaborate pulpit, the main altar, and the *retablo de la pasión,* the altar which depicts the crucifixion. That one is just to the left of the main altar as one faces it.

The outside is brick at the bottom, with a more modern whitewashed tower planted incongruously on top. A glacier-paced renovation of the church has restored the whole outside to a semblance of its former glory.

To get to the church, make a right turn off the main road to Santa Fé at the police station. Make another right upon entering town. The church will be straight ahead.

Refresquería y Quesería El Mirador (tel. 954-2128, 9 a.m.–8 p.m. daily) is a snack bar and cheese shop by the side of the road two kilometers north of San Francisco. It makes decent flavored yogurt and cheese (think cream cheese and cottage cheese, not fancy *fromage*) on the premises and sells it at the counter. The menu also includes burgers and such, to be consumed on a large terrace with views of the surrounding valley and hills. It's a good place to stop on the way to or from Santa Fé.

GETTING THERE AND AROUND

The road is good all the way from Santiago to Santa Fé, and in 2012 new bridges were going up along every river crossing all the way up. The same bus passes by San Francisco and can drop passengers off; just tell the driver ahead of time. After visiting the church, catch another bus the rest of the way to Santa Fé (US$2, 45 minutes) or back down to Santiago.

To get to San Francisco and Santa Fé by car, turn north off the Interamericana at the crossroads just west of Santiago. The turn is right before the overpass, but may not be marked. Head up into the hills for 17 kilometers and turn right at the police station to get to San Francisco. Stay straight on the main road for another 37 kilometers to get to Santa Fé. The road has now been paved all the way to Alto de

Piedra, the most popular area for hikes. It's five kilometers up from Santa Fé, and the route is well signposted. After that the road is still mud and requires a four-wheel drive. The road is gradually being extended and paved down the Caribbean slope.

Archipiélago de las Perlas

Ninety named islands and more than 130 unnamed islets make up this archipelago, which begins just 15 minutes by plane or a couple of hours by fast boat from Panama City. *Perlas* is Spanish for pearls, and pearls are what first brought these beautiful islands international fame. When Vasco Nuñez de Balboa crossed the Darién looking for the South Sea, one of his motives was to find and conquer the islands he had heard were overflowing with the precious little oyster byproducts. The conquistadors did just that. In the process, they wiped out the islands' indigenous people. According to Spanish accounts, the islands were densely populated when they first arrived. There is evidence the islands were inhabited in A.D. 600 and perhaps 500 years earlier than that.

The archipelago has a way of periodically achieving brief international notoriety. In 1983, the island of Contadora was the site of the first meeting of the Contadora Group, formed by the leaders of several Latin American countries to try to promote democracy in Central America and influence U.S. foreign policy in El Salvador, Nicaragua, and Guatemala, which were being torn apart by bloody military conflicts. In 1979, the same island briefly played host to the exiled shah of Iran. In more recent years, the archipelago has hosted wave after wave of *Survivor,* the reality-TV series, and its spinoffs and imitators.

There are lush forests on the islands, lovely sandy beaches on their shores, and healthy coral reefs a short swim away. The latter attract a wealth of brilliant small fish and impressive larger creatures, including sea turtles, manta rays, white-tipped reef sharks, and moray eels.

The Perlas are considered one of the better spots in the country for divers in search of big fish.

None of the islands in the archipelago, including Contadora, have ATMs or banks. Bring all the cash you may need with you.

CONTADORA

By far the most developed and visited of the islands is Contadora, named for its role as the countinghouse island for the Spanish pearl trade. Wealthy Panamanians have beach homes here, and it has nearly all the accommodations, places to eat, and tour operations in the archipelago. It's a small island—just 1.2 square kilometers, with a population of 359 people. It's easy to explore just about all of it on foot in a couple of hours, or scoot around it in a golf cart, which can be rented near the airstrip. The roads are quiet and scenic enough to make this a surprisingly fun way to get around.

The setting is beautiful, but the island is pricey, even though many of its facilities have seen better days. Contadora was Panama's first true resort island; it had its heyday in the 1980s and went into decline when the tourist trade moved on. However, things are in flux, and the island seems to be on a bit of an upswing at the moment.

Sports and Recreation

Contadora has several nice beaches, including one, **Playa de las Suecas** (Swedish Women's Beach), where you can sunbathe nude. My favorite, **Playa Cacique,** is a pretty, secluded beach behind Villa Romántica and away from the crowds. Contadora's largest and busiest beach, the aptly named **Playa Larga,** is somewhat rocky at low tide. **Snorkeling** is possible

CENTRAL PANAMA

ARCHIPIÉLAGO DE LAS PERLAS

Isla Pacheca

Saboga
Isla Saboga · Isla Contadora
Isla Chapera
Isla Mogo Mogo

0   5 mi
0   5 km

Isla Bayoneta · Isla Casaya

Isla Viveros · San Miguel

Isla Pedro González

Isla del Rey

Bahía del Rey

Bahía San Telmo

Isla San Telmo

Isla San José

Golfo de Panamá

Isla Galera

© AVALON TRAVEL

just off Playa de las Suecas, Playa Galeón, Playa Ejecutiva, and Playa Larga. There's very little else to do on the island, though.

Boat tours of Contadora and the surrounding islands are a popular activity, as are snorkeling, diving, and deep-sea fishing. Those on a budget can negotiate for a tour with a boatman (try Playa Larga or Playa Galeón), but don't expect life jackets or well-maintained crafts.

Dive operators can take guests to nearly two dozen **scuba-diving** spots within a 45-minute boat ride from Contadora. Most are only 10 minutes away. The diving in the Perlas can be impressive, especially for those fond of big fish: There's quite a good chance of spotting white-tipped reef sharks, manta rays, and moray eels. Among the many other critters you may come across are angelfish, parrotfish, grunts, snappers, amberjack, sergeant majors, and trigger-fish. Personal-watercraft rental is also available for those who feel the need to shatter the peace of the fish and fellow visitors.

Dive shops come and go on Contadora. **Coral Dreams** (cell 6536-1776, www.coral-dreams.com) has been around for a while now, however. It offers snorkeling and diving tours, as well as courses ranging from Discover Scuba to divemaster. It's right next to the Contadora airstrip. Look for the Dive Center sign.

Accommodations

Lodging options are severely limited on Contadora. **Contadora Island Inn Bed and Breakfast** (cell 6699-4614, www.contadoraislandinn.com, starts at US$94 s/d, including breakfast and transfers to and from the airstrip, a/c) consists of a vacation home that was converted into a bed-and-breakfast. It's in a residential area on the west side of the island. The B&B is in the interior of the island, not on a beach.

The house features a large deck, a spacious living room with TV/DVD player and stereo, and a kitchen guests can use. It sleeps up to 12 people in five plain but okay bedrooms. All the rooms are different and priced accordingly; prices are per room, not per guest. All rooms have ceiling fans, hot-water bathrooms, in-room safes, and outdoor sitting areas. Entire houses can also be reserved. Golf carts are available for US$40/day, but you have to fill them up with fuel at a station near the airstrip.

This has long been considered the best hotel on the island, but it appears to be on the decline. Staff seem generally grumpy and indifferent to their guests. There is air-conditioning, but the machines rattle and management is averse to using it in the common areas.

Villa Romántica (tel. 250-4067, www.villa-romantica.com, starts at US$125.40 s/d in the main house, US$105.60 s/d in the old annex, a/c) is a quirky place that has to be approached with the right attitude to be enjoyed. It's on the south side of the island right above beautiful Playa Cacique and offers 12 rooms in two houses. Two of the rather glitzy rooms in the main house have waterbeds. Potential guests should look at the photos on Villa Romántica's website before deciding to book here; the hedonistic-1970s vibe is not for everyone.

Rooms in the main house are nicer and closer to the beach than those in the separate guesthouse, which in turn has a bit more privacy. The owner is going for a romantic getaway vibe, as the name of the place suggests. That atmosphere is helped by the large veranda and open-air restaurant, Restaurante Romántico, that looks right out on the secluded beach. But it's diminished by the clutter and air of cheerful chaos about the place. The Austrian owner is an enthusiastic, effusive, and friendly character named Charley who offers boat tours.

Punta Galeón Resort and Spa (tel. 250-4234 or 250-4221, www.hotelpuntagaleon.com, starts at US$135.30 s/d, a/c) has a lovely location on a low, rocky point above Playa Galeón, as its name suggests. Rooms are in a series of white-washed one-story buildings and perched on the edge of the point. Rooms are simple but cheerful and attractive. All have TVs and in-room safes. It's gone through rocky times in the past, with complaints about service, maintenance, and, especially, food. Even if the hotel disappoints, the location is great. It's above an attractive but often crowded beach.

Food

Contadora is not known for good restaurants. What's worse, diners have to pay quite a bit even for mediocre food, since everything has to be brought over from the mainland. Expect to pay US$20 or more for an entrée that costs half that in Panama City. There are grocery stores near the airstrip. Contadora is a good place to arrive with lots of snacks stashed in the luggage.

Gerald's (no phone, noon–3 P.M. and

6–11 P.M. or so daily), in a large, attractive *rancho* on a hill just above the airstrip, is known for its seafood and steaks. It's a pleasant place to hang out in the evenings.

Restaurante Romántico (tel. 250-4067, www.villa-romantica.com, roughly 8 A.M.–3 P.M. and 6–10 P.M. daily, most mains US$12–20), the restaurant attached to Villa Romántica, offers expensive food in a good location: It's an open-air place right above a pretty beach that's likely to be deserted when you visit. The view is gorgeous. Offerings include prawns, shrimp, fondue, German sausages (including real, tasty bratwurst), and sandwiches. The food here is pretty good. Try the shrimp. This place is a bit of a hike from the main hotels, but the staff get around that these days by picking up and dropping off diners for free on request.

Fonda Sagitario (6:30 A.M.–8:30 P.M. daily), near the police station, is a basic but clean locals' hangout that serves simple food at cheap prices. Anglers take note: This place will cook your catch for a few dollars.

Getting There and Around

Most come to Contadora by small plane. The flight lasts about 20 minutes and costs US$62 each way. **Air Panama** (tel. 316-9000, www.fly-airpanama.com) flies to Contadora at 9:30 A.M. Monday–Saturday and 4:30 P.M. daily. Return flights are a half hour later.

Ferry services from Panama City to Contadora have been started and abandoned many times over the years. After a couple of false starts, a new service, **Sea Las Perlas** (tel. 263-5044, cell 6780-8000, http://sealasperlas.com) was up and running at the time of writing, though it was still looking for a permanent dock. Its final home will probably be somewhere in Amador, though it's been bouncing back and forth between the area near the Balboa Yacht Club, near the entrance to Amador, and the Brisas de Amador development on Isla

Perico, which is toward the end of the Amador Causeway. Be sure to confirm the current location at the time of booking.

The ferry ride is on a modern if utilitarian 54-foot catamaran and is quite a pleasant trip, if not particularly comfortable. There are great views of the Causeway and Panama City skyline coming and going. Be sure to keep an eye out for marine life. There are life jackets on the ferry, which is a good thing as the ride is on open ocean. They also sell overpriced beer and soft drinks on board. There is no ferry landing on Contadora. Passengers must climb down the side of the ferry onto small *pangas,* which then take passengers to the beach. This is not an easy way to go for disabled or elderly people. Expect to get your feet wet; wear shorts and shoes you don't mind soaking in seawater.

The ultimate ambition is to make the ferry a daily service, which would be a first for the islands, which in the past have not had enough visitors during the week, particularly during the rainy season, to sustain a daily operation. For now, at least, the service runs Thursday–Sunday. The ferry leaves at 8 A.M. from the mainland, dropping passengers off on Contadora by the Punta Galeón Resort and Spa. It makes the return trip to the mainland at 3 P.M. The ride takes about an hour and 45 minutes, and the fare is US$38/person.

ISLA SAN JOSÉ

This remote, 44-square-kilometer private island, the second-largest in the archipelago, saw few visitors before the opening of the 17-room **Hacienda del Mar** (Panama tel. 269-6634 or 269-6613, U.S. toll-free tel. 866/433-5627, www.haciendadelmar.net, starts at US$207 for up to four people). It's easily the most exclusive place to stay in the archipelago.

The cabanas look rather rustic from the outside, with their cane walls and red zinc roofs. But inside they're quite modern and feature hot-water bathrooms, in-room safes, ceiling fans, and balconies. The resort's clubhouse has a sports bar with satellite TV, pool table, sauna, and so on. It leads out to an attractive swimming pool. All this is on the southeast side of the island, perched above a sandy beach.

Hacienda del Mar offers 14 beachfront cabanas and three rooms. The 10 standard cabanas have two double beds and sleep up to four people. The most expensive accommodations are in the main building, where the two-bedroom Almiral Suite goes for US$385.

Possible activities at Hacienda del Mar include hikes or ATV tours through the island's forests, snorkeling and scuba diving, mountain biking, and deep-sea fishing. All these activities are extra, as are lunch and dinner. There's an extensive trail system through the island's forests, which are home to white brocket deer, peccaries, iguanas, anteaters, and other wildlife.

Most guests arrive by plane from Panama City, 90 kilometers away. The flight takes about 20 minutes. The resort handles the plane reservations. The round-trip fare is US$135 per person.

Beautiful as Isla San José is, it has a less than peaceful history. During and immediately after World War II, the United States, with support from Canada and Great Britain, dropped or detonated thousands of chemical weapons on the island to test their use in tropical warfare.

A 2001 inspection team found several unexploded chemical bombs on the island. The Panamanian government temporarily placed the island in quarantine, but a more thorough inspection to search for other weapons has not taken place. A conflict between the United States and Panama over who should pay for the inspection and possible cleanup has dragged on for years and has yet to be resolved. Resort management says all these weapons tests took place many kilometers from Hacienda del Mar. I have heard no reports of guests being harmed in any way.

OTHER ISLANDS

The islands listed here are just a sampling of what else the archipelago has to offer. However, most of the islands are not easily accessible. There's no commercial air or ferry service among the islands (except for the ferry between Contadora and Saboga). Most visitors use Contadora or San José as a base to explore the nearest islands on a boat tour.

Saboga is just a few minutes west of Contadora by boat. There is little on it, but a major residential and tourism project is in the works that, if it happens, would develop its entire coastline.

Pacheca, immediately north of Contadora, is also known as Isla de Los Pájaros (Bird Island) because it's a sanctuary for magnificent frigate birds, brown pelicans, and cormorants, among other seabirds.

Mogo Mogo, less than five kilometers south of Contadora, is a picturesque island with nice beaches.

Casaya, about three kilometers farther south, still has a small village of pearl divers. One can shop for pearls here, but don't expect any great treasures; those days are long over.

Isla del Rey is, at nearly 240 square kilometers, the giant of the islands, with the most inhabitants (about 2,000). To its south is **San Telmo**, a private nature reserve owned by the nonprofit environmental group ANCON. It's home to a large brown pelican colony as well as to boobies, cormorants, magnificent frigate birds, and endangered moist premontane forest.

WESTERN HIGHLANDS AND BEACHES

Western Panama offers some of the country's most spectacular, and diverse, attractions. There are the verdant highlands, home to the country's tallest mountain and the picturesque town of Boquete, which rivals Bocas del Toro as Panama's hottest destination. There are the remote Pacific islands and beaches of the Golfo de Chiriquí, which is so large and species-rich some consider it a small sea, as well as those of the Golfo de Montijo farther east.

The region also includes Panama's second-largest city, David, near the coast not far from the Costa Rican border. Most visitors simply pass through David on the way to somewhere else, usually the highlands, but it has all the services you would expect of a busy, modern provincial capital. There are a few large beaches within a couple hours' drive of David, the most popular of which are Playa Barqueta and Playa Las Lajas. The coastline and islands around the fishing village of Boca Chica are beautiful and beginning to take off as a tourist destination, though getting to them can be a bit of an adventure. Farther east, remote Playa Santa Catalina is internationally famous as one of the best surfing spots in Latin America.

The western highlands are a different world, one filled with powerful rivers, gigantic waterfalls, imposing mountains, secluded hot springs, and green forests bursting with life. The highlands are also home to Volcán Barú, a dormant volcano that, at 3,475

© WILLIAM FRIAR

HIGHLIGHTS

LOOK FOR ◖ TO FIND RECOMMENDED SIGHTS, ACTIVITIES, DINING, AND LODGING.

◖ **Finca Lérida:** This highland coffee farm is one of the best places anywhere to see the resplendent quetzal (page 315).

◖ **Parque Nacional Volcán Barú:** Panama's tallest mountain is visible from everywhere in the western highlands; on a clear day adventurous hikers can see both oceans from its summit. Don't miss Sendero Los Quetzales, the most popular hike in the highlands (page 324).

◖ **Parque Internacional La Amistad:** This gigantic international park has some of the most diverse flora and fauna in Panama (page 343).

◖ **Cañon Macho de Monte:** This impressive and accessible canyon appeals both to birdwatchers and inner-tube rafters (page 354).

◖ **Parque Nacional Marino Golfo de Chiriquí:** A remote and still little-known tropical paradise, this marine park is lightly peppered with deserted islands, bohemian hangouts, and exclusive resorts (page 363).

◖ **Playa Santa Catalina:** Panama's top spot for surfers, remote Catalina has one of the most consistent breaks in all of Latin America (page 375).

◖ **Parque Nacional Coiba:** Panama's answer to the Galapagos, Coiba is the crown jewel of the country's islands, with virgin forest, rich sealife, and a Devil's Island mystique (page 387).

meters, is Panama's biggest and most dramatic mountain.

There's plenty to keep outdoorsy types busy, including hiking, horseback riding, biking, the country's best white-water rafting, kayaking, even rock climbing and rappelling. The western highlands are popular with bird-watchers, since the forests attract hundreds of species, including many spectacular ones.

Most of the highland sights are clustered on the west and east sides of Volcán Barú. While the west side of Barú is a bit cooler and more dramatic looking, the east side has both great beauty and something its western neighbor lacks: a charming little town called Boquete.

Boquete is booming. As a result, there are more options for lodging, food, outfitters, and guided tours on this side of the mountain. The west side of Barú is quieter, less densely populated, and more rugged. It also has easily accessible trails through the enormous Parque Internacional La Amistad.

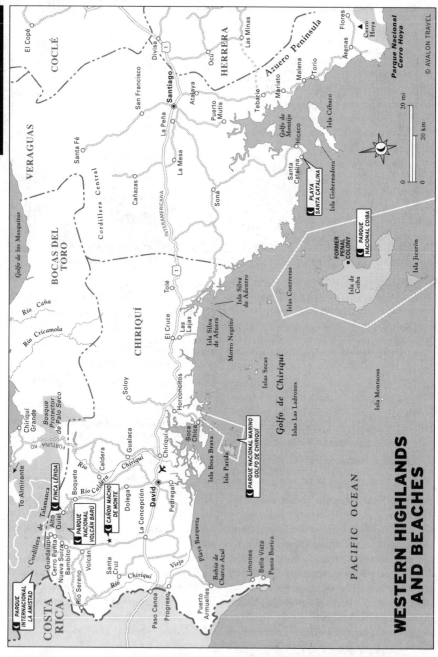

WESTERN HIGHLANDS AND BEACHES

© AVALON TRAVEL

PLANNING YOUR TIME

Most visitors to western Panama choose to spend their time in the highlands, either on the west side or the east side of **Volcán Barú.** To truly do justice to both sides of the mountain would require up to a week. The eastern side, centered around **Boquete,** is more popular. Allow at least three days to explore the town, go for a hike, and do at least one of the activities the area is known for, such as a coffee tour, white-water rafting trip, or search for quetzals. The highlights of the western side, including a long hike, can be covered in two days. Physically fit visitors who want to see both sides of the mountain may want to hike the **Sendero Los Quetzales** from one side to the other when they're ready to relocate; allow a full day for this. Note: This trail has been closed for the last few years following severe storm damage. Do not attempt to hike it until it is officially reopened.

It's fun to combine a trip to the highlands with a visit to the beaches and islands of the Golfo de Chiriquí and the smaller Golfo de Montijo. It's quite a contrast. Those who just want a little beach time can spend a night or two at the mainland beaches of **Barqueta** or **Las Lajas,** or make day trips there from **David.** David itself can be explored in half a day, and most people give it even less time than that. Getting just about anywhere else in the Golfo de Chiriquí takes time and planning, especially for those of us who don't own private yachts.

Parque Nacional Coiba is about two hours by boat from the nearest mainland ports; only private planes can fly there, and only then with special permission. Reaching **Playa Santa Catalina** or **Parque Nacional Marino Golfo de Chiriquí** usually means a fair amount of driving, but the roads to both places have recently been paved and are now much more accessible.

Few will have the time or inclination to visit both marine parks. Coiba and its surrounding waters and islands are stunning, at the top of most visitors' wish lists. The most accessible parts of Parque Nacional Marino Golfo de Chiriquí are not as uniquely impressive as Coiba, but the park has plenty of small, deserted islands to explore, and it's easier and cheaper to get to.

Most people go to the islands through a tour, dive, surf, or fishing operator, though some areas close to shore can be reached by taking a taxi, bus, or private vehicle to the coast, where fishing boats can generally be hired. Even Coiba can be reached this way, though it's not the safest and certainly not the fastest way to go. Plan to spend at least two nights on the islands to enjoy the surroundings and recover from the hassle of getting there.

Exploring the **Fortuna Road area** makes most sense for travelers who are going to or from Bocas del Toro by land. Otherwise, combining it with a visit to the western beaches and other highlands may mean more traveling time than most are likely to want.

THE NATURAL TREASURES OF THE WESTERN HIGHLANDS

The western highlands of Panama start at the Costa Rican border and run east for hundreds of kilometers along the Cordillera de Talamanca and the Cordillera Central. Much of Parque Internacional La Amistad and all of Parque Nacional Volcán Barú are in the highlands.

This chapter deals mainly with the Pacific slopes of the Continental Divide, since the parks and other sights are more accessible from that side. But the highlands extend north into Bocas del Toro province, where they descend toward the Caribbean.

The western highlands harbor more virgin forest than any other region of Panama. The area's huge national parks are home to a bewildering array of plant and animal life, much of it endemic and some of it endangered. The mountain forests are threatened by encroaching farmland, which in turn is threatened by erosion. But there's a growing sense among highland dwellers that they're surrounded by something special that needs to be carefully preserved.

Spend any time up here, and you'll soon know how cloud forests got their name. At the highest elevations you are literally in the clouds, and it's quite a dramatic sight to see puffy white billows blowing through the moss-draped trees in the afternoons.

Some parts of the woods may remind you of a temperate forest, but don't be fooled; you are still in the tropics. The forest has many of the same dangers and attractions as the lowland jungles, including venomous snakes.

This is one of the best places in the Americas to see the resplendent quetzal, an absolutely stunning bird. In the dry season, visitors often see several on a single outing. You're likely to see several species of jewel-toned hummingbirds among the hundreds of other bird species that make their home here.

Though you'd be very lucky to spot one, the forests are home to all five species of endangered felines found in Panama, including the jaguar. They are also home to one of the last stands of the endangered Baird's tapir, the largest land mammal in Central America.

Boquete is famous for its coffee and oranges, and the streams on the west side of Barú are filled with human-introduced trout. Flowers, strawberries, racehorses, and dairy cows are also raised in the highlands.

It's refreshingly cool in the highlands, with temperatures that dip down to 7°C and sometimes lower. And it's wet: Rainfall can exceed five meters. Even in the dry season, the mountains and valleys are often shrouded in what's affectionately known as *bajareque*, a foggy drizzle that can create photogenic rainbows. No matter when you come, bring rain gear.

David

Depending on where one draws the boundaries, David (dah-VEED), the provincial capital of Chiriquí province, is the second- or third-largest city in Panama (pop. 140,000). It's the lowland hub for visits to the highlands and other parts of western Panama and has the largest concentration of visitor services in the region.

David is a bustling, congested commerce and transportation center for Chiriquí province, which has the most productive farmland in the country. Every year the city hosts the Feria Internacional de David, an enormous agriculture and livestock fair that draws participants from around Latin America, Europe, and even Asia. It is also the only major, modern urban center in western Panama. With each passing year, residents of western Panama have less need to venture to Panama City to meet their shopping needs.

Few foreign visitors who aren't into farming or business spend much time in the city. Though David was settled by the Spanish in

© WILLIAM FRIAR

the national flag and the Chiriquí provincial flag

has not kept pace with this growth, and there's a severe lack of stoplights, stop signs, and street-lights. If possible, avoid driving in David. Even though the city is more or less on a grid sys-tem, even locals can get lost and confused on its streets. Drivers and pedestrians should be extremely careful at all intersections, as some drivers blast right through where stop signs have recently been installed.

Even for those used to the heat and humidity of Panama, David's climate can be pretty brutal. It's easily one of the hottest spots in the country. David is most bearable when the dry-season winds blow, but it's back in the frying pan the second they die down. Those exploring on foot should aim to do so in the early morning or evening. The heat starts getting intense as early as 8:30 A.M. Drink lots of water and consider doing what some locals do even in the dry season: use an umbrella as a parasol.

SIGHTS

David is not a pretty town, and it has little that qualifies as a true sight. The best way to get a feel for the place and its people is to wander around, especially near **Parque Cervantes,** the plaza at the center of town.

It's also fun to explore the streets just west and south of the **bus terminal area.** This is the commercial hub of the city, with kiosks and lit-tle stores selling everything from cheap clothes to saddles, and where street vendors still pre-pare and sell anything that can be deep-fried. This bustling area can be a bit intimidating at first, but it's really not a threatening part of town, particularly during the daytime. The people-watching here is great.

Be sure also to visit **Barrio Bolívar,** the best-preserved part of a city that is rapidly losing all signs of its past. The attractions here are mod-est but are worth a visit. Local preservation-ists are doing all they can to protect this area with very little funding. Few foreign visitors or Panamanians even know it's there, and that's a shame.

1602 and has a history of indigenous habita-tion far older than that, few traces of all that rich history remain, and most of the contem-porary buildings and byways are utilitarian at best. Its lowland location that's close, but not close enough, to the coast can also make it wilt-ingly hot and humid. David has some decent places to stay and eat, and even a few city-style diversions. It can be a good change of pace after time spent in the boonies.

SAFETY CONSIDERATIONS

David is a pretty safe and mellow town. Davideños are generally easygoing and cordial. But David is a growing city, and visitors should keep their city smarts about them, particularly women traveling alone. Streets beyond the cen-ter of town are poorly lit and deserted at night.

The roads pose the greatest risk to travel-ers and residents alike. David is booming, and more cars, trucks, and buses clog its already congested streets every day. The infrastructure

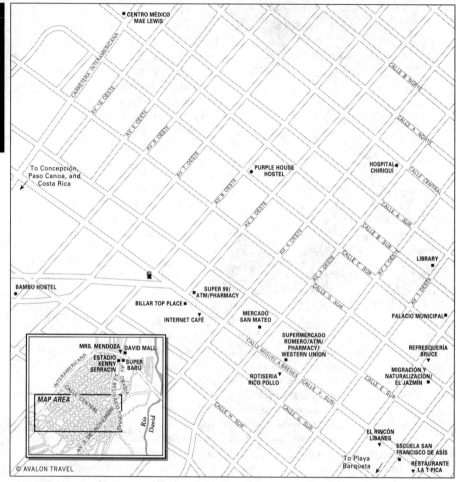

© AVALON TRAVEL

Parque Cervantes

As one might expect, the town plaza is the symbolic heart of the city. The "park" (really just a square block, most of which is paved) features a weird, diamond-shaped metal fountain, but it's a spacious and inviting area.

The church on the northwest side of the plaza, **Iglesia de la Sagrada Familia,** dates from the 19th century, but the current interior is newish and generic.

Barrio Bolívar

There are some colonial-era buildings on the southeast side of town in an area of a few square blocks known as Barrio Bolívar. This area is also sometimes known as **El Peligro** (The Danger). Don't let the name put you off: It's worth roaming around a bit here.

MUSEO DE HISTORIA Y DE ARTE JOSÉ DE OBALDÍA

Most notable of the buildings in Barrio Bolívar is the Museo de Historia y de Arte José de

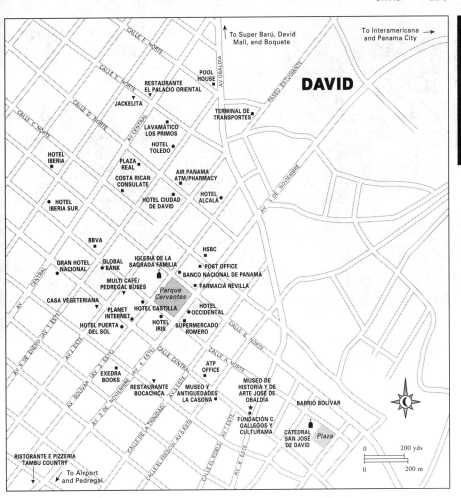

To Super Barú, David Mall, and Boquete

To Interamericana and Panama City →

DAVID

Obaldía (Avenida 8 Este between Calle Central and Calle A Norte, tel. 775-7839), a small museum housed in the crumbling remains of the 19th-century wooden, red tile–roofed home of José de Obaldía (1806–1889). An important figure in 19th century Panamanian history, Obaldía was instrumental in the founding of Chiriquí province in 1849. Among his other notable accomplishments was a stint as acting president of New Granada, which encompassed Panama and Colombia, 1854–1855.

The museum has been closed for restoration for years; the government announced plans to begin restoration work in May 2012, but the renovations will likely take years.

This history and art museum is an extremely modest place. When it was open, displays included a metate (a flat stone used for grinding corn) and a broken statue from the ancient Barriles culture, whose roots in Chiriquí date to 734 B.C. There were also some Spanish colonial swords and wooden

Parque Cervantes, David

© WILLIAM FRIAR

church figures. Some mementos from the War of a Thousand Days are upstairs.

FUNDACIÓN C. GALLEGOS Y CULTURAMA

Next to the Obaldía museum is Fundación C. Gallegos y Culturama (Avenida 8 Este and Calle Central, tel. 774-0536, 8 a.m.–noon and 1–5 p.m. Mon.–Fri., 8 a.m.–5 p.m. Sat.). It's a nonprofit foundation and cultural center that's recording the history, including oral histories, of as much of Chiriquí as it can. This is all too rare in Panama, and the commitment of the participants is inspiring. The place is of possible interest to visitors because it's another 19th-century building with character, it contains historic photos of David and its leading residents, and it has a substantial library of historic books and documents. Visitors are welcome, and the friendly, enthusiastic members have interesting information to share on the history of the area (at least with those who speak Spanish).

CATEDRAL SAN JOSÉ DE DAVID

Near Avenida 10 Este and Calle A Norte is the crumbling tower of the Catedral San José de David, which was consecrated in 1891. The cathedral was built on the site of a shrine that first appears in the historical record in 1722, but repeated restorations over the years have destroyed the building's personality. It now looks like a warehouse, though it's still a hub of civic activity; worshippers often gather in the evening while families play with their children in the neighboring park. The tower is the only part of the cathedral that's more or less intact, though it seems fragile and still bears the scars from bullets that struck it during the War of a Thousand Days. The cathedral bell hasn't rung since Panama's centennial celebration in 2003, but the local padre says that has nothing to do with fear the tower might collapse.

MUSEO Y ANTIGUEDADES LA CASONA

Be sure to stop by the Museo y Antiguedades La Casona (Calle Central between Avenida 6 Este and Avenida 7 Este, tel. 775-2239, cell 6676-5761 or 6675-7245, 9:30 A.M.–12:30 P.M. and 2:30–5:30 P.M. Mon.–Fri., 9 A.M.–1 P.M. Sat., free). The museum contains a curious mixture of antique furniture, religious artifacts, and displays illustrating traditional *chiricano* life, all housed in a private home that dates from the 19th century. The museum has a more interesting collection of historic pieces than many of the country's public museums.

ENTERTAINMENT AND EVENTS
Nightlife

The best place to try to find nightlife here would be Calle Miguel A. Brenes/F Sur, which is a booming commercial corridor. Also check out Avenida Obaldía, the main entrance into the city. Live dance-music shows are sometimes held in venues on or near the Interamericana. Taxi drivers will know the current hot spots (but be sure to ask for a "disco" rather than a "nightclub"—the latter is usually a euphemism for strip clubs and brothels).

A good place to mix with locals is **Pool House** (corner of Avenida Obaldía, Calle F Norte, and Avenida 9 de Enero, tel. 774-2364, 3 P.M.–late Mon.–Fri., 1:30 P.M.–late Sat.). Part of the charm of this place is its utter lack of charm: It's just a big, bare air-conditioned pool hall with a balcony overlooking two of David's busiest streets. Its lack of pretension and abundance of cheap beer ($0.80 per bottle) makes it a popular destination for twenty-somethings, local college kids, and blue-collar workers alike. It's a mellow place managed by Joey Charles, the gringo surfer who runs the river-tubing outfit in David and Boquete. It's the kind of place where single foreign women can feel safe going for a drink. A security guard downstairs checks out potential clients before buzzing them in.

Joey has plans to expand the balcony, which is the most appealing spot. It's pleasant to sit out there in the evening to catch the breeze, eavesdrop on neighboring tables, and watch the manic street scene below. Wednesday is ladies night; women can shoot pool for free from 6–9 P.M. There's Atlas on tap, a rarity for a country that hasn't quite discovered draft beer. Pool House is a block northwest of the bus station overlooking Avenida Obaldía, the main drag leading into David.

Pool players can also knock balls around at one of the growing number of **Billar Top Place** locations, including one on Calle Miguel A. Brenes/F Sur and Avenida 5 Oeste, next to Restaurante Jenny #19.

A slightly more upscale place to soak up the local scene and the local beer is **Restaurante Bocachica** (Calle A Sur between Avenida 3 de Noviembre and Avenida 5 Este, tel. 730-4057, noon–10 P.M. Sun.–Thurs., noon–11 P.M. Fri. and Sat., most mains US$8–12). It's a seafood restaurant a couple of blocks south of Parque Cervantes. This is a good spot to have a beer, which is automatically accompanied by a shot glass full of quite tasty ceviche, a nice gimmick. The place is nothing fancy, but it's authentically local. The restaurant is in one of the oldest surviving houses in David, a simple one-story affair with a red-tiled roof. There's a small air-conditioned room, but the atmosphere and crowd are more fun in the open-air main room. Try to get a table on the front terrace if you can put up with cigarette smoke. The place seems popular with upwardly mobile twentysomethings, as well as a somewhat older, artsy set, but it doesn't have an obnoxious vibe.

Festivals and Events

The **Feria Internacional de San José de David** (www.feriadedavid.com), usually shortened to Feria Internacional de David or simply Feria de David, is a huge trade fair that draws thousands of attendees from all over the country and abroad for 10 days in mid-March. It's essentially a giant agriculture, livestock, and commerce convention, though it does make room for folkloric crafts and dances. The fairgrounds take up 12 hectares on the western outskirts of town near Avenida 9 de Enero/1 Este, the road that leads to Playa Barqueta. In recent years it's drawn 500 exhibitors from around Panama, Latin America, and beyond, including some from Europe and Asia, as well as 600 prize livestock specimens. It's said to draw a staggering 300,000 attendees a year.

David's Barrio Bolívar celebrates the **Festival del Tambor** at the end of November, around the time of Panama's celebration of its independence from Spain on November 28. This is a traditional festival that features *tambores* (drums), *tunas* (marching bands), folkloric dances in colorful local costumes, and traditional *chiricano* food.

David and its surrounding communities celebrate **Carnaval** along with the rest of the country. A particularly popular place to go for the celebration is Dolega, a small town about midway between David and Boquete. It's less than 20 kilometers up the David–Boquete road and a more mellow affair than Carnaval in Las Tablas and Panama City.

March 19 is the *fiesta patronal de San José,* David's patron saint's day.

SHOPPING

Avenida 3 de Noviembre (Avenida 4 Este), which runs past Parque Cervantes northeast toward Avenida Obaldía, is a crowded commercial street with many shops hawking inexpensive clothes, household goods, and such.

There is an ever-expanding **mall** on the Interamericana at the crossroads with the road to Boquete. It's officially called Centro Commercial el Terronal, but no one uses that name. In English, it's usually referred to as the David mall. If going by taxi, tell the driver to take you to *"El Rey cerca de la Interamericana"* (the El Rey supermarket near the Interamericana). Stores include a big Farmacia Arrocha, electronics retailers, banks, and home-goods outlets. The **Do-It Center** (Interamericana, tel. 775-3648,

9 A.M.–8 P.M. daily), a DIY store next to the El Rey, carries outdoor gear such as rain ponchos, lightweight sleeping bags, rather flimsy life jackets, and cheap tents.

A slightly older shopping center, **Chiriquí Mall,** is a few kilometers west of David on the Interamericana. It's never really taken off, but it has a multiplex, a branch of **El Hombre de la Mancha bookstore** (tel. 774-1174, 10 A.M.–7 P.M. daily), fast-food stalls, clothing stores, and so on.

A small branch of the Panama City bookstore **Exedra Books** (Calle A Sur between Avenida Bolívar/3 Este and Avenida 3 de Noviembre, tel. 730-7662, www.exedrabooks.com, 10 A.M.–6 P.M. Mon.–Sat.) is in downtown David.

Those who'd like to take back some goodquality Chiriquí highland coffee without going to the Chiriquí highlands can buy gourmet-roast Café Ruiz coffee, one of the finest in Panama, at the **Super Barú** supermarket (Interamericana and Avenida Obaldía, 7 A.M.–midnight Mon.–Sat., 8 A.M.–10 P.M. Sun.). It's one of the few stores in Panama that carry the gourmet roast. Other kinds of Café Ruiz are more widely available.

SPORTS AND RECREATION

Regional and youth baseball games are held in **Estadio Kenny Serracín** (tel. 260-6916, http://chiriquibeis.com, tickets US$5), a stadium two blocks south of the Interamericana between Avenida Obaldía and Avenida Belisario Porras. *Béisbol* games are held only in the dry season, from January to around early May. Tickets can be bought at the gate. Schedules are not well publicized, but some information is available from the official website.

The most popular beach within easy driving distance of David is **Playa Barqueta,** a wide, black-sand beach with pounding surf that's usually far too rough for swimming.

To get to Playa Barqueta by public transit, take the Guarumal bus from the David bus terminal. For those driving, the main turnoff from David to Playa Barqueta is at the Escuela San Francisco de Asís, a large school at the corner of Calle Miguel A. Brenes/F Sur and Avenida 9 de Enero/1 Este. There's no name on it, so look for the statue of St. Francis in front. Head southwest on Avenida 9 de Enero and keep on going. The trip is about 30 kilometers long and takes about half an hour.

ACCOMMODATIONS

There are good lodging options both for budget travelers and those with a bit more to spend. Accommodations tend to be clustered around Parque Cervantes, in the heart of town. Another cluster is located on the east side of town near the bus terminal. The number of hostels is also slowly growing; these tend to be outside the center of town.

Under US$25

Opened in 2002, the **Purple House Hostel** (Calle C Sur and Avenida 6 Oeste, tel. 774-4059, www.purplehousehostel.com, US$9.90 pp for fan-cooled dorm, US$23–25 s/d or US$27 with private bath) was one of the first true hostels in Panama. It's located in a—you guessed it—purple house. Though it's 10 hot blocks from the heart of the city, it's within easy walking distance of a commercial district with all kinds of services and good transportation connections. The hostel offers 21 spaces in a configuration that's constantly changing. The house is simple but clean and comfortable and totally geared toward the budget traveler. There is a backyard garden with beach chairs and sprinklers when guests need to cool off. The hostel still has its original owner, Andrea, a former U.S. Peace Corps volunteer from New York. She is a great source of useful area information and budget traveling tips. Staying here gives guests access to lots of extras, including a book exchange, lockers, use of the kitchen, luggage storage, free wireless Internet access

and use of a computer terminal, all the fresh orange juice you can squeeze (in season), free coffee and tea, and discounts on some area services, restaurants, and transportation. All these amenities are available only to guests. English and Spanish are spoken. There's no curfew, but quiet time starts around 11:30 P.M. This is not a wild-party kind of place. The house is in a residential neighborhood, and hostelers are guests in Andrea's home.

Air-conditioners are available in the private rooms for US$5 at night or US$10 all day. Hot water and laundry service are available for an extra fee. In early 2012, Andrea was beginning work on a cement "splash pad," a fountain in the side yard where guests will be able to cool down on a hot afternoon. Guests can also use the pool at the nearby Plaza Mirage Hotel and Casino for US$2 a day. Availability is limited in October; call ahead if you plan to be in David at that time.

With advance notice, Andrea will try to arrange dance (salsa, merengue, and *típico*) and Spanish language lessons for guests. The Purple House also sometimes offers a free or discounted bed in exchange for volunteering at the hostel. Andrea can sometimes arrange transfers to Boca Chica if there's enough guest interest.

Bambu Hostel (Calle de La Virgencita, San Mateo Abajo, tel. 730-2961, www.bambuhostel.com, dorm beds US$12 pp, US$28–35 s/d with a/c), which opened in 2008, is in a rather bare house with a big backyard close to the Interamericana. The main building offers 8-bed and 12-bed dorms with thin mattresses and floor fans as well as four private rooms, some with private bathrooms. The hostel recently built a "jungle lodge," a large bamboo hut on stilts in its backyard, with 8 more beds (US$10 pp). The best thing about this place is its swimming pool, which measures about 4 by 6 meters. There's free wireless access, Internet computers for guest use, lockers, a shared kitchen, and a barbecue in the backyard. The hostel is a little tricky to find. It's close to the Santa Rosa sugar factory.

US$25-50

Hotel Toledo (Avenida 9 de Enero/1 Este between Calle D Norte and Calle E Norte, tel. 774-6732, 774-6733, 775-0694, or 775-2446, starts at US$30.25 s/d, US$35 for two beds, a/c) has 39 old but well-maintained rooms, some with good beds. The place isn't much to look at—it's a featureless building with aluminum siding—but it's long been a staple of the budget-hotel offerings in David. Try the mattresses in several rooms. All rooms have a phone and cable TV. There's a restaurant/bar attached.

The **Hotel Iris** (Calle A Norte between Avenida Bolívar/3 Este and Avenida 3 de Noviembre/4 Este, tel. 775-2251, hotel_irispanama@hotmail.com, US$25 s/d with fan, US$35 with a/c, US$5 for two beds) has decent rooms with okay beds, telephones, and slightly grungy but passable bathrooms. The best thing about it is its location right on Parque Cervantes, with balconies from which to people-watch. Rooms 223, 245, 346, and 266 overlook the park, but they're also likely to be the loudest rooms in the place. Since the balcony is shared and the bar/restaurant also has a balcony, it might be better to go for a room at the back of the hotel and sit outside when the spirit moves you. Rooms are fairly small, but there are bigger ones for a few dollars more. This is a good value for budget travelers, especially if you can do without air-conditioning, which is tough in David.

Hotel Occidental (Avenida 3 de Noviembre/4 Este between Calle A Norte and Calle B Norte, tel. 775-4695 or 775-8340, fax 775-7424, US$26.40 s, US$31.90 d, a/c), on the southeast side of Parque Cervantes, seems older than its twenty-something years, but it offers 61 well-maintained and clean rooms with phones. One nice feature is the spacious balcony that overlooks the plaza. There's an authentically retro vibe about the place that gives it character.

Hotel Alcalá (Avenida Bolívar/3 Este between Avenida Obaldía and Calle D Norte, tel. 774-9018, 774-9019, or 774-9020, fax 774-9021, http://hotelalcalapanama.com, US$34.10 s, 37.40 d, a/c) is a modern hotel that offers 55 pleasant rooms with cable TV and phones. The mattresses aren't very comfortable. The hotel is close to the public market and has a restaurant that's open until around 10:30 P.M. daily.

Hotel Iberia (Calle B Norte and Avenida 1 Oeste, tel. 777-2002 or 775-7395, fax 774-1950, hoteliberia@hotmail.com, US$42 s/d, a/c) opened in 2002 with 34 spare but comfortable and clean rooms with cable TV, free wireless Internet access, and telephones. The hotel has a bar and restaurant. In 2007, the Iberia opened a second "wing" of the hotel in a separate building around the corner. It's called Iberia Sur, but it's part of the same operation.

◖ **Hotel Castilla** (Calle A Norte between Avenida 2 Este and Avenida Bolívar/3 Este, tel. 774-5236, 774-5260, 774-5261, or 774-5262, fax 774-5262, www.hotelcastillapanama.com, US$50.60 s/d, a/c) remains popular with business travelers and is the best option for those who want a quiet, comfortable place in the heart of town (it's across the street from Parque Cervantes). The Castilla offers 68 pleasant, clean rooms with phones, cable TV, and wireless Internet access.

This hotel is spotless, well-maintained, and a good deal. (In practice, rates are often less than those listed, especially for singles.) The water is never more than lukewarm, though that doesn't matter too much in a sweltering place like David. A few rooms have balconies. The hotel has an underground, gated car park, which is a plus for those driving these busy streets. The restaurant here is decent but nothing special. This place fills up, so make reservations at least a day ahead of time if possible.

US$50-100

The **Gran Hotel Nacional** (Calle Central

between Avenida Central and Avenida 9 de Enero/1 Este, tel. 775-2221 or 775-2222, fax 775-7729, http://hotelnacionalpanama.com, starts at US$93.50 s/d in standard room, $121 s/d poolside, including breakfast buffet) was for decades the fanciest place in town, with 75 rooms and suites, a swimming pool, a casino, a poolside barbecue restaurant, a cafeteria, a pizzeria, and a six-screen theater that shows first-run movies. It's designed to vaguely resemble a Spanish-colonial hacienda, with red-tile roofs, whitewashed walls, and breezy corridors.

Rooms have finally gotten a long overdue makeover and gained flat-screen TVs, in-room safes, and free wireless Internet access. Oddly, the furniture looks old and cheap, though it's in good shape. The only rooms that have been completely transformed, however, are those along the good-size pool, which is kept clean and attractive but could use some landscaping around its stark perimeter. These rooms have been completely redone in a modern style and are, unsurprisingly, significantly more expensive than the standard rooms. The service is friendly, attentive, and professional. Those who can afford it may want to cough up the extra money to get a poolside room.

The food is edible but mediocre. Everything but the swimming pool is open to the public, so there's no reason to stay here just for the extras.

The Hotel Nacional has more local character than the Hotel Ciudad de David. It is also in a less-congested part of the city without being any farther away from Parque Cervantes. Its comparatively large and sprawling campus will appeal to anyone feeling crowded in David.

The most luxurious place in town is the ◖ **Hotel Ciudad de David** (Calle D Norte between Avenida 9 de Enero/1 Este and Avenida 2 Este, tel. 774-3333, www.hotelciudaddedavid.com, starts at US$95 s/d, including buffet breakfast, a/c), a six-story, twin-towered, mirrored-glass business hotel with 103 rooms. Opened in late 2009, it's a quiet oasis in the

middle of busy, muggy David. The service from the staff, clearly proud to work at the best hotel in town, is a tad formal but perfectly gracious. From the outside, the hotel is rather odd looking; the architect must have thought he was designing a high-tech computer factory. But inside, even the standard rooms are good-size, modern, tastefully decorated, and exceptionally comfortable, with 32-inch flat-screen TVs, minibars, in-room safes, and free wireless Internet access. Rooms have high ceilings and plate-glass windows overlooking what view there is, which makes them feel especially spacious. Security is good here: a card key is needed to operate the elevators, and rooms are equipped with smoke detectors and sprinklers. One of the rooms is equipped with disability aids.

A fairly good-size and attractive pool nestles between the towers on the third floor. Other amenities include a business center, an attractive restaurant and bar, and a small gym, complete with a sauna. Food is the one thing that needs work here; it ranges from tasty but unexceptional to subpar for a hotel in this category. However, it's still better than that at any other hotel in David.

This is a great deal for the money, offering an experience better than most hotels charging twice as much in Panama City.

FOOD
Restaurants and Cafés

Dining options are slowly getting better in David. The best you can hope for at most places is to fill up with cheap, inoffensive fare. There are also lots of gringo and local fast-food outlets. Most are located along Calle Miguel A. Brenes, which is quite a hike from downtown. Closer to Parque Cervantes, in central David, most dining options are in the hotels.

The casinos serve a full lunch, including drink, for about US$3.30. These are popular with budget travelers. The Fiesta Casino, across the street from the Gran Hotel Nacional, is centrally located.

HIDDEN FAVORITE

Though it's not conveniently located close to anything, especially for those without their own transportation, **Marisquería Nueva Sol de Mar** (tel. 770-6841, 11:30 A.M.-midnight or later daily, US$5-10) is a great place for well-prepared but reasonably priced seafood. It's an open-air venue on the north side of the Interamericana just west of Concepción and almost exactly midway between David and the Costa Rican border (about 23 kilometers from either). The *langostinos* (prawns) are delicious. It's a rather cozy place with a large bar area in the back.

Opened in late 2010, 🟥 **Cuatro** (Avenida Obaldía and Calle Estudiante, tel. 730-5639, cell 6613-3581, info@restaurantecuatro.com, www.restaurantecuatro.com, noon–3 P.M. and 6:30–10:30 P.M. Tues.–Sat., noon–8 P.M. Sun., mains US$10–20) is by far the best restaurant in David. Cuatro could hold its own with the best Panama City has to offer as well. The restaurant is in a converted one-story house near the baseball stadium on busy Avenida Obaldía, the main thoroughfare into the city. (Driving into David from the Interamericana, it'll be on the left 600 meters past the Super Barú supermarket.) Be sure to take a look at the photos on the wall, which show fascinating street scenes of David a hundred years ago, when mud-walled buildings were the norm. There's an open-air side terrace, but it looks out on a busy, none-too-scenic street.

The food here is outstanding. The young chef/owner is Luis Mendizábal, and his deep connection with his David and Chiriquí roots is reflected in his cooking, which Luis describes as "authentic but not traditional." (Even the name of the restaurant is a reference to Chiriquí; the number four is code for the province of Chiriquí on national ID cards.)

The menu changes but includes Luis's twist on a variety of Panamanian staples, such as *corvina ceviche* with passion fruit and a soy reduction, light and flaky empanadas with a Dijon mustard sauce, *platanos maduros* with gouda cheese and guava ketchup, red snapper in spiced shrimp sauce, *arroz con pollo* with chorizo and cilantro, and coffee-rubbed beef fillet. Groups should consider ordering several appetizers to share. The cuisine tends to rely on sweet flavors, which can get a bit overwhelming. Luis uses the freshest local ingredients he can find, such as hydroponic lettuce from Boquete, from which he makes the best green salad in Panama.

Desserts include haute cuisine takes on Latin American staples such as flan, which is served as four mini flans of different flavors: cheese, *dulce de leche* (milk caramel), coffee, and Nutella. The wine list is decent and reasonably priced, but consider trying one of the five different kinds of sangria on offer, including such unusual concoctions as white sangria with vanilla vodka and pineapple.

Luis is a professionally trained chef, a rarity in this part of Panama. He is a graduate of the Culinary Institute of America in New York and cooked at restaurants in Miami and Panama City (he did a stint at 10 Bistro) before returning to David. The restaurant is strict about its opening hours, which reflects its effort to deliver professional standards to its clients. If you show up at two minutes past 8 P.M., do not expect to be seated. Reservations are a good idea.

One of the best places to eat in David is, bizarrely enough, at the airport. 🟥 **Bernard's** (cell 6751-5628 or 6656-2750, 6:30 A.M.–5 P.M. Mon.–Sat., under US$10) is a simple but attractive international café, the most recent creation of Bernard Bahary, an Iranian expat who for many years was the chef/owner of one of the best restaurants in Bocas. The menu is eclectic, ranging from Thai and Middle Eastern cuisine to pasta, burgers, Panamanian food, and daily specials. The prices are a bargain for the quality offered. Breakfast with a bottomless cup of coffee or tea is served all day. Breakfast offerings are equally wide-ranging, from waffles with fresh fruit to a hearty Panamanian country breakfast.

Because the restaurant has to close when the airport does, it's not a place for dinner (unless you dine before 5 P.M.). Call ahead of time if possible, as the restaurant's actual opening hours seem to depend on Bernard's mercurial moods.

The restaurant in the Hotel Ciudad de David, officially known as **Stylo Resto-bar** (D Norte between Avenida 9 de Enero/1 Este and Avenida 2 Este, tel. 774-3333, www.hotel-ciudaddedavid.com, US$9–25) offers a shiny, air-conditioned oasis from the busy, broiling streets. It's a large, modern, and attractive, if somewhat sterile, restaurant with a long bar. The food, however, is hit-or-miss and overpriced given the quality. The best time to give it a shot is during the all-you-can-eat lunch buffet, noon–3 P.M. daily. There's a reasonable selection, and it's decent value at US$12. Take a look at what's on offer before you commit, as the selection changes daily.

Restaurante El Palacio Oriental (Calle E Norte and Avenida Central, tel. 777-2410, 10 A.M.–11 P.M. daily, most mains US$5–8) is a longtime favorite for Chinese food, served in a bustling atmosphere. The menu is huge.

There are three dining options at the **Gran Hotel Nacional** (Calle Central between Avenida Central and Avenida 9 de Enero/1 Este, tel. 775-2221 or 775-2222). They aren't great, but they aren't bad either. The cafeteria (6:30 A.M.–11 P.M. daily, most mains US$5–8.50) offers pizza, pasta, and fancier than usual meats and fish. Monday–Saturday, from noon to 2 P.M., the cafeteria offers a good deal: an all-you-can-eat buffet of pretty good food and a glass of wine for US$7.25. The buffet includes several salads, a variety of meat and fish dishes, some veggies, and several desserts. On Sunday noon–2:30 P.M., there's a popular

brunch buffet for US$8.50. The hotel's pizzeria is open 11 A.M.–11 P.M. daily. At night there's a pleasant open-air barbecue (5–11 P.M. daily, around US$15) under a *rancho* by the pool, with a variety of grilled meats.

The restaurant at the **Hotel Castilla** (Calle A Norte between Avenida 2 Este and Avenida 3 Este/Bolívar, tel. 774-5236 or 774-5260, 7 A.M.–10 P.M. Mon.–Sat., 7 A.M.–3 P.M. Sun., US$5–10) is pleasant enough and the food is decent. It's worth eating here just for the fascinating English translations of the dishes. You can feast on such mysterious delicacies as "beef steak in the horse," "rice with sailor," or "filet of fish in the white lady." Breakfasts are big and edible, but the coffee is awful.

El Rincón Libanes (Calle Miguel A. Brenes, Calle F Sur, and Avenida 9 de Enero/Avenida 1 Este, tel. 774-2700, 11 A.M.–midnight daily, full meals around US$8, sandwiches around US$5) offers a reasonable approximation of Lebanese food in a pleasant and lovingly decorated, air-conditioned setting. It's not uncommon to see a table of Middle Eastern immigrants discussing business and sucking on hookahs at the table next to you. The breads here are reheated in the microwave, which turns them into leather as they cool.

Lots of cheap *pollo a la leña* (rotisserie chicken) and snack places come and go along this same busy corridor, near El Rincón Libanes. A popular option is **Rostiseria Rico Pollo** (tel. 775-7494, noon–midnight daily), which offers a roasted half-chicken with *patacones* or yuca for US$4. This place has changed names at least once; it's the relatively large, clean-looking place across the street from Supermercado Romero.

Restaurante La Típica (Calle Miguel A. Brenes and Avenida Bolívar, tel. 777-1078, 24 hours daily) is a popular open-air place which serves cheap local food 24 hours a day on the busy Calle Miguel A. Brenes corridor near where it meets the road leading to the airport.

It serves cafeteria-style *comida corriente* (fast food) during breakfast and lunch, with most items US$2.50 for lunch and less than US$2 for breakfast. In the evenings and night diners order from the menu, where the average price for a main is US$7.

◖ **Jackelita** (Calle E Norte between Avenida 1 Oeste and Avenida Central, tel. 774-6574, 7:30 A.M.–10 P.M. Sun.–Fri., 4–10:30 P.M. Sat.) is an open-air drive-in with zero atmosphere near Restaurante El Palacio Oriental that's locally famous for its homemade ice cream, yogurt, and juices. They're all made with fresh fruit, including *zarzamora* (blackberry), *guanábana* (usually called soursop in English, if that helps), *piña* (pineapple), mango, *fresa* (strawberry), and both *pipa* and *coco* (fresh and dry coconut). The yogurt isn't on the menu, oddly enough, but the place has got tons of it. This is a great place on a hot day. Try the *yogurt de fresa*—it's delicious. It also carries *duros,* a kind of fruit popsicle in a cup. Jackelita makes cheap breakfasts and fast food, including burgers and chicken, as well. Nearly everything on the menu is less than US$2. There are now several other Jackelita outlets, including one at the end of the *Terminal de Transportes* (bus terminal) closest to Avenida Obaldía.

Kotowa Coffee (Plaza Real shopping center, Calle D Norte between Avenida Central and Avenida 9 de Enero, cell 6674-3023, 7 A.M.–8:30 P.M. Mon.–Sat., 1–8 P.M. Sat.) has a branch of its ever-expanding Panama coffeehouse empire in a little shopping center one block northwest of Hotel Ciudad de David. They serve iced coffee and the usual blended concoctions as well as hot espresso drinks.

Refresquería Bruce (Avenida Central and Calle D Sur, tel. 730-1102, 5:30 A.M.–10 P.M. Mon.–Sat., US$1.7 or less) is a clean, simple open-air snack bar with a couple of tables set outside on the street. It's not a place one would make a special trip to, but for those who need to pay a visit to the immigration office around the corner, it's a good place to escape for a soda and a cheap meal while waiting for the wheels of bureaucracy to grind slowly and painfully on. Burgers, hotdogs, nachos, and fruit shakes are usually on offer; the breakfast varies. The little college across the street provides the bulk of the clientele, which accounts for the low prices. The snack bar stays open later when college is in session. The Bruce for which the place is named is a cordial Spaniard with a kind smile.

The Taiwanese-owned **Casa Vegeteriana** (Calle Central and Avenida 2 Este, 7 A.M.–4 P.M. Mon.–Sat.) is a dubious-looking hole in the wall, but it's long-established and a godsend for vegetarian backpackers and other adventurous souls. Some find the offerings on the bland side, especially since the cooks don't use onions or garlic. You'll find it two blocks west of Parque Cervantes between the Hotel Nacional and Hotel Puerta del Sol.

Markets and Supermarkets

The two city markets downtown closed in 2010, scattering vendors around the city, at least temporarily. Until they find a permanent home, the vendors can be found in makeshift stalls around the Terminal de Transportes and the Palacio Municipal.

However, **Mercado San Mateo** (Calle Miguel A. Brenes/Calle F Sur between Avenida 3 Oeste and Avenida 4 Oeste, 5 A.M.–9 P.M. daily) has relocated to a new building right behind its old home. It's a fresh fruit and vegetable market within walking distance of the Purple House Hostel. At night vendors set up huge vats of oil and cook fried snacks until 5 the next morning.

Super Barú (Interamericana and Avenida Obaldía, 7 A.M.–midnight Mon.–Sat., 8 A.M.–10 P.M. Sun.) is a large grocery store with a bakery, gringo-oriented packaged foods, and good veggies. It also has a pharmacy and a bank with an ATM.

There's a 24-hour **El Rey** supermarket with a pharmacy across the Interamericana from Super Barú.

Super 99 (Calle Miguel A. Brenes/F Sur near Avenida 5 Oeste, 24 hours daily) is a large grocery store with a pharmacy and ATM.

Supermercado Romero (a half block northeast of Calle Miguel A. Brenes/F Sur between Avenida 2 Oeste and Avenida 3 Oeste, 24 hours daily) is a grocery and dry goods store behind the McDonald's on Calle Miguel A. Brenes. It has a bakery, pharmacy, and ATM. It cashes travelers checks.

There's another **Romero** (Calle A Norte and Avenida 3 de Noviembre/Avenida 4 Este, 8 a.m.–midnight Mon.–Sat., 9 a.m.–6 p.m. Sun.) at the south end of Parque Cervantes. It's mainly a department store, but it has an attached grocery and pharmacy that are open 24 hours a day.

INFORMATION AND SERVICES
Tourist Information
The local **ATP office** (Avenida Central and Calle 6 Este, tel. 775-4120, 8:30 a.m.–4:30 p.m. Mon.–Fri.) is in the Barrio Bolívar, near the Museo de Historia y de Arte José de Obaldía, but don't expect much from it. There's also an ATP booth at the airport.

The regional office for **ANAM** (tel. 775-2055 or 775-3163, 8 a.m.–4 p.m. Mon.–Fri.) is on the road to the airport. Heading into town from the airport, it'll be on the right. Hikers can get permits to visit Parque Internacional La Amistad and Parque Nacional Volcán Barú here (US$5 to enter, another US$5 to camp), but it usually makes more sense to get them at the ranger stations in the highlands.

Medical Services
There's a huge **Farmacia Arrocha** (7 a.m.–10 p.m. daily) on the Interamericana next to the Do-It Center and El Rey (a supermarket that also has a pharmacy, which is open 24 hours a day).

Farmacia Revilla (Calle B Norte between Avenida 3 Este/Bolívar and Avenida 3 de Noviembre/4 Este, tel. 775-3711, 7 a.m.–11 p.m. Mon.–Sat., 11 a.m.–6 p.m. Sun.) is a

large pharmacy on the northeast side of Parque Cervantes that sells lots of general goods as well.

Hospital Chiriquí (Calle Central and Avenida 3 Oeste, tel. 774-0128 or 775-8999, fax 774-0144, hchiriqui@pananet.com) is a modern hospital with a 24-hour pharmacy. A comparable option is **Centro Médico Mae Lewis** (Interamericana near Calle B Sur, tel. 775-4616).

Money
There are now ATMs pretty much everywhere in David, as well as tons of banks. A branch of **HSBC** (8 a.m.–3:30 p.m. Mon.–Fri., 9 a.m.–noon Sat.) is across the street from the post office. It has an ATM.

A **Banco Nacional de Panamá** (Calle B Norte between Avenida 3 Este/Bolívar and Avenida 3 de Noviembre/4 Este, 8 a.m.–3 p.m. Mon.–Fri., 9 a.m.–noon Sat.) with an ATM is at the northeast side of Parque Cervantes.

Global Bank (Calle A Norte between Avenida 9 de Enero/1 Este and Avenida 2 Este, 9 a.m.–3 p.m. Mon.–Fri., 9 a.m.–noon Sat.; ATM booth 10 a.m.–5 p.m. Mon.–Fri., 9 a.m.–2 p.m. Sat.) is near the Hotel Castilla.

Post Office
The post office (Avenida 3 de Noviembre/4 Este and Calle C Norte, 7 a.m.–5:30 p.m. Mon.–Fri., 7 a.m.–4:30 p.m. Sat.) is one block northeast of the plaza.

Internet Access
Internet places open and close all the time in David. Most charge US$0.75–0.80 an hour. Two long-established places are **Planet Internet** (Avenida Bolívar/3 Este and Calle Central/E. Pérez Ballardares, 7 a.m.–midnight daily), across the street from the Hotel Puerta del Sol, and **Pars Computer Technology** (Calle Miguel A. Brenes/F Sur near Avenida 5 Oeste, tel. 774-7510, 24 hours daily), next to Restaurante Jenny #19. Service at the latter is incredibly slow and uncaring when the place gets busy. If these go

out of business, there are others nearby. Many hotels also have Internet computers, and, increasingly, free wireless access.

Visas and Officialdom

Those who need their visa extended can apply at the **Migración y Naturalización office** (Calle C Sur and Avenida Central, tel. 775-4515 or 794-1332, fax 775-6823, 9 A.M.–4 P.M. Mon.–Fri.). It's in a residential area southwest of downtown. It's worth calling or visiting the office to get the latest requirements before starting on the laborious process since the particulars seem to change depending on the government in power, the immigration office, and the mood of the bureaucrat dealing with you. Come first thing in the morning, do not wear shorts or sandals, bring a snack and something to read, and be prepared to spend at least half the day there.

El Jazmín (tel. 775-1084 and 774-6514, 9 A.M.–4 P.M. Mon.–Fri.) right next door to the immigration office, takes visa-size carnet photos for US$2 for two, US$3 for four. They provide fax services as well. The store also sells water and soft drinks, which will most likely be welcome while you wait (and wait) at the immigration office.

The **Costa Rican consulate** (Consulado de Costa Rica in Spanish, Calle C Norte and Avenida 9 de Enero/1 Este) has moved from the suburbs to the 2nd floor of a three-story office building downtown. It's now across the street from the *policlínica*.

Laundry

There are few launderettes in the center of David, so it's worth checking the prices at your hotel to see if it'd be better just to let them do it. There are, however, a few launderettes near the Hotel Toledo, not too far from the bus station. **Lavamático Los Primos** (Calle E Norte between Avenida Central and Avenida 9 de Enero/1 Este, no phone, 7 A.M.–8 P.M. Mon.–Sat., 9 A.M.–8 P.M. Sun.) is long-established and is the most likely one to still be around when you visit.

GETTING THERE AND AROUND

David is the transportation hub for all of western Panama, with good connections to the highlands around Volcán Barú, Bocas del Toro, the Costa Rican border, and Panama City. It has a large bus terminal, a small but growing international airport, and outlets for major rental car agencies.

By Air

David's **airport** (off Avenida 3 de Noviembre/Avenida 4 Este, on the way to Pedregal), formally known as Aeropuerto Internacional de David "Enrique Malek," is less than five kilometers south of downtown. The airstrip has been lengthened with the idea of making the airport a true international hub. The new international terminal was nearing completion in 2012. If all goes as planned, flights between David and the United States may be offered by the time you visit. This may affect the schedule of regional flights as well; be sure to check ahead of time.

Airlines have added and dropped flights between David and Bocas del Toro in recent years. At the time of writing, the only domestic service was between David and Panama City (about one hour, US$113).

Air Panama (tel. 316-9000, www.flyairpanama.com) flies from Panama City to David at 6:30 A.M., 9:15 A.M., and 4 P.M. Monday–Friday; at 9:15 A.M. and 4 P.M. on Saturday; and at 8:30 A.M. and 4 P.M. on Sunday.

The airline flies from David to Panama City at 7:45 A.M., 1:15 P.M., and 5:15 P.M. Monday–Friday; 10:30 A.M. and 5:15 P.M. on Saturday; and 9:45 A.M. and 5:15 P.M. on Sunday.

Air Panama also flies between David and San José, Costa Rica, on Mondays, Wednesdays, and Fridays. The flight costs US$106 and takes about an hour. Flights leave David at 10:30 A.M. and return from San José at 11 A.M. (Costa Rican time, which is one hour earlier than Panamanian time.)

Major U.S. rental car companies, and a local

one or two, have their offices in a building in the airport car park. They also have desks in the terminal itself.

Café Kotowa, a gourmet coffee producer based in the Chiriquí highlands, has a coffee bar at the airport with Starbucks-style drinks and prices. There's a café upstairs called Bernard's (cell 6751-5628 or 6656-2750, 6:30 A.M.–5 P.M. Mon.–Sat., under US$10) that is one of the best places to eat in David. There is also an ATM.

By Bus

David's busy Terminal de Transportes is east of downtown on Avenida Estudiante, which begins near the corner of Avenida 2 Este and Avenida Obaldía. Buses for destinations throughout Chiriquí province and the rest of the country leave from here.

There's a left-luggage facility (6 A.M.–8 P.M. daily) near the Caldera bus stall. Travelers can leave backpacks here for US$0.50, US$1 for larger suitcases.

The following are some of the more popular routes:

Almirante (Bocas del Toro): Almirante is a port town, the jumping-off point for water taxis to the archipelago of Bocas del Toro. Buses run every 30 minutes, 3:15 A.M.–7 P.M., but to catch the last water taxi to Bocas (they run only during daylight hours) take the 1 P.M. bus at the very latest. Even that is cutting it close; to be safe, take an earlier bus. Those who miss the last water taxi will have to spend the night in or around Almirante, which has severely limited accommodations and appeal. The trip takes about 4.5 hours and costs US$8.45. The bus stops at the crossroads outside of Almirante, and it's a long walk to the water-taxi pier. A taxi from the crossroads costs US$0.50 per person and is well worth it. Passengers crossing the Costa Rican border at Guabito-Sixaola can continue on to Changuinola for another

© WILLIAM FRIAR

Ngöbe-Buglé coffee pickers wait at the David bus terminal.

US$1.25. Trips are made in minibuses that are often crowded and stop frequently. The trip between David and Bocas is made via the Fortuna Road, which crosses over the Continental Divide. It's a wonderfully scenic drive, though the road is windy, prone to washouts, and a bit white-knuckle at times.

Boca Chica: No buses go all the way to Boca Chica, the jumping-off point for Boca Brava and Parque Nacional Marino Golfo de Chiriquí. The best way to get there by public transportation is to take a bus east along the Interamericana and get off at the crossroads that lead into the town of Horconcitos ("*el cruce de Horconcitos*"). The fare is US$2. Do not take the bus all the way to Horconcitos itself, where it'll be much harder to get a ride to Boca Chica. There are six daily Horconcitos buses, but any bus that goes at least that far will drop passengers off at the Horconcitos crossroads. From David, these include the Tolé, San Felix, Las Lajas, and Remedios buses. *Colectivos* and taxis wait next to the Interamericana to take passengers to Boca Chica. Be sure to travel during daylight hours, as these are remote areas and it will be much harder to find transport at night.

Boquete: Buses run every 20–25 minutes, 5:25 A.M.–9:45 P.M., though slightly less frequently in the evenings and more frequently during Boquete's annual flower fair. The trip takes 45 minutes and costs US$1.75. The buses on this run are mostly converted yellow school buses, making them easy to spot.

Changuinola: Those crossing into Costa Rica at the Guabito-Sixaola crossing must first get to Changuinola. Buses run every 30 minutes, 3:15 A.M.–7 P.M. The trip takes about 4.5 hours and costs US$8. (Same schedule on the way back.)

Horconcitos: Buses to Horconcitos leave at 7 A.M., 9:30 A.M., noon, 1 P.M., 4 P.M., and 5 P.M. They return to David at 7 A.M., 10:30 A.M., 1 P.M., 2:30 P.M., and 5 P.M.

Las Lajas (town): Buses leave at 11:45 A.M., 12:45 P.M., 4:25 P.M., and 5:20 P.M. and return

at 2:15 P.M. and 3:15 P.M. The trip takes 1.5 hours and costs US$3. The town is eight kilometers from the beach, which means you'll have to take a taxi, if you can find one. The bus timing doesn't work well for beachgoers, especially those who don't plan to spend the night. A better option is to take a San Felix or Tolé bus to El Cruce de San Felix (US$3), the crossroads that leads into Las Lajas, and then take a taxi (US$6) to the beach from there. San Felix and Tolé buses leave about every hour, 7 A.M.–6:50 P.M., but their schedules are staggered so there's a departure every 30 minutes most of the day. Buses are somewhat more frequent on the weekend.

Panama City: Three companies run large air-conditioned buses between David and Panama City. The fare is US$15.20 one way, or US$18.15 for an express bus. The trip is supposed to take about 6.5 hours, but buses often run late. The bus makes stops at provincial towns along the Interamericana, most notably Aguadulce, Penonomé, and Santiago. Other stops are made by request. In Santiago, buses generally take a half-hour break at the Hotel Pyramidal or Centros Los Tucanes complex, each of which has a cafeteria, restaurant, bathrooms, pharmacy, ATM, and other services.

Especially on the expresses, those heading somewhere short of Panama City should ask the ticket seller—and double-check with the driver—that the bus will, in fact, stop at that destination.

These companies frequently shift their schedules, so call ahead if you want to ensure getting the bus you need. However, there's almost always a bus to Panama City within the hour, especially during the day. **Terminales David-Panama** (tel. 775-7074 or 775-2974, tel. 775-2923 for cargo, terminal@cwpanama. net) is a large bus company and the main way those without their own wheels travel between David and Panama City. It has its own air-conditioned waiting room at the bus terminal. Its schedule changes slightly from time to time, but it generally departs every 1–1.5 hours, 3 A.M.–midnight. The 3 A.M., 10:45 P.M., and midnight buses are expresses. **Padafront** (tel. 774-9205) has departures every 1–2 hours, 7:15 A.M.–midnight. The 11 P.M. and midnight buses are expresses. A newer company, **Panafrom,** makes the trip six times a day.

Paso Canoa: This is the main border crossing with Costa Rica, and buses have *frontera* (border) written on the front. They run continuously 6 A.M.–8 or 9 P.M. daily. The trip takes about 75 minutes and costs US$2. The Padafront buses from Panama City also continue from David to the border.

Puerto Armuelles: Those heading to Punta Burica must first get to this port town. Look for buses simply marked Armuelles. Buses run every 15–30 minutes, 4 A.M.–10 P.M. The trip takes about 2.5 hours and costs US$3.60.

Playa Barqueta: Take a Guarumal bus at 7 A.M., 8:20 A.M., 11:20 A.M., 1:20 P.M., 3:20 P.M., or 6:20 P.M. Check with driver about return times, as these vary during the year.

Río Sereno: This little-used border crossing with Costa Rica is in the Chiriquí highlands. Take this bus to get to Finca Hartmann (about 2.5 hours into the trip, US$4.50). The trip all the way to Río Sereno takes a little under three hours and costs US$5.10.

San José, Costa Rica: Agencia Tracopa (David tel. 775-7269 or 775-0585, Paso Canoa tel. 506/2732-2119, San José, Costa Rica tel. 506/2221-4214 or 506/2258-8939, www.tracopacr.com) has two bus departures to San José daily, at 8:30 A.M. and 12:30 P.M. The trip takes about eight hours and costs US$21 each way. The bus lets passengers off at the Coca-Cola bus terminal in San José. Be careful on arrival in San José, as the area around the terminal is considered unsafe. Costa Rican time is always one hour behind Panamanian time. The Tracopa office in the David bus terminal (7:30 A.M.–noon and 1–4 P.M. Mon.–Fri., 7:30 A.M.–2 P.M. Sat., and 7:30 A.M.–noon Sun.) is next to where the Cerro Punta buses stop.

Volcán, Bambito, Cerro Punta, and Guadalupe: Look for the minibuses with Cerro Punta on the windshield. These make all the highland stops on the west side of Volcán Barú. Buses generally continue past Cerro Punta all the way up to Guadalupe, but ask to be sure. Fares are US$3 to Volcán, US$3.30 to Bambito, and US$3.50 to Cerro Punta/Guadalupe. The trip all the way up takes about two hours. Buses run every 15 minutes, 5 A.M.–8 P.M. daily.

By Car

David is just south of the Interamericana. Depending on road conditions, it takes about 7–8 hours to drive the nearly 450 kilometers between David and Panama City at a reasonable clip with few stops. It takes a little over an hour to drive between David and the Costa Rican border crossing at Paso Canoa.

The road is a mostly well-maintained divided highway from between Panama City and Santiago. Between Santiago and David, it's mostly a two-lane road, though it has the occasional passing lane.

The drive between David and Santiago is through lovely countryside, with little but farmland, blue sky, and, close to David, rolling hills that lead to fog-shrouded mountain ranges in the distance. Passengers should keep their eyes open for the occasional mammoth waterfall pouring down from those mountains.

Consider stopping for a break east of David at the Ngöbe-Buglé artisan stands set up along the Interamericana near the town of Tolé. There is a police/agricultural checkpoint seven kilometers west of Tolé, so make sure your papers are in order.

There are few gas stations between Santiago and David; fill up before driving anywhere in western Panama.

RENTAL CARS

It's easy to rent a car in David. Those wanting a four-wheel drive should book a reservation as

ROAD SAFETY

Many of the highland roads are newly re-surfaced and in great shape. Ironically, that can make them even more dangerous than usual. New roads are oily, and the lack of potholes encourages drivers to see how fast they can take those hairpin turns. If you drive, be extremely careful. Honk the horn at blind curves. Drive with low beams and hazard lights even in the daytime. (Don't forget to turn them off when you park.) If you're visiting in the rainy season, try to drive in the morning, when you're less likely to encounter torrential rains. If at all possible, stay off the roads at night or when it's foggy. If you take a taxi, don't be shy about asking your driver to slow down. Remember, you're paying. A firm *"Despacio, por favor"* (des-PAW-see-o, por-fah-VOR) should get results.

One road in the highlands – fortunately, not one you're likely to take – is nicknamed La Carretera de la Muerte (Death High-way). Another one has a sign tallying the dozens of annual fatalities along a single stretch. I learned to drive on Panamanian roads and have the local survival skills, yet on a trip to Cerro Punta a few years back, my car was totaled by a speeding, hydro-planing truck coming down the mountain. The 3.5-hour wait for the police on a dark, rainy night gave me ample time to wonder what would have happened if someone had been hurt, which luckily no one was.

far ahead of time as possible, as these are pop-ular and can be in limited supply. Rental cars cannot be taken across the Costa Rican border. The companies listed have outlets both in town and at the airport.

- **Avis:** tel. 774-7075 or 774-7076, airport tel. 771-0844, fax 774-7250, www.avis.com.pa
- **Budget Rent A Car:** tel. 775-5597 or 775-1667, airport tel. 721-0845, fax 775-1667, www.budgetpanama.com
- **Dollar:** tel. 721-1103, www.dollarpanama.com

- **Hertz:** tel. 775-8471, www.rentacarpanama.com
- **Hilary Rent A Car:** tel. 775-5459 (no website)
- **National Car Rental:** tel. 721-0974, www.nationalpanama.com
- **Thrifty Car Rental:** tel. 721-2477, airport tel. 721-2478, www.thrifty.com

GETTING AROUND

Downtown David is concentrated in a small, con-gested area, so walking is the most practical way to get around. The rest of the town is sprawling, how-ever, and those who walk for any distance in the daytime can get broiled quickly. The best way to get to places away from downtown is by taxis, which are everywhere (there were 2,000 at last count). A ride most places costs US$1.50 for one person. The fare between the bus terminal and center of town is US$2. The fare from the town center to the airport is US$3 per person. A trip to Pedregal, David's en-tryway to the Pacific Ocean, is US$3.

Additional passengers in a taxi are an extra US$0.25 per person. Drivers are also allowed to add a US$0.25 surcharge for at night, on Sundays, and during holidays.

The only area bus you may want to deal with goes to the riverside port of Pedregal, though its importance to travelers has greatly dimin-ished as Boca Chica has taken off as the main jumping-off point to the Gulf of Chiriquí. Buses leave outside the Multi Café near the town center, at Calle A Norte and Avenida 2 Este. They run constantly 6 A.M.–11 P.M. The fare for any bus in town is US$0.35.

WEST OF DAVID

There are a few notable places between David and the Costa Rican border, though they are not high on most people's list of tourist attrac-tions. The industrial port of Puerto Armuelles is important in the shipment of bananas and oil, Paso Canoa is the major border crossing with Costa Rica, and Punta Burica is an ex-traordinarily remote spot for surfers who truly want to get away from absolutely everything.

Paso Canoa

This grim little frontier outpost has nothing to interest visitors, nowhere to stay, and sketchy-looking greasy spoons that will appeal only to the brave or starving. But many tourists are forced to visit it every day, as it is the main border crossing with Costa Rica.

As with the two other border crossings in western Panama, it's hard to tell where Costa Rica ends and Panama begins. A barren stretch of road is the only thing separating the two.

Immigration, customs, and an ATP government tourism office are housed in a cement monolith at the border. The main function of the **ATP office** (tel. 727-6524, 7 A.M.–11 P.M. daily) is to sell tourist cards for those entering from Costa Rica. As usual, it has little tourist information to offer.

There are two banks, a pharmacy, and a few places to eat down the road leading to Puerto Armuelles. As one faces Costa Rica, the road is on the left at the intersection just before the border crossing. Everything of interest is within a few hundred meters of the intersection. The **Banco Nacional de Panamá** (8 A.M.–3 P.M. Mon.–Fri., 9 A.M.–noon Sat.) is across the street from the Zona Libre Mall. Farther down the same street is a branch of **Banco Universal** (9 A.M.–5 P.M. Mon.–Fri., 9 A.M.–2 P.M. Sat.). Both banks have ATMs, but neither exchanges money.

Farmacia Tiffany #3 (no phone, 7:30 A.M.–10 P.M. daily) is up the street from Banco Nacional de Panamá.

GETTING THERE

There's a bus and taxi stand on the Panamanian side just east of the immigration/customs building. A taxi between Paso Canoa and David costs about US$25, but, if business is slow, haggling may be possible. However, bus service to downtown David is frequent and fairly quick. Buses run continuously 6 A.M.–8 or 9 P.M. The trip takes about 1.25 hours and costs US$2.

Padafront (Paso Canoa tel. 727-7230, David tel. 774-9205) has multiple buses to Panama City, with intermediate stops along the Interamericana. The trip takes 8–9 hours, somewhat less for an express. The fare is US$14, or US$17 for an express. Alternatively, travelers can take any bus to David and board a bus to Panama City there.

There's a small **Tracopa bus office** (7–11:30 A.M. and 12:30–4 P.M. Mon.–Sat., 7–11 A.M. Sun. and holidays) on the north side of the street between the Costa Rican and Panamanian immigration offices. It sells tickets to San José, Costa Rica, for US$9.50 (depending on number of stops). Buses leave at 4 A.M., 8:30 A.M., 9 A.M., 1 P.M., and 4:30 P.M. Costa Rican time (one hour earlier than Panamanian time). But this office is mainly of interest to travelers looking to meet the proof of onward travel requirement to enter Panama.

For those heading to Costa Rica who need colones (Costa Rican currency), next to the Tracopa office is a branch of **Banco de Costa Rica** (8 A.M.–5 P.M. Mon.–Sat., 8 A.M.–noon Sun.). It has an ATM that dispenses colones. Other ATMs are nearby.

Those with their own transportation can just drive straight onto the Interamericana to get to David and points east.

Panamanian police routinely stop cars on the highway between the Costa Rican border and David to check for smugglers, illegal immigrants, and, more prosaically, drunk or unlicensed drivers. This happens throughout the country but is more common west of Santiago. These checks are normal and no cause for alarm. Just make sure your papers are in order.

Punta Burica and Puerto Armuelles

The Burica Peninsula is a finger of land that separates Panama's Pacific coast from Costa Rica's. Most of the peninsula falls on the Panamanian side. At its very tip is Punta Burica, which consists of a stretch of sandy beach broken by occasional wide slabs of striated rock that reach out to sea. The shoreline is fringed by palm trees and the occasional fisherman's house. That's about it.

The beach itself isn't all that great. The only draw for visitors—other than the area's extreme isolation and the adventure of getting there—is the surf. This is still a spot little known to all but a few pioneering surf dudes and dudettes. Long, tubing waves break left along the tip of the point. Some say the waves are overhyped, though, so have some kind of backup entertainment planned in case the surf's not happening, as there is absolutely nothing else out there but sand and sea.

GETTING THERE

Access to Punta Burica is through Puerto Armuelles, a surprisingly tidy little town considering the especially rough times this backwater has been through in recent years. It holds little of interest for visitors, though it has been the center of quite a bit of international economic activity as a port town fueled by the banana business and a nearby oil pipeline. This area is near the border, so remember to have all your papers in order, as there are frequent checkpoints along the Interamericana.

Buses to Puerto Armuelles leave from the David bus terminal every 15–30 minutes, 4 A.M.–10 P.M. (US$3.60, 2.5 hours). Buses make the return trip to David 4 A.M.–9:30 P.M. Those driving should head west toward the border. At Paso Canoa, about 50 kilometers from David, make a left. Puerto Armuelles is another 40 kilometers south.

From Puerto Armuelles there are two ways to get to Punta Burica: by boat and by car. At the waterfront in Puerto Armuelles, it should be possible to hire a fisherman and his boat to go down to Punta Burica. Expect to pay about US$50 each way, just to get to the point. The trip takes about 1.5 hours.

It's also possible to get to Punta Burica by land, but this is even more of an adventure than a boat trip. A road is gradually being extended

toward Punta Burica, but chances are good at least part of the trip will still involve driving on the beach itself.

There's a big old Ford pickup "bus" that makes the trip between Puerto Armuelles and Punta Burica at low tide. In central Puerto Armuelles, ask around for *el carro de la costa*. The fare is US$1.50.

It's also possible to drive, but until and unless the road is completed the whole way, this requires some tricky off-road maneuvering. Only attempt it in a high-clearance four-wheel drive with a powerful engine. Don't go alone.

Drive west from Puerto Armuelles through the Petroterminal complex. The road ends at the beach. Drive on the damp sand, which is more solid and holds traction better. To make the trip the whole way, the tide has to be quite far out. Otherwise, you'll round a bend and find your way blocked by the sea. This is a hairy drive at times. There are some wide stretches of slippery, jagged, volcanic rock that have to be navigated.

Some of the worst bits toward the end can be avoided by taking a detour up a dirt loop road between the microscopic villages of Limones and Puerto Balsa. Ask anyone you see to point out the road, which can be hard to spot from the beach. The road is rough and steep, leading through some desolate fields, but it's better than the rock obstacle course. Be sure to park well above the high-tide line.

Punta Burica itself is the tip of the peninsula. Costa Rica begins on the western side of the tip. This is a rather pretty spot, and it's certainly away from it all, but there's just about nothing here except a palm-lined beach and the sea. It may be possible to hire a fisherman at Puerto Balsa to run you out to Isla Burica, if you're so inclined.

There are two places to stay way out here. The first is a simple nature reserve called **Mono Feliz** (juancho_3@hotmail.com or mono_feliz@hotmail.com) run by a gringo character named John Garvey, better known locally as "Juancho." Try emailing Juancho to make a reservation, or just show up and take your chances.

A newer place is **Tigre Salvaje** (davidteichmann@yahoo.com, vielkateichmann@hotmail.com, www.tigresalvaje.com, US$50/person, including meals), a wildlife reserve and rehabilitation project at the end of Punta Burica. Its aim is to help endangered species, particularly sea turtles and the red-backed squirrel monkey. The couple who run it are only able to check their email every couple of weeks; they say they will accommodate anyone who shows up unannounced, which is the spirit of adventure and flexibility you'll need to visit this remote spot. After driving along the beach to the village of Bella Vista, it's a 45-minute hike or horseback ride to the reserve.

Those planning just to camp on the beach should bring a tent, food, water, and supplies. There are no stores or restaurants of any kind in the area.

Boquete

The main attraction on the east side of Volcán Barú is Boquete (pop. 4,493 in central Boquete, 21,370 in the district), a cute little town and one of Panama's top tourist draws.

Boquete has long been famous in Panama for its coffee and oranges, and for a flower fair which draws thousands of visitors from around the country each year. As with Bocas del Toro, it was finally discovered in the late 1990s by foreign backpackers and other adventurous travelers, who were soon followed by older North Americans looking for a pleasant place to retire—and by developers and land speculators. In recent years, real-estate madness had reached such a pitch that some land in downtown Boquete was going for the same price as prime real estate in San Francisco, California.

The gold-rush atmosphere has calmed down a bit, but Boquete is still booming and its few streets are now busy with too many cars in a hurry, but it stubbornly retains its charm. It's a peculiar kind of charm, as most of the buildings downtown are jumbled together. But the setting makes it beautiful. It's in the middle of a picturesque valley surrounded by forested mountains and bordered on the east by the churning waters of the Río Caldera.

On a clear day, the Barú volcano dominates the landscape to the northwest. And those who venture beyond Boquete's main streets will discover the town itself is still laid-back, a relaxing place to hang out and plan day trips to the many attractions nearby.

At a little over a kilometer above sea level, it doesn't get quite as chilly here as it does in the higher mountain towns on the west side of Barú, but it's still pleasantly cool compared to most of Panama, and it can sometimes get surprisingly cold. Expect the foggy drizzle known as *bajareque* year-round, which can be quite refreshing and produce stunning rainbows. Again, bring warm, waterproof clothes.

What most people think of as Boquete is officially **Bajo Boquete** (Lower Boquete). Its main drag is **Avenida Central,** which descends from Alto Boquete (Upper Boquete), runs north through town, and continues past a small church to the hills beyond.

The plaza midway through town, on the east side of Avenida Central, is the town hub. It's where buses to and from David stop, and where everyone passes through eventually. It's not exactly photogenic—it feels as jumbled-up and unplanned as the rest of town—but it was expanded recently and is a good spot for people-watching. The latest addition is a fountain in the northwest corner of the plaza which was seemingly made from bathroom tiles. However,

© WILLIAM FRIAR

Boquete is one of Panama's most charming and scenic towns.

the cascades of water do cool things down on a warm day. On the east side of the plaza is a government building which houses the post office. This used to be Boquete's train station, in the bygone era when a narrow-gauge railway ran between the town and David. A vintage train car from those days is in front of the post office.

One block northeast of the plaza is a little square, **Parque de Las Madres,** with a statue depicting a mother with two small children who appear to be squirming in agony.

A coffee tour, a stroll through Boquete's surreal gardens, a hike along a mountain trail, and a quest for quetzals are all worthwhile ways to spend time in this area. Try to find an opportunity to do them all. The most popular activities for outdoorsy types are white-water rafting, hiking the **Sendero Los Quetzales,** scaling **Volcán Barú,** horseback riding, and, increasingly, learning to rock climb on the unusual basalt formations of **Los Ladrillos.** Areas near Boquete of possible interest to

visitors include **Bajo Mono,** northwest of Bajo Boquete, which has a lovely loop road and the trailhead for Sendero Los Quetzales; **Caldera,** which is southeast of Boquete and has good hot springs, some petroglyphs, and a bunch of little waterfalls; and the road to **Volcancito,** which starts near the CEFATI building in Alto Boquete and has a couple of attractions, including lovely views. **Alto Boquete** could not be more different from the rest of Boquete. It's mostly a hot, barren plain and is of interest to visitors mainly because the David–Boquete highway runs right through it. But there are a few roadside attractions worth stopping for, including spectacular, unobstructed views of the surrounding mountains.

SIGHTS

There aren't that many real "sights" in Boquete proper—the town itself is the sight. But there are a couple of bizarre gardens that have been popular with Panamanian tourists for years and

BOQUETE

To **C** *PARQUE NACIONAL VOLCÁN BARÚ*

To Sendero Los Quetzales

To Jaramillo Arriba

▼ LA POSADA BOQUETEÑA

ZANZIBAR

■ FOLKLÓRICA MUSEO

▼ ART CAFE LA CREPE

CHURCH

■ ESTILO CAMPO   LA CABAÑA ▼

ORGANICA ■   HSBC ■

MULTIBANK ■   ■ FARMACIA REVILLA

DELI BARÚ ▼   ▼ RESTAURANTE EL SABROSON

LAVANDERÍA   ■ FARMACIA ANY
LA MEJOR ■

■ SUPER CENTRO BRUÑA

BISTRO BOQUETE ▼   CALLE 1 SUR
AREA BUSES AND TAXIS   *Parque de las Madres*

● NOMBA

■ MAILBOXES ETC.   ★ FAIRGROUNDS

SUPERCENTRO ■   ■ SUPERMERCADO ROMERO
EL MANDARÍN

BUS STOP (DAVID) ■   ■ MERCADO MUNICIPAL   ■ HOSTAL BOQUETE

SOUVENIR EL CACIQUE/FARMACIA DANKA   *Plaza* ■ POST OFFICE

HOSTEL MAMALLENA ■   ■ COMMUNITY CENTER

HASTOR COMPUTERS ■   ▼ BOQUETE BAR RESTAURANT AND BAR

BILLARES ESPINOSA ■   ■ FIRE STATION

ISLA VERDE ●   ■ POLICE STATION   EL OASIS B&B ●

PLAZA LOS ESTABLOS/   ■ LAVAMÁTICO
BOQUETE TREE TREK/
BANCO GENERAL ■   CHOKO CHETTA ▼

RESTAURANTE ▼   CALLE 5 SUR
NELVI'S   ■ BANCO NACIONAL
DE PANAMA

DELTA ■

GLOBAL BANK ■   ▼ RESTAURANTE
MACHU PICCHU

BIG DADDY'S GRILL ▼   ● HOTEL REBEQUET

CAFÉ PUNTO   PENSIÓN
DE ENCUENTRO   MARILÓS

SUGAR   PENSIÓN
AND   TOPAS
SPICE

TEXACO ■

HOTEL LOS FUNDADORES ●   ■ LAVAMÁTICO

BIBLIOTECA ■

To Valle Escondido

AV A OESTE

AV CENTRAL

AV A OESTE

CALLE CENTRAL

AV B OESTE

CALLE 1 SUR

CALLE 2 SUR

AV C OESTE

CALLE 3 SUR

CALLE 4 SUR

AV CENTRAL

AV A ESTE

Río Caldera

0   200 yds
0   200 m

To Cefati,
Volcancito, Caldera,
and David

© AVALON TRAVEL

COFFEE 101: MADE IN THE SHADE

Boquete is coffee country, but as you look around, you may wonder where they're hiding the farms. Scanning the hillsides, all you see are shady trees, particularly orange trees. Look closer: If it's a coffee farm, you'll see tall shrubs below the trees. In the picking season, these will have ripe, cherry-red berries. The seeds are coffee beans.

Most of the coffee here is shade-grown, a traditional method in which coffee bushes are sheltered in the shade of a forest or among trees planted by farmers. Farther west, especially around Río Sereno near the Costa Rican border, coffee is grown in open fields. This method produces a greater yield, but conservationists say it's a poor trade-off.

They argue that trees protect the crop from pests, produce natural mulch, preserve the chemical balance of the soil, and prevent erosion. Shade-grown coffee therefore requires less pesticide and fertilizer and is less disruptive to the environment. The money saved on fertilizer helps offset the lower productivity. Also, the trees provide a habitat for mammals and hundreds of bird species, particularly migratory birds. This habitat becomes ever more important as forests are cleared in coffee-producing countries. It's a pretty efficient system.

The pulp of the berry that surrounds the bean is even used as compost, and the dried husk encasing the bean is used as fuel.

In Boquete, orange trees are commonly planted along with coffee and provide an extra source of income for the farmers. This also helps make up for the lower productivity of the shade-grown method. You can almost always find good oranges in Boquete. Navel oranges grow eight or nine months out of the year. Valencias take over February–March.

But even ecofriendly coffee processing has its limitations. Processing uses a great deal of water, which is then flushed into the rivers. The runoff is filled with pulp and sugar compounds that upset the biological balance of the rivers and streams. In 2006, Panama enacted a law requiring the local coffee industry to purify their runoff before dumping it.

It's also hard to grow coffee completely organically. Few farms in Boquete use herbicides, but the orange trees attract Mediterranean fruit flies, which farmers do fight with pesticides. Still, the main enemy in the highlands is fungal disease, not insects. Because it's so wet up here, farmers plant coffee so that air flows through the rows of bushes, keeping everything a bit drier.

are worth a visit for those with a fondness for the offbeat. A visit to a coffee farm, which is more like a nature walk than an agricultural tour, is a must. A dip in the Caldera hot springs is also popular, though they're a significant drive away from downtown Boquete.

El Explorador

This peculiar private garden (tel. 720-1989, cell 6627-6908, 9:30 A.M.–6 P.M. Fri.–Sun., US$5 adults, US$2 kids) in the hills above town is worth a visit if approached with a sense of humor. A winding path leads through two hectares of terraced land with orange and lemon trees, a rose garden, stands of papyrus, a bonsai nursery, and much more. But the human touches one stumbles upon are what's most

striking about this place. All kinds of junk—shoes, bottles, shopping carts, TVs—have been turned into planters. Cartoon eyes peer out from trees and topiary shrubs. Classical music is pumped throughout the place. And dotted around the garden are wise sayings and encouraging words in Spanish. One sign leads the way to the "greatest miracle in the world." When you get there, you find a mirror. What starts off seeming kitschy ends up making you feel rather loved. This is a good place to recharge your batteries, and a fun place for kids to explore since it has something of the feel of a treasure hunt (the name of the garden is Spanish for explorer). If you see gardeners, thank them: They take great pride in the place. There's a great view of the valley from the rose garden.

El Explorador is about three kilometers northeast of town, near La Montaña y el Valle: The Coffee Estate Inn. It's possible to walk from town, but it's uphill most of the way, and steep at times. On days when the garden is officially closed, it may be possible to get in by appointment. There's a small food stand on the premises.

Mi Jardín Es Su Jardín

There must be something about the Boquete air that makes gardens come out a little wacky. Mi Jardín Es Su Jardín (9 A.M.–5 P.M. daily, free)—My Garden Is Your Garden—is a formal garden as it might have been conceived by the designer of a miniature golf course. We're talking a topiary dinosaur, brightly painted cow statues, and a toy windmill, set on a sloping lawn crisscrossed by fountains and artificial streams. There's an impressive view of the valley and surrounding mountains from the observation tower. It's a toss-up whether this garden or El Explorador is quirkier. The garden is on private land, but it's open to the public, no reservations necessary. From the plaza, head north on Avenida Central past the church, keeping left at the fork. You'll soon see the entrance on the right. Drivers must park outside. The gardens shut down during the Feria de las Flores y El Café, a flower fair that takes over Boquete for 10 days every January.

◖ Finca Lérida

This is one of the more famous birding spots in Panama. Though a working coffee plantation that produces some of the finest coffee in Panama, Finca Lérida (tel. 720-1111, www.fincalerida.com) contains 650 acres of primary and secondary forest that is home to hundreds of species of birds, as well as howler monkeys, peccaries, deer, and other mammals. There's a good chance of seeing resplendent quetzals here January–August. The finca is up in the hills of Alto Quiel northwest of town, in a setting so picturesquely alpine you may find yourself

humming the theme from *The Sound of Music*. That's part of the secret of the coffee's success: It's grown at elevations of up to 1,600 meters, on the highest plantations in Panama.

There is now a rapidly expanding hotel and restaurant on a part of the property. Confusingly, the hotel is simply known as Finca Lérida, but the main birding area is some distance away from the hotel and its grounds. Most birding tours go to a part of Lérida above the main coffee estate, along a brutal road that leads through coffee and vegetable plantations that give way to dense, beautiful secondary cloud forest. The road ends at an even more gorgeous grove of primary forest, where you're likely to encounter quetzals, howler monkeys, and nasty mosquitoes.

Because Finca Lérida is private property and visitors must go with an authorized guide, this entry does not contain directions on how to get to the bird-watching spots at the finca. These are usually arranged through tour guides. Visitors can also book a tour directly through the finca that includes bird-watching, a nature walk, a tour of the coffee facilities, and lunch. Visitors can also hike a five-kilometer trail system (using a trail map) on the finca. The chances of spotting quetzals without a good guide, however, are not great.

Coffee Tours

A tour of one of Boquete's many coffee operations is a pleasant way to spend a few hours, and it'll deepen your appreciation of the area and its people, not to mention the incredible amount of work that goes into that morning caffeine buzz. It's not necessary to be a coffee addict to enjoy one of these tours, but it does help.

The tour of **Café Ruiz** (just north of town on Avenida Central, tel. 720-1000, cell 6672-3786 and 6642-3786, www.caferuiz-boquete.com or www.caferuiz.com), Panama's largest producer of gourmet coffee, is best for those who want a real nuts-and-bolts look at the whole coffee production process.

COFFEE 101: DON'T BURN THE BEANS

Like many a wannabe coffee snob, I'd always preferred hearty dark-roast coffee over the bitter stuff Americans traditionally consumed or the scorched water they now drink at Starbucks. As true coffee connoisseurs in Boquete will point out, though, dark roasts are often used to mask low-quality coffee. Gourmet coffees tend to get a lighter roast, allowing you, in the catchphrase of one Boquete grower, to "taste the coffee, not the roast." If you like your coffee strong, just brew more beans per cup. Those with sensitive stomachs should also note that dark roasts are more acidic. Another tip: Coffee made from somewhat coarse grounds often tastes better than finely ground stuff.

The full tour (three hours, US$30 pp, 9 A.M. and 1 P.M. Mon.–Sat. or by special arrangement) takes visitors to one of Ruiz's coffee farms; through its impressive mill in Palmira, near Alto Boquete; and ends up at its roasting facility/coffee shop, where visitors can taste some of its coffees and see how the beans are roasted, ground, and packaged. Sign up at the Ruiz coffeehouse or call for a reservation.

Visitors can also opt just for a 45-minute tour (US$9) of the roasting facility. These are more frequently available; it may be possible just to stop by the coffee shop and get an ad hoc tour, though reservations are a good idea just to be sure.

Café Kotowa (tel. 720-1430, www.kotowa-coffee.com) offers a tour that is on a smaller scale but more charming and scenic. Its small mill is up in Palo Alto, a few kilometers north of Boquete. It faces a breathtaking view of Barú across rolling pasture. Behind the mill, coffee farms run far up the steep slopes of emerald hills until they're lost in the clouds. This is cloud-forest country, and it gets quite wet up here.

Kotowa is the Ngöbe word for mountain, and the company is named in recognition of the indigenous people who work the farms. It's widely considered to make some of the finest coffee in Panama. The operation is owned by Ricardo Koyner MacIntyre, the grandson of a Scot who moved here from Canada after reading a newspaper article about Boquete in 1918. The original wooden coffee mill, powered by water and brought all the way over from Scotland, has been lovingly preserved and is part of the tour, as is the modern-day mill.

The tour concludes at an espresso bar in the wooden mill. **Coffee Adventures** (tel. 720-3852, cell 6634-4698, http://coffeeadventures.net, 2 P.M. Mon.–Sat.) is the official tour operator for Café Kotowa. The excellent coffee tours are given by a Dutch couple, Hans van der Vooren and Terry van Niekerk. Hans's enthusiasm and good humor make learning about coffee beans a surprisingly entertaining experience. Tours last three hours and cost US$35 per person, two-person minimum, and include transportation from and to hotels and a coffee cupping at the end. Contact Coffee Adventures for reservations.

Finca Lérida (tel./fax 720-1111, www.fincalerida.com) also offers tours of its coffee facilities, which consist of several quaint wooden buildings that house the old coffee mill and a newer hotel, set in a pretty, mountain garden setting. It's a highly photogenic place.

Los Pozos de Caldera

These hot springs are a fair haul southeast of Boquete near the town of Caldera, famous in Panama as a home of cowboys and witches. Those who love hot springs will enjoy the Pozos de Caldera. Those who can take them or leave them will find the trip here a bit of a hassle for the payoff. The springs are attractive, situated in a secluded stretch of forest near the bank of the roaring Río Chiriquí.

Unlike hot springs that belch forth a

COFFEE 101: IT'S ALL IN THE TIMING

Coffee in Boquete is normally harvested from October to February. The beans of the best coffee are sun dried, a process that takes 8-12 days. They are then stored for at least three months to cure them. The whole process is delicate; any misstep from bush to roaster can degrade the quality of the coffee.

Coffee is ready to sell in late March or early April. That's when the buyers come and the "cupping," the coffee equivalent of wine-tasting, begins. The different farms compete to see who will have the highest-rated crop that year.

April to June is the best time to visit to Boquete if you want to taste ultra-fresh coffee. Even then, you should aim for coffee that's been roasted within the last two weeks, if possible. If you grind the beans, you've got two days to taste it at its best.

sulfurous stench, these barely smell at all. There are four pools. The first one is the warmest, supposedly 42°C (108°F). There's one closer to the river that's hard to spot but quite nice. It's not as warm as the first one, but it's surrounded by trees and less developed (the others are lined with large, flat rocks).

Not far from the springs is a tributary to the Río Chiriquí that, if you don't mind quite a bit of scrambling over slippery rocks and muddy banks, you can follow upriver to five waterfalls, each more picturesque than the one before. This hike is best done with a guide. At the very least, as with any other forest hike in Panama, don't go alone. A dip in the hot springs is especially pleasant after splashing about in these brisk waters. A hydroelectric dam was recently built in this area, though thankfully it has not affected the hot springs except to improve the road that leads to them.

To get to the *pozos* from Boquete, head

south out of town on Avenida Central. After about 12 kilometers look for a blue sign that says Caldera. Turn left here and continue past the town of Caldera. The drive this far takes about half an hour. Another blue sign indicates a right onto a gravel road. Those with a four-wheel drive can follow this road to within a 15-minute walk of the springs. Otherwise, park by the side of the road and hike the rest of the way, about a 40-minute walk. Do not leave anything of value in your car. After crossing the cable-and-plank bridge, make a left turn uphill (there should be a sign). Make the first left at the barbed-wire gate, which is easy to miss because there's no sign. From here the springs are about 15 minutes straight down the trail. Admission is US$1, which goes to keeping the area clean. The caretaker will most likely find you. Warning: I've heard reports of an unscrupulous guy posing as the caretaker and collecting the admission, meaning that people have had to pay twice. If this happens to you, report it to the police and to the ATP staff at the CEFATI in Alto Boquete. After a dip in the hot springs, head back downhill and turn left. There's a surprisingly pleasant sandy beach right by the refreshingly cool river. It's a nice spot for a cold plunge.

On the way to the hot springs, it's worth stopping to check out the **Piedra Pintada.** This is a riverside boulder etched with mysterious squiggles by a pre-Columbian people about which little is known. These petroglyphs are found all over Panama. Just before downtown Caldera, look for a Piedra Pintada sign on the right side of the road. Pull over and park. Duck under the barbed wire and bamboo fence behind the beer garden and walk across a pasture toward the water. Head in the direction of a metal post with the number 80 painted on it. On the left as you face the river is a three-meter-high boulder just above the river that is covered with crude faces and figures (and some modern-day graffiti).

© WILLIAM FRIAR

Piedra Pintada, near Caldera

A minibus service runs between downtown Boquete and Caldera. Ask the driver to drop you off at the turnoff to the *pozos* (PO-sohs). For the return trip, flag down a Boquete-bound bus at the same spot. It takes about 40 minutes to walk from the turnoff to the hot springs. The bus ride costs US$1.50 per person each way. Buses leave Boquete at 7 A.M., 10:45 A.M., 1 P.M., and 5 P.M., returning 8:30 A.M., 1:30 P.M., and 4 P.M. Double-check the return schedule with the bus driver to be on the safe side.

Taxis from downtown Boquete to Caldera charge US$18 each way for one or two people, US$6 more for each additional person. How close the taxi can get to the hot springs depends on the condition of the road, and the taxi, at the time. Arrange a pickup time for the return trip, as few taxis hang around this area. This is a good place to bring a cell phone, in case the driver forgets about you. Alternatively, hike back to the main road after your soak and cross your fingers you'll spot a passing cab.

ENTERTAINMENT AND EVENTS

The most important time of the year for partiers comes during the 10 days in January when the annual flower fair, the **Feria de las Flores y El Café,** descends on the town.

Nightlife

Boquete has traditionally been a place for daytime pursuits; when the sun goes down, the streets grow quiet. But the city is finally threatening to become a place where one can talk about "the nightlife scene" without bursting into laughter. Mostly, however, the scene amounts to hanging out in a bar.

For several years now **Zanzibar** (Avenida Central, no phone, 5 P.M.–midnight or later daily), at the north end of Avenida Central, has been a staple of the evening bar scene. It's a cute and cozy place with an African safari theme. Regular entertainment includes belly dancing on Wednesdays, house music DJs on Fridays, and live music on Saturdays.

Another popular place is **La Cabaña** (no phone), on the east side of the Caldera just north of the fairgrounds. It has a faux log-cabin look and keeps erratic hours. It's usually open on weekends starting at 9 P.M. and going all night long, much to the chagrin of everyone trying to sleep on that side of the river.

The nicest watering hole in town is the bar at the **Panamonte Inn and Spa** (tel. 720-1324, noon–11 P.M. daily), which is now both cozy and sleek. It's quite relaxing to sit with a drink at either of its two stone fireplaces (one indoors, one out). Be sure to check out all the antiques. The only unwelcome addition is a big-screen TV.

Right across the river from the Panamonte (though one has to go over the downtown bridge to get to it, as the closer bridge is gone), the bar of the **Hotel Ladera** (tel. 730-9000, 10 A.M.–11 P.M.) is much more in harmony with its surroundings than the hotel itself is. (Remember not to confuse this place with Finca Lérida.) It has a mountain-lodge feel, complete with (gas) fireplace. The bar opens onto a terrace right above a brook. It's a fine place to sit and be serenaded by the sound of rushing water and the songs of frogs in the forest. The menu is blissfully brief and the French-Italian cuisine (most mains US$12–18) is appealing.

Boquete Barú Restaurant and Bar (Calle 4 Sur, tel. 730-9294, www.restaurante-baru.com, 11 A.M.–midnight Mon.–Thurs., 11 A.M.–2 A.M. Fri.–Sat.), on the town plaza next to Hostel Mamallena, attracts a nice mixture of backpackers, Panamanian tourists, locals, and assorted weirdos. If the weather is cooperating, it's pleasant to have a drink out on the large, breezy patio overlooking the town plaza, away from the Latin power ballads blasting out of the bar and dining room. The food here is sub-par, but it's a good spot for a drink and people-watching.

Bistro Boquete (Avenida Central, tel. 720-1016, noon–10 P.M. Wed.–Mon.) is a popular gringo hangout. It's an airy, high-ceilinged place with large windows that open right onto Avenida Central and a mural depicting coffee pickers along one wall. The menu is ambitious, but both the food and the service were unsatisfactory. But the building is handsome, and the upstairs terrace overlooking the main street can be a good place to have a drink. If you do eat here, keep it simple.

On my most recent visit **Hostal Nomba** (Ave. A Oeste, cell 6920-4169 or 6497-5672, www.nombapanama.com), a friendly hostel west of downtown, was about to launch a nightly happy hour (6 P.M.–midnight) open to guests and nonguests alike.

A pool hall, **Billares Espinosa** (Avenida Central, no phone, 3 P.M.–midnight Mon.–Fri., 10 A.M.–midnight Sat.–Sun.) is on Avenida Central just south of the plaza.

Festivals and Events

The **Feria de las Flores y El Café** (Fair of Flowers and Coffee) is Boquete's showplace event. The flower fair draws tens of thousands of people from all over Panama to view the pretty flowers that carpet Boquete's fairgrounds on the east side of the Río Caldera. The fair has its roots in a celebration first held in 1950. Though gardens all over Boquete are spruced up for the event, the fairgrounds are the epicenter, transformed each year into a floral playground with fanciful landscaping. It's held for 10 days in the middle of January, but exact dates change annually. Locals say it has a knack of taking place just as the weather turns rainy and blustery. Check www.visitpanama.com for dates.

The fair also includes concerts, folkloric dancers, handicraft exhibits, and a chance to sip gourmet coffee and chug vast amounts of other liquids. During those 10 days, the town is overrun with drunken revelers and ear-shattering music performed by DJs and live bands late into the night.

This is either the best or worst time to be in Boquete, depending on one's perspective. Those who plan to visit Boquete in January should consider whether they want to be in town during the madness, and if so book accommodations well ahead of time. Those who'd like to see the flowers without the crowds should visit sometime in the last few weeks leading up to the festival, as most of the exhibitions are in place by then. Don't come expecting anything too spectacular. While a big deal for Panama, the flower displays aren't much more than what one would expect to find in a well-tended city park in the States on an average day.

After the Feria de las Flores y El Café in January, the fairgrounds remain open until late March or early April, when a smaller fair, the **Feria de las Orquídeas** (Orchid Fair) closes out the season with a four-day celebration. Again, check with ATP (CEFATI, tel. 720-4060) for exact dates.

The **Boquete Jazz Festival** (http://boquetejazzfestival.com) was held for the first time in 2007 and has become an annual event, bringing Panamanian and international jazz musicians to town for three days of performances in February.

The entire country celebrates Panama's independence from Spain on November 28, but Boquete's celebration is the biggest, presided over by the president of Panama and drawing people from far beyond the highlands for a huge party.

SHOPPING

The noteworthy souvenir item in these parts is coffee. The best bet for finding a decent tchotchke or bit of memorabilia with a Boquete connection is to explore the little art and souvenir shops that come and go along the stretch of Avenida Central between the church and the turnoff to the Panamonte Inn and Spa. It's just north of downtown and easily explored on foot.

Los Establos Plaza, on the left at the entrance to downtown Boquete, is a mini-mall with a few shops selling handicrafts, jewelry, souvenirs, and the like.

Packages of good coffee are easy to come by in Boquete, as you might imagine, in an overwhelming variety of roasts, qualities, and flavors. You can choose either whole bean or ground coffee, though whole beans preserve the coffee's flavor longer. Attractive souvenir packs are often available, which make for nice gifts. Finca Lérida, Café Ruiz, and Café Kotowa are safe bets for excellent coffee.

Panama's most widely available boutique coffee is **Café Ruiz** (tel. 720-1392, www.caferuiz.com, 7 A.M.–6 P.M. Mon.–Sat., 10 A.M.–6 P.M. Sun.). The best-quality Ruiz is the gourmet, which is a lighter roast and is sold in gold bags. Ruiz coffee is increasingly easy to come by throughout Panama, but its gourmet coffee is sold only at its Boquete shop (just north of town on Avenida Central), its shop in Panama City, and a few gourmet stores and upscale supermarkets, including Super Barú in David. La Berlina Estate is arguably the best of the gourmet varieties. Those interested can pay for a tour of the roasting facility or sign up for a more extensive tour of the entire coffee-making process.

To get to Café Ruiz, keep left at the fork past the church. It's the white complex on the right, near Mi Jardín Es Su Jardín.

Café Kotowa (tel. 720-1430, www.kotowacoffee.com, 7 A.M.–7 P.M. daily) is becoming the mini-Starbucks of Panama. Kotowa cafécum-store outlets and bags of coffee are popping up around the country. Kotowa has two outlets in Boquete, one at the CEFATI and one at Los Establos Plaza.

Some companies will ship coffee overseas. Several have also made their coffee available for online sale, either directly through their websites (Kotowa and Ruiz) or through international distributors (Finca Lérida). A growing number of online stores buy and sell Boquete coffee. However, it's far cheaper to buy coffee in person in Boquete. Shipping costs alone can exceed the cost of the coffee itself.

Estilo Campo (Avenida Central next to the church, tel. 730-9322, 8:30 A.M.–6 P.M. daily) sells birdhouses, signs, baby rocking chairs, and other small items handpainted with images of flowers in vibrant colors. The birdhouses are especially cute.

Souvenir El Cacique (tel. 720-2217, 10 A.M.–7 P.M. Mon.–Sat., 10 A.M.–2 P.M. Sun.) sells Ngöbe-Buglé necklaces, *molas* (handcrafted blouses), cocobolo statues, and other crafts from Panama, as well as a few things from Guatemala and Peru. The staff speak English here. It's on the south side of the town plaza.

The Bookmark (tel. 776-1688, dembook@ yahoo.com, 9 A.M.–5 P.M. Tues.–Sun.) is in Dolega, a small town about midway between David and Boquete. Though not a large place, it has the largest collection of English-language books in the country. It has a little bit of everything, mostly used: best sellers, true crime, science fiction, nonfiction, history, romance, and so on. There are some rare, out-of-print books on Panama, including some from the old Canal Zone library, and a small Spanish-language section. This is a good place to sell or swap that tattered beach book. It's worth stopping by even if the place seems closed. As you head up toward Boquete, look for it on the left 17 kilometers after the turnoff from the Interamericana.

SPORTS AND RECREATION

There are plenty of options for outdoor activities around Boquete. The most popular and impressive of these are a zipline ride, white-water rafting, hiking the Sendero Los Quetzales, and climbing Volcán Barú.

The zipline company, **Boquete Tree Trek** (Los Establos Plaza, tel. 720-1635, www.aventurist.com), also rents **mountain bikes** (US$15 a day) and offers tours and outings, including **mountain-biking trips** (US$35 pp), **horseback rides** (US$35 pp), and **rock climbing** at **Los Ladrillos** (US$40 pp), an unusual rock wall north of town on the Bajo Mono loop. These all last roughly 3.5 hours.

A couple of local outfitters offer boating, fishing, and sea-kayaking packages off the

Pacific coast, about an hour away. Those primarily interested in sea-kayaking should contact **Boquete Outdoor Adventures** (tel. 720-2284, www.boqueteoutdooradventures.com).

Mirador Adventures (Ave. A Oeste, tel. 720-2864, cell 6920-4169, ryan@miradoradventures. com, www.nombapanama.com) is the resident tour operator and outfitter for Hostal Nomba. They offer river-kayaking trips for US$45 (half day) or US$90 (whole day), including transportation and lunch. They also have a whole raft of other outdoor trips, ranging from guided, overnight hikes to the summit of Barú (US$75 pp, minimum two people), daily early evening trips to the Caldera hot springs (US$32 pp, including entrance fee and wine/beer), combination hiking and mountain-bike adventures (US$85 pp), and more. Those staying at the hostel get discounts on trips.

For those who prefer to go it alone, Mirador Adventures also rents a wide range of good-quality gear, including inflatable and hardshell kayaks, sleeping bags, backpacks, camping gear, mountain bikes, surfboards, and snorkel gear. If needed, the company can store luggage for anyone renting their gear.

Zipline Rides

Zipline rides are beginning to pop up all around Panama, but **Boquete Tree Trek** (Los Establos Plaza, tel. 720-1635, www.aventurist.com, US$65 pp) is particularly impressive, and the longest one to date. On a zipline, riders wear harnesses connected to pulleys that are then attached to a series of cables stretched between trees at a slight downward angle. Riders shoot along the cable, braking manually. The Boquete Tree Trek features 12 stages and 14 platforms spread over three kilometers and passing over two waterfalls. The longest run is 360 meters, during which you can reach speeds of up to 18 kilometers an hour. One stretch of the ride is about 90 meters above the forest floor. It's an exhilarating, scenic experience that is over much too quickly.

THE BEST COFFEE IN THE WORLD?

© WILLIAM FRIAR

coffee beans drying the old-fashioned way: in the sun

Three years in a row, 2005–2007, a Panamanian coffee was voted the best in the world by the Specialty Coffee Association of America, the industry's largest trade association. It came in second in the two years after that. It also won the Best of Panama competition every year but one between 2004 and 2010. And so on.

The marketplace has taken notice: The price of the coffee, La Esmeralda Especial, keeps setting world records. In 2007, 10 132-pound bags of the coffee sold at auction for an astonishing US$130 a pound. By comparison, the coffee voted second best went for US$11.80 a pound. In 2010, Esmeralda Especial broke the record again, selling for US$170 a pound. The coffee has become so popular the grower sells the entire crop at auction each year.

Today, it remains among the most sought-after coffee in the world.

Why all the fuss? La Esmeralda Especial is grown by the Peterson family, longtime Boquete residents whose Hacienda Esmeralda is one of Panama's finest coffee producers. Several years ago the family discovered it could brew an unusual-tasting cup of coffee from an ara-bica variety called geisha (sometimes spelled "gesha") that had been growing wild on one of its farms. Originally from Ethiopia, geisha was introduced to Central America in the 1950s because it is disease resistant, but it never caught on because the plants are low yielding. But in the age of the coffee aficionado, there is a market for low-yield, high-quality premium coffee.

Those who've sampled geisha coffee say it has a floral, citrusy taste that is strikingly different from that of other coffees. Hacienda Esmeralda produces about 200 132-pound bags of the Especial a year. Two other growers in Boquete, Garrido and Don Pachi, produce a small amount of geisha, but the total world supply is still tiny. Coffeehouses in the United States and other countries lucky enough to score some have been known to sell it for US$15 or more a cup. Not surprisingly, other Boquete growers are now planting their own geisha.

Prices are so high it's hard to find geisha in Panama; nearly all of it gets exported. If none is available in Boquete, visit www.haciendaesmeralda.com for a list of retailers. The various growers' geisha is sometimes available by mail order as well.

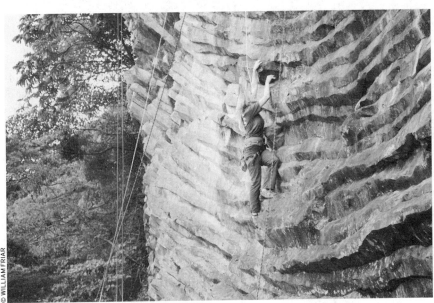

© WILLIAM FRIAR

Los Ladrillos is an unusual basalt formation that is popular with rock climbers.

The natural beauty is impressive—the zipline is in a cloud forest right below the Continental Divide, and on a clear day there's a view of Volcán Barú—and by the guides. Without exception they are friendly, enthusiastic, and highly professional. All are bilingual. There's an attractive lodge (with bathrooms) that serves food and drinks before and after the ride. For outdoor types who'd like a longer visit, there are 10 rooms in the lodge and several log cabins dotted around the attractive grounds. These provide a picturesque, if isolated, lodging option. There are lots of hiking possibilities in the area, but little else to do.

This ride requires somewhat more upper-body strength than other ziplines in Panama, particularly if the lines are wet. Riders must be able to apply enough pressure with their gloved hands to slow down, and be able to pull themselves along if they stop short of a platform.

The ride starts at an elevation of nearly 1,900 meters, in an area up the mountain from the Café Kotowa mill in Palo Alto, but the guides pick guests up from the Boquete Tree Trek office, which is in Los Establos Plaza in downtown Boquete. Pickup times are 8 A.M. and 1 P.M. daily. The whole thing, including transportation from downtown, lasts about four hours. The ride itself lasts about 1.5 hours.

White-Water Rafting

Western Panama has fantastic white water, some of it truly world class. The longest-established commercially run rivers are the powerful **Río Chiriquí** (east of Boquete) and **Río Chiriquí Viejo** (west of Boquete, near the Costa Rican border). Even experienced rafters will likely find these thrilling. They feature very long wave trains, relentless runs, hair-raising moments, and lots of variety. There are also much more peaceful sections of the river where timid beginners can get their feet wet.

One of the great things about rafting on these rivers is the sense of solitude. Yours may be

COURTESY OF CHIRIQUÍ RIVER RAFTING

The western highlands offer world-class river rafting.

the only raft on the river, and you may not see a soul along the banks. Other than the occasional cow, rafters are likely to find little but trees, gorges, tributaries, and huge, beautiful birds.

Gentler rides, featuring Class II and III rapids, are available on the nearby Río Gariché, Río Dolega, and Río Majagua.

Some of the rivers can only be run during the height of the rainy season, approximately June–November. The water level is too low at other times. There's always water in the Chiriquí Viejo, but during times of heavy rainfall it can be too rough to run.

Sadly, part of the Río Chiriquí has been dammed, and only parts of it can now be run. The Panamanian government is authorizing dams all over western Panama, and other wild rivers are endangered, including the Chiriquí Viejo, one of Central America's most spectacular white-water rivers. If you have an opinion about this, send an email to ANCON,

Panama's largest environmental nonprofit (ancon@ancon.org). The Habla Ya website (www.hablayapanama.com) has detailed information on the endangered rivers and other suggestions about how to make your voice heard.

Boquete Outdoor Adventures (Los Establos Plaza, cell 6474-0274, www.boqueteoutdooradventures.com) offers full-day rafting trips for US$90 per person (three-person minimum). A kayak sampler trip on gentle rapids is US$80 per person, two-person minimum.

The company also offers guided overnight hikes to the summit of Barú, multiday white-water and sea-kayaking trips, deep-sea fishing excursions, and other outdoor adventures.

◖ PARQUE NACIONAL VOLCÁN BARÚ

The most popular activities in this national park are hiking the gorgeous Sendero Los Quetzales, which skirts the north side of Barú and links Boquete with Cerro Punta, and climbing Volcán Barú. Neither of these trails is appropriate for small children. It's possible to hire trail guides for these and other hikes in the area. Try to find a guide who is also a skilled birder; even those not particularly into birding will have a richer experience when guided by someone attuned to the natural surroundings.

Hiking Sendero Los Quetzales

Cerro Punta is nearly a kilometer higher in elevation than Boquete, so you'll be walking uphill most of the way. Because of that, most people choose to hike in the other direction. Some reckon the uphill hike, though strenuous, is actually easier than hiking downhill since the steep descent is rough on the knees and can set you up for a case of the "wobbles," which is no fun when you still have hours of downhill hiking ahead of you. And some of those who regularly hike the trail claim there's a better chance of outrunning the rain hiking uphill, since it often rains in the morning on the Cerro Punta side and in the afternoon on the Boquete side. Besides not getting wet, you'll have a much better chance of seeing birds.

The trail was closed and not being maintained as of early 2012. All the information below assumes the trail has been repaired and reopened, which is slated to happen in 2013. Do not attempt to hike it if it hasn't been opened. Hiking on the closed trail is against the law as well as dangerous. Since its closure, the trail has been dubbed a *trampa de muerte* (death trap) in the Panamanian press. Some who have disregarded the warnings have had tragic accidents. The trail is crisscrossed by rivers and streams along its entire length, and with bridges down it's all too easy to slip and get washed away in a storm while trying to ford a stream. Since the trail is off-limits, if you do hurt yourself and a search party manages to save you, you'll pay the entire cost of the rescue. Those determined to hike the trail regardless of these warnings should at the very least tell someone of their plans and leave instructions to call for help if they go missing.

It's best to go with a guide when hiking the trail up to Cerro Punta, as there are a couple of places where it's easy to miss a turn. Get an early start.

Allow six hours just to hike between the two ANAM ranger stations—Alto Chiquero (Boquete side) and El Respingo (Cerro Punta side). And bear in mind the stations are a long way from any town. It's possible to camp or stay in a dorm room at the stations.

Access to the Boquete entrance is from the scenic Bajo Mono loop road. A road branches off the loop toward the trailhead. The road is marked, but in a rather confusing way. Take the road that's bordered by a pipeline.

From this point it's a three-kilometer uphill walk to the Alto Chiquero ranger station, a walk that will add at least 1.5 hours to the hike. It's possible to hire a taxi to go all the way to the ranger station, but it'll be significantly more expensive than just being dropped off at the start of the road, where it meets the Bajo Mono loop. Buses only go as far as the Bajo Mono loop.

Pay the park admission fee (US$5) at the station. The trail officially starts here. Those with their own vehicles can park at the station. Don't leave any valuables in the car. There's a US$1 parking fee.

From the station, hike down the dirt road for about 45 minutes. The Los Quetzales trailhead is on the left. There may be a sign marking it, but don't count on it; keep your eyes open, as it's possible to miss the turnoff and walk too far on the dirt road.

The trail gets far steeper about 2.5 hours into the hike. After another hour, there's a campsite with vista points but few facilities. This is a good place to take a break and eat lunch.

Once at El Respingo, where the trail ends on the Cerro Punta side of the volcano, it's still another 1.5-hour hike downhill to the road linking Cerro Punta and Guadalupe. From here you may be able to flag down a bus or taxi. If this doesn't sound like a fun way to end a hike, consider arranging for a taxi to meet you at El Respingo station. Because the road is so rough, the fare to Cerro Punta will be about US$30.

Those who choose to start their hike from the Bajo Mono turnoff and end it all the way in Guadalupe or Cerro Punta are looking at a nine-hour hike. This is the only option for those who want to get to or from the trails by bus, as buses do not go all the way to the ranger stations. When hiring a guide, be sure to ask where the tour begins and ends.

Arrange transportation back to Boquete ahead of time or plan to spend the night in the Cerro Punta area. The trip by bus takes at least three hours, not including waiting time in David, where travelers must change buses. One-way trippers: Consider shipping luggage ahead to meet you. Hire a taxi to do so, or make arrangements through your hotel or guide. Those who choose one of the latter options should find out how the luggage will be sent and when it will arrive. There have been cases of tourists getting stuck waiting for bags that had been sent by courier services that make the trip only once a day. No fun.

Climbing Volcán Barú

The summit of the dormant volcano that gives the park its name is, at 3,475 meters, the highest point in Panama. Those wanting to climb to the top of Barú will find the Boquete summit trail easier to manage than the one on the west side of Barú. When the road is in slightly less horrendous shape than normal, which means the dry season, it may even be possible to drive to the summit from this side. Even then, however, this requires a good four-wheel drive with a winch. The road more closely resembles a steep riverbed. It's an absolutely brutal drive.

Hikers should allow at least 4–5 hours up and 3–4 hours back down. The hike is strenuous but not technically difficult.

On a clear day, it's possible to see both the Pacific and Atlantic oceans from the summit. The best chance of having this unusual experience is to be at the summit at dawn; clouds tend to blanket everything shortly thereafter. This means either hiking through the night or camping near the summit. Bear in mind that even when the volcano itself is free from fog, the distant coasts may be shrouded in cloud.

Locals shake their heads when they see tourists attempting this hike in shorts. Those who do this inevitably regret it bitterly. Even when it's warm in Boquete, it can be near freezing in the upper reaches of the mountain. Snow flurries are not unheard of near the summit. It also rains a lot, and being cold and wet is a recipe for hypothermia.

Dress warmly in waterproof clothes, and if you plan to camp, bring a good tent and a second set of clothes. Bring plenty of water, as there are no facilities anywhere near the summit. Also, bear in mind that the elevation is high enough for altitude sickness to be a possibility. If you feel nauseated or get a bad headache, head down the mountain immediately.

One bummer about this hike is that people have scrawled graffiti all over the rocks near the summit and left their trash behind. Try to ignore this, and maybe pack up some of the trash for your return journey. Then concentrate on the view and the accomplishment of having made it to the top.

Take a cell phone if you have one. There are communication towers at the summit, so it might be possible to find a signal if you get into trouble.

Unless you're looking for a marathon hike, drive or hire a taxi (US$8 for one or two people) to the ranger station at the trailhead. A four-wheel drive is needed even to get this far. From Boquete, head north through town and take the second left past the church (look for the blue Volcán Barú sign). Continue straight past the first intersection, then head uphill. There's a fork after 6.7 kilometers. Take the right fork. The road forks again in about 800 meters. Take the left fork. After another 600 meters, take the right fork up the very steep gravel road.

Entrance is US$5, payable at the little ranger station (if there's someone there) at the entrance to the park, which is in an area called Camiseta. There's an outhouse at the station. It's another US$5 to camp in the park, but there are no facilities. From the station (elevation 1,840 meters) it's another 13.5 kilometers to the top. The trail is fairly steep and very rocky. Those determined to start their trek in downtown Boquete should add another nine kilometers to the total.

Other Hikes

A less-ambitious hike is along a stretch of the **Bajo Mono Loop,** a scenic, 20-kilometer paved, circular road that begins and ends just north of downtown Boquete and loops through lovely countryside. It features lush forest, dramatic volcanic cliffs, and a valley with a pretty river flowing through it. It's easy to flag down a bus if you get tired. Be careful—many of the truckers plying these roads seem to have a death wish. Take food and water, as there's no

© WILLIAM FRIAR

waterfall along the Bajo Mono Loop

place to buy them during this hike. The Bajo Mono loop starts north of Boquete. Follow Avenida Central and keep left at the fork past the church. The loop is well marked. It's also possible to bike or drive the road.

Nature Tours

A guide is a good idea for more ambitious hikes, such as summiting Volcán Barú or hiking the Sendero Los Quetzales. A knowledgeable birding guide also greatly increases the chance of spotting quetzals. Many guides have access to four-wheel-drive vehicles, a plus for those without their own transportation. Several of the hotels, especially the more upscale ones, can arrange tours for their guests. So can **Boquete Tree Trek** (Los Establos Plaza, tel. 720-1635, www.aventurist.com).

Though most of the guides in Boquete are good, safe, and reliable people, there have been occasional complaints about dangerous practices as well as inappropriate behavior toward women. If possible, try not to take guided tours alone. No matter what a tour guide might tell you, a hike to the top of Volcán Barú or the length of Sendero Los Quetzales is too much for young children, not to mention adults who aren't in reasonably good shape.

The guides listed here are all pros with good reputations. I have known nearly all of them for quite a few years and have had a blast on their tours.

Coffee Adventures (tel. 720-3852, cell 6634-4698, http://coffeeadventures.net) is a guide outfit that consists of Terry van Niekerk and Hans van der Vooren, the warm and eminently dependable Dutch couple who own Tinamou Cottage. They offer several excellent, well-organized guided hikes. These include half-day private birding or hiking trips (US$55 pp). They can design birding trips for visitors seeking specific birds. Full-day birding or hiking trips are also available, both in the Boquete area and as far away as the Fortuna Road. In addition, they can combine a birding or hiking trip or visit to a Ngöbe settlement with ground transportation to or from Almirante in Bocas del Toro (US$149 pp). This is a great option for those needing to travel between Bocas and Boquete, as Hans and Terry are safe and reliable drivers, and it's a good way to combine transportation with a mini-adventure.

Some of these tours are not at all strenuous. All tours include transportation and snacks. The birding tours are usually led by Terry, an accomplished birder, and the hiking tours by Hans. Both guides speak English, Dutch, and Spanish. Terry and Hans take a first-aid kit and cell phone along on all their hikes. As the name Coffee Adventures suggests, they also offer excellent tours of coffee facilities.

Mirador Adventures (Ave. A Oeste, tel. 720-2864, cell 6920-4169, ryan@mirador-adventures.com, www.nombapanama.com), which operates out of Hostal Nomba, offers a range of guided outdoor adventures, including overnight hikes to the summit of Barú (US$75 pp, minimum two people), daily early evening trips to the Caldera hot springs (US$32 pp, including entrance fee and wine/beer), a hike to five waterfalls (US$50 pp), and combination hiking and mountain-bike adventures (US$85 pp). Those staying at the hostel get discounted rates. The company also arranges kayaking and white-water rafting trips and rents a wide range of outdoor gear.

Santiago "Chago" Caballero (cell 6626-2200) has been guiding people in the highlands for 18 years and is often employed by top guide outfits. He is generally acknowledged as the best quetzal spotter around; if your main aim is to see a quetzal, he's your guy. He's a kind, gentle man and can be depended on to show up on time. He's got his own four-wheel drive and is a careful driver. His bird-watching tours cost US$120 for 1–2 people, US$150 for 3–4 people.

Chago also takes guests on Sendero Los Quetzales (US$170 for 1–2 people, US$60 pp for 3–5 people). Other offerings include tours of the Cerro Punta side of the mountain, including either Parque Internacional La Amistad or Cañon Macho de Monte and the Lagunas de Volcán (both US$140 1–2 people, US$50 pp for 3–5 people). All tours include a box lunch and transportation. Chago also offers transfers to David (US$30), Cerro Punta (US$70), and Almirante (US$180), which is the jumping-off point for Bocas del Toro.

Massages and Spa Treatments

Those who would like some pampering have several options. A quite opulent spa called **The Haven** (tel. 730-9345, www.boquetespa.com) aims to be a destination spa. It offers a full range of massage therapies, facials, and clinical treatments including acupuncture, all priced at more or less what you'd expect to pay in the United States. It also has state-of-the-art exercise equipment and six small but well-appointed guest rooms. I've had one massage here, which was skilled if rather coldly efficient.

The **Panamonte Inn and Spa** (off Avenida Central, north of town center, tel. 720-1324, 8 A.M.–7 P.M. daily) has a quaint and airy day spa where you can relax to the tune of the Río Caldera rushing by. It offers massages (US$68–78 for 55 minutes), facials, mud therapy, and the like.

ACCOMMODATIONS

Lodging is in or near downtown Boquete unless otherwise specified. There are some good options in the outlying area, but those without their own transportation may find getting around inconvenient. Hostels and other backpacker-friendly places are more plentiful than they used to be, and there are quite a few pleasant, economical options for those on a modest budget. Private homes are increasingly posting room-for-rent signs in front of their houses. These tend to be pretty basic. A number of the more upscale places periodically offer great rates for those who book through their websites; be sure to check. Hotel rooms can get booked up in Boquete, particularly during major festivals. Make reservations well in advance.

Under US$10

◖ **Pensión Marilós** (Avenida E Este, tel. 720-1380, www.pension-marilos.com, US$6.95 s or US$9.90 d with shared bath; US$9.90 s or US$15.95 d with private bath) remains the best deal in all of Panama. Marilós offers seven simple but clean and tidy rooms at bargain prices. It's two blocks south of the plaza, on Avenida E Este, which is parallel to and two blocks east of Avenida Central. Guests can use the kitchen and dining room. The prices here haven't gone up in years.

US$10–25

Hostal Nomba (Ave. A Oeste, tel. 720-2864, cell 6920-4169, ryan@miradoradventures.com, www.nombapanama.com, dorm rooms US$8–9 pp, private rooms US$15 s, US$22 d, including breakfast and good local coffee) is a friendly hostel in a residential area just west of downtown Boquete.

Rooms are clean and range in size from 2–6 beds. There are no private bathrooms, but the three shared bathrooms have hot water. There are two shared kitchens, a hammock lounge, laundry facilities, a foosball table, and other extras. The hostel's bar just started a nightly happy hour (6 P.M.–midnight) open both to guests and the general public.

The hostel is run by a warm couple (he's from Colorado; she's from Boquete) who offer their guests much more than a bed for the night. It's an especially good option for those interested in outdoor adventures. The hostel is literally attached to Mirador Adventures, and has good-quality outdoor equipment for rent, ranging from tents and sleeping bags to warm socks. You don't have to stay at the hostel to rent the equipment, and they'll stash your luggage for free while you use it. The owners also lead free hikes twice a week. This is the best place for backpackers interested in climbing Barú, as they can equip and prepare guests and give them good advice on how to tackle it. The hostel can also arrange volunteer opportunities.

Hostal Nomba is one block west of Avenida Central. If you're heading uphill from the town plaza, turn left at Supercentro El Mandarín and make the next right. The hostel is the third house on the right and is painted bright green.

US$25-50

Hostal Boquete (Calle 4a Sur, tel. 720-2573, US$33–38 s/d), near the west bank of the Río Caldera and just north of the bridge spanning it, offers 15 basic but cheerful rooms with private bath and cable TV. It has a picturesque location on the banks of the Río Caldera, with a view of the fairgrounds on the east bank. Even if you could get a room here during the flower fair, you probably wouldn't want to—the music blasting across the river from the fairgrounds would render you deaf in seconds. There's a riverside deck with a small restaurant. This place is popular with gringo travelers on a budget.

The 40-room **Hotel Los Fundadores** (Avenida Central, tel. 720-2354 or 720-1298, info@hotel-fundadores, starts at US$35 s/d) is a Boquete stalwart. It's on the left side of Avenida Central just before downtown; its faux Arthurian-castle facade is hard to miss. Rooms here are small, drab, musty, and well past their prime, but a babbling creek runs right through the middle of the building, which makes up for a lot.

The German-run **Pensión Topas** (Avenida Belisario Porras, tel./fax 720-1005, schoeb@cwpanama.net, starts at US$24 s, US$35 d) is three blocks south of the plaza on Avenida Belisario Porras, which is parallel to and one block east of Avenida Central. This is a cheerful place with eight rooms set in a garden filled with flowering trees. A simple breakfast (8–11 A.M.) on the terrace is US$5.90. The owner, Axel Shöb, speaks English and is helpful on advice about where to go and what to see. There's a volleyball net and small swimming pool on the premises. The pension can also help arrange tours. There are a few cheaper rooms, which are very simple and small with a shared bath. Allow 10 days for an answer to email; Axel hates computers.

Hostel Mamallena (tel. 720-1260, www.mamallenaboquete.com, starts at US$11 pp dorm rooms, US$27.50–33 s/d private rooms, including pancake breakfast) is the sister of the hostel of the same name in Panama City. This one is in a two-story wooden building that dates from the 1950s and has tons of charm. It's right on the south side of the town plaza. It offers 23 dormitory beds with new and clean shared bathrooms, of different sizes and shapes. Private rooms are available for US$27.50 s/d with shared bath or US$33 s/d with private bath. There's free wireless Internet access and computers for guest use. It's managed by friendly people who speak Spanish and English and have voluminous amounts of local information to share and can set up a number of low-price tours, including a popular visit to a small local coffee farm. Advice and access to a thick binder are available to anyone who passes by. This is a great addition to the local backpacker scene.

US$50-100

The best thing about **El Oasis B&B** (tel. 720-1586 and 720-1625, info@oasisboquete.com, www.oasisboquete.com, standard rooms US$71.50–88 s/d) is its location. It's in a residential area right on the east bank of the Río Caldera, set in a garden just south of the grounds of the Feria de las Flores y El Café. A recent extension added six suites (US$110–165; weekly rates available). El Oasis is a clean and tidy place with firm beds, a shared terrace strung with hammocks, and free wireless Internet. There's also an Internet-connected computer in the common room that guests are welcome to use. Rooms are simple but newish. The cheapest rooms are dark and have no view. Try to get a room away from the common areas, which can get noisy.

Isla Verde (Calle 5a Sur, tel. 720-2533, fax 720-2751, http://islaverdepanama.com, starts at US$99 s/d), two blocks west of Avenida Central on the south end of town, is an unusual place. Its most notable features are the six hexagonal roundhouses set in a garden and connected by paths. Each roundhouse has a comfortable bed downstairs, another one up in a loft in the center of the cabin, and a kitchenette. Three of the roundhouses sleep a maximum of four people; the other three sleep six, have a more extensive kitchen area, and are wheelchair-accessible. The decor in all is bright and cheerful. Six newer suites, in rectangular two-story buildings, have kitchenettes and balconies. All accommodations have cable TV and free wireless Internet. Rates are US$99 s/d in the smaller roundhouses and lower suites and US$121 s/d in the larger roundhouses, and US$121–165 in the upper suites. Additional people are US$22 each. Breakfasts to order are served in an open-sided geodesic dome in the middle of the village. The owners speak English, Spanish, and German. If you're heading into Boquete from the south, Isla Verde is a left turn off Avenida Central onto Calle 5a Sur just as you enter downtown. Look for it on the right after two blocks.

Panamonte Inn and Spa (tel. 720-1327 or 720-1324, fax 720-2055, www.panamonte.com, starts at US$93.50 s/d) is a Boquete institution—it dates from the early 20th century and has lots of old-world charm. Famous guests have included Charles Lindbergh and Admiral Richard Byrd, who wrote an article about his Arctic exploits for *National Geographic* while relaxing here. The hotel's charming, semiformal restaurant makes it worth a visit even for those who don't stay here. The spa is lovely, too.

The Panamonte's 16 rooms are quaint and clean. The least expensive ones are on the small side, but there are also four spacious garden cabanas (US$152.80 s/d) and an especially appealing three-bedroom apartment (US$264, sleeps six), El Fresal, with a wraparound porch across the street from the main hotel. There's a Honeymoon Suite (US$126.50 s/d) on the 2nd floor that once hosted Ingrid Bergman. All rooms have a safe, cable TV, telephone, air-conditioner, and other amenities. The Panamonte Inn and Spa is about 0.7 kilometers north of the town center. Follow Avenida Central past the church and head right when you come to a fork. It's the blue wooden building on the left.

Finca Lérida Ecolodge (tel./fax 720-2285, cell 6450-3848, www.fincalerida.com, US$90–99 s/d) is a nice addition to the Boquete lodging scene. The finca has long been famous for birdwatching and gourmet coffee, and even those not particularly interested in either will likely find there's something magical about the place and its natural beauty. Now overnight guests have a chance to soak up the scenery.

The main lodge consists of a row of rooms in a long building up on a hill with a view of the gardens, coffee plantation, and surrounding mountains. The rooms are rather luxurious, with hardwood floors, firm beds, massive flat-screen TVs, and plate-glass windows that look out on the view. All the rooms are on the ground floor and have a front patio with a hammock and sitting area. In the middle of the building is a mountain-lodge-style bar with a fireplace. During my most recent visit a second row of rooms was being built farther down the hill, close to the lodge's appealing restaurant, Restaurante Monniche.

At the base of the hill, the old board-and-batten family homestead was built in 1917 by Tollef B. Mönniche, a Norwegian engineer who was an important figure in the construction of the Panama Canal. It's very cool to see the Norwegian-style stone fireplace he built in one of the common rooms and to thumb through the books in his personal library. In recent years, quetzals have been spotted in the backyard of the house mid-January–end of February, but there is of course no guarantee you'll see one. Guides lead hikes around the property, including one to a waterfall.

All this is located in a single compound in the community of Alto Quiel, about a 10-minute drive above Boquete. To get there, drive north on Avenida Central and continue straight past Café Ruiz and the stadium. At the next intersection, follow the road leading to Callejon Seco. Follow the steep, winding road up into the mountains for about another five kilometers. Look for a Finca Lérida sign on the right. A taxi from downtown Boquete is US$7.25.

US$100-150

Hotel Ladera (tel. 730-9000, www.hotel-ladera.com, rack rates start at US$223.50 s/d), not to be confused with Finca Lérida, is essentially a business hotel that's gone on holiday in the country. It's just across the bridge from the Panamonte, on the east bank of the Río Caldera and offers formal service and rooms that have firm beds, terraces, TVs, and a vaguely Japanese-minimalist air. There's a

rather austere restaurant and much cozier bar, the latter of which opens onto a brook and has a ski-lodge ambiance. The hotel offers significant discounts for those booking through its website, and rates can plummet in the low season.

Boquete Garden Inn (tel. 720-2376, www.boquetegardeninn.com, starts at US$108.90–119.90 s/d) is one of the most popular places to stay in Boquete. It consists of 10 units in five peach-colored, two-story hexagonal cabanas in a pleasant garden setting along the Río Palo Alto. There's a *rancho* bar right by the river. Rooms have attractive furnishings, good mattresses, kitchenettes, cable TV, stylish bathrooms (with hot water in the shower, though not in the sink), free wireless Internet, and the sound of the rushing river. Stays include a continental breakfast and an evening drink in the *rancho* by the river. This place has a friendly vibe. The hotel is about 2.5 kilometers northwest of downtown. Cross over the downtown bridge over the Río Caldera and make a left. Stay on this road, heading north toward Palo Alto, for 1.5 kilometers past Hotel Ladera. The hotel is on the left past the Rock restaurant. They speak English and Spanish here.

Tinamou Cottage (tel. 720-3852, cell 6634-4698, www.coffeeadventures.net, starts at US$127.60 s/d) actually consists of three cottages on a coffee farm, Finca Habbus de Kwie. It's southeast of Boquete in Jaramillo Abajo, a little more than five minutes by car or a hefty hike from downtown. It belongs to Hans van der Vooren and Terry van Niekerk, a charming and friendly Dutch couple who also are among the best tour guides in Boquete.

Of the 8.5-hectare finca, a little under half of it still grows coffee. The rest has been allowed to revert to nature, and the couple has built 1.5–2 hours of trails through the secondary growth, through which run several creeks and little waterfalls. There's some good birding here.

Little Tinamou (US$127.60 s/d) is cozy and cheerful, offering a queen-size canopy bed, a sitting area, and a kitchenette with fridge, oven, and sink. This room was recently remodeled and modernized. A sofa bed in the sitting area can accommodate a third guest (US$22). The owners' home is just next door, as are their three good-natured dogs. The other two cottages, Highland Tinamou and Great Tinamou (US$184.80 s/d, US$22 for each additional person) are more secluded, situated deeper into the plantation and surrounded by forest. They each have two bedrooms, an open kitchen/living room, and a porch looking out on the view. These cottages can sleep 4–5 people. All cottages have cable TV. Guests get a substantial discount if they book through www.coffeeadventures.net; the longer the stay, the greater the discount.

A breakfast basket with bread and pastries is left outside each cottage in the morning. Hans and Terry will pick up arriving guests from downtown Boquete for free. Guests can hike to the farm. It takes about an hour from downtown. The owners can arrange hikes to any of the area's attractions, some of which they lead themselves. They speak Dutch, English, Spanish, and some German. This has long been one of the most appealing places to stay in Boquete, and Hans and Terry are great people as well as great hosts.

Just up the street from Pensión Marilós is **Hotel Rebequet** (tel. 720-1365, info@rebequet.com, www.rebequet.com, US$96.80 s, US$121 d), which offers nine large, clean, pleasant rooms set around an interior courtyard. All have small TVs and refrigerators. Prices for this place have doubled in recent years, so it's not the great deal it once was. Boquete hotels in this price range generally offer more. But the Rebequet is a consistently solid option, and it's worth calling to see if deals are available.

Hotel Los Establos (tel. 720-2685, U.S./Canada toll-free tel. 888/481-0656, www.losestablos.net, US$165 s/d, US$308 for suites) was originally part of the Valle Escondido empire, with similar Spanish-mission decor, but is now under new management. It's 0.7 kilometers farther up the hill from La Montaña y El Valle: The Coffee Estate Inn. As its name suggests, it was originally meant to be a horse stables but became a hotel instead. Its pastoral setting is stunning: It has a panoramic view of Volcán Barú and the surrounding countryside. On its four hectares, a spacious bar area with pool table looks out on a large garden. Breakfast is available from 7–10 A.M.

There are just four rooms downstairs and two suites upstairs in the main building. Two newer rooms have been added in a separate building. The suites consist of a small bedroom attached to a small sitting room, though the latter is glass-enclosed and gets a lot of light.

Each of the downstairs rooms has a tiny terrace, but, oddly enough, only one of them looks out on the volcano. All the rooms have cable TV and a DVD player; guests need to bring their own DVDs (they can be rented in downtown Boquete). The **Riverside Inn** (tel. 720-1076, www.riversideinnboquete.com, start at US$137.50 s/d, including breakfast), consists of six opulent rooms in a lovely wooden house by the Río Palo Alto. The best of the bunch (and, naturally, the most expensive) is the Orchidea, which features a handsome, king-size four-poster bed and a large bathroom with a whirlpool tub, both of which look out on the Río Palo Alto. All rooms have free wireless Internet access and televisions with cable TV and DVD players. The common areas feature a cozy sitting room with stone fireplace and a TV room/solarium. Rack rates are double what's listed here, but in practice the lower rates appear to be the norm. The hotel is under the same management as the Rock restaurant, which is just next door. The hotel is a couple of kilometers northwest of downtown. Cross over the downtown bridge over the Río Caldera and make a left. Stay on this road, heading north toward Palo Alto. The Riverside Inn will be on the left, just past the Rock. If you reach the Boquete Garden Inn, you've gone too far.

Over US$150

Some innkeepers have hospitality wired into their genetic code. Meet Jane Walker and Barry Robbins, Canadian expatriates who have turned their 2.5 hectares of forested land above Boquete valley into one of the most appealing places to stay in the country. They call it ❰ **La Montaña y El Valle: The Coffee Estate Inn** (tel./fax 720-2211, www.coffeeestateinn.com, US$198 s/d). You get a sense of the couple's obsessive attention to detail as soon as you make a reservation. (And it's a popular place, so advance reservations are a must.) They immediately send out a large information package with solid advice on what to do and how to get around in Boquete and other parts of Panama.

The inn consists of three large, modern, immaculate bungalows set on a hillside just northeast of Boquete. They're essentially small apartments, and they're tastefully decorated. Each has a balcony, sitting room, kitchenette, flat-screen TV with cable TV and DVD player, safe, wireless Internet access, and a terrific view of Barú and the valley. (The estate is at 1,300 meters.)

Barry and Jane are always finding ways to make a great place even better. There are heated floors in the bathroom, probably the only place in Panama with them. Guests can enjoy Barry's homemade breads and scones for breakfast, and twice a week those who are interested can dine by candlelight in their bungalows (US$19–25 for main dishes). Offerings include rack of lamb, braised halibut, five-spice roasted duck, and so on. This is incredibly romantic for couples and a treat for anyone else, as the staff festoon the whole bungalow with candles and artful flower arrangements. Appetizers and simpler suppers are available every other night of the week. Options include a smoked salmon platter, vegetarian moussaka, and cannelloni stuffed with spinach and beef (US$10–12 pp).

The property is a working coffee farm that produces more than 2,000 kilos of coffee a year. The coffee grows in the shade of a pretty, well-tended little forest that attracts more than 100 species of birds and lots of other highland critters. More than 50 indigenous trees have been identified so far. As usual, though, orange trees are especially well-represented. They produce thousands of oranges a year, so help yourself to as many as you like.

Stays of three nights or more include a free, optional tour of the owners' coffee operation from soil to cup. The (free) coffee you drink here has never been out of the roaster more than two days. You can buy souvenir packs to take home. They have also concocted a delicious coffee liqueur, called Barubica, which is also for sale.

Barry and Jane are a great source of information on the area's attractions. Guests are invited to walk through the couple's lovely gardens and more than a kilometer of trails on the property and use their extensive library, which also has a computer with free Internet access.

Barry and Jane run a tight, gleaming ship. The inn has more in common with a modern country getaway than some bohemian tree house. But this is a great place to pamper yourself, which can be especially fun if you've been roughing it for a while. This is a popular place with honeymooners.

To get there from town, take the downtown bridge over the Río Caldera and make a left. The entrance gate is past El Explorador. The last stretch of road is rough and rocky but doesn't require a four-wheel drive if driven carefully. A third person in the room is another US$55. Children must be 14 or older.

Valle Escondido Resort Golf and Spa (tel. 240-2454, www.veresort.com, starts at US$220 s/d), also known as Hotel Escondido, is part of the Valle Escondido gated community. Accommodations include rooms in the hotel, bungalows dotted about the complex, and, for longer stays, condominiums. The rooms are pleasant and feature patios, flat-screen TVs with cable TV and DVD players, and free wireless Internet. If you stay here, try to get a room that looks out on the lovely river. Guests are welcome to use Valle Escondido's pools and fitness center. Golfers must pay to use the nine-hole golf course. There's a formal restaurant, Sabor Escondido, on the grounds, and a café that features a riverside deck shaded by a banyan tree. I've found food at both places inconsistent, depending on the quality of the ingredients available. Valle Escondido is close to but feels quite separate from the rest of Boquete.

As the name suggests, ◖ **Rancho de Caldera** (tel. 772-4225, U.S./Canada toll-free tel. 877/810-0898, cell 6612-2147, contact@ ranchodecaldera.com, www.ranchodecaldera. com, standard rooms US$176 s/d, junior suites US$198 s/d) is in Caldera, about a 25-minute drive from Boquete. This is one of the nicest places to stay in western Panama, but it has a very different feel from Boquete proper: There's no *bajareque,* no view of the volcano, and no cool mountain air. There is, however, a lovely pool and deck next to the restaurant, with a view of the surrounding hills.

The main accommodations consist of three sets of three rooms set along a rise with a view of the 20-hectare former cattle and horse ranch as well as the hills in the distance. Rooms are very large, cheerful, and decorated simply. The east-facing wall of each is a six-meter-wide sliding-glass door that opens onto a private porch; guests can watch the sun rise over the hills in the morning if they can manage to wake up early in such comfortable surroundings.

The standard rooms have a king or two queen beds, a well-stocked modern kitchenette, flat-screen satellite TV, air-conditioning, and an iPod docking station. Some rooms have bathtubs; see the ranch's website, which lists each room's features in detail. The junior suites add a full kitchen, dining/living area, and massage chair. Rooms and suites closer to the pool and restaurant are US$44 more per night. Free wireless Internet is available throughout the property.

For those on a tighter budget, there are also two far smaller and more modest rooms in the main house. They have no TV, no air-conditioning, and share a bathroom, and the owner's home is on the floor above, but they are perfectly nice and a fantastic deal at US$66 s/d, especially since all the ranch's public facilities are available to guests in these rooms.

There are still some horses at the ranch which are available for hire; some find this a pleasant way to get to and from the Caldera hot springs. The owner sometimes invites guests up to watch a movie in her lovely home, which has a large movie screen that lowers from the ceiling.

It's not easy to get to the ranch by public transportation, so those without a car should either be prepared to walk the last couple of kilometers to the ranch or be willing to pay around US$25 for a taxi to or from Boquete. Heading south from Boquete, make a left at the Caldera turnoff and continue straight towards Caldera for 10 kilometers. Do not confuse Rancho de Caldera with Montañas de Caldera, a gated residential community between it and Boquete. As you reach Caldera, you'll see a church and soccer field on the left. Turn left here and head uphill for two kilometers. The last 700 meters is on a one-lane track, so drive cautiously. A couple of large, friendly dogs greet new arrivals.

Another incentive to make the trip: The restaurant, Madre Tierra, serves some of the finest food in Panama. It's open to the public and offers some great deals.

Camping

Though it's not as cold around Boquete as it is in the higher elevations on the west side of Barú, it can still get plenty chilly. As always in the highlands, campers should bring plenty of warm, waterproof clothing and a waterproof tent. Expect drizzle even in the dry season.

Camping is possible in **Parque Nacional Volcán Barú,** but those who pitch their tents high up should be prepared for weather that can approach freezing.

Campers can get a camping permit from the ranger station at the start of the Volcán Barú summit trail. Camping permits are US$5, plus the US$5 park entrance fee. It's also possible to camp at the **ANAM ranger station** at Alto Chiquero, the Boquete-side end of the Sendero Los Quetzales. The station has two dorm rooms upstairs, each of which has four bunk beds and lockers for storing gear. There's also a kitchenette. The cost is US$5 per bed. Parking is US$1.

FOOD
Restaurants

The restaurant at the ◖ **Panamonte Inn and Spa** (off Avenida Central, north of town center, tel. 720-1327 or 720-1324, www.panamonte. com, 6–10 A.M., noon–3 P.M., and 6–9 P.M. Mon.–Fri.; 7:30–11 A.M., noon–3 P.M., and 6–9 P.M. Sat.–Sun., US$8–12) is the fanciest in town, with tablecloths, fresh flowers,

The margaritas at Big Daddy's Grill are the best in Panama.

candles, fine china, and lots of fascinating antiques. It's got an almost dollhouse charm, and the waitresses serve guests in frilly old-country uniforms. When everything comes together, this is the best restaurant in Boquete. However, it suffers from the usual Boquete problem of inconsistency, which has been exacerbated recently since its celebrated chef, Charlie Collins, has been focusing his attentions on a new cooking school. The food tends toward continental cuisine. There are also vegetarian options and a budget menu of burgers and sandwiches. The soups can be delicious—try the spicy pumpkin soup if it's available—and this is a good place to sample the highland trout. Save room for dessert, as it tends to be done well. The rum cake is excellent, as is the Chocolate Decadence.

Don't let the name or appearance of ◖ **Big Daddy's Grill** (Avenida Central, cell 6683-3354, noon–9 P.M. Tues.–Sat., noon–8 P.M., Sun.) put you off. From the outside, it looks like a plain *fonda* right above the busy main road on the way into downtown. But there's a much more attractive terrace hidden in a garden behind the restaurant, and—much more important—the food is great. It's run by Larry and Elizabeth Slagle, a couple from Sarasota, Florida, where Larry had a long career in restaurants. This is the place to come for fish, which is fresh and carefully selected, as Larry goes down to the Pacific coast every morning for the catch of the day. Elizabeth is a friendly and super-attentive hostess. Be sure to ask about the fish tacos, which are not on the regular menu but are out of this world. They are the best I've ever had: smoky, grilled to perfection, huge, and served with equally delicious black beans and rice. There's also lots of gringo favorites on the menu, including burgers, fried chicken, and corn dogs. This is a popular place with in-the-know resident expats.

The owners boast they've got the best margaritas in Panama, and they're right. They use homemade sour mix and sprinkle the rim

© WILLIAM FRIAR

not just with salt but with chilis shipped from Elizabeth's sister in the States. They're fantastic. The grill gets its name, by the way, from Larry's nickname, given to him by homeless kids in Panama City with whom he used to volunteer as a sports coach.

◖ **Machu Picchu** (tel. 720-1502, noon–11 P.M. Mon.–Sat., noon–9 P.M. Sun.) is the sister of the popular Machu Picchu in Panama City, and some reckon this is actually the better of the two. The seafood here is good. The teak furniture, blue tablecloths, and Peruvian music on the stereo contribute to the pleasant atmosphere, as does the friendly service. Save room for dessert: The lemon pie is tasty. The restaurant is at the south end of downtown, one block east of Avenida Central and half a block south of Calle 5 Sur.

◖ **Ristorante y Pizzeria Il Pianista** (tel. 720-2728, noon–10 P.M. Tues.–Sun.) is just insanely cute. It's a stone-walled little place with a handful of tables that look out on a gushing waterfall just a few feet beyond the windows. The waterfall is lighted at night. This is easily the best place in Boquete for Italian food, and one of the best restaurants, period. The (Italian) chef makes his own pastas and uses the best and freshest ingredients he can find, and it shows. Offerings include pizzas, calzones, and bruschettas, all served by the chef's friendly *bocatoreña* wife. The restaurant is about four kilometers north of downtown on the Palo Alto road. Head toward the Boquete Garden Inn and continue straight for another 1.6 kilometers. The restaurant is on the right, on the ground floor of the owners' house. Parking is a bit tricky, and the restaurant is near a somewhat sketchy coffee workers' barracks. If you drive, lock the doors and don't leave valuables in the car.

◖ **Madre Tierra** (cell 6604-9028, contact@ranchodecaldera.com, www.ranchodecaldera.com, lunch noon–2 P.M., and dinner at 6:30 P.M. Thurs.–Mon.) is at Rancho de Caldera, an appealing inn a 25-minute drive from Boquete. It's worth making the trip, or gathering a group to share the US$25 cab ride, for a meal at this place.

For one thing, the food is outstanding. The chef, Craig Miller, insists he plans to stick around, which is probably a good thing for the famous names in Panama City's fancy restaurants, as he would immediately outshine most of them. Whenever possible he uses local ingredients, and he combines them in innovative ways. The menu changes constantly, but keep an eye out for the watermelon salad with kalamata olives, feta, red onion, mint, and harissa dressing, as well as for the Thai pulled pork sandwich with green papaya slaw and some of the best fries I've ever had. No alcohol or soft drinks are served. Instead, Craig makes innovative drinks such as a Thai Citrus Sparkler (fresh orange and lime juice, honey, a pinch of cayenne, and sparkling water), or the fresh Basil and Lime Fizz.

For another, the setting is gorgeous: It's a simple but attractive place that opens onto a pool deck and has a view of the surrounding mountains.

Finally, there are good deals to be had. For US$15, diners not staying at the ranch can have lunch and all-day access to the pool. This makes it a reasonable indulgence even for those on tight budgets, particularly if they're willing to take a bus from Boquete to Caldera and hoof it for the last two kilometers up to the ranch.

In the evenings, a fixed-price menu for US$23 is served at 6:30 P.M. Reservations are required, which can be made through a form on www.ranchodecaldera.com, by phone, or by email. These are themed (e.g., Mexican, Indian, Italian, Thai, etc.) and change nightly.

Heading south from Boquete, make a left at the Caldera turnoff and continue straight towards Caldera for 10 kilometers. You'll pass the Montañas de Caldera gated community along the way; continue straight past it. As you reach Caldera proper, you'll see a church and soccer field on the left. Look for the sign for Rancho de Caldera. Turn left here and head uphill for two kilometers. The last 700 meters is on a one-lane track, so drive carefully.

If you have an irresistible craving for pizza and don't want to go all the way up to Ristorante y Pizzeria Il Pianista, **La Posada Boqueteña** (Avenida Central, tel. 730-9440, http://laposadaboquetena.com, 11:30 A.M.–10 P.M. daily, occasionally closed Mon.) has a reputation for serving the best pizza in town. La Posada is on the main road just north of downtown. Heading north past the church, it'll be on the right at the turnoff to the Panamonte.

Pizzeria La Volcánica (Avenida Central, 12:30–10 P.M. Tues.–Sun.) serves fairly tasty but greasy pizzas with thin cracker crusts ranging in size from *chica* to *gigante*. A *chica* will feed two moderately hungry adults for around five bucks. Other offerings include sandwiches and half or whole roast chickens. The pizzeria is one block before the park on the main road.

Restaurante El Sabrosón (Avenida Central, tel. 720-2147, 6:30 A.M.–10 P.M. Mon.–Fri., 6:30 A.M.–midnight Sat.–Sun., under US$4) is a popular place with low-budget diners. It's on the east side of Avenida Central at the north end of town, just down from where the road forks at the church. Its steam-table offerings include the usual, plus some Chinese dishes. It's best known for its fresh trout, which the cook will prepare however you like. It's good.

Restaurante Nelvi's (cell 6578-6528, 7 A.M.–3 P.M. Mon.–Sat., under US$3) is a newer *comida corriente* (fast food) place that has quickly become a favorite among locals looking for cheap decent food. It's my hole-in-the-wall of choice in Boquete. It's behind Los Establos Plaza on the road to Valle Escondido. Daily offerings may include various preparations of chicken, pork, spaghetti, mystery meat, and, happily enough, salads. The fried chicken is decent; the rice with *guandu* (a legume) is not. (Pay after you eat.) They'll pack food to go if you like. A second, much-more attractive branch is in Alto Boquete (cell 6414-1393, 7 A.M.–7 P.M. daily).

The restaurant at Finca Lérida keeps changing its name, but when I last visited it was called **Restaurante Monniche** (tel. 720-1111 or 720-2285, 7:30 A.M.–9 P.M., US$14–24). The dining room resembles that at the Panamonte, which used to be owned by the same family. The French-Italian cuisine is a bit hit-and-miss, but the sweeping view of the Boquete valley almost makes the quality of the food irrelevant in any case. It's quite pleasant to sit out on the terrace during the day. Stick to the Italian-influenced stuff, such as the homemade ravioli or the perfectly cooked shrimp risotto. Breakfast options include traditional Panamanian fare such as *bistec* (grilled beef). They serve Lérida's own gourmet coffee but, oddly, they burn it.

The Rock (tel. 720-2516, www.therock-boquete.com, 11:30 A.M.–9:30 P.M. daily, US$11.50–24), on the east bank of the Río Caldera northeast of downtown, makes more of an effort than most restaurants in Boquete to create a cozy atmosphere. The dining hall has a canopied ceiling, which makes for a warm feel. The lighting is subdued, it has an attractive gas fireplace, and it has an outdoor terrace with a glass windbreak right above the river. The small but eclectic menu includes jambalaya, trout, beef kabobs, veggie Thai curry, burgers, and angel-hair pasta. The restaurant uses good-quality produce and meat, though the execution doesn't always live up to the attractive presentation. The Rock produces its own nutty, creamy microbrew, which is still a rarity for Panama. It's quite decent.

The Rock is popular, particularly on Thursdays from 5 to 8 P.M., when the restaurant has an all-you-can-eat ribs special. Reservations are a must at those times. There's live jazz on Monday.

The Rock is a couple of kilometers northwest of downtown. Cross over the downtown bridge over the Río Caldera and make a left. Stay on this road, heading north toward Palo Alto. The restaurant will be on the left just before the Riverside Inn.

Cafés

☾ Art Cafe La Crepe (Avenida Central next to Zanzibar, tel. 720-1821, 11 A.M.–3 P.M. and 5–9 P.M. Tues.–Sun.) is on everyone's list of favorite places to eat in Boquete these days. It offers excellent savory and sweet crepes, as well as a range of salads, seafood, and meat dishes. Most crepes are around US$7. A daily three-course set menu is US$14. Service is gracious and the atmosphere is cheerful, with vibrantly painted café furnishings.

Café Kotowa (tel. 720-1430, www.kotowa-coffee.com, 7 A.M.–7 P.M. daily) has two coffee shops in Boquete. The one in Los Establos Plaza shares space with Boquete Tree Trek. The other is in the CEFATI building in Alto Boquete. Both offer a full range of espresso drinks and a handful of snacks. Brightly colored, gift-worthy packages of coffee are sold in both shops.

The gourmet coffee company **☾ Café Ruiz** (Avenida Central, tel. 720-100, www.caferuiz.com, 8 A.M.–5 P.M. Mon.–Sat., 9 A.M.–6 P.M. Sun. and holidays) has a coffee shop that serves espresso drinks, cakes, snacks, and other goodies at its roasting and packaging plant just north of town on Avenida Central. Keep left at the fork past the church. It's the white complex on the right, near Mi Jardín Es Su Jardín. The espresso here is among the best I've ever tasted—strong but not bitter. You can also buy a wide range of packaged coffees fresh from the plant. They come whole bean (*grano*) or ground (*molido*), sealed in plain packaging or a variety of gift packs. There are a few tables outside, and inside is a new seating area where one can see the roasting facility through plate-glass windows while sipping coffee. Tours of the facility, as well as the entire growing and processing operation, are available.

Café Punto de Encuentro (7 A.M.–noon daily, most US$2.50–5.50), one block west of Pensión Marilós, is a cute little outdoor breakfast café attached to a home. Also known as Olga's, in honor of its proprietor, it's long been a local favorite spot for breakfast. It serves pancakes, French toast, well-stuffed omelets, and other breakfast goodies. It's a simple, friendly place.

Choko Chetta (Avenida Central and Calle 5 Sur, tel. 720-1997, 10:30 A.M.–9:30 P.M. daily, US$3–9), across from Plaza Los Establos, gets its peculiar name from its dessert-on-a-stick shtick: It offers goodies such as strawberries and marshmallows on a brochette, usually drowned in chocolate and ice cream. Dessert purists can go for the brownie with ice cream, which is delicious. Other offerings range from salads and sandwiches to full meals. The mod decor—all glass and steel—is something new for Boquete. A plus here is they'll deliver to your hotel.

Anyone can come for breakfast on the terrace at **Pensión Topas** (Avenida Belisario Porras, tel./fax 720-1005, 8–11 A.M. daily, US$2.50–7), but guests staying at the pension get priority. The pension does not serve other meals.

Sugar and Spice (Avenida Central, 8 A.M.–6 A.M. Thurs.–Tues.) is locally popular for its fresh bread, soups, sandwiches, cakes, and cookies. You're unlikely to find a better bakery in Panama. This is also a good place to pick up a sandwich to go before an all-day excursion. It's on the right side of the main road as you drive into town, a block and a half past the Texaco station.

Pastelería Alemana Marianne's Café (approximately 12:30–8 P.M. Thurs.–Mon., usually closed Tues. and Wed.), a little German pastry shop on the main road through Alto Boquete, is a popular place to stop for a sugar fix on the way to or from downtown Boquete. Its pies, cakes, and other sweets are delicious, and the prices are good—about US$1.25 for a slice, or US$5 for an entire pie. Try the lemon meringue pie, the pineapple pie, the choco-vanilla cake, or the chocolate chip cookies. It's about a kilometer south of the CEFATI building. The café is closed in June.

☾ Fresas Mary (tel. 720-3394, 10 A.M.–7 P.M. daily, US$2.50 or less) is an attractive snack kiosk built into the front of a house just a half kilometer down the Volcancito road from the turnoff at the CEFATI building. It'll be on the left as you head toward Volcancito. The strawberry *batidos* (milk shakes) here are so good and fresh they'll make your knees buckle. The other nine flavors of *helados caseros* (homemade ice cream) include papaya, banana, *zarzamora* (blackberry), and *guanábana* (a tropical fruit sometimes known in English as soursop). Hamburgers and other hot bites, coffee, and sweets are also available. There's a comfortable indoor sitting area if it's raining.

Markets

A produce and meat market, the **Mercado Municipal** (also known as the Mercado Público, 6:30 A.M.–6 P.M. daily), is on the northeast corner of the plaza. There are two entrances, one on the south side and one on the east side of the building. It's worth exploring the whole complex to see who's got the best stuff that day.

There are several supermarkets within a couple of blocks of the plaza. Besides groceries, **Supercentro El Mandarín** (Avenida Central at the Calle 2a Sur) carries a range of toiletries, hardware, and other dry goods. The 24-hour **Supermercado Romero,** behind the post office, has a bakery and pharmacy. They also sell used books in English.

Deli Barú (8 A.M.–8 P.M. daily) offers a modest selection of imported cheese, deli meats, chocolate, and other goodies that are normally hard to find up here.

Organica (Calle Central off Avenida Central, tel. 720-2575, 9 A.M.–6 P.M. Mon.–Sat.) carries a small selection of health-food and ecofriendly products.

INFORMATION AND SERVICES
Tourist Information

ATP's **Centro de Facilidades Turísticas e Interpretación Volcán Barú-Boquete** (CEFATI, tel. 720-4060, 9:30 A.M.–5:30 P.M. daily) is in Alto Boquete on the main road just before it heads downhill into the town of Boquete. The place, almost as imposing as its name, was a costly undertaking for a glorified information booth, especially since the information it offers is negligible. Three good things about it: It has bathrooms, there's a great view of the Boquete valley and Río Caldera behind the building, and there's a Café Kotowa shop (7 A.M.–7 P.M. daily) next door. A decent museum display upstairs contains some background on the region's culture, history, and coffee industry.

Boquete Tree Trek (Los Establos Plaza, tel. 720-1635, cell 6615-3300, www.aventurist.com) is a better source of local tourist information, even for those who don't book one of their tours.

If the CEFATI doesn't have a decent Boquete map, try Boquete Tree Trek, Café Ruiz, or one of the Café Kotowa outlets.

Boquete's new and rather flashy **library** (tel. 720-2879, 10 A.M.–7 P.M. Mon.–Sat.) opened in 2012 after several years of construction. It's three stories tall, air-conditioned, and modern—easily the most impressive-looking *biblioteca* in the country (that's the Spanish word for a library; a *librería* is a bookstore). It features rows of Internet-connected computers, exhibition spaces, disabled access, and actual lending privileges, the last of which is unheard of in Panama. What it seems to have a shortage of, at least so far, are books. Still, there appears to be at least a little bit of everything, including a modest collection of English-language fiction. It's south of downtown, on the east side of the main road.

Banks

Banco Nacional de Panamá and **Banco General** are on Avenida Central at the entrance to downtown (both open 8 A.M.–3 P.M. Mon.–Fri., 9 A.M.–noon Sat.). **HSBC** (8:30 A.M.–3:30 P.M. Mon.–Fri., 9 A.M.–noon Sat.) is at the north end of town, across Avenida Central from the church.

Communications

The **post office** (tel. 720-1265, 8 A.M.–2:45 P.M. Mon.–Fri., 8 A.M.–12:45 P.M. Sat.) is on the east side of the plaza. The building that houses it used to the terminal for the little railroad that ran between Boquete and David, a fact now commemorated by the train car outside the entrance.

Hastor Computers (tel. 720-2855, 8 A.M.–11 P.M. Mon.–Sat., 10 A.M.–11 P.M. Sun.), next to the Chiriquí River Rafting office, charges US$1 an hour for Internet access. Travelers can also make international calls here.

Mail Boxes Etc. (Avenida Central, tel. 720-2684, 8:30 A.M.–6 P.M. Mon.–Fri., 8:30 A.M.–12:30 P.M. Sat.), across from La Reina, offers a variety of communication services, including sending and receiving faxes. Internet access is US$1 an hour.

Pharmacies

A branch of **Farmacia Revilla** (tel. 720-2995, 7 A.M.–9 P.M. Mon.–Sat., 10 A.M.–6 P.M. Sun.) is at the north end of town near the church.

Farmacia Danka (Calle 3 Sur, tel. 720-2367, 8 A.M.–8:30 P.M. Mon.–Sat., 8:30 A.M.–6:30 P.M. Sun.) is a pharmacy next to Hostel Mamallena. **Farmacia Any** (Avenida Central, tel. 720-1296, 8 A.M.–9 P.M. daily) is just north of Super Centro Bruña on the east side of Avenida Central.

Laundry

Lavandería La Mejor (Calle 1 Sur, tel. 720-1280, 8 A.M.–5 P.M. Mon.–Sat., 9 A.M.–1 P.M. Sun.) charges US$4.28 to wash and dry a load. It's a half block west of Avenida Central on Calle 1 Sur.

Spanish-Language Courses

The **Habla Ya Language School** (Los Establos Plaza, tel. 720-1294, cell 6480-4506, www.hablayapanama.com, 8 A.M.–8 P.M. Mon.–Fri., 9 A.M.–2 P.M. Sat.) offers a flexible menu of Spanish courses that includes an ultra-compressed "Spanish for travelers" package (10–20 hours over 2–5 days), beginner crash courses, and longer-term, total-immersion packages that can include homestays with local families. Prices are per hour, starting at US$8.75–12.75 (group class) or US$13.75–17.75 (private lessons). Special offers are sometimes available. Free extras at the school include a café with wireless Internet, Wednesday-night Spanish-language movies, conversation sessions, and Saturday afternoon salsa and merengue lessons. The school also arranges lodging, field trips, and outdoor adventures.

Spanish by the River (tel. 720-3456, cell 6759-5753, spanishbytheriverboquete@gmail.com, www.spanishatlocations.com) is actually by a road, not the river. Specifically, it's in Alto Boquete just off the main road, on the turnoff that leads to Palmira. However, it's a pleasant spot, and it's a quick bus ride or US$0.60 shared cab ride to downtown. Instruction is given in open-air classrooms in the school's spacious and surprisingly quiet backyard. Prices start at US$185 per week for small group classes.

Students can spend part of their course at the school's sister facilities, Spanish by the Sea in Bocas del Toro and in Turrialba, Costa Rica. The school can also arrange tours, horseback riding trips, and volunteer work.

The staff can arrange home stays, and there are also four small, spotless rooms with good beds at the school itself. (Prices range US$10–30.) Priority is given to students, but anyone can stay here when there's no demand. Most people don't realize this, so it's possible to find a room here even when more expensive and less appealing accommodations are full in downtown Boquete.

GETTING THERE

The city of David, in the lowlands, is less than 40 kilometers from Boquete and is the transportation hub for buses and planes to and from other parts of the country, most notably Bocas del Toro and Panama City. Some hotels and guides offer transportation to David, the west side of Barú, the Costa Rican border, and Almirante, the port of entry for the archipelago of Bocas del Toro. Fees for this service generally range US$20–30 for David–Boquete up to US$150–200 for Boquete–Almirante.

Boquete is 45 minutes by car from David, seven hours from Panama City. Those driving west from Panama City should turn right at the first major intersection upon entering David. It's a straight shot up to Boquete on a road that is being widened to a four-lane divided highway which is being completed ahead of schedule and may be finished by the time you read this.

Boquete-bound buses leave the David bus terminal about every 20–25 minutes, 5:15 A.M.–9 P.M., with a final bus at 9:45 P.M. David-bound buses leave Boquete approximately every 20–25 minutes, 4:15 A.M.–7 P.M. Buses are slightly less frequent in the evenings, but more frequent during the flower fair. Catch the bus to David in front of the Hostal Palacio on the northwest side of the plaza. The trip costs US$1.75 each way and takes about 45 minutes. The buses are mostly converted yellow school buses, so they're hard to miss.

Boquete Tree Trek (Los Establos Plaza, tel. 720-1635, www.aventurist.com) offers a shuttle service between David or David's airport (US$10). It can also help arrange car rentals and plane tickets. Some hotels offer pickup and drop-off service, usually for an extra fee.

Taxis between Boquete and David cost US$25 (downtown or bus station) and US$30 (airport). Expect to pay US$40–60 for trips to Cerro Punta or the Costa Rican border. A trip to the Respingo entrance to Sendero Los Quetzales, on the Cerro Punta side of Barú, costs US$80. It's also possible to arrange a taxi between Boquete and Almirante, the jumping-off point for the islands of Bocas del Toro. Expect to pay anywhere from US$135–180.

Those transferring to Bocas who have a spirit of adventure should also consider contacting **Lost and Found Eco-Resort** (cell 6432-8182 or 6920-3036, lflodge@gmail.com or info@ lostandfoundlodge.com, www.lostandfound-lodge.com), a hostel east of Boquete on the Fortuna Road. Anyone going between Bocas and Boquete by road passes by the hostel, which is near the Continental Divide. Lately the hostel has been offering a transfer service between Boquete and Bocas that can be combined with tours of the attractions along the way, outdoor adventures, and/or overnight stays. The cost for pure transportation ranges US$40–70 per person, two-person minimum. The per-person rate depends on the number of people in the group.

Driving between Boquete and the Volcán/Cerro Punta side of the mountain has until recently meant heading down the mountain towards David, traveling down the Interamericana, and then heading back up the mountain. But a new road now connects Cerro Punta with the Boquete side of the mountain near Dolega. It's a windy, two-lane road through cattle country, so, surprisingly, taking this route doesn't save time, particularly if one gets stuck behind a herd of cows: the trip between downtown Boquete and Cerro Punta takes about 1.5 hours. The road is new and the drive is lovely, with spectacular views of the mountains and wide valleys. Until road signs are installed, though, it's a bit tricky to find one's way, particularly when traveling from Cerro Punta to Boquete. A good local tip is to, at any intersection, choose the road with a yellow lane line.

To find the road from Boquete, head south for 22 kilometers past the CEFATI. At the intersection near Dolega, make a sharp right turn at the gas station. Stay left when the road forks and follow the yellow-lined road. The road ends in a T-intersection at Cuesta de Piedra, about two kilometers south of Cerro Punta. Turn right for Cerro Punta or left to head down the mountain towards Volcán.

GETTING AROUND

You probably won't need transportation in town since it's easy to walk from one end of Boquete to another in just a few minutes. Buses and taxis to surrounding areas are plentiful and cheap. Taxis can be hard to come by at night.

Drivers should be careful at night. The streets outside of town are dark and have no sidewalks. Pedestrians often walk down the middle of the streets at night.

Urbana minibuses that roam around the nearby hills leave from Avenida Central just north of the plaza. Their destinations are written on their windows. ("El Bajo" refers to Bajo Boquete, not Bajo Mono.)

Since taxis here are reasonable, you may want to try them first for nearby destinations. It's easy to get one along Avenida Central. Taxis within town shouldn't cost more than US$1.50. Taxis to places just outside of Boquete, such as El Explorador and Mi Jardín Es Su Jardín, should be around US$3 or less. A taxi to Alto Boquete should be less than US$2. The drive to the ranger station *caseta* for the climb up Volcán Barú is US$8 for one or two people and should be made in a pickup taxi. The fare to the beginning of the Bajo Mono loop is US$6.05.

The fare is also at least US$10 to the Alto Chiquero ranger station, near the Boquete-side trailhead for Sendero Los Quetzales. Expect to pay US$15 to get within walking distance of the Pozos de Caldera.

Daniel Higgins (cell 6617-0570) is a fully bilingual Panamanian taxi driver with an excellent reputation. He is punctual, good-natured, friendly, interesting to talk to, and, most important, a safe and skilled driver. He'll drive you around in his late-model four-wheel drive for US$20 an hour, which includes a commentary on the history of the area. Longer trips include Cerro Punta (US$65) and Almirante (US$150), the jumping-off point for the islands of Bocas del Toro.

Juan Carlos Contreras (cell 6709-5369, tel. 720-1140—ask the dispatcher for Juan Carlos), is another option. He doesn't speak English but understands a fair amount. He charges US$15 an hour. Both Higgins and Contreras also offer regular taxi service to the surrounding areas for the going rates.

Cerro Punta and Vicinity

The west side of Volcán Barú looks like a pastoral paradise. As the road winds its way up the foggy mountains, it passes one tranquil dairy farm after another. Soon there are neat quilts of green-and-brown farmland clinging at impossible angles to mountain slopes. Down in the valleys, racehorses romp in vast pastures. It's all so picturesque it's easy to overlook the fact that intensive farming is damaging this beautiful area. Erosion and pesticide overuse are serious problems. The developed land also borders two of Panama's most spectacular parks, and in some cases encroaches on them. Illegal logging, farming, and even cattle ranching still take place in them.

Environmentalists have made some difference here, though, including stopping an ill-conceived plan a few years back to build a road right through the heart of one of the national parks. Hikes through these parks are thus still among the great attractions of the area. Cerro Punta has the most accessible entry into Parque Internacional La Amistad, a park so important UNESCO declared it a World Heritage Site in 1990.

All the towns and tourist sights on the west side of Barú are linked by a single road that starts in the lowland town of Concepción and ends at Guadalupe, elevation 2,130 meters. The first town is Volcán, officially known as Hato de Volcán, which has most of the visitor services, but little else.

The road forks here. Straight leads to a little-used Costa Rican border crossing at Río Sereno. A right turn leads farther up the mountain toward Bambito, Cerro Punta, and Guadalupe. Bambito has hotels and a few places to eat, but the town itself is really just a few roadside stands. The vistas open up at little Cerro Punta and tiny Guadalupe just beyond it. You're up in the clouds here, and you may feel you've found Shangri-la.

The town of Cerro Punta consists of little more than a small commercial strip in the middle of a heavily developed agricultural area. There are gas stations, a couple of dreary bars and pool halls, a few greasy-spoon restaurants, small grocery stores, and a launderette.

SIGHTS

Natural beauty is the major draw of this area, particularly for those looking to hike in the mammoth Parque Internacional La Amistad or along the popular Sendero Los Quetzales. Visitors will get more out of the hikes with the help of a naturalist guide; it also greatly improves the chances of spotting quetzals. Those with extra time should consider a visit to the impressive Finca Dracula orchid farm. The horse, strawberry, and flower farms are also worth a quick visit.

◖ Parque Internacional La Amistad

The enormous and magnificent Parque Internacional La Amistad (PILA), which lies along the Talamanca mountain range, was established in September 1988 and declared a UNESCO World Heritage Site in 1990. A little less than half of it is in Costa Rica, which leaves 207,000 hectares on the Panama side. Nearly all of this land is in the province of Bocas del Toro, but the 3 percent of it that pokes into Chiriquí province is far more accessible.

The park's plant and animal life are among the most diverse in Panama. The forests vary from lowland tropical to subalpine, and much of the vegetation is virgin. Five of the six species of Central American felines—the jaguar, puma, ocelot, jaguarundi, and margay—are still hanging on here, as is the also-endangered Baird's tapir. Among the nearly 600 types of birds identified in the area are such spectacular species as the resplendent quetzal, the three-wattled bellbird, and the rarely seen bare-necked umbrellabird.

All that said, you may not see much wildlife other than birds on a day hike near Cerro Punta. But the park is well worth a visit even if you're not a birding fanatic. The forests are dense and varied, and there are several kilometers of well-maintained trails near town.

The main entrance to the park is at Las Nubes, about seven kilometers west of Cerro Punta. Heading up to Cerro Punta from the south, look for the sign indicating a left turn off the main road just before one enters downtown. Make another left at the Las Nubes sign. The road from this point on can sometimes be brutal. Ask about its current state before venturing here without a four-wheel drive. Round-trip taxi fare from Cerro Punta is US$5–7.

An **ANAM ranger station** (regional office tel. 775-3163 or 775-2055; there's a radio but no phone at the station itself; 8 or 8:30 A.M.–4 P.M. daily) is on the right at the end of the road, where the trails start. Follow the signs to the *sede administrativa*. Pay the entrance fee (US$5) here and get trail maps from the friendly staff. There's a small display on the park and its flora and fauna.

There's also a *comida corriente* (fast food) restaurant next door. Camping is possible in the park for an additional US$6 a night; some choose just to pitch a tent in the grassy field by the ranger station, which also has dorm beds, cooking facilities, and a common room with a large fireplace (US$15 pp).

Finca Dracula

Don't worry, you don't need to bring garlic.

© WILLIAM FRIAR

one of the more than 2,000 species of orchids at Finca Dracula

Finca Dracula (tel. 771-2070, www.fincadracula.com) is named for the 30 varieties of the *Telipogon vampirus* that are among the more than 2,000 species of orchids found in this famous botanical garden. It has one of the most important collections in Latin America—it claims to be one of the 10 largest in the world—and is known for its experiments in propagating endangered species. The lovely landscaped grounds, which are crisscrossed with streams and ponds, make for a pleasant walk.

The collections at the finca are contained in three areas, separated according to climate, from those that thrive at the local temperature of 14–20°C up to those that need a temperature of 25°C or higher. Specimens include carnivorous orchids, orchids the size of a nail head, orchids that disguise themselves as bees, orchids with a delicious fragrance, and orchids that bloom for only one day.

Finca Dracula is in Guadalupe, about a 20-minute walk or very short car ride past Los Quetzales Lodge and Spa. When the road splits past the hotel, take the right fork and then turn left onto the gravel road. You'll need a four-wheel drive if you're driving. You'll see a sign across the gate of the finca on the left, at the turnoff to the entrance to the dirt road that leads to the Los Quetzales cabanas.

Contact Finca Dracula to reserve a tour and get a 10 percent discount, or just drop by. Guides speak little English. Minimum tour length is half an hour, but it can go quite a bit longer depending on the level of detail you're interested in. Tours are available 8–11:30 A.M. and 1–4 P.M. daily. The cost is US$10 per person.

Farms

Those who want to get a closer look at some of the crops the rich volcanic soil and mild weather of this region produce may be interested in paying a quick visit to the flower and strawberry farms. They're more photogenic and interesting than you might think. Several of them are located along the road that links Guadalupe and the turnoff to Parque Internacional La Amistad. There's no need to make an appointment. Just stop by during regular business hours and ask if you can poke around. They might think you're a little strange, but they'll probably let you.

Haras Cerro Punta (tel. 771-2057, www.harascerropunta.com) breeds some of Panama's best racehorses in one of Panama's prettiest spots. The *haras* (stud farm) comprises wide-open pastureland ringed by mountains. Visitors are welcome to tour the farm with advance notice. The main entrance is just before Guadalupe on the Cerro Punta–Guadalupe road, but visitors should come through the entrance on the opposite, downhill side of the farm.

SPORTS AND RECREATION

Hiking and looking for quetzals in the national parks are the big activities here, but there are

© WILLIAM FRIAR

The fertile hills around Cerro Punta are farmed intensively.

a few other outdoor possibilities. White-water companies are headquartered in Boquete, on the other side of Barú, but they can usually pick clients up here for trips on either side of the mountain. Cerro Punta produces the finest horses in the country. Visitors can arrange rides on much more modest steeds for around US$5–6 an hour. **Los Quetzales Lodge and Spa** (tel. 771-2182 or 771-2291, fax 771-2226, www.losquetzales.com) charges US$8 an hour to hire a horse, with an extra US$5 for a guide. The hotel also rents mountain bikes for US$5 an hour.

Genover "Ito" Santamaria (cell 6501-1621) is a friendly, reliable guide who works with some of the local hotels. He specializes in long hikes, including ones to the summit of Volcán Barú (US$80 for two people) and Sendero Los Quetzales to Boquete (US$40 for two people). He's also available for multiday treks. Call him directly, or ask about him through your hotel.

A good guide is essential on wilderness trails,

particularly up Volcán Barú. But for nearby, less rugged destinations, it's simpler to make arrangements on your own than to go through a guide. This is especially true of visits to Finca Dracula, which supplies its own tour guides for a fraction of what third-party outfits charge.

Hiking in Parque Internacional La Amistad

Three main trails start from the ANAM ranger station at Parque Internacional La Amistad. **Sendero La Cascada** is a 3.4-kilometer, two-hour round-trip hike that leads to a picture-perfect 55-meter waterfall. The trail is wide and well maintained. It's a 1.7-kilometer uphill hike to the falls, with the elevation climbing from 2,180 to about 2,500 meters. There are three miradors along the trail with sweeping views of the mountains and valleys. However, if it's a foggy day, you won't see a thing from them.

The first platform is unmarked, but it's on the right as the trail levels off and comes out of the woods. Mirador La Nevera is on the left a little farther on. The trail forks at Mirador El Barranco. To get to the falls, head down the steep wooden staircase to the right. (Some of the stairs are loose and slippery. Watch your step.) Those in the mood for more exercise can take the left fork. If it's a clear day, a two-hour hike from here offers a view of the Caribbean.

Sendero El Retoño, a two-kilometer loop trail, is much less strenuous but even more beautiful. The trail is mostly level and remarkably varied. It leads through lush green forest, over bridges spanning rushing streams, and into a tunnel formed from leaning stands of bamboo. The hike takes about an hour at a very leisurely pace.

There are a few forks along the trail: To stay on the main trail, just take every left fork. For a longer hike, there's a loop within the loop that starts halfway down the trail at a marked fork to the right. It ends near the exit to the main trail.

A newer trail, **Vereda La Montaña,** leads

up the side of Cerro Picacho. According to the rangers, this rustic trail (*vereda* is Spanish for footpath) is four kilometers long and a quite strenuous uphill trek, though there's a wooden cabin with a kitchen and bathroom at the top. Ask the rangers about it before attempting this hike. Allow six hours for the trip up and back.

For those who just want to take a little stroll, **Sendero Panamá Verde** is a 400-meter walk near the ranger station that takes about 15 minutes to walk. Do not attempt any of the longer hikes without a good guide. The forest here is rugged wilderness, and it's very easy to get lost. Those who speak Spanish can ask the forest ranger at Las Nubes for guidance. It's possible to camp in the park or stay in a dormitory at the ANAM station.

Serious trekkers may be interested to know there's an unmarked eight-hour hike through the forest to some hot springs, though this should not be attempted without an experienced guide. That's one-way; you'd have to camp out by the springs.

For the truly hard core, there's also the possibility of multiday treks over the cordillera toward the Caribbean coast. Los Quetzales Lodge and Spa may be able to help arrange an eight-day trek for those feeling brave. This is an extremely hard-core trip through mountainous wilderness and deep mud. You'll spend the last two days traveling in *cayucos* (dugout canoes) through Naso (also called Teribe) territory. For food and shelter you'll mostly rely on friendly folk living in huts in the woods. Trekkers must have their own tents, sleeping bags, and all other equipment. Los Quetzales has booked this trip only once. Even the Naso who live in this forest will probably think you're nuts.

Sendero Los Quetzales

This popular trail through Parque Nacional Volcán Barú curves around the north side of Barú, linking Cerro Punta with Boquete to the east. Hiking it in either direction is far less challenging than a climb to the top of Barú, but it's still a serious hike.

Note: The trail was closed and not being maintained as of early 2012. All the information below assumes the trail has been repaired and reopened, which is scheduled to happen by 2013. If it hasn't been, do not attempt to hike it. For one thing, it's against the law. For another, when the trail is bad, it's dangerous. Since its closure, it's been dubbed a *trampa de muerte* (death trap) in the Panamanian press. Without bridges and a well-defined trail, it's all too easy to get swept away attempting to ford a stream that a sudden rainstorm has turned into a flooded, raging river. Finally, if you do hurt yourself and have to be rescued, you'll pay the entire cost of the rescue.

It's not essential to have a guide, at least in this direction, but do not attempt it alone. Bring a first-aid kit. Do not hike the trail in shorts; it's cool in the forest, and if it rains it gets downright cold. A walking stick can come in handy.

The Sendero Los Quetzales gives a taste of real wilderness, but when it's maintained, it's well-defined enough that it's not technically difficult to walk. And, because of the rapid change in elevation, it offers a vivid lesson in life zones, starting with mossy cloud forest dotted with towering oaks and picture-postcard streams that quickly give way to palms, bamboo, and serpentine lianas and vines. You'll encounter some forest giants, but most of the forest is secondary growth. Despite its name, this trail is not the best place to see quetzals.

There are lots of signs along the trail, though whoever put them up has a fanciful sense of distance; don't pay much attention to them. About a third of the way down, there's a designated campsite with few facilities other than an open-sided wooden shelter and some rotting benches. The ground slopes at a pretty steep angle; campers who want to pitch a tent here are best off doing it in the relatively level shelter. A short walk behind this campsite leads to a couple of miradors, the second of which has a beautiful, expansive view down toward Boquete. The red-roofed building off in the distance is the little ranger station at the Boquete entrance to the trail.

It's less grueling to hike the trail from Cerro Punta to Boquete than vice versa since it's downhill most of the way, descending nearly a kilometer in altitude (though there is an uphill stretch at the end, just when you think you're literally out of the woods).

The hike requires some planning since hikers end up far away from Cerro Punta, on the other side of the mountain. The bus ride back takes at least three hours, not including waiting time in David, where you have to switch buses. The best strategy is to leave early in the morning and either have someone meet you with a car at the end of the trail or plan to spend the night in Boquete. Some who choose the latter option arrange to have their luggage shipped ahead to Boquete, usually through their hotel or guide, but be sure to nail down exactly when the luggage will arrive. Some tourists have had their luggage sent by couriers who only make the trip once a day, leaving them stranded without their belongings, waiting for their luggage to catch up with them.

So how long will the hike down take? This question trips up a lot of hikers, who end up with a much longer outing than they bargained for. It takes an average of five hours to get from El Respingo ranger station (near Cerro Punta) to the Alto Chiquero ranger station (near Boquete, sometimes known as La Roca), but that doesn't take into account getting to and from the ranger stations.

El Respingo station is at the end of 5.5 kilometers of uphill road that branches off the main road that links Cerro Punta and Guadalupe. The turnoff is halfway between Cerro Punta and Guadalupe, or about 1.5 kilometers past the Hotel Cerro Punta. As you head toward Guadalupe, there's a huge trail sign on the right just after a little bridge. Turn here and follow

the road toward the Bajo Grande area. The road soon turns brutal and drivers must have a four-wheel drive with high clearance.

If you want to walk to the station from the turnoff, add about two hours to the hiking estimate. You may want to opt instead for a taxi, which will cost about US$30 from Cerro Punta to the station. Guests at Los Quetzales Lodge and Spa can get a ride to or from the El Respingo station for the same price, in a van that can carry up to 10 people. An alternative is to hire a taxi to take you to the end of the paved road (US$3) and then hike the rest of the way to the station, which cuts the two-hour walk in half.

Those with a vehicle can park near the station. Don't leave anything of value in the car. Park entrance is US$5, US$1 to park, US$6 to camp, or US$15 for a bunk bed in the quite nice ranger station.

From the Alto Chiquero ranger station at the Boquete end it's another 1.5-hour hike to get to the Bajo Mono loop road. From there you can catch one of the frequent buses to downtown Boquete for US$1.

Finca Fernández, on the road to Sendero Los Quetzales, has long been famous as a prime place to see quetzals. Sadly, there have been so many reports of thefts from tourists' cars here over the years that it is not recommended as a safe place to visit. There are plenty of other places to see quetzals and plenty of other guides to find them for you.

ACCOMMODATIONS

There are only a few, widely scattered places to stay around Cerro Punta. Fortunately, these include a couple of appealing possibilities. There is now a hostel in Cerro Punta, though backpackers may find the dorm options at Los Quetzales Lodge and Spa more appealing, if more expensive.

US$25-50

Hostal Elvita (tel. 771-2014, US$15 pp), on the main road next to Hotel Cerro Punta, has three pleasant dorms with wooden floors and dirty shared bathrooms. It's in an attractive old country house that has a communal kitchen and a common area with a large stone fireplace and plate-glass windows overlooking the mountains. The framed photo on the mantelpiece is a tribute to the old owner of the house, for whom the hostel is named. There's an Internet-wired computer that guests can use for US$1/hour.

Hotel Cerro Punta (tel. 771-2020, US$45 s/d) is on the left just as one approaches downtown Cerro Punta. It offers 10 decent rooms with okay beds. Six of the rooms are in an annex facing a gorgeous view of the mountains. Perversely, the windows are in the back, looking out on nothing. The rooms in the main building are nicer, and two have a good view for no extra charge. The service here is friendly.

US$50-100

Las Orquídeas B&B (Bajo Grande Road, tel. 771-2687, http://lasorquideaspanama.com, starts at US$62.50 s/d, including breakfast) is on the way to the El Respingo entrance to Sendero Los Quetzales. It's 400 meters up a narrow road above the huge trail sign. It's a small B&B wedged between the road and a pretty brook with three plain, dark rooms with squishy mattresses. Rooms are US$62.50–88 depending on size and the number of beds; the largest room sleeps four. There's also a split-level cabin, but it's not very appealing. Facilities are fairly basic, but there's a friendly, homey vibe to the place, which is run a young Brazilian-Panamanian man, his Chinese-Panamanian wife, and her mother, who has lived in Panama for more than two decades but is still very shy about her Spanish. The mother is the namesake of Mama Jenny's Chinese Cuisine, the B&B's little restaurant. This place does not yet see many foreign tourists and is mainly patronized by visiting Panamanians looking for a reasonable place to sleep.

Easily the best-run place to stay on this side

of the mountain is ◀ **Hostal Cielito Sur Bed and Breakfast** (tel./fax 771-2038, cell 6602-3008, www.cielitosur.com, starts at US$104.50 s/d, closed in Oct., two-night minimum in high season). Along with Los Quetzales Lodge and Spa, it is also the coziest and most pleasant. Actually 4 kilometers south of Cerro Punta and 10 kilometers north of Volcán in a postage stamp–size community called Nueva Suiza, Cielito Sur sits by itself on 2.5 hectares of land just off the main road, but within easy driving distance of most of the area's attractions. It consists of four comfortable, spacious rooms, each with decor inspired by one of Panama's indigenous peoples—the Guna and Teribe rooms (US$104.50 s/d), and the larger Ngöbe-Buglé and Wounaan-Emberá rooms (US$115.50 s/d), which also have a minifridge and microwave. Even if you don't stay in the Wounaan-Emberá room, you should ask to check out the especially beautiful specimens of their woven baskets mounted on the wall. Janet and Glenn have recently added a self-catering option, Casita Margarita, which has two bedrooms and a full kitchen. It can accommodate up to four guests for US$126.50. Breakfast is not included, and there's a three-night minimum with this option.

Beds are very firm and the bathrooms and other fixtures are getting a bit dated, but the rooms are clean and well-maintained. In fact, everything here is done right. The back patio of the bed-and-breakfast overlooks a spring-fed stream that runs through a carefully tended garden that attracts 10 species of hummingbirds. A stay includes an enormous breakfast (try the delicious French toast, which is made with banana-nut bread) in a sunny dining room and use of a private, enclosed hot tub. There's a common lounge with a fireplace, CD player and CDs, library, wireless Internet access, and Internet-connected computer (free).

Your hosts are Janet and Glenn Lee, a Panamanian-American couple who speak fluent

English and Spanish and are a good source of information on just about anything you'd like to know about the whole area. They can arrange transfers to or from David for US$35 each way, and ground transportation to or from just about anywhere else in western Panama, including Bocas and the Costa Rican border, as well as make domestic plane reservations and ground-transfer arrangements to or from Panama City. Rates depend on the destination.

Los Quetzales Lodge and Spa (tel. 771-2291 or 774-5555, www.losquetzales.com, starts at US$85 s/d/t, including breakfast at the lodge) is really a destination in itself. Mostly this is because some of the accommodations are in a 350-acre private cloud-forest reserve that's inside both a national park (Parque Nacional Volcán Barú) and an international one (Parque Internacional La Amistad). The owner bought land here in 1968, before the parks were founded. Los Quetzales was one of Panama's first ecotourism operations and remains among its most committed.

As the name suggests, there are actually two Los Quetzales: a hotel in the little town of Guadalupe, three kilometers past Cerro Punta, and five large cabins in a forest farther uphill. The hotel is an attractive place with lots of handsome woodwork, on the edge of a fast-flowing river. It features 10 rooms next to the main building and five large suites and dorm rooms in a nearby annex. The main building resembles a comfy ski lodge, and the smells wafting up from the bakery/pizzeria on the 1st floor add to the cozy feel. There's an Internet café, bar, restaurant, and rec room on the 2nd floor. The paintings everywhere, some of them rather spooky, are by Brooke "Cookie" Alfaro, the host's brother and one of Panama's most famous artists.

Small rooms have one queen and one single bed and a shower for US$85 s/d/t. Larger, considerably nicer and brighter rooms with bathtubs and terraces are US$95 s/d/t. Suites go for US$115–130 and sleep up to four people.

These are quite large and have fireplaces, sitting rooms, and balconies. One of the suites is wheelchair accessible. All the rooms have orthopedic beds and phones that can be used for local and international calls.

There are also three dorm rooms crowded with bunk beds, featuring the same warm wood as the private rooms. Each has a shared toilet and shower. The smallest dorm room has lockers. Dorm beds are US$18, or US$7 more with continental breakfast. One of the cabins in the park also has dorm beds, for US$20 pp. Transportation between the lodge and the cabins is US$10 each way.

A health spa right next to the river helps guests recover from a grueling hike with a massage, sauna, or dip in an outdoor hot tub. Packages are available that include various combinations of accommodations, spa treatments and/or hikes, and meals. All packages include use of the sauna, and some include free horse hire and use of mountain bikes and fishing gear.

Cabins are slightly rustic, but they're comfortable and nicely designed. None of the cabins has electricity, but all have wood-burning stoves or fireplaces, hot water, and a kitchen. Ten kinds of colorful hummingbirds are among the more than 100 species of birds identified near here. You'll see them buzzing around like mosquitoes.

The cabins are built at more than 2,020 meters above sea level, right in the middle of a stunning cloud forest. The Chiriquí Viejo River runs through the property.

Rates for the cabins are US$140–180, sleeping between three and eight people. Most of the cabins offer enough privacy that friendly acquaintances can share to save money. An "Estate House" with eight bedrooms and five bathrooms is outside the park. It can accommodate up to 22 people for US$230.

Daily guided hikes in the park are included with stays in the cabin or Estate House. Eight trails originate from the area around the cabins. Foggy mountains, trees draped in moss, waterfalls, orchids, the lovely songs of countless birds—it's like a fairy kingdom up there. Daily tours, led by Ngöbe-Buglé guides who speak only Spanish, are available. Los Quetzales can supply boots, rain jackets, and horses. There's a good chance of seeing quetzals here January–May.

The park cabins are only 2.5 kilometers from the main hotel in Guadalupe, but the road is so ferociously bad it takes about 25 minutes to get there by four-wheel-drive vehicle. (Transportation is included with cabin rental, except for those staying in the cabin dorms.) Among other things, vehicles must ford a shallow river. That's something to bear in mind if you decide to hike in. Even if you go by four-wheel drive, it's a short but steep walk up to some of the cabins.

Camping

It's possible to camp in **Parque Internacional La Amistad** for US$6, but as usual with Panamanian parks, don't expect developed campsites, though there is a lawn around the ranger station where some choose to pitch a tent. There's also a surprisingly pleasant dormitory at the **ANAM station** at the main entrance to the park for US$15 pp. It offers bunk beds in shared rooms, a large fireplace, and a kitchen. Bring your own bedding. Some campers choose to pitch their tent on the lawn next to the station car park, which gives them access to the station facilities, including bathroom and kitchen, for the US$6 camping fee. For more information, ask at the station, or call the ANAM regional office in David (tel. 775-3163).

There's a similar setup at **El Respingo ranger station** at the trailhead for Sendero Los Quetzales. It'll cost US$6 to camp or US$15 for a bunk bed in the quite decent ranger station, which is on a hill surrounded by nicely landscaped grounds. The view from here is stunning, and it's a great place to pitch a tent. The bunks are in a small, dark wooden room that's quite okay and has lockers.

FOOD

There are few dining options this far up the mountain. More possibilities are farther down, around Bambito and Volcán. Many small kiosks also offer fruit shakes, burgers, and the like for a couple of dollars along the road from Volcán all the way to Guadalupe. Most of them are between Bambito and Cerro Punta. There are also some fruit and vegetable stands for those who want to stock up on fresh produce.

Meals are a roll of the dice at **Los Quetzales Lodge and Spa** (tel. 771-2291 or 774-5555, 6–10 A.M., noon–2 P.M., and 6–10 P.M. daily). Chefs come and go, and the only constant here is inconsistency. However, the surroundings are pleasant and the restaurant typically features trout from Los Quetzales's own pond, produce from its own garden, dairy from its own cow, and pizza made in its own wood-burning pizza oven.

The little [C] **Mama Jenny's Chinese Cuisine** (Bajo Grande Road, tel. 771-2687, cell 6464-6688, www.lasorquideaspanama.com, 11 A.M.–8 P.M. Mon.–Sat., US$6–8), in Las Orquídeas B&B, serves the best Chinese food in Chiriquí. The cook is Chinese, the mother of one of the young owners of the B&B, and the "restaurant" is three tables in her kitchen, plus a few more on a glassed-in terrace above a rushing brook with a lovely view of a well-tended garden and the forested slope of a hill. The food is hearty, tasty, and somewhat greasy Chinese home-cooking.

The decor is plain in the dining room of the **Hotel Cerro Punta** (on the left as you approach downtown Cerro Punta, tel. 771-2020, US$10 or less), but the food is surprisingly tasty and the service is refreshingly warm and friendly. The veggie rice dish (*arroz jardinero*) is a godsend for those tired of meat and deep-fried starches. There's also the usual assortment of meats and fish. The fresh-fruit shakes (*batidos*) are pretty good.

INFORMATION AND SERVICES

Services are limited on this side of the mountain and become sparser the higher up you go. Cerro Punta has some basic necessities, but for many things (such as an ATM) visitors have to go down at least as far as Volcán. The main road through town has hole-in-the-wall restaurants, a grocery store, a produce market, a couple of gas stations, and, midway down, a police station.

Many services are on an unmarked loop road toward the Las Nubes entrance to PILA that leads off this downtown strip. Heading up toward Guadalupe, turn left off the main road at Restaurante La Fé. It's the first left turn after Hotel Cerro Punta. **Fernando Cyber Café** (tel. 771-2778, 8:30 A.M.–early evening daily) charges US$0.65/hour for Internet access. The local **Centro de Salud** (public health clinic) is next door. Across the road is the minimal but helpful **Farmacia Omaira** (tel. 771-2012, 8 A.M.–7 P.M. Mon.–Sat., 11 A.M.–7 P.M. Sun.)

Supercentro Cerro Punta (7 A.M.–10 P.M., daily) is a large but basic supermarket and general store next to Hostel Elvita on the main road.

Lavandería Cerro Punta (8 A.M.–7 P.M. Sun.–Fri.) is on the left as one drives through Cerro Punta on the way to Guadalupe. It charges US$3 to wash and dry a load.

GETTING THERE

The lowland city of David is the bus and airline hub for the western highlands. It takes 6–7 hours by car to get from Panama City to David. From there it's about a two-hour drive to Cerro Punta. If you're driving from David, take the Interamericana west to Concepción, 26 kilometers away. Turn right and head uphill. After another 34 kilometers you'll come to Volcán. Turn right at the fork to get to Bambito, Cerro Punta, and Guadalupe. There may be no sign at the intersection except one pointing toward Hotel Bambito. Follow it. Bambito is the first

place you'll come to, about six kilometers north of Volcán. Cerro Punta is about another eight winding kilometers farther up the mountain.

In all, Cerro Punta is about 74 kilometers from David. The village of Guadalupe is three kilometers farther uphill.

Bus fare from David is US$3.50 to Cerro Punta or Guadalupe. Look for the bus with Cerro Punta painted on the windshield; it stops at all the towns along the way. The Cerro Punta bus should go all the way to Guadalupe, but ask to make sure. If not, taxi fare from Cerro Punta to Guadalupe is US$1. Buses bound for Cerro Punta leave David 5 A.M.–8 P.M.; David-bound buses leave Cerro Punta 4:45 A.M.–6:45 P.M. Buses run every 15 minutes. Those coming from Costa Rica can also catch the Cerro Punta bus at Concepción rather than go all the way to the David bus terminal. Taxis between David and Cerro Punta charge around US$35 one way. Taxis between Volcán and Cerro Punta are US$8; it's US$9 between Volcán and Guadalupe.

GETTING AROUND

This is a pleasant place to go for a walk, though attractions, hotels, and restaurants tend to be rather spread out. You can flag down any long-distance minibus running along the main road, since they all make stops between Cerro Punta/Guadalupe and Volcán on their way to or from David. For destinations off the main road, taxis are the best way to go. Sample fares include US$1 between Cerro Punta and Guadalupe, around US$5–7 between Cerro Punta and the Las Nubes entrance to PILA, and US$30 from Cerro Punta up the brutal road to El Respingo, the trailhead for Sendero Los Quetzales.

Volcán and Vicinity

Volcán is what passes for an urban center on the west side of Barú. It's really little more than a crossroads, but there are several sights and an entrance to Parque Nacional Volcán Barú nearby. It also has the only banks and ATMs for many kilometers, as well as most of the dining options.

Volcán definitely has its charms, though most of them are natural ones outside the town itself and can be explored easily by those who make their base elsewhere. There are a couple of decent places to stay between Volcán and Bambito, but for the most part the choice is between lousy budget hotels that charge too much and overpriced luxury hotels that aren't that luxurious. Unless you plan to explore the area extensively, you may want to head up toward Cerro Punta, 14 kilometers up the mountain, where the lodging and scenery are more attractive.

SIGHTS
Parque Nacional Volcán Barú

Though only a fraction the size of its imposing neighbor, La Amistad, this park is still plenty impressive. Its centerpiece is the dormant volcano that gives the park its name and whose summit, at 3,475 meters, is the highest point in Panama. The park was founded in 1976.

This is a good place for long hikes, camping, and bird-watching. Because of the change in elevation, the park has quite a range of life zones for its size (14,000 hectares). You'll pass through several different kinds of forests before reaching its barren and rocky summit. In the bushes near the top you can spot the rather plain-looking volcano junco. This is its only Panamanian habitat. Other birds you might encounter at the higher elevations before the forest ends include the timberline wren, black-and-yellow silky-flycatcher, and large-footed finch.

Lagunas de Volcán

These picturesque lakes are part of a protected area comprising Panama's highest wetlands (the elevation is 1,200 meters). They're famous for good bird-watching. On the lakes there's a chance of seeing masked ducks and northern jacanas. Look for pale-billed woodpeckers, flycatchers, antbirds, and the rare rose-throated becard in the woods.

To get to the *lagunas,* turn left off the main road toward Río Sereno at the sign for the Volcán Inn. Pass the hotel and go straight for 0.9 kilometers. Turn right at Mini Super Casa Elsa and continue straight for 1.7 kilometers on the severely potholed road until you get to the old airstrip. Here you have two choices. You can cross the airstrip and continue straight, but the road is awful. You'll need a powerful four-wheel drive with high clearance. A better option is to head over to La Torcaza Estate and ask to use the shortcut on a better road that runs behind the facility. Ask nicely, because someone has to unlock a gate for you. It might help your cause if you buy some coffee and take their coffee tour.

The *lagunas* are a 15-minute drive from downtown Volcán, more if the road's in bad shape (which it usually is), and requires a four-wheel drive in the rainy season. Taxi fare from downtown Volcán is US$5. Vehicles have been broken into here. If you drive, keep an eye on the car. Admission is free, and there are no facilities.

La Torcaza Estate

This mill and farm (tel. 771-4306, www.estate-cafe.com, tours: 8:30 A.M.–noon, 1–5:30 P.M. Mon.–Sat., open Sun. by arrangement only, free), near Volcán's decaying and more-or-less abandoned airstrip, offers free tours of its facilities, in English or Spanish. It's run by the Janson family and is still known to some as Janson Family Coffee. There's also an espresso bar/shop on the premises where one can sip a cup and watch the beans roast. Buy souvenir packages of coffee here or, if you want to avoid schlepping kilos of coffee around the country, wait until you get home and buy it (for a heftier price) through the Internet. To get to the mill, turn left off the main road toward Río Sereno about 300 meters past the crossroads, at the sign for the Volcán Inn. Pass the hotel and go straight for 0.9 kilometers. Turn right at Mini Super Casa Elsa and continue straight for 1.7 kilometers on the torn-up road until you get to the old airstrip. Turn right onto the airstrip and drive for another kilometer. Look for a gate marked Janson's Coffee House, which leads to a large building off in the distance to the right. That's your destination. A taxi from central Volcán costs about US$3 each way.

Sitio Barriles

This field, on Finca Landau near central Volcán, is one of Panama's most important archaeological sites, but as usual the site (no phone, 7 A.M.–6:30 P.M. daily, free) itself has little to offer visitors but a view of some holes in the ground. Most of the items recovered here are now in Panama City's anthropology museum, which makes for a better visit. Still, those with an archaeological bent may want to take a quick look to help them connect the pieces with their place of origin.

The Barriles culture is intriguing, mostly because so little is known about it. It's believed to have been an agrarian, warrior-dominated society with roots extending back to 734 B.C.

It consisted of about four dozen human settlements that extended from this area to the north and east as far as Cerro Punta. The highland settlements are the most ancient. The relatively lowland Barriles site is much more recent, dating from around 60 B.C. It was the ceremonial center of the Barriles society.

The pieces found here are mysterious. The most numerous are odd stone statues depicting a proud figure wearing a conical hat who is being carried on the shoulders of a stockier

man. Because these pieces were discovered in 1947–1948 through *huaquería* (grave robbing) rather than professional excavation, nearly all their historic context has been lost. But later research has helped to date the site and its treasures. An authorized archaeology dig in 2001 uncovered more pieces.

Barú's last major eruption, in A.D. 600, scattered the Barriles culture, though the Barriles site itself was far enough away from the volcano that it may have remained populated until A.D. 800. There's some evidence it was recolonized in A.D. 1200.

Just about the only remnants of all that history are some petroglyphs near the home of the Landau family, which owns the finca farm the site is on. They're trying to make it a tourist attraction—including neatly embedding some pottery into the walls of a hole in an attempt to simulate what a dig might look like.

If you're pressed for time, you can easily skip this place. They do have some tasty homemade cheese and jams to sell, though.

To get to the site from Volcán, head toward Río Sereno for one kilometer past the crossroads. (If you get to Hotel Don Tavo, you've gone too far.) You should see a sign on the left; make a left turn onto that road. The site is just down the road; look for the sign. A taxi from downtown Volcán shouldn't cost more than US$5.

Los Pozos Termales de Tisingal

These undeveloped hot springs are set in countryside within easy driving distance of Volcán. The road is in surprisingly good shape the whole way, though there are mud traps and steep sections that require a four-wheel drive. A creek runs right across the road near the hot springs, and in the rainy season it can rise high enough to be impassable. If the creek's not too high, park on the near side and wade across, hiking the rest of the way.

The turnoff to the hot springs is 10 kilometers from the Volcán crossroads on the road to

Río Sereno. Look for a sign on the right as you crest a hill. Turn right and follow the winding road until you come to the springs.

C Cañon Macho de Monte

This dramatic canyon, which features sheer faces, waterfalls, and the boulder-choked Río Macho de Monte at the bottom, is a prime bird-watching area. You have a decent chance of spotting orange-collared manakins, riverside wrens, fiery-billed aracaris, and orange-bellied trogons. The turnoff to Macho de Monte is about 12 kilometers south of Volcán at the tiny community of Cuesta de Piedra. If you're heading downhill, the unmarked turn will be on the left. Look for Restaurante El Porvenir and Mini Super Meinor; the road to the canyon is between them. Head down this road for less than three kilometers, past the guardhouse for the hydroelectric plant. You'll cross two bridges. Park by the tin-roofed *rancho* on the right. For a spectacular vista, walk down the slippery path, climb over the barbed wire fence (there to keep cattle in, not you out, and not hard to climb over), and scramble over a few boulders until you come to a vertiginous drop-off. A path near the guardhouse leads down to the river. Ask the guard to point it out.

Truchas de Bambito

If shooting fish in a barrel sounds too challenging, Truchas de Bambito (north of Volcán, tel. 771-4373 or 771-4374, www.hotelbambito.com, 7 A.M.–4 P.M. daily) is for you. This is the Hotel Bambito's trout farm (*trucha* is Spanish for trout). Tons of the big guys swim about in a series of concrete tanks, and you're welcome to fish one out or ask the workers to catch one for you. Catch and release is not allowed.

The trout farm is on the left 0.4 kilometers past Hotel Bambito as you head uphill. Fishing poles are available for rent, and you have to pay for what you catch.

SHOPPING

The **Mercado Horticola, Artesanal, y Turístico de Tierras Altas** (7 A.M.–7 P.M. daily) is a produce and crafts market housed in a warehouse on the right just after one turns off the main road onto the road leading to Cerro Punta. Don't go with high expectations, as the offerings are rather sparse and not great quality. Some of the booths do carry a few traditional Ngöbe crafts. **Volcán Lodge** hosts a community market on Friday mornings.

SPORTS AND RECREATION

The tourist infrastructure on this side of the mountain is far less developed than it is around Boquete. Guiding operations are more casual because there is simply less business.

The same guides who work with hotels in Cerro Punta, such as Genover "Ito" Santamaria, work with hotels down here. One long-established Volcán-based outfit is **Highland Adventures** (tel. 771-4413, ecoaizpurua@hotmail.com), run by Gonzalo Aizpurua. He has been guiding hikers up to the top of Barú for years and offers a range of other hikes and outdoor adventures.

It's usually best to make arrangements through your hotel, particularly if you're staying at Los Quetzales Lodge and Spa or Hostal Cielito Sur in Cerro Punta; these two places should know the best available guides. Another option is to arrange a package with an outside tour operator that employs naturalist guides, such as Ancon Expeditions.

Summiting Volcán Barú is the big physical challenge around here, but there are plenty of other high-adrenaline possibilities, as well as gentler options. **Hostal Cielito Sur** (tel./fax 771-2038, cell 6602-3008, www.cielitosur.com) in Cerro Punta rents mountain bikes for US$5 an hour or US$20 a day. **Hotel Bambito** (tel. 771-4373 or 771-4374, www.hotelbambito.com) rents mountain bikes for US$5 an hour and horses for US$8 an hour.

Hiking

There are three major trails in **Parque Nacional Volcán Barú.** One of these is Sendero Los Quetzales. The other two lead to the summit of Barú from either side of the mountain. On a clear day you can see both oceans from the summit.

From either of these last two trails, reaching the summit takes about five or six hours up and four or five hours down. It's a strenuous climb, but not technically difficult. A very rough road serves as a trail on the east (Boquete) side of the mountain. Neither trail is suitable for children.

Do not attempt the summit trail on this side of the mountain without a safety-conscious and knowledgeable guide. There are lots of forks, and it's easy to get lost, especially when the fog rolls in. It's also essential that you plan well. The average temperature at the higher elevations is 7.2°C (45°F) and it can get down to freezing; hypothermia is a real possibility. And, like every place else in the highlands, it's often incredibly wet. Plan either to start very early or else camp out on the mountain. As an incentive, the best chance of a clear view is to be at the top close to dawn. Bear in mind that even when the volcano itself is free from fog, the distant coasts may be shrouded in cloud.

Dress warmly in waterproof clothes, and if you plan to camp, bring a good tent and a second set of clothes. Bring plenty of water, as there are no facilities anywhere near the summit. Also, bear in mind that the elevation is high enough for altitude sickness to be a possibility. If you feel nauseated or get a bad headache, head down the mountain immediately.

If you have a cell phone that works in this part of Panama, bring it. There are communication towers at the summit, so it might be possible to make a call if you get into trouble.

For the hike to the summit of Barú, drive to the trailhead, unless you're up for a marathon trek. The trailhead is at the end of 7.4 kilometers of dirt and gravel road, half of it horrible, that heads east across the plains from the main road between Volcán and Bambito. The road is not marked but your guide will know the way.

Admission to the park is theoretically US$5, US$6 more to camp, but there are usually no rangers around to collect it. This is yet another reason to exercise caution in climbing the mountain; don't expect the Mounties to come to the rescue if you get in trouble. Make sure there's someone back in town who knows where you are and is prepared to call for some sort of help if you don't return at a specified time. Again, a summit climb is absolutely not appropriate for young children.

Birding Tours

Birding guides who operate farther up the mountain in Cerro Punta and Guadalupe also work with clients down here, so birders staying around Volcán can book directly through them or through your hotels. The best places to try are Hostal Cielito Sur in Nueva Suiza and Los Quetzales Lodge and Spa in Guadalupe.

Rafting

A number of hotels and guides offer **whitewater rafting trips.** All of them contract out to rafting companies in Boquete, on the east side of Barú, so find out if the tour planner is charging you a premium just to book the trip for you. You might do better to contact the company directly. The companies can usually pick rafters up and take them to rivers on either side of the mountain. Organized guide services and outfitters have been slow to take hold on this side of the mountain. Going through your hotel is the best bet for now.

ACCOMMODATIONS

Lodging around Volcán is generally unsatisfying. Consider heading farther up the mountain to the area around Cerro Punta. There are a couple of places worth checking out, however. (Don't confuse the rustic but rather charming Volcán Lodge with the large but drab Volcán Inn.)

US$25-50

Hotel y Restaurante Don Tavo (tel./fax

WESTERN HIGHLANDS

© WILLIAM FRIAR

Restaurante Maná in the Volcán Lodge is a great place to have dinner.

771-5144, starts at US$28.88 s, US$38.12 d) is on the right just past downtown. It's set around a pretty courtyard and offers 16 simple but clean rooms with TV. It's by far the best moderately priced place to stay in the area, and the best value overall.

US$50-100

Volcán Lodge (tel. 771-4709, www.volcanlodge. webs.com/, US$55 s/d, including full breakfast) opened in late 2010 in one of the last old wooden country houses in town. It's a two-story place with six rooms and two balconies. There's hot water and free wireless Internet. This is a rustic place—rooms are plain, dark, and have thin mattresses—but it has tons of character, a cute little garden out front, and one of the best restaurants on this side of the mountain. Volcán Lodge is in a residential area with barking dogs, crowing roosters, and neighbors fond of loud music, so the best chance of a quiet night is to

get a room upstairs and in the back. There's also a cabin on the grounds behind the house that's available for long-term stays. The lodge hosts a community market on Friday mornings.

Heading into Volcán from the lowlands, turn right off the main road 200 meters before the gas station. The lodge will be on the right less than 200 meters down this road.

Hotel Dos Ríos (tel. 771-5555, www.dosrios. com.pa, starts at $77 s/d, including a minimal continental breakfast), on the outskirts of the Volcán area, 2.7 kilometers from the crossroads on the road to Río Sereno, was renovated in 2000 by its former owner, the Spanish Barceló chain. It's an attractive place consisting of 14 rooms, two suites, and two casitas (here meaning tiny bungalows with bunk beds) set in a garden with a creek flowing by. Rooms are dark but have cheerful touches, especially the painted vines and startled-looking toucans that adorn the walls. Windows can't be opened, so forget about ventilation. Rooms have TVs that get fuzzy local channels. All the polished wood everywhere is a mixed blessing. It looks nice, but it makes the place resonate like the sound box of a guitar, ensuring that anyone who walks by sounds like an army of storm troopers. Try to get a room on the 2nd floor.

You can choose from 19 quaint cottages at **Cabañas Kucikas** (Bambito tel./fax 771-4245, www.kucikas.com, US$72.60 s/d), 0.7 kilometers up from Hotel Bambito, just past the trout farm. It's on the left, but there's no sign so it's easy to miss the turn. The cottages are on forested grounds snug up against the mountains. It's a pleasant, if aging, place. All the cottages are different, with some more cheerful and well appointed than others. There's no restaurant on the premises, but all the cottages have full kitchens. This place is a good deal for larger groups. There's a fancy honeymoon cottage with a queen-size bed for US$72.60 s/d. Rates for the other cabins, which are intended for groups, run US$72.60–181.50 for 6–10 people.

US$100-150

Hotel Bambito Resort (tel. 771-4373 or 771-4374, www.hotelbambito.com, starts at US$82.50 s/d, including breakfast), about six kilometers north of Volcán, is an aging resort that's pretty imposing, but which you may find out of keeping with the natural beauty of the surroundings. It was built in 1981, and almost nothing about it has been changed since then, including the *Last Days of Disco* decor. It offers surprisingly plain standard rooms and several varieties of large suites. The place has seen better days. There are tennis courts, an indoor/outdoor swimming pool, sauna, hot tub, and a few pieces of gym equipment. There are frequent promotional deals; check the hotel's website and ads in national newspapers.

Camping

Be sure to bring plenty of warm clothing and a good tent if you camp out. It can get quite cold and drizzly even in the dry season.

It's possible to camp in **Parque Nacional Volcán Barú,** which you may want to do if you hike to the summit. The fee is US$6, but good luck finding someone to pay it to. If you want to do things by the book, buy a permit ahead of time at the ANAM office in David or Panama City.

FOOD

Several of the better dining options are located away from the center of town, which is a bit of a nuisance for those without transportation. Any place not within walking distance shouldn't be more than a US$1 cab ride away.

C **Restaurante Maná** (tel. 771-4709, www.volcanlodge.webs.com, 11 A.M.–8 P.M. daily, US$8–13) is the best restaurant not only in Volcán but on this entire side of the mountain. It's a cozy, wood-paneled place with the feel of a ski lodge dining room, on the ground floor of the Volcán Lodge. Offerings range from filet mignon to Thai chicken to pasta, plus the occasional local delicacy, such as *gallo pinto*.

Lighter fare includes soups, salads, sandwiches, and wraps. The food is tasty and well prepared.

Café Cerro Brujo (cell 6669-9196, noon–9 P.M. daily, US$9–12) is now located down a bumpy dirt about one kilometer north of downtown. It's amazing this place is still around, as it has stylish, relatively haute cuisine aspirations that you wouldn't expect out here. It has a small menu that changes but might include unexpected dishes like chicken in a Thai curry sauce and bananas Foster for dessert. Soup and salads tend to be quite good and are probably the safest bet. To get there, turn north off the main drag at the American Shop. The road forks after one kilometer. Turn right. The last 500 meters of this road is very rough. The restaurant is on the right, in a house that's been converted into a simple but pleasant-looking café with a back patio.

Some think **Ristorante Il Forno** (tel. 771-5731, cell 6827-0621 or 6748-9060, noon–9 P.M. Thurs.–Sun.) is one of the better Italian restaurants in Panama, but I was disappointed by the food on a recent visit. Pizza is baked in a brick oven (though one fired by gas, not wood). Il Forno is in a wooden house just down a side street near the crossroads. As you head in the direction of Río Sereno, it's a left turn just past the Banco Nacional de Panamá.

Restaurante Las Truchas (in the Hotel Bambito, tel. 771-4265, US$10–15) features plate-glass windows that look out on the artificial terraced pond in front of the hotel and the side of a mountain right across the street. The house specialty, as the name of the restaurant implies, is trout from its own trout farm up the street, prepared any way you can think of.

For those who'd rather fend for themselves, there's a 24-hour **Supermercado Romero** (tel. 771-4524) at the Volcán–Cerro Punta crossroads.

INFORMATION AND SERVICES

The 24-hour **Supermercado Romero** (tel. 771-4524) at the turnoff to the road to Cerro Punta has a pharmacy, and the pharmacist can be called day or night in an emergency. **Farmacia Don Bosco** (tel. 771-4317, 8 A.M.–8 P.M. daily) is near the HSBC bank. **Farmacia Volcán** (tel. 771-4651, 7:30 A.M.–9 P.M. Sun.–Thurs., 7:30 A.M.–6 P.M. Fri.) is on the left, one kilometer from the crossroads on the way to Río Sereno. There are several other pharmacies in town, but these are the most well-established and likeliest to still be around.

The only banks on the west side of Barú are in the town of Volcán. As you head up from the lowlands, **HSBC** (8 A.M.–3:30 P.M. Mon.–Fri., 9 A.M.–noon Sat.) is on the right shortly before the road forks. A branch of the **Banco Nacional de Panamá** (8 A.M.–3 P.M. Mon.–Fri., 9 A.M.–noon Sat.) is on the left, straight past the fork on the road to Río Sereno. Both banks have ATMs and will cash travelers checks.

A 24-hour **Internet café** (tel. 771-4461 or 771-4055) is attached to the Hotel y Restaurante Don Tavo. It charges US$1/hour.

GETTING THERE

Buses from David to Cerro Punta all stop in Volcán (US$3) and Bambito (US$3.30). Bus fare just between Volcán and destinations farther up the volcano include US$0.90 to Bambito, US$1 to Nueva Suiza, and US$1.35 to Cerro Punta or Guadalupe. Buses to all these destinations will most likely just have Cerro Punta painted on the windshield.

David-bound buses leave Cerro Punta 4:45 A.M.–6:45 P.M., arriving in Volcán, 14 kilometers down the mountain a quarter of an hour or so later. Buses run every 15 minutes. Those coming to Volcán from Costa Rica can catch the Cerro Punta bus at Concepción, rather than going all the way to the David bus terminal, and get off in Volcán.

Buses run between Volcán and Río Sereno about once an hour, 5 A.M.–5 P.M. daily. The fare is US$3.30. Look for the bus with Sereno on the windscreen. It stops at Finca Hartmann (US$2.25) by request.

Taxi fare from David to Volcán is about US$30, a bit more to go farther up the mountain. Some of the highland hotels will arrange pickup at the airport or bus terminal, for a fee. Check with your hotel. Taxi fare from Volcán to Finca Hartmann is US$20, or US$25 all the way to Río Sereno.

Buses and taxis to all these places can be found at the Volcán–Cerro Punta crossroads.

A new, winding mountain road now connects Cerro Punta and Boquete. This is an option for those who want to avoid going the traditional roundabout away via David. The entrance is at Cuesta de Piedra, two kilometers south of Cerro Punta. However, the entrance to the road is unmarked and hard to find, and few people choose to go this way. Those who want to take this route should follow my directions for the Boquete–Cerro Punta route (in reverse, of course). The drive takes about 1.5 hours.

GETTING AROUND

It's easy to walk around central Volcán, but those staying at a hotel on the road to Río Sereno who don't have their own transportation will probably have to rely on taxis. There's a taxi stand at the crossroads, next to Supermercado Romero. Taxis anywhere within the vicinity of Volcán are US$0.75. Between Volcán and Cerro Punta the fare is US$5, US$3 more to get to Las Nubes entrance to PILA. Other fares include Sitio Barriles (US$4), Lagunas de Volcán (US$5), and Los Pozos Termales de Tisingal (US$15). Catch the Cerro Punta–David bus if you want to take a bus between Volcán and the Bambito area.

WEST OF VOLCÁN

If you stay straight on the road through Volcán rather than turning right toward Cerro Punta, you'll head west and eventually end up in **Río Sereno,** a tiny town (pop. 3,289) with nothing to offer visitors but a little-used border crossing with Costa Rica that is not always open to foreign travelers. The main reason to come this way is to visit Finca Hartmann, a combination gourmet coffee farm and private forest reserve with a couple of cabins for birders and other nature lovers. It's 27 kilometers west of Volcán, 15 kilometers east of Río Sereno.

The road to Río Sereno is one of the prettiest in Panama. Bright, tiny flowers dot the shoulders. The road crosses over rivers and winds past splashing waterfalls, forested hills, coffee plantations, tall stands of evergreens, and plump cows grazing in fields.

But the road also features blind curves and trucks that barrel down the hills without a thought for what might lie around the bend. Count on landslides and washouts in the rainy season, though the road should be in good shape.

Though the countryside is attractive, Río Sereno itself isn't. It consists of a couple of basic stores (the best bet for food), a central plaza, a bank, the border crossing, and little else. There's an open-air market by the plaza with modest offerings, catering to Costa Rican day-trippers. Given the limited services here, and the fact that even the immigration officials don't quite know what to make of tourists, visitors should enter or exit Panama through the far less attractive but much more convenient crossing at Paso Canoa.

Finca Hartmann

This family-owned coffee farm (tel./fax 775-5223, cell 6450-1833, tourism@fincahartmann.com, www.fincahartmann.com) is a great favorite with birders—more than 280 bird species have been identified—but even if that's not your thing, you may want to consider visiting for its away-from-it-all natural beauty, for a tour of its coffee operation, or just for a cup of coffee with some friendly folks. The Hartmanns have two remote cabins, one of them surprisingly comfortable, for guests who want to stay overnight. The finca is in the community of Santa Clara, 27 kilometers from Volcán on the road to Río Sereno.

The Hartmanns offer tours of their small coffee mill. The coffee here is excellent, and there's a small coffee shop with an attractive wooden *rancho* where you can buy a cup or pick up some souvenir packs to take home. A tour of the coffee operation and access to the grounds for birding or hiking will be US$15 per person.

The patriarch of the clan is the friendly and gregarious Ratibor "Chicho" Hartmann, now in his eighties but in fantastic shape. He's an entomology enthusiast who worked for years in the Canal Zone at Gorgas Hospital, an important center for tropical medicine. Research scientists have been studying the farm's rich flora and fauna for years. Their gratitude has included naming two new beetle species and a new species of cloud-forest bee after Hartmann.

Reflecting his hobby, he has built a tiny museum in the compound that contains an impressive insect collection from the area and around the world. There's also a small collection of pre-Columbian pottery and stone figures, mostly from Chiriquí.

The real treasure of the place is the fragmented primary cloud forest 3.7 kilometers up from the main finca on a brutal road that requires a four-wheel drive with high clearance. It's called **Ojo de Agua** (eye of water) for the spring that runs between the two cabins in a clearing at the end of the road. Besides the incredible array of birds, the lucky might encounter a few of the 62 species of mammals that have so far been identified on the finca, including red brocket (a kind of deer), peccaries, armadillos, porcupines, opossums, and close to 20 species of mice, as well as white-faced capuchin, red spider, and howler monkeys.

Ojo de Agua borders Parque Internacional La Amistad (PILA). To the west one can see clear to Costa Rica. Five trails start from near the cabin: a one-kilometer uphill one that connects with the road, a three-kilometer trail that leads up a hill and that skirts PILA, another three-kilometer one that leads to a small river, a 350-meter walk to a 50-meter waterfall, and a 500-meter trail that leads to an enormous ficus tree.

The two cabins are quite different. The larger one is a two-story building that's been used as a research station, so creature comforts have not been a main concern. It's a basic place with a concrete floor, kitchen with gas stove, dining/sitting area, fireplace, and five bedrooms. There's no electricity, just kerosene lamps, but it does have hot-water showers. The smaller cabin is quite a bit nicer. It's still rustic, but it features finished wood, a snug bedroom, a kitchenette, and hot-water bathroom. Electricity is on the way; expect prices to go up when it arrives.

Rates run from US$20–35 for a bunk bed to US$70 for a cabana for two. Optional food service is available. If you need transportation from the finca to the cabins, the Hartmanns will take you there for US$20 round-trip.

Río Sereno Practicalities

The **Posada Los Andes** (no phone, US$20 s/d) is the only option for those stranded in Río Sereno on the way to someplace more interesting. It's in the building that looks like a factory looming over the plaza; rooms are upstairs from the shops. Don't expect the Ritz. Finca Hartmann is a better, but remoter, alternative.

A branch of **Banco Nacional de Panamá** (8 A.M.–3 P.M. Mon.–Fri., 9 A.M.–noon Sat.) is next to the plaza in the center of Río Sereno.

Getting There and Around

To drive to Finca Hartmann from Volcán, continue straight at the crossroads instead of turning right toward Cerro Punta. The drive takes about a half hour. You'll see a sign on the left side of the road; make a quick right onto the gravel road here. The 42 kilometers from Volcán all the way to Río Sereno takes about 45 minutes by car. Just stay straight on the main road.

Buses run between Volcán and Río Sereno about once an hour, 5 A.M.–5 P.M. daily. The fare is US$3.30. The bus will stop at Finca Hartmann (US$2.25) if requested. Taxi fare from Volcán is US$15–20 to either place.

Buses between David and Río Sereno run every 45 minutes, 5 A.M.–5 P.M. The trip takes nearly three hours and costs US$5.10. Tell the driver if you want to get off at Finca Hartmann (about 2.5 hours, US$4.50).

Río Sereno is tiny. You can walk from one end of downtown to the other in five minutes. You can also wander right over to Costa Rica for a minute, if you want that weird little thrill of crossing a border. The crossing is wide open and not even marked; you'll only know which country you're in from the flags flying at the tiny *migración* offices.

Buses run between Volcán and Río Sereno about once an hour, 5 A.M.–5 P.M. daily. The fare is US$3.30. Look for the bus with Sereno on the windscreen. It stops at Finca Hartmann (US$2.25) by request.

Taxi fare from David to Volcán is about US$30, a bit more to go farther up the mountain. Some of the highland hotels will arrange pickup at the airport or bus terminal, for a fee. Check with your hotel. Taxi fare from Volcán to Finca Hartmann is US$20, or US$25 all the way to Río Sereno.

ALONG THE FORTUNA ROAD

The area around the Fortuna reservoir, farther east along the cordillera, is known for its sweeping vistas and great bird-watching, but so far it doesn't see many visitors or even have that many residents.

Because the Fortuna Dam generates more than 30 percent of Panama's electricity, there's an economic incentive to keep its watershed well protected. That's good news for nature lovers, as the forests here are overflowing with life. It can get cool at the higher elevations, down to about 14°C (57°F), but it's significantly warmer than the area around Volcán Barú.

The reservoir, just south of the Continental Divide, is surrounded by the **Reserva Forestal**

Fortuna (Fortuna Forest Reserve, 19,500 hectares), which in turn is bordered by the enormous **Bosque Protector de Palo Seco** (Palo Seco Buffer Forest, 244,000 hectares) to the northwest. The Continental Divide marks the border between the provinces of Chiriquí and Bocas del Toro.

A good road—usually referred to as the Fortuna Road—cuts north across the mountains from the town of Chiriquí on the Interamericana to the oil port of Chiriquí Grande on the Caribbean coast, less than 100 kilometers away (this road can be dangerous in bad weather). A fairly new road links Chiriquí Grande with Almirante, the jumping-off point for water taxis and ferries to the archipelago of Bocas del Toro. Along the way there are rugged access roads into the forest, making it relatively easy to explore the area.

More than 1,000 plant species have been identified just in the Fortuna Forest Reserve, which is also home to 40 mammal and 70 amphibian and reptile species. Endangered mammals here include the white-lipped peccary and Baird's tapir. The area has some of the best bird-watching in Panama. Besides the ever-popular resplendent quetzal, there's a chance of seeing such spectacular specimens as the bare-necked umbrellabird, azure-hooded jay, black-bellied hummingbird, lattice-tailed trogon, and yellow-eared toucanet, to name just a few. Some of these are rare and nearly impossible to spot, so you'll get a lot more out of a hike if you go with a good guide.

Accommodations

Until recently there were three appealing places to stay aimed at ecotourists. As of this writing, sadly, only one remains. Finca La Suiza, the pioneering lodging of the area, closed suddenly in 2012 following the death of one of its owners. It was for sale at the time of writing, so there's hope that new owners will eventually reopen it.

Lost and Found Eco-Resort (cell 6432-8182 or 6920-3036, lflodge@gmail.com or info@lostandfoundlodge.com, www.lostandfoundlodge.com, US$12 dorm beds, US$30 s/d private room) is, depending on your perspective, either an ecolodge for the backpacking set or a hostel for nature lovers. Opened in 2007 by a couple of Canadians named Andrew and Patrick, it's got a great location on 30 acres of hilly, forested land just south of the Continental Divide at 1,255 meters above sea level. Lost and Found is aptly named, as it's not visible from the Fortuna Road but rather in the woods above it. Getting there requires a 10-minute climb up steep stairs carved into the side of a hill; those lugging a heavy backpack will get their day's exercise.

The hostel consists of a series of terraced platforms that hold an open-air kitchen/dining area, a dorm, private rooms, a "chill-out" room, and outhouses with clean, hot-water showers and flush toilets. The wooden dorm has multiple tiers of bunk beds with double mattresses. Every third night is free. There are also three bare but perfectly adequate private rooms for US$30 s/d. Two of these have a view of Volcán Barú. Guests are welcome to use the communal kitchen (and provisions are sold on-site) or pay US$4–7 for a prepared meal.

The hostel is a pleasant, friendly, and well-equipped place, especially given its isolation, but the surroundings are the star attraction. Guests can watch the sun set behind Volcán Barú and go for day and night hikes on the network of trails, which connect with trails used by the Smithsonian Tropical Research Institute. Hikers can sometimes glimpse the Pacific from the trails, which climb as high as 1,800 meters above sea level. There's a onetime US$3 fee to use the trails. A guided hike is US$7 per person or US$24 for groups. Guests don't always have to go hiking to spot wildlife. Kinkajous and sloths sometimes come to the hostel looking for food, and white-faced capuchins are occasionally spotted on the property as well.

The hostel offers a variety of tours, including

The Lost and Found Eco-Resort is a forest hostel near the Continental Divide.

a coffee tour (US$25), a jungle tour led by an indigenous guide, including lunch with his family (US$18); a trip to the Caldera hot springs (US$14), beach excursions (US $20–25, depending on destination), and horseback riding (US$40). These guys are always coming up with new ideas for trips and adventures. For the more sedentary, the chill-out room has a foosball table, book exchange, karaoke machine, and a TV and DVD player with 200 movies available to rent.

The hostel also offers a variety of transportation options between Bocas and Boquete. For those who just want transportation, the price for this ranges from US$40 to US$70 per person, two-person minimum, depending on the number of people in the group. Other options add on tours of interesting places en route, outdoor adventures, overnight stays, or some combination thereof.

Lost and Found is just beyond kilometer marker 42 on the Fortuna Road. It's north of the weigh station and the sign for Valle de la Mina. Keep an eye out for the sign. Those coming by bus (US$3 from David, US$6 from Almirante) can ask the bus driver to stop at the *casa amarilla* on the Fortuna Road. Those with their own transportation can park at a neighbor's house for US$2.50 per night. The hostel can sometimes pick up guests from David (US$40), Boquete (US$60), or Almirante (US$90). The rate is per carload, not per person, with a maximum of four passengers.

Information and Services

This is a remote area with few services of any kind and certainly no tourist information booths. The best bet for information and guides is at Lost and Found Eco-Resort. Don't attempt a hike into the forest without a guide.

Getting There

The Fortuna Road begins at the town of Chiriquí, 15 kilometers east of David on the

Interamericana. Turn north off the highway at Chiriquí and head straight past town. Keep left when you come to the fork at Gualaca. The two-lane route, unofficially known as the Fortuna Road, soon starts winding through the highlands, and the views become spectacular. Beware of landslides, washouts, and sudden dips and bumps in the road caused by soil erosion below it. Returning to the Interamericana on the way back down can be a bit confusing. At Gualaca, be sure to turn left at the crossroads, following the signs that say "CPA" (for Carretera Pan-Americana, or the Interamericana).

Any bus running between David and Chiriquí

Grande or Almirante uses this road and can drop off and pick up passengers anywhere along it. To return to David or Almirante you'll have to flag down a bus by the side of the road.

Note to those driving to or from Boquete: A road links Caldera and the Fortuna Road that can potentially shorten the trip considerably since it spares you from having to drive all the way down to the Interamericana. It was recently paved most of the way and should be in good shape. However, it's prone to landslides and washouts, so ask locals about conditions before attempting. The road is about 38 kilometers long. It's a pretty drive.

Golfo de Chiriquí and Golfo de Montijo

The western Pacific coast of Panama arcs around two gulfs. The larger one is Golfo de Chiriquí, which extends from Punta Burica at the western edge of Panama toward the Azuero Peninsula to the east, encompassing the entire coast of Chiriquí province and much of the Pacific coast of Veraguas. Just east of it is a much smaller gulf, the Golfo de Montijo, which is roughly bounded by the west coast of the Azuero Peninsula to the east, the river port of Puerto Mutis to the north, the surfers' paradise of Playa Santa Catalina to the west, and the large and lovely Isla Cébaco to the south.

This is a region of superlatives. It contains the richest mangrove forests in Central America, the largest island in Panama, and one of the largest coral reefs in the Pacific. It offers truly world-class diving, surfing, and sportfishing.

Conservation organizations have targeted this area as one of the most ecologically important in Central America. This area has seen less development than other parts of Panama, but human pressures are mounting. Panama has reacted by establishing protected areas, most notably two huge marine parks: Parque Nacional

Marino Golfo de Chiriquí and, more recently, Parque Nacional Coiba. The Golfo de Montijo is also recognized by the Ramsar Convention as a "wetlands of international importance."

Because this region is still relatively remote and untouched, it's only now beginning to take off as a tourist destination. There are now half a dozen good options, plus decent places to eat and reliable tour operators. More are on the way. Playa Santa Catalina is also growing fast, both because it's the best surfing spot in Panama and because it's a convenient jumping-off point for Parque Nacional Coiba. All these places are much more accessible than ever before.

◖ PARQUE NACIONAL MARINO GOLFO DE CHIRIQUÍ

Parque Nacional Marino Golfo de Chiriquí is a 14,740-hectare marine park that encompasses two dozen islands and their surrounding waters. The park is a refuge for all kinds of wildlife, including howler monkeys, leatherback and hawksbill turtles, and tiger-herons. Humpback whales come here to calve between August and November. This area was for

© WILLIAM FRIAR

The remote volcanic islands of Parque Nacional Marino Golfo de Chiriquí offer pristine nature and spectacular diving.

years the well-kept secret of backpackers and deep-sea anglers, but in the last few years it's begun to take off as a more mainstream tourist destination.

As this region becomes better known, the shorthand to refer to it is shaping up to be either **Boca Chica,** which technically is just the fishing village and anchorage that are the gateway to the islands, or **Boca Brava,** which is actually just one of the islands.

It's still a bit of an adventure to get to the islands that start just off the coast east of David; that's half the fun of visiting this area. You get the sense of being in the middle of nowhere without actually being that far from civilization or having to spend a lot of money to get there. The only population center nearby is the little fishing village of Boca Chica, which is more than an hour by road or sea from David. Accommodations and places to eat are near Boca Chica and out on the islands a short boat ride away.

If all this sounds more like fun than hassle, you have the right attitude to visit this place. The islands and ocean here are beautiful and still feel like an undiscovered paradise. Another plus about this whole region: Dry season tends to start earlier than in other parts of Panama, around November, and ends at about the same time, in April.

Nearby Islands and Coast

There is an endless maze of mangroves to explore in the estuaries of several rivers that empty into the sea near Boca Chica. But most come here to enjoy the islands. **Isla Boca Brava** is the closest to Boca Chica. The island is 14 kilometers long, six kilometers wide, and overflowing with wildlife. It's right on the edge of the park.

Because of the rivers on the mainland, the water gets clearer the farther away one gets from shore. The closest uninhabited islands are **Linarte, Saino,** and **Las Ventanas** (*ventana* means window; the name refers to the caverns that run straight through their rocky sides).

But the best islands are farther out. The snorkeling is decent around **Isla San José,** a short boat trip away, but it's definitely worthwhile to head out even farther. **Isla Bolaños** is 13 kilometers from Boca Brava, about 45 minutes by a small boat equipped with a decent outboard motor. This is a lovely little deserted island with a couple of sandy beaches, lots of coconut palms, and snorkeling when the tide's low. This is one of the best places to see humpback whales and their young between August or September and November. Twenty minutes from Bolaños is **Isla Gámez** (sometimes spelled Gámes), also lovely and even smaller. This one, however, tends to attract yachts and the weekend personal watercraft crowd, while Bolaños is rarely visited. Both these islands are tended by the nonprofit environmental group ANCON. **Isla Parida,** just across from Gámez, is a big island with a few inhabitants. The aptly named Playa Grande, a kilometer-long stretch of sandy beach, is quite inviting. At one end of the beach is a stunningly picturesque point, Punta La Trinidad, which is covered with a forest of enormous trees.

There's an ANAM station on Parida next to a bunch of ramshackle huts and a dirty beach. You can spend the night at the station, but it's hard to see why you'd want to.

Remote Islands

The scuba diving is said to be terrific around **Islas Las Ladrones** and **Islas Secas,** where the water is clearest and the sealife richest. The diving visibility can be up to 30 meters at Las Ladrones. The islands are very far away: Las Ladrones islands are 40 kilometers southwest and the Islas Secas 30 kilometers southeast of Boca Brava. Do not attempt to go this far on the open sea without something more substantial than the little *pangas* common around here. Divers and snorkelers need to be strong

swimmers in some of the dive spots, as powerful waves smash on the rocky volcanic shores of the islands and barely submerged rocks.

Sports and Recreation

Even with the sudden growth, this area is not exactly crawling with tour operators and recreational facilities. Guests generally arrange excursions through their hotels, some of which offer tours for nonguests as well. There is one dive operator based in the area. There's a US$5 per-person fee to enter the marine park, usually collected by the tour operator.

The best bet for an economical boat tour is **Hotel Boca Brava** (tel. 851-0017, fax 700-0250 or 676-3244, www.hotelbocabrava.com), which offers a wide variety of tours to all the attractions in the area. Round-trip excursions to the nearest islands, for instance, are US$4–7 a person. A half-day snorkeling and hiking trip to Isla San José costs US$35 total for up to four people. The hotel has a more substantial excursion boat it can use for day trips to distant destinations, such as Islas Secas (US$280 for up to six people, including snorkeling gear and lunch). The hotel also rents snorkels and masks for US$2. Single sea kayaks are US$3 an hour or US$15 a day; two-person kayaks are US$4.50 an hour or US$22.50 a day.

Diving in the region is best during the dry season, December–April. Divers should try to make it all the way out to Islas Secas or Islas Ladrones.

Boca Brava Divers (tel. 775-3185, cell 6600-6191) is run by Carlos Spragge, who has a highly professional operation. A full day of diving costs US$150 per diver, including boat, divemaster, tanks, weights, and a picnic lunch. Trips are limited to 4–8 divers.

Carlos converted a 46-foot commercial vessel into a somewhat spartan live-aboard, *Miss Bessy,* that he uses for day trips to Islas Secas and Islas Ladrones, as well as for cruises that last up to seven days. Per-person prices are US$150 for the first day and US$250 for each additional

© WILLIAM FRIAR

The view from Seagull Cove Lodge changes throughout the day.

day, including a berth, three daily meals, divemaster, tanks, and weights. Overnight trips are limited to 4–5 people.

Accommodations and Food

The area now has a surprisingly diverse range of accommodations, catering to those on budgets ranging from starvation to luxury. Prices here tend to be significantly cheaper in the low season, but if this place really takes off, be prepared for the rapidly rising prices Boquete and Bocas del Toro have experienced.

Chitras (sand flies) and occasionally mosquitoes can be a nuisance all around here in the evenings, but much less so during the breezy dry season. That's the price of having healthy mangroves. For the last few years there have been only two places to stay on the mainland: they are Gone Fishing Panama Resort and Seagull Cove Lodge.

Other places are accessible only by boat, though in the case of Restaurante y Cabañas

Boca Brava and Panama Big Game Fishing Club, the boat ride is a stone's throw across the harbor and costs US$3 by fishing boat water taxi. They are next to each other on the inland side of Isla Boca Brava. Cala Mia is significantly farther away, on the ocean-facing side about a 20-minute, US$25 *panga* ride from Boca Chica on open seas. Pacific Bay Resort is perched on the tip of Punta Bejuco, which is on the mainland but accessible only by sea. The trip from Boca Chica by *panga* takes about 25 minutes and costs around US$20 one way.

There's also an ANAM ranger station on distant Isla Parida that can provide lodging for a small fee, but the island is inhabited and quite junked up. There's no reason to stay here when you can sleep in a hammock at Hotel Boca Brava for US$7.70, or camp for free on a deserted island with a little planning.

Boca Chica and Horconcitos have a couple of rock-bottom places to eat, but most people dine where they stay. The restaurants at Seagull

Cove Lodge and Hotel Boca Brava are easily accessible and open to the public.

Hotel Boca Brava (tel. 851-0017, fax 700-0250, hotelbocabrava@yahoo.com, www.hotelbocabrava.com, US$7.70 pp in a hammock, US$11 pp in dorm, rooms start at US$38 s/d) was the first, and for several years the only, hotel in the whole region. It's a cool place to stay or visit and I have a soft spot for it, but it's definitely not for everyone. The place is a good deal so long as you don't mind some rusticity and living close to nature. However, for the last few years the place has been managed by a service-oriented gringo couple, Brad and Kelly, who have worked in tourism in Mexico and the United States and are gradually making the place more comfortable.

The cabins and restaurant are on a cliff 20 meters and a long flight of stairs above the ocean on the eastern edge of the island, giving it striking views of the Pacific and the surrounding islands.

There are more than 10 kilometers of trails that lead into the forest and down to the island's beaches. The forest is home to monkeys, anteaters, coatimundis, all kinds of birds, and a wealth of trees and plants. The previous manager, who still owns the place, proudly maintained that the island has "no poisonous spiders, but every kind of poisonous snake." He always insisted they're mellow, but don't go for a forest hike without good boots, and watch your step.

In recent years some (relatively) upscale rooms have been added. These deluxe rooms are still pretty basic but have air-conditioning, hot water, a terrace, tile floors, satellite TV, and two queen-size beds (US$71.50 s/d). The midrange "standard" rooms (US$49.50 s/d) all have private cold-water baths and fans. These are very simple rooms—mattresses lie on raised platforms on the floor—but perfectly fine.

A step down in quality and price are the hostel rooms with shared shower and toilet. Dorm beds are in an open-air room. Those on a tight budget can also rent a hammock in an open-sided room. The price for the dorm beds and hammocks includes access to the showers and toilet. This place has become well known on the backpackers' circuit and sometimes fills up. Call for reservations.

The restaurant and bar are a peculiar open-air, two-story affair on the edge of the cliff. The panoramic view is terrific, and there's now a little "crow's nest" above the 2nd floor where the view's even better.

It's a tough call, but █ **Pacific Bay Resort** (cell 6695-1651, U.S. tel. 617/782-3228, www.pacificbayresort.net, $65 s, US$110 d, including all meals) has arguably the best scenery in the region. It certainly has the most: It extends over 65 hilly hectares, fewer than 10 of which are developed. The rest is covered with tropical forest that runs down to three long, brown-sand beaches. South Beach, as it's come to be known, is especially lovely, a crescent-shaped expanse of sand with an islet just offshore that keeps the surf tranquil. It's backed by shallow, vine-draped caves. Very *Treasure Island.*

The presence of the resort has discouraged hunters and encouraged wildlife to return, including howler monkeys, white-faced capuchins, hawks, deer, ocelots, white-nosed coatis, iguanas, anteaters, and sloths. During any visit, don't be disappointed if you only see birds and hear howlers in the distance.

The owner, Frank, was born in Panama but grew up in Boston. He's a friendly, easygoing guy who seems to genuinely love this place and be more interested in sharing it with like-minded visitors than making a fast buck.

Facilities are more basic than at the higher-end places in this area. There are nine cabins on the property, five of which are intended for guests. The cabins are borderline rustic but roomy and perfectly adequate. Each cabin has a queen and full-size bed, fan and screened windows, bathrooms with showers, and a small patio with hammock. All of them have a view of the ocean. Cabins are set in gardens and spaced far enough apart for privacy, so long as there's no one in the room next door (the cabins are duplexes).

Each cabin is named for a province of Panama, arranged to roughly correspond to the geographic position and, even more roughly, the characteristics of the province. My favorites are Veraguas and Chiriquí, which are set on hilly terrain that leads down to the beach, not unlike their provincial namesakes.

An open-air restaurant/bar is on the edge of a cliff with sweeping views of the ocean and coast. With advance notice, Frank can arrange a sunset barbecue out on nearby Turtle Point, named for the large sea turtles that sometimes make an appearance. The price does not include transportation, which runs about US$60 round-trip per group. The resort can arrange that transportation, or just hire a fishermen in Boca Chica. Each cabin can accommodate two more people for an additional US$40 each, including meals.

Activities available include kayaking, horseback riding, and boat trips to the islands. Telephone communications way out here are unreliable, and email is the best way to make reservations. The U.S. telephone number reaches a college bar Frank owns in Boston, which can result in some baffling conversations. Bring shoes with good traction, as the paths are paved and can get slippery.

Seagull Cove Lodge (tel. 700-0236, U.S. tel. 786/735-1475, www.seagullcovelodge.com, $181.50 s/d, a/c), also opened in 2006, offers a little bit of everything: It's comfortable, it has striking views, it's accessible, and you don't have to take out a second mortgage to stay here. It's on the mainland just a few minutes uphill from the village of Boca Chica.

Seagull Cove features six roomy, red-tile-roof bungalows staggered on a hillside and linked by a steep staircase that leads to a pier and small beach. The lodge rents kayaks for US$8/hour and snorkeling gear for US$10/day. A little

public bar (11 A.M.–9 P.M. Tues.–Sat. if there's demand) has recently been added to the end of the pier. Four of the bungalows have queen-size beds and two have two double beds each. They are otherwise identical, with modern furnishings, sliding-glass doors, a terrace, firm mattresses, cable TV, safe, walk-in closet, and large, attractive bathrooms. The 7,500-square-meter property is steep but narrow, which means guests must close their curtains to have privacy from their neighbors and those passing by on the stairs. The *chitras* and mosquitoes are less of a nuisance here than elsewhere in the area, thanks to the air-conditioning.

Five of the bungalows have great views of the tranquil anchorage, ocean, and surrounding islands. The sixth is at the top of the hill closest to the restaurant, and it looks out mainly on forest. But it's also the most secluded of the bungalows, and the trees around it are filled with oropendola nests. (Oropendolas are large, flamboyant birds known for their hanging nests.)

The lodge's restaurant (11:30 A.M.–2 P.M. and 5:30–8 P.M. Tues.–Sun., most mains US$14.95–16.95) is a large, comfortable, Italian-style terrace at the top of the hill with a terrific ocean view. Breakfast is for guests only, but the restaurant is open to the public for lunch and dinner, serving food ranging from burgers and chicken wings to pastas and quite good seafood. There's a small plunge pool next to the terrace that's a nice spot to soak and watch the ocean on a hot day. (Hotel guests only.) The place is managed by a South African couple, Avril and Derek, and their attentive staff.

Opened in 2006, **Cala Mia** (tel. 851-0059 or 851-0025, cell 6617-5352, hotelcalamia@gmail.com, www.boutiquehotelcalamia.com, starts at US$242 s, US$264 d) is one of the loveliest places to stay in Panama. It consists of 11 modern, elegant bungalows on a narrow, rocky spit of land on the far side of Boca Brava, about 15 minutes by boat from Boca Chica. It's flanked by two deserted beaches, a short stroll down the hill from the bungalows. The beaches aren't the loveliest in the area, but gorgeous ones are a short boat ride away. Behind the beaches is tropical forest, home to howler monkeys and plenty of other small critters, which guests are free to explore. (A one-hour trail leads over the island to Restaurante y Cabañas Boca Brava.)

The bungalows are large and comfortable, with plate-glass sliding doors that look out on a private, thatch-roofed terrace and a view of the ocean and surrounding islands. The well-appointed bathrooms feature circular glass-block showers. The bungalows do not have air-conditioning, and it can get a bit warm in there, but they do have ceiling fans and screened windows.

At the tip of the little peninsula is an artfully decorated bar and dining room; a circular staircase leads to a mirador with 360-degree views. Outside is a small but appealing infinity pool, and across a rope bridge is an islet with a tiny crow's nest of a spa that seems to float above the sea. The whole place has an air of bohemian elegance, and everything is done so tastefully it's hard to believe the Italian-Dutch couple who own the place designed it without any background in architecture.

Stays include free use of kayaks, snorkeling equipment, and sailboards. Half-day and full-day excursions to the islands are possible, including trips as far away as Islas Secas (US$400 for up to four people). Scuba and snorkeling packages are also available, as are deep-sea fishing trips to the waters near Isla Coiba. Horseback riding in the forest is US$38 per person. The spa offers massages, manicures/pedicures, and exfoliation treatments. Yoga packages are also sometimes available. Cala Mia currently offers Mediterranean cuisine, including three-course dinners. Packages that include all meals are available, or guests can pay as they go.

Chitras (sand flies) can be a nuisance out here, though less so in the dry season, when the breezes keep them at bay. One impressive thing about this place is that the owner states flat out in the promotional literature that they know their very presence in such a pristine area causes harm. It certainly causes a lot less than most hotels, and they try to minimize the damage not only by ecofriendly practices such as using solar power, but by doing something for the community—they say that five percent of their proceeds go to community-service projects in the area.

The **Panama Big Game Fishing Club** (tel. 6674-4824, U.S. tel. 786/200-1672, U.K. tel. +44 (0)203/287-2672, www.panamabiggamefishingclub.com, a/c) shares the same general idea as Restaurante y Cabañas Boca Brava—cabins and a restaurant/bar perched high up on the edge of Isla Boca Brava—but the result couldn't be more different. The Big Game Fishing Club is an upscale, all-inclusive sportfishing lodge.

The four modern, cheerful cottages are similar except for the bright, hand-painted murals. Each cottage is 600 square feet, big enough for two queen-size beds in different wings of the cottage. The beds are separated from each other by a partial partition (but not doors). The cottages have huge, glass block–walled showers. Each cottage can sleep up to six people.

At the top of the hill is an attractive, semicircular bar and restaurant with plate-glass windows overlooking the sea, nearby islands, and the forested mainland. Above the restaurant, a ladder leads to an observation tower with an even more sweeping view and, if you're lucky, a chance to eavesdrop on howler monkeys in the treetops.

The club offers fishing packages that last 4–6 days starting at US$3,553–4,596 per person for groups of four anglers, not including taxes and tips. Packages include in-country transport and all meals and drinks. Rates are higher for smaller groups and lower in the rainy season. This place is quite upscale.

Getting There

Some of the hotels will help arrange transport

from David. Transfers are included with stays at Panama Big Game Fishing Club. Cala Mia offers a variety of transfer options from David and Boca Chica to its resort. The cheapest is simply a boat trip between the Boca Chica dock and Cala Mia, which is US$32 per group each way, or free with a minimum three-night stay. The Purple House Hostel in David sometimes arranges transport for its guests.

BY BUS

Any bus plying the Interamericana, including the long-distance ones that run between David and Panama City, can drop passengers off at the Horconcitos turnoff so long as the bus runs past that point. From David, these include a few buses with Horconcitos as the final destination, as well as the Tolé, San Felix, Las Lajas, and Remedios buses. The fare from David is US$2. Get off at the crossroads leading into Horconcitos (*el cruce de Horconcitos*), not Horconcitos itself, where it'll be much harder to get a ride to Boca Chica. There's now an occasional *colectivo* taxi service during daylight hours (US$3 pp). Show up early in the day to improve chances of getting a ride.

Six buses a day travel between Horconcitos proper and David (US$2). The last one leaves either location at 5 P.M.

BY TAXI

Taxi prices from David to Boca Chica fluctuate depending on the state of the road and the price of fuel. Expect to pay at least US$40 for one or two people, a bit more for additional passengers.

It's also possible to get a taxi by the side of the Interamericana at the Horconcitos crossroads (it's significantly harder to find one in "downtown" Horconcitos itself) to Boca Chica. There are now several that hang out at the crossroads, so you have a pretty good chance of finding one if you just show up during the day. Expect to pay around US$15 per ride, depending on the state of the road.

DRIVING TO BOCA CHICA

For those coming on their own, the easiest access to the islands is through the little town of Horconcitos, the turnoff to which is about 40 kilometers east of David on the Interamericana. The turnoff is poorly marked; if you're coming from David, it'll be on the right—look for signs advertising hotels and water sports. Horconcitos itself is five kilometers from the Interamericana on a good road. The road forks at the town center. Continue straight, then make the next left; the turn will probably not be marked. Then it's a 16-kilometer drive south to the fishing village of Boca Chica. This road used to be horrendous, but the last 16 kilometers were finally paved in 2008, turning what was once a brutal trek of an hour to a spectacularly scenic drive of around 20 minutes on a good day. About 10 kilometers from Horconcitos, the road forks. The left fork leads to a beach, Playa Hermosa. Straight continues to Boca Chica. The road dead-ends at a pier. Parking by the pier is US$2 a night.

FROM BOCA CHICA TO THE HOTELS

Gone Fishing and Seagull Cove Lodge are on the mainland just up the hill from Boca Chica. Make a left turn just before arriving in Boca Chica and head uphill less than 500 meters. The road is rough but navigable in a regular car, at least during the dry season.

To get to Boca Chica itself, just stay straight on the main road, which dead-ends suddenly at the water. Those heading to the islands from Boca Chica usually hire fishermen to make the trip unless a hotel or tour operator has arranged to meet them. Rates are US$3 per person for nearby destinations, US$25–30 or more per boatload for distant ones. There's a pay phone at the pier in case you get stranded and need to call for assistance.

ISLA PARIDITA

There's no place in Panama I'm more eager to go back and spend a week than Paridita, which is one of Panama's best-kept secrets. It's 40 minutes by fast boat from Boca Chica, in the middle of Parque Nacional Marino Golfo de Chiriquí, surrounded by nothing but clear blue water and volcanic islands with enormous trees clinging to their rocky cliffs.

There is only one rustic place to stay on the island, which has many natural attractions and is a great base for exploring the surrounding islands and waters. There is almost nothing and no one else out here.

Paridita has five beaches to choose from, a total of eight kilometers in all, ranging from black to gray sand. Powerful waves smash black coral off one of the beaches, turning it into a coral mine when it washes onshore.

About a half-mile away is the far larger Isla Parida, a bustling metropolis in comparison, as it has about 15 residents. The shorelines of Paridita and Parida form a calm, sheltered bay, making it easy for beginning kayakers to paddle around. Parida has a number of beaches of its own, including the appealing, half-mile-long Playa Grande.

This is a great spot for whale-watching between August and November. Visitors have spotted as many as 20 humpback whales in a single go.

Leatherback turtles nest on the island, which also has anteaters and sea turtles. A meter-long crocodile lives in one of the two freshwater lagoons on the island. You can find bird nests on the grounds, as they have no natural predators and no fear of humans. Visitors can explore tide pools at low tide.

Those who know the island well say it has no poisonous snakes. In the 1920s the island was used as a pig farm, and supposedly the pigs killed all the snakes.

For such a deserted spot, Paridita has seen a lot of action. The island has been a spot for making and repairing boats and ships for many hundreds of years. The trees along the shore are perfect for making dugout canoes, and convenient; canoe-makers chop the trees down into the ocean, then float the logs to shore. During the days of the Spanish Empire, galleons going to and from the Philippines would repair their ships in the protected bay, Bahía Baradero, to avoid attacks by natives and pirates on the mainland and inland islands. Visitors are constantly turning up artifacts from these different eras, including very ancient-looking indigenous statuettes and tools.

Several trails cross the island through secondary forest. The forest has been left relatively undisturbed for a long time, so there are plenty of huge trees. There is also a lot to discover that hints at the many waves of human visitors who have come through over many hundreds of years: the remains of a sugarcane press carved into a tree, old roof tiles the builders made by shaping the wet clay over their thighs, a stone wall that was erected who knows when.

The longer one spends out here, the more one discovers. But those who get restless can visit the Islas Secas, about 20 minutes away by fast boat, which has some of the clearest water for snorkeling in Panama. Los Ladrones (14 miles away, about half an hour by fast boat) has excellent scuba diving, but is only appropriate for strong, experienced divers because of powerful currents.

Accommodations and Food

The only place to stay on Isla Paridita is known as **Isla Paridita** (cell 6464-2510, info@expeditionpanama.com, https://sites.google.com/site/islaparidita, all-inclusive rates are US$150 pp double occupancy, three-night minimum). It's perfectly designed for what the island and its surroundings have to offer. The property is owned by George Ravenscroft and his family, who are originally from San Diego. They bought 65 hectares of land on Paridita in 1995, before the national marine park was established. It was originally a family retreat, but in the last few years they have begun to share it with other visitors. It is managed by George's son Grant and his Nicaraguan wife, Marbel, who live on the island with their baby. Grant is a trained emergency medical technician and a licensed boat captain, both of which are reassuring since this place is far away from any hospitals.

The family is quick to emphasize this is by no means a resort. Accommodations are rustic, consisting of four thatched-roof, wood-and-cane cabins, two of which are on a black-sand beach and two a short walk away on a little cliff overlooking the ocean. However, the cabins have solar power so there's light at night and small fans over the mosquito-net-covered beds. The cabins also have flush toilets and attractive stone-walled, hot-water showers. They're reminiscent of Al Natural in Bocas del Toro or the Art Lodge on Isla Gubernadora. A kitchen and restaurant/bar is in another *rancho*. There are no more than eight guests at any time, and the vibe is Swiss Family Robinson–style adventure. One gets the sense that the family is as excited about this special place as their guests are, and that they enjoy showing it to others. It feels very much like a labor of love.

The rate of US$150 per person may seem a bit steep for such a rustic place, but it's actually quite a reasonable deal given that this includes not just the cabin but meals, activities, and transfers between the island and Boca Chica, which takes about 40 minutes in their large, sturdy, and high-powered boat. If you hired a boat to come out for the day, the cost of fuel alone would cost nearly as much as a night's stay.

Activities include a boat trip to neighboring islands, a "jungle tour" of Paridita, and unlimited access to kayaks and snorkeling equipment. There's an extra fee for scuba-diving trips. In season, guests in the beach cabins can watch sea turtles nesting right below their feet, and guests in the cliff cabins can watch from the comfort of their bed as humpback whales cavort offshore.

The owners have also built a walkway that leads to a thatched-roof hut in the middle of one of the lagoons; stand here in silence for a few minutes and wait for your surroundings to start humming with bird and aquatic life. Grant and Marbel can supply a military-style hammock for those who want to string it up in the hut and spend the night communing with the swamp life.

ISLAS SECAS

The **Islas Secas Resort** (U.S. tel. 805/729-2737, www.islassecas.com, starts at US$639 s, US$855 d, three-night minimum, including all activities and meals) is one of the most exclusive places to stay in all of Panama. It consists of 16 small private islands far away from just about everything. The resort itself is on Isla Cavada, where there are six casitas for guests, a dining/lounging area, and a spa. There are generally no more than 14 guests at a time. The casitas are on a cove facing the ocean and are circular, yurt-style buildings that provide a panoramic view of the surroundings. Each has a queen-size bed, minibar, and bathroom. The largest, the Casita Grande, has a full kitchen.

While it's possible to do nothing but relax on a deserted beach, the resort's location is spectacular and lends itself to lots of nature activities. Possibilities include scuba diving or snorkeling, surfing near Morro Negrito, ocean kayaking, deep-sea and inshore fishing, and hiking on the islands. Diving and fishing in this region are outstanding.

Both "R&R" and considerably more expensive sportfishing packages are available, either by the night (three-night minimum) or by the week. All guests either arrive or depart on a Sunday, no matter which package they select. All stays includes room, all meals, and daily excursions and activities. These include scuba-diving, snorkeling, surfing, and boat trips to surrounding islands. Those opting for an R&R package can book sportfishing by the day for an extra fee. Spa services are extra, as are transfers to and from the island.

There is a short—and, for many, adrenaline-inducing—airstrip on Isla Cavada. Round-trip charter flights between Tocumen International

Airport in Panama City and the resort are available as an add-on to the weekly packages for US$600 per person. Those paying by the night only have access to a charter flight one way, either to or from the resort; transfers in the other direction are by boat to or from Boca Chica and then by road to or from David. This costs US$450 per person. Both transfer fees include land transportation between hotels and airports in David and Panama City.

ALOUATTA SANCTUARY AND ECO-LODGE

The Alouatta Sanctuary and Eco-Lodge (cell 6236-5336, www.alouattasanctuary.org, US$100 s, US$190 d in the lodge) is a monkey sanctuary 27 kilometers east of David. It was created by a couple of expat horticulturalists who originally intended simply to create a botanical garden on their 40 acres of former pastureland. They sold the sanctuary in 2012, but the new owners intend to keep the sanctuary going.

There are 200 types of palm and 25 types of heliconia here. There are also five wide, well-maintained trails for those who'd like to stroll the grounds.

In 2012, Alouatta had six mantler howler monkeys, three tamarins, and one kittenish coati cub. The tamarins are rescued pets and have to be kept in an enclosure; familiarity with humans has made them too aggressive to be released back into the wild. The other animals are free to wander the grounds and leave altogether when they're ready. The new owners will offer guests opportunities to observe the sanctuary's wildlife up close, with staff present.

Day visitors are welcome with advance notice. The price for a day visit ranges US$10–55, depending on what is included (lunch, guided nature hike, yoga, and so on).

In addition to staying in the lodge, overnight guests can also opt to stay in a basic, rustic jungle hut that is entirely screened in (US$60 s, US$100 d). It features two single beds and nothing else. Visitors can also spend the night in an enclosed, military-style hammock (US$45 pp), with a shared bathroom. A less-rustic cabin with a private bathroom was nearing completion in 2012 (US$130 s, US$260 d). The overnight rates seem steep for the rustic accommodations, but perhaps the finished product offered by the new owners will justify the rates.

A large deck with a stunning view of the ocean and surrounding countryside was nearing completion in 2012. Next to it is a large fire pit for cookouts. The owners rely as little as possible on electricity, which is supplied only by a generator.

The turnoff for Alouatta is on the Interamericana 27 kilometers east of David or 12 kilometers west of the Herconcitos crossroads. There is a yellow sign for the lodge at the turnoff, but it's only visible from the eastbound lane. The lodge is three kilometers uphill on a rough dirt road that requires four-wheel-drive. After 2.7 kilometers, turn left at the Alouatta Lodge and park at the grass lot 300 meters farther uphill. The grounds of the lodge are high enough up to have fantastic views of the Gulf of Chiriquí and Isla Boca Brava.

LAS LAJAS

The most popular mainland beach in the region is at Las Lajas, the turnoff to which is about 75 kilometers east of David (or 35 kilometers east of Horconcitos) on the Interamericana. It's a long, wide, gray-sand beach with few facilities. It's not all that pretty or otherwise special, but it's the most accessible large expanse of sand around, and it's big enough to offer seclusion even on busy dry-season weekends.

The crossroads of the Interamericana and the road leading down to Las Lajas is known as **El Cruce de San Felix.** This is a common pit stop for buses and private cars making the long haul across the country. It has a gas station, but skip the hole-in-the-wall greasy spoon and hotel, and don't take your eyes off your stuff for a second.

The beach is a 13-kilometer drive south

HIDDEN HANDICRAFTS

The town of **Tolé**, about 25 kilometers east of El Cruce de San Felix, is worth a visit if you're in the area. During the day, Ngöbe-Buglé vendors set up roadside stands along the Interamericana just east of town. This is a good place to buy their crafts, including popular handwoven *chácaras* (bags), traditional dresses, and *chaquiras* (necklaces made from bright beads). The best of the necklaces are suitable for framing.

down a paved but pitted road from El Cruce, a drive that leads through the town of Las Lajas itself. Curve right when the road forks at a small yellow building in the center of town; if the road turns to dirt, you've missed the turn. The road ends at the beach.

Accommodations and Food

The road to the beach ends in a T-intersection. A few rustic places to stay and eat are scattered along the dirt roads to the left and right of this intersection, and there is now one rather appealing hotel. Most visitors just come for the day, hiring a *rancho* at one of several compounds in the area which provide shade, a parking spot, bathrooms, and usually a simple place to eat and drink. You'll probably need a four-wheel drive to get down these roads in the rainy season.

A good option for backpackers is **Cabañas Panamá** (cell 6561-9470, starts at US$20/cabin), in a secluded spot about 700 meters down the dirt road to the right as you face the beach. It's been here for years, and it never seems to change. (This place has had a variety of names over the years, and you may just see a sign for cabanas). It's a fenced-off property with nine cabins—bamboo huts, really—right on a long, wide, peaceful beach. Each has foam mattresses, cement floors, a loft for sleeping bags, and a picnic

table outside. They're super-rustic but adequate for a no-frills stay. They don't have bathrooms; a separate building houses basic shared toilets and showers. There are also six rooms in a building set back from the beach. These do have cold-water bathrooms but zero charm: They're basically four concrete walls, bunk beds, and a cement floor, and they're next door to a garbage dump. A restaurant and bar on the premises prepares meals when there are enough guests, which usually means the dry season. At other times, dinner is whatever you bring yourself.

Rates are per accommodation, not per person. High-season rates are US$20 for the cabins and US$40 for the rooms back from the beach. Prices are halved in the rainy season. If you stuff more than a car's worth of people into either, though, they'll charge another US$5 for the second car. That buys a 24-hour stay. Camping on the property is US$10 per group (US$5 in the rainy season). Day use of the facilities is US$5; the fee is waived for overnight guests. Again, a group is defined as a carload.

Las Lajas Beach Resort (cell 6790-1972, www.laslajasbeachresort.com, US$99 s/d, a/c) is a new and pleasant place to stay. Rooms are in a bright-yellow hacienda-style building set on a garden right above the beach. Rooms are simply decorated but cheerful, with two queen beds, hot water, cable TV, in-room safes, high ceilings, and nature scenes painted on the walls. There's an attractive, good-size pool and an open-air restaurant/bar that looks out on the beach. Service here seems friendly and attentive. This is a popular place in the dry season.

Getting There and Around

Buses to the town of Las Lajas leave the David bus terminal at 11:45 A.M., 12:45 P.M., 4:25 P.M., and 5:20 P.M. and return at 2:15 P.M. and 3:15 P.M. The trip takes 1.5 hours and costs US$3.

The beach is eight kilometers from the town, and the only way to get to the beach from town is to take a taxi, which may be hard to find in town. A better option is to take any bus running along the Interamericana that goes as far as the Las Lajas crossroads, which is called El Cruce de San Felix. The fare is US$3. Get off there and take a taxi (US$6) to the beach, which is 13 kilometers from the Interamericana. Long-distance buses from David that go at least as far as El Cruce de San Felix include the San Felix and Tolé buses, which run about every 20 minutes. Getting back to El Cruce de San Felix from the beach can be tricky during the week and in the rainy season, when few taxis may be hanging around. Consider arranging a pickup time with the taxi driver, or asking for a contact phone number.

For those who don't want to bother with buses, taxis between the Las Lajas beach and David cost US$45.

MORRO NEGRITO SURF CAMP

Started in June 1998, Morro Negrito Surf Camp (www.surferparadise.com) is on two islands in the Gulf of Chiriquí east of Las Lajas. The actual surf camp, Morro Negrito, is on an island that the locals call **Ensenada.** The camp has rustic cabanas, running water, and a dining area. Electricity is generated in the evenings. The waves here are smaller than on the second island, with faces that range 1.5–2.5 meters on average. The other island is **Isla Silva de Afuera,** a half hour away by boat. This is the main surfing island, with wave faces that average 3.5–5.5 meters. There are both left and right breaks on both islands. Ten breaks have been discovered so far. The best time to find big waves is April–October. For non-surfers there's a long beach, ocean kayaking, horseback riding, snorkeling, and fishing (bring your own gear for the last two). It's also possible to hike to a 15-meter waterfall.

Only weeklong packages are offered (Saturday to Saturday). Packages cost US$640 per person and include all food, local transfers to and from the mainland, and daily boat trips for surfing, snorkeling, or fishing.

■ PLAYA SANTA CATALINA

Santa Catalina is the best surfing spot in Panama, with one of the most consistent breaks in Central or South America. There's something to ride here every month of the year. While Santa Catalina is of greatest interest to serious surfers, it's a pretty place even for those who just want to watch the rollers from a distance, and it's becoming the prime jumping-off spot for trips to Coiba. However, much of the beach is strewn with rocks and boulders, and it's a remote and isolated spot west of the Azuero Peninsula, at the tip of sparsely settled farmland. Most lodging and dining options are still basic, though facilities are improving rapidly. There are just enough appealing and reasonably priced things to do, places to stay, and spots to eat and drink to attract adventurous, fun-loving travelers, but it has not yet been discovered by the masses. Those who want to get off the beaten track should consider a visit. Those who just want some beach time, though, will find better and more accessible spots elsewhere.

The main surfing season is March–October, though the surf is consistent year-round. Historically, January–February has the smallest swell. Wave faces can get as high as 6–9 meters at *la Punta* (the Point), Santa Clara's most famous break. There are several other breaks, some requiring a boat ride to reach, that can get even bigger.

National and international surf competitions are sometimes held in Santa Catalina, during which the place gets packed and advance reservations are a must. Those not participating may want to avoid the area during these times. Check www.santacatalinabeach.com or local hotels to see if a contest is scheduled during your visit.

The nearest sizable settlement on the drive down to the beach is Soná, an unattractive crossroads town with little to offer travelers. You can get some provisions there, but you're better off stocking up back in Santiago, on the Interamericana, a two-hour drive from the beach.

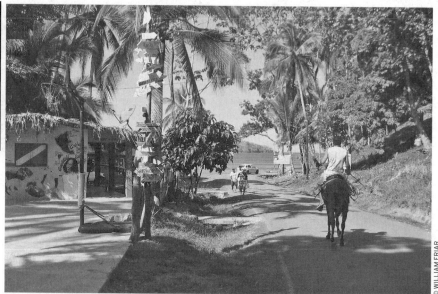

© WILLIAM FRIAR

Playa Santa Catalina

The road ends right at the beach. Along the road are several places to stay, a few dive operators and a kayak operation, and some houses. This is part fishing village, part surfers' hangout. A left turn onto a newly paved road leads to most of the surf camps and restaurants.

Surfing

The internationally famous surf break at Santa Catalina, **La Punta** (The Point), has been described as a perfect point break with long, powerful hollow waves that break left and right. The sea bottom is volcanic rock, so bring booties. This place is strictly for experienced surfers; it's all too easy to bust a board or a head on those rocks. It can only be surfed within two hours of high tide. There's also a **sand beach break** with hollow lefts and rights that are smaller than waves at the point and popular with beginners.

Several other breaks in the area are less well known. **Punta Brava,** about a half-hour walk southeast of Santa Catalina point, is a hollow left-hand, rock-bottom which can get twice as big as those at Santa Catalina. **Punta Roca,** about a half-hour walk northeast of Catalina, is another left-hand point break, about the same size as Catalina. Except for the Santa Catalina point break, which can be surfed at medium or high tide, experienced surfers say these other waves can be ridden only at medium to low tide.

Isla Cebaco, which is accessible only by boat, is an island with a beach break and point break, with left- and right-breaking waves that tend to be somewhat bigger than Catalina point. The truly ambitious can opt for a trip to **Isla Montuosa,** 3–4 hours west of Coiba. The waves here have five-meter faces and are shallow, hollow, and powerful. Do not attempt to surf them unless you really know what you're doing. Surfers should plan on a two-day trip, including a night on the island.

Some of the surf camps rent surfboards, though expect these to be pretty banged up. The going daily rate is US$10 for a short board or US$15 for a long board. **Surf and Shakes** (cell 6451-9939, 9 a.m.–6 p.m. daily) is a surf shop in a house a few minutes' walk up the road that leads to the surf camps. Surfboards are US$12, or US$20 with a surf lesson. Beach gear is also for sale. As the name suggests, they also serve milk shakes and other snacks. The cheapest place to rent surfboards at the time of writing was Santa Catalina Surf Point, at the end of the surf-camp road, just before the estuary.

Scuba, Snorkeling, Sea Kayaking, and Nature Tours

There are plenty of beautiful islands and dive spots to explore. Nearby islands include **Isla Cebaco,** known for clear waters and good coral. But the biggest draw is **Parque Nacional Coiba,** at the heart of which is the astonishing **Isla de Coiba,** about a 1.5-hour trip away by fast boat. Given the distance and how amazing Coiba is, those with the time and money should consider staying overnight on the island. Still, you may not have to go nearly that far to encounter spectacular sea life.

Some of the hotels and surf camps offer trips to the islands, usually on pretty basic *pangas.* These should be fine for trips to nearby islands, but I don't recommend them for trips on the open ocean. For trips to Coiba and other distant destinations, stick with substantial boats that have life preservers, an emergency radio, and, preferably, a spare motor. The seas can quickly turn rough out here, and the ride to Coiba is bumpy year-round.

Those who choose to go this route should expect to pay about US$75 per person for snorkeling trips to Coiba, with a minimum group size. Boats set off for Coiba around 8 a.m., so make arrangements at least a day ahead of time, ideally more, to avoid disappointment. Those who want to hire a private boat should expect to pay a minimum of US$250 just for the boat ride to Coiba and back.

A better option is to go with one of the dive outfits or a more organized tour operator. These can accommodate snorkelers and those who want to explore the island of Coiba itself. Be sure to ask for the itinerary of these trips, as the area around the ranger station is a popular first stop, but only a taste of what the island and its waters have to offer. A good introduction to the area would also include a visit to the Bahía Damas area, on the east side of the island.

Prices for trips to Parque Nacional Coiba, which includes the island of Coiba and its surrounding waters, generally do not include the park entrance fee. This is US$20 per person, payable at the ranger station on the island.

There are now three dive operators in Santa Catalina. They're on the main road near the town beach, making it easy to do comparison-shopping.

They offer dives on 25-foot boats at a number of spots close to Santa Catalina and around Parque Nacional Coiba, which is about a 90-minute boat ride away. The cheapest scuba trips are a two-tank dive at nearby spots (about US$60–65 pp). A two-tank trip to Parque Nacional Coiba starts at US$105–110. Rates include guide, tanks, and weights, but not the US$20 per person park entrance fee. Add US$10 to the prices to rent full diving gear.

The dive operators tend to offer a calendar of multiday dive trips to Coiba. These typically include transportation, all meals, lodging at the ranger station, and fees. Expect to pay around US$480 for two-day, six-dive trips and about US$650 for three-day, nine-dive trips. Nondivers pay around US$270 for a two-day trip and US$375–390 for a three-day trip. There's usually a two-person minimum for all these trips.

Besides Coiba and the local area, **Coiba Dive Center** (cell 6780-1141 or 6774-0808, www.coibadivecenter.com or www.scuba-charters.com) makes trips all over the Golfo de Chiriquí, including Islas Secas, Islas Ladrones, and Isla Montuosa. There's a three-person minimum on all dive trips.

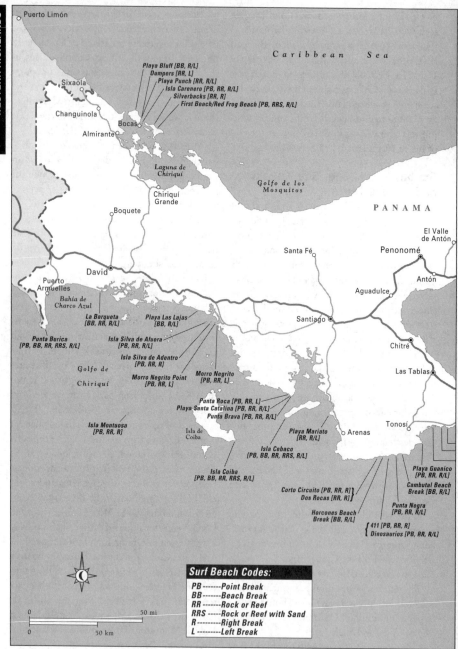

Puerto Limón

Caribbean Sea

Playa Bluff [BB, R/L]
Dumpers [RR, L]
Playa Punch [RR, R/L]
Isla Carenero [PB, RR, R/L]
Silverbacks [RR, R]
First Beach/Red Frog Beach [PB, RRS, R/L]

Sixaola

Changuinola

Bocas

Almirante

Laguna de Chiriquí

Golfo de los Mosquitos

Chiriquí Grande

Boquete

PANAMA

El Valle de Antón

Santa Fé

Penonomé

David

Antón

Puerto Armuelles

Aguadulce

Bahía de Charco Azul

La Barqueta [BB, RR, R/L]
Playa Las Lajas [BB, R/L]

Santiago

Punta Burica [PB, BB, RR, RRS, R/L]

Isla Silva de Afuera [PB, RR, R/L]

Chitré

Isla Silva de Adentro [PB, RR, R]

Las Tablas

Golfo de Chiriquí

Morro Negrito [PB, RR, L]

Morro Negrito Point [PB, RR, L]

Punta Roca [PB, RR, L]
Playa Santa Catalina [PB, RR, R/L]
Punta Brava [PB, RR, R/L]

Tonosí

Isla Montuosa [PB, RR, R]

Isla de Coiba

Playa Mariato [RR, R/L]

Arenas

Isla Cebaco [PB, BB, RR, RRS, R/L]

Isla Coiba [PB, BB, RR, RRS, R/L]

Playa Guanico [PB, RR, R/L]

Corto Circuito [PB, RR, R]
Dos Rocas [RR, R]

Cambutal Beach Break [BB, R/L]

Punta Negra [PB, RR, R/L]

Horcones Beach Break [BB, R/L]

411 [PB, RR, R]
Dinosaurios [PB, RR, R/L]

Surf Beach Codes:

PB --------Point Break
BB --------Beach Break
RR --------Rock or Reef
RRS -----Rock or Reef with Sand
R ----------Right Break
L ----------Left Break

0   50 mi
0   50 km

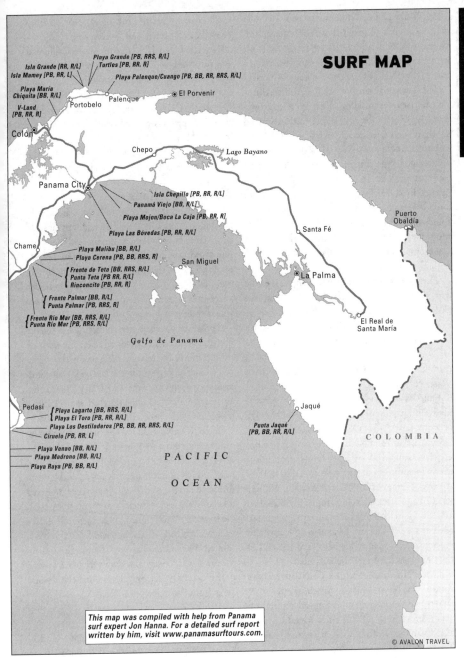

SURF MAP

Isla Grande [RR, R/L]
Isla Mamey [PB, RR, L]

Playa Grande [PB, RRS, R/L]
Turtles [PB, RR, R]

Playa Palenque/Cuango [PB, BB, RR, RRS, R/L]

Playa María
Chiquita [BB, R/L]

V-Land
[PB, RR, R]

Portobelo

Palenque

El Porvenir

Colón

Chepo

Lago Bayano

Panama City

Isla Chepillo [PB, RR, R/L]
Panamá Viejo [BB, R/L]
Playa Mojon/Boca La Caja [PB, RR, R]

Playa Las Bóvedas [PB, RR, R/L]

Santa Fé

Puerto
Obaldía

Chame

Playa Malibu [BB, R/L]
Playa Cerena [PB, BB, RRS, R]

Frente de Teta [BB, RRS, R/L]
Punta Teta [PB RR, R/L]
Rinconcito [PB, RR, R]

Frente Palmar [BB, R/L]
Punta Palmar [PB, RRS, R]

Frente Río Mar [BB, RRS, R/L]
Punta Río Mar [PB, RRS, R/L]

San Miguel

La Palma

El Real de
Santa María

Golfo de Panamá

Pedasí

Playa Lagarto [BB, RRS, R/L]
Playa El Toro [PB, RR, R/L]

Playa Los Destiladeros [PB, BB, RR, RRS, R/L]

Ciruelo [PB, RR, L]

Playa Venao [BB, R/L]
Playa Madrono [BB, R/L]
Playa Raya [PB, BB, R/L]

Jaqué

Punta Jaqué
[PB, BB, RR, R/L]

COLOMBIA

PACIFIC

OCEAN

This map was compiled with help from Panama surf expert Jon Hanna. For a detailed surf report written by him, visit www.panamasurftours.com.

© AVALON TRAVEL

A full-day Coiba snorkeling trip costs US$55 per person, but consider the US$65 per person Coiba tour, which includes a half day of snorkeling and a half day on the island, including a tour of what's left of the penal colony. All prices include gear and transportation. PADI certification courses start at US$115 for a one-day, one-dive Discover Scuba course. A PADI Advanced Open Water certification course is US$325.

Scuba Coiba (cell 6980-7122 or 6575-0122, www.scubacoiba.com) was the first land-based scuba operation in Santa Catalina, having opened in 2003. They speak English, Spanish, and German here. Besides its day trips to local spots and Parque Nacional Coiba, it also offers multiday Coiba trips, with overnight stays on Isla Coiba, and packages that combine diving with hotel stays.

There's a two-diver minimum on most of the trips, but singles can arrange a two-tank dive close to Santa Catalina for US$90. PADI certification courses start with a one-day, one-tank Discover Scuba courses around Santa Catalina or Coiba. Other courses range from a scuba tune-up to Open Water and Advanced Open Water certification.

Fluid Adventures (cell 6560-6558, http://fluidadventurespanama.com) offers a whole range of water-based adventures. These include seakayak trips around Santa Catalina (US$50 pp) and Isla Coiba (US$105 pp, four-person minimum, including boat transport to Coiba but not the park entrance fee). Overnight and multiday kayak trips are available. Single (US$35/day) and double (US$55/day) kayaks are available to rent, as are surfboards. They also offer surf and yoga classes. Their office is toward the end of the main road, next to Scuba Coiba.

Javier Elizondo of **Coiba Eco-Tours/Casa Kenia** (cell 6544-1806, www.casakenia.com, javier@casakenia.com) has a good reputation as a professional, reliable tour operator. He is also the only birding guide in Santa Catalina. Tours include one-day and multiday trips to Coiba for snorkeling, hiking, and/or birding, as well as surf tours and fishing trips.

Javier is bilingual (he's from Southern California) and runs the business along with his Panamanian wife, Kenia. Their house, Casa Kenia, has rooms for guests starting at US$32 s/d with private bath. Day trips to Coiba without stays in Casa Kenia start at US$225 pp for two people, though the rate drops to US$100 pp for groups of six. Coiba Eco-Tours/Casa Kenia is just off the main road, uphill on the right just before the road dead-ends at the beach.

Accommodations

More comfortable accommodations are slowly coming to Santa Catalina. The relatively upscale places are primarily along the main road that leads into the village. Most of the surf camps (and restaurants) are off the road that intersects the town's main (and only) street. The sea view gets better and better at each place to stay along the road, which ends at an estuary 1.6 kilometers away.

Those without their own transportation should note that it's a considerable walk between most of the surf camps and town. It takes about 20 minutes at a good clip to get from the last one, Oasis Surf camp, to the town's main road. Carry a flashlight, as there are no lights along the road and without a moon you'll literally be stumbling about in the dark.

The surf-camp road is a left turn off the main road as one comes into town. It was paved in late 2011 and is now a breeze to drive, though the road has no shoulders and is bordered by deep drainage ditches which are all too easy to drive, bike, or walk into, especially at night; some people have. The surf camps are at the ends of private, mainly dirt, roads that lead from this road toward the water. These can be rough, and in the rainy season very muddy. Every place to stay in this area is either right above or a short walk away from the main point break.

US$10-25

It's been fun over the years to watch the evolution of **Cabañas Rolo** (cell 6494-3916 or

6598-9926, cabinasrolo@yahoo.com, www. rolocabins.net, dorm beds US$10 pp, private rooms US$20–40 s/d). Other surfers' hangouts come and go, but Rolo just keeps getting bigger, better, and more popular. The dorm rooms are in two motel-style rows near the end of the main road and just up from the beach. Most of the dorms have single beds and sleep two to four people, but there's one private room with a double bed for couples. The dorm rooms are simple but cheerful and clean, cooled only with rotary floor fans and equipped with hammocks to lounge in on the front terrace. There are shared toilets and showers next door. There's a communal kitchen and a little restaurant that's open from the morning to 9 P.M.

Rolo in recent years has added two two-story hacienda-style buildings with fancier air-conditioned rooms, one on each floor. All have a double and single bed with okay mattresses, satellite TV, private bathrooms, and a front terrace with table. These are US$40 s/d, US$10 more for a third person.

The Blue Zone Surf and Dive Hostel (www. bluezonepanama.com, US$12 s, US$24 d) consists of a hive of rooms in a long, funky adobe-style building near the edge of a bluff just above the rocky beach and surf break. Its five fan-cooled rooms are rustic, a bit snug, and have foam beds, but are pleasant enough for the price. The walls are made from cinderblocks and don't have screens, but the beds have mosquito nets. There are three shared bathrooms, a shared kitchen and dining room, and laundry facilities. It's located just past and on the same road as Pizzeria Jamming.

Boarder's Haven (cell 6572-0664, starts at US$10 pp) is a tiny surf hostel with three rooms next to and managed by La Buena Vida on the main road. The mattresses are decent, and there are hot-water shared bathrooms. The roof is corrugated zinc, so it can get boiling hot in this little place during the day. The doorways here are shaped like surfboards. This place is a fair walk to the nearest surf break.

The most popular surfers' hostel at the time of writing was **Santa Catalina Surf Point** (cell 6550-5555, info@santacatalinasurfpoint.com, www.santacatalinasurfpoint.com, dorm beds US$8–10 pp). It's next to Rancho Estero, right before the surf-camp road ends at the estuary. It's run by a Frenchman, his Panamanian wife, and their family members and has a friendly family vibe. Fan-cooled dorm rooms are US$8–10 per person; if the room is full enough, they turn on the air-conditioning. Small private rooms are US$10–12 pp with shared bath or US$30 s/d with air-conditioning and private bath. The more expensive rooms are not very attractive, but they're new. More rooms are on the way. Tents are available for those who would prefer to camp on the grounds (US$5 pp). This is also a cheap place to rent surfboards. Guests pay US$5/$10 half/full day. Nonguests pay US$2 more.

US$25-50

At the end of the dirt road that runs past the other surf camps is 🄲 **Oasis Surf Camp** (cell 6588-7077, www.oasissurfcamp.com, US$38.50 s/d with fan, US$49.50 s/d with air-conditioning). It's past the end of the road, on Playa El Estero, a beach at the estuary of a small river. It's actually nicer than the phrase "surf camp" suggests, but the best thing about this place, which opened in 2002, is that it's right on a wide, black-sand beach rather than on a hill looking down on rocks. It's the nicest spot for those who just want to sunbathe or splash about, and the surf here is much better for beginners, thanks to gentler waves and sand bottoms. Oasis Surf Camp rents boards (US$10–15/day) and offers lessons (US$25 per hour, including board). Airport transfers and boat excursions are sometimes available.

Oasis offers six somewhat rustic but pleasant rooms, three with double beds and three with two single beds, in cabanas on the edge of the beach. Each can sleep up to three people

© WILLIAM FRIAR

The Gecko Villa is the most whimsical and charming of the cabañas at La Buena Vida.

and has a cold-water bathroom, fan, and front patio with a hammock facing the beach. Air-conditioning is available for US$11 more. A larger casa can sleep up to six. Campers can pitch a tent on the spacious grounds for US$5 pp. The place is owned by an Italian family from Rome and is run by the younger members of the family: Silvia and David.

Breakfast, lunch, and dinner are available. Dinner is the highlight, with David and Silvia cooking authentic Italian food. Meals are served in an attractive *rancho* restaurant/bar behind the cabins. Oasis Surf Camp is on the far side of the estuary from town. A four-wheel drive can ford it in the dry season, but those with regular cars will have to park and splash across year-round. The surf camp recently opened a hostel **Hostal Oasis** (cell 6588-7077, US$10 pp) back in town on the main road near the turnoff to the surf-camp road. It's in a wooden, red-tile-roofed building with a shared kitchen and wraparound terrace.

The newly renovated **Rancho Estero** (cell 6562-9747, www.ranchoestero.com, starts at US$15 s, US$20 d) consists of cane-walled, thatched-roof cabins on a rise just above the estuary, toward the end of the surf-camp road. The grounds are well tended, the cabins are rustic but pleasant, and the view is spectacular. A bar/restaurant in a *rancho* on the edge of the hill is perched right above the surf. The place is managed by the same folks who run Fluid Adventures, so it's easy to rent kayaks (US$35/day) and surfboards (US$15/day) and arrange tours.

US$50-100

Surfside (cell 6929-2996, surfsidepanama@gmail.com, www.dospalmascatalina.com, starts at US$44 s/d, US$16.50 pp dorms) is a new incarnation of an old surf camp, now under the management of the same folks who've taken over the running of Hotel Boca Brava in the Boca Chica area. As with that hotel, they're gradually upgrading what had been a quite basic place as finances allow. For instance, they've put in new, semi-orthopedic mattresses, done some decoration, and generally spruced up the place. The main building has three rooms upstairs (US$55 s/d, US$66 for two-bedroom suite with terrace), and four rooms downstairs (US$49.50 s/d) with AC and hot water. A motel-style building right above La Punta has the cheapest private rooms and dorms. Air-conditioning should be installed in all the rooms by the time you visit. This place is very much a work in progress, but it's definitely on the way up.

Cabañas Sol y Mar (cell 6920-2631, www.solymarpanama.com, US$72.60 s/d, a/c) which opened in 2005, sits on a steep hill on the main road leading into Santa Catalina, just a few minutes' walk from the ocean, but a fair distance from the surf breaks. There are six rooms in three duplex corrugated-roof cabins on the hillside. Each room has two okay double beds and a sitting area with two foam-rubber foldout futons. A third and fourth person in each room is about US$12 each. The rooms are fairly bare, but they have cable TV, a minifridge, hot water, and a front porch with hammock. The latest addition is an open-air restaurant at the top of the property, which is as popular for its food as it is for its views, especially at sunset.

Sol y Mar is cheerful and appealing. The place is managed by Luis Manuel Marques de Silva, a capable Portuguese guy, who one suspects will continue to upgrade the place as finances allow. He can arrange transfers to and from Panama City for US$230 each way for groups of up to four people.

◖ **La Buena Vida** (cell 6572-0664, www. labuenavida.biz, starts at US$66 s/d, US$11 more for each additional person, US$5 children under 18, a/c) opened in 2007 and has just three cabanas, but the owners are planning to build more eventually. This is my favorite place to stay in Santa Catalina. It's just down the street from Cabañas Sol y Mar, and is just a few minutes' walk from the ocean, but a bit of a hike to the nearest surf break. It's a cute little complex that includes a gift shop selling handicrafts made by local women and kids (75 percent of the proceeds go to the artists), and a terrace café/restaurant that's a pleasant spot for a meal or a drink. Food is good and includes lots of healthy options. The place is owned and operated by Mike and Michelle, a friendly, mellow couple from Alaska. Michelle is also a massage therapist and yoga instructor whose spa/yoga studio is a breezy covered deck on a hill at the top of the property.

The cabanas have different designs, but are equally pleasant. The two-story Bird Villa (US$77 s/d) has two double beds and a terrace on both floors. It can sleep up to four people. The Butterfly Villa (US$66 s/d) accommodates up to five; its most memorable feature is the outdoor (but private) shower. The newest is the Gecko Villa (US$88 s/d), which is the most whimsical and charming yet. Geckos feature throughout, from a giant tile gecko along the shower to another one right above the bed; its eyes are reading lights. All are spacious and have a ceiling fan, screened windows, a fridge, and a private terrace and hammocks.

Guests also have access to a binder stuffed with local tips about anything you could possibly ask. There are loving touches throughout the complex, such as pretty mosaic-tile designs and tree branches that have been left alone to grow in and around the buildings.

Mike and Michelle have also started renting out "Casa de Mar," a little one-bedroom house on the property where they used to live. It has two double beds, one set of bunk beds, a full kitchen, a private outdoor shower, air-conditioning, and a barbecue on a covered patio. It goes for US$121 for up to four people.

◖ **Hotel Santa Catalina** (cell 6571-4387 or 6781-4847, www.hotelsantacatalinapanama. com, US$70 s/d, a/c) is the most upscale place to stay in Santa Catalina. Formerly home to Kenny's Surf camp, it's on a spacious, grassy property looking out on the boulder-strewn point and has six spotless, well-maintained rooms with high ceilings, memory-foam beds, and minifridges. The rooms are pretty much unadorned, but they feature lots of handsome teak and pine. Each room sleeps up to four people; one oddity of the place is that each room features a bunk bed as well as either two singles or one king-size bed. Rooms are in a Spanish-style, red-tile-roofed building set on a lawn quite a ways back from the water. A large thatch-roofed *rancho* houses a restaurant (7 A.M.–3 P.M. daily), which is open to the public. This place is managed in conjunction with Los Pibes restaurant next door, where guests are encouraged to go for dinner. The property is surrounded by a wall on one end and the ocean on the other; the gate is locked at night. The beach is too rocky to be inviting or even scenic, but the breaking surf is wonderfully photogenic. A swimming pool is in the works. Surfboards are available for US$10–15, or US$25 with a lesson. Bikes are available for free. Spanish, French, and Italian are spoken here.

VICINITY OF PLAYA SANTA CATALINA

There is one place to stay on the way to Santa Catalina worth considering, especially for nature lovers who don't need to be on a sandy beach with crashing breakers. **Hibiscus Garden** (no phone, info@hibiskusgarten.de, www.hibiscusgarden.com, US$10–30 pp) is run by two friendly German couples from Munich who offer eight rooms along a stretch of beach on the Golfo de Montijo. The rooms are a bit bare, but the nicest (and most expensive) have air-conditioning, hot-water bathrooms, and bed frames and bathroom sinks made from polished driftwood. Those on a tighter budget can opt for rooms with bunk beds, fans, and shared bathrooms for US$10 pp. The place is near the mouth of the Río Lagatero, and the beach ends in mudflats that stretch out 600 meters before meeting the sea at low tide. The tide here is six meters, so twice a day it comes rushing right up to the property line in half an hour. This is an isolated spot so those who come here should be looking for peace and quiet.

Breakfast, lunch, and dinner are served in a *rancho* nearby, which is equipped with a pizza oven. They make German bread here.

Daily surfboard rentals are US$10 for short boards or US$15 for long boards, but surf breaks are a boat or car ride away. The owners offer a shuttle service to Playa Catalina (US$3 pp), which is about 11 kilometers away.

Things to do here include horseback riding and bird-watching (especially shorebirds). Snorkeling and fishing trips to Isla Cebaco include lunch. Trips to nearby mangroves to go caiman-spotting are also possible.

There's a communal kitchen on the property. Those coming by bus will be dropped off along the main road at the flyspeck village of Lagatero. From there it's a kilometer walk along a cattle path; those driving need a four-wheel drive, particularly in the rainy season. The turnoff is three kilometers before Hicaco on the way to Santa Catalina.

CAMPING

Camping is best done in the dry season, as it can get awfully wet and mucky around here in the rainy season. The nicest and safest place to camp is **Oasis Surf Camp** (tel. 202-1022, cell 6588-7077, www.oasissurfcamp.com, US$5 pp) on Playa El Estero. A close second is **Santa Catalina Surf Point** (cell 6550-5555, www.santacatalinasurfpoint.com), which is on the other side of the estuary, at the end of the surf-camp road. They also charge US$5 pp, and can provide tents at no extra charge.

Campers can also pitch a tent for free on the beach, but it might be better to work out a deal at one of the surfing camps or with a farmer to camp on their land. It doesn't always feel safe to camp on this beach, at least near the village itself.

Food

Like the accommodations, dining options are improving in Santa Catalina. There are now 22 places to eat in Santa Catalina; this would have been unbelievable just a couple of years ago. Of that 22, however, only a handful are particularly appealing. This is still a good place to come with a cooler and supplies, if possible, especially since the nearest grocery store of any size is back in Soná, about 70 kilometers away. A small general store and a fruit and vegetable stand are along the main road, however.

Because the entire area is oriented toward surfers, divers, and other outdoor adventurers (not to mention the fact it's a fishing village), Santa Catalina gets up and goes to bed early. Restaurants tend to open for breakfast at 7 A.M., and few stay open late. Most people have dinner around sundown, and late diners run a risk of going hungry.

A new town regulation allows places to sell booze until midnight, but few do so thus far.

Santa Catalina is not yet a late-night party spot. The most popular watering hole is **No Worries** (no phone, opens at 6 P.M. daily), a thatched-roof *rancho* close to Donde Viancka on the surf-camp road near town.

With a couple of notable exceptions, nearly all the appealing restaurants are located along the surf-camp road about a 10–15-minute walk from town. There are no streetlights; take a flashlight.

La Buena Vida (cell 6572-0664, 7 A.M.–2 P.M., US$6–7.50) is a cute open-air spot on the main road, and the food is good and features lots of healthier options that are hard to come by in Santa Catalina. Breakfast is US$2.50–5 and includes fruit salad, pancakes, homemade granola, breakfast burritos, delicious fresh-fruit smoothies and milk shakes, and a Greek scramble. Lunch includes salads, Mexican tacos, and sandwiches. A more exotic daily lunch special might include Thai, Indian, Mexican, or Italian fare. They can also make a to-go lunch for those going on excursions if the order is placed the night before. La Buena Vida has options for vegetarians, a rarity in the region.

The well-established **Pinguino Café** (cell 6477-8023, 7 A.M.–10 P.M. daily, US$8–14) is a rustic but appealing Italian-run place right above the town beach at the end of the main road. It's a great place to come at sundown. It serves both Italian and Panamanian food, but don't be in a hurry to get either; service is glacial. The pasta here is good.

The popular **Restaurante Donde Viancka** (cell 6585-9787, noon–9 P.M. daily, US$7–10) is a cozy place a few minutes' walk down the dirt road leading to the surf camps. The menu changes daily depending on what's fresh, but includes seafood, pasta, and Panamanian fare. It looks out on a field rather than the ocean, but there's a breezy upstairs balcony where groups can sit and catch a glimpse of the sea. The best thing about the restaurant is Viancka herself. Panama's 2001 surfing champion, she's a warm and friendly hostess who goes out of her way to make her clients happy.

Chili Rojo (cell 6872-3117, 7–10:30 A.M. and 6–10 P.M. daily, most mains US$15–19) is mainly a place to go for seafood, but the small menu also includes pasta and a few meat dishes. Food here is expensive but tasty, and the portions are huge. The "seafood rain" (US$14) is a heaping plate of all kinds of seafood in a wine and passion-fruit sauce; it could easily serve two. The restaurant is sometimes open for lunch, but only by reservation. The restaurant plays soft rock at hard-rock volumes and is in a thatched-roof *rancho* at the beginning of the beach road. As you crest the hill, it'll be on the right.

Some say **☐ Pizzeria Jamming** (cell 6447-1373, 6:30–10:30 P.M. Tues.–Sun., US$5.50–10) has the best pizza in Panama. That's hyperbole, but the place does serve real Italian pizza baked in a real wood-burning brick oven by real Italians (from Florence, to be exact). It's an open-air place near the edge of a bluff leading down to the surf break. There's a bar scene, and one end of the pizzeria is strung with hammocks where battered surfers can recover from their battles with monster waves. It's a cozy, relaxing spot to hang out in the evening.

Chano's (cell 6736-1652, US$10–16) is basically a wooden shack with three tables and a couple of counter spots next to Pizzeria Jamming, but it has a well-deserved local reputation for good seafood. The owner/chef is an intimidating-looking but kindly Venezuelan man who serves excellent clams and thick-cut french fries. The small menu focuses on seafood but also includes pasta and some meats. Breakfast can include huevos rancheros and pancakes. Chano doesn't have set hours, but he's usually open mornings until early–mid evenings. Call ahead for a reservation.

Those with a meat craving should stop by the Argentinean-owned **Los Pibes** (no phone, 6:30 P.M.–until guests leave daily, US$6.50–8), which has great burgers. It's a friendly, open-air place about a 15-minute walk from town, down the dirt road in the surf-camp area. To get there, head past Restaurante Donde Viancka and turn right at the sign. Another plus here is if you show up with a freshly caught fish, they'll cook it for you in their outdoor oven for free. The owners speak English, Spanish, and French.

A nameless **bakery** (no phone, 5–9 A.M. and 1–9 P.M. or so daily) is across the main road from La Buena Vida and offers delicious smells and warm smiles. The baked goods are rather bland, but they're fresh and cheap.

Information and Services

There are few services of any kind in Santa Catalina. For anything more than the basics, most people have to go to Soná or Santiago. Even basic communications have been slow to come to Santa Catalina. There is no home telephone service and there are no ATMs (the nearest is in Soná). The dive shops and a few hotels now accept credit cards, but most other businesses are cash only. The area finally has mobile-phone reception, but it can still be spotty. Come with enough cash to cover your stay and activities. There are two pay phones, on the main street near the beach.

A good website, www.santacatalinabeach.com, provides all kinds of useful information, and maps, on Santa Catalina and its accommodations, restaurants, and attractions. A giant area map is also signposted on the main road near the beach, but is not kept current.

Wireless Internet is gradually coming to Santa Catalina, which is a good thing because the only Internet café these days is inconveniently located one kilometer before town, along the main road. It's called **Los Tecales** (8 A.M.–9 P.M. daily, US$2/half-hour, US$3/hour). It also has a simple restaurant.

Getting There

There is an airstrip in Santa Catalina, but so far only private planes use it. For the foreseeable future, getting here means a long road trip, except for those few who come by private boat.

BY BUS

There are no direct bus connections to Playa Santa Catalina from major towns or cities. Travelers must first get to Soná, usually by way of Santiago, then take a bus or taxi to Santa Catalina, about 50 kilometers away. Get an early start to avoid having to overnight in Soná.

Buses from Panama City to Soná (US$9.70, about 4.5 hours) leave at 8:20 A.M., 10:20 A.M., 12:45 A.M., 2:20 P.M., 4:20 P.M., and 5:45 P.M. from the Gran Terminal Nacional de Transportes.

A better alternative for breaking one's journey is to go first to Santiago, switch to a Soná-bound bus from there, and then take another bus from Soná to Santa Catalina.

Buses to Santiago run constantly from Panama City, David, and other major cities. Any bus going at least as far as Santiago can drop passengers at the Pyramidal or Los Tucanes terminals outside of Santiago. Passengers will then have to go to the bus terminal in downtown Santiago, Terminal de Transporte de Veraguas, to catch the bus to Soná. Some buses go into Santiago and stop at this terminal, avoiding this nuisance transfer; be sure to ask. Best bets are the long-haul buses between David and Panama City. The fare between Panama City and Santiago is US$9.10.

Buses from Santiago to Soná leave from Santiago's Terminal de Transportes every 20 minutes, 5:30 A.M.–9:15 P.M. Mon.–Fri., 6 A.M.–8 P.M. Sat.–Sun. (US$2.10, a little under an hour).

Buses from Soná to Santa Catalina (US$4.85) leave at 5 A.M., 11 A.M., 2 P.M., and 4 P.M.

Plan ahead to make sure the different legs of your return journey from Santa Catalina link up; Soná is not an appealing place to get stranded. The return bus from Santa Catalina to Soná leaves from the main road in Santa Catalina at 7:15 A.M., 8:15 A.M., 1:15 P.M., and 3:15 P.M. From there, travelers can take one of the frequent buses to Santiago, which has good connections to other parts of Panama. Direct buses from Soná to Panama City leave Soná at 1:30 A.M., 4 A.M., 8:30 A.M., 10:30 A.M., 1:30 P.M., and 4 P.M.

BY TAXI

Travelers who decide to take a taxi from Santiago to Santa Catalina should expect to pay US$60–90; this is not a common trip, so there aren't really established prices. Taxis between Santa Catalina and Soná are US$30–40. There are better deals to be had going from Santa Catalina to Santiago than vice versa. Those with more money than time or patience can hire a taxi between Panama City and Santa Catalina for US$250–300.

DRIVING TO SANTA CATALINA

Those coming by car must pass through Santiago, the provincial capital of Veraguas. It's on the Interamericana between Panama City (250 km, about 3.5 hours) and David (190 km, about 4 hours). As you drive west, the highway forks just before Santiago. Take the left fork and drive into Santiago. This road forks at the church. Drive past the right side of the church and make the first right. Continue past the Museo Regional de Veraguas. Make a left at the first four-way intersection. You should see a communications tower on the left. It's possible to get this far through a second route that bypasses Santiago, but it's unmarked. Heading west on the Interamericana, drive eight kilometers past the overpass and make a left off the highway to the town of La Peña. Three kilometers on there'll be a T-intersection. Make a sharp right.

Continue straight to Soná, which is 50 kilometers southwest of Santiago on a scenic road that was recently repaved and has new bridges.

To continue to Santa Catalina, make a left at the gas station just before Soná; the turn is marked. Make a note of the mileage here. Continue on this okay road another 48 kilometers. This stretch has been plagued by potholes in the past, but it was being entirely resurfaced in 2012 so should be in good shape when you

visit. At the 48-kilometer mark, make a left turn. The turnoff may not be signposted, so keep an eye on the odometer. The road from this point on to Santa Catalina used to be brutal but was paved a few years ago and is in good shape.

The village of Hicaco is nine kilometers down this road. Make a right at the Hicaco police station. The road ends at Playa Santa Catalina, eight kilometers away. Driving straight through, the entire trip from either Panama City or David takes about five hours.

◧ PARQUE NACIONAL COIBA

Everything about Parque Nacional Coiba is big. It's one of the largest marine parks in the world. The island at the center of the park, **Coiba** (pronounced KWOY-buh), is Panama's largest—a massive 493 square kilometers. It has the second-largest coral reef in the eastern Pacific Ocean. And the waters are filled with big fish—very big fish, as in orcas, dolphins, humpback whales, whale sharks, manta rays, barracudas, amberjack, big snappers, three kinds of marlin, moray eels, and white-tip, hammerhead, and tiger sharks. A total of 760 species of fish and 33 species of shark have been recorded. Sharks and mantas are plentiful, and there's a decent chance of coming face to face with a sea turtle. Visibility can be unpredictable, but even on bad days one is likely to see some impressive creatures. The diving here has been described as a cross between that off the Galapagos Islands in Ecuador and the Cocos Islands in Costa Rica.

The park became even larger in 2004 when Panama enacted a law that raised its status and nearly doubled its area, to 430,821 hectares. Besides Coiba, the park includes the comparatively tiny (242-hectare) island of **Coibita** just off its northeast tip, the 20-square-kilometer island of **Jicarón,** the **Islas Contreras,** and 35 other islands and their surrounding waters, mangroves, and coral reefs. UNESCO declared it a World Heritage Site in 2005.

Coiba itself is still mainly covered in virgin forest—it's reportedly 85 percent intact—though there has been some deforestation and forest disruption. Rare moist tropical forest is the most common vegetation. As on most islands, there isn't a huge diversity of animal species on Coiba itself, but there are at least 36 species of mammals, including howler monkeys, and dozens of amphibians and reptiles, including the deadly fer-de-lance snake. You're much more likely to come across beautiful birds, however, of which there are about 150 known species. Coiba is just about the last stand in Panama of the gorgeous scarlet macaw, which are concentrated in an area called **Barco Quebrado.** Other impressive birds common on Coiba include the bicolored hawk and the enormous king vulture. Coiba also has several endemic species, including the Coiba spinetail (a bird—*Cranioleuca dissita*), Coiba agouti *(Dasyprocta coibensi),* and a local variety of howler monkey *(Alouatta palliata coibensis).*

Coiba attracts visitors largely on the strength of its world-class diving and deep-sea fishing. But the impact of human pressures, including the appearance of commercial fishing vessels that trawl these waters illegally, is beginning to mount.

Two things have so far kept nature more or less intact on and around Coiba: It's quite remote and hard to get to, and from 1919 to 2004 it was the home of a Devil's Island–style penal colony housing serious criminals. Prisoners were confined to a series of colonies around the massive island, but they were not locked in. Instead, guards locked themselves in their quarters with their guns at night. The island jungle and shark-filled ocean kept prisoners from straying too far.

The prison camp, along with its legacy of horror and misery, has been slowly phased out in recent years. Officially, the last 25 prisoners were removed from the island in 2004, but a few guards and model prisoners were left behind to maintain the area.

The island of Coiba is still relatively little known even by scientists. It's hilly in the center and crisscrossed by many rivers, including the 20-kilometer Río Negro. But because of the penal colony, access to the island itself is only now loosening up. Most visitors only come ashore in the area around an ANAM field station on the northeast tip of the island, which still has the only guest accommodations. The guest cabins are rustic but okay, and the station is on a sandy cove. However, tour operators are increasingly venturing to **Bahía Damas,** on the east side of the island, to visit the spooky ruins of the penal colony and dive among spectacular coral reefs.

There is a landing strip on Coiba, but only charter flights make the trip. Otherwise, access to the island is a long haul by land and sea. The logistical hassles in getting to Coiba almost force travelers to go with some kind of tour operator. This can get expensive, but you'll see a lot more and have a far more comfortable—and safe—trip than if you tried to get there on your own or by hiring a local fisherman.

Sports and Recreation

Dry season is the best time to see monkeys and other animals on shore. **Diving** can be good year-round, though visibility can vary dramatically day to day.

The waters off **Bahía Damas,** a bay on the east side of the island, have the largest coral reef in Central America (135 hectares) and the second-largest in the eastern Pacific. That and the density and diversity of large sea creatures have made the park famous among scuba divers. The sea life includes turtles, orcas, humpback whales, and sharks that zip right past divers. Because of the fragility of the environment here, and the necessity of knowing these waters well, diving trips should be arranged through reputable professionals.

A good and accessible spot for **snorkeling** is **Granito de Oro,** a lovely islet a short boat ride from the ANAM field station. There are coral fields, including brain and fan coral, and schools of pretty little tropical fish just off the islet's sandy beach. The current becomes very strong just beyond the rocky cove—even strong swimmers should be careful not to venture out too far. This spot is sometimes visited by small cruise ships that bring passengers over for a snorkel.

There are two trails—short walks, really—around the ANAM ranger station. The **Sendero del Observatorio** (Observatory Trail) is a 15-minute walk at a very slow pace that leads to an elevated bird-watching station. It's not a particularly good place to watch birds, but the view is nice. The trail starts behind cabin 6. Note the sign that says the trail is "approximately" 527.81 meters long. Another brief walk behind the kitchen leads up to a second lookout point on a small hill. It has a lovely view of the sea and Isla Coibita.

The **Sendero de Los Monos** (Monkey Trail) is not accessible from the ranger station. It requires a boat ride to the area near the Granito de Oro islet. It takes about an hour to walk and curves inland from one beach to another. There are howlers and white-faced capuchins along the trail, but you'd be lucky to spot them; best bet is in the dry season. Other flora and fauna found along the trail include fiddler and hermit crabs, coconut trees, the guinea pig–like ñeque de Coiba *(Dasyprocta coibae),* boa constrictors, and fer-de-lance snakes.

Sportfishing within the park limits is catch-and-release only and requires a permit, and the government has finally begun to enforce this law. **Hannibal Bank,** between Isla de Coiba and Isla Montuosa, is an especially famous fishing spot.

Tour Operators

Because Coiba is in the middle of a national park, there are no tour operators or private enterprises of any kind on or near the island. The closest tour operators are on the Pacific mainland coast, particularly in Playa Santa Catalina.

Diving and snorkeling trips are offered by **Boca Brava Divers** (tel. 775-3185, cell 6600-6191, www.scubadiving-panama.com) in Boca Chica and by **Coiba Dive Center** (tel. 938-0007 or 202-9214, www.coibadivecenter.com or www.scuba-charters.com), **Scuba Coiba** (tel. 202-2172, www.scubacoiba.com), and **Panama Dive Center** (cell 6665-7879, www.panama-divecenter.com) in Playa Santa Catalina. **Fluid Adventures** (cell 6560-6558, http://fluidadventurespanama.com), also based in Playa Santa Catalina, offers sea-kayak trips in the waters around Isla Coiba. These and other tour operators in Santa Catalina offer multiday trips to the park that include overnight stays at the ranger station on Isla Coiba and tours around the island. **Javier Elizondo of Coiba Eco-Tours** (cell 6544-1806, www.casakenia.com, javier@casakenia.com), a naturalist guide based in Santa Catalina, has a solid reputation and is popular with birders.

Tanager Tourism (cell 6676-0220, http://tanagertourism.com), which is operated by the couple who own Heliconia Bed and Breakfast on the west coast of the Azuero Peninsula, offers multiday hiking and snorkeling trips to Coiba. Their trips have proved popular in part because they are more economical than those offered in Santa Catalina.

The **Art Lodge** on Isla Gobernadora can arrange Coiba tours for its guests. Some of the national tour operators based in Panama City offer trips to Coiba. A good place to start is **Ancon Expeditions** (tel. 269-9415, www.anconexpeditions.com).

Several companies offer multiday deep-sea fishing trips to the waters around Coiba. It's worth doing some research before settling on a package, as they tend to be quite expensive and some of the operations are not well run and either use dilapidated boats or go out of business overnight. Operations tend to be run out of either Puerto Mutis, a port 24 kilometers southwest of Santiago, or Pedregal, David's port.

A fishing group that enjoys a good reputation is **Coiba Adventure Sportfishing** (U.S./Canada toll-free tel. 800/800-0907, U.S. tel. 636/405-1200, www.coibadventure.com). The operation is run by Tom Yust, who has been organizing fishing trips to Coiba since 1991 and was the skipper on the original *Coiba Explorer* mother ship. His current operation uses a 31-foot Bertram and a 22-foot Mako.

The outfit offers two- to six-day fishing trips. Rates depend on the trip length, number of anglers, and choice of boats, but count on spending more than US$3,500 per person. Prices include a round-trip charter flight between Panama City and Coiba, all meals, and an air-conditioned room at the ranger station.

The **Panama Big Game Fishing Club** (tel. 6674-4824, U.S./Canada toll-free tel. 866/281-1225, www.panamabiggamefishingclub.com) offers several fishing packages. Guests stay at their high-end cabins on Isla Boca Brava.

Another group to consider is **Pesca Panama** (U.S./Canada toll-free tel. 800/946-3474, U.S. tel. 501/946-3474, www.pescapanama.com). This fishing operation is run out of Pedregal and uses a cozy 70-foot barge as a mother ship. It sleeps up to 16 in four air-conditioned guest cabins. Fishing is from 27-foot Ocean Masters. The standard package consists of six days of fishing. Per-person rates are US$2,995–3,895 depending on the number of anglers per boat. The package includes two nights in a hotel in Panama City and food and accommodations during the four nights on the barge. Transportation and food in Panama City and transfers to David are not included in the rate.

Practicalities

The most commonly visited part of the island has an **ANAM field station** on a pretty, sandy cove backed by hills. Even day visitors must register here and pay a US$20-per-person national park entrance fee. The complex includes a boat anchorage, guest cabins, a kitchen and dining area, and a small museum. The museum contains the skeleton of a humpback whale and specimens of other critters recovered from the park, including pickled fer-de-lance and coral snakes.

Each of the cabins for guests has two rooms with separate entrances. The cabins are quite basic and bare-bones, but they're perfectly fine, especially given the extreme isolation of this place. They're even air-conditioned. Rates are US$20 per person, plus the onetime US$20 per-person park entrance fee.

It is much less of a hassle to arrange a visit through a tour operator that frequents the island, but to set up a visit on your own, contact ANAM in Santiago (tel. 998-4271). You can also try calling the field station on the island (tel. 999-8103).

The station supplies diesel for electricity 6 P.M.–midnight. Those who want air-conditioning through the night have to bring their own diesel supply. About 15 gallons of diesel per cabin should last through two nights.

Independent travelers should also note the need to bring not only food but also the gas to prepare it (stoves are provided). Meals are eaten in an open-air *rancho*. Be prepared for mosquitoes and *chitras* (sand flies), which are fierce around here. There's nothing to do in the evenings but enjoy the tranquility.

Though this place is paradise, it's easy to see that life here could get a bit tedious. No wonder the rangers have befriended some of the local wildlife. The most impressive is Tito, a three-meter crocodile that emerges from the water when called to dinner. Another is Pancho, a Geoffroy's tamarin. Sara is a fat and lazy deer.

Getting There

There's a landing strip on Coiba, but only charter flights make the trip. Nearly everyone comes by boat. Playa Santa Catalina has emerged as the primary gateway to Parque Nacional Coiba. It takes about 90 minutes by fast boat to get to the island from there. Some folks come out from Puerto Mutis, Santiago's port, which is much closer to Panama City but a longer boat ride: 2–3 hours, depending on the boat. Other trips originate from Pedregal or the west coast of the Azuero Peninsula. Wherever the starting point, be careful whom you travel with. It's best to go with an experienced, safety-conscious tour operator with a substantial boat and good equipment.

ISLA GOBERNADORA

A far smaller and less-well-known island, Isla Gobernadora is in the Golfo de Montijo a half-hour by boat from Santa Catalina. It's next to the huge Isla Cébaco. On the side facing the mainland is the tidiest, most appealing fishing village I've ever seen in Panama. The village itself is not particularly charming—most houses are made from cinderblocks and linked by a cement path—but the views of the sparkling ocean and forested mainland are gorgeous, the

villagers have left plenty of trees intact, and one just gets a sense of a people who take pride in their village.

A fifteen-minute walk down the island from the village brings one to the **Art Lodge** (cell tel. 6636-5180, info@artlodgepanama.com, www.artlodgepanama.com, starts at US$120 pp), the only tourist lodgings on the island. Run by a warm and friendly French couple and their equally inviting staff, it features four rustic but attractive guest *ranchos* with thatched roofs. The bungalows are open-sided but have mosquito nets over the beds, flush toilets, and showers. Each *rancho* is decorated differently, with whimsical Swiss Family Robinson touches such as shower curtains made from strung-together shells and showerheads fashioned from coconut shells. There's a common area where guests can eat, drink, and socialize or just soak up the tranquil atmosphere. There's solar power, but facilities are generally rustic.

© WILLIAM FRIAR

The rustic but charming Art Lodge features lots of playful arts and crafts.

The owners are artists, and their love of art is evident everywhere from sculptures they've installed on the grounds through their work to help set up an artists' cooperative in the village.

Stays here start at US$120 pp, including meals, nonalcoholic drinks, daily boat trips, and transfers to and from Santa Catalina (transfers from the more distant Puerto Mutis, near Santiago, are possible for an extra fee). There's usually a 2–3 night minimum stay. Things to do here include hanging out on the beach (the one closest to the lodge is rocky, but a huge, deserted black-sand beach is just a few minutes away), visiting Isla Cebaco, snorkeling/diving or hiking trips to Coiba and other spots, birding, and going for a hike on a three-hour trail on Gobernadora itself. There's whale-watching in July and August. The lodge also sometimes hosts yoga retreats and surfing tours.

It's also possible to visit Gobernadora on a day trip from Playa Santa Catalina, Hicaco, or Puerto Mutis. Expect to pay about US$90 per boat for a trip on a fisherman's *lancha,* or less if arranged through a fisherman in Hicaco, which doesn't see as much tourist traffic. But consider going through a tour operator, who will probably charge more but should be a safer way to go (e.g., life jackets, radio) on these open waters, which can get quite choppy when the wind picks up. A tour operator will also be more likely to arrange things to do and see; a fisherman will just provide transport.

THE AZUERO PENINSULA

The Azuero Peninsula is a paradoxical place. It's a heavily settled, terribly deforested land where wilderness has largely been supplanted by farms. In some places erosion has transformed forest into wasteland. Yet it still feels isolated from modern Panama, frozen in an idyllic past, and there's lots of charm and natural beauty left. Oddly enough, it's even home to one of Panama's most pristine national parks. The Azuero is a land both much beloved and much abused.

The Azuero is inevitably called Panama's heartland, a designation that slights the country's widely scattered indigenous populations, not to mention, for instance, those of African descent.

Still, the peninsula occupies an important, almost mythological, place in the Panamanian psyche. It is the wellspring of Panama's favorite folkloric traditions, many of which originated in Spain but have taken on a uniquely Panamanian form—often thanks, ironically enough, to borrowings from the above-mentioned indigenous and African peoples.

Beautiful traditional clothing, such as the stunning *pollera* (hand-embroidered dress), and handicrafts, such as ceramics based on pre-Columbian designs, originated and are still made on the Azuero. The same is true of some important musical and literary traditions. Even Panama's national drink, the sugarcane liquor known as *seco,* is made here. Traces of Spanish-colonial Panama—rows of houses with red-tile roofs and ornate ironwork, centuries-old

© BONNIE KAY SPINDLER

THE AZUERO PENINSULA

HIGHLIGHTS

LOOK FOR ◖ TO FIND RECOMMENDED SIGHTS, ACTIVITIES, DINING, AND LODGING.

◖ **La Catedral de San Juan Bautista:** Chitré's cathedral, at the heart of this cozy provincial town, has an understated elegance that's rare in Panama (page 400).

◖ **La Arena:** This entire town is devoted to making pottery, with pre-Columbian designs, that is eternally popular around the country (page 401).

◖ **Parita:** Visiting this immaculately preserved Spanish colonial town is like stepping through a time portal to the Azuero of a hundred years ago (page 402).

◖ **Carnaval in Las Tablas:** Here you'll find the biggest pre-Lent party north of Rio de Janeiro (page 418).

◖ **Pedasí:** This Spanish colonial town is on the verge of becoming a hot beach destination (page 422).

◖ **Parque Nacional Cerro Hoya:** Panama's most isolated and unexplored national park, it is finally accessible (page 444).

churches overlooking quiet plazas—are easy to find, especially in well-preserved little towns such as Parita and Pedasí.

Most of all, the Azuero is known for its festivals. It has the biggest and best in the country, from all-night bacchanals to sober religious rituals. At the top of the heap is Carnaval, held during the four days leading up to Ash Wednesday. No Latin American country outside of Brazil is more passionate about Carnaval than Panama, and no part of Panama is more passionate about it than the Azuero. Those who can't—or don't want to—experience Carnaval madness on the Azuero will likely have plenty

of other spectacles to choose from. It's rare for a single week to go by without some festival, fair, holy day, or other excuse for a major party somewhere on the peninsula.

For all the affection the Azuero inspires among Panamanians, most who live outside the peninsula know it only as a place to come for festivals. It flies below the radar of most foreign visitors altogether. But those who want a taste of an older, more stately Panama should consider a visit. In some places, it's as though the 20th century never happened.

The Azuero is large enough to be shared by three provinces. The nearly landlocked

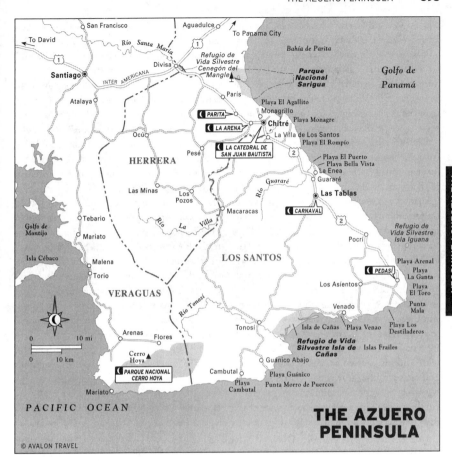

Herrera province, Panama's smallest, is to the north; Los Santos to the southeast has an extensive coastline ringing the eastern and southern sides of the peninsula; and huge Veraguas, the only province with a Caribbean and a Pacific coast, dips into the western side of the Azuero.

The Azuero is a region of farmers, cattle ranchers, and, on the coast, fishermen. Slash-and-burn agriculture and logging have been more extensive on the Azuero than in any other part of Panama, and the inevitable result has been both dramatic and sad. Deforestation has turned some parts of this region into barren desert, and most of the rest of it is pastureland.

Residents of Los Santos province are especially well-known for their tree-chopping prowess. Having cut down most of the trees in their own province, *santeño* farmers and cattle ranchers have spread out to deforest other parts of the country, including, most sadly of all, the forests of the Darién.

The hilly southwestern tip of the Azuero is the least developed, with a few patches of unspoiled wilderness left. These have until recently been extremely hard to get to, which is why they're still lovely. The accessible lowland areas are now mostly farm country.

The east coast of the Azuero, as well as a strip of coast in Coclé province to the north, is known as the *arco seco* (dry arc), because of its lack of rainfall. While good news for sunbathers, that scarcity is bad news for the environment, showing the effects of creeping desertification.

The east-coast beaches resemble those within a couple of hours of Panama City, minus 30 years of development. They're easy to get to, yet for dozens of kilometers at a stretch there's little sign of human habitation. However, tourism has finally arrived in the area, though on a rather small scale so far. The most popular tourist destinations are Pedasí, Playa Venao, and, most recently, Cambutal. Some of the lodgings and tour operations are appealing. Others seem to exist primarily to create a market for real-estate sales. Buyer beware.

Don't expect pure white sand on the Azuero. But those who don't mind brown, gray, and in some cases black sand will have no trouble finding a deserted seaside paradise. The beaches are wide and long, often backed by rugged cliffs and facing rolling surf. Their waters are filled with big fish and, in some places, extensive coral. Isla de Cañas, off the south coast of the Azuero, is the most important nesting spot for sea turtles on Panama's Pacific coast: Tens of thousands lay their eggs there each year.

The interior of the peninsula is taken up mostly by farmland, cattle pasture, and towns. There are few facilities for visitors there, but visiting this heart of the heartland is like stepping back in time.

The people of the Azuero are among the friendliest in Panama, and the percentage of smiles per capita seems to go up the farther south you head. People seem not just content but genuinely happy. It'll probably rub off on you.

PLANNING YOUR TIME

It's possible to explore the biggest towns of the Azuero—**Chitré** and **Las Tablas,** which by Panamanian scale qualify as "cities"—and their surrounding attractions in a couple of days. It's a straight shot, for instance, to pull off the road to take a quick look at **Parita,** shop for pottery in **La Arena,** visit **La Catedral de San Juan Bautista** and **El Museo de Herrera** in Chitré, then pop by La Villa de Los Santos before ending up in Las Tablas for dinner. Those who have their own transportation can do all that in a day. Those relying on buses and taxis, however, should plan on spending at least two days in the area, probably making Chitré home base for excursions to the surrounding area. And those who arrive during festival times should plan to stay longer than that, as many of the festivals last several days. The biggest **Carnaval** celebration is in Las Tablas; Chitré runs a close second. Bear in mind that just about everything shuts down during big celebrations. Add at least one more day to visit more remote destinations, especially along the coast, where you'll want time to enjoy the beach.

The west coast of the Azuero is rather cut off from the rest of the peninsula, as there is only one main road, and it runs north-south between the outskirts of the city of Santiago down to **Parque Nacional Cerro Hoya.** The easiest and fastest way to travel between the east and west coasts of the Azuero is to head all the way back up to the Interamericana. The other option is to take the winding back roads which link the small towns and villages in the interior of the peninsula. It's a more scenic but more time-consuming way to go.

Nearly the entire Azuero is well served by buses. Bus service between the peninsula and other parts of Panama is also good. Buses run constantly, for instance, to and from Panama City and Chitré and Las Tablas.

Las Tablas and Chitré are the major transportation hubs on the Azuero. They can be used as bases for exploring the east coast of the peninsula, but those looking for good beaches should head all the way down to **Pedasí,** near the southeast tip of the Azuero.

To drive to the Azuero Peninsula from Panama City, head west on the Interamericana until Divisa, which is little more than a crossroads. Divisa is about 215 kilometers from Panama City, a drive that takes around three hours. There's an overpass across the highway there. Head south (left) here. Straight leads to Santiago and from there to western Panama.

Most of the notable towns in the Azuero are on a single main road, an ambitiously named *carretera nacional* (national highway) that runs down the east coast of the peninsula. The stretch of road from Divisa all the way to Pedasí is about 100 kilometers long and takes a little under two hours to drive. From Divisa as far as Las Tablas the road is a four-lane divided highway.

As is so often the case in Panama, it's easy to drive right by a town that time forgot without noticing it. That's because the part of the town abutting the main road is often quite ugly and industrial. It's worth pulling off the highway or hopping off the bus from time to time to explore the older parts of the towns, which are set back from the road. The best bet for finding a slice of colonial quaintness is to head for the church and check out the buildings set around its plaza.

The interior of the peninsula has a confusing network of roads of various quality. But a closer look reveals reasonably well-maintained loops that link up the towns of most interest to travelers. These are also served by buses. The largest of the loops connects Chitré, Las Tablas, Pedasí, Tonosí, and Macaracas (a tiny town whose sole claim to national fame is its Epiphany Festival, held around January 6, during which it stages a reenactment of the gift of the Magis to the baby Jesus). The loop ends back at Chitré.

FESTIVALS

Carnaval is celebrated throughout the country, but those who can get away try to come to the Azuero during those four days of partying. The Carnaval celebration held in the town of Las Tablas, in southeastern Azuero, is the most famous in the country. For those who don't mind a madhouse, this is the place to be. Smaller but no less enthusiastic Carnaval celebrations are held in other towns and villages throughout the peninsula.

Another big event is the **Festival de Corpus Christi,** which takes over the tiny town of La Villa de Los Santos for two weeks between May and July every year. As with Carnaval, specific dates depend on the Catholic religious calendar and vary from year to year. Ostensibly an allegory about the triumph of Christ over evil, it's most notable for its myriad dances, especially those featuring revelers in fiendishly elaborate devil costumes. Then there's the **Festival Nacional de la Mejorana,** Panama's largest folkloric festival, which takes over the sleepy town of Guararé each September. It draws performers and spectators from around the country.

That's just for starters. Los Santos alone has more religious festivals than any other province in the country.

Dates for some of these festivals change yearly. ATP, Panama's ministry of tourism, publishes updated lists of festival dates and details each year. Stop by any of the several ATP offices scattered throughout the Azuero. This is one part of the country ATP does a decent job of covering, especially when it comes to the parties.

It sometimes feels as though the entire peninsula is dedicated to preserving the past, at least symbolically. This includes maintaining the charming but definitely antiquated custom of the *junta de embarre* (rough translation: the mudding meeting), in which neighbors gather to build a rustic mud home, called a *casa de quincha,* for newlyweds. Miniature versions of these are sometimes made during folkloric events. Some tradition-minded music festivals go so far as to ban, by town decree, the use of newfangled instruments—such as the six-string classical guitar.

HISTORY

The Azuero Peninsula has an incredibly ancient history. Evidence of an 11,000-year-old fishing settlement, the earliest sign of human habitation in all of Panama, has been found in what is now Parque Nacional Sarigua. Ceramics found around Monagrillo date to at least 2800 B.C., possibly much earlier. It's the oldest known pottery in all of Latin America.

Excavations at Cerro Juan Díaz, near La Villa de Los Santos, indicate the site was used as a burial and ceremonial ground off and on for 1,800 years, from 200 B.C. until the arrival of the Spanish brought a bloody end to the indigenous civilizations.

Just how complete that victory was can be seen in the modern-day residents of the Azuero.

They are by and large the most Spanish-looking people in Panama, with lighter skin and eyes than residents of most other parts of the country.

The Azuero has continued to play an important role in the history of the country into the modern era. On November 10, 1821, for instance, residents of the little town of La Villa de Los Santos wrote a letter to Simón Bolívar asking to join in his revolution against the Spanish. This Primer Grito de la Independencia (First Cry for Independence) is still commemorated today. It was the first step in Panama's independence from Spain and union with Colombia.

Chitré

The provincial capital of Herrera province, Chitré (pop. 7,756 in town, 42,467 in district; pronounced sort of like chee-TRAY) has now surpassed Las Tablas as the busiest urban hub on the Azuero Peninsula. I've always found Chitré more attractive and charming than Las Tablas, since what's left of its historic center is more compact and better preserved than that of its more sprawling neighbor to the south. However, Chitré is rapidly growing out of its quaintness, kind of like a cute kid hitting awkward adolescence. Malls are popping up on its perimeter, and even on a Sunday the streets are congested with cars in a mad rush to get who knows where. Las Tablas may not be as physically appealing as Chitré, but, at least for now, it still has the old Azuero mellowness and slower pace of life which accounts for much of the charm of the peninsula.

However, Chitré is still clinging to the last vestiges of its Spanish colonial past. The high-curbed streets near the cathedral are still lined with row houses that have red-tile roofs and ornate iron window screens. Each of these houses is tiny and melds seamlessly with its neighbors. Life is still lived and observed in the front rooms and porches of these modest homes, which overlook the increasingly congested streets.

Many men still wear traditional hats, without affectation, as they go about their daily business. On dry-season evenings, people still gather in the town plazas to sit and enjoy the breeze, though now they're more likely to be staring at their smartphones and laptops than chatting with their friends.

Chitré was founded October 19, 1848, though according to some historians it was first settled by the conquistadors in 1558, which would make it one of the oldest surviving towns on the isthmus.

There isn't much to see in Chitré beyond its attractive cathedral and small museum. But it's a pleasant place for people-watching and to get a sense of life on the Azuero. It's also a good base for exploring the surrounding area, including the well-preserved Spanish colonial town of Parita, the pottery shops of neighboring La Arena, and a few unusual natural attractions. La Villa de Los Santos is just four kilometers south, which makes this a convenient place to stay during that town's Festival de Corpus Christi and other big events.

THE AZUERO PENINSULA

CHITRÉ

© AVALON TRAVEL

For those coming from the north, the main road into Chitré starts at the little town of La Arena, about two kilometers west of Chitré. The road forks here.

To get to downtown Chitré, keep going straight. The road will lead through La Arena past the big Paseo Central shopping mall into Chitré, where it becomes Paseo Enrique Geenzier, the main west–east promenade, before morphing into Calle Manuel María Correa near the cathedral downtown.

The right fork circumvents downtown and heads toward Los Santos province. This is the more direct route to Chitré's ATP information center, Hotel Guayacanes, and the bus terminal. They are all on Calle 19 de Octubre (also called Avenida Roberto Ramírez de Diego and Vía Circunvalación) before the road links up again with the main road leading south toward La Villa de Los Santos and Las Tablas.

The cathedral is at the heart of downtown Chitré, and most of the town's hotels, restaurants, and services are within a few blocks of it.

Avenida Herrera cuts across town from north to south. It starts near the ocean, at Playa El Agallito, then runs down past the airport and the east side of Chitré's cathedral. Several of the cheaper places to stay are on this avenue, near the cathedral.

SIGHTS

Sightseers can take in Chitré's few landmarks in a couple of hours. The best way to do this is on foot, if the heat's bearable. Soaking up the street life on the way is at least as interesting as seeing the landmarks.

To get a quick overview of Chitré, start at the cathedral, then head west past Parque Union (the church plaza) on Calle Melitón Martín. Turn right on Avenida Julio Arjona and walk north one block, to the Museo de Herrera. After visiting the museum, head east down Calle Manuel María Correa, a busy shopping street. Finish the tour by wandering up

and down Avenida Herrera, another shopping street. There may be a vendor or two selling (real, not Ecuadorian) Panama hats here. The tour ends back at the cathedral. That's pretty much downtown Chitré.

The ceramic shops of La Arena, the historic towns of Monagrillo and Parita, and the natural attractions of Playa El Agallito, Parque Nacional Saringua, and the Refugio de Vida Silvestre Cenegón del Mangle are all outside of Chitré. They're accessible by car or bus.

◀ La Catedral de San Juan Bautista

Chitré's cathedral was built between 1896 and 1910 on the site of an earlier church (on the east end of Parque Union). With its tall twin towers, it's an easily spotted landmark. Inside, it's most notable for what it lacks: overwrought decorations. Instead, it makes restrained use of dark woods, gold trim, attractive frescoes, and stained glass. An arched ceiling of thick beams, some of them hand-hewn, gives the cathedral a cozy feel.

In recent years it underwent a tasteful restoration that, among other things, exposed the handsome stone walls of the exterior. The cathedral looks especially attractive at night, when it's illuminated. This is also a good time to people-watch, as families and disaffected youth alike gravitate to the cathedral grounds and the park to enjoy the evening breezes and check their email on the free wireless Internet.

Museo de Herrera

Chitré's museum (Calle Manuel María Correa and Avenida Julio Arjona, tel. 996-0077, 8 A.M.–noon and 1–4 P.M. Tues.–Sat., 8–11 A.M. Sun., US$1 adults, US$0.25 children) is housed in a lovingly preserved Spanish colonial building. The collection downstairs is devoted to archaeological finds from all around the central provinces, including stone tools from Monagrillo dating 2400–1000 B.C. Be sure to check out the collection of ancient ceramics. Local artisans are still inspired by

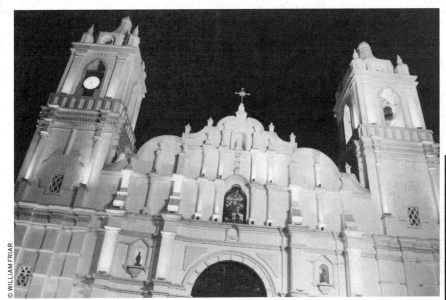

© WILLIAM FRIAR

La Catedral de San Juan Bautista looks especially attractive at night.

the same designs the indigenous peoples used more than 1,500 years ago. In the middle of the ground floor is a re-creation of the burial site of a *cacique* (tribal chief) found by the Spanish in 1517, including exact replicas of beautifully wrought gold jewelry, made by the Reprosa jewelry company in Panama City.

The displays upstairs are devoted to the history of Herrera province, from Spanish times to the modern era, represented by a signed baseball and Chicago White Sox cap donated by major-leaguer Olmedo Sáenz, who is from Chitré. Other exhibits include devil masks, *polleras* (hand-embroidered dresses), and traditional musical instruments from the area. A diorama outside depicts a traditional local kitchen garden and sugarcane press. As small and simple as this museum is, it's one of the better ones in the country.

La Arena

This town, two kilometers west of Chitré,

could be renamed Ceramics City. All along the main street that passes through the little locale (pop. 6,429), which is practically a suburb of Chitré, are small shops selling the pottery this area is famous for throughout Panama. These include pots, mugs, ashtrays, plates, vases, pitchers, and even entire sets of tableware.

The pottery is based on designs created thousands of years ago by the indigenous residents of this area. The most traditional piece is the *tinaja* (pot) that was once used to store household water. These are now used as decorative items all over Panama. One of the country's most famous painters, Sheila Lichacz, made a career out of her pastel images of and montages using these *tinajas,* which fascinate her.

The oldest designs made in La Arena are based on pre-Columbian patterns, mostly abstract, painted in earth tones on the reddish-brown piece. More modern designs incorporate bright colors, glazes, and representational images, and these have become popular in recent

© BONNIE KAY SPINDLER

Chitré's little Museo de Herrera is one of the country's best museums.

years. It can now be difficult to find more traditional pieces. The factories are constantly experimenting. After a little comparison shopping it's easy to spot the distinctive style of each *taller* (workshop/factory).

La Arena is also known for its bread. If you're curious to try some of La Arena's famous baked goods, stop by **Panaderia la Arena** (tel. 974-4788, 5:30 A.M.–9 P.M. daily), which boasts it's been making the best bread in the world since 1948. The bakery is right across the street from the Presidente John F. Kennedy school, though there are lots of other *panaderias* among the ceramics places all along the road.

Monagrillo

One of the most ancient inhabited spots on the isthmus can be reached from Chitré by heading north on Avenida Pérez two kilometers from where it intersects Paseo Enrique Geenzier. Avenida Pérez runs past the Cable

and Wireless office; look for the tall communications towers. Ceramics found in this area date from at least 2500 B.C., the oldest found in Central America and among the oldest anywhere in the Americas. There are no archaeological displays or other traces of that ancient history, but those with spare time who just like the idea of being near that much history should consider a quick drive-through. The town (pop. 9,549) does have a quaint little church with some well-preserved old homes with red-tile roofs. It's similar to Parita, though not quite as scenic. The taxi ride from Chitré should cost around US$2. Buses also make the run between Monagrillo and Chitré, and if it's not too hot, you can even walk it.

◖ Parita

This amazingly well-preserved Spanish colonial town is 10 kilometers northwest of Chitré. As you drive up from Chitré, the turnoff is on the left at a gas station. Those without their own transportation can visit the town by bus on the way to or from Chitré. Any bus heading between Chitré and the Interamericana can stop there. The fare is US$0.65 from Chitré's bus terminal.

There's nothing much to do here but walk around and take photos, but Parita hints at what towns on the Azuero must have been like in olden days. It's also home to a nationally famous devil-mask maker.

Parita was founded in 1556 as Santa Elena and was later renamed. Work began on the town church, **Iglesia Santo Domingo de Guzmán,** a century later. It's a simple but attractive church filled with ornately carved woodwork. It's worth a quick visit.

The townspeople live next to each other in narrow, block-long buildings with red-tile roofs set around the plaza and church. The pride residents take in the place is evident in the spotless streets and the riot of flowering plants that cover the whole front of some buildings. It's a supremely mellow place, and so removed from the flow of modern life that many Panamanians don't know it exists.

Parque Nacional Sariqua

This 8,000-hectare national park (tel. 996-7679 in Chitré, no local phone, 8 A.M.–4 P.M. daily, US$5) stretches east toward the coast and out to sea. It's 10 kilometers northwest of Chitré, near Parita.

Sariqua was the site of a fishing settlement an astonishing 11,000 years ago. That's the oldest trace of human habitation on the entire isthmus. It was also home to the country's earliest-known farming community, which tilled the land here up until about 1,500 years ago.

That long history makes it all the sadder to realize what modern humans have done to this area in just a few decades in the 20th century. Sometimes tourist officials try to bill this place as a desert. That misses the point entirely. It's not a desert: It's a wasteland. It's a vivid, horrifying example of just what deforestation in the tropics can look like. This area used to be covered by species-rich mangroves and dry coastal forest. They were chopped and burned away. Strong winds blow here in the dry season; without the buffer of the mangroves, the wind blew sand inland, hastening the deforestation.

The average temperature now is around 36°C (97°F), far above the norm for the surrounding areas that still have vegetation, and it can get even hotter. The area gets less than a meter of rain yearly, a fraction of the precipitation in other parts of the Pacific coast. Note the garbage sticking out of the mounds around the ranger station; Parita used the area as a dump before 1980.

There's a mirador near the station that visitors can climb to get a good view of the sweeping nothingness. The ranger will probably come up and give a little lecture and may speak a little English.

It's possible to drive around here even when the ranger station is closed, but it's not a good idea to come by in the late afternoon in any case. It's too hot. Visitors can drive only about two kilometers into the park. After that there's a private shrimp farm that's not open to the public.

To get to the park from Chitré, head northwest on the main road toward Parita for about 10 kilometers. Turn right before Parita at the large park sign. After about three kilometers, turn left onto the dirt road and follow some more signs into the park.

Refugio de Vida Silvestre Cenegón del Mangle

Cenegón del Mangle is a 776-hectare wildlife refuge that's worth a quick visit on the way to or from Chitré or Las Tablas. There's no admission fee or set opening hours. It's best to go in a four-wheel-drive vehicle.

The part that's accessible to visitors consists of a half-kilometer-long boardwalk that loops through tall black mangroves near the shore. It makes for a short, scenic walk that's halfway between spooky and pretty, since it's easy to imagine all kinds of creatures in the mangroves and the murky marsh below one's feet.

This is a major heron hangout. In fact, some of the herons that grace the fountain in the Palacio de las Garzas (Palace of the Herons), the presidential palace in Panama City, are captured here. The area attracts what birders call "mixed colonies" of herons, including the great egret, tricolored heron, and cattle egret.

It's also easy to spot caimans here, especially when some of the herons nest, June–September. The toothy critters wait patiently under the nests, like dogs by the dinner table, in hopes the odd egg will fall from a nest and into the marsh. Yum. Also be on the lookout for iguanas and the occasional crocodile. Herons can be spotted year-round.

Access to the refuge is from the village of **París**, the turnoff to which is at a gas station seven kilometers north of Parita. If you're heading up from Chitré, which is 17 kilometers southeast of París, the turnoff is to the right.

There's no sign marking the turn from this direction. París is one kilometer down this road.

Once in París, which won't remind you of the one in France, take the right fork when the road splits at the church. Then make a right turn 0.3 kilometers past this fork onto a road that quickly turns to dirt. Go six kilometers, until the road forks at the none-too-scenic garbage dump.

The left fork leads to the mangroves. Park just past the dump. There's a dirt trail on the left. Follow this to the boardwalk, about a five-minute walk away. This area is parched in the dry season, but even then there are plenty of marshy areas as one gets closer to the shore.

If you have trouble finding all this, ask around back in París. A local kid will probably hop in your car and show the way for a quarter or two.

The right fork back at the dump, by the way, leads to some so-called thermal pools said to have medicinal properties. These consist of shallow, foot-wide puddles with nasty-looking stagnant water. They look like boils on the face of a sunbaked patch of earth. To say this is easily skipped is a wild understatement.

It takes about 45 minutes to drive to the refuge from Chitré.

Playa El Agallito

This is not a bathing beach, though Chitré has made a halfhearted attempt to dress it up as one. Rather, it consists of mudflats that lead into mangroves. This becomes obvious at low tide, when the muck stretches nearly two kilometers out into the distance. The tide varies by six meters from high to low. You can literally see it coming in and going out.

The beach, such as it is, is artificial. It dates from 1967, when the residents of Chitré decided they wanted a town beach and cut down mangroves to create one. The main reason to come out here is to watch the impressive bird life. Playa El Agallito attracts 35 species of shorebirds, including sandpipers, black-bellied plovers, willets, whimbrels, American oystercatchers, yellowlegs, ospreys, and warblers. Most of all, it attracts *Calidris mauri*, the western sandpiper. According to Franciso Delgado, a dedicated local ornithologist, about 10,000 of these shorebirds come to the beach each year. They start showing up in late October and leave in early March.

To get to Playa El Agallito from downtown Chitré, head north on Avenida Herrera for six kilometers past the cathedral. The road ends in the beach. A taxi ride from Chitré should cost around US$3–4.

ENTERTAINMENT AND EVENTS
Nightlife

Nightlife when no festival takes over the town is normally very limited, consisting mainly of some grimy bars. There's a large **casino** (Calle 19 de Octubre, tel. 996-9758 or 996-8093, www.losguayacanes.com) at the Hotel Guayacanes and another one two blocks south of the cathedral.

La Castañuela (corner of Calle Manuel María Correa and Avenida Herrera, tel. 996-8719, 9 A.M.–11 P.M. Mon.–Sat., 10 A.M.–6 P.M. Sun.), next to Hotel Santa Rita, is a bar with a few slot machines and occasional live music.

The **Cines Modernos** (tel. 996-6121, Paseo Enrique Geenzier) is a gringo-style multiplex complete with Hollywood blockbusters and the mall rats they attract. It's west of and across the street from Hotel Versalles.

Festivals and Events

The **Carnaval** celebration in Chitré is the biggest on the Azuero after Las Tablas. As always, it takes place in the four days leading up to Ash Wednesday. The festivities are similar to those at Las Tablas.

The town celebrates two events tied to its origins. The first is **October 19,** the day on which the district of Chitré was founded in 1848. This is cause for a big parade and festivities. The other event commemorates the town's patron saint, **San Juan Bautista** (John

© WILLIAM FRIAR

dragon decorations from one of the Azuero Peninsula's many festivals

are welcome to step back into the workshop to see the wood-burning ovens, the drying rooms, the painting workshops, and so on. **Cerámica Marcelino** (tel. 974-4801, 7:30 A.M.–6 P.M. daily) is at the west end of La Arena, where the road from Chitré meets the road from Los Santos. I especially like the work at **Cerámica Calderón** (tel. 974-4946 or 974-4157, early morning–late evening daily), a few houses closer to Chitré on the main road. Pieces here are well made, with clean designs and striking patterns. Those with the time can design their own pieces and have them made here. Proprietor and lead designer Angel Calderón and his son, also called Angel, pull out books of photos and sketches of actual pre-Columbian ceramics, some of them museum pieces, and let you pick and choose designs you like. It's possible to order a full, custom-made 12-piece dinner set for less than US$300. They deliver to Panama City, but you may have to make your own arrangements to ship the pieces out of the country. Sadly, I can't recommend any shipping company. A gringa I know used a highly regarded one and ended up with nothing but shards when the crate arrived in the United States. If possible, pack the dishes carefully and take them with you. Making a set takes several weeks.

Those interested in Panama-style Panama hats can sometimes find a street vendor with a good selection on Avenida Herrera near the cathedral.

While in Parita, pay a visit to the home workshop of **Darío López** (tel. 974-2015, 7 A.M.–5 P.M. daily). He's nationally famous for his fearsome *diablicos* (devil masks), which are worn by dancers during the Corpus Christi Festival in nearby Villa de Los Santos. He's been making them for 40 years, helped out in recent years by his nine children.

The large masks cost around US$30 and take two days to make. Don't expect to find them in stock close to Corpus Christi or other festivals, when they're much in demand, but smaller models—including ones barely big

the Baptist), on June 24. This latter celebration also dates from the 19th century, when an image of St. John was brought to town.

The **Festival de Corpus Christi** is held in neighboring La Villa de Los Santos sometime between May and July. The dates change yearly.

SHOPPING

The best place in La Arena to get a sampling of the range of available ceramics is at the **Mercado de Artesanías de Herrera** (8:30 A.M.–4:30 P.M. daily), the white two-story building at the fork in the middle of town. It sells pieces from a variety of *talleres* (workshops). The prices are highly reasonable; a small pot costs a couple of dollars or less.

It's also possible to stop by the workshops themselves during business hours, and this is where you can find the best pieces. The most garish pieces are displayed outside. Don't be dissuaded by this; go in and poke around. Visitors enough to mask a finger—are usually on sale for significantly less.

López's house, which is also his workshop, is on the highway, across the street from and north of the Shell station, near Calle José Angel Bosquez B. His home is next to Kiosco Chely. Look for devil masks hanging on the front of the house.

A new three-story mall, **Paseo Central,** has gone up on the outskirts of Chitré on the main road leading from La Arena. The 24-hour El Rey supermarket and a massive Farmacia Arrocha are the anchor stores and the only two likely to be of much interest to travelers. The Arrocha has some camping and snorkeling equipment. There are ATMs in the mall.

ACCOMMODATIONS

Chitré has the biggest array of accommodations on the Azuero. These include a number of budget hotels and *hospedajes,* as well as a few relatively upscale choices. Those planning to visit during Carnaval, the Corpus Christi festival, or other big events should book several months in advance and expect to pay premium prices. At other times, there should be plenty of options available.

US$10-25

The centrally located **Miami Mike's** (Avenida Herrera and Calle Manuel Correa above Panadería Chiquita, tel. 910-0628, cell 6603-9711, www.miamimikeshostel.com, US$7 hammock, US$9.90 dorm, US$13 private room) is a godsend for backpackers whose only cheap lodging options in Chitré used to be by-the-hour *pensions* and glorified toolsheds. Like most Panama hostels, it's been converted from a fairly grungy old apartment, and it's on the 2nd floor of a building above one of Chitré's busiest, and hence noisiest, intersections. There are two four-bed dorms and one private room, all with shared bathroom, lockers, and floor fans, which you'll definitely need in this hot town. Besides the price, there are two things to recommend

the hostel. The first is its access to the roof of the building, which gets a great breeze in the dry season and has the best views in town of the cathedral, especially at night when it's all lit up. Guests can choose to string a hammock up here for US$7 a night (tents are available in the rainy season). The second is Mike himself, who is a sweet, sincere teddy bear of a guy who is eager to help his clients in any way he can.

The 18-room **Hotel Santa Rita** (Calle Manuel María Correa near Avenida Herrera, tel. 996-4610, fax 996-2404, US$11 s, US$15.40 d with fan; US$15.40 s, US$19.80 d with a/c) is a clean, neat, old-fashioned place with character. Rooms are dark and offer thin mattresses, tiny TVs, and cold-water bathrooms that must be shared with the room next door. That aside, they are pleasant enough. Some have balconies overlooking the loud, busy commercial street below. Rates during festivals are higher (US$23.10 s/d with fan; US$30.80 s/d with a/c).

US$25-50

The popular and centrally located ◖ **Hotel Rex** (just north of the cathedral on Calle Melitón Martín, tel. 996-4310 or 996-2408, US$44 s/d, including breakfast, a/c) has 37 bright, simple rooms with hot-water bathrooms and satellite TV. The rooms on the top floor are the cheeriest. A pleasant terrace upstairs overlooks the cathedral plaza. There's a restaurant and Internet café on the premises. Though the Rex is not as fancy as some of the other hotels, its location right in the heart of Chitré will appeal to those who want to soak up the local atmosphere. This is the best of the budget hotels.

Hotel Hong Kong (Calle Carmelo Spadafora A., tel. 996-4483 or 996-9180, www.hotelhong-kongpanama.com, starts at US$26.50 s, US$48 d, a/c), on the southern outskirts of town, once offered two kinds of rooms: old and older, but a face-lift has improved things considerably. It's still a tad gloomy and the beds are on the soft side, but it's one of the better options in town.

There are 32 rooms in all, all with satellite TV and telephones. There's a 24-hour Internet café, a bar, and a Chinese restaurant. The decor is vaguely Chinese. The hotel has a somewhat surreal mini aquatic park—a waterslide and three small pools, dominated by a Buddha statue—that's extremely popular with kids.

Hotel Balí Panama (Avenida Herrera, tel. 996-4620, www.hotelbalipanama.com, US$30 s, US$35 d), formerly Hotel Prado, is a plain and basic 27-room hotel saved by a generally pleasant and friendly atmosphere. (Some of the photos on its website are, shall we say, more aspirational than realistic.) Ask for the corporate rates, which are half the normal ones. Rooms have thin mattresses, satellite TV, and hot-water bathrooms. Some have safes. The place is moderately clean and has a spacious open-air lobby/restaurant/sitting area overlooking a busy street. The attached restaurant serves breakfast, lunch, and dinner.

☾Hotel Versalles (Paseo Enrique Geenzier, tel. 996-4422, 996-3133, or 996-4563, www.hotelversalles.com, starts at US$50 s, US$58 d, a/c) has gotten a bit of a makeover recently, perhaps to compete with the new Hotel Gran Azuero next door. As a result, prices nearly doubled in two years. It lacks its neighbor's flashy pretensions, but it is a clean and fairly pleasant place with 80 plain rooms featuring decent mattresses, satellite TV, and wireless Internet. There's a small pool in an inner courtyard, which also contains an attractive lobby, bar, and restaurant. The inward-looking design of the hotel complex tends to insulate this place from street noise and creates a peaceful oasis in the city (so long as no one's partying in the hotel itself). The best, and most expensive, rooms are in a new extension, with room numbers ending in 27 through 32. These are larger, with two double beds, flat-screen TVs, newer air-conditioners, and slightly nicer fittings. These go for US$76 s/d. This place fills up; make reservations as far ahead of time as

possible. Reservations for Carnaval should be made by October. The hotel's one real drawback is its isolated location on the west end of Paseo Enrique Geenzier, the main avenue that heads east into town.

US$50-100

Hotel Guayacanes (Calle 19 de Octubre, tel. 996-9758 or 996-8093, www.losguayacanes.com, US$88 s, US$99 d, including welcome cocktail and full breakfast) is the second-fanciest place to stay in town, after Hotel Gran Azuero. Until recently it was a member of the Spanish Barceló chain. Built in 2001, it's kind of an odd place. Rooms are in several two-story buildings set around an artificial duck pond with an artificial waterfall. The hotel has a pool that's popular with day groups, plus a restaurant, bar, large casino, and little garden in back. It started having problems, such as perpetual shortages of hot water, within its first year of opening. During my last stay, the duck pond was turning into a swamp, the infrastructure was already crumbling, and the room I stayed in was invaded by tiny ants. In spite of all that, it was still an okay place. The hotel is in a sparsely populated area a short drive from downtown Chitré. It's quite insulated from its surroundings, which will not appeal to those who come to the Azuero to mix with the locals. Prices have doubled in the last few years, and it is now distinctly overpriced.

The new **Hotel Gran Azuero** (Paseo Enrique Geenzier, tel. 970-1000, www.hotelazuero.com, starts at US$75 s/d) looks nice at first glance, with its large swimming pool, polished stone waterfall decorated with orchids, and polite service, but a closer look reveals a hurried and cheaply assembled place. The beds feature thin foam pads instead of mattresses, the water pressure is erratic, the restaurant food is grim, and the service there is poor. The place is aging very quickly, and neither maintenance nor cleanliness appear to be a top priority.

However, the place is still reasonably comfortable, and the gracious hotel staff does try hard. Only stay here during a promotion, as the rack rates (US$155–175) are extortionate. If you do stay here, request a pool-view room with a balcony, as the outside rooms look out onto a roof, which may invite burglars.

FOOD

Restaurants are generally mediocre at best in Chitré. I've been visiting the town for years and have never had a genuinely satisfying meal there. If none of the options below appeal to you, there are several places to buy groceries, and there are lots of fast-food options. For instance, there's a 24-hour El Rey supermarket and a food court in the Paseo Central mall, a grocery store on Paseo Enrique Geenzier, and a Super 99 supermarket across the Carretera Nacional from Hotel Hong Kong.

ROADSIDE FAST FOOD, AZUERO STYLE

Toward the weekend, a rustic but fun place to eat on the road between Chitré and Las Tablas is **Fonda El Ciruelo** (tel. 966-7910, 6 A.M.–8 P.M. Thurs.-Sun.). It's 4.5 kilometers southeast of La Villa on the road to Las Tablas; look to the left for a large, open-air shed with a corrugated zinc roof. Food is cooked in an old-fashioned wood oven fueled by a mountain of wood stacked at the back of the place. Everything on the menu is US$2 or less. The *sancocho* (a classic Panamanian chicken stew) is disappointingly bland, but that's not why people come here. They come instead for the delicious tamales, which go for US$0.50 each. Bet you can't eat just one.

The place has a lot of character. Chickens wander through the restaurant, waiting for their turn to end up in the pot. It's easy to imagine food being prepared the same way at the same spot a hundred years ago.

One of the most popular places to eat in Chitré is not actually in Chitré at all but rather on the road to La Arena. The open-air **Restaurant El Mirador** (tel. 974-4647, 4–10 P.M. Mon., 10 A.M.–11 P.M. Tues.–Sat., noon–10 P.M. Sun., under US$6) gets packed with local families on the weekend, who come for the seafood and for the view, as the restaurant is on one of the highest points in the region. (This area is quite flat and not particularly scenic, so don't expect a mountain vista. The restaurant is on a little hill.) It's hardly fine dining, but the food is tasty and the people-watching great. Those who don't like seafood should give the smoked pork chops a try; they're not bad. Vegetarians are out of luck. This is an authentically "local" experience; gringos are not a common sight here. To drive to the restaurant from Chitré, head toward La Arena down Paseo Enrique Geenzier. A half kilometer past El Rey, turn left onto the road that runs past Jorón Corotu (a beer garden that is itself a popular hangout). Head uphill 400 meters until the road dead-ends. Every taxi driver in Chitré knows El Mirador. A taxi ride to or from central Chitré should cost US$2 for the first person, US$0.30 for each additional person.

The restaurant in the Hotel Guayacanes, **Restaurante Las Brisas** (Calle 19 de Octubre, tel. 996-9758, 7 A.M.–11 P.M. Sun.–Thurs., 7 A.M.–midnight Fri.–Sat., under US$10), has an outdoor dining room covered by a large wooden roof held up by massive wooden pillars. There's also a fancier, air-conditioned dining room, but no one ever seems to use it. A few years ago, management built office space along one side of the outdoor area, blocking what had been best feature: a strong, pleasant breeze that gave the restaurant its name. The menu is limited—pastas in addition to the usual assortment of meats—and the dishes are hit or miss. The spaghetti marinara and spaghetti bolognese, for instance, are fairly good, while the *hongos al ajillo* (garlic mushrooms) are vulcanized rubber.

The restaurant at **Hotel Versalles** (Paseo Enrique Geenzier, tel. 996-4422 or 996-3133, 6:30 A.M.–10 P.M. daily, US$10) is pricey by Chitré standards, but the food is decent. The grilled chicken and the *patacones* (twice-fried green plantains) are good.

Panadería Chiquita (two blocks north of the cathedral on Avenida Herrera, tel. 996-2411, 5 A.M.–10 P.M. daily, less than US$6) serves pastries, coffee, and juices as well as fast-food options that include sandwiches, chicken, burgers, and pizza.

Restaurante El Mesón (just north of the cathedral on Calle Melitón Martín, tel. 996-4310, 7 A.M.–11 P.M. daily, under US$7), on the ground floor of the Hotel Rex, has an extensive menu that varies from burritos and tacos to lasagna and pastas to seafood, meats, and salads. It also offers two dozen sandwiches. Patrons can sit outside on a front deck overlooking the church or in the nicely air-conditioned dining room. The food's pretty good, definitely one of the better fancy dining options in town. I always go for the tacos, which actually taste like tacos. They're not spicy, but they're pretty yummy. The daily lunch special goes for US$3 and is an especially good deal. Sample menu: grilled chicken, rice, beans, and salad.

Restaurante El Aire Libre (Avenida Obaldía, tel. 996-3639, 6:30 A.M.–10 P.M. daily, US$6.50 or less) is, as the name suggests, an open-air place. It's a pretty basic *fonda,* but it's popular and serves decent food. Options include sandwiches, grilled chicken, and chow mein. The menu is a bit pricey by Chitré *fonda* standards, but it's right across the street from Parque Unión, just west of the cathedral.

Restaurante La Estrella (Avenida Herrera and Calle Melitón Martín, no phone, 6 A.M.–10 P.M. daily, US$3–4.50) is a *comida corriente* (fast food) place in an attractive building that dates from 1913. It's across the street from the northeast corner of the cathedral. It offers cafeteria items, pizzas, and sandwiches for a couple of bucks. Frankly, I wouldn't eat here myself, but I love the building and it's one of the cheaper places to eat in central Chitré. Come early before the food gets too old and scary-looking.

Pizzeria Trevi (Avenida Herrera, tel. 918-0818, 9 A.M.–midnight Mon.–Sat., 6 P.M.–midnight Sun.) is a new, Chinese-run open-air place that looks out on the cathedral, which is one block north. It's moderately clean and spacious, though the best thing that can be said of the pizza is it has no flavor at all. Small pizzas run US$3–4.50. *Comida corriente* lunches run US$2.50 or less. Chow mein and other noodle Chinese dishes are also on the menu.

INFORMATION

The attractive **CEFATI tourist information center** (Calle 19 de Octubre, tel. 974-4532, 8:30 A.M.–4:30 P.M. daily, including holidays) actually has some tourist information. The staff are friendly and eager to help.

The CEFATI is one kilometer east of the Los Santos/Chitré fork at La Arena. Take the right fork toward Los Santos. The CEFATI is off the road to the right. It's a two-story building with a red-tile roof.

SERVICES
Banks

HSBC (Paseo Enrique Geenzier, 8 A.M.–3:30 P.M. Mon.–Fri., 9 A.M.–noon Sat.) is across the street from Pension Chitré, near the museum. The **Caja de Ahorros,** just east of the cathedral across Avenida Herrera, has a 24-hour ATM. There are plenty of other banks on Paseo Enrique Geenzier or downtown.

Communications

The **post office** (Avenida Perez, tel. 996-4974, 7 A.M.–6 P.M. Mon.–Fri., 7 A.M.–5 P.M. Sat.) is a long block north of the museum. It's around the corner from, but in the same building as, the main **Cable and Wireless** office.

Sanchi Computer (Avenida Herrera, tel. 996-2134, 8 A.M.–midnight daily) offers Internet access for US$0.60 an hour. It's across the street from Pension Central, close to the cathedral. The Internet café at the **Hotel Rex** (just north of the cathedral on Calle Melitón Martín, tel. 996-4310 or 996-2408) charges US$0.50 an hour.

Laundry

Lavandería La Nacional (Avenida Herrera, tel. 996-4696 or 996-8131, 7 A.M.–5:30 P.M. Mon.–Sat.) charges US$2.50–4 to wash and dry a load. It's across the street and down from Panadería Chiquita as one walks away from the cathedral. They offer free home delivery, which presumably extends to hotel as well.

Pharmacies

Farmacia Universal (Calle Melitón Martín and Avenida Herrera, tel. 996-4608, 8 A.M.–8 P.M. Mon.–Sat., 8 A.M.–noon Sun.) is a drugstore across the street from the north end of the cathedral. **Metro RX** (Paseo Enrique Geenzier, tel. 996-7119, 7 A.M.–10 P.M. Mon.–Sat., 8 A.M.–10:20 P.M. Sun.) is a pharmacy between Hotel Versalles and downtown. There's a giant **Farmacia Arrocha** (Paseo Enrique Geenzier, 7 A.M.–10 P.M. daily) in the Paseo Central mall at the entrance to town.

GETTING THERE
By Bus

The **Terminal de Transportes de Herrera** is a large regional bus terminal two kilometers south of downtown on Calle 19 de Octubre (also called Avenida Roberto Ramírez de Diego), the street that runs past Hotel Guayacanes. It has a 24-hour greasy spoon, an ATM, and a few little shops selling snacks, pharmaceuticals, and knickknacks.

Some of the more common destinations include:

Las Minas: Every 30 minutes, 6 A.M.–6:15 P.M. The trip takes an hour and costs US$3.

Las Tablas: Every 10 minutes, 6 A.M.–9 P.M. Monday–Friday, until 8 P.M. Saturday–Sunday. The trip takes about 45 minutes and costs US$1.50. The bus also stops in **Guararé** (US$1.20). Those heading to **Pedasí** have to take a bus to Las Tablas and catch a Pedasí-bound bus there.

Parita: Every 20 minutes, 6:30 A.M.–6:30 P.M. daily. The trip takes 15 minutes and costs US$0.65.

Los Pozos: Every 25 minutes, 6 A.M.–7:25 P.M. Monday–Friday and 6:40 A.M.–7:25 P.M. Saturday–Sunday. The trip takes 45 minutes and costs US$2.

Ocú: Every 30 minutes, 6:30 A.M.–7 P.M. The trip takes an hour and costs US$2.50.

Panama City: The Tuasa bus company (tel. 996-8652) has a departure every 45 minutes in the morning and every hour in the afternoon, 1:30 A.M.–6 P.M. The trip takes 3.5 hours and costs US$9.05. Look for the ticket booth with the *boletería* sign.

Pesé: Every 15 minutes, 6:40 A.M.–6:45 P.M. The trip takes 30 minutes and costs US$1.10.

Santiago: Every 30 minutes, 5 A.M.–6:30 P.M. The trip takes about 1.25 hours and costs US$3. Note that there are no direct buses to **David** from Chitré at the time of writing. Instead, take a bus to Santiago and board a David-bound bus there; these leave constantly. The alternative is to take a bus from Chitré to **Divisa** (US$1.50). It lets passengers out near the Interamericana, where it's easy to flag down a west-bound bus to Santiago or David.

Tonosí: Every 1.5–2 hours, 7:30 A.M.–4 P.M. The trip takes two hours and costs US$5. The usual route these days goes through Macaracas, not down the east coast through Pedasí. When direct buses aren't available, it should be possible to take a bus to Macaracas and switch to a Tonosí-bound bus there. Start early in the day to avoid getting stranded.

By Air

The airport is three kilometers north of

downtown on Avenida Herrera, the avenue running by the east side of the church. Due to the sudden collapse of Aeroperlas in 2012, no airlines currently fly to or from Chitré.

GETTING AROUND

A taxi ride between the bus terminal and most places in town costs US$1.40. Other destinations include La Arena (US$2), the airport (US$2.50), La Villa de Los Santos (US$2), Parque Nacional Sariguá (at least US$8), Playa Monagre (US$10), and Las Tablas (US$15).

All these prices are for one person. Each additional person in a taxi is US$0.30. Taxi drivers are authorized to charge an additional US$0.30 at nights and on weekends and holidays.

Buses between Chitré and La Villa de Los Santos, four kilometers away, run constantly. The fare is US$0.30.

La Villa de Los Santos

Four kilometers south of Chitré lies La Villa de Los Santos, which, as the name suggests, is in Los Santos province. Río La Villa, which the road crosses just northwest of town, marks the border between Los Santos and Herrera provinces.

La Villa de Los Santos is commonly known simply as La Villa. It's also sometimes called Los Santos, which makes it easy to confuse with the whole province.

This tiny town has played a big role in Panama's history through the years. Founded by the conquistadors, its moment of glory came on November 10, 1821. On that date a group of La Villa residents wrote a letter to Simón Bolívar, who had recently defeated the Spanish and won independence for Gran Colombia. In the letter, they complained of exploitation by the Spanish governor and voiced their wish to sign on to Bolívar's revolution. The letter is considered a proud moment in Panama's independence struggle, but some feel the tone is rather petulant and seems more like a rather self-serving plea to be rescued than a bold pledge to join in a revolutionary movement.

This Primer Grito de la Independencia (First Cry for Independence) was followed just 18 days later by Panama's actual declaration of independence from Spain and union with Gran Colombia, decided at a meeting in Panama City. The house in which this letter was signed is now a museum, where each year La Villa commemorates the *primer grito,* also known as La Grita de La Villa (The Cry of La Villa), with a solemn ceremony attended by dignitaries, often including the president of Panama.

The area's history goes much deeper than that, though. Indigenous peoples used nearby Cerro Juan Díaz, a hill at the edge of the Río La Villa, both as a village and as a burial and ceremonial ground off and on for 1,800 years, from 200 B.C. until the arrival of the Spanish. There's an archaeological dig at the site, but it's not set up for tourists. Ornaments made from gold, shells, pearls, and the like have been excavated, along with a more grisly find: human jawbones from which the teeth were pried (postmortem, thankfully). Because teeth with holes drilled in them have been found at other sites, it's believed the missing teeth were used to make grim necklaces.

The main town of La Villa de Los Santos consists of just a few blocks of homes and businesses, some quite old and well-preserved, on the northeast side of the Chitré–Las Tablas road. Places to stay and eat are in the newer suburban area directly across from town, on the southeast side of the road. Any of the many buses plying the road between Chitré and Las Tablas can drop passengers off in La Villa. The fare from Chitré is US$0.30.

SIGHTS

Most of La Villa's few sights surround Parque Simón Bolívar, the town plaza. Unless a festival has taken over the town, which happens pretty frequently, visitors can see La Villa's attractions in about an hour.

Iglesia de San Atanasio

La Villa's church, sometimes spelled Iglesia de San Atanacio, was declared a national monument in 1938, though what's inside is more impressive than the building itself. It has a huge main altar, an ornate wooden affair in gold and blue that was erected in 1733. That makes it older than the current church, whose beginnings date from 1773. The altar and other fixtures underwent a major restoration in recent years. (The decaying church building itself did not.) Among the church's other features is a tall, fantastically ornate archway, also erected in 1733, that is covered with gold arabesques and splashes of reds and blues. It looks almost Chinese. The church is in the center of town, next to the plaza.

El Museo de la Nacionalidad

This little museum (tel. 966-8192, 8:30 a.m.–4 p.m. Tues.–Sat., 9 a.m.–noon Sun.) is on the northwest side of the church plaza. As is so often the case with Panama's museums, its name (The Museum of Nationality) is far grander than its offerings. Ostensibly tracing the history of the area from its earliest days to its role as the first town in Panama to call for independence from Spain, it makes the most it can out of a few scraps of history and little explanation of their significance.

The museum is installed in the house where the town leaders signed their famous letter to Bolívar, declaring they wanted in on his revolutionary movement. The centerpiece is a display commemorating this letter, La Grita de La Villa. It attempts to replicate the room where the letter was signed, using furniture from the

period. Other than that, the displays consist mainly of a few pieces of pre-Columbian pottery, some random 18th-century religious objects, rusty conquistador swords, and the like.

Centro de Estudios Superiores de Folklore Dora Pérez de Zárate

This school for students of folklore is run by the Instituto Nacional de Cultura (INAC). While not set up to receive tourists, it's housed in an old, attractive blue and white building that's worth a quick peek. Lucky visitors might hear, through the upstairs balcony doors, the strains of students practicing traditional music. It's a couple of blocks southwest of the plaza, toward the highway.

ENTERTAINMENT AND EVENTS

La Villa lives for its festivals. At other times, there's little in the way of entertainment in this sleepy town. The main party is the Festival de Corpus Christi. La Grita de La Villa, the town's other nationally known event, is a more serious affair.

Festival de Corpus Christi

This is the biggest celebration in La Villa, drawing revelers from all over Panama. Though it's celebrated elsewhere, no place can compete with La Villa. The festival lasts nearly two weeks and is quite a production.

Pope Urban IV sanctioned the Corpus Christi (Body of Christ) festival in A.D. 1264, though its origins go back even further. It is still celebrated throughout the Catholic world, with lots of local variation.

The festival officially commemorates the Eucharist, but in La Villa it is far more elaborate and far-reaching than that. By incorporating "pagan" dances into the celebration, Spanish colonial priests in Panama used the celebration both as a colorful way to attract converts and as a graphic lesson in the church's views on good versus evil.

These dances are at the heart of the festival

and have evolved through the years. Keeping them alive is practically the main industry of La Villa. The dances include **El Gran Diablo, El Torito, Los Diablícos Sucios, La Montezuma Española, La Montezuma Cabezona, El Zacarundé,** and several others.

Many of these seemingly have little or nothing to do with the Eucharist, the sacrament in which Catholics consume the body and blood of Christ. El Zacarundé, for instance, remembers the African slaves who escaped from the Spanish in the Darién. La Montezuma Española is about the conquest of Mexico. El Torito involves a predawn search for a bull effigy.

The main story line that holds the two-week celebration together is the battle between the forces of evil, led by the Gran Diablo, and the forces of good, led by the Archangel Michael. The diabolical side of the struggle tends to get most attention and energy. Artisans compete to outdo each other in making the most frightening and horrendous devil masks for the dancers.

The two-week celebration always kicks off at noon on the first day with huge explosions and music and the appearance of a band of devils. They have a plot to terrorize the world and carve up the cosmos into four pieces they will then divvy up among themselves. Eventually, of course, the forces of good prevail.

The whole thing involves more than 100 dancers, actors, and musicians. The festivities take place up and down the streets of La Villa, in people's homes, and inside the town church. At one point, the devils ask and receive permission from the Archangel Michael to enter the church, something that fascinates scholars.

By tradition, only men are allowed to perform. However, in a mild concession to the excluded, there's a *día de la mujer* (woman's day) tacked on to the end of the celebration during which women are allowed to dance. In recent years a *día del turismo* (tourism day) has also been added to the end of the festivities. It compresses the highlights into a single day for those unable to get away for two weeks of partying.

The dates of the celebration vary considerably from year to year, since they're based on several Catholic holy days. Generally it's held sometime between late May and early July. Check with ATP for dates. The **CEFATI** (Calle 19 de Octubre, tel. 974-4532, 8:30 A.M.–4:30 P.M. daily, including holidays) tourist information center in Chitré should also be able to provide information.

La Grita de La Villa

Every November 10 local and national dignitaries, often including the president of Panama, gather to reenact La Grita de La Villa, the town's call for independence from Spain on November 10, 1821. This date is a national holiday. The ceremony starts in the morning at El Museo de la Nacionalidad, the house in La Villa where the historic letter was signed. It's a pretty solemn occasion, but a parade and music performances have been added to the event in recent years. Santeños love to party.

ACCOMMODATIONS AND FOOD

La Villa is so close to Chitré that visitors can easily stay in either town. In fact, those who like to party but want to get away from the action when it's time to sleep should consider staying in Chitré for the big La Villa events, such as the Corpus Christi festival, and staying in La Villa for the big Chitré festivals, such as Carnaval. On festival days, of course, visitors may feel lucky to get a room anywhere.

🄲 **Hotel La Villa** (tel. 966-9321, fax 966-8201, www.hotellavillapanama.com, starts at US$16.50 s, US$20 d, a/c) has 38 rooms with satellite TV in a quite pleasant garden setting. There's also an attractive restaurant attached that serves breakfast, lunch, and dinner daily.

The place is clean, the beds are firm, and this is generally one of the better lodging options in the whole area. The place is decorated with love. The owner is high on folkloric art, particularly *tinajas* (the earthenware pots this part of the Azuero is famous for). They're everywhere: in the lobby, hanging from the rafters, used as planters, on the tables, and so on. It's no surprise to see a poster in the lobby signed by Sheila Lichacz, the local artist internationally famous for her depictions of *tinajas.*

Prices start low for the most basic rooms and can be twice that for the nicer ones. Add a few dollars for weekend visits and take off a few for longer stays. You can probably haggle here. The newer rooms are significantly more pleasant than older ones, which have tired furniture and fake-wood paneling.

The hotel is at the end of a quiet cul-de-sac 700 meters southwest of the main road. To get there from Chitré, look for the signs as you enter La Villa; it's a right turn off the road.

Loop Road: Pesé to Ocú

Those who want to truly immerse themselves in the culture and rhythms of the Azuero Peninsula should consider exploring the loop road that circles through the heart of the peninsula. Even though the wilderness long ago surrendered to cattle pasture, farms, and teak plantations, the drive is still scenic and the rolling countryside quite pretty. The road is in good shape most of the way, and new stretches continue to be paved.

One festival or another always seems to be happening in one of these towns. A few are discussed below, but, since many of them change yearly, check with ATP (the main office is near the start of the road, on the outskirts of Chitré) for a current calendar of the major events. Unless some sort of festival is taking place, the towns themselves don't hold much interest.

The loop starts at Pesé, about 25 kilometers west of Chitré. To get to Pesé, turn west off the main road just north of La Arena (north of where the main road forks at Cerámica Marcelino). The turn is marked.

From Pesé traveling clockwise, the road leads through the towns of Los Pozos, Las Minas, and Ocú. Note that these are also names of districts, of which the towns are the *cabecera,* sort of the Panama equivalent of a county seat. The loop can also be driven counterclockwise. Those without wheels can explore this area by bus. They run frequently between each of the towns and Chitré.

The clock itself seems to turn back with every kilometer along the road. Towns here—really rural villages—probably don't look much different than they did 100 years ago. This is the real heartland of the heartland. Be prepared for curious stares. Not many foreigners make it this far into the interior.

Distances below assume driving the loop clockwise. Even though the distances aren't great, allow a half day just to drive the loop, or a full day to stop and explore what the towns have to offer. Each has some claim to fame.

PESÉ

The cutest of the towns is Pesé (pop. 2,547), 19 kilometers from the turnoff. It has a quaint little church surrounded by red-roofed buildings half-hidden behind flowering trees. Horse carts are still used to haul goods around here.

In the odd juxtaposition one sometimes sees in small Panamanian towns, across the street from the church is a Seco Herrerano factory. *Seco* is sugarcane liquor, and Panama's national drink. There are no official tours of the factory, but curious visitors who show up on a normal workday, which also includes Saturday before noon, can probably convince someone to let them poke around.

Given this cozy combination of the sacred and profane, it's only fitting that Pesé is noted for a live reenactment of the suffering and final days of Jesus Christ during Semana Santa (Holy Week), the week leading up to Easter. This may sound pretty somber, but in recent years the Catholic Church has chided the town for, essentially, having too much fun during what is supposed to be a religious observance.

LOS POZOS AND LAS MINAS

There's really not much to see in Los Pozos (pop. 2,268), the next significant town. It's 19 kilometers south of Pesé. Las Minas (pop. 2,209), 13 kilometers west of Los Pozos or 51 kilometers from the start of the loop, is kind of attractive, though not as appealing as Pesé. At this point, the road has turned hillier and the surrounding countryside greener and more lush. The big party in Las Minas is on December 4, in honor of the village's patron saint, Santa Barbara.

OCÚ

Ocú (pop. 8,150), 21 kilometers farther north on a potholed road, is not quaint. The houses and church are made from cinderblocks, for instance. But the town works hard to preserve the old ways, and it's often considered the folkloric center of Herrera province. The town and its namesake district are known for producing lovely *polleras* that are quite unlike those made in Los Santos province. The area is also known for producing distinctive white hats with a black band that more closely resemble the famous "Panamas" made in Ecuador than do other traditional Panamanian hats. A national folkloric festival, the **Festival del Manito,** is held here annually on the second weekend in August. A highlight of the festival is the chance to see a traditional country wedding, with the bride on horseback in a beautiful white *pollera,* her proud groom mounted behind her, protecting her from the sun with an umbrella. The town's other big multiday celebration is the **Feria de San Sebastián,** a country fair that takes place in the week leading up to and including January 20, the town's patron saint day.

BACK TO CHITRÉ

The fastest way back to Chitré is to finish the loop to Pesé, 30 kilometers away. From there it's a 19-kilometer drive to the main road leading into Chitré. Getting back to Pesé from Ocú can be a bit tricky. Don't be shy about asking for directions if you get lost; the people are friendly, and they know roads get confusing out here.

The road to Pesé starts past a supermarket to the east of downtown. The road is paved and should be in good shape. After 13 kilometers, make a right. This will lead south into Pesé. From there just continue east to Chitré.

Those wanting to go straight from Chitré to Ocú can take this more direct route rather than drive the whole loop. Those not already on the Azuero Peninsula can also drive directly to Ocú from the Interamericana. The turnoff is west of Divisa.

Guararé

This small, not particularly scenic town (pop. 3,883) is famous throughout Panama for the Festival Nacional de la Mejorana, a huge folkloric festival held annually in September. There's little reason to plan an overnight trip between festivals.

Guararé is right on the main highway linking Chitré, 25 kilometers to the north, and Las Tablas, 5 kilometers to the south. The main town is just east of the highway. It boasts a tiny folkloric museum, a couple of fireworks factories that are probably worth staying well clear of on a hot day, and an elaborate open-air stage on the church plaza that was built for the Mejorana.

A quite decent hotel is on the west side of the highway. It's the best bet for food, though there are some other basic eateries in town.

La Enea (pop. 1,128), sometimes called La Enea de Guararé, is an even tinier town tucked away just north of Guararé, toward the coast. It's sort of a suburb of Guararé and is famous for producing beautiful *polleras* (hand-embroidered dresses). Beyond it are a couple of mediocre beaches, Playa Bella Vista and Playa El Puerto, that aren't worth a special trip. That's just about it.

SIGHTS

This backwater town holds a few surprises even when no festival has invaded the place. While there's not enough to justify an overnight stay between festivals, those with a spare hour or two should consider exploring the town's modest attractions. At the top of the list is the chance to see a master *pollera* maker at work.

Casa-Museo Manuel F. Zárate

Two blocks past the church as you head into Guararé from the highway, a small folkloric museum (tel. 994-5644, 8 A.M.–4 P.M. Mon.–Sat., 8 A.M.–noon Sun., US$0.75 adults, US$0.25 children) was installed in the home of the late Manuel F. Zárate. He was a chemistry professor who, along with his wife, Dora Pérez de Zárate, and a few colleagues founded the Mejorana Festival in 1949. He is nationally known for his work to revive and preserve Panama's folkloric traditions.

The museum's offerings are meager. Displays consist mainly of folkloric costumes, including some old but not especially fine *polleras,* as well as photos of traditional homes, a few impressive devil masks, and so on. It's worth a very quick visit.

ENTERTAINMENT AND EVENTS

Guararé is synonymous with the Mejorana Festival, which is just about the only reason visitors come to this remote town. There's little in the way of entertainment at nonfestival times.

Every September, Guararé hosts **La Festival Nacional de la Mejorana,** Panama's biggest and most important folkloric festival. The weeklong festival was started in 1949 by a small group of local folklore preservationists, and through the years it has ballooned into one major party.

The festival is named in honor of a Panamanian song form called the *mejorana,* which is played on a small, five-string guitar called a *mejoranera.* Just to make things confusing, the instrument itself is sometimes called a *mejorana,* as is a traditional dance that it accompanies.

The festival's celebrants are so determined to preserve tradition that the town banned by law all modern or foreign music and dance during the festival. Even playing a six-string guitar is forbidden.

However, the festival does attract hundreds of folkloric dancers and musicians whose styles diverge from the *mejorana* tradition. They come from far beyond the Azuero heartland, ranging from performers from Bocas del Toro in western Panama to the African-inspired *congos* dancers of Colón in eastern Panama.

THE ART OF THE *POLLERA*

One of Panama's most famous *pollera* makers, **Ildaura S. de Espino** (tel. 994-5527), lives in La Enea, the teeny town between Guararé and the beaches. It takes her six months to make one of these heavily embroidered national dresses, and each sells for US$1,500-2,000. She takes orders, but be prepared for a long wait. Those just curious to see an artist at work are welcome to stop by for a visit.

La Enea is about two kilometers past Guararé on the way to Playa El Puerto. Look for the church steeple in the distance on the right. That's where the town square is.

Once in La Enea, look for the house with a green-tile front right on the town square, near the statue of the Virgin Mary. Don't be shy about asking for directions—everyone knows Ildaura and will probably point her out without prompting; she's the main reason out-of-towners stop by. She's gracious and happy to show visitors her work. She's now in a wheelchair and looking a bit frail, but she still spends her days making beautiful costumes.

THE AZUERO PENINSULA

Competitions are held for the best performer in all kinds of categories, including competitions for both the best spoken-word and song-form *décima,* a traditional Spanish poem consisting of 10 eight-syllable lines, and a *saloma* competition for the best Panamanian-style yodeler.

A queen is chosen each year. She wears a pointed crown and presides over the festivities from her throne when not dancing with different groups in her gorgeous *pollera.*

Other attractions include bullfights, a parade of super-elaborate floats pulled by oxcarts, fireworks, strolling musicians, and handicraft booths. Each day an *abandadero* (standard-bearer) is chosen to lead that day's events.

Probably the wackiest part of the festival is **La Atolladera,** which very loosely translates to Day of the Mud Fight. It's a day to sling mud at your friends. The queen and her court show up in pure white outfits just so winging mud balls at them is all the more satisfying. Good times.

The festival is a big deal and attracts Panamanian tourists from all over the country. Give up all hope of finding lodging in Guararé without a reservation made months in advance. Las Tablas is the nearest town, but it may be necessary to look for a place in Chitré, 25 kilometers away, or maybe even farther afield.

The Mejorana Festival is always held in September, though the dates and length of the festival vary yearly. It's always pegged to the town's commemoration of its patron saint, La Virgen de las Mercedes, which lasts for nine days, climaxing on September 23–24. The Mejorana generally dovetails with the end of that religious observance and lasts about a week. Check with ATP for exact dates and a schedule of events.

ACCOMMODATIONS AND FOOD

The red-tile-roofed **Hotel La Mejorana** (tel. 994-5794, fax 994-5796, US$12.10 s, US$14.30 d small rooms; US$22 s/d larger rooms, a/c) is lovingly decorated with Guararé's role as a folkloric center in mind. The walls of the common areas are adorned with devil masks, sketches of women in *polleras,* paintings of sugarcane presses—all the traditional touchstones. Its 22 rooms are much simpler and dark, with tiny windows, but they're clean and pleasant enough, with pretty good beds, hot-water bathrooms, local TV, and telephones. Reserve 2–3 months in advance for all festivals.

The cheerful open-air restaurant at the hotel serves most of the usuals, but it also offers a surprisingly extensive seafood selection.

Las Tablas

Las Tablas (pop. 7,980 in town, 24,298 in the district) has more sprawl and less charm than Chitré, its sister town 30 kilometers north in Herrera province. However, Chitré has now surpassed Las Tablas in urban bustle, and I've reluctantly had to concede that *tableños* now have the more mellow, easygoing town, even if it has less to offer tourists in terms of accommodations, food, and scenic appeal.

Most visitors come here for exactly one reason: Carnaval. Las Tablas hosts Panama's biggest, wildest celebration, which is saying a lot for a country known for the fervor of its Carnaval spirit.

Las Tablas is built up around an L formed by two roads. The first is the stretch of highway that runs north to south from Chitré to Las Tablas. It intersects in downtown Las Tablas with Avenida Belisario Porras, which runs east through town and turns back into highway outside the town limits.

Most of the restaurants, hotels, and services are along these two streets or within a block or two of them. At the base of the L is the town church, plaza, and a museum dedicated to favorite son Belisario Porras, a three-time president of Panama. A stroll from the plaza east down Avenida Belisario Porras is a good way to get a sense of town life.

As is true of every town in Panama, most streets have multiple names, none of which may appear on a road sign or be known even by those who live on the street. The only street that people may know by name is Avenida Belisario Porras, which is basically the town's main drag.

SIGHTS

Though Las Tablas is an important provincial city, it has very little in the way of sights. After taking in the museum and church around Parque Porras in downtown Las Tablas, there's little left to do but wander around and people-watch. A good place to start is along Avenida Belisario Porras, which begins at Parque Porras and heads east.

Museo Belisario Porras

The town museum (Avenida Belisario Porras and Calle 8 de Noviembre, tel. 994-6326, 8:30 A.M.–5 P.M. Mon.–Fri., 9:30 A.M.–5 P.M. Sat.–Sun., US$0.50 adults, US$0.25 children), on the south side of the church plaza, contains personal effects, important documents, and memorabilia from the life of Porras, a national hero who is considered one of Panama's founding fathers and was its president three times. He was born in Las Tablas in 1856 and died in 1942. The displays have been damaged in recent years, according to preservationists, through neglect and smoke from Carnaval fireworks.

Parque Porras and Iglesia Santa Librada

The name of the town plaza is Parque Porras, though it contains more *cemento* than *parque.* It's at the heart of Las Tablas, where the north–south highway into town intersects Avenida Belisario Porras, which runs west–east. This is ground zero during Carnaval.

The town church, Iglesia Santa Librada, on the west side of the plaza, is more notable for the constant devotion of the worshippers inside than for the building itself. The centerpiece is a large altar covered with gold leaf.

◖ CARNAVAL

To say that the Carnaval celebration in Las Tablas is its biggest annual party is putting it far too mildly. It's one of the biggest parties in the entire country. Other major Carnaval locations on the Azuero include Chitré, Parita, Ocú, and Villa de Los Santos, but none can compete with Las Tablas.

Carnaval officially lasts from the Saturday before Ash Wednesday until what we gringos call Fat Tuesday, the last hurrah before the 40 abstemious days of Lent.

In Las Tablas, though, things get started on Friday, with the coronation of the town's two Carnaval queens. Las Tablas's first queen was crowned in 1937, but since 1950 the town has had two rival queens and their attendant courts, or *tunas:* that of Calle Arriba (high street) and Calle Abajo (low street).

Throughout Carnaval, the two retinues try to outdo each other in the beauty, opulence, splendor, and ingenuity of their costumes and floats *(carros alegóricos).* More resources seem to go into creating these than the entire town produces in a year. The competing courts compose songs, called *tonadas,* that, among other things, praise the beauty and grace of their chosen queen and mock the supposed ugliness and witchiness of the rival one. These *puyas* (taunts) are part of the fun and usually taken in stride, but the *tonadas* are approved ahead of time by a censorship board to make sure they don't get too nasty and personal.

Both *tunas* take to the streets every day for a

huge parade, with different jaw-dropping floats and costumes for each one. These are usually incredibly flamboyant and elaborate, reminiscent of those found at Rio de Janeiro's Carnaval.

Neither costumes nor behavior tends to get as risqué as that at Rio's Carnaval or even New Orleans's Mardi Gras. Carnaval everywhere in Panama, while it certainly has a lot of booze and steaminess, is still considered a family affair.

Still, this is a decidedly secular celebration with deep pagan roots. The reigning deity is Momo, also known as Momus, the Greek god of laughter and mockery. Carnaval is a huge party, the goal of which seems to be to make sure everyone has something to atone for come Lent.

Though masks were featured in Panama's early Carnaval celebrations, which were officially recognized nationwide in 1910, they quickly faded out and are rarely seen during Panama's Carnaval today. One Panamanian addition is for the queens to include stunning *polleras*—Panama's flowing, embroidered national dress—among their many costumes.

Another important part of the Carnaval celebration, in Las Tablas and throughout the country, is the *culecos*. Each morning of Carnaval, to the cry of *¡agua, agua!,* large water trucks with hoses spray revelers with thousands of gallons of water, cooling them off as they dance in the heat. Some participants also flirtatiously squirt each other with water guns. The tradition is somewhere between a mild version of a wet T-shirt contest and the ritual opening of fire hydrants during a summer heat wave in a U.S. city.

The *culecos* are such a beloved part of the celebration they're officially sanctioned even during water shortages, though officials urge residents to conserve water in the days leading up to the celebration.

Music played at maximum volume is an important part of the proceedings, as it is at every Panamanian festivity. Temporary discos sprout up, and *murgas* (strolling musicians) march in the processions. At night, fireworks light the skies—and maybe houses and partiers, too, given the drunken knuckleheads that sometimes fire off rockets in the middle of downtown.

The celebration climaxes on Tuesday night. Or rather, it climaxes at dawn on Ash Wednesday, since the final party goes all night long.

There's a saying in Panama, kept alive by its own citizens, that the only thing Panamanians take seriously is Carnaval. In that sense *tableños* are the most serious people in the country.

No sooner is Carnaval over than plans begin to select the following year's queens. These are introduced on **New Year's Eve,** another huge party that resembles the last night of Carnaval. The two new queens are greeted and the two retiring queens seen off with fireworks and a parade.

ACCOMMODATIONS

For a place that attracts what seems like the entire country for Carnaval, Las Tablas has few hotel rooms. Most visiting Carnavalites stay with friends or family, or else rent houses during the nearly weeklong celebration. At that time, residents looking to make some quick bucks rent out even the most modest homes to eager revelers. Unless things improve, it's best to spend the night elsewhere. Hotel La Mejorana in nearby Guararé is much nicer than any option in Las Tablas.

Just south of the town center is **Hotel Sol del Pacífico** (Calle Agustin Cano Castillero, tel. 994-1280, US$30 s/d, a/c); it has 13 rooms and three apartments, with 18 more rooms on the way. Rooms are spartan but okay, with local TV and private baths. The hotel is on Calle Agustin Cano Castillero, which runs west–east at the southern end of downtown Las Tablas. It's two blocks south of Belisario Porras and about two blocks southeast of the town plaza. Note: For some reason, this place is also sometimes referred to as Hotel Costa del Pacífico.

FOOD

Dining options are severely limited in Las Tablas. The following are the best bets. Main dishes at just about anyplace in Las Tablas should be less than US$10.

Restaurante y Bar Jorón Moravel

(Avenida Rogelio Gáez, tel. 994-7250, 7 A.M.– 11 P.M. daily), two blocks southwest of the bus terminal, is a cute little place that, with its thatched roof, resembles a giant *rancho*. Lunch offerings include lasagna, chicken, spaghetti, and *sancocho* (stew). The lasagna is pretty good. It also does seafood, meat, Chinese fried rice, pizza, and sandwiches. Breakfast costs just a couple of bucks. The place does a thriving takeout business. The name is sometimes also spelled Restaurante Morabel.

Housed in an old home in the center of town, **Restaurante Los Portales** (Avenida Belisario Porras, 6 A.M.–10 P.M. Mon.–Sat., 6 A.M.–3 P.M. Sun.) has a certain rustic charm. It features high ceilings, arched doorways, a sloping red-tile roof, and tables set around a porch right on Avenida Belisario Porras. It's a basic place but offers a wide range of food, including prawns, calamari, octopus, corvina, spaghetti, and various meats. The *bistec picado* comes in a kind of sweet-and-sour sauce and is surprisingly tasty.

Restaurante El Caserón (Avenida Moises Espino, tel. 994-6066, 7 A.M.–11 P.M. daily, US$10 or less) is a semi-pleasant open-air place known for its heaps of meat. The *parrillada mixta* (mixed grilled meat) offers a pile of chicken, pork, beef, and local sausage. It's reasonably tasty, especially the sausage, though meals here are a good way to use up a whole year's quota of grease and cholesterol. The restaurant also serves pizza, seafood, chow mein, pasta, and more meat. The restaurant is on Avenida Moises Espino, which is parallel to and one block north of Avenida Belisario Porras. It's about two blocks northeast of Hotel y Restaurante Manolo.

INFORMATION AND SERVICES

Farmacia Miriam (Calle Bolívar, tel. 994-0735, 7:30 A.M.–10:30 P.M. Mon.–Sat., 8 A.M.–8 P.M. Sun.) is on the northwest corner of the town plaza.

Most banks are set around or close to the town plaza. Other services are spread out around the downtown area.

A branch of **Banco Nacional de Panamá** (Avenida Carlos L. Lopez, 8 A.M.–3 P.M. Mon.–Fri., 9 A.M.–noon Sat.) is next to the bus terminal on the main street running south into downtown. **HSBC** (Avenida Belisario Porras and Calle 8 de Noviembre, 7:30 A.M.–3:30 P.M. Mon.–Fri., 9 A.M.–noon Sat.) is at the intersection of Las Tablas's two main streets. It has an ATM.

The main **post office** (Calle Ramón Mora, tel. 994-6611, 7 A.M.–6 P.M. Mon.–Fri., 7 A.M.–5 P.M. Sat.) is a block and a half west of the bus terminal.

Cyberworld (Calle 8 de Noviembre, tel. 994-1319, 8 A.M.–10 P.M. daily, US$0.75/hour) is an Internet café across the street from the southeast corner of the town plaza.

There's a self-service **launderette** (Calle 3 de Noviembre, 7 A.M.–6 P.M. Mon.–Sat., 8 A.M.–noon Sun.) a block north and east of Hotel Sol del Pacífico.

GETTING THERE AND AROUND

Taxis are easy to find in Las Tablas, and there are taxi stands all over. The **taxi stand** (tel. 994-8532 or 994-8533) near the launderette on Calle 3 de Noviembre is open 24 hours a day. Taxis within town should cost around US$1.40 for one or two people. A taxi to Guararé is US$3.

A bus as far as Pedasí will probably cost at least US$20. For those who can't afford the cab fare, buses to Guararé leave from downtown every 10 minutes (US$0.30) from early morning to evening. They can be flagged down on Avenida Carlos L. Lopez, the main road heading north out of Las Tablas.

Buses to more distant locations leave from the town bus terminal at the north end of town, shortly after the national highway morphs into Avenida Carlos L. Lopez. The cross street is Avenida Emilio Castro. There's a taxi stand at the bus terminal. Though it's just a half kilometer to the center of town, it can feel like a major hike in the heat when you're toting luggage. Avoid the misery and cough up the US$1.40 cab fare.

There is no direct bus service to Santiago or David. Go to Divisa (US$3.35) or the Chitré bus terminal (US$1.50) and catch a bus from there. A few of the most important bus routes from Las Tablas include:

Panama City: The first bus leaves at 6 A.M. every day. After that, buses leave every hour on the half hour, 7:30 A.M.–4:30 P.M. There are two additional early departures at 2 A.M. and 4 A.M. Monday–Friday. On Friday and Sunday there's a final departure at 5:30 P.M. Got all that? Never mind—all times are more theoretical than real in any case. The fare is US$9.70 and the trip takes 4.5 hours.

Pedasí: Buses run every 45 minutes, 6 A.M.–7 P.M. The trip takes 45 minutes and costs US$2.40. These buses also stop along Avenida Belisario Porras in the heart of town.

Buses to **Tonosí** leave from a second terminal in downtown Las Tablas, one block south of Hotel Sol del Pacífico. They leave every hour from about 6 A.M.–5:30 P.M. The trip takes about an hour and 20 minutes and costs US$3.60. Note that this is an inland route and does not lead down the coast near Pedasí, Playa Venao, or Isla de Cañas.

Pedasí and Vicinity

C PEDASÍ

I'm so proud of Pedasí (pop. 1,830). When I first visited in 1999, it was a sleepy, idyllic little town that time forgot. Time has now remembered Pedasí, but despite the best efforts of real-estate developers, speculators, and others who have been trying to turn it into a tourist trap, it retains its special charm.

Pedasí is growing and developing, but it retains the same kind of architecture and the same civic pride in keeping the place clean and quaint as in Parita.

There are always new hotels and places to eat, including some you would never expect to find way out here.

The is the hometown of Mireya Moscoso, Panama's president from 1999 to 2004. The presidential connection led to road improvements, a large branch of Banco Nacional de Panamá that looks bigger than the town itself, and an influx of development dollars that spruced up the whole town.

But the charm of this friendly little town is still intact, and it doesn't yet look like a museum exhibit. Townspeople still live in town. Its main road is busier now, but Pedasí is still a haven of tranquility surrounded by natural beauty. I can't think of a more pleasant place to discover heartland Panama.

Most of Pedasí is on either side of a one-kilometer stretch of two-lane road that runs north–south through the town. The ocean is just a couple of kilometers to the east. The town church and plaza are on the southeast side of town.

Visitors can take in the town itself in less than an hour. The main attractions are its nearby beaches; a couple of unusual islands, Isla Iguana and Isla de Cañas, that aren't too hard to get to; and a surfing spot, Playa El Venao, about 30 kilometers south of town that's especially good for beginners. The waters off Pedasí offer good diving and fishing. Humpback whales can be spotted offshore from around August–October or November.

November 25 is the celebration of Pedasí's patron saint, Santa Catalina. The town also has its own elaborate Carnaval celebration. This is a saner place than most to celebrate Carnaval on the Azuero. Pedasí has a big *desfile de carreta* (parade with floats) in November; dates vary.

Sports and Recreation

Pedasí still feels as though it has more beaches

than tourists, which is one of its charms. It's also a good base for planning trips to nearby diving, snorkeling, and surfing spots. There are not yet many tour operators and outfitters, however. I've seen quite a few come and go over the last 10 years or so, and this will probably continue until tourism is more firmly established.

NEARBY BEACHES

Pedasí is only a couple of kilometers from the ocean, and its beaches are easily accessible. **Playa Arenal** is three kilometers east of town on a good road. To get there, follow the road behind the gas station that leads past the CEFATI. Arenal is absolutely massive. You have to take a short hike across the sand just to get to the water, and it stretches along the coast farther than the eye can see. Fisherfolk anchor their boats here, but there's more than enough beach and surf to go around.

One of my favorite beaches in the area is **Playa Los Destiladeros,** 10 kilometers south of town. Head south down the main road through town until you get to Limón, three kilometers away. The turn will be on the left.

When that road forks, take the right fork. The road dead-ends at Los Destiladeros, seven kilometers away. It's a wide brown beach with a great view. Locals don't tend to come here since there are no facilities or shade, but it's shaping up to be the main tourist beach. There are a couple of little beach hotels, and major construction on the French-owned real-estate development. A taxi trip to Los Destiladeros should run US$8.

For those willing to go a little farther south, there's a little-known beach just south of Villa Romana. It's a bit out of the way and requires either four-wheel drive or a bit of hiking to get to, which means you're likely to have it all to yourself. It's a huge, arcing beach on an undeveloped stretch of coast. To get there, follow the directions to Villa Romana and then continue past it on a dirt road with rocky, hilly sections.

The road will fork; the left fork takes you to a stretch of beach used by fishing boats. Take the right fork to get to the nicer stretch. The beach will be easiest to get to for those staying near Playa Los Destiladeros.

DIVING AND SPORTFISHING

The main dive destinations are the waters around **Isla Iguana** and the **Islas Frailes.**

Isla Iguana has extensive coral fields, though human pressures and El Niños have damaged them. The Islas Frailes, considerably farther out, off the southeast tip of the Azuero, are a pair of rock outcroppings that offer good open-water diving. There is no beach on either of the Frailes; all diving is from the boat. There are also two wrecks south of Punta Mala, in 20-meter-deep waters: a U.S. Navy ammunition ship that dates from before World War II and a shrimper.

Diving is best during the rainy season, April–December. In December–mid-March, dry-season winds stir up the sea and limit visibility. Wetsuits are necessary in January as protection from the cold waters of the Humboldt Current. They also fend off the stings of tiny jellyfish.

There's more demand for sportfishing than diving around here. This area has been nicknamed the Tuna Coast, and there's even a major international tuna research facility, Laboratorio Achotines, on the coast 30 kilometers south of Pedasí. Other big fish found in these waters include sailfish, wahoo, and black, blue, and striped marlin.

It's possible to hire a local fisherman to take you sportfishing, but as this will be in a fairly small *panga,* you'll probably need to bring your own fishing gear, and there's a decent chance your captain may be tippling even in the early morning. Only go this route if you get a local recommendation from someone you trust; the recommended hotels should be good sources. Expect to pay US$150–200 for this adventure.

Sportfishing trips with a professional operation that has a well-equipped boat and good gear are increasingly easy to come by, but expect to pay upward of US$700 for a day out. **Buzos de Azuero** (tel. 995-2405 or 995-2894, www.dive-n-fishpanama.com) is the only diving and deep-sea fishing operator in town. It's also known as Dive-N-Fish Pedasí. It offers weeklong packages that include four nights in a Pedasí hotel, two nights in Panama City, transfers, gear, and breakfasts. Packages that include three days of sportfishing or diving are US$795 per person, two-person minimum. It also offers tours of area attractions including horseback riding, snorkeling at Isla Iguana, whale-watching, a visit to Laboratorio Achotines, and turtle-watching at Isla de Cañas for US$45 per person, two-person minimum. It's located between the Accel gas station and the CEFATI building at the north end of town. It recently built the Pedasí Sports Club (www.pedasisportsclub.com).

Pucha's (no phone, www.puchagarcia.com.pa, 8 A.M.–5 P.M. Tues.–Sun.), next to the gas station at the entrance to town, rents snorkel gear (US$12/day) and bikes (US$7–10 for half–full day). It's owned by Pucha Garcia, a 10-time national surf champion who is nearly as famous for her pinup calendars as for her board skills. Her store includes a gallery commemorating her career.

Accommodations

Try to call ahead for hotel reservations in the rainy season. The risk is not so much that places will fill up as that no one might be around to let you in if you just show up when business is slow. Most of the places listed here are in town, but there are a few others either on or near the beach. Three of the nicest accommodations are near Playa Los Destiladeros, south of town.

US$10-25

Peak Hostel Pedasí (tel. 995-2776, www.peakhostel.com, dorm beds US$10 pp, US$45–55), on the town plaza, was putting the final touches on a little place with both dorm beds

and six private rooms (US$45–55 s/d, depending on size) last time I visited. The private rooms are simple, with mattresses on cement pedestals, but they're surprisingly attractive, more so than those in some comparably priced "boutique" hotels in the area. There's a little restaurant on the back patio, with most mains US$5–6. The place is run by friendly Israeli surfers, and it seemed likely this place was going to rent surfboards and other outdoor gear. They rent bikes for US$10/day.

Hotel Residencial Pedasí (tel. 995-2490, www.residencialpedasi.com, US$20 s, US$25 d, a/c), on the main road at the north end of town, offers 14 clean, spartan rooms with wireless Internet. The beds are a bit saggy and the rooms tend to be somewhat dark, but the spot is nice and quiet. There's an open-air restaurant that is in service when the hotel has guests.

US$25-50

Dim's Hostel (tel. 995-2303, cell 6664-1900, mirely@iname.com, US$27 s, US$33 d, including breakfast, a/c) is on the west side of the main road about midway through town. It's actually a simple bed-and-breakfast, not a hostel. Accommodations consist of eight rooms with private baths in the aging home of the owner, Mirna Batista. Rooms are basic, but they have character and were recently renovated. None of the rooms has hot water but most have satellite TV. Guests are served full breakfasts out of on an attractive thatch-roofed patio area with a massive mango tree as the centerpiece. Guests can bring their own food for lunch and dinner and use the backyard kitchen to prepare it. Out back there's a traditional *casa de quincha*—an adobe house built during community festivals. Mirna now lives out there. The guesthouse has an Internet-wired computer (first half hour free, then US$1/hour).

Mirna is an energetic, attentive, and helpful host who speaks pretty good English. She's very friendly and will cheerfully take guests under her wing if they want her to. She's the go-to person for help setting up a trip to Isla de Cañas and other area attractions. Expect to pay US$30 for transportation and US$15 for a guide. This place is popular, so make reservations as far in advance as possible, especially during the dry season and holidays.

Rosa de Vientos (cell 6778-0627, www.bedandbreakfastpedasi.com, US$40–45 s/d) does not offer air-conditioning or even electricity. (The latter, at least, is allegedly working its way to the property.) What it does offer are three clean, simple rooms with firm beds and high ceilings, 700 meters from the coast. It's run by a Swiss woman who has lived in Pedasí since 2005. It's about two kilometers from downtown Pedasí on the road to Playa Toro, which is popular with locals.

Breakfast is available for US$4. This place is a good value.

US$50-100

The popular **Casita Margarita** (tel. 995-2898, www.pedasihotel.com, US$99 s/d, including buffet breakfast, a/c) is in a two-story yellow building on the south end of town, on the main road and the corner of Calle José A. Carrasquilla. It offers five clean, spacious rooms with flat-screen TVs, good beds, and wireless Internet. Flowering vines shelter a front terrace, and a second, glassed-in terrace is strung with hammocks for guests who'd like a snooze. The inn is run by a family from Pennsylvania and has a friendly, relaxed atmosphere. The small restaurant is open to the public on Friday and Saturday nights, but private dinners can be arranged for guests staying at the inn on other nights. Tours are available, including boat trips to Isla Iguana (US$25–40 pp, depending on group size) and a variety of fishing packages. Prices are significantly higher during major holidays but drop by about US$10 in the low season. There is a two-night minimum for weekend stays.

Posada Los Destiladeros (tel. 995-2771,

cell 6673-9262, www.panamabambu.net, starts at US$75 s/d, including breakfast) is south of Pedasí on a ridge just above Playa Los Destiladeros. It consists of 12 attractive bungalows in a garden compound with a swimming pool, sundecks, and comfortable common areas including a large dining room and a breakfast *rancho*. Each bungalow is different, ranging from little cabanas to split-level A-frame affairs. Some have thatched roofs, and others resemble traditional adobe Azuero houses with red-tile roofs. They're fairly rustic but comfortable, with a castaway bohemian vibe like four-poster beds made of bamboo or driftwood.

The whole place has a certain funky elegance about it. The cheapest bungalows, Sophie and Julie (US$75 s/d), are set back from the beach but still have a view of the ocean. My favorites, especially for a romantic getaway, are the small but cozy Virginia and Bouboulina (US$150 s/d), the redtile-roofed cottages right above the beach. Each has a ceiling fan, air-conditioning, double beds, bathrooms, and a porch where one can sit and watch the sea. Breakfast is included with stays, and dinner is available for US$20. One thing to note about this place is that the eccentric French owner has been known to wander around naked on the grounds. Think of it as part of the local color.

The Israeli-owned **Pedasito** (Calle Agustín Moscoso, tel. 995-2121, www.pedasitohotel.com, rooms start at US$60.50 s/d, a/c) means "little Pedasí" and is a play on a word meaning "small piece." It's an appropriate name for this 10-room place, where just about everything is small, including the rooms and the swimming pool, which is really a giant bathtub. Rooms are quite plain but have satellite TV. Rooms around the pool are larger (US$93.50 s/d) though the small rooms with no view (US$60.50 s/d) are actually more attractive. Guests in these rooms are not allowed in the pool. All rooms are US$11 more on the weekend. There are also a restaurant, also called Pedasito, and a small spa (massages start at US$40 for 50 minutes).

© WILLIAM FRIAR

Casa de Campo Pedasí is one of the most stylish boutique hotels in the country.

OVER US$100

Casa de Campo Pedasí (tel. 995-2733, cell 6780-5280, www.casacampopedasi.com, starts at US$94.50 s/d) is a special place. The owners, Ovidin, who is from Pedasí, and his wife, Koby, who is from Guararé, have taken their spacious family home and transformed it into a chic B&B. It's the loveliest place of its kind I've yet encountered in my travels around the country.

The property is right on the main road leading into town, but it's a quiet, peaceful spot because it's in a 7,000-square-meter compound, much of which is given over to trees and a burgeoning organic garden.

The design was the work of the same Moroccan designer behind Villa Camilla and shares a similar aesthetic: modern, eclectic, and luxurious, and as open as possible. The ceilings are high and the common areas all flow into each other and into an interior courtyard with half-century-old trees, including a particularly massive mango tree.

Four rooms sit apart from the rest of the house around a fairly large and lovely swimming pool. Another two family rooms (US$137.50, including breakfast) are available in the main house when needed. The cabanas (US$94.50 s/d) are the smallest, with two single beds, but these two have high ceilings, plus a view of the pool. The Junior Suite Irene (US$110 s/d) is quite spacious, and the Master Suite Marina (US$137.50) has two bathroom sinks, a shower, and separate stone bathtub. All the rooms are decorated in good taste with elegant bathroom fixtures, free wireless Internet, and comfortable beds. The entire B&B can be rented out for a week (six nights) for US$2,500 in high season or US$2,000 in low season. Expect all the rates to go up as this place is discovered.

The only thing that still needs some improvement is the food, which is authentically local but not as gourmet as its elegant surroundings demand. The owners are working on that.

The staff can arrange tours and a range of

© WILLIAM FRIAR

As the name suggests, Hotel Villa Romana resembles a lovely Roman villa.

outdoor activities, including boat trips for around US$50 and whale-watching (in season) for US$125.

There are lots of nice touches here—meals on the terrace, a retro-mod bar by the pool, *ranchos* for snoozing or socializing—but best of all are the hosts themselves. They make guests feel at home and care deeply both about the history and folkloric traditions of the Azuero. They are constantly trying to make their place even better. Take time to chat with them, especially if you speak Spanish (Ovidin's English is quite good; Koby is a bit shy about hers). They are good hosts, and Koby in particular is utterly charming. I love this place.

◖**Hotel Villa Romana** (tel. 848-3004, 848-3002, or 995-2922, U.S. tel. 786/264-1387, www.villapedasi.com, starts at US$109 s/d), which opened in April 2009, is on a rocky bluff near Puerto Escondido, which is on the western edge of Playa Los Destiladeros (the side farther from town). As the hotel's name suggests, it resembles a lovely Roman villa and was formerly the home of the Italian owner (who speaks fluent English) and his Colombian wife. On my most recent visit a young Panamanian-gringo couple was managing it. Because the place is a bit south of town and is tucked away down a somewhat rough road near the aptly named Puerto Escondido (Hidden Port), it's quiet and secluded and feels like a well-kept secret.

There were a total of 10 rooms of different kinds on my most recent visit, all of which are attractive and have air-conditioning, stocked mini-bars, well-appointed bathrooms, comfortable beds, TVs, and ocean views. Accommodations range from the small but pleasant junior suites (US$109 s/d) with two single beds, up to spacious master suites (US$219) for up to four people. The latter have a queen bed, a single, and a sofa bed. My favorite among these is Master Suite 1, a split-level room in a separate building with a wraparound terrace, though Master Suite 2 is slightly larger. More units were under construction on my most recent visit; fingers crossed it doesn't get too big and lose its quiet boutique-hotel charm.

There is a restaurant and bar in the main, two-story building, which is on the edge of the bluff and has great views, especially from the upstairs terrace. (Check out the house on the distant point to the right: It's owned by a member of Liechtenstein's royal family.) Villa Romana also has a lovely, good-size swimming pool.

The restaurant is open to the public for dinner (6–10 P.M. Mon.–Sat., mains average US$10–12), but reservations are a must to make sure there's enough food and the chef is definitely around. The small menu includes some tasty Italian dishes, and it's pleasant to dine alfresco on the cliffside terrace, which has a fantastic view of the ocean and coastline.

The hotel is above a boulder-strewn stretch of coast, but beaches are a short walk away. The *chitras* (sand flies) get a bit nippy around here when the breeze dies down.

Hotel Villa Romana is south of Pedasí, 7.5 kilometers from the turnoff to Playa Los Destiladeros. Getting there requires driving through the Azueros housing development, which is still under construction. The road can get rough and trucks use this road, so drive carefully. It's best attempted with four-wheel drive, particularly in the rainy season. There are signs pointing the way, but it's still possible to get lost at night. A taxi from Pedasí is US$8; it's US$2 more in the other direction. This place is a great find and often books up.

Villa Camilla (tel. 232-6721, www.azueros. com, US$300–450 s/d) is one of the most beautiful little hotels in all of Panama. It consists of just seven rooms: all different, all exquisitely designed and decorated. Little wonder: It was created by Gilles Saint-Gilles, a celebrated French architect, as a guesthouse for visitors to his incredibly ambitious Azueros project: up to 300 homes on a 357-hectare property surrounding Playa Los Destiladeros. Quite a few houses have been built, and the developers are renting out split-level lofts in addition to rooms at the villa.

Unhappy with the level of local construction available, Saint-Gilles created his own construction company and trained plumbers, builders, electricians, and craftspeople to work on the project and this boutique hotel. Most of the furnishings were created on-site, though a few items were brought from China, in keeping with the aesthetic of the place, which blends formal Chinese and casual Mediterranean elements to create an eminently comfortable place to stay that harmonizes well with its environment.

Every room at the villa is gorgeous, and each has unique elements: one has a bathroom sink carved out of a single block of polished cocobolo (rosewood); another has an enormous, two-headed shower. Of the smaller rooms, Saffron (US$300 s/d) is my favorite because it's next to a breezy rooftop terrace and sundeck and has a good view of the ocean. It's also the brightest room at the villa; the one quibble about this place is that most of the rooms seem designed to keep light out, which keeps things cool but is not ideal for a beach villa. Common areas blend seamlessly into a breezy terrace where delicious meals are served. A three-meal plan is US$50 per person per day. Meals can also be bought separately. The dinner, at US$25, is well worth it; the breakfast, when presumably the French chef is not in the kitchen, is not. An infinity pool sits on the edge of a hill that rolls down to the sea in the distance. Villa Camilla is about a 10-minute walk from the beach.

Food

Pedasí is not the place for fine dining. In fact, sometimes it's not the place for any kind of dining. Many places are closed on Monday, and quite a few are closed on Tuesday. Despite restaurants' alleged opening hours, it's also quite possible to find every eatery in town closed at mealtimes.

However, things are gradually changing, with Italian, Spanish, and other international dishes on offer, though most of the relatively upscale restaurants are only open for dinner. In addition to the places listed below, there are a few cafés and simple restaurants on the town plaza.

Hotel Villa Romana (tel. 843-3002 or 995-2922, U.S. tel. 786/264-1387, www.villapedasi.com, 6–10 P.M. Mon.–Sat., mains average US$10–12), on the coast south of town, serves dinner to outside guests, by reservation only, who are willing to drive or cab it to Puerto Escondido. The ambience and sea view are great.

Pedasito (Calle Agustín Moscoso, tel. 995-2121, www.pedasitohotel.com, mains US$8.50–10), the restaurant at the hotel of the same name, offers soups, salads, sandwiches, and somewhat more ambitious fare. Locals reckon on a good night it's one of the better options in town. When I ate there the chicken parmigiana was quite tasty, and the (good) mashed potatoes were made from actual potatoes. The place has café ambience, with a good-size bar, air-conditioning inside, and a front terrace overlooking the street. It looks a bit dingy during the day, but at night when it's candlelit, it's considerably more attractive. On Fridays there's sushi by the tiny pool.

Casita Margarita (on the main road and the corner of Calle José A. Carrasquilla, tel. 995-2898, www.pedasihotel.com) serves dinner to the public on Friday and Saturday.

Pasta e Vino (6:30–10:30 P.M. Wed.–Sun., US$5) is an Italian place that serves (you guessed it) pasta and wine in a house on the road to Playa Toro. I always seem to show up in Pedasí when it's closed, but many people (including Italians) tell me that both the pasta and the wine are good. To get there, walk or drive down the road to Playa Toro, turning right about two blocks past the *Centro de Salud* (health center).

◖**Maundy's** (cell 6911-7999 or 6090-7251, 8 A.M.–5 P.M. daily) is my and many locals' favorite spot for breakfast. It's a little kiosk with a few tables on the main road, at the intersection with Calle Policía #1, popular for its delicious smoothies (most US$2.25–3.50). Maundy herself, who is from the Netherlands, is a friendly and hospitable host. There's free wireless Internet too.

The Bakery (tel. 995-2878, 7 A.M.–10 P.M. daily), on the main road opposite the Palacio Municipal, serves bread that actually has some flavor, though you'll pay for it. A small round loaf of sourdough, for instance, goes for US$5. The chocolate-chip cookies are a bit dry but tasty. I haven't dared try their croissants yet, which look like they were made by Franken-Baker. If you're French, don't look. They make their own jam here.

Refresquería y Dulcería Yely (9 A.M.–8 P.M. daily, and maybe open until 9 P.M. on Sat.), across the street from and south of Residencial Moscoso, is a sweets shop locally famous for its cakes. Slices are less than a buck. The *nueces* (nut) cake is good; the rum one is just so-so. Other temptations include flan and *tres leches*.

It also offers cheap sandwiches, empanadas, and other snacks.

◖**Café Limón** (tel. 995-2942, 7 A.M.–8:30 P.M., full breakfast US$4) is a pleasant place to stop for breakfast, particularly for those going to or from the Playa Los Destiladeros area. It's right at the Limón crossroads, which is the turnoff to Los Destiladeros from the main road. It's three kilometers south of Pedasí. It's a cheerful little café surrounded by flowering bushes and serves coffee, smoothies, cakes, or a full breakfast. There's free wireless Internet, and the service is friendly.

Information and Services

The ATP tourist office in Pedasí may be open when you visit, or it may be utterly abandoned and dilapidated. I've seen it both ways; seems to depend on the mood of the government. In any case, the best sources of information are likely to be the hotels. Dim's Hostel, Casita Margarita, and Casa de Campo Pedasí are good sources. Casita Margarita has a notice board with useful information in its reception area.

The mammoth **Banco Nacional de Panamá** (8 A.M.–3 P.M. Mon.–Fri., 9 A.M.–noon Sat.) is hard to miss at the north end of town. It has an ATM. There's another ATM at the **Caja de Ahorros** (8 A.M.–3 P.M. Mon.–Fri., 9 A.M.–noon Sat.) next to The Bakery on the main street.

You should be able to find Internet-enabled computers at the **public library** (town plaza, 9 A.M.–noon and 1–5 P.M. Mon.–Fri., 8 A.M.–1 P.M. Sat.). However, free wireless access in the town plaza just next door may finish off this service. While in the library, check out the historic photos of Pedasí.

There's a small **grocery and general store** (6:30 A.M.–9 P.M. daily) at the gas station at the entrance to town. The gas station is also home to a self-service *lavamático* (8 A.M.–4 P.M. daily, US$1.75 wash, US$2 dry).

The **post office** (tel. 995-2221, 7 A.M.–6 P.M. Mon.–Fri., 7 A.M.–5 P.M. Sat.)

is behind the ambitiously named Palacio Municipal on the main road.

Getting There and Around

Las Tablas has direct buses to Pedasí. They leave every 45 minutes, 6 A.M.–7 P.M. The trip takes 45 minutes and costs US$2. Catch the return bus on Pedasí's main street, 6 A.M.–5 P.M. There is no longer bus service between Pedasí and Tonosí, though a bus goes as far as Cañas, the jumping-off point for Isla de Cañas, at 8 A.M. and 4 P.M. The fare is US$2.25. The bus stop in Pedasí is opposite Restaurante Angela.

There are now commercial flights to Pedasí. Air Panama flies there at 1:15 P.M. on Wednesday and 3 P.M. Friday and Sunday. Return flights are at 2:25 P.M. and 4 P.M. Friday and Sunday. The flight takes about 35 minutes and costs US$77 each way.

The town is easily walkable; the main street is just a kilometer long. There's a taxi stand (tel. 995-2275; the phone is at the stand itself, so there's not always someone there to answer it) on that street just north of Residencial Moscoso for longer trips. One-way fares are less than US$5 to nearby beaches, US$25 to Playa Venao and Las Tablas, US$30 to Tonosí, and US$40 to Cambutal.

Pucha's (8 A.M.–5 P.M. Tues.–Sun.), rents bikes for US$7–10 for a half–full day. It's next to the gas station at the entrance to town. Peak Hostel, on the town plaza, also rents bikes for US$10/day.

Those on a tight budget can also hike to Playa Arenal, Playa Toro, or Playa Garita without much trouble. They're about three kilometers from the center of town.

REFUGIO DE VIDA SILVESTRE ISLA IGUANA

Isla Iguana is a small, narrow island that, along with its surrounding waters, was declared a wildlife sanctuary in 1981. It's accessible by boat from Playa El Arenal in Pedasí. The island is a popular spot for snorkeling since it has the biggest (15 hectares) and oldest (500 years) coral reef in the Gulf of Panama, and it's the only one that's nominally protected. It contains more than a dozen species of coral and attracts about 200 species of reef fish.

Among the dozens of bird species drawn to the island, the most important is a colony of 5,000 magnificent frigate birds, the largest colony on the eastern Azuero.

Sadly, the island and its waters are far from pristine. The current brings garbage from as far away as Panama City, as do some thoughtless visitors who junk up the beach, drop anchors on the coral, and take back souvenirs.

Also, the U.S. military used this island for target practice during World War II, as evidenced by the craters in the middle of the island. More than half a dozen bombs have been found and detonated on the island since then; there may be more that haven't been discovered, so don't wander off the trail.

Still, there's lots of natural beauty left that humans and coral-damaging El Niños haven't yet destroyed.

Snorkeling is best off the west side of the island, where the longest beach is. Known as **Playa El Cirial** or simply La Playa, it's a pretty, long, light-sand beach, as long as you ignore the motor-oil bottles, tires, plastic buckets, and so on that can wash up and spoil the scene. Swimmers should not venture out past the reef, as the water quickly turns rough.

Divers may be able to find moray eels off the north end of the island, octopus and large jewfish around the rocky outcroppings on the southern end, and big schools of fish among the mushroom coral fields off the southeast side. The waters around the island can get quite turbulent.

The boat ride takes about 20 minutes from Playa El Arenal, 30 minutes if the water is choppy. Be prepared for one hell of a bouncy adventure on a windy dry-season morning; it feels more like a watery roller-coaster ride than a boat trip. On those days, the return trip can be much faster, as the wind and waves practically blast the boat back to shore.

Since Isla Iguana is a government wildlife refuge, there's a US$10 charge to visit, collected on the island.

Fishermen charge about US$40 round-trip for the boat ride to Isla Iguana from Arenal. **Iguana Tours** (tel. 226-8738, www.nvmundo. com/iguanatours/index.htm), specializes in trips to the island from Panama City and may be able to tell you about current reef conditions.

PLAYA VENAO

Also called Playa Venado, this beach, 34 kilometers southwest of Pedasí, is popular with surfers, and it's easy to see why. The beach describes a huge, easy arc, and the surf offers an exceptionally long and gentle ride that breaks left and right. It's a good place for beginners.

Practicalities

Heading south, Playa Venao is a left turn 1.4 kilometers south of La Playita Resort turnoff.

The road is good, and it's possible to drive right up to the beach. A taxi here costs about US$12–15 one way from Pedasí.

Facilities have improved vastly in this area in the last few years, though some of these look better from a distance than close up. The new places are overcharging for what they offer, but this may shake out as the tourism market becomes established in this up-and-coming area.

Hotel El Sitio (tel. 832-1010, elsitiopv@ gmail.com, US$140 s/d, a/c) is a new beach hotel with a restaurant/bar in an attractive *rancho* right on the beach. The hotel is a two-story affair with a red-tile roof and modern-looking rooms with TVs and beds with foam mattresses (the kind you would normally expect to find in a hostel). For this and a view of the ocean, US$140 a night is very high for this area and will probably go down once things shake out. The surf shop at the hotel charges US$25 to rent a surfboard or take a surf lesson, which is

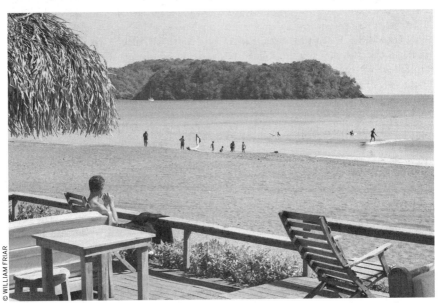

© WILLIAM FRIAR

Playa Venao, on the Azuero Peninsula, is a favorite with surfers.

THE AZUERO PENINSULA

nearly twice the going rate at other surf spots throughout Panama.

On the opposite side of the beach is **Bar y Restaurante Playa Venao** (no phone, 8 A.M.–9 P.M. daily, US$10–14), which popped up in 2010 on the site of what was for many years a very basic beach beer garden with a few rustic sheds for surfers. The new place is a major improvement, with wooden lounge chairs on an attractive deck. Surfboard rentals here are US$5 an hour, maxing out at US$25 for the day. In 2012 some new upscale-looking bungalows, **Resort Playa Venao** were being built behind a wall away from the beach. They appeared designed to have as little view of the ocean and beach as possible.

There are public toilets at both El Sitio and Bar y Restaurante Playa Venao. Campers should remember that anyone can pitch a tent on the beach for free; report anyone who says otherwise to the police.

Eco Venao (tel. 202-0530, cell 6507-0726, www.ecovenao.com, US$12 for dorm bed, US$27.50 s/d) is a friendly surf camp on a hill above Playa Venao. It's on a 135-hectare reforestation project, which makes this a quiet and secluded place to crash. The main building sits on the edge of a bluff and catches the breeze. Accommodations consist of a dorm with eight bunk beds and good mattresses, and two small private rooms with fans and double beds. The rooms are rustic but pleasant, and guests have access to a full kitchen, a volleyball court, and lots of hammocks that are strung about the place. There are also three houses for rent and a campsite (between December and May). The place is run by an Englishman named Nicholas and a Panamanian caretaker named Pablo. It offers surf lessons (US$10/hour), board rentals (US$20/day), and horseback riding (US$15/tour). A restaurant is open to the public from about 8 A.M. to 8 P.M. Eco Venao is about one kilometer from Playa Venao by road.

Villa Marina (tel. 263-6555, www. villamarinapanama.com, US $165 s/d, including continental breakfast, a/c) is on the beach about a kilometer north of the turn-off to the surf break. It offers nine simple but pleasant rooms with hot water, satellite TV, and wireless Internet. There's an attractive stone-lined swimming pool, and the beach is just a few paces away. This is a private spot, so this stretch of beach is essentially secluded. There's a restaurant and bar. However, the place is rather pricey for what it offers, and if you're not sportfishing, you may feel out of place here. The hotel offers five-hour fishing trips on *pangas* for US$150. Horses can be had for US$8 an hour.

REFUGIO DE VIDA SILVESTRE ISLA DE CAÑAS

Isla de Cañas is the most important nesting site for sea turtles on Panama's Pacific coast. Five species can be found here. By far the most numerous is the olive ridley *(Lepidochelys olivacea),* the smallest of the turtles that come to Panama, weighing in at about 35–45 kilograms and with a shell about 70 centimeters long. The second-most frequent visitor is the Pacific green *(Chelonia mydas),* followed, in very limited numbers, by the loggerhead *(Caretta caretta),* leatherback *(Dermochelys coriacea),* and hawksbill *(Eretmochelys imbricata).*

To make things confusing, the green turtle is known colloquially in Panama as the *tortuga negra* (black turtle) and the olive ridley as the *tortuga mulata* (mulatto turtle).

Every year 20,000–30,000 turtles show up to lay their eggs in successive waves, which makes for a spectacular sight if you time a visit right. That's not necessarily an easy thing to do, since no one seems to agree on the best time to come. Visitors should be able to see the best action between September and November, though nesting season can begin as early as April or May, and islanders say that massive inundations of turtles have occurred as late as the end of December. Very few turtles nest during the dry-season months of January–March.

Getting to the island is kind of complicated, but the trip is fun. From Pedasí, head south on the main road to the town of Cañas, about 40 kilometers away, or 11 kilometers south of Playa Venao. The turnoff is on the left, and it's easy to miss because the sign faces the northbound traffic. Head down the rocky but okay road until it dead-ends at the shore, 2.5 kilometers away. Isla de Cañas is a long, narrow barrier island parallel to and quite close to shore. It's an unusual island: Its ocean-facing beach is 13 kilometers long, but the island is just 175 meters wide at its narrowest point.

From the landing it's a five-minute boat ride through mangroves to the island (US$0.50 pp each way). Go at high tide if you don't want to slop around in muck. If there's no boat waiting, call the island's one phone (tel. 995-8002); it's a pay phone. Ask for Neyla or for a *lancha* or *bote*. The closest pay phone to make the call is back in Cañas.

The biggest pain in all this is getting to the flyspeck village of Cañas, on the mainland. The area is not well served by buses, especially since a route running between Pedasí and Tonosí was dropped in recent years. Only two buses make the trip from Pedasí, at 8 A.M. and 4 P.M. The fare is US$2.25. Taxis from Pedasí are about US$20 each way; make sure to arrange a pickup time, try not to pay until the return trip, and hope for the best.

Given the logistical hassles involved in getting here, many will find it worthwhile to arrange a guided trip. Most of these will have to be set up with a tour operator back in Panama City, but those near Pedasí should contact Mirna Batista at Dim's Hostel (tel. 995-2303, cell 6664-1900, mirely@iname.com), who, if she has time, may be able to arrange a trip for a quite reasonable fee, probably no more than the cost of a taxi. She knows the area well.

The island is a colorful place with a population of about 900, most of whom live in cane houses. The community has been here since the 1920s, drawn from mainland towns and the surrounding countryside. They protect the turtles and their eggs, in exchange for which they're legally allowed to harvest some eggs (but not the turtles).

There are a few ultra-basic, no-name huts for rent near the beach for US$10–15 per night, but those who want to hang out here are better off pitching a tent on the beach for free. The beach where the turtles do their thing is just a five-minute walk across the island.

Sea turtles lay their eggs only late at night, but trying to get to the island alone after dark can be tricky, not to mention spooky. Camping on the beach is probably the best bet for those not traveling with a guide. Do not use flashlights or wear light-colored clothing at night; the turtles are easily disoriented and scared off by anything brighter than moonlight.

Those visiting the island without a guide should still hire a villager to guide them to the turtles. It likely will cost less than US$10 per group (arrange the price ahead of time), and the tourism dollars help ensure the turtles are left in peace to procreate rather than end up on someone's dinner plate.

Southeast Azuero

The road stays in fairly good shape south and west of Playa Venao, but until recently there was little reason for most people to come all this way. The only sizable town is the backwater of Tonosí, and the two main beaches, Playa Guánico and Playa Cambutal, have mainly been of interest to adventurous surfers.

However, Playa Cambutal suddenly seems on the verge of taking off. When I first visited the area circa 1998, it saw few visitors, and the coastal road was a riverbed that could only be traversed in the dry season.

Now, however, it's got a few quite nice places to stay and is just waiting to be discovered. It's still mainly of interest to surfers and deepsea anglers, but with beaches as attractive as Playa Venao and not much farther to drive, it should also appeal to those who think surf is just meant to be looked at. It's more attractive than Playa Guánico, which has black sand and is probably only of interest to surfers.

Tantalizingly close to this area is a fantastic national park, Parque Nacional Cerro Hoya. But on this side of the peninsula it's accessible only by boat on seas that are often rough. There is now good land access to the park on the west coast of the Azuero Peninsula, but to date no good east–west roads link the peninsula's coasts. To get to the park from the east side of the peninsula requires heading back north toward Santiago and then traveling down the peninsula's west coast. (It's absolutely worth the effort, though.)

TONOSÍ

Really little more than a glorified crossroads, Tonosí (pop. 2,272) for most people is merely a place to pass through on the way to nearby Playa Guánico and Playa Cambutal. It's not a pretty town, though it does have some facilities, including two surprisingly okay places to stay.

Other services include a post office, a bank with an ATM, a couple of small groceries, and a few gas stations and pharmacies. Most everything in town is built around a Y-shaped intersection.

Only one thing passes for a sight in Tonosí. One kilometer south of town on the road to the beaches, make a quick stop at the overpass over the Río Tonosí. Look left down at the pond: It's absolutely crawling with caimans. Locals sometimes feed them bread as though they were ducks. Those who have trouble spotting the pond should ask in town where to find the *lagartos*.

Practicalities

Pensión Boamy (tel. 995-8142, US$18–25 s/d, a/c), a pleasant surprise on the road to Playa Cambutal, has 11 rooms with TVs and hot-water bathrooms. It's a clean, perfectly fine place by a church on the edge of town. It also has a cheerful little restaurant. The hotel is on the main road just before the turnoff to Playa Cambutal.

The newer **Hotel Mi Valle** (tel. 995-8089, cell 6063-1521, hotelmivalle@gmail.com, US$32 s/d, a/c) offers 24 plain but clean rooms on the 2nd floor of a building overlooking the main street with TV and good beds. There's a shared balcony in front. Try to get a room at the back of the building, away from the noisy main road. There's a restaurant downstairs and a parking lot in back.

An **Infoplaza,** next door to Hotel Mi Valle, offers free access to the Internet 9 A.M.–9 P.M. Monday–Friday.

Banco Nacional de Panamá (8 A.M.–3 P.M. Mon.–Fri., 9 A.M.–noon Sat.), near the center of town, now has an ATM.

There are a couple of pharmacies in town. **Farmacia Danka** (tel. 995-8851, 7:30 A.M.–8:30 P.M. Mon.–Sat., noon–4:30 P.M. Sun.) is near the Bancon Nacional de Panamá.

Getting There and Around

A loop road connects Tonosí with the northeast

of the Azuero Peninsula. (Look at a map to get your bearings.) It links Las Tablas, Pedasí, Playa Venao, and Isla de Cañas and ends six kilometers north of Tonosí.

If heading north out of Tonosí, when the road forks, stay right to take the loop counterclockwise, towards the coast. Take the left fork to head clockwise up the loop, which is a more direct way to Las Tablas that cuts out the intermediate stops.

In Tonosí itself, the road splits at a Y-intersection in the center of town. The south fork heads to Playa Cambutal and Playa Guánico on the south coast of the peninsula. (If you're coming into Tonosí from the north, it's a left turn. It'll lead past the police station and over a bridge.)

The west fork at the Y-intersection heads into the interior of the peninsula up toward the town of Macaracas. This road starts out hilly, with sweeping views of deforested but still scenic hills, passes through Macaracas, and ends up in the flatlands as it gets close to Chitré, about 100 kilometers away. Those who drive this way should watch out for tire-eating potholes and one-way bridges.

Buses to Las Tablas leave from the center of Tonosí every hour and a half or so (6 A.M.–4 P.M. Mon.–Sat. and 7:30 A.M.–4:30 P.M. Sun.). The trip costs US$3 and takes an hour and 20 minutes. Buses no longer run between Tonosí and Pedasí, oddly enough. Note that these buses take the inland route, not the coastal one, so do not pass through Pedasí. Two daily long-distance buses also run from Panama City to Tonosí, leaving Panama City at 7:45 A.M. and 1 P.M.

PLAYA CAMBUTAL AND VICINITY

Those who make it all the way down here will find accommodations ranging from a basic

© WILLIAM FRIAR

fisher mending a net, Playa Cambutal

surf camp to a quite appealing boutique hotel. This is definitely a place to come with a cooler, though, as there are few places to eat outside of the handful of lodgings.

All the places to stay are on a 1.5-kilometer stretch of beach just beyond the town of Cambutal.

Practicalities

The town of Cambutal has virtually nothing but a phone booth and a real-estate office that lets visitors piggyback on its wireless signal. The lodgings here are listed in order of their distance from town, with the closest first. They begin about 1.5 kilometers from town.

C Hotel Playa Cambutal (tel. 832-0948, Skype: Hotel Playa Cambutal, www.hotel-playacambutal.com, starts at US$135 s/d, including breakfast, a/c) is a modern, two-story boutique hotel that opened in January 2010. The 10 rooms face the ocean and have a balcony, simple but tasteful decor, good beds, and handsome hot-water showers. It's one of the most attractive hotels on the Azuero. Kayak, surfing, fishing, and horseback-riding tours are available. It has a restaurant and bar.

Next door is **Boom Shiva** (cell 6745-4745, boomshiva@gmail.com, US$100 s/d) which consists of three attractive teak bungalows on the beach. Each has a loft bedroom, warm-water bathrooms, a minifridge, and seating area. Air-conditioning has been installed, which is essential, since these things are hot boxes during the day. There's a little pizza and pasta restaurant on the premises.

About 1,300 meters beyond these is **Hotel y Restaurante Cambutal Beach Club** (tel. 994-1547, www.losbuzos.net, starts at US$65 s/d, a/c), which offers six rooms with private baths in a one-story building across the road from the beach. The property looks nice, with two large, attractive *ranchos* to house a bar grill and a reception area. Other vacation rental villas are available, with prices ranging from US$110–200 a night. The restaurant serves a buffet breakfast, lunch, and dinner for US$10–15. The main focus of this project seems to be real-estate development and sportfishing.

On the beach directly opposite Cambutal Beach Club is a little place called **Gonzales Surf Camp** (no phone), run by champion Panamanian surfer Gonzalo Gonzales and his extremely proud mother. This is a casual and friendly spot. Everytime I visit, I ask Doña Gonzales how much she charges for campers. Her answer is always the same: a shrug. In a way that's fair enough, since camping on the beach is free. But pitching a tent here gives campers the protection of a well-known local family. Give whatever donation seems right, but bear in mind these are hardly well-off people. Far too often, surfers and backpackers mistake the dignified reticence of people who are living a hand-to-mouth existence as a free pass to take what little they have. At a minimum, contribute US$5 per tent per night. Those who pay them for food and drink, however, may feel okay about camping for free. Surf lessons are sometimes available; again, make an offer. A breakfast, lunch, or dinner of whatever's on her stove goes for a buck or two and is served in a cute little *rancho* on the beach. This is not a pristine spot—there's junk in the yard and horse droppings on the beach—but the price is certainly right. It's safer than just pitching a tent at a remote spot on the beach.

C Hostal Kambutaleko (cell 6677-0229, kambutaleko@gmail.com, http://kambutaleko.blogspot.com, dorm beds US$15, private rooms US$35–45 s/d) is a welcome addition to the area, as it's the first midrange place in Cambutal. It's on a ridge above the beach, offering six rooms in a new two-story house with a wraparound terrace. Rooms are small and simple, with fans and thin but okay mattresses. Rooms are US35 s/d, US$40 s/d with a minifridge, and US$45 s/d with a view. The view is lovely: nothing but ocean and coastline. The place has a warm, family vibe. It's run by a French-Spanish couple, and, unsur-prisingly, the first people to discover it are French or Spanish. Cell-phone signals are just coming to this area, so try emailing if you can't get through by phone. The turnoff to Kambutaleko is opposite Boom Shiva. From there it's 200 meters up a dirt road.

Getting There and Around

The nearest sizable town with regular transpor-tation connections is Tonosí, about 11 kilome-ters north.

There is no regular public transportation be-tween Pedasí and this area. Playa Guánico is about 75 kilometers from Pedasí, or around an hour by car. Playa Cambutal is a little under 100 kilometers from Pedasí, which takes around 1.5 hours by car. There is no bus service to either place. The closest bus stop is Tonosí, where it's also possible to get a taxi. There are direct buses to Tonosí from Panama City, leav-ing daily at 7:45 A.M. and 1 P.M.

To get to either beach by car from Tonosí, head south out of town. After about 15 kilo-meters there'll be a marked left turn into the town of Guánico, for those who want to visit that beach. Otherwise, take the left fork that appears 5 kilometers past the Guánico turn-off. (The right fork leads towards Parque Nacional Cerro Hoya, which is nearly inacces-sible from this side of the peninsula.) The town of Cambutal is 10 kilometers past the turnoff. Drive through it to get to the beach and lodg-ings. The road remains in pretty good shape until Gonzales Surf Camp, after which only four-wheel drives can continue.

Western Azuero

The most exciting thing about compiling this edi-tion has been seeing the beginnings of accessible nature tourism coming to the west coast of the Azuero Peninsula. What's especially exciting is that for the first time ever, it is relatively easy and inexpensive to visit Parque Nacional Cerro Hoya.

Paradoxically, this national park is among the most pristine and unexplored pockets of wilder-ness left in Panama, set as it is within some of the longest-settled, most heavily worked land in the country. Few have explored Cerro Hoya because it's always been so hard to get to. In the past, just making it to the park entrance meant a boat ride over open ocean that can quickly turn quite rough, a long trek by horse, and/or hours of hiking over rivers and rough terrain.

Now, however, one can spend the night in a comfortable inn or simple hostel near the ocean, drive or be driv on decent roads to the park, take a guide   hrough primary for-est, and (if one can t .r :self away) be back in more-or-less civilizat: time for a hot lunch.

This is also an economical jumping-off point for boat trips to Parque Nacional Isla Coiba, Isla Cébaco, and Isla Gobernadora. Those who just want a little beach time have kilometer after kilometer of sand to choose from, most of them deserted. There are 26 beaches in total. As elsewhere on the Azuero, though, expect slate-gray rather than gleaming-white sand.

Just driving along the coast is breathtaking, especially on the hills. Take time to pull over and enjoy some of the most spectacular and wide-open views of the ocean and coastline in Panama. From the highlands on the way to Cerro Hoya, it's possible to clearly distinguish the coastline of the peninsula from that of the main coast as well as get a bird's-eye view of the emerald forests of Isla Cébaco.

The west coast of the Azuero Peninsula is al-most inaccessible from elsewhere on the penin-sula. (There is one road that connects through Ocú, but it's brutal.) One gets to this area via the Interamericana. The turnoff is at Atalaya,

THE AZUERO PENINSULA

© WILLIAM FRIAR

Rodeos are hugely popular in the western Azuero.

29 kilometers west of Divisa or five kilometers east of the outskirts of Santiago. From Atalaya, a single road runs nearly due south through several population centers—one can barely call most of them villages, let alone towns. These include Mariato, Malena, and Torio, continuing south through hilly terrain until Arenas, when the road turns sharply east along the outskirts of Parque Nacional Cerro Hoya before coming to a dead end at Flores.

The western Azuero is largely deforested but still lightly settled. This is a region of cattle ranchers, farmers, fishers, and not much else. In 2012, there were five places to stay and about the same number of places to eat along the entire coast, and only a couple of these were likely to appeal to most visitors. Tourism of any kind is new to the area, but this may change soon. Developers and property speculators have discovered the western Azuero, and bulldozers are clearing hillsides to create entire neighborhoods of vacation/retirement homes. Land

prices on the west coast of the Azuero were around US$7 per square meter in 2012 versus US$30 in Pedasí, on the east coast. This has piqued the interest of speculators. The development is confined to a small area at the moment, mainly around Torio, and there is little happening along most of the coast. Those who want to explore the area in a more low-impact way will be pioneers for the foreseeable future.

Mariato is the largest town along the coast, with a few services. The area in and around Torio, with the most development, has a couple of places to eat and sleep and the largest concentration of resident expats. Most travelers interested in nature and outdoor adventure base themselves between these two population centers. There is an appealing inn, a hostel, and access to guide services in this area. In the western Azuero cell-phone coverage is spotty, Internet access is rare, and home phone service a distant dream. Be patient when trying to make bookings, and be prepared to be pretty cut off from the rest of the world during a visit.

Though generally a quiet part of the country, with little traffic, the roads can be surprisingly busy with rumbling trucks even at night during the rice harvest, in December and January. Given that virtually all accommodations are by the main road, evenings can be a bit noisier than one might expect.

It rains an awful lot out here, especially given how deforested the Azuero is: about 180 days a year, during which a total of 4.5 meters of rain falls. October is the wettest month, but there can be heavy rainfalls in late January, when much of the rest of the country is in the middle of a dry summer. However, the rain tends to fall in the late afternoon and not last long.

MARIATO

The district of Mariato (pop. 5,778) was only created in 2001, and the little town of the same name at its heart, officially known as El Llano de Mariato or Llano de Catival, has a population of just 2,490 people and is not particularly developed. It's pleasant enough and has more facilities than anywhere else along the coast, but there isn't much to lure visitors, who will mostly be interested in continuing on south.

Practicalities

There are no hotels and only one restaurant in Mariato, though there are three cantinas. **Restaurante Maria** is just north of town near the gas station and serves simple food for a couple of bucks. There's a **Banco Nacional de Panamá** (8 A.M.–3 P.M. Mon.–Fri., 9 A.M.–noon Sat.) with an ATM along the main road. A nameless **pharmacy** (cell 6102-0744, 8 A.M.–5 P.M. Mon.–Sat.) is on the right as one heads into town from the north. There's also a **gas station, minisuper, police station** (cell 6744-6455), and **Centro de Salud** (government health clinic; 7 A.M.–3 P.M. during the week) in town. The number of the public telephone is tel. 999-8135.

Getting There and Around

Mariato is 50 kilometers south of the well-cared-for little town of Atalaya, a drive that takes about an hour. The turnoff in Atalaya to the west coast road is not well marked. After turning off the Interamericana, head straight 3.7 kilometers. There'll be a minisuper at an intersection on the right. There may be a small sign that says Playas. Turn right here and head south. (If you get to the Instituto Agripecuario, you've gone too far.) The road is in decent shape, but watch out for potholes.

Buses run frequently between Santiago and Mariato during daylight hours (US$4, about an hour). Buses leave as soon as they fill up, and they're more likely to fill up in the late afternoon so try to travel early to avoid getting stranded. Ten of these buses continue south down the coast to places you're more likely to want to visit. Buses heading south as far as Torio run every 1.5–2 hours, again only during daylight hours. The more frequent buses run in the morning.

There is one **taxi** (cell 6934-8387) in Mariato. The driver charges US$4 between Mariato and Hotel Heliconia. The fare between Santiago and Mariato is about US$50.

MALENA AND VICINITY

Things start to get more interesting as one continues to head down the peninsula. Nine kilometers south of Mariato is the Hotel Heliconia, the most appealing place to stay on the west coast and the best source of information on its natural attractions. There's no sign but it's easy to spot, as it's in a large modern house on the right as one heads south. Even those not staying at Heliconia should stop by; the owners can book tours with local guides and give visitors tips on getting around. Two kilometers farther south past Hotel Heliconia is the mellow fishing village of Malena (pop. 140), which has a hostel, a place to eat, a kiosk selling a few supplies, and a turtle conservation project. There's little else in it, not even a bar. In fact, drinking and smoking are frowned upon in the village, which has a strong evangelical Christian influence. There is one **public telephone** (tel. 999-8301) in Malena, which you can try calling if you're unable to make contact any other way.

Sports and Recreation

Boat trips to the islands of **Coiba, Cébaco,** and **Gobernadora** can be arranged in this area, as can hikes to **Parque Nacional Cerro Hoya,** visits to nearby **waterfalls, horseback riding,** and (in season) visits to **turtle nesting** spots. Ask about any of these at Hotel Heliconia, whose Tanager Tourism wing (cell 6676-0220, http://tanagertourism.com) works with local guides, fishermen, and turtle-conservation projects in the community.

Adventurous sorts have discovered that boat trips to Coiba from here take longer but are cheaper than going via Playa Santa Catalina. The trip to Coiba takes three hours on a local fishing boat equipped with a 60 hp motor. I don't normally recommend travelers hire these boats because of the risk of going adrift on the ocean, which indeed does happen around here. But when these trips are arranged through Tanager Tourism, one of the capable owners goes along on the boat and handles the logistics, which is somewhat reassuring if something goes wrong.

Heliconia/Tanager Tourism offers two-night trips to Coiba for US$150 per person (groups of four or more). This includes all costs for transportation, the boat captain and anchorage, but it does not include the national park entrance fee of US$20 per person, the US$20 per person per night fee to stay in the ranger station cabins, nor food. Heliconia can arrange food for an extra fee. The boat has a canopy, life vests, and radio.

Boat trips to closer spots can also be arranged. These include the closest part of Isla Cébaco (20 minutes), Isla Gobernadora (45 minutes), and Playa Santa Catalina (about an hour). Expect to pay a minimum of $100 to hire a boat for the day; longer trips take more fuel and cost more; a trip to Santa Catalina will cost about US$150. If the fishing is good, however, it may be hard to find a boat. Again, Heliconia can arrange these trips. The boats they hire tend to leave from a boat landing, Puerto Palo Seco, between Hotel Heliconia and Mariato.

Horseback riding is US$10 an hour. There's a popular two-hour loop route that includes a stretch of riding along the beach. Rides can be booked through Heliconia/Tanager or directly through Raquel Ortega, whose **Caballeriza Eben-Ezer** (cell 6933-5520 or 6933-9784, raquelortega63@yahoo.com) is the only outfit in the area. **Playa Reina,** a couple kilometers north of Malena, is a popular **surfing** spot; there's a basic cantina/restaurant at the beach, and camping is possible there. For those who'd like to go for a splash in a river, the **Río Negro** is locally popular. It's accessible from a bridge over the river just south of Mariato.

This whole stretch of coast is crazy about **rodeos,** and each town and village has its own team of calf ropers. Arenas and Flores tend to have the best teams, each of which consists of 10 riders and two reserves. The roping I've seen out here is less aggressive than that typically practiced in the States: the aim is only to get the lasso around the calf's neck, with no trussing up of the legs. Cattle are precious out here, and the last thing the ranchers want is to injure a calf. The dry season is rodeo season, and teams practice constantly, so it's easy to see them in action even if you visit between rodeos. It's definitely worth stopping by a rodeo if one's in town, though. It really gives one a window into the local cowboy and community spirit, and the photo opportunities are outstanding.

The community of Malena supports a local turtle-conservation project **La Associación Conservacionista de Playa Malena** (cell 6685-8908, 6863-6228, or 6865-8924, playamalena@gmail.com, www.playamalena.org). Nearly half the population of the town is directly involved in the project. Its turtle hatchery is on the beach right next to town. Logically enough, the beach is called Playa Malena. It's also possible to swim here at low tide. Heading into Malena from the north, take a right turn just before town and head 300 meters to the beach.

This area attracts mostly olive ridley turtles, though some hawksbills occasionally show up. The females come to the beach to lay their eggs from mid-July to September or October. The conservation project protects these and, when they hatch, releases them one or two at a time in the morning before sunrise or in the early evening. October is the best chance of seeing the baby turtles make their way into the ocean. If you visit, please consider making a donation of at least US$5 to the project.

The conservation association also accepts volunteers from about May to December. Would-be volunteers should only consider this if they can spend at least a week. Otherwise, the time the association has to invest in the volunteer will not be repaid by enough useful work. The project especially needs people with specific skills, including carpenters, builders, and trained conservationists. A basic command of Spanish is helpful but not mandatory. The association can arrange food and a homestay for volunteers for US$150 a week. Inquiries in English can be sent to **Tanager Tourism** (cell 6676-0220, http://tanagertourism.com, tanagertourism@gmail.com).

There are waterfalls about a 10-minute hike from Malena, but finding them will require a local guide from the village (about US$1). This can be arranged through the turtle-conservation project.

Hikes in Parque Nacional Cerro Hoya can be arranged through Heliconia/Tanager, but the guide lives 50 kilometers south of here, near the park boundary, and there's no phone reception out there. Heliconia needs at least a day's notice to arrange a hike, as the only way to book the tour is to drive to the guide's house and talk with him.

Accommodations and Food

◖ **Hotel Heliconia** (cell 6676-0220, http://

hotelheliconiapanama.com, US$44 s, US$66 d, including breakfast) is the best place to stay in the entire western Azuero. It's run by a warm and capable Dutch couple, Kees (pronounced "case") and Loes (pronounced "loose"). They're both biologists, and they arrived in Panama in 2006 and set about planting trees on eight hectares of former pastureland and building their surprisingly modern house by the side of the road. They may be relatively new to running a tourism operation, but they've spent years working on sustainable-development projects in Mozambique and Angola; making things happen in Panama must seem like a breeze in comparison.

The four large guestrooms are simple but clean, bright, and cheerful, with ceiling fans, screen windows, and sliding glass doors that open onto a covered patio hung with hammocks. Some rooms have air-conditioning for an extra US$5 a night. Rooms have either one double or two single beds. Extra beds in a room are US$22 each. Laundry service is available for US$3.

Bathrooms are modern and have hot-water showers. About the only thing I'd change in the rooms are the somewhat thin mattresses; I suspect these will be upgraded as finances allow.

Fruit bats like to snooze under the eaves outside the rooms; it's pretty cool to see them up close, and they're harmless.

Kees and Loes have also set up two rustic *ranchos* (US$16.50 s, US$27.50 d, US$33 t) with tents and raised wooden floors on the eight kilometers of land that comprise their backyard. The *ranchos* are about a 10-minute walk from the inn. It's pretty much scrub brush back there at the moment, but the couple's hard work reforesting it is gradually becoming more apparent. The *ranchos* are a good option for those on a budget or who just want to be closer to nature but within a short walk of flush toilets, electricity, and hot food.

There is an outdoor, cold-water shower, toilets, and a common-kitchen *rancho* with gas stove that guests are free to use. But those feeling lazy can pay for lunch or dinner in the main house. (Unlike hotel guests, *rancho* dwellers must also pay for breakfast; US$2.50–3.50 per person.)

The roofs and wooden floors do a pretty good job of protecting guests from the elements, but the *ranchos* aren't rented out during the heaviest parts of the rainy season, as it'd just be too miserable out there.

Meals are served family style on the veranda of the main house. Food is simple but tasty and focuses on fresh, healthy food. A two-course lunch is around US$8 and a three-course dinner around US$15. Hearty eaters may find the portions on the small side.

The other lodging option in the area is **Hostel Iguana Verde** (cell 6865-8908 or 6469-3520, Anagonz1960@yahoo.com, US$10 pp, including breakfast), in "downtown" Malena. It offers three rooms jammed with okay beds in a little house owned by a Malena resident, Anna, whose own house is on the property. Rooms have floor fans and Miami windows but no air-conditioning. The hostel will be on the left just past the bridge as one drives south into Malena.

Restaurante Tortuga (cell 6865-8924, cholitotortuga@yahoo.com, 7 A.M.–9 P.M. daily) serves a menu of the day that will likely feature fried fish, *guandu,* and rice for around US$3. The food is surprisingly tasty and nongreasy. This is the only restaurant in the flyspeck village of Malena. It's in the front porch of a house on the road through town, and it's impossible to miss. It's across the street from Hostel Iguana Verde. There's no better way to get to know the locals than to chow down here. Tipplers should note that Malena is a dry village (as in, no booze served). Mariato is the closest place to buy anything harder than soda pop.

Getting There and Around

The 10 daily buses that run between Santiago and Torio pass right by Hotel Heliconia and Hostel Iguana Verde and can be flagged down as they pass; everything around Malena is built right next to the one road. Buses run only during daylight hours, about every 1.5 hours in the morning and about every 2 hours in the afternoon. Try to avoid late afternoon buses, which may fill up and have no room for you. The only taxi in the area is in Mariato (cell 6934-8387). He charges US$4 for the trip between Mariato and Hotel Heliconia. Expect to pay around US$50 to go all the way to Santiago.

TORIO

Though it's little more than a crossroads at a top of a hill, Torio is what passes for a hub of activity on the west side of the peninsula. It's 15 kilometers south of Mariato (of, if you prefer, 6 kilometers south of Hotel Heliconia). There are two places to stay and three places to get food. Options will probably increase soon, as this is ground zero for expat building projects in the area; a housing development is going up right behind the main hotel/restaurant. Keep an eye out for bulldozers and other heavy equipment. Just past the hotels, at the crest of the hill, is the turnoff to **Playa Torio,** which is popular with families with small kids, as it's quite flat and lacks pounding surf. But it's not the most appealing beach in the area, as it's at the mouth of the river, and among other things there's gold mining going on upriver. Hopefully they're not using dangerous chemicals, but the seawater tends to be reddish brown with silt, and after a storm all kinds of debris washes downriver onto the soil. The rocky road to the beach is only half a kilometer long, so it's a bumpy but okay ride for a regular car.

Practicalities

The few lodging and food options are also clustered near each other on or near a hill that's one of the highest vantage points in this lowland country.

Panadería y Dulcería El Cruce de Torio (no phone, 7:30 A.M.–9 P.M. daily) is on a rise just above the main road. It's a little bakery/sweet shop that serves sandwiches, desserts, *chichas* (fruit juice), and such for US$2.50. Cakes here are a bit dry but okay, and those with a sweet tooth don't have many other options out here.

You'll hear a lot of English spoken at **Ludvig's Tower** (cell 6864-1541 or 6441-3626, edilsagh@hotmail.com, www.panamaoceanview.com, most US$38.50–48.50 s/d), much of it about real estate. It's a hotel/restaurant just off the main road that's the most popular gringo hangout on the west side of the Azuero, though Ludvig himself is Norwegian. It doesn't have much competition, as there are few restaurants or bars of any kind on this side of the peninsula, but it's a pleasant place to while away the hours over a beer or three. The restaurant is a basic open-air covered terrace perched on the side of a hill with sweeping views of the ocean and surrounding country. A *comida del dia* lunch is US$3. Fish and seafood ranges US$5–10. A pretty tasty plate of grilled chicken and fries goes for US$8. Rather slow wireless, via satellite, is free for diners, US$2 for everyone else. The restaurant serves food from 7 A.M. daily, staying open as late as 10 P.M. in the dry season.

Ludvig's Tower offers 10 rooms of varying price and quality. The cheapest are two tiny cell-like rooms with ceiling fans in a building next to the restaurant for US$16.50 s/d. Stand-alone casitas on the side of the hill are significantly nicer, with decent beds, air-conditioning, minifridges, and small TVs. They're a bit lacking in charm, but they're modern and clean. Some of these are crammed with beds, which is handy for friendly groups and a bit cumbersome for couples. These go for US$38.50–US$48.50, or US$55 for a casita with a balcony overlooking the sea.

The other option in Torio is **Cabañas Torio** (cell 6939-1436, www.torioresort.com, US$31.90–38 per cabin), just north of and downhill from Ludvig's Tower and the bakery. It consists of a row of A-frame cabins, an open-air *rancho* restaurant, a volleyball court, and an artificial pond in a compound completely ringed by a rather uninviting-looking wall. The grounds are pleasant enough, but the cabins are the size of a postage stamp and nearly as sticky looking. Somehow the owners have managed to squeeze a TV, minifridge, and coffeemaker into the cabins. The restaurant (7–10 A.M. and 3–10 P.M.) serves chicken, burgers, seafood, and the like for around US$5–8. It's only open in the dry season.

Getting There and Around

There are 9–10 daily buses that run between Santiago and Torio. The trip takes about an hour and a half and costs US$5. Buses run only during daylight hours. They leave Santiago at 6 A.M., 7:30 A.M., 9 A.M., 10:30 A.M., noon, 1:15 P.M., 2:30 P.M., 4:30 P.M., and 5:30 P.M. On Mondays, the first bus leaves Santiago at 5:30 A.M., and there's an extra bus at 11 A.M. The schedule is similar for the ride back to Santiago. Buses leave when they fill up, so arrive early to be sure of getting a seat. This is especially true of the last couple of buses of the day. Drivers should stay alert, as the road becomes quite potholed south of Malena.

PLAYA MATA OSCURA

About 13 kilometers south of Torio there's a bus stop with turtles painted on the side. This is Mata Oscura, another little community with a turtle project. The project started in 2011 with the help of a Peace Corps volunteer. In 2012, the last coats of paint were drying on a modest but cheerful visitors center that has two six-bed dorms for visitors and volunteers. The dorms are quite basic, with a zinc roof, shared bathrooms, and walls that don't reach all the way to the ceiling. Beds are US$10 per night. Breakfast (US$3.50), lunch (US$5), and dinner (US$8) can also be arranged. The managers live right next door. Volunteers with the turtle-nesting project get discounted rates. The group planned to offer a variety of tours, including a short hike to a nearby waterfall or a more ambitious horseback ride to primary forest and

© WILLIAM FRIAR

Parque Nacional Cerro Hoya has some of the most unspoiled wilderness in Panama.

a waterfall an hour away. In the summer, the group can arrange tours of a traditional sugarcane processing operation. Wildlife that visitors have a chance of seeing in the area include capuchin and howler monkeys, poison-dart frogs, and, of course, turtles. The association offers tours of the turtle hatcheries, in season, for US$25 per group; they're located a 15-minute walk from the visitors' center. It's not terribly easy to get to this area without one's own transportation. Only three buses a day run between here and Mariato.

The road that turns off from the turtle-covered bus stop also leads to a five-kilometer-long gray-sand beach, **Playa Murillo.** The road is a bit rough but should be drivable in a regular car, at least during the dry season. The road forks 300 meters down the road. Take the right fork. The beach starts 700 meters down this road. If the beach here doesn't appeal, it's possible to follow a beach road just above the shoreline to the left for about another 1.5 kilometers

until you find a spot that does. The beach road is sand and dirt and can get quite rutted; only attempt it in a four-wheel drive.

◖ PARQUE NACIONAL CERRO HOYA

This dramatic national park is named for the tallest mountain on the Azuero Peninsula, Cerro Hoya. Bear in mind that the Azuero is distinctly flat, so "tallest mountain" here means 1,559 meters. Cerro Hoya is of volcanic origin; its rocks are the oldest ever found in Panama.

The park is sometimes known as Tres Cerros, since Cerro Hoya has two neighbors, Cerro Moya (1,534 meters), and Cerro Soya (1,478 meters). Created in 1984, it consists of 32,557 hectares of mountainous forest on the southwest tip of the peninsula as well as the waters that surround it. Traditionally the most isolated and unexplored national park in Panama, it contains some of the last primary forest on the peninsula. None of these mountains is actually visible until one has hiked deeply into the park; they're behind the highlands visible from the road.

The park is still rich in flora and fauna. It is one of the last habitats in Panama for the endangered scarlet macaw, though the chances of actually seeing one are slim; only a handful are known to survive in the park. Chances of seeing great green macaws are far better, particularly in the dry season. They start nesting in December. The macaws have a regular feeding pattern so the best time to get a glimpse of them on the move is early morning or late afternoon. Plan to be in the park by 6 A.M. if spotting one is important to you. Serious birders visit the park, however, to look for the Azuero parakeet *(Pyrrhura picta eisenmanni)*, the indigenous subspecies of the painted parakeet. Only about 2,000 of these are known to exist, but because they are concentrated in a small area, birders have a good chance of spotting them. They appear in the lowlands around the end of April to early July, depending on when the figs and nances they feed on ripen.

Jaguars still roam these forests, though, as always, seeing one would require extraordinary luck. Other critters of interest include the enormous king vulture, white-tailed deer, the mangrove black hawk, ospreys, *conejos pintados* (pacas), ocelots, and five species of monkeys. The best time to see wildlife is late in the dry season, when animals come down from the highlands to the few remaining water sources. They're easiest to spot around rivers. Wildlife viewing can also be good in the early rainy season, when everything is just starting to turn green again.

There is an official entrance to the park at the mouth of the Río Restingue, but it's very hard to get to. By far the easiest way to enter the park is from the buffer zone that starts just outside the village of Flores, which is where the main road ends. This access is through private land, but fortunately the owner of the land, Juan Velázquez, is also a forest guide who welcomes visits, if arranged in advance.

The approach to the park from this direction is dramatic. When one drives south from Mariato, the road crosses over the Río Pavo then makes a sharp left turn at the settlement of Arenas, the last spot on this side of the peninsula with a gas station, though it sometimes runs out of fuel. The landscape around here is flat, deforested cattle pasture and farmland. Then suddenly there are forest-covered hills jutting straight into the sky. The contrast could not be starker.

The way into the park here is not marked. As one approaches the village of Flores, where the road ends, there is a line of fences along the pasture on the right side of the road, broken by the occasional gate. Enter through the last gate before Flores. This is about an hour's drive south of Malena. Once through the gate, head in the direction of the mountains. There are a whole series of gates after this one, including some consisting of vertical poles strung together with barbed wire. Be careful with these, as they're tricky to manage and it's easy to cut oneself. There are eight gates in total before the road ends at Juan's family's house, right above the Río Playita.

Leave each gate as you find it: if it's closed, close it behind you after passing through. Otherwise you may let someone's cows into someone else's pasture, which will not make you popular. Note that all of this is private land, and you should not just show up unannounced. It's also not a good idea to walk through this land on one's own, as it's easy to end up in a field alone with a bull. Those with their own transportation should note that the drive is over dirt paths which are not always easy to make out, and which get muddy during the rainy season, when a four-wheel drive is essential.

Guide Services

The only experienced forest guide in the region is Juan ("Juancho") Velázquez, whose land opens onto the national park. Juan owns 152 hectares of woodland in the park in addition to 22.5 hectares of farm and pastureland just outside of it. He is authorized by ANAM, Panama's national environmental authority, to act as a kind of forest guard and guide. He is not a naturalist, but he has very sharp eyes and knows the area intimately. He charges small groups US$20/US$40 for a half/full-day hike. Birders come to the area to spot the Azuero parakeet and other endemic species, which are often visible in the area immediately around the house; for these non-hiking visits, Juan charges US$10 per person. Campers can also pitch a tent here for a modest fee. Note that the family are Jehovah's Witnesses, so please do not bring any alcohol onto the property.

Don't just show up expecting to hike or camp; arrangements should be made in advance, preferably at least a week ahead of time. This is a bit tricky since Juan has no phone or email. Hotel Heliconia/Tanager Tourism (cell 6676-0220, http://tanagertourism.com) works with Juan and can make the arrangements. This takes at least a day, since Kees or Loes has to drive all the way down to let Juan know.

Some travelers hire villagers in Flores to take them on a guided hike to the national park. The only way they can do this is through Juan's land, which means either paying Juan for his services anyway or trespassing on his property. But it's possible to hire someone in Flores to explore the general area outside the park for about US$5, or to show the way to Juan's house.

Hiking

Hiking in the park is challenging. There are no real trails, no facilities of any kind, and it's steeply uphill to get nearly anywhere. I don't recommend going without a knowledgeable guide, and as always, hiking alone is foolish and dangerous.

There are two main options for entering the buffer zone and the park itself through Juan's land. The first option is a steep uphill hike through secondary forest behind the family's house. Primary forest starts after about 40

minutes of climbing, when the path levels off briefly at around 350 meters. There's a good chance of coming upon capuchin monkeys during this hike. On my first visit to the park, I arrived here at noon, when there's little chance of seeing wildlife, and was chatting loudly with my companions. We still managed to see capuchins, a toucan, and a trogon without even trying. There's a beautiful waterfall in this area which is a good place to stop for a break and a snack. Juan has cut rough trails into the side of the hills, but expect to do a fair amount of scrambling. A walking stick is useful on this hike, especially on the way down. This is a real workout and shouldn't be attempted by anyone who isn't reasonably fit, but it's stunningly beautiful and unspoiled up there, with tremendously tall trees and plentiful wildlife to see, if one's lucky. Try to arrive as early in the morning as possible and plan on at least half a day in the forest.

Another option is to follow the Río Playita a three-hour hike upriver to a 20-meter waterfall with a deep pool at its base. This involves crossing the riverbed 10 times, so it's only possible in the dry season when the river is low.

Those who want to climb to the top of Cerro Hoya will have to camp overnight in the park. The extremely fit could theoretically rush to the summit and back in a day, but bear in mind this is a tough, steep climb through tropical forest with no real trails. The vegetation changes to cloud forest at around 800–1,200 meters. Bring warm, waterproof clothing and a tent. Do not attempt to camp during the rainy season, when it's far too muddy and difficult to get around.

The truly adventurous can plan a hike through the park that ends in the ocean. This requires 2–3 days of trekking over very steep, mountainous terrain with no trails. At the coast, a boat can then take hikers back to civilization. This has to be organized ahead of time, with a captain one can absolutely trust to show up, as

© WILLIAM FRIAR

The end of the road on the western Azuero Peninsula is in the small village of Flores.

there will be no way to communicate with him once one enters the park. Anyone interested in this adventure would do well to speak to Kees and Loes at Hotel Heliconia for advice.

FLORES

The western Azuero road comes to an abrupt end at a T-intersection at the entrance to the tiny village of Flores. Turn right to a find a little *refresquería* under a gorgeous old tree, right across the street from the local school. Drinks and snacks are available here. Take time to chat with the owner, Miguel Angel Moreno Bravo, who is the author of a little book on the area called *Las Flores de Arenas y Su Iglesia*. He can arrange tours of the area, and he may also be able to put visitors in touch with Juan Velázquez, who leads hikes to Parque Nacional Cerro Hoya.

Next to the *refresquería* is a private house with a room for visitors. The room is quite basic, with a double bed, corrugated zinc roof, and nearly clean bathroom. Staying here costs US$15 s, US$20 d and includes a very modest breakfast—a cup of coffee and some bread.

There is no phone, so the best way to find out if the room is available is to ask the driver of the Flores bus before heading down this far; he'll know if there's someone already there. Alternatively, call the Arenas public phone (tel. 999-8143) and ask to be speak to Toca Barrios (the nickname of the owner of the house; his real name is Ezekiel, but no one calls him that) or Miguel, the owner of the *refresquería*. On the other side of the T-intersection is a little *fonda* that constitutes the only dining option in town. Let them know ahead of time if you're looking for a meal, as otherwise they may not stay open or have enough food on hand.

Getting There and Around

Flores is about 50 kilometers south of Malena. Only two buses run between Santiago and Flores in the dry season. They leave Santiago at 6 A.M. and 8 A.M. and return from Flores at 11 A.M. and noon. In the rainy season there's just one daily bus, leaving Santiago at 7 A.M. and returning at 2 P.M. The fare is US$7 and the ride takes about two hours.

GUNA YALA

Welcome to paradise. Cartoonists who draw tropical islands as small discs of soft sand with a coconut palm or two could have gotten the idea from Guna Yala, otherwise known as the San Blas Islands. That image fits countless idyllic spots in this archipelago of nearly 400 islands off the eastern Caribbean coast of Panama. When the sun hits the sea, you'll think of emeralds and sapphires.

The islands are just part of the Comarca de Guna Yala, a semiautonomous homeland of the Guna people. Guna territory also encompasses a mountainous strip of mostly virgin forest on the mainland, along the Caribbean slope of the Darién. It runs the length of the archipelago, ending at the Colombian border.

You will no doubt see the Gunas referred to as the Kunas in Panama (and just about everywhere, for that matter). But in October 2011 the Gunas managed to get the Panamanian government to officially recognize them as the Guna people, and the *comarca* as Guna Yala. They argued that there is no "K" in the Guna language and therefore things needed to change. This is going to take some getting used to. It wasn't that long ago that Kuna was commonly spelled Cuna, and Guna Yala is still more commonly known as the San Blas Islands in many circles. Funnily enough, the Guna don't refer to themselves as the Kuna or the Guna: They know themselves as the Tule (pronounced TOO-lay). Kuna (now Guna) is

© WILLIAM FRIAR

HIGHLIGHTS

© AVALON TRAVEL

LOOK FOR ☾ TO FIND RECOMMENDED SIGHTS, ACTIVITIES, DINING, AND LODGING.

☾ **Achutupu:** You'll find easy and accessible snorkeling in crystalline waters by this island (page 460).

☾ **Cartí:** This cluster of islands near El Porvenir has an interesting blend of traditional and modern Guna life, as well as a museum that offers insight into that life (page 461).

☾ **Isla Maquina:** The vibrant Guna culture is going strong on Isla Maquina, one of the most traditional, charming, and attractive inhabited islands in the archipelago (page 465).

☾ **Cayos Holandéses and Cayos Coco Bandero:** These cays are among the archipelago's most remote and stunning string of sparsely inhabited islands, with clear water and spectacular coral (page 471).

just the name they let the *huaga* (foreigners) call them. Spend any amount of time out here, and these kinds of sudden shifts and confusions will start seeming awfully familiar.

Most visitors prefer to hang out on the islands. Nearly all the estimated 40,000 Guna who live in the *comarca* (reservation) inhabit just 40 of the islands, none of which is very large. As one might imagine, things get pretty crowded: On many islands, the thatch roofs of the Gunas' cane huts almost touch, making walking around a bit of a challenge. Even if you feel the allure of the uninhabited islands, be sure to visit a village. The chance to meet the Guna, who have one of the most vibrant indigenous cultures in Latin America, is reason enough to stop in.

If you're looking for an island resort, Guna Yala is emphatically not for you. Even the most exclusive accommodations are quite simple, and there's little to do on the islands except swim, snorkel, laze in hammocks, and visit villages. The food on the islands is generally bland and basic. Coral Lodge is the only place out here with a modern infrastructure, and it's not actually in the archipelago.

More disturbing, any lingering romantic notions one has about indigenous people's harmonious relationship with nature gets a jolt upon realizing how severely the Guna are overfishing their own waters, or seeing the garbage and sewage they routinely dump into pristine blue waters.

On the other hand, there are still plenty of

GUNA YALA

lovely, uninhabited islands in the archipelago, more than anyone could possibly see during a visit. A big part of the charm of these islands is their very simplicity: no time-share condos or tacky T-shirt shops here. Nodding off in a hammock slung between coconut palms, watching a Guna woman sewing a *mola* (handcrafted blouse), and showering by the light of a kerosene lantern can soon seem like a pretty good way to spend the day.

PLANNING YOUR TIME

The Comarca de Guna Yala consists of a strip of mountainous coast and a nearby archipelago that stretch 226 kilometers down the eastern Caribbean side of the isthmus to the Colombian border. Nearly all the islands are within five kilometers of the mainland. Only a handful of the inhabited ones have much in the way of visitor facilities. Few tourists visit the coast, which is home primarily to Guna farms and dense tropical forest.

The islands most popular with and accessible to visitors are organized into five clusters in this chapter. It's possible to visit more than one of these island clusters during a visit. However, distances are too great and the sea sometimes too rough to make a day trip from one cluster to another practical by the chief means of transportation: small wooden boats powered by outboard motors. Unless you have access to a large powerboat or yacht, choose just one area to explore. If your schedule allows, you can also fly to a second area and spend one or more nights there, but that will increase the logistical hassles significantly; interisland flights are tricky to arrange.

Visitors will get the most out of their stay if they take time both to explore Guna villages and to escape to one of the uninhabited islands for snorkeling or sunbathing. Most island groups offer an attractive combination of both. Those who stay around the busy hubs of **El Porvenir** and **Cartí,** for instance, have easy access to the uninhabited island of **Achutupu** and other pristine spots. Those who stay on the tranquil hotel islands around **Río Sidra,** on the other hand, can take a day trip to explore the nearby village islands, including traditional and picturesque **Isla Maquina.**

Try to stay a bare minimum of two nights on the islands. That allows enough time to explore a Guna village, go snorkeling, shop for *molas* (handcrafted blouses), and lounge in a hammock. A three-night or longer stay gives visitors a better sense of the rhythms and beauty of life on the islands. Time will go much faster than you expect.

WHEN TO GO

Late in the dry season, late February–March, is generally reckoned to be the best time to visit the islands. The winds are calmer, improving snorkeling visibility. This calmer weather can last until mid-April. There are strong trade winds December–February, which create lots of chop in the sea. It also tends to be cloudy then, which drops snorkeling visibility even more.

There's less wind in the rainy season, which begins around mid-April and lasts until the end of the year. This calms the water, but underwater visibility near land can be poor because of runoff from the rivers. The lack of wind can also make it quite hot and humid. On the other hand, the seas are calm enough to go exploring by boat outside the reef that protects the western half of the archipelago from the open ocean. The fishing is also better then, and there are fewer tourists. The high season for tourists is December–March. According to experienced sailors, if there are hurricanes out in the Caribbean (Panama is beyond the hurricane belt), the weather in Guna Yala tends to be good.

Holidays in Guna Yala include the anniversary of the Revolución Tule (the Guna war against Panama in 1925) on February 21, which is celebrated throughout the archipelago, and the honoring of Charles Robinson, an important figure in the revolution, which is observed only on his native island of Narganá.

Visiting the Guna Yala Islands

The island clusters of the *comarca* (reservation) are covered in geographical order in this chapter, starting with the westernmost one and heading southeast down the archipelago. This is followed by a description of the most popular of the lovely, remote, and sparsely inhabited outer cays.

Farther down the archipelago, east of Corazón de Jesús, the reef ends and the islands are subject to higher seas. This area sees few tourists.

Island names are confusing. Some have both Spanish and Guna names, and there is rarely agreement on how to spell them in either language. Different islands sometimes have the same name. The most common names and their alternatives are used in this chapter.

SPORTS AND RECREATION
Water Activities

Underwater visibility in these crystalline waters can be better than 30 meters on a good day. The best **snorkeling** is found among the sparsely inhabited outer cays at the western end of the archipelago, where the coral is extensive and indescribably beautiful. The most popular of these are the **Cayos Holandéses.**

The hotels typically have snorkeling equipment to rent or borrow, but it's usually not in good shape. Bring your own if possible. The Gunas have banned scuba diving in their waters.

Several groups now offer **kayak** adventures, which can be a great way to explore the islands. When conditions are right, you can see many meters down, and, if you're lucky, dolphins will swim along the kayak. Groups to consider include **Aventuras Panama** (tel. 260-0044, info@aventuraspanama.com, www.aventuraspanama.com) and **Expediciones Tropicales** (tel. 317-1279, info@xtrop.com, www.xtrop.com).

Don't swim around inhabited islands, as human and animal waste is allowed to flow out to sea; try even to avoid sea-spray during boat rides near them.

Hiking Tours

Some hotels now offer tours of the rainforest near the coast for an extra fee. These usually go to a waterfall or Guna cemetery. The more ambitious of these can be hikes through true jungle. Come prepared, and do not attempt to explore the forests without a Guna guide.

ACCOMMODATIONS AND FOOD

Most of the phone numbers listed for lodgings are in Panama City, where nearly all the hotels have offices. Typical hotel packages include room, meals, pickup and drop-off at the airstrip, and one or two daily boat tours to a snorkeling spot or Guna village. Some will also arrange plane reservations.

Some hotels allow guests to opt out of the full package and fend for themselves for meals and transport. However, unless you have your own boat, you'll probably find it cheaper, and certainly simpler, to go with a package deal. Remember that nearly all accommodations out here vary from fairly rustic to very rustic. Also, there are no true restaurants in Guna Yala.

PHOTOS OF THE GUNA

It's tempting to take photos of the Guna, especially the colorfully dressed women. But always ask first, and expect to pay for the privilege. If the Guna are going to be treated as curiosities, they figure the least tourists can do is compensate them for it. Note that the going rate is US$1 per subject, *not* per photo, as some try to claim. A Guna woman you've just bought something from is more likely to let you snap her photo, and she may not even charge you. Photos of village scenes that don't focus on an individual are free.

Most visitors eat all their meals in their hotel's simple dining area.

The food is usually mediocre at best. Bear in mind that lobster, once a subsistence food for the Guna, has been so commercially overexploited it's in danger of local extinction. At the very least, do not eat lobster during the mating season, which runs March–July, when it is against Guna law to serve or eat it. Also, even those with a package deal will probably pay extra for lobster, something you may not realize until you're presented the bill.

It's probably also wise to avoid squid. Guna fishermen typically chase squid out of aquatic caves by squeezing bleach into the cave entrance. It's bad for the environment and bad for you.

Do not camp on a deserted island without permission from the island's owner—every island belongs to a person or community. Even then, don't camp except with an organized group. Smugglers, including drug traffickers, run these waters. You really wouldn't want them to stumble upon you in the middle of the night.

INFORMATION AND SERVICES

There are few modern services of any kind on the islands. Bring just about anything you'll need during your stay, as only the most basic supplies are sold anywhere.

Bring enough cash to cover any expenses you expect to incur on the islands. That means lots of small bills (US$1 and US$5); anything larger than a US$10 is hard to break. There's only one bank in the archipelago, on Narganá, and it doesn't have an ATM.

The inhabited islands usually have telephone booths that accept calling cards, and mobile phone signals now reach some of the inhabited islands. But expect to be more or less cut off from the rest of the world during your stay.

One of the most maddening things about visiting the islands is trying to get in touch with people. Even the longest-established hotels and services are perpetually changing their phone numbers, names, and email addresses. I list as many as possible in the hope that at least one of them will still work by the time you read this.

More places now have websites, but how long they'll stick around is anyone's guess, and most give a far more idealized image of what they offer than what they actually deliver. Again, don't come expecting a resort, or even a Motel 6. Think Robinson Crusoe and you might be pleasantly surprised, or at least not too disappointed.

GETTING THERE AND AROUND

Traveling to and around Guna Yala can be a bit of a hassle. The islands' isolation and the logistics involved in visiting them help keep them relatively undeveloped and the Guna culture more or less intact. Most visitors traditionally have arrived by small plane from Panama City, or by yacht. But a road now connects the western borders of the *comarca* with the rest of Panama. Driving to the Caribbean coast and catching a Guna boat to the islands has become the favored way to visit, at least for budget travelers and those who want to explore the westernmost islands, which have always had the most tourists. A Guna shuttle service of sorts runs between Panama City and the Caribbean coast, where travelers are met by Guna boatmen who ferry them to the islands.

In recent times land and sea have been the only ways to get to the western islands, as the airstrips in this part of the archipelago, most notably those on El Porvenir and on the mainland near Cartí and Río Sidra, have been closed, ostensibly for repairs.

The El Porvenir strip reopened and commercial flights resumed in the spring of 2012. There was no indication when or if the other western airstrips would be reopening as well.

Flights still serve the main population centers in the central and eastern islands. The only other way to reach these distant islands is on a substantial, oceangoing vessel (e.g., a yacht).

GUNA YALA

THE GUNA PEOPLE

Some still refer to the Guna as the San Blas, because of the Spanish name for the archipelago where most Guna live. But Guna is the preferred term, and the archipelago is increasingly known by its official name, Guna Yala (Land of the Guna). To confuse matters, the Guna call themselves the Tule (pronounced "TOO-lay"), though they refer to themselves as Guna when dealing with *uagas* (outsiders).

No one knows for sure where the Guna originally came from, but surprisingly enough they have only been on the islands a few hundred years. Before that they lived in the Darién forest. Wars with the Spanish, the Emberá-Wounaan, and descendants of escaped African slaves gradually pushed them toward the Caribbean coast and islands. Some Darién rivers that are now part of Emberá and Wounaan territory still bear Guna names.

Some Guna remain in the mainland forests, mostly in two other *comarcas* (reservations), Madungandí and Wargandí. The mainland Guna were historically known as the Guna Bravo (fierce Guna, for their warriorlike ways). The remotest of these see few visitors, cling especially tightly to their traditional ways, and tend to exclude outsiders, whom they view with considerable suspicion. A distinction is still made between the more open and adaptable "island Guna" and the traditional "mainland Guna."

Most of the inhabitants of the Comarca de Guna Yala are island Guna, but even they travel by *cayuco* (dugout canoe) to the mainland to farm, hunt, and bury their dead. About 40,000 of the estimated 61,700 Guna live on the islands. The rest live in the mainland forests, in Panama City, and scattered around the country.

The Guna have done a remarkable job over the centuries of keeping invaders out and holding on to their rich culture. They even fought and won a revolt against the Republic of Panama in 1925, which eventually earned them their semiautonomous status. Today, no foreigner is allowed to own land in Guna territory.

Gunas have gained a greater voice in Panamanian government in recent years. In 1999 a Guna, Enrique Garrido, became the head of Panama's general assembly.

Visitors are inevitably struck by the beautiful traditional dress of the Guna women, which is not worn to impress tourists. The Guna themselves cite the preservation of women's traditional clothing and ornamentation as vital to maintaining their culture.

The most famous parts of this dress are the panels of intricately worked cloth that decorate the front and back of the woman's blouse. Known as *molas* (*mola* is Guna for blouse), these panels are prized by collectors around the world. Older women in particular also wear gold rings through the bottoms of their noses and tight strings of beads around their forearms and lower legs.

Gunas have the highest rate of albinism in the world for reasons that are still not well understood. Known as "moon children," albinos are treated as special people but, sadly, have a shortened life expectancy because of their susceptibility to skin cancer. Why a people so close to the equator should have such a high rate of albinism has fascinated scientists for years.

The Guna have always been wary of outsiders, and that's a major reason they still exist. One can have a relatively inexpensive stay in the San Blas Islands, but nothing is free; even taking a photo of a Guna usually costs a dollar. The Gunas' reticence, and a belief that visitors should pay for the privilege of visiting their homeland, can be off-putting to those who come with stereotyped notions of fun-loving, generous people. It's not hard to see the Gunas' point of view, though. Outsiders have been trying to take their home away from them for centuries, and even visitors with more benign intentions often treat them as colorful parts of the scenery.

Try to bear that in mind during your stay. At the very least, never take a photo of a Guna without asking permission first. You'll probably find that if you're willing to accept the Guna on their own terms, you'll get a glimpse of a fascinating world.

RESORT COMFORT NEAR GUNA YALA

The best place to stay in Guna Yala is not actually in Guna Yala. **Coral Lodge** (tel. 836-5434, U.S./Canada toll-free tel. 888/499-2497, www.corallodge.com, high-season rates start at US$170 pp), which opened in 2006, is on a lovely cove on Escribano Point, right about where the province of Colón stops and Guna Yala begins. It's accessible only by sea – in a powerful motorboat. It's about a 45-minute ride from El Porvenir or a half hour from Miramar, in Costa Arriba.

Accommodations consist of six water villas – spacious and comfortable modern bungalows over the water – that are linked by a boardwalk to a small half-moon beach. A larger beach is a short walk away. The bungalows have tall thatched ceilings, air-conditioning, ceiling fans, excellent beds, simple but tasteful teak and rattan furnishings, and small sundecks. Spa bathtubs are in the bedroom right next to windows that look out on the ocean; showers are in the attached bathroom. All the bungalows are angled for maximum privacy, but number 6, at the end of the boardwalk, has the best unobstructed view – there's nothing in front of it but sea.

On the beach is a large swimming pool that's illuminated at night. Meals are served next door in a large modern dining room with a thatched roof, 20 meters above the tile floors. The lodge also has a couple of Internet computers and a little game room with a TV and DVD player. There's an open-air bar over the water. The chef is Peruvian.

Most guests get to the lodge by traveling first by land to Miramar, near the end of the road in Colón province, and then transferring to Coral Lodge on its boat.

High-season rates start at US$170 per person, but that only includes the room. Packages are available that include meals, transfers, tours, or some combination thereof. Possible activities range from forest hikes or horseback riding on the mainland to overnight stays in Guna Yala and scuba diving. The Gunas do not allow diving in the *comarca* (reservation) itself, but there's a divemaster at the lodge who can take guests to little-visited spots just outside Guna territory. The Escribano reef, for instance, is just two kilometers away.

The American-Peruvian owner, who owns two well-regarded hotels in Peru, plans eventually to add 12 lower-cost accommodations on the beach for divers on a budget.

This is one of my favorite places in all of Panama, but it is not for everyone. The accommodations are luxurious enough to convince potential guests they're coming to a premiere resort where everything works perfectly. That's impossible out here; this is a remote spot surrounded by nothing but sea and tropical forest. The boat ride to and from the lodge can be bumpy when the wind picks up, and diving and fishing conditions can change without warning. The diving and fishing are best Easter–October, which is also the rainy season. And the *chitras* (sand flies) can be voracious when the wind dies, since there's a healthy mangrove system near the lodge. To be happy out here you have to be easygoing and have at least a slight sense of adventure. This is a great spot even during a thunderstorm; the view is gorgeous and the sound of rain falling on the thatch can induce blissful afternoon naps.

GUNA YALA

Attempting to travel by Guna *panga* that far is quite expensive and potentially very dangerous.

However you choose to visit the islands, the chances are good that not all will go according to plan. Flight schedules can change overnight, the road can get washed out in a storm, or the Guna may suddenly decide a certain kind of tourism is not to their liking (this is what happened years ago, when the Guna banned scuba diving entirely from their waters, a ban which they've never lifted). More than just about anywhere else in Panama, Guna Yala is a place to come equipped with a travel insurance policy that has good trip disruption and cancelation provisions.

By Sea

The best way to explore the islands is by yacht. A few tour companies based in Panama City

PARADISE UNDER PRESSURE

The spectacularly clear water around the islands makes the underwater flora and fauna of the *comarca* (reservation) the big draw for most visitors. For starters, consider the coral reefs that can make navigating these waters so treacherous: According to the Smithsonian Tropical Research Institute, which until recently had a research facility on the islands, Guna Yala has more coral species than just about anywhere else in the Caribbean. It's easy to spot colorful staghorn, brain, fan, and leaf coral, among many others. Nearly 60 species of marine sponges grow on the western side of the *comarca*.

Sadly, however, overfishing and reef destruction have decimated marine life. Five types of lobster are found here, but they are in danger of local extinction because Guna divers catch them to sell to outside commercial interests. The same thing is happening with other marine creatures, including sea turtles and, beginning in the early 1990s, even small tropical fish, which are ending up in household aquariums in the United States. Marine life in the region, while still impressive, is not what it was even a decade ago.

The Guna also lost nearly 80 percent of their remaining coral in the last three decades of the 20th century, according to a study conducted in 2003, due mainly to coral mining to build seawalls and landfill to expand islands, as well as some natural causes.

About 90 percent of the territory of the *comarca* on the mainland is still covered with forest. Though these forests are under pressure, animals found in them include the collared and white-lipped peccary, Baird's tapir, red brocket deer, and iguana.

organize charter trips with sailing-yacht owners and captains. As this book went to press, charter companies were negotiating with the Guna the right to continue offering these trips. This kind of haggling happens from time to time, and presumably this hiccup will be resolved by the time you read this. Check with the companies below to make sure, however.

Prices for charters depends on the number of people, the length of the cruise, and the type of yacht hired. Expect to pay a minimum of US$125 per person per day, including meals and tours. The shortest cruise is typically three days, but that barely gives one time to settle in and see much of anything. In my opinion, four days is the minimum to truly unwind and enjoy what the islands have to offer when visited by boat. You'll be amazed how quickly a week can slip by out here.

Charter groups typically tailor itineraries to a group's interests. I recommend a combination of visits to village islands and to the remoter and more unspoiled parts of the archipelago, such as the Cayos Holandéses. Forest hikes on the mainland to waterfalls and traditional Guna cemeteries can sometimes be arranged. Even in the more inhabited parts of the archipelago, it should be possible to visit a village by day but then spend the night onboard the yacht in an uninhabited anchorage.

There may be a range of vessels to choose from. Bigger and/or more luxurious yachts cost more, naturally; balance your need for comfort against the number of days you plan to travel. I personally favor catamarans since they have a very shallow draft, meaning they can explore a wide variety of remote and beautiful spots, including coral reefs, that would damage the hull of many monohull yachts. I'm also happy to go fairly rustic if it means being able to afford a longer trip and more time to explore. Many people find they're quite happy with basic accommodations in such lovely and interesting surroundings.

Whatever the choice, make sure the yacht is equipped with life vests, a radio, and a dinghy

© BONNIE KAY SPINDLER

Guna trading vessels run up and down the archipelago.

with an outboard motor. Onboard kayaks are a major plus, as it's a blast to go for a paddle in calm and sheltered waters, stopping for a snorkel from time to time. On one of my kayak paddles I was lucky enough to have a close encounter with a pod of curious dolphins.

Be sure to ask if snorkel equipment will be available onboard or if guests are expected to provide their own. Also, find out what languages the captain speaks; occasionally guests who speak only English get paired with a captain who doesn't speak any, which can be tricky. Travelers who don't speak Spanish should consider bringing a phrasebook just in case.

Two experienced companies to consider: **Panama Travel Unlimited** (Edificio Stela, Calle 1, Perejil, Panama City, tel. 395-5014, http://panamatravelunlimited.com) is the tour-company wing of the Mamallena youth hostel in Panama City. They regularly run a number of different kinds of trips in Guna Yala so are

well placed to know current conditions. Their yacht trips start at US$125 per person per day. **San Blas Sailing** (tel. 314-1800 or 314-1288, www.sanblassailing.com) has been organizing yacht charters in Guna Yala for a number of years. They work with a number of yachts, ranging from a quite simple 34-foot catamaran to a rather upscale 55-foot one, plus a number of monohulls. Rates start at US$125 per person per day for groups of four in the 34-footer, three-day minimum. Smaller groups pay higher per-person rates.

The second-best way to explore the islands is by small, adventure-type cruise ship. These cruises can be very pricey, but they often feature academic and naturalist guides who can deepen the experience. And they're certainly a comfortable way to go. Among the outfits that regularly include Guna Yala in their itineraries are **Tauck World Discovery** (U.S. toll-free tel. 800/788-7885, www.tauck.com) and **Star Clippers** (U.S. tel. 305/442-0550, U.S./

Canada toll-free tel. 800/442-0551, www.
starclippers.com).

Several of the huge cruise ships that transit the Panama Canal also stop in the islands.
Tourists can outnumber Gunas during these brief visits, which are hardly the ideal way to experience the islands or Guna culture.

Some tourists are under the misapprehension it's easy to buy passage on a boat from El Porvenir to Colombia. This is not true. Though I don't recommend hitching a ride in these waters, which are known drug-trafficking routes, it's far easier to do so from Colón or Isla Grande. Tourists have been known to get stranded on Porvenir for days waiting for a ride, if they get one at all. It may be possible to buy passage down the archipelago or trade a ride for work on a private yacht, a Colombian trader, or a 75-foot-long Guna supply boat. The latter two options are quite rustic, slow, and most likely unsafe. It's also possible to arrange boat transportation from the area around Nombre de Dios, but this is generally on small motorized fishing boats and is a quite risky way to get to the islands. A less risky and far more comfortable option is to book a berth on a private yacht that's going to or from Cartagena, Colombia; these stop over in the islands. This is an informal arrangement and can be quite affordable, but it is not without its dangers. There is no approved commercial boat transport to and from the islands.

By Air

For many years the main way to get to the islands was by small plane from Panama City. The paving of the road to the west end of the *comarca* (reservation) has rapidly changed this, however, and at the time of writing no commercial flights were running to most of the airstrips that serve the western islands, including Cartí and Río Sidra. However, small planes are still the main way to get to the islands farther down the archipelago.

Flying on these tiny, sometimes aged-looking contraptions can be an adventure in itself, especially while crossing the coastal range. But on a clear day the views are breathtaking, and the flights are mercifully short.

The sudden collapse of Aeroperlas in February 2012 left just one airline serving the islands. **Air Panama** (tel. 316-9000, www.fly-airpanama.com), flies from Panama City to the islands and coastal airstrips. There is generally one daily, early-morning flight between Panama City and the major island groups.

The planes usually make several stops, so be careful to get off at the right place—I've been out there when travelers disembarked at the wrong place and were unable to meet up with a yacht they'd chartered, spoiling their entire trip. Nonstop flights to most destinations are around 30–45 minutes, but with stops they can last longer than an hour, not including delays.

For those staying at one of the island hotels, transportation by small boat between the closest airstrip and the hotel is included with a stay. There are no true airline offices in the archipelago, but hotels can sometimes make or change reservations for guests. However, it's best to come to the islands with a round-trip ticket and stick to the itinerary. And despite the airplane island-hopping, it's not easy to arrange flights between one island group and another; ticketing is geared for travel between Panama City and the islands, not among them.

Airfare is quite reasonable. However, rising fuel prices are making fares go up faster than in the past. As this book went to press, the longest and most expensive flight cost about US$110 one-way and took an hour of nonstop flying. That was to Puerto Obaldía, near the Colombian border. Air Panama currently makes that trip only on Tuesdays, Thursdays, and Sundays. The only travelers who go there are attempting to cross over into Colombia. (The conflict in Colombia has made Puerto Obaldía a dicey place, and visitors are being advised to stay well away from it.) Shorter flights cost proportionately less. The round-trip fare to all destinations is double the one-way fare.

By Land

Shortly before Lago Bayano is the **El Llano-Cartí Road,** which heads north over the Continental Divide and down into the Comarca de Guna Yala. It is the only land access to the islands, and most of its 30-kilometer length was recently paved. However, as one approaches the Caribbean coast, vehicles must still ford a river and there can be washouts, particularly during the rainy season. There are also hairpin turns with sheer drops. Do not attempt this trip without a good four-wheel-drive vehicle with high clearance and, preferably, a winch.

I do not advise that travelers drive themselves, even when the road is in good shape (when it's in poor shape, private vehicles are not allowed). It is far better, and probably cheaper, to go with a Guna transport service. These are gradually becoming more professional operations, but they still basically amount to a driver with a four-wheel drive and a mobile phone. They have experience on this road, will know its condition, and will be able to help with the logistics of getting into and around Guna territory. The base price is US$25–30 per person each way from Panama City, which is a good deal. They typically pick up clients from their lodgings before dawn, usually around 5 A.M. The trip takes about three or four hours, including brief stops to admire the spectacular views.

Once you arrive at the coast near Cartí, the Guna taxes begin. Expect to pay at least US$7 tourist tax and US$2 port tax (the rate fluctuates), plus boat fare to whichever island you're going to if you're not being met by a boat from your hotel. Boat transport to the Islas Robinson, the most common backpacker destinations, is US$20 round-trip. In other words,

total round-trip transportation costs per person from Panama City to the islands will be at least US$80 per person; still cheaper than flying (when flying is an option), but not as much as many initially think.

One advantage of going by road is you're not limited by the strict baggage-weight allowance of the small planes. Consider bringing a medium-size cooler stocked with ice, food, snacks, and drinks—though concentrate on things that are safe and pleasant to consume at room temperature, because you won't find any ice on the islands. (The last real stores you're likely to encounter on the road are at 24 de Diciembre, on the eastern outskirts of Panama City, and they may not be open by the time you pass through in the morning.) Also, bring large jugs of water to limit having to buy bottled water on the islands.

For those who want—or need—to break their land journey, there is an appealing ecolodge, **Burbayar Lodge** (tel. 393-7340, cell 6674-2964, www.burbayar.com) up in the mountains along the El Llano–Cartí Road.

I recommend booking ground transport through one of the Guna hotels, a reputable hostel, or a tour operator. Reliable youth hostels are an especially good bet, as they send clients out all the time and will have the latest information on road conditions and reliable drivers. They also get constant feedback from their guests. A group to try is **Panama Travel Unlimited** (Edificio Stela, Calle 1, Perejil, Panama City, tel. 395-5014, http://panamatravelunlimited.com), which is affiliated with the Mamallena youth hostel in Panama City. They organize a good range of different trips for budget-minded travelers and can book accommodations as well, ranging from rustic homestays to rooms at the most upscale places to yacht charters.

Another good hostel option is **Luna's Castle** (Calle 9 Este and Avenida Eloy Alfaro, Casco Viejo, Panama City, tel. 262-1540, www.lunascastlehostel.com). They send backpackers to the islands by land all the time, booking transportation and accommodations for them. Land transportation is by Jeep and costs US$25 each way; book by 7 P.M. the evening before you want to go at the very latest. The Jeep picks travelers up in front of Luna's Castle at 5 A.M.

Even those who decide not to travel with either outfit should check out their websites, which have useful, detailed information on the islands.

Tours

No formal tour operators are based on the islands. Visitors usually arrange tours and boat trips through their hotels, which offer one or two daily excursions in their standard packages. It's also easy to hire Guna boatmen and guides, but almost none of them speaks English, and some don't even speak much Spanish. Agree on a price and itinerary ahead of time.

The prices listed here may rise, as the cost of tours is mainly driven by the cost of boat fuel. That also goes for lodging packages that include daily boat tours, which most do.

You may find it simpler to arrange a trip to the islands through a tour operator in Panama City, who will book the flights or land transport, make room reservations, and make sure a boatman's there to meet the plane.

Panama Travel Unlimited (Edificio Stela, Calle 1, Perejil, Panama City, tel. 395-5014, http://panamatravelunlimited.com), the Mamallena-affiliated travel company mentioned elsewhere in this chapter, offers a day trip to Guna Yala for those who'd like to get a taste of Guna culture and the islands but aren't up to spending the night. The tour includes land and boat transportation, a guide, meals, and a visit to one of the inhabited islands and one of the beach islands around the Cartí/El Porvenir area. The cost is US$120–130 per person, including everything but the Guna taxes, which are around US$8–10. One thing I like about these guys is they don't oversell Guna Yala; they do a conscientious job of informing visitors of exactly what to expect, both the good and the not-so-great.

El Porvenir and Vicinity

EL PORVENIR

The small island of El Porvenir is the western point of entry for the archipelago. It has a landing strip, a couple of government offices, and a basic hotel. There's also an **artisans' cooperative** that sells *molas* (handcrafted blouses) and other arts and crafts. The two-story yellow building housing the **Museo de la Nación Guna** (Museum of the Guna Nation) is on the far side of the island. I've yet to find it open, but it's supposed to have displays on Guna art, history, and culture. There's little else on the island, but because it's isolated from the densely populated islands nearby, El Porvenir's little beach is clean and pleasant. For most people, though, this island is just a transit point.

◖ ACHUTUPU

Also known as **Isla de los Perros** (Dog Island), Achutupu is a private island a short boat ride to the east that is inhabited only by a family of caretakers. Visitors must pay them a US$2 entrance fee. (Don't confuse this Achutupu with the large, crowded island of the same name much farther east.) Everything about this pristine speck of sand and palm trees is straight out of a postcard. The water is calm and crystalline, with great snorkeling visibility. There's an old shipwreck in shallow water just off the south side of the island. It's overgrown with brilliant coral and has become a playground for a variety of small and medium-size tropical fish.

Achutupu is surrounded by other lovely islands, with rustic Guna sailboats and the occasional sleek foreign yacht gliding around them. If Achutupu isn't perfect enough, ask the boatman to do some more exploring.

◖ CARTÍ

South of the Porvenir area, about a 40-minute motorized boat ride away, is a cluster of islands and a bit of coast known collectively as Cartí (Gardi). There's a large, vibrant village on **Cartí Suitupu** (Gardi Sugdup), which makes it a popular cruise-ship destination. This place sees more foreigners than any other part of the archipelago, so it's perhaps not surprising it has an estimated two dozen bars/soda stands. There's an ultra-basic dormitory and three private rooms, **Cartí Homestay** (cell 6734-3454 Germain, in Panama City; or 6517-9850 Eulogio, in Cartí; info@cartihomestay. info, sanblasadventures@yahoo.com, www.cartihomestay.info, US$40 pp, including meals and a boat trip), for those who get stranded going to or from the islands by the El Llano–Cartí Road or want to stay on a busy inhabited island with a relatively modern infrastructure. There is generator-powered electricity 6 P.M.–midnight. This place is growing in ambition with the influx of tourists coming by road. They can arrange road transportation to and from Pamama City (US$25 pp) and trips to Puerto Obaldía by cargo boat ($150 pp).

Especially noteworthy is a small **Guna museum** (tel. 299-9002 or 299-9074, 8 A.M.–4 P.M. daily, US$2) housed in a thatch-roofed hut. It has its own dock, so small boats can go there directly. The displays are modest but include an interesting mix of traditional implements, exhibits on the Guna puberty ritual (only girls go through this, and it's a huge, drunken party for the whole village), vintage *molas* (handcrafted blouses), and so on. It gives a glimpse into the mythology, history, rituals, and daily life of the Guna. A Guna man named José Davis, who established the museum along with his father, gives guided tours

of the exhibits in English and Spanish, with lots of intricate and sometimes hard-to-follow explanations of Guna history and religion. One of the more interesting tidbits is a description of Guna burials. (The cemeteries are on the mainland, where the Gunas dig underground rooms and string them with hammocks into which the deceased are placed.)

Visitors are welcome to stop by the other islands in the group as well, which are not quite as modernized or heavily touristed as Cartí Suitupu.

OTHER ISLANDS

Clustered just to the south of El Porvenir are Wichub-Huala (WITCH-ub WAH-la), Ukuptupu (ook-oop-TOO-puu), Nalunega (nah-loo-NEH-gah), and Isla Corbisky. All but Ukuptupu have villages. All have generator-powered electricity 6 P.M.–midnight, and it's much easier to find English speakers here than elsewhere in the archipelago. They are just a couple of minutes from each other by motorized boat.

Ukuptupu is entirely covered with a sprawling wooden complex connected by boardwalks that was the home of a Smithsonian Tropical Research Institute facility for 21 years. The Guna, ever suspicious of foreigners in their *comarca* (reservation), finally kicked the researchers out of Guna Yala in 1998. The research facility is now a rustic hotel. **Nalunega** is home to the Hotel San Blas, the oldest hotel in the archipelago. **Wichub-Huala** has the attractive Hotel Kuna Niskua, a health center, and a small community. A kiosk near the pier sells beer, water, soda, and other basic goods.

Isla Corbisky, sometimes spelled Corbiski, offers a chance for visitors to live with a Guna family.

ACCOMMODATIONS AND FOOD

Nearly all visitors fly into El Porvenir and stay at one of the basic hotels on the surrounding islands. Hotel stays generally include all meals, transfers to and from the airstrip on El Porvenir, and daily boat trips. These trips

GUNA YALA

are generally to Achutupu or Cartí, but jungle hikes on the mainland or boat rides to the Cayos Limónes, Cayos Grullos, or the remote Cayos Holandéses are sometimes possible for an extra fee. Boat trips to more distant locations, such as the Cayos Holandéses, can cost well over US$100 just for fuel.

The **Hotel San Blas** (cell 6538-1141 Karina I. Burgos, in Panama City; tel. 257-3310 or 257-3311; hotelsanblas@hotmail.com, US$50 pp, including all meals and a daily boat trip), on Nalunega, is the old stalwart among the archipelago's hotels. Sometimes known as Cabañas San Blas, it consists of 30 rooms with shared bathrooms on the southern side of Nalunega. There are several kinds of accommodations here. The four huts right on the beach have sand floors and offer slightly more privacy, as they are a few centimeters away from their neighbors. If a breeze is more important than privacy, for the same price one can get a room in the large two-story building behind the huts. Be warned, though, that this is essentially a dormitory with cane dividers that don't reach all the way to the very tall thatch roof.

Meals are served in a large, unadorned cement-block dining room. A few more rooms are upstairs. The ones by the terrace have a view of the sea. Avoid the one right above the kitchen.

The hotel was started decades ago by Luis Burgos, a laid-back Guna who speaks English and Spanish, and is still owned by the Burgos family.

The rest of the island is taken up by a village of about 450 inhabitants. One of the charms of this place is staying in such close proximity to the Guna. There's a general store with basic supplies and several kiosks that sell sodas, cookies, beer, and such.

As with other Guna villages, this one is none too clean, but the hotel staff rake the sand around the hotel every day, ensuring its little patch is tidy (but not free of outhouses over the water). Rats are a fact of life on the islands, and they tend to make an appearance here more often than at some other Guna hotels. I've never heard of anyone being bitten, but the rustling critters have been known to upset a good night's sleep.

Hotel Kuna Niskua (tel. 259-3471 or 259-9136, cell 6709-4484 or 6537-3071, www .kunaniskuahotel.com, US$55 pp, based on double occupancy, including transfers, all meals and a daily boat tour, US$10 extra for those traveling alone), on Wichub-Huala, is the most attractive of the simple hotels. It's still quite basic, but it's a tidy, well-cared-for place. The main building is concrete, but softened by intricately woven cane walls. More rooms are on the 2nd floor of a second building, which also has a terrace strung with hammocks. There are 10 rooms with private bathrooms and 3 with shared ones. There's no difference in price. The rooms in the second building (also with shared bath) are darker and offer less privacy. Most have just a single window, so try to get the corner room overlooking the water; it has more windows.

Kuna Niskua recently completed a new place, **Kuna Niskua Isla Wailidup** (contact Hotel Kuna Niskua, bungalows start at US$125 pp first night, US$95 after first night, including all meals and a daily boat tour), a short boat ride to the east of Wichub-Huala. Also known as Waily Lodge, it's on pretty, uninhabited Wailydup (pronounced WHY-lee-doop), a sandy island just a few hundred meters long. It offers two rustic wood-floored, thatched-roofed cabins, each with a good double bed, private shower, flush toilet, and a little back porch overlooking the sea and nearby islands. There's electricity at night. The snorkeling around here is good. A sand-floored dining hall is nearby, and four more cabins are in the works. There's nothing else on the island. The one problem with this place is the abundance of *chitras* (sand flies): When I was there, a nice breeze was blowing and they weren't a problem, but I'm told that when the wind dies, they're ferocious.

Though the location is great, prices are steep

for such a simple place. The owners plan to offer packages that combine stays here and at Kuna Niskua; they might be more economical. Those not staying here can visit for US$10 per person.

There are two reasons to stay at **Hotel Corbiski** (tel. 257-7189, cell 6708-5254, 6703-8378, or 6682-0625, Panama City tel. 257-7189, eliasperezmartinez@yahoo.com, http://hospedajecorbiskikunayala.blogspot.co.uk, $55 pp, including all meals and a daily boat trip). The first is the owner, Elías Pérez. He's a warm, friendly guy who speaks Spanish and quite a bit of English and has a great deal of experience as a tour guide. He can sometimes offer special trips for an extra fee, including kayak expeditions and forest hikes on the mainland. The second is the chance to live close to a Guna family in the heart of a Guna community. The rooms are basic, even by the standard of Guna accommodations, but cane-walled rooms over the water have been built that at least have some charm and a bit more privacy, even if they are still quite rustic. There are a total of 12 rooms. The proximity to a Guna village is not for everyone. Other houses are crammed nearby, as are outhouses that empty into the sea. Elías works with the guys who run Cartí Homestay, so if you have trouble reaching them or want to stay at both places, get in touch with him. Elías can also arrange land transportation to and from Panama City. This place is sometimes known as Hospedaje Corbiski, and as with the island, is sometimes spelled Corbisky.

While this is a thriving Guna community, it's a fairly modern one; expect cinderblock buildings and electricity at night.

Cabañas Ukuptupu (tel. 293-7893, 293-8709, or 299-9011, cell 6746-5088 or 6744-7511, www.ukuptupu.com, US$55 pp, including transfers, all meals and a daily boat trip) is the only thing on the rocky island of Ukuptupu, nestled between Wichub-Huala and Nalunega. The hotel, which until 1998 was a Smithsonian research facility, consists of

15 basic, but spacious, cane-and-wood rooms over shallow water, connected to each other by boardwalks. Because it's very easy to walk off the boardwalks into the ocean, this is not a place to bring small children. The hotel completely covers the tiny island, so it's more private and isolated than the other hotels in this region, without the pros and cons of sharing an island with a Guna village. Service can be pretty disorganized. Beds consist of foam mattresses in a wooden frame. Bathrooms are shared but have flush toilets. Guests take bucket baths from barrels filled with rainwater. There's an open-air bar and a little library with battered books. The hotel has good views of the ocean and the surrounding inhabited islands. Hammocks are strung up around the place, which tends to get a nice breeze. An underwater rock corral houses the lobsters, crab, and other sea creatures guests may be offered for dinner. The elderly owner, Juan García, worked in a U.S. military mess hall for five years and speaks fluent English.

The **Hotel Kikirdub** (tel. 396-1223, cell 6029-8563, www.hotelkikirdub.com, US$150 pp, including transfers, all meals, and daily boat trip), on a tiny islet between El Porvenir and nearby Wichub-Huala, is the first lodging in the archipelago with truly modern infrastructure. It can sleep up to 12 people in four rooms. Some of the rooms are in the house, but the nicest and most private one has a separate entrance with a hammock-strung terrace. All the rooms have dark wood floors and paneling, modern bathrooms, and thin mattresses. There's electricity 6 P.M.–6 A.M.

This is the home of Enrique Garrido, formerly the president, and still a member, of Panama's general assembly. There is no beach on the island, which is not much bigger than the house itself, and the only other things on it are a thatched-roofed kitchen and bar and an artificial pond with turtles and other wild creatures. The staff are friendly. The hotel also offers day trips from Panama City, including all land and boat transport, lunch, and a tour of a local community, for US$50 per person, minimum eight people, though why anyone would want to make such a long trip without staying at least one night is a mystery to me.

If all accommodations are full, the 13-room **Hotel El Porvenir** (cell 6692-3542 or 6718-2826, Panama City tel. 221-1397, 262-9922, or 292-4543, http://hotelporvenir.com, US$60 pp, including all meals and two daily boat tours) may have to do. Rooms here are drab, dark, and run-down, and they have worn mattresses and zero charm. The staff are friendly, though, and there are toilets and showers in the rooms, though they're not especially clean. As the name suggests, the hotel is on the island of El Porvenir, which is also home to the area's airstrip and some small government offices. There's nothing else on the island, which means you'll have plenty of peace and quiet—at least until an airplane lands, since the hotel is almost on the airstrip. The little beach here is pleasant, and the water seems much cleaner than that surrounding the crowded islands nearby. But you'll likely feel quite isolated.

GETTING THERE

The traditional way to get to this area is to fly into El Porvenir and transfer to the surrounding islands. However, the land route has been supplanting it, and got a major boost when all the airstrips in the area shut down simultaneously for a slow renovation. This is the easiest and most economical part of the archipelago to get to by road and local boat.

Most of the hotels in the region offer packages that include transportation to and from the islands from Panama City. These days that's usually by land, and usually at the standard US$25 per person rate each way.

The El Porvenir airstrip finally reopened and flights resumed in the spring of 2012; how long these will continue this time is anyone's guess.

For now, though, flights from Panama City to El Porvenir cost US$59 each way. Air Panama has a daily flight that leaves from Albrook around 6:45 A.M. daily. Return flights leave El Porvenir at about 7:25 A.M. on the same days. The flight takes as little as 25 minutes or as much as an hour, depending on the number of stops.

Río Sidra and Vicinity

RÍO SIDRA

Río Sidra is a densely packed island of about 2,000 inhabitants that has seen more and more visitors in recent years thanks to a growing range of accommodations in the area.

Río Sidra actually comprises two communities, **Mamartupo** and **Urgandí,** that have distinctive identities. The school is the unofficial dividing line between the two. Mamartupo faces the sea; Urgandí faces the land. The island is quite crowded, with huts packed tightly together over the entire surface of the island. Some of the inhabitants sport modern clothing.

KUANIDUP

Kuanidup is a gorgeous private island a half hour away by motorized boat from Río Sidra.

Actually, there are two Kuanidups. The first is Kuanidup Grande, which is home just to Cabañas Kuanidup, a sandy beach, a sand volleyball court, and hammocks strung between coconut palms. About the same size as tiny Isla Robinson, it's *grande* only in comparison to its little sister, Kuanidup Chico. There's nothing but a single hut, sand, and palm trees on Kuanidup Chico, which is an easy swim away (maybe 300 meters) for a moderately fit swimmer. The hotel staff on Kuanidup Grande can also ferry guests over. Nonguests should ask permission to visit either island; expect to pay a fee.

There's pretty good snorkeling around the islands. It's fun to circumnavigate Kuanidup Chico and explore the coral shelf that rings the

THE ART OF THE *MOLA*

© WILLIAM FRIAR

Mola **sales are an important source of income for the Guna.**

Molas (handcrafted blouses) are made from several layers of brightly colored cotton cloth. Guna women create these works of art using a technique of cutting and sewing sometimes referred to as reverse appliqué. The way the cloth is cut reveals the layers beneath, which all go into creating the overall design. Designs can be abstract or representational. The best designs are such works of art that *mola*-making has been described as painting with a needle.

What should you look for in a *mola*? Anthropologist Mari Lyn Salvador conducted a study in which she asked Guna women themselves that question. A few of her findings:

- The design should be balanced and all the spaces filled.

- The lines should be thin and evenly spaced, with smooth edges.

- Stitches should be small, even, and nearly invisible.

- The design should stand out and be easy to see, which is largely a matter of the proper use of contrast and color.

For more information on Guna arts and culture, see *The Art of Being Guna: Layers of Meaning Among the Guna of Panama* (UCLA Fowler Museum of Cultural History), edited by Mari Lyn Salvador.

island; it has surprisingly diverse species. Take it slow and really check things out: There are lots of small, hidden natural treasures. Watch out for sea urchins, fire coral, and sudden shallows. Visibility plummets after a rain because of the proximity to mainland rivers.

◖ ISLA MAQUINA

One island well worth a visit is Isla Maquina (**Mormarketupo** in Guna), about a 10-minute boat ride from Río Sidra. It's the quietest and most purely traditional of the islands in the region and one of the most traditional in the archipelago. It's known for its *mola* (handcrafted blouse) makers. Huts aren't as squashed together, and it's quite tidy and significantly cleaner than other islands. It has a school and an aqueduct, but very little else in the way of facilities—no hotel, no health center. It's pleasant to wander around the narrow paths lined

with cane fences that border homes. There are a few places to buy sodas and snacks.

OTHER ISLANDS

Other islands in the area include **Nusatupo (Isla Ratón),** a populated island next to Río Sidra, and the small, private **Islas Robinson,** between Río Sidra and Kuanidup.

ACCOMMODATIONS AND FOOD

There are a few basic places to stay on and around Río Sidra, but the most appealing options are on uninhabited islands farther out to sea. As usual, hotel stays generally include all meals and daily boat tours, though room-only options are available. Typical tours go to Achutupu (the uninhabited one with the shipwreck, not the one farther down the archipelago) or Río Sidra. With at least one day's notice and permission from local authorities, it's possible to

GUNA YALA

visit a mainland cemetery. This requires a guide, which will probably be an extra fee. Visitors are not allowed to take photos at the cemetery.

Thanks to the El Llano–Cartí Road, the cheaper accommodations in this area are surging in popularity with backpackers and more-adventurous Panamanians. They are scattered among a few small private islands known collectively as the **Islas Robinson**—piggybacking on the success of the pioneering backpacker cabins that went by that name. Names, contact information, quality, and life span of accommodations are more in flux here than anywhere else in the islands, and it's likely to be a while before everything shakes out.

Visitors can normally expect to pay around US$25–30 for private rooms and meals. Dorm rooms usually go for around US$4–5 less. Camping is sometimes available for around US$15, including meals. Typical accommodations are cane-walled, thatched-roof huts with hammocks and sand floors on an island with an outhouse over the water, a communal outdoor shower, a common sitting/dining area, spectacular views, and nothing else. Boat tours can be arranged for an extra fee. These are places for those who don't need much more than a rustic shelter from the elements.

If all this sounds appealing, the best way to ensure a decent place to stay is to go through a Panama City hostel. Usually this service is only available to guests, but **Luna's Castle** (Calle 9 Este and Avenida Eloy Alfaro, Casco Viejo, Panama City, tel. 262-1540, www.lunascastle-hostel.com) may be willing to book the land transfer and trip to the islands for nonguests: Go by or give them a call. They also try hard to keep current with what the islands are offering, and they get reports back from the many guests they send out there. Try not to go during national holidays in Panama, as these places can fill up. In fact, if possible you might want to try to keep your plans loose; the lodgings are close enough together that for a few dollars

you can survey several and choose the one that looks most appealing when you arrive, or perhaps transfer to after the first night. Expect to pay at least US$10 per person one-way for the boat trip from Cartí to these islands.

The best place to stay in the region, ◖**Cabañas Kuanidup** (cell 6635-6737, 6742-7656, or 6656-4673, http://kuanidup.8k.com or http://kuanidup.com, US$95 pp, including transfers, meals, and daily boat tour) is a good bet for those who want the beauty of a remote island without spending a fortune for the privilege of living simply. The location is gorgeous. Because the nearest sizable settlement is a half-hour boat ride away, the sea here is clean and the beaches free of trash. There are 10 cabanas with foam mattresses, sand floors, and the usual thatched roofs and cane walls. They are spaced a few feet away from each other to offer a bit of privacy. Accommodations vary from a small cabana with a double bed to a couple of large ones with four single beds. The cabanas are rustic but comfortable. There are shared toilets and showers with very weak water pressure in a separate hut and a small open-sided dining room on the opposite end of the island. Guests can buy beer, wine, water, and *seco* at a little bar area. Lights in the dining room are powered by solar panels, but the cabanas are lit only by kerosene lanterns. The standard package includes daily boat trips to tour Río Sidra or snorkel and laze around Achutupu. The only other entertainment will be looking at the blue ocean, the occasional small fishing boat, and the islands off in the distance. You have to be truly in the mood to get away from everything to come here.

Cabañas Kuanidup can sometimes be hard to contact. If you don't manage to get through to them directly, book through a travel agency, such as **Panama Travel Unlimited** (Edificio Stela, Calle 1, Perejil, Panama City, tel. 395-5014, http://panama-travelunlimited.com).

GETTING THERE

Río Sidra is about an hour from the Porvenir/ Cartí area by motorized boat. It has a well-established airstrip, but there have been no scheduled flights there for a few years. Most tourist traffic these days consists of backpackers taking the land route to Cartí and then going by boat to the Islas Robinson. Those who'd prefer to fly to this region should check with Air Panama, as flight schedules change frequently and with no advance notice. The Río Sidra airstrip is actually on the mainland coast rather than the island itself.

Corazón de Jesús and Narganá

Another hub of island life lies about 40 kilometers east of El Porvenir, centered around the inhabited islands of Corazón de Jesús and Narganá (pop. 12,685), which are linked by a footbridge. These are the least traditional islands in the archipelago. There are more concrete buildings than thatch-roofed huts, and most younger women do not wear traditional clothing. There's electricity around the clock, and at night residents gather in the homes and stores of those with TVs to watch shows, with great enthusiasm.

These islands are unlikely to interest most travelers. Since the closing a few years back of the Kwadule Eco-Lodge, once the archipelago's most upscale hotel, there is no appealing place to stay here. Only those who've spent a great deal of time on the more traditional islands are likely to find these more modern and less colorful ones of great interest, and only then for the contrast they provide.

The more southerly island, Narganá, has the archipelago's one true bank, a small branch of the Banco Nacional de Panamá. The central square has a statue of Charles Robinson, a pivotal figure in Guna Yala's 1925 war against Panama. Public phones are at the side of the square, and a hospital, school, church, and police station are nearby. It also has the best place to eat and the only hotel. With quite a bit of humor, residents have named the *barrios* of this small island after those in Panama City—the vicinity of the lone bank thus becomes the *area bancaria* (banking area), the posher homes are in Paitilla, the poorer ones are in Chorrillo, the main walkway is Avenida Central, and so on.

Corazón de Jesús is across a short footbridge (watch for loose planks) on the seaward-facing side of the island. It has the airstrip, a simple restaurant, a pool hall, and little else.

Isla Tigre, also called Río Tigre, is a few kilometers east. A visit to the traditional Guna community here is the most common day trip for visitors.

PRACTICALITIES

The only hotel on either island is **Hotel Noris** (public phones tel. 299-9009 or 299-9090, US$10 s, US$15 d with fan; US$15 s, US$20 d with a/c), a pink, two-story concrete building facing the mainland that has seven spartan but okay rooms. Some have air-conditioning and private toilets and showers; the rest are more basic, with fans and shared baths. Room 1 is the nicest. The location isn't very nice, however—it's right on a somewhat swampy shore that smells of sewage. Boat rides to a nearby beach are US$5 per person; trips to Isla Tigre are US$15. Meals can also be arranged. Laundry is US$3 a load. Call one of the public phones and ask for Paco, the half-Guna, half-Spanish owner of the place.

Restaurante Nali's Café (6:30 A.M.– 10:30 P.M. daily) is the nicest place to eat on either island. A full seafood meal costs no more than US$4, and the food is both good and nicely presented. More basic dinners cost US$2.50. Breakfast offerings include eggs, ham, and sausage. Diners, if they want, can rent a film at the café and watch it on the TV inside. But most will probably prefer to sit in the open-air area, which is right on the beach overlooking the channel between Narganá and Corazón de Jesús.

A couple of *minisupers* in town carry basic supplies. There's a pleasant-looking *fonda* (tavern) just after the bridge over on Corazón de Jesús. It's next to the pool hall, **Billar Akuanusa,** which can look intimidating from the outside but is actually a friendly place to have a beer and knock balls around.

Narganá has a small branch of the **Banco Nacional de Panamá** (8 A.M.–2 P.M. Mon.–Fri., 9 A.M.–noon Sat.). It has no ATM, but it does cash travelers checks.

It takes about 2.5 hours by motorized *cayuco* (dugout canoe) to reach these islands from El Porvenir. Unless you've got a yacht, it's much more practical, and most probably safer, to come by plane. The airstrip is on Corazón de Jesús. Air Panama has daily flights that leave Panama City at 6 A.M. The return flight leaves around 6:35 A.M. Airfare is US$61 each way. The flight takes about half an hour if it's non-stop and can last longer than an hour if not.

Playon Chico and Vicinity

PLAYON CHICO

Playon Chico (Ukupseni in Guna) is a fairly large, somewhat bedraggled village island of about 3,000 inhabitants. It's a relatively modern community with a two-story health center, the churches and missionaries of a half dozen religions, some houses made of concrete, and even a group of allegedly drug-dealing teens who hang out in a graffiti-covered youth hall. But there are still lots of traditional huts and traditional ways. Though none too tidy, Playon Chico is full of life, and it's fascinating to walk down the main drag and watch kids romping, a father playing a flute for his children, local dancers practicing for a festival, women sewing *molas* (handcrafted blouses) and old men playing dominoes. A concrete footbridge connects the island with an airstrip on the mainland.

ISLA IGUANA

Isla Iguana (Arridup) is a private island 20 minutes by boat from the hotel island Sapibenega. It's cared for by the hotel, whose staff rake the sand and clear debris and trash to make it appealing for guests. It's a nice place to hang out on the beach by a coconut palm and look at the sea or the forest-covered mountains, but the snorkeling isn't good. The coral has been decimated, the water is often turbulent and cloudy, especially after a rain, and the fish are scarce.

OTHER ISLANDS

There are two hotel islands, **Sapibenega** and **Yandup,** a few minutes' boat ride away from Playon Chico.

There are other islands nearby, both uninhabited and with traditional villages, which can be visited with guides. Trips to the nearby cemetery or a waterfall on the mainland can also be arranged, as can more ambitious forest hikes.

ACCOMMODATIONS AND FOOD

There are few facilities, no hotels, and no appealing places to eat on Playon Chico. Visitors generally stay on one of the two hotel islands.

C Yandup (tel. 202-0854 or 394-1409, www.yandupisland.com, starts at US$140 s, US$200 d, including transfers, meals, and two daily tours), a small island about five minutes by boat from Playon Chico, offers five bungalows over the water with wooden floors, bamboo walls, decent mattresses, private bathroom, mosquito nets, and wraparound porches overlooking the sea. There are two other bungalows on the edge of the water with private bathrooms, and one smaller cabin with a shared bathroom. There's an open-air dining room. This place was significantly upgraded a few years ago and now features some of the most spacious and comfortable accommodations on the islands (though, as always, they're still quite simple). The main problem is it's near a mangrove forest, and the *chitras* (sand flies) can be a serious nuisance. Over-the-water bungalows cost US$15 more per person, and it's worth it. There's also a one-time payment of US$10 per person community tax just to set foot on the island.

Sapibenega: The Kuna Lodge (tel. 215-1406, Skype: sapibenega.s.a, www.sapibenega.com, US$251 s, US$364 d, US$423 t, including transfers, all meals and two daily boat tours; there are discounts for children), just a few minutes by boat from Playon Chico, has some of the best—not to mention most expensive—accommodations and service in Guna Yala. Formerly known as Iskardup, it's a small island with nothing much on it but guest cabins, each of which has two units. Most have double beds, but some can accommodate three or four people in each unit. The cabins are spacious, with wooden floors, cane walls, comfortable beds, flush toilets, ceiling fans, and tiled showers with hot water and good water pressure. All look out on the sea, and hammocks are strung up just outside the back doors, on the edge of the water. Like everyplace else in Guna Yala, though, accommodations are still rustic and close to nature. Don't be surprised to find small crabs in the shower or geckos hiding in the soap dish.

Sapibenega has an attractive dining room, a bar, and a lounge area with rough-hewn furniture inside a large thatched-roof building with high ceilings and open sides. Another bar is in a little *rancho* set on pilings above the water, connected by a walkway with the island. There is electricity 24 hours a day, supplied by solar cells and a generator. Food here can be good, and tiki torches are set up on the grounds at night so guests can dine under the stars. The island is within hailing distance of the shore, but far enough away from everything to feel remote and tranquil.

GETTING THERE AND AROUND

Playon Chico is far down the archipelago, and most people arrive and leave by airplane. The airstrip is on the mainland, connected by a footbridge with Playon Chico. Air Panama has daily flights that leave Panama City at 6 A.M., and return from Playon Chico around 7 A.M. The fare is US$66 each way. The flight takes about 45 minutes nonstop, or nearly 90 minutes with lots of puddle-jumping.

Mamitupu, Achutupu, and Vicinity

Quite a bit farther south and east down the archipelago, less than 100 kilometers from the Colombian border, is yet another island cluster with several inhabited, fairly traditional islands and a number of small, uninhabited private islands. The former include Mamitupu, Achutupu, and, farther away, Ailigandí.

Don't confuse the Achutupu here with the little snorkeling spot near El Porvenir. This one is a densely inhabited island, in the middle of which is a huge gathering house. These long thatch-roofed buildings are the center of community life in Guna villages. If you're lucky, a puberty ceremony or community meeting will be taking place on the island during your stay. If you're very lucky, you'll be allowed to observe some of it.

Immediately to the east of Achutupu, about a

© BONNIE KAY SPINDLER

hanging on the dock at Mamitupu

minute away by boat, is **Uaguitupu,** also known as Dolphin Island. About half the island is taken up by Guna huts, while the other half is home to the long-established Dolphin Island Lodge, also known as Uaguinega. The island is pretty and offers tranquil views. However, it doesn't offer much in the way of a beach. This is primarily a place to collapse in a hammock for hours on end, and for that it's just about perfect. There are two newer places to stay in the area, Akwadup Lodge and Dad Ibe Lodge, adding to the sense of this area as a center for relatively upscale lodging. Each is on a private island a short boat ride away from the mainland.

About 20 minutes north of these islands are a series of coral heads. If the sea is calm and the visibility good, the snorkeling here is okay. Sadly, though, intensive fishing in the area makes it unlikely you'll see much besides tiny fish. In fact, I've found the snorkeling in this densely populated part of the archipelago to be disappointing in general. The area's charm

comes from the beauty and peace of the surroundings and the proximity to more-or-less traditional inhabited islands.

Other tour possibilities include trips to the nearby inhabited islands of **Ailigandí** or **Mamitupu,** forest hikes, and a tour of a Guna cemetery. Several tours to more distant locations are available for an extra fee.

ACCOMMODATIONS AND FOOD

Uaguinega Ecoresort, also known as ◖ **Dolphin Island Lodge** (tel. 396-4805, cell 6090-8990 or 6137-7668, U.S. tel. 213/533-2211, www.uaguinega.com, starts at US$155 s, US$250 d, US$300 t, including transfers, all meals, and two daily boat trips), is in some ways a good blend of the other accommodations in the archipelago. It offers seclusion and comfortable accommodations, yet there's an interesting Guna village just minutes away on Achutupu. Try to make reservations as far ahead of time as possible, as this place fills up.

The only thing on Uaguitupu (Dolphin Island, pronounced wah-ghee-TOO-poo) is the lodge and quarters for the staff. The lodge's name, Uaguinega (WAH-ghee-NEH-guh), literally means dolphin house. It consists of large, attractive, and comfortable bungalows and a common dining area. The bungalows have hardwood floors, cold-water showers, sinks, and toilets. Most have a back porch right on the water. Solar panels provide 24-hour electricity.

The open-air dining room is on the northern edge of the island, looking out on open sea.

The lodge is owned and run by a Guna family called the de la Ossas, and service is personal and friendly. One of the sons, Horacio, learned English during a three-month visit to the hippie enclave of Bolinas in Northern California, which he found a fascinating anthropological experience.

The owners of Uaguinega have opened a somewhat more upscale sister hotel, **Akwadup Lodge** (tel. 396-4805, U.S. tel. 213/533-2211, www.sanblaslodge.com, US$185 s, US$3520 d, US$390 t, including transfers, meals, and two daily boat tours). It's on the small island of Akwadup (OCK-wah-doop), about a 10-minute boat ride away from Achutupu. This one consists of seven thatched-roof, wooden-floored cabins on pilings right over the ocean. Each has mosquito netting, a ceiling fan, a terrace with hammocks, private bathrooms, and 24-hour electricity. There is also a bar/dining room. Rates drop around US$15 per person after the first night, depending on group size.

The newish **Dad Ibe Lodge** (tel. 293-8795, cell 6112-5448 www.dadibelodge.net, US$145 s, US$245 d, US$300 t, including transfers, all meals, and two daily boat tours) consists of three substantial cane-walled, thatched-roof cabins on a small private island about 10 minutes by boat from Ailigandí. Dad Ibe (dodd-EE-bay) appears similar to the other upscale accommodations in the archipelago: relatively comfortable but still basic cabins on a small private island. Cabins are over the water, with balconies and private bathrooms with flush toilets. There's an open-air dining room above the water. Tour possibilities include two nearby uninhabited islands with beaches and a visit to the village on Ailigandí or the mangroves around it. Rates drop US$10 per person after the first night.

GETTING THERE AND AROUND

This section of the archipelago is quite a hike from more commonly visited areas, and distances are much too great to take a small boat from any of them. The closest airstrip is on Achutupu (again, do not confuse this Achutupu with the tiny beach island at the west end of the archipelago). Air Panama flies from Panama City to Achutupu daily around 6 A.M. and returns at about 6:50 A.M. The flight takes around an hour, and airfare is US$68.27 each way to either place. Destinations are confusing down here; make sure you get off at the right place.

The Uninhabited Cays

The loveliest and most unspoiled islands in the archipelago are fairly remote, and they can be difficult to visit. There are no accommodations on these remote cays. However, it is possible to arrange budget camping trips to some of them.

◖ CAYOS HOLANDÉSES

The Cayos Holandéses are the best known of the many gorgeous uninhabited and lightly populated islands toward the western end of the archipelago. They are 15 kilometers north of the mainland, farther offshore than any others in the archipelago. Yachts like to hang out here, as do snorkelers. The coral in some areas is beautiful, though even out here the waters have been overfished and the coral damaged.

To the west of the Holandéses, and closer to the Porvenir area, are the also lovely **Cayos** Chichime, the **Cayos Limónes,** and, farther south, the **Cayos Los Grullos.**

◖ CAYOS COCO BANDERO

About 40 minutes east of the Holandéses by large motorboat (the smallest thing one should be in this far out) are the Cayos Coco Bandero (**Ordupuquip** in Guna). It's a pristine group of more than a half dozen islets that's rarely visited by anyone other than yachters. It's stunningly beautiful out here. A Spanish galleon supposedly sank around this area, but neither the ship nor the gold has ever been found. There's also a modern-day wreck, a cargo ship, that's lodged upright on the nearby reef. It makes for quite a haunting sight. The waters are calm, protected by the same reef that snagged the ship, making it an appealing spot for snorkelers.

GUNA YALA

THE SPIRIT OF THE UAGA

All things come from Mother Earth. Nothing exists that is more necessary than she is. Without her, life is not possible. Our ancestors fought for her because they recognized her value. "I am nothing without the earth. I would be poor without her," so they said. . . .

We always left medicinal plants in the fields when we cleared and cut trees. The elders give us advice about how to take care of useful plants. Therefore, in Kuna Yala we still have forests. The foreigners don't do this. They thoughtlessly destroy nature for their livestock.

The jungle and the forests provide us with meat, as well as wines, poles, and medicinal plants. In them lie our history and our culture. We know that Europeans don't have the same resources because their scientists come to the comarca (reservation) to see what is in our forests. I want it to stay this way, but I'm afraid that one of them will arrive with a chainsaw.

The lobster traders are responsible for the deterioration of our main resources – only for the money. Even if we want to control the fishing of lobsters, we won't succeed, because the young people who are involved in this activity are making their living from it.

Our tradition of working together no longer exists. Once, when a decision was made to address a problem, everyone complied unanimously. Now they follow money. We are acquiring the spirit of the uaga (foreigner, outsider).

Once everything is evaluated in terms of money, it changes one's way of being, it makes one selfish. So said our forefathers. Thus we are beginning to deceive our forefathers. That's what I think.

From The Spirit of the Uaga by Cacique General Carlos López, recorded by Valerio Núñez from *Plants and Animals in the Life of the Kuna,* by Jorge Ventocilla, Heraclio Herrera, Valerio Núñez, edited by Hans Roeder, translated by Elisabeth King, 1995. Courtesy of the University of Texas Press.

GETTING THERE AND AROUND

The Cayos Holandéses are accessible by boat from the Porvenir, Río Sidra, and Corazón de Jesús/Narganá areas, but it's quite a haul on open sea. Coco Bandero is much closer to Corazón de Jesús/Narganá. No hotels offer a visit to the more distant of these island groups as part of their standard packages, but they may be able to arrange a trip for an extra fee.

The cost of a boat trip obviously depends on where you're coming from and how many islands you want to explore. From El Porvenir, for instance, the trip to the Cayos Holandéses is several hundred dollars. For those who can afford it, a far better way to explore this area is by private yacht.

One travel agency in Panama City has pioneered an affordable three-night camping trip to the Cayos Holandéses and Cayos Limónes. **Panama Travel Unlimited** (Edificio Stela, Calle 1, Perejil, Panama City, tel. 395-5014, http://panamatravelunlimited.com) arranges trips that include land transportation between Panama City and Cartí, a night camping on Achutupu (the uninhabited one), and two nights camping on an island in the cays. All meals and a guide are included. Guests have the option to spend one of the nights in the home of a Guna family in a traditional village. The rate is US$240 per person, plus Guna taxes of around $10 per person. Entrance fee to some of the islands is another US$2. There is a four-person minimum on these trips, but the travel agency can generally put together groups. Most trips depart on Mondays and Fridays.

This is a bare-bones, rustic trip. Guests must bring their own water, they'll be camping on blow-up mattresses in tents, and toilets will be basic or nonexistent. Panama Travel Unlimited can only make the arrangements; the tour itself is entirely run by Gunas. But this is a unique opportunity to get to some of the most beautiful islands in Guna Yala at a very reasonable rate.

THE DARIÉN

The Darién: There's something magical about the name. In many people's minds the magic is of a dark and sinister kind. The Darién has historically been seen as a foreboding, dangerous place, a Conradian wilderness into which explorers venture, never to return. But the Darién is magical in many more positive ways as well. It is one of planet Earth's last great bastions of pristine tropical nature. Its biodiversity is so incredible it's been named both a World Biosphere Reserve and a Natural World Heritage Site by UNESCO.

The province of Darién is, at 16,671 square kilometers, by far the largest in Panama. It's extremely sparsely inhabited; only 40,000 people live in the entire area. Parque Nacional Darién alone is enormous, covering 579,000 hectares of wilderness that sprawl across the isthmus near the Colombian border. It contains the most extensive lowland tropical forest left along Central America's Pacific coast. Balboa stepped out of this forest in 1513 and became the first European to set eyes on the South Sea.

The great attraction of the Darién is its magnificent forests and the incredible biodiversity they contain. Hiking, trekking, and birdwatching are what draw most nature tourists. But there are a couple of places along the coast of the Darién with accessible beaches and coral reefs. And the waters off Piñas Bay offer world-class deep-sea fishing.

What's commonly thought of as the Darién

© WILLIAM FRIAR

HIGHLIGHTS

LOOK FOR **◖** TO FIND RECOMMENDED SIGHTS, ACTIVITIES, DINING, AND LODGING.

◖ Santa Cruz de Cana: Cana is the most remote part of Panama, and one of the most beautiful, with extensive trails through pristine foothills up to a cool cloud forest. It's also one of the world's top birding destinations (page 492).

◖ Pirre Station: This is a relatively accessible entrance to the fabled Parque Nacional Darién, Central America's grandest tropical forest (page 495).

◖ Punta Patiño Nature Reserve: Patiño is the largest private nature reserve in the country, and the gateway to the coast and rivers bordering the Golfo de San Miguel (page 497).

◖ Mogue: This is the best bet for those who'd like to spend the night in an Emberá village (page 502).

◖ Bahía de Piñas: Considered the best deep-sea fishing destination on the planet, the Piñas area also has stunning forests, colorful villages, and the only luxury hotel in the Darién (page 504).

extends beyond Darién province itself. It encompasses all of eastern Panama except the islands of Guna Yala.

The part of the Darién of most interest to visitors lies toward the southeast section of the province, where there are no roads. The only way to get around here is by plane, boat, and foot. This contains the most accessible entry points into Parque Nacional Darién. Two of the best spots in the park are Cana, on the east side of 1,615-meter-high Cerro Pirre, and Pirre Station, on its west side. These are right in the middle of barely inhabited tropical forest. Cana, the most remote point in Panama, is especially impressive.

The most popular coastal areas are Punta Patiño, on the Golfo de San Miguel, and the Bahía de Piñas, farther down the coast near the Colombian border. Those looking for a trip up a Darién river usually find themselves on the Sambú, Mogue, Balsas, Pirre, or Tuira, though innumerable others crisscross this part of the Darién.

For every tree in the forest there's a saying about the Darién. My favorite, and one likely to resonate with any visitor, is this: Though many have come before you, you'll feel as though you're the first to enter the Darién.

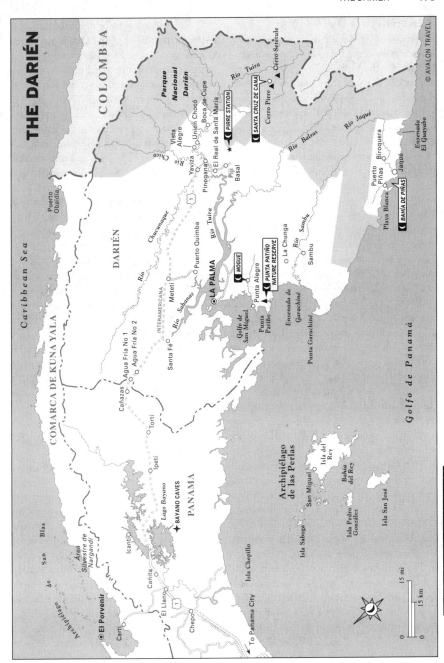

THE DARIÉN

COLOMBIA

Caribbean Sea

COMARCA DE KUNA YALA

Archipiélago de San Blas

Área Silvestre de Nargandí

Puerto Obaldía

DARIÉN

Parque Nacional Darién

Río Tuira

Cerro Seteule

★ PIRRE STATION

◄ SANTA CRUZ DE CANA

Cerro Pirre ▲

Vista Alegre

Unión Chocó

Boca de Cupe

Río Chico

Yaviza

Pinogana

El Real de Santa María

Piji Basal

Río Tuira

Río Balsas

Río Jaqué

Puerto Piñas

Biroquera

Ensenada El Guayabo

Playa Blanca

Jaqué

◄ BAHÍA DE PIÑAS

Chucunaque

Río

Río Sabanas

Puerto Quimba

INTERAMERICANA

Metetí

Santa Fé

Agua Fría No 1

Agua Fría No 2

Cañazas

Torti

Ipetí

●LA PALMA

★ MOGUE

Punta Alegre

◄ PUNTA PATIÑO NATURE RESERVE

Punta Patiño

Golfo de San Miguel

Ensenada de Garachiné

Punta Garachiné

La Chunga

Río Sambú

Sambú

Río Sambú

BAYANO CAVES ★

Lago Bayano

PANAMA

Icantí

Cañita

El Llano

Chepo

To Panamá City

Golfo de Panamá

Archipiélago de las Perlas

Isla Chepillo

Isla Saboga

Isla San Miguel

Isla del Rey

Bahía del Rey

Isla Pedro González

Isla San José

Carti

●El Porvenir

0   15 mi

0   15 km

© AVALON TRAVEL

THE DARIÉN

PLANNING YOUR TIME

Where you go and how long you choose to stay in the Darién depends on how deeply you want to enter into this formidable world. It may help to think in terms of three Dariéns: the coast, the rivers, and the foothills and highlands of Parque Nacional Darién. Ecosystems, accommodations, and the overall experience are quite different in each.

Assuming travel restrictions have been lifted, those with the time and ability for serious trekking should consider an organized trip that touches on all three Dariéns. This requires at least a week and perhaps two and involves all-day hikes in rugged, hot, and humid conditions. These trips are really mini-expeditions and do not come cheap. The best way to arrange one is through a good tour operator that can provide qualified guides, keep trekkers safe, and handle the considerable logistics.

Visiting just one part of the Darién can be done in as little as two or three days, particularly if you fly. Given the time and expense involved in getting around this part of the country, visitors will not get much out of the experience if they attempt a stay shorter than that. Visitors to Tropic Star Lodge, the only true resort in the entire Darién, generally stay for a week, though half-week packages are sometimes available.

The only parts of the Darién you can consider visiting without a guide are the towns along the Interamericana or those that can be reached by air, which also happen to be among the least appealing and least attractive places in the Darién. No one should set foot in the forest or venture far on a river without experienced guides.

The coast is the most accessible part of the Darién, and the least rugged. The most comfortable accommodations are found here. This area includes the **Bahía de Piñas, Jaqué,** and **Punta Patiño,** as well as the town of **La Palma,** the provincial capital of the Darién. Most people fly in or come by oceangoing vessel.

The rivers are the main means of transportation in the interior of the Darién, and most visitors spend at least a little time on them. It can be a pleasant way to get around, and it's certainly scenic, but boat travel can also be hot, humid, and wet. Most transport is by long dugout canoes called *piraguas,* which can get uncomfortable after an hour or two. Getting any distance by boat can take a long time, depending on conditions: The crew may need to clear tree falls or drag the *piragua* through shallow stretches of some rivers. Rivers worth considering include the **Río Sambú, Río Balsas, Río Mogue,** and **Río Marea,** all of which have Emberá-Wounaan villages along their banks.

The **Río Pirre** is far less densely settled and quite beautiful. The **Río Tuira** is wide and lightly populated between La Palma and El Real, then narrows and is lined by villages as it flows farther east. For their own safety, visitors have not been allowed to travel up the Tuira past the village of **Boca de Cupe,** for a number of years. Those who want to spend a night on the river will probably camp in a village with few facilities. Only **Mogue** and the Río Sambú area have true visitors' accommodations; staying in any other village requires negotiating for a spot in someone's hut or a place to pitch one's tent. The town of **El Real,** on the Río Tuira near the Río Pirre, also has guest accommodations and a couple of basic places to eat and drink.

The foothills and highlands of Parque Nacional Darién are among the wildest and most beautiful parts of the country. Most visitors go to the area around **Cerro Pirre,** usually making their base at **Rancho Frío,** in the lowlands just northwest of the mountain, or **Cana,** on its eastern slope. Hikers can stay at **Pirre Station** (the ranger station at Rancho Frío) or the rustic lodge at Cana. This area is particularly treasured by bird-watchers, but the magnificent primary and secondary forests will impress anyone.

Cana has more trails and facilities, it's more comfortable, and it has a nifty cloud-forest camp.

Conditions at Pirre Station are more rustic, but a trip there can be arranged far more cheaply. Those on a moderate budget will find Pirre Station the most accessible part of the national park. (Pirre Station and Cana are only about 20 kilometers apart, but no trails connect them.)

The average temperature in the Darién is 26°C (79°F), but as usual in the tropics that average sounds milder than it feels. The Darién lowlands are hot and humid year-round. Be prepared to feel wet and sticky even in the dry season, and don't expect ever to get completely dry in the rainy season. The Pacific and central parts of the Darién can see as much as 2.5 meters of rain a year. The Caribbean side gets up to 3.5 meters a year. Trekkers on long expeditions often take just two sets of clothing, which after the first day can be categorized as "wet" and "wetter." Sleep in the former; hike in the latter.

The highlands, however, can get surprisingly cool at night. You'll probably need a light jacket or windbreaker, for instance, at Cana's cloud-forest camp.

With few exceptions, transactions are cash only in the Darién, and there are no ATMs anywhere east of Meretí. Those traveling independently should calculate a rough budget ahead of time and bring a stash of cash with them, including lots of small bills.

SAFETY CONCERNS AND TRAVEL RESTRICTIONS

When traveling to the Darién, it is expected you will go only with experienced, respected nature guides. I strongly urge you to do so.

Those who don't speak Spanish and know the area will find it hard to get logistics set up for a Darién trek. A naturalist guide can spot and describe animals and plants the uninitiated will miss. Most important, those who venture off by themselves have a great chance of getting lost and dying. The Darién is a fantastic place and definitely worth visiting, but it must be treated with respect.

There are human hazards as well. Colombia's civil war has spilled over the border into the Darién, and there are guerrillas and paramilitaries working in some areas. Drug traffickers, kidnappers, and bandits also hide out in the forest (they're often indistinguishable from the military fighters). All these baddies have done unwitting good for conservation: Even hunters with guns are afraid to enter some areas.

Knowing which regions are unsafe is tricky. Again, experienced guides can be helpful, since it's in their interest to know the dangerous spots. Border police and park rangers are also sources of information. Be sure to check the U.S. State Department's travel warnings and Consular Information Sheet at www.travel.state.gov. However, it's important to note that these advisories are not always accurate or up to date.

Sadly, it is possible the national park and other areas of interest to adventurous travelers may be off-limits during your visit. There have been multiple clashes between Panamanian border police and Colombian guerrillas in the last few years, and things seemed to have been heating up in late 2011 and early 2012.

All this conflict is making travel in the Darién more restricted and unpredictable than it has been in some time. It is unlikely travelers will find themselves in a conflict zone, at least so long as they do not try to slip into restricted areas without permission. But they may not be able to get to some of the most appealing places in the Darién. It's worth getting good travel insurance that includes trip cancellation and delay coverage, but look at the fine print to make sure a trip delay in the Darién won't trigger a "war zone" or "terrorist act" exclusion.

In the past, a general rule of thumb has been that the eastern parts of the Darién close to the Colombian border were the areas to avoid. Look at a map of the Darién and picture an imaginary line drawn from Punta Carreto (west of Puerto Obaldía in the Comarca de Guna Yala, on the Caribbean coast) through the town of Yaviza in the heart of the Darién, down to Punta Piñas on

DARIÉN SURVIVAL TIPS

Those going on a multiday trek in the Darién, versus staying in a lodge with screens, should start taking antimalarial medication in advance of the trip.

There are three hospitals in the Darién: in Yaviza, La Palma, and El Real. There are also six *centros de salud* (health centers), in Boca de Cupe, Metetí, Santa Fé, Garachiné, Jaqué, and Sambú, plus a subcenter on the Río Balsas. All should have antivenin for venomous snakes. The El Real hospital sees 12-15 snakebites a year, mostly fer-de-lance. The hospitals are reasonably well stocked, but serious cases are stabilized and flown to Panama City.

Be careful in the forest during and after a rain. Tropical trees have shallow roots and fall all the time. You can hear them crashing all around you.

Keep your passport with you at all times. There are police checkpoints throughout the Darién, and you'll be asked repeatedly to present your papers. As always in Panama, be respectful toward the police. To keep the passport dry, double-bag it in Ziploc plastic bags.

The Darién is one of the few places in Pan-ama where water can be unsafe. Bring a good water purifier or water purification tablets.

Campers should always sleep in tents. Always. Among the dangers of sleeping in the open are malaria, which is endemic to the Darién, and rabies from vampire bat bites. There is no cure for rabies, and only one person in history has survived it (though taking a series of vaccinations after exposure can usually prevent infection). On one trek, an experienced Darién guide got so hot he ignored his own advice and unzipped his tent a speck. He woke up the next morning with congealed blood in his hair and little bite marks on his scalp — a vampire bat had gotten into his tent. Back in Panama City a doctor gave him his shots and told him the only thing else he could do was wait. For what? To see whether he died. He didn't, but he'll never leave his tent open again.

Some cell phone networks reach only as far as Chepo. Others carry as far as Punta Patiño. None penetrates deep into the forest. But even some remote villages have a pay phone. Buy a prepaid local phone card in Panama City, as these phones get choked with change.

the Pacific coast. Travel east of this imaginary line is usually considered dangerous.

But as this book went to press, the U.S. State Department's travel advisory warned visitors to avoid basically any part of the province that's not on the Interamericana:

> While the number of actual incidents remains low, U.S. citizens, other foreign nationals and Panamanian citizens are potentially at risk of violent crime, kidnapping, and murder in this general area. Moreover, all around the Panama-Colombia border area the presence of Colombian terrorist groups, drug traffickers and other criminals is common, increasing the danger to travelers. The Revolutionary Armed Forces of Colombia (FARC) operates in Pana-ma's Darien Province, including in areas far removed from the immediate vicinity of the Panamanian-Colombian border.

In the past, those who know the area well have felt the risk was overstated, particularly for remote parts of Parque Nacional Darién, such as Cana and Pirre Station. Panamanian authorities seemingly agreed, as they did not prohibit travel to these spots. But the border police were not allowing visitors into the national park as of the spring of 2012. Travelers trying to enter the park via Yaviza were being turned back, and charter flights were not running to Cana.

There are also fewer commercial flights anywhere in the Darién than there have been in years, making it harder to get around regardless of official restrictions.

Travel up the Río Tuira beyond Boca de Cupe is considered dangerous and has been off-limits for several years. Boca de Cupe itself has a border-police post, but that doesn't necessarily make it safe. It's best to avoid trips on the upper Tuira (Alto Tuira) for now. Other areas that have seen guerrilla activity recently include the Río Balsas, the upper reaches of the Río Tuira around Cerro Pirre, and the Guna *comarca* of Madungandí.

Violence in recent years near the village of Jaquí on the Pacific coast near the Colombian border has made this a place best avoided. Travel to Puerto Obaldía, on the Caribbean coast, is also considered unsafe.

There have also been major busts of drug-smuggling operations on the Interamericana itself, at Metetí and Agua Fría.

The situation in the Darién is fluid, and a quiet spot today can be an area of concern tomorrow, and vice versa. This chapter is written under the assumption that things will have calmed down by the time you visit and that restrictions on visiting the national park will be lifted.

Going nearly anywhere in the Darién requires registering at police checkpoints. This is a good way for travelers to learn if any area they're going into is reasonably safe, as they will not be allowed to proceed if not. It's also a good way for officials to track your last-known location if anything does go wrong.

If at any point the police refuse permission to go any farther into the Darién, do not argue and do not try to slip past them. If these beefy, heavily armed characters don't think it's safe to go somewhere, it really isn't.

HISTORY

The earliest known inhabitants of the Darién were the Cuevas, who were wiped out by the conquistadors. The Gunas moved in to fill the void and managed to resist the Spanish, in part by helping English and French pirates in their constant raids against the Spanish forts, towns, and gold mines. Many of the rivers in the Darién still bear Guna names.

In the 18th century, a new group of indigenous peoples, traditional enemies of the Guna, moved into the region. Once known collectively as the Chocó, because they came from the Chocó region of Colombia, they were actually two linguistically distinct but culturally similar peoples, the Emberá and the Wounaan. They spoke the same language an estimated 3,000 years ago and a third of their vocabulary still overlaps. But their languages have grown so far apart that today the Emberá and Wounaan speak Spanish when they want to communicate with each other.

Centuries of conflict with the Spanish, Emberá-Wounaan, and so-called Afro-Colonials pushed the Guna north toward the Caribbean coasts and islands, though some tradition-minded Guna still live in the Darién. The Emberá-Wounaan triumphed in their wars, some believe, because of superior war technology: They, unlike the Guna, knew how to use blowgun darts tipped with the toxin from the tiny golden poison frog *(Phyllobates terribilis)*. It's the most lethal poison of any known land animal; the toxin on the skin of a single frog is said to be powerful enough to kill 100 adult humans.

There are an estimated 22,000 Emberá and 7,000 Wounaan in Panama, though some place their numbers at just half that. Most still live in the Darién, generally along rivers that flow into the Golfo de San Miguel. Other villages are inhabited by Afro-Colonials, the descendants of African slaves who escaped from the Spanish. They are also known as *darienitas* or *costeños*. The Emberá-Wounaan have integrated into some of these villages.

The Emberá-Wounaan tend to live in thatched-roof, open-sided huts on stilts. The stairway leading up to the living quarters is a log with steps chopped into the side. If the log is inverted, with the notched steps pointing down, it's a sign the family wants privacy. The log is pulled up at night to keep out unwelcome visitors, both two- and four-legged. As befits the climate, the people traditionally wear very few clothes, but the influx of "civilization" has eroded this practice.

Village life is a relatively new thing for the Emberá and Wounaan. Traditionally, families set up house along a river in relative isolation from others. The patriarch of a clan would live upriver, with his children in homes some distance away downriver. They followed a seminomadic existence, settling into an area and practicing slash-and-burn agriculture and hunting, then moving away to fresh territory, allowing the depleted area to recover. This worked as long as the human pressures on the land were small. This mobile way of life changed in the 20th century, when the Panamanian government pressured the Emberá-Wounaan to form villages.

The Emberá-Wounaan continue to have land conflicts with loggers, cattle ranchers, poachers, and small farmers from outside the Darién who followed the building of the Interamericana and devastated the rainforest in western Darién from Chepo to Yaviza. The subsistence ranchers and farmers are known as *colonos,* many of whom moved to the Darién from heavily deforested Los Santos province.

The Panamanian government established about 25 percent of the Darién as Emberá-Wounaan *comarcas,* semiautonomous reservations, giving them much greater control over their land and lives. The issues of land stewardship are complex. Parts of the *comarcas* as well as other areas the Emberá-Wounaan have traditionally seen as theirs overlap with the boundaries of the Parque Nacional Darién, where they are no longer legally allowed to hunt, farm, or extract timber. Poor Emberá-Wounaan increasingly log their own land and sell the timber, helping them survive in the short run but endangering their future.

FLORA AND FAUNA

From rainforests to sandy beaches to cloud forests to mangroves, the Darién has a greater variety of ecosystems than any other place in tropical America. Lush doesn't even begin to cover it. Those who fly over the Darién see an endless expanse of forest, broken only by an occasional snaking river or a lone flowering tree trying to add a splash of bright red, orange, or yellow to the sea of green.

The wildlife is spectacular. Mammals alone include jaguars, ocelots, pumas, margays, jaguarundi, giant anteaters, capybaras, white-lipped and collared peccaries, howler monkeys, white-faced capuchins, spider monkeys, Geoffroy's tamarins, two- and three-toed sloths, and Baird's tapirs. And unlike so many other places in the neotropics, there's a fair chance of spotting at least a couple of these.

The Darién is one of the best places in the world to spot birds. More than 400 species have been identified, including plenty to impress those who don't normally give a hoot about birds. In some places it's actually hard not to see flocks of flamboyant blue-and-yellow, red-and-green, great green, and chestnut-fronted macaws. The rare harpy eagle, the world's most powerful bird of prey, lives here, as does the lovely golden-headed quetzal.

Reptiles and amphibians abound as well, including caimans, crocodiles, and jewel-like poison-arrow frogs. And yes, there are lots of snakes, including some very venomous ones. The wisdom is it's rare to spot them, and those who do should count themselves lucky. My experience is that if you do any amount of serious hiking in the tropics, you will eventually come across at least one, probably several. Most are not aggressive, and if you leave them alone, they won't bother you.

The most common venomous snake in the Darién is also one of the most lethal: the fer-de-lance, a tan pit viper with a diamond pattern on its skin. They are everywhere in the Darién, though you probably won't see one. If you do, stay away.

GOD'S HANDS

Cuando entres al Darién, encomiéndate a María. En tu mano está la entrada; en la de Dios la salida.

An anonymous bit of verse, said to have been carved into the walls of a Spanish fort at the edge of the Darién. It reads: "When you enter the Darién, commend your soul to the Virgin Mary. In your hands lies the way in; in God's, the way out."

GETTING THERE AND AROUND

Traditionally, the Darién starts at the town of Chepo, just 50 kilometers east of Panama City, though the city has expanded so much it's hard to believe this area was pure wilderness less than three decades ago. It's possible to drive into the Darién as far as the town of Yaviza, but it's not pleasant. Though the road was recently much improved, the drive still takes a solid day, and all one encounters along the way are vast expanses of deforested land.

By Air

For most travelers, flying into the Darién is the only reasonable option. Except to places served only by charter planes, such as Cana, flights are reasonably priced, and flying is a much faster and less tiring way to get to the most interesting parts of the Darién. Flight times in the Darién are rough approximations at best. Planes often run late out here, sometimes by many hours. But arrive at the airstrip at least an hour early on the way back. If by some miracle the plane shows up early, it'll leave early, with or without you.

With the sudden collapse of Aeroperlas in February 2012, flights to the Darién, always limited, are now especially scarce. At the time of writing, **Air Panama** (tel. 316-9000, www.flyairpanama.com) had regular scheduled flights only to the Bahía de Piñas, Jaqué, and Garachiné.

By Land

The Interamericana (Interamerican Highway) extends east from Panama City to Yaviza, about 270 kilometers away. Here the highway—really a two-lane road nearly all the way from Panama City—comes to an abrupt end about 50 kilometers from the Colombian border, and the famous Darién Gap begins.

Going into the Darién by four-wheel drive or bus is becoming increasingly common. The road was mostly paved all the way to Yaviza in 2012, but is still a long, tiring trip through unlovely countryside. Roads deteriorate quickly out here, and when it's in sad shape, you can expect an all-day, vehicle-punishing journey. It can take up to eight hours by four-wheel drive, including stops for breakfast and lunch, to cover the approximately 270 kilometers from Panama City to Yaviza in the dry season, which gives some sense of the road conditions.

Traveling by bus is the cheapest way to get into the Darién. There are frequent daily buses from Panama City that go at least as far as Metetí and make interim stops at all the towns and villages along the highway.

Budget travelers can take a bus from Panama City to Metetí, switch buses to the nearby river port of Puerto Quimba, and then cross the wide mouth of the Río Tuira to La Palma, the capital of Darién province. From there it's possible to arrange expeditions to explore the Emberá-Wounaan and Afro-Colonial villages and the coasts and lowland forests of southwestern Darién province. It's also possible to hire a boat to go far up the Río Tuira toward Parque Nacional Darién.

Alternatively, when road conditions and safety considerations allow, those on a budget can travel by land all the way to Yaviza, take a motorized *piragua* (long dugout canoe) to the nearby town of El Real, and from there plan trips to visit villages up the Río Tuira or to Pirre Station, the most accessible part of Parque Nacional Darién.

By River

Because there are (thankfully) still few roads in the Darién, most travel within the province is done the old-fashioned way: on the river. Spend much time in the Darién and you'll become intimately familiar with *piraguas*, 30- to 45-foot-long dugout canoes that are still the best way to get around on the rivers. Their shallow drafts and tough bottoms allow them to skim over water that's just a few centimeters deep or be dragged across rocks without springing a leak. The only concession to modernity is the outboard motor, to make upriver trips much easier.

Travel by *piragua* is nothing fancy. You sit on a wooden plank along the bottom, often in a puddle of water. They're completely exposed to the elements, which means it can be broiling hot and humid in the sun and startlingly chilly in the rain. Some sort of cushion to sit on and, in the rainy season, a poncho with hood will make long *piragua* trips more comfortable. Consider bringing a life jacket; flash floods are possible on some rivers. And stay alert: Tree falls and other obstacles can suddenly appear on a fast-flowing river, requiring a quick limbo to avoid getting knocked out of the boat.

It's possible to arrange a river trip on your own, but it will entail a great deal of planning and hassle, particularly for those who don't speak decent Spanish. Life will be a lot easier and safer if you go with a qualified guide who knows the good boaters and can make all the arrangements.

If you do decide to go it alone, the main points of entry for the rivers discussed here are El Real, La Palma, Punta Patiño, and the area around Sambú.

How much a river trip costs depends primarily on how far you want to go, as the main expense is fuel. Expect to pay at least US$120 one-way per group for a solid couple of hours of motoring, which will probably be as far as you'd like to go in a day. Note that this just covers the cost of the boat, fuel, and crew. Food, supplies,

guides, porters, and tips are all extra, as is lodging for those who plan to spend the night.

The best cultural rivers, which give a taste of Emberá-Wounaan village life, are the Río Sambú and the Río Balsas. The farther upriver you go, the more traditional the villages are. Other possibilities are the Río Mogue and Río Marea. The sparsely inhabited Río Pirre is a good bet for sheer natural beauty; those venturing up to Pirre Station in Parque Nacional Darién can take the river most of the way to the station in the rainy season.

Rivers to avoid because of violent activity include the upper reaches of the Río Jaqué, the stretch of the Río Tuira upriver from Boca de Cupe, and possibly the Río Balsas. As with all travel in the Darién, the closer one gets to the Colombian border, the greater the risk of coming across a dangerous situation.

It's possible to travel between La Palma and El Real by boat on the Río Tuira, but it's not cheap. It takes about two hours and can cost more than US$200 per group to hire a boat, though it may be possible to hitch a ride for considerably less. It's a different kind of river experience, as the Tuira is quite wide for most of the way, especially the closer you get to La Palma. Being out on open water near the ocean is incredibly refreshing after the heat and humidity of the forests and towns.

The Tuira is the longest river in Panama (with the possible exception of the unbelievably tortuous Chucunaque) and carries the greatest volume of water. The water is brown with sediment, and the river too wide to see much wildlife, though when I last took this trip we spotted a four-meter-long American crocodile sunning itself on a sandbar.

Note: Be sure any boat you take on the Tuira between El Real and La Palma has an extra outboard motor. There is virtually nothing and no one on this part of the river, so it's not a great place to get stranded.

Western and Central Darién

The western Darién is fairly accessible by road from Panama City. The Lago Bayano area is particularly easy to get to, and it's now also possible to drive north across the western Darién all the way to Guna Yala. Most people heading farther east than that prefer to fly, when possible. However, travelers with more time than money can get to La Palma, El Real, and parts of Parque Nacional Darién by road and boat.

LAGO BAYANO

Even those who'll pass on a drive all the way into the Darién might be interested in going at least as far as the Bayano Dam area. It's about 90 kilometers east of Panama City. Note that there's an active police checkpoint at Bayano, and your papers will definitely be scrutinized here.

Lago Bayano is an artificial lake, created when the Río Bayano was dammed in 1976. It flooded

Exploring the caves of Lago Bayano makes for an exciting day trip.

© WILLIAM FRIAR

350 square kilometers of tropical forest and displaced thousands of Guna and Emberá. It is the second-largest source of power in the country, after the Fortuna Dam in western Panama.

The 10 Guna communities in this area banded together and in 1996 gained *comarca* (semiautonomous reservation) status. Called the **Comarca Guna de Madungandí,** its government office is right at the checkpoint, along with a little stand selling (rather poorly made) *molas* (handcrafted blouses). They have clashed in recent years with the Panamanian government over compensation for land lost with the building of the dam.

Bayano Caves

There are three caves here, though nearly everyone just explores the first one. The second one requires crawling through narrow passages on hands and knees—pretty intense. I haven't yet met anyone who has explored the third.

The first has a river flowing through it, the Río Seco, which is fed by creeks and underground springs. At the height of the rainy season, it's possible to steer a boat a fair distance inside the cave. At other times visitors have to get out of the boat and wade in through chest-high water—make sure valuables are sealed in plastic bags and be prepared to carry them over your head, or else leave them behind. Carrying a camera is a pain, and it's hard to get good photos in here; it's dark, and the humidity fogs up the lens.

This trip requires lots of scrambling over slippery rocks, so be careful not to break an ankle or crack your head. Scuba or surfing booties work well here. Second-best are sneakers with good traction.

Wear a bandanna or T-shirt over your nose and mouth. There are lots of bats in this cave, and that means an outside chance of contracting something unpleasant from the droppings, such

THE DARIÉN

as histoplasmosis, a potentially serious or even fatal infection. Chances of this are minimized by the fast-flowing river that washes out the cave.

Flashlights are a must; it's utterly dark in some sections. After a couple of minutes you'll hear a roar of water and the squeaking of thousands of wings. Shine the flashlight straight ahead and you'll likely see a solid wall of agitated bats. This is what a guide friend of mine likes to call "a high-adrenaline moment." Some may have second thoughts at this point. Those who continue shouldn't be bothered by the bats—they'll flit right by—and will be rewarded by a large open area, with shafts of light streaming down from high above. Impossibly long tree roots hang through the cracks overhead, and otherworldly mounds formed by calcium deposits cling to the walls. It's all very Indiana Jones.

The cave is about two kilometers long, though the water is usually too deep to go the whole way except at the height of the dry season. It's a spooky but beautiful place.

On my most recent visit, this trip was being offered by some Panama City hostels and was catching on with the backpacking set. The caves are best explored with a good guide. **Burbayar Lodge** (tel. 236-6061, cell 6949-5700, www.burbayar.com, reservas@green-citypanama.com), an ecolodge in the highlands above the lake, runs a popular tour that includes pickup and drop-off in Panama City.

Practicalities

Those coming on their own can drive or take any Darién-bound bus to Lago Bayano, getting off at the checkpoint just before the bridge, Puente Bayano. Buses from Panama City that go only as far as Lago Bayano leave from the Gran Terminal in Albrook daily every 40 or so minutes, 3:20 A.M.–6 P.M. The fare is US$3 and the trip takes about 2.5 hours.

Cañita (pop. 2,140), a little over 20 kilometers east of the Chepo turnoff, is a good place to stop for a break on the way to or from the Darién. It has a few basic restaurants and stores and a couple of rustic places to spend the night.

El Descanso, a pleasant open-air restaurant on the north side of the road, is a popular place to eat. It's owned by immigrants from Los Santos province and is known for its soups, such as *sancocho* (stew) and *sopa de carne* (beef soup). A breakfast of steak, tortilla, juice, and coffee costs about US$3. The old ocelot, jaguar, and peccary pelts hanging from the rafters are disturbing reminders of the toll humans have taken on nature in this area, and the endangered turtle eggs that may be for sale proves it's not a thing of the past. Please don't buy them; for one thing, it's against the law. In fact, if they're being sold, you can boycott the place and tell the management why you're doing so.

EL LLANO-CARTÍ ROAD

Shortly before reaching Lago Bayano there's a turnoff to a road that leads all the way down to the Comarca de Guna Yala. This is the 30-kilometer long El Llano–Cartí Road, which heads north over the Continental Divide to the Caribbean coast, ending at the Guna town of Cartí. It is the only land access to the islands, and it has finally been paved. There are still some rough spots, and storms can wash entire lanes right off the mountain. The road shouldn't be attempted without a high-clearance four-wheel-drive vehicle and a competent driver. But this access has opened up the islands to a whole new group of travelers. Enterprising Gunas have set up a low-cost transportation service from Panama City to Guna Yala via this road.

The Guna established a nearly 100,000-hectare forest reserve in this area called the **Área Silvestre de Narganá.** There is an ecolodge, **Burbayar Lodge,** along the road that attracts birders and other nature lovers. The lodge is used by hikers trekking the length of the road or exploring the forests along it. This area is popular because it offers a true taste of the Darién surprisingly close to Panama City, and the lodge and road make a visit relatively affordable, accessible, and comfortable.

Practicalities

The unmarked turnoff to El Llano–Cartí is about 15 kilometers east of Chepo, just before the flyspeck town of El Llano (pop. 2,839). There's a rice field on the right. Turn left onto the unpaved road. It's possible to pick up some provisions in El Llano, but Cañita, eight kilometers farther east, is better stocked.

There is one appealing place to stay along the road. **Burbayar Lodge** (tel. 236-6061, cell 6949-5700, www.burbayar.com, reservas@greencitypanama.com, US$190 pp for the first night, including all meals, transportation from and to Panama City, and a guided hike; US$155 pp for subsequent nights) lies along the San Blas mountain range 14.5 kilometers north of the Interamericana and 22 kilometers south of the Caribbean coast. There is electricity and running water, and the accommodations are simple but comfortable. The lodge can accommodate just 14 people at a time, in shared rooms. Meals are served family-style on a terrace in the main lodge.

The lodge borders the Narganá forest reserve and offers six forest trails of varying degrees of difficulty. The lodge also offers tour packages. These include visits to Lago Bayano and the Bayano caves as well as a tough all-day hike to Cartí, in Guna Yala. Once there, hikers can spend the night in a Guna hotel on one of the islands. Tour packages generally include transportation to and from Panama City, boat transportation, a local guide, and meals.

This area has the finest birding in eastern Panama after Cana and Pirre Station. This is the best place in Panama, for instance, to see the speckled antshrike, black-headed antthrush, and black-crowned antpitta. An estimated 400 bird species pass through the area, of which birders at Burbayar have so far counted about 300. The dry season is the best time for birding.

Those who choose not to stay at the lodge can also do some exploring along the road on a day trip. The view from even a few kilometers above the Interamericana is sweeping and lovely.

It's also possible to hike from the highway all the way to Cartí, on the Caribbean coast, but this means two long days of trekking. Cartí is the coastal area where tourists from Panama City are dropped off and picked up by the four-wheel-drive transport service run by the Guna. Here they meet Guna boats that shuttle visitors between the shore and the islands of Guna Yala. Hikers who want to visit the islands should plan to arrive at Cartí in the morning. Later in the day there may not be anyone to take hikers to the islands until the next day. It's possible to do this hike without a guide, but it's not a good idea. In any case, the usual mantra applies: Do not hike alone. Only truly fit people should attempt this one.

SPENDING THE NIGHT IN A VILLAGE

It's generally possible to spend the night in an Emberá-Wounaan village, though I don't recommend it. Malaria is endemic, and you'll probably be sleeping in an open-sided hut without screens. If you do stay in a village, sleep in a tent, no matter how hot it gets, stay indoors in the evenings (or as close to indoors as feasible), and douse yourself with insect repellent. Also, plan to start taking antimalarial medicine well before a visit; it takes several weeks to kick in. You must ask permission to stay in a village, and you'll probably have to pay. Ask to speak to the *dirigente* (leader, pronounced dir-ee-HEN-tay); US$10 per night for a couple should do it.

ON THE ROAD TO YAVIZA

With the exception of El Llano–Cartí Road and the area around Lago Bayano, there's little to interest travelers on the road to Yaviza. Leave Panama City as early in the morning as possible to improve the chances of getting to your destination the same day. Breakdowns and missed connections on the road are common.

Attempt the drive only in a four-wheel drive with high clearance, a couple of spare tires, a winch, and plenty of fuel. The whole length of road is tough or impossible to navigate in the rainy season, and even in the dry season there can be rough patches. Still, there are tire-repair stands at regular intervals, which may very well come in handy. Note also that, while there are police checkpoints all along the highway, these are at widely spaced intervals. Those who get stranded or have an accident are in for a long wait before help arrives. There is exactly one transit police station along the entire 200 kilometers between Chepo and Yaviza, and it doesn't even have a phone. It's in the tiny town of Zapallal, just east of Santa Fé, about 80 kilometers from the end of the road.

From Panama City, take the Corredor Sur toward Tocumen until it peters out, then follow the signs east to Chepo and the Darién. If you forget something, stop at the town of 24 de Diciembre, at the turnoff to Cerro Azul. There's a mall here with a supermarket, gas station, and the last McDonald's until Colombia (talk about entering the wilderness).

The highway passes through or close to all the towns listed. There are several other small towns and Guna, Emberá, and Wounaan villages along the way, some of which have *minisupers* (convenience stores), pay phones, rustic places to stay, and little else. Any bus going at least as far as Metetí stops by them all.

Chepo

Though actually in eastern Panama province, Chepo (pop. 12,734) has traditionally been thought of as the starting point for the Darién. This view persists today, despite the fact that Panama City has grown so far east and this area has been so heavily settled Chepo now seems more like a suburb of the city. It's a big, sprawling town with a hospital, filling station, ATM, and stores where travelers can stock up on provisions.

The first police checkpoint on the road is just before the turnoff to town. Chepo itself is five kilometers south of the Interamericana. It's not a scenic place, however, and because it's just 50 kilometers from Panama City, there's little reason to stop here on the way to or from the Darién. It's locally popular during Carnaval, though.

The **Río Mamoní** crosses the Interamericana just east of Chepo. At the beginning of the 1970s, it marked the beginning of the Darién Gap. There was solid rainforest from this point east, pure wilderness. It's sobering how quickly and completely all that has vanished.

Darién province actually starts about 85 kilometers east of the Bayano Dam, at **Agua Fría No. 1.** The only things there are a couple of houses, an agriculture checkpoint, some transit police, and an ANAM office.

Santa Fé

Santa Fé (pop. 5,764), about 200 kilometers east of Panama City, is a surprisingly large and lively town, though not a scenic one. It has a long history thanks to its accessibility: It's possible to navigate from the Pacific all the way to Santa Fé by river.

Though the place can draw an interesting mix of people from neighboring areas during a festival, there isn't much reason to visit it. It does, however, have a hospital and other services you would expect to find in a remote provincial town. All buses going at least as far as Metetí pass by it. There are a few basic places to stay for stranded visitors.

Metetí

The last real town before Yaviza is Metetí (pop.

6,244). Most residents are colonists from the province of Chiriquí, of all places—it's clear on the other side of Panama, on the Costa Rican border.

Metetí is mainly of interest to travelers as the crossroads to Puerto Quimba on the Río Tuira. From there it's possible to take a water taxi to La Palma or, with more difficulty, arrange boat trips to El Real and Yaviza. Along with other services, there are several hole-in-the-wall restaurants and places to stay.

Hotel Felicidad (tel. 299-6544 or 264-9985, hotel_felicidad@yahoo.com. US$20 s/d, a/c), the most substantial and best-run hotel in the region, is on the Interamericana just before the crossroads. There are a couple of other, more rustic places to stay at the crossroads.

There's a branch of **Banco Nacional de Panamá** (tel. 299-6052 or 299-6054, 8 A.M.–3 P.M. Mon.–Fri., 9 A.M.–noon Sat.) at the Metetí crossroads. It has an ATM and can supposedly cash American Express travelers checks. There's also a large police post and checkpoint, filling station, and pay phones. There's an ANAM station a right turn off the road before the crossroads as one heads toward Yaviza, though the staff aren't very helpful.

Most services are at the crossroads outside Metetí rather than in the town itself. To get to the town, turn south off the Interamericana. The road continues to Puerto Quimba.

Puerto Quimba (KEEM-buh) is Metetí's port. It's sometimes spelled Puerto Kimba or even Kimball. Pickup "buses" link Puerto Quimba and Metetí.

A water taxi runs from Puerto Quimba to La Palma, 7:30 A.M.–6:30 P.M., and from La Palma to Puerto Quimba, 5:30 A.M.–5 P.M. Theoretically it runs every 60–75 minutes, but after the first trip of the day, the boat leaves when it gets a full load. It's US$3 one-way and takes about 30–45 minutes.

Those who need a boat up the Río Tuira to El Real, Yaviza, or Parque Nacional Darién may find someone willing to make the trip at Puerto Quimba, but the chances are better in La Palma. How much this will cost depends on the number of passengers and whether the boat was already going that way. It may be possible to hitch a ride for about US$10 per person, but expect to pay US$100 or more to hire your own boat.

YAVIZA

Welcome to the end of the road. And not just any road: Yaviza (yaw-VEE-sa, pop. 3,177) marks the abrupt end of the Interamericana, which those in a less environmentally aware time once dreamed would link North and South America. Fortunately, sanity has so far prevailed, and the road has been indefinitely halted, which is at least delaying the ecological destruction that would inevitably follow. The famous Darién Gap begins here. Depending on how one measures it, the gap consists of about 100 kilometers of unbroken wilderness near the borders of Panama and Colombia, through which no road has ever been built.

Yaviza is certainly colorful, and it's an interesting place to spend an hour or so on the way to somewhere better. That's all the time needed to get the flavor of this tiny town. Those who need to spend the night in the area are better off in the nearby (and much friendlier) town of El Real, if the border police in Yaziva allow travelers to continue on, or in Metetí, back west along the Interamericana. That said, if you get stuck here there is one semi-okay place to stay.

A Spanish fort, **Fuerte San Jerónimo de Yaviza,** was built by the Spanish in the 18th century to prevent pirates from raiding the gold mines of Cana by river. What's left of the fort's crumbling walls can still be seen perched on the edge of the Río Chucunaque. Erosion is wearing away the riverbanks, and this haunting bit of history is slowly tumbling into the murky waters, with no attempt to preserve it. It's the only real sight in town and is worth a quick visit. It's easy to find, but if you have trouble ask anyone where the *fuerte* is.

The Chucunaque snakes around the edge of

THE DARIÉN

THE END OF THE ROAD...AT LEAST FOR NOW

No road has ever penetrated all the way through the Darién, and many hope none ever will. The Interamericana (Interamerican Highway) comes to a complete stop in Yaviza, and from there the road doesn't pick up again for another 100 kilometers, well inside Colombia. The Darién Gap is the only missing piece in a system of roads that links North and South America from Alaska to Patagonia.

The completion of the highway was long stalled by fears that hoof-and-mouth disease would spread from South America to Central and North America. Those fears have abated, but environmental ones have grown.

Wherever there is a road, massive deforestation has followed. Logging, ranching, farming, and hunting have decimated enormous tracts of the Darién. If the Interamericana is completed, it is all but certain the days of the Darién as a magical place will be numbered.

So far, building those last 100 kilometers of road continues to be put on hold, due to conservation concerns, the war in Colombia, and worries about giving drug traffickers yet another route to the north.

But even without the road, the Darién is under enormous pressure. How well protected the Darién, and particularly Parque Nacional Darién, is depends on the whim of the particular government in power. The consensus among environmentalists is that in the first few years of the 21st century, the Darién has been sadly neglected at best.

Even in better times, Parque Nacional Darién never had more than about a dozen rangers to protect an area the size of some countries. Now there are only two ranger stations being staffed in the entire park, Pirre Station and Balsas Station. The Cruce de Mono Station (Cruzamono Station) was abandoned, and poachers have moved in. There have been reports of hunters almost all the way to Cana, which is among the remotest and most pristine areas in the entire country. Wild peccary meat is being sold everywhere, illegally.

For now, however, the Darién remains a fantastic nature destination. Try to get there if you possibly can.

Yaviza, making for a natural boundary. There's a **boat landing,** on the right at the entrance to town, where 45-foot-long *piraguas* (dugout canoes) loaded with *plátanos* (plantains) and *ñames* (yams) from riverside plantations unload their cargo onto trucks, which carry them to Panama City. These same boats are the main source of transportation for those venturing deeper into the Darién.

Watching the *piraguas* in port is just about the only other entertainment in town. The wiry stevedores who do the unloading are impressive guys. They carry huge, handwoven baskets on their backs up a slippery incline to the trucks. There the baskets are weighed on a mechanical scale, and the weight is shouted to a supervisor sitting comfortably in the shade, who makes a note in his ledger. Each basketful weighs 60–90 kilos.

Party days in Yaviza include the Festival de San Francisco Javier, the town's patron saint, on March 12, and the Festival de la Virgen del Carmen, usually celebrated throughout the province and the country on July 16, though sometimes it comes earlier here.

Practicalities

The town consists mainly of dilapidated two-story wooden buildings, incongruously well-paved streets, and a large, fenced-in police station. Ask for the *cuartel* (police station). Drivers can park their vehicles at the station, where they should be safe. Travelers should register their passport information and intended destination at the station as soon as they arrive. It's the law, and it's an excellent idea in any case. The police will also be able to tell you if it's safe to continue farther into the Darién. Do not attempt to continue on without official permission. Travelers will need to register at every town, village, or checkpoint they pass through from this point on.

Hotel Tres Americas (no phone, US$15 s/d with fan, US$20 s/d with a/c) is the only real option for those who get stuck in Yaviza, and it's not a great one. It's by the basketball courts in the plaza at the center of town. A couple of the rooms are okay; the others aren't. The shared bathroom is less than appealing. Air-conditioned rooms are in a separate building behind the main hotel. These are actually grimmer and literally stink. The hotel also has a basic bar and restaurant. The bar can get raucous at night—don't expect to get much sleep on the weekends or holidays.

Those who forgot something in Panama City can find all kinds of basic provisions at hole-in-the-wall stores in Yaviza: food, equipment, machetes, rope, ammo—everything one needs for a Darién expedition. Yaviza also has a small hospital.

Getting There and Around

If the road is especially bad, which is likelier in the rainy season, buses make it only as far as Metetí. In that case, getting to Yaviza from there means traveling up the Río Tuira.

It takes about eight hours by four-wheel drive, including stops for breakfast and lunch, to cover the approximately 270 kilometers from Panama City to Yaviza in the dry season.

If you're able to convince a taxi driver with a four-wheel drive to make the trip to the end of the road, expect to pay at least US$200 one-way from Panama City, depending on the condition of the road and fuel prices.

There are only two ways to venture farther into the Darién from Yaviza: by foot or by river. The best option is to head southwest by boat, first on the Chucunaque and then onto the mighty Río Tuira, to El Real. It's a good base for reaching the national park and other parts of the Darién. The closest airport in this whole region is in El Real.

Cargo-carrying *piraguas* charge about US$5 a head to El Real, a trip that takes less than an hour with a 30-horsepower motor. Those attempting this trip on their own should note that *piraguas* aren't always available, and even when they are, it can take hours to unload the thousands of kilos of produce before the boatmen are ready to head back out.

EL REAL DE SANTA MARÍA

Known by everyone simply as El Real, this sleepy town (pop. 1,185) sits on the edge of the Río Tuira and is mainly of interest to travelers as the staging ground for trips into Parque Nacional Darién or up and down the enormous Río Tuira. The town is friendlier and more laid-back than nearby Yaviza. Still, few visitors use El Real as anything other than a stepping-stone to someplace else.

The Spanish founded El Real in the early 17th century. Today it boasts little more than an airstrip, a small hospital, a couple of places to stay, three basic restaurants, a few bars, and one billion roosters, all of which are eager to rouse exhausted travelers insanely early.

A big party day around here is August 15, the festival of La Virgen Santa María la Antigua. It's considered a good excuse for cockfighting and drinking.

Practicalities

El Real's ramshackle houses are connected by a short network of streets and footpaths. It takes maybe 10 minutes to see the whole place. All the spots listed here are within shouting distance of each other. If any are closed when you arrive, ask around: The owner is probably nearby and would be happy to open up for a potential customer.

Cana Blanca (no phone) is the most attractive and interesting of the town's bars. It's a 60-year-old cantina with a thatched roof and cane walls, a local institution that's a popular place to begin or end an expedition.

Hotel El Nazareno (tel. 299-6567 or

299-6548, US$10 s, US$12 d) is an old wooden tinderbox of a place on what passes for the main street in what passes for downtown. It's rustic, and the plumbing doesn't work well—one flushes the toilets by dumping a bucket of water down them. Rooms are equipped with fans, and some have private baths. The best rooms are on the balcony facing the street. Reception is at the small general store next door.

A better, though not more attractive, lodging option is the very basic rooms rented out by **Narciso "Chicho" Bristán** (tel. 299-6566, US$8 pp). However, these are generally only available to those using Chicho's expert boatman services. Rooms have foam mattresses, plywood walls that don't extend all the way to the ceiling, fans, and that's about it. Showers and toilets are down the hall. This is basically a rustic barracks, but it's about as good as it gets in this part of the Darién.

The most appealing of the three hole-in-the-wall eateries in town, **Fonda Maná** (no phone), consists of a few tables in what is essentially someone's living room. The food is pretty good, considering, and as in all *fondas* (taverns) consists of whatever's on hand that day. Nothing costs more than a buck or two.

The general store next to Hotel El Nazareno and a similar store just up the street carry the bare necessities for a Darién adventure, from machetes to dry noodles.

Those heading into the national park, including Pirre Station, must pay the US$5 park entrance fee at the **ANAM office** (tel. 299-6965, 8 A.M.–4 P.M. Mon.–Fri.) in town. A bed in the dormitory at Pirre Station costs US$10 per person per night. Make that US$5 if you just want to pitch a tent on the grounds. It may be possible to hire an ANAM forest guard to guide you for about US$10 each way.

There's an office of the **Servicio Nacional para la Eradicación de Malaria** (SNEM, tel. 299-6299) in town. It can supply antimalaria pills for free if you're running low.

Getting There and Around

Thanks to the improvement of the road from Panama City to Yaviza, there are no longer flights to El Real, at least for now. Most visitors now travel by four-wheel drive or bus to Yaviza and then travel by boat to El Real.

El Real is the closest transportation hub to Pirre Station, an ANAM ranger station in the most accessible part of Parque Nacional Darién. There are two ways to get to Pirre Station from El Real: by boat up the Río Pirre and on foot along a forest trail.

Most transportation around here is by river. It shouldn't be tough to hitch a ride on a *piragua* (long dugout canoe) to or from Yaviza, where the Interamericana begins. The fare is US$5 a head.

Narciso "Chicho" Bristán (tel. 299-6566) has a well-deserved reputation as the most able boatman in the Darién. He's a sharp, serious guy who shows up on time and hires a top crew. He lives in El Real; everyone knows him. Chicho charges US$75 each way for a trip up the Río Pirre to Piji Basal, the closest village to Pirre Station. A day trip up the Río Tuira to visit the villages along the river costs US$160 round-trip to go as far as Union Chocó. A voyage down the Río Tuira to La Palma, the provincial capital of Darién province, costs at least US$200 one-way (the high cost is because he has to go back to El Real at the end of the trip). All prices are for up to five people and do not include tips.

Caution: The steps leading down to El Real's port are incredibly slippery.

UP THE RÍO TUIRA TOWARD BOCA DE CUPE

This section is included in the hope that guerrilla activity along the upper Río Tuira (Alto Tuira) will have died down by the time you read this. Even at the best of times, it's long been unsafe to continue upriver past Boca de Cupe.

The riverbanks past El Real are dotted with small communities of Emberá, Wounaan and *darienitas* (descendants of African slaves).

THE ART OF THE *JAGUA*

Emberá-Wounaan men, women, and children sometimes decorate themselves with a black dye drawn from the *jagua* fruit *(Genipa americana)*, creating a kind of temporary tattoo. The fruit is pulped, and the liquid from the pulp is painted onto the face and body. The liquid appears clear at first, but as it dries, it gradually turns black and the pattern emerges. Traditionally this consists of a geometric pattern across the body up to the lower jaw.

These days Emberá-Wounaan typically only go in for *jagua* decoration at festivals or special occasions. But they've discovered that offering to paint tourists is a good way to entertain them when they visit.

One little catch, though: The dye doesn't wash off. It wears off gradually, usually in a week to 10 days. Sheepish-looking tourists heading home with their faces tattooed-up like Maori warriors can be an amusing sight at the airport. One wonders what the immigration officials make of them back home.

Maybe the Emberá-Wounaan actually came up with a way to entertain *themselves*, not the tourists.

If you decide to get painted, think about where you have to go and what you have to do in the next two weeks. At the very least, you might want to skip the face.

These villages have far too much contact with the modern world to be particularly traditional. Their narrow streets tend to be paved, for instance, and the Emberá and Wounaan do not traditionally live in villages, period. Those who want to immerse themselves in an older era of indigenous life should consider an expedition far up the Río Sambú.

This stretch of river is certainly colorful and interesting, but it's too densely populated to be particularly pretty. The river is brown with silt, which is probably a good thing since everything gets dumped in the river. It's not clogged with trash, but it's disheartening to see bottles and foam cups floating by in what used to be Eden. I once even saw a cooler bobbing along. Villagers bathe in the river, which is not something you'll want to try.

Still, green forest lines the banks, unbroken except for the occasional little rice and plantain field. Towering cuipo trees and bizarre-looking kapoks, which can have a crown broader than the tree is tall, jut up from time to time, and majestic neotropical cormorants and other waterbirds fish along the banks.

Boats are welcome to put in at any community. Villages here tend to be laid-back to the point of torpor, and visitors will likely be looked upon with mild curiosity but little enthusiasm. As always, be respectful and courteous. Do not, for instance, take a photo of anyone without asking permission.

Travelers must register at every police outpost along the river. This means regularly scrambling up muddy banks to present passports and answer a few questions. This is not meant as harassment but rather as a way to tightly monitor all movement in the area. Any boatman with sense will automatically pull in at every post.

Heading up the Tuira means getting closer and closer to the frontier with Colombia and thus to areas frequented by guerrillas, paramilitary troops, and other characters you won't want to meet. Traveling east past **Boca de Cupe** (pop. 902), about four hours upriver from El Real, is dangerous. Boca de Cupe, sometimes known as Boca de Cupé, has the last police post on the river, and thus the last semblance of law and order.

The main reason visitors come here is to hike into or out of Cana, a two-day trek southwest. Boca de Cupe was once the supply town for the gold-mining camp in Cana, and though it's hard to believe today, a railroad once linked the two areas.

At the height of the dry season, the river level

THE DARIÉN

can drop so low that boat transportation all the way to Boca de Cupe is impossible. Most day-trippers will probably be satisfied with touring the river and the villages closer to El Real.

It's easy to distinguish Emberá and Wounaan villages from Afro-Colonial ones. The houses of the former, made either of planks or (more traditionally) cane, are built on stilts. The latter are built right on the ground. There are representative examples of each well before Boca de Cupe.

Pinoganá, an Afro-Colonial village about a half hour upriver from El Real by motorized *piragua* (long dugout canoe), is the first village. Though it has a population of only about 350, that's apparently big enough to support three cockfighting rings, which offer pretty much the only entertainment option in town unless you arrive on a festival day. The Fiesta de la Virgen de la Candelaria, held around the end of January and beginning of February, is a big one. There's a tiny place to eat and no official place to sleep. There's also a police checkpoint.

Vista Alegre, about an hour farther upriver, is a Wounaan village that has another police checkpoint. This is a good place to buy one of the Wounaan's world-famous handwoven baskets, since every girl in the village age 12 and older makes them. Expect to pay US$60–70 for one the size of a bowling ball. Before haggling too much, look around at how poor this place is and bear in mind it takes two months to weave a basket that size. Baskets are about all the place has to offer.

Union Chocó, less than half an hour farther up, is most notable for the sizable police station in the heart of the village.

All these villages have pay telephones. Remember to bring calling cards in case of an emergency; phones tend to fill up with coins.

The trip back downriver is much faster, thanks to the current. A *piragua* with a 30-horsepower motor can cut trip time in half on the way out.

Parque Nacional Darién

This magnificent national park has long been thought by those who know the Darién well to be one of the least likely places to encounter guerrillas and other scary folk. The wildest parts of it are just too far away from everything to appeal even to those hiding in the jungle. But the flare-up in clashes between Panamanian government forces and guerrillas has led to a clampdown on travel throughout the Darién, including the park. This entire section is written under the assumption that things will have calmed down and trips to the national park will be back to normal by the time you visit.

◐ SANTA CRUZ DE CANA

More commonly known simply as Cana, this is the most remote spot in all of Panama: The nearest human settlement, Boca de Cupe, is 2–3 days away on foot, and there are no roads. Cana

is a truly amazing place that offers genuine wilderness amid relative comfort—a rare combination. It's my favorite spot in the Darién.

Cana sits in a forested valley up against the eastern slope of the 1,615-meter-high Cerro Pirre. Given its extremely isolated location in the middle of dense, uninhabited forest, it's hard to believe Cana has been a major player in the history of the isthmus for at least 500 years. Even more astonishing is that at various times in that period it has hosted large, important settlements. During the Spanish colonial era it grew to be a town of 20,000. Later, it became the first place in all of Panama to have electricity, not to mention an ice plant.

The reason for all this attention was gold. The early conquistadors founded a settlement here and named it Santa Cruz de Cana, but it wasn't until 1665 that they discovered the area's fabulous gold deposits. "The richest gold mines ever yet found in America," the buccaneer historian William Dampier called them in 1684. You can almost hear him drooling.

The Spaniards forced slaves to work the mines, which came to be known as Las Minas del Espíritu Santo de Cana. At their height, they produced 100,000 troy ounces of gold a year. But repeated attacks by English pirates, rebellions, and disease forced the Spanish to abandon the mines in 1727.

They were lost to the jungle for many years before they were reopened in the 19th century. Their most productive period was 1887–1912, when they were run by an Anglo-French outfit called the Darien Gold Mining Company. During this era there was a railroad linking Cana with Boca de Cupe, and from there to the outside world.

The mines were abandoned once again, and once again the jungle swallowed up most traces of human habitation. But in 1962 the last survivor of the Anglo-French operation, a hearty 73-year-old named Medardo Murillo, guided an expedition to the mines. He had started working as a mule driver in 1904, when he was 15, and he still remembered the way. The whole place was overgrown, naturally, but they did find one house still completely intact and stocked with viable dynamite.

Though mining was revived once again for a spell starting in the 1960s, today Cana is treasured for different kinds of natural riches: amazingly diverse and abundant flora and fauna. Two of Murillo's grandsons now work at an ecological field station at Cana, which, except for a tiny border-police post, is the only inhabited facility of any kind in the entire region. Though in the middle of Parque Nacional Darién, Cana is operated by ANCON, a nonprofit environmental organization, and the tourist concession is operated by Ancon Expeditions, its for-profit tour-operator sister.

Other tour operators can use the facilities, but arrangements have to be made through Ancon Expeditions. The imposing abandoned mines (do not try to explore them; for one thing, it's the perfect lair for jaguars and other beasties) and rusted mining equipment overwhelmed by vegetation give the place a slightly spooky *Heart of Darkness* feel. But for the most part it's an open, airy, and inviting spot that doesn't square with stereotypes that the uninitiated may harbor about the forbidding jungle.

Flora and Fauna

The wildlife here is breathtaking. As usual, the only things you're guaranteed to see are some of the most gorgeous birds in the world. But, there's a better chance of coming across impressive land animals than in most parts of Panama. Spider monkeys are likely, and it's a near certainty you'll be surrounded by the uncanny bark of howler monkeys. It's not uncommon to come across fresh jaguar prints. Jaguars have been known to take a leisurely stroll down Cana's landing strip, but you'd be extremely lucky to spot one during a brief visit.

Herds of literally hundreds of white-lipped peccaries sometimes descend on the station and tear up the turf, rooting for food. When this happens, everyone locks themselves in the lodge. Peccaries, the only creature I've seen Darién guides get nervous about, can be aggressive; they have sharp teeth, and they run faster than you do. Don't make the mistake of thinking they're just cute little pigs.

The very lucky few might also come across a Baird's tapir, the largest land mammal in Central America. At the cloud-forest camp above Cana, a tapir once sat on a guide's tent while the guide was sleeping in it, much to the surprise of both of them.

Cana has been called one of the 10 greatest bird-watching spots on the planet. Even those with only the slightest interest in feathered creatures will likely be bowled over.

THE DARIÉN

Blue-and-yellow, red-and-green, great green, and chestnut-fronted macaws streak across the valley all day long. Keel-billed toucans, looking as if they just flew off a Froot Loops box, peer down at visitors from the trees.

The lodge is a barely converted mining-camp building that dates from the 1960s. It's a rustic wooden structure containing six basic rooms with little in them besides a bed and a few shelves. Fresh linens are supplied, and there are screens on the windows. There are shared bathrooms and showers with running water. A generator provides electricity 7–9 P.M., after which everyone switches to candles and flashlights. A plan to upgrade the facilities is on indefinite hold because there are not yet enough visitors to justify the cost.

Hiking

Since Cana's elevation is nearly 500 meters, the forest here is premontane, and it's neither as hot nor as buggy as one might expect. The valley offers beautiful views of the surrounding hills, which are covered with lush virgin forest. There's also a cloud-forest camp on the mountain itself, at 1,280 meters, where it can get cool in the evenings.

Five main trails originate from Cana, not counting a short trail near the station that follows railroad tracks to an abandoned locomotive. The **Boca de Cupe Trail** is the longest. It continues for a solid two days, all the way to the village of Boca de Cupe. Hiking in for at least a few kilometers is well worthwhile. It's a mostly flat trail offering spectacular birding and the chance of seeing larger wildlife. The **Machinery Garden Trail** is a lovely and exotic two-kilometer loop that features both nature and the rusting remains of the 19th-century mining operation. The **Seteganti Trail** leads down to the Río Seteganti. Visitors can easily explore all these trails during a brief visit.

The **Pirre Mountain Trail** is a somewhat strenuous nine-kilometer hike that leads

three-quarters of the way up Cerro Pirre to the cloud-forest camp. The hike takes 4–5 hours at a reasonable clip. The hike down takes about three hours.

It's absolutely worth the effort. The trail itself leads through beautiful primary forest alive with animals. On a single trip I encountered large groups of spider monkeys crashing through the trees, a fer-de-lance snake, and, of course, dozens upon dozens of flamboyant birds.

The cloud-forest camp itself is a pretty impressive operation. A full field kitchen is set up in one large thatch-roofed hut, and tents with pads are set up in another. The camp can accommodate about two dozen guests. It's relatively cushy for its location. Generally all you have to take is a day pack; the cook and staff bring the food and water and set up the tents. (Tips are much appreciated; the guides can suggest amounts.) The view of nearby Cerro Setetule and the forested valley is breathtaking, and the nights are a riot of forest sounds. Big animals have been known to wander through camp at night.

The truly dedicated can continue a bit farther up the mountain on the **Cloudforest Trail,** but the summit can't be reached from this side of the mountain. There's a slim chance of spotting the rare golden-headed quetzal on this trail. Guides lead all these hikes. Do not attempt to venture out anywhere alone.

It's hard to exaggerate just how special the Cana area is. It's an enormous expanse of nearly pristine tropical forest, an overwhelming oasis of biodiversity. It's not cheap to get there and the trip is a bit of an adventure, but nature lovers will likely find it the highlight of their stay in Panama.

Getting There

The easiest, though by far the most expensive, way to visit Cana is by airplane, since only small chartered planes make the trip. Visits are generally arranged through tour operators, who offer package deals that include airfare. The trip over takes about 1.25 hours. The view is incredible. Planes land on a grass landing strip that ends in the mountain, which makes take-offs and landings adventures in themselves.

Ancon Expeditions (tel. 269-9415 or 269-9415, fax 264-3713, www.anconexpeditions.com) offers a five-day all-inclusive package to Cana, "The Ultimate Darién Experience," for US$1,595 per person. Larger groups pay significantly lower per-person rates. Prices do not include sales tax, currently 7 percent. A visit to Cana is sometimes included as part of other packages.

A far cheaper, though far more strenuous, way to visit is on foot. It's a two- to three-day trek from Boca de Cupe, when the security situation allows, following the route of the old railroad. Most get to Boca de Cupe by river from El Real or Yaviza. This is a popular leg of many multiday Darién treks and definitely something to be tried only with well-equipped, knowledgeable guides.

◖ PIRRE STATION

The area around Pirre Station, an ANAM ranger station in Parque Nacional Darién, offers an experience similar to Cana at a fraction of the cost. While Pirre is in the lowlands and Cana is in the foothills, they are on opposite sides of Cerro Pirre and share many of the same birds and other wildlife. Both have good trails, including ones that lead up onto Cerro Pirre.

Pirre Station is just within the boundaries of Parque Nacional Darién, in an area known as **Rancho Frío.** The forest here is lush and primeval; it has never been cut. The birding is excellent. Specialties include such beauties as lemon-spectacled and scarlet-browed tanagers, white-fronted nunbirds, and crimson-bellied woodpeckers. Those who wouldn't know a white-fronted nunbird from a nun should keep their eyes and ears open for flocks of macaws, an impressive sight by anyone's standards. Mammals include sloths, spider and howler monkeys, white-faced capuchins, and Geoffroy's tamarins. A 150-kilogram jaguar has

been seen in the area, but as usual the chances of spotting it are extremely slim.

The station is surrounded by primary forest and little else. Facilities are minimal, consisting of a dormitory, an outhouse with flush toilets and showers, a field kitchen, and a couple of picnic tables. The dormitory is basic, to say the least. It consists of two bedrooms and a bare common area with concrete floors. Visitors sleep on bunk beds that are nothing more than foam mattresses on wooden frames. The rangers sleep in the second bedroom. There is no electricity at the station.

The site itself, however, is beautiful. The crystal waters of the Río Peresenico run by the camp, which sits in a clearing ringed by verdant forest.

Hiking

Two main trails originate from the station. One is an easy two-kilometer **loop trail** that leads to a series of waterfalls just 15 minutes away from the station. It's a real *Blue Lagoon* scene.

© WILLIAM FRIAR

THE DARIÉN

The trails around Cerro Pirre offer some of the best bird-watching in the world.

The first waterfall is about five meters tall and pours into a deep pool filled with cold, clear water and surrounded by deep green vegetation.

Those feeling adventurous or foolish or both can climb the sheer, slippery face of the first waterfall and follow the river to two more falls. Be aware that there are several ways to get seriously hurt doing this, and it's a long, long way to a hospital from here.

So don't attempt to clamber around without a good, strong guide to help you. Throw rocks into the brush at the side of the falls to scare away venomous snakes. Watch your step at the higher falls; it's easy to step out into space and fall into a chasm. Be prepared to swim hard when you slide back down the first waterfall, especially if wearing lots of jungle gear. And make sure someone's always nearby in case of an emergency.

A fork in the middle of the loop trail leads up to a clearing that has a communications tower, but it's a tough, two-hour climb up a steep incline, and clouds usually obscure the view.

The **Cerro Pirre trail** leads up the mountain, starting in the forest and coming out onto an exposed ridge that skirts the mountain, rather than climbing to its summit. It's a fairly steep hike, very steep at times, with lots of ups and downs. Expect the trail to be muddy and slippery. It's a moderately strenuous trail, and only reasonably fit hikers should attempt it.

It takes about two hours at a rapid clip to get to **Rancho Plástico,** which, despite its name, is only a reference point and has no facilities. It offers a view of the Río Balsas. Theoretically one could continue along the ridge for two days before turning back. This trail does not link up with Cana's Cloudforest Trail on the other side of the mountain. It's possible to camp along the ridge, but there are no facilities.

It's especially important to have a guide on this hike. The trail is not well defined and is not being maintained. It's easy to get lost, and tree falls sometimes completely block the way.

If you're alone and get lost or hurt, there's a real chance you won't make it out.

Practicalities

Pirre Station is too far from El Real, or anywhere else, for a day trip. Plan to spend at least one night here, two if possible.

Visitors must bring their own towels and will probably want to bring sheets, though the latter can be rented at the station for US$3. Because there is no electricity, or even kerosene lanterns, bringing lots of extra flashlight batteries is a good idea. Bring a good water purifier or purification tablets unless you don't mind toting water all the way from El Real.

The rangers keep the grounds of the station well groomed and clear of debris. But within about 100 meters of the station the forest is literally crawling with venomous fer-de-lance snakes. You're unlikely to come upon one, but never wear sandals and shorts outside the immediate station area. In the Darién, I generally wear boots and long pants even in camp, especially at night.

Visitors should pay the national park fees ahead of time at the **ANAM office** (tel. 299-6965, 8 A.M.–4 P.M. Mon.–Fri.) in El Real.

Travelers must bring their own food, usually from El Real. The rangers will cook and wash dishes for a small tip. Around US$5 a day for a small group is about right. It'd be a nice gesture to bring enough food for the rangers, too. Remember that these are forest guards, not hotel staff. They're your hosts, and you'll have a more enjoyable time if you've won their goodwill. If you arrive without a guide, consider hiring a ranger to take you on the trails, though their wilderness skills and knowledge of the area vary. Again, do not venture far on a trail without a competent guide.

Getting There

Unlike many places in the Darién, it's possible to visit Pirre Station on your own without tremendous hassle or expense. However, I recommend going with a good tour operator, as you're likely to have a safer, more enlightening trip and won't have to deal with making all the considerable arrangements.

Getting to Pirre Station can be an adventure. The usual point of entry is El Real. There are two ways to get to Pirre Station from El Real, when the authorities allow: by boat up the Río Pirre and on foot along a forest trail.

The trail leads directly to Pirre Station. Do not hike it without a knowledgeable guide. Hiking in takes about 2.5 hours in the dry season, when it is generally the only option because the Río Pirre drops to an unnavigable trickle. In the rainy season, though, the trail to Pirre Station turns into a boot-sucking ribbon of mud and the hike becomes a four-hour slog.

When it's runnable, the river is definitely the way to go for those who can afford it. **Narciso "Chicho" Bristán** (tel. 299-6566) in El Real

is an excellent boatman and the obvious first choice. The trip costs US$75 for up to five people each way and takes travelers up the Río Pirre to the poor little Emberá village of Piji Basal. This leg of the journey can take up to three hours if the river is choked with fallen trees, which it frequently is. Watching a boatman chainsawing a massive trunk in the middle of a fast-flowing river suddenly makes the fare seem quite reasonable.

It takes about 90 minutes to hike the trail from Piji Basal to Pirre Station, a little less if you take an overgrown shortcut for the first part of it. Again, go with a knowledgeable guide. It's good politics (and karma) to hire a porter in Piji Basal. It'll cost about US$5 up to Pirre. Don't count on the porter knowing the way, oddly enough.

The trip back down the Río Pirre is much faster. Stay alert throughout the lovely ride. It's remarkably easy to get your head taken off by tree falls if you're dozing.

Coastal and Upriver Darién

PUNTA PATIÑO NATURE RESERVE

Punta Patiño is, at 30,000 hectares, the largest private reserve in the country. It's owned by ANCON, a Panamanian environmental nonprofit, and operated by its for-profit sister organization, Ancon Expeditions. It's a great place to come to get a taste of "coastal Darién," which has a much different feel from the interior. Punta Patiño offers quite a range of vegetation and wildlife, and it's the most comfortable place to stay in the Darién outside of the Tropic Star Lodge. It's on the Golfo de San Miguel, a little under an hour by boat from La Palma.

Large swaths of Patiño, about a third of the reserve, were used for a cattle, coconut, and lumber operations before it became a protected area. The coconut plantation is still standing, but nothing is being done with it. Nature is

making a surprisingly strong recovery in the disturbed areas. A large reforestation project is under way, and ANCON is also working to preserve red and black mangroves here.

Punta means "point." The point is off to the left as you face the beach, where the lighthouse is. The closest settlements from here are the small Afro-Colonial town of Punta Alegre, between Punta Patiño and La Palma, and an Emberá village up the Río Mogue.

Flora and Fauna

The forest around the lodge is secondary growth, but primary forest isn't far away. Notable trees include the massive cuipo, whose blossoms burst into bright red or orange at the end of the dry season, and the spiny cedar, which has sharp spikes covering its trunk.

THE DARIÉN

© WILLIAM FRIAR

Coastal Darién is a different world from the forests of the interior.

There's a decent chance of seeing at least one kind of exotic critter that doesn't have wings here. You're almost guaranteed to see capybara, the world's largest rodent (picture a giant guinea pig), and gray foxes at night toward the end of the rainy season (late December–January). Sightings drop off thereafter. Other largish mammals include *tayras* (a lanky weasel with a long, bushy tail), Geoffroy's tamarins, night monkeys, and collared peccaries. Caimans lurk in the swampier areas, and there are also lots of iguanas. Pilot and humpback whales and bottlenose dolphins can sometimes be spotted in the Golfo de San Miguel. Bird specialties at Patiño include black-tailed trogons, boat-billed herons, and night herons. A jaguar has been known to hunt capybara in the area, but don't expect to see it.

Sports and Recreation

There are several well-developed trails—in some cases they lead to old roads—wandering into a variety of ecosystems.

The **Sendero Piedra de Candela (Flintstone Trail)** is named for the reddish quartzes along this stretch; striking them with a machete sets off sparks. It's a loop trail that takes about an hour to walk. It goes through secondary-growth coastal forest where birders can hunt for mannakins, common black hawks, woodpeckers, and tanagers. It's also a good place to spot Geoffroy's tamarin and, at night, red-eyed tree frogs. It's a flat, easy trail. After 2.5 kilometers it meets a coastal road that eventually leads to the Afro-Colonial town of Punta Alegre in one direction and back to the lodge in the other.

A trail that starts behind Cabin 10 merges with a road leading to the back part of the reserve, which consists of primary lowland forest. There's also a road/trail that leads through the coconut plantation into some wetlands, and another short one leading onto the airstrip.

While walking the trails is the main activity here, don't forget the beach just down the hill from the lodge. It's black sand, but pleasant,

THE HARPY EAGLE

© JIM GUY

Luigi, a harpy eagle at the Peregrine Fund's conservation program at Clayton

The Darién is one of the last Panamanian homes of the harpy eagle *(Harpia harpyja),* the world's most powerful bird of prey. It is Panama's national bird. Deforestation has endangered this magnificent creature, which inhabits lowland tropical forests from southeastern Mexico to parts of Argentina and Brazil. So has hunting, especially since harpy eagles don't generally fear humans. It doesn't help that they produce at most one chick for every nesting attempt, and that they nest only once every three years. This is the longest known breeding period for any raptor.

Conservation programs are underway in Panama, including a breeding program to reintroduce harpy eagles into wilderness areas where they've disappeared. The first harpy eagle bred in captivity in Panama, or anywhere else in Central America, was born in January 2002 at the Peregrine Fund's Neotropical Raptor Center near Panama City.

The eagle can grow to over a meter long from fierce hooked bill to tail, more than half the height of a tall man. Its wingspan can reach 2.1 meters, as wide as a basketball player is tall. Its talons are the size of a grizzly bear's claws. Adults have a distinctive two-pronged crest, making them easy to distinguish from other eagles.

You'd be extremely lucky to spot a harpy eagle even in the Darién, as they rarely soar above the treetops. They hunt within the canopy with remarkable agility given their great size. They favor monkeys, sloths, and other hefty mammals, which they scoop up in their powerful talons at speeds of up to 80 kilometers per hour.

---

and you'll have it all to yourself. There's a second beach a 10-minute boat ride away.

Accommodations

Guests stay in **ANCON's lodge,** high on a hill behind a long, deserted beach. It's a steep walk, but the reserve has a tractor taxi, a tractor with a wagon hitched to it, to transport guests and luggage. The lodge has a dining hall with a wraparound balcony fitted with strategically placed hammocks. There's a mirador upstairs. The balcony and observation platform have gorgeous views of the Golfo de San Miguel and the point where historians believe Balboa stepped out of the forest and became the first European to see the Pacific. On the left there's a sweeping view of the old coconut plantation. Sunsets can be spectacular here, especially during the dry season. The lodge is high enough to watch mangrove black hawks sail by at eye level. It's an incredibly tranquil spot, especially when it's breezy.

The 10 simple but pleasant cabins are behind the lodge. They're surrounded by flowering trees, and all are air-conditioned and have a view out over the coconut plantation from their balconies. Each has two beds, high ceilings, and a private cold-water shower and toilet. Towels and soap are provided. A generator supplies electricity in the lodge and cabins 6 P.M.–6 A.M.

The place is well managed and guest-oriented. Thoughtful touches include being greeted with a *pipa* (fresh coconut), finding fresh-cut flowers in the cabin, and discovering that a staff member has fired up the air-conditioner in the cabin before you turn in for the night. Lime trees are everywhere, so there's always plenty of fresh limeade to cool you off.

However, because Patiño is surrounded by mangroves, it's much buggier than places such as Pirre Station and especially Cana. The mosquitoes are intense in the late rainy season, and insect repellent just seems to make them thirstier. As annoying as this is, Patiño has so many charms that it's worth a little crazed scratching and a welt or two.

This place is a good compromise for those who'd like a taste of the Darién, but don't want to rough it too much.

Getting There and Around

There is a private airstrip at Punta Patiño, but only chartered aircraft land there. The nearest commercial airstrip is in La Palma. From La Palma it's about an hour down to Patiño by boat, which will be arranged for those who go with a tour operator. **Ancon Expeditions** (tel. 269-9415 or 269-9415, fax 264-3713, www.anconexpeditions.com) offers a four-day, three-night package to Patiño for US$750 per person. The price includes lodging, airfare, guided hikes in the forest, tours of the Emberá village on the Río Mogue, and meals.

Sales tax is not included. The company also includes a visit to Punta Patiño as part of other trips.

LA PALMA

La Palma (pop. 3,884) is the provincial capital of the Darién, with the emphasis squarely on "provincial." Branches of the major government offices are here, including ANAM (the environmental regulatory agency), a police headquarters, a grim jail, and even an outpost of the national lottery.

La Palma's location is striking. It's at the wide mouth of the Río Tuira, just where it races into the Golfo de San Miguel. Balboa became the first European to discover the Pacific near here. The ruins of Spanish fortifications are on craggy islets topped with emerald vegetation a few minutes' boat ride away. It's a natural launching point for trips by water into the heart of the Darién.

Look away from the water, though, and the view becomes less appealing. La Palma is a hot, humid town where garbage piles up on the side of the road or is just chucked into the fast-flowing river. It consists of a strip of road wedged between an unbroken chain of hole-in-the-wall restaurants, bars, stores, and hotels perched above the rivermouth on one side and a steep hill crowded with shanties on the other side. A remarkable number of minibuses ply this single road, which leads to the village of Setegantí, about 20 kilometers south of the airstrip. Walking the length of downtown, from the airstrip at one end to the Cable and Wireless office at the other, takes about 10 minutes at a slow pace. The town does not have a friendly vibe. Be prepared for lots of poker-faced stares.

As with Yaviza and El Real, most visitors use La Palma as a way station and provisioning post en route to somewhere else. Still, town life in La Palma can be fascinating for an hour or two: a drunk staggering around at 10 in the morning, a surly Colombian shop owner grumbling about being ostracized by the locals, a tailor working his foot-pedaled Singer on the street, kids setting off to school in neat blue-and-white uniforms.

An important festival day here is the Fiesta de San José, held on March 19.

Sights

Other than the town itself, the only thing in the

area that constitutes a sight is **El Fuerte de San Carlos de Boca Chica,** the ruins of which are five minutes by motorboat from La Palma on the island of Boca Chica. It should be easy to find a boatman willing to make the trip. Ask down by the boat ramps about *el fuerte de Boca Chica.* About US$10 for a small group should do it.

There's a small battery on a neighboring islet, but the main fortifications are on Boca Chica. The Spanish built El Fuerte de San Carlos de Boca Chica in the mid-18th century as part of their network of defenses for the Espiritu Santo gold mines in Cana. It's not a big fort, and the jungle has devoured much of it—a strangler fig has practically melded with what's left. But it's an impressive, photogenic sight, and it brings history vividly to life. It doesn't take much imagination to picture a poor, homesick Spanish soldier on lookout here, sweating in the jungle and keeping an eye out for pirates. The fort is a couple of minutes uphill from shore and so shrouded by forest it's no longer easy to see from the water.

There are two Afro-Colonial towns a few minutes by boat from La Palma: Punta Alegre on the Golfo de San Miguel to the southwest and Chepigana near the mouth of the Río Tuira to the southeast, though they're little more than collections of zinc-roofed shanties on the water's edge.

Accommodations and Food

Hotel Biaquirú Bagará (tel. 299-6224, US$10 s, US$15 d for a room with fan and shared bath; US$20 s, US$30 d with a/c and private bath), near the end of town heading away from the airstrip, is by far the best place to stay in La Palma. The place is a local institution and has been the home base of many expeditions. It offers 13 tidy little rooms, some of which are surprisingly cheerful. A few have balconies. The two best rooms have air-conditioning and private bathrooms. Amenities include satellite TV, a pay phone, and free drinking water. It's by no means a fancy place, but after spending time

in the jungle, it'll feel like the Ritz. There's a lovely view of the river from the balcony. Meals can be arranged at the hotel with notice. Price depends on what you want. A few other places in town will do in a pinch.

All the restaurants in La Palma are *fondas,* little holes-in-the-wall that serve whatever they happen to have on hand that day for a buck or two. Sometimes this includes peccary (usually called *puerco de monte,* mountain pig). Hunting and eating peccaries and other wild animals are illegal and punishable by jail time. Do not order it.

Information and Services

All the services in town are squeezed together one after another on La Palma's main road. The exception is the hospital, which is now in a new structure on the hill at the far side of the town's airstrip, outside of town. Every bus running between La Palma and Setegantí drives near the place.

La Palma carries just about anything you'd need for a Darién expedition. It's also one of the few places in the Darién with fresh produce. There are a couple of general stores, offering provisions ranging from sodas to machetes.

Banco Nacional de Panamá (8 A.M.–3 P.M. Mon.–Fri., 9 A.M.–noon Sat.), near the airstrip, cashes American Express travelers checks.

The **Cable and Wireless office** (8:30 A.M.– 4:30 P.M. Mon.–Fri.), at the far end of town from the airstrip, sells phone cards.

Getting There and Around

The crumbling airport at the edge of town doesn't inspire much confidence, and Panama's one remaining domestic airline was not running scheduled flights to La Palma at the time of writing. Contact **Air Panama** (tel. 316-9000, www.flyairpanama.com) to see if this has changed by the time you visit. The flight takes around an hour. Even if flights do resume, don't count on them arriving or leaving anywhere close to on time.

The only other way to get to La Palma is by

THE DARIÉN

boat. A water taxi runs from Puerto Quimba to La Palma, 7:30 A.M.–6:30 P.M., and from La Palma to Puerto Quimba, 5:30 A.M.–5 P.M. The water taxi to La Palma theoretically runs every 60–75 minutes, but in reality only the first one of the day is reliable. After that, the boat leaves when it gets a full load. The trip costs US$3 one-way and takes about 30–45 minutes. A bus shuttles passengers between Puerto Quimba to the side of the Interamericana at Metetí, where it's possible, if one times it right, to get a bus to Panama City and sometimes to Yaviza.

◉ MOGUE

The Emberá village of Mogue (MOE-gay), up the river that gives it its name, welcomes visitors and in fact has become a tourist destination for the area. It's about midway between Punta Patiño and La Palma.

It takes about a half hour by boat from either Patiño or La Palma to get to the mouth of the Río Mogue. It's a potentially bumpy boat ride on the ocean. The Mogue is a beautiful river, in a slightly spooky, Conradian sense; it's swampy, still, and serpentine, with towering black mangroves on either side.

Boats have to take it slow up this murky river to avoid damaging the engine. It's about a 25-minute cruise from the mouth of the river to Mogue village. On the river and the trails around the village, birders might spot white ibises, willets, whimbrels, mangrove black hawks, roseate spoonbills, red-throated caracaras, laughing falcons, black oropendolas, orange-crowned orioles, and other gorgeous birds. You'll know the village is near when the mangroves give way to plantain fields. It's a 15-minute walk from where the boat puts in to Paraíso Mogue (Mogue Paradise), as a welcome sign in the village puts it.

The Emberá established Mogue in the late 1960s. It's a relatively pretty little village that caters to tourists, putting on traditional dances and opening handicraft stalls when groups arrive.

But it feels relatively traditional, given that the Emberá do not traditionally live in villages at all.

It's possible to spend the night in Mogue in relative comfort. There's a huge version of a *tambo,* a traditional Emberá open-sided thatched-roof hut raised on stilts about 15 feet off the ground, where visitors can pitch tents and relax in hammocks. It's breezy up there and has an eavesdropper's view of the surrounding village, as well as a vista of the forest-covered hills in the distance. If you stay here, drown yourself in insect repellent and be prepared to be awakened early by roosters and crying babies.

Primary forest starts 15 minutes from the village. An hour hike from here leads to a harpy eagle nest. An hour hike in the opposite direction leads to the nest of a crested eagle. You'll need a guide to show the way in either case.

A big festival in these parts is held on November 14, the anniversary of the building of the local school.

Practicalities

Because of Mogue's proximity to Punta Patiño, most visitors come here with **Ancon Expeditions** (tel. 269-9414 or 269-9415, fax 264-3713, www.anconexpeditions.com) as part of a stay at Patiño. Ancon Expeditions brings in food, which the villagers cook. Depending on the itinerary, visitors either spend the night or just pay a short day visit. Mogue has showers for tourists that may actually work, and a rather scary-looking latrine.

UP THE RÍO SAMBÚ

The Río Sambú makes for a memorable boat ride. Its wide, muddy mouth opens into the Ensenada de Garachiné, a cove that in turn opens into the Pacific Ocean. The mouth is about midway between Punta Garachiné to the south and Punta Patiño to the north. The river is bordered by an intricate tangle of mangroves, behind which rise lush green towering trees. It's a beautiful sight. Even though there are settlements along the banks and many small fishing boats plying the waters, there's no doubt you're in Mother Nature's living room here.

It's easy to spot birds sailing overhead or hanging by the water as you motor upriver, particularly such water-loving fowl as herons, egrets, frigate birds, pelicans, and cormorants. You'll probably see at least a couple of hawks perched high atop the tallest trees. Toucans and parrots are a bit harder to spot, but they're around. And the occasional splash and burble in the river will set your mind wondering exactly what is lurking in there.

La Chunga and Sambú

The touristy Emberá village of La Chunga (la CHOON-guh) is about an hour upriver. It's along the banks of the Río Chunga, a sluggish but no less scenic little river that empties into the Sambú. A *chunga* is a kind of black palm with sharp spines, used by the Emberá-Wounaan to make decorative baskets. Ask a villager to point one out. The village is about a 20-minute walk down a wide, flat path from where the boat lands.

You may have mixed feelings about visiting La Chunga. The village, which has a population of about 300 people, has obviously been shaped with tourists in mind. Most of the tourists come from small cruise ships that offer a taste of the Darién as part of a transcanal itinerary. Those who slip into the village ahead of a tour group may see women taking off their blouses and bras and men kicking off their jeans to look appropriately native for their visitors. Decked out in little more than short skirts or loin coverings, they dance around as tourists snap photos. The whole thing looks as uncomfortable for the villagers as it will probably feel to you.

When a tour group is expected, Emberá and Wounaan come from nearby settlements to join the villagers in selling handicrafts at tables set up around the village. It's possible to get some well-made souvenirs at good prices, and the money is going right to the needy source. Popular items include cocobolo (rosewood) figurines, tightly woven baskets and bowls, and tagua nuts (also known as ivory nuts) carved in the shape of forest animals.

The airstrip for the area is in the tiny, ramshackle town of Sambú, whose residents are a mixture of Afro-Colonials, Emberá, and Wounaan. There are a couple of new guesthouses in town.

Accommodations

The residents of La Chunga managed to turn their village into one of the more comfortable places to stay in the Darién. "Comfort" is a relative term where the Darién is concerned, but amazingly enough this place has real flush toilets and running water. Four solid thatch-roofed, bamboo-sided cabins on stilts are rented out to visitors. The rooms, officially known as the **Hotel Emberá,** are a short walk from the village proper, set in a little clearing where medicinal plants are grown for the edification of visitors. The cabins have two rooms, each equipped just with two wooden beds topped by foam mattresses and mosquito nets. One of the cabins has double beds; the rest are singles. Showers are in a neighboring hut and consist of a cold-water spigot. Rates are US$150 for one person, US$60 for each additional person. This includes lodging, meals, and tours, but not airfare to Sambú.

Your host is Ricardo Cabrera, *cacique* (chief) of La Chunga and 11 other villages. Ricardo is a friendly guy who speaks English well. (He's the only one in the village who speaks more than a word or two.) He can arrange guided hikes on which you might see all kinds of critters, including crocodiles in a nearby lake, golden-headed quetzals, peccaries, and, of course, snakes. Ricardo has recently opened a second, three-room guesthouse, **Villa Siesta,** in the tiny town of Sambú itself. Rates are US$20 for the room alone. He's also working on a third place farther up the river.

To stay at Hotel Emberá or Villa Siesta, get in touch with Ricardo Cabrera, which can be tricky. Start by calling Ricardo's sister in Panama City (tel. 234-8281). Ricardo has a mobile phone (cell 6687-2271), but he's often out of range. There is one public telephone in the village (tel. 299-6083); ask for Ricardo. However, be advised that the phone is often out of order. If all else fails, send a telegram from a post office to: Ricardo Cabrera, La Chunga, Darién, Zona 4. List your contact information, proposed date of arrival, number in the party, and how long you want to stay. If Ricardo knows you're coming, he'll arrange to meet you at the airstrip, but don't be surprised if you have to wait around for a while.

A surprisingly decent place in Sambú is **Sambú Hause** (tel. 268-6905, cell 6766-5102, sambuhause@yahoo.com, http://sambuhause-darienpanama.com, US$125 s/d, including meals), consisting of four rooms in a simple wooden house about 500 meters from the airstrip. One of the rooms has a private bathroom; the rest share bathrooms. The house has electricity, mosquito screening, modern fixtures, a TV/DVD player, a deck and front porch, an outdoor barbecue, and a fully equipped kitchen. It is by no means a luxurious place, but these things alone mean it offers by far the best-equipped village accommodations in the Darién.

It's the creation of Michael Harrington, an American married to a *darienita,* and managed by his sister-in-law, María Asprilla and her daughter, Mabel. It is still a work in progress: Everything must be brought in by boat or plane, so construction is slow and expensive. But it appears to be a good midrange option for those who want a bit of comfort during a Darién trip, but have an adventurous spirit, are comfortable with rustic surroundings, and like the idea of staying in the heart of a hand-to-mouth Darién community.

Sambú Hause can arrange guided forest hikes (about US$15/hour) and river trips on motorized *piraguas* (about US$35/hour). As at La Chunga, the local indigenous people perform Emberá-Wounaan dances (no charge, but a US$20 tip is expected and appreciated) and sell baskets, tagua carvings, and other handicrafts.

Sambú Hause offers adventurous overnight treks, arranged through a man named Juancito, who can also come up with cheaper, more rustic accommodations for those who can't afford Sambú Hause.

Getting There and Around

With the exception of those who come by boat from Punta Patiño or elsewhere, most visitors fly to this area. At the time of writing, **Air Panama** (tel. 316-9000, www.flyairpanama.com) was not flying to Sambú, but it was flying to Garachiné nearby. Visitors can hire a boat from there to Sambú or La Chunga if they haven't arranged for someone to meet them. Air Panama flies from Panama City to Garachiné at 10:30 A.M. on Wednesday and Saturday and returns to Panama City at 11:45 A.M. on Tuesday and Thursday.

◖ BAHÍA DE PIÑAS

The Bahía de Piñas (Piñas Bay) is far down the Pacific coast of Panama, southeast of the Golfo de San Miguel and just 56 kilometers from the Colombian border. It is world-famous for deep-sea fishing, but the area is so extraordinarily beautiful that even those who don't want to go near a fish will likely enjoy a visit. It's also a culturally interesting area.

Approximately 200 deep-sea fishing world records have been set in this area, more than anywhere else on the planet. Most of these are for black, blue, or striped marlin and Pacific sailfish.

What accounts for this? It has a lot to do with **Zane Grey Reef,** a dramatic seamount (underwater mountain) that rises from the 100-meter-deep sea bottom in three peaks, two of which top out within 45 meters of the surface. The current sweeps plankton around the reef, which feeds huge amounts of baitfish, which in turn attract large predators. The area is a giant natural aquarium filled with, among other things, sharks, rays, jacks, snappers, dorado, tuna, and, of course, billfish. The reef is particularly renowned among anglers for black marlin. The area is carefully protected: Panama enforces a 32-kilometer exclusion zone around the bay, into which commercial fishing vessels with their huge nets are not allowed. Panama's marine authority keeps a small ship stationed in the area that investigates any suspected infractions; violators are fined and can lose their fishing licenses.

The Bahía de Piñas itself is a small, narrow bay formed by two fingers of land that jut out to sea. Between are the landscaped grounds of Tropic Star Lodge. Close to 6,000 hectares of the surrounding land is owned by Tropic Star, and nearly all of this has been left undeveloped and pristine. It is heart-stoppingly gorgeous: Emerald forests filled with massive trees spill down the hilly countryside to the very edge of the coast, which ends in sheer, rocky cliffs broken by the occasional waterfall. Dolphins like to romp around inside the bay, and humpback whales are sometimes spotted outside it. Indigenous people still pan for, and sometimes find, gold nuggets on the Río Piñas.

Playa Blanca, a small but gorgeous white-sand beach just north of the bay, offers clear blue water and snorkeling near a coral reef just offshore. It's on property owned by Tropic Star Lodge, but as with all beaches in Panama, it's open to the public. However, only guests of the lodge may hike into the forest.

Nearby are two small coastal towns, **Puerto Piñas** and **Jaqué,** which have a mixed population of Afro-Colonial and Emberá inhabitants. Several indigenous villages are up the Río Jaqué, one of which, the Wounaan village of **Biroquera,** is open to day visitors.

Puerto Piñas

To the southeast of the lodge, about 10 minutes by boat, is the small fishing village of Puerto Piñas (pop. 819). It's a dilapidated place, but the people are friendly and laid-back and it's right on a gray sandy beach. A little more than half its residents are estimated to be Emberá and the rest Afro-Colonial. Dwellings consist of modest cinderblock houses next to traditional cane or plank thatch-roofed huts. There is also a good airstrip, a police bunker, an ultrabasic place to stay, a couple of equally basic places to eat and drink, a primary school, a tiny general store, several churches, a volleyball court, a sand soccer field, and not a whole lot else. An odd little factoid: The town and its environs have a dog population of about 400, one for every two residents.

Past the soccer field, on the far end of the village, is an enormous open-sided thatched-roof hut used for village meetings and Emberá dances presented to tourists. About half of the adult residents of the village work at Tropic Star during the fishing season. Otherwise, they sustain themselves through fishing and subsistence agriculture, especially bananas, plantains, and rice.

The area surrounding Puerto Piñas has been turned into farmland. It and the neighboring village of Jaqué are both at the edge of swampy plains backed by hills; the flatlands have largely been deforested, but the hills are mostly intact.

Jaqué

The area around the town of Jaqué (ha-KAY; pop. 2,244) is even more deforested. They actually graze cattle here—thankfully the only place along this stretch of coast that does. They mainly fish and grow crops that include rice, plantains, yuca, and yams. It's considerably larger and relatively more affluent-looking than Puerto Piñas, with some fairly substantial houses, but it's still a place where people live pretty close to the bone. There's an airstrip, a hospital, two *hospedajes,* a soccer field, and a handful of basic places to get a bite or a drink. A police bunker is at the edge of town near the

THE DARIÉN

mouth of the Río Jaqué, and there's a camouflage netting–covered main *cuartel* (police station) in the center of town.

In 2000, the Colombian civil war pushed hundreds of refugees from the Colombian town of Juradó over the border into Jaqué and its surroundings. Due to the general unrest of the civil war, the police presence in town and up the Río Jaqué was increased, keeping the situation under control for several years. There was increased unrest starting in 2010, so I strongly advise visitors to avoid Jaqué and the surrounding area.

Normally, the town is mellow and the people are friendly to strangers. Those who come to Jaqué by boat must get from open sea to the mouth of the Río Jaqué, and doing so often means riding waves that can be three meters high or even bigger. Managing this requires an experienced captain with a feel for surfing, and no one should attempt it without life jackets. This wave actually can be surfed, though few have made it all the way down here with their boards.

Near Jaqué

Before heading upriver, check in with the police station in town to make sure it's safe to do so. There are four indigenous villages on the Río Jaqué within about 20 kilometers of the town of Jaqué: Biroquera, Lucas, El Coco, and El Mamey. There are police posts in each village, but the upper reaches of the Río Jaqué beyond El Mamey are not patrolled and are supposedly used as a rest spot by combatants in the Colombian civil war. All the villages are Emberá except the first one, Biroquera, which is Wounaan. It's about 15 minutes by fast boat from Jaqué and is the only village Panamanian authorities are allowing foreign travelers to visit. For your own safety, do not attempt to travel farther upriver. Getting to the Río Jaqué by sea can be rough.

© WILLIAM FRIAR

There are a number of indigenous villages up the Río Jacqué.

Biroquera is a fairly tidy and spacious village built right on the edge of the river. It's worth a quick visit. Houses are a mixture of traditional white cane–walled huts on stilts and more modern huts with walls made of wooden planks. A concrete path winds through the village, which is lit for a couple of hours in the evening by a small generator. The Wounaan are renowned for their crafts, and it should be possible to buy directly from the makers here. Hiring a boat from Jaqué to Biroquera should cost about US$40 for a small group.

About 20 kilometers southeast of Jaqué there's a small bay, **Ensenada El Guayabo,** that has a white sand beach that's said to be even prettier than Playa Blanca. All that's there is a handful of indigenous huts. It makes for an easy day trip from Jaqué or Piñas. Visitors can trade fishing hooks and sodas with the residents for fresh coconut milk. It's probably not a good idea to head much farther down toward the Colombian border.

Tropic Star Lodge

Most foreign visitors to this area stay at the Tropic Star Lodge (U.S. toll-free tel. 800/682-3424, U.S. tel. 407/843-0125, www.tropicstar. com), a four-decades-old institution that looms large over the area and has made the Bahía de Piñas world-famous in fishing circles.

An exclusive fishing resort that can accommodate no more than 36 guests at a time, the lodge is set on lovely, landscaped land right above the bay. There's a small beach in front, flowering trees all around, a swimming pool with a bar, and a river that cuts across the grounds.

It's the kind of place pop stars, screen idols, and famous athletes frequent—notable guests have ranged from John Wayne to Walter Peyton to George Strait. Ask about the time Lee Marvin was kicked out for throwing a chair through the restaurant window. It's entertaining to thumb through the old guest books looking for familiar names.

This was originally the vacation home of a Texas oil millionaire named Ray Smith, who turned it into a fishing lodge in 1965. It has been owned by the Kittredge family since 1976. The current owners are Terri Kittredge Andrews and her husband, Mike Andrews.

Accommodations are, as one might expect, quite comfortable, though this is definitely a fishing lodge and not an ultraposh hotel. Given the lodge's remote location, however, it is remarkably well maintained and filled with creature comforts. It's easy to forget the nearest road is more than 100 kilometers away.

Most rooms are in two-unit cabins with wraparound wooden porches or in a single long building near the beach. The rooms are spacious, with air-conditioning, twin beds, and large private bathrooms/dressing rooms. All have a view of the bay. Up the hill is El Palacio, a three-bedroom house with a sunken living room that was the original owner's home. It can accommodate up to six guests. It's reachable by climbing 122 stairs or taking the more popular cable car.

The food is delicious, with multicourse candlelit dinners served at night in the circular, air-conditioned restaurant/bar or out on the veranda. There are no telephones, fax machines, or televisions at the lodge, so guests can have a true sense of getting away from it all. Expect pampering: A staff of 80 serve the 36 guests.

The lodge still has a 1960s vibe about it, though a 2004 updating of the facilities has meant some welcome changes—such as replacing wall-to-wall carpet in the cabins with tile—while retaining the vintage feel of the place.

Daily fishing trips are made on 31-foot Bertrams, of which the lodge owns 14. The prime black marlin season runs mid-December–April. Pacific sailfish are caught year-round, with April–July especially good months. The lodge is open December–September. Guests have free use of kayaks to explore the bay or travel up the Río Piñas.

THE DARIÉN

Several kilometers of trails wind through primary and secondary forest. These are well worth walking, especially in the early morning when there's the best chance of spotting wildlife. I came across a group of curious coatimundis during a hike shortly after dawn. Don't expect to see many animals, as hunters from surrounding villages have taken their toll through the years. But pumas, three-toed sloths, and foxes have been spotted near the lodge, and the staff have found jaguar prints on the beach.

The staff can also arrange a trip up the Río Jaqué to visit the Wounaan village of Biroquera.

None of this comes cheap, of course. The basic fishing package in the high season starts at about US$5,350 per person, including seven nights of lodging, six days of fishing, and three meals a day, but not tips or transport from Panama City. Rates vary depending on the season, length of stay, and number of people in the boat. Nonfishing packages are sometimes available. Charter airfare to and from Panama City is US$500 per person. The lodge is small and popular, with lots of repeat business. Reservations must often be made a year or two in advance.

Practicalities

Again, until conflicts in this area die down again, I do not advise staying in or around Jaqué. Tropic Star Lodge is quite separate from the area on a large stretch of private land, so presumably it will remain relatively insulated from the conflict. However, you should contact the lodge for current conditions before visiting (it's in their interest to make sure their guests remain safe and happy, and they have years of experience in doing so).

There are two basic *hospedajes* (lodgings) in Jaqué and an ultrabasic one in Puerto Piñas. Enterprising souls can probably strike a bargain to rent a room in someone's house upon arrival. The only places to eat are rustic to say the least; this is a good place to come with one's own food supply.

Aventuras Anamar (tel. 233-5976 or 221-7423; ask for Señor Herman Torres or Señora Praxedes Torres, US$10 s/d) in Jaqué offers the best rooms in either town. The *hospedaje* is a two-story building on a rather attractive stretch of beach past the east edge of town. It's completely basic but surprisingly okay, with three rooms that look out on a porch facing the ocean and four darker ones behind them. Room 1 is the nicest. It's a corner room with lots of glass windows and a partial view of the ocean. Bathrooms are shared. Management here is friendly and animated and should be able to arrange food.

Food and booze are available at a handful of nondescript kiosks, *fondas* (taverns), and cantinas in Jaqué. Near the river is a tiny general store with an airless little bar next door.

Getting There and Around

Commercial flights from Panama City often stop at both Jaqué and Puerto Piñas (sometimes known to the airlines as Bahía Piñas), though the order of arrival varies. The two airstrips are about two minutes' flight time away.

Air Panama flies to Bahía Piñas and Jaqué at 10:30 A.M. Monday and Friday. The return flights leave Piñas at 11:35 A.M. and Jaqué around 11:55 A.M.

The flights take about an hour. Make sure to get off at the right airstrip. All these departure times are optimistic estimates. The fare is US$78.97 each way to Piñas; it's about US$2 cheaper each way to Jaqué.

The new concrete airstrip at Piñas is in great shape. The Jaqué airstrip is not, and it gets quite muddy in the rainy season—an acquaintance compared landing here to an off-road adventure in a four-wheel drive.

BACKGROUND

The Land

The Republic of Panama covers 75,517 square kilometers, which makes it slightly bigger than Ireland and slightly smaller than South Carolina. Panama is young in geological terms. It emerged from the sea just 2.5 million years ago, dividing the Atlantic from the Pacific and forming a natural bridge that connects the North and South American continents. The bridge has allowed North and South American species to intermingle. Known as the Great American Interchange, this mingling had a profound effect on the ecology of South America.

Panama's peculiar shape—like the letter S turned on its side—causes confusion for many visitors. It takes a while to get used to the notion that the Caribbean Sea is to the north and the Pacific Ocean to the south. Many also find it strange to be able to watch the sun rising over the Pacific and setting in the Caribbean, or to realize that when a ship transits the Panama Canal from the Pacific to the Caribbean it actually ends up slightly west of where it started.

Panama is at the eastern end of Central America, bordered to the west by Costa Rica and to the east by Colombia. It's far longer than it is wide. The oceans are just 80 kilometers

© WILLIAM FRIAR

apart at the Panama Canal, near the middle of the country, and that isn't even the narrowest spot on the isthmus. But the country stretches surprisingly far to the east and west; Panama has nearly 3,000 kilometers of coastline along its Caribbean and Pacific flanks.

People often wonder which body of water is the higher of the two. The reality is that there's no difference in elevation—sea level is sea level. A locks canal was necessary in Panama not to keep the oceans from spilling into each other, but to carry ships over the landmass of the isthmus. But there is a dramatic difference between the tides on each side. The Caribbean tide averages less than half a meter; Pacific tides can be more than five meters high.

Many visitors are surprised to discover how mountainous Panama is. The most impressive mountain range is the Cordillera Central, which bisects the western half of the country, extending from the Costa Rican border east toward the canal. It contains Panama's highest mountain, Volcán Barú, a dormant volcano that is 3,475 meters high. Another impressive range runs along Panama's eastern Caribbean coast, starting at the Comarca de Guna Yala and ending at the Colombian border. It officially comprises the Serranía de San Blas to the west and the Serranía del Darién to the east, where it enters Darién province.

Most parts of Panama experience few significant earthquakes, which is one of the reasons it was chosen as the site of an interoceanic canal. However, western Panama, particularly Bocas del Toro and Chiriquí, is far more seismically active. In 1991, an earthquake measuring 7.5 on the Richter scale struck along the Costa Rica–Panama border, leaving two dozen people dead in Bocas del Toro and thousands homeless.

Besides the humid tropical forests that people expect to find, which compose a third of Panama's remaining forests, Panama has a great variety of other ecosystems, ranging from cloud forests to an artificially made desert. Extensive

AN ABUNDANCE OF THEORIES

The country of Panama gets its name from the city of Panama, but what does "Panama" mean? No one knows for sure.

The Spanish first used the name in conjunction with a native fishing village they soon claimed as the cornerstone of their new capital. It's little wonder, then, that the most common explanation is that Panama (or, to be proper, Panamá) is a forgotten indigenous word for "abundance of fishes." Another theory is that the word means "abundance of butterflies." Yet another posits that the striking (and abundant) Panama tree lent its name to the city and then the republic. Some say the word just meant "abundance," hence the odd variety of plentiful things associated with it. A personal favorite is that it means "to rock in a hammock." Take your pick: All definitions still fit.

mangroves, coral reefs, and hundreds of islands can be found on both the Pacific and Caribbean sides of the isthmus. Panama also has at least 500 rivers.

CLIMATE

Panama lies between 7 and 10 degrees north of the equator. The climate is mainly tropical, and days and nights are almost equally long throughout the year. Sunrise and sunset vary by only about half an hour during the year: The sun rises approximately 6–6:30 A.M. and sets approximately 6–6:30 P.M.

Temperatures in Panama are fairly constant year-round. In the lowlands, these range from about 32°C (90°F) in the day down to 21°C (70°F) in the evening. It never gets cold in the lowlands, and dry-season breezes are very pleasant there in the evenings. It gets considerably cooler in the highlands. At the top of Volcán Barú temperatures can dip below freezing.

Humidity tends to be quite high year-round, but especially so in the rainy season, when it approaches 100 percent.

Most of Panama has two seasons, the rainy and the dry. The dry season, also known as summer *(verano)*, lasts from about mid-December to mid-April. Rain stops completely in many parts then, especially on the Pacific side. Flowering trees burst into bloom around the country at the start of this season. Toward the end, vegetation turns brown or dies, and smoke from slash-and-burn agriculture and the burning of sugarcane fields can make the skies hazy.

The rainy season, also known as winter *(invierno)*, generally lasts from about mid-April to mid-December. The rains tend to be heaviest and longest at the end of the season, as though the heavens were wringing out every last drop of moisture. October, November, and the beginning of December are especially heavy. Thunderstorms are a near daily occurrence during the rainy season.

Some parts of Panama, including Bocas del Toro and the western highlands, have microclimates that differ from this general dry season/rainy season pattern.

Yearly rainfall averages around three meters. It's far wetter on the Caribbean side than the Pacific side. The rains in most parts of Panama tend to come in powerful bursts in the afternoon or early evening. Mornings are usually dry on the Pacific side.

Dirt roads and trails can become impassable in the interior during the rainy season, and paved roads and bridges are often washed out by mudslides and rising rivers. Flooding is a serious problem in parts of the interior, such as Bocas del Toro and Chiriquí.

The rain never stops completely along the Caribbean coast, in the western highlands, and on the islands of Bocas del Toro. Rainfall patterns in Bocas are quite different from other parts of Panama. It has no true dry season, but generally little rain falls September–October and February–March.

Panama is south of the hurricane zone, so it's spared those terrible storms.

Flora and Fauna

Panama's shape and location—at the southernmost range of many North American species and the northernmost range of many South American species—makes it home to a particularly rich variety of plant and animal life. Sadly, the future of this abundant life is by no means secure: The World Conservation Monitoring Centre's Red List of threatened animals includes 112 species found in Panama.

A total of 972 species of birds have been identified so far, more than are found in the United States and Canada combined. The country is also home to well over 200 mammal and 200 reptile species, close to 200 amphibian species, and more than 10,000 species of plants. Some of these are found nowhere else on earth.

TREES AND PLANTS

Panama's plant life is among the most diverse in the world. The country contains 12 of the planet's 30 Holdridge life zones. By far the most common is humid tropical forest, which accounts for about a third of Panama's remaining forest cover. All of these zones but one, humid premontane forest, are represented in a system of protected areas. Of Panama's estimated 10,000 species of plants, about 1,500 of them are found nowhere else on the planet. Panama also has extensive wetlands, mangroves, and coral reefs.

Panamanian environmentalists like to point out that, per square kilometer, Panama has 21 times the plant diversity of Brazil. Trying to identify the plants even in a small patch of rainforest

© HOTSHOTSWORLDWIDE/WWW.123RF.COM

quetzal

is daunting. There are 480 species of trees just on the 15 square kilometers of Isla Barro Colorado, more than are found in all of Europe.

The Panama tree *(Sterculia apetala)* is widely thought of as the national tree, and some maintain it gave the country its name. It has a straight trunk that can grow up to 35 meters tall, with vertical buttresses around its base.

The ceiba or kapok *(Ceiba pentandra)* can reach 60 meters and often juts above other trees in the forest. One kapok specimen on Isla Barro Colorado is so huge other trees grow on its branches.

The *espavé* or wild cashew *(Anacardium excelsum)* has a trunk so straight and tall that indigenous peoples use it to make dugout canoes. One explanation of its name is that *espavé* is a contraction of *es para ver* ("it's for seeing"), meaning it's a good tree to climb to see what's off in the distance.

The *mata palo* or strangler fig *(Ficus obtusifolia)* starts as a seedling on a host tree that it eventually surrounds and engulfs. The mature strangler fig can be hollow inside, its original host completely decomposed. It's easy to spot because of its enormously thick strangler roots, which can also engulf boulders and the ruins of buildings.

The massively thick trunk of the abundant cuipo *(Cavanillesia platanifolia)* also makes it easy to identify it in the forest.

In the dry season, flowering trees burst into bloom around the isthmus, dotting the green canopy with brilliant colors.

Panama has more than 1,000 species of orchids, many of them endemic. The delicate white *espíritu santo* (holy ghost) orchid, also known as the dove orchid, is considered Panama's national flower.

BIRDS

Panama is especially well known for its incredible number and diversity of bird species. Besides its vast local populations, more than 120 species are migrants that regularly cross the isthmus on the way to and from their winter homes.

The famous (among birders) raptor migration of broad-winged hawks, Swainson's hawks, and turkey vultures is absolutely spectacular. During the fall and spring, particularly October–mid-November and March–early April, they pass overhead in flocks that can number in the many thousands. It's an unbelievable sight. The first comprehensive study of the migration was conducted in fall 2004, when researchers tallied more than 2.7 million raptors. One researcher counted 92,000 in a single day. They are easiest to spot around the former Canal Zone. Good places to see them include Cerro Ancón, the Canopy Tower, and the top of the aerial tram at the Gamboa Rainforest Resort.

Other species likely to impress non-birders include five species of macaws (blue-and-yellow, chestnut-fronted, great green, red-and-green, and the rare scarlet); several species of toucans and toucanets; the harpy eagle, the world's most powerful bird of prey; and the

howler monkey

resplendent quetzal, which has been called the most beautiful bird on the planet.

LAND MAMMALS

The country's national parks are filled with animals that thrill foreign visitors, though many are hard to spot. There are five species of big cats on the isthmus—jaguars, jaguarundis, pumas, margays, and ocelots—but finding one in the wild is exceedingly hard. The forests harbor every species of nonhuman primate found in Central America: western night monkeys, mantled howler monkeys, white-faced capuchins, several types of spider monkeys, and Geoffroy's tamarins. Howlers are generally the easiest to spot (or at least hear) in the wild, but a few years ago a wildlife rescue project introduced four species of primates to islands in Lago Gatún, where the night monkey still occurs naturally. It's easy to spot several species during a boat tour of the lake.

Many visitors find white-nosed coatis (coatimundis) and kinkajous, with their long tails and furry bodies, terribly cute. They're reasonably easy to find, especially around Gamboa.

Capybaras are the world's largest rodents, but they more closely resemble giant guinea pigs than rats. They can grow up to a meter long and weigh up to 45 kilograms. They're shy, but they're pretty easy to spot in Gamboa and Punta Patiño.

Far smaller but equally cute are Central American agoutis, known locally as *ñeques.* They're generally less than half a meter long and weigh just 3–4 kilograms. They're covered in fur and have a rather large rump. They're among the easiest mammals to spot in Panama; they're diurnal and found just about anywhere there's forest. Agoutis are sometimes confused with pacas because of the latter's scientific name, *Agouti paca.* But pacas are quite a bit larger, and their brown fur is marked with rows of white spots, giving rise to their local name, *conejo pintado* (painted rabbit).

Small red brocket and white-tailed deer are common. Isla San José is the only place in Central America where gray brockets are found. Other notable land mammals include giant anteaters, white-lipped and collared peccaries, two- and three-toed sloths, and Baird's tapirs, the largest land mammal in Central America. The last can weigh up to 300 kilograms and are rather odd-looking creatures with a trunk-like nose.

SEA LIFE

Five species of sea turtles can be found in Panama's waters, and four of them lay their eggs on its islands and coasts. They are the hawksbill, leatherback, loggerhead, olive ridley, and green.

Sea turtles are easiest to find in mating season on the islands and coasts of Bocas del Toro in the Caribbean (roughly March–October, with most activity in the later months) and on Isla Cañas in the Pacific (most numerous September–November). Nesting season varies

COURTESY OF CLEA EFHIMIADAS

Iguanas are officially protected in Panama.

by species, location, and the mood of the turtles, but dry season is generally the worst time to see them.

The hawksbill and leatherback are the most abundant in Bocas. All five species make their way to Isla Cañas, but by far the most numerous are the olive ridley. Many thousands come to the long island every year, making for a dramatic spectacle at night. The loggerhead rarely, if ever, lays eggs in Panama. (It's a subject of some debate.)

The West Indian manatee can be found in the Panama Canal, most easily seen around the Gatún Yacht Club and, to a lesser extent, the rivers and channels of Bocas del Toro.

The seas are filled with brilliant tropical fish as well as impressive large specimens, including orcas, several species of dolphins, humpback whales, marlins, manta rays, jewfish, moray eels, barracudas, big snappers, and white-tip, hammerhead, tiger, and whale sharks. The biggest creatures are found in the Pacific,

especially around the Islas Perlas, the Golfo de Chiriquí, and the Bahía de Piñas, where dozens of deep-sea fishing records have been set. Small, radiant tropical fish are easiest to find among the coral gardens in the clear waters off the Caribbean islands.

AMPHIBIANS

Of the nearly 200 species of amphibians in Panama, the best loved and studied are the frogs and toads. Bocas del Toro is especially well known for its many different morphs, or forms, of strawberry poison-dart frogs *(Oophaga pumilio,* though until recently classified as *Dendrobates pumilio).* In addition to the distinctive red morphs that give the species its common name, these tiny frogs come in green, yellow, purple, orange, black, white, and multicolor forms, sometimes within a surprisingly small area. Panama is also known for its nearly extinct golden frogs *(Atelopus zeteki),* which are easiest to find in El Valle.

REPTILES

The country's many reptile species contain several that make visitors most nervous about the tropics: venomous snakes. It's unlikely you'll encounter any snakes at all during a hike, and highly unlikely any will bother you if you don't bother them.

That said, one of the country's most venomous snakes is also one of the most prolific: the fer-de-lance *(Bothrops asper),* a pit viper more commonly known in Panama as an *equis* (X, for the diamond or X-pattern on its brown skin) or a *terciopelo* (which means velvet). A full-grown adult can be more than 2 meters long. The females give birth to up to 50 young at a time, which are born venomous and can actually be more deadly than an adult because they have not learned to regulate their venom. Fer-de-lance can be aggressive, especially during mating season.

Another forbidding creature is the bushmaster *(Lachesis acrochorda, Lachesis muta,* and *Lachesis stenophrys),* the world's largest viper and the largest venomous snake in the western hemisphere. Known locally as a *verrugosa* (the warty one), it can grow up to three meters long, but is much more rarely encountered. That's a good thing, since its bite has a high fatality rate. The eyelash palm pit viper *(Bothriechis schlegelli)* comes in an assortment of brilliant colors. It's quite beautiful and sinister-looking at the same time (a snake fancier in Panama once described its visage as "unmasked malice in pure form"). Panama also has several species of coral snake. Assume any coral snake you encounter is dangerous—the rhymes used to distinguish venomous from nonvenomous corals in the United States do not work in Panama. Other notable venomous snakes include jumping pit vipers *(Atropoides nummifer* and *Atropoides picadori),* known locally as *mano de piedra* (hand of stone) and *patoca.* The yellow-bellied sea snake *(Pelamus platorus)* is commonly known as the Pacific sea snake since they only occur in the Pacific and Indian Oceans (the risk of it spreading to the Atlantic was an argument against building a sea-level canal). Its venom is deadly, but it is not aggressive and is rarely encountered.

Nonvenomous but potentially dangerous snakes include the boa constrictor, which averages a little under two meters long and can bite if provoked. There are also plenty of harmless snakes, including a variety of vine snakes.

Caimans *(Caiman crocodilus)* are, despite their scientific name, a kind of alligator found in great abundance in some of Panama's rivers. They're easy to spot in Gamboa. They are generally small and rather placid, though some can grow to be about 2.5 meters long. There have been reports of the far larger American crocodile *(Crocodylus acutus)* in the waters of the Panama Canal, especially around Gamboa, though this endangered species can be hard to find. It spends most of its time in estuaries on the Pacific side of the isthmus. On a recent trip to the Darién, I encountered an enormous one on a sandbank on the Río Tuira.

Green iguanas are a protected species in Panama, but they are sometimes still hunted as food. Efforts are being made to reintroduce iguanas in various parts of the country.

INSECTS, ARACHNIDS, AND OTHER SMALL CREATURES

Visitors will most certainly have some encounters with insects, but many parts of Panama are not nearly as buggy as one might think. The mosquito population, for instance, is strictly controlled because of the risk of disease.

But the variety of insects found on the isthmus is staggering. It's estimated there are at least 10,000 species of beetles alone.

Most visitors would just as soon not encounter some of these insects, such as chiggers, bullet and army ants, giant cockroaches, Africanized bees, and stinging centipedes, not to mention the vast array of impressive arachnids, which include such creepy-crawlies as scorpions, tarantulas, and the stunning golden

COURTESY OF THE COFFEE ESTATE INN

giant moth, Boquete

orb spider. But Panama is home to plenty of less-intimidating little creatures, such as 16,000 species of butterflies. One of the most spectacular of these is the huge and luminous blue morpho, which can often be seen floating slowly through the forest canopy.

Environmental Issues

Environmental destruction in the tropics is a terrible, disheartening thing to witness—and there's plenty of it going on in Panama. Panama and its friends woke up to the problem toward the end of the 20th century and took several encouraging steps, including the creation of new protected areas, the introduction of environmental protection laws, and the establishment of environmental nonprofits. However, new roads, real-estate developments, mining operations, and the usual ranches and farms are pushing ever farther into pristine countryside.

Government and nonprofit environmental watchdog agencies are often either toothless or end up accused of rubber-stamping destructive projects. However, while it's still far too common to see citizens trash their own country, there are also people out there cleaning up the mess—or at least refusing to add to it. It may have limited resources and often lacks the power to create real, lasting change, but there is now a fledgling environmental movement in Panama, a claim that would have been hard to make 20 years ago.

DEFORESTATION

About 40 percent of the Republic of Panama was still covered by primary forest at the beginning of the 21st century. That's the good news.

The bad news is that 50 years ago, the figure

was 70 percent. In other words, in the last half of the 20th century Panama lost nearly half its remaining primary forests—about 2.2 million hectares (5.4 million acres) of wild, species-rich nature wiped out.

Even more disturbing, the trend continues in an era of increased environmental awareness. Though estimates vary, deforestation is believed to claim up to 50,000 hectares (123,500 acres) of forest a year. That's a loss of more than one percent each year.

These forests have mostly been converted into farms and cattle ranches or paved over to make way for cities and towns. There is intense pressure on the remaining forests from subsistence farmers, ranchers, and large commercial interests. They have almost completely deforested the heartland provinces of Los Santos and Herrera on the Azuero Peninsula, as well as the Pacific slopes of western and central Panama. Eventually this land becomes useless and barren—there is even an artificially made desert on the Azuero Peninsula. This has driven people north to the Caribbean slopes and east and west to forests that were once nearly inaccessible.

Whenever a road enters a forest, the forest begins to disappear. So-called *colonos* (colonists)—slash-and-burn farmers in need of new land—follow the road. So do timber interests in search of magnificent old-growth giants. Once the forest cover is gone, the soil erodes easily under Panama's incredible downpours. This is worsened by the fact that nearly 78 percent of Panama's land is mountainous, with a high potential for erosion. The soil is generally of poor quality in any case—nearly all the nutrients in a tropical forest are contained in the trees themselves, not the soil—and is quickly overexploited, leading to the need for more land and thus more deforestation. Within just a few years the soil is exhausted, and ranchers bring in cattle to graze on what is now sparse pastureland. The farmers, loggers, and ranchers move farther into the forest, and the cycle continues.

Deforestation is proceeding at a particularly alarming rate in the Darién, Bocas del Toro, Colón province, and the new Ngöbe-Buglé *comarca* (reservation), all of which are rich in biodiversity and primary forests. Even the Guna, who traditionally have been successful in keeping invaders off their land, have in recent years protested the incursion of *colonos* onto their mainland reservations in the Darién.

While much of the deforestation is driven by the needs of impoverished subsistence farmers, Panamanian and multinational commercial interests have also done substantial damage to the environment. Banana, coffee, and sugarcane plantations, for instance, wiped out forests and contaminated rivers with pesticides and other kinds of chemical runoff. The government continues to grant gold- and copper-mining concessions to corporations in the heart of important ecosystems. And large hydroelectric dams that flood forests, disrupt rivers, and displace indigenous people are being built.

To cite just one example, a few years back Panama granted concessions for four large hydroelectric dams—three on the Río Changuinola and one on the Río Bonyic, a tributary to the Río Teribe—in the buffer zone for Parque Internacional La Amistad (PILA) in western Panama. PILA is a World Heritage Site and one of the most important protected areas in the Americas. If these dams are built, the destructive impact on the park's biodiversity and watershed, and the indigenous peoples who live near the park, will be profound. It is likely to threaten the very existence of the Naso people.

Some efforts have been made in the last two decades to reforest parts of Panama where the soil has not become too degraded. Tax incentives have helped turn tree planting into a popular get-rich-quick scheme throughout the country.

Critics, including Panama's own environmental protection agency, point out that the policy has several flaws. The one most frequently cited is that about two-thirds of the trees planted so far are teak, a nonnative species that Panama's birds, animals, and other flora and fauna seem to have little use for. Teak is most often grown in plantations instead of being planted alongside native species, creating monocultures that do little for the local environment and, according to some, actually degrade it further. There have even been reports of species-rich native forest being illegally cleared to make way for teak plantations.

By the beginning of the 21st century, a total of 46,000 hectares (114,000 acres) of land had been reforested, less than is lost every year through deforestation.

The difference between the still-intact Caribbean and heavily deforested Pacific slopes is startling, especially when seen from the air. But deforestation is creeping toward the Caribbean as well. New roads and even open-pit mines are being built right in the heart of it. The loss or fragmentation of these last forests, which some see as all but inevitable unless immediate steps are taken, will have profound, far-reaching effects. Panama is a vital part of the Mesoamerican Biological Corridor that links the ecosystems of North and South America. Consider birds alone: 122 migratory bird species regularly pass through Panama. What happens to them if the biological corridor disappears?

WATER RESOURCES

Water pollution and the shrinking of Panama's watersheds are also serious problems. Raw sewage and industrial waste are dumped directly into the Bahía de Panamá (Panama Bay), for instance, turning parts of what was once a tremendously vital body of water into toxic zones. Some older folks still remember swimming in Panama Bay right across the street from bustling Panama City. Now doing so is a serious health risk. Fishing in the bay has long been banned. At low tide, the smell wafting off the bay can be overpowering. After decades of discussion, a plan to treat sewage and clean up the bay was finally approved in 2006. The project is expected to cost at least US$350 million, and will take years.

The most remote, untouched islands and beaches of Panama sometimes have a ring of trash on the shores, carried there by currents that pass near cities and towns where garbage is dumped indiscriminately. Pollution and deliberate destruction are also decimating coral reefs, and overfishing is doing even more damage to the biodiversity of the seas.

Mangroves are a vital and fragile component of marine ecosystems, and they help prevent coastal erosion. Panama has the most extensive mangrove forests in Central America. But in the last three decades, Panama lost well over half its mangroves, which were cut down to make way for construction projects, resorts, cattle ranches, shrimp farms, and the like. Mangroves have also been lost through pollution.

The Panama Canal watershed is the most important in Panama. It supplies the water needed to run the Panama Canal and provides drinking water to the greater metropolitan areas of Panama City and Colón, where most of the country's people live. Slash-and-burn agriculture, urbanization, and pollution have done considerable damage to the watershed, diminishing the quantity and quality of its fresh water.

The purity of Panama's drinking water, a legacy of the Panama Canal Company's strict hygiene standards, has long been a source of pride. One can turn on a tap almost anywhere in the country and be sure the water is safe to drink. However, studies have concluded that if immediate steps aren't taken to curtail pollution, city dwellers may soon find themselves forced to drink bottled water.

AIR QUALITY

Those who've traveled extensively in the developing world will not be overwhelmed by air pollution even in Panama's most congested urban areas. But this problem is growing, particularly as more and more cars clog Panama's roads. Parts of Panama City register well above acceptable limits for airborne toxins. In the past, strong winds kept Panama City's air relatively fresh. In recent years, however, a brown haze hangs over the city more and more often.

PARKS AND PROTECTED AREAS

Panama has set aside 76 protected areas covering nearly two million hectares (close to five million acres) of land, or about 25 percent of Panama's total area, and a substantial portion of its territorial waters. Most of these protected areas are part of an extensive system of 13 national parks and marine parks and one international park, the giant Parque Internacional La Amistad (PILA) that extends over the border into Costa Rica. There are numerous wildlife refuges, buffer forests, protected wetlands, and

© WILLIAM FRIAR

sea turtle eggs being sold illegally along the main road near Chitré

so on. There are also laws on the books to protect endangered or threatened animals.

The protected areas are a relatively new phenomenon. The first national park, Parque Nacional Altos de Campana, was set aside in 1966, and all the others have been created just in the last 25 years. The parks and other protected areas are managed by the Autoridad Nacional del Ambiente (ANAM), which translates as National Environmental Authority.

As anyone who travels extensively in Panama's national parks will soon discover, just being named a protected area does not confer much protection. Illegal hunting, fishing, logging, and even farming continue in many of the protected areas.

All the parks have at least rudimentary ranger stations, but few have much in the way of visitors' facilities or developed trails. Large sections of some parks, notably the Caribbean slope of PILA and almost all of Parque Nacional Cerro Hoya, are almost inaccessible, which is the main reason they're still intact.

ANAM has only a couple hundred workers spread throughout the entire system of protected areas; there's an average of about one employee for every 7,000 hectares. Sometimes they're spread far more thinly than that: There are only a handful of rangers at two rustic ranger stations to guard the entire 579,000 hectares of Parque Nacional Darién. A third of the protected areas do not have a single ranger assigned to them.

Anyone who witnesses poaching, the sale or captivity of endangered species, habitat destruction, or other kinds of illegal environmental damage can report it to ANAM's hotline (tel. 500-0855, ext. 1111). These *denuncias* can also be made online (www.anam.gob.pa/denuncia_web/default.asp).

CONSERVATION GROUPS

Panama's largest conservation group is the nonprofit **Asociación Nacional para la Conservación de la Naturaleza** (National

Association for the Conservation of Nature, tel. 314-0052, www.ancon.org), or ANCON. Since its founding in 1985, it has played an important role in Panama's attempts to protect its environment by taking on such basic but critical projects as demarcating park boundaries and training park rangers. ANCON does have its critics, who sometimes accuse it of giving a seal of approval to big development projects that are destructive to the environment.

ANCON owns the country's largest private nature reserve, the 65,000-hectare Punta Patiño Reserve on the Darién coast. Its other holdings include Isla San Telmo, in the Archipiélago de las Perlas, which protects endangered moist premontane forest and is a sanctuary for brown pelicans and other animals. It also owns several nature lodges around the country that are managed by Ancon Expeditions, a private for-profit organization that spun off as a separate entity. ANCON welcomes foreign volunteers to its projects.

The U.S.-based Nature Conservancy works with local organizations on several projects in Panama. For more information contact the **Nature Conservancy** (4245 N. Fairfax Dr., Arlington, VA 22203-1606, tel. 800/628-6860, http://nature.org).

The prestigious **Smithsonian Tropical Research Institute** (STRI, www.stri. org) is based in Panama. STRI is one of the leading centers for the study of tropical animals, plants, marine life, evolution, conservation, and much more.

The **Sociedad Audubon de Panamá** (Panama Audubon Society, tel. 232-5977, www.panamaaudubon.org) hosts regular bird-watching tours, and nonmembers are invited to come along. The society is also a good source of information on nature hikes and backcountry places to stay, and some of its members are freelance guides.

History

There is hardly another place in the world, as a Panama historian once pointed out, where so much has happened yet left so little trace behind. The jungle swallowed up whole civilizations, and grave robbers made away with the crumbs.

But some of the earliest evidence of human habitation in the Americas has been found in Panama. Remarkably advanced cultures flourished millennia after that. And since Spanish explorers discovered the isthmus, it has played an important role in determining the shape of the modern world. Over the last 500 years, Panama helped establish Spain and the United States as great world powers, nearly bankrupted France, and forced Scotland to give up its sovereignty and become part of the United Kingdom.

ANCIENT HISTORY

Archaeologists estimate that humans have lived on the isthmus of Panama for 12,000 years, possibly longer. No massive structures, such as

the pyramids found elsewhere in the Americas, have been discovered, and knowledge of the ancient inhabitants of Panama is sketchy. Many of the archaeological sites that have been uncovered have been damaged by the elements, looters, and amateur excavations. But the surviving indigenous peoples of western Panama still tell intriguing if fanciful tales of lost cities in little-known and nearly inaccessible mountain forests—so who knows what may turn up one day? Archaeology in Panama is still in many ways in its infancy.

The earliest evidence of human habitation found to date is Clovis-type arrowheads found near what is now Lago Alajuela (Madden Lake) in the Panama Canal. Archaeologists dated them to about 9000 B.C. Agriculture appears on the Pacific coast of central Panama at around 5000 B.C. Ceramics appear around 3000 B.C. A particularly rich site was Monagrillo, on the

There may have been as many as two million indigenous Panamanians when the Spanish arrived.

Azuero Peninsula, where archaeologists uncovered large numbers of decorated ceramics dating from at least 2500 B.C., the oldest in Central America and among the oldest known in the Americas.

Most of the archaeological treasures dug up in Panama are far more recent. The roots of the Barriles culture of western Panama are believed to go back to at least 700 B.C., but the culture reached its zenith between about A.D. 400 and A.D. 600, when the eruption of Volcán Barú dispersed it. Intriguing, mysterious stone sculptures have been dug up that depict what appear to be chiefs or priests being carried piggyback by other men, as well as an elaborate and oversize metate (stone used to grind corn) that may have been used for sacrifices. Some of these are on display at Panama City's anthropology museum, Museo Antropológico Reina Torres de Araúz.

But the bulk of the evidence of advanced civilizations, at least so far, is found in central Panama. One of the most famous pre-Columbian archaeological sites in the Americas, Sitio Conte, was found between the Río Grande and Río Coclé near the town of Penonomé.

The site was a cemetery used for hundreds of years, approximately A.D. 750–950. It was discovered when the Río Grande changed its course in the early 20th century and washed gold ornaments and pottery from the riverbanks. Excavated by scientists from Harvard in the 1930s, most of its treasures are scattered among museums in the United States and Europe. It's considered the richest pre-Columbian site ever discovered in Central America. About 60 graves, more than 1,000 gold ornaments, and literally tons of pottery and carved stone were dug up there. One tomb, apparently that of a great leader buried around A.D. 750, contained about half the gold found at the site, as well as the remains of 22 followers. Nothing is left at the site today, which is on a private farm and cattle ranch and is not open to the public.

Another important archaeological site that raises more questions than it answers is Parque Arqueológico del Caño, on the outskirts of the town of Natá, not far from Sitio Conte. It contained a cemetery and a large circular field marked off by carved stone columns in the shape of animal and human figures. Some of these statues are six meters high, and they may have been used to demarcate a ceremonial ground or playing field. Unfortunately, nearly all these figures were removed in the 1920s by an American adventurer and taken to museums in the United States. Only their pedestals remain. The site dates from about A.D. 800–1100.

Mysterious petroglyphs carved into boulders have been found near streams and rivers at dozens of sites around the country, including remote forests and islands. They consist mainly of abstract designs, especially spirals and squiggles, as well as crude animal and human figures. No one knows their purpose or when they were carved, but archaeologists have speculated they could be anything from ceremonial or sacrificial sites to "no trespassing" warnings. Wishful thinkers speculate they're maps to buried treasure awaiting someone clever enough to crack the code.

THE SPANISH CONQUEST

The arrival of the Spanish in 1501 spelled the end of the indigenous peoples' dominion over the isthmus and the beginning of the European conquest. The first to come here was an explorer named Rodrigo de Bastidas, who sailed along the Caribbean coast from the Darién at least as far west as Nombre de Dios. His crew included a sailor by the name of Vasco Núñez de Balboa; 12 years later Balboa would become the first European to hack his way through the Darién and lay eyes on the "Southern Sea," the Pacific Ocean.

Christopher Columbus came to the isthmus during his fourth and final voyage to the New World, which left Spain on May 11, 1502. His most glorious days behind him, Columbus had the use of four dilapidated ships to explore the Caribbean coastline that Bastidas had not seen, from Bocas del Toro in the far west of the isthmus to Nombre de Dios in the east. In Bocas he came across indigenous people wearing gold jewelry, a discovery that excited his crew far more than the quest for a passage to Asia.

During the voyage, Columbus's ships anchored near the mouth of the Río Belén, on the border between the modern-day provinces of Colón and Veraguas. It was here, on Epiphany, January 6, 1503, that Columbus established the first European settlement on the isthmus, Santa María de Belén. Almost immediately, however, battles with the indigenous population, led by a chief known to history only as "the Quibián," brought this first Spanish foothold in Panama to a bloody end. Columbus sailed back to Jamaica with two barely seaworthy ships, having been forced to abandon the other two: the *Gallega* at the mouth of the Belén and the *Vizcaina* somewhere near Portobelo.

Balboa and the Discovery of the Pacific

Balboa's career as a great explorer began inauspiciously. Though he was among the first Europeans to explore Panama, when he was a crew member on Bastidas's voyage of discovery in 1501, he spent the next eight years in Hispaniola (modern-day Haiti and the Dominican Republic) getting into financial trouble. Determined to change his fortunes, he stowed away on a ship bound for the isthmus, slipping past his creditors by hiding in a cask that was loaded onto the ship. When he was discovered, the angry captain almost left him marooned on a desert island, but he soon made himself indispensable because of his knowledge of the isthmus.

When the early settlements began to fall apart, Balboa suggested a new colony be founded at a place in the Darién he remembered from his early days with Bastidas. This became Santa María de la Antigua del Darién, or Antigua, the first lasting European settlement. It was established in 1510 and eventually became the first capital of Castilla del Oro.

Balboa proved to be popular with the men and quickly moved into a position of power. He became the administrative head of Antigua and acting governor of Castilla del Oro, subjugating any indigenous peoples who opposed him. Though his methods were vicious, Balboa became known for his strategy of making peace with the indigenous peoples who submitted to him. By the standards of his day, he was considered fair and merciful, particularly compared to his murderous contemporaries and successors.

Told by native allies of a sea to the south along whose coast were cities of gold, Balboa set out from Antigua on September 1, 1513, with 190 of his men, an estimated (and probably exaggerated) 1,000 indigenous peoples, and a pack of dogs. Among his men was Francisco Pizarro. Along the way they had to fight both the hardships of the jungle and indigenous peoples on whose land they were trespassing. At 10 A.M. on September 25, Balboa told the 67 of his men who had survived the brutal trek to wait while he climbed one last hill and became the first European to lay eyes on the "Southern Sea"—the Pacific Ocean. When he finally made it down to the shore four days later, he found himself on the edge of a large gulf off the Pacific coast of the Darién that he named the Golfo de San Miguel. He waded out into the water in full armor and promptly claimed the entire sea and all the lands touching it for the Spanish crown, no doubt the biggest land grab in history.

The Founding of Panama City

Meanwhile, King Ferdinand of Spain had appointed a new governor of the isthmus, Pedro Arias de Ávila, better known as Pedrarias. On the isthmus, he had an even more fitting designation: Furor Domini (the wrath of God). He saw the popular and resourceful Balboa

as a rival and had him beheaded for treason in January 1519 at Aclá, a settlement on the Caribbean coast of the Darién.

Pedrarias decided to move the capital from Antigua to the site of a fishing village called Panama, on the central Pacific coast of the isthmus. He founded Panama City, the first European settlement on the Pacific coast of the Americas, on August 15, 1519. He also proceeded to slaughter the indigenous inhabitants of the isthmus.

His men met fierce resistance and sometimes suffered losses at the hands of warriors led by rulers impressive enough to have made it into Spanish records, such as París and Urracá. It was, of course, just a matter of time before the Spanish prevailed. París, for instance, died of natural causes, but he was hounded even in death: The Spaniards looted his grave of its gold. Urracá made peace with the Spaniards, but his people have long since vanished and his only lasting legacy is his profile on Panama's one-centavo coin.

Panama was home to large, diverse populations of indigenous peoples when the Spanish arrived at the turn of the 16th century. Some put the population of the isthmus at that time at two million or even higher, two-thirds the modern-day population. The Spanish decimated these original inhabitants through war and disease. Today only eight groups of indigenous peoples remain, and three of these are barely hanging on.

COLONIAL ERA

During the colonial period, Panama's greatest importance to Spain was as a transshipment point for the silver, gold, pearls, and other treasures plundered from South America once the conquest spread to include the Incan Empire. These riches were taken to Panama City, and then had to be carried over to the Caribbean coast, where Spanish ships transported them to Europe. They were carried across the isthmus by two main routes, both of which had their Pacific terminus at Panama City and were established by the Spanish in the early 16th century.

The Camino Real and the Camino de Cruces

The first route was the Camino Real, an overland route that linked Panama City with Nombre de Dios (and with Portobelo, when Nombre de Dios was abandoned in 1597). Its name, which translates to "royal road," was rather regal for what was essentially a mule trail, only part of which was paved. It was brutal and muddy, and where it crossed over the foothills, it grew so steep that travelers had to climb through the muck on their hands and knees.

The second was the Camino de Cruces, known in English as Las Cruces Trail. This was an overland route from Panama City to Venta de Cruces, a village on the Río Chagres about a third of the way across the isthmus. The trail was wider than a person is tall during the Spanish colonial era, and it was paved with flat stones. From Venta de Cruces, it became a water route, with cargo moved by boat or barge up and down the Chagres, which flows into the Caribbean. Fuerte San Lorenzo was built at the mouth of the Chagres to defend it. Because this route was considerably farther west than the Camino Real, goods had to be transported by sea between the mouth of the Chagres and Nombre de Dios or Portobelo to the east. The whole trip took 1–2 weeks each way.

Though an easier and cheaper route, especially for shipping heavy loads, the Camino de Cruces was more vulnerable to pirate attack than the Camino Real, which had the natural protection of the jungle for much of its length.

The Spanish established the Camino de Cruces in 1527, and it was still being used up until the mid-19th century. The 49ers used it in their own hunt for treasure, as they rushed to the goldfields of California. It was finally abandoned with the building of the Panama Railroad in the 1850s. The village of Venta de Cruces is now at the bottom of the Panama Canal, but part of the Camino de Cruces is still intact and can be walked. The Camino Real was abandoned in 1826.

Gold gets all the attention in romantic tales of Caribbean pirates and Spanish galleons, but silver made up the bulk of the riches Spain looted from South America, mostly from the mines of Peru. By the end of the 17th century, Spain had tripled the amount of silver in circulation throughout the world. An estimated 60 percent of it came through Portobelo alone.

Trade Fairs

This silver, and other treasures from the New World, were traded at massive fairs held at Nombre de Dios and Portobelo. Spanish merchants from Europe and South America converged at the fairs for several weeks each year, more or less, during which they exchanged treasure for European finished goods, which included everything from nails to fine cloth. Merchant ships heading across the Atlantic to and from Spain were escorted by the Spanish navy.

The first organized fair was held in 1537. At their peak, the fairs surpassed those held anywhere else in the world. Bars of silver were stacked high in the streets, but the presence of the heavily armed Spanish fleet kept pirates away.

Not so between fairs. Despite its great importance to the Spanish Empire, the isthmus was neglected and never adequately defended against pirates. Panama was always treated as a notch below, say, Peru, a wealthy and powerful viceroyalty. Panama had the lower administrative rank of *audencia* and was governed by a president.

The trade fairs and treasure shipments marked the first time Panama became a crucial link in world commerce, a role it has continued to play over the years—as a route for the 49ers, as the site of the Panama Canal, and as an international banking capital. One can even see the Colón Free Zone, along the coast where the ruins of the Spanish fortifications still stand, as a kind of descendant of the Spanish trade fairs.

JOHAN MORGAN.
geboren in de Provincie van s' illes in Engeland.
Generaal van de Roovers or Jamaica.

Henry Morgan sacked Panama City in 1671.

After 1628, these fairs diminished in importance along with the declining fortunes of the Spanish Empire. They were finally abandoned in 1739.

Elizabethan Pirates and Privateers

Lack of funds, poor planning, and procrastination have been blamed for the fact that Panama was constantly sacked and looted throughout the Spanish era.

Nombre de Dios was always a bad choice for a port—the harbor was shallow and exposed, and it would have been hard to defend even if it had had better fortifications. Sir Francis Drake attacked it in 1572 and would likely have sacked it then if he had not been wounded during the conflict. Still, he and his men went on to ambush a mule train on the Camino Real loaded down with so many tons of silver they couldn't carry it away. They buried it instead and made off with some gold. The Spanish dug up the silver before Drake could return for it.

Drake's many exploits on the isthmus as a young adventurer during this period read like something straight out of *Treasure Island*. As historians have pointed out, one gets a sense he had an enormously good time tweaking the Spanish. He had help in his adventures from *cimarrones,* escaped African slaves who lived in hidden towns in the jungle and also delighted in harrying their former Spanish masters.

Drake returned to the isthmus years later for more adventures, but he fell sick and died on January 28, 1596, and was buried at sea in a lead-lined coffin near Portobelo. Expeditions have searched for that coffin, but it has never been found.

The Spanish abandoned Nombre de Dios and moved west to Portobelo in 1597, before the fortifications were even completed. Portobelo was a far better location for an important port town. The harbor was long and narrow, surrounded by hills. The Spanish fortified it heavily, but the design was poor from the beginning and constant redesigns over the years didn't seem to help matters much.

Portobelo was barely completed by the time the English pirate William Parker attacked and looted it in 1601. It was sacked and rebuilt several times over the next 200 years.

Morgan and the Sacking of Panama City

The Welsh buccaneer Henry Morgan took Portobelo and held it for ransom in 1668. He did so by landing his troops at night some distance from Portobelo and attacking the fortifications by land. The defenders' cannons, pointing out to sea, were useless. Still, it was a vicious battle. At one point, Morgan's men used Spanish priests and nuns as human shields, forcing them to erect scaling ladders against the fort walls. The Spanish governor ordered the poor hostages shot down. When Morgan captured the city, he tortured its inhabitants if they refused to reveal where they had hidden their goods. The Spanish finally paid him a ransom of 100,000 pieces of eight to get him to leave.

As this tale suggests, the buccaneers of the 17th century earned a reputation as a far crueler, bloodier, and less dashing lot than the Elizabethan privateers of the previous century.

Morgan was determined to sack and loot Panama City, and he knew where to start his raid. There was another Caribbean fort, Castillo de San Lorenzo el Real, better known today as Fuerte San Lorenzo. It was built near the mouth of the Río Chagres. An imposing cliff there overlooks the rivermouth and the sea, the perfect place for a fortress. Oddly, however, the fort was made of wood and its buildings had thatched roofs. As bizarre as it sounds, even the fort's gunpowder was stored in a thatched hut. When Morgan invaded the isthmus, he was able to sack and destroy San Lorenzo, even though the Spanish knew he was coming, by shooting flaming arrows over the walls. He then proceeded up the Chagres by canoe and sacked Panama City. The city was burned to the ground—whether by Morgan or the Spanish is still a matter of debate—and later rebuilt at a more defensible location eight kilometers farther west. This second Panama City still stands, as a historical part of modern-day Panama City known as Casco Viejo or Casco Antiguo.

The Scottish Colony

One of the stranger and more tragic episodes during this period was the doomed Scottish colony of New Edinburgh. It was the dream of an entrepreneur named William Paterson, who convinced the Company of Scotland, an overseas trading company created by the Scottish parliament, to invest hundreds of thousands of pounds in his scheme to establish a colony on the Caribbean coast of the Darién. He argued the colony would be ideally situated to become a trading center between Europe and Asia and would help transform Scotland's struggling economy. In July of 1698, Paterson and 1,200 colonists set sail for the Darién. Those who survived the crossing arrived in the Darién on November 2. They built a fort, Fort Saint Andrew, on a long, narrow bay they named Calidonia, a name it retains to this day. The colonists were completely unprepared for life in the tropical rainforest, and the venture was a debacle. The first attempt at settlement was abandoned in less than a year, and only a third of the colonists made it back to Scotland. Attempts were tried to reestablish the colony, but incompetence, infighting, battles with the Spanish, opposition from the English, shipwrecks, and disease brought an end to New Edinburgh by 1700. Scotland, deeply in debt, was forced in 1707 to give up dreams of independence and empire, and joined England to form Great Britain.

THE TUMULTUOUS 19TH CENTURY

With the decline of the Spanish Empire and the drying up of the treasures of the Incan Empire, Panama became a colonial backwater. When independence movements swept through Latin America, Panama eventually got caught up in the tide.

Independence from Spain

On November 10, 1821, residents of the little town of La Villa de Los Santos on the Azuero Peninsula wrote a letter to Simón Bolívar complaining of mistreatment by the Spanish governor and asking for his help. This Primer Grito de la Independencia (First Cry for Independence) is commemorated as a national holiday in Panama.

This was followed 18 days later by a meeting in Panama City in which Panama broke away from Spain and joined Colombia in an uneasy union that for a while included Venezuela and Ecuador. November 28 is celebrated in Panama today as the first of several steps toward independence.

In 1826, Bolívar called a congress, held in what is now the Casco Viejo section of Panama City, in an attempt to create a union of Latin American republics. The Congress of Panama took place June 22–July 15. Though Bolívar himself did not attend and the talks ended in failure, the attempt is still considered an important moment in Latin American history.

The isthmus of Panama was in turmoil through much of the 19th century. It attempted three times between 1831 and 1841 to break away from Colombia, but each time it failed.

The Prestán Uprising

One of the bloodiest incidents of the 19th century in Panama was the so-called Prestán Uprising of 1885. Depending on whom one chooses to believe, Pedro Prestán was either a revolutionary martyred in the cause of freedom or a rabble-rousing mulatto with an irrational hatred of foreigners, especially white ones. When a former president of the department of Panama, Rafael Aizpuru, tried to seize power in Panama City, Colombian troops were dispatched to the city from the Caribbean side of the isthmus, leaving the city of Colón largely undefended. Prestán took advantage of this, reportedly leading a band of machete-wielding men in a looting spree along Front Street. He then took hostages, whom he threatened to kill if the U.S. warship *Galena,* at port in Colón, landed troops. He also demanded he be given a shipment of arms that had been smuggled in by steamer and was waiting for him in the harbor.

The commander of the *Galena* had been ordered not to interfere in Panama's domestic affairs unless the Panama Railroad was threatened, which so far it hadn't. The American consul, one of Prestán's hostages, promised to turn over the weapons. Prestán released the hostages, but the *Galena* towed the steamer with the cargo of guns away from shore before Prestán could get access to them.

On March 31, Colombian troops returned from Panama City and battled Prestán's men at Monkey Hill, just outside the city. Routed, Prestán allegedly set fire to Colón as his men retreated. The city, which was built almost entirely of wood, burned to the ground, leaving at least 18 dead and thousands homeless. The Colombian troops rounded up dozens of Prestán's men and executed them. Prestán himself was tried and hanged in Colón, above the railroad tracks. Aizpuru, whose own failed rebellion in Panama City left dozens dead, was sentenced to 10 years in exile.

The War of a Thousand Days

The isthmus was also the scene of major battles in the War of a Thousand Days (1899–1902), a Colombian civil war fought between the Liberal and Conservative parties.

One of the most important of these was the battle of La Vieja Negra, fought outside the city of David in western Panama on March 31, 1900. Liberals who had taken refuge in Nicaragua from the ruling Conservative party invaded Panama from the west, captured David, and defeated better-trained and equipped Conservative forces at La Vieja Negra, after which they marched on Panama City and were defeated. A peace treaty was signed on July 26, 1900, but was quickly broken. Bloody battles continued to flare up around the isthmus. Colombia called on the United States to intervene, and the war finally came to an end with the signing of a peace treaty aboard the warship U.S.S. *Wisconsin* on November 19, 1902.

Though the Liberals lost the war, Panama considers the leaders of the Liberal forces to be heroes and founding fathers of the country. These include Belisario Porras, the civilian head of the isthmian forces, and Victoriano Lorenzo, who commanded an army of his fellow *cholos* (people of indigenous descent but Latino culture) that played a key role in many of the battles. Porras would later serve as president three times when Panama finally became an independent country. Although the peace treaty was supposed to grant the combatants amnesty, Lorenzo was executed by firing squad on May 15, 1903, which Panama remembers as one of the darker days in its history.

GOLD RUSH DAYS

The California gold rush brought Panama back onto the world stage in another quest for treasure. The fastest way to get to the goldfields was to cross at Panama, but it was hardly the easiest. Thousands made their way by foot or mule over the 50 miles of the isthmus by way of the muddy, brutal Camino de Cruces, the same trail used by the Spanish during their own bout of gold fever. Untold others died attempting it, of cholera, dysentery, yellow fever, malaria, and the other dangers that made the Panama route notorious.

If a railway could be built across the isthmus, it would make the crossing faster and far safer for the 49ers who, not incidentally, would be willing to pay a small fortune for the privilege. A forward-thinking U.S. merchant named William Henry Aspinwall negotiated a treaty with Nueva Granada to build just such a railway shortly before the California gold rush began.

Though only 47.5 miles long, the railroad was an incredibly costly undertaking, both in dollars and lives. It was said that every railroad tie represented one worker dead from disease. That's a wild exaggeration, but thousands did die building the little railroad through the jungle. In 1852, a cholera epidemic struck so quickly that workers died on the tracks, to be eaten by ants and land crabs. So many died that the Panama Railroad Company started a lucrative side business shipping cadavers preserved in barrels to medical schools and hospitals around the world. Engineers had to contend with the powerful Río Chagres, which could rise 40 feet overnight, and with obstacles such as the seemingly bottomless Black Swamp. When the railroad was completed in 1855, it included 304 bridges and culverts. The company was able to charge US$25 in gold for a one-way trip, a huge sum for the day.

The massive influx of foreigners on the isthmus, some of them rather rough characters, caused some conflicts. The worst incident occurred in April of 1856, when an allegedly drunk train passenger who had just arrived in Panama City grabbed a slice of watermelon from a black vendor and refused to pay for it. This sparked the so-called Watermelon War, a day of rioting that had racial, anti-U.S., and class overtones. It left at least 16 dead, almost all North Americans, and caused extensive damage to railroad property.

THE PANAMA CANAL AND INDEPENDENCE FROM COLOMBIA

For hundreds of years, visionaries had dreamed of building a canal across the isthmus. Even the early Spanish colonists toyed with the idea until King Philip II allegedly declared that if God had wanted a canal joining the oceans, God would have put one there himself.

The French Canal

The French were the first to undertake the challenge, in 1882. The moving force behind the effort was Ferdinand de Lesseps, a charismatic diplomat with no engineering background who was basking in the glory of leading the successful effort to build the Suez Canal. He insisted that building a sea-level canal at Panama would be far easier. After all, Suez was twice as long.

But this was Panama, and a sea-level canal here meant digging through mountains, not sand, and contending with its tropical diseases, fierce heat, torrential rains, and forbidding terrain.

The French failed disastrously. It has been estimated that 20,000 workers died, mostly of disease, during the seven-year French effort. The French canal company ran out of money in 1889, and the ensuing financial crisis nearly bankrupted France.

The U.S. Canal

The United States had long toyed with building its own canal. It bought out the French concession, but clashed with the government of Nueva Granada (i.e., Colombia) over payments and the

testing Gatún Locks, June 11, 1914

granting of rights over the proposed waterway. When negotiations stalled, the United States, under President Theodore Roosevelt, decided to support a small independence movement in Panama spearheaded by a few prominent Panamanians and Panama Railroad officials. In a display of literal "gunboat diplomacy," the United States sent a warship to Panama to intimidate the Colombian forces on the isthmus. On November 3, 1903, Panama declared its independence from Nueva Granada.

It was a remarkably peaceful civil war. Bloodshed was likely averted by a fast-thinking Panama Railroad official. He convinced a Colombian general who had just landed in Colón with his troops that it was only fitting that he and his officers should ride in a special train car ahead of his men, who were left stranded in Colón. When the officers arrived in Panama City, Panama-based Colombian soldiers who had been bought off by the revolutionaries took them prisoner. The only casualty

during the whole conflict was a Chinese shopkeeper, asleep in his bed, who was killed by an errant shell from a Colombian gunboat. A second shell killed a donkey in a slaughterhouse. By November 6, the revolution was over.

The United States immediately signed the controversial Hay–Bunau-Varilla Treaty with the new Panamanian government, which gave America the right to build a canal in Panama. It would become a source of contention for decades to come that no Panamanian signed the treaty. The official signatory for Panama was a Frenchman, Philippe Bunau-Varilla, the former director of and major shareholder in the French canal effort. The revolutionaries had reluctantly agreed to let him negotiate with Washington on their behalf as an "envoy extraordinary." He signed the treaty in New York before the Panamanian delegation even arrived.

The treaty granted the United States control in perpetuity over the canal and a 50-by-10-mile strip of land surrounding it. The United States paid the new country of Panama US$10 million, plus an annual payment of US$250,000. The French canal company received US$40 million for all the equipment, infrastructure, and excavation it left behind, much of which proved useful to the new enterprise.

The U.S. effort was quite different from the French one. Instead of a sea-level ditch, the U.S. plan called for a lock canal that would lift ships over the isthmian landmass. The plan was designed by John Stevens, a brilliant railway engineer, and seen to completion by his successor as chief engineer, George W. Goethals. All work on the canal had to be halted, however, until disease could be controlled. Under the leadership of a forward-looking sanitary officer named Dr. William Gorgas, the U.S. canal effort eliminated yellow fever from Panama, brought malaria and other deadly diseases under control, and introduced clean water and modern sanitation to the isthmus.

The canal was a colossal task. It required an excavation three times as massive as that at Suez. And among other challenges, the builders had to cut right through nine miles of mountains at the Continental Divide, a job overseen by David Gaillard, for whom the resulting Gaillard Cut is named. The lock chambers were among the largest structures ever made by humans. The mighty Río Chagres was contained by the largest earthen dam in history, forming the largest artificially made lake in the world. The canal is still considered one of the most extraordinary engineering feats of all time.

The U.S. canal effort cost US$352 million and took 5,600 lives, most of them West Indians who made up the bulk of the labor force. But the canal opened for business on August 15, 1914, under budget and ahead of schedule.

THE NEW NATION

The first president of the new Republic of Panama was Dr. Manuel Amador Guerrero, an elderly, well-respected medical doctor from a prominent Panamanian family and the leader of the little band of revolutionaries. Panama was a kind of democracy, but leaders inevitably came from the wealthiest families of European descent.

One of the biggest challenges to the new republic was an independence movement among the Gunas of the San Blas Islands. The Gunas declared their independence from Panama in February of 1925 and announced the creation of their own country, the Republic of Tule. A brief war ensued that left about two dozen dead. The United States intervened and presided over a peace treaty between Panama and the Gunas that gave the latter the semiautonomous status they retain to this day. The other indigenous peoples of Panama have slowly gained similar control over their ancestral lands over the years through the establishment of *comarcas* (reservations). Some are still fighting for *comarca* status.

Arnulfo Arias

A figure who loomed large in Panamanian politics through much of the 20th century was Arnulfo Arias Madrid, a Harvard Medical School graduate from a family of provincial farmers. Along with his brother, Harmodio Arias Madrid, he was a leading figure in a group called Acción Comunal that overthrew the president, Florencio Harmodio Arosemena, in a bloody assault on the presidential palace in 1931. (Note: Many of the major figures in Panamanian politics have similar names, including many who are not remotely related.) Arosemena was replaced by Ricardo J. Alfaro, a choice acceptable to Acción Comunal. The following year, Arnulfo's brother was elected president. The United States decided not to intervene in any of this. It was the country's first successful coup.

But it was hardly the last. Arnulfo Arias himself, ironically enough, endured them incessantly. He was elected president of Panama at least four times (voter fraud makes the official outcome in two elections hard to confirm) between 1940 and 1984. Each time he was either deposed or forbidden to take office by the Policía Nacional (National Police) or its successor, the Guardia Nacional (National Guard).

Arnulfo, as he is known in Panama, was a charismatic populist who espoused a vehement brand of nationalism known as *panameñismo*. He was also a fascist sympathizer during World War II who was determined not only to rid the isthmus of North Americans but also of fellow citizens he deemed undesirables. Nevertheless, he was beloved by many of Panama's poor and disenfranchised, who saw him as a counterweight to the power of the oligarchy.

In 1941, at the beginning of his first aborted administration, he introduced a new constitution that replaced the one instituted in 1904. Among other things, it increased the presidential term of office to six years. But it's most notorious for blatantly racist provisions that forbade the immigration of blacks from non-Spanish-speaking countries, as well as Chinese, Indians, and Arabs. It also stripped those already in the country of their citizenship. It was replaced with yet another constitution five years later, after he was overthrown the first time. But Arias is also credited with establishing many of Panama's most important institutions, such as the social security system, and expanding the rights of some of its citizens.

The Rise of the National Guard

The commander of the National Police, José Antonio Remón Cantera, militarized and increased the power of the force and served as kingmaker (and breaker) for several Panamanian presidents before running for president himself. In a strange series of events, he first opposed and then installed Arnulfo Arias as president in 1949, declaring, without presenting evidence, that the election of the year before should have found Arias the victor. Arias's second attempt at wielding power deteriorated rapidly, and demonstrations against him turned so violent he was forced to hole up in the presidential palace with his most loyal supporters. Two officers of the National Police were shot dead on the steps of the palace under mysterious circumstances. The murders were to prove emblematic of the enmity that would exist for the rest of the century between the *arnulfistas* and the National Police, later the National Guard. Arias was removed from power a second time.

Remón decided it was time to become president himself. He was elected in 1952 and began a campaign of social and economic reforms that was cut short in 1955 when he was machine-gunned to death at a horse-racing track on the outskirts of Panama City. All kinds of conspiracy theories have been put forth about who was behind the assassination. One even points the finger at the American mobster "Lucky" Luciano. Panama City's racetrack was renamed in Remón's honor.

EMERGING NATIONALISM

Tensions between Panama and the United States flared up repeatedly through much of the 20th century. Again and again, especially in the early days of the republic, the United States intervened in the domestic affairs of the country. Because of the strategic and economic importance of first the Panama Railroad and then the Panama Canal, the United States insisted on reserving the right to play a hand in the destiny of the isthmus in treaty after treaty.

Tensions occasionally erupted in violence. When the Panamanian national legislature met in 1947 to consider a treaty that would allow the United States to continue to use military bases outside the Canal Zone, 10,000 protesters took to the streets and clashed with Panama's National Police, with deaths on both sides. The legislature rejected the treaty unanimously. Violent anti-U.S. demonstrations flared up again in 1958 and 1959.

The Flag Riots

The most infamous incident, though, was

termed the Flag Riots of 1964. The United States had agreed to fly the Panamanian flag alongside the U.S. one in a few places in the Canal Zone, even though some feared (and others hoped) this would throw U.S. sovereignty over the zone into doubt. In an attempt to avoid controversy, the governor of the Canal Zone decided to take down some flagpoles in the zone altogether. One of these spots was Balboa High School. A group of high school students objected to this, and before the pole could be removed, they raised a U.S. flag themselves. When a group of Panamanian college students heard of this, they organized a march to the high school and attempted to lower the U.S. and raise the Panamanian one. A scuffle broke out, during which the Panamanian students claimed their flag had been torn.

What happened after that will probably forever be a source of passionate debate, depending on one's sympathies and prejudices. What everyone can agree on is that rioting, looting, and destruction followed, mostly along Fourth of July Avenue, which separated Panama City from the Canal Zone. In the end, two dozen people were killed and millions of dollars of property destroyed. The Panamanians who died are officially considered martyrs in Panama, and January 9 is still a national day of mourning in their honor. Fourth of July Avenue was renamed Avenida de los Mártires.

In the wake of this terrible clash, President Lyndon B. Johnson announced that the United States would undertake negotiations with Panama on an entirely new canal treaty.

A NEW TREATY

In 1968 Arnulfo Arias was again elected president. He took office on October 1 and immediately called for the turnover of the canal to Panama and attempted to take control of the National Guard. The second move was a mistake. A military junta deposed him on October 11, and, ironically enough, he fled to the Canal Zone for protection. He had served 11 days in office, his shortest term yet.

Omar Torrijos

After a period of chaos and demonstrations, a National Guard colonel named Omar Torrijos Herrera assumed power. He was himself the subject of an attempted coup by three rival colonels when he took a trip to Mexico early in his rule. When he learned of this, he returned to Panama, rallied supporters in the western city of David, and marched on the capital. He regained power and sent the colonels into exile.

Torrijos had himself promoted to general and became a remarkably popular figure. Though a military dictator, he was also a populist who flirted with socialist ideas—he had a friendly relationship with Fidel Castro—and instituted sweeping social reforms. Though he installed a figurehead president, Demétrios Lakas, everyone knew who was really in charge. In 1972 he introduced yet another new constitution that confirmed him as head of a powerful central government and curtailed civil rights. He ordered the redistribution of land to the campesinos, greatly expanded public health programs, reformed the school system, built roads and bridges in rural areas, and laid the groundwork for Panama's emergence as an international banking center. Some of these changes came at the expense of the oligarchy.

For all these accomplishments, however, corruption and nepotism blossomed under Torrijos, and the bodies of his political enemies are still being dug up around the country.

One of the things that helped ensure Torrijos's popularity was his focus on a new treaty that would turn control of the canal over to Panama. Negotiations began with the Nixon and Ford administrations, but progress was slow until Jimmy Carter took office in 1977. On September 7 of that year, Torrijos met Carter in Washington, D.C., to sign two new Panama Canal treaties. The first called for a gradual turnover of the canal to Panamanian control, to allow the small country time to absorb the massive undertaking. Panama gained complete jurisdiction over the canal and former Canal Zone at noon on December 31, 1999. The second one, the Neutrality Treaty, bound the United States and Panama to guarantee the canal's neutrality in peace or war and allow unimpeded transit of the ships of all nations. The United States reserved the right to act against any perceived threat to the canal, but not otherwise intervene in the domestic affairs of Panama. This second treaty was open-ended and is still in effect, and it continues to be a source of discontent in Panama from time to time. Two-thirds of the Panamanian people voted in favor of the new treaties, a weaker show of support than expected.

To gain support in Washington for the treaties, Torrijos had agreed to begin a process of democratization. He stepped down as the official head of government but retained ultimate authority by holding on to his position as head of the National Guard. He allowed Arnulfo Arias to return to Panama and start rebuilding his political support. The constitution was amended in October 1978 to weaken the power of the executive branch somewhat and increase that of the Asamblea Legislativa, the national legislature. The legislature voted in Aristides Royo, a candidate backed by Torrijos, as president.

The first political party granted official recognition was the Partido Revolucionario Democrático (Democratic Revolutionary Party) or PRD, which was controlled by Torrijos and his supporters and would come to be known as the National Guard's party. National elections were held in 1980. Opposition parties gained some representation in the national legislature, but Torrijos ensured that most seats were reserved for the PRD.

Noriega Takes Power

On July 31, 1981, Torrijos died in a small plane that crashed in the mountains above El Copé in central Panama. The area has since been turned into a national park named in his honor. Rumors that the crash was arranged by one of his political rivals circulated immediately. A period of turmoil followed, with a parade of military figures succeeding each other in power.

By 1983, General Manuel Antonio Noriega had firm control of the National Guard, which he soon renamed the Fuerzas de Defensa de Panamá (Panama Defense Forces), and the country as a whole. Torrijos had spotted Noriega's potential early in his own military career, and when he became dictator he had put Noriega in charge of military intelligence. Despite this long association, some speculated that Noriega was behind the death of Torrijos. The contrast between the two dictators could not have been starker. Torrijos was a handsome, charismatic man who inspired loyalty among his supporters and enacted many popular programs. Noriega's pockmarked face earned him the nickname *cara de piña* (pineapple face), and he ruled through fear.

In the 1984 elections, the Noriega-controlled PRD nominated Nicolás Ardito Barletta Vallarino, a former World Bank vice president with a degree in economics from the University of Chicago. Opposing him was the indefatigable Arnulfo Arias. Barletta was elected president in what was widely agreed to be a fraudulent vote count. The United States decided to recognize him anyway.

But in September 1985 a horrific event occurred that began Noriega's spectacular fall from power. Dr. Hugo Spadafora, a colorful and charismatic Noriega opponent who had been a guerrilla fighter in Africa and a protégé of Torrijos, decided to return to Panama by bus to challenge Noriega's hold on power. He claimed to have information on Noriega's illegal dealings throughout Latin America that would force him from power. He took a bus from the Costa Rican border toward Panama

City on September 13, but he was stopped near the town of Concepción and forced off the bus. He was subsequently tortured and beheaded, his decapitated body later found in a river across the border in Costa Rica. Suspicion immediately fell on Noriega.

The following year, the Pulitzer Prize–winning investigative reporter Seymour Hersh began breaking stories in *The New York Times* that detailed a laundry list of shady dealings by Noriega: that he had long been a CIA asset, that he was deeply involved in drug dealing and money laundering, that he'd rigged the 1984 election, that he did intelligence work for Cuba, that he was implicated in the murder of Spadafora. When the Iran-Contra scandal broke, Noriega emerged as a vital player who was said to have a cozy relationship with Oliver North, CIA director William Casey, and other Iran-Contra figures. He was accused of helping the Contras with everything from shipping arms to planning sabotage operations in Nicaragua. Noriega was proving an increasing embarrassment, first to President Ronald Reagan and then to President George H. W. Bush, whom Noriega had known since Bush's days as CIA director in the 1970s.

Operation Just Cause

A new election was held on May 7, 1989, with a Noriega-backed candidate named Carlos Duque running against Guillermo Endara, a lawyer and protégé of Arnulfo Arias, whose long political career had finally ended the year before, when he died at age 86. Panama always elects two vice presidents, and Endara's running mates were Guillermo "Billy" Ford and Ricardo Arias Calderón.

The election was a sham: votes were bought; eligible voters were turned away from the polls; ballots were destroyed. Jimmy Carter, who had flown to Panama as an election observer, held a press conference at a Panama City hotel and declared, "The government is taking the election by fraud." He said the opposition had won by a margin of three to one.

Endara and his two running mates led a protest march three days later that was attacked by Panama Defense Forces troops and Noriega goons. Demonstrators were blasted with buckshot and tear gas. Endara was knocked unconscious by an attacker wielding a steel pipe, and Arias Calderón and Ford were beaten and shot at. Images of the bloodied candidates were beamed around the world.

By now, some officers of the Panama Defense Forces were becoming nervous at what seemed to be Noriega's increasingly erratic behavior. Major Moises Giroldi decided to mount a coup, with tentative support from a suspicious Washington. On October 3, 1989, Giroldi and his supporters took Noriega hostage at his headquarters, the Comandancia, but hesitation and confusion allowed Noriega time to phone his most loyal troops, who surrounded the Comandancia and engaged in a firefight with the rebels. Noriega prevailed, and the coup plotters were tortured and executed. The Bush administration denied having any involvement with the coup attempt, despite considerable evidence it had encouraged the coup, then declined to give it support at the vital moment.

Periodic violent clashes between the Panama Defense Forces and U.S. military personnel traveling outside the Canal Zone reached a low point when a U.S. Marine Corps lieutenant, Robert Paz, was shot dead in Panama City on December 17. Three days later, on December 20, 1989, President Bush ordered an invasion of Panama, dubbed Operation Just Cause. It left somewhere between 200 and 4,000 civilians dead. The true number may never be known, as it was in the interest of the United States and the subsequent Panamanian government to downplay the number, and of those with other political agendas to inflate it. The hardest-hit area was El Chorrillo, an impoverished neighborhood of wooden tenements and anti-Noriega sentiment that lay right next to the Comandancia. It was swept by a fire that left an untold number dead and thousands homeless.

Noriega escaped and sought asylum at the residence of the papal nuncio, the representative of the Vatican in Panama, on Christmas Eve. U.S. troops surrounded the house and "psychological operations" personnel blasted loud rock music to keep him from getting any rest. He surrendered on January 3, 1990, and was flown to Florida. On July 2, 1992, he was sentenced to 40 years in a Miami prison on drug and racketeering charges. The sentence was later reduced.

With time off for good behavior, Noriega completed his sentence on September 9, 2007, having served 17 years in prison. He remained in custody in Florida until 2010, however, while he fought extradition to France, where he faced charges of laundering drug money. He was finally extradited, and in July 2010 was tried and sentenced to seven years in a French prison.

The Panamanian government has called for his extradition to Panama, where he was convicted in absentia of a number of crimes, including murdering the leaders of the 1989 coup attempt. What would actually happen to Noriega if he is ever returned to Panama is unclear. He is now in his 70s, and under a new law convicts older than 70 can serve their sentences under house arrest.

A NEW DEMOCRACY

Guillermo Endara, who had been robbed by Noriega of the presidency in 1989 and brutally beaten along with his vice-presidential candidates in the protests that followed, was finally sworn in as president during the invasion. His term was a period of instability, as Panama worked to recover from the devastation of the invasion and the U.S. economic sanctions that preceded it. A final military coup was attempted and failed. The Panama Defense Forces were disbanded, and today Panama no longer has a military. But crime increased in Panama while order was restored and a new civilian police force organized.

Endara—a figure of some fun in Panama because of his obesity, lack of political experience, and infatuation with his young, attractive wife—managed to serve out his term, and democracy took hold in Panama.

Endara was succeeded in 1994 by Ernesto Pérez Balladares, a member of the PRD, the party of Noriega and Torrijos. He won with 33 percent of the vote in an election that also featured Mireya Moscoso, the widow of Arnulfo Arias, and Rubén Blades, the famous salsa singer and actor. The election was considered fair.

The PRD attempted to distance itself from the Noriega years, but during the Balladares administration it continued to face accusations of drug trafficking, money laundering, and corruption. Balladares, popularly known as El Toro (The Bull), enacted free-market reforms that sparked protest in Panama and caused his popularity to suffer. He attempted to change the constitution to allow him to run for a second term, but Panamanian voters defeated the proposal by a two-to-one margin.

In 1999, Moscoso ran again for the presidency on the ticket of the Partido Arnulfista (PA) or Arnulfista Party. This time her main opponent was Martín Torrijos, the young son of the late dictator, who represented the PRD. Moscoso won and became Panama's first female president. A peaceful democracy proved to be well established as full control of the Panama Canal was turned over to Panama at noon on December 31, 1999.

The new millennium began with things looking pretty bright for Panama. The Panama Canal was in the middle of a billion-dollar expansion and was increasingly being run as a business, its raised tolls making a major contribution to the economy. New construction was transforming the Panama City skyline, and thanks to Balladares, the road system throughout the country was greatly improved.

But a downturn in the world economy hit Panama's services sector hard. Moscoso also generated a great deal of animosity, and not just from her political rivals. Her administration, like the one before it, was plagued by accusations of corruption. She did little to endear herself to the poor people among her supporters when, early in her administration, she presented each of the 72 members of the national legislature with a Cartier watch as a Christmas present.

Environmentalists also complained that her policies were wreaking immeasurable damage for short-term gain. Her support for a road linking Cerro Punta and Boquete, for instance, sparked public outrage. Her critics maintained that a rough road already existed farther down the mountain and, if improved, would help many impoverished communities along the route with minimal harm to the environment. Moscoso favored building a new road right through the heart of Parque Nacional Volcán Barú; public protests and a negative environmental impact study halted the plan.

Some of Moscoso's actions were applauded, however. In 2001 her administration established a Comisión de la Verdad (Truth Commission) to investigate the disappearance of 110 people under the Torrijos and Noriega dictatorships. Forensic anthropologists dug up human remains all over the country, and in its final report the commission concluded that at least 70 of the cases it investigated were murders.

Throughout her term in office, Moscoso and her government continued to be hounded by impassioned accusations of corruption and incompetence that were striking for Panama, which traditionally has had a cynical attitude toward the actions of those in power. A widely quoted poll of Latin American countries, conducted toward the end of her time in office, put her approval rating among Panamanians at 15 percent, the second-lowest for a Central American leader at the time.

Moscoso's term ended in 2004. Martín Torrijos ran a second time for the presidency and this time was elected. He took office on September 1, 2004—as always, to a single, five-year term.

Torrijos's term had its share of troubles. A 2005 overhaul of the Caja de Seguro Social, Panama's ailing social security system, led to sometimes-violent protests, including a monthlong strike. Under the new law, workers' required contributions were increased, and the retirement age was raised by five years. It also faced repeated protests from Suntracs (Sindicato Único de Trabjadores de la Construcción y Similares), Panama's powerful construction workers' union, over pay, benefits, and safety.

In 2006, the government was widely criticized for a public-health crisis that led to the deaths of at least 115 patients poisoned by cough syrup. Panamanian public-health officials made the syrup using what they believed to be glycerin, but which was actually diethylene glycol, an industrial solvent used in antifreeze. The counterfeit glycerin was supplied by a Chinese company that did not have a license to sell drug ingredients. Chinese companies have been blamed for similar cases around the world. Investigations into the tragedy, including how the chemical ended up in the public-hospital system, continue. Officials doubt the true number of those killed or injured by the tainted medicine will ever be known. Victims' families have slammed the government for not being aggressive enough in its investigation.

But many things also went well during Torrijos's watch. Most notably, Panama's economy boomed. That may help account for his relatively high approval rating, which remained above 50 percent throughout most of his term. On the other hand, rival politicians and some among the public complained that the Torrijos administration deferred tough decisions and spent too much time and money on public relations. Polls suggested that Panamanians were increasingly worried about issues they feel are not receiving enough attention, such as a perceived rise in violent crime, the increasing cost of living, and inadequate public transportation in congested Panama City.

If nothing else, Torrijos will be remembered for his support of the third-locks project at the Panama Canal, which was approved in a national referendum on October 22, 2006. Work on the project officially began on September 3, 2007, and is expected to be finished by 2014. Officials expect the project to cost US$5.3 billion, to be funded largely through increased tolls. Critics, however, believe the final figure could be twice as high, and they worry about where all that money will end up coming from. In any case, if and when the project is finally completed it should greatly expand the canal's capacity.

On May 3, 2009, Ricardo Martinelli, the leader of the *Cambio Democrático* (Democratic Change), was elected president of Panama in a landslide. He received 60 percent of the vote, far ahead of his closest rival, Balbina Herrera of the PRD, who received about 36 percent.

The wealthy owner of a supermarket chain, Martinelli immediately set about cracking down on corruption, investigating former leaders, firing public workers who were not performing, and launching a plan to bring a modern transportation system to Panama City. For a while, he was the most popular leader in Latin America. His approval ratings slipped in the second half of his term, however, with many complaining that he was trying to accumulate too much power. International monitoring groups and internal critics voiced concerns over alleged corruption scandals, erosion of civil rights, and curtailing of press freedoms.

Government and Economy

Panama is a constitutional democracy. The chief executive is the president, traditionally assisted by two vice presidents, all of whom are elected to a single five-year term. A change to the constitution in 2004 reduced the number of vice presidents to one, starting with the 2009 election. The popularly elected Asamblea Nacional, formerly the Asamblea Legislativa, is the national legislature. It's a unicameral (one house) body. The number of legislators has fluctuated in the past, but the constitutional reforms of 2004 fixed it at 71, starting with the 2009 election. Legislators serve five-year terms that run concurrently with the presidential term. There is also a supreme court consisting of nine justices who serve 10-year terms, along with several superior courts and courts of appeal.

For much of Panama's history, however, the government was essentially controlled by the oligarchy, the military, or both. Especially during the military dictatorship that lasted from the 1968 coup to the 1989 U.S. invasion that removed Noriega from power, the president was often a figurehead, and neither the legislature nor the courts held much independent power.

Every election from 1994 on has been widely considered free and fair, with less controversy surrounding them than, for instance, recent U.S. elections. Though corruption and influence peddling are still acknowledged to be problems, Panama's democracy appears healthier and more firmly entrenched than ever before. Suffrage is universal and compulsory—that is, everyone 18 years and older is required to vote in all national elections.

Panama either adopted a new constitution or amended an existing one several times during its first 100 years, usually motivated by expanding or contracting the government's power and citizens' rights or realigning its relationship with the United States, particularly concerning U.S. intervention in Panama's affairs and its

A sustained surge in highrise construction in Panama City has given Panama's economy a major boost.

© WILLIAM FRIAR

rights in the Canal Zone. In 2004, it amended the constitution again, making a total of 67 changes. Significant changes included approving the expansion of the Panama Canal.

The central government loosened its control over large sections of the country through the creation of *comarcas,* or semiautonomous reservations for the country's indigenous peoples.

Panama's nominal gross domestic product (GDP) in 2009 was US$24.75 billion. Unlike its Central American neighbors, Panama's economy depends mainly on an extensive services sector, not agriculture. About three-quarters of its GDP comes from the Colón Free Zone, international banking, the Panama Canal, ports, ship registry, tourism, and related services. Agriculture comprises less than 7 percent of GDP. The main agricultural exports are bananas, rice, coffee, sugarcane, and shrimp. Panama's largest trading partner, by far, is the United States.

Panama has always been a dollar-based economy, meaning its currency is tied to the U.S. dollar. In fact, Panama's paper currency, officially known as the balboa, *is* the dollar.

The economy took a major hit toward the end of the 1990s with the departure of U.S. military personnel and their dependents (and dollars), but Panama Canal profits have helped soften the blow since 2000. Canal revenues in fiscal year 2009 were US$1.96 billion.

Panama has experienced impressive economic growth in recent years, driven in large part by a boom in construction. This in turn has been fueled in part by an influx of foreigners, especially North American retirees, tourists, and affluent Colombians and Venezuelans fleeing instability and social upheaval in their home countries.

Panama has had one the fastest-growing economies in the Americas in recent years, for several years posting GDP growth greater than 7 percent and sometimes in the double figures. In 2009, GDP growth dropped to 2.4 percent as a result of the worldwide recession, which Panama was weathering better than most Latin American economies thanks to a stable and cautious financial sector that did not take the same risks as some of its neighbors, coupled with a construction boom that just kept on booming.

A healthy economy has also cut the unemployment rate in recent years. The official rate was estimated at 7.1 percent in 2009. Canal construction is expected to create thousands of new jobs.

Panama historically has had quite low inflation, estimated at 2.9 percent in 2009. It fluctuated a bit more in recent years, but remains lower than most other Latin American countries.

Though one of the region's most affluent countries, Panama has one of the most unequal distributions of wealth in the world. Despite the strong economy, nearly 40 percent of the population still lives in poverty. Half of these people live in extreme poverty, trying to get by on less than US$1 a day. At the other extreme, a widely quoted study claimed in 2004 that just 80 individuals accounted for half of Panama's total GDP.

People and Culture

Panama's 1911 census, the country's first, estimated its population at just 336,742. By the 2010 census it had grown to 3,322,576. Panama is a young country: Nearly one-third of the population is 14 years or younger and just six percent are older than 64.

Despite widespread poverty and high unemployment, Panamanians remain prosperous by Latin American standards. A primary-school education is compulsory, and more than 93 percent of the population aged 10 and older can read and write. Average life expectancy at birth is 75 years, about the same as in Poland. Women outlive men by nearly five years.

Panamanians often identify themselves by their family's province of origin, each of which has regional stereotypes associated with it. There are nine provinces: Bocas del Toro, Chiriquí, Veraguas, Herrera, Los Santos, Coclé, Panamá, Colón, and Darién. There are also a number of *comarcas* (indigenous reservations), and in recent years the national legislature has been adding more by carving out territory from existing provinces.

More than two-thirds of Panama's people live in urban areas. The most densely inhabited part of the country borders the Panama Canal, an area that encompasses Panama City and Colón and the most developed parts of the provinces (Panamá and Colón) that contain them.

Most of the rest of Panama's population is concentrated on the Pacific hills and lowlands of the isthmus, particularly in the so-called central provinces of Coclé, Herrera, Los Santos, and Veraguas. This area, particularly the Azuero Peninsula, is considered by many Panamanians to be their heartland because of its preservation of traditional folklore and crafts, the Spanish colonial architecture that can still be found in its provincial cities and towns, and its long agricultural history. It occupies in the Panamanian imagination a place somewhere between that occupied by the Old West and the Great Plains in the gringo one. Not surprisingly, given its early settlement, it's also the most severely deforested part of Panama.

The province of Chiriquí contains the fertile mountains of western Panama and the country's second-largest city, David (pop. 77,734 in the central city, 124,280 in the entire district), in its humid lowlands. Chiricanos have a strong regional identity and are proud of their beautiful homeland. It's sometimes said that they consider themselves Chiricanos first and Panamanians second. Stickers depicting the provincial flag adorn the windows of many

COURTESY OF PAUL SABAN

The Ngöbe-Buglé are the largest indigenous group in Panama.

INDIGENOUS PEOPLES

While pockets of the indigenous peoples of the isthmus can be found all over the country, either clinging to vestiges of their way of life or assimilating fully into the Panamanian mainstream, most still live on their ancestral lands. *Comarcas* (semiautonomous reservations) are still being established.

Most Guna (pop. 62,000) live in one of three *comarcas*. The largest of these is Guna Yala, or the San Blas Archipelago, which includes a strip of mainland and a string of nearly 400 coral islands that extends down the eastern Caribbean coast from Colón province to the Colombian border. The other two Guna *comarcas,* Madungandí and Wargandí, are on the Caribbean slope of the Darién rainforest. The Gunas refer to themselves as Tule, though they recognize the name Guna as well.

The Emberá (pop. 22,000) and Wounaan (pop. 7,000) live in *comarcas* on both the Caribbean and Pacific slopes of the Darién. They are culturally similar, but speak different languages. In the past they have been known collectively as the Chocos, but the name is seldom used today. Emberá-Wounaan is preferred when speaking of them as a group.

The Ngöbe (pop. 170,000) and Buglé (pop. 18,000) have traditionally been known as the Guaymí, but the name is increasingly falling out of favor. Ngöbe-Buglé (pronounced NO-bay BOO-glay) is preferred when speaking of them collectively. Like the Emberá and Wounaan, they are culturally similar but speak different languages. They are by far the largest indigenous group in Panama. Most live in the mountains of western Panama. In 1997, they gained their own, enormous *comarca,* carved out of the provinces of Chiriquí, Bocas del Toro, and Veraguas.

The remaining recognized indigenous people are the Naso, also known as the Teribe (pop. 3,800), who live along the rivers on the mainland of Bocas del Toro and are trying to gain

homes and the bumpers of many cars, and fake Chiriquí passports are sometimes sold as novelties in stores. The area around Volcán Barú, Panama's highest mountain, has been experiencing a tourist boom in recent years, particularly the cozy town of Boquete.

Bocas del Toro also feels somehow separate from the rest of Panama, but here it takes the form of neglect. Bocatoreños often complain of their region being treated as a backwater province. It is one of the few places in Panama that still cannot rely on a steady supply of clean water, which is one of the grievances that spark occasional demonstrations. Paradoxically, the islands of Bocas del Toro are developing rapidly thanks to a tourism explosion.

The Darién (which traditionally includes both Darién province and the eastern side of Panamá province) to the east and the Caribbean slope to the north are still mostly forested and lightly populated, though that's changing rapidly.

comarca status; the Bri Bri (pop. 2,500), who also live in Bocas del Toro; and the Bokota (pop. 993), whose few surviving members live in eastern Bocas del Toro and northwest Veraguas.

Most indigenous people make a living through subsistence farming, fishing, and hunting. The Guna and Emberá-Wounaan are also able to bring in some cash through the sale of their handicrafts, which are prized by collectors around the world. Many Ngöbe-Buglé work on coffee plantations in the Chiriquí highlands. Indigenous peoples are increasingly experimenting with tourism, especially ecotourism, to improve their economic conditions. By far the most experienced at this are the Guna, who have allowed foreign tourists on their islands for decades.

Unemployment, poverty, illiteracy, and poor health are consistently highest among the indigenous people. An estimated 95 percent live in poverty, most in extreme poverty, defined as trying to get by on less than US$1 a day. Poorest of all are the Ngöbe-Buglé.

DEMOGRAPHY

Panama is a remarkably diverse country by Central American standards, thanks to its surviving indigenous peoples and its status as an important transit point for international commerce for more than 500 years. While most of the arrivals during that time came from Spain and sub-Saharan Africa, Panama also has a substantial population of immigrants from around the world, especially from China, India, the Middle East, Central Europe, and North America.

Of these, the longest-established group is the Chinese, who first came over to build the Panama Railroad in the 19th century. Many stayed to open shops and restaurants, and today they are in all walks of life. The traditional community is cohesive enough in Panama City to support three newspapers, three temples, a small Chinatown, a cultural center, and a radio station. People of Chinese descent also can be found throughout the country. Some estimates put their number as high as 150,000, or 5 percent of the total population.

People of African origin have lived on the isthmus since the 16th century. In Panama, a distinction is made between Afro-Colonials, the descendants of Spanish slaves, and Afro-Antillanos, who came later from the Caribbean islands. The latter are generally referred to as West Indians by English-speakers on the isthmus.

Afro-Colonials who escaped from their Spanish masters were known as *cimarrones,* and they built secluded villages, or *palenques,* along the eastern Caribbean coast and the Darién jungle. Some of these still exist today.

The Afro-Antillanos include Jamaicans brought over to dig the French Canal, banana-plantation workers from Jamaica and the Colombian islands of San Andrés and Providencia who settled in Bocas del Toro, and workers from around the West Indies who supplied most of the labor for the Panama Canal. Most of this last group, which numbered 20,000 in all, came from Barbados.

The ethnic breakdown of Panama is generally thought of as being about 65–70 percent mestizo (mixed Amerindian and Caucasian) and 8–10 percent Amerindian, with the bulk of the remaining population consisting of those of African and/or European descent. These estimates are quite rough and have recently been called into question, with one local DNA study concluding that 75 percent of Panama's common gene pool is of African and Amerindian origin and just 25 percent from Europe. Estimates of the number of smaller minorities, such as those of Chinese, Indian, and Middle Eastern ancestry, are even more unreliable.

Race relations on the isthmus are complex. Most Panamanians, whether officially mestizo or not, are the product of a mixture of different ethnicities, and the country is increasingly proud of being a *crisol de razas* (racial melting pot). Some of the country's legendary national heroes are of African and Amerindian descent.

But a racial pecking order lingers, tied closely to socioeconomic class. The country has traditionally been ruled by an oligarchy drawn from the elite families, many of whom have lighter skin and European features and can trace their ancestry back to Spain. They still wield a great deal of power in Panama and tend to marry within other elite families. They are known disparagingly by other Panamanians as *rabiblancos* (white tails).

The indigenous peoples and those of African descent are among the nation's poorest, and they still find it difficult to move up in society. As late as 2002, Panama found it necessary to pass a law forbidding discrimination against minorities in commercial establishments, sparked by repeated incidents of blacks being turned away at the door of bars, discos, and restaurants.

In 1941 the national legislature passed a new constitution that stripped English-speaking blacks (meaning the Afro-Antillanos or West Indians) and other non-Latino minorities of their Panamanian citizenship. It also outlawed the immigration of new arrivals from the English-speaking West Indies, as well as China, India, and the Middle East. The constitution was overturned in 1946.

Afro-Antillanos in particular had an uneasy existence on the isthmus during much of the 20th century. They faced discrimination both in the Canal Zone and Panama, but had largely lost their ties to the Caribbean islands from which they came. As the years have gone by, most have adopted Spanish as their first language and assimilated more fully into mainstream Panamanian society. The process sped up with the decline and disappearance of the U.S. Canal Zone, where many families had lived and worked since canal construction days.

The military dictatorship that took power in 1968 was the most serious challenge to the rule of the oligarchy, opening up opportunities for those of different ethnicities and lower socioeconomic classes to rise to positions of power. A relatively large middle class began to emerge. In modern times especially, academic achievement, professional success, and other new sources of societal clout can sometimes overcome the traditional obstacles of race and family connections.

CULTURE

In part because of the long U.S. presence in Panama and in part because of its even longer role in world commerce, Panama has been quicker to globalize than many of its Latin American neighbors. Siestas, for instance, are not really a part of daily life, and in many ways Panama City today has more in common with Miami than it does with, say, Madrid.

But for all Panama's diversity, the country's dominant culture does derive directly from Spain. The extended family is by far the most important social unit. Taking care of one's family comes first, and family-oriented occasions such as baptisms, Mother's Day, and birthdays are treated as important celebrations. Most hotels, especially outside Panama City, are still oriented to accommodate fairly large Panamanian families that share the same room for a weekend or holiday retreat, rather than foreign couples or singles exploring the country. Panama is also a quite child-friendly country, all the more so since such a high percentage of the population is younger than 14.

There is a strong feeling of national pride in Panama. Panamanians often express a sense that their country is somehow different from others in the region, in part because of Panama's unique geographical position and unusually rich history for such a small place. Many, for instance, don't really consider Panama a part of Central America, whatever a map might say. The sense of Panama as someplace special is best summed up in the popular phrase that is in essence Panama's national motto: *puente del mundo, corazón del universo* (bridge of the world, heart of the universe).

first day of school, Playa Santa Catalina

Family and Society

Home is sacrosanct, and it's quite possible to be friends with a Panamanian for years without setting foot in his or her home. Dining with the middle and upper classes of Panama City usually means meeting at a restaurant. To be invited to someone's house or weekend country home is something special and can mean you're considered family. Outside Panama City, especially among the campesinos, entertaining at home is more typical.

Whom one is related to is still extremely important in determining status in Panamanian society. Panama is a small enough country that the names of the prominent families are widely known. Even in nonelite circles, the names of one's father and mother can help one get ahead or hold one back.

Men and Women

Machismo is a fact of life in Panama. But it's not as pronounced as in some other Latin American countries, and stereotypical sex roles have begun to break down in modern times. Women are now in more positions of power outside the home; in 1999, Panama even elected its first female president (albeit one best known for being the widow of a popular male politician). Still, boys tend to be given more freedom during their upbringing, in rural areas men work in the fields and women in the home, and the tradition of married men having a mistress and even an entirely separate family has not died out; women are still expected to dress and act in "feminine" ways, and men on the street think nothing of openly ogling any attractive woman who passes by.

Manners and Mores

Foreigners often comment on how laid-back and peaceful Panamanians are—except behind the wheel. One word any visitor is likely to hear often is *tranquilo* (calm, peaceful, easygoing), used both as an injunction (as in, "take it easy") and as an expression of praise (as in, "what a peaceful place"). It says a lot about what's valued in Panama.

But boisterous celebrations are also extremely popular. Panamanians take time off seriously, and the calendar is filled with national holidays, religious observances, and other excuses to party. The entire country comes to a halt for big celebrations, such as Carnaval. Parties often last all night and feature music played at ear-shattering volumes. Those who can afford it have cottages at the beach or in the mountains, or fincas that they use for weekend getaways or extended holidays.

Another important word to know is *dignidad* (dignity). Treating others with politeness and respect is extremely important in Panama, and slights are taken seriously.

On the other hand, Panama is also quite a tolerant place, and a laissez-faire attitude prevails. While, just as in any other country, there is racism and discrimination, people of different nationalities, religions, and lifestyles have generally been left in peace. Open homosexuality is still a thing of the future, but gay and lesbian people have begun to assert their rights, and gay bars and clubs aren't subject to raids and official harassment. While abortion is officially illegal in this Catholic country (punishable by up to three years in jail for the woman and up to six years for the practitioner), it's surreptitiously available at some clinics. Birth control is practiced by a majority of the sexually active. Prostitution is legal and regulated by the government.

Perceptions of Time

Among the hardest things for visitors to adjust to, especially those from North America and northern Europe, are local attitudes toward time. As in many other Latin American countries, showing up later than an agreed-upon time is normal, even expected. It's not unusual for guests at a sit-down dinner party to show up an hour or two after the appointed hour.

There's also ample opportunity for culture clashes concerning appointments. As in other Latin American countries, foreigners trying to do business in Panama often complain of the *mañana* syndrome: putting off for a vague future time what would seem possible to do right now. Miscommunications are common. What a visitor may interpret as a commitment to call or show up somewhere without fail may actually have been intended only as a polite expression of intent to help out if nothing more urgent comes up.

Panama and the United States

Not surprisingly, the United States generates a range of feelings in Panama. The United States has intervened in the affairs of the isthmus constantly since its own early days as a republic. It often has used the isthmus to further its own strategic and commercial interests, and for most of the 20th century had military bases and a largely foreign community planted in a 500-square-mile zone that bisected the country and over which Panama had little control.

Students, politicians, activists, and nationalistic citizens regularly denounced the U.S. presence on the isthmus as imperialistic and paternalistic, quite often with good cause, though sometimes Panama's leaders used the U.S. presence as a bogeyman to deflect attention from domestic problems.

Though some in Panama were violently opposed to the U.S. presence, others had largely positive attitudes toward it. Many others were ambivalent, seeing the United States as instrumental in helping Panama gain independence but selfishly robbing it of true self-determination, in spurring great improvements in health and welfare on the isthmus but keeping most of the spoils for itself, and in propping up but finally removing the military dictatorships that ruled the country for decades.

What most can now agree on is that the end of the Canal Zone and the closing of the U.S.

military bases have made possible a healthier and more equal relationship between the two nations. There's a widespread sentiment in Panama that the country did not gain full sovereignty until December 31, 1999, when it gained full control of the Panama Canal. *Soberanía* (sovereignty) is still a word one hears often in Panama, and its importance to many is undeniable. When the Panamanian government created a new national park through a swath of the Panama Canal's watershed, it named it Parque Nacional Soberanía. Evidence of the U.S. presence in the former Canal Zone has been steadily eroded, with streets renamed and English-language signs removed.

Panama and the United States generally enjoy good relations these days. The U.S. Congress finally passed a free trade agreement on October 12, 2011. Panamanian officials announced in 2012 that they expect it to come into effect by the end of the year.

American pop culture took hold long ago, apparent in everything from the Hollywood movies playing at the multiplexes to the popularity of American fast-food franchises, to the clothing and musical tastes of young people. Baseball, basketball, and, to a more limited extent, American football have long been popular in Panama. European football (soccer) has only come into its own in recent years. For wealthier Panamanians, Florida is a popular shopping destination, and U.S.-style malls sprouted up in and around the major cities. Middle- and upper-class students often go to the United States for college and graduate school.

SPORTS

Panama has produced a considerable number of outstanding world athletes and a few bona fide legends. Many of them have come from the ranks of Panama's poorest families.

Panama is known for producing great boxers, the best known of whom is Roberto Durán. Nicknamed Manos de Piedra (Hands of Stone),

he held world titles in four weight categories: lightweight, welterweight, junior middleweight, and middleweight. He earned the welterweight title in a famous match against "Sugar" Ray Leonard in June 1980. But his career took a sharp downward turn during a rematch with Leonard in November of that same year. Durán, after being taunted repeatedly by a fast-moving Leonard, told the referee during the eighth round that he wanted to stop the fight. The two words he spoke to end the match, *no más* (no more), would haunt the rest of his career and cause an uproar back home. The words are better remembered today than the fact Durán went on to win two more world titles. His best days behind him, a car accident finally forced him to retire in 2002 at the age of 51. He is considered one of the best boxers in history, with 104 wins in 120 fights, 69 of them knockouts.

Panama has also produced champion horseracing jockeys, by far the most famous of whom is Laffit Pincay Jr. In 1999, Pincay broke Willie Shoemaker's record for career wins. He rode until April 2003, when a fall during a race left him with a broken neck and forced him to retire at the age of 56. By then, he had racked up an astonishing 9,530 victories.

But in sheer volume of great athletes, Panama's biggest contribution to world sports has been the disproportionate number of major-league baseball players. These include Hall-of-Fame first baseman Rod Carew, who retired in 1986 with 3,053 career hits. He was born on a train going from Colón to Panama City and was named Rodney after the doctor who delivered him. Stars include New York Yankees relief pitcher Mariano Rivera and Houston Astros left fielder Carlos Lee.

Panama's greatest international football (soccer) star to date is forward Julio César Dely Valdés, who earned the nickname "Panagol" for his prowess as a striker while playing for Nacional de Montevideo in Uruguay. He spent much of his career playing in Spain and

Uruguay before retiring in 2004 at the age of 37. He's considered one of the best football players to come out of Central America.

Panama has also had some track-and-field stars. Long-jumper Irving Saladino won a gold medal at the 2008 Olympic Games, Panama's first.

THE ARTS

Panama takes great pains to preserve its traditional music forms, dances, costumes, crafts, and customs. It also has a vibrant contemporary arts and entertainment scene with roots in its unique history.

While music and dance are extremely popular, one often hears complaints in Panama that the fine arts and literature play far too small a role in daily life.

A number of painters have received at least some international recognition, though Panama's most widely known artistic creations are the work of anonymous indigenous artists, especially the Guna with their *molas* (handcrafted blouses) and the Emberá-Wounaan with their tagua and cocobolo carvings and woven baskets.

Music and Dance

Given its geographical location, it's not surprising that a wide variety of music is popular in Panama. Dance clubs may spin a salsa, cumbia, merengue, or reggae number, then follow it up with a Latin pop music hit, a bit of electronic dance music, or a rock song in English or Spanish. What may be more surprising is how strong a hold Panamanian folkloric music still has on the country, both in purist and modernized forms.

Important instruments in folkloric music include the accordion, *los tambores* (wooden drums with the top covered by cowhide), *la caja* (a small wooden drum with both sides covered with hide), *la mejoranera* (a small, five-stringed guitar), *la bocona* or *socabón* (a four-stringed guitar), *la guáchara* or *churuca* (a gourd-shaped instrument played by scraping an implement across notches carved into it), maracas, and violins. Folkloric music can be instrumental or feature singing, the most distinctive element of which is the *saloma,* a Panamanian form of yodeling. The music is an acquired taste for those who didn't grow up listening to it.

Folkloric music is often accompanied by traditional dances, the most famous of which is the drum-based *el tamborito.* This is Panama's national dance, with many regional variations, and is usually what is performed for visitors or on other special occasions when there is a folkloric dance performance. Women dress in beautiful hand-embroidered *polleras* (formal hand-embroidered dresses) and the men in either long-sleeved white *camisillas* (shirts) and black pants or a colorful embroidered shirt and pants cut off below the knees. In either case, the man wears some variety of traditional Panama hat, often the *sombrero pintado* (painted hat). All of these hats are quite different from the so-called Panama hats that are made in Ecuador.

Other important dance-music forms include the *mejorana,* a type of song accompanied by the *mejoranera,* and the festive dance music performed by *murgas* (strolling bands of musicians) during Carnaval.

All these folkloric traditions come from Panama's central provinces, particularly the Azuero Peninsula. Other traditional dance forms include the *congos,* derived from Africa and still performed occasionally by descendants of African slaves, and the *balsería,* which is really something between a festival and an extreme sport performed by the indigenous Ngöbe-Buglé peoples; it involves throwing balsa poles at the legs of participants, often with painful results.

Music rooted in Panama's folkloric traditions has changed with the times and evolved into what is known as *música típica* or simply *típico,* a dance-music form that features traditional elements such as accordion and yodeling, but has a livelier beat, modern lyrics, and an almost pop sensibility. It's enormously popular in Panama. Its biggest stars include the accordionists Osvaldo Ayala and Ulpiano Vergara and the brother-sister duo Samy and Sandra Sandoval.

Panama's most famous musician outside its own borders is the salsa star, actor, and politician Rubén Blades. He first gained fame for his work with salsa legend Willie Colón before launching a solo career notable for both his politically conscious lyrics and musical innovation. He ran an unsuccessful campaign for the presidency of Panama in 1994. He is currently the director minister of tourism.

Another international music star is Danilo Pérez, an innovative jazz pianist noted for blending Latin, African, and other influences with established jazz forms. Both he and Blades spend a great deal of their performance time abroad, and concerts in Panama are special events.

El General (born Edgardo A. Franco) had some reggae-influenced, Spanish-language dance hits in parts of the United States and Latin America in the early 1990s. He is now considered one of the forefathers of reggaeton, a hugely popular blend of rap, reggae, rock, dancehall, and calypso that has become hugely popular in the last few years. Nando Boom, a Panamanian reggae star, is also considered an early influence.

Reggaeton is usually characterized by a driving, syncopated snare-drum rhythm that's come to be known as "Dem Bow." It's a notoriously controversial genre, both because nonfans tend to find the music irritating at best and because the lyrics of many songs are deemed misogynistic, violent, pornographic (often through innuendo), racist, or all the above. Perhaps fortunately, many don't have a clue what the lyrics are, since they tend to be delivered in heavily accented Spanish, English, or patois. Despite or because of all this, it has a large audience around the Spanish-speaking world.

Many trace reggaeton's roots to Panama, though most of the genre's stars are Puerto Rican. The biggest Panamanian star is El Roockie (sometimes spelled El Rookie), who has so much street cred he once made a video that featured rival street gangs. Félix Danilo Gómez, who records under the name Nigga, had a major hit in Mexico in 2007–2008. He plans to record under the less controversial name Flex to try to crack the U.S. market. Nearly all reggaeton's hitmakers so far are male. But Panama's Lorna (Lorna Zarina Aponte) had an international hit a couple years back with "Papi Chulo," which was many European club-goers' first exposure to reggaeton.

Panama has a sizable rock scene, with a number of bands of varying skill performing original songs and covers in Spanish and English. The veteran band Los Rabanes has met with the greatest success outside of Panama, with tours in Latin America and the United States. Cage9, which records in both English and Spanish, plays modern hard rock and seems poised to gain an international audience as well. Other popular bands include Son Miserables, Os Almirantes, Señor Loop, the long-established Los 33, newcomer Filtro Medusa, and the band formerly known as Big Fat Hen, which in 2003 wisely changed its name to Polyphase.

Jazz and classical music draw urban sophisticates to occasional performances at concert halls and restaurants in Panama City. Panama has also been trying to establish regular music festivals, including an annual Panama Jazz Festival, held in Panama City during the dry season.

High-toned cultural events—such as performances by the 60-person national symphony orchestra, the national ballet, and visiting arts groups—are generally held in the Teatro Nacional or Teatro Balboa. Smaller groups sometimes perform in the intimate Teatro Anita Villalaz. These kinds of performances are rare outside of Panama City.

Fine Arts

Panama has a number of notable artists. An important early figure is the painter and sculptor

Roberto Lewis (1874–1949), known for his paintings of Isla Taboga and his sweeping murals, which depict romantic scenes drawn from history and mythology. The latter still adorn the Teatro Nacional, the presidential palace, and the Escuela Normal Juan Demóstenes Arosemena in the provincial city of Santiago.

Alfredo Sinclair (b. 1915) and Guillermo Trujillo (b. 1927) are widely considered to be two of Panama's great master painters. Their work has been displayed around the world. Other major figures include Manuel Chong Neto (b. 1927), whose paintings often feature fleshy women with birds, and Juan Manuel Cedeño (1914–1997), a disciple of Lewis. Important younger artists include Isabel de Obaldía (b. 1957), noted for her paintings as well as her glass art, and Brooke Alfaro (b. 1949), whose subjects include the marginalized of Panamanian society and who now works mainly in video.

Making generalizations about any diverse group of artists is difficult, but it's striking how many of Panama's best-known painters make use of warm, vivid colors and dreamlike or primitive elements in their work.

Other popular and widely collected artists include Sheila Lichacz (b. 1942), whose main subjects are the *tinajas* (clay pots) that date from pre-Columbian days and are folkloric icons throughout Panama. She is relatively well known outside of Panama, but some art aficionados in her home country were surprised in 2003 when her work was exhibited at the Smithsonian in Washington, D.C. Al Sprague (b. 1938), a Panama-born American who was an art teacher at Balboa High School in the former Canal Zone, is popular locally and among former zone residents for his paintings, drawings, and prints of the Panama Canal, the Canal Zone, and daily life in Panama.

Some of Panama's finest art is made by its indigenous people, though these works are usually made anonymously and sold as souvenirs. The carved tagua nuts, cocobolo statues, and woven baskets of the Emberá-Wounaan have begun to receive the international fame long accorded the *molas* of the Guna people. A few Emberá, Wounaan, and Guna artists now sign their work.

Literature

Panamanian literature has made a small splash beyond the country's borders, in part, perhaps, because much of it has been inward-looking, drawing inspiration from distinctly Panamanian themes of national identity and history, the country's natural beauty, and daily life on the isthmus. Even in Panama it can be hard to find books by Panamanian authors, whose works are often printed cheaply in modest, limited editions. Panama's literary output leans heavily toward poetry and short stories, followed by novels and essays and, to a far lesser extent, plays. Nearly all of it is in Spanish.

Ricardo Miró (1883–1940) is the country's most revered poet, often referred to as "El Poeta de Panamá" and for whom the country's most prestigious literary awards are named. His most famous poem is "Patria," an ode to his beloved country. He also produced short stories and novels. Other notable early poets include María Olimpia de Obaldía (1891–1985), whose main theme was family life, and Amelia Denis de Icaza (1836–1911), most famous for her patriotic "Al Cerro Ancón."

One of the country's most important literary figures in the 20th century was Rogelio Sinán (1902–1994), the pen name of Bernardo Domínguez Alba. Sinán is remembered for the breadth and quality of his work, which included short stories (particularly "A la Orilla de Las Estatuas Maduras"), novels (most notably *Penilunio*), poetry, and even a children's play, *La Cucarachita Mandinga*. Other major figures of the period included the poets Ricardo J. Bemúdez (1914–2000), Demetrio Korsí (1899–1957), Demetrio Herrera Sevillano (1902–1950), and Stella Sierra (1917–1997).

Novelists and short-story writers have come to the forefront in the modern era. Prominent contemporary authors include Ernesto Endara (b. 1932), known especially for his short stories and plays; Rosa María Britton (b. 1936), a physician whose novels include *El Señor de las Lluvias y el Viento* (1984) and *Todas Íbamos a Ser Reinas* (1997); and the prolific Enrique Jaramillo Levi (b. 1944), whose works include the short-story collection *Duplicaciones* (1990) and many other short stories, poems, and essays. He is also a scholar and cultural promoter who has probably done more than any other living person to draw attention to Panamanian literature. He is the editor of *Maga,* a Panamanian literary review.

The historical novels of Jorge Thomas, the pen name of the lawyer Juan David Morgan (b. 1942), are relatively easy to find in Panama, especially *Con Ardientes Fulgores de Gloria* (1999). *El Caballo de Oro* (2005), about the building of the Panama Railroad, is his first novel published under his real name.

In 2006, Cristina Henríquez, whose father is Panamanian, published *Come Together, Fall Apart,* a collection of short stories about life in Panama. It met with glowing reviews in U.S. newspapers and found a fan in Isabel Allende. In 2010 she published her first novel, *The World in Half.* Both are easy to find internationally.

Panama City has an active theater scene, and works by Panamanian and foreign playwrights are staged frequently. Plays range from hoary classics to experimental pieces. One playhouse, the aging Teatro Guild de Ancón in the former Canal Zone, still offers works in English.

RELIGION

An estimated 85 percent of Panamanians are Roman Catholic. Various sects of Protestantism have made inroads over the years, accounting for most of Panama's other followers of organized religion.

Catholicism is taught in public schools unless parents request that their children be exempted. Catholic holidays, festivals, and rites are widely observed. However, many Panamanian Catholics take a "cafeteria" approach to church doctrine. Birth control, for instance, is widely available and practiced throughout the country. And Panama has a long history of religious freedom and tolerance.

Judaism and Islam have significant minority followings and a long history in Panama, particularly in the cities. Islam is believed to have first come to the isthmus with African slaves in the 16th century. The first Jewish congregation in Panama, Kol Shearith, was founded in 1876. Panama City has one of the world's seven Baha'i Houses of Worship, as well as a prominent Hindu temple. The Greek Orthodox Metropolitanate of Central America is based in Panama. Many of Panama's indigenous peoples still practice their traditional religions to some degree.

LANGUAGE

The official language of Panama is Spanish. English is the major second language, but it's not as widely spoken as one might think given the long U.S. presence in the country and Panama's role in world commerce and finance. In fact, even in Panama City it seems harder to find someone fluent in English than it was 25 years ago.

A nationalistic emphasis on Spanish, combined with the exodus of U.S. civilians and military personnel when the Canal Zone disappeared, has led to a steady erosion in English on the isthmus. Even the large English-speaking West Indian immigrant populations, which learned Spanish as a second language when they came to the isthmus, are gradually losing their English skills as they become fully assimilated into the Panamanian mainstream.

The role of English in Panamanian life is still a touchy subject. A major controversy erupted in 2002 when a proposal to make English an official second language of business was floated in the national legislature, with many denouncing it as unconstitutional and impractical.

But the greatly diminished U.S. presence on the isthmus has helped make English less of a political hot potato. There's a growing belief in Panama that English skills are crucial to the survival of its services-oriented economy. The point was driven home in 2002 when the HSBC Bank tried to open a 600-person call center in Panama. Of the 1,600 applicants, only 41 were fully bilingual in English and Spanish. The bank set up the call center in Malaysia instead. That same year, a Panamanian official estimated that only about two percent of government employees speak English well.

In 2003 the Panamanian government passed a law requiring the teaching of English in all primary and secondary schools. Private schools of English have sprung up all over the country. Suddenly, everyone wants to learn English, but progress has been slow.

All that said, English-speaking visitors usually have little trouble getting around even if they don't speak Spanish. It's not hard to find someone who speaks at least some English, especially in the fancier hotels and restaurants.

Outside of Panama City, English is mostly widely spoken along the Caribbean coast, particularly in Bocas del Toro. There are few English speakers in the rural areas and *comarcas* (semiautonomous reservations). In some of the *comarcas*, even Spanish is not universally spoken.

Panama's indigenous people still speak their traditional languages to varying degrees. Ngöbere (spoken by the Ngöbe) and Guna (spoken by the Guna) are probably the least endangered, mostly because of the sheer number of speakers.

Those who speak neither Spanish nor English will have a harder time getting around, as no other European languages are widely spoken on the isthmus, let alone languages from other parts of the world. Panama City, Bocas town on Bocas del Toro, and, to a lesser extent, Boquete have the greatest mix of international residents and visitors.

Some descendants of Chinese immigrants in Panama City and larger towns in the interior still speak their ancestral languages, especially Hakka and Yue (Cantonese). Arabic and Hebrew are among the other languages with a foothold in cosmopolitan Panama City.

So-called Panamanian Creole English (PCE) is still spoken among the descendants of immigrants from Jamaica, Barbados, San Andrés, Providencia, and other West Indian islands. Most speakers live in Colón, the former canal area, Panama City, and Bocas del Toro, whose distinctive regional variation of PCE is called Guari-Guari. It's almost impossible for uninitiated speakers of standard English to understand PCE.

ESSENTIALS

Getting There

Most visitors come to Panama by air, and it's rarely a bargain. Except for occasional promotions, such as an airline inaugurating a new route, standard fares don't change much.

The cheapest way to get to Panama from North and Central America is by bus, so long as one has lots of time and doesn't mind a bit of adventure and discomfort. Driving from North America to Panama, even all the way to the Darién Gap, is a popular adventure for intrepid road warriors that requires considerable planning and resourcefulness. There are no roads between Colombia and Panama, and no ferry service. The only safe way to travel between Panama and South America is by air. Panama has no international rail service.

Make reservations far in advance for travel around holidays and festivals, particularly Christmas and Carnaval. Planes and buses are generally more crowded during the dry season, which is high season for both in-country and foreign tourists and summer vacation for Panamanian students. November is filled with national holidays, which can make travel logistics trickier. There are typically fewer flights and buses on Sundays. Domestic and regional

© WILLIAM FRIAR

airlines typically revert to a Sunday schedule for holidays, sometimes without notice. On a recent trip, a couple had to cancel their visit from San José, Costa Rica, to Panama because they held a ticket for a weekday flight that turned out not to exist—the date fell on a national holiday. The airline didn't notice the problem when it booked their reservation and sold them the ticket for the imaginary flight.

Remember that visitors to Panama must be able to show proof of onward travel. This is enforced more often than it used to be, and visitors without proof can be turned away at the border.

The departure tax to leave the country is US$40. It is now included in the price of air tickets.

CHARTER FLIGHTS AND PACKAGE DEALS

All-inclusive packages, sometimes including charter flights, are popular, especially with Canadians, Europeans, and Latin Americans. They can be a good deal for those who don't mind traveling with the herd and like having accommodations, meals, and activities concentrated in one place.

The all-inclusive resorts generally offer tours of the surrounding attractions for an extra fee, but visitors should expect to spend most of their time at or near the hotel.

BY AIR

Panama has good air connections with destinations throughout the Americas and parts of the Caribbean and western Europe.

Travel to and from anywhere farther east, including Australia and Asia, is more complicated and will probably require at least one change of plane and/or airline. Generally, few European and no Asian, African, Middle Eastern, or Australian airlines offer passenger service to Panama.

Carriers add and drop service to Panama frequently. However, routes dropped by one airline are generally picked up by another.

In mid-2004, Panama regained its Category 1 International Civil Aviation Organization (ICAO) rating following an inspection by the U.S. Federal Aviation Administration. This means Panama's civil aviation authority again meets all international safety standards (its ratings slipped in 2001), which paved the way for new flights to the United States.

Carriers serving Panama include:

- U.S. airlines: American, Continental, and Delta
- European airlines: Iberia and KLM
- Central American and Caribbean airlines: Copa, TACA, LACSA, and Cubana
- South American airlines: Avianca, Aero República, and Aires

Most of the airlines have so-called "code share" agreements with other carriers, meaning flights booked on one airline may actually be operated by a partner airline that's supposed to meet similar standards of quality and safety. For instance, Copa, Panama's national airline, has code share agreements with several airlines, including a well-established alliance with Continental Airlines and a new one with KLM. Copa's own fleet, fairly large by Latin American standards, flies to 40 destinations in 21 countries. It's a growing airline with a good reputation.

Grupo TACA, a consortium of major Central American airlines that includes El Salvador's TACA and Costa Rica's LACSA, has code share agreements with a number of carriers, including United Airlines, Air France, Iberia, Lufthansa, and Avianca.

International Airports

Panama's main international airport is **Aeropuerto Internacional de Tocumen** (tel. 238-2761, www.tocumenpanama.aero). Its airport code is PTY. Commonly referred to simply as Tocumen (toe-KOO-men), it's about 25 kilometers east of downtown Panama City. A multimillion-dollar expansion and modernization have improved it considerably. There is now a

TWO PANAMA CITIES

When booking a flight, make sure it's for Panama City in the Republic of Panama, and not Panama City, Florida. I've heard more than one tale of visitors from the United States and United Kingdom ending up in that Florida beach town. They were—briefly—pleasantly surprised at how short the flight from Miami was, though they wondered why the plane was so small. When making a reservation, be sure to verify the correct destination. And when the ticket or e-ticket arrives, double-check that it has the airport code for Tocumen International in Panama City, Republic of Panama: PTY.

Those who use the Internet to search for flights should also note that pull-down menus on airline websites, especially those in Spanish, sometimes list Panama under "Ciudad de Panamá," "Tocumen," "Aeropuerto Omar Torrijos Herrera" (the international airport's erstwhile name), and so on.

---

small domestic terminal at the airport (it's the building on the right as one faces the front of the international terminal), which is supposedly going to be increasingly used by international travelers connecting directly to destinations in western Panama, sparing them having to make a land transfer between Tocumen and the main domestic airport at Albrook.

The airport has a branch of the Banco Nacional de Panamá (tel. 238-4161 or 238-4178, 7 A.M.–11 P.M. daily). It used to exchange major currencies, but in 2012 this service had been at least temporarily suspended. Panacambios in Panama City carries a wide variety of currencies. There is also an ATM in the arrivals lounge.

There are ATP information booths between the *aduana* (customs) area and in the arrivals lounge that may or may not be staffed. They carry a few hotel flyers but little else. There are also a couple of airport information booths in the terminal.

A 24-hour left luggage office is on the ground floor of the arrivals lounge. It's to the right as one exits customs. Look for the *consigna de equipaje* sign. The rate for suitcases is US$4 per day.

There's a Cable and Wireless office (7 A.M.–7 P.M. daily) near the ticket counters upstairs that sells phone cards and has fax, Internet, and long-distance calling services.

A number of duty-free and other shops are in the departure lounge. They carry electronics, liquor, clothing, some souvenirs, and so on. There are two new coffeehouses, one in the terminal and one in the departure lounge. They are the only sit-down restaurants. The branch in the terminal is larger and more pleasant.

David, in western Panama, is expanding its runway in the hopes of attracting international flights, which to date have not really taken off there (pardon the pun). Officially known as Aeropuerto Internacional de David "Enrique Malek," this airport is coded DAV.

There are also a few flights between Costa Rica and the small airport on Isla Colón in Bocas del Toro. Its airport code is BOC.

Airport Transportation

Though Panama City is just a 25-kilometer drive from Tocumen, there's no satisfactory public transportation to or from it.

To be sure of getting a licensed taxi driver, book through the taxi-information booth in the arrivals lounge (ground floor). The fare to Panama City is US$28 for one or two persons. The fare for two people sharing a cab but with different destinations is US$32. Groups of three or more can share a *colectivo* van ride for US$11 per person. There's an extra charge to take the toll road, but it's well worth the savings in time. Most destinations in the former Canal Zone—including Amador, Albrook, Clayton, and "Kobby" (Kobbe Beach, home to

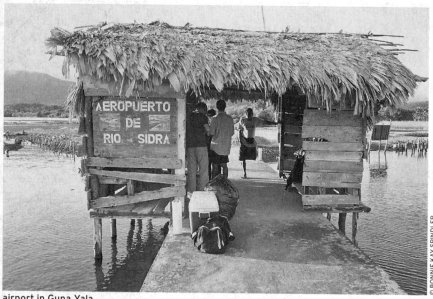

airport in Guna Yala

Playa Bonita Resort and Spa)—run US$30–35 for one or two people. Other fares available at the booth include Gamboa (US$45) and Colón (US$65) for up to four people. Those passing through Panama who have a long layover can get a tour of the Panama Canal for US$60. More ambitious tours are also offered. Add US$10 to most of these fares for a third person. Pay at the booth and take the receipt. It's not customary to tip taxi drivers in Panama.

Your driver will be pointed out to you, most likely a neatly dressed man with a clean, late-model car. Groups are transported in white minivans. These should have "SET" license plates, which means they are so-called "tourism taxis." This is the one occasion when I do recommend using a tourism taxi, as their rates from the airport are controlled and reasonable. (Usually they're allowed to charge much more than regular cab fare.)

It may be possible to save a few dollars by negotiating with other taxi drivers, licensed or otherwise, who hang around the terminal, but there's a risk of getting ripped off or worse by an unscrupulous character. These guys often try to take tourists to hotels that pay them commissions.

Regular Panama City taxis should charge about US$20–25 for the trip back to the airport, but settle on the price before getting in the cab.

A few hotels in Panama City offer airport pickup and drop-off for less than the cost of a taxi; ask when making room reservations. The Riande Airport hotel, which is a short drive from the airport, offers a free shuttle service. There is also a free shuttle bus between the airport and Metromall, aimed at transit passengers who get feverish if they have to go more than an hour or two without shopping.

It's possible to take a bus into the city, but it's a hassle and should only be attempted by those on a tight budget. Buses do not stop at the terminal. To catch one requires hauling your luggage outside the grounds of the airport. There's a bus shelter on the roundabout a hot and humid half-kilometer away on the main road. Look for the white and orange Metro Bus. The Tocumen-Albrook bus travels along the Corredor Sur (a toll highway) and the Cinta Costera next to Panama Bay, with stops in Paitilla, Marbella, Bella Vista, and Calidonia before ending at the Gran Terminal de Transportes in Albrook. From there, visitors can catch canal-area buses, long-distance buses, and taxis to other destinations. The whole trip can take more than an hour, depending on traffic. The fare is US$1.45.

Buses run frequently but erratically. There is no luggage storage compartment; you'll have to squeeze on with all your gear. I don't recommend attempting all this at night, which is quite likely when your plane will arrive. However, the Gran Terminal de Transportes is busy and well lit day and night, and is the safest place to start or end this trip.

Rental cars are available at the airport. All the major companies have offices there. Only those planning road trips outside Panama City should fool with them, though, because driving and parking in the city is a hassle.

The quickest route between Tocumen and Panama City is by way of the Corredor Sur, a toll highway to the airport that starts on the eastern outskirts of the city, rather than on the congested surface streets. The toll is US$2.40 to the end of the line. The Corredor Sur section of the drive takes only a few minutes, but heavy traffic in Panama City can slow getting to or from the highway. Allow at least an hour to drive between Tocumen and most parts of the city, more during the height of morning and evening rush hours.

From the United States and Canada

Panama's gateway cities in the United States are Atlanta, Houston, Dallas/Fort Worth, Los Angeles, Miami, Newark, New York City (JFK), Orlando, and Washington, D.C. There are nonstop flights between all of them and Panama City. Those coming from other U.S. cities will have to make one stop en route, and in some cases more.

Allow at least two hours to connect through any U.S. airport when returning from Panama City; clearing U.S. customs and immigrations can take a long time.

The busiest route is Miami–Panama City, with several daily nonstop flights each way. The flight takes a little less than three hours. Copa is the only airline that flies nonstop to Orlando, with 11 weekly flights.

The major carriers offering nonstop service from U.S. gateway cities are American (from Miami and Dallas/Fort Worth), Continental (Houston and Newark), Copa (Miami, New York City, Washington-Dulles, Los Angeles, and Orlando), and Delta (Atlanta and New York). The discount airline Spirit Air introduced daily flights between Fort Lauderdale and Panama City in 2008.

Many visitors from the West Coast of the United States are surprised to discover they have to fly not just south but considerably east to get to Panama—Panama City is actually slightly east of Miami. Those traveling from the San Francisco Bay Area, for instance, most often take connecting flights through Houston, Atlanta, or Miami.

Airfares between the United States and Panama fluctuate, though bargain fares and packages are not as easy to come by as they are in, for instance, tourist-saturated parts of the Caribbean. Expect to pay around US$400–700 round-trip from most U.S. cities. Flights out of Miami and Houston tend to be on the cheaper end of the scale. The least expensive West Coast flights usually originate in Los Angeles, though the difference is generally not great enough to make it worthwhile for those outside of Southern California to route their trip through Los Angeles International Airport (LAX).

Except for charters, there are no direct flights from Canada to Panama. Those flying to or from Canada will most likely have a stop in the United States or Mexico. Advance-purchase fares hover around C$1,000. Flights out of Toronto are generally cheaper than from other cities. Canadians are a major market for package deals that often include charter airfare. These can be very good value for those who like all-inclusive resorts. Check with a travel agent or contact any resort hotel listed in this book for current offers.

From Mexico

The U.S. carriers that fly into Panama City also fly into Mexico City, but that doesn't mean they fly *between* Panama City and Mexico City. At least, not directly: American's Mexico–Panama flights require a circuitous stop in Miami or Dallas, for instance. It makes more sense to fly with the Latin American carriers. Expect to pay US$400–600 round-trip; non-stops are more expensive.

Copa offers two daily nonstops between Panama City and Mexico City, as well as 10 weekly nonstops to and from Cancún, and five weekly nonstops to and from Guadalajara. Copa also has a code share agreement with Aeroméxico. Mexicana has two daily flights to and from Mexico City. The airlines of Grupo TACA also fly out of Mexico City, usually with at least one Central American stop en route.

From Central America and the Caribbean

Getting to Panama by air from most Central American capitals generally means taking the "milk run" down the Central American isthmus; expect to make at least one stop en route, possibly more. The exceptions are Costa Rica and El Salvador, both of which have regular nonstop flights to and from Panama City.

The major carriers for flights within Central America are Grupo TACA and Copa. Both airlines fly between most Central American capitals and Panama City. Advance-purchase round-trip fares to and from most places are around US$500–700, though prices vary quite a bit and deals are often available through the airlines' websites.

FROM COSTA RICA

There are plenty of nonstop flights between Panama City and San José, Costa Rica. For such a nearby destination and popular route, prices can be steep. Advance-purchase fares are about US$350–500 round-trip, with the cheaper fares available through website deals and other promotions. The flight takes about an hour, or closer to two on a small plane. Note that Costa Rican time is always an hour behind Panamanian time.

Copa has the most flights between the two capitals—five daily each way. Air Panama, which is primarily a domestic airline, flies three times a week between Panama City and San José.

There are also several flights between San José and David, in western Panama. Air Panama flies three times a week. Grupo TACA makes the trip four times a week. More flights may be coming.

There are also a few flights between Costa Rica and Bocas del Toro. Air Panama and the Costa Rica–based Nature Air offer this service.

FROM THE CARIBBEAN

Copa flies between Panama City and Cuba, Jamaica, Puerto Rico, Haiti, the Dominican Republic, and Trinidad and Tobago. TACA flies to Cuba. Cubana, Cuba's national airline, has daily flights to Panama City. Travel to and from other parts of the Caribbean generally requires flying through Miami or doing some island-hopping by small plane after arriving at one of the gateway islands.

A visit to Cuba is a popular add-on for travelers to Panama. Standard round-trip airfare from Panama starts at around US$550, but package deals that include airfare, three nights' accommodation, some meals, airport transfers, and tours are widely available and popular.

European and Canadian visitors sometimes route their trips to Panama to include a visit to Cuba on the way over or back. There are severe restrictions on visits to Cuba by U.S. citizens. Air Caraïbes flies to the French-speaking islands of the Caribbean. It's possible to fly to Aruba or Curacao on Avianca, but this requires going through the airline's hub in Bogotá, Colombia.

From South America

Panama has good connections with much of South America, particularly Colombia. Flights will most likely be on a Central American or South American airline. Few other carriers fly directly between South America and Panama, but tickets can be booked through an airline's code share partners. American Airlines has an especially extensive network of South American flights operated either by itself or its partners.

Copa flies between Panama City and Colombia (Bogotá, Barranquilla, Cali, Cartagena, and San Andrés), Argentina, Venezuela, Peru, Chile, Brazil, and Ecuador (Quito and Guayaquil). Other airlines that fly between Panama and South America include Avianca, Grupo TACA, and Aero República.

Colombia and Ecuador are less than two hours from Panama City, and standard round-trip, advance-purchase fares to these and other relatively close destinations run about US$500–800. Promotional deals can cut fares in half, especially for popular routes. Nonstop flights to or from the most distant locations, such as Argentina and Brazil, take at least seven hours and can cost well over US$1,000 for advance-purchase fares.

From Europe and the United Kingdom

KLM and Iberia are the only European airlines offering direct service to Panama. KLM offers three weekly nonstops from its hub in Amsterdam. Iberia flies between its hub in Madrid and Panama City, usually connecting through Miami or San José, Costa Rica. The best deals are sometimes available through carriers that don't fly directly between Europe and Central America. Often this requires no more than one stop. U.S. carriers that fly to both Europe and Panama offer connecting flights through their East Coast hubs in the United States. British Airways, Virgin Atlantic, and Air France offer flights in conjunction with code share partners.

Expect to pay around €800–950 for round-trip tickets between most European countries and Panama. Lower fares may start to appear if Panama becomes a hot tourist destination, as many are gambling it will. Consider buying an air pass if you plan to travel elsewhere in the Americas.

A good way to compare all current routes and fares is through an Internet travel search service such as www.kayak.co.uk or www.expedia.co.uk. Those in the United Kingdom should also check out **Journey Latin America** (tel. 020/8747-3108, www.journeylatinamerica.co.uk), a knowledgeable, London-based tour operator and travel agency that books flights to Panama, sells several kinds of air passes, and offers a few adventure-oriented Panama tours. Its website has lots of current information.

From Elsewhere in the World

There is currently no direct service between Panama and Asia, Australia, Africa, and the Pacific. However, Asian carriers attempt Panama routes from time to time, so this may well change. Getting to Panama from points east of Europe generally means flying to San Francisco, Los Angeles, or Mexico City and connecting there with Panama-bound flights. It's usually a quite expensive proposition. Try to find a good travel agent or be prepared to do a fair amount of independent research to find reasonable fares. Round-the-world tickets or travel using an air pass may prove to be the most economical way to go.

BY LAND

There are three border crossings between Panama and Costa Rica: at Paso Canoa on the Pacific side of the isthmus, at Río Sereno in the highlands, and at Guabito-Sixaola on the Caribbean coast. Paso Canoa, which is on the Interamericana (Interamerican Highway), is by far the most traveled. The Guabito-Sixaola crossing is used mainly by those traveling to and from Bocas del Toro. The Río Sereno crossing is rarely used and is not always open to foreign visitors.

The Interamericana comes to an end at the town of Yaviza in eastern Panama, where the famous Darién Gap begins. There are no roads linking Panama with Colombia and the rest of South America, and no car-ferry services. Travelers generally must fly from Panama to Colombia and continue their journey from there.

By Private Vehicle

It's possible to drive the entire length of the Interamericana (often referred to as the Pan-American Highway outside of Central America) from North America to Panama, but this is a long, serious trek and there's always some risk of encountering bandits, brutal roads, and dyspeptic border guards. Making the trip requires serious planning and a well-equipped vehicle. Allow about three weeks from the Mexican border to Panama at a reasonable pace. Bear in mind that North American auto insurance policies don't apply south of the border.

Cars rented in Costa Rica cannot be driven in Panama, and vice versa. Even trying to drive cars registered in one of the countries across the border into the other is a nuisance and a source of continuing squabbles. It's not worth the hassle for a short trip; take the bus instead.

RV convoys occasionally make pilgrimages down the Interamericana. The only true RV park in Panama is **XS Memories** (tel. 993-3096, fax 993-3069, www.xsmemories.com) in Santa Clara, about a two-hour drive west of Panama City. It has 22 hookups for campers and mobile homes and can provide current information for those interested in shipping vehicles to South America.

By Bus

Inexpensive, relatively comfortable buses make daily trips from southern Mexico, Guatemala, Honduras, El Salvador, Nicaragua, and Costa Rica to Panama. This is, obviously, quite a long haul—nearly four solid days from the Mexico-Guatemala border, including two overnight stays in El Salvador and Nicaragua. Few take buses the whole way. Buses between San José, Costa Rica, and Panama City are popular, however.

Two bus companies, Tica Bus and Panaline, make one daily trip between Panama City and San José, Costa Rica. Both leave from the Gran Terminal de Transportes, Panama City's main bus terminal in Albrook. Try to make reservations at least a month ahead of time during the dry season and on holidays. At other times, booking about four days ahead of time should be fine. Reservations can be made by phone or email, but they must be bought in person at the Albrook bus terminal, with cash. Travelers can check two pieces of luggage and take one carry-on at no extra charge.

Transport is by large, long-haul air-conditioned buses with toilets and reclining seats. The trip costs US$35.10/US$70.10 one-way/round-trip on either line and takes about 16 hours, which usually includes a lengthy stop at the Paso Canoa border crossing to go through immigration and customs, as well as a half-hour or so break in Santiago, about halfway across Panama, where travelers have access to a cafeteria, restaurant, pharmacy, ATM, and other services.

Costa Rican time is always one hour behind Panamanian time. Times listed here are all local.

Tica Bus (Panama City tel. 314-6385, San José tel. 506/222-8680, www.ticabus.com) leaves from the Albrook bus terminal at 11 A.M. daily, arriving on Paseo Colón in San José around 4 A.M. the next day.

The bus from San José to Panama City leaves at noon daily, arriving at Panama City's Gran Terminal de Transportes at 4 A.M. the next day.

Panaline (Panama City tel. 314-6383, San

José tel. 506/256-8721, www.panalinecr.com) leaves from the Albrook bus terminal at 10 P.M. daily, arriving in San José around 3:30 P.M. the next day. The bus drops off passengers in San José, 200 meters north of Hospital San Juan de Dios, near Terminal Coca Cola. Note that this is a rough part of San José.

Buses from San José leave from the same spot at 1 P.M. daily and arrive around 5 A.M. the next morning at the Albrook bus terminal.

A third bus company, **Agencia Tracopa** (David tel. 775-7269 or 775-0585, Paso Canoa tel. 727-6581, San José tel. 506/222-2666), has one bus departure from David to San José daily, at 8:30 A.M. The trip takes about eight hours and costs US$12.50.

Tica Bus also links Panama with Nicaragua, Honduras, Guatemala, and Tapachula, Mexico, which is near the Guatemalan border. Connections are pretty good between Panama and Nicaragua. Theoretically, one could make the trip to or from Managua in a brutal 30 hours or so either way, including a layover of just an hour or two in San José if timed right. Trips to or from El Salvador, however, require an overnight stay in Nicaragua, and trips starting or ending anyplace farther north require overnight stays in both Nicaragua and El Salvador. Travelers must find their own accommodations, so consider booking rooms ahead of time. Passengers are free to break their travel anywhere and catch a bus on another day, but they must book reservations ahead of time for the onward journey. The longest trip, between Mexico and Panama, costs around US$120 one way.

BY SEA
Cruise Ships

The Panama Canal is one of the top cruising destinations in the world, though "destination" is not really the right word. More than 150,000 people transit the canal each year, but most never set foot in Panama itself. Panama has been trying to change that. It now has two cruise-ship ports on the Caribbean side of the isthmus near Colón. A cruise-ship terminal and other facilities have been completed at Amador on the Pacific side, though ships must bring passengers ashore by tender boats.

Royal Caribbean Cruise Line was the first major cruise line to make Panama a home port, meaning it offers cruises that originate in Panama. It offers one-week cruises on its massive *Enchantment of the Seas,* departing from the Colón 2000 port.

The main Panama Canal cruise season begins in October, when ships end their Alaska cruises. They head down south and transit the canal to position themselves for their Caribbean and Panama Canal cruises. The main season lasts until the end of the dry season, around mid-April. A canal transit takes 8–10 hours. Ships sometimes visit Panama's islands, especially those of Guna Yala.

By Yacht and Cargo Boat

Panama has long been a haven for yachters, who come to transit the canal and explore the islands and beaches. It may come as a surprise, then, that facilities for yachts are still quite limited. Slips are scarce and haul-out facilities can be quite crude. However, this is beginning to change. Marinas near the canal include the Panama Canal Yacht Club, at Cristóbal near the Caribbean entrance to the canal, and the Balboa Yacht Club and Flamenco Yacht Club, at Amador near the Pacific entrance to the canal. The famous and funky wooden clubhouse at the Balboa Yacht Club, alas, burned down a while back. Today it consists of little more than moorings, a dock, and a burger stand. The newish Flamenco Yacht Club has extensive, modern facilities, but they're expensive. A new marina, Shelter Bay, recently opened on the site of the old Fort Sherman, near the Caribbean entrance to the canal.

Long-established ports and anchorages include Pedregal, Boca Brava, Puerto Mutis, and

Isla Taboga on the Pacific side of the isthmus and Bocas del Toro, Portobelo, Isla Linton, and José del Mar (aka José Pobre) on the Caribbean side. Yachts also frequent the Islas Perlas and several islands in the Golfo de Chiriquí, but with the exception of Contadora and a few other islands, most of these spots are uninhabited and lack even rudimentary marinas.

Facilities vary dramatically outside the canal area. The two marinas in Bocas del Toro can accommodate large yachts and perform limited maintenance work, and both are right in the middle of all the Bocas action. José del Mar and Boca Brava, on the other hand, are remote though lovely spots offering little more than a place to anchor and get a bite and a beer. A new marina has been proposed for Boca Brava, however, as have others around the country. How many of these actually materialize remains to be seen, but there may be more options by the time you read this.

The San Blas Islands (Guna Yala) are a popular yachting destination, but yachters should be prepared to pay a small fee when anchoring off islands in the archipelago. The waters out there can be treacherous; this is a place for skilled, experienced sailors. Transiting the canal by yacht is a complex and time-consuming process. An increase in tolls has made transiting a quite expensive proposition. The minimum cost is US$600 for yachts up to 50 feet. Many yachts need to take on additional crew at the canal to help handle lines.

Joining a Crew

Landlubbers looking for a free canal transit can sometimes join a yacht as a line handler. This is not a pleasure cruise, however. Don't consider this unless you're fairly strong, respond quickly to orders, and are prepared to get a little training. Yachters sometimes pay for the service, but not if there are enough volunteers around. Yachts are sometimes required to stop in the middle of the canal, sometimes for the night, so be prepared

for the possibility of sleeping onboard. The transit is a one-way trip; so if you need to get back, figure out ahead of time how you're going to do it. The yacht owner sometimes coughs up the bus (US$2) or cab fare (about US$40).

The best places to look for needy yachts are the Balboa Yacht Club or the Flamenco Yacht Club, on the Pacific side of the isthmus, and the Panama Canal Yacht Club or Shelter Bay, on the Caribbean side. Ask around. Note: The Panama Canal Yacht club is right next to Colón. It's dangerous to wander anywhere outside the grounds of the club. Panama City hostels may be able to help connect line handlers and yachts.

It may also be possible to sign on as a crew member on a yacht for a longer trip, but this is not common, especially for those who aren't experienced sailors. Ask around at any of the yacht clubs. The dock master will likely know who's going where and/or is in need of new crew members. It's also sometimes possible to pay for passage. Local authorities are keeping a wary eye on this practice, however, out of concern people are slipping illegally in and out of the country.

To Colombia by Sea

There is no commercial ferry service between Panama and Colombia, but the adventurous occasionally book passage on yachts to or from Cartagena. Some yachts make this trip often enough that it's become a commercial service for them, albeit an informal one. Most yachts charge US$400–500 per person, including meals. The trip takes 4–5 days, most of which is spent sailing among the uninhabited islands of Guna Yala. Yachts typically anchor near the beautiful, remote islands of Chichime, Coco Bandero, or Cayos Holandéses. An itinerary like this would normally cost many times what these yachts charge, though of course this is not a luxury cruise.

Think carefully before making this trip, as there are many risks to consider. The seas around

Guna Yala can turn rough very quickly. They are also notoriously dangerous because of shallow reefs that lurk like depth charges throughout the archipelago. There are lots of shipwrecks there to prove it, and at least two lives have been lost from yachts out there in the last few years. The winds blow so strongly in the dry season that many boats won't even make the trip.

Also, Panama is a popular transshipment point for drugs coming up from South America. If you're unlucky enough to be aboard a vessel intercepted with a few tons of cocaine in the hold, you'll have some tricky explaining to do. Boats are also sometimes caught with less-sinister but no-less-illegal contraband.

The truly adventurous sometimes strike a deal for passage on a cargo boat, such as the Colombian trading vessels that ply the waters of Guna Yala or the Guna-owned boats that travel the same route. I strongly advise against this. For one thing, some of these boats are barely seaworthy rust buckets. Those who insist on hitching a ride should know it's tough to join a boat in Guna Yala. Many a tourist ends up stranded in El Porvenir because they've heard that's the place to hop on a boat. It's much easier to arrange from Colón. Even here, I've heard tales of passengers having to wait 10 days for their boat to get even as far as Isla Grande, which is less than 50 kilometers east of Colón. Those still interested should start by asking around at Panama City hostels, like Mamallena or Luna's Castle.

Finally, some people fly from Panama City to the border town of Puerto Obaldía, on the Caribbean coast, and take a launch to Colombia from there.

However you go, don't board any boat that doesn't have life jackets, well-equipped lifeboats, communication equipment, and a captain who inspires confidence.

Getting Around

It's easy to get almost anywhere in Panama by bus or small plane. Commercial boat service, ironically for a country that owes so much to its waterways, is harder to come by.

The main roads in Panama are generally in good shape, and they've been much improved in recent years. The nation's major artery is the Interamerican Highway, or Interamericana, which in Panama stretches from the Costa Rican border along the Pacific slope of the isthmus all the way to the town of Yaviza in the Darién, where all roads stop.

The Interamericana is a divided highway in mostly good shape from just west of Panama City to around Santiago, halfway across the isthmus. From there to the city of David there are poorly maintained, two-lane sections with monster potholes, detours, and washouts. However, work is proceeding on extending the divided highway all the way to David.

The easternmost section of the highway to the Darién is not paved all the way. It is drivable all the way to Yaviza only in the dry season, and then only with great effort and a good four-wheel drive or bus. At other times it's almost impossible to get much beyond Meteti.

Buses offer the cheapest way to explore most parts of Panama and are the best option for many travelers. Rental cars are a viable option for those who can afford it, are in a hurry, plan to travel extensively beyond the cities, and are up for the many hazards of driving in Panama. Domestic flights offer the fastest way to get from point A to point B in many parts of Panama, and for some remote spots they're the only reasonable option.

BY AIR

Panama is dotted with airstrips served by a network of small commercial prop planes and jets.

The longest flights take a little over an hour (not including interim stops). There are several flights a day along some popular routes.

The planes are essentially air taxis that often make several stops, and not always in the order you expect. Planes to Guna Yala often go island-hopping down the archipelago, landing at several airstrips. Make sure to get off in the right place.

Panama City has the country's main domestic airport, Aeropuerto Marcos A. Gelabert, in the Albrook neighborhood a short drive from downtown. Most taxi drivers won't know it by name: Ask to go to the **Aeropuerto de Albrook.** Most flights originate from and end at Albrook, with a few exceptions. There is now a domestic terminal at Tocumen International Airport, though at least so far it's used primarily (and even then not that often) to connect international travelers with destinations in western Panama. This allows travelers to avoid a land transfer between Albrook and Tocumen, which are on opposite outskirts of Panama City.

David's airport was finishing a dramatic expansion in 2012 with the aim of becoming the international hub for western Panama. Flights between Bocas del Toro and David have been added and dropped over the years. It's also occasionally possible to fly between islands in Guna Yala (San Blas Islands).

But at least for now, most travelers have to go through Albrook on the way to anywhere else. Panama's domestic carriers are not really set up for complicated itineraries. It's usually best to think of Panama City as your flight hub and plan trips that begin and end there.

Also, beware of flying on holidays. Flight schedules automatically revert to a Sunday schedule on these days, but this is not always accounted for in the airline's reservation system. If you fly on a holiday, be sure to confirm with a live person that your flight exists. To be safe, don't book a holiday flight that isn't also listed for a Sunday.

The sudden closure of Aeroperlas, Panama's oldest domestic airline, in March 2012 left Panama with just one regular domestic carrier: Air Panama. It's hard to believe some new airline won't step into the breach at some point; this may have happened by the time you visit.

Air Panama (tel. 316-9000, www.flyairpanama.com) flies to most of the same destinations as Aeroperlas did, plus Chitré and San José, Costa Rica. Frequent fliers grumble that its flights often run late.

Flying within Panama is hardly risk-free. Passengers have traditionally complained about questionable maintenance, aging aircraft, deteriorating runways, and a casual attitude toward air safety. On the other hand, the views are spectacular, and the flights don't last long. These pilots fly constantly and, at least from my lay perspective, often have impressive skills. Flying is quite likely the safest way to get around, given the hazards of traveling by road and sea.

Weight Limits

The baggage weight limit on domestic flights is about 12 kilograms. This is total weight, including both checked luggage and carry-ons. Do not try to slip by with more; planes are sometimes dangerously overloaded. Passengers are sometimes also asked to report their own body weight. Err on the side of exaggerating your weight.

Fares

Domestic airline fares are regulated by the government. Standard fares are the same regardless of airline or season. They tend to go up only very slowly from year to year, though the recent rise in fuel prices is exerting unusual upward pressure. But in 2010, the most expensive one-way domestic fare was still just over US$100. The round-trip fare is always double the one-way fare. There are usually discounts for young children. Try to make reservations at least several days in advance, and reconfirm the reservation 72 hours before the flight. Be at the airport at least an hour before the scheduled departure time.

local Panama City buses

BY BUS

Panama's buses are the backbone of its transportation system. Except for the relatively few able to afford cars, Panamanians rely on buses to get just about everywhere. They're cheap, run frequently, and are generally fast—sometimes too fast. The only ones not worth fooling with, except for those on a starvation budget, are buses within Panama City. They crawl across the city's congested streets, and anyone who can afford it takes the inexpensive taxis instead.

Many buses, especially in rural areas, run from dawn to dusk. There are few night buses except in the cities and along a few major long-distance routes. Few buses are expresses. Generally you can take any bus that goes at least as far as your destination. For instance, to get from Panama City to Penonomé, you can take a bus with a final destination of, say, Aguadulce or Santiago, both of which pass by Penonomé.

Panama's biggest bus terminal, not surprisingly, is in Panama City: the Gran Terminal de Transportes, in the Albrook neighborhood not far from downtown. Buses leave from there to every part of the republic, often without any changes.

The other major hubs are Santiago and David. The hubs on the Azuero Peninsula are in Chitré and Las Tablas.

Reservations are seldom necessary (and not always possible). On most popular routes, if a bus fills up, there's usually another one shortly thereafter. However, a reservation or at least an early arrival at the station is a good idea if you need to make specific connections. In Bocas del Toro, for instance, travelers need to arrive in time to get a water taxi to the islands.

BY BOAT

Organized ferry and water-taxi service is available between Panama City and Isla Taboga and sometimes Contadora, and between the mainland and Isla Colón in Bocas del Toro province. Other than these services, boat transportation for travelers is generally more casual and arranged ad hoc.

Boats are the main means of regional transportation within the archipelagos of Bocas del Toro and Guna Yala (San Blas Islands). They are also the main way to get around the densely forested parts of the Darién and mainland Bocas close to rivers, especially in the rainy season when the rivers are more easily navigable.

The Bocas archipelago is the only place with anything resembling scheduled, cheap, commercial boat transportation among the islands. Boat transportation everyplace else is usually a matter of tracking down a fisherman or enterprising local boat owner and negotiating a price for a tour or extended trip. This can get expensive quickly. Tours are generally charged by the hour per group; the price for longer trips is based on distance, with gasoline the biggest expense. The price always includes the boat, a captain (and crew, if needed), and fuel. As always, agree on a price ahead of time.

Transportation is generally in exceptionally long wooden dugouts called *piraguas,* though fiberglass boats *(botes)* are also used in some places. Both come equipped with outboard motors. For long trips especially, check the horsepower of the motor, and ask if there's a backup motor and life jackets *(salvavidas). Piraguas* are actually the preferred form of transportation on the river. Long dugouts used on the ocean are similar, but they have higher sides and an angled prow to break the waves. Short dugouts called *cayucos* are powered by a single wooden paddle and are all too easy for inexperienced paddlers to flip; it's unlikely you'll find yourself in one except for a very short trip.

Chartered sailboats, fishing or diving trips, and other outdoor activities on more substantial boats are easy to come by, but they tend to be quite expensive. It's possible to take a partial or complete transit of the Panama Canal every Saturday via small vessel.

BY RAIL

The only passenger rail service in the country is on the recently rebuilt Panama Canal Railway,

---

A REAL LIFESAVER

If you know ahead of time you'll be making trips on open ocean or even fast-flowing rivers, bring a life jacket with you to be on the safe side. Few boats are equipped with them, and even the larger ferry services don't always have enough for all passengers. These are light and easy to carry in your luggage, and during safe stretches of water they make a convenient cushion over the hard wooden planks that serve as seats. At the end of the trip, donate the jacket to the boatman; hopefully someone else will use it to make their own trip safer. This leaves extra room in your luggage for souvenirs on the way back home. Those who forget to bring one down to Panama should be able to find them in a sporting goods, home-supply, or department store in the larger cities. Try Novey or a Do-It Center in Panama City.

---

which runs between Corozal, a few minutes' drive north of downtown Panama City, and Colón. Some Panamanian businesspeople use it as a commuter service, but for most travelers it's a day excursion, and getting there is all the fun.

BY TAXI

Taxis are everywhere in Panama, especially Panama City. They're clearly marked and nearly always small Japanese cars. By law, taxis must be painted bright yellow. Fares are based either on a series of zones established by law or on long-established prices for particular routes. There are no metered taxis in Panama.

Taxis are cheap, and drivers do not expect a tip. Always ask for the price ahead of time, and clarify whether the price quoted is per person or the total amount. Fares are typically based on a single person in a taxi, with a small surcharge added for each additional passenger. Taxis are often allowed to charge a bit more late at night, on Sunday, or during holidays.

It's rare to pay more than US$2 or US$3 even for long rides in Panama City. Fares within other cities generally top out at US$1. Rides outside the cities are more negotiable and more expensive, though it's rare to pay more than US$20 even for a long trip on bad roads. Most shouldn't cost more than US$5–10.

In rural areas, the taxis are sometimes pickup trucks, occasionally converted into a kind of homemade minibus. These *colectivos* are especially useful for travel on dirt or badly maintained roads. Some taxis running specific routes, especially the converted pickups, operate more like buses than taxis and charge by the head.

Taxis can be hired by the hour for tours, though few taxi drivers speak much English. This can be a good option for those who want to cover a lot of ground in a short amount of time and would like the driver to wait between stops. There are no set prices for this service, but expect to pay about US$7 an hour within Panama City, or considerably more for long trips. Again, agree on a price ahead of time and don't pay until the end of the tour.

In Panama City, so-called "tourist taxis" (they have "SET" license plates) hover around the more expensive hotels. These are larger, air-conditioned cars that are authorized to charge several times the going rate. It's a pricey way to go, but may be of interest to those who want a more comfortable ride and the security of a lot more metal around them on the capital's chaotic streets. Those who want the cheaper ride can just walk down to a main street and hail a cab.

Taxi drivers tend to drive fast and aggressively, and their cars have the dents to prove it. Buckle in and hope for the best. If a driver is making you uncomfortable, a firm but polite *"despacio, por favor"* ("slow, please") should help a bit. If it doesn't, demand to be let out and get another taxi.

It's usually easy to find a cab night or day, and the international hailing sign of the raised arm works just fine. At night, it can be worth calling for a radio taxi rather than waiting on the street. Many hotels, restaurants, and bars will be happy to call one for you.

RENTAL CARS AND DRIVING LAWS

Do not bother with rental cars for travel within Panama City or any other urban area. It's far easier, cheaper, and more convenient to take taxis. But renting a car is a reasonable option for longer trips. There is a standard charge of US$180 to drop a car off in a different city from the one you rented it in.

Visitors can drive in Panama for 90 days with a driver's license from their home country; there's no need to get an international or Panamanian driver's license or permit. Be prepared to present both your driver's license and passport if stopped by the transit police for any reason.

Two kinds of insurance are obligatory when driving a rental car in Panama. Different rental companies call them by different names, but they're essentially collision and robbery insurance (called *cobertura de colisión y robo* and comparable to collision damage waiver—CDW—in the United States) and insurance against liability for harm to third parties (called *cobertura de daños a terceros o responsabilidad civil* or *suplemento de seguro de responsabilidad contra terceros*). Other kinds of insurance are optional. Your credit card, home auto insurance, or travelers' insurance may include some car-rental protection, but be sure to check ahead of time that it covers driving in Panama.

Drivers and passengers are required by law to wear seat belts. Cars are not yet required to have airbags, so ask if your car has them.

It's against the law to drive while talking on a cell phone. If you need to make a call, pull over. It's also illegal to drive without a shirt—seriously, you'll get ticketed for this.

Rental car agencies in Panama do not allow customers to take cars out of the country. Visitors are allowed to drive foreign-registered vehicles within Panama for up to 90 days.

COURTESY OF THOMAS GORISSEN/WWW.THOMASGORISSEN.COM

Panama City's streets are perpetually jammed.

Panama's streets are increasingly choked with enormous SUVs, so consider that when contemplating renting a subcompact car. For some remoter, rugged areas, a four-wheel-drive vehicle with high clearance is a must to navigate rough, rocky dirt roads and small streams. In the rainy season, some roads will be impassable no matter what you're driving. Four-wheel drives are popular, so be sure to make a reservation for these well ahead of time. If you're unused to driving these vehicles, bear in mind many have a high center of gravity and it's disturbingly easy to flip them over on sharp turns or when dodging road obstacles, both of which pop up often on Panama's roads. Four-wheel drives are known in Panama as *cuatro por cuartos* (four by fours), *vehículos con doble traccion* (vehicle with double traction), or simply *dobles*.

Rental cars are most widely available in Panama City, but they can also be found in David and a few other places. In Panama City, the highest concentration of offices is in the Vía España area, though there are branches dotted around the city and at the international airport. Rates are about the same and sometimes cheaper than they are in the United States, and promotions are often available, including packages that combine a car rental with domestic flights and/or hotel stays. These can be great deals.

The major companies are Hertz, Avis, Thrifty, Dollar, Alamo, National, and Budget. Which company is best changes so rapidly, depending on current local management, it's impossible to recommend one over another. Vehicles rented in Panama City should be reasonably well maintained. Outside the capital things are dicier.

Toll Roads

Panama has three toll highways: the Corredor Norte, the Corredor Sur, and the Autopista Arraiján–La Chorrera. The Corredor Sur links Tocumen International Airport and central Panama City. The Corredor Norte extends

© WILLIAM FRIAR

Traffic accidents are all too common in Panama.

north from Panama City across the isthmus toward Colón. Both of these latter highways were begun in the 1990s and are still works in progress to some degree. The Corredor Norte is being extended to Sabanitas, not far from Colón.

Tolls on the *corredores* are based on distance driven, the amount collected in increments at toll plazas along the way. Payments are made in cash or through an electronic debit system that only regular commuters bother with. Most tolls are around US$1 or less.

The Autopista Arraiján–La Chorrera, completed in 1981, is Panama's oldest toll road. It's on the Interamericana west of Panama City. The toll plaza is about 30 kilometers west of Panama City. The toll for a passenger car is US$0.50.

Tolls on all three highways are collected in either direction. Take the receipt the attendant hands you and hold on to it until you exit the highway. Tolls are higher for larger vehicles.

BY BICYCLE

Panama is not a bicycle-friendly country. There are no bike lanes, few places to rent bikes, and only a handful of areas where it's even marginally safe to venture out on a bike. A trailblazing friend is determined to build a bike trail through Parque Natural Metropolitano in Panama City, and it may actually exist by the time you visit.

If not, the best bet for a reasonably safe workout are the hilly loop roads above Boquete, though even here it's important to keep a sharp eye out for speeding trucks and cars. The Calzada de Amador is a good place for a flat, leisurely ride with great views. Isla Colón in Bocas del Toro is pretty much the only place that lends itself to biking as a sightseeing activity.

There are few bike shops and rental places in the country. The main place in Panama City to rent bikes is **Bicicletas Moses** (tel. 211-2579, 8 A.M.–9 P.M. daily) on the Calzada de Amador, which not coincidentally is pretty much the only place in Panama City where it's safe to ride them. Bikes can also be rented in Gamboa, Santa Clara, Farallón, El Valle, Boquete, Bambito, and Bocas del Toro. Do not expect high-quality bicycles at any of these locations. Rentals tend to be basic mountain bikes or clunky old road bikes. Bike rentals are usually around US$2–5 an hour. Some true adventurers have biked all the way from North America to the Darién Gap.

HIKING

Panama is a great place for hikes, both casual day trips and major backcountry treks. There are very few developed campsites in the country, however, and few rangers to help out stranded hikers. Trails are often rugged and rudimentary.

Never, ever hike in the forest alone. Go with a qualified naturalist guide. It's surprisingly easy to get lost, and in some parts of Panama—such as the Darién—getting lost can be fatal. Also,

IF THE CHICKEN CROSSES THE ROAD

Among the many road obstacles intrepid drivers are likely to encounter on the back roads of Panama are suicidal chickens. Chickens are definitely free range in the countryside, and they have a way of blundering out into the road with no notice. If you hit one, you are expected to find the owner and pay him or her for the pummeled poultry. Seriously. Make the effort to do the right thing, since for many people chickens are an important means of subsistence. You are, of course, then welcome to take the roadkill with you, if you have a means of preparing it. More likely you'll turn the deceased over to the grieving farmer. Also be on the lookout for dogs.

rainforest trails can be very slippery, and you don't want to be stuck alone in the forest with even a twisted ankle. I'm embarrassed to admit how many times I've wiped out on what looked like an easy trail or gentle stream crossing.

Appropriate gear is key to a safe, enjoyable hike in the tropics. Always camp in a tent, even on the beach, to prevent insect and possible vampire-bat bites. Treat even small scratches with antibiotics; wounds quickly become infected in the tropics.

ORGANIZED TOURS

Panama has many tour operators and guides, of wildly different quality. Companies appear and disappear constantly, and I've encountered many a guide who hasn't a clue what he or she is talking about. Even the more established companies can be hit-and-miss.

The ones included here are among the most prominent and well established, and I have indicated the ones I recommend highly. In addition to setting up tours, many operators can also make hotel and travel arrangements. Those especially interested in nature travel should be

sure to sign up with a group that uses qualified naturalist guides; ask about credentials.

In addition to the guides and services described here, a couple of other individuals are worth mentioning. A naturalist guide and environmental activist named Guido Berguido works with a guide outfit called **Advantage Tours** (tel. 232-6944, www.advantagepanama. com). They typically offer 10-day birding trips, but other tours are available. They have a field station in Gamboa and can take groups to two sites in the Darién.

Iann Sanchez (kayakinn@hotmail.com), the son of Hector Sanchez of Chiriquí River Rafting fame, also has a good reputation. He's worked as a U.S. park ranger and a rafting guide in the United States and Panama, and he is known for being knowledgeable and safety-conscious. He offers some unusual trips, including kayaking tours around Lago Gatún. He is completely bilingual.

Ancon Expeditions

Ancon Expeditions (P.O. Box 0832-1509 WTC, Panama City, Republic of Panama, tel. 269-9414 or 269-9415, fax 264-3713, www.anconexpeditions.com) is Panama's top nature-tour company. It's known for employing some of Panama's best naturalist guides, particularly in the Darién.

These include Hernan Araúz (www.hernanarauz.com), Rich Cahill (www.richardjcahill.com), Iván Hoyos (ivan@panamensis.com), and Rick Morales (morales.rick@gmail.com), all of whom I've traveled with and can recommend. They're all fluent in both English and Spanish. Hernan (one of Panama's top birding guides and Darién experts) and Rich are particularly experienced, with multiple trans-Darién treks and many shorter adventures to their credit. They're a blast to travel with: filled with a sense of fun and adventure, but always responsible and safety-conscious. Ancon Expeditions also runs some unique ecolodges, including ones in Cana, Punta Patiño, and Bocas del Toro.

Tours range from easy day trips to ambitious, multiday treks through the forest. The company occasionally organizes ocean-to-ocean adventures through the heart of the Darién. It also offers a weeklong trip that includes a multiday hike along what remains of the historic Camino Real, which once stretched from Panamá La Vieja across the isthmus to Portobelo.

Boquete Outdoor Adventures

This is a fairly new operation led by John Miller (cell 6474-0274, www.boqueteoutdooradventures.com), who worked for 10 years at the Nantahala Outdoor Center as a rafting guide and kayak instructor. It offers a variety of trips but specializes in weeklong white-water kayaking adventures in western Panama.

Ecocircuitos

This company (tel./fax 314-1586, www.ecocircuitos.com), based at the Country Inn and Suites in Amador, offers a wide range of short and multiday tours around the country. It hires friendly and accommodating guides who speak English and Spanish.

Exotics Adventures

This group (tel. 223-9283, www.panamaexoticsadventures.com) is led by a Frenchman named Michel Peuch who comes highly recommended. Unusual offerings include a fast and arduous ocean-to-ocean Darién trek and a kayak trip in Bocas del Toro. His Darién trips focus on the western end, relatively close to Panama City and far from the dangers of the Darién Gap. These include hikes along the El Llano–Cartí Road to Guna Yala. Other offerings include a day hike along a part of the Camino de Cruces.

Gold Coast Expeditions

This operation (tel. 441-4339, cell 6635-2292, http://goldcoastpanama.homestead.com) is run by Skipper and Jill Berger, longtime residents of the Caribbean side of the former Canal Zone.

They offer a variety of snorkeling/diving, sailing, and sightseeing trips around Panama, with the Caribbean side of the canal area their specialty. Popular trips include kayaking excursions around Portobelo and the lower Río Chagres.

Iguana Tours

Iguana Tours (tel. 226-8738, 226-1667, or 226-4516, fax 226-4736, www.nvmundo.com/iguanatours) specializes in trips to Isla Iguana off the Azuero Peninsula, but it offers a range of tours all over the country.

José Saenz

José (based in Panama City, tel./fax 399-4003 or 251-0698, cell 6614-7811, www.goldenfrog.net) is a taxi driver, but if you spend any amount of time in Panama, you'll realize he's an important part of the tourist infrastructure. I highly recommend him. He's punctual, responsible, polite, dependable—and a safe driver. These are qualities to prize among Panama taxi drivers. He charges US$25 for transfers to and from Tocumen International Airport. Transfers to or from most Panama City hotels to the domestic airport at Albrook is US$5. With enough notice, he can make hotel and domestic airline reservations. He charges US$12 an hour for Panama City tours. These prices are for one or two people. José also offers tours all over Panama, including Chiriquí, the Azuero Peninsula (his specialty; that's where he's from), and Bocas del Toro. Rates for this vary. Besides his air-conditioned cab, he has access to a minibus and pickup truck. He speaks pretty good English.

Panama Travel Experts

Many offerings from Panama Travel Experts (tel. 265-5323, fax 265-5324, U.S. tel. 877/836-5300 or 707/226-2640, www.panamatravelexperts.com) are higher-end multiday packages that include stays at luxury hotels, but the group also offers less expensive day tours.

Pesantez Tours

Pesantez (tel. 223-5374 or 263-7577, www. pesantez-tours.com) is a long-established company that enjoys a solid reputation. It specializes in tours of Panama City and cultural tours, rather than nature trips.

San Blas Sailing

This outfit (tel. 314-1800 or 314-1288, www. sanblassailing.com) arranges memorable multi-day yacht tours of Guna Yala (San Blas Islands).

Though not cheap, these trips are not as expensive as one might expect and offer good value. For those who don't have yachts of their own, it's the best way to explore and enjoy the islands.

Scubapanama

Scubapanama (tel. 261-3841 or 261-4064, www.scubapanama.com) is Panama's biggest dive operator. Common offerings include diving around Portobelo, a dive in both oceans in a single day, and diving in the Panama Canal.

Visas and Officialdom

Tourist-entry requirements for Panama are a muddle. Rules are in flux, and government officials often seem the last people you can count on for accurate information. It's possible to call a half dozen consulates and get a half dozen contradictory answers to basic questions. Things got immeasurably worse in 2007 with the introduction of a new tourist-entry law that confused everyone. In 2010, the confusion got worse when Panama eliminated *tarjetas de turismo* (tourist cards), which those from the United States, Canada, Australia, and a few other countries had to buy from their airline or at the border. Now tourists from these countries are allowed to enter with just their passports, but Panama officialdom has not yet updated its websites and documentation accordingly; some forms issued by the Panamanian government still have the old rules printed on them.

The website of Panama's immigration and naturalization office (http://migracion.gob.pa/) is the best place to go for current information if it's ever working properly, but even it is not the final word. All that ultimately matters is what the immigration official who greets you in Panama says the rules are.

That said, it's not hard for most people to enter Panama as tourists, especially by air. With all the changes, two things have remained

constant: Tourists can normally stay in Panama at least 30 days, and U.S. citizens need only their passport to enter.

All foreign nationals need to present a passport that is valid for at least six months from their date of entry. Tourists must also be able to show proof of having at least US$500 (a credit card or travelers checks are usually good enough) and a return or onward travel ticket out of Panama. In practice, this rule will probably not be enforced, especially for clean, neatly dressed North Americans and Western Europeans. Bedraggled backpackers may get more attention. Bus passengers arriving at Paso Canoa without proof of onward travel are usually required to buy a bus ticket back to Costa Rica, whether they intend to use it or not.

VISAS

Panama divides foreign tourists into two categories, depending on nationality: those who need a tourist visa; and those who don't need anything but a passport to enter Panama. Tourist visas are further broken down into "stamped visas" and the more restrictive "authorized visas."

Countries whose citizens need only a passport to enter Panama include: Argentina, Australia, Austria, Belgium, Canada, Chile, Colombia, Costa Rica, Cyprus, the Czech

Republic, Denmark, Estonia, Finland, France, Germany, Great Britain, Greece, Hungary, Iceland, Ireland, Israel, Italy, Japan, Luxembourg, Mexico, the Netherlands, New Zealand, Norway, Poland, Portugal, Slovakia, South Korea, Spain, Sweden, Switzerland, Singapore, Taiwan, and the United States. Note: This list changes often; check with the consulate or embassy in your country for current requirements.

Stamped Visa

Panama issues a so-called "stamped visa," a kind of tourist visa that lets some travelers enter the country multiple times over the course of a year. It is available only through a Panamanian consulate or embassy, and as the name implies, it consists of a stamp placed in the traveler's passport. Length of stay is at the discretion of the Panamanian authorities, but is generally 30 days for each visit.

Anyone eligible to travel to Panama on a tourist card can choose to apply for a stamped visa instead, if they want. Citizens of some countries are required to get a stamped visa.

Countries whose citizens must have a stamped visa to travel to Panama include the Dominican Republic, Ecuador, Georgia, Peru, Russia, Ukraine, Vietnam, and Zimbabwe. Remember, these lists are subject to change.

Authorized Visa

Citizens of some countries need a so-called *visa autorizada* (authorized visa). This is the most restrictive kind of tourist visa. It is available only through a Panamanian consulate or embassy, which decides whether to approve the visa application and determines the length of stay. Most countries on this list are in Africa, the Middle East, eastern Europe, and Asia.

Confusingly, stated requirements can vary by consulate, so double-check with the nearest one before beginning the process to make sure to have all the required documents in order.

But even the loosest interpretation of the rules makes applying a lengthy hassle, and they sure aren't designed to make the applicant feel welcomed with open arms. Begin the process at least 30 days before the start of travel.

Applicants will probably need to present:

- A completed one-page application form
- A valid passport
- A copy of the passport including pages showing entry and exit stamps
- A letter from a local sponsor in Panama, as well as a recent bank statement and utility bill from the sponsor. (It may be worth arranging at least one tour with a Panamanian guide company or tour operator and have them supply this letter for you—again, start this process well in advance, as getting this letter may be a nuisance. Don't pay for the tour until the letter's supplied.)
- A copy of your most recent Panama visa (if applicable)
- A copy of your residence or identification card from your home country
- Two passport-size photographs

Some consulates require proof of a round-trip. If so, make sure the ticket's refundable in case the application is turned down.

Not surprisingly, many prefer to apply for this visa through a lawyer or visa service.

Countries whose citizens can travel to Panama only with an authorized visa include: Bangladesh, Cuba, Haiti, India, Pakistan, the People's Republic of China, and South Africa. Again, this list changes frequently.

Extended Stays

How long can one stay in Panama as a tourist? Excellent question. It's a major source of confusion these days. Everyone agrees that tourists can generally stay for at least 30 days. The upper limit for most tourist stays is 90 days, but this is discretionary. When a tourist enters the country, the immigration official now asks for length of intended stay and, if he or she agrees, writes that number on the entry stamp in your passport. If you think you may stay longer than 30 days, say so and hope the official approves.

Tourists who want to extend their stay beyond that authorized when they entered the country must apply for a *prórroga de turista* (tourist extension) at an immigration office. Just who's eligible for a *prórroga* these days is a matter of debate.

Getting a *prórroga* is a serious nuisance. Gather all the materials needed and start the application process about four working days before the visa or tourist card expires. Wear your nicest clothes and be unfailingly polite.

Applicants must submit:

- Their passport and tourist card or visa
- A photocopy of the passport pages that show the applicant's photo, personal details, and latest entry stamp for Panama
- A photocopy of the tourist card or visa
- A sponsorship letter from a Panamanian or foreign resident, along with a photocopy of the sponsor's *cédula* (national identity card) and a photocopy of his or her latest telephone or utilities bill
- A photocopy of a return or onward-travel ticket that's valid for a year
- Proof of one's own financial solvency (e.g., travelers checks, credit cards, or US$500 in cash)
- Two passport-size photos
- A payment of US$1 to open a file and US$15 to make the *carnet de prórroga* (ID card)

Applicants need to fill out a simple Spanish form (those who don't speak Spanish may want to bring a phrasebook). The whole procedure can sometimes be completed in a day but can take longer. Applicants are required to leave their passport (be sure to make an extra photocopy or two for yourself).

Tourists can get up to 60 more days in Panama through this process. Note that getting the full extension is not guaranteed. The number of days granted is at the discretion of immigration authorities.

After the extension expires, tourists have a two-day grace period to leave the country. The penalty for staying beyond that, interestingly, is not that bad. Tourists whose stay has expired are required to pay a *multa* (fine) before leaving the country. The fine is US$25 for overstaying a month, and it goes up slowly from there, topping out at US$300 for a year or more. Still, it's not a good idea to get enmeshed in the cogs of the Panamanian bureaucracy by overstaying your official welcome.

The main immigration office is in Panama City. It's formally known as the **Ministerio de Gobierno y Justicia, Dirección de Migración y Naturalización** (Avenida Cuba and Calle 29 Este, tel. 207-1800, 777-7777, or 227-1077, tel./fax 227-1227, 8 A.M.–3 P.M. Mon.–Fri.). The influx of foreigners has made this place a jam-packed nightmare. It's so crowded the line to get in forms at 6 A.M. The first thing one needs to do is take a number: This being Panama, enterprising locals show up early, take the numbers, and sell them to foreigners who chose to sleep in. If you can't get to the office by about 10 A.M., you might as well not bother; go the next day.

A street kiosk next to the office, Kiosca Yolanda, makes photocopies for US$0.10. Just up the street is an Internet café (8 A.M.–10 P.M. Mon.–Fri., 10 A.M.–1 P.M. Sat.–Sun.) that also makes photocopies. There are other immigration offices around the country, including one in David, one in Chitré, and two in Bocas del Toro.

LIVING AND WORKING IN PANAMA

It's tough to get a permit to work in Panama. The country has high unemployment, and the government wants jobs to go to Panamanians, not foreigners. However, foreign investors, entrepreneurs, and retirees are welcome to make their home in Panama if they meet certain conditions.

Coming to Panama as anything other than a

PROHIBIDO
TOMAR LICOR, FUMAR
JUGAR DOMINÓ, FUTBOL
Y VULGARIDADES SE MULTARA CON B/. 10.00

© WILLIAM FRIAR

regulations for water-taxi drivers, Bocas del Toro

tourist requires considerable paperwork, the services of a Panamanian lawyer, and certification by a Panamanian consulate. The process is time-consuming. Allow several months for the paperwork to make its way through the system, and try to get a lawyer who specializes in immigration law.

The biggest and most established law firms include: Morgan and Morgan; Galindo, Arias, and López; Arias, Fábrega, and Fábrega (ARIFA); and Icaza, González-Ruiz, y Alemán (IGRA).

A useful book for those planning a move to Panama is *Living in Panama,* by Sandra Snyder. It covers the daily realities of life in Panama, particularly Panama City, and includes tips on everything from registering a car to choosing a school to how to pay the phone bill. It's widely available in Panama or can be ordered online; visit www.livinginpanama.net. (Full disclosure: Sandra is a family friend, but her knowledge is solid. She has lived for years in Panama and is so plugged into the local scene some Panamanians turn to her for tips.)

Residency for Foreign Retirees

Foreign retirees who want to make their home in Panama must get a *visa de turista pensionado* (pensioned tourist visa). Retirees are required to hire a lawyer to handle the process. Fortunately, Panama wants relatively affluent retirees, so the requirements are not nearly as onerous as in some other countries. These include a recent medical evaluation certifying the applicant is in good health, an HIV test, proof of retiree status, and a monthly pension of at least US$500, plus US$100 for each dependent the retiree wants to bring along. The dependents also need a clean bill of health. The applicant must also show proof of not having a police record back home. The lawyer will explain the kind of documentation needed, as well as the photos, passport photocopies, and other bureaucratic fodder that must be supplied.

Benefits of *turista pensionado* status, besides the right to live in Panama, include the right to import up to US$10,000 worth of possessions for personal use duty-free, as well as the duty-free import of a vehicle every two years. A huge plus for retirees, both foreign and domestic, is discounts at restaurants and hotels, for transportation and many medical services, and for some financial dealings. These can range from 10 percent to 50 percent.

Retirees are allowed to invest in Panama, but are not allowed to work except under certain special circumstances.

Work Permits, Temporary Visitor Visas, and Immigrant Visas

Work permits are generally only granted if a Panamanian company has offered the applicant a job, and even then only if it can be proved no Panamanian could do that job. The permits are issued by Panama's labor ministry, El Ministerio de Trabajo y Desarrollo Laboral, and getting one requires a good Panamanian attorney. The applicant must then apply for a temporary visitor visa, again with legal help. Executives who want to work in the Zona Libre de Colón, technical and scientific experts, and qualified candidates interested in working at one of the Ciudad del Saber (City of Knowledge) projects have the best chance of being approved.

Investors who want to live and do business in Panama must meet several other conditions, not the least of which is a commitment to invest at least US$40,000 in capital and hire at least three Panamanian employees.

Anyone with assets of at least US$200,000 in a Panamanian bank account can apply for an immigrant visa, even without job prospects.

EMBASSIES AND CONSULATES

Panama City is home to the embassies and consulates of quite a number of countries. But some major nations are missing: Australia, for instance, advises its citizens to contact the Australian embassy in Mexico if they need help. A few countries with embassies or consulates in Panama City include:

Canada: World Trade Center, Calle 53 Este in Marbella, tel. 264-9731, fax 263-8083, www.dfait-maeci.gc.ca/panama/menu-en.asp

Colombia: World Trade Center, Calle 53 Este in Marbella, tel. 264-9513 or 264-9266 (embassy), tel. 223-3535 (consul general), fax 223-1134, www.embajadadecolombia.org.pa/

Costa Rica: Avenida 2 Sur/Samuel Lewis, tel. 264-2980 or 758-9128 (consulate), fax 264-6348 (Costa Rica also has a consulate in David: Calle C Sur and Avenida 2 Este Avenida, tel. 774-1923.)

Cuba: Avenida Cuba and Ecuador, tel. 227-5277 or 227-0359, fax 225-6681

El Salvador: Calle 58 and Avenida Samuel Lewis, tel. 223-3020

France: Plaza de Francia in Casco Viejo, tel. 211-6200, fax 211-6235

Germany: World Trade Center, Calle 53 Este in Marbella, tel. 263-7733, fax 223-6664, www.panama.diplo.de

Great Britain: MMG Tower, Calle 53 Este in Marbella, tel. 269-0866, fax 223-0730, www.britishembassy.gov.uk/panama

Guatemala: Vía Argentina, tel. 269-3406, fax 223-1922

Mexico: ADR Tower, Calle 58 and Avenida Samuel Lewis, tel. 263-4900 or 263-2159, www.sre.gob.mx/panama

Nicaragua: Vía España y Calle Elvira Mendez, Edificio Torre Delta, tel. 269-6721 or 264-6431, consulnicpa@cableonda.net

Spain: Calle 33 and Avenida Perú, tel. 227-5122, fax 227-6284, http://emb.panama@mae.es

United States: The U.S. embassy recently moved from central Panama City to an enormous, fortresslike compound in Clayton, in the former Canal Zone. The American Citizens Service Unit (Building 520, Clayton, tel. 207-7030, fax 207-7303, http://panama.usembassy.gov, 8 A.M.–noon Mon.–Fri.) is closed on the last Wednesday of every month and on all U.S. and Panamanian holidays. The main embassy phone number is 207-7000.

BORDER CROSSINGS

There are three border crossings between Panama and Costa Rica: at Paso Canoa on the Pacific side of the isthmus, at Río Sereno in the highlands, and at Sixaola-Guabito on the Caribbean coast. Paso Canoa, which is on the Interamericana, is by far the most traveled. The Sixaola-Guabito crossing is used mainly by those traveling to and from Bocas del Toro. The Río Sereno crossing is rarely used, and foreign travelers are not always allowed across.

The Interamericana comes to an end at the town of Yaviza in eastern Panama, where the famous Darién Gap begins. There are no roads linking Panama with Colombia and the rest of South America. There is a border crossing at Puerto Obaldía, at the very eastern tip of the Caribbean coast, but the civil war in Colombia sometimes makes crossing here too dangerous to attempt even when it's actually open. Flying is the safest way to travel between Colombia and Panama.

General Considerations

Panama is trying, not always successfully, to strike a balance between retaining control over its borders and encouraging tourists and potential investors to visit. This includes cracking down on foreign nationals who are living in Panama without changing their tourist status; they merely pop across the border for 72 hours, then come back.

On arrival at any border crossing, be prepared to present immigration officials with an onward ticket out of Panama and evidence of having US$500. Except at Paso Canoa these aren't often asked for, but officials have the right to refuse entry to anyone without them. Arriving at the border looking clean and neatly dressed in long pants and good shoes (no sneakers, flip-flops, sandals, etc.) increases one's chances of being waved through without incident.

Try to arrive at border crossings during regular business hours to avoid a lengthy wait at the border for immigrations and customs officials to show up. Borders are open every day.

Paso Canoa

The border crossing at the decaying town of Paso Canoa (sometimes also know as Paso Canoas) is on the Interamericana and is the route taken by the great majority of visitors coming from or going to Costa Rica by land. It's about an hour by bus or car west of David, the provincial capital of Chiriquí province. It tends to be the strictest border crossing.

Going through formalities on both sides can be surprisingly quick or painfully slow, especially when a bus arrives. Count on an hour or two for the whole process and hope for the best. Panamanian time is always one hour ahead of Costa Rican time.

Panama immigration, customs, and an ATP government tourism office are housed in a new cement monolith at the border. The **ATP office** (tel. 727-6524, 7 A.M.–11 P.M. daily) has very little to offer tourists. Don't expect much tourist information.

Those arriving by bus tend to encounter the most inconvenience. Passengers are generally expected to hand-carry their luggage across the border for inspection on either side. Also, processing a busload of visitors takes time, especially if the bus arrives early in the morning.

It's impossible to get lost crossing over, but the offices aren't well marked. Streetwise little boys may offer to help navigate for a small tip. This may be worthwhile if the procedures are baffling or if you just want to stop the other kids from bugging you. About US$0.25–0.50 should make your assistant happy.

Men wearing money pouches hang around the immigration office offering to buy or sell Costa Rican colones. If changing money on the streets of a grungy border town doesn't sound like a smart thing to do, exchange money before arriving at the border. There are ATMs between the two borders that dispense both colones and dollars.

There are plenty of buses and taxis about 50 meters past immigration/customs.

Sixaola-Guabito

This border crossing is used primarily by those traveling between Costa Rica and Bocas del Toro. Sixaola is the border town on the Costa Rican side; Guabito is on the Panamanian side. The border itself runs down the middle of the Río Sixaola. Travelers must cross over a short, rickety railroad bridge, either by foot or in a vehicle. Pedestrians should look out for traffic, missing handrails, and gaps in the planking.

Travelers usually find border formalities here quick and laid-back. The Panamanian border post is on an elevated railway trestle on the edge of the Río Sixaola. The **immigration office** (tel. 759-7019, 8 A.M.–noon and 12:30 P.M. to 6 P.M. daily) is right on the train tracks next to the bridge that crosses the river. Travelers can enter and leave Panama only when the office is open. An ATP representative at the post sells tourist cards to those eligible. Remember that Panamanian time is always one hour ahead of Costa Rican time.

There are no hotels, no appealing places to eat, and almost no services in Guabito. The nearest place with significant services is Changuinola, about a 20-minute drive away.

Those entering Panama without onward transportation should walk down from the railroad tracks to get a bus or taxi after clearing customs and immigration. Taxi drivers and unofficial tour guides sometimes try to overcharge new arrivals or take them to hotels that pay them a commission, so be cautious.

Río Sereno

This little-used border crossing is a possible alternative to Paso Canoa for those coming from or going to the western highlands of Panama. However, it's rarely used and is not always open to foreigners. There's nothing much of interest for tourists there, and you're likely to be the only foreigner in town. It's a far prettier spot than Paso Canoa, but it's not really set up to deal well with foreign visitors, it's out of the way for any destination but the area around Volcán, and the road leading east into Panama is dangerous. It's a better idea all around to cross over at Paso Canoa.

The Panamanian **immigration/customs office** (tel. 722-8054, 7 A.M.–7 P.M. daily) in Río Sereno is on a hill above the town plaza. It's near the radio tower and shares a building with the police station.

The nearest major junction for onward travel in Panama is at Volcán, 42 kilometers east of the border. The drive, on a beautiful but dangerous road, takes nearly two hours. The pickup-taxi ride costs about US$20, and you'll be sharing the ride. Buses from Río Sereno run 5 A.M.–5 P.M. every 45 minutes to Volcán and David.

There is one basic but okay place to stay for those unlucky enough to get stranded at the border: Posada Los Andes (next to the plaza, no phone, US$20 s/d).

Puerto Obaldía

The only marginally safe way to cross the Colombia-Panama border by land is to go through the grim border town of Puerto Obaldía, on the Caribbean coast. Because of the civil war in Colombia, even this border crossing is not always open or safe.

Even at the best of times, this route is only for the adventurous. I do not recommend it. Traveling by boat and bus through western Colombia can be dangerous, and the trip can take days. It's the cheapest way to go, but the modest savings aren't worth the effort and risk.

Flights operating between Panama City and Puerto Obaldía are offered intermittently. From Puerto Obaldía, travelers must hire a launch to Capurganá, a beach resort on the Colombian side. The fare is US$10 per person, but there's a minimum; single travelers may have to pay as much as US$30 if no one else is going. The trip takes about an hour and is a bumpy ride, especially in the dry season. Expect to get wet. The boat does have life jackets, though. A boat between Capurganá and Turbo takes about two hours and costs about US$20. Again, this tends to be a wet, wild ride. Turbo has bus connections with other parts of Colombia, notably Cartagena and Medellín. Turbo has historically been a hotbed of paramilitary activity. Be careful, and travel only in the daytime.

Travelers must seek out the immigration officials in Puerto Obaldía and Capurganá to get their exit/entry clearance. Expect also to be interviewed and possibly searched by border police. Exchange currency ahead of time, as it can be tough to do so near the border. Those entering Panama via this route must have an onward ticket out of Panama. Proof of a yellow fever vaccination is no longer officially required but is probably still a good idea, just in case the officials out here in the boonies haven't yet gotten the memo. Those flying from Puerto Obaldía to Panama City will probably have to go through a second grilling upon arrival at Albrook to make sure they're not drug traffickers, Colombian fighters, or illegal aliens.

Getting through all this in a single day requires plane reservations, documents in perfect order, and luck, particularly with connections. It's not unusual to get stuck on either side of the border for at least a night. Capurganá is a popular beach resort and has a wide range of accommodations. Puerto Obaldía, however, is a backwater, though rock-bottom rooms are available for about US$5.

CORRUPTION, BRIBES, AND SCAMS

Nepotism, corruption, *amiguismo* (cronyism), and conflicts of interest have been serious problems in Panama throughout its history. In 2002, Panama's then-president, Mireya Moscoso, repeatedly defended nepotism as a long-established tradition in Panama. Panamanians place little faith in their legal system or political parties. Panama has also long been notorious as a transshipment point for drugs and a haven for money launderers.

There have been attempts in recent years to address these problems through new anticorruption commissions, press exposés, stricter banking laws to crack down on money laundering, transparency laws designed to stop illegal deals, subjecting once-secret government and business negotiations to public scrutiny, and removing from the public payroll so-called *botellas* (literally, "bottles"—well-connected appointees without the skill or inclination to do their assigned jobs).

Many of these efforts have been dismissed as cynical or halfhearted. Reformers in Panama maintain that an attitude of *juega vivo* (roughly, "live game" or "the game of life") is still firmly rooted in daily life. *Juega vivo* refers to a belief that one should grab any opportunity life presents, even if ethically or legally shaky.

Corruption does remain a fact of life in Panama. But societal attitudes seem to be shifting. It's much more common these days to hear people assert that putting the interests of family and self first can hurt society as a whole, and that Panama cannot be a modern, successful country without trustworthy public institutions.

It's unlikely most tourists will find themselves in a situation where a bribe is expected. The possible exception is being stopped by a police officer, usually for a traffic violation, and being encouraged to pay the fine on the spot instead of going to the trouble of paying it at the courthouse. How to handle this is a judgment call. Some adamantly refuse to pay a bribe out of principle. Sometimes the officer will lose interest and let the violator go; other times this leads to a time-wasting visit to the local courthouse. Paying or offering a bribe is illegal, and theoretically it can get a visitor in far more serious trouble. Others find paying a few dollars the easiest way to deal with the nuisance.

In recent years, there have been reports of travelers being stopped by police repeatedly while driving in western Panama. This occurs between Divisa and David on the Interamericana. They are accused, rightly or not, of speeding or not staying within the lane and then told to pay a fine of US$20. Some have refused to pay and are let go; others pay, only to be stopped again farther down the road. The police reportedly spot likely looking tourists as they drive by and radio ahead to their confederates to stop them. Those driving in western Panama should obey the speed limit and all other traffic rules and try as much as possible not to look too touristy.

More recently, there have been reports of bribe demands at the Paso Canoa bordering crossing with Costa Rica.

Those interested in Panamanian real estate should proceed carefully. Land scams are a problem, especially since the start of the tourist and retiree boom in Bocas del Toro and Boquete. Be especially cautious with timber plantations and other get-rich-quick schemes. If it looks too good to be true, it is. A great deal of land in Panama is untitled, which makes buying it tricky and in some cases legally precarious—don't buy a piece of land from someone who doesn't actually own it. Some people have been buying into Panama sight unseen, which is nuts. Besides the danger of getting ripped off, Panama is not a place everyone would want to live or invest in. To avoid disappointment, get to know the country first.

Scams against regular tourists are still not much of a problem, though touts and taxi drivers sometimes steer visitors to hotels and services that pay them a commission. Most visitors are more likely to be ripped off by a fellow foreigner than by a Panamanian. But stay alert and be cautious with overly friendly strangers.

POLICE

Panama's police force is a lot less intimidating now than in the days of the military dictatorship. Law-abiding visitors are unlikely to have any bad dealings with the police. In fact, Panama is so eager to protect tourists and give them a positive impression of the country there's a whole detachment of police officers, known as the policía de turismo (tourist police), dedicated to watching out for them in Panama City. They're generally bicycle cops, easy to spot in their khaki uniforms with short pants. They're most visible in the Casco Viejo section of the city, where the force is headquartered.

Transit police sometimes crack down on certain offenses on busy stretches of road. They're usually on the lookout for speeders, those making illegal turns, drivers talking on cell phones, and so on. Drivers signal that the transit police are staking out an area by flashing headlights at each other. I sometimes flash lights to slow down reckless drivers even when no cops are around.

The police sometimes set up roadblocks to check drivers' licenses and registrations. This is normal and no cause for alarm. If a police officer stops you, be unfailingly polite and friendly. Be prepared to hand over your passport and driver's license. Police officers rarely speak English, which some use to their advantage when stopped for a traffic violation, feigning an inability to speak Spanish in the hopes the officer will lose patience and just wave the driver on instead of handing out a ticket.

Conduct and Customs

Despite Panama's undeserved reputation among those who've never been there as a dangerous country, you'll likely find it a remarkably mellow and low-key place to travel. It's extremely rare to encounter hostility or belligerence. Courtesy is considered quite important, however. Panamanians may take offense if they feel they're not being treated with proper dignity and respect.

Foreigners sometimes complain that the Panamanians they encounter in stores and offices seem unfriendly or sullen. This complaint is most often made about Panama City; in the countryside, visitors are frequently overwhelmed by the warmth and friendliness they encounter. If you feel you're being treated rudely, do not raise your voice or snap at the offending party—this will get you absolutely nowhere. Be patient and polite, and take your business elsewhere next time. Similarly, the less you expect punctuality and speediness the happier you will be.

As in other Latin American countries, machismo is a fact of life in Panama. Women may find they have to deal with unwanted male attention.

DRESS AND APPEARANCE

It's tempting to wear skimpy, sloppy clothes in the Panamanian heat. Resist the temptation. Panama is not Margaritaville; it is in some ways a rather formal and conservative country. Neat dress, good grooming, and cleanliness are expected.

The influx of foreign tourists and retirees has led to a proliferation of Hawaiian shirts, T-shirts, shorts, baseball caps, tank tops, sneakers, sandals, and the like on city streets and even in fancy restaurants. This is a no-no in Panama. Many businesses will look the other way, out of politeness or a desire for dollars. But it's considered disrespectful and inappropriate to dress like this anywhere other than the beach. Even the poorest Panamanians dress neatly and cleanly; imagine how rude it must seem that far more affluent foreigners, who don't have to work in the fields and can afford nice clothes, won't make the same effort.

If offending local sentiments is not enough of a disincentive, bear in mind that people are judged by their appearance to a greater extent in Panama than in more casual countries. Well-groomed, well-dressed people get better, more courteous service. And just wearing shorts or a Hawaiian shirt on the streets instantly marks you as a clueless foreigner for the unscrupulous to take advantage of, or worse. Few longtime expatriates dress like that, and not coincidentally they are far less likely to be hassled in dodgy parts of town. Overly casual dress also limits where you can go. Those wearing sneakers, sandals, or shorts are not allowed in nightclubs or government offices, and they can be turned away from churches.

It's actually against the law to drive or walk down a city street without a shirt; violators are subject to fines. What constitutes a city street is broadly defined: Shirtless travelers have been ticketed for walking down the main street in Bocas town, a place that hardly qualifies as an urban setting in most people's minds.

Neat clothing made from cotton, linen, and other lightweight fabrics can be quite comfortable, and it provides better protection from the sun and bugs than beachwear does.

Suits have largely replaced guayabera shirts as business and semiformal wear for middle- and upper-class Panamanian men, made practical by the widespread use of air-conditioning in the cities. Women tend to dress as elegantly as their budget will allow, and two-piece suits or conservative dresses are the norm for professional women.

One funny side effect of the recent influx of gringos and other tourists is that it's now more common to see Ecuadorian-style "Panama hats" on the streets. They were popular during the gold rush and canal-construction days, but they've never been made in Panama and haven't been seen around in many decades. When tourists arrived and demanded to buy what they thought of as Panama hats, the market responded, just as it did more than a century ago.

Children wear uniforms to school, and, though spiky modern hairstyles and casual clothes have made some inroads in recent years, it's rare to see even teenagers take their fashion sense too far. (Chances are excellent that the Spanish-speaking dude you see in shorts and a baseball cap is actually not Panamanian but rather a visitor from another Latin American country.) But long-haired kids are no longer hauled off by the police for a haircut, as they were during the military dictatorship of the 1970s.

Mochileros (backpackers) sometimes get a bad rap in Panama as an unkempt and disreputable lot that add little to the economy. There's little animosity, but one occasionally senses a mild distrust. To this day, most tourism efforts are pitched at the affluent, and some shudder at the thought of Panama being overrun with foreign backpackers, as they believe Costa Rica has been. This attitude has softened somewhat as real backpackers proved to be less scary than feared. Still, those traveling on a frugal budget will feel more welcome if they do their best to look especially neat and respectable, and if they stash the backpack in a safe place when possible.

ETIQUETTE

Formality extends to etiquette as well. Titles are taken seriously (such as *doctor* for a physician, *licenciado* for an attorney or even someone who holds a bachelor's degree, *profesor* or *maestro* for a teacher, *ingeniero* for an engineer, etc.). If known, they should be used in introductions and correspondence. Courtesies in writing and speech tend to be more elaborate in Panama than in English-speaking countries. Some allowances are made for foreigners, but try to make up for any gaps in eloquence with cordial body language.

Women often greet each other and men with air kisses. Unlike in some other Latin American countries, men rarely greet each other with an *abrazo* (hug) unless they are on quite friendly terms. Handshakes are the norm, but these tend to be far lighter than in other countries. A crushing handshake is considered aggressive.

It's not typical in Panama to greet someone with an *hola* (hello). This is considered quite casual and, especially if the person is unknown to you, not very polite. The main greetings are *buenos días* (good morning), *buenas tardes* (good afternoon), and *buenas noches* (good evening). In casual situations this is often shortened to a simple *buenas,* which conveys a tone somewhere between "hey" and "howdy." It's become fashionable in recent years, for some reason, to say *"ciao"* when parting.

Courtesy may be less elaborate among the working classes of the city and the country, but being polite is just as important. Even more so, in some ways. It's considered extremely insulting to address someone of perceived lesser status as though they're inferior. When in doubt, use formal terms of address (such as *usted* instead of *tú*) with strangers, and be especially sensitive about not lapsing into casual forms with someone who's performing a service for you.

Many Panamanians are proud of their country and do not take kindly to criticism of Panama and things Panamanian. Complaints they may make to each other are one thing, complaints from a foreigner are quite another. This is especially true when it comes from U.S. citizens, not surprising given the long and complicated relationship between the two countries.

Food

Traditional Panamanian food relies heavily on starches and red meat, chicken, and pork. Green vegetables do not grow well in the tropics, so outside of better restaurants in the cities, don't be surprised if fried plantain is as close as you'll come to a veggie side dish. Vegetarians will have a tough time finding a balanced meal even in cosmopolitan Panama City. Their best bet is usually Chinese restaurants, which are found throughout the country.

Fish is excellent in Panama. The most common on the menu is also one of the most delicious: corvina, a delicately flavored saltwater fish. Restaurants often prepare it a dozen different ways, but usually simplest is best. Prepared well, *corvina a la plancha* (grilled corvina) is hard to beat. *Guabina* is similar to corvina; it tends to be found at the fancier restaurants.

Other seafood includes shrimp *(camarones)*, prawns *(langostinos)*, squid *(calamares)*, octopus *(pulpo)*, crab *(cangrejo)*, red snapper *(pargo rojo)*, and lobster *(langosta)*. Think twice about eating lobster in Panama since it's terribly overfished.

Ceviche in Panama is delicious. Traditionally it consists of raw corvina marinated in lime juice, peppers, and onions, which chemically "cook" the fish. It's increasingly common to find shrimp or octopus ceviche, or ceviche made from a combination of all three.

A staple of the Panamanian diet is yuca or manioc. (Don't confuse yuca with yucca, the desert plant.) It's a root vegetable prepared in a variety of ways. Most common is deep-fried yuca, which when done right is crispy and golden brown on the outside and chewy on the inside. *Carimañolas* are a kind of roll made from ground and boiled yuca that is generally stuffed with meat then deep fried.

Plantains *(plátanos)*, which are similar to bananas, are even more common. By the end of your trip you will probably have had more than your fill of *patacones*, which are green plantains cut crossways into discs, fried, pressed, and then fried again. These can be tasty when hot; they turn into concrete when cold. Ripe plantains are typically sliced lengthwise and then either fried or sprinkled with cinnamon and baked, or broiled with butter. Fried plantains are called *tajadas;* the baked or broiled plantain dish is known as *plátanos maduros* or *plátanos en tentación*.

Other typical treats include empanadas, a kind of turnover made with flour or corn pastry that is stuffed with spiced ground meat and fried; tamales, which are made from boiled ground corn stuffed with chicken or pork and spices, then wrapped in banana leaves and boiled; and tortillas, which in Panama are thick, fried corncakes often served with breakfast in the countryside.

The Panamanian palate doesn't tend to favor lots of spices, and you may find some of your meals rather bland. But done well, even the simplest country fare can be delicious. Try *sancocho*, a thick and hearty soup usually made with chicken, yuca, and whatever vegetables are around. *Ropa vieja* (literally, old clothes) is also good; it consists of spiced shredded beef served over rice. *Arroz con pollo* (rice with chicken) is also a common dish. Food is spicier in parts of Caribbean Panama, where hot sauce and dishes made with coconut milk are sometimes available.

Outside of Panama City, the menu can get monotonous. Main dishes will typically involve beef (usually referred to as *carne*, though literally this just means meat), chicken *(pollo)*, and pork *(puerco)*. A good strategy to keep from getting jaded is to take advantage of the very good international restaurants in Panama City and save traditional fare for trips into the hinterland.

Panamanians tend to like hot lunches. Lunchtime traffic in Panama City can be almost as bad as rush hour, as the streets get

Mexican food is catching on in Panama.

© WILLIAM FRIAR

jammed with drivers eager to go home or out to a restaurant for a hot meal. Even workers (and travelers) on a tight budget partake when they can, filling hole-in-the-wall restaurants called *fondas,* which serve big plates of *comida corriente.* This is the traditional Panamanian equivalent of fast food, generally consisting of a variety of local dishes *(comida criolla)* served from steam tables in a cafeteria setting. It's easy to fill up for less than US$2 at these places, which are often open for breakfast and dinner as well.

Tips for Travelers

WHAT TO TAKE

Plan to travel light, especially if your itinerary calls for domestic flights, where there's a severe **weight restriction on luggage.** Launderettes aren't hard to come by once clean clothes are exhausted.

Most parts of Panama are hot and humid year-round. Bring lots of **thin cotton or breathable, moisture-wicking synthetic clothing.** Keep in mind that dress in Panama is conservative.

It can cool off significantly in some regions of Panama, and air-conditioning can raise goose bumps in the lowland cities. A **light sweater or fleece** along with a **waterproof windbreaker or parka** is a useful combination. Consider taking along a **small umbrella** for use in town.

If you think you'll spend much time island-hopping, consider bringing a **life jacket.** These are often not standard equipment.

Consider bringing a **bedroll or light sleeping bag** even if you're not planning on doing serious camping. It can come in handy if you have to spend a night in a place without decent linens. And don't forget the **binoculars.**

OPPORTUNITIES FOR STUDY

The easiest way to study in Panama is through an exchange program through one's university back home. With the possible exception of casual, short-term programs, visiting students must travel with a special visa. Student visas are a kind of temporary visitor visa, with many of the same requirements as other visas (HIV test, criminal record report, medical certificate of good health, letter of sponsorship, etc.). Applicants must also show proof of acceptance into the academic program and evidence of economic solvency. The process generally requires a lawyer, but presumably the academic institution will help that.

For several decades **Florida State University** has had a satellite program in Panama (tel. 314-0367, http://panama.fsu.edu/) that draws students from Latin America, the United States, and Canada. Instruction is in English. Students can enroll in bachelor's and associate's degree programs in environmental studies, international affairs, Latin American and Caribbean studies, computer science, information studies, and the social sciences, offered in collaboration with the Ciudad del Saber (City of Knowledge) at Clayton. FSU Panama now occupies what was once the campus of Canal Zone College, a community college at the foot of the Bridge of the Americas near the Pacific entrance to the Panama Canal. Note: Don't confuse this program with the FSU campus in Panama City, Florida.

The **Smithsonian Tropical Research Institute** (STRI) coordinates a variety of short-term and long-term fellowships for undergraduate, graduate, and postdoctoral students that are offered either through STRI itself or by the Smithsonian Institution. Information on STRI fellowships is available through the Smithsonian Tropical Research Institute, Office of Education (www.stri.org). For information on Smithsonian Institution fellowships in Panama, contact the Smithsonian Institution's Office of Research Training and Services in Washington, D.C. (www.si.edu).

The **Ciudad del Saber** (City of Knowledge, www.cdspanama.org) in Clayton hosts a variety of academic programs in a number of disciplines.

Panama has several universities, the most prominent of which is the **Universidad de Panamá** (tel. 523-5000, www.up.ac.pa), opened in 1935, which offers a wide array of degree programs. Through its main campus in Panama City and extension programs around the country, it has about 74,000 students. Instruction is in Spanish. Foreigners interested in attending must apply through the university's Secretario General three months before the start of term.

A Florida-based nonprofit called the **Institute for Tropical Ecology and Conservation** (ITEC, U.S. tel. 352/367-9128, www.itec-edu.org) has a biological field station in Bocas del Toro.

VOLUNTEER OPPORTUNITIES

Those interested in doing volunteer work in Panama will most likely have to come up with a scheme of their own. Few formal volunteer programs exist as of yet. The best way to start is to find a place or a cause one is interested in and then pitch a volunteer plan to the director, highlighting your skills. Many will be happy for the free labor.

The **Canopy Tower** (tel. 264-5720, U.S. toll-free tel. 800/930-3397, www.canopytower. com) accepts volunteers willing to work at the tower in exchange for room, board, and a stipend of about US$400 a month. Volunteers are expected to take on a full range of responsibilities at the tower. Management prefers volunteers willing to stay at least three months. Those interested should send an email to the tower's owner, Raúl Arias de Para, at birding@canopytower.com. He speaks fluent English.

Los Quetzales Lodge and Spa (tel. 771-2182 or 771-2291, fax 771-2226, www.

losquetzales.com) sometimes uses volunteers to help run the hotel. Panama City hostels and the **Purple House Hostel** (Calle C Sur and Avenida 6 Oeste, 774-4059, www.purplehousehostel. com) in David are other possibilities. Those interested can also try one of the universities or research institutes.

The environmental nonprofit **ANCON** (tel. 314-0052, www.ancon.org) sometimes takes volunteers as well. The best approach is to send ANCON a letter or email detailing skills and saying when you'd like to come down and how long you'd like to stay. Try to be as specific as possible about what you can contribute.

The **Spanish by the Sea** (tel. 757-9518, www. spanishbythesea.com) program in Bocas del Toro can sometimes organize volunteer work. Possibilities include a sea-turtle conservation project.

WOMEN TRAVELING ALONE

This is a tough one. Women who travel alone in Panama are likely to be safer than in many other countries, but it's still not the safest way to go. On the one hand, it's unusual for any traveler to face serious harassment in Panama. It's an easygoing, live-and-let-live kind of place. On the other hand, it is a macho country, and women are subject to lots of cat-calling, honking horns, smooching noises, and other obnoxious behavior from dudes on the street. Generally, that's as aggressive at it gets, but it can certainly make women who travel alone feel unsafe, sometimes with good reason.

Women are most likely to encounter this nonsense in Panama City. Some women have also reported unwanted attention in Bocas del Toro and Boquete, where a sudden influx of foreign tourists has collided with provincial attitudes. A woman friend was practically stalked in Bocas by a few eager guys a couple years back, so much so she cut her visit short. More recently, there have been reports of attempted rapes in Bocas. In one case, a woman woke up to find men she'd met earlier had gotten into her room; screams scared them off. Rape is punishable by 1–5 years in jail, but convictions are rare.

Common sense can reduce the risk of ugly encounters. Never tell a casual acquaintance the name of your hotel, and certainly not your room number. Women who travel alone should be especially alert in Bocas and Panama City. The Calidonia and Casco Viejo neighborhoods of Panama City are not the best places for women traveling on their own.

Panamanian women who get bothered on the street tend to ignore the culprits completely. That's probably the best tack to try at first. Try not to lose your cool. Knowing at least some Spanish and appearing confident and at home can also help diffuse unpleasant encounters. Befriend fellow visitors and travel in groups if possible. Cabs are probably safer than walking at night, but avoid taking them alone. Women who go to bars and discos alone are often assumed to be looking for sex, and there will be no shortage of guys eager to help them find it. Especially outside sophisticated circles in Panama City, the same goes for a woman who agrees to visit a man's home or allows him into her room late at night.

GAY AND LESBIAN TRAVELERS

Panama is a quite tolerant and open-minded place for a predominantly Roman Catholic Latin American country. I've yet to hear a story, for instance, about a police raid on a gay club. However, gays and lesbians are still for the most part closeted. Same-sex affection on the streets would cause a sensation at best, an ugly encounter at worst. Homosexuality is not illegal in Panama, but neither is it legally protected.

Foreigner status helps protect gay and lesbian travelers from harassment. Gay and lesbian acquaintances in Panama say they've never felt threatened, but it's hard to know how much of this is just the natural immunity that comes from having power in a society that's sharply divided between the haves and have-nots. Poorer

TIPS FOR RESPONSIBLE TRAVEL

Visitors will get more out of Panama and help keep it an enjoyable destination for others if they make an effort to get to know the place and how their actions may affect it.

Start by reading up on the fascinating history of Panama, which for hundreds of years has earned its reputation as the crossroads of the world, and by learning a bit about its flora and fauna.

SOUVENIRS

Buying souvenirs made from the body parts of endangered animals – jaguar teeth, tortoiseshell jewelry – is a big no-no. Remember that possessing these products is a serious crime in Panama, punishable by fines and jail time. Trafficking in *vida silvestre* (wildlife) is punishable by six months to two years in jail. Note this includes *all* animals found in the wild, not just endangered species. The same thing goes for possession of pre-Columbian pottery and other historic artifacts. Collecting these is known as *huaquería* (roughly, "grave robbing") and is illegal. Obviously, it's also illegal to eat endangered animals; do not partake of tortoise eggs or the like. Do not buy jewelry made from coral, which is being severely damaged in Panama. Leave intact shells on the beach; they're potential homes for a variety of sea creatures.

FOOD

Think about what you eat in Panama. Lobster, for instance, has been terribly overharvested in the San Blas Islands (Guna Yala). You'll be tempted to try one on the islands, but bear in mind that what was once a subsistence food for the Guna is now in danger of extinction, which would have serious consequences for the Guna and their environment. And it's not just in the San Blas you should consider this: Poor lobster divers sell their catch to fancy restaurants in Panama City. If nothing else, avoid lobster during the mating season, which runs March–July. Consider that a female lobster carries thousands of eggs, but divers scoop up the expectant moms right along with the other lobsters. It'd be a shame if your dinner meant the end of a whole generation of baby lobsters.

Among the many other reasons not to eat beef is the fact that cattle ranching is not at all sustainable in Panama. It has led to massive deforestation and the destruction of entire habitats. Carnivores should cut down in Panama.

ECO-ACTIVITIES AND RESORTS

Personal recreational watercraft (Jet Skis and the like) panic marine life, shatter the tranquility of other beachgoers, and pollute the environment. Resist the temptation to go for a spin.

Be skeptical of tour operators and hotels that advertise themselves as eco-conscious. Ask them exactly what they mean by that and what kind of environmentally conscious services they offer.

Because hotels and tour operators know that "eco" can spell money for them, they have an incentive to exaggerate just how ecologically sound their operations are. This has begun to happen in Panama, with just about any place that has a view labeling itself an "eco-resort" no matter how many resources it gobbles. To help readers make informed decisions about who to go with, this book attempts to highlight the features of a place or an operation likely to appeal to a low-impact tourist (e.g., small-scale, locally owned hotels that tread lightly on their surroundings) as well as those features that may be off-putting (e.g., a private zoo on the property).

Environmentally sensitive tourism is so new to Panama it's hard for tourists to be entirely pure about where they stay and how they travel. Probably the most useful thing to do is to seek out those that are on the right track, and through our own actions to encourage those qualities we like and discourage those we don't. Most of the best operations are owned and run by intelligent businesspeople who take great pride in what they're trying to accomplish. Don't be afraid to give them feedback, including criticisms. They're all still trying to figure out just what it is low-impact tourists want, and they'll likely be eager to hear your comments.

Nature tourists to Panama in the next few years may well play a critical role in shaping the future of the Panamanian industry. If entrepreneurs see a demand for responsible, low-impact nature travel, and they are shown that it can pay, in a few years there may be more simple ecolodges and fewer sprawling five-star resorts.

gays do sometimes get beaten and harassed, and they have little protection or legal recourse.

In 2001, after a three-year battle, Panama gave legal recognition to its first gay and lesbian organization, **La Asociación de Hombres y Mujeres Nuevos de Panamá** (AHMNP, The Association of New Men and Women of Panama, tel. 264-2670, www.ahmnpanama. org). AHMNP advocates the rights of "sexual minorities," including gays, lesbians, bisexuals, and transgendered people. It also aims to provide education about preventing sexually transmitted diseases and support for those infected with HIV.

In 2007, activists from 14 countries in the Americas met in Panama for a conference that ran parallel to a meeting of the general assembly of the Organization of American States (OAS). The meeting was meant to encourage greater participation of gays, lesbians, and other sexual minorities in the OAS. Among the speakers was Aristides Royo, a former president of Panama and the country's chief representative to the OAS.

The visibility of gays and lesbians in popular culture is also increasing. Local soap operas, enormously popular in Panama, have introduced gay characters who are portrayed in a positive light, and a few years back one of the hosts of a popular TV chat program, *La Cocoa*, was an openly gay man. Gays have also been allowed to enter floats in Panama's Carnaval celebration in recent years, complete with a Carnaval queen in drag. However, Panama was not quite ready for this: Cross-dressing in Carnaval parades has now been banned throughout the country on "moral grounds." In 2008, gay groups withdrew from the parades in protest.

For more information on international gay rights issues, check out the International Gay and Lesbian Human Rights Commission (www.iglhrc.org), the International Lesbian and Gay Association (www.ilga.org), and http://gaynewswatch.com. Information on gay-run

and gay-friendly accommodations can be found at www.purpleroofs.com. None of these groups has much information on Panama, however.

Information on parties, clubs, and events in Panama aimed at the GLBT crowd is available at www.farraurbana.com.

ACCESSIBILITY FOR TRAVELERS WITH DISABILITIES

Travelers with disabilities will not find Panama an easy country to maneuver around. Accessibility and rights for people with disabilities are new concepts in Panama.

In 1999, Panama passed Ley 42 (Law 42), which guarantees equal opportunity for and makes it illegal to discriminate against people with disabilities in employment, education, services, transportation, health services, and so on. That same year, Panama signed the Organization of American States' Inter-American Convention on the Elimination of all Forms of Discrimination Against Persons with Disabilities.

However, Panama has been slow to enforce compliance with either and other disability-rights laws on the books.

Even in the fanciest hotels and restaurants it's still unusual to encounter ramps, handrails, and other accommodations for people with disabilities. Ley 42 requires making both public and private buildings accessible, but advocacy groups estimate that to date only about 5 percent of public buildings meet the requirements.

Awareness of disability issues, at least, improved under the Martín Torrijos administration (2004–2009). He and his wife, Vivian Fernández de Torrijos, have a daughter with disabilities. The first lady made the rights of people with disabilities one of her priorities.

In recent years the government has installed ramps and "mainstreamed" some kids in public schools, but facilities are still inadequate. By law, at least 2 percent of a company's employees must be people with disabilities, but the actual number is nowhere near that, and those with disabilities tend to get paid less than non-disabled people doing the same job. The organization responsible for placing workers with disabilities held a job fair in 2007; 100 companies were invited, but only 8 showed up.

That same year, the government gave greater autonomy and a separate budget to the agency responsible for protecting the rights of people with disabilities, La Secretaría Nacional para la Integración de las Personas con Discapacidad (SENADIS, The National Secretariat for the Integration of People with Disabilities). Funding for disability programs has increased, but it is still modest compared with the need.

The modern infrastructure of Panama City makes it perhaps the easiest place for visitors with disabilities to get around. The abundant elevators and taxis help, though almost all taxis are rather cramped and there are no taxi services geared toward those with wheelchairs. Conditions quickly become difficult in the countryside, particularly in the Darién or any of the island groups, where paved roads disappear, transportation is often by small boat, and it can be somewhat challenging for just about anyone to get around.

Some information on accessible travel worldwide is available at www.access-able.com, though there are no Panama-specific tips.

SENIORS

Seniors are treated with deference and respect in Panama, where the old-fashioned honorifics *don* and *doña* are sometimes still used for venerable older people. Panamanian seniors and foreign residents are entitled to discounts as high as 50 percent on a whole range of services, but these are not available to visitors.

TRAVELING WITH CHILDREN

Panama is a child-friendly country. There are many young families in the country, so lodgings often include little playgrounds, child-oriented activities, and guest rooms with multiple beds.

Vaccination recommendations and other preventative-care measures are often different for small children than for adults. Visit the U.S. Centers for Disease Control's website (www.cdc.gov/travel) or ask your doctor for information.

Panama's warm weather and abundance of outdoor-recreation possibilities make the country a great place for kids. But parents need to be especially alert when traveling around Panama given the comparatively fewer safeguards for children than in more developed countries (missing handrails, sudden drop-offs, chaotic traffic, etc.).

Kids are welcome just about everywhere; only a few hotels and other establishments do not allow or at least discourage bringing children. These are usually ecolodges that don't want the wildlife disturbed or are concerned about children falling off boardwalks into the water. I do not recommend taking small children to most parts of the Darién or to Guna Yala (San Blas Islands) because of the rugged conditions and possible dangers from wildlife. Rats, for instance, are a fact of life in the San Blas Islands, and while the risk of a bite is small, rustling in the rafters has been known to shatter more than one worried parent's rest.

Since 1995 Panama City has had a nighttime curfew for those under age 18. Unattended minors are supposed to be off the streets 8 P.M.–6 A.M. Sunday–Thursday and 11 P.M.–6 A.M. Friday–Saturday. Exceptions are made for students and young workers, but only with proper documentation. The curfew is aimed at residents, but theoretically foreign minors could be stopped by the police if unaccompanied by a parent or legal guardian. Violators are taken to a police station until picked up by their parents, who are subject to a fine.

TRAVELING WITH PETS

Bringing a pet to Panama is a bad idea unless one is planning a lengthy or permanent stay. Dogs and cats must be quarantined for 30 days, though a recent law allows for home quarantine in lieu of a stay in a kennel. Travelers on the road will obviously not be able to provide a home in which to quarantine the pets, so kenneling at the quarantine office may be the only option. There is also considerable paperwork involved that may require the help of a lawyer or at least a relocation-service agent. (José Saenz—based in Panama City, tel./fax 399-4003 or 251-0698, cell 6614-7811, www.goldenfrog. net—provides such a service.) The process can't be started any sooner than 10 days before the pets are shipped, because all documents must be as up-to-date as possible. Leaving the country with a pet requires a whole other round of permissions. Requirements are more stringent for birds and other animals. Contact a Panamanian consulate for current requirements.

Health and Safety

It's extremely unlikely you'll contract a serious disease in Panama. Health conditions are generally good, especially for a developing nation. For instance, the country has not had a single report of polio since 1972, yellow fever since 1974, diphtheria since 1981, or cholera since 1993. Panama City and the former Canal Zone are particularly safe.

However, those planning to spend a considerable amount of time in rural areas, especially if camping, can do several things to stay healthy.

The most important of these is to avoid insect bites as much as possible. Always use insect repellent in the countryside, particularly in the evenings and early mornings. Sleep in screened-in rooms or use mosquito netting. Wearing long-sleeved shirts and long pants will also reduce insect bites. If you're only planning to spend a few days in these areas and know you'll be sleeping under mosquito nets or in screened-in rooms, you may not want to fool with malaria prophylaxis.

For current information on health conditions in Panama, contact the Centers for Disease Control in Atlanta, Georgia (U.S. tel. 877/394-8747, www.cdc.gov/travel).

BEFORE YOU GO

Make preparations for any needed vaccinations or antimalarial medication as far ahead of time as possible. Some vaccinations can't be administered at the same time, and some antimalaria meds need to be started a week or two before traveling.

The information that follows is meant to give travelers general guidelines on staying healthy in Panama. It's drawn from a number of public-health sources, but it's not intended as medical advice and is certainly no substitute for profession medical care in case of emergency. Do not attempt to diagnose or treat yourself for any illness.

Vaccinations

Note that many physicians unfamiliar with Panama except for a vague and dated notion that the place is synonymous with "tropical disease" go overboard in prescribing all kinds of unneeded preventative measures. Many a visitor who plans only to visit Panama City and the Panama Canal area comes loaded with expensive antimalaria medications that serve no purpose other than to amuse their fellow travelers and hosts. Some travelers also worry about official warnings they see about disease risk in Bocas del Toro and Guna Yala. These warnings are generally based on remote areas of the mainland, not the islands that tourists visit.

What kind of precautions to take depends largely on where travelers plan to go and what they plan to do. Those who will spend most of their time in Panama City and the Panama Canal area probably do not need more than minimal protection. Those planning a trek across the Darién may want every defense against disease they can find.

Health conditions and vaccination recommendations can change quickly, so check current requirements and advisories through the CDC (www.cdc.gov/travel) or your doctor.

All visitors should make sure their routine immunizations are up to date, especially against measles-mumps-rubella and tetanus-diphtheria. The incidence of these diseases in Panama is low to nonexistent, but the CDC recommends everyone stay current on their immunizations against them, including nontravelers.

The CDC also recommends that travelers to Central America be vaccinated against hepatitis A and, in some cases, hepatitis B. A rabies vaccination is recommended for those who expect to spend a lot of time outdoors, particularly in rural areas. The CDC suggests typhoid fever vaccinations for those traveling in Central America, though the chance of contracting it in Panama seems remote.

Those planning to travel to rural parts of Panama, especially near the Costa Rican or Colombian border, should probably be vaccinated against yellow fever and may want to consider antimalaria medication.

There is a far greater risk of someone bringing yellow fever to Panama than of catching it there (the last known case in Panama was in 1974). Until recently, Panama required proof of a current yellow-fever vaccination from travelers entering the country from anyplace where yellow fever is endemic. This regulation comes and goes, so it's probably a good idea to have the vaccination if coming from an endemic area, just in case. This means tropical South America, including Colombia, and most of sub-Saharan Africa. Check the CDC website for current information and for a list of U.S. clinics that administer the vaccinations.

Beware: Panamanian authorities have been known to vaccinate those arriving from infected countries at the airport if the traveler cannot present a yellow-fever certificate. Better to take care of this before leaving home. Be sure to bring a properly stamped and signed international yellow-fever certificate, which the person administering the vaccine should give you.

There is no vaccine for malaria, but there are several kinds of antimalarial drugs meant to be taken daily or weekly before, during, and after travel to an endemic area.

Visitors to most parts of Panama should not need to take them. However, outside of Panama City and the area around the former Canal Zone, there is a slight risk of contracting malaria. The risk is greatest in the Darién and the Comarca de Guna Yala (San Blas Islands and mainland). The highest-risk areas west of the Panama Canal are the rural parts of Bocas del Toro and Veraguas provinces.

Many travelers even to these areas don't take antimalarial medication unless they plan to spend a fair amount of time in remote villages or sleep somewhere that doesn't have screened-in rooms. The true risk is almost impossible to measure, so think about the kind of traveling you want to do and discuss options with your physician.

There is a chloroquine-resistant strain of malaria in the Darién and Guna Yala. Mefloquine, doxycycline, or atovaquone/proguanil is recommended for those planning to spend a significant amount of time in these regions. Chloroquine is considered effective against any strains found west of the Panama Canal.

These medications go by an assortment of brand names, which can cause confusion. Some antimalarial medications have serious side effects and are not recommended for everyone (pregnant or breast-feeding women should avoid them). They can also make one more susceptible to sunburn. Some of the contraindications are unusual—mefloquine, for instance, is not recommended for those with a history of depression—so do some research and quiz your doctor carefully. To be effective, travelers must continue to take the medications anywhere from a week to a month after returning home.

INSECTS AND ARACHNIDS

Insects generally come second (after snakes) in the list of creatures tropical neophytes worry about. But most parts of Panama are not nearly as buggy as one might think, and certainly can't compare to, say, the mosquito swarms of an Alaskan summer.

Mosquito populations are kept down around populated areas because of the potential risk of mosquito-borne diseases. Still, mosquitoes can be a nuisance in certain places, especially in the rainy season. Dusk and dawn tend to be active times. Insect repellent and long-sleeved shirts and pants are effective at keeping mosquitoes at bay. Sleep in tents or screened-in rooms to avoid bites at night.

Sand flies (aka sand fleas or no-see-ums) are locally known as *chitras* and can be a real irritation. They love to bite feet and ankles and can cause itching for hours. To avoid infection, try not to scratch. Mosquito repellent helps. They tend to like beach spots without breezes, especially near mangroves, and dine in force in the early evenings. They can be a nuisance in Boca Brava, parts of Bocas del Toro (there's actually a Sand Fly Bay off Isla Colón), and Guna Yala. They're worse during the rainy season; dry-season breezes keep them at bay. Some claim *chitras* like pale skin, so consider working on a leg tan. Keeping feet covered with shoes and socks provides some protection. Anti-inflammatory and itch-relieving creams, such as hydrocortisone, can help with the irritation after bites. Eurax is locally popular for the itching, as is coconut oil. I've found the Pure Tree Natural Body Products (cell 6607-8962 and 6570-8277, www.upinthehill.com) made in Bocas del Toro effective in controlling the itching. They also make a *chitra* repellent, but I haven't tried it yet. *Chitras* can spread leishmaniasis, so it's a good idea to minimize exposure as much as possible.

Chiggers are a type of parasitic mite that hikers can pick up wandering through a field or grassy area. They often climb up the hikers' legs and like to burrow into the skin around the elastic bands of underwear or pants. Once they latch on, they stay attached for days and cause their hosts to itch like crazy. Insect repellent on the clothes, especially around the legs and feet, can offer some protection. Experienced hikers often tuck their pants into their boots and seal them off with masking tape to keep the things out. Some also sprinkle powdered sulfur into their boots to ward them off.

In general, be careful where you put your hands and feet when hiking. Many plants have sharp spines and the like and may harbor aggressive ants, poisonous caterpillars, and other nasties.

There's a reasonable chance of coming across a scorpion, especially in rural and semirural areas. Except for small children the sting is rarely life-threatening, but it's quite painful. Ditto for some spider bites. To be on the safe side, shake out your shoes and clothes before putting them on. When I'm traveling in the countryside, I stuff my socks into my shoes before going to bed at night and shake them out in the morning. In the canal construction days, workers slept with their boots under their pillows. Tarantulas and other large spiders sometimes make an appearance, which is more startling than dangerous; if you leave them alone, they'll do likewise.

Panama has Africanized bees—the so-called "killer bees"—which can be aggressive and dangerous. Keep well away from any bees you come across. If you disturb them and they start chasing you, try to run through dense brush. They will have a hard time following. Do not jump into a body of water to escape them; they will wait for you to surface.

Stay out of the way of ants. Some, such as the bullet ant, have ferocious stings, and less-nasty ones can still swarm over an unsuspecting hiker remarkably quickly.

INSECT-BORNE DISEASES
Dengue Fever

Dengue fever is a viral infection that gets little press but is becoming an increasingly serious public health threat around the world, including the Americas. It's spread through a bite from infected mosquitoes, and so far the only way to prevent it is to keep mosquito populations down and avoid mosquito bites as much as possible. There is no vaccine against the disease and no specific medications to treat it, but anyone who suspects an infection should get medical attention immediately. It's a serious illness, and in some cases can be fatal if untreated.

The main carrier is the *Aedes aegypti,* the same mosquito responsible for yellow fever, but it is also carried by the *Aedes albopictus,* a resilient, adaptable mosquito colloquially known as the Asian tiger mosquito because of its coloration: black with white stripes.

Aedes aegypti is endemic to Panama, but *Aedes albopictus* originated in Asia and has only recently spread to other parts of the world, including the United States. It was not discovered in Panama until 2002.

The disease comes in two forms. Classic dengue fever is characterized by high fever, nausea, vomiting, headache, and pain in the back, joints, and eyes. Pain can be intense, which is how the disease earned the ominous nickname "breakbone fever." Symptoms are often milder for younger children. Recommended treatment includes pain medications, rest, and drinking lots of fluids under a doctor's care while the virus runs its course.

Dengue hemorrhagic fever (DHF) is a far more serious form of the disease. It can be fatal if not properly recognized and treated. With good medical care, however, the mortality rate is generally less than 1 percent. Symptoms include a fever that lasts 2–7 days, accompanied by symptoms that are easily confused with those of other illnesses, such as nausea, vomiting, headache, and stomach pain. This stage is followed by signs of hemorrhage, including a tendency to bruise easily, bleeding nose or gums, and sometimes internal bleeding. Without treatment, this stage can be followed by circulatory failure, shock, and death.

Both dengue fever and DHF are caused by four distinct but closely related viruses. All four now exist in Panama. Infection by one type provides no immunity against later infection by another type.

Dengue epidemics are becoming increasingly common in the Americas. In 1993 Panama had its first reported case of dengue in nearly 50 years. In 2007, there were more than 1,000 dengue cases, and 2 cases of DHF. (By way of comparison, Costa Rica reported more than 25,000 cases of dengue and 300 of DHF in 2007. The population of Costa Rica is about 4.1 million vs. 3.3 million for Panama.)

Dengue thrives in poorer urban areas, and by far the largest concentration of cases has occurred in the sprawling San Miguelito district on the outskirts of Panama City. But dengue is a risk anywhere mosquitoes are found. I was surprised during my last visit at the number of people in comfortable (though usually rural) surroundings I met who'd had a bout of dengue. Mosquito populations are kept down through removing or covering standing pools of water and through fumigation. Panamanian officials have been lax about this in recent years, but they have ramped up their sanitation and fumigation efforts recently. Anyone with uncovered water containers on their property can be fined.

Yellow Fever

Yellow fever was the most dreaded disease in Panama until a massive sanitation and public health program eliminated it from the isthmus in 1906. While it has never had a serious resurgence in Panama (the most recent known case was in 1974), the country has to be constantly on guard against the possibility.

Panama provides a perfect home for the disease and its local vector, the *Aedes aegypti* mosquito. Relaxed sanitation standards helped the mosquito reestablish itself on the isthmus in 1985, which sparked a new public-health push to control it. So far, the mosquito has brought with it dengue fever but not yellow fever.

The biggest concern is that the disease will be brought to the country by foreign visitors from a neighboring country that still has the disease, such as Colombia, which experienced a yellow-fever outbreak in 2004 that killed several people.

Yellow fever symptoms typically come in two phases. The first is characterized by fever, intense muscle pain, nausea, headache, chills, and vomiting. For about 15 percent of sufferers, there is a drop-off in symptoms that is followed in a few days by a return of the fever, and sometimes jaundice (hence the name "yellow fever"), stomach cramps, vomiting, and hemorrhaging. About half of these latter patients die within 10–14 days after the onset of the first symptoms. There is no cure, but most people do survive a yellow-fever attack. Those who do are immune to the disease thereafter, which is a mild consolation. Seek medical help immediately at the first sign of symptoms.

Malaria

Malaria is a tenacious disease that has not been entirely eradicated either in Panama or most of the rest of the world where it's endemic. But it was drastically reduced during Panama Canal construction days as a result of the same sanitation program that eradicated yellow fever. It's been kept at bay ever since.

Chloroquine-resistant strains of the disease exist in eastern Panama, but any strain found west of the Panama Canal is not believed to have acquired immunity to this medication.

Symptoms of malaria usually do not appear until at least a week after infection from the bite of an *Anopheles* mosquito. Flu-like symptoms such as fever, chills, headache, muscle pain, and fatigue are common. Malaria can also cause anemia and jaundice. Symptoms can be intense or quite mild. Those infected may not realize it for some time, which is dangerous. Malaria is a serious disease and potentially fatal if not treated quickly. The U.S. Centers for Disease Control urge any traveler to an endemic area to get medical care immediately at the first sign of fever or flu-like symptoms for a full year after returning home. Be sure to tell the doctor where you've been.

Leishmaniasis

Leishmaniasis is a parasitic disease spread by bites from infected sand flies. The type most commonly found in Latin America is known as cutaneous leishmaniasis, which is characterized by skin sores and is far less serious than visceral leishmaniasis, which attacks the internal organs but is found primarily in Brazil, Africa, and southern Asia.

There is no vaccine for leishmaniasis; the best way to avoid the small chance of contracting it in Panama is to reduce contact with sand flies as much as possible. The only travelers likely to be at risk in Panama are adventurous types who travel far off the beaten track.

Sores develop weeks or even months after the victim is bitten by an infected sand fly. The sores may be painless, and they may or may not scab over. Untreated sores can last from weeks to years and develop into prominent craters on the skin. Anyone who suspects an infection should see a tropical-medicine specialist for diagnosis and treatment.

American Trypanosomiasis (Chagas' Disease)

Chagas' disease is a parasitic infection carried by triatomine bugs (blood-sucking insects sometimes known as the assassin, cone nose, or kissing bug). The parasite, *Trypanosoma cruzi*, often produces a small sore at the point where it enters the body. If this happens around the eye, the eyelid may become swollen. Other symptoms can include a fever and swollen lymph nodes, but infection can be asymptomatic. There is no vaccine against the disease. Those who suspect they might be infected should see a tropical-medicine specialist for diagnosis and treatment. Chronic infections can cause damage to the heart and intestines and even death.

It's rare for travelers to contract Chagas' disease, in Panama or anywhere else. The bugs tend to infest ramshackle buildings made of palm thatch, mud, or adobe, especially those with lots of nooks and crannies in the walls and roof. The disease can also be spread through transfusions of blood that has not been screened for the parasite.

Panama has found about 500 cases of Chagas' disease in the entire country in the last 25 years, and the Pan American Health Organization has noted a marked decline in the presence of the disease since 1993. Central Panama seems more vulnerable to the disease than other parts of the country.

RABIES

The chance of catching rabies is remote, but the consequences of doing so are extreme. There is no cure for rabies, and it's fatal. Only one person in history has ever recovered from a full-blown case of rabies: a girl who was bitten by a bat in the rural United States in late 2004 and treated with a bold experimental technique that could easily have killed her.

Rabies is almost always transmitted by an animal bite. Any mammal can be a carrier, but in Central America one should be particularly wary of vampire bats, feral or aggressive dogs and cats, and monkeys.

In Panama, most cases of rabies in humans are caused by bat bites. In 2002, a 69-year-old woman and her daughter, residents of the community of San Juan Demóstenes Arosemena in Colón province, died from rabies after being bitten by a vampire bat. The last confirmed rabies cases before that occurred in 1995, again from bat bites.

The CDC recommends rabies vaccines for travelers to Latin America who expect to spend considerable time outdoors in rural areas at night or in the evening, even if the trip is brief. This is especially true for those who like to explore caves.

Anyone bitten or scratched by an animal should immediately wash the wound with plenty of soap and water and iodine, if available. Don't panic: Most suspect mammals, even violent ones, do *not* have rabies. The animal should be captured—if possible to do so without risking further attacks—and taken to a medical center for testing. Those potentially exposed to rabies need a series of shots, usually given over the course of a month. This is true even if the victim has had a pre-exposure rabies vaccine. The recommended injections these days are no more painful than flu shots. Prompt treatment after exposure can nearly always prevent rabies infection.

Most people bitten by vampire bats do not realize it at the time. The bat usually approaches its victims at night, while they're sleeping (yes, just like in all those B movies). It lands next to the victim and waddles over to a vulnerable spot. The bat drools onto the site before biting it. The saliva contains an anesthetic and an anticoagulant that lets the bat bite its victim without waking it and lap up the blood that trickles steadily out. Human victims generally don't discover they've been bitten until the next morning, when they find a clump of dried blood near the wound site.

Disgusting? You bet. That's why I recommend travelers sleep only in a tent or screened-in room in rural areas, including beaches and forests. This is especially true around cattle, a favorite blood supply for vampire bats.

Endemic zones for rabies in Panama include Chilibre, eastern Panamá province, La Chorrera, the Darién, the district of David in western Panama, and various spots along the Interamericana.

Symptoms of rabies include paralysis, spasms

of the swallowing muscles in the presence of water (hydrophobia), delirium, and convulsions, followed by coma and death.

STOMACH AILMENTS

Gastrointestinal complaints such as dysentery, giardia, E. coli infections, and even so-called "traveler's diarrhea" are far less common among travelers to Panama than in most parts of Latin America.

It's safe to drink water out of the tap almost everywhere in the country. The destination chapters alert you to the few places where that still isn't a good idea, such as some parts of the Darién and Bocas del Toro. Never drink untreated water from a stream or lake, no matter how pristine it looks.

Hygiene standards in restaurants tend to be fairly high, particularly in Panama City. You're unlikely to get so much as a stomachache. But if a place looks dirty or unpopular, you're probably better off going elsewhere. Street-vendor fare is somewhat riskier. Make sure whatever you munch has just been fried at high temperature. It's not a good idea to eat ice cream and other milk- or water-based sweets sold by street vendors.

The CDC warns that certain fish and shellfish served in tropical countries can contain biotoxins even when well cooked. Barracuda has the highest level of these toxins and should always be avoided. Other possibilities include red snapper and sea bass. I've never heard of anyone in Panama being poisoned by these delicious fish, but if you experience stomach distress accompanied by a sudden change of temperature, weakness, or other unusual symptoms after eating fish, get medical help.

Mild traveler's diarrhea doesn't usually need to be treated with anything more than fluids, rest, and a modest diet of bland foods. Anything more serious, such as bacterial or amoebic dysentery, needs to be treated with drugs and requires a visit to the doctor.

HANTAVIRUS

There was an outbreak of hantavirus pulmonary syndrome in Las Tablas and Guararé in Los Santos province in late 1999 and early 2000 that infected a dozen people and left three dead. It forced the cancellation of the Carnaval celebration in Las Tablas that year. Panama's biggest Carnaval is held in Las Tablas, and so that was a major blow to the local economy.

Hantavirus is an infectious disease most often spread through the inhalation of particles from the feces, urine, or saliva of infected rodents. However, person-to-person infection is also possible. The disease is characterized by fever, headache, and muscle pain followed by hypotension, shock, difficulty breathing, and pulmonary edema (fluid in the lungs). It's a serious disease, and the fatality rate can be above 50 percent. There is no treatment, cure, or vaccine. However, getting health care immediately, especially oxygen therapy, greatly increases one's chance of recovery. Anyone who has been around rodents and experiences shortness of breath and fever should tell a doctor immediately.

Hantavirus was first discovered in the Four Corners region of the western United States in 1993, and before the Las Tablas outbreak it had not been diagnosed in Central America. A major public-health push, in coordination with the U.S. Centers for Disease Control, appears to have largely contained the disease so far, though officials remain vigilant about the possibility of a major flare-up, especially around Carnaval time. There have been a handful of cases both on and outside the Azuero in the years since the initial outbreak. In 2007, five people nationwide were diagnosed with the virus, two of whom died.

The chance of contracting hantavirus is exceedingly low, especially for those who avoid contact with rodents. Mice and rats infest some lodgings in the Panamanian countryside, especially the cheaper places. It's probably worth splurging for better digs in Los Santos province, since that's where the disease erupted in Panama. Rats are a fact of life in Guna Yala, unfortunately, and it's not unusual to hear them rustling in the rafters of tourist huts or running along the beach at night. Clean up messes and keep all food packed away at night.

SEXUALLY TRANSMITTED INFECTIONS

Estimates of the number of people living with HIV in Panama range from 17,000 to more than 30,000. Given the country's small population, that makes it the third-highest rate in Central America. HIV in Panama is more often transmitted through heterosexual than homosexual sex. According to a United Nations agency in Panama, HIV rates have skyrocketed in recent years.

The sexually adventurous should also remember that other STIs are serious and not necessarily easily treatable. An antibiotic-resistant strain of gonorrhea, for instance, is on the rise. Be sure to get a hepatitis B vaccination and always use condoms and other safer-sex methods.

OTHER DISEASES

Panama has seen flare-ups of viral meningitis, pertussis (whooping cough), and tuberculosis in recent years, but travelers are at little risk of contracting them.

SUNBURN

Remember that Panama is just 8 degrees north of the equator, and it's easy to get sunburned amazingly fast. Pale northerners have been known to get a nasty sunburn after just a half hour out in the noonday sun. Try to stay in the shade noon–3 P.M. Don't be fooled by mild or cloudy days. Even if you don't feel hot, ultraviolet rays are frying you. Always wear sunscreen. Be especially careful when out on the water, which reflects sun rays like a mirror. (Ever had a chin burn?) Sunglasses and a hat are also a good idea. Drink lots of water to avoid dehydration even when it feels humid.

OCEAN DANGERS

A rip current, sometimes erroneously referred to as an "undertow," is created when surf gets trapped on its way back out to sea, often by a sandbar. Pressure builds up until a concentrated stream of water rips a hole in the sandbar and water surges back out in a narrow channel, sometimes at impressive speed. It's similar in effect to pulling the plug on a bathroom drain.

Be on the lookout for patches of muddy, dark, or disturbed water, which can indicate a rip. If you feel yourself being pulled out to sea, don't panic and don't try to fight against the current—it's stronger than you are. Instead, swim with the current but try to veer off at a 45-degree angle to it. Contrary to popular belief, rip currents don't drag swimmers under or sweep them out to sea. They are typically short and narrow and swimmers should be able to swim out of the channel fairly quickly. Tired or poor swimmers should just float with the current until it weakens, then swim parallel to shore to escape it. Stay calm and conserve your strength. Once you escape the rip current, swim back to shore.

Panamanians often prefer to bathe along stretches of beach with muddy sand and little surf, knowing from experience how powerful those majestic, rolling waves on the picture postcard beaches can be. Waves can get enormous on some of Panama's beaches and give swimmers a real pounding. Use common sense and don't wade in past your shins when the surf is high, and look out for hidden rocks and reefs.

Shark attacks are highly unlikely, particularly in the Caribbean. The Pacific sea snake is one of the most toxic creatures in the world, but the chances of coming across one are slim. Barracudas may be scary-looking, but they're not generally aggressive toward humans. However, do not wear shiny jewelry while swimming or diving. The flash of the sun off jewelry looks to a barracuda like the scales of a fish, and they may dart in the direction of it.

Look out for sea urchins and fire coral, and never touch any other kind of coral; it'll scrape you up and cause serious damage to the coral.

Shuffle your feet on entering or exiting the water to avoid stepping on a hidden ray.

HYPOTHERMIA

The chance of contracting hypothermia in a tropical country such as Panama may seem slim, but it can get quite chilly in the highlands, even in the Darién, something not all travelers are prepared for. Do not go hiking in the highlands, particularly around Volcán Barú, in just shorts and a T-shirt. It can get down to freezing at the top of Barú even when it's sweltering hot far down the volcano. Bring warm, waterproof clothing to change into if it gets wet and chilly, which it often does.

Hypothermia is caused by a drop in the body's core temperature, so it's possible to become hypothermic even in milder conditions. To avoid hypothermia, stay dry, dress warmly, avoid alcohol and rapid changes of temperature, and drink lots of water.

Early warning signs of hypothermia include loss of coordination, inability to concentrate, and involuntary shivering. If the afflicted person continues to shiver even when bundled up, the hypothermia is more serious.

WILD ANIMALS

Almost every hiker new to the tropics worries about snakes. As has been mentioned several times throughout the book, it's rare to come across a snake while hiking and extremely rare to be bothered by one. The chances of coming across one near any population center are even smaller, partly because Panamanians are aggressive about exterminating snakes in their midst. However, be cautious around leaf and trash piles even in the cities, just in case.

There are several things hikers can do to make it even less likely they'll be bothered by a slithering critter.

First, be careful stepping over tree falls, which attract snakes (not to mention stinging insects). Also be careful around piles of dried leaves. Before gathering any to start a fire, shuffle boot-clad feet through them.

This should go without saying, but don't play with snakes in the tropics. Some people seem irresistibly drawn to disturbing the creatures, which usually just want to be left alone. A European tourist I was hiking with in the Darién once tried to use his walking stick to prod a baby fer-de-lance we came across. The fer-de-lance is a deadly pit viper, and even the babies can be lethal. They can also be extremely aggressive and quick when disturbed. The guide and I managed to save the guy from his foolish, possibly suicidal, curiosity.

In the extremely unlikely event of being bitten, try not to panic. All that accomplishes is to increase one's heart rate and pump any injected venom faster through one's system. Poisonous snakes don't always inject venom when they strike. Obviously, get to the nearest hospital as soon as possible. If possible without risking further bites, kill the snake and take it with you to be identified. Do not try slashing at the wound and sucking out the poison, as usually this is ineffective and can actually make things worse. Keep the site of the wound below the heart and head if possible.

Do not feed, tease, or get too close to monkeys. Some can be aggressive if they feel threatened and will fling feces, bite, or otherwise attack. If bitten by a monkey, get medical help immediately. They can carry rabies and other nasty diseases.

Peccaries, a kind of wild pig, are a concern in the more remote forests, particularly in the Darién. Because their natural predator, the jaguar, has been hunted to near extinction, peccary populations have exploded in some areas. They sometimes descend on a spot by the hundreds and tear everything up. They can run surprisingly fast and have fearsomely sharp teeth. Those unlucky enough to get in the path of a herd should climb the nearest tall tree and stay there until they move on.

TRAFFIC ACCIDENTS

Traffic accidents pose by far the greatest hazard for visitors to Panama. Traffic in Panama tends to be chaotic, road conditions poor, and enforcement of driving laws lax. About one person a day is killed on the roads, which is a lot for a country of 3.3 million people, many of whom don't have cars. Be alert at all times on the road, and if you're a passenger, don't be shy about asking a speeding driver to slow down.

If you're involved in an accident, do not move the cars—it's against the law. Stay on the scene until the *tránsito* (transit police) arrive. If someone is injured or it's otherwise an emergency, call the police emergency number (104) or the fire department (103). Panama has been gradually rolling out an ambulance dispatch service (911) in urban areas. Once the *tránsito* arrive, they'll fill out a report that will include your description of the accident. Be fully cooperative and polite. Contact your insurance company or the car-rental agency as soon as possible.

Panamanian attitudes toward safety in general tend to be far more relaxed than those in, say, Northern Europe and North America. Accidents, including traffic accidents, are the second leading cause of death in Panama, after cancer.

LOCAL DOCTORS, CLINICS, AND HOSPITALS

Panama has world-class medical facilities and doctors, many of whom were trained in the United States and speak English. Even those without medical insurance can receive good care for far less than it would cost them in the United States. It's possible to get a checkup from, say, a specialist trained at Johns Hopkins for about US$35. The best medical facilities are in Panama City. The hospitals in David also have a good reputation.

Condoms and other nonprescription means of birth control are available at pharmacies.

Centros de salud (health centers) and small rural hospitals are scattered throughout the country, though they can be poorly staffed and equipped. Serious medical problems should be treated in Panama City if at all possible. Those

planning adventurous travel in remote spots may want to consider buying travel insurance that includes emergency evacuation provisions. I strongly advise all travelers to buy at least basic travel insurance.

ILLEGAL DRUGS

Panama is famous for its marijuana (the "Panama Red" of hippie anthems) and notorious as a transshipment point for cocaine. Don't let that fool you into thinking the consumption of illegal drugs is treated casually in Panama. If you're caught with any, you could very well find yourself spending years in a squalid, overcrowded prison.

Simple possession of even a small amount of marijuana or any other drug is punishable by a minimum of one year in prison. Those caught with more than a tiny bit of a drug are assumed to be trafficking in it, and punishment is correspondingly harsh. Anyone caught buying or selling drugs is looking at 5–10 years behind bars.

Dealers have been known to set up gullible tourists for a bust, sometimes in the hope of sharing a bribe with a corrupt cop. Resist all temptations to sample the local products. It's an extremely foolish risk to take.

CRIME

Panama is by and large a peaceful, mellow place despite its undeserved reputation as some sort of danger zone. You'll likely be safer in Panama City than you would in any city of comparable size back home. Violent crime against tourists and affluent Panamanians is still so unusual that when it does happen it's huge news and causes lots of local hand-wringing about the decline of Panamanian society.

Property theft and other kinds of nonviolent crime are the main concern for the haves, and even this is mainly a problem for those who live in the cities, not travelers.

However, violent crime is on the rise. Most of this is gang-on-gang or drug-related violence in areas few travelers visit. Extreme unemployment and poverty make Colón, historically Panama's second-most important city, unsafe for any outsider. There's an excellent chance of getting mugged if you wander around here. Avoid that city altogether for the foreseeable future.

Even in Panama City, avoid the poorest neighborhoods, such as El Chorrillo and Curundu, and be alert in transitional ones, such as the historic Casco Viejo area.

Because of reports of robberies at the secluded Madden Dam (on Lago Alajuela), I do not recommend that travelers visit it even in groups. I have also heard the occasional unconfirmed report of robberies in the national parks around Panama City, but this does not yet appear to be a major problem. Just do not hike alone, which is never a good idea anyway.

Rural areas are generally quite safe, but do not leave valuables even in a locked car when going for a hike in remote spots.

As tourism increases, it's probably inevitable that scams and crimes against tourists will increase as well. More tourists are complaining of thefts from their rooms at both budget and luxury hotels, particularly in Panama City. In the last few years, hotels around the country have added in-room safes; use them. There are also reports of thefts from beaches while tourists are swimming or surfing. These generally occur at the more popular surfing spots, such as the northern side of Bastimentos in Bocas del Toro. Again, this is not a major problem, at least not yet. Even the scams usually amount to being overcharged for a taxi ride or taken to a hotel one is not interested in. Be alert and use common sense when traveling in the relatively more touristed parts of Panama.

Money

Panama's currency is the balboa. The balboa's rate of exchange has always been tied to the dollar, with one dollar equal to one balboa. In fact, Panama does not print paper money, so the U.S. dollar is legal tender in Panama. Panamanian coins (1-, 5-, 10-, 25-, and 50-cent pieces) are the same size, weight, and color as the U.S. ones and are used interchangeably with them. The only difference is what is printed on the faces; except for the one-centavo coin and special-edition coins, heads is always a portrait of Balboa and tails is always the shield of Panama. The one-centavo coin has Urracá, a fierce indigenous chief who won many battles against the conquistadors. You may see prices quoted with either a "B/" or "$" before them. Both mean the same thing.

Despite Panama's status as a world banking capital, it's tough to exchange foreign currencies almost everywhere in Panama. Try to bring only dollars to Panama.

CHANGING MONEY

Those who can't avoid changing money in Panama have only a few options, and most are in Panama City. Changing money at the border is difficult to impossible except at Tocumen International Airport and Paso Canoa, on the Costa Rican border. Even there options are limited.

BANKS

Banks are generally open 8 A.M.–2 or 3 P.M. Monday–Friday and 9 A.M.–noon Saturday. ATMs are located throughout Panama and are by far the easiest way to access cash; look for red signs that read Sistema Clave. Some find service at the state-run Banco Nacional de Panamá (BNP) to be slower and more bureaucratic than at private banks, but BNP is sometimes the only option in remoter areas.

FINANCIAL SERVICES

Panama's extensive financial services sector is focused on offshore banking, not serving short-term visitors. Try not to get involved with bank transfers and such during your stay, as it'll most likely be an expensive exercise in bureaucratic frustration. For those who must wire money to or from Panama, the best option is to use Western Union or Moneygram, which have many outlets throughout the country.

TRAVELERS CHECKS

Travelers checks are difficult to cash in Panama. Merchants are reluctant to accept them since banks treat them as foreign checks and put a 45-day hold on them before the merchants' accounts get credited. Travelers checks are generally more nuisance than they are worth. Often banks are the only place to cash them, and some banks have begun to refuse them. Trying to cash anything other than American Express checks is even more difficult. Given the ubiquity of ATMs, it's better to rely on cash cards than travelers checks in Panama. It's still a good idea, however, to bring some travelers checks as a backup, or as way to prove economic solvency when crossing borders.

CREDIT CARDS

Credit cards are widely accepted in the cities, especially in the more upscale hotels and restaurants and most stores of any size. Visa and Mastercard are the most widely accepted. Other cards can generally only be used in the most cosmopolitan establishments, such as five-star hotels. Simpler hotels and restaurants are often cash only, as are most personal services (taxis, tour guides, small outfitters, etc). The farther away one gets from an urban center, the less likely it is credit cards will be accepted. Bring lots of small bills to more remote parts of Panama, such as the Comarca de Guna Yala (San Blas Islands), where credit cards are not accepted and larger denominations are hard to break. Casinos can be a good place to break larger bills. Some businesses in Bocas del Toro still impose a surcharge on credit-card purchases; ask ahead of time.

TAXES AND TIPPING

A 10 percent tourism tax is added to hotel room bills. Room prices quoted in this book include the tax unless specified. Panama sales tax is 7 percent. The airport departure tax for those leaving the country is US$40; it is now generally included in the price of the air ticket.

It's customary to tip 10 percent in restaurants. Bellhops, porters, and others who perform special services should be tipped. How much to tip depends on the service and the discretion of the tipper. Anywhere from US$0.25 to US$1 should do it for minor services. Porters at the international airport expect a buck a bag. Taxi drivers do not expect a tip.

In rural areas, park rangers and other workers sometimes provide guide services, cook food, tote luggage, etc., for campers and hikers. It's good karma to tip at least US$5 a day for these services on top of the camping or transportation fees.

BARGAINING AND DISCOUNTS

Haggling is not the norm in Panama. It's sometimes possible to get a slight break on major purchases, such as expensive electronics, or on handicrafts, such as *molas* (blouses), but don't expect much. Crafts sellers will sometimes start out with an inflated price, but they quickly come down to a firm offer and are unlikely to budge. It's always worth asking if there's some kind of *descuento* (discount), though. There may be a price break for buying more than one item; those willing to buy two or more *molas,* for instance, can sometimes get a break.

Senior and student discounts are generally only available to Panamanians and resident expatriates, not visitors. In fact, in some places, such as the national parks, there is a two-tier system of fees, with foreigners expected to pay more than residents. It may be possible to get a student or senior discount at museums and the like, though the entrance fee is usually so small to begin with it's probably not worth bothering with.

Maps and Tourist Information

MAPS

Tourist maps of Panama and Panama City are getting better, but even the best ones are instantly out of date. New roads, bridges, and buildings just go up too fast. The maps recommended here are widely available online, especially through online bookstores such as Amazon.com.

National Geographic's **Panama Adventure Map** (http://shop.nationalgeographic.com), part of its "adventureMAP" series, is the best map of the entire country. It's especially useful for outdoorsy types, as it shows elevations clearly and marks all the protected areas.

A map entitled **Panamá: Mapa Guía,** put out by Distribudora Lewis in Panama, has easy-to-read street maps of Panama City, with insets of the areas of most interest to visitors, including Panamá La Vieja. There are also inset maps of David, Santiago, Chitré, and the Panama Canal. There's a decent country map that highlights beaches, main roads, protected areas, and major towns. It's quite useful and will meet the needs of most travelers.

International Travel Maps and Books (ITMB) has made good Panama maps in the past, but they are not updated frequently.

Every issue of the freebie tourist magazine **Focus Panama** contains fold-out maps of the country, Panama City, Colón, and David. The city maps aren't terribly detailed, but they can be useful. The magazine is widely distributed to hotels, restaurants, and shops frequented by tourists.

Other maps of various quality are available in Panama, especially Panama City. Best bets in Panama City include Exedra Books, Librería Argosy, and El Hombre de la Mancha bookstores, Farmacia Arrocha drugstores, or Gran Morrison department-store outlets.

The **Instituto Geográfico Nacional Tommy Guardia** (Vía Simon Bolívar/Transístmica, tel.

236-2444 or 236-1844, fax 235-1841, www.mop.gob.pa, 8 A.M.–3:30 P.M. Mon.–Fri.) in Panama City sells a wide variety of physical, political, and topographical maps of the country, including a nine-sheet 1:12,500 scale map just of Panama City. The prices are low, but most of its maps are too large and detailed to be of use to most visitors. Many of the more popular maps, including ones of central Panama City, are frequently unavailable. The place is affectionately known as "Tommy Guardia," and most taxi drivers should know it. It's on the north side of the Transístmica directly across the street from the Universidad de Panamá. The **Islamorada Internacional** (Bldg. 808, Avenida Arnulfo Arias Madrid/Balboa Road, tel. 228-4348 or 228-6069, www.islamorada.com, 8 A.M.–5 P.M. Mon.–Fri.) store in Balboa is an excellent resource for those who need nautical charts.

TOURIST INFORMATION

Large-scale tourism is still a new concept for Panama, and getting good, accurate, and current tourist information in the country is not always easy. Take everything you read and hear with a grain of salt, as much of the material out there is more interested in promoting tourism and selling real estate than giving balanced information.

The best way to get current information on Panama before a trip is through the Internet. A good place to start is **www.panamainfo.com,** an enthusiastically pro-Panama-tourism site that consistently has the most up-to-date information of any of the overview sites. It's written in both English and Spanish. Panama's government tourism sites are **www.visitpanama.com** and **www.atp.gob.pa.** They contain some useful information, such as an updated schedule of festivals and holidays.

The Panamanian newspaper with the best

and most extensive coverage of tourist destinations and promotional deals is *La Prensa,* a daily widely available throughout the country. It has a good website that gives free access to most of its content, including its archives: www.prensa.com.

Panama's government tourism agency, the **Autoidad de Turismo de Panameño** (www. visitpanama.com), widely known as ATP, provides little actual information to tourists. Each change of government brings new optimism that ATP will be galvanized into action, usually with mixed results at best.

ATP has both small information booths and massive tourist-information complexes known as CEFATIs (Centros de Facilidades Turísticas e Interpretación, which roughly translates to tourist and interpretive centers) dotted around the country. These sometimes have minimally informative printed information, but the attendants often know surprisingly little about the area's attractions and rarely speak anything other than Spanish. CEFATIs are sometimes worth a visit for their displays on the history and culture of the given area.

Film and Photography

EQUIPMENT

Good-quality cameras are widely available around Panama, particularly Panama City. Don't expect great deals, though—the equipment is probably at least as expensive as it is back home. Good places to shop for photo equipment in Panama City are the walking section of Avenida Central, along Vía España, and at the huge Panafoto store on Calle 50. The latter is also a good bet for photo processing for you nondigital types. It's not worth shopping for photo equipment in the Colón Free Zone unless you're in the market for a dozen cameras or so. Film is easy to come by; try any of the pharmacy chains, such as the omnipresent Farmacia Arrocha.

Disposable cameras are widely available, waterproof disposable cameras less so. Bring a disposable underwater camera or a waterproof case from home if you expect to spend much time snorkeling or diving; the photo possibilities can be spectacular.

TIPS

Bring a couple of large, sturdy plastic bags to wrap the camera in to protect it from Panama's sudden torrential downpours and sloshing from boat trips, as well as sand and salt near the ocean. The country's heat and humidity are hard on cameras, film, and memory sticks; try to keep them in as cool a place as possible. Also, allow time for the camera to adjust from the air-conditioned indoors to the steamy outdoors.

The light is usually best in the early morning and late afternoon, but the sun rises and sets fast near the equator, so work quickly. The scenery can get washed out by the sun around midday.

PHOTO ETIQUETTE

Always ask permission before taking someone's picture. Snapping away at a "colorful local" is a good way to offend someone's dignity. Do not take photos of police or sensitive government installations. In a Guna village, always ask first and expect to pay for the privilege of taking someone's photo. The going rate is US$1 per subject.

Communications and Media

Panama has a relatively free and aggressive press, certainly in comparison with the days of the military dictatorship, which controlled and censored the press either directly or through intimidation and violence. But Panama continues to be widely criticized for restrictive and antiquated laws that, for instance, make it a criminal offense for a journalist to insult public officials, even if the criticism is factually accurate. Newspaper reporters, TV journalists, and editorial cartoonists continue to be arrested and fined for these and other offenses. While journalists are usually released quickly, international press-freedom organizations have denounced the laws and worry about the chilling effect it has on the media. Physical attacks, threats, and harassment of journalists sometimes occur as well. Despite new transparency laws, it remains difficult for journalists to get access to many government documents and records that are publicly available in other countries.

NEWSPAPERS

Panama has an abundance of Spanish-language daily newspapers, all headquartered in Panama City, but most are widely available throughout the country. Panama's various news outlets tend to have allegiances to parties, political stances, and families, which can color what they cover and how they cover it.

The best of the bunch is *La Prensa,* which is comparable to a major U.S. daily. It has a bewildering array of weekly supplements, on everything from fashion to health, and does the best job of any paper in covering tourism and other topics likely to be of interest to visitors. *El Panamá América* and *La Estrella de Panamá* are fallbacks if *La Prensa* is sold out. Panama also has popular tabloids, notably *La Crítica* and *El Siglo,* which specialize in gory, sensationalist crime stories and inflammatory political topics.

Panama no longer has a major daily English-language paper. In 2007, *La Estrella* introduced an English-language supplement, the *Panama Star,* in all but its Sunday editions. The best sources for English-language news are online, particularly www.panama-guide.com. Bocas del Toro (the *Bocas Breeze*) and Boquete (the *Bajarque Times*) now have small, local newspapers in English.

There are also three well-established Chinese-language newspapers that cater to the large Chinese immigrant population.

TELEVISION AND RADIO

For years Panama had just two television stations: RPC (channel 4) and TVN (channel 2), as well as the U.S. armed forces station (SCN, channel 8 on the Pacific side of the isthmus and channel 11 on the Caribbean side). The armed forces stations disappeared with the closing of the American bases, but several other networks, including Telemetro (channel 13, which is owned by the company that owns RPC) have popped up in recent years. The entire country is increasingly plugging into cable television—actually satellite TV—through DirecTV and the plethora of Spanish- and English-language stations it offers.

The country's airwaves are crammed with the sounds of radio stations, most offering *típico,* Latin pop, and mainstream American rock. English-language talk shows, usually aimed at older expatriate residents, are beginning to appear. Radio Metropolis (93.5 FM) has a Sunday night show 6–10 P.M. that can also be heard online at www.pbcpanama.com. Ultra Stereo (98.9 FM) has a morning talk and music show 8–10 A.M. Monday–Friday.

TELEPHONE SERVICES

The country code for Panama is 507. Do not dial 507 when making calls within the country.

Cellular phone numbers begin with the number six and have eight digits (landlines have seven digits). These can be more expensive to call, but they're often the best way to contact someone. The emergency number for the **police** *(policía nacional)* is 104. The emergency number for the **fire department** *(bomberos)* is 103. In smaller communities, these numbers don't always work; you have to dial a local number instead. Ask a resident or call directory assistance for help. **Directory assistance** *(asistencia al directorio)* is 102. The **national operator** can be reached at 101. To reach the **international operator,** dial 106.

Panama is finally rolling out an official emergency medical response service, starting with the major urban areas. Dial 911 to call an ambulance (note that this is only for medical help; dial 104 for the police). This service, *Sistema Único de Manejo de Emergencias* (translation: Unified System for the Management of Emergencies, www.sume911.pa/) is new, and how well it works will take time to ascertain. If an ambulance doesn't come fast, your best bet may be to grab a taxi and get to the closest hospital.

Pay phones pop up in the most unlikely places, including dirt-poor villages and islands in the middle of nowhere. Long-distance calls within the country generally cost no more than US$0.15 per minute. Instructions on using modern pay phones are in English and several other languages, but finding one that actually works can sometimes be a problem. Also, many of these phones accept only prepaid calling cards.

Those with an unlocked cell phone should consider buying a local SIM card. They're available from outlets of Panama's main telephone service provider, Cable and Wireless (C&W), and from a competing company, Movistar. They cost about US$1 and usually include a usage credit. They're used in conjunction with C&W's prepaid Móvil phone cards in denominations up to US$50. These disposable cards contain a code that the user enters into the phone, which is then credited for the amount (instructions are in Spanish and English). Calling rates are quite reasonable, so don't buy a larger denomination than you're likely to need. The Móvil cards are easy to find, as they're sold in stores and vending machines around the country. However, low-denomination credits expire more quickly.

Some Internet cafés offer international calling and fax services. Calls can be quite reasonable, but check carefully before sending or receiving a fax. International fax service isn't that common at most of these places, and the charges can be steep, especially to send. It's not unusual to be charged US$1 a page to receive and up to US$5 a page to send, plus international dialing charges. The high-end hotels tend to have business centers with computer and phone services.

The international access code for placing direct calls from Panama is 00 followed by the country code. The country code for the continental United States or Canada is 1, the United Kingdom is 44, Spain is 34, Germany is 49, France is 33, Australia is 61, Costa Rica is 506, Nicaragua is 505, Colombia is 57, and Mexico is 52. Check a local phone book or call the international operator (106) for other access codes and for help making a call.

MAIL SERVICE

Mail between Panama and other countries is not too speedy. A postcard sent from Panama takes at least 5–10 days to reach the United States, and longer to more distant destinations. Postcards to the United States cost US$0.25. Airmail letters weighing up to 20 grams (0.7 ounce) cost US$0.35. Add US$0.05 to postcards and airmail letters for Canada addresses, US$0.10 for European ones, and US$0.15 for addresses in Asia, Africa, and Oceania. Some of the more expensive hotels sell stamps. Note that bulky packages sent to or from Panama sometimes get lost in the mail.

Do not put tape on an envelope; the post

office may refuse to accept it or return international mail that has tape on it. One explanation for this strange rule may be that it discourages thieves from opening mail and then resealing the envelope to hide the crime.

Post office hours are generally 7 A.M.–6 P.M. Monday–Friday, 7 A.M.–5 P.M. Saturday. Post offices are closed on Sunday.

Another oddity about mail in Panama is there is no home delivery; even in modern Panama City, everyone must have mail sent to an *apartado postal* (post-office box). Frustration with slow and sometimes unreliable postal service has driven many who can afford it to subscribe to private mail and courier services, some of which are only slightly more satisfying.

There are a number of international mailing and shipping stores in Panama City. Mail Boxes Etc. has outlets around the city, including one at Vía España and Calle 61 and one in the Albrook Mall next to the Gran Terminal de Transportes. They also have fax services.

INTERNET ACCESS

Internet cafés are everywhere in Panama. You will have little trouble finding one in the cities, and they're beginning to pop up in fairly remote areas as well. Charges are rarely more than a dollar or two an hour, often less. Most of these cafés use Windows-based machines. Free wireless Internet is proliferating all over the country, particularly in mid-price hotels and businesses that cater to tourists. Macintoshes are sometimes available as well.

Weights and Measures

Panama uses the metric system, though auto fuel is sold by the gallon, and pounds, inches, and feet are still sometimes used interchangeably with their metric equivalents.

ELECTRICITY

Panama's voltage is almost universally the same as it is in the United States: 110 volts. Sockets are two-pronged, and U.S. appliances don't need an adapter. There are still a few remote places that use 220 volts, however, so if there's any doubt, ask before plugging in. Note that short blackouts and power surges are common in Panama. Those traveling with sensitive equipment, such as a laptop computer, may want to bring a surge suppresser.

TIME ZONE

Panama is on eastern standard time. There is no daylight savings time in Panama, so the time difference with U.S. destinations changes by an hour during daylight savings time in the United States. Put another way, Panama time is five hours behind Greenwich Mean Time. Panama is always one hour ahead of Costa Rica, something to remember when crossing the border.

Holidays

If you are in Panama around Christmas, New Year's, Carnaval, Semana Santa (the week leading up to Easter), or the November independence holidays, be prepared for celebrations and business closures even on days that are not officially listed as holidays. Also note that when holidays fall on a weekday they are often celebrated on a Monday to create a long weekend. In October–November every city, town, and tiny village has a drum corps and marching band that practices incessantly. Some will find the incessant drumming colorful. Others will find it maddening. Check with ATP (www.visitpanama.com) for exact dates of holidays that change yearly, and for a current list of the many other festivals, fairs, religious observances, and regional celebrations that take place somewhere in the country just about every week. The major national holidays are:

- January 1: Año Nuevo (New Year's Day)
- January 9: Día de los Mártires (Martyrs' Day)
- The four days leading up to Ash Wednesday: Los Carnavales (Carnival Week)
- Friday before Easter Sunday: Viernes Santo (Good Friday)
- May 1: Día del Trabajo (Worker's Day)
- November 3: Separación de Panamá de Colombia (Independence from Colombia)
- November 4: Día Nacional de la Bandera (Flag Day)
- November 10: Primer Grito de Independencia de España (First Call for Independence from Spain)
- November 28: Independencia de Panamá de España (Independence from Spain)
- December 8: Día de Las Madres (Mother's Day)
- December 25: Navidad (Christmas)

RESOURCES

Glossary

abrazo: a hug

Afro-Antillano: Panamanian of African descent from the West Indies

Afro-Colonial: Panamanian of African descent from the Spanish colonial era

águila: eagle

apartado postal: post office box, often abbreviated to *apartado*

aparthotel: apartment-style hotel designed for long-term stays

ardilla: squirrel

arnulfista: supporter of the Partido Arnulfista, a political party started by Arnulfo Arias

arrecife: reef

artesanías: handicraft

baina: thing (colloquial)

banco: bank

barco: ship

batido: milk and/or fruit shake

biblioteca: library

bicicleta: bicycle

bienes raices: real estate

bohío: a thatched-roof, open-sided hut; also called a *rancho*

bombero: firefighter

bote: boat

botero: boatman

brisa: breeze

bucero: diver

buho: owl

caballero: gentleman

cacique: chief

campesino: country person, farmer

cangrejo: crab

canoa: canoe

caracol: shell

carimañola: a kind of roll made from ground and boiled yuca that is generally stuffed with meat and then deep fried

carro: car

cascada: waterfall (also *chorro*)

catedral: cathedral

cayo: cay, small island

cayuco: small dugout canoe

chakara: handwoven bag made by the Ngöbe-Buglé

chaquira: necklaces made by the Ngöbe-Buglé

chicha: fresh juice, usually made from fruit or corn; sometimes alcoholic

chitra: sandflea, sand fly, no-see-um

chiva: small, often makeshift bus

churro: tube-shaped, doughnut-like fried snack

cimarron: escaped African slave during Spanish colonial era

colectivo: shared taxi or van

colono: settler, often used in Panama to refer to farmers and ranchers on recently deforested land

comarca: in Panama, a semiautonomous reservation for indigenous people

comida corriente: fast food

conejo: rabbit

conejo pintado: agouti paca (literally, painted rabbit)

congos: traditional dances performed by Afro-Colonials on special occasions

criollo: native, local

crucero: cruise ship
culebra: snake
delfín: dolphin
desfile: parade
dueño: owner
equis: fer-de-lance snake (literally, "x")
estrella: star
extranjero: foreigner
finca: farm; also, country house
fonda: basic restaurant serving comida corriente
fuerte: fort
gato: cat
gato solo: coatimundi, white-nosed coati (literally, lone cat)
gavilán: hawk
gerente: manager
guandu: a small, pea-like legume
gucamayo: macaw
hojaldre: fry bread; a breakfast dish
hospedaje: guesthouse; often a low-cost one
hostal: a hostel, but can refer to more upscale inns as well
huaca: ceremonial treasures buried with the dead; in Panama, usually refers to pre-Columbian gold figurines or modern replicas
iglesia: church
joven: young person
kiosco: kiosk, usually a food or grocery stand
lagarto: alligator, usually refers to caiman
lago: lake
lancha: (boat) launch
lavamático: launderette
lavandería: a cleaners, especially dry cleaners
librería: bookstore
loro: parrot
macho de monte: Baird's tapir (literally, man of the mountain)
maleantes: thugs, troublemakers, thieves
malpache: raccoon
manigordo: ocelot
minisuper: convenience store
mola: Guna blouse, but generally refers to front panel of mola blouse, which is sold as a handicraft made from layers of brightly colored cloth

mono: monkey
mono araña: spider monkey
mono aullador: howler monkey
mono cariblanco: white-faced capuchin (monkey)
mono tití: Geoffroy's tamarin (monkey)
moto: motor scooter
museo: museum
naturaleza: nature
oso perezoso: sloth (literally, lazy bear)
panadería: bakery
panga: boat, usually a fiberglass boat with an electric motor
parque: park
patacones: twice-fried green plantains
patoca: jumping pit viper; also mano de piedra (literally, hand of stone)
perro: dog
pesca: fishing
pescado: fish
piedra pintada: boulder with petroglyphs (literally, painted stone)
piragua: large dugout canoe
piscina: swimming pool
pollera: formal, embroidered dress
puerta: door
puerto: port
pushboton: a hotel designed for private sexual encounters; also called a push (from the English "push button," so-called because patrons have little contact with management)
quebrada: brook, ravine
rabiblanco: pejorative term for Panama's white ruling elite (literally, white tail)
rana: frog
rancho: thatched roof, open-sided hut; also called a bohío
refresquería: snack or refreshment bar
reggaeton: music form that blends reggae, rap, and dancehall
residencial: low-cost accommodations, similar to hospedaje
restaurante: restaurant
saíno: peccary; also called puerco de monte (literally, mountain pork)

saludos: greetings; usually used in letters
salvavidas: life jacket or lifeguard
sapo: toad
seco: dry; also the name of a popular Panamanian alcohol made from sugarcane
sendero: trail
serpente: serpent
tagua: ivory nut
taller: workshop
tigre: tiger, but often used in Panama to refer to jaguar
típico: literally, typical, but in Panama also refers to *música típica,* a dance-music form that features traditional elements such as accordion and yodeling
tortuga: turtle
vegetariano: vegetarian
velero: sailboat
verrugosa: bushmaster snake
viento: wind

COMMONLY USED ABBREVIATIONS

ANAM: Autoridad Nacional del Ambiente; Panama's national environmental authority

ATP: Autoidad de Turismo de Panameño; Panama's government tourism institute, formerly known as IPAT

CEFATI: Centro de Facilidades Turísticas e Interpretación; large tourist-information centers run by ATP (roughly, tourist and interpretative center)

INAC: Instituto National de Cultura (Panama's national institute of culture); government agency that runs the country's museums and other cultural institutions and events

PA: Partido Arnulfista; a political party

PILA: Parque Internacional La Amistad; an international park shared by Panama and Costa Rica

PRD: Partido Revolucionario Democrático; a political party

STRI: Smithsonian Tropical Research Institute

Suntracs: Sindicato Único de Trabjadores de la Construcción y Similares; a construction workers' union

Spanish Phrasebook

Your Panamanian adventure will be more fun if you use a little Spanish. Panamanian folks, although they may smile at your funny accent, will appreciate your halting efforts to break the ice and transform yourself from a foreigner to a potential friend.

Spanish commonly uses 30 letters—the familiar English 26, plus four straightforward additions: ch, ll, ñ, and rr, which are explained in "Consonants," below.

PRONUNCIATION

Once you learn them, Spanish pronunciation rules—in contrast to English—don't change. Spanish vowels generally sound softer than in English. (Note: The capitalized syllables receive stronger accents.)

Vowels

a like ah, as in "hah": *agua* AH-gooah (water), *pan* PAHN (bread), and *casa* CAH-sah (house)

e like ay, as in "may": *mesa* MAY-sah (table), *tela* TAY-lah (cloth), and *de* DAY (of, from)

i like ee, as in "need": *diez* dee-AYZ (ten), *comida* ko-MEE-dah (meal), and *fin* FEEN (end)

o like oh, as in "go": *peso* PAY-soh (weight), *ocho* OH-choh (eight), and *poco* POH-koh (a bit)

u like oo, as in "cool": *uno* OO-noh (one), *cuarto* KOOAHR-toh (room), and *usted* oos-TAYD (you); when it follows a "q" the **u** is silent; when it follows an "h" or has an umlaut, it's pronounced like "w"

Consonants

b, d, f, k, l, m, n, p, q, s, t, v, w, x, y, z, and ch pronounced almost as in English; **h** occurs, but is silent—not pronounced at all

c like k as in "keep": *cuarto* KOOAR-toh (room), *Tepic* tay-PEEK (capital of Nayarit state); when it precedes "e" or "i," pronounce **c** like s, as in "sit": *cerveza* sayr-VAY-sah (beer), *encima* ayn-SEE-mah (atop)

g like g as in "gift" when it precedes "a," "o," "u," or a consonant: *gato* GAH-toh (cat), *hago* AH-goh (I do, make); otherwise, pronounce **g** like h as in "hat": *giro* HEE-roh (money order), *gente* HAYN-tay (people)

j like h, as in "has": *Jueves* HOOAY-vays (Thursday), *mejor* may-HOR (better)

ll like y, as in "yes": *toalla* toh-AH-yah (towel), *ellos* AY-yohs (they, them)

ñ like ny, as in "canyon": *año* AH-nyo (year), *señor* SAY-nyor (Mr., sir)

r is lightly trilled, with tongue at the roof of your mouth like a very light English d, as in "ready": *pero* PAY-doh (but), *tres* TDAYS (three), *cuatro* KOOAH-tdoh (four)

rr like a Spanish r, but with much more emphasis and trill. Let your tongue flap. Practice with *burro* (donkey), *carretera* (highway), and Carrillo (proper name), then really let go with *ferrocarril* (railroad)

Note: The single small but common exception to all of the above is the pronunciation of Spanish **y** when it's being used as the Spanish word for "and," as in "Ron y Kathy." In such case, pronounce it like the English ee, as in "keep": Ron "ee" Kathy (Ron and Kathy).

Accent

The rule for accent, the relative stress given to syllables within a given word, is straightforward. If a word ends in a vowel, an n, or an s, accent the next-to-last syllable; if not, accent the last syllable.

Pronounce *gracias* GRAH-seeahs (thank you), *orden* OHR-dayn (order), and *carretera* kah-ray-TAY-rah (highway) with stress on the next-to-last syllable.

Otherwise, accent the last syllable: *venir* vay-NEER (to come), *ferrocarril* fay-roh-cah-REEL (railroad), and *edad* ay-DAHD (age).

Exceptions to the accent rule are always marked with an accent sign: (á, é, í, ó, or ú), such as *teléfono* tay-LAY-foh-noh (telephone), *jabón* hah-BON (soap), and *rápido* RAH-pee-doh (rapid).

BASIC AND COURTEOUS EXPRESSIONS

Most Spanish-speaking people consider formalities important. Whenever approaching anyone for information or some other reason, do not forget the appropriate salutation—good morning, good evening, etc. Standing alone, the greeting *hola* (hello) can sound brusque.

Hello. *Hola.* In Panama, *buenas* is more commonly used in informal greetings.

Good morning. *Buenos días.*

Good afternoon. *Buenas tardes.*

Good evening. *Buenas noches.*

How are you? *¿Cómo está usted?*

Very well, thank you. *Muy bien, gracias.*

Okay; good. *Bien.*

Not okay; bad. *Mal or feo.*

So-so. *Más o menos.*

And you? *¿Y usted?*

Thank you. *Gracias.*

Thank you very much. *Muchas gracias.*

You're very kind. *Muy amable.*

You're welcome. *De nada.*

Goodbye. *Adios.*

See you later. *Hasta luego.*

please *por favor*

yes *sí*

no *no*

I don't know. *No sé.*

Just a moment, please. *Momentito, por favor.*

Excuse me, please (when you're trying to get attention). *Disculpe or Con permiso.*

Excuse me (when you've made a boo-boo). *Lo siento.*

Pleased to meet you. *Mucho gusto.*

closed *cerrado*

open *abierto*

How do you say... in Spanish? *¿Cómo se dice... en español?*

What is your name? ¿Cómo se llama usted?
My name is... Me llamo...
Do you speak English? ¿Habla usted inglés?
Is English spoken here? (Does anyone here speak English?) ¿Se habla inglés?
I don't speak Spanish well. No hablo bien el español.
I don't understand. No entiendo.
Would you like... ¿Quisiera usted...
Let's go to... Vamos a...

TERMS OF ADDRESS

When in doubt, use the formal usted (you) as a form of address.

I yo
you (formal) usted
you (familiar) tú
he/him él
she/her ella
we/us nosotros
you (plural) ustedes
they/them ellos (all males or mixed gender); ellas (all females)
Mr., sir señor
Mrs., madam señora
miss, young lady señorita
wife esposa
husband esposo
friend amigo (male); amiga (female)
sweetheart novio (male); novia (female)
son; daughter hijo; hija
brother; sister hermano; hermana
father; mother padre; madre
grandfather; grandmother abuelo; abuela

TRANSPORTATION

Where is...? ¿Dónde está...?
How far is it to...? ¿A cuánto está...?
from... to... de... a...
How many blocks? ¿Cuántas cuadras?
Where (Which) is the way to...? ¿Dónde está el camino a...?
the bus station la terminal de autobuses
the bus stop la parada de autobuses

Where is this bus going? ¿Adónde va este autobús?
the taxi stand la parada de taxis
the train station la estación de ferrocarril
the ship el barco
the airport el aeropuerto
I'd like a ticket to... Quisiera un boleto a...
first (second) class primera (segunda) clase
roundtrip ida y vuelta
reservation reservación
baggage equipaje
Stop here, please. Pare aquí, por favor.
the entrance la entrada
the exit la salida
the ticket office la oficina de boletos
(very) near; far (muy) cerca; lejos
to; toward a
by; through por
from de
the right la derecha
the left la izquierda
straight ahead derecho; directo
in front en frente
beside al lado
behind atrás
the corner la esquina
the stoplight la semáforo
a turn una vuelta
right here aquí
somewhere around here por acá
right there allí
somewhere around there por allá
road el camino
street calle
avenue avenida
highway carretera
toll road autopista; corredor
bridge; toll puente; cuota
address dirección
north; south norte; sur
east; west este; oeste

ACCOMMODATIONS

hotel hotel

room *habitación; cuarto*
standard room *habitación estandar*
Is there a room? *¿Hay habitación?*
May I (may we) see it? *¿Puedo (podemos) verlo?*
What is the rate? *¿Cuál es el precio?*
Is that your best rate? *¿Es su mejor precio?*
Is there something cheaper? *¿Hay algo más económico?*
a single room *un cuarto sencillo*
a double room *una habitación sencilla*
double bed *cama matrimonial*
twin beds *camas gemelas*
with private bath *con baño*
hot water *agua caliente*
luxury *lujo*
shower *ducha*
towels *toallas*
soap *jabón*
toilet paper *papel higiénico*
blanket *frazada; manta*
sheets *sábanas*
air-conditioned *aire acondicionado*
fan *abanico; ventilador*
key *llave*
manager *gerente*

FOOD

I'm hungry *Tengo hambre.*
I'm thirsty. *Tengo sed.*
kitchen *cocina*
menu *lista; menú*
order *orden*
glass *vaso*
plate *plato*
fork *tenedor*
knife *cuchillo*
spoon *cuchara*
napkin *servilleta*
soft drink *refresco*
coffee *café*
tea *té*
drinking water *agua pura; agua potable*
bottled carbonated water *agua mineral*

bottled uncarbonated water *agua sin gas*
beer *cerveza*
wine *vino*
milk *leche*
juice *jugo*
cream *crema*
sugar *azúcar*
cheese *queso*
snack *antojo; botana*
breakfast *desayuno*
lunch *almuerzo*
dinner *cena*
the check *la cuenta*
eggs *huevos*
bread *pan*
salad *ensalada*
fruit *fruta*
mango *mango*
watermelon *sandía*
papaya *papaya*
passion fruit *maracuya*
banana *plátano*
blackberry *zarzamora*
guava *guayaba*
apple *manzana*
orange *naranja*
lemon *limón*
lime *lima*
strawberry *fresa*
soursop *guanábana*
fish *pescado*
grouper *mero*
red snapper *pargo rojo*
shellfish *mariscos*
trout *trucha*
shrimp *camarones*
meat (without) *(sin) carne*
chicken *pollo*
pork *puerco*
beef; steak *res; bistec*
bacon; ham *tocino; jamón*
fried *frito*
spicy *picante (caliente means hot only in regard to temperature, not "hot" with chilis)*

roasted asada
grilled a la parilla
barbecue; barbecued barbacoa; al carbón

SHOPPING

money dinero
money-exchange bureau casa de cambio
I would like to exchange traveler's checks. Quisiera cambiar cheques de viajero.
What is the exchange rate? ¿Cuál es el tipo de cambio?
How much is the commission? ¿Cuánto cuesta la comisión?
Do you accept credit cards? ¿Aceptan tarjetas de crédito?
money order giro
How much does it cost? ¿Cuánto cuesta?
What is your final price? ¿Cuál es su último precio?
expensive caro
cheap barato; económico
more más
less menos
a little un poco
too much demasiado
clothing ropa
jewelry joyas

HEALTH

Help me please. Ayúdeme por favor.
I am ill. Estoy enfermo.
Call a doctor. Llame un doctor.
Take me to... Lléveme a...
hospital hospital
drugstore farmacia
pain dolor
fever fiebre
headache dolor de cabeza
stomachache dolor de estómago
burn quemadura
cramp calambre
nausea náusea
vomiting vomitar

medicine medicina
antibiotic antibiótico
pill; tablet pastilla
aspirin aspirina
ointment; cream pomada; crema
bandage venda
cotton algodón
sanitary napkins use brand name, e.g., Kotex
birth control pills pastillas anticonceptivas
contraceptive foam espuma anticonceptiva
condoms preservativos; condones
toothbrush cepilla dental
dental floss hilo dental
toothpaste crema dental
dentist dentista
toothache dolor de muelas

POST OFFICE AND COMMUNICATIONS

long-distance telephone teléfono larga distancia
I would like to call... Quisiera llamar a...
collect por cobrar
station to station a quien contesta
person to person persona a persona
credit card tarjeta de crédito
post office correo
general delivery entrega general
letter carta
stamp estampilla, timbre
postcard tarjeta
aerogram aerograma
airmail correo aereo
registered registrado
money order giro
package; box paquete; caja
string; tape cuerda; cinta

AT THE BORDER

border frontera
customs aduana
immigration migración
tourist card tarjeta de turista
inspection inspección; revisión

passport *pasaporte*
profession *profesión*
marital status *estado civil*
single *soltero*
married; divorced *casado; divorciado*
widowed *viudado*
insurance *seguros*
title *título*
driver's license *licencia de manejar*

AT THE GAS STATION

gas station *gasolinera*
gasoline *gasolina*
unleaded *sin plomo*
full, please *lleno, por favor*
tire *llanta*
tire repair *reparación de llantas*
air *aire*
water *agua*
oil (change) *aceite (cambio)*
grease *grasa*
My... doesn't work. *Mi... no sirve.*
battery *batería*
radiator *radiador*
alternator *alternador*
generator *generador*
repair shop *taller mecánico*

VERBS

Verbs are the key to getting along in Spanish. They employ mostly predictable forms and come in three classes, which end in *ar*, *er*, and *ir*, respectively:

to buy *comprar*
I buy, you (he, she, it) buys *compro, compra*
we buy, you (they) buy *compramos, compran*

to eat *comer*
I eat, you (he, she, it) eats *como, come*
we eat, you (they) eat *comemos, comen*

to climb *subir*
I climb, you (he, she, it) climbs *subo, sube*
we climb, you (they) climb *subimos, suben*

Got the idea? Here are more (with irregularities indicated):

to do or make *hacer* (regular except for *hago*, I do or make)
to go *ir* (very irregular: *voy, va, vamos, van*)
to go (walk) *andar*
to love *amar*
to work *trabajar*
to want *desear, querer*
to need *necesitar*
to read *leer*
to write *escribir*
to repair *reparar*
to stop *parar*
to get off (the bus) *bajar*
to arrive *llegar*
to stay (remain) *quedar*
to stay (lodge) *hospedar*
to leave *salir* (regular except for *salgo*, I leave)
to look at *mirar*
to look for *buscar*
to give *dar* (regular except for *doy*, I give)
to carry *llevar*
to have *tener* (irregular but important: *tengo, tiene, tenemos, tienen*)
to come *venir* (similarly irregular: *vengo, viene, venimos, vienen*)

Spanish has two forms of "to be":

to be *estar* (regular except for *estoy*, I am)
to be *ser* (very irregular: *soy, es, somos, son*)

Use *estar* when speaking of location or a temporary state of being: "I am at home." "*Estoy en casa.*" "I'm sick." "*Estoy enfermo.*" Use *ser* for a permanent state of being: "I am a doctor." "*Soy doctora.*"

NUMBERS

zero *cero*

one *uno*
two *dos*
three *tres*
four *cuatro*
five *cinco*
six *seis*
seven *siete*
eight *ocho*
nine *nueve*
10 *diez*
11 *once*
12 *doce*
13 *trece*
14 *catorce*
15 *quince*
16 *dieciseis*
17 *diecisiete*
18 *dieciocho*
19 *diecinueve*
20 *veinte*
21 *veinte y uno* or *veintiuno*
30 *treinta*
40 *cuarenta*
50 *cincuenta*
60 *sesenta*
70 *setenta*
80 *ochenta*
90 *noventa*
100 *ciento*
101 *ciento y uno* or *cientiuno*
200 *doscientos*
500 *quinientos*
1,000 *mil*
10,000 *diez mil*
100,000 *cien mil*
1,000,000 *millón*
one half *medio*
one third *un tercio*
one fourth *un cuarto*

TIME

What time is it? *¿Qué hora es?*
It's one o'clock. *Es la una.*
It's three in the afternoon. *Son las tres de la tarde.*
It's 4 a.m. *Son las cuatro de la mañana.*
six-thirty *seis y media*
a quarter till eleven *un cuarto para las once*
a quarter past five *las cinco y cuarto*
an hour *una hora*

DAYS AND MONTHS

Monday *lunes*
Tuesday *martes*
Wednesday *miércoles*
Thursday *jueves*
Friday *viernes*
Saturday *sábado*
Sunday *domingo*
today *hoy*
tomorrow *mañana*
yesterday *ayer*
January *enero*
February *febrero*
March *marzo*
April *abril*
May *mayo*
June *junio*
July *julio*
August *agosto*
September *septiembre*
October *octubre*
November *noviembre*
December *diciembre*
a week *una semana*
a month *un mes*
after *después*
before *antes*

(Adapted from *Moon Pacific Mexico*. Courtesy of Bruce Whipperman.)

Suggested Reading

Some of the books listed are out of print or most readily available in Panama, but even these can generally be special-ordered through bookstores or the Internet.

GENERAL INFORMATION

Espriella III, Ricardo de la. *Panamá: Resumen Histórico Illustrado del Istmo, 1501–1994.* Colombia: Antigua Films, 1994. A slender coffee-table book with historic photos and brief summaries of major events in Panama's history. In Spanish.

Friar, William. *Portrait of the Panama Canal: From Construction to the Twenty-First Century.* Portland, Oregon: Graphic Arts Center Publishing, 2003. A photo-essay book by the author of this travel guide.

Navarro Q., Juan Carlos. *Panama National Parks.* Panama: Ediciones Balboa. A beautiful coffee-table book depicting Panama's national parks. In English and Spanish.

Salvador, Mari Lyn (ed.). *The Art of Being Kuna: Layers of Meaning Among the Kuna of Panama.* University of Washington Press: October 1997. A hefty coffee-table book with fascinating photos and scholarly essays on Guna life, culture, art, beliefs, and history. The best introduction to the Gunas and their *molas* (blouses).

HISTORY, POLITICS, AND CURRENT EVENTS

Anderson, Dr. C. L. G. *Old Panama and Castilla del Oro.* New York: North River Press, 1911. A fascinating, in-depth account of the Spanish conquest and pirate history of Panama, written by a medical doctor who worked for the Panama Canal during its construction.

Buckley, Kevin. *Panama: The Whole Story.* New York: Simon and Schuster, 1991. Solidly reported and well written, this is the most reliable account of the U.S. invasion that removed Noriega from power in 1989.

Díaz Espino, Ovidio. *How Wall Street Created a Nation: J. P. Morgan, Teddy Roosevelt, and the Panama Canal.* New York: Four Walls Eight Windows, 2001. An impassioned polemic about behind-the-scenes dealings leading to Panama's separation from Colombia and the 1903 Panama Canal treaties.

Dyke, Tom Hart, and Paul Winder. *The Cloud Garden: A True Story of Adventure, Survival, and Extreme Horticulture.* Guilford, Connecticut: Lyons Press, 2004. An alternately funny and horrifying account of two backpackers kidnapped by guerrillas in the Darién jungle in 2000.

Howarth, David. *The Golden Isthmus.* London: Collins, 1966. Also published as *Panama: Four Hundred Years of Dreams and Cruelty.* Contains fascinating tidbits on the exploits of Spanish conquistadors, Elizabethan adventurers, and bloody buccaneers. Becomes unreliable as it enters the modern era.

Howe, James. *A People Who Would Not Kneel: Panama, the United States, and the San Blas Kuna.* Washington: Smithsonian, 1998. Gives interesting insights into the history and culture of the Guna.

Lindsay-Poland, John. *Emperors in the Jungle: The Hidden History of the U.S. in Panama.* Durham, North Carolina: Duke University Press, 2003. Investigative journalism examining the history of U.S. military involvement in Panama.

McCullough, David. *The Path Between the Seas: The Creation of the Panama Canal, 1870–1914.* New York: Simon and Schuster, 1977. The definitive history of the Panama Canal. An astonishing book that reads like a thriller.

Prebble, John. *The Darien Disaster: A Scots Colony in the New World, 1698–1700.* New York: Holt, Rinehart, and Winston, 1968. A readable account of the doomed Scottish attempt to establish a colony in the Darién jungle.

PANAMA CITY HISTORY

Spanish-speakers interested in learning more about Panama City's history will have their best chance of finding locally written books at local bookstores. However, these generally are academic works produced on a minimal budget and containing far more minute detail than the average reader will have much use for.

Castillero Reyes, Ernesto J. *Leyendas e Historias de Panamá la Vieja.* Panama City: Producciones Erlizca, 2nd edition 1998. The history and legends of Old Panama from its founding to its sacking by Henry Morgan, with crude illustrations and a blurry map of the city during its heyday.

de La Espriella III, Ricardo. *Panamá: Resumen Histórico Ilustrado del Istmo, 1501–1994.* Bogotá: Antigua Films, 1994. A slender coffee-table book with historic photos and brief summaries of major events in Panama's history.

Díaz Szmirnov, Damaris. *Génesis de la Ciudad Republicana.* Panama City: Agenda del Centenario, 2001. A detailed account of the emergence of modern Panama City in the late 19th and early 20th centuries. Though likely to be of most interest to residents, it fills in many gaps in Panama's recent history, something that has not been well documented, especially from a Panamanian perspective. It contains some small but interesting historical photos.

NATURE AND WILDLIFE

Forsyth, Adrian, and Ken Miyata. *Tropical Nature: Life and Death in the Rain Forests of Central and South America.* New York: Simon and Schuster, 1995. An introduction to tropical ecology.

Kircher, John. *A Neotropical Companion: An Introduction to the Animals, Plants, & Ecosystems of the New World Tropics.* Princeton, New Jersey: Princeton University Press, 1999. A detailed explanation of just about anything you'd like to know about the New World tropics. Reading it will deepen hikers' experience of the forest.

Ventocilla, Jorge, Heraclio Herrera, and Valerio Nunez. Elisabeth King, trans. *Plants & Animals in the Life of the Kuna.* Austin, Texas: University of Texas, 1995. This book is notable for describing flora and fauna, forest life, and environmental destruction in Guna Yala from the point of view of the Guna themselves, often in their own words.

Wong, Marina, and Jorge Ventocilla. *A Day on Barro Colorado Island.* Panama: Smithsonian, 1995. A slim volume that contains an overview of the flora and fauna of the island and a detailed trail map.

FIELD GUIDES

Reid, Fiona A. *A Field Guide to the Mammals of Central America and Southeast Mexico.* New York: Oxford University Press, 1998. Comprehensive illustrated guide to mammals found in Panama, including aquatic ones. Includes range maps, descriptions, habitats, and habits. The English and Spanish names, nicknames, and regional names of species are included, which is a nice touch.

Ridgely, Robert S., and John A. Gwynne Jr. *A Guide to the Birds of Panama.* Princeton, New Jersey: Princeton University Press, 1989. Though overdue for an update, this is still the bible of Panama bird-watching. Also contains information on birds found in Costa Rica, Nicaragua, and Honduras.

TRAVEL GUIDES

Pritchard, Raymond, and Audrey Pritchard. *Driving the Pan-American Highway to Mexico and Central America.* Costa Rica: Costa Rica Books, 1997. Quite out of date, but at the time of writing the only guidebook on driving to Panama from North America.

Zydler, Nancy Schwalbe, and Tom Zydler. *The Panama Guide: A Cruising Guide to the Isthmus of Panama.* Port Washington, Wisconsin: Seaworthy Publications, 2001. A guide to yachting destinations along both sides of the isthmus, with detailed tips and 187 charts.

LIFE IN PANAMA

Henderson, Malcolm. *Don't Kill the Cow Too Quick: An Englishman's Adventures Homesteading in Panama.* Lincoln, Nebraska: iUniverse, 2004. Homespun account of an expatriate couple's adventures building their retirement dream in Bocas del Toro.

Henríquez, Cristina. *Come Together, Fall Apart: A Novella and Stories.* New York: Riverhead Books, 2006. Though fiction, this well-written and widely praised collection of short stories will give English-language readers some insight into modern Panamanian life. Henríquez, who has a Panamanian father and gringa mother, grew up in the United States. The best stories explore how it feels to be an expat Panamanian trying to reconnect with one's roots.

Knapp, Herbert, and Mary Knapp. *Red, White, and Blue Paradise: The American Canal Zone in Panama.* New York: Harcourt Brace Jovanovich, 1984. An account of life in the old Canal Zone from a couple who lived it.

Snyder, Sandra. *Living in Panama.* Panama: Tantoes, S.A., 2007 (2nd ed.). A thorough guide for expatriates moving to Panama, covering everything from dinner-party etiquette to registering cars.

Internet Resources

There is at last a fair amount of useful information about Panama on the web. However, most websites are badly designed, rarely get updated, and don't work well with any browser other than Internet Explorer. Be especially wary of booking through websites, as their forms often don't function smoothly. There are also plenty of easy-to-find community forums on the web by and for tourists and resident expatriates.

TRAVEL

Bocas del Toro
www.bocas.com
This visitor-information site for Bocas del Toro contains listings for many hotels, restaurants, and services as well as some background information on Bocas.

Bocas Marine & Tours, S.A.
www.bocasmarinetours.com
Bocas Marine & Tours is a Bocas del Toro water-taxi service, but its site also contains useful, updated maps of the Bocas archipelago and

mainland, transportation schedules, and facts about Bocas. However, it is no longer regularly updated.

Boomers Abroad
www.boomersabroad.com/panama.html
This is an overview site for those interested in retiring or investing in Panama. It takes a more measured approach than similar sites, which can be aggressive about hyping Panama.

Journey Latin America
www.journeylatinamerica.co.uk
Journey Latin America is a London-based tour operator and travel agency that's a good place to start for those going to Panama from Europe and points east.

LegalInfo Panamá
www.legalinfo-panama.com
This site contains detailed legal information for those interested in moving to or doing business in Panama, as well as listings of lawyers and law firms. It's in Spanish with some English content.

Panama
www.visitpanama.com
The official site of Panama's government tourism institute, ATP. It's in English and Spanish.

Panamainfo
www.panamainfo.com
Panamainfo is a frequently updated Panama-promotion site that accentuates the positive; it's not the place to go for critical reviews of places or services. Its visitor information is geared primarily toward traveling on a moderate-to-high budget, but it also contains general information for various regions of Panama.

TransPanamá
www.transpanama.org
This is the website for a very cool volunteer-run project to build a trail across Panama from Costa Rica to Colombia. It is also creating a GPS map of the route, which hopefully it will eventually put on this bilingual site. The project welcomes volunteers.

U.S. Department of State
http://travel.state.gov
The website of the U.S. State Department contains general entry requirements and travel warnings for U.S. citizens traveling abroad, listed by country.

The Visitor
www.thevisitorpanama.com
The Visitor/El Visitante is a bilingual tourist newspaper published every two weeks and widely available at tourist haunts in Panama City. Contents include information on upcoming festivals and events, features on destinations, and reviews of restaurants, primarily in Panama City. Current and back issues are on its website.

ECOTOURISM

Almanaque Azul
www.almanaqueazul.org
The "blue almanac" is a wiki-style guide to the beaches and coasts of Panama meant to raise awareness of conservation issues while providing useful practical information for visiting even the remotest beaches. Anyone can add to the almanac. In Spanish only.

ANCON
www.ancon.org
ANCON is Panama's largest environmental organization. The site contains some information on the country's national parks and a list of endangered species. In Spanish only.

Panama Audubon Society
www.panamaaudubon.org
The Panama Audubon Society organizes frequent bird-watching trips that are open to

foreign visitors and listed on its site, which is in Spanish and English.

Planeta
www.planeta.com
Long-established, thoughtful website on eco-tourism issues, with practical advice on low-impact travel. It contains some Panama-specific information.

Smithsonian Tropical Research Institute
www.stri.org
The website of the Smithsonian Tropical Research Institute (STRI) contains information on its projects and installations, including Barro Colorado Island. It also shows live video from user-controllable webcams set up on Barro Colorado and Parque Natural Metropolitano.

NEWS SITES

Bajareque Times
www.boquete-bajareque-times.com
Similar to the *Bocas Breeze,* but covering Boquete and the surrounding area.

The Bocas Breeze
www.thebocasbreeze.com
A print and online newspaper run by resident expatriates living in Bocas del Toro. It covers tourism and environmental issues likely to interest visitors. Stories are in English and Spanish. The print edition appears monthly.

Panama-Guide
www.panama-guide.com
The best and most balanced online source for news articles in English, including articles translated from Spanish-language Panamanian newspapers. It's the place to start for information on Panama that is neither promotional nor overly cynical. Though it grinds its share of axes and engages in occasional online feuds, it does a good job of separating news and opinion.

La Prensa
www.prensa.com
Panama's best Spanish-language newspaper. Free registration allows access to its extensive archives.

Rob Rivera
www.rob-rivera.com
Interesting and articulate English-language blog by an up-and-coming Panamanian writer. Rivera offers rare insight into Panamanian life from the perspective of a well-educated young guy who speaks perfect English. Or, as his blog's tagline puts it, "This is where first-world mentality meets a third-world country."

GOVERNMENT

Dirrección Nacional de Migración y Naturalización
http://migracion.gob.pa
The official website of Panama's immigration and naturalization service contains useful information (in English!) on visa laws and procedures. The pulldown menus for which country's citizens need which visa can make errors, producing misleading results.

Panama Canal Authority
www.pancanal.com
The website for the Panama Canal Authority contains news and history about the Panama Canal, and tide tables for Balboa and Cristóbal. But its coolest features are the live video feeds from the webcams set up at Miraflores Locks, Gatún Locks, and the Centennial Bridge over Gaillard Cut.

República de Panamá
www.pa
General Panamanian government site with telephone listings and links to government ministries and organizations, including the tourism and culture institutes. In Spanish.

MISCELLANEOUS INFORMATION

Centers for Disease Control and Prevention
wwwn.cdc.gov/travel
The U.S. Centers for Disease Control lists comprehensive immunization information and health advisories for destinations around the world.

Central Intelligence Agency
www.cia.gov/library/publications/
the-world-factbook
The U.S. Central Intelligence Agency lists statistics and background information on Panama here.

CZBrats and the Lost Paradise
www.czbrats.com, http://lostparadise.com
Nostalgia sites for Zonians, containing photos, stories, and memorabilia from the former Canal Zone.

Paginas Amarillas
www.paginasamarillas.com
Online telephone book for Panama and other Latin American countries.

Index

List of Maps

Acknowledgments

For Karen

Writing a guidebook restores your faith in humanity; you meet so many people who are generous with their time, knowledge, and hospitality. The following are just a few of the many people who made this new edition possible.

I am fortunate to have in my family one of the foremost experts on the Panama Canal: my mother, Willie K. Friar. Her expertise and support—not to mention her networking prowess—were invaluable as always. I don't know how I could ever keep up with the lightning changes in Panama City without help from Mary Coffey, Sandra Snyder, and David Wilson year after year. And trying to do so would be much more difficult and far less pleasant without Clotilde O. de la Guerra and Tony Barrios.

The list of people to thank around the country is now too long for this small space, but I am especially indebted once again to Jane Walker and Barry Robbins in Boquete, Andrea Aster in David, and Carla Rankin in Bocas. Paul Saban and Jim Guy were kind enough to donate terrific photos to the cause. I also am grateful for the many readers who took the time to contact me with tips, updates, and kind remarks.

My colleagues at Avalon Travel once again had to be as patient with me as they are professional. Those who made sure this edition finally saw print include Leah Gordon, Tabitha Lahr, and Mike Morgenfeld.

Most of all, I need to thank my wife, Karen, who not only kept the home fires burning during this endless project but also cut and hauled the firewood. I couldn't have done it without her kind heart, patience, wisdom, and loving support.